COMPOSITION·AND·LITERATURE
EXPLORING HUMAN EXPERIENCE

COMPOSITION ·AND· LITERATURE

Exploring Human Experience

JESSE JONES
Richland College
(Dallas Community College District)

VEVA VONLER
Texas Woman's University

JANET HARRIS
University of Texas at Dallas

HARCOURT BRACE JOVANOVICH, PUBLISHERS
San Diego   New York   Chicago   Austin   Washington, D.C.
London   Sydney   Tokyo   Toronto

Preface

Composition and Literature: Exploring Human Experience will help students improve their skills as writers, develop keener perceptions and greater sophistication as readers, and grow in awareness, understanding, and appreciation of the human experience. Distinctive features which will assist students and instructors in achieving these goals include the following:

- ☐ The integration of composition and literature
- ☐ A stages-of-life arrangement of chapters, writing activities, and reading selections
- ☐ For each chapter, an organization featuring a preliminary list of terms and topics, an overview paragraph, sections of assignable length, and a concluding summary and review
- ☐ A "user friendly" tone
- ☐ An *Instructor's Manual* containing additional suggestions, strategies, and resources

These features combine to create a strong composition text and a strong introduction to literature text in a single book.

"Composition and Literature . . ."

The two major distinctive features of this book are reflected in its title. *Composition and Literature* presents composition as the process of writing— of generating ideas, organizing, drafting, and revising. It defines literature as any product of that writing process, whether prose or poetry, fiction or nonfiction, student essay or Shakespearean play. This integration of composition and literature encourages students to focus on and practice the shared compositional characteristics of all writing, even as they note differences between belletristic and functional writing. They see that the basic processes and techniques of all writers—including famous authors of poetry, plays, and fiction—are pertinent to their own writing for college, career, and personal expression.

Writing and reading activities in the book underscore the inseparability of composition and literature; they also stress the interrelated, complementary relationship of writing, reading, thinking, speaking, and listening skills. Writing activities are presented in three formats:

1. "Writing ↔ Reading ↔ Thinking Activities." These questions and suggestions are designed to generate personal reflection, brief writings, and classroom discussion. Most chapters include several "Writing ↔ Reading ↔ Thinking Activities" sections.

2. "Expanding Your Writing Skills." These exercises—at least one in each chapter, two or three in most chapters—pose questions or problems requiring essay-length responses. These thinking and writing situations generally bring together the principal points of an entire chapter or a major portion of a chapter.

3. A Research Paper Appendix. This supplemental section traces the steps in preparing a research paper, from choosing a subject to writing a final draft.

Reading selections also foster reading, writing, thinking, speaking, and listening skills. Reading aloud is encouraged. The many prereading, reading, and rereading questions and suggestions in the textbook and the *Instructor's Manual* prompt individual and group analysis. Readings include (a) a wide variety of nonfiction prose, poetry, short fiction, and drama, and (b) readings created by students themselves. These selections appear in three formats:

1. Integrated readings. Part 1 includes 43 selections interwoven in Chapters 1 through 6 as models for writing and as subject matter for written and oral analysis and discussion.

2. Readings composed by students. Periodically, students are asked to critique their own essays and those of classmates. In Chapter 7 each student is asked to analyze the portfolio of literature that he or she has composed during the semester.

3. Additional readings. Part 2 provides 118 supplemental readings grouped to correspond to Chapters 1 through 6.

"... Exploring Human Experience"

The second major distinctive feature of *Composition and Literature* is its life-cycle organization. Except for the introductory and concluding chapters, the book is arranged according to the stages of life: childhood, adolescence, adulthood, old age, and death. This pattern provides a refreshing change from the typical sentence-paragraph-essay format of composition texts and from the usual poetry-fiction-drama or plot-character-theme organization of literature anthologies. Furthermore, presenting composition and literature in a "lifetime" format relevant to each student, at whatever age, demonstrates that all writing and literature are interwoven threads in the fabric of life, contributing to and commenting on the human experience. This organization also effectively complements the teaching of writing and reading skills. Movement in the book, as in life, is generally from the simple to the complex, from the subjective to the objective. For example, early writing activities are subjective, internal, writer-centered; later assignments include objective, external, reader-centered activities.

In *Composition and Literature: Exploring Human Experience* students of all ages and backgrounds will find engaging writing and reading activities, a relevant "lifetime" organization, and a challenging, supportive tone which will appeal to them and encourage thoughtful self-expression as they study writing, literature, and life.

Acknowledgments

We can now attest to the truth of Winston Churchill's observation that "writing a book is an adventure. To begin with, it is a toy and an amusement. Then it becomes a mistress, then it becomes a master, and then it becomes a tyrant. The last phase is just as you are about to be reconciled to your servitude, you kill the monster, and fling him to the public." As we finally fling our toy-turned-tyrant to students and instructors, we wish also to fling grateful acknowledgments to those who have provided personal and professional challenge and support.

First and foremost to our mates, Terri Kennedy Jones and Charles Vonler, for abiding faith, hope, love—and patience.

To our secretaries, Sarah Clay and Kathryn Virgin, for innumerable services and constant assistance.

To colleagues who read early drafts and provided valuable criticism and guidance: Lee Miller—mentor, friend, Professor Emeritus of English at North Texas State University; Eugene Garber, State University of New York at Albany; John Heyda, Miami University (Ohio); Gary A. Olson, University of South Florida; and Myron Tuman, University of Alabama.

To the fine, friendly professionals at Harcourt Brace Jovanovich: Bill McLane, senior acquisitions editor, for his intuition, insights, and insistence; Craig Avery, manuscript editor, for his astute emendations; and Amy Dunn, James Chadwick, Don Fujimoto, and Kim Turner for the textbook's design and production.

And finally to each other, for the friendship and respect and affection which led us into this adventure and sustained us throughout.

JESSE JONES

VEVA VONLER

JANET HARRIS

Contents

3

Awakenings 63

4

Making Connections   **139**

5

Coming to Terms with Life   231

6

Coming to Terms with Death   261

7

The Literate Mind at Work:
Writing as Re-Vision   307

PART TWO
ADDITIONAL READINGS

1
On Literacy, Literature, and Life   321

2
Beginnings   329

3

Awakenings   425

4

Making Connections   461

5

Coming to Terms with Life   **661**

6

Coming to Terms with Death   823

COMPOSITION·AND·LITERATURE
EXPLORING HUMAN EXPERIENCE

PART 1

EXPLORING
HUMAN
EXPERIENCE

1

On Literacy, Literature, and Life

"Writing is a metaphor for life."*

□ Why This Textbook?   □ You as Writer   □ You as Writer and Reader   □ You as Writer, Reader, and Explorer of Human Experience   □ Checking Your "Literacy Level"   □ Journal Writing

Who are you, and why are you reading this book? How literate are you as a writer and reader? How can you improve your "literacy level"? The answers to these questions in Chapter 1 will clarify the purpose, organization, and audience for this book. As a point of departure in this course—an exploration of writing, literature, and human experience—you will begin reading about life as viewed by various writers and begin recording your own views.

Who, What, Where, Why?

This book focuses on composition, the art and craft of writing. It presents works of literature in various forms as examples and products of that writing. And, through the writing and reading opportunities provided, it encour-

*Elaine Maimon and others, *Writing in the Arts and Sciences* (Cambridge, Mass.: Winthrop Publishers, Inc., 1981) v.

ages the exploration of human experience. In other words, this textbook emphasizes the interrelatedness of writing, literature, and life. The student who finishes Chapter 7 should write better, read the writing of others better, and know a bit more about self and others than the student who is just beginning the book.

And who is this student, the "you" of page 4, Chapter 1? What assumptions are we making about where you are, who you are, what you know, and why you are reading Chapter 1 with the intent of concluding Chapter 7?

The first and last points, the "where" and the "why," are easy enough. You are on a college campus as an undergraduate, and you are currently enrolled in a course for which this textbook is required. Whether the course is a composition course, an introduction to literature course, a combination of the two, or something slightly different, it surely is designed to improve your writing skills by exercising your ability to read, write, think, talk, and listen.

Your instructor standing at the front of the class surveying the group will probably see the following:

- Young students just out of high school, still in their teens
- Older students returning to college or beginning college after several years away from school who can barely remember their teens
- Dropout/drop-in students of various ages who began college in their teens, dropped out along the way for various reasons, and are now back in school
- Students of various ethnic backgrounds
- Students from several geographical regions

In the past, most students on most college campuses would have been teenagers just out of high school. Today, however, such uniform classes and campuses are more the exception than the rule. Not only are there ethnic, geographical, and age diversities in your class, but also diversities in interests, major fields of study, familial responsibilities such as spouses and children, career stages, and educational backgrounds. In short, the class your instructor faces is a motley crew (expressed negatively) or a richly diversified group (expressed positively).

What does this richly diversified group know? What have your varied educational backgrounds provided to build on in this course? To a great extent, you already possess the very skills this book is designed to develop. You know how to read, write, think, talk, and listen—but *not* as well as you would like. You surely consider yourself literate in the sense that you are "able to read and write." But you probably do not consider yourself literate in the sense of being "well-educated; having or showing extensive knowledge, learning, or culture."* None of us can really lay claim in any definitive way to being literate in this latter sense; perhaps the best we can aim for is to be more literate as college seniors than as college freshmen, more literate still five years after college graduation, and so on.

You have been working toward your current literacy level formally and informally since you began to recognize letters of the alphabet on building blocks and to duplicate those letters in crayon on your bedroom walls. In elementary school you learned how to print, then how to connect letters in cursive handwriting. You struggled through beginning readers. Later you studied English grammar, mechanics, punctuation, spelling, and diction. Writing became an important skill used almost daily in composing sentences, paragraphs, essays, and secret notes to classmates. You transferred your wall-writing talents to classroom blackboards. Your reading ability expanded to textbooks, plays, short stories, novels, poems, and—at the corner drugstore or drive-in grocery—comic books and true romance and sex magazines. For a long time now, you have been able to write and read, but probably not as well as you want to or feel you need to. Studying this book should move you up the literacy ladder of writing and reading skills.

You as Writer

The approach to composition, the first priority of this book, builds on your background, acknowledges your individuality, and focuses on the kinds of writing that will be required of you from now on:

☐ You will write in college. During your college career, you will take classroom notes and write essay exams, write journals, write critical reviews, write outlines, write lab reports, write case studies, write paraphrases, write summaries, write short essays, write long essays, write research papers; in short, you will *write* in college. (The more writing, the better the college education.)

☐ You will write on the job. Most jobs require some of the following some of the time: memos, reports, surveys, letters, proposals, summaries, analyses, guidelines, and instructions.

*The quoted definitions of *literate*, and of *literature* later in the chapter, are from *Webster's New World Dictionary of the American Language*, Second College Edition (Cleveland: William Collins Publishers, Inc., 1979).

□ You will write in your personal life. There will be all kinds of functional writing: fill-in-the-blank-line types such as writing checks and filling out application forms; grocery lists; brief notes stuck on the refrigerator door for family members; longer letters to friends and family; lengthy responses to the county appraisal review board explaining why their proposed increase in the tax appraisal value of your house is ridiculously high, and so on and on.

What you need in order to improve your handling of all this present and future writing is familiarity with and practice of a variety of writing forms, techniques, and purposes. The questions, suggestions, directions, explanations, and exercises in each chapter should help you realize that you have something to say and should provide numerous opportunities for you to say it on paper.

You as Writer and Reader

An additional way this book will help you is by providing examples of writing forms, techniques, and purposes in a variety of reading selections. These selections appear in each chapter and as additional readings at the end of the book. They serve several purposes:

□ They provide models of writing types and techniques for illustration, analysis, and writing practice. Any "reading" can just as well be called a "writing," since it is the product of a writer's creative process. The focus will be on that writing process, as well as on the product.

□ They provide interesting, challenging, and rewarding reading; they also serve as a means toward the end of improving your writing. (The more you read, the better you read; the better you read, the better you write.)

□ They will stimulate thought and discussion not only about their writing form and style, but also about their substance and ideas. This thinking and talking will also carry over as a positive force in your writing.

□ Finally, they illustrate various types and characteristics of literature, and we think that a basic knowledge of literary types, techniques, and terminology is essential to one's being literate in both the sense of being "able to read and write" and of being "well-educated."

The emphasis on literature, the second priority, will be an outgrowth of the emphasis on composition. In a general sense, you cannot read without reading literature, and you cannot write without writing literature. Literature is frequently defined as "fiction, poetry, drama, etc. as distinguished from technical and scientific writings," but this definition seems unnecessarily narrow. Literature can also be defined as "all writings in prose or verse." For our purposes we choose the latter definition.

This expanded definition includes not only poetry and fiction and drama but also essays, autobiography, biography, newspaper articles, scholarly articles, chapters from scientific works, and letters—selections composed by others and selections composed by you. As you work through this text, you will accumulate a portfolio or notebook of your writings, "literature" of your own creation. You, your classmates, and your instructor will read and discuss and critique your literature as well as the selections in the book.

This approach to literature will treat all these writings and readings as general examples of writing in addition to their specific classifications as types of literature. When a writer like Walt Whitman is creating a poem, he does some poetry-creating things as a writer that only poets must worry about, but things that readers of the finished poem should be able to perceive and appreciate. He also uses more general writing techniques which readers and writers can perceive, appreciate, and *practice* as well.

You as Writer, Reader, and Explorer of Human Experience

As all writing is in some sense literature, so all writing and literature are in some sense a record of human experience. Our third priority, exploring human experience, grows out of priorities one and two—composition and literature. All writers record something of themselves—their experiences, their knowledge, their perceptions. And when they read others' writing, they expand their own experiences, knowledge, and perceptions.

This book has been organized, the readings selected, and the writing activities created to encourage exploration of human experience. The organizing principle is that of the human life cycle; the book begins with childhood and ends with death. The thread running through all the chapters and weaving them together is the thread of human existence: human growth, human development, human interests, human thought, human feeling, human experience. This organization means that a portion of the book deals with your past, a portion deals with your present, and a portion deals with your future. In Chapter 2, you will be looking back at an earlier stage in life. Somewhere in Chapter 3, 4, or 5 you will come to your current stage. Chapter 6 will be for you a looking ahead.

Much of your writing for this course will be about your own experiences, remembrances, perceptions, and anticipations; about those you know and *their* experiences, remembrances, perceptions, and anticipations; and about people you encounter in the reading selections in this book. Such writing about yourself and real and imagined others is a way of exploring and expanding your awareness of the individuality and universality of humankind.

It is also a way of introducing, practicing, and analyzing the kinds of writing you will be doing from now on. By the time you finish Chapter 7, you will have written journal entries, lists, autobiographical and biographical notes and descriptions, narratives, essays, outlines, summaries, paraphrases, letters, reports, and critical analyses. You will have studied and practiced techniques needed for academic, professional, and personal writing. You should write better, know more about literature, and have an expanded awareness and appreciation of human experience. The result should be a more literate you.

You can check your current literacy level with a few introductory reading and writing exercises. We begin with four selections which serve as keynote commentaries on life—with the fourth also a keynote summary of the goals for this book.

Checking Your Current Literacy Level

In the history of modern English, two works of literature have been more widely read and quoted than any others. The first is the Bible, especially the King James Bible published in 1611; the second is the collection of plays by William Shakespeare. To begin a book on writing, literature, and human experience with a passage from each seems especially fitting. First, here is the biblical comment on "a time to every purpose":

The Bible (King James Version)

Ecclesiastes 3:1–8

1 To everything there is a season, and a time to every
    purpose under the heaven:
2 a time to be born, and a time to die;
  a time to plant, and a time to pluck up that which is planted;

3 a time to kill, and a time to heal;
      a time to break down, and a time to build up;
4 a time to weep, and a time to laugh;
      a time to mourn, and a time to dance;
5 a time to cast away stones, and a time to gather stones together;
      a time to embrace, and a time to refrain from embracing;
6 a time to get, and a time to lose;
      a time to keep, and a time to cast away;
7 a time to rend, and a time to sew;
      a time to keep silence, and a time to speak;
8 a time to love, and a time to hate;
      a time of war, and a time of peace.

The author seems to be saying that during a person's lifetime there is an appropriate moment for "every purpose," even for purposes that are contradictory. At a given time, in a given situation, one action may be appropriate. At another time, in another situation, the opposite response may be appropriate. And a single life encompasses many such opposites and contradictions.

A single life also encompasses many phases, as Shakespeare tells us.

William Shakespeare (1564–1616)
As You Like It

Act 2, Scene 7, lines 139–66

All the world's a stage,	
And all the men and women merely players:	140
They have their exits and their entrances;	
And one man in his time plays many parts,	
His acts being seven ages. At first the infant,	
Mewling and puking in the nurse's arms.	
And then the whining schoolboy, with his satchel	145
And shining morning face, creeping like snail	
Unwillingly to school. And then the lover,	
Sighing like furnace, with a woeful ballad	
Made to his mistress' eyebrow. Then a soldier,	
Full of strange oaths, and bearded like the pard,	150
Jealous in honour, sudden and quick in quarrel,	
Seeking the bubble reputation	

Even in the cannon's mouth. And then the justice,
In fair round belly with good capon lined,
With eyes severe and beard of formal cut,   155
Full of wise saws and modern instances;
And so he plays his part. The sixth age shifts
Into the lean and slipper'd pantaloon,
With spectacles on nose and pouch on side,
His youthful hose, well saved, a world too wide   160
For his shrunk shank; and his big manly voice,
Turning again toward childish treble, pipes
And whistles in his sound. Last scene of all,
That ends this strange eventful history,
Is second childishness and mere oblivion,   165
Sans teeth, sans eyes, sans taste, sans every thing.

Life is a drama in which each person plays a series of chronological and career roles. For all the struggles and aspirations, the ending is similar to the beginning of "this strange eventful history"—a "second childishness."

Another way of describing life is as a journey. One well-known life-journey comparison appears in the following poem by the twentieth-century American poet Robert Frost.

Robert Frost (1875–1963)
The Road Not Taken

Two roads diverged in a yellow wood,
And sorry I could not travel both
And be one traveler, long I stood
And looked down one as far as I could
To where it bent in the undergrowth;   5

Then took the other, as just as fair,
And having perhaps the better claim,
Because it was grassy and wanted wear;
Though as for that the passing there
Had worn them really about the same,   10

And both that morning equally lay
In leaves no step had trodden black.
Oh, I kept the first for another day!
Yet knowing how way leads on to way,
I doubted if I should ever come back.   15

I shall be telling this with a sigh
Somewhere ages and ages hence:
Two roads diverged in a wood, and I—
I took the one less traveled by,
And that has made all the difference.   20

In this poem the emphasis is not so much on the journey of life as it is on the importance of one's choices, the decisions an individual makes when faced with alternative routes along the way.

In the next selection, Oliver Wendell Holmes describes human development as an upward spiral into ever more spacious quarters, "more stately mansions."

Oliver Wendell Holmes (1809–1894)
The Chambered Nautilus

This is the ship of pearl, which, poets feign,
  Sails the unshadowed main,—
  The venturous bark that flings
On the sweet summer wind its purpled wings
In gulfs enchanted, where the Siren sings.   5
  And coral reefs lie bare,
Where the cold sea-maids rise to sun their streaming hair.

Its webs of living gauze no more unfurl;
  Wrecked is the ship of pearl!
  And every chambered cell,   10
Where its dim dreaming life was wont to dwell,
As the frail tenant shaped his growing shell,
  Before thee lies revealed,—
Its irised ceiling rent, its sunless crypt unsealed!

Year after year beheld the silent toil   15
  That spread his lustrous coil;
  Still, as the spiral grew,
He left the past year's dwelling for the new,
Stole with soft step its shining archway through,
  Built up its idle door,   20
Stretched in his last-found home, and knew the old no more.

Thanks for the heavenly message brought by thee,
  Child of the wandering sea,
  Cast from her lap, forlorn!

From thy dead lips a clearer note is born   25
Than ever Triton blew from wreathèd horn!
    While on mine ear it rings,
Through the deep caves of thought I hear a voice that sings: —

Build thee more stately mansions, O my soul,
    As the swift seasons roll!   30
    Leave thy low-vaulted past!
Let each new temple, nobler than the last,
Shut thee from heaven with a dome more vast,
    Till thou at length art free,
Leaving thine outgrown shell by life's unresting sea!   35

In this poem Holmes sees in the spiraling development of the sea creature's shell a "heavenly message," nature's pattern and prototype for the
desirable growth and expansion of the individual human being.

In a way, Holmes's poem also summarizes the purposes and goals of this
textbook: to challenge and support you in an upward spiral of expanding
writing ability and literary knowledge and human awareness.

But where are you now, before you start spiraling upward? Here is a
series of questions for you and your instructor to document your current
literacy level. The purpose of these questions is simply to prompt you to
think a bit, record your thoughts on paper, and thereby begin what we hope
proves a pleasant and growing working relationship between your mind and
your hand.

□ WRITING ↔ READING ↔ THINKING ACTIVITIES □
Determining Your Literacy Level

1. The passage from Ecclesiastes lists several human actions and feelings,
    but it is not all-inclusive. Extend it by writing two or three additional
    verses; maintain the same pattern but avoid repeating actions or emo-
    tions already mentioned.

2. Shakespeare includes both sexes when he begins by saying that "all men
    and women" are "merely players," but he lists the seven "parts" or
    "ages" only for the male. List seven corresponding parts or ages for a
    female; include a descriptive phrase or two for each part.

3. Surely you have already traveled life's road far enough to have come to
    a point where "two roads diverged" and you made a choice or decision of
    importance. Explain one such life-choice you have made.

4. Shakespeare, Frost, and Holmes compare life to a play, to a journey, and to a seashell. Can you think of three additional comparisons?

□ EXPANDING YOUR WRITING SKILLS □
Composing a First Writing

The Additional Readings for Chapter 1 toward the back of the book are brief writings commenting on humankind, on the nature of life, or on man and nature. Select one which appeals to you; read it aloud repeatedly; then write as much about the form, the style, and the ideas as you can without looking up any additional information. Which ideas do you agree with or find personally relevant? Which do you reject? Are there passages that puzzle you, that you do not understand?

This longer writing exercise provides written calisthenics for your mind and hand so your instructor can gain some idea of your current writing strengths. But more importantly, the purpose is to focus on what you think and do in producing this writing (and, by extension, any writing). As you begin, be aware of what you are actually doing—what you are thinking, how you are composing and creating. Try to sense something of the process as you write.

Retain the writing you produce in the assignments above. Start a notebook, a folder, or a portfolio in which you keep *all* the writing you compose for this course. You will be building a body of literature (in the broader sense of the term) which you composed and created, and which will serve in its own way as the primary text for the course. From time to time you will be referring to your work—analyzing it, revising an earlier piece, building on and improving earlier efforts. So hang on to everything: notes, drafts, and finished copies.

"Dear Daybook, . . ."

One of the most enjoyable and rewarding ways to write regularly while feeling minimal anxiety about grades or "correctness" is to keep a journal. You have probably already done something of the sort at one time or another in the form of a diary, personal notes, or private records of your innermost thoughts and feelings. Because journal writing can serve as an important rung in your climb up the literacy ladder, we strongly encourage you to keep a journal throughout this course. As preparation, read the following discussion regarding the nature and benefits of a journal. (This selection originally served as an introduction to several passages from journals, including the one by Ralph Waldo Emerson which is mentioned.)

Arthur Eastman (born 1918)
Prose Forms: Journals

Occasionally one catches oneself having said something aloud, obviously with no concern to be heard, even by oneself. And all of us have overheard, perhaps while walking, a solitary person muttering or laughing softly or exclaiming abruptly. Something floats up from the world within, forces itself to be expressed, takes no real account of the time or the place, and certainly intends no conscious communication.

With more self-consciousness, and yet without a specific audience, one sometimes speaks out at something that has momentarily filled his attention from the world without. A sharp play at the ball game, the twist of a political speech, an old photograph—something from the outer world impresses the mind, stimulates it, focuses certain of its memories and values, interests and needs. Thus stimulated, one may wish to share an experience with another, to inform or amuse that person, to rouse him or her to action or persuade someone to a certain belief. Often, though, the person experiencing may want most to talk to himself, to give a public shape in words to thoughts and feelings but for the sake of a kind of private dialogue. Communication to another may be an ultimate desire, but the immediate motive is to articulate the experience for oneself.

To articulate, to shape the experience in language for one's own sake, one may keep a journal. Literally a daybook, the journal enables one to write down something about the experiences of a day which for a great variety of reasons may have been especially memorable or impressive. The journal entry may be merely a few words to call to mind a thing done, a person seen, a menu enjoyed at a dinner party. It may be concerned at length with a political crisis in the community, or a personal crisis in the home. It may even be as noble as it was with some pious people in the past who used the journal to keep a record of their consciences, a periodic reckoning of their moral and spiritual accounts. In its most public aspect, the idea of a journal calls to mind the newspaper or the record of proceedings like the U.S. *Congressional Record* and the Canadian *Hansard*. In its most closely private form, the journal becomes the diary.

For the person keeping a journal, whatever he experiences and wants to hold he can write down. But to get it down on paper begins another adventure. For he has to focus on what he has experienced, and to be able to say what, in fact, the experience is. What of it is new? What of it is remarkable because of associations in the memory it stirs up? Is this like anything I—or others—have experienced before? Is it a good or a bad thing to have happened? And why, specifically? The questions multiply themselves quickly, and as the journalist seeks to answer the appropriate ones, he begins to know what it is he contemplates. As one tries to find the words that best represent this discovery, the experience becomes even more clear in its shape and meaning. We can imagine Emerson going to the ballet, being absorbed in the spectacle, thinking casually of this or that association the dancer and the movements suggest. When he writes about the experience in his journal, a good many questions, judgments, and speculations get tied up with the spectacle, and it is this complex of event and his total relation to it that becomes the experience he records. The simple facts of time, place, people, and actions drop down into one's consciousness and set in motion ideas and feelings which give those facts their real meaning to oneself.

Once this consciousness of events is formulated in words, the journal-keeper has it, not only in the sense of understanding what has been seen or felt or thought, but also in the sense of having it there before him to contemplate long after the event itself. When we read a carefully kept journal covering a long period and varied experiences, we have the pleasure of a small world re-created for us in the consciousness of one who experienced it. Even more, we feel the continuity, the wholeness, of the writer. Something of the same feeling is there for the person who kept the journal: a whole world of events preserved in the form of their experienced reality, and with it the persistent self in the midst of that world. That world and that self are always accessible on the page, and ultimately, therefore, usably real.

Beyond the value of the journal as record, there is the instructive value of the habit of mind and hand journal keeping can assure. One begins to attend more carefully to what happens to and around oneself. One learns the resources of language as a means of representing what one sees, and gains skill and certainty in doing justice to experience and to one's own consciousness. And the journal represents a discipline. It brings together an individual and a complex environment in a relation that teaches the individual something of himself or herself, something of the world, and something of the meaning of their relation. There is scarcely a moment in a person's life when he is not poised for the lesson. When it comes with the promise of special force, there is the almost irresistible temptation to catch the impulse, give it form, make it permanent, assert its meaning. And so one commits oneself to language. To have given up one's experience to words is to have begun marking out the limits and potential of its meaning. In the journal that meaning is developed and clarified to oneself primarily. When the whole intention of the development and the clarification is the consideration of another reader, the method of the journal redirects itself to become that of the essay.

Arthur Eastman's comments should give you a good idea of why we encourage you to keep a journal. Before you actually begin, your instructor may provide more specific details regarding these aspects of journal writing:

- ☐ The length of entries
- ☐ The frequency of entries
- ☐ The type of notebook or writing materials to use
- ☐ The manner in which your journal may be reviewed or checked or graded
- ☐ Any additional suggestions or guidelines or requirements

Choose a time, a place, and a process that will assure your writing regularly and often, and that will make journal writing more enjoyment than drudgery. But even when it does seem like hard work and your writing sounds stupid and deadly dull to you, keep at it. Some of the entries you will eventually like best and find most valuable will be among those that seemed like dreary, drab dronings at the time. And with writing, as with anything else, there is value in making yourself perform when you do not want to.

More often than not, though, you will probably enjoy your written dialogue with yourself, your "thinking aloud on paper." Before long, you should begin to experience, in Eastman's words, "the instructive value of the habit of mind and hand journal keeping can assure." You will perceive and appreciate how your journal "brings together an individual and a complex environment in a relation that teaches the individual something of himself or herself, something of the world, and something of the meaning of their relation." In the future, you will also discover "the value of the journal as record."

Summary and Review

At the conclusion of each chapter there is a Summary and Review section that highlights primary points and activities. In this chapter, those points and activities have included a discussion of the purposes, audience, and organization of the book; a few "literacy level" reading and writing exercises; the beginning of a semester-long personal portfolio of your writing; and, ideally, the beginning of a journal.

By way of looking backward and forward, this chapter concludes with an essay on student writing by a college English teacher.

Toby Fulwiler (born 1942)

Freshman Writing: It's the Best Course in the University to Teach

Some English teachers believe that teaching freshman English is the worst chore in the university. So bad, in fact, that only part-timers and graduate students should have to do it. Or so bad that everyone on the faculty should share The English Teacher's Burden. But there's another way of looking at it.

An English teacher myself, I've always considered teaching writing to be among the very best jobs in the university—best, that is, if you value teaching small classes where your primary business is helping students learn to think imaginatively, reason critically, and express themselves clearly, and where it matters who your students are, where they come from, and what they believe.

Many 18-year-olds arrive at college unprepared for the academic community, where they will be expected to reason dispassionately and autonomously about a wide range of ideas. Instead, they expect 13th grade, where they will be told once again what to do. I'm not quite sure where their misconception comes from, but I have my suspicions. This past fall, for instance, as my freshmen talked with me about writing, they told me a lot about how they viewed learning, as well.

• They described their own writing ability in clear, correct, coherent sentences that began with the words "I can't write because . . ." Why do they believe that writing is a skill they cannot master?

• They asked me to teach them about "thesis statements" and "topic sentences." When I asked them what those were, they taught me. Where did they learn that English classes are an endless series of repetitions?

• Early in the term, they told me that they had nothing important to say about their schools, jobs, families, friends, experiences, ideas, lives; later, they wrote pages about those same subjects. Why did they come to college believing they had nothing to say?

• When I asked them to define good writing, they wrote that it was detailed, focused, supported, and aimed well at an audience; they told me all that in writing that was general, unfocused, unsupported, and aimed at no audience at all. Why did they not practice what they preached?

• They came to my class after being schooled for 12 years, yet they had never learned to write for one another; to read their own writing to others; to listen seriously to what their classmates wrote; to give and receive positive criticism. Who or what taught them that learning is a one-way street?

Freshmen arrive at college with a badly distorted view of writing because they have seldom written anything that mattered to them. Instead, in the name of writing, they have been asked to memorize spelling lists; to fill in blanks in vocabulary workbooks; to compose fragments of thought into practice sentences; to write in arbitrary formats, such as five-paragraph themes. They have been drilled in those activities in spite of research by such scholars as James Britton at the University of London, Janet Emig at Rutgers University, and Donald Graves at the University of New Hampshire, indicating that students, from the first grade through college, learn to write best when they write and rewrite whole compositions on subjects they care about, for audiences who take them seriously.

Freshmen arrive at college believing writing has more to do with correctness than with communication, with prescription than with imagination, with drill than with critical thought. They believe that writing serves the teacher, not themselves. And they certainly do not believe that the act of writing is either creative or fun. Unfortunately, they expect yet another round of the debilitating criticism that has sapped their confidence and taught them that they have nothing to say. After 18 years of teaching college writing, I've come to believe that American schools do more to discourage serious writing (and learning) than to encourage it.

First-year college students show up in class behaving just like first-year college students. Their writing is not only full of faulty spelling, clumsy grammar, and careless diction; it is also full of sloppy reasoning, unsupported assertions, and weak logic. Those who lament that freshmen write and think like freshmen consider such a course a burden. Those that see the first year of college as a starting point, and understand that all sophomores must be freshmen first, consider freshman English an opportunity.

If writing is the academic activity most likely to reveal faulty reasoning, and insufficient knowledge, then re-writing is the activity most likely to correct the inconsistencies and supply the knowledge. A good freshman writing course is essentially a re-reading and re-writing course.

Teaching writing is not the same as teaching subjects such as literature, history, or economics, and that difference is what causes most of the problems for teachers of first-year writing courses. Writing teachers cannot lean on a vast accumulation of bibliographic knowledge or even on last year's lecture notes. Instead, they need to study and understand their own writing process in order to help the students with theirs. The primary "texts" in their classroom will not be published textbooks, but rather the corpus of each student's own writing.

For writing classes to work, teachers must surrender some of the authority to which they are accustomed and pass it, along with the responsibility to use it well, to the students. Teachers must stop taking home their student writing to "correct" or "grade," and start taking it home to read and respond to. Of course, for this to be possible, the students' writing must become interesting to read.

And now we've come full circle. Writing becomes interesting to read only when it becomes interesting to write; and it becomes interesting to write only when the writer has a stake in his or her topic, thinks it's important, and believes someone else will think so, too. When that happens, as it often does, the transition from passive trainee to active learner occurs.

What is a freshman writing course actually like? My current class is fairly typical: I meet 22 students twice a week for 80 minutes. They bring drafts of writing to nearly every class, some of which I read and respond to, some of which they read and respond to among themselves, none of which is graded until the end of the term. In 15 weeks, I ask my freshmen to complete three or four pieces of writing, but for the first seven weeks they write and rewrite only one piece, a personal narrative.

I expect drafts written early in the term to be sketchy and superficial, as the writers try to find out what is expected of them. I tell them that I expect their narratives to recreate for the reader, as believably as possible, each writer's private experience. They are to recast general memories into articulated experience, refocus it, describe it, fill in relevant detail—show, rather than tell—and always answer the question, So what?

Each draft comes in clipped to the previous drafts; each time I read a draft I notice the changes from one to the next. I want revision to become a habit of mind, and so encourage major changes, additions, re-starts—all the time trying to react honestly to what I read. When drafts work right away, the students try out new angles, expand what's there, and work continually on their editing skills. When drafts are not working, I encourage the students to start again, and encourage them to try until something clicks. We pay serious attention to all the work that's written seri-ously. We use one another's writing—mine as well as theirs—to demonstrate what-ever lessons (about leads, titles, editing, for example) we need to learn.

During the second half of the course we study the relationship between personal experience and more objective, research-based academic writing. In the latter form, too, the problem is believability, but for objective writing the resources are external to the writer. Now they depend on libraries, interviews, and site visits to create credibility, whereas before they relied upon their own experience.

As students write and revise, they learn to shape and reshape meaning in both their personal and their academic lives. In the act of seemingly endless revision, usually without precedent in their secondary-school experience, students begin to transform their understanding of knowledge from something fixed and rigid to some-thing fluid and relative. By the end of the term, they have revised their way to new interpretations of their own experience. They have refocused and reshaped their research projects several times, making it difficult for them to continue to see things as black or white, right or wrong. ("No, what you say here isn't wrong—but what if you approached it this way next time?")

At the end of the term, the students hand in portfolios containing all their written work. They receive one grade on a combination of process (amount of serious revision and risk-taking) and product (completeness, neatness, correctness, and coherence of the final draft).

The opportunity in freshman English, then, is to help students learn to write in their own voices about a variety of issues for different audiences, and to help one another along the way. Not all of them succeed completely, of course, but they are well started. When they do succeed, they have become mature and independent writers. And they have become mature and independent thinkers, as well, members of the academic community at last.

Professor Fulwiler is describing his own courses and classes, his own university, his own approach, and his own attitudes. So, in a sense, he speaks only for himself. No two campuses are the same, no two classes are identical, and certainly no two college English teachers have quite the same perspective and philosophy. This book will differ in some respects from the course described by Fulwiler, and no doubt your instructor's teaching will differ at times from both the Fulwiler version and the one presented here.

But in another sense, Professor Fulwiler speaks not only for himself but also for us as textbook writers and for your instructor. He sets forth some basic tenets to which we all pledge allegiance, some fundamental goals toward which we all strive. Here are some of them to keep in mind:

- □ An instructor's "primary business is helping students learn to think imaginatively, reason critically, and express themselves clearly."
- □ You have a great deal to say that is important—about your "schools, jobs, families, friends, experiences, ideas, lives."
- □ Good writing is "detailed, focused, supported, and aimed well at an audience."
- □ In a writing course, you should learn "to write for one another; to read . . . [your] writing to others; to listen seriously to what . . . [your] classmates . . . [write]; to give and receive positive criticism."
- □ "A good freshman writing course is essentially a re-reading and re-writing course."
- □ "The primary 'texts' . . . [should be] the corpus of each student's own writing."
- □ "Writing becomes interesting to read only when it becomes interesting to write; and it becomes interesting to write only when the writer has a stake in his or her topic, thinks it's important, and believes someone else will think so, too."
- □ "As students write and revise, they learn to shape and reshape meaning in both their personal and their academic lives."

Keep these points in mind in Chapter 2, which contains selections and exercises designed "to shape and reshape" the meaning of your younger years.

2
Beginnings

"The Child is father of the Man"*

□ Writing and Speaking   □ Prose and Poetry   □ Purposes for Writing
□ Audience   □ Style   □ Process and Product   □ Introduction, Development,
Conclusion   □ Fiction and Nonfiction   □ Autobiography   □ Paragraph
Structure   □ Paragraph Transition   □ Planning, Drafting, and Revising
□ Literature: the Particular and the Universal

What are some of your clearest, keenest recollections from childhood? As you "go forth" in this chapter with Walt Whitman's child, you will recall some of your favorite childhood haunts and habits, some of your special places and special people.

Some Fundamentals about Your Writing

Writing and Speaking

Writing is a substitute for speaking. The letters of the alphabet you write represent sounds, and the arrangement and joining of those letters-representing-sounds results in words. Those words, in turn, symbolize any

*William Wordsworth, "My Heart Leaps Up" (in the Additional Readings for Chapter 1).

number of things: objects, ideas, persons, actions. In this sense, your writing is a symbolic arrangement of sounds. Effective writers are usually keenly aware of this close kinship of writing and speaking. They develop a good ear, a sound-sensitivity, for their own writing and the writing of others. They "listen" as they write. They also listen by reading aloud—both their own writings and the writings of others. Reading aloud and listening often aid both readers and writers in understanding, testing clarity of expression, following the development of ideas, and appreciating the music and flow of sounds. Listen to your words and thoughts as you write; listen to the words and thoughts of others as you read.

Prose and Poetry

This sound-symbolism called writing is always one of two general types: it is either *prose* or *poetry*. What differentiates one from the other is the form each takes on the page. Prose is written in *sentences* and *paragraphs*. Most of your everyday writing and reading will be in prose form.

If you write poetry, you usually also write sentences.
But the units of structure and organization
Are first the *line*, then the *stanza*.
Individual lines of poetry may be long
Or short,
And are grouped together to form a stanza.

Purpose and Audience

Whether writing prose or poetry, you should be aware of your *purpose*. Ask yourself, "Why am I writing this? What am I trying to do? What is the best way to convey my purpose to the reader?" The same questions should be asked in reading the writing of others: "What is Whitman trying to do in this poem? What is Thomas's purpose in his essay? How does he convey his purpose?" Sometimes, whether you are writer or reader, your answers to these questions will be simple, single-purpose ones. At other times the purpose may be more complex; it may actually be two, three, or more purposes. At various times in your writing, your purpose may be to record, to remember, to learn, to clarify, to discover, to describe, to entertain, to explain, to praise, to condemn, to create, to play, to narrate, to persuade, to evaluate, to reminisce, or any combination of these reasons, plus a great many others.

Whenever you write, then, you choose a form. You determine your purpose. And you adapt your writing to your *audience*, to those for whom the writing is intended. Writers usually determine in advance the audience they are addressing with a particular piece of writing. The newspaper columnist, the manager preparing a report, the student writing a research paper, the preacher writing a sermon, the banker writing a "payment overdue" letter, and the college administrator writing a memo all have a clear picture of the person or persons who will be reading (or hearing) and reacting to their work. They compose or create with this audience in mind. They adapt their writing to this individual or group in order to communicate most clearly and effectively. One of the basic questions to be answered when you write is "Who is my audience?"

Style

Whether you write prose or poetry, whatever your purpose, whoever your audience, you will demonstrate in your writing an individual *style*. A writer's style manifests itself in a variety of ways: through the form of writing chosen, the topic addressed, the ideas presented and developed, the organization, the voice or tone, the sentence or stanza structure, the word choice, the use of grammatical conventions. Your style of writing is as unique as your signature.

Through reading the selections in this book, you will discover how Robert Frost, Alice Walker, Carl Sagan, and other writers use the compositional tools and techniques of the English language to convey ideas and feelings in their individual styles. Through writing and analyzing your writing, you will discover the distinct traits of *your* writing style and work to improve and enrich that style.

Process and Product

Finally, with any writing there is the *process* and the *product*. The process is the cause, the means; the product is the effect, the end result. The process includes, among other things, selecting a form, determining purpose, and considering audience. It also includes organizing, writing, and revising. If freshman Kathy Staton is writing a note to leave in Professor Scott's mailbox explaining why she missed class yesterday, the writing process will be shorter and simpler than when she composes her term paper for the course. Even so, perhaps without really thinking about it, she will choose the form of a written note, will identify Dr. Scott as her audience, and will realize that her dual purpose is to explain her absence and persuade her instructor not to drop her from the course. As she writes, she will choose her words carefully so as to convey the appropriate apologetic tone. She will surely reread and may even rewrite her initial effort. Finally, when the process is complete, she will drop the product in her teacher's box.

The Child Goes Forth

Our first selection is by the nineteenth-century American writer Walt Whitman. Read it more than once, at least one time aloud, preferably to someone else.

Walt Whitman (1819–1892)

There Was a Child Went Forth

There was a child went forth every day,
And the first object he looked upon, that object he became,
And that object became part of him for the day or a certain part of the day,
Or for many years or stretching cycles of years.

The early lilacs became part of this child,   5
And grass and white and red morning-glories, and white and red clover, and the
    song of the phoebe-bird,
And the Third-month lambs and the sow's pink-faint litter, and the mare's foal
    and the cow's calf,
And the noisy brood of the barnyard or by the mire of the pond-side,
And the fish suspending themselves so curiously below there, and the beautiful
    curious liquid,
And the water-plants with their graceful flat heads, all became part of him.   10

The field-sprouts of Fourth-month and Fifth-month became part of him,
Winter-grain sprouts and those of the light-yellow corn, and the esculent roots
    of the garden,
And the apple-trees covered with blossoms and the fruit afterward, and wood-
    berries, and the commonest weeds by the road,
And the old drunkard staggering home from the outhouse of the tavern whence
    he had lately risen,
And the schoolmistress that passed on her way to the school,   15
And the friendly boys that passed, and the quarrelsome boys,
And the tidy and fresh-cheeked girls, and the barefoot negro boy and girl,
And all the changes of city and country wherever he went.

His own parents, he that had fathered him and she that had conceived him in her
    womb and birthed him,

They gave this child more of themselves than that,   20
They gave him afterward every day, they became part of him.

The mother at home quietly placing the dishes on the supper-table,
The mother with mild words, clean her cap and gown, a wholesome odor falling
    off her person and clothes as she walks by,
The father, strong, self-sufficient, manly, mean, angered, unjust,
The blow, the quick loud word, the tight bargain, the crafty lure,   25
The family usages, the language, the company, the furniture, the yearning and
    swelling heart,
Affection that will not be gainsayed, the sense of what is real, the thought if after
    all it should prove unreal,
The doubts of day-time and the doubts of night-time, the curious whether and
    how,
Whether that which appears so is so, or is it all flashes and specks?
Men and women crowding fast in the streets, if they are not flashes and specks
    what are they?   30
The streets themselves and the façades of houses, and goods in the windows,
Vehicles, teams, the heavy-planked wharves, the huge crossing at the ferries,
The village on the highland seen from afar at sunset, the river between,
Shadows, aureola and mist, the light falling on roofs and gables of white or brown
    two miles off,
The schooner near by sleepily dropping down the tide, the little boat slack-towed
    astern,   35
The hurrying tumbling waves, quick-broken crests, slapping,
The strata of colored clouds, the long bar of maroon-tint away solitary by itself,
    the spread of purity it lies motionless in,
The horizon's edge, the flying sea-crow, the fragrance of salt marsh and shore
    mud,
These became part of that child who went forth every day, and who now goes,
    and will always go forth every day.

□ WRITING ↔ READING ↔ THINKING ACTIVITIES □
Recalling Childhood Memories

1.   Assume that you are the child going forth in this poem; list some of your
    childhood memories or "objects" randomly as you remember them.
    Either list until you reach 25 items or until you have written for 15
    minutes. Before you pick up a pen to write, give yourself some time to
    recall memories from your younger years.

Here is part of a list of remembrances composed in response to this assignment:

- My anguish as a young child when my mother left me in the mornings to go to work
- My collie Lucky
- Shooting my brother Mike in the head with an arrow
- My asthma attacks
- The smell of my dad and mother when I crawled in bed with them
- My parents' squeaky bedsprings
- Smoking grapevine
- Eating canned dog food on a dare
- Trading comic books
- Crying uncontrollably and creating a minor crisis at school in Waco
- Our first TV
- My father's death
- Spitwad fights
- Killing a bird with a slingshot
- Ghost stories in the summer under the street lamp
- Sneaking and smoking cigarettes from Aunt Donna's and Uncle Greg's packages
- The empty feeling of despair every time we moved as a result of my dad's changing jobs
- Saturday movies at the Rosewin and Texas theatres in Oak Cliff
- Mashing my fingers while cleaning my BB gun

2. Once you have composed your list, look back at the sample list above. Each entry should suggest to you, as a reader, something of how the writer might flesh out the recollection if asked to.

- Shooting my brother Mike in the head with an arrow

(Here is a story to be narrated, with touches of explanation and description. You would expect the writer to answer some obvious questions: How old were you and Mike? What was the situation? Was it a real bow and arrow? Was the shooting accidental? How serious was it? What did Mike do? What did your *parents* do?)

- My collie Lucky

(Sounds like description, maybe involving narration of a special event or two involving the dog, maybe also involving explanation. Here are some questions you would probably expect the writer to answer if he developed his recollection into a paragraph or an essay: Did you acquire the dog as a newborn pup, or when he was older? What did he look like?

Did he have any special markings? Any special tricks or habits or quirks of behavior? Did you have any outstanding adventures, exploits, occurrences with Lucky? How long did you have him? How did he die?)

Here are two other entries from the list. For each, indicate what you would expect a fuller version to contain, and what questions you would expect the writer to answer:

- Crying uncontrollably and creating a minor crisis at school in Waco
- My father's death

3. Now pick two or three remembrances from your own list. For each, explain what details a reader would expect a fuller version to include.

Introduction, Development, and Conclusion

In Whitman's poem, his own long list of childhood recollections constitutes almost the entire work. There is the four-line introductory stanza. There are his listed memories of childhood. And there is the concluding line suggesting that his (and your) going forth is not only an action of the past, but of the present and the future as well: the child "went forth," "now goes," and "will always go forth every day." As a writer alert to the techniques of authors, especially as they may aid in improving your own writing, you can easily see how the poet is organizing and presenting his writing for his audience of readers:

☐ He introduces his topic and indicates his intent with a general statement.

☐ He develops his topic through specific examples.

☐ He concludes his comments with a general wrap-up statement.

☐ WRITING ↔ READING ↔ THINKING ACTIVITIES ☐
Looking Closely at ". . . A Child Went Forth"

What writing techniques or elements of style seem to characterize this poem?

☐ Do you see anything unusual about the length of Whitman's sentences?

☐ Is there any relationship between sentence structure and stanza structure?

☐ Is the vocabulary simple or complex, or a mixture of the two?

- □   What senses does the poet appeal to in his descriptions and listings? How specific and how effective are these appeals?
- □   Why do you think he begins most lines with either *the* or *and*?
- □   Is there any discernible effect in his listing pairs in the several lines beginning with line 14 (drunkard and schoolmistress, "friendly boys" and "quarrelsome boys," and so on)?
- □   Whitman usually writes in a poetic form called *free verse*. Taking this poem as an example of the form, can you construct a tentative definition of free verse?

Haunts and Habits

Walt Whitman was born on Long Island, and the "changes of city and country" which he records are those of the Brooklyn area in the early nineteenth century. The first of the following two prose selections is by another nineteenth-century American author, Mark Twain, whose real name was Samuel Clemens. Twain grew up in Hannibal, Missouri, on the banks of the Mississippi River. The second composition is by the Welsh poet Dylan Thomas. Thomas was born in Swansea, Wales, in 1914. Each of these writers records unique childhood experiences in different times and places. But their writing also reveals universal feelings and relationships which you will recognize from your own childhood.

Mark Twain (1835–1910)
The Boys' Ambition

When I was a boy, there was but one permanent ambition among my comrades in our village on the west bank of the Mississippi River. That was, to be a steamboatman. We had transient ambitions of other sorts, but they were only transient. When a circus came and went, it left us all burning to become clowns; the first negro minstrel show that ever came to our section left us all suffering to try that kind of life; now and then we had a hope that, if we lived and were good, God would permit us to be pirates. These ambitions faded out, each in its turn; but the ambition to be a steamboatman always remained.

Once a day a cheap, gaudy packet arrived upward from St. Louis, and another downward from Keokuk. Before these events, the day was glorious with expectancy; after them, the day was a dead and empty thing. Not only the boys, but the whole village, felt this. After all these years I can picture that old time to myself now, just as it was then: the white town drowsing in the sunshine of a summer's morning; the streets empty, or pretty nearly so; one or two clerks sitting in front of the Water Street stores, with their splint-bottomed chairs tilted back against the walls, chins on breasts, hats slouched over their faces, asleep—with shingle-shavings enough around to show what broke them down; a sow and a litter of pigs loafing along the sidewalk, doing a good business in watermelon rinds and seeds; two or three lonely little freight piles scattered about the "levee"; a pile of "skids" on the slope of the stone-paved wharf, and the fragrant town drunkard asleep in the shadow of them; two or three wood flats at the head of the wharf, but nobody to listen to the peaceful lapping of the wavelets against them; the great Mississippi, the majestic, the magnificent Mississippi, rolling its mile-wide tide along, shining in the sun; the dense forest away on the other side; the "point" above the town, and the "point" below, bounding the river-glimpse and turning it into a sort of sea, and withal a very still and brilliant and lonely one. Presently a film of dark smoke appears above one of those remote "points"; instantly a negro drayman, famous for his quick eye and prodigious voice, lifts up the cry, "S-t-e-a-m-boat a-comin'!" and the scene changes! The town drunkard stirs, the clerks wake up, a furious clatter of drays follows, every house and store pours out a human contribution, and all in a twinkling the dead town is alive and moving. Drays, carts, men, boys, all go hurrying from many quarters to a common center, the wharf. Assembled there, the people fasten their eyes upon the coming boat as upon a wonder they are seeing for the first time. And the boat *is* rather a handsome sight, too. She is long and sharp and trim and pretty; she has two tall, fancy-topped chimneys, with a gilded device of some kind swung between them; a fanciful pilot-house, all glass and "gingerbread," perched on top of the "texas" deck behind them; the paddle-boxes are gorgeous with a picture or with gilded rays above the boat's name; the boiler-deck, the hurricane-deck, and the texas deck are fenced and ornamented with clean white railings; there is a flag gallantly flying from the jack-staff; the furnace doors are open and the fires glaring bravely; the upper decks are black with passengers; the captain stands by the big bell, calm, imposing, the envy of all; great volumes of the blackest smoke are rolling and tumbling out of the chimneys—a husbanded grandeur created with a bit of pitch-pine just before arriving at a town; the crew are grouped on the forecastle; the broad stage is run far out over the port bow, and an envied deck-hand stands picturesquely on the end of it with a coil of rope in his hand; the pent steam is screaming through the gauge-cocks; the captain lifts his hand, a bell rings, the wheels stop; then they turn back, churning the water to foam, and the steamer is at rest. Then such a scramble as there is to get aboard, and to get ashore, and to take in freight and to discharge freight, all at one and the same time; and such a yelling and cursing as the mates facilitate it all with! Ten minutes later the steamer is under way again, with no flag on the jack-staff and no black smoke issuing from the chimneys. After ten more minutes the town is dead again, and the town drunkard asleep by the skids once more.

My father was a justice of the peace, and I supposed he possessed the power of life and death over all men, and could hang anybody that offended him. This was distinction enough for me as a general thing; but the desire to be a steamboatman kept intruding, nevertheless. I first wanted to be a cabin-boy, so that I could come out with a white apron on and shake a table-cloth over the side, where all my old comrades could see me; later I thought I would rather be the deck-hand who stood on the end of the stage-plank with the coil of rope in his hand, because he was particularly conspicuous. But these were only day-dreams—they were too heavenly to be contemplated as real possibilities. By and by one of our boys went away. He was not heard of for a long time. At last he turned up as apprentice engineer or "striker" on a steamboat. This thing shook the bottom out of all my Sunday-school teachings. That boy had been notoriously worldly, and I just the reverse; yet he was exalted to this eminence, and I left in obscurity and misery. There was nothing generous about this fellow in his greatness. He would always manage to have a rusty bolt to scrub while his boat tarried at our town, and would sit on the inside guard and scrub it, where we all could see him and envy him and loathe him. And whenever his boat was laid up he would come home and swell around the town in his blackest and greasiest clothes, so that nobody could help remembering that he was a steamboat-man; and he used all sorts of steamboat technicalities in his talk, as if he were so used to them that he forgot common people could not understand them. He would speak of the "labboard" side of a horse in an easy, natural way that would make one wish he was dead. And he was always talking about "St. Looy" like an old citizen; he would refer casually to occasions when he was "coming down Fourth Street," or when he was "passing by the Planter's House," or when there was a fire and he took a turn on the brakes of "the old Big Missouri"; and then he would go on and lie about how many towns the size of ours were burned down there that day. Two or three of the boys had long been persons of consideration among us because they had been to St. Louis once and had a vague general knowledge of its wonders, but the day of their glory was over now. They lapsed into a humble silence, and learned to disappear when the ruthless "cub"-engineer approached. This fellow had money, too, and hair-oil. Also an ignorant silver watch and a showy brass watch-chain. He wore a leather belt and used no suspenders. If ever a youth was cordially admired and hated by his comrades, this one was. No girl could withstand his charms. He "cut out" every boy in the village. When his boat blew up at last, it diffused a tranquil contentment among us such as we had not known for months. But when he came home the next week, alive, renowned, and appeared in church all battered up and bandaged, a shining hero, stared at and wondered over by everybody, it seemed to us that the partiality of Providence for an undeserving reptile had reached a point where it was open to criticism.

This creature's career could produce but one result, and it speedily followed. Boy after boy managed to get on the river. The minister's son became an engineer. The doctor's and the postmaster's sons became "mud clerks"; the wholesale liquor dealer's son became a barkeeper on a boat; four sons of the chief merchant, and two sons of the county judge, became pilots. Pilot was the grandest position of all. The pilot, even in those days of trivial wages, had a princely salary—from a hundred and fifty to two hundred and fifty dollars a month, and no board to pay. Two months of his wages would pay a preacher's salary for a year. Now some of us were left disconsolate. We could not get on the river—at least our parents would not let us.

So, by and by, I ran away. I said I would never come home again till I was a pilot and could come in glory. But somehow I could not manage it. I went meekly aboard a few of the boats that lay packed together like sardines at the long St. Louis wharf, and humbly inquired for the pilots, but got only a cold shoulder and short words from mates and clerks. I had to make the best of this sort of treatment for the time being, but I had comforting day-dreams of a future when I should be a great and honored pilot, with plenty of money, and could kill some of these mates and clerks and pay for them.

Dylan Thomas (1914–1953)
Reminiscences of Childhood

I like very much people telling me about their childhood, but they'll have to be quick or else I'll be telling them about mine.

I was born in a large Welsh town at the beginning of the Great War—an ugly, lovely town (or so it was and is to me), crawling, sprawling by a long and splendid curving shore where truant boys and sandfield boys and old men from nowhere, beachcombed, idled and paddled, watched the dock-bound ships or the ships steaming away into wonder and India, magic and China, countries bright with oranges and loud with lions; threw stones into the sea for the barking outcast dogs; made castles and forts and harbours and race tracks in the sand; and on Saturday summer afternoons listened to the brass band, watched the Punch and Judy, or hung about on the fringes of the crowd to hear the fierce religious speakers who shouted at the sea, as though it were wicked and wrong to roll in and out like that, white-horsed and full of fishes.

One man, I remember, used to take off his hat and set fire to his hair every now and then, but I do not remember what it proved, if it proved anything at all, except that he was a very interesting man.

This sea-town was my world; outside a strange Wales, coal-pitted, mountained, river-run, full, so far as I knew, of choirs and football teams and sheep and storybook tall hats and red flannel petticoats, moved about its business which was none of mine.

Beyond that unknown Wales with its wild names like peals of bells in the darkness, and its mountain men clothed in the skins of animals perhaps and always singing, lay England which was London and the country called the Front, from which many of our neighbours never came back. It was a country to which only young men travelled.

At the beginning, the only "front" I knew was the little lobby before our front door. I could not understand how so many people never returned from there, but later I grew to know more, though still without understanding, and carried a wooden rifle in the park and shot down the invisible unknown enemy like a flock of wild birds. And the park itself was a world within the world of the sea-town. Quite near where I lived, so near that on summer evenings I could listen in my bed to the voices of older children playing ball on the sloping paper-littered bank, the park was full of terrors and treasures. Though it was only a little park, it held within its borders of old tall trees, notched with our names and shabby from our climbing, as many secret places, caverns and forests, prairies and deserts, as a country somewhere at the end of the sea.

And though we would explore it one day, armed and desperate, from end to end, from the robbers' den to the pirates' cabin, the highwayman's inn to the cattle ranch, or the hidden room in the undergrowth, where we held beetle races, and lit the wood fires and roasted potatoes and talked about Africa, and the makes of motor cars, yet still the next day, it remained as unexplored as the Poles—a country just born and always changing.

There were many secret societies but you could belong only to one; and in blood or red ink, and a rusty pocketknife, with, of course, an instrument to remove stones from horses' feet, you signed your name at the foot of a terrible document, swore death to all the other societies, crossed your heart that you would divulge no secret and that if you did, you would consent to torture by slow fire, and undertook to carry out by yourself a feat of either daring or endurance. You could take your choice: would you climb to the top of the tallest and most dangerous tree, and from there hurl stones and insults at grown-up passers-by, especially postmen, or any other men in uniform? Or would you ring every doorbell in the terrace, not forgetting the doorbell of the man with the red face who kept dogs and ran fast? Or would you swim in the reservoir, which was forbidden and had angry swans, or would you eat a whole old jam jar full of mud?

There were many more alternatives. I chose one of endurance and for half an hour, it may have been longer or shorter, held up off the ground a very heavy broken pram we had found in a bush. I thought my back would break and the half hour felt like a day, but I preferred it to braving the red face and the dogs, or to swallowing tadpoles.

We knew every inhabitant of the park, every regular visitor, every nursemaid, every gardener, every old man. We knew the hour when the alarming retired policeman came in to look at the dahlias and the hour when the old lady arrived in the Bath chair with six Pekinese, and a pale girl to read aloud to her. I think she read the newspaper, but we always said she read the *Wizard*. The face of the old man who sat summer and winter on the bench looking over the reservoir, I can see clearly now and I wrote a poem long long after I'd left the park and the seatown called:

The Hunchback in the Park

The hunchback in the park
A solitary mister
Propped between trees and water
From the opening of the garden lock
That lets the trees and water enter
Until the Sunday sombre ball at dark

Eating bread from a newspaper
Drinking water from the chained cup
That the children filled with gravel
In the fountain basin where I sailed my ship
Slept at night in a dog kennel
But nobody chained him up.

Like the park birds he came early
Like the water he sat down
And Mister they called Hey mister
The truant boys from the town
Running when he had heard them clearly
On out of sound

Past lake and rockery
Laughing when he shook his paper
Hunchbacked in mockery
Through the loud zoo of the willow groves
Dodging the park-keeper
With his stick that picked up leaves.

And the old dog sleeper
Alone between nurses and swans
While the boys among willows
Made the tigers jump out of their eyes
To roar on the rockery stones
And the groves were blue with sailors

> Made all day until bell-time
> A woman figure without fault
> Straight as a young elm
> Straight and tall from his crooked bones
> That she might stand in the night
> After the locks and the chains
>
> All night in the unmade park
> After the railings and shrubberies
> The birds the grass the trees and the lake
> And the wild boys innocent as strawberries
> Had followed the hunchback
> To his kennel in the dark.

And that park grew up with me; that small world widened as I learned its secrets and boundaries, as I discovered new refuges and ambushes in its woods and jungles; hidden homes and lairs for the multitudes of imagination, for cowboys and Indians, and the tall terrible half-people who rode on nightmares through my bedroom. But it was not the only world—that world of rockery, gravel path, playbank, bowling green, bandstands, reservoir, dahlia garden, where an ancient keeper, known as Smoky, was the whiskered snake in the grass one must keep off. There was another world where with my friends I used to dawdle on half holidays along the bent and Devon-facing sea-shore, hoping for gold watches or the skull of a sheep or a message in a bottle to be washed up with the tide; and another where we used to wander whistling through the packed streets, stale as station sandwiches, round the impressive gas-works and the slaughter house, past by the blackened monuments and the museum that should have been in a museum. Or we scratched at a kind of cricket on the bald and cindery surface of the recreation ground, or we took a tram that shook like an iron jelly down to the gaunt pier, there to clamber under the pier, hanging perilously on to its skeleton legs or to run along to the end where patient men with the seaward eyes of the dockside unemployed capped and mufflered, dangling from their mouths pipes that had long gone out, angled over the edge for unpleasant tasting fish.

Never was there such a town as ours, I thought, as we fought on the sandhills with rough boys or dared each other to climb up the scaffolding of half-built houses soon to be called Laburnum Beaches. Never was there such a town, I thought, for the smell of fish and chips on Saturday evenings; for the Saturday afternoon cinema matinees where we shouted and hissed our threepences away; for the crowds in the streets with leeks in their hats on international nights; for the park, the inexhaustible and mysterious, bushy red-Indian hiding park where the hunchback sat alone and the groves were blue with sailors. The memories of childhood have no order, and so I remember that never was there such a dame school as ours, so firm and kind and smelling of galoshes, with the sweet and fumbled music of the piano lessons drifting down from upstairs to the lonely schoolroom, where only the sometimes tearful wicked sat over undone sums, or to repeat a little crime—the pulling of a girl's hair during geography, the sly shin kick under the table during English literature. Behind the school was a narrow lane where only the oldest and boldest threw pebbles at windows, scuffled and boasted, fibbed about their relations—

"My father's got a chauffeur."

"What's he want a chauffeur for? He hasn't got a car."

"My father's the richest man in the town."

"My father's the richest man in Wales."

"My father owns the world."

And swapped gob-stoppers for slings, old knives for marbles, kite strings for foreign stamps.

The lane was always the place to tell your secrets; if you did not have any, you invented them. Occasionally now I dream that I am turning out of school into the lane of confidences when I say to the boys of my class, "At last, I have a real secret."

"What is it—what is it?"

"I can fly."

And when they do not believe me, I flap my arms and slowly leave the ground only a few inches at first, then gaining air until I fly waving my cap level with the upper windows of the school, peering in until the mistress at the piano screams and the metronome falls to the ground and stops, and there is no more time.

And I fly over the trees and chimneys of my town, over the dockyards skimming the masts and tunnels, over Inkerman Street, Sebastopol Street, and the street where all the women wear men's caps, over the trees of the everlasting park, where a brass band shakes the leaves and sends them showering down on to the nurses and the children, the cripples and the idlers, and the gardeners, and the shouting boys: over the yellow seashore, and the stone-chasing dogs, and the old men, and the singing sea.

The memories of childhood have no order, and no end.

□ WRITING ↔ READING ↔ THINKING ACTIVITIES □
Comparing Writers' Recollections

1. Whitman recalls an "old drunkard staggering home" in line 14. Twain refers to a "fragrant town drunkard" near the beginning of the second paragraph. And Thomas was so struck by the "solitary mister," the "hunchback in the park," that he later wrote a poem about him. Was there in your childhood any such noteworthy, alienated person; any person whom you and others taunted? If so, jot down as many facts and feelings about him or her as you can easily remember. What are your adult feelings or thoughts now about the individual?

2. Thomas begins paragraph 12 expressing a feeling of fondness and pride that surely Whitman and Twain and all of us have felt: "Never was there such a town as ours." He begins the next sentence by repeating the same claim—"Never was there such a town, I thought"—and then listing several specific details to support that claim. (Writers must be sensitive to the reader's predictable response of "Prove it" or "Show me" or "Convince me." Specific details help to answer such questions, to support the writer's claims.) In that paragraph he structures his sentence this way: an opening claim of uniqueness is followed by a list of proofs, each introduced by *for* and separated by semicolons.

   Using that same introductory statement and structure, list in one sentence some details about *your* town or neighborhood that you especially remember. Here is the skeleton of your sentence: "Never was there such a town [or neighborhood], I thought, for the . . . ; for . . . ; for . . ." and so on.

3. In that same paragraph Thomas repeats the basic pattern, this time without using *for* and semicolons. He claims special status for his school, then lists specific details, anticipating the reader's reaction of "*How* was it special?" or "What made it so special?": "I remember that never was there such a dame school as ours, so firm and kind and smelling of galoshes, with the sweet and fumbled music of the piano lessons drifting down from upstairs to the lonely schoolroom," and so on. Using Thomas's sentence structure, complete your own sentence about a school you attended as a child—what sights, sounds, smells, people, and events stand out most vividly in your mind? Here is one student's recollections:

   > There never was a school like Westcliff Elementary for Miss Austin's perfect circles and push-pulls during handwriting exercise (she could do them flawlessly on the board with chalk and on paper with her Esterbrook pen); for the stolen moments in the cloak room with Carolyn Ann Brown ("True or False?"); for the stomach-turning, permeating smell of lunchroom soup and duplicating fluid; for the woman principal; for the constant clicking in the workroom of the duplicating machine (boy, would I hate to be named A. B. Dick!); for notes given to and received from Carolyn Ann Brown; for the Farrington Field Relays (we all ran barefoot); for the spelling bee competition with the sixth-grade girl ("sandal" was the word she finally missed); for the private, grown-up talks with Miss Willie C. Austin, that most wise, warm, and wonderful of teachers.

4. There was also in Thomas's childhood a park "full of terrors and treasures," a park that he says "grew up with me." Was there in your own early life such a place of wonder, mystery, and fun—a park, an open field, a wooded area, a barn, a playground? If you had such a special

place, write down as many things as you can recall about it. "Prove" to your reader how and why it was special to you.

As Dylan Thomas poignantly observes, "The memories of childhood have no end," so you could probably reminisce and write on and on about special memories of early years, flitting from one time and place and memory to another.

Recollections: Autobiography and the Autobiographical

Thomas's essay, Twain's chapter from *Life on the Mississippi*, and the writings you have been composing in this chapter are all examples of prose. All prose can be further classified as either *fiction* or *nonfiction*. Fiction prose is imagined, created, or "made-up." Examples are novels and short stories. Nonfiction prose is "real," based on fact or occurrence. Newspaper articles, works of history, psychology, philosophy, personal journals, essays, textbooks, biographies, and autobiographies are some examples of nonfiction.

An *autobiography* (literally "written self-life") is a nonfiction prose account of a person's life or portion of that life written by the individual himself or herself. (If someone else writes the account, it is *biography*.) Since Thomas writes of his own childhood in Wales, Twain of his childhood in Hannibal, and you of your own childhood locale, all these compositions are nonfiction prose, *autobiographical* writings.

But "autobiographical" can refer not only to actual autobiographies, but also to any work of prose or poetry which includes experiences, events, people, or places drawn from the writer's life. Whitman's poem, then, is also "autobiographical," meaning that he writes into his poem experiences and recollections from his own childhood—although his purpose is not to provide an actual account of his life.

☐ WRITING ↔ READING ↔ THINKING ACTIVITIES ☐
Comparing Writers' Recollections

1. The introduction–development–conclusion (or beginning–middle–end) structure of Whitman's poem is the basic organizational principle of almost all writing. In either Twain's or Thomas's essay, can you identify those three structural sections?
2. All three writers recall the streets of their towns or villages. Whitman refers to "the streets themselves and the façades of houses, and goods in the windows, / Vehicles, teams." Twain describes the streets of his home town before, during, and after the arrival of the steamboat. And Thomas

remembers both the "packed streets, stale as station sandwiches" and the "lane of confidences." Usually, the more specific the descriptive details, the better the writing. Using this criterion, determine which of the three writers does the best job of describing the streets of his town.

3.   Is it fair to the writers to judge their effectiveness in this way? Does it make any difference that Whitman is writing poetry while the other two are writing prose? Can the differences in the way each uses description be accounted for by differences in purpose? In style?

If you were to read more of the writings of Whitman, Twain, and Thomas, you could learn to distinguish easily among them even if the authors were not identified. But how? On what basis? If the selection is in free verse, is it by Whitman? If it consists of one-sentence paragraphs, is it by Thomas? What would characterize Twain's style—the Mississippi River subject matter? His droll humorous touches like "Now and then we had a hope that, if we lived and were good, God would permit us to be pirates"? Or is it his word choice, his sentence structure, or a combination of all of these traits as well as others?

Mothers and Fathers

The central relationship during one's early years is usually that of a child and parent. Of the writings studied so far in this chapter, only Whitman's poem mentions mother or father at any length.

The mother at home quietly placing the dishes on the supper-table,
The mother with mild words, clean her cap and gown, a wholesome odor falling
   off her person and clothes as she walks by,
The father, strong, self-sufficient, manly, mean, angered, unjust,
The blow, the quick loud word, the tight bargain, the crafty lure, . . .

These descriptions primarily *contrast*, or highlight differences between, the two parents; they also suggest Whitman's relationship and dealings with each—especially with the father.

□ WRITING ↔ READING ↔ THINKING ACTIVITIES □
Remembering Parents

How about your relationship with your own mother and father? Here are a few questions to prompt recollection of descriptive details (in the manner of Whitman) and scenes of interaction involving you and one or both parents. If you were reared by a single parent, or by a guardian, make the questions and answers fit your situation.

1. Can you cite a funny incident involving you and one (or both) of your parents?
2. Do you recall a sad or painful incident?
3. Did you ever have the feeling that one (or both) of your parents was ashamed of you or embarrassed by you? What was the situation?
4. As the other side of that coin, do you ever recall being ashamed of or embarrassed by your parents? When and why?
5. What was the angriest you can recall being at one of your parents?
6. List five adjectives or phrases describing your mother; describing your father. Do the two descriptions compare or contrast?
7. What traits listed in the question above do you think you have inherited from each parent? What characteristic of each parent would you *most* like to possess? *Least* like to possess?
8. Can you recall a time when you felt particularly close to your parents?
9. When were you particularly alienated from one or both of them?
10. If you lost one or both parents by death when you were a child, what do you remember thinking and feeling at the time? What details of the event do you most clearly recall?
11. If your parents divorced when you were young, what were your feelings toward each at the time? What are your feelings now?
12. What did your mother and father look like when you were young? Write a brief physical description of each.
13. Can you write a brief personality sketch of one or both of your parents?
14. Do you recall any occasion when one of your parents was particularly distraught? What was the cause?

Emerging from answers to these questions should be a distinct recollection of your relationship with your mother and father. Here is one more question to consider while reading the following selection: how do the parental specifics of your own childhood compare or contrast with this psychological explanation by Erich Fromm of the mother–child and father–child relationship?

Erich Fromm (1900–1980)

Love Between Parent and Child

The infant, at the moment of birth, would feel the fear of dying, if a gracious fate did not preserve it from any awareness of the anxiety involved in the separation from mother, and from intra-uterine existence. Even after being born, the infant is hardly different from what it was before birth; it cannot recognize objects, it is not yet aware of itself, and of the world as being outside of itself. It only feels the positive stimulation of warmth and food, and it does not yet differentiate warmth and food from its source: mother. Mother *is* warmth, mother *is* food, mother *is* the euphoric state of satisfaction and security. This state is one of narcissism, to use Freud's term. The outside reality, persons and things, have meaning only in terms of their satisfying or frustrating the inner state of the body. Real is only what is within; what is outside is real only in terms of my needs—never in terms of its own qualities or needs.

When the child grows and develops, he becomes capable of perceiving things as they are; the satisfaction in being fed becomes differentiated from the nipple, the breast from the mother. Eventually the child experiences his thirst, the satisfying milk, the breast and the mother, as different entities. He learns to perceive many other things as being different, as having an existence of their own. At this point he learns to give them names. At the same time he learns to handle them; learns that fire is hot and painful, that mother's body is warm and pleasureful, that wood is hard and heavy, that paper is light and can be torn. He learns how to handle people; that mother will smile when I eat; that she will take me in her arms when I cry; that she will praise me when I have a bowel movement. All these experiences become crystallized and integrated in the experience: *I am loved.* I am loved because I am mother's child. I am loved because I am helpless. I am loved because I am beautiful, admirable. I am loved because mother needs me. To put it in a more general formula: *I am loved for what I am,* or perhaps more accurately, *I am loved because I am.* This experience of being loved by mother is a passive one. There is nothing I have to do in order to be loved—mother's love is unconditional. All I have to do is *to be*—to be her child. Mother's love is bliss, is peace, it need not be acquired, it need not be deserved. But there is a negative side, too, to the unconditional quality of mother's love. Not only does it not need to be deserved—it also *cannot* be acquired, produced, controlled. If it is there, it is like a blessing; if it is not there, it is as if all beauty had gone out of life—and there is nothing I can do to create it.

For most children before the age from eight and a half to ten, the problem is almost exclusively that of *being loved*—of being loved for what one is. The child up to this age does not yet love; he responds gratefully, joyfully to being loved. At this point of the child's development a new factor enters into the picture: that of a new feeling of producing love by one's own activity. For the first time, the child thinks of *giving* something to mother (or to father), of producing something—a poem, a drawing, or whatever it may be. For the first time in the child's life the idea of love is transformed from being loved into loving; into creating love. It takes many years from this first beginning to the maturing of love. Eventually the child, who may now be an adolescent, has overcome his egocentricity; the other person is not any more primarily a means to the satisfaction of his own needs. The needs of the other person are as important as his own—in fact, they have become more important. To give has become more satisfactory, more joyous, than to receive; to love, more important even than being loved. By loving, he has left the prison cell of aloneness and isolation which was constituted by the state of narcissism and self-centeredness. He feels a sense of new union, of sharing, of oneness. More than that, he feels the potency of producing love by loving—rather than the dependence of receiving by being loved—and for that reason having to be small, helpless, sick—or "good." Infantile love follows the principle: *"I love because I am loved."* Mature love follows the principle: *"I am loved because I love."* Immature love says: *"I love you because I need you."* Mature love says: *"I need you because I love you."*

Closely related to the development of the *capacity* of love is the development of the *object* of love. The first months and years of the child are those where his closest attachment is to the mother. This attachment begins before the moment of birth, when mother and child are still one, although they are two. Birth changes the situation in some respects, but not as much as it would appear. The child, while now living outside of the womb, is still completely dependent on mother. But daily he becomes more independent: he learns to walk, to talk, to explore the world on his own; the relationship to mother loses some of its vital significance, and instead the relationship to father becomes more and more important.

In order to understand this shift from mother to father, we must consider the essential differences in quality between motherly and fatherly love. We have already spoken about motherly love. Motherly love by its very nature is unconditional. Mother loves the newborn infant because it is her child, not because the child has fulfilled any specific condition, or lived up to any specific expectation. (Of course, when I speak here of mother's and father's love, I speak of the "ideal types"—in Max Weber's sense or of an archetype in Jung's sense—and do not imply that every mother and father loves in that way. I refer to the fatherly and motherly principle, which is represented in the motherly and fatherly person.) Unconditional love corresponds to one of the deepest longings, not only of the child, but of every human being; on the other hand, to be loved because of one's merit, because one deserves it, always leaves doubt; maybe I did not please the person whom I want to love me, maybe this, or that—there is always a fear that love could disappear. Furthermore, "deserved" love easily leaves a bitter feeling that one is not loved for oneself, that one is loved *only* because one pleases, that one is, in the last analysis, not loved at all but used. No wonder that we all cling to the longing for motherly love, as children and also as adults. Most children are lucky enough to receive motherly love (to what extent will be discussed later). As adults the same longing is much more difficult to fulfill. In the most satisfactory development it remains a component of normal erotic love; often it finds expression in religious forms, more often in neurotic forms.

The relationship to father is quite different. Mother is the home we come from, she is nature, soil, the ocean; father does not represent any such natural home. He has little connection with the child in the first years of its life, and his importance for the child in this early period cannot be compared with that of mother. But while father does not represent the natural world, he represents the other pole of human existence; the world of thought, of man-made things, of law and order, of discipline, of travel and adventure. Father is the one who teaches the child, who shows him the road into the world.

Closely related to this function is one which is connected with socio-economic development. When private property came into existence, and when private property could be inherited by one of the sons, father began to look for that son to whom he could leave his property. Naturally, that was the one whom father thought best fitted to become his successor, the son who was most like him, and consequently whom he liked the most. Fatherly love is conditional love. Its principle is "I love you *because* you fulfill my expectations, because you do your duty, because you are like me." In conditional fatherly love we find, as with unconditional motherly love, a negative and a positive aspect. The negative aspect is the very fact that fatherly love has to be deserved, that it can be lost if one does not do what is expected. In the nature of fatherly love lies the fact that obedience becomes the main virtue, that disobedience is the main sin—and its punishment the withdrawal of fatherly love. The positive side is equally important. Since his love is conditioned, I can do something to acquire it, I can work for it; his love is not outside of my control as motherly love is.

The mother's and the father's attitudes toward the child correspond to the child's own needs. The infant needs mother's unconditional love and care physiologically as well as psychically. The child, after six, begins to need father's love, his authority and guidance. Mother has the function of making him secure in life, father has the function of teaching him, guiding him to cope with those problems with which the particular society the child has been born into confronts him. In the ideal case, mother's love does not try to prevent the child from growing up, does not try to put a premium on helplessness. Mother should have faith in life, hence not be overanxious, and thus not infect the child with her anxiety. Part of her life should be the wish that the child become independent and eventually separate from her. Father's love should be guided by principles and expectations; it should be patient and tolerant, rather than threatening and authoritarian. It should give the growing child an increasing sense of competence and eventually permit him to become his own authority and to dispense with that of father.

Eventually, the mature person has come to the point where he is his own mother and his own father. He has, as it were, a motherly and a fatherly conscience. Motherly conscience says: "There is no misdeed, no crime which could deprive you of my love, of my wish for your life and happiness." Fatherly conscience says: "You did wrong, you cannot avoid accepting certain consequences of your wrongdoing, and most of all you must change your ways if I am to like you." The mature person has become free from the outside mother and father figures, and has built them up inside. In contrast to Freud's concept of the super-ego, however, he has built them inside not by *incorporating* mother and father, but by building a motherly conscience on his own capacity for love, and a fatherly conscience on his reason and judgment. Furthermore, the mature person loves with both the motherly and the fatherly conscience, in spite of the fact that they seem to contradict each other. If he would only retain his fatherly conscience, he would become harsh and inhuman. If he would only retain his motherly conscience, he would be apt to lose judgment and to hinder himself and others in their development.

In this development from mother-centered to father-centered attachment, and their eventual synthesis, lies the basis for mental health and the achievement of maturity. In the failure of this development lies the basic cause for neurosis. While it is beyond the scope of this book to develop this trend of thought more fully, some brief remarks may serve to clarify this statement.

One cause for neurotic development can lie in the fact that a boy has a loving, but overindulgent or domineering mother, and a weak and uninterested father. In this case he may remain fixed at an early mother attachment, and develop into a person who is dependent on mother, feels helpless, has the strivings characteristic of the receptive person, that is, to receive, to be protected, to be taken care of, and who has a lack of fatherly qualities—discipline, independence, an ability to master life by himself. He may try to find "mothers" in everybody, sometimes in women and sometimes in men in a position of authority and power. If, on the other hand, the mother is cold, unresponsive and domineering, he may either transfer the need for motherly protection to his father, and subsequent father figures—in which case the end result is similar to the former case—or he will develop into a one-sidedly father-oriented person, completely given to the principles of law, order and authority, and lacking in the ability to expect or to receive unconditional love. This development is further intensified if the father is authoritarian and at the same time strongly attached to the son. What is characteristic of all these neurotic developments is the fact that one principle, the fatherly or the motherly, fails to develop or—and this is the case in the more severe neurotic development—that the roles of mother and father become confused both with regard to persons outside and with regard to these roles within the person. Further examination may show that certain types of neurosis, like obsessional neurosis, develop more on the basis of a one-sided father attachment, while others, like hysteria, alcoholism, inability to assert oneself and to cope with life realistically, and depressions, result from mother-centeredness.

□ WRITING ↔ READING ↔ THINKING ACTIVITIES □
Summarizing a Paragraph

Use Fromm's eleven-paragraph passage to test his ability as a writer to convey clearly a thought or stage in each of his paragraphs, and your ability as a reader to detect that thought. Summarize the thought of each paragraph in a single sentence. If there is already a sentence in the paragraph which serves as focus or summary, use that sentence. But place it in quotation marks to indicate that the wording is Erich Fromm's and not yours. When finished, you should have eleven sentences that summarize the main points in Fromm's selection, sentences that should not have been hard to develop if he has taken pains to be sure his reader follows and understands his thinking.

Paragraph Structure

A paragraph composed as a complete piece of writing in itself is usually a miniature of the same kind of general structure that Whitman, Twain, and Thomas used in their poem and essays: introduction, development, and conclusion. Any extended piece of writing, even if it is only a single paragraph, must convey to the reader the basic message, expand on that basic idea, and conclude logically and clearly.

In a writing longer than a single paragraph, the process becomes more complicated. Each paragraph should still stand alone as an idea-conveying unit, but it also must be linked with the paragraph before and the paragraph after so that the longer passage proceeds in a logical flow from one paragraph to the next. The writer makes the link with the preceding paragraph at the same time that he or she launches the idea that will be the focus of the new paragraph. Although there are an infinite number of ways to achieve this *transition* from paragraph to paragraph, usually the first sentence in a paragraph will serve as a "hook" to attach the new paragraph to the preceding one in some effective way.

□ WRITING ↔ READING ↔ THINKING ACTIVITIES □
Analyzing Paragraph Transition

To see if Fromm's writing actually corresponds in practice to our observations in theory, we can write an *analysis* of the first sentence of each of his paragraphs, looking closely at the organizational and transitional functions of those first sentences.

First Sentence of Each Paragraph	Analysis
1. "The *infant, at the moment of birth*, would feel the fear of dying, if a gracious fate did **not** preserve it from **any awareness** of the anxiety involved in the separation from mother, and from intra-uterine existence."	As he begins, Fromm seems to set forth a twofold organizational progression—physical growth and psychological development. Physical growth is signaled by the phrase "infant at the moment of birth"; psychological development is suggested by

the phrase "not . . . any awareness." (To highlight these two structural movements from paragraph to paragraph, the key words suggesting physical growth have been italicized, and those words signifying psychological development have been printed in boldface italics.)

2. "When the *child grows and develops*, he becomes **capable of perceiving things** as they are; the **satisfaction** in being fed **becomes differentiated** from the nipple, the breast from the mother."

Readers know that physical growth and psychological development are the patterns of progression when in paragraph 2 he writes, "When the child grows and develops [physical growth], he becomes capable of perceiving . . . ; satisfaction . . . becomes differentiated . . . [psychological development]." Note also how the sentence begins with the time-passage word *when*.

3. "For most children *before the age from eight and a half to ten*, the **problem** is almost exclusively that **of being loved**—of being loved for what one is."

The initial sentence in paragraph 3 further confirms and advances this twofold movement. The chronological age is extended to include the period "before the age from eight and a half to ten," and the development problem of that period is identified as "being loved."

4. "Closely **related** to the development of the capacity of love is the **development of the object of love**."

The first sentence in paragraph 4 is a deft transitional touch. The phrase "Closely related" is the signal that the author is shifting topics; the remainder of the sentence reminds the reader that Fromm has been considering "development of the capacity of love," but now he is shifting to another "closely related" kind of development, "development of the object of love." Having traced one type of development from the stage of infant through age eight and a half,

Fromm will now go back and trace a second type of "closely related" development during those same years.

5. "In order to understand this shift from mother to father, we must consider the essential differences in quality between motherly and fatherly love."

[Your turn! From this point on let's alternate. Identify the key words in the sentence which indicate physical growth or psychological development. Then analyze the structural and transitional features of this sentence and those of paragraphs 7, 9, and 11.]

6. "The *relationship to father* is quite different."

After having paused in paragraph 5 to consider the mother-love, father-love contrast, Fromm begins paragraph 6 by alerting the reader that he is now moving ahead again. He had analyzed the relationship to mother in paragraph 4, paused in paragraph 5 to contrast maternal and paternal love, and is now proceeding to consider "the relationship to father."

7. "Closely related to this function is one which is connected with socio-economic development."

8. "The mother's and the father's *attitudes* toward the *child correspond to* the child's own *needs*."

Paragraph 8 begins more straightforwardly, without benefit of any "closely related" or "in order to understand" transitional phrases. Nevertheless, in this first sentence Fromm still looks back and links the thoughts together, then looks forward and indicates the next focus, just as he has before. The "mother's and the father's attitudes" have already been considered in the discussion of each parent's relationship to the child. Now Fromm will go a step further, indicating how these attitudes of each parent "correspond to the child's own needs."

9. "Eventually, the mature person has come to the point where he is his own mother and his own father."

10. "In this *development from mother-centered to father-centered attachment*, and their eventual synthesis, lies the *basis for mental health and the achievement of maturity*."

The first sentence in paragraph 10 is a good example of an opening sentence which provides transition and progression: transition by summarizing the thoughts just covered, and progression by previewing the upcoming thoughts in the rest of the paragraph. The linking summary is a reference to the entire psychological process Fromm has traced: "this development from mother-centered to father-centered attachment, and their eventual synthesis." The preview summarizing the emphasis in this paragraph is deftly shown as a progression of already discussed ideas: "In this development . . . lies the basis for mental health and the achievement of maturity."

11. "One cause for neurotic development can lie in the fact that a boy has a loving, but overindulgent or domineering mother, and a weak and uninterested father."

An attentive reader can clearly perceive and easily follow Fromm's organization and progression. His key words identifying growth and psychological development; his time-passage words like "when" and "eventually"; the summarizing and linking phrases like "this shift," "this function," and "this development"; his indicators of shifts in thought like "closely related," "in order to understand," and "quite different"—all serve as essential signals at the beginning of his paragraphs.

The Process of Writing

Fromm's essay should pose no comprehension problem for you as a careful reader. But it may pose a compositional difficulty for you as a writer, a reaction which might be expressed as follows: "Okay, so all these organizational and transitional signals are there, tying paragraphs together and announcing progressions and shifts in thought. How much of this did the writer plan in advance, and how much is accidental? As a writer myself, how can I possibly be this conscious of structure, transition, and progression and still *say* anything? Won't I be spending all my time diddling with outlines instead of writing anything? And, unless my writing somehow winds up being dissected in a textbook by English teachers, who is going to look that closely anyway?"

Such questions are legitimate, and the answers lie in a brief consideration of the writing process which Fromm probably engaged in, the process resulting in this eleven-paragraph product. It is the same general process any writer would (or should) follow for any extended piece of writing.

The process consists of three general stages:

1. Planning and organizing
2. Writing or drafting
3. Rewriting or revising

As you surely know from your own writing experiences, it is oversimplifying things to speak of three clear-cut steps, as though writing were a rigidly sequential process. Sometimes you do not know what you want to say until you start writing, and your ideas and organization may come to you as you are composing. In revising you are still generating new ideas, and you may discover a different, more effective organization. Writing is often a sort of looping, recursive, discover-as-you-go individual process. Nevertheless, it is helpful to talk about progressive steps or stages in that general process—so long as we do not insist on their being strictly sequential and mutually exclusive.

Planning and organizing the writing task is a way of determining what you want to say (purpose), whom you are saying it to (audience), the type of writing to use in saying it (form), and how to get from beginning point A to concluding point Z in a manner which will enable the average attentive reader to follow along, seeing when you move from B to C to D, noting that F is really a summary of A through E, with G launching out in a new direction, and so on. It is determining where you want to go, and why, and how to get there.

If you are writing a short memo, any planning usually takes place in your head; if you are writing an essay, you probably generate something on paper, perhaps a brief outline of major points arranged in some kind of logical order; if you are writing a book, as Fromm was, the outline is usually more lengthy and more detailed. He probably laid out his basic growth-and-development progression during this prewriting process, determining the order of treatment of each stage and the most effective placement of each closely related idea.

More often than not, the structural skeleton or "map" will develop as you use certain writing techniques that correspond to the purpose of the moment. When Twain is narrating—story-telling, really—he uses *time movement*—first the town was asleep, then it came to life, then it settled back into slumber. When he is describing his home town, he uses *space movement*. In citing descriptive details, for example, Twain moves down Water Street to the levee to the wharf to the head of the wharf to "the majestic, the magnificent Mississippi." If you are attempting to argue or persuade, or if you are explaining, as Erich Fromm is, you might use any number of possible techniques: comparison, contrast, definition, analysis, classification, cause to effect, general to specific, and so on.

Once the basic map is laid out, or sometimes as a way of discovering what the map will look like, the writer sets out on the journey and begins an actual draft. During the composing process, as ideas, descriptions, events, and explanations unfold, the writer also creates on the spur of the moment many transitional words, phrases, and sentences. Most of Fromm's phrases like "closely related" and "in order to understand," and his summarizing references to "this function," may well have sprung into being during an early draft.

If Professor Fromm is like most writers, he did not immediately turn out a product that satisfied him, but moved into the rewriting or revising process. Perhaps he shifted a paragraph to a more logical position, improved punctuation and grammar, changed words for clearer meaning, deleted a sentence, provided smoother transition between thoughts, or completely rewrote passages. In other words, he produced a more finished draft—or drafts.

In this stage the writer is still the composer, but he also assumes the role of attentive reader, trying to read and listen to the writing with the eyes and ears of the intended audience: "This doesn't make sense; I need to show explicitly the relationship between A and B. Hmm! I need to put a comma there so as to prevent ambiguous reading. Oops—wrote 'bother' when I meant 'mother.' This sentence doesn't make sense," and so on.

Sometimes in the case of brief writings like notes or memos, little or no rewriting takes place. And sometimes, as with essay exams, there is no opportunity to revise. With longer pieces, however, when you are particularly concerned about communicating concisely, clearly, and correctly, multiple drafting and revising is essential.

We can now give better answers to those perplexing questions: "How much of this structuring and transition is conscious on the author's part?" Virtually *all* is conscious, but a good writer like Fromm usually achieves organizational and transitional tightness through a multiple-draft process. "Can't structuring become an all-consuming process in itself?" It can become all-consuming, but it should not. Time spent determining the purpose, identifying the audience, choosing the appropriate form, jotting down ideas, and arranging those ideas into some logical sequence before actually writing is usually time wisely invested. And revising or redrafting for further improvement simply makes good sense. The British writer Oscar Wilde once remarked, "I was working on the proof of one of my poems all the morning, and took out a comma. In the afternoon I put it back again."* Since few writers can afford quite that much time for that little an effect, it makes sense for you to move through the planning, drafting, and revising process expeditiously.

As a result of the exercise with Fromm's paragraphs, you should have a good grasp of his basic ideas. Try the following activities as an application of your new knowledge.

□ WRITING ↔ READING ↔ THINKING ACTIVITIES □
Applying Fromm's Concepts

1. How closely do you think Whitman's parents approximated Fromm's "ideal types," based on the poet's description of each in lines 22 to 25 of his poem?
2. How does your mother, her love for you, and your relationship to her during your early years compare or contrast with Fromm's "ideal type"?
3. How about Fromm's "ideal" father and your father?
4. Assuming the validity of Fromm's ideas, can you make any observations about yourself as an adult based on your relationship as a child with your parents?

Brothers, Sisters, and Grandparents

Each of the following two selections addresses the same religious experience in the life of a youngster. In fact, they have the same title—"First Confession." The first, by X. J. Kennedy, is a brief poem; the second, by Frank O'Connor, is a short story. As you read the selections, consider why Kennedy chose one form and O'Connor chose a very different form.

*Alvin Redman, ed., *The Wit and Humor of Oscar Wilde* (New York: Dover, 1959) 218.

X. J. Kennedy (born 1929)
First Confession

Blood thudded in my ears. I scuffed,
    Steps stubborn, to the telltale booth
Beyond whose curtained portal coughed
    The robed repositor of truth.

The slat shot back. The universe   5
    Bowed down his cratered dome to hear
Enumerated my each curse,
    The sip snitched from my old man's beer,

My sloth pride envy lechery,
    The dime held back from Peter's Pence   10
With which I'd bribed my girl to pee
    That I might spy her instruments.

Hovering scale-pans when I'd done
    Settled their balance slow as silt
While in the restless dark I burned   15
    Bright as a brimstone in my guilt

Until as one feeds birds he doled
    Seven Our Fathers and a Hail
Which I to double-scrub my soul
    Intoned twice at the altar rail   20

Where Sunday in seraphic light
    I knelt, as full of grace as most,
And stuck my tongue out at the priest:
    A fresh roost for the Holy Ghost.

Frank O'Connor (1903–1966)
First Confession

    All the trouble began when my grandfather died and my grandmother—my father's mother—came to live with us. Relations in the one house are a strain at the best of times, but, to make matters worse, my grandmother was a real old countrywoman and quite unsuited to the life in town. She had a fat, wrinkled old face, and, to Mother's great indignation, went round the house in bare feet—the boots had her crippled, she said. For dinner she had a jug of porter and a pot of potatoes with— sometimes—a bit of salt fish, and she poured out the potatoes on the table and ate them slowly, with great relish, using her fingers by way of a fork.

Now, girls are supposed to be fastidious, but I was the one who suffered most from this. Nora, my sister, just sucked up to the old woman for the penny she got every Friday out of the old-age pension, a thing I could not do. I was too honest, that was my trouble; and when I was playing with Bill Connell, the sergeant-major's son, and saw my grandmother steering up the path with the jug of porter sticking out from beneath her shawl I was mortified. I made excuses not to let him come into the house, because I could never be sure what she would be up to when we went in.

When Mother was at work and my grandmother made the dinner I wouldn't touch it. Nora once tried to make me, but I hid under the table from her and took the bread-knife with me for protection. Nora let on to be very indignant (she wasn't, of course, but she knew Mother saw through her, so she sided with Gran) and came after me. I lashed out at her with the bread-knife, and after that she left me alone. I stayed there till Mother came in from work and made my dinner, but when Father came in later Nora said in a shocked voice: "Oh, Dadda, do you know what Jackie did at dinner-time?" Then, of course, it all came out; Father gave me a flaking; Mother interfered, and for days after that he didn't speak to me and Mother barely spoke to Nora. And all because of that old woman! God knows, I was heartscalded.

Then, to crown my misfortunes, I had to make my first confession and communion. It was an old woman called Ryan who prepared us for these. She was about the one age with Gran; she was well-to-do, lived in a big house on Montenotte, wore a black cloak and bonnet, and came every day to school at three o'clock when we should have been going home, and talked to us of hell. She may have mentioned the other place as well, but that could only have been by accident, for hell had the first place in her heart.

She lit a candle, took out a new half-crown, and offered it to the first boy who would hold one finger—only one finger!—in the flame for five minutes by the school clock. Being always very ambitious I was tempted to volunteer, but I thought it might look greedy. Then she asked were we afraid of holding one finger—only one finger!— in a little candle flame for five minutes and not afraid of burning all over in roasting hot furnaces for all eternity. "All eternity! Just think of that! A whole lifetime goes by and it's nothing, not even a drop in the ocean of your sufferings." The woman was really interesting about hell, but my attention was all fixed on the half-crown. At the end of the lesson she put it back in her purse. It was a great disappointment; a religious woman like that, you wouldn't think she'd bother about a thing like a half-crown.

Another day she said she knew a priest who woke one night to find a fellow he didn't recognize leaning over the end of his bed. The priest was a bit frightened— naturally enough—but he asked the fellow what he wanted, and the fellow said in a deep, husky voice that he wanted to go to confession. The priest said it was an awkward time and wouldn't it do in the morning, but the fellow said that last time he went to confession, there was one sin he kept back, being ashamed to mention it, and now it was always on his mind. Then the priest knew it was a bad case, because the fellow was after making a bad confession and committing a mortal sin. He got up to dress, and just then the cock crew in the yard outside, and—lo and behold!—when the priest looked round there was no sign of the fellow, only a smell of burning timber, and when the priest looked at his bed didn't he see the print of two hands burned in it? That was because the fellow had made a bad confession. This story made a shocking impression on me.

But the worst of all was when she showed us how to examine our conscience. Did we take the name of the Lord, our God, in vain? Did we honour our father and mother? (I asked her did this include grandmothers and she said it did.) Did we love our neighbours as ourselves? Did we covet our neighbour's goods? (I thought of the way I felt about the penny that Nora got every Friday.) I decided that, between one thing and another, I must have broken the whole ten commandments, all on account of that old woman, and so far as I could see, so long as she remained in the house I had no hope of ever doing anything else.

I was scared to death of confession. The day the whole class went I let on to have a toothache, hoping my absence wouldn't be noticed; but at three o'clock, just as I was feeling safe, along comes a chap with a message from Mrs. Ryan that I was to go to confession myself on Saturday and be at the chapel for communion with the rest. To make it worse, Mother couldn't come with me and sent Nora instead.

Now, that girl had ways of tormenting me that Mother never knew of. She held my hand as we went down the hill, smiling sadly and saying how sorry she was for me, as if she were bringing me to the hospital for an operation.

"Oh, God help us!" she moaned. "Isn't it a terrible pity you weren't a good boy? Oh, Jackie, my heart bleeds for you! How will you ever think of all your sins? Don't forget you have to tell him about the time you kicked Gran on the shin."

"Lemme go!" I said, trying to drag myself free of her. "I don't want to go to confession at all."

"But sure, you'll have to go to confession, Jackie," she replied in the same regretful tone. "Sure, if you didn't, the parish priest would be up to the house, looking for you. 'Tisn't, God knows, that I'm not sorry for you. Do you remember the time you tried to kill me with the bread-knife under the table? And the language you used to me? I don't know what he'll do with you at all, Jackie. He might have to send you up to the bishop."

I remember thinking bitterly that she didn't know the half of what I had to tell— if I told it. I knew I couldn't tell it, and understood perfectly why the fellow in Mrs. Ryan's story made a bad confession; it seemed to me a great shame that people wouldn't stop criticizing him. I remember that steep hill down to the church, and the sunlit hillsides beyond the valley of the river, which I saw in the gaps between the houses like Adam's last glimpse of Paradise.

Then, when she had manoeuvred me down the long flight of steps to the chapel yard, Nora suddenly changed her tone. She became the raging malicious devil she really was.

"There you are!" she said with a yelp of triumph, hurling me through the church door. "And I hope he'll give you the penitential psalms, you dirty little caffler."

I knew then I was lost, given up to eternal justice. The door with the coloured-glass panels swung shut behind me, the sunlight went out and gave place to deep shadow, and the wind whistled outside so that the silence within seemed to crackle like ice under my feet. Nora sat in front of me by the confession box. There were a couple of old women ahead of her, and then a miserable-looking poor devil came and wedged me in at the other side, so that I couldn't escape even if I had the courage. He joined his hands and rolled his eyes in the direction of the roof, muttering aspirations in an anguished tone, and I wondered had he a grandmother too. Only a grandmother could account for a fellow behaving in that heart-broken way, but he was better off than I, for he at least could go and confess his sins; while I would make a bad confession and then die in the night and be continually coming back and burning people's furniture.

Nora's turn came, and I heard the sound of something slamming, and then her voice as if butter wouldn't melt in her mouth, and then another slam, and out she came. God, the hypocrisy of women. Her eyes were lowered, her head was bowed, and her hands were joined very low down on her stomach, and she walked up the aisle to the side altar looking like a saint. You never saw such an exhibition of devotion; and I remembered the devilish malice with which she had tormented me all the way from our door, and wondered were all religious people like that, really. It was my turn now. With the fear of damnation in my soul I went in, and the confessional door closed of itself behind me.

It was pitch-dark and I couldn't see priest or anything else. Then I really began to be frightened. In the darkness it was a matter between God and me, and He had all the odds. He knew what my intentions were before I even started; I had no chance. All I had ever been told about confession got mixed up in my mind, and I knelt to one wall and said: "Bless me, father, for I have sinned; this is my first confession." I waited for a few minutes, but nothing happened, so I tried it on the other wall. Nothing happened there either. He had me spotted all right.

It must have been then that I noticed the shelf at about one height with my head. It was really a place for grown-up people to rest their elbows, but in my distracted state I thought it was probably the place you were supposed to kneel. Of course, it was on the high side and not very deep, but I was always good at climbing and managed to get up all right. Staying up was the trouble. There was room only for my knees, and nothing you could get a grip on but a sort of wooden moulding a bit above it. I held on to the moulding and repeated the words a little louder, and this time something happened all right. A slide was slammed back; a little light entered the box, and a man's voice said: "Who's there?"

"'Tis me, father," I said for fear he mightn't see me and go away again. I couldn't see him at all. The place the voice came from was under the moulding, about level with my knees, so I took a good grip of the moulding and swung myself down till I saw the astonished face of a young priest looking up at me. He had to put his head on one side to see me, and I had to put mine on one side to see him, so we were more or less talking to one another upside down. It struck me as a queer way of hearing confessions, but I didn't feel it my place to criticize.

"Bless me, father, for I have sinned; this is my first confession," I rattled off all in one breath, and swung myself down the least shade more to make it easier for him.

"What are you doing up there?" he shouted in an angry voice, and the strain the politeness was putting on my hold of the moulding, and the shock of being addressed in such an uncivil tone, were too much for me. I lost my grip, tumbled, and hit the door an unmerciful wallop before I found myself flat on my back in the middle of the aisle. The people who had been waiting stood up with their mouths open. The priest opened the door of the middle box and came out, pushing his biretta back from his forehead; he looked something terrible. Then Nora came scampering down the aisle.

"Oh, you dirty little caffler!" she said. "I might have known you'd do it. I might have known you'd disgrace me. I can't leave you out of my sight for one minute."

Before I could even get to my feet to defend myself she bent down and gave me a clip across the ear. This reminded me that I was so stunned I had even forgotten to cry, so that people might think I wasn't hurt at all, when in fact I was probably maimed for life. I gave a roar out of me.

"What's all this about?" the priest hissed, getting angrier than ever and pushing Nora off me. "How dare you hit the child like that, you little vixen?"

"But I can't do my penance with him, father," Nora cried, cocking an outraged eye up at him.

"Well, go and do it, or I'll give you some more to do," he said, giving me a hand up. "Was it coming to confession you were, my poor man?" he asked me.

"'Twas, father," said I with a sob.

"Oh," he said respectfully, "a big hefty fellow like you must have terrible sins. Is this your first?"

"'Tis, father," said I.

"Worse and worse," he said gloomily. "The crimes of a lifetime. I don't know will I get rid of you at all today. You'd better wait now till I'm finished with these old ones. You can see by the looks of them they haven't much to tell."

"I will, father," I said with something approaching joy.

The relief of it was really enormous. Nora stuck out her tongue at me from behind his back, but I couldn't even be bothered retorting. I knew from the very moment that man opened his mouth that he was intelligent above the ordinary. When I had time to think, I saw how right I was. It only stood to reason that a fellow confessing after seven years would have more to tell than people that went every week. The crimes of a lifetime, exactly as he said. It was only what he expected, and the rest was the cackle of old women and girls with their talk of hell, the bishop, and the penitential psalms. That was all they knew. I started to make my examination of conscience, and barring the one bad business of my grandmother it didn't seem so bad.

The next time, the priest steered me into the confession box himself and left the shutter back the way I could see him get in and sit down at the further side of the grille from me.

"Well, now," he said, "what do they call you?"

"Jackie, father," said I.

"And what's a-trouble to you, Jackie?"

"Father," I said, feeling I might as well get it over while I had him in good humour, "I had it all arranged to kill my grandmother."

He seemed a bit shaken by that, all right, because he said nothing for quite a while.

"My goodness," he said at last, "that'd be a shocking thing to do. What put that into your head?"

"Father," I said, feeling very sorry for myself, "she's an awful woman."

"Is she?" he asked. "What way is she awful?"

"She takes porter, father," I said, knowing well from the way Mother talked of it that this was a mortal sin, and hoping it would make the priest take a more favourable view of my case.

"Oh, my!" he said, and I could see he was impressed.

"And snuff, father," said I.

"That's a bad case, sure enough, Jackie," he said.

"And she goes round in her bare feet, father," I went on in a rush of self-pity, "and she knows I don't like her, and she gives pennies to Nora and none to me, and my dad sides with her and flakes me, and one night I was so heartscalded I made up my mind I'd have to kill her."

"And what would you do with the body?" he asked with great interest.

"I was thinking I could chop that up and carry it away in a barrow I have," I said.

"Begor, Jackie," he said, "do you know you're a terrible child?"

"I know, father," I said, for I was just thinking the same thing myself. "I tried to kill Nora too with a bread-knife under the table, only I missed her."

"Is that the little girl that was beating you just now?" he asked.

"'Tis, father."

"Someone will go for her with a bread-knife one day, and he won't miss her," he said rather cryptically. "You must have great courage. Between ourselves, there's a lot of people I'd like to do the same to but I'd never have the nerve. Hanging is an awful death."

"Is it, father?" I asked with the deeper interest—I was always very keen on hanging. "Did you ever see a fellow hanged?"

"Dozens of them," he said solemnly. "And they all died roaring."

"Jay!" I said.

"Oh, a horrible death!" he said with great satisfaction. "Lots of the fellows I saw killed their grandmothers too, but they all said 'twas never worth it."

He had me there for a full ten minutes talking, and then walked out the chapel yard with me. I was genuinely sorry to part with him, because he was the most entertaining character I'd ever met in the religious line. Outside, after the shadow of the church, the sunlight was like the roaring of waves on a beach; it dazzled me; and when the frozen silence melted and I heard the screech of trams on the road my heart soared. I knew now I wouldn't die in the night and come back, leaving marks on my mother's furniture. It would be a great worry to her, and the poor soul had enough.

Nora was sitting on the railing, waiting for me, and she put on a very sour puss when she saw the priest with me. She was mad jealous because a priest had never come out of the church with her.

"Well," she asked coldly, after he left me, "what did he give you?"

"Three Hail Marys," I said.

"Three Hail Marys," she repeated incredulously. "You mustn't have told him anything."

"I told him everything," I said confidently.

"About Gran and all?"

"About Gran and all."

(All she wanted was to be able to go home and say I'd made a bad confession.)

"Did you tell him you went for me with the bread-knife?" she asked with a frown.

"I did to be sure."

"And he only gave you three Hail Marys?"

"That's all."

She slowly got down from the railing with a baffled air. Clearly, this was beyond her. As we mounted the steps back to the main road she looked at me suspiciously.

"What are you sucking?" she asked.

"Bullseyes."

"Was it the priest gave them to you?"

"'Twas."

"Lord God," she wailed bitterly, "some people have all the luck! 'Tis no advantage to anybody trying to be good. I might just as well be a sinner like you."

☐ WRITING ↔ READING ↔ THINKING ACTIVITIES ☐
Exploring Form and Style

1. Why do you think X. J. Kennedy chose the form of a brief poem to relate the speaker's experience? Do you think his purpose prompted, or even dictated, his choice? What exactly *is* his purpose?

2. Consider the same questions for O'Connor. What may be the reason for

his choosing the prose form of the short story? What do you think was the extent to which his purpose played a role in his choice of that form?

3. How would you compare or contrast Kennedy's and O'Connor's writing with regard to (a) length? (b) number of characters? (c) details provided about each character? (d) humor? (e) the effect on the reader? (f) other categories you can think of? Do your comparisons or contrasts provide further commentary on questions 1 and 2 regarding form and purpose?

4. Based on your reading of O'Connor's short story, can you venture a guess about the characteristics of his writing—the elements of his style—that you would expect to find in other of O'Connor's writings? (Once you have composed your list, try testing it by reading O'Connor's "My Oedipus Complex" in the Additional Readings for Chapter 2.)

Kinships

In O'Connor's story, for the first time in our writing selections, there are familial kinships which will probably foster more memories from your childhood: the brother–sister and child–grandparent relationships. Much of the story's substance springs from these relationships. Jackie's grandmother and sister are not only the bane of his home life, but they also burden the prospect of his first confession. His blackest "sins," those which he most fears confessing, are committed or contemplated against Gran and Nora.

□ WRITING ↔ READING ↔ THINKING ACTIVITIES □
Remembering Kinships

You probably have some vivid memories from your childhood years of your own grandparents and brothers or sisters.

1. Try to convey, through physical description and details of personality, your childhood impression of one of your grandparents.

2. Can you recall one particularly memorable incident regarding you and a grandparent? Is there a story told by your parents about your grandparents which you found particularly interesting, unusual, or memorable?

3. Describe a disagreement or fight you had with a brother or sister. What was the cause? How was it resolved? Were parents involved? If so, how?

4. Describe an older or younger brother or sister as you perceived him or her when you were a child. Include both a physical description and a personality sketch.

5. Can you describe briefly the relationships between parents and children in your home when you were young? Did your parents favor one child over another or consistently take sides?
6. Which child were you—oldest, middle, youngest? Only boy, only girl? Did your sex or age make any notable difference in parental expectation and treatment of you?
7. If you were an only child, what advantages and disadvantages do you think you enjoyed or suffered?
8. If the recollection, incident, or impression you most vividly and emotionally recall about a brother or sister is something our questions have not touched on, what is it?

Literature: The Particular and the Universal

The subject matter of both Kennedy's poem and O'Connor's short story is distinctly Catholic. The poem describes a Catholic youngster's experience from title to last line, and the short story focuses on an Irish Catholic family and a Catholic child's first confession. Are these selections more appropriate or significant for the Catholic reader than for the Jewish reader or the Southern Baptist or other non-Catholic reader?

In one sense, the reader coming from a Catholic background does have an edge. He or she will have personally "been there," will react to the religious context with a sense of familiarity not fully shared by other readers. This reader will have no trouble at all understanding instantly what Kennedy means when he refers to "the telltale booth," the "curtained portal," and the "robed repositor of truth." When the speaker says "I . . . stuck my tongue out at the priest," the reader familiar with Catholic communion will not misread or be confused by the statement. He or she will have an initial advantage, an immediate sense of relevance.

In another sense, the non-Catholic reader has the edge. He or she will gain the experience of having "been there" vicariously through the poem, will catch a glimpse of and incorporate into his or her experience a valuable dimension that was formerly nonexistent. That expansion of experience, understanding, knowledge, and insight is a primary reason for reading literature.

There is another sense in which the poem transcends altogether its religious particulars. All readers, regardless of their religious orientation, will recognize and appreciate from personal experience the young boy's hesitance, fear, and uncertainty in the face of authority and the unexperienced. Most readers will also remember the sense of challenge and anxiety when they were required to perform grown-up acts formally and in public for the first time.

There is also much for all readers to appreciate in the poem's richness of texture and technique. For example, read each line of the first stanza aloud and note the sound repetitions. Note that each line has exactly the same number of syllables. Note the figures of speech, the similes and metaphors. (These techniques will be discussed in later chapters.)

Whatever your background, then, whether or not you can personally relate to the specific context of a writing, you can certainly experience it in a universal sense. Whitman's child ventured forth in and around nineteenth-century Brooklyn; Twain lived in "a village on the west bank of the Mississippi"; Thomas reminisced about "a large Welsh town at the beginning of the Great War"; and Jackie suffered at the hands of his sister in Ireland. Because of these different settings, you gain insight about different times and places and contexts. But you also gain from recognizing and responding to underlying human universals that transcend time and place.

Summary and Review

Here are a few of the principal points from this chapter you should have in mind as you read Chapter 3:

- ☐ Writing is a substitute for speaking. *Listen* as you write and read.
- ☐ All writing is either prose or poetry. If you write in prose form, you write sentences and paragraphs. If you write in poetic form, you write lines and stanzas.
- ☐ All prose writing is either fiction or nonfiction.
- ☐ Be mindful of your purpose in writing.
- ☐ Also consider your audience, those for whom your writing is intended.
- ☐ Each writer has a unique, individual style.
- ☐ Writing is a process that results in a product.
- ☐ The usual structure of a piece of writing is threefold: introduction, development, and conclusion.
- ☐ To compare in writing is generally to point out similarities; to contrast is to point out differences.
- ☐ Autobiographical writing contains personal experiences of the writer.
- ☐ You can usually summarize the central idea of a paragraph in a single sentence.

☐   When your writing is longer than a single paragraph, each new paragraph must be linked effectively with the preceding paragraph.

☐   The writing process consists of three (sometimes overlapping) stages: planning (or prewriting), drafting, and revising.

☐   In poems and short stories and many other types of writing, there are the specifics of time, place, and context which the reader may be exploring for the first time. There are also human feelings and attitudes the reader readily recognizes as universal.

The writing and reading activities in this chapter were intended to provide a practical awareness of most of these points. Perhaps writing about the precious and sometimes painful years of your childhood has served to emphasize just how much "the child is father of the man," how the past is present with you and in you, how "these became part of that child who went forth every day, and who now goes, and will always go forth every day."

3

Awakenings

"I want to know why."*

□ Narration   □ Reading and Writing the Short Story   □ Plot   □ Character
□ Theme   □ Writing a Plot Summary   □ Analyzing a Short Story   □ Setting
□ Point of View   □ Writing Narration   □ Narrative Style   □ Symbolism
□ Irony   □ Literary Criticism as Argumentation   □ Primary Source
□ Secondary Source   □ Writing Argumentation

As children carry their accumulated experience into adolescence, the period from puberty to early adulthood, the world seems to change—or perhaps only the children change. In this chapter, adolescents venture into the adult world, sometimes with brashness, often with insecurity, and always with naiveté. The writings you will read are short stories which record accounts of that uncertain time of growing, of exploring, of reaching out for maturity. Before you read the first selection, try to remember the first time you were "on your own" away from your parents or guardians—perhaps going to camp, taking your first trip by plane, starting your first job, driving the family car alone for the first time, enrolling in college, moving into your own apartment. Whatever the occasion, do you recall that peculiar mixture of bravado at being independent and terror at the possibility you might not "make it" on your own?

*Sherwood Anderson, "I Want to Know Why" (in the Additional Readings for Chapter 3).

Venturing into the World of Adulthood

Throughout this chapter, the focus will be on narration and narrative techniques. *Narration* is writing which relates a happening or event: someone doing something. Narrative skills can be used in composing poems, short stories, novels, and plays, but they can also be useful in summarizing a meeting, writing a news story, reporting on a vacation, telling a joke, and even making credible excuses. If you can appreciate the narrative elements of plot, character, theme, setting, and point of view, you not only gain a better understanding of literary works but also become aware of these elements in everyday reading and writing. The abilities to arrange events in logical sequence, to narrate in sufficient detail to provide an accurate record, to characterize individuals in order to present a true picture of their motivations, to perceive and state the main purpose or theme of a piece of writing, to analyze point of view—these are skills necessary for effective written communication.

Narration and the Short Story

For purposes of illustration and analysis of narrative writing, the form of prose fiction called the *short story* is most helpful. In a short story, the writer imagines or creates one main incident or closely connected series of events. If the writer imagines or creates numerous incidents and extends the story to book length, a novel is the result, but the basic narrative elements and techniques found in short stories are still present.

One way to approach the reading or writing of narration is to pose the same questions a journalist tries to answer when writing another form of narrative, a news story: "Who? What? Where? When? How? Why?" Since the first short story is Nathaniel Hawthorne's "My Kinsman, Major Molineux," here are those basic questions applied to that narrative:

1. *Who* is Robin? What do you know about his age, background, and appearance? In what sense is he an adolescent?
2. *What* does he do? Can you trace his journey episode by episode?
3. *Where* does he come from? Where does he go? Can you identify the geographical location of the story? How many different places within the town are described?
4. *When* does Robin make his journey? At what point in his life do these events occur? What is the historical period of the story?
5. *How* does the author tell the story? From what perspective or angle of vision does the reader witness the events? Is a specific individual narrating the story?

6. *Why* does Robin leave home? Why does he want to return home at the
    end of the story? Why does Hawthorne link the historical events de-
    scribed in the introduction to the story of Robin's journey?

As you read "My Kinsman," look for Hawthorne's answers to these
questions.

Nathaniel Hawthorne (1804–1864)

My Kinsman, Major Molineux

After the kings of Great Britain had assumed the right of appointing the colonial
governors, the measures of the latter seldom met with the ready and general approbation, which had been paid to those of their predecessors, under the original char-
ters. The people looked with most jealous scrutiny to the exercise of power, which
did not emanate from themselves, and they usually rewarded the rulers with slender
gratitude, for the compliances, by which, in softening their instructions from beyond
the sea, they had incurred the reprehension of those who gave them. The annals of
Massachusetts Bay will inform us, that of six governors, in the space of about forty
years from the surrender of the old charter, under James II, two were imprisoned by
a popular insurrection; a third, as Hutchinson inclines to believe, was driven from the
province by the whizzing of a musket ball; a fourth, in the opinion of the same
historian, was hastened to his grave by continual bickerings with the House of Representatives; and the remaining two, as well as their successors, till the Revolution,
were favored with few and brief intervals of peaceful sway. The inferior members of
the court party, in times of high political excitement, led scarcely a more desirable
life. These remarks may serve as preface to the following adventures, which chanced
upon a summer night, not far from a hundred years ago. The reader, in order to avoid
a long and dry detail of colonial affairs, is requested to dispense with an account of
the train of circumstances, that had caused much temporary inflammation of the
popular mind.

It was near nine o'clock of a moonlight evening, when a boat crossed the ferry
with a single passenger, who had obtained his conveyance, at that unusual hour, by
the promise of an extra fare. While he stood on the landing-place, searching in either
pocket for the means of fulfilling his agreement, the ferryman lifted a lantern, by the
aid of which, and the newly risen moon, he took a very accurate survey of the
stranger's figure. He was a youth of barely eighteen years, evidently country-bred,
and now, as it should seem, upon his first visit to town. He was clad in a coarse grey
coat, well worn, but in excellent repair; his under garments were durably constructed
of leather, and sat tight to a pair of serviceable and well-shaped limbs; his stockings
of blue yarn, were the incontrovertible handiwork of a mother or a sister; and on his
head was a three-cornered hat, which in its better days had perhaps sheltered the

graver brow of the lad's father. Under his left arm was a heavy cudgel, formed of an oak sapling, and retaining a part of the hardened root; and his equipment was completed by a wallet, not so abundantly stocked as to incommode the vigorous shoulders on which it hung. Brown, curly hair, well-shaped features, and bright, cheerful eyes, were nature's gifts, and worth all that art could have done for his adornment.

The youth, one of whose names was Robin, finally drew from his pocket the half of a little province-bill of five shillings, which, in the depreciation of that sort of currency, did but satisfy the ferryman's demand, with the surplus of a sexangular piece of parchment valued at three pence. He then walked forward into the town, with as light a step, as if his day's journey had not already exceeded thirty miles, and with as eager an eye, as if he were entering London city, instead of the little metropolis of a New England colony. Before Robin had proceeded far, however, it occurred to him, that he knew not whither to direct his steps; so he paused, and looked up and down the narrow street, scrutinizing the small and mean wooden buildings, that were scattered on either side.

"This low hovel cannot be my kinsman's dwelling," thought he, "nor yonder old house, where the moonlight enters at the broken casement; and truly I see none hereabouts that might be worthy of him. It would have been wise to inquire my way of the ferryman, and doubtless he would have gone with me, and earned a shilling from the Major for his pains. But the next man I meet will do as well."

He resumed his walk, and was glad to perceive that the street now became wider, and the houses more respectable in their appearance. He soon discerned a figure moving on moderately in advance, and hastened his steps to overtake it. As Robin drew nigh, he saw that the passenger was a man in years, with a full periwig of grey hair, a wide-skirted coat of dark cloth, and silk stockings rolled about his knees. He carried a long and polished cane, which he struck down perpendicularly before him, at every step; and at regular intervals he uttered two successive hems, of a peculiarly solemn and sepulchral intonation. Having made these observations, Robin laid hold of the skirt of the old man's coat, just when the light from the open door and windows of a barber's shop, fell upon both their figures.

"Good evening to you, honored Sir," said he, making a low bow, and still retaining his hold of the skirt. "I pray you to tell me whereabouts is the dwelling of my kinsman, Major Molineux?"

The youth's question was uttered very loudly; and one of the barbers, whose razor was descending on a well-soaped chin, and another who was dressing a Ramillies wig, left their occupations, and came to the door. The citizen, in the meantime, turned a long favored countenance upon Robin, and answered him in a tone of excessive anger and annoyance. His two sepulchral hems, however, broke into the very centre of his rebuke, with most singular effect, like a thought of the cold grave obtruding among wrathful passions.

"Let go my garment, fellow! I tell you, I know not the man you speak of. What! I have authority, I have—hem, hem—authority; and if this be the respect you show your betters, your feet shall be brought acquainted with the stocks, by daylight, tomorrow morning!"

Robin released the old man's skirt, and hastened away, pursued by an ill-mannered roar of laughter from the barber's shop. He was at first considerably surprised by the result of his question, but, being a shrewd youth, soon thought himself able to account for the mystery.

"This is some country representative," was his conclusion, "who has never seen the inside of my kinsman's door, and lacks the breeding to answer a stranger civilly. The man is old, or verily—I might be tempted to turn back and smite him on the nose. Ah, Robin, Robin! even the barber's boys laugh at you, for choosing such a guide! You will be wiser in time, friend Robin."

He now became entangled in a succession of crooked and narrow streets, which crossed each other, and meandered at no great distance from the water-side. The smell of tar was obvious to his nostrils, the masts of vessels pierced the moonlight above the tops of the buildings, and the numerous signs, which Robin paused to read, informed him that he was near the centre of business. But the streets were empty, the shops were closed, and lights were visible only in the second stories of a few dwelling-houses. At length, on the corner of a narrow lane, through which he was passing, he beheld the broad countenance of a British hero swinging before the door of an inn, whence proceeded the voices of many guests. The casement of one of the lower windows was thrown back, and a very thin curtain permitted Robin to distinguish a party at supper, round a well-furnished table. The fragrance of the good cheer steamed forth into the outer air, and the youth could not fail to recollect, that the last remnant of his travelling stock of provision had yielded to his morning appetite, and that noon had found, and left him, dinnerless.

"Oh, that a parchment three-penny might give me a right to sit down at yonder table," said Robin, with a sigh. "But the Major will make me welcome to the best of his victuals; so I will even step boldly in, and inquire my way to his dwelling."

He entered the tavern, and was guided by the murmur of voices, and fumes of tobacco, to the public room. It was a long and low apartment, with oaken walls, grown dark in the continual smoke, and a floor, which was thickly sanded, but of no immaculate purity. A number of persons, the larger part of whom appeared to be mariners, or in some way connected with the sea, occupied the wooden benches, or leather-bottomed chairs, conversing on various matters, and occasionally lending their attention to some topic of general interest. Three or four little groups were draining as many bowls of punch, which the great West India trade had long since made a familiar drink in the colony. Others, who had the aspect of men who lived by regular and laborious handicraft, preferred the insulated bliss of an unshared potation, and became more taciturn under its influence. Nearly all, in short, evinced a predilection for the Good Creature in some of its various shapes, for this is a vice, to which, as the Fast-day sermons of a hundred years ago will testify, we have a long hereditary claim. The only guests to whom Robin's sympathies inclined him, were two or three sheepish countrymen, who were using the inn somewhat after the fashion of a Turkish Cara-vansary; they had gotten themselves into the darkest corner of the room, and, heedless of the Nicotian atmosphere, were supping on the bread of their own ovens, and the bacon cured in their own chimney-smoke. But though Robin felt a sort of brotherhood with these strangers, his eyes were attracted from them, to a person who stood near the door, holding whispered conversation with a group of ill-dressed associates. His features were separately striking almost to grotesqueness, and the whole face left a deep impression in memory. The forehead bulged out into a double prominence, with a vale between; the nose came boldly forth in an irregular curve, and its bridge was of more than a finger's breadth; the eyebrows were deep and shaggy, and the eyes glowed beneath them like fire in a cave.

While Robin deliberated of whom to inquire respecting his kinsman's dwelling, he was accosted by the innkeeper, a little man in a stained white apron, who had come to pay his professional welcome to the stranger. Being in the second generation from a French Protestant, he seemed to have inherited the courtesy of his parent nation; but no variety of circumstance was ever known to change his voice from the one shrill note in which he now addressed Robin.

"From the country, I presume, Sir?" said he, with a profound bow. "Beg to congratulate you on your arrival, and trust you intend a long stay with us. Fine town here, Sir, beautiful buildings, and much that may interest a stranger. May I hope for the honor of your commands in respect to supper?"

"The man sees a family likeness! the rogue has guessed that I am related to the Major!" thought Robin, who had hitherto experienced little superfluous civility.

All eyes were now turned on the country lad, standing at the door, in his worn three-cornered hat, grey coat, leather breeches, and blue yarn stockings, leaning on an oaken cudgel, and bearing a wallet on his back.

Robin replied to the courteous innkeeper, with such an assumption of conse-quence, as befitted the Major's relative.

"My honest friend," he said, "I shall make it a point to patronize your house on some occasion, when—" here he could not help lowering his voice—"I may have more than a parchment three-pence in my pocket. My present business," continued he, speaking with lofty confidence, "is merely to inquire the way to the dwelling of my kinsman, Major Molineux."

There was a sudden and general movement in the room, which Robin interpreted as expressing the eagerness of each individual to become his guide. But the innkeeper turned his eyes to a written paper on the wall, which he read, or seemed to read, with occasional recurrences to the young man's figure.

"What have we here?" said he, breaking his speech into little dry fragments. "'Left the house of the subscriber, bounden servant. Hezekiah Mudge—had on, when he went away, grey coat, leather breeches, master's third best hat. One pound currency reward to whoever shall lodge him in any jail in the province.' Better trudge, boy, better trudge!"

Robin had begun to draw his hand towards the lighter end of the oak cudgel, but a strange hostility in every countenance, induced him to relinquish his purpose of breaking the courteous innkeeper's head. As he turned to leave the room, he encountered a sneering glance from the bold-featured personage whom he had before noticed; and no sooner was he beyond the door, than he heard a general laugh, in which the innkeeper's voice might be distinguished, like the dropping of small stones into a kettle.

"Now is it not strange," thought Robin, with his usual shrewdness, "is it not strange, that the confession of an empty pocket, should outweigh the name of my kinsman, Major Molineux? Oh, if I had one of these grinning rascals in the woods, where I and my oak sapling grew up together, I would teach him that my arm is heavy, though my purse be light!"

On turning the corner of the narrow lane, Robin found himself in a spacious street, with an unbroken line of lofty houses on each side, and a steepled building at the upper end, whence the ringing of a bell announced the hour of nine. The light of the moon, and the lamps from numerous shop windows, discovered people promenading on the pavement, and amongst them, Robin hoped to recognize his hitherto inscrutable relative. The result of his former inquiries made him unwilling to hazard another, in a scene of such publicity, and he determined to walk slowly and silently up the street, thrusting his face close to that of every elderly gentleman, in search of the Major's lineaments. In his progress, Robin encountered many gay and gallant figures. Embroidered garments, of showy colors, enormous periwigs, gold-laced hats, and silver hilted swords, glided past him and dazzled his optics. Travelled youths, imitators of the European fine gentlemen of the period, trod jauntily along, half-dancing to the fashionable tunes which they hummed, and making poor Robin ashamed of his quiet and natural gait. At length, after many pauses to examine the gorgeous display of goods in the shop windows, and after suffering some rebukes for the impertinence of his scrutiny into people's faces, the Major's kinsman found himself near the steepled building, still unsuccessful in his search. As yet, however, he had seen only one side of the thronged street; so Robin crossed, and continued the same sort of inquisition down the opposite pavement, with stronger hopes than the philosopher seeking an honest man, but with no better fortune. He had arrived about midway towards the lower end, from which his course began, when he overheard the approach of some one, who struck down a cane on the flag-stones at every step, uttering, at regular intervals, two sepulchral hems.

"Mercy on us!" quoth Robin, recognizing the sound.

Turning a corner, which chanced to be close at his right hand, he hastened to pursue his researches, in some other part of the town. His patience was now wearing low, and he seemed to feel more fatigue from his rambles since he crossed the ferry, than from his journey of several days on the other side. Hunger also pleaded loudly within him, and Robin began to balance the propriety of demanding, violently and with lifted cudgel, the necessary guidance from the first solitary passenger, whom he should meet. While a resolution to this effect was gaining strength, he entered a street of mean appearance, on either side of which, a row of ill-built houses was straggling towards the harbor. The moonlight fell upon no passenger along the whole extent, but in the third domicile which Robin passed, there was a half-opened door, and his keen glance detected a woman's garment within.

"My luck may be better here," said he to himself.

Accordingly, he approached the door, and beheld it shut closer as he did so; yet an open space remained, sufficing for the fair occupant to observe the stranger, without a corresponding display on her part. All that Robin could discern was a strip of scarlet petticoat, and the occasional sparkle of an eye, as if the moonbeams were trembling on some bright thing.

"Pretty mistress,"—for I may call her so with a good conscience, thought the shrewd youth, since I know nothing to the contrary—"my sweet pretty mistress, will you be kind enough to tell me whereabouts I must seek the dwelling of my kinsman, Major Molineux?"

Robin's voice was plaintive and winning, and the female, seeing nothing to be shunned in the handsome country youth, thrust open the door, and came forth into the moonlight. She was a dainty little figure, with a white neck, round arms, and a slender waist, at the extremity of which her scarlet petticoat jutted out over a hoop, as if she were standing in a balloon. Moreover, her face was oval and pretty, her hair dark beneath the little cap, and her bright eyes possessed a sly freedom, which triumphed over those of Robin.

"Major Molineux dwells here," said this fair woman.

Now her voice was the sweetest Robin had heard that night, the airy counterpart of a stream of melted silver; yet he could not help doubting whether that sweet voice spoke Gospel truth. He looked up and down the mean street, and then surveyed the house before which they stood. It was a small, dark edifice of two stories, the second of which projected over the lower floor; and the front apartment had the aspect of a shop for petty commodities.

"Now truly I am in luck," replied Robin, cunningly, "and so indeed is my kinsman, the Major, in having so pretty a housekeeper. But I prithee trouble him to step to the door; I will deliver him a message from his friends in the country, and then go back to my lodgings at the inn."

"Nay, the Major has been a-bed this hour or more," said the lady of the scarlet petticoat; "and it would be to little purpose to disturb him to-night, seeing his evening draught was of the strongest. But he is a kind-hearted man, and it would be as much as my life's worth, to let a kinsman of his turn away from the door. You are the good old gentleman's very picture, and I could swear that was his rainy-weather hat. Also, he has garments very much resembling those leather—But come in, I pray, for I bid you hearty welcome in his name."

So saying, the fair and hospitable dame took our hero by the hand; and though the touch was light, and the force was gentleness, and though Robin read in her eyes what he did not hear in her words, yet the slender waisted woman, in the scarlet petticoat, proved stronger than the athletic country youth. She had drawn his half-willing footsteps nearly to the threshold, when the opening of a door in the neighborhood, startled the Major's housekeeper, and, leaving the Major's kinsman, she vanished speedily into her own domicile. A heavy yawn preceded the appearance of a man, who, like the Moonshine of Pyramus and Thisbe, carried a lantern, needlessly aiding his sister luminary in the heavens. As he walked sleepily up the street, he turned his broad, dull face on Robin, and displayed a long staff, spiked at the end.

"Home, vagabond, home!" said the watchman, in accents that seemed to fall asleep as soon as they were uttered. "Home, or we'll set you in the stocks by peep of day!"

"This is the second hint of the kind," thought Robin. "I wish they would end my difficulties, by setting me there to-night."

Nevertheless, the youth felt an instinctive antipathy towards the guardian of midnight order, which at first prevented him from asking his usual question. But just when the man was about to vanish behind the corner, Robin resolved not to lose the opportunity, and shouted lustily after him—

"I say, friend! will you guide me to the house of my kinsman, Major Molineux?"

The watchman made no reply, but turned the corner and was gone; yet Robin seemed to hear the sound of drowsy laughter stealing along the solitary street. At that moment, also, a pleasant titter saluted him from the open window above his head; he looked up, and caught the sparkle of a saucy eye; a round arm beckoned to him, and next he heard light footsteps descending the staircase within. But Robin, being of the household of a New England clergyman, was a good youth, as well as a shrewd one; so he resisted temptation, and fled away.

He now roamed desperately, and at random, through the town, almost ready to believe that a spell was on him, like that, by which a wizard of his country, had once kept three pursuers wandering, a whole winter night, within twenty paces of the cottage which they sought. The streets lay before him, strange and desolate, and the lights were extinguished in almost every house. Twice, however, little parties of men, among whom Robin distinguished individuals in outlandish attire, came hurrying along, but though on both occasions they paused to address him, such intercourse did not at all enlighten his perplexity. They did but utter a few words in some language of which Robin knew nothing, and perceiving his inability to answer, bestowed a curse upon him in plain English, and hastened away. Finally, the lad determined to knock at the door of every mansion that might appear worthy to be occupied by his kinsman, trusting that perserverance would overcome the fatality which had hitherto thwarted him. Firm in this resolve, he was passing beneath the walls of a church, which formed the corner of two streets, when, as he turned into the shade of its steeple, he encountered a bulky stranger, muffled in a cloak. The man was proceeding with the speed of earnest business, but Robin planted himself full before him, holding the oak cudgel with both hands across his body, as a bar to further passage.

"Halt, honest man, and answer me a question," said he, very resolutely. "Tell me, this instant, whereabouts is the dwelling of my kinsman, Major Molineux?"

"Keep your tongue between your teeth, fool, and let me pass," said a deep, gruff voice, which Robin partly remembered. "Let me pass, I say, or I'll strike you to the earth!"

"No, no, neighbor!" cried Robin, flourishing his cudgel, and then thrusting its larger end close to the man's muffled face. "No, no, I'm not the fool you take me for, nor do you pass, till I have an answer to my question. Whereabouts is the dwelling of my kinsman, Major Molineux?"

The stranger, instead of attempting to force his passage, stept back into the moonlight, unmuffled his own face and stared full into that of Robin.

"Watch here an hour, and Major Molineux will pass by," said he.

Robin gazed with dismay and astonishment, on the unprecedented physiognomy of the speaker. The forehead with its double prominence, the broad-hooked nose, the shaggy eyebrows, and fiery eyes, were those which he had noticed at the inn, but the man's complexion had undergone a singular, or, more properly, a two-fold change. One side of the face blazed of an intense red, while the other was black as midnight, the division line being in the broad bridge of the nose; and a mouth, which seemed to extend from ear to ear, was black or red, in contrast to the color of the cheek. The effect was as if two individual devils, a fiend of fire and a fiend of darkness, had united themselves to form this infernal visage. The stranger grinned in Robin's face, muffled his parti-colored features, and was out of sight in a moment.

"Strange things we travellers see!" ejaculated Robin.

He seated himself, however, upon the steps of the church-door, resolving to wait the appointed time for his kinsman's appearance. A few moments were consumed in philosophical speculations, upon the species of the *genus homo*, who had just left him, but having settled this point shrewdly, rationally, and satisfactorily, he was compelled to look elsewhere for amusement. And first he threw his eyes along the street; it was of more respectable appearance than most of those into which he had wandered, and the moon, "creating, like the imaginative power, a beautiful strangeness in familiar objects," gave something of romance to a scene, that might not have possessed it in the light of day. The irregular, and often quaint architecture of the houses, some of whose roofs were broken into numerous little peaks; while others ascended, steep and narrow, into a single point; and others again were square; the pure milk-white of some of their complexions, the aged darkness of others, and the thousand sparklings, reflected from bright substances in the plastered walls of many; these matters engaged Robin's attention for awhile, and then began to grow wearisome. Next he endeavored to define the forms of distant objects, starting away with almost ghostly indistinctness, just as his eye appeared to grasp them; and finally he took a minute survey of an edifice, which stood on the opposite side of the street, directly in front of the church-door, where he was stationed. It was a large square mansion, distinguished from its neighbors by a balcony, which rested on tall pillars, and by an elaborate Gothic window, communicating therewith.

"Perhaps this is the very house I have been seeking," thought Robin.

Then he strove to speed away the time, by listening to a murmur, which swept continually along the street, yet was scarcely audible, except to an unaccustomed ear like his; it was a low, dull, dreamy sound, compounded of many noises, each of which was at too great a distance to be separately heard. Robin marvelled at this snore of a sleeping town, and marvelled more, whenever its continuity was broken, by now and then a distant shout, apparently loud where it originated. But altogether it was a sleep-inspiring sound, and to shake off its drowsy influence, Robin arose, and climbed a window-frame, that he might view the interior of the church. There the moonbeams came trembling in, and fell down upon the deserted pews, and extended along the quiet aisles. A fainter, yet more awful radiance, was hovering round the pulpit, and one solitary ray had dared to rest upon the opened page of the great Bible. Had Nature, in that deep hour, become a worshipper in the house, which man had builded? Or was that heavenly light the visible sanctity of the place, visible because no earthly and impure feet were within the walls? The scene made Robin's heart shiver with a sensation of loneliness, stronger than he had ever felt in the remotest depths of his native woods; so he turned away, and sat down again before the door. There were graves around the church, and now an uneasy thought obtruded into Robin's breast. What if the object of his search, which had been so often and so strangely thwarted, were all the time mouldering in his shroud? What if his kinsman should glide through yonder gate, and nod and smile to him in passing dimly by?

"Oh, that any breathing thing were here with me!" said Robin.

Recalling his thoughts from this uncomfortable track, he sent them over forest, hill, and stream, and attempted to imagine how that evening of ambiguity and weariness, had been spent by his father's household. He pictured them assembled at the door, beneath the tree, the great old tree, which had been spared for its huge twisted trunk, and venerable shade, when a thousand leafy brethren fell. There, at the going down of the summer sun, it was his father's custom to perform domestic worship, that the neighbors might come and join with him like brothers of the family, and that the wayfaring man might pause to drink at that fountain, and keep his heart pure by freshening the memory of home. Robin distinguished the seat of every individual of the little audience; he saw the good man in the midst, holding the Scriptures in the golden light that shone from the western clouds; he beheld him close the book, and all rise up to pray. He heard the old thanksgivings for daily mercies, the old supplications for their continuance, to which he had so often listened in weariness, but which were now among his dear remembrances. He perceived the slight inequality of his father's voice when he came to speak of the Absent One; he noted how his mother turned her face to the broad and knotted trunk; how his elder brother scorned, because the beard was rough upon his upper lip, to permit his features to be moved;

how his younger sister drew down a low hanging branch before her eyes; and how the little one of all, whose sports had hitherto broken the decorum of the scene, understood the prayer for her playmate, and burst into clamorous grief. Then he saw them go in at the door; and when Robin would have entered also, the latch tinkled into its place, and he was excluded from his home.

"Am I here, or there?" cried Robin, starting; for all at once, when his thoughts had become visible and audible in a dream, the long, wide, solitary street shone out before him.

He aroused himself, and endeavored to fix his attention steadily upon the large edifice which he had surveyed before. But still his mind kept vibrating between fancy and reality; by turns, the pillars of the balcony lengthened into the tall, bare stems of pines, dwindled down to human figures, settled again in their true shape and size, and then commenced a new succession of changes. For a single moment, when he deemed himself awake, he could have sworn that a visage, one which he seemed to remember, yet could not absolutely name as his kinsman's, was looking towards him from the Gothic window. A deeper sleep wrestled with, and nearly overcame him, but fled at the sound of footsteps along the opposite pavement. Robin rubbed his eyes, discerned a man passing at the foot of the balcony, and addressed him in a loud, peevish, and lamentable cry.

"Halloo, friend! must I wait here all night for my kinsman, Major Molineux?"

The sleeping echoes awoke, and answered the voice; and the passenger, barely able to discern a figure sitting in the oblique shade of the steeple, traversed the street to obtain a nearer view. He was himself a gentleman in his prime, of open, intelligent, cheerful, and altogether prepossessing countenance. Perceiving a country youth, apparently homeless and without friends, he accosted him in a tone of real kindness, which had become strange to Robin's ears.

"Well, my good lad, why are you sitting here?" inquired he. "Can I be of service to you in any way?"

"I am afraid not, Sir," replied Robin, despondingly; "yet I shall take it kindly, if you'll answer me a single question. I've been searching half the night for one Major Molineux; now, Sir, is there really such a person in these parts, or am I dreaming?"

"Major Molineux. The name is not altogether strange to me," said the gentleman, smiling. "Have you any objection to telling me the nature of your business with him?"

Then Robin briefly related that his father was a clergyman, settled on a small salary, at a long distance back in the country, and that he and Major Molineux were brothers' children. The Major, having inherited riches, and acquired civil and military rank, had visited his cousin in great pomp a year or two before; had manifested much interest in Robin and an elder brother, and, being childless himself, had thrown out hints respecting the future establishment of one of them in life. The elder brother was destined to succeed to the farm, which his father cultivated, in the interval of sacred duties; it was therefore determined that Robin should profit by his kinsman's generous intentions, especially as he had seemed to be rather the favorite, and was thought to possess other necessary endowments.

"For I have the name of being a shrewd youth," observed Robin, in this part of his story.

"I doubt not you deserve it," replied his new friend, good naturedly; "but pray proceed."

"Well, Sir, being nearly eighteen years old, and well grown, as you see," continued Robin, raising himself to his full height, "I thought it high time to begin the world. So my mother and sister put me in handsome trim, and my father gave me half the remnant of his last year's salary, and five days ago I started for this place, to pay the Major a visit. But would you believe it, Sir? I crossed the ferry a little after dusk, and have yet found nobody that would show me the way to his dwelling; only an hour or two since, I was told to wait here, and Major Molineux would pass by."

"Can you describe the man who told you this?" inquired the gentleman.

"Oh, he was a very ill-favored fellow, Sir," replied Robin, "with two great bumps on his forehead, a hook nose, fiery eyes, and, what struck me as the strangest, his face was of two different colors. Do you happen to know such a man, Sir?"

"Not intimately," answered the stranger, "but I chanced to meet him a little time previous to your stopping me. I believe you may trust his word, and that the Major will very shortly pass through this street. In the mean time, as I have a singular curiosity to witness your meeting, I will sit down here upon the steps, and bear you company."

He seated himself accordingly, and soon engaged his companion in animated discourse. It was but of brief continuance, however, for a noise of shouting, which had long been remotely audible, drew so much nearer, that Robin inquired its cause.

"What may be the meaning of this uproar?" asked he. "Truly, if your town be always as noisy, I shall find little sleep, while I am an inhabitant."

"Why, indeed, friend Robin, there do appear to be three or four riotous fellows abroad to-night," replied the gentleman. "You must not expect all the stillness of your native woods, here in our streets. But the watch will shortly be at the heels of these lads, and—"

"Aye, and set them in the stocks by peep of day," interrupted Robin, recollecting his own encounter with the drowsy lantern-bearer. "But, dear Sir, if I may trust my ears, an army of watchmen would never make head against such a multitude of rioters. There were at least a thousand voices went to make up that one shout."

"May not one man have several voices, Robin, as well as two complexions?" said his friend.

"Perhaps a man may; but Heaven forbid that a woman should!" responded the shrewd youth, thinking of the seductive tones of the Major's housekeeper.

The sounds of a trumpet in some neighboring street now became so evident and continual, that Robin's curiosity was strongly excited. In addition to the shouts, he heard frequent bursts from many instruments of discord, and a wild and confused laughter filled up the intervals. Robin rose from the steps, and looked wistfully towards a point, whither several people seemed to be hastening.

"Surely some prodigious merrymaking is going on," exclaimed he. "I have laughed very little since I left home, Sir, and should be sorry to lose an opportunity. Shall we just step round the corner by that darkish house, and take our share of the fun?"

"Sit down again, sit down, good Robin," replied the gentleman, laying his hand on the skirt of the grey coat. "You forget that we must wait here for your kinsman; and there is reason to believe that he will pass by, in the course of a very few moments."

The near approach of the uproar had now disturbed the neighborhood; windows flew open on all sides; and many heads, in the attire of the pillow, and confused by sleep suddenly broken, were protruded to the gaze of whoever had leisure to observe them. Eager voices hailed each other from house to house, all demanding the explanation, which not a soul could give. Half-dressed men hurried towards the unknown commotion, stumbling as they went over the stone steps, that thrust themselves into the narrow foot-walk. The shouts, the laughter, and the tuneless bray, the antipodes of music, came onward with increasing din, till scattered individuals, and then denser bodies, began to appear round a corner, at the distance of a hundred yards.

"Will you recognize your kinsman, Robin, if he passes in the crowd?" inquired the gentleman.

"Indeed, I can't warrant it, Sir; but I'll take my stand here, and keep a bright look out," answered Robin, descending to the outer edge of the pavement.

A mighty stream of people now emptied into the street, and came rolling slowly towards the church. A single horseman wheeled the corner in the midst of them, and close behind him came a band of fearful wind-instruments, sending forth a fresher discord, now that no intervening buildings kept it from the ear. Then a redder light disturbed the moonbeams, and a dense multitude of torches shone along the street, concealing by their glare whatever object they illuminated. The single horseman, clad in a military dress, and bearing a drawn sword, rode onward as the leader, and, by his fierce and variegated countenance, appeared like war personified; the red of one cheek was an emblem of fire and sword; the blackness of the other betokened the mourning which attends them. In his train, were wild figures in the Indian dress, and many fantastic shapes without a model, giving the whole march a visionary air, as if a dream had broken forth from some feverish brain, and were sweeping visibly through the midnight streets. A mass of people, inactive, except as applauding spectators, hemmed the procession in, and several women ran along the sidewalks, piercing the confusion of heavier sounds, with their shrill voices of mirth or terror.

"The double-faced fellow has his eye upon me," muttered Robin, with an indefinite but uncomfortable idea, that he was himself to bear a part in the pageantry.

The leader turned himself in the saddle, and fixed his glance full upon the country youth, as the steed went slowly by. When Robin had freed his eyes from those fiery

locations (for example, what the parents are saying, doing, and thinking while worrying about where the boys and the dog are, as well as what the boys are saying, doing, and thinking). This all-knowing or *omniscient* point of view is one approach to third-person narration. Or the writer may decide to limit the point of view to one character's consciousness. For example, Hawthorne's narrator or narrative voice relates "My Kinsman" from Robin's perspective, even though Robin does not relate the story himself. Instead we hear *about* him but only what *he* sees, thinks, imagines, or dreams. The choice you, or a writer like Hawthorne or Conrad, make about point of view dramatically affects the story.

"Youth" offers an excellent opportunity to study point of view because of the unusual narrative technique Conrad selects. An unidentified narrator sets the stage with his reference to the sea and then introduces Marlow, who tells the story. This first narrator "frames" Marlow's story by appearing at the beginning and the end. In other works by Conrad, this type of frame appears so frequently that like the sea setting it becomes characteristic of Conrad's narrative technique. But even so, a reader should never assume that a narrator like Marlow, or even the first narrator in "Youth," *is* the writer and that what he says is exactly what the writer is thinking. Conrad may create a narrator who has many characteristics in common with himself, but there is always some distance or difference between a writer and the created narrator.

□ WRITING ↔ READING ↔ THINKING ACTIVITIES □
Considering Details of Setting and Point of View

Examining point of view in any story (or any real-life situation) requires not only determining who tells the story but also noting details which affect the telling. For example, how may the fact that Marlow is speaking directly to an audience in the story influence the tale he tells? What specifically may be the effect of the following:

- □ The five men sitting around the table share a bond of experience at sea. ("All began life in the merchant service.")
- □ They are drinking as they reminisce. ("Pass the bottle.")
- □ Marlow is forty-two remembering his experience at twenty. (Does he consistently speak from the perspective of forty-two?)
- □ All the men at the table have left the sea.

By creating this particular setting for Marlow's narrative, Conrad offers the reader a special perspective of a story of initiation. But he might have chosen another approach. How would the tale differ if Marlow had been testifying at a board of inquiry immediately following the loss of the ship? reminiscing at Captain Beard's eighty-second birthday party?

Bridging the Generations

Numerous short stories have been written about the initiation of boys into manhood, but relatively few have been written about girls growing into womanhood. The next two stories were written by women, include three generations of women, and have as major characters and first-person narrators women recalling experiences from their adolescence. Do these stories indicate that the transformation into adulthood is similar for both sexes, or are there genuine differences? Do males and females relate differently to their parents? to their grandparents? How might these stories differ if the narrators had been men relating events from their adolescence?

Shirley Jackson (1919–1965)
Dorothy and My Grandmother and the Sailors

There used to be a time of year in San Francisco—in late March, I believe—when there was fine long windy weather, and the air all over the city had a touch of salt and the freshness of the sea. And then, some time after the wind first started, you could look around Market Street and Van Ness and Kearney, and the fleet was in. That, of course, was some time ago, but you could look out around the Golden Gate, unbridged at that time, and there would be the battleships. There may have been aircraft carriers and destroyers, and I believe I recall one submarine, but to Dot and me then they were battleships, all of them. They would be riding out there on the water, quiet and competently grey, and the streets would be full of sailors, walking with the roll of the sea and looking in shop windows.

I never knew what the fleet came in for; my grandmother said positively that it was for refueling; but from the time the wind first started, Dot and I would become more aware, walking closer together, and dropping our voices when we talked.

Although we were all of thirty miles from where the fleet lay, when we walked with our backs to the ocean we could feel the battleships riding somewhere behind and beyond us, and when we looked toward the ocean we narrowed our eyes, almost able to see across thirty miles and into a sailor's face.

It *was* sailors, of course. My mother told us about the kind of girls who followed sailors, and my grandmother told us about the kind of sailors who followed girls. When we told Dot's mother the fleet was in, she would say earnestly, "Don't go near any sailors, you two." Once, when Dot and I were about twelve, and the fleet was in, my mother stood us up and looked at us intently for a minute, and then she turned around to my grandmother and said, "I don't approve of young girls going to the movies alone at night," and my grandmother said, "Nonsense, they won't come this far down the peninsula; I *know* sailors."

Dot and I were permitted only one movie at night a week, anyway, and even then they sent my ten-year-old brother along with us. The first time the three of us started off to the movies together my mother looked at Dot and me again and then speculatively at my brother, who had red curly hair, and started to say something, and then looked at my grandmother and changed her mind.

We lived in Burlingame, which is far enough away from San Francisco to have palm trees in the gardens, but near enough so that Dot and I were taken into San Francisco, to the Emporium, to get our spring coats each year. Dot's mother usually gave Dot her coat money, which Dot handed over to my mother, and then Dot and I got identical coats, with my mother officiating. This was because Dot's mother was never well enough to go into San Francisco shopping, and particularly not with Dot and me. Consequently every year, sometime after the wind started and the fleet came in, Dot and I, in service-weight silk stockings which we kept for the occasion, and each with a cardboard pocketbook containing a mirror, a dime for luck, and a chiffon handkerchief caught at one side and hanging down, got into the back seat of my mother's car with my mother and grandmother in the front, and headed for San Francisco and the fleet.

We always got our coats in the morning, went to the Pig'n'Whistle for lunch, and then, while Dot and I were finishing our chocolate ice cream with chocolate sauce and walnuts, my grandmother phoned my Uncle Oliver and arranged to meet him at the launch which took us out to the fleet.

My Uncle Oliver was taken along partly because he was a man and partly because in the previous war he had been a radio operator on a battleship and partly because another uncle of mine, an Uncle Paul, was still with the Navy (my grandmother thought he had something to do with a battleship named the *Santa Volita*, or *Bonita*, or possibly *Carmelita*) and my Uncle Oliver was handy for asking people who looked like they might know my Uncle Paul if they did know him. As soon as we got on a boat my grandmother would say, as though she had never thought of it before, "Look, that one over there seems to be an officer; Ollie, just go over casually and ask him if he knows old Paul."

Oliver, having been one himself, didn't think that sailors were particularly dangerous to Dot and me if we had my mother and my grandmother with us, but he loved ships, and so he went with us and left us the minute we were on board; while we stepped cautiously over the clean decks eyeing the lifeboats apprehensively, my Uncle Oliver would touch the grey paint affectionately and go off in search of the radio apparatus.

When we met my Uncle Oliver at the launch he would usually buy Dot and me an ice cream cone each and on the launch he would point out various boats around and name them for us. He usually got into a conversation with the sailor running the launch, and sooner or later he managed to say modestly, "I was to sea, back in '17," and the sailor would nod respectfully. When it came time for us to leave the launch and go up a stairway on to the battleship, my mother whispered to Dot and me, "Keep your skirts down," and Dot and I climbed the ladder, holding on with one hand and with the other wrapping our skirts tight around us into a bunch in front which we held on to. My grandmother always preceded us onto the battleship and my mother and Uncle Oliver followed us. When we got on board my mother took one of us by the arm and my grandmother took the other and we walked slowly around all of the ship they allowed us to see, excepting only the lowest levels, which alarmed my grandmother. We looked solemnly at cabins, decks which my grandmother said were aft, and lights which she said were port (both sides were port to my grandmother; she believed that starboard was up, in the sense that the highest mast always pointed at the north star). Usually we saw cannon—all guns were cannon—which my Uncle Oliver, on what must have been harmless teasing, assured my grandmother were kept loaded all the time. "In case of mutiny," he told my grandmother.

There were always a great many sightseers on the battleships and my Uncle Oliver was fond of gathering a little group of boys and young men around him to explain how the radio system worked. When he said he had been a radio operator back in '17 someone was sure to ask him, "Did you ever send out an S.O.S.?" and my Uncle Oliver would nod heavily, and say, "But I'm still here to tell about it."

Once, while my Uncle Oliver was telling about '17 and my mother and my grandmother and Dot were looking over the rail at the ocean, I saw a dress that looked like my mother's and followed it for quite a way down the battleship before the lady turned around and I realized that it was not my mother and I was lost. Remembering what my grandmother had told me, that I was always safe if I didn't lose my head, I stood still and looked around until I isolated a tall man in a uniform with lots of braid. That will be a captain, I thought, and he will certainly take care of me. He was very polite. I told him I was lost and thought my mother and my grandmother and my friend Dot and my Uncle Oliver were down the boat a ways but I was afraid to go back alone. He said he would help me find them, and he took my arm and led me down the boat. Before very long we met my mother and my grandmother hurrying along looking for me with Dot coming along behind them as fast as she could. When my grandmother saw me she ran forward and seized my arm, pulling me away from the captain and shaking me. "You gave us the scare of our lives," she said.

"She was just lost, that's all," the captain said.

"I'm glad we found her in time," my grandmother said, walking backward with me to my mother.

The captain bowed and went away, and my mother took my other arm and shook me. "Aren't you ashamed?" she said. Dot stared at me solemnly.

"But he was a captain—" I began.

"He might have *said* he was a captain," my grandmother said, "but he was a marine."

"A marine!" my mother said, looking over the side to see if the launch was there to take us back. "Get Oliver and tell him we've seen enough," she said to my grandmother.

Because of what happened that evening, that was the last year we were allowed to see the fleet. We dropped Uncle Oliver off at home, as usual, and my mother and my grandmother took Dot and me to the Merry-Go-Round for dinner. We always had dinner in San Francisco after the fleet, and went to a movie and got home to Burlingame late in the evening. We always had dinner in the Merry-Go-Round, where the food came along on a moving platform and you grabbed it as it went by. We went there because Dot and I loved it, and next to battleships it was the most dangerous place in San Francisco, because you had to pay fifteen cents for every dish you took and didn't finish, and Dot and I were expected to pay for these mistakes out of our allowances. This last evening Dot and I lost forty-five cents, mainly because of a mocha cream dessert that Dot hadn't known was full of coconut. The movie Dot and I chose was full, although the usher outside told my grandmother there were plenty of seats. My mother refused to wait in line to get our money back, so my grandmother said we had to go on in and take our chances on seats. As soon as two seats were vacant my grandmother shoved Dot and me toward them, and we sat down. The picture was well under way when the two seats next to Dot emptied, and we were looking for my grandmother and mother when Dot looked around suddenly and then grabbed my arm. "Look," she said in a sort of groan, and there were two sailors coming along the row of seats toward the empty ones. They reached the seats just as my mother and grandmother got down to the other end of the row, and my grandmother had just time to say loudly, "You leave those girls alone," when two seats a few aisles away were vacated and they had to go sit down.

Dot moved far over in her seat next to me and clung to my arm.

"What are they doing?" I whispered.

"They're just sitting there," Dot said. "What do you think I ought to do?"

I leaned cautiously around Dot and looked. "Don't pay any attention," I said. "Maybe they'll go away."

"*You* can talk," Dot said tragically, "they're not next to *you.*"

"I am next to *you*," I said reasonably, "that's pretty close."

"What are they doing now?" Dot asked.

I leaned forward again. "They're looking at the picture," I said.

"I can't stand it," Dot said. "I want to go home."

Panic overwhelmed both of us at once, and fortunately my mother and grandmother saw us running up the aisle and caught us outside.

"What did they say?" my grandmother demanded. "I'll tell the usher."

My mother said if Dot would calm down enough to talk she would take us into the tea room next door and get us each a hot chocolate. When we got inside and were sitting down we told my mother and my grandmother we were fine now and instead of a hot chocolate we would have a chocolate sundae apiece. Dot had even started to cheer up a little when the door of the tea room opened and two sailors walked in. With one wild bound Dot was in back of my grandmother's chair, cowering and clutching my grandmother's arm. "Don't let them get me," she wailed.

"They followed us," my mother said tautly.

My grandmother put her arms around Dot. "Poor child," she said, "you're safe with us."

Dot had to stay at my house that night. We sent my brother over to Dot's mother to tell her that Dot was staying with me and that Dot had bought a grey tweed coat with princess lines, very practical and warmly interlined. She wore it all that year.

Elizabeth Forsythe Hailey (born 1938)
His Children

As a child it did not seem strange to me to hear my grandmother speak reverently of her first husband in the presence of her second. I was still at an age when it seemed reasonable that an adult was entitled to more than one of everything, including husbands.

Until I was twelve my favorite story was her description of the day her first husband had come home from work and hugged her so tightly one of her ribs had actually cracked. But during the space of time the term adolescence attempts to dignify, I began to suffer for her second husband—the only grandfather I had ever known. Though my own attitude changed, however, I could detect no difference in my grandfather.

Carefully insuring her comfort by the arrangement of pillows behind her back, my grandmother would delight in recalling the day her first husband celebrated a successful business deal by coming home with a new horse and buggy for her. Then, with a significant look at my grandfather, she would murmur, "He was such a generous man. He gave me everything I wanted."

I would look at my grandfather, hoping somehow her concluding sentence had escaped him. But instead of being offended, my grandfather would add his own confirmation: "He was a dynamo in business. Would have made a fortune if he had lived. Everyone said so." I was the only one who seemed able to imagine what these words cost my grandfather. My grandmother took it for granted that the final seal on this particular story would come from him, as it always had.

I used to search old photograph albums for hours, trying to find what there was about this gentle man that kept him from ever emerging favorably in comparison with my "real grandfather." (This was my grandmother's term for her first husband when talking to her grandchildren. It was a distinction impossible for me to conceive. How could a portrait in her bedroom be more real to me than the man who took movies of my first steps and taught me to play tennis and every Christmas played a faltering flute to accompany the family Christmas carols? No matter how many husbands my grandmother had had, I only had one grandfather, real or otherwise.) After a certain age, when my grandmother spoke to me of my "real grandfather," I would counter by referring to him as "your first husband." She never acknowledged the distinction, but it made me feel better.

There was an undercurrent of feeling among the grandchildren that our grandfather was a victim of discrimination at the hands of our grandmother but, being the oldest grandchild, I was the first to put it into words. One day I approached my mother, "Didn't Granddaddy want children of his own?"

"Howard?" she asked, and hearing the name made me realize that she had never thought of him as her father despite the fact that she was only seven when he married her mother. Her own father had died before she had any memory of him.

My mother hesitated and I insisted, "Well, didn't he? They were still young, weren't they?"

"I don't remember hearing it discussed," she said finally, as if the possibility that my grandfather might have expected more from his marriage had never occurred to her before.

It remained a mystery to me why my grandfather—obviously an eligible bachelor with unlimited prospects—had married a widow with three children who would never call him father. Finally, about the time I went away to college, I decided the answer had to be a matter of money. My grandmother had been left a substantial amount by her first husband (even my grandfather acknowledged that the man was on his way to being a tycoon). This must have enticed my grandfather to marry her, knowing that he would be her second husband and nothing more—to her or her children.

With this explanation in mind, I called on my grandparents the afternoon I arrived home for Christmas vacation of my freshman year. My grandmother was waiting for me, holding my Christmas check in her hand. She could never endure having to share a holiday with the rest of the civilized world. She presented her gifts and garnered her gratitude several days before the occasion—and usually succeeded in creating the impression that everyone else was a little late.

I took the check—which was generous—and thanked her. My grandfather watched the exchange without comment but my grandmother felt that his silence should be explained: "Your grandfather will be giving his checks Christmas Day," she said, implying that she would have to spend the intervening time coaxing him to his checkbook.

Their checks were always for an equal amount but my grandmother was careful to build the impression that she set a goal my grandfather was obliged to match. Without her check as a guide, she implied that he would settle for a smaller amount—and consequently we would all be a great deal poorer. In this way she assumed the credit not only for what she gave but for a large part of what he gave. And we came away with the vague impression that she was the source of all the money we received. However, I had begun to suspect that her wealth was so much greater than what my grandfather could have accumulated through a life of steady but quiet industry that his gifts came at a much greater cost to him.

And so this year, when she presented her check and commented, as usual, that my grandfather, as usual, had chosen to wait until Christmas Day, I was bold enough to reply, "Why, this check is large enough for both of you. I don't expect anything else."

My reply must have betrayed my attitude more than I realized because this time, instead of accepting the gratitude she was due, my grandmother looked at me sharply and changed the topic. A few moments later when my grandfather left the room, I saw that the conversation had only been momentarily diverted. My grandmother had more to say, and suddenly revealed a startling fact. "Howard has three times as much money as I do. But I never see it. I own this house, and what he gives me each month doesn't even pay for the servants."

What I had assumed to be a marriage of convenience was even less—on either part. Every question of fact had now been answered. My grandfather had not married my grandmother for the children they would have or the fortune he would share. He made no claim on either. What then did he hope to gain? If I had asked him, he would not have understood the question. As for my grandmother, she clearly felt he was already getting more than he deserved.

Then came the summer I graduated from college and in one afternoon on a road trip my education became complete. I had become a favorite traveling companion for my grandparents from the time I earned my driver's license, and we made frequent weekend trips.

This particular afternoon they were sitting together in the back seat arguing about the mileage to our destination, ignoring maps that might have settled the question. I was driving. I knew the exact mileage but I also knew better than to deny them the pleasure of their argument. Then, not at all in the nature of a confession but rather as a familiar fact, my grandfather referred to his first wife.

The car swerved. I will never know whether my grandfather was aware that this was my initiation into the fact of his first marriage, but it was my grandmother who sensed the need to explain: "She was a very ambitious woman. Her career mattered more to her than anything—her home, her husband."

My grandfather listened in agreement but for once the official version of an event was not to rest wholly with my grandmother. "She was very beautiful," he added in the same way he added details to my grandmother's stories of her first husband, "and she was unfaithful to me."

Though silent, my grandmother made her judgment of this unspeakable act loud in my mind. This was the first time I had seen her give unqualified support to my grandfather on any question and I could sense him drawing comfort from it.

The conversation soon returned to the number of miles saved by the new interstate highway, but now I knew that what my grandmother could give my grandfather was what his first wife had taken from him. In most marriages faithfulness is an obligation. To my grandfather it was a gift and it overshadowed any question of children or money.

In his last years, sitting peacefully in the garden of the nursing home where he had lived since a stroke had left him almost helpless, able to speak only in disconnected words, my grandfather listened while my grandmother spoke my name.

"Nancy has come to see you and she has brought the baby."

I had been living in another state when my first child was born, so this was my grandfather's first look at his first greatgrandchild. My grandfather looked at me without recognition, as if I were at best a concerned stranger, then he turned to the baby and with a delighted smile held out his arms and said, "Come here, Nancy."

I quietly put the baby in his lap. My grandmother adjusted his laprobe and I suddenly knew how wrong I had been ever to think she had denied him children of his own.

□ WRITING ↔ READING ↔ THINKING ACTIVITIES □
Comparing Elements of Narration

You have now read examples of short fiction and considered plot, character, theme, setting, and point of view. Preparing a summary chart which highlights the similarities and differences in the stories can be an aid in analyzing the narrative style of each writer. Review the entries for "My Kinsman, Major Molineux" and "Youth," then expand the chart on your own paper to include the two stories you have just read. Although reducing any work of fiction, or indeed any writing, to chart form does not reflect the writer's artistry, pinpointing essential narrative techniques can be a useful basis for comparison.

Elements of Narration

	"My Kinsman, Major Molineux"	"Youth"	"Dorothy and My Grandmother and the Sailors"	"His Children"
Writer	Nathaniel Hawthorne	Joseph Conrad		
Plot Structure	Journey from country to town	Voyage		
Main Character	Country boy aged 18	Second mate aged 20		
Theme	Initiation (abrupt revelation)	Initiation (test of responsibility and manhood)		
Time of Story (Chronological Setting)	Colonial period prior to American Revolution	Time of East Indian trade		
Place (Geographical Setting)	New England village	English ship in port and at sea		
Point of View	Third person	First person(s)		

☐ EXPANDING YOUR WRITING SKILLS ☐
Composing a Narrative

Now that you have studied the major elements of fiction, especially short fiction, compose your own narrative. This assignment has three distinct parts:

1. Review your journal entries or select some other personal experience from adolescence and narrate it in writing for your classmates in 500 to 600 words. You may wish to consider the following possible topics:
   a. Your first trip away from home to experience life "on your own"

  b. A particular experience which revealed something to you about your
   parents or grandparents you had not previously suspected
  c. An occurrence in which a childhood hero was revealed to be, after all,
   human and imperfect
  d. Any experience which had a significant impact on your initiation into
   adulthood

2. Although you are not writing a short story, you are dealing in this essay
with the major elements of narration: plot, character, theme, setting,
and point of view. As you plan your narrative, as you write it, and as
you revise it, record in your journal your observations about the process.
For example, as you think about how to begin, what topics do you consider and reject? Why do you select the one you do? In planning the
essay, how do you deal with the questions of who, what, when, where,
how, and why? What particular difficulties do you have in writing the
narrative? What types of revisions do you make in successive drafts?

3. When you have a satisfactory draft, ask a classmate or two to read your
account and to prepare a narrative elements chart like the one for the
first four stories in this chapter. Reviewing and discussing this chart
with your reader may reveal a great deal about what you meant to say
and what someone else thinks you said.

Questioning Appearances

  Your familiarity with Hawthorne's "My Kinsman, Major Molineux"
should assist you in understanding the next story, also by Hawthorne. Although a reader should not expect two stories by a writer to be too much
alike, an author like Conrad or Hawthorne usually has a distinct range of
interests, favorite subject matter, and a personal storytelling and writing
style.

Nathaniel Hawthorne (1804–1864)
Young Goodman Brown

  Young Goodman Brown came forth, at sunset, into the street of Salem village,
but put his head back, after crossing the threshold, to exchange a parting kiss with
his young wife. And Faith, as the wife was aptly named, thrust her own pretty head

into the street, letting the wind play with the pink ribbons of her cap, while she called to Goodman Brown.

"Dearest heart," whispered she, softly and rather sadly, when her lips were close to his ear, "pr'y thee, put off your journey until sunrise, and sleep in your own bed to-night. A lone woman is troubled with such dreams and such thoughts, that she's afeard of herself, sometimes. Pray, tarry with me this night, dear husband, of all nights in the year!"

"My love and my Faith," replied young Goodman Brown, "of all nights in the year, this one night must I tarry away from thee. My journey, as thou callest it, forth and back again, must needs be done 'twixt now and sunrise. What, my sweet, pretty wife, dost thou doubt me already, and we but three months married!"

"Then, God bless you!" said Faith, with the pink ribbons, "and may you find all well, when you come back."

"Amen!" cried Goodman Brown. "Say thy prayers, dear Faith, and go to bed at dusk, and no harm will come to thee."

So they parted; and the young man pursued his way, until, being about to turn the corner by the meeting-house, he looked back, and saw the head of Faith still peeping after him, with a melancholy air, in spite of her pink ribbons.

"Poor little Faith!" thought he, for his heart smote him. "What a wretch am I, to leave her on such an errand! She talks of dreams, too. Methought, as she spoke, there was trouble in her face, as if a dream had warned her what work is to be done to-night. But, no, no! 'twould kill her to think it. Well; she's a blessed angel on earth; and after this one night, I'll cling to her skirts and follow her to Heaven."

With this excellent resolve for the future, Goodman Brown felt himself justified in making more haste on his present evil purpose. He had taken a dreary road, darkened by all the gloomiest trees of the forest, which barely stood aside to let the narrow path creep through, and closed immediately behind. It was all as lonely as could be; and there is this peculiarity in such a solitude, that the traveller knows not who may be concealed by the innumerable trunks and the thick boughs overhead; so that, with lonely footsteps, he may yet be passing through an unseen multitude.

"There may be a devilish Indian behind every tree," said Goodman Brown, to himself; and he glanced fearfully behind him, as he added, "What if the devil himself should be at my very elbow!"

His head being turned back, he passed a crook of the road, and looking forward again, beheld the figure of a man, in grave and decent attire, seated at the foot of an old tree. He arose, at Goodman Brown's approach, and walked onward, side by side with him.

"You are late, Goodman Brown," said he. "The clock of the Old South was striking as I came through Boston; and that is full fifteen minutes agone."

"Faith kept me back awhile," replied the young man, with a tremor in his voice, caused by the sudden appearance of his companion, though not wholly unexpected.

It was now deep dusk in the forest, and deepest in that part of it where these two were journeying. As nearly as could be discerned, the second traveller was about fifty years old, apparently in the same rank of life as Goodman Brown, and bearing a considerable resemblance to him, though perhaps more in expression than features. Still, they might have been taken for father and son. And yet, though the elder person was as simply clad as the younger, and as simple in manner too, he had an indescribable air of one who knew the world, and would not have felt abashed at the governor's dinnertable, or in King William's court, were it possible that his affairs should call him thither. But the only thing about him, that could be fixed upon as remarkable, was his staff, which bore the likeness of a great black snake, so curiously wrought, that it might almost be seen to twist and wriggle itself, like a living serpent. This, of course, must have been an ocular deception, assisted by the uncertain light.

"Come, Goodman Brown!" cried his fellow-traveller, "this is a dull pace for the beginning of a journey. Take my staff, if you are so soon weary."

"Friend," said the other, exchanging his slow pace for a full stop, "having kept covenant by meeting thee here, it is my purpose now to return whence I came. I have scruples, touching the matter thou wot'st of."

"Sayest thou so?" replied he of the serpent, smiling apart. "Let us walk on, nevertheless, reasoning as we go, and if I convince thee not, thou shalt turn back. We are but a little way in the forest, yet."

"Too far, too far!" exclaimed the goodman, unconsciously resuming his walk. "My father never went into the woods on such an errand, nor his father before him. We have been a race of honest men and good Christians, since the days of the martyrs. And shall I be the first of the name of Brown, that ever took this path, and kept—"

"Such company, thou wouldst say," observed the elder person, interpreting his pause. "Well said, Goodman Brown! I have been as well acquainted with your family as with ever a one among the Puritans; and that's no trifle to say. I helped your grandfather, the constable, when he lashed the Quaker woman so smartly through the streets of Salem. And it was I that brought your father a pitch-pine knot, kindled at my own hearth, to set fire to an Indian village, in King Philip's war. They were my good friends, both; and many a pleasant walk have we had along this path, and returned merrily after midnight. I would fain be friends with you, for their sake."

"If it be as thou sayest," replied Goodman Brown, "I marvel they never spoke of these matters. Or, verily, I marvel not, seeing that the least rumor of the sort would have driven them from New-England. We are a people of prayer, and good works, to boot, and abide no such wickedness."

"Wickedness or not," said the traveller with the twisted staff, "I have a very general acquaintance here in New-England. The deacons of many a church have drunk the communion wine with me; the selectmen, of divers towns, make me their chairman; and a majority of the Great and General Court are firm supporters of my interest. The governor and I, too—but these are state-secrets."

"Can this be so!" cried Goodman Brown, with a stare of amazement at his undisturbed companion. "Howbeit, I have nothing to do with the governor and council; they have their own ways, and are no rule for a simple husbandman, like me. But, were I to go on with thee, how should I meet the eye of that good old man, our minister, at Salem village? Oh, his voice would make me tremble, both Sabbath-day and lecture-day!"

Thus far, the elder traveller had listened with due gravity, but now burst into a fit of irrepressible mirth, shaking himself so violently, that his snake-like staff actually seemed to wriggle in sympathy.

"Ha! ha! ha!" shouted he, again and again; then composing himself, "Well, go on, Goodman Brown, go on; but pr'y thee, don't kill me with laughing!"

"Well, then, to end the matter at once," said Goodman Brown, considerably nettled, "there is my wife, Faith. It would break her dear little heart; and I'd rather break my own!"

"Nay, if that be the case," answered the other, "e'en go thy ways, Goodman Brown. I would not, for twenty old women like the one hobbling before us, that Faith should come to any harm."

As he spoke, he pointed his staff at a female figure on the path, in whom Goodman Brown recognized a very pious and exemplary dame, who had taught him his catechism, in youth, and was still his moral and spiritual adviser, jointly with the minister and Deacon Gookin.

"A marvel, truly, that Goody Cloyse should be so far in the wilderness, at nightfall!" said he. "But, with your leave, friend, I shall take a cut through the woods, until we have left this Christian woman behind. Being a stranger to you, she might ask whom I was consorting with, and whither I was going."

"Be it so," said his fellow-traveller. "Betake you to the woods, and let me keep the path."

Accordingly, the young man turned aside, but took care to watch his companion, who advanced softly along the road, until he had come within a staff's length of the old dame. She, meanwhile, was making the best of her way, with singular speed for so aged a woman, and mumbling some indistinct words, a prayer, doubtless, as she went. The traveller put forth his staff, and touched her withered neck with what seemed the serpent's tail.

"The devil!" screamed the pious old lady.

"Then Goody Cloyse knows her old friend?" observed the traveller, confronting her, and leaning on his writhing stick.

"Ah, forsooth, and is it your worship, indeed?" cried the good dame. "Yea, truly is it, and in the very image of my old gossip, Goodman Brown, the grandfather of the silly fellow that now is. But—would your worship believe it?—my broomstick hath strangely disappeared, stolen, as I suspect, by that unhanged witch, Goody Cory, and that, too, when I was all anointed with the juice of smallage and cinque-foil and wolf's-bane—"

"Mingled with fine wheat and the fat of a new-born babe," said the shape of old Goodman Brown.

"Ah, your worship knows the receipt," cried the old lady, cackling aloud. "So, as I was saying, being all ready for the meeting, and no horse to ride on, I made up my mind to foot it; for they tell me, there is a nice young man to be taken into communion to-night. But now your good worship will lend me your arm, and we shall be there in a twinkling."

"That can hardly be," answered her friend. "I may not spare you my arm, Goody Cloyse, but here is my staff, if you will."

So saying, he threw it down at her feet, where, perhaps, it assumed life, being one of the rods which its owner had formerly lent to the Egyptian Magi. Of this fact, however, Goodman Brown could not take cognizance. He had cast up his eyes in astonishment, and looking down again, beheld neither Goody Cloyse nor the serpentine staff, but his fellow-traveller alone, who waited for him as calmly as if nothing had happened.

"That old woman taught me my catechism!" said the young man; and there was a world of meaning in this simple comment.

They continued to walk onward, while the elder traveller exhorted his companion to make good speed and persevere in the path, discoursing so aptly, that his arguments seemed rather to spring up in the bosom of his auditor, than to be suggested by himself. As they went, he plucked a branch of maple, to serve for a walking-stick, and began to strip it of the twigs and little boughs, which were wet with evening dew. The moment his fingers touched them, they became strangely withered and dried up, as with a week's sunshine. Thus the pair proceeded, at a good free pace, until suddenly, in a gloomy hollow of the road, Goodman Brown sat himself down on the stump of a tree, and refused to go any farther.

"Friend," said he, stubbornly, "my mind is made up. Not another step will I budge on this errand. What if a wretched old woman do choose to go to the devil, when I thought she was going to Heaven! Is that any reason why I should quit my dear Faith, and go after her?"

"You will think better of this, by-and-by," said his acquaintance, composedly. "Sit here and rest yourself awhile; and when you feel like moving again, there is my staff to help you along."

Without more words, he threw his companion the maple stick, and was as speedily out of sight, as if he had vanished into the deepening gloom. The young man sat a few moments, by the road-side, applauding himself greatly, and thinking with how clear a conscience he should meet the minister, in his morning walk, nor shrink from the eye of good old Deacon Gookin. And what calm sleep would be his, that very night, which was to have been spent so wickedly, but purely and sweetly now, in the arms of Faith! Amidst these pleasant and praiseworthy meditations, Goodman Brown heard the tramp of horses along the road, and deemed it advisable to conceal himself within the verge of the forest, conscious of the guilty purpose that had brought him thither, though now so happily turned from it.

On came the hoof-tramps and the voices of the riders, two grave old voices, conversing soberly as they drew near. These mingled sounds appeared to pass along the road, within a few yards of the young man's hiding-place; but owing, doubtless, to the depth of the gloom, at that particular spot, neither the travellers nor their steeds were visible. Though their figures brushed the small boughs by the way-side, it could not be seen that they intercepted, even for a moment, the faint gleam from the strip of bright sky, athwart which they must have passed. Goodman Brown alternately crouched and stood on tip-toe, pulling aside the branches, and thrusting forth his head as far as he durst, without discerning so much as a shadow. It vexed him the more, because he could have sworn, were such a thing possible, that he recognized the voices of the minister and Deacon Gookin, jogging along quietly, as they were wont to do, when bound to some ordination or ecclesiastical council. While yet within hearing, one of the riders stopped to pluck a switch.

"Of the two, reverend Sir," said the voice like the deacon's, "I had rather miss an ordination-dinner than to-night's meeting. They tell me that some of our community are to be here from Falmouth and beyond, and others from Connecticut and Rhode-Island; besides several of the Indian powows, who, after their fashion, know almost as much deviltry as the best of us. Moreover, there is a goodly young woman to be taken into communion."

"Mighty well, Deacon Gookin!" replied the solemn old tones of the minister. "Spur up, or we shall be late. Nothing can be done, you know, until I get on the ground."

The hoofs clattered again, and the voices, talking so strangely in the empty air, passed on through the forest, where no church had ever been gathered, nor solitary Christian prayed. Whither, then, could these holy men be journeying, so deep into the heathen wilderness? Young Goodman Brown caught hold of a tree, for support, being ready to sink down on the ground, faint and overburthened with the heavy sickness of his heart. He looked up to the sky, doubting whether there really was a Heaven above him. Yet, there was the blue arch, and the stars brightening in it.

"With Heaven above, and Faith below, I will yet stand firm against the devil!" cried Goodman Brown.

While he still gazed upward, into the deep arch of the firmament, and had lifted his hands to pray, a cloud, though no wind was stirring, hurried across the zenith, and hid the brightening stars. The blue sky was still visible, except directly overhead, where this black mass of cloud was sweeping swiftly northward. Aloft in the air, as if from the depths of the cloud, came a confused and doubtful sound of voices. Once, the listener fancied that he could distinguish the accents of town's-people of his own, men and women, both pious and ungodly, many of whom he had met at the communion-table, and had seen others rioting at the tavern. The next moment, so indistinct were the sounds, he doubted whether he had heard aught but the murmur of the old forest, whispering without a wind. Then came a stronger swell of those familiar tones, heard daily in the sunshine, at Salem village, but never, until now, from a cloud of night. There was one voice, of a young woman, uttering lamentations, yet with an uncertain sorrow, and entreating for some favor, which, perhaps, it would grieve her to obtain. And all the unseen multitude, both saints and sinners, seemed to encourage her onward.

"Faith!" shouted Goodman Brown, in a voice of agony and desperation; and the echoes of the forest mocked him, crying—"Faith! Faith!" as if bewildered wretches were seeking her, all through the wilderness.

The cry of grief, rage, and terror, was yet piercing the night, when the unhappy husband held his breath for a response. There was a scream, drowned immediately in a louder murmur of voices, fading into far-off laughter, as the dark cloud swept away, leaving the clear and silent sky above Goodman Brown. But something fluttered lightly down through the air, and caught on the branch of a tree. The young man seized it, and beheld a pink ribbon.

"My Faith is gone!" cried he, after one stupefied moment. "There is no good on earth; and sin is but a name. Come, devil! for to thee is this world given."

And maddened with despair, so that he laughed loud and long, did Goodman Brown grasp his staff and set forth again, at such a rate, that he seemed to fly along the forest-path, rather than to walk or run. The road grew wilder and drearier, and more faintly traced, and vanished at length, leaving him in the heart of the dark wilderness, still rushing onward, with the instinct that guides mortal man to evil. The whole forest was peopled with frightful sounds; the creaking of trees, the howling of wild beasts, and the yell of Indians; while, sometimes, the wind tolled like a distant church-bell, and sometimes gave a broad roar around the traveller, as if all Nature were laughing him to scorn. But he was himself the chief horror of the scene, and shrank not from its other horrors.

"Ha! ha! ha!" roared Goodman Brown, when the wind laughed at him. "Let us hear which will laugh loudest! Think not to frighten me with your deviltry! Come witch, come wizard, come Indian powow, come devil himself! and here comes Goodman Brown. You may as well fear him as he fear you!"

In truth, all through the haunted forest, there could be nothing more frightful than the figure of Goodman Brown. On he flew, among the black pines, brandishing his staff with frenzied gestures, now giving vent to an inspiration of horrid blasphemy, and now shouting forth such laughter, as set all the echoes of the forest laughing like demons around him. The fiend in his own shape is less hideous, than when he rages in the breast of man. Thus sped the demoniac on his course, until, quivering among the trees, he saw a red light before him, as when the felled trunks and branches of a clearing have been set on fire, and throw up their lurid blaze against the sky, at the hour of midnight. He paused, in a lull of the tempest that had driven him onward, and heard the swell of what seemed a hymn, rolling solemnly from a distance, with the weight of many voices. He knew the tune; it was a familiar one in the choir of the village meeting-house. The verse died heavily away, and was lengthened by a chorus, not of human voices, but of all the sounds of the benighted wilderness, pealing in awful harmony together. Goodman Brown cried out; and his cry was lost to his own ear, by its unison with the cry of the desert.

In the interval of silence, he stole forward, until the light glared full upon his eyes. At one extremity of an open space, hemmed in by the dark wall of the forest, arose a rock, bearing some rude, natural resemblance either to an altar or a pulpit, and surrounded by four blazing pines, their tops aflame, their stems untouched, like candles at an evening meeting. The mass of foliage, that had overgrown the summit of the rock, was all on fire, blazing high into the night, and fitfully illuminating the whole field. Each pendent twig and leafy festoon was in a blaze. As the red light arose and fell, a numerous congregation alternately shone forth, then disappeared in shadow, and again grew, as it were, out of the darkness, peopling the heart of the solitary woods at once.

"A grave and dark-clad company!" quoth Goodman Brown.

In truth, they were such. Among them, quivering to-and-fro, between gloom and splendor, appeared faces that would be seen, next day, at the council-board of the province, and others which, Sabbath after Sabbath, looked devoutly heavenward, and benignantly over the crowded pews, from the holiest pulpits in the land. Some affirm, that the lady of the governor was there. At least, there were high dames well known to her, and wives of honored husbands, and widows, a great multitude, and ancient maidens, all of excellent repute, and fair young girls, who trembled, lest their mothers should espy them. Either the sudden gleams of light, flashing over the obscure field, bedazzled Goodman Brown, or he recognized a score of the church-members of Salem village, famous for their especial sanctity. Good old Deacon Gookin had arrived, and waited at the skirts of that venerable saint, his revered pastor. But, irreverently consorting with these grave, reputable, and pious people, these elders of the church, these chaste dames and dewy virgins, there were men of dissolute lives and women of spotted fame, wretches given over to all mean and filthy vice, and suspected even of horrid crimes. It was strange to see, that the good shrank not from the wicked, nor were the sinners abashed by the saints. Scattered, also, among their pale-faced enemies, were the Indian priests, or powows, who had often scared their native forest with more hideous incantations than any known to English witchcraft.

"But, where is Faith?" thought Goodman Brown; and, as hope came into his heart, he trembled.

Another verse of the hymn arose, a slow and mournful strain, such as the pious love, but joined to words which expressed all that our nature can conceive of sin, and darkly hinted at far more. Unfathomable to mere mortals is the lore of fiends. Verse after verse was sung, and still the chorus of the desert swelled between, like the deepest tone of a mighty organ. And, with the final peal of that dreadful anthem, there came a sound, as if the roaring wind, the rushing streams, the howling beasts, and every other voice of the unconverted wilderness, were mingling and according with the voice of guilty man, in homage to the prince of all. The four blazing pines threw up a loftier flame, and obscurely discovered shapes and visages of horror on the smoke-wreaths, above the impious assembly. At the same moment, the fire on the rock shot redly forth, and formed a glowing arch above its base, where now appeared a figure. With reverence be it spoken, the figure bore no slight similitude, both in garb and manner, to some grave divine of the New England churches.

"Bring forth the converts!" cried a voice, that echoed through the field and rolled into the forest.

At the word, Goodman Brown stept forth from the shadow of the trees, and approached the congregation, with whom he felt a loathful brotherhood, by the sympathy of all that was wicked in his heart. He could have well nigh sworn, that the shape of his own dead father beckoned him to advance, looking downward from a smoke-wreath, while a woman, with dim features of despair, threw out her hand to warn him back. Was it his mother? But he had no power to retreat one step, nor to resist, even in thought, when the minister and good old Deacon Gookin seized his arms, and led him to the blazing rock. Thither came also the slender form of a veiled female, led between Goody Cloyse, that pious teacher of the catechism, and Martha Carrier, who had received the devil's promise to be queen of hell. A rampant hag was she! And there stood the proselytes, beneath the canopy of fire.

"Welcome, my children," said the dark figure, "to the communion of your race! Ye have found, thus young, your nature and your destiny. My children, look behind you!"

They turned; and flashing forth, as it were, in a sheet of flame, the fiend-worshippers were seen; the smile of welcome gleamed darkly on every visage.

"There," resumed the sable form, "are all whom ye have reverenced from youth. Ye deemed them holier than yourselves, and shrank from your own sin, contrasting it with their lives of righteousness, and prayerful aspirations heavenward. Yet, here are they all, in my worshipping assembly! This night it shall be granted you to know their secret deeds; how hoary-bearded elders of the church have whispered wanton words to the young maids of their households; how many a woman, eager for widow's weeds, has given her husband a drink at bed-time, and let him sleep his last sleep in her bosom; how beardless youths have made haste to inherit their fathers' wealth; and how fair damsels—blush not, sweet ones!—have dug little graves in the garden, and bidden me, the sole guest, to an infant's funeral. By the sympathy of your human hearts for sin, ye shall scent out all the places—whether in church, bed-chamber, street, field, or forest—where crime has been committed, and shall exult to behold the whole earth one stain of guilt, one mighty blood-spot. Far more than this! It shall be yours to penetrate, in every bosom, the deep mystery of sin, the fountain of all wicked arts, and which inexhaustibly supplies more evil impulses than human power—than my power, at its utmost!—can make manifest in deeds. And now, my children, look upon each other."

They did so; and, by the blaze of the hell-kindled torches, the wretched man beheld his Faith, and the wife her husband, trembling before that unhallowed altar.

"Lo! there ye stand, my children," said the figure, in a deep and solemn tone, almost sad, with its despairing awfulness, as if his once angelic nature could yet mourn for our miserable race. "Depending upon one another's hearts, ye had still hoped, that virtue were not all a dream. Now are ye undeceived! Evil is the nature of mankind. Evil must be your only happiness. Welcome, again, my children, to the communion of your race!"

"Welcome!" repeated the fiend-worshippers, in one cry of despair and triumph.

And there they stood, the only pair, as it seemed, who were yet hesitating on the verge of wickedness, in this dark world. A basin was hollowed, naturally, in the rock. Did it contain water, reddened by the lurid light? or was it blood? or, perchance, a liquid flame? Herein did the Shape of Evil dip his hand, and prepare to lay the mark of baptism upon their foreheads, that they might be partakers of the mystery of sin, more conscious of the secret guilt of others, both in deed and thought, than they could now be of their own. The husband cast one look at his pale wife, and Faith at him. What polluted wretches would the next glance shew them to each other, shuddering alike at what they disclosed and what they saw!

"Faith! Faith!" cried the husband. "Look up to Heaven, and resist the Wicked One!"

Whether Faith obeyed, he knew not. Hardly had he spoken, when he found himself amid calm night and solitude, listening to a roar of the wind, which died heavily away through the forest. He staggered against the rock and felt it chill and damp, while a hanging twig, that had been all on fire, besprinkled his cheek with the coldest dew.

The next morning, young Goodman Brown came slowly into the street of Salem village, staring around him like a bewildered man. The good old minister was taking a walk along the grave-yard, to get an appetite for breakfast and meditate his sermon, and bestowed a blessing, as he passed, on Goodman Brown. He shrank from the venerable saint, as if to avoid an anathema. Old Deacon Gookin was at domestic worship, and the holy words of his prayer were heard through the open window. "What God doth the wizard pray to?" quoth Goodman Brown. Goody Cloyse, that excellent old Christian, stood in the early sunshine, at her own lattice, catechising a little girl, who had brought her a pint of morning's milk. Goodman Brown snatched away the child, as from the grasp of the fiend himself. Turning the corner by the meeting-house, he spied the head of Faith, with the pink ribbons, gazing anxiously forth, and bursting into such joy at sight of him, that she skipt along the street, and almost kissed her husband before the whole village. But, Goodman Brown looked sternly and sadly into her face, and passed on without a greeting.

Had Goodman Brown fallen asleep in the forest, and only dreamed a wild dream of a witch-meeting?

Be it so, if you will. But, alas! it was a dream of evil omen for young Goodman Brown. A stern, a sad, a darkly meditative, a distrustful, if not a desperate man, did he become, from the night of that fearful dream. On the Sabbath-day, when the congregation were singing a holy psalm, he could not listen, because an anthem of sin rushed loudly upon his ear, and drowned all the blessed strain. When the minister spoke from the pulpit, with power and fervid eloquence, and, with his hand on the open Bible, of the sacred truths of our religion, and of saint-like lives and triumphant deaths, and of future bliss or misery unutterable, then did Goodman Brown turn pale, dreading, lest the roof should thunder down upon the gray blasphemer and his hearers. Often, awakening suddenly at midnight, he shrank from the bosom of Faith, and at morning or eventide, when the family knelt down at prayer, he scowled, and muttered to himself, and gazed sternly at his wife, and turned away. And when he had lived long, and was borne to his grave, a hoary corpse, followed by Faith, an aged woman, and children and grandchildren, a goodly procession, besides neighbors, not a few, they carved no hopeful verse upon his tomb-stone; for his dying hour was gloom.

□ WRITING ↔ READING ↔ THINKING ACTIVITIES □
Comparing Hawthorne's Stories

1. Compare Hawthorne's method of narrating "Young Goodman Brown" with his storytelling style in "My Kinsman, Major Molineux" by completing a narrative elements chart for "Young Goodman Brown."
2. What other features of the two stories contribute to Hawthorne's special way of narrating a tale? For example, what observations can you make about the way he uses laughter, color, dreams, and wizardry in the two stories? What other features can you identify?

Symbols

One special characteristic of Hawthorne's storytelling style is his frequent use of *symbols*. Objects, characters, and actions can have both a literal and an abstract meaning. In "My Kinsman, Major Molineux," for example, an object like Robin's cap, a character like Major Molineux, and an event like Robin's dream contribute to the progression of the story and can be read in a literal sense. But a writer like Hawthorne often gives things, people, and actions an abstract meaning to reinforce the theme of a story. For instance, Robin's cap is a literal part of his country clothes, but it also symbolically represents his childhood view of the world which he brings with him. Major Molineux is Robin's uncle who will give him an opportunity to "rise" in the world, but the major is also a substitute father. Robin's dream about his family illustrates natural homesickness, but the closing door in the dream symbolically signifies his exclusion from that childhood environment. With these and other symbols, Hawthorne adds another dimension or level of meaning to the literal events in his story.

☐ WRITING ↔ READING ↔ THINKING ACTIVITIES ☐
Identifying Symbols

1. Symbols appear not only in literature; they occur also in other kinds of writing and in your daily life. What abstract qualities do you associate with the following objects you probably see frequently? What does each symbolize to you?
   a. a cross in front of a church
   b. a U.S. flag
   c. a rainbow
   d. a wedding ring
   e. a clock
   f. a policeman in uniform
2. Extend the above list by naming five additional people, places, objects, or actions from your daily experiences that can be seen as symbolic. What does each represent to you?
3. Since each reader interprets symbols, as well as other aspects of writing, in light of personal experience, you and your classmates may have different explanations for a symbol. From the two lists above, pick three symbols from the first and three from the second and compare your interpretation to that of a classmate. Can you see several possible explanations for the same symbol?
4. In the works you have already read, what do you think the symbolic meanings are of the following:
   a. The road in "The Road Not Taken"
   b. The shell in "The Chambered Nautilus"
   c. The child in "There Was a Child Went Forth"
   d. The river in "The Boys' Ambition"
   e. The cudgel in "My Kinsman, Major Molineux"
   f. The voyage in "Youth"
5. Identify as many symbols as you can in "Young Goodman Brown." Determine in each case what the symbol is, what it stands for, and what its purpose is. When you have finished your list, share it with the rest of the class to develop a longer combined list.

Irony

Another component of Hawthorne's storytelling method is *irony*. Irony results when a character expects something to occur or be spoken but the unexpected happens or the opposite is said. When irony relies on an event or circumstance, *situational irony* occurs. If the ironic effect depends on speech, it is *irony of statement*. In "My Kinsman," for example, Robin expects to find a relative who is highly regarded. When instead he sees his uncle tarred and feathered, that is situational irony. And when Robin insists that he is a "shrewd" youth when all around him have evidence of his lack of perception, that is irony which hinges on the use of a single word.

□ WRITING ↔ READING ↔ THINKING ACTIVITIES □
Recognizing Irony

1. Can you recall some recent situation in your life that you consider ironic? Did your ironic interpretation depend on an event or on what was said? How much did point of view contribute to your sense of irony? In other words, from the perspective of someone else involved, was the occurrence ironic?
2. What examples of situational and verbal irony can you identify in "First Confession" by O'Connor?
3. Hawthorne uses irony in "My Kinsman" to characterize Robin. Skim the story, noting each time "shrewd" or some variation of the word is used and by whom. Then determine whether each example is situational or verbal.
4. Explain the irony of the following in "Youth":
    a. Captain Beard leaving the ship
    b. Incidents involving rats
    c. Marlow's attitude toward each "disaster"
5. What uses of irony does Hawthorne make in his development of plot, character, and theme in "Young Goodman Brown"? Are they verbal? Are they situational?
6. What relationship do you see between irony and symbolism in this tale?

Literary Criticism as Argumentation

Now compare your interpretation of Hawthorne's story with that of another reader. Knowledgeable readers, among them college professors and literary critics, often react to a work of literature by writing their interpretations for publication in literary magazines or journals in order to share their insights. Out of these sometimes conflicting explanations grows a better understanding of a complex work like "Young Goodman Brown." Such interpretations and explanations are referred to as *literary criticism*, and the writers are called *literary critics*. In this literary context, *criticism* simply means "interpretation" and not something necessarily negative. Critics may at times point out what they perceive as shortcomings, but the overall purpose of literary criticism and analysis is to provide readers with insights, to assist them in appreciating the richness of the story. The following essay by D. M. McKeithan is a brief example of literary criticism.

D. M. McKeithan (1902–1985)
Hawthorne's "Young Goodman Brown": An Interpretation

The majority of Hawthorne critics feel that "Young Goodman Brown"[1] is one of the very best of Hawthorne's tales, but there is somewhat less certainty as to its meaning. The theme of the story has been variously stated as the reality of sin, the pervasiveness of evil, the secret sin and hypocrisy of all persons, the hypocrisy of Puritanism, the results of doubt or disbelief, the devastating effects of moral scepticism, or the demoralizing effects of the discovery that all men are sinners and hypocrites.[2]

Mark Van Doren, in the fullest and most recent criticism, gives a thorough analysis of the tale both as to its artistry and as to its meaning. I quote briefly from his discussion of its meaning:

> "Young Goodman Brown" means exactly what it says, namely that its hero left his pretty young wife one evening . . . to walk by himself in the primitive New England woods, the Devil's territory, . . . and either to dream or actually to experience (Hawthorne will not say) the discovery that evil exists in every human heart. . . . Brown is changed. He thinks there is no good on earth. . . . Brown, waking from his dream, if it was a dream, . . . sees evil even where it is not. . . . He had stumbled upon that "mystery of sin" which, rightly understood, provides the only sane and cheerful view of life there is. Understood in Brown's fashion, it darkens and sours the world, withering hope and charity, and perverting whatever is truly good until it looks like evil at its worst: like blasphemy and hypocrisy.[3]

[1] Published in *The New England Magazine* for April, 1835, and collected in *Mosses from an Old Manse* in 1846.

[2] See, among others, George Parsons Lathrop, *A Study of Hawthorne* (Boston, 1876), p. 203; George E. Woodberry, *Nathaniel Hawthorne* (Boston and New York, 1902), p. 146; Frank Preston Stearns, *The Life and Genius of Nathaniel Hawthorne* (Boston, 1906), p. 181; Newton Arvin, *Hawthorne* (Boston, 1929), pp. 61–62; Austin Warren, *Nathaniel Hawthorne: Representative Selections* (New York, 1934), pp. xxviii, lxix, 362; Randall Stewart, *Nathaniel Hawthorne: A Biography* (New Haven, 1948), p. 262.

[3] Mark Van Doren, *Nathaniel Hawthorne* (New York, 1949), pp. 77–79.

This survey of critical opinion is not complete, but it is all I have space for in this brief note. All of these interpretations are plausible, and a good case might be made for each. Some of them agree essentially, and the interpretation which I present below partly coincides with some of them, though it points out certain truths so obvious that I marvel at the critics' neglect of them.

At the end of Chapter VIII of *The House of the Seven Gables* Hawthorne discusses the effects on various types of mind of the discovery or suspicion that "judges, clergymen, and other characters of that eminent stamp and respectability, could really, in any single instance, be otherwise than just and upright men." But to those critics who think they have discovered in this or in similar passages the theme of "Young Goodman Brown" I would suggest that it would be more logical to look for the theme of "Young Goodman Brown" in "Young Goodman Brown" itself. One should carefully guard against reading into the story what is not there. Moreover, elsewhere Hawthorne frequently said that there is evil in every human heart (though evil impulses or desires may not lead to evil deeds), but he does not, in his own person, say so in this story, and that is not, I think, its meaning. The theme is Hawthorne's favorite one: sin and its blighting effects. Goodman Brown's sin is not identified, but its horrible effects are most impressively described. At the end of the story he is full of cynicism and moral scepticism; they are not his sin but merely its effects. The distinction, it seems to me, is essential to a correct interpretation of the story.

Goodman Brown is everyman of average intelligence who is striving to live the good life. For three months he had been married to a lovely young woman symbolizing religious faith. He was not loyal to Faith, though he fully expected to be loyal after just one more indulgence in sin. At some earlier time he had met Satan and had promised to meet him in the forest at night. It is doubtful that he recognized Satan at first, but he knew that his journey was an evil one, and his conscience hurt him because of his disloyalty to Faith. He had confidence in his ability to indulge in the sin—whatever it was—once more and then resist all future temptations. He did not know in advance how far into the forest he would be persuaded to go or what the results would be.

Faith urged him to postpone his journey until the next day, but he said it had to be made between sunset and sunrise. His heart smote him and he called himself a wretch to leave her on such an errand; he believed it would kill her to know what work was to be done that night—and it would have appalled him too if he had known. He thought of her as a blessed angel on earth and said, "After this one night I'll cling to her skirts and follow her to heaven." This "excellent resolve" did not prevent his making haste "on his present evil purpose." It is clear that before Brown had any suspicions concerning the sincerity of supposedly pious people—that is, before he had entered the forest—he was himself deliberately and knowingly indulging in sin, though with the intention of reforming soon.

In the body of the story Satan is the main speaker. In two disguises—first as the man with the serpent staff and second as the priest who presides at the meeting of sinners—Satan poisons the mind of Brown and destroys his belief in virtue and piety. But the reader should not make Brown's mistake: he should not suppose that Satan always speaks the truth—nor need he suppose that Satan always expresses Hawthorne's own opinions.

Satan denies the existence of virtue and piety in the world. It is a consequence and a punishment of Brown's sin that he believes Satan and thus becomes cynical. Hawthorne himself believed that evil impulses visit every human heart, but he did not believe that most men are mainly evil or that most men convert any considerable proportion of their evil impulses into evil deeds. In *Fancy's Show-Box* he said:

> It is not until the crime is accomplished that guilt clinches its grip upon the guilty heart, and claims it for its own. . . . In truth, there is no such thing in man's nature as a settled and full resolve, either for good or evil, except at the very moment of execution.[4]

In short, Hawthorne himself does not share the black pessimism that finally came to Goodman Brown as a result of his sin. Hawthorne greatly admired many people with whom he was personally acquainted, and many good characters are pictured in his tales and romances.

Goodman Brown became cynical as a result of his sin and thought he saw evil even where none existed. This is not a story of the disillusionment that comes to a person when he discovers that many supposedly religious and virtuous people are really sinful; it is, rather, a story of a man whose sin led him to consider all other people sinful. Brown came eventually to judge others by himself: he thought them sinful and hypocritical because he was sinful and hypocritical himself. He did not judge them accurately: he misjudged them. The minister of Salem village, Deacon Gookin, Goody Cloyse, and Faith were all good in spite of what Goodman Brown eventually came to think of them.

Moreover, it is not necessary to choose between interpreting the story literally and taking it as a dream. "Young Goodman Brown" is an allegory—which is what Hawthorne meant when he suggested that it might have been a dream—and an allegory is a fictitious story designed to teach an abstract truth. In reality, Brown did not go into a forest at night nor did he dream that he did. What Brown did was to indulge in sin (represented by the journey into the forest at night—and of course the indulgence might have lasted much longer than a night: weeks, months, even years) under the mistaken notion that he could break off whenever he wanted to. Instead of breaking off promptly, he continued to indulge in sin longer than he had expected and suffered the consequences, which were the loss of religious faith and faith in all other human beings.

[4] See Austin Warren, *op. cit.*, p. 62.

What Brown's sin was at the beginning of the story Hawthorne does not say, but it was not cynicism: at that time he was not cynical, although he was already engaged in evil dealings with Satan. Cynicism was merely the result of the sin and came later and gradually. By not identifying the sin Hawthorne gives the story a wider application. Which sin it was does not greatly matter: what Hawthorne puts the stress on is the idea that this sin had evil consequences.

McKeithan's article illustrates *argumentation*, the attempt to explain his reading of the story and to convince his readers to accept that explanation. In his introduction, he states his basic thesis or idea. Then he presents evidence from the story as proof and concludes by restating his point. As a writer, you usually argue or attempt to persuade in one of three ways: by providing evidence, by reasoning, or by appealing to emotions. You may offer facts or cite examples, as McKeithan does, or you may try to show the logical connection between what you say is true and some benefit to the reader or society. You may also choose to appeal to the reader's sense of beauty, sympathy, or morality so that he or she becomes emotionally involved in your "cause."

Notice how McKeithan introduces his argument. Knowing that numerous other readers have already written about "Young Goodman Brown," he lists several of these writers and then indicates how his interpretation will be different. Only after he has reviewed and politely dismissed these other possibilities does he state his own thesis or controlling idea: "The theme is Hawthorne's favorite one: sin and its blighting effects." Throughout the rest of his essay, McKeithan interprets the events and characters of the story in light of his thesis and presents evidence to support his opinion. His approach of presenting arguments offered by other recognized authorities or experts is useful when you are writing on a subject on which much material has already been published or for which there are some current widely accepted opinions that you plan to refute.

To convince his readers that "Young Goodman Brown" is a story about the consequences of sin, McKeithan uses evidence from two sources. First, he refers to the *primary source*, the story itself, summarizing and quoting to illustrate his interpretations. For example, to show that Brown's disloyalty to Faith is the sin which weighs on his conscience, McKeithan quotes Brown's comment: "After this one night, I'll cling to her skirts and follow her to heaven." To reinforce his references to the story, McKeithan quotes from a *secondary source*, another work by Hawthorne. McKeithan argues that not the evil nature of others but Brown's own belief in the vision of evil leads to his cynicism. For support he offers a quotation from Hawthorne's *Fancy's Show-Box*: "In truth, there is no such thing in man's nature as a settled and full resolve, either for good or evil, except at the very moment of execution." By applying this statement of Hawthorne's attitude about human nature to "Young Goodman Brown," McKeithan argues that his interpretation of the story is valid.

□ EXPANDING YOUR WRITING SKILLS □
Writing Literary Criticism

When you write literary criticism, you explain your interpretation of a literary work and cite evidence to prove that your interpretation is valid. Such an essay can focus on any aspect of a work: theme, plot, characterization, point of view, or some other characteristic of the writer's storytelling technique. The following steps offer one way to prepare for this kind of writing opportunity:

1. Select and read a short story from the Additional Readings for Chapter 2 or Chapter 3. As you read, keep in mind the questions of who, what, when, where, how, and why.
2. Search for a topic for your essay, focusing on an element of the story that attracts you or that you particularly noticed. Perhaps it will be the way the writer shapes the plot; or it might be the narrative point of view. Possibly you noted some special feature of the writer's style; or, like McKeithan, you may want to focus on the theme, the writer's message in the story.
3. Once you identify a focal point, read the story again, taking note of all evidence you can cite to illustrate and prove that your interpretation, or "reading," is correct.
4. Shape that evidence around your central idea and write a first draft of the essay. Be sure to illustrate or prove your ideas by referring to the story. Show the reader that what you say is true by citing specific points and quoting key passages.

Summary and Review

Adolescence is a time for reaching out—for new experiences, for new discoveries about the self, and for new confidence in abilities as individuals. In this chapter, you too have "reached out" as reader and writer. The following are some of the significant points which will be useful in your future experiences with composition and literature:

□ In creating fiction, news stories, reports, and in everyday writing of various kinds, writers use narration to relate events.

□ A short story is a fictional narrative involving one main incident or closely connected series of events.

□ Five basic elements of narration are plot, character, theme, setting, and point of view.

□ Asking the questions "Who? What? When? Where? How? Why?" can be helpful as you read and write narration.

□ The structure of a short story includes an introduction, a complication, a climax, and a conclusion.

□ When writing a summary of a plot, select only the most important incidents, relate the events in present tense and active voice, and try to convey the "flavor" of the original.

□ One way of determining the central character in a narrative is to ask, "Whose story is it?"

□ To state the theme of the work of fiction, convey the universal significance or meaning of the specific events.

□ A story may be narrated from first-person or third-person point of view.

□ Each writer of fiction develops a particular storytelling style.

□ Symbols are people, objects, or actions which represent abstract ideas or qualities.

□ Irony of situation occurs when the opposite of the expected happens. Irony of statement occurs when what is said is contrary to fact or to the action.

□ Literary criticism, usually in the form of argumentation, offers a reader assistance with interpreting and appreciating a literary work.

The writing techniques you have observed in short fiction and practiced in this chapter will make your everyday writing more effective. In Chapter 4, you will discover that the elements of narration you have studied will also be useful in understanding poetry, drama, and nonfiction.

4
Making Connections

"Till the gossamer thread you
fling catch somewhere, O my soul"*

□ Metaphor   □ Simile   □ Connotation   □ The Writer's Persona or Voice
□ Tone   □ Narrative Elements in Drama   □ Argument in Drama   □ Interviewing   □ Dialogue and Quotation

Breaking away from childhood usually involves a separation from family, especially parents. Ideally this estrangement is only temporary, and adults later reforge each familial relationship at the same time they develop strong new ties with persons outside the family circle. In this chapter you will examine various adult relationships. These "connections" are set forth by writers who may have lived far away from you in place and time but whose writings will probably reveal familiar thoughts and experiences. You will begin by reading another poem by Walt Whitman and then build upon your recent experiences with narration by observing its use in essay and drama forms.

*Walt Whitman, "A Noiseless Patient Spider," in this chapter.

Looking for Connections

For most people, the need for connections with others results in a wide variety of relationships. Some of these bonds are more satisfying than others. Some last a lifetime, others a short while. Some break down and are severed permanently; others are reshaped and reestablished under new conditions. Passionate lovers may marry, later become indifferent mates, then change into antagonistic ex-spouses. Or they may marry and grow closer as time passes. Some relationships appear to be mutually beneficial, others mutually destructive to those involved.

□ WRITING ↔ READING ↔ THINKING ACTIVITIES □
Perceiving Your Connections

Writers often deal with the basic human need for connections with others in both fiction and nonfiction. Before reading other writers' observations, however, use some of your journal-writing time to reflect upon the connections in your life.

1. Do you see yourself as a person who makes friends easily, or are you slow to move beyond superficial acquaintance?
2. Do you consciously work at improving relationships, or do you assume that they will take care of themselves?
3. Are you aware of significant changes over time in your relationships with family members or long-standing friends?
4. What do you consider to be basic obligations of friendship?
5. Of love?
6. Of parenthood?
7. Of marriage?
8. Do you know anyone who does not seem to need intimate relationships?

As a first excursion into reading and writing about connections, here is a brief poem by Walt Whitman, "A Noiseless Patient Spider." Before reading it carefully, recall or reread the poems by Shakespeare, Frost, and Holmes in Chapter 1. Each of those writers compares a human life to something else, something basically dissimilar—a stage play, a journey, or a seashell. When writers make such skillful comparisons of unlike things, the reader sees the parallel and appreciates its significance, knowing that life is neither a play nor a journey nor a shell. These figures of speech (a general term referring to the nonliteral, or figurative, use of language) are called metaphors. See whether Whitman the writer conveys clearly to you the metaphor and its significance in "A Noiseless Patient Spider."

Walt Whitman (1819–1892)
A Noiseless Patient Spider

A noiseless patient spider,
I marked where on a little promontory it stood isolated,
Marked how to explore the vacant vast surrounding,
It launched forth filament, filament, filament, out of itself,
Ever unreeling them, ever tirelessly speeding them.   5

And you O my soul where you stand,
Surrounded, detached, in measureless oceans of space,
Ceaselessly musing, venturing, throwing, seeking the spheres to connect them,
Till the bridge you will need be formed, till the ductile anchor hold,
Till the gossamer thread you fling catch somewhere, O my soul.   10

Metaphor and Simile

To explain the metaphor in this poem, begin by identifying the two elements being compared. You might summarize the comparison and its significance in a sentence such as this: "A spider's throwing out its web in a ceaseless attempt to attach itself to something is like my soul's reaching out for human connections." Notice the phrase *is like*. In the poem itself, Whitman never explicitly says "is like"; rather, he implicitly identifies the soul with the spider by referring to the "gossamer thread" which the soul "flings." When such a comparison is implied, like Whitman's, it is called a *metaphor*; when explicitly stated with the words *as* or *like*, as in the summary sentence above, it is called a *simile*.

□ WRITING ↔ READING ↔ THINKING ACTIVITIES □
Identifying Similes and Metaphors

1. Similes and metaphors are common in both prose and poetry. Here are a few examples from the selections included in this book. Which are similes, and which are metaphors? In each case, what two things are being compared? What is the writer's purpose in making the comparison? What is the significance of the comparison?
    a. "Poplars stood up like delicate green brooms." ("Tears, Idle Tears," Elizabeth Bowen)
    b. "He had a nutcracker face." ("Youth," Joseph Conrad)

    c. "All the world's a stage." (from *As You Like It*, Shakespeare)

    d. "[His hair] lies on his skull like paint." ("The Names and Faces of Heroes," Reynolds Price)

    e. "The universe / Bowed down his cratered dome to hear." ("First Confession," X. J. Kennedy)

    f. ". . . The evening is spread out against the sky / Like a patient etherized upon a table. . . ." ("The Love Song of J. Alfred Prufrock," T. S. Eliot)

    g. ". . . we used to wander whistling through the packed streets, stale as station sandwiches. . . ." ("Reminiscences of Childhood," Dylan Thomas)

2. If the basis for Whitman's poem is a metaphor, what might he be trying to convey metaphorically to readers about his view of human life? Why did he choose this particular metaphor? How and why might such a comparison suggest itself to the poet in the first place? List three other metaphors he might have used.

Figurative Language and Clichés

Figurative language is often found in poetry, but it is important in other kinds of writing as well. A fresh comparison can enliven your writing, can strengthen an argument, can capture your reader's attention, can make your reader "see" your point vividly. Whitman's unusual spider–soul metaphor lends force to his idea because of its freshness and originality.

This freshness is essential for force. Casual conversations and routine writings may be sprinkled with similes and metaphors, but too often these comparisons have lost their power through overuse. Saying that something is as "old as the hills," for example, was at one time an effective simile; but the expression has been so overused that listeners or readers probably no longer think about the comparison at all. Nor are your listeners or readers likely to react with strong mental images when they hear (or read) "quiet as a mouse," "red as a beet," "stone cold," or "thin as a reed." Such tired phrases are called *clichés*; careful writers generally avoid using them.

□ WRITING ↔ READING ↔ THINKING ACTIVITIES □
Creating Vivid Comparisons

1. On your own paper, try completing each of the following similes with a vivid comparison rather than with the usual clichés. Consider also the effect you want to create, the reaction you want your reader to have. For example, "as soft as the wing of a dove" creates a totally different image and reaction from that evoked by "as soft as an overripe peach."

a. As old as _____   f. As strong as _____
b. As quiet as _____   g. As sweet as _____
c. As red as _____   h. As flat as _____
d. As thin as _____   i. As easy as _____
e. As nervous as _____ j. As smooth as _____

2. Now complete the following sentences with fresh comparisons.
   a. My teacher is as _____ as _____.
   b. My _____'s clothes are as _____ as _____.
   c. This textbook is as _____ as _____.
   d. Writing this exercise is like _____.

Connotations

By using metaphor and simile in your writing, you can help your reader see your point clearly. You can also create a positive or negative impression, leading the reader to share your opinion about some person or thing. In other words, figurative language allows you to express your judgment and, by generating an emotional response, to encourage the reader to agree with you.

Closely akin to the use of figurative language is the deliberate use of certain words that carry *connotations*, nuances of meaning in addition to their explicit dictionary definitions. For example, depending on the intended effect and reaction, you might describe a small room as "cozy," or you might describe the same room as "cramped." Through purposeful selection of connotative terms, you create your desired images and reactions in the reader's mind. Whitman's use of the adjective *gossamer*—rather than, say, *delicate*—reinforces his image of a spider because the word *gossamer* is associated specifically with cobwebs. Why do you suppose he used the word *catch* rather than *stick* or *adhere* in the last line of the poem?

☐ EXPANDING YOUR WRITING SKILLS ☐
Revising Earlier Writing

In Chapter 1 you selected one of the Additional Readings and wrote about it. Rework that assignment now in light of the reading and writing you have done since then. For instance, you may now be more aware of the writer's use of figurative language, symbols, irony, and connotation; you may feel more comfortable pointing out examples of such devices. You may also be more conscious of structure in your own writing: how do your introduction and conclusion support your purpose? Are your ideas presented methodically and clearly enough for your audience to follow easily the progression of your thoughts? In other words, look at that earlier paper with a critical eye and see what you can do to make it clearer, more interesting, more finely crafted.

Disconnections and Reconnections

The next two selections make an interesting pair because of the writers' relationships to each other—they were married for many years, and now they are divorced. Some writers dealing with emotion-laden autobiographical experiences use fiction to create distance and anonymity, but Jo Brans chooses to deal directly with incidents from her personal life. Similarly, Bill Porterfield, who figures prominently in Brans's essay, uses events from *his* own life as nonfiction subject matter for a newspaper column.

In Brans's essay you read of her original "connection" with Porterfield through friendship and marriage, their "disconnection" through divorce, and their eventual "reconnection" as friends. In his briefer article, Porterfield focuses on his "reconnections" of remarriage and life-affirming parenthood.

As you read, consider how these writers treat autobiographical matters. How much does each reveal about his or her personal life? How does their approach compare with the autobiographical revelations of Whitman or Conrad?

Jo Brans (born 1933)
A Divorce Made in Heaven

In 1973, the fifteenth and last year of my marriage to Bill Porterfield, Bill, wanting out, wrote me a letter that began, "José, why fight it? After all, everything in nature changes, nothing is permanent." I, wanting to stay in, answered with a reversal: "Bill, how can you say that? *Nothing* in nature changes, everything is permanent." As usual in our arguments, then and now, we were both right. Our divorce, when it came, was a no-fault divorce.

Having lunch at The Grape in Dallas last week, Bill and I laughed over the desperate sophistry in that exchange at the end of our marriage. "You could always make everything you wanted to do so—so literary," I complained.

"And you were a damned clever Jesuit—still are," he said.

We had another glass of wine and agreed that if "Divorces are made in Heaven," as Oscar Wilde wrote, some friendships are, too. What for both of us finally became an unendurable marriage has become, mysteriously and miraculously, a satisfying friendship.

Maybe it always was a friendship, I say, and our problems came when we imposed the conventions of marriage upon it. Maybe we didn't fail. Maybe, as

Margaret Mead suggests, marriage as an institution has failed us, has caused us to live in bad faith—publicly honoring a contract while privately disliking it or reneging on it. Maybe divorce is as creative and necessary for twentieth-century Americans as marriage was sustaining and vital for early Christians. Maybe.

I'm being Jesuitical again.

"It's your turn to pick up the tab," Bill pointed out. "But you didn't finish your sole."

I'm working on it. Let's call this an essay, in the sense of Montaigne's *"essai,"* or "trial," in the completion of my soul. When I last wrote about the divorce, I still regretted the marriage, still saw myself as the victim, a sacrificial lamb on the altar of masculine frailty. Four years later, that view seems shortsighted, even silly. I gained quite as much as I lost in the crucible of that marriage. I'm glad we married. I'm also glad we divorced. Plenty of good came from both, including two children and this friendship. The children are *ours*: two people who have children are always married in a way. I'm leaving the children out of this story, however, to focus on the changes in relationship between that original pair, Adam and Eve stumbling around in the Garden. As real friends we have outlasted other mates, money muddles, and the malaise of monotony. After twenty-five years, together and apart, we feel like blood kin.

Raise your glasses, then. Here's looking at the happily divorced couple.

THIS CERTIFIES
that on the 24th day of August
in the Year of our Lord 1958
Billy Mack Porterfield
and Miss Mary Jo Reid
were by me united in
MARRIAGE
at Houston, according to the
Laws of the State of Texas.

Billy Mack Porterfield was the oldest child of an oil field worker and a woman who had never held a job outside her home in the forty-five years of her marriage. Bill grew up with a full crop of curly hair of which he was inordinately vain, a talent and love for fine words, and a wispy notion that all women were like his mother and the little Mexican girls he'd dated in high school.

He was wrong.

Miss Mary Jo Reid was the oldest child of a dragline operator and a history teacher. She grew up with skinny legs, a passion for books, and a desire to marry a tall bookish Harvard man in horn-rimmed glasses and a gray sweater.

She didn't.

Bill wore black muscle shirts, black pants, and lifted weights. He didn't wear underwear. His last two years at Southwest Texas, he fed on Thomas Wolfe and drank Tchaikovsky, and brooded because it was pathetic that he couldn't go home again. Not that he wanted to, really.

As a cub police reporter at the *Houston Chronicle,* he pulled down the curtains in his one-room apartment to use for blankets when his college friends came to visit, and offered them the *Chronicle* as toilet paper. He read all the time that he wasn't drinking and dancing with pretty girls. His refrigerator contained a six-pack of Carta Blanca and something furry. When his car stopped one night, he pushed it to a Humble station, left it, and never went back. For twenty-one days one winter, a banana peel lay in the middle of his kitchen floor.

He was, of course, an atheist.

Jo wore saddle shoes, a red sweater, and her green gym shorts from Belhaven College, where she'd majored in English, what else? At seventeen, she and a Mississippi girl friend had once gotten drunk on gin and lime sherbet. At Belhaven, a girls' school, Jo went in for drama, playing Ariel, junior misses, and old ladies; she was too short to play men and not pretty enough for ingenues. She was asked to sing more quietly in the Singing Christmas Tree.

Teaching seventh-grade English in Houston for $3500 per annum, she took long walks at night—throwing a mouton jacket over her gym shorts in cool weather—left a large number of ungraded student papers in the back seat of her 1951 Oldsmobile, and wrote sonnets about the city.

Though not an atheist, she insisted, she was, of course, an agnostic. Nevertheless, she tithed ($350 per annum) to the First Baptist Church of Houston. She was always a girl to hedge her bets.

She loved newspapermen, she said. Loving newspapermen is not hedging your bets.

> Americans are dreamers. We marry out of hope, and we hope that our dreams will come true.
>
> That is why we continue to marry even though the United States has the largest divorce rate in the world. We are a mobile and unauthoritarian people, increasingly rootless, shedding our past, evading our future. We live for today and shut out the reality of tomorrow in the same way that we shut out the reality of death.
>
> People marry when there is a curious and too often temporary alignment of expectations and need between a man and a woman.
>
> Sheresky and Mannes, *Uncoupling*

Bill and I got acquainted through a couple of Mexican babies. Like many young people, we came together largely because of proximity.

My second year of teaching, 1957, I blithely decided to write a novel, and moved to my own apartment for "privacy," as well as to separate myself from what I smugly considered the terminal messiness of my roommates. I chose to live in a second-floor triplex behind a Venetian blind factory on West Alabama, because it was, as I recall, $65 a month, bills paid, and because on the early fall day I looked at it, the tiny courtyard was inhabited by a tall bookish man wearing hornrimmed glasses and a gray sweater and reading *Ulysses*.

He was not Bill Porterfield.

Bill lived downstairs. I thumbtacked my magenta-and-green William Steig prints to the living room walls, arranged Pier 1 pillows on my sofa *cum* bed, and decorated the kitchen simply by naming the views from the two windows. One, which over-looked the tile roof of the Venetian blind factory, I dubbed "Paris Roofs"; the other, a close-up of the brick wall next door, was "Infinity" or "Eternity"—I can't remember which. I was home. I was also apparently noisy.

Ulysses introduced himself to me one day to inform me that when I hit the floor every morning at six to get to Jane Long Junior High by seven-thirty, I sounded like "a herd of water buffalo." His real name was Burt Schoor, he worked nights as a reporter for the old *Houston Press*, and he didn't much like my morning stampede. We became good friends—he later married one of my supremely messy room-mates—but we were doomed as lovers from the beginning. He wanted romance, of course, and he would look at me and shake his head in wonder: How can 105 pounds sound like that? He introduced me to Bill, a shadowy figure who seemed rarely to be home, so never noticed my galumphing.

About nine o'clock one early October evening, I was slumped in my ratty green Morris chair, poetically contemplating the human condition in *The Myth of Sisyphus*. "There is no sun without shadow, and it is essential to know the night. The absurd man says yes and his effort will henceforth be unceasing. If there is a personal fate. . . ."

I looked up, exalted. Someone was rapping lightly at my door—Bill, hair curlier and T-shirt blacker than usual. Oh, I was flustered and flattered, but soon set straight. Two of his old friends were visiting from South Texas, and they wanted to go out dancing. Would I sit with the babies while he cha-chaed with the mamas? I carried Camus downstairs and watched Bill whirl off with two pretty young señoras. The disorderly apartment smelled of pee and perfume. As I studied the sleeping brown babies, I couldn't get back to my book, though I tried. "I leave Sisyphus at the foot of the mountain! One always finds one's burden again."

But there were some mountain tops in our ten-month courtship (I'm smiling as I use the lovely old-fashioned word; I'm not sure we ever knew who was courting whom). We both pored over Camus, both read Dylan Thomas aloud, both felt populist surges listening to Cisco Houston, Woody Guthrie, and Jimmie Rodgers, the Missis-sippi brakeman:

> Standin' around the water tank
> A-waitin' for a train
> A thousand miles away from home
> A-standin' in the rain.

Bill taught me about progressive jazz, and I taught him prosody, condescendingly assuring him he could never be a poet till he mastered the double dactyl.

In those first halcyon days of a new friendship, the two of us formed The West Alabama Amalgamated Poets and Artists League, taking as our credo a line from Siegfried Sassoon I'd learned at Belhaven: "You've got your limitations? Let *them* sing!" We planned to meet every week, each bringing a manuscript to read and discuss. But the first week Bill had to skip because he had a date, the second week I did. Nevertheless we fed each other's dreams of literary success.

I think I first realized he had different dreams about me when he invited me to his aunt's house for Thanksgiving dinner. I accepted a little shyly and reluctantly; it sounded like the kind of family do a self-respecting bohemian would avoid. "Just wear your green shorts," Bill urged. "That'll be fine, José. They're easygoing people; this is no big deal."

Something—my mother's training?—told me better. I wore my sometime church dress, printed silk with a wool jersey jacket, as well as hose, heels, and the whole respectable bit, and saw his aunt give me the once-over. I passed muster— hard to argue against a schoolteacher—and Bill told me later a widowed uncle present had mournfully compared my skinny frame to his dead wife's.

Our biggest arguments came—how funny it seems now!—over my dancing. Four years at Belhaven of dancing with other girls or with imported boys at our twice- yearly proms hadn't prepared me to please Bill with my sensuous poise at Rosalie's, the beer joint on South Main where we drank Champale and danced. I was about as conscious of my body as my Morris chair was, and a lot less comfortable with it. Bill, accustomed to the dark-eyed verve of a lithe Lola or a buoyant Bertha, was fairly appalled by my Anglo-Saxon decorum.

"Where's your lilt, José?" he would demand sotto voce, immediately driving my poor beleaguered lilt into hiding, like a holed fox. The more he exhorted me to relax and flash, the stiffer and duller I became. Under the blue lights that turned white into ultraviolet, I turned coward, and our evenings on the town often ended with me sunk in Champale and misery and him at once contrite and disgusted. We should have paid attention, but we didn't.

> But I should get married I should be good
> How nice it'd be to come home to her
> and sit by the fireplace and she in the kitchen
> aproned young and lovely wanting my baby
> and so happy about me she burns the roast beef
> and comes crying to me and I get up from my big papa chair
> saying Christmas teeth! Radiant brains! Apple deaf!
> God what a husband I'd make! Yes, I should get married!
>
> Gregory Corso, "Marriage"

As winter turned into the ephemeral Houston spring, we began to see that we were, to use our terminology, "serious." I made no bones about it: I wanted marriage. Everything in my background and experience advised me to translate our relationship into marriage, the sooner the better. Bohemian be damned, marriage was what people *did*, certainly all the people I knew. Bill was reluctant. Marriage hardly suited his image of free young manhood, and what about Lola and Bertha? To prove to himself I was worth the sacrifice, he, probably unconsciously, imposed a series of tests on me. He called me in the middle of the night to get out of the Pier 1 pillows and come pick him up at the *Chronicle* office or the bar across from it. When he worked the night police beat, I'd sit all night in the press room at the station with him and John Harris and Jim Maloney, drinking salty dogs and playing gin rummy. Fidelity and strength—those were the tests.

Finally in June when school was out and I went to work downtown for an independent oil producer, the acid test came. "Let's not see each other for a while," he suggested one afternoon. "We need to find out how we really feel about each other." I agreed.

The next morning early he called me. "Can you have breakfast at One's-A-Meal?" he asked.

"I thought we weren't seeing each other."

"It's okay when *I* ask *you*," he explained, with the mad illogic of cornered men.

But it was the wrestler who did the trick. All that summer I swam at the apartment pool of my ex-roommates, getting thinner and browner daily. There I met a professional wrestler, a sweet slow guy with the mentality of King Kong and the body of—metaphors fail me. He lay on his towel, tanning his perfect body and watching me with a sweet slow smile on his sweet slow face. He adored me. "You're a real lady," he told me—he almost but not quite said "duh"—"much too good for someone like me." I smiled mysteriously; secretly I agreed. He didn't appeal to me at all.

One afternoon, Bill, all strutting machismo, came over to pick me up at the pool, and got a good look at my sweet, slow swain. An intellectual he could have resisted, a wrestler, never. I had him in a full nelson. In a month we were married.

Why? As Will Rogers says about being born, "I was born because it was the custom in those days. People didn't know any better." Bill and I didn't know any better. We liked, maybe loved, each other—I, this cocky little man who could squeeze the juices out of life; he, a fragile, poetic but above all good woman who deserved to be cherished and protected.

We had our ulterior motives, of course. I wanted security, someone to matter to; I also suspect now I thought I could handle him. He wanted "a completely independent woman who needs me," the mirage for men everywhere. Probably we both wanted to be grown-up, solid citizens, married therefore real. It was the custom in those days.

> ". . . whatever being in love means."
>
> Charles, Prince of Wales

Unlike Princess Diana, I was married in a rosy-flowered cotton satin chemise, very high style the summer of '58. Bill was torn between pride at my fashion progressiveness and dismay at the dress's cut; he liked women in clothes that fit.

That first year we were married, my mother made some dresses for me, with Bill directing the tailoring. At his instructions, she got the skirts so snug that I literally couldn't go to the bathroom in them. In the highly scented lavender restroom at Rosalie's, I virtually undressed to answer the call of nature. I've sometimes wondered what my Baptist mother thought when Bill had her sewing rose sequins or gold braid on the shoulders of my sundresses. She never said a word, perhaps because my parents loved Bill from the beginning. Besides, he was so happy, so much the young husband: I was female, I was pretty enough, I was his. My chemise days were over, at least for a while.

As for me, my immediate campaign after marriage was to get Bill out of black muscle shirts and into underwear. I was quite sure all Harvard men in horn-rimmed glasses wore athletic-looking jockey shorts, and thinking of Bill so naked under his pants shocked my wifely sensibilities. The horn-rimmed glasses were out, obviously—he had 20/30 vision or something. But we would see the dentist twice a year, and those damned weights could go into a closet!

Bill, who had never had a cavity in his life, was puzzled by all this. But he wanted to please me, so he tried. For most of the fifteen years we were married, he signed his paychecks over to me. Gone were the bachelor pleasures of cashing his check, walking around flush till the money ran out, then living on Grapenuts till payday again—always filthy rich or cleanly poor. I reduced him to what I considered the golden mean.

Then he painted our door gold. I came home from school one afternoon to discover a brightly gilded surface, still wet, on our massive apartment door.

"My god, it's pure South Texas," I groaned to myself, but I didn't say a word.

Bill smiled at me proudly as I slipped gingerly in. "Did you see it, José? Just thought I'd give the place some class."

As we sat down that night to our Weiner Surprise, a long irate peal of the doorbell announced that Parker Edwards, the aging interior decorator we rented the place from, had noticed the new paint job. When we let him in, an apoplectic Parker was quivering with distaste.

"Off!" he squealed. "I want it off. When you finish that ungodly mess you're eating, get it off!" The door slammed.

"Never mind, honey," I said to my crestfallen husband. "We'll go to Rosalie's, and I'll wear my new pink springolators."

I submerged myself in marriage. We had not been married a week when I began darning Bill's socks. I bought an ironing board and ironed his shirts. At my insistence he bought me a sewing machine for Christmas, a domestic tool that seemed to certify me as a genuine housewife—my mother had always sewed. Now, when his shirt collars were worn, I turned them, an act of frugality and patience even my mother had never done. I would beat my mother. I would be the best wife ever. We would have an ideal marriage.

Bill, of course, would have to acquire my father's virtues, along with underwear and a gray sweater. My father, a quiet, gentle man, was as predictable as sunset. He came straight home from work; supper was on the table, hot and waiting for him. It never got cold. Poor Bill. When he was having fun, he had no more sense of time than a cat. He could never be my father, but he tried.

We bought a house in the suburbs, acquired a station wagon and a VW sedan, a daughter, Erin, then a son, Winton. I quit teaching, of course, when Erin was born. We had good friends, other newspapermen and their wives, for whom I learned to cook charming Friday and Saturday night dinners. I sewed; it was fun to dress my little girl, my little doll.

Some of this domesticity pleased Bill, I think, else why would he have supported me all those years, allowing me the luxury of staying at home when we often badly needed my salary? He took his role as paterfamilias seriously. He made a patio outside our den, spading the groundwork so earnestly that our neighbor asked if he were digging a well. In spite of our religious rebellion, he learned a grace for big family meals. The Selkirk grace, it placated my Protestant parents, yet nicely accommodated our atheism/agnosticism. As well as I remember, it went:

> Some ha' meat and canna eat
> And some would eat that want it,
> But we ha' meat and we can eat,
> And so the Lord be thankit.

When I visited my parents in Mississippi, he wrote me:

city room
Wed, Apr. 10, '62

Dear José,

After I wrote you yesterday morning, I toiled until almost dark in our little green yard. I never did get around to ordering bank sand, but I planted two new trees—white ash, which grow as fast as Erin; more fig ivy on the front bedroom outside wall, and some evergreen grass around the edges of the front yard trees. I mowed, spread some extra fill dirt around the clothesline. For dinner, Puck and I had barbecued beef. God, it was hot, 92. I got a little sunburn and burnt off some suet around my midriff. It was Kaopectate for breakfast this a.m.

Frank Agee and me and Jack across the street are going in together to buy a motor-powered lawn edger. It'll cost about $15 apiece, and we'll all have access to it. That hand thing I got was a waste, and no matter how often you mow a lawn, it still looks lousy without edging.

I ran out of gas on the way to work this morning.

Tonight, I'll give the whole house a good scrubbing and wash the mountain of dirty towels. Tomorrow night, I'll go to the ballgame with Gene—he got free passes.

I plan on putting the car in the garage early Friday, so it'll be ready by Sat. morning. Sat. afternoon, I'll spread the bank sand, and then get a good night's sleep.

Plan to drive to Austin Sunday, leave there Monday for Olive Branch, in hope of missing Easter weekend traffic.

That's about it right now. Got to write some 2nd final stories. I look forward to Tuesday and seeing my girls, whom I miss VERY much.

> love,
> bill

The only part of the old Bill here is the running out of gas—but he wouldn't dare abandon this car at the nearest Humble station. It was my car too.

Staying home, I began to use Bill as my index of reality. I had no opinions of the outside world that weren't his first. If, as he says now, in those years I was often a mystery to him, I was a mystery to myself as well. Put it less flatteringly: not a mystery, a big blank. I failed us both by losing myself.

Oh, there were good times—often, oddly enough, in the midst of calamity. We were never so close as we were in the fall of 1962 driving to Arkansas to see Bill's family at the peak of the Cuban missile crisis. Horribly, Thomas Wolfe seemed literally right. Sure that we could never go home again, we saw each action as a symbolic last. I knew Bill's would be the face I saw as I died. At some point during that fearful week, we came up with ninety-three years as an image of permanence, and all our notes to each other afterward pledge fidelity and strength for ninety-three years.

They didn't last that long.

> The ache of marriage:
>
> thigh and tongue, beloved,
> are heavy with it,
> it throbs in the teeth
>
> We look for communion
> and are turned away, beloved,
> each and each
>
> It is leviathan and we
> in its belly
> looking for joy, some joy
> not to be known outside it
>
> two by two in the ark of
> the ache of it.
>
> Denise Levertov, "The Ache Of Marriage"

Most of the harm we did to each other in those years we did in completely unconscious response—abreaction, to use Freud's word. When I commented enthusiastically on Johnny Cash's raw masculine sexiness on late-night television, Bill (wondering, was I remembering the wrestler?) told me Cash was only five feet, two inches and stood on boxes hidden from the camera to sing. I believed him, and he never told me better for years.

When Bill acted the least bit irresponsible, occasionally calling me from bar after bar as he pursued his snail's path homeward, instead of laughing about it as I'd done during courtship, I made him pay for it dearly. The more he loved the world, the less love I suspected was there for me. The looser he was, the tighter I became. As Saul Bellow's Herzog says of his first wife, Daisy, "By my irregularity and turbulence of spirit I brought out the very worst in Daisy. I caused the seams of her stockings to be so straight, and the buttons to be buttoned so symmetrically." I was another Daisy.

And I quit ever dreaming of sonnets and double dactyls. Perhaps I believed to have my father as a husband I had to be my mother. Who knows? It is a fact that for the first ten years we were married, I never wrote anything but recipes and letters. But let Bill tell it. In a *Times Herald* column on "the writing mamas of Dallas" in 1979 he wrote:

> I'll close with this proud confession. Jo Brans is the mother of my kids. She's never owned up to this in her columns in *D* Magazine, though it's obvious this subtle Southern lady bard loves to dwell on the past. She's more circumspect than her readers think. When we first met, some 21 years ago, I was convinced she was going to be more of a writer than me. But in all the years we were married I don't think she ever wrote a line. Now I realize she was just biding her time, and sparing me the embarrassment of being an also-ran.

Actually, the fears were all on my side. That changed.

> Girls sometimes make passes
> At men who wear glasses
>
> Ogden Nash, revised

When Bill, the children, and I moved to Austin in the summer of 1968, we had a dream: Bill would support us by freelancing, and I would at last get the graduate degree in English I'd planned for years. Beyond the degree I didn't think. After ten years out of a classroom, I had no idea whether I'd succeed or fail in graduate school.

We bought an old house near the university with a basement Bill converted into his office. Timidly, I enrolled in some classes, and with him to babysit as the need arose, we put our plan to work. It worked all right, but with completely unexpected results.

For the first time in almost a decade, our roles were reversed. I was out in the world, in a dazzling university atmosphere where multitudes of male intellectuals strolled around wearing gray T-shirts with peace symbols, or bent over *Ulysses* with horn-rimmed specs. Austin in those last two years of the Sixties was a hot place to be: demonstrators, hippies, dopers. You could buy anything but a sewing machine on the Drag, lovers copulated at dusk in crannies on the front campus, a gentle haze of grass smoke sometimes drifted through the library stacks in the Tower.

I loved it. I really didn't pay too much attention to the hippie shenanigans. My courses excited me enough. I had William Arrowsmith for classical civ, Gould for Plato, Mills for symbolism—hard stuff, I thought. At first I sweated and trembled in class, and I never learned to speak up much. But the atmosphere of tolerance gradually affected me. I was made to realize that here I was not José, not Mommy, not a 35-year-old wife and mother, but just Jo, someone I'd misplaced a while back, who was now accepted with the serene smile we students reserved for each other. Everything was okay except oppression and war. Carl Rogers was in vogue, and we practiced being "significant others" in the rarefied air of the post-couple era.

Meanwhile Bill was in the basement. Toiling away grimly, he missed the pressures of the cityroom he'd maligned, the raw oysters or hot pastrami and beer for lunch, the five o'clock camaraderie at his favorite haunt across the street he'd so often called me from. Now I would come home, chattering away endlessly, endlessly, about the admirable Arrowsmith or the marvelous Mills, and find him sunk in gloom and wads of yellow copy paper. If he pulled me down, I drove him mad.

Once again, as with all our dreams, we tried to make this one come true. Most of the people we knew in Austin were figures from Bill's turf, so I brought my new friends home. Ten years younger than we, they seemed raw youths to Bill. Caught up in the Austin aura, I knew age didn't matter. Most of them were male, as, for that matter, most of Bill's newspaper friends had been. Bill and the young wives made conversation or shot each other glances while the scholar/husbands and I talked about signs versus symbols or the Ideal versus the Real. There were plenty of signs, most of them more Real than I was aware.

Bill did take pride in my work, as I always had in his. He read my tentative papers, declared them all publishable, thought I was the smartest thing at Texas in years. But as I got closer and closer to becoming the girl he'd first met, he became more and more uneasy. We were both relieved when he decided in December to go to Dallas to work for KERA's new Newsroom show. I would stay in Austin to finish my degree. Neither of us thought of it as a "separation."

But it did give us both what he'd requested all those years ago, "time to see how we really feel." I soon discovered I needed freedom, movement, adventure; I'd had it with the pumpkin shell. No one could supplant Bill in my heart, and I never meant to break up my marriage, but "the soul wants what it wants," Bellow says, and I was in a tizzy with wanting.

Bill, seeing me wing it, felt differently. Early in January of 1970 he wrote me from the Tolltec:

José,

Special paper for you. Bond. The one between us.

   How can I tell you the fresh, urgent way I feel about you and have you believe me? After 11 years of marriage, of intimacy and alienation and compromise. It isn't just that I'm alone and blue in Dallas. I suppose it started with your liberation, via the U of T, and my seeing you not in four wall wifely terms but as a swinging young woman who can make it very well on her own, and on her own terms.

Your going free has been hard on me and my primordial instincts as a sentinel at the cave door. I knew that as long as I had you cloistered, you would grow faint on my musk and remain meekly mine. I didn't think this out, and intellectually I would have denied it, but it is probably so, and reason enough for our both growing stale. We both breathed one another's carbon monoxide too long. But now you are out of the cage, the cave, and can take true measure of your man. And that is how it should be.

I'm saying that, I hope I'm strong enough to say this, you are a free woman, responsible to me only as you see fit to be or want to be, that I expect no more than you want to give me. You too, woman, have rights in the matter. Having said that brave-new-world thing . . .

He wasn't at all sure he meant it. And when he came to Austin on weekends, unable to take his own tumultuous and conflicting feelings, often as not he escaped from the house to go off and drink with friends, tramp around the hills, get away. We were a mess.

If I'd been more proportionate, closer to that golden mean I'd once extolled, able to "worship freedom in moderation," as some idiot counsels in a Euripides play, we'd have been okay perhaps. But freedom is free, it doesn't follow rules; revolution is violent; and I simply couldn't help myself.

Or if Bill had been more secure, able to give the little woman a silken cord instead of enough rope to hang herself, we'd have been okay. I didn't want a showdown certainly.

If. The sad thing about human beings is that we can't be smarter than we are. The showdown lurked on the next page.

Easter came early that year. One Sunday afternoon right after Easter, I sat out on a red-checked bedspread on the lawn, wearing a green bikini, my books and notes spread around me. I was getting a tan and studying for my qualifying exams. The children were playing on the swings, the cat ambled over to my side, Bill sat nearby reading the paper, all seemed, for the moment, well. Bill got up, stretched. "Think I'll drive out to Bob's for a while," he said.

"Sure, you go ahead," I answered, deep in a closed couplet. "See you later."

It was later. Afternoon died slowly, lazily, deepened to evening. The children took naps, had supper, watched television. No Bill, not even a call.

I felt cold in my green bikini, took a warm shower, dressed in jeans and T-shirt, put my books away. Waited.

By now it was eight o'clock and I knew he had to drive back to Dallas. One part of my mind said, "This is what he does when you only have weekends!" The other part answered coolly, "Who gives a damn?"

At last he came in carrying a beer, smiling, making us drinks, making up. "Hey, José, you look brown." The liberal, liberated me disappeared, and I found myself screaming at him, crying out wildly, "You're trying to do it, you're trying to break up this marriage!"

He turned, foolishly holding out a gin and tonic, studied my face. Then he very deliberately hurled the drink in his hand across the kitchen floor. We faced each other over the shards of broken glass.

> That a marriage ends is less than ideal; but all things end under heaven, and if temporality is held to be invalidating, then nothing real succeeds.
>
> John Updike, *Too Far to Go*

Let us look at these two young people, as they stand locked in mortal combat. He is going gray a bit, steely hairs visible in his moustache and the sparse curly locks on his head. His sharp brown eyes are squinted as if against the sun and his face is very red. Her brown hair is straight and center-parted, her shirt reads, "Make Love, Not War," and her face is filled with passion. How angry they are! How misunderstood they feel! How can two people so far apart ever get back together? Simple. They got a divorce.

It took us three years.

NO. 73-8710-DR/3

IN THE MATTER OF

THE MARRIAGE OF

MARY JO PORTERFIELD AND

BILLY MACK PORTERFIELD

IN THE DOMESTIC RELATIONS

COURT NUMBER THREE

OF

DALLAS COUNTY, TEXAS

DECREE OF DIVORCE

ON THIS 4th day of October, 1973, came on to be heard the above styled and numbered cause, and came the Petitioner in person and by attorney and announced ready for trial, and the Respondent having waived issuance and service of citation by waiver duly filed herein did not appear but wholly made default. All matters of fact and of law were submitted to the Court and the Court having examined the pleadings filed herein and having determined that the same are in due form and contain all the allegations and information required by law; and having heard the evidence and argument of counsel, and being of the opinion that the material allegations of such pleadings are supported by the evidence and are true, and that all prerequisites of the law have been complied with, and that the following judgment should be rendered herein.

It is, therefore, ORDERED, ADJUDGED AND DECREED by the Court that the bonds of matrimony existing between the Petitioner and the Respondent be and the same are hereby dissolved.

I brought the petition. Bill never would have. In the comic opera routines of those ensuing three years—painful and tragic at the time, of course, but funny now—Bill learned that a living wife was great protection against the predatory attentions of women smitten with TV stars. He loved the attention, but was not eager to marry again.

When we had finished all the hysterical melodrama of intercepted letters, strange keys "found" on the mantel, whining into a phone to our friends, the marriage counselor who cried over us, "But you have everything! If I ever saw a couple I hate to see get a divorce, it's you," we discovered we could talk again. We were legally, technically separated for seventeen months, from May of 1972 to October of 1973, when, a few days before Bill's forty-first birthday, the divorce came through. During those seventeen months, we let go. We discovered we no longer wanted to—nor even could—be married to each other, but we also learned to see each other again as individuals, not as partners in some script written in the heavens.

Freed from the necessity of having supper hot and waiting for him, once again I could delight in Bill's ability to immerse himself in the moment. I didn't care when he came home, since I didn't live there, and I've often been guilty of detaining him.

After the divorce, his fecklessness with money was peripheral to my life. When he paid child support from a wad of $100 bills, I realized he had cashed his paycheck and was temporarily rich. But I didn't have to worry about the end of the month. I was lucky that the children's money came first in his mind; statistics indicate that, after two years, eighty percent of husbands stop paying child support.

Having no legal claims on me, Bill genuinely rejoiced in my independence as much as he'd bravely promised to three years earlier. Out of sheer generosity, he put a down payment on a car for me just as the divorce became final, and on Valentine's Day I got a card that read: "Dear José, love that's shared grows deeper in tender quiet ways." That's good, I thought: I'm glad we're back to tender quiet ways.

I don't mean to gloss over the difficulties of divorce. We both suffered a great deal through the changes in our lives. We inflicted suffering on each other. Because it was Bill who finally pulled out, he carried a heavy load of guilt, evident in this note he wrote the children in 1976:

Dear Erin and Wink,
Babies I am very tired and sore right now and I may have to leave for awhile and rest. My mother is dying and I want to go and be with her. That way I can rest and redeem myself with her at the same time. I feel very strongly right now all the times I have failed her as a son. I feel my failures to you as a father. It hurts me to think about it. But I must say it so that you understand how deeply I love you. You know a man can be a fool and still love with all his heart.

And a woman, too.

The children suffered too, and though I haven't meant to make this their story, obviously their suffering and their health have been our greatest common concern. Whenever either one of them screws up now, I hear a little voice go off: "If you hadn't divorced." Maybe somewhere in the stratosphere the Ideal exists, but human children are born into an imperfect world, to imperfect parents, and they have to take their lumps. History has no record of Plato's progeny.

Bill and I have tried to keep the sense of family for them, and for ourselves. We live within blocks of each other in Dallas, and we've put together some pretty odd Thanksgiving and Christmas tables over the past eight years, with children and stepchildren, husbands and ex-husbands, wives and ex-wives, grandparents, and step-grandparents, all sitting down to, sometimes, the Selkirk grace. One of Bill's subsequent ladies pronounced the whole scene "decadent," but she didn't last long, and my second husband calls Bill "a great soul."

I married again first. I believe in marriage. I'd never agree with my wise older friend who said, "In my next life I think I will have outgrown marriage and I'll be able to go it alone." I like to be married, especially to my husband, a tall bookish man with horn-rimmed glasses and a gray sweater who wrote his thesis on *Ulysses*.

My successors with Bill have been beautiful, voluptuous women with a great deal of lilt and not a double dactyl among them. I don't want Bill to be a lonely old man with dirty underwear—notice my continuing obsession with this article of clothing—but I have mixed feelings about these women. Their presence seems to say that Bill and I were an aberration in each other's lives. But such an aberration.

One more comment. You read a lot these days about "the failure to communicate" in marriage. That was rarely our problem. Bill and I have communicated long, hard, and insistently for the last 25 years. Take this recent communication, for example.

I had written most of this piece when I gave it to Bill to read.

"Unh," he said when he finished it. "That's quite a story, José."

"Is it us?" I asked nervously.

"A lot of it," he said. "But what amazes me is how dumb we were, how much smarter we are now. Thank god, people grow up and change. After all, nothing in nature stays the same."

"How can you say that, Bill?" I began. "We're the same underneath as we always were. People don't really change all that much. Nature appears to change, but everything in nature is perman—"

I broke off, suspiciously. Sure enough, he was laughing at me.

Well, it's a start.

Bill Porterfield (born 1932)

Rye Observations

This is the day *after* you should have filed your 1983 income tax with Uncle Sam. I'm really talking to myself rather than you, good citizens. I missed the deadline again. A day late and a dollar short. That was my father's favorite expression. He applied it first to himself and then, with amazement and chagrin, to my brother and me. There was clearly no breaking of the mold. His mark was upon us. We would always be a day late and a dollar short.

I see it now in my almost adult children, and I shudder. How long do these negative hand-me-downs continue? And how does nature cull them? Do we go down with our genetic weaknesses or do we shake them off and triumph? So far, about the best you can say about a Porterfield is that they have survived. And I suppose that is something in itself, given the cut of the caul.

The other day, Laurie Garrett said something out of the blue of an airy conversation that I'll never forget. She said of this mutual friend that "he never got to the soft middle." Laurie has a habit of saying things that go the heart of the matter. It struck me this friend of which she spoke must be a blood brother. To test the kinship, I called him last midnight and asked if he had filed with the IRS.

"No," he said, "I'm a day . . ."

". . . Late and a dollar short," I finished for him.

And yet one persists, even procreates.

By this time tomorrow, I should be a father again, for the first time in 20 years. The sonogram suggested it will be a big, healthy girl. Certainly she's a kicker. Oren is her name. I have stared over and over at the almost opaque yet transparent picture of her the sound waves recorded as she squirmed in her mother's womb.

I fancy she has my round head and her mother's large, dark eyes. The nose looks like it has a slight Lebanese hook in it, which I, with my Irish pug, welcome. Beauty is in the bones, not the flesh, and surely that kind of angular architecture will elevate the line, which in my side of the family has tended toward the round and the squat.

Those who know my history and who creak with me into the far side of middle age think I am daft for "starting all over again." Any experienced parent can recite testament and verse the pain of mothering and fathering, especially those of us who have lived through the assault of puberty upon our young. There is nothing more selfish or demanding than a child, unless it's an adolescent or a new adult. And they are like cats. They give little in return. Eventually they come around, usually when they themselves are becoming parents, but often it's too late. You're already on the edge of the grave. Thanks a lot, kid, thanks for the funeral flowers.

But still, they are more than worth the sacrifice and grief, in and of themselves. And it's nice for the ego that they carry on some of you and your beloved. One has to agree with Germaine Greer, that barren and beautiful old feminist who now concludes, with surely some rue, that "Most of the pleasure in the world is still provided by children" and not by the sterile "genital dabbling" of the childless modern.

They pull you out, children. They make you get up and go with them. They make you see the world anew as they are seeing it. They also pull you in, children. They make you lie down and snuggle with them. They make you feel life new and wondrous as they are feeling it. This isn't simply sentiment. It's the shrewdness of Mother Nature. She makes the young so cuddly, even hyena and jackal cubs, even tender Porterfields, that parents cannot but coddle and protect them.

I need this at 51. And I will be a better parent than I was at 28. That is for sure. I am a better gardener now. There's been little sun this spring and many storms, but my carrots and corn fairly burst through the sod. And now that I've committed myself, strewn my seed after all these years, the genes will have to take care of themselves, just as Oren's half-sister and half-brother are about to take care of themselves as they come, at last, through the rye.

There is, of course, more to a person than genes, and the part of Oren that reaches out to Daddy I will happily care for, as Holden Caulfield did for his sister Phoebe and all children in J. D. Salinger's *The Catcher in the Rye.*

At one point in the novel, Holden says: "I keep picturing all these little kids in this big field of rye. . . . If they're running and they don't look where they're going I have to come out from somewhere and catch them. That's all I do all day. I'd just be the catcher in the rye and all. I know it's crazy."

Beautifully, affirmatively crazy.

Persona, Voice, and Tone

"A Divorce Made in Heaven" and "Rye Observations" have much in common besides the former marriage of the two writers. Each selection has an air of sincerity about it; each expresses the writer's earnest desire to communicate some hard-won discovery about the business of being human and forming bonds with loved ones and with life; and each openly reveals the writer's personal feelings and experiences.

In your own writing you sometimes have to make a decision: to what extent do you want to reveal yourself, and how do you wish that self to be perceived? Your purpose, your audience, and the form of writing you choose will, to some extent, determine the nature of your "presence" in your writing; you will adopt a "voice" or *persona* accordingly. This voice also establishes the *tone*, which reveals your attitude toward your subject and your audience. Persona, subject matter, and tone combine to create the audience's impression of you-as-writer. That impression should, therefore, be appropriate to your purpose. For instance, if you wish to convince a skeptical audience that your position on a controversial issue is correct, your persona will probably exhibit unshakeable conviction. On the other hand, if your purpose is to encourage your audience to consider all sides of the issue, your persona will probably acknowledge the difficulty of reaching a decision.

□ WRITING ↔ READING ↔ THINKING ACTIVITIES □
Recognizing Tone, Narration, and Figurative Language

1. What effects would the following conditions have on your writing voice and the tone of that voice in these three writing situations?
    a. Your purpose is to clarify a situation in your own mind.
    b. Your audience is a highly judgmental professor.
    c. Your form is a skit for the college talent show.
2. How does the personal, openly autobiographical approach of Brans and Porterfield differ from the autobiographical approach of Walt Whitman in "There Was a Child Went Forth" or of Joseph Conrad in "Youth"? Is there a difference in your reaction as reader? Would you rather read Conrad's autobiography or his fiction? Why?
3. Brans herself refers to her writing as an essay, but "A Divorce Made in Heaven" seems to follow the form of a short story. Trace the narrative flow, which closely resembles a plot. Where do you find the exposition? the climax? the denouement? Is characterization a strong element? Are the characters static or dynamic? How does the use of dialogue contribute to the effectiveness of the writing?
4. Both Brans and Porterfield obviously enjoy wordplay and figurative language. Point out an example of a pun (a humorous play on words that sound alike but have different meanings) in each work. Locate and explain at least one metaphor in each.
5. Do you note any stylistic differences? Does either writer use more difficult words than the other? Does either write longer paragraphs or longer sentences? Are any differences in writing possibly due to differences between intended audiences?

□ EXPANDING YOUR WRITING SKILLS □
Composing a Narrative: Form and Tone

For your next writing assignment, deal with one of your own "connections" using the form of either Brans or Porterfield: a nonfiction narrative with yourself as a main character, or a newspaper column essay. Whichever form you choose, incorporate into your account some truth you have discovered or some perception you have acquired about that particular relationship or about relationships in general. Here are some topics to consider, and perhaps to write about in your journal as a means of clarifying their meaning to yourself:

1. The early days of a "best friendship"
2. A conflict that damaged a friendship
3. The early days of courtship
4. A relationship with a former spouse
5. Your reaction to the birth of a child
6. A description of your as-yet-undiscovered ideal mate.

If you choose to emulate Brans's form, you will be free to let the story dictate the length needed to tell it. If you decide on Porterfield's newspaper column form, however, you will know that the length of your essay is predetermined by the space some imaginary editor has allocated for your column. (Assume your editor has assigned you a minimum of 500 and a maximum of 600 words.)

In either case, give some thought to your attitude and the emotional state associated with your topic—euphoria, sorrow, yearning, anger, quiet happiness, or whatever; choose your words carefully to convey that tone to your reader. Keep in mind the structural necessities of an introduction and a conclusion, but concentrate on conveying the tone of this particular writing, on establishing the desired persona, and on using figurative language.

Faulty Connections

Just as harmonious relationships with other people can provide a human being's greatest happiness and satisfaction, so discordant relationships can lead to misery for all concerned. In the next selection, the writer invites you to consider such issues as hypocrisy, sincerity, loyalty, manipulation, honesty, tactfulness, and tolerance in social interactions. Is tactfulness really another name for lying? Is diplomacy merely hypocrisy? Could society exist if people were always totally honest with one another? These are some questions he poses for your consideration.

The work is a French play by Molière, entitled *The Misanthrope*. A play, as a form of writing, is different in many ways from the other selections included so far in this book. First, a play, or drama, is normally written to be performed and viewed onstage. Although the actors and the director must certainly read the play closely in order to create an appropriate performance, the playwright's primary audience is not a reader at all but the spectators at the theater. This fact makes drama a unique form of writing. Although it includes the same narrative elements as fiction—plot, character, setting, point of view, and theme—it also has its own characteristics and terminology.

□ WRITING ↔ READING ↔ THINKING ACTIVITIES □
Comparing Drama and Narrative Fiction

1. You are already familiar with dialogue as one element of a short story or other type of writing; but in a play, dialogue conveys everything: exposition, plot development, and characterization. What effect does this fact have on point of view in a play? How is a playwright more limited in using point of view than the writer of a short story?

2. Why would a writer choose to write a play rather than a short story or a novel? Would purpose be a determinant? Would intended audience be a factor? Would some stories be more difficult than others to write as a play?

Another difference between *The Misanthrope* and most other writings in this book is that the version here is a translation. Molière, who lived during the 1600s, wrote in French; Richard Wilbur, a noted American poet of the twentieth century, has translated *The Misanthrope* into English, going so far as to duplicate Molière's use of couplets, or rhymed pairs of poetic lines.

You may find yourself initially put off by the idea of dialogue written in verse. "People don't talk that way," you might object, especially if your taste in television shows and movies runs to the more realistic variety. But the fact is that most of the great drama of the past was written in verse. Sophocles, Euripides, and Shakespeare all have their greatest characters—Oedipus, Medea, Hamlet—speak with the majesty of poetry.

When you bring your twentieth-century sensibilities to a verse drama, however, you may have to work a bit to achieve what Samuel Taylor Coleridge, in his *Biographia Literaria*, called a "willing suspension of disbelief." In order to enjoy *The Misanthrope* and enter into its world, you must allow yourself to believe, for its duration, that people really *can* talk that way, just as your enjoyment of *The Wizard of Oz* is dependent upon your ability to suspend your disbelief in Munchkins and witches.

The Misanthrope is a play concerned with the society of Molière's time, with the way people behaved toward one another. This type of play is called a *comedy of manners*. Its conflict and comedy grow out of the customs and morals of a specific cultural setting, but the natural human foibles it depicts are as prevalent today as they were in seventeenth-century France. In drama, as in fiction and poetry, the universal truth transcends the specifics of time and place.

Now read the first act of *The Misanthrope*, in which the playwright provides exposition, introduces the main characters, and sets up the conflict. Reading some of the speeches aloud may help you enjoy the poetry and assist you in following the action. Before you begin reading, determine the meaning of the title term *misanthrope*.

Molière (1622–1673)

The Misanthrope

Translated by Richard Wilbur (born 1921)

CHARACTERS

ALCESTE *In love with Célimène*
PHILINTE *Alceste's friend*
ORONTE *In love with Célimène*
CELIMENE *Alceste's beloved*
ELIANTE *Célimène's cousin*
ARSINOE *A friend of Célimène's*
ACASTE ⎫
CLITANDRE ⎭ *marquesses*
BASQUE *Célimène's servant*
A GUARD *of the Marshalsea*
DUBOIS *Alceste's valet*

The scene throughout is in Célimène's house at Paris.

ACT I

Scene 1

(PHILINTE, ALCESTE)

PHILINTE   Now, what's got into you?
ALCESTE (*Seated*)   Kindly leave me alone.
PHILINTE   Come, come, what is it? This lugubrious tone . . .
ALCESTE   Leave me, I said; you spoil my solitude.
PHILINTE   Oh, listen to me, now, and don't be rude.   5

ALCESTE   I choose to be rude, Sir, and to be hard of hearing.

PHILINTE   These ugly moods of yours are not endearing;
   Friends though we are, I really must insist . . .

ALCESTE (*Abruptly rising*)   Friends? Friends, you say? Well, cross me off your list.
   I've been your friend till now, as you well know;   10
   But after what I saw a moment ago
   I tell you flatly that our ways must part.
   I wish no place in a dishonest heart.

PHILINTE   Why, what have I done, Alceste? Is this quite just?

ALCESTE   My God, you ought to die of self-disgust.   15
   I call your conduct inexcusable, Sir,
   And every man of honor will concur.
   I see you almost hug a man to death,
   Exclaim for joy until you're out of breath,
   And supplement these loving demonstrations   20
   With endless offers, vows, and protestations;
   Then when I ask you "Who was that?", I find
   That you can barely bring his name to mind!
   Once the man's back is turned, you cease to love him,
   And speak with absolute indifference of him!   25
   By God, I say it's base and scandalous
   To falsify the heart's affections thus;
   If I caught myself behaving in such a way,
   I'd hang myself for shame, without delay.

PHILINTE   It hardly seems a hanging matter to me;   30
   I hope that you will take it graciously
   If I extend myself a slight reprieve,
   And live a little longer, by your leave.

ALCESTE   How dare you joke about a crime so grave?

PHILINTE   What crime? How else are people to behave?   35

ALCESTE   I'd have them be sincere, and never part
   With any word that isn't from the heart.

PHILINTE   When someone greets us with a show of pleasure,
   It's but polite to give him equal measure,
   Return his love the best that we know how,   40
   And trade him offer for offer, vow for vow.

ALCESTE   No, no, this formula you'd have me follow,
   However fashionable, is false and hollow,
   And I despise the frenzied operations
   Of all these barterers of protestations,   45
   These lavishers of meaningless embraces,
   These utterers of obliging commonplaces,

Who court and flatter everyone on earth
And praise the fool no less than the man of worth.
Should you rejoice that someone fondles you,   50
Offers his love and service, swears to be true,
And fills your ears with praises of your name,
When to the first damned fop he'll say the same?
No, no: no self-respecting heart would dream
Of prizing so promiscuous an esteem;   55
However high the praise, there's nothing worse
Than sharing honors with the universe.
Esteem is founded on comparison:
To honor all men is to honor none.
Since you embrace this indiscriminative vice,   60
Your friendship comes at far too cheap a price;
I spurn the easy tribute of a heart
Which will not set the worthy man apart:
I choose, Sir, to be chosen; and in fine,
The friend of mankind is no friend of mine.   65
PHILINTE   But in polite society, custom decrees
That we show certain outward courtesies. . . .
ALCESTE   Ah, no! we should condemn with all our force
Such false and artificial intercourse.
Let men behave like men; let them display   70
Their inmost hearts in everything they say;
Let the heart speak, and let our sentiments
Not mask themselves in silly compliments.
PHILINTE   In certain cases it would be uncouth
And most absurd to speak the naked truth;   75
With all respect to your exalted notions,
It's often best to veil one's true emotions.
Wouldn't the social fabric come undone
If we were wholly frank with everyone?
Suppose you met with someone you couldn't bear;   80
Would you inform him of it then and there?
ALCESTE   Yes.
PHILINTE   Then you'd tell old Emilie it's pathetic
The way she daubs her features with cosmetic
And plays the gay coquette at sixty-four?
ALCESTE   I would.
PHILINTE   And you'd call Dorilas a bore,   85
And tell him every ear at court is lame

From hearing him brag about his noble name?
ALCESTE   Precisely.
PHILINTE   Ah, you're joking.
ALCESTE   *Au contraire:*
In this regard there's none I'd choose to spare.
All are corrupt! there's nothing to be seen   90
In court or town but aggravates my spleen.
I fall into deep gloom and melancholy
When I survey the scene of human folly,
Finding on every hand base flattery,
Injustice, fraud, self-interest, treachery. . . .   95
Ah, it's too much; mankind has grown so base,
I mean to break with the whole human race.
PHILINTE   This philosophic rage is a bit extreme;
You've no idea how comical you seem;
Indeed, we're like those brothers in the play   100
Called *School for Husbands,* one of whom was prey . . .
ALCESTE   Enough, now! None of your stupid similes.
PHILINTE   Then let's have no more tirades, if you please.
The world won't change, whatever you say or do;
And since plain speaking means so much to you,   105
I'll tell you plainly that by being frank
You've earned the reputation of a crank,
And that you're thought ridiculous when you rage
And rant against the manners of the age.
ALCESTE   So much the better; just what I wish to hear.   110
No news could be more grateful to my ear.
All men are so detestable in my eyes,
I should be sorry if they thought me wise.
PHILINTE   Your hatred's very sweeping, is it not?
ALCESTE   Quite right: I hate the whole degraded lot.   115
PHILINTE   Must all poor human creatures be embraced,
Without distinction, by your vast distaste?
Even in these bad times, there are surely a few . . .
ALCESTE   No, I include all men in one dim view:
Some men I hate for being rogues; the others   120
I hate because they treat the rogues like brothers,
And lacking a virtuous scorn for what is vile,
Receive the villain with a complaisant smile.
Notice how tolerant people choose to be
Toward that bold rascal who's at law with me.   125

His social polish can't conceal his nature;
One sees at once that he's a treacherous creature;
No one could possibly be taken in
By those soft speeches and that sugary grin.
The whole world knows the shady means by which   130
The low-brow's grown so powerful and rich,
And risen to a rank so bright and high
That virtue can but blush, and merit sigh.
Whenever his name comes up in conversation,
None will defend his wretched reputation;   135
Call him knave, liar, scoundrel, and all the rest,
Each head will nod, and no one will protest.
And yet his smirk is seen in every house,
He's greeted everywhere with smiles and bows,
And when there's any honor that can be got   140
By pulling strings, he'll get it, like as not.
My God! It chills my heart to see the ways
Men come to terms with evil nowadays;
Sometimes, I swear, I'm moved to flee and find
Some desert land unfouled by humankind.   145
PHILINTE   Come, let's forget the follies of the times
And pardon mankind for its petty crimes;
Let's have an end of rantings and of railings,
And show some leniency toward human failings.
This world requires a pliant rectitude;   150
Too stern a virtue makes one stiff and rude;
Good sense views all extremes with detestation,
And bids us to be noble in moderation.
The rigid virtues of the ancient days
Are not for us; they jar with all our ways   155
And ask of us too lofty a perfection.
Wise men accept their times without objection,
And there's no greater folly, if you ask me,
Than trying to reform society.
Like you, I see each day a hundred and one   160
Unhandsome deeds that might be better done,
But still, for all the faults that meet my view,
I'm never known to storm and rave like you.
I take men as they are, or let them be,
And teach my soul to bear their frailty;   165
And whether in court or town, whatever the scene,

My phlegm's as philosophic as your spleen.
ALCESTE   This phlegm which you so eloquently commend,
Does nothing ever rile it up, my friend?
Suppose some man you trust should treacherously   170
Conspire to rob you of your property,
And do his best to wreck your reputation?
Wouldn't you feel a certain indignation?
PHILINTE   Why, no. These faults of which you so complain
Are part of human nature, I maintain,   175
And it's no more a matter for disgust
That men are knavish, selfish and unjust,
Than that the vulture dines upon the dead,
And wolves are furious, and apes ill-bred.
ALCESTE   Shall I see myself betrayed, robbed, torn to bits,   180
And not . . . Oh, let's be still and rest our wits.
Enough of reasoning, now. I've had my fill.
PHILINTE   Indeed, you would do well, Sir, to be still.
Rage less at your opponent, and give some thought
To how you'll win this lawsuit that he's brought.   185
ALCESTE   I assure you I'll do nothing of the sort.
PHILINTE   Then who will plead your case before the court?
ALCESTE   Reason and right and justice will plead for me.
PHILINTE   Oh, Lord. What judges do you plan to see?
ALCESTE   Why, none. The justice of my cause is clear.   190
PHILINTE   Of course, man; but there's politics to fear. . . .
ALCESTE   No, I refuse to lift a hand. That's flat.
I'm either right, or wrong.
PHILINTE   Don't count on that.
ALCESTE   No, I'll do nothing.
PHILINTE   Your enemy's influence
Is great you know . . .
ALCESTE   That makes no difference.   195
PHILINTE   It will; you'll see.
ALCESTE   Must honor bow to guile?
If so, I shall be proud to lose the trial.
PHILINTE   Oh, really . . .
ALCESTE   I'll discover by this case
Whether or not men are sufficiently base
And impudent and villainous and perverse   200
To do me wrong before the universe.
PHILINTE   What a man!

ALCESTE   Oh, I could wish, whatever the cost,
   Just for the beauty of it, that my trial were lost.
PHILINTE   If people heard you talking so, Alceste,
   They'd split their sides. Your name would be a jest.   205
ALCESTE   So much the worse for jesters.
PHILINTE   May I enquire
   Whether this rectitude you so admire,
   And these hard virtues you're enamored of
   Are qualities of the lady whom you love?
   It much surprises me that you, who seem   210
   To view mankind with furious disesteem,
   Have yet found something to enchant your eyes
   Amidst a species which you so despise.
   And what is more amazing, I'm afraid,
   Is the most curious choice your heart has made.   215
   The honest Eliante is fond of you,
   Arsinoé, the prude, admires you too;
   And yet your spirit's been perversely led
   To choose the flighty Célimène instead,
   Whose brittle malice and coquettish ways   220
   So typify the manners of our days.
   How is it that the traits you most abhor
   Are bearable in this lady you adore?
   Are you so blind with love that you can't find them?
   Or do you contrive, in her case, not to mind them?   225
ALCESTE   My love for that young widow's not the kind
   That can't perceive defects; no, I'm not blind.
   I see her faults, despite my ardent love,
   And all I see I fervently reprove.
   And yet I'm weak; for all her falsity,   230
   That woman knows the art of pleasing me,
   And though I never cease complaining of her,
   I swear I cannot manage not to love her.
   Her charm outweighs her faults; I can but aim
   To cleanse her spirit in my love's pure flame.   235
PHILINTE   That's no small task; I wish you all success.
   You think then that she loves you?
ALCESTE   Heavens, yes!
   I wouldn't love her did she not love me.
PHILINTE   Well, if her taste for you is plain to see,
   Why do these rivals cause you such despair?   240

ALCESTE   True love, Sir, is possessive, and cannot bear
   To share with all the world. I'm here today
   To tell her she must send that mob away.
PHILINTE   If I were you, and had your choice to make,
   Eliante, her cousin, would be the one I'd take;   245
   That honest heart, which cares for you alone,
   Would harmonize far better with your own.
ALCESTE   True, true: each day my reason tells me so;
   But reason doesn't rule in love, you know.
PHILINTE   I fear some bitter sorrow is in store;   250
   This love . . .

Scene 2

(ORONTE, ALCESTE, PHILINTE)

ORONTE (*To* ALCESTE)   The servants told me at the door
   That Eliante and Célimène were out,
   But when I heard, dear Sir, that you were about,
   I came to say, without exaggeration,
   That I hold you in the vastest admiration,   5
   And that it's always been my dearest desire
   To be the friend of one I so admire.
   I hope to see my love of merit requited,
   And you and I in friendship's bond united.
   I'm sure you won't refuse—if I may be frank—   10
   A friend of my devotedness—and rank.

(*During this speech of* ORONTE'S, ALCESTE *is abstracted, and seems unaware that he is being spoken to. He only breaks off his reverie when* ORONTE *says*)

   It was for you, if you please, that my words were intended.
ALCESTE   For me, Sir?
ORONTE   Yes, for you. You're not offended?
ALCESTE   By no means. But this much surprises me. . . .
   The honor comes most unexpectedly. . . .   15
ORONTE   My high regard should not astonish you;
   The whole world feels the same. It is your due.
ALCESTE   Sir . . .
ORONTE   Why, in all the State there isn't one
   Can match your merits; they shine, Sir, like the sun.
ALCESTE   Sir . . .

ORONTE   You are higher in my estimation   20
  Than all that's most illustrious in the nation.
ALCESTE   Sir . . .
ORONTE   If I lie, may heaven strike me dead!
  To show you that I mean what I have said,
  Permit me, Sir, to embrace you most sincerely,
  And swear that I will prize our friendship dearly.   25
  Give me your hand. And now, Sir, if you choose,
  We'll make our vows.
ALCESTE   Sir . . .
ORONTE   What! You refuse?
ALCESTE   Sir, it's a very great honor you extend:
  But friendship is a sacred thing, my friend;
  It would be profanation to bestow   30
  The name of friend on one you hardly know.
  All parts are better played when well-rehearsed;
  Let's put off friendship, and get acquainted first.
  We may discover it would be unwise
  To try to make our natures harmonize.   35
ORONTE   By heaven! You're sagacious to the core;
  This speech has made me admire you even more.
  Let time, then, bring us closer day by day;
  Meanwhile, I shall be yours in every way.
  If, for example, there should be anything   40
  You wish at court, I'll mention it to the King.
  I have his ear, of course; it's quite well known
  That I am much in favor with the throne.
  In short, I am your servant. And now, dear friend,
  Since you have such fine judgment, I intend   45
  To please you, if I can, with a small sonnet
  I wrote not long ago. Please comment on it,
  And tell me whether I ought to publish it.
ALCESTE   You must excuse me, Sir; I'm hardly fit
  To judge such matters.
ORONTE   Why not?
ALCESTE   I am, I fear,   50
  Inclined to be unfashionably sincere.
ORONTE   Just what I ask; I'd take no satisfaction
  In anything but your sincere reaction.
  I beg you not to dream of being kind.
ALCESTE   Since you desire it, Sir, I'll speak my mind.   55

ORONTE   *Sonnet.* It's a sonnet. . . . *Hope* . . . The poem's addressed
   To a lady who wakened hopes within my breast.
   Hope . . . this is not the pompous sort of thing,
   Just modest little verses, with a tender ring.
ALCESTE   Well, we shall see.
ORONTE   *Hope* . . . I'm anxious to hear   60
   Whether the style seems properly smooth and clear,
   And whether the choice of words is good or bad.
ALCESTE   Well, we shall see.
ORONTE   Perhaps I ought to add
   That it took me only a quarter-hour to write it.
ALCESTE   The time's irrelevant, Sir: kindly recite it.   65
ORONTE (*Reading*)

   Hope comforts us awhile, 'tis true,
   Lulling our cares with careless laughter,
   And yet such joy is full of rue,
   My Phyllis, if nothing follows after.

PHILINTE   I'm charmed by this already; the style's delightful.   70
ALCESTE (*Sotto voce to* PHILINTE)   How can you say that? Why, the thing is frightful.
ORONTE

   Your fair face smiled on me awhile,
   But was it kindness so to enchant me?
   'Twould have been fairer not to smile,   75
   If hope was all you meant to grant me.

PHILINTE   What a clever thought! How handsomely you phrase it!
ALCESTE (*Sotto voce to* PHILINTE)   You know the thing is trash.
   How dare you praise it?
ORONTE

   If it's to be my passion's fate   80
   Thus everlastingly to wait,
   Then death will come to set me free:
   For death is fairer than the fair;
   Phyllis, to hope is to despair
   When one must hope eternally.   85

PHILINTE   The close is exquisite—full of feeling and grace.
ALCESTE (*Sotto voce, aside*)   Oh, blast the close; you'd better close your face
   Before you send your lying soul to hell.
PHILINTE   I can't remember a poem I've liked so well.   90

ALCESTE (*Sotto voce, aside*)   Good Lord!

ORONTE   I fear you're flattering me a bit.

PHILINTE   Oh, no!

ALCESTE (*Sotto voce, aside*)   What else d'you call it, you hypocrite?

ORONTE (*To* ALCESTE)   But you, Sir, keep your promise now: don't shrink

From telling me sincerely what you think.   95

ALCESTE   Sir, these are delicate matters: we all desire

To be told that we've the true poetic fire.

But once, to one whose name I shall not mention,

I said, regarding some verse of his invention,

That gentlemen should rigorously control   100

That itch to write which often afflicts the soul;

That one should curb the heady inclination

To publicize one's little avocation;

And that in showing off one's works of art

One often plays a very clownish part.   105

ORONTE   Are you suggesting in a devious way

That I ought not . . .

ALCESTE   Oh, that I do not say.

Further, I told him that no fault is worse

Than that of writing frigid, lifeless verse,

And that the merest whisper of such a shame   110

Suffices to destroy a man's good name.

ORONTE   D'you mean to say my sonnet's dull and trite?

ALCESTE   I don't say that. But I went on to cite

Numerous cases of once-respected men

Who came to grief by taking up the pen.   115

ORONTE   And am I like them? Do I write so poorly?

ALCESTE   I don't say that. But I told this person, "Surely

You're under no necessity to compose;

Why you should wish to publish, heaven knows.

There's no excuse for printing tedious rot   120

Unless one writes for bread, as you do not.

Resist temptation, then, I beg of you;

Conceal your pastimes from the public view;

And don't give up, on any provocation,

Your present high and courtly reputation,   125

To purchase at a greedy printer's shop

The name of silly author and scribbling fop."

These were the points I tried to make him see.

ORONTE   I sense that they are also aimed at me;

But now—about my sonnet—I'd like to be told . . .   130

ALCESTE   Frankly, that sonnet should be pigeonholed.
  You've chosen the worst models to imitate.
  The style's unnatural. Let me illustrate:

> For example, *Your fair face smiled on me awhile,*
> Followed by, *'Twould have been fairer not to smile!*   135
> Or this: *such joy is full of rue;*
> Or this: *For death is fairer than the fair;*
> Or, *Phyllis, to hope is to despair*
>   *When one must hope eternally!*

This artificial style, that's all the fashion,   140
Has neither taste, nor honesty, nor passion;
It's nothing but a sort of wordy play,
And nature never spoke in such a way.
What, in this shallow age, is not debased?
Our fathers, though less refined, had better taste;   145
I'd barter all that men admire today
For one old love-song I shall try to say:

> If the King had given me for my own
> Paris, his citadel,
> And I for that must leave alone   150
> Her whom I love so well,
> I'd say then to the Crown,
> Take back your glittering town;
> My darling is more fair, I swear,
> My darling is more fair.   155

The rhyme's not rich, the style is rough and old,
But don't you see that it's the purest gold
Beside the tinsel nonsense now preferred,
And that there's passion in its every word?

> If the King had given me for my own   160
> Paris, his citadel,
> And I for that must leave alone
> Her whom I love so well,
> I'd say then to the Crown,
> Take back your glittering town;   165
> My darling is more fair, I swear,
> My darling is more fair.

There speaks a loving heart. (*To* PHILINTE) You're laughing, eh?
Laugh on, my precious wit. Whatever you say,

I hold that song's worth all the bibelots   170
  That people hail today with ah's and oh's.

ORONTE   And I maintain my sonnet's very good.

ALCESTE   It's not at all surprising that you should.
  You have your reasons; permit me to have mine
  For thinking that you cannot write a line.   175

ORONTE   Others have praised my sonnet to the skies.

ALCESTE   I lack their art of telling pleasant lies.

ORONTE   You seem to think you've got no end of wit.

ALCESTE   To praise your verse, I'd need still more of it.

ORONTE   I'm not in need of your approval, Sir.   180

ALCESTE   That's good; you couldn't have it if you were.

ORONTE   Come now, I'll lend you the subject of my sonnet;
  I'd like to see you try to improve upon it.

ALCESTE   I might, by chance, write something just as shoddy;
  But then I wouldn't show it to everybody.   185

ORONTE   You're most opinionated and conceited.

ALCESTE   Go find your flatterers, and be better treated.

ORONTE   Look here, my little fellow, pray watch your tone.

ALCESTE   My great big fellow, you'd better watch your own.

PHILINTE (*Stepping between them*)   Oh, please, please, gentlemen!   190
  This will never do.

ORONTE   The fault is mine, and I leave the field to you.
  I am your servant, Sir, in every way.

ALCESTE   And I, Sir, am your most abject valet.

Scene 3

(PHILINTE, ALCESTE)

PHILINTE   Well, as you see, sincerity in excess
  Can get you into a very pretty mess;
  Oronte was hungry for appreciation. . . .

ALCESTE   Don't speak to me.

PHILINTE   What?

ALCESTE   No more conversation.

PHILINTE   Really, now . . .

ALCESTE   Leave me alone.

PHILINTE   If I . . .

ALCESTE   Out of my sight!   5

PHILINTE   But what . . .

ALCESTE   I won't listen.

PHILINTE   But . . .

ALCESTE   Silence!
PHILINTE   Now, is it polite . . .
ALCESTE   By heaven, I've had enough. Don't follow me.
PHILINTE   Ah, you're just joking. I'll keep you company.

□ WRITING ↔ READING ↔ THINKING ACTIVITIES □
Understanding Act I

1. Act I is divided into three scenes, even though we are told at the begin-
    ning of the play that "The scene throughout is in Célimène's house at
    Paris." Explain the difference between the two uses of the word *scene*.
2. The arrival or departure of characters appears to be the signal for a new
    scene in this play. What character's arrival or departure creates scene
    2? scene 3?
3. Scene 1 reveals three conflicts in Alceste's life. What are they?
4. What are Philinte's observations about each of the conflicts?
5. In scene 2, Oronte introduces a complication relating to which of the
    three conflicts set out in scene 1?
6. What does the exchange in the last two lines of act I reveal about
    Alceste's and Philinte's personalities and the nature of their friendship?
7. How much of act I is devoted to exposition?
8. Write a paragraph explaining how you would respond to a fellow class-
    mate's request for your opinion of his or her expensive new clothes,
    which in your judgment are completely unattractive. Would you be ab-
    solutely honest, or would you tell a lie to spare your classmate's feel-
    ings? Why?

ACT II

Scene 1

(ALCESTE, CELIMENE)

ALCESTE   Shall I speak plainly, Madam? I confess
Your conduct gives me infinite distress,
And my resentment's grown too hot to smother.
Soon, I foresee, we'll break with one another.
If I said otherwise, I should deceive you;
Sooner or later, I shall be forced to leave you,
And if I swore that we shall never part,
I should misread the omens of my heart.

5

CELIMENE   You kindly saw me home, it would appear,
So as to pour invectives in my ear.   10
ALCESTE   I've no desire to quarrel. But I deplore
Your inability to shut the door
On all these suitors who beset you so.
There's what annoys me, if you care to know.
CELIMENE   Is it my fault that all these men pursue me?   15
Am I to blame if they're attracted to me?
And when they gently beg an audience,
Ought I to take a stick and drive them hence?
ALCESTE   Madam, there's no necessity for a stick;
A less responsive heart would do the trick.   20
Of your attractiveness I don't complain;
But those your charms attract, you then detain
By a most melting and receptive manner,
And so enlist their hearts beneath your banner.
It's the agreeable hopes which you excite   25
That keep these lovers round you day and night;
Were they less liberally smiled upon,
That sighing troop would very soon be gone.
But tell me, Madam, why it is that lately
This man Clitandre interests you so greatly?   30
Because of what high merits do you deem
Him worthy of the honor of your esteem?
Is it that your admiring glances linger
On the splendidly long nail of his little finger?
Or do you share the general deep respect   35
For the blond wig he chooses to affect?
Are you in love with his embroidered hose?
Do you adore his ribbons and his bows?
Or is it that this paragon bewitches
Your tasteful eye with his vast German breeches?   40
Perhaps his giggle, or his falsetto voice,
Makes him the latest gallant of your choice?
CELIMENE   You're much mistaken to resent him so.
Why I put up with him you surely know:
My lawsuit's very shortly to be tried,   45
And I must have his influence on my side.
ALCESTE   Then lose your lawsuit, Madam, or let it drop;
Don't torture me by humoring such a fop.
CELIMENE   You're jealous of the whole world, Sir.
ALCESTE   That's true,
Since the whole world is well-received by you.   50

CELIMENE   That my good nature is so unconfined
   Should serve to pacify your jealous mind;
   Were I to smile on one, and scorn the rest,
   Then you might have some cause to be distressed.
ALCESTE   Well, if I mustn't be jealous, tell me, then,   55
   Just how I'm better treated than other men.
CELIMENE   You know you have my love. Will that not do?
ALCESTE   What proof have I that what you say is true?
CLEIMENE   I would expect, Sir, that my having said it
   Might give the statement a sufficient credit.   60
ALCESTE   But how can I be sure that you don't tell
   The selfsame thing to other men as well?
CELIMENE   What a gallant speech! How flattering to me!
   What a sweet creature you make me out to be!
   Well then, to save you from the pangs of doubt,   65
   All that I've said I hereby cancel out;
   Now, none but yourself shall make a monkey of you:
   Are you content?
ALCESTE   Why, why am I doomed to love you?
   I swear that I shall bless the blissful hour
   When this poor heart's no longer in your power!   70
   I make no secret of it: I've done my best
   To exorcise this passion from my breast;
   But thus far all in vain; it will not go;
   It's for my sins that I must love you so.
CELIMENE   Your love for me is matchless, Sir; that's clear.   75
ALCESTE   Indeed, in all the world it has no peer;
   Words can't describe the nature of my passion,
   And no man ever loved in such a fashion.
CELIMENE   Yes, it's a brand-new fashion, I agree;
   You show your love by castigating me.   80
   And all your speeches are enraged and rude.
   I've never been so furiously wooed.
ALCESTE   Yet you could calm that fury, if you chose.
   Come, shall we bring our quarrels to a close?
   Let's speak with open hearts, then, and begin . . .   85

Scene 2

(CELIMENE, ALCESTE, BASQUE)

CELIMENE   What is it?
BASQUE   Acaste is here.
CELIMENE   Well, send him in.

Scene 3

(CELIMENE, ALCESTE)

ALCESTE   What! Shall we never be alone at all?
   You're always ready to receive a call.
   And you can't bear, for ten ticks of the clock,
   Not to keep open house for all who knock.
CELIMENE   I couldn't refuse him: he'd be most put out.   5
ALCESTE   Surely that's not worth worrying about.
CELIMENE   Acaste wouldn't ever forgive me if he guessed
   That I consider him a dreadful pest.
ALCESTE   If he's a pest, why bother with him then?
CELIMENE   Heavens! One can't antagonize such men;   10
   Why, they're the chartered gossips of the court,
   And have a say in things of every sort.
   One must receive them, and be full of charm;
   They're no great help, but they can do you harm,
   And though your influence be ever so great,   15
   They're hardly the best people to alienate.
ALCESTE   I see, dear lady, that you could make a case
   For putting up with the whole human race;
   These friendships that you calculate so nicely . . .

Scene 4

(ALCESTE, CELIMENE, BASQUE)

BASQUE   Madam, Clitandre is here as well.
ALCESTE   Precisely.
CELIMENE   Where are you going?
ALCESTE   Elsewhere.
CELIMENE   Stay.
ALCESTE   No, no.
CELIMENE   Stay, Sir.
ALCESTE   I can't.
CELIMENE   I wish it.
ALCESTE   No, I must go.
   I beg you, Madam, not to press the matter;
   You know I have no taste for idle chatter.   5
CELIMENE   Stay: I command you.

ALCESTE No, I cannot stay.

CELIMENE Very well; you have my leave to go away.

Scene 5

(ELIANTE, PHILINTE, ACASTE, CLITANDRE, ALCESTE, CELIMENE, BASQUE)

ELIANTE (*To* CELIMENE) The Marquesses have kindly come to call. Were they
    announced?

CELIMENE Yes. Basque, bring chairs for all.

(BASQUE *provides the chairs, and exits*)

(*To* ALCESTE)

You haven't gone?

ALCESTE No; and I shan't depart
    Till you decide who's foremost in your heart.

CELIMENE Oh, hush.

ALCESTE It's time to choose; take them, or me.   5

CELIMENE You're mad.

ALCESTE I'm not, as you shall shortly see.

CELIMENE Oh?

ALCESTE You'll decide.

CELIMENE You're joking now, dear friend.

ALCESTE No, no; you'll choose; my patience is at an end.

CLITANDRE Madam, I come from court, where poor Cléonte   10
    Behaved like a perfect fool, as is his wont.
    Has he no friend to counsel him, I wonder,
    And teach him less unerringly to blunder?

CELIMENE It's true, the man's a most accomplished dunce;
    His gauche behavior strikes the eye at once;   15
    And every time one sees him, on my word,
    His manner's grown a trifle more absurd.

ACASTE Speaking of dunces, I've just now conversed
    With old Damon, who's one of the very worst;
    I stood a lifetime in the broiling sun   20
    Before his dreary monologue was done.

CELIMENE Oh, he's a wondrous talker, and has the power
    To tell you nothing hour after hour:
    If, by mistake, he ever came to the point,
    The shock would put his jawbone out of joint.   25

ELIANTE (*To* PHILINTE)   The conversation takes its usual turn,
   And all our dear friends' ears will shortly burn.
CLITANDRE   Timante's a character, Madam.
CELIMENE   Isn't he, though?
   A man of mystery from top to toe,
   Who moves about in a romantic mist   30
   On secret missions which do not exist.
   His talk is full of eyebrows and grimaces;
   How tired one gets of his momentous faces;
   He's always whispering something confidential
   Which turns out to be quite inconsequential;   35
   Nothing's too slight for him to mystify;
   He even whispers when he says "good-by."
ACASTE   Tell us about Géralde.
CELIMENE   That tiresome ass.
   He mixes only with the titled class,
   And fawns on dukes and princes, and is bored   40
   With anyone who's not at least a lord.
   The man's obsessed with rank, and his discourses
   Are all of hounds and carriages and horses;
   He uses Christian names with all the great,
   And the word Milord, with him, is out of date.   45
CLITANDRE   He's very taken with Bélise, I hear.
CELIMENE   She is the dreariest company, poor dear.
   Whenever she comes to call, I grope about
   To find some topic which will draw her out,
   But, owing to her dry and faint replies,   50
   The conversation wilts, and droops, and dies.
   In vain one hopes to animate her face
   By mentioning the ultimate commonplace;
   But sun or shower, even hail or frost
   Are matters she can instantly exhaust.   55
   Meanwhile her visit, painful though it is,
   Drags on and on through mute eternities,
   And though you ask the time, and yawn, and yawn,
   She sits there like a stone and won't be gone.
ACASTE   Now for Adraste.
CELIMENE   Oh, that conceited elf   60
   Has a gigantic passion for himself.
   He rails against the court, and cannot bear it
   That none will recognize his hidden merit;
   All honors given to others give offense
   To his imaginary excellence.   65

CLITANDRE   What about young Cléon? His house, they say,
  Is full of the best society, night and day.
CELIMENE   His cook has made him popular, not he:
  It's Cléon's table that people come to see.
ELIANTE   He gives a splendid dinner, you must admit.   70
CELIMENE   But must he serve himself along with it?
  For my taste, he's a most insipid dish
  Whose presence sours the wine and spoils the fish.
PHILINTE   Damis, his uncle, is admired no end.
  What's your opinion, Madam?
CELIMENE   Why, he's my friend.   75
PHILINTE   He seems a decent fellow, and rather clever.
CELIMENE   He works too hard at cleverness, however.
  I hate to see him sweat and struggle so
  To fill his conversation with bon mots.
  Since he's decided to become a wit   80
  His taste's so pure that nothing pleases it;
  He scolds at all the latest books and plays,
  Thinking that wit must never stoop to praise,
  That finding fault's a sign of intellect,
  That all appreciation is abject,   85
  And that by damning everything in sight
  One shows oneself in a distinguished light,
  He's scornful even of our conversations:
  Their trivial nature sorely tries his patience;
  He folds his arms, and stands above the battle,   90
  And listens sadly to our childish prattle.
ACASTE   Wonderful, Madam! You've hit him off precisely.
CLITANDRE   No one can sketch a character so nicely.
ALCESTE   How bravely, Sirs, you cut and thrust at all
  These absent fools, till one by one they fall: 95
  But let one come in sight, and you'll at once
  Embrace the man you lately called a dunce,
  Telling him in a tone sincere and fervent
  How proud you are to be his humble servant.
CLITANDRE   Why pick on us? Madame's been speaking, Sir,   100
  And you should quarrel, if you must, with her.
ALCESTE   No, no, by God, the fault is yours, because
  You lead her on with laughter and applause,
  And make her think that she's the more delightful
  The more her talk is scandalous and spiteful.   105
  Oh, she would stoop to malice far, far less
  If no such claque approved her cleverness.

It's flatterers like you whose foolish praise
Nourishes all the vices of these days.
PHILINTE   But why protest when someone ridicules   110
Those you'd condemn, yourself, as knaves or fools?
CELIMENE   Why, Sir? Because he loves to make a fuss.
You don't expect him to agree with us,
When there's an opportunity to express
His heaven-sent spirit of contrariness?   115
What other people think, he can't abide;
Whatever they say, he's on the other side;
He lives in deadly terror of agreeing;
'Twould make him seem an ordinary being.
Indeed, he's so in love with contradiction,   120
He'll turn against his most profound conviction
And with a furious eloquence deplore it,
If only someone else is speaking for it.
ALCESTE   Go on, dear lady, mock me as you please;
You have your audience in ecstasies.   125
PHILINTE   But what she says is true: you have a way
Of bridling at whatever people say;
Whether they praise or blame, your angry spirit
Is equally unsatisfied to hear it.
ALCESTE   Men, Sir, are always wrong, and that's the reason   130
That righteous anger's never out of season;
All that I hear in all their conversation
Is flattering praise or reckless condemnation.
CELIMENE   But . . .
ALCESTE   No, no, Madam, I am forced to state
That you have pleasures which I deprecate,   135
And that these others, here, are much to blame
For nourishing the faults which are your shame.
CLITANDRE   I shan't defend myself, Sir; but I vow
I'd thought this lady faultless until now.
ACASTE   I see her charms and graces, which are many;   140
But as for faults, I've never noticed any.
ALCESTE   I see them, Sir; and rather than ignore them,
I strenuously criticize her for them.
The more one loves, the more one should object
To every blemish, every least defect.   145
Were I this lady, I would soon get rid
Of lovers who approved of all I did,

And by their slack indulgence and applause
Endorsed my follies and excused my flaws.
CELIMENE   If all hearts beat according to your measure, 150
   The dawn of love would be the end of pleasure;
   And love would find its perfect consummation
   In ecstasies of rage and reprobation.
ELIANTE   Love, as a rule, affects men otherwise,
   And lovers rarely love to criticize. 155
   They see their lady as a charming blur,
   And find all things commendable in her.
   If she has any blemish, fault, or shame,
   They will redeem it by a pleasing name.
   The pale-faced lady's lily-white, perforce; 160
   The swarthy one's a sweet brunette, of course;
   The spindly lady has a slender grace;
   The fat one has a most majestic pace;
   The plain one, with her dress in disarray,
   They classify as *beauté négligée*; 165
   The hulking one's a goddess in their eyes,
   The dwarf, a concentrate of Paradise;
   The haughty lady has a noble mind;
   The mean one's witty, and the dull one's kind;
   The chatterbox has liveliness and verve, 170
   The mute one has a virtuous reserve.
   So lovers manage, in their passion's cause,
   To love their ladies even for their flaws.
ALCESTE   But I will say . . .
CELIMENE   I think it would be nice.
   To stroll around the gallery once or twice. 175
   What! You're not going, Sirs?
CLITANDRE AND ACASTE   No, Madam, no.
ALCESTE   You seem to be in terror lest they go.
   Do what you will, Sirs; leave, or linger on,
   But I shan't go till after you are gone.
ACASTE   I'm free to linger, unless I should perceive 180
   Madame is tired, and wishes me to leave.
CLITANDRE   And as for me, I needn't go today
   Until the hour of the King's *coucher*.
CELIMENE (*To* ALCESTE)   You're joking, surely?
ALCESTE   Not in the least; we'll see
   Whether you'd rather part with them, or me. 185

Scene 6

(ALCESTE, CELIMENE, ELIANTE, ACASTE, PHILINTE, CLITANDRE, BASQUE)

BASQUE (*To* ALCESTE)   Sir, there's a fellow here who bids me state
   That he must see you, and that it can't wait.
ALCESTE   Tell him that I have no such pressing affairs.
BASQUE   It's a long tailcoat that this fellow wears,
   With gold all over.
CELIMENE (*To* ALCESTE)   You'd best go down and see.   5
   Or—have him enter.

Scene 7

(ALCESTE, CELIMENE, ELIANTE, ACASTE, PHILINTE, CLITANDRE, A GUARD *of the
Marshalsea*)

ALCESTE (*Confronting the* GUARD)   Well, what do you want with me?
   Come in, Sir.
GUARD   I've a word, Sir, for your ear.
ALCESTE   Speak it aloud, Sir; I shall strive to hear.
GUARD   The Marshals have instructed me to say
   You must report to them without delay.   5
ALCESTE   Who? Me, Sir?
GUARD   Yes, Sir; you.
ALCESTE   But what do they want?
PHILINTE (*To* ALCESTE)   To scotch your silly quarrel with Oronte.
CELIMENE (*To* PHILINTE)   What quarrel?
PHILINTE   Oronte and he have fallen out
   Over some verse he spoke his mind about;
   The Marshals wish to arbitrate the matter.   10
ALCESTE   Never shall I equivocate or flatter!
PHILINTE   You'd best obey their summons; come, let's go.
ALCESTE   How can they mend our quarrel, I'd like to know?
   Am I to make a cowardly retraction,
   And praise those jingles to his satisfaction?   15
   I'll not recant; I've judged that sonnet rightly.
   It's bad.
PHILINTE   But you might say so more politely. . . .
ALCESTE   I'll not back down; his verses make me sick.
PHILINTE   If only you could be more politic!
   But come, let's go.
ALCESTE   I'll go, but I won't unsay   20
   A single word.

PHILINTE   Well, let's be on our way.

ALCESTE   Till I am ordered by my lord the King
  To praise that poem, I shall say the thing
  Is scandalous, by God, and that the poet
  Ought to be hanged for having the nerve to show it.   25

  (*To* CLITANDRE *and* ACASTE, *who are laughing*)

  By heaven, Sirs, I really didn't know
  That I was being humorous.

CELIMENE   Go, Sir, go;
  Settle your business.

ALCESTE   I shall, and when I'm through,
  I shall return to settle things with you.

☐ WRITING ↔ READING ↔ THINKING ACTIVITIES ☐
Understanding Act II

1. Philinte describes the character of Célimène in act I; she does not appear
    until act II. In what specific ways does the playwright reveal her char-
    acter? How does the audience learn about characters in a play? Does
    Molière use techniques different from those a short story writer uses?
2. On what grounds does Alceste defend Célimène in scene 5?
3. Scene 7 further develops the conflict with Oronte which was begun in
    act I. Oronte is apparently threatening to challenge Alceste to a duel.
    What is the issue?

ACT III

Scene 1

(CLITANDRE, ACASTE)

CLITANDRE   Dear Marquess, how contented you appear;
  All things delight you, nothing mars your cheer.
  Can you, in perfect honesty, declare
  That you've a right to be so debonair?

ACASTE   By Jove, when I survey myself, I find   5
  No cause whatever for distress of mind.
  I'm young and rich; I can in modesty
  Lay claim to an exalted pedigree;

And owing to my name and my condition
I shall not want for honors and position.   10
Then as to courage, that most precious trait,
I seem to have it, as was proved of late
Upon the field of honor, where my bearing,
They say, was very cool and rather daring.
I've wit, of course; and taste in such perfection   15
That I can judge without the least reflection,
And at the theater, which is my delight,
Can make or break a play on opening night,
And lead the crowd in hisses or bravos,
And generally be known as one who knows.   20
I'm clever, handsome, gracefully polite;
My waist is small, my teeth are strong and white;
As for my dress, the world's astonished eyes
Assure me that I bear away the prize.
I find myself in favor everywhere,   25
Honored by men, and worshipped by the fair;
And since these things are so, it seems to me
I'm justified in my complacency.
CLITANDRE   Well, if so many ladies hold you dear,
Why do you press a hopeless courtship here?   30
ACASTE   Hopeless, you say? I'm not the sort of fool
That likes his ladies difficult and cool.
Men who are awkward, shy, and peasantish
May pine for heartless beauties, if they wish,
Grovel before them, bear their cruelties,   35
Woo them with tears and sighs and bended knees,
And hope by dogged faithfulness to gain
What their poor merits never could obtain.
For men like me, however, it makes no sense
To love on trust, and foot the whole expense.   40
Whatever any lady's merits be,
I think, thank God, that I'm as choice as she;
That if my heart is kind enough to burn
For her, she owes me something in return;
And that in any proper love affair   45
The partners must invest an equal share.
CLITANDRE   You think, then, that our hostess favors you?
ACASTE   I've reason to believe that that is true.
CLITANDRE   How did you come to such a mad conclusion?
You're blind, dear fellow. This is sheer delusion.   50

ACASTE   All right, then: I'm deluded and I'm blind.

CLITANDRE   Whatever put the notion in your mind?

ACASTE   Delusion.

CLITANDRE   What persuades you that you're right?

ACASTE   I'm blind.

CLITANDRE   But have you any proofs to cite?

ACASTE   I tell you I'm deluded.

CLITANDRE   Have you, then,   55
    Received some secret pledge from Célimène?

ACASTE   Oh, no: she scorns me.

CLITANDRE   Tell me the truth, I beg.

ACASTE   She just can't bear me.

CLITANDRE   Ah, don't pull my leg.
    Tell me what hope she's given you, I pray.

ACASTE   I'm hopeless, and it's you who win the day.   60
    She hates me thoroughly, and I'm so vexed
    I mean to hang myself on Tuesday next.

CLITANDRE   Dear Marquess, let us have an armistice
    And make a treaty. What do you say to this?
    If ever one of us can plainly prove   65
    That Célimène encourages his love,
    The other must abandon hope, and yield,
    And leave him in possession of the field.

ACASTE   Now, there's a bargain that appeals to me;
    With all my heart, dear Marquess, I agree.   70
    But hush.

Scene 2

(CELIMENE, ACASTE, CLITANDRE)

CELIMENE   Still here?

CLITANDRE   'Twas love that stayed our feet.

CELIMENE   I think I heard a carriage in the street.
    Whose is it? D'you know?

Scene 3

(CELIMENE, ACASTE, CLITANDRE, BASQUE)

BASQUE   Arsinoé is here,
    Madame.

CELIMENE   Arsinoé, you say? Oh, dear.

BASQUE   Eliante is entertaining her below.

CELIMENE   What brings the creature here, I'd like to know?   5

ACASTE   They say she's dreadfully prudish, but in fact
  I think her piety . . .
CELIMENE   It's all an act.
  At heart she's worldly, and her poor success
  In snaring men explains her prudishness.
  It breaks her heart to see the beaux and gallants   10
  Engrossed by other women's charms and talents,
  And so she's always in a jealous rage
  Against the faulty standards of the age.
  She lets the world believe that she's a prude
  To justify her loveless solitude,   15
  And strives to put a brand of moral shame
  On all the graces that she cannot claim.
  But still she'd love a lover; and Alceste
  Appears to be the one she'd love the best.
  His visits here are poison to her pride;   20
  She seems to think I've lured him from her side;
  The spiteful, envious woman runs me down.
  In short, she's just as stupid as can be,
  Vicious and arrogant in the last degree,   25
  And . . .

Scene 4

(ARSINOE, CELIMENE, CLITANDRE, ACASTE)

CELIMENE   Ah! What happy chance has brought you here?
  I've thought about you ever so much, my dear.
ARSINOE   I've come to tell you something you should know.
CELIMENE   How good of you to think of doing so!

(CLITANDRE *and* ACASTE *go out, laughing*)

Scene 5

(ARSINOE, CELIMENE)

ARSINOE   It's just as well those gentlemen didn't tarry.
CELIMENE   Shall we sit down?
ARSINOE   That won't be necessary.
  Madam, the flame of friendship ought to burn
  Brightest in matters of the most concern,
  And as there's nothing which concerns us more   5
  Than honor, I have hastened to your door
  To bring you, as your friend, some information
  About the status of your reputation.

I visited, last night, some virtuous folk,
And, quite by chance, it was of you they spoke;   10
There was, I fear, no tendency to praise
Your light behavior and your dashing ways.
The quantity of gentlemen you see
And your by now notorious coquetry
Were both so vehemently criticized   15
By everyone, that I was much surprised.
Of course, I needn't tell you where I stood;
I came to your defense as best I could,
Assured them you were harmless, and declared
Your soul was absolutely unimpaired.   20
But there are some things, you must realize,
One can't excuse, however hard one tries,
And I was forced at last into conceding
That your behavior, Madam, is misleading,
That it makes a bad impression, giving rise   25
To ugly gossip and obscene surmise,
And that if you were more *overtly* good,
You wouldn't be so much misunderstood.
Not that I think you've been unchaste—no! no!
The saints preserve me from a thought so low!   30
But mere good conscience never did suffice:
One must avoid the outward show of vice.
Madam, you're too intelligent, I'm sure,
To think my motives anything but pure
In offering you this counsel—which I do   35
Out of zealous interest in you.

CELIMENE   Madam, I haven't taken you amiss;
I'm very much obliged to you for this;
And I'll at once discharge the obligation
By telling you about *your* reputation.   40
You've been so friendly as to let me know
What certain people say of me, and so
I mean to follow your benign example
By offering you a somewhat similar sample.
The other day, I went to an affair   45
And found some most distinguished people there
Discussing piety, both false and true.
The conversation soon came round to you.
Alas! Your prudery and bustling zeal
Appeared to have a very slight appeal.   50
Your affectation of grave demeanor,

Your endless talk of virtue and of honor,
The aptitude of your suspicious mind
For finding sin where there is none to find,
Your towering self-esteem, that pitying face   55
With which you contemplate the human race,
Your sermonizings and your sharp aspersions
On people's pure and innocent diversions—
All these were mentioned, Madam, and, in fact,
Were roundly and concertedly attacked.   60
"What good," they said, "are all these outward shows,
When everything belies her pious pose?
She prays incessantly; but then, they say,
She beats her maids and cheats them of their pay;
She shows her zeal in every holy place,   65
But still she's vain enough to paint her face;
She holds that naked statues are immoral,
But with a naked *man* she'd have no quarrel."
Of course, I said to everybody there
That they were being viciously unfair;   70
But still they were disposed to criticize you,
And all agreed that someone should advise you
To leave the morals of the world alone,
And worry rather more about your own.
They felt that one's self-knowledge should be great   75
Before one thinks of setting others straight;
That one should learn the art of living well
Before one threatens other men with hell,
And that the Church is best equipped, no doubt,
To guide our souls and root our vices out.   80
Madam, you're too intelligent, I'm sure,
To think my motives anything but pure
In offering you this counsel—which I do
Out of a zealous interest in you.
ARSINOE   I dared not hope for gratitude, but I   85
Did not expect so acid a reply;
I judge, since you've been so extremely tart,
That my good counsel pierced you to the heart.
CELIMENE   Far from it, Madam. Indeed, it seems to me
We ought to trade advice more frequently.   90
One's vision of oneself is so defective
That it would be an excellent corrective.
If you are willing, Madam, let's arrange

Shortly to have another frank exchange
In which we'll tell each other, *entre nous,*   95
What you've heard tell of me, and I of you.
ARSINOE   Oh, people never censure you, my dear;
It's me they criticize. Or so I hear.
CELIMENE   Madam, I think we either blame or praise
According to our taste and length of days.   100
There is a time of life for coquetry,
And there's a season, too, for prudery.
When all one's charms are gone, it is, I'm sure,
Good strategy to be devout and pure:
It makes one seem a little less forsaken.   105
Some day, perhaps, I'll take the road you've taken:
Time brings all things. But I have time aplenty,
And see no cause to be a prude at twenty.
ARSINOE   You give your age in such a gloating tone
That one would think I was an ancient crone;   110
We're not so far apart, in sober truth,
That you can mock me with a boast of youth!
Madam, you baffle me. I wish I knew
What moves you to provoke me as you do.
CELIMENE   For my part, Madam, I should like to know   115
Why you abuse me everywhere you go.
Is it my fault, dear lady, that your hand
Is not, alas, in very great demand?
If men admire me, if they pay me court
And daily make me offers of the sort   120
You'd dearly love to have them make to you,
How can I help it? What would you have me do?
If what you want is lovers, please feel free
To take as many as you can from me.
ARSINOE   Oh, come. D'you think the world is losing sleep   125
Over that flock of lovers which you keep,
Or that we find it difficult to guess
What price you pay for their devotedness?
Surely you don't expect us to suppose
Mere merit could attract so many beaux?   130
It's not your virtue that they're dazzled by;
Nor is it virtuous love for which they sigh.
You're fooling no one, Madam; the world's not blind;
There's many a lady heaven has designed
To call men's noblest tenderest feelings out,   135

Who has no lovers dogging her about;
From which it's plain that lovers nowadays
Must be acquired in bold and shameless ways,
And only pay one court for such reward
As modesty and virtue can't afford. 140
Then don't be quite so puffed up, if you please,
About your tawdry little victories;
Try, if you can, to be a shade less vain,
And treat the world with somewhat less disdain.
If one were envious of your amours, 145
One soon could have a following like yours;
Lovers are no great trouble to collect
If one prefers them to one's self-respect.
CELIMENE   Collect them then, my dear; I'd love to see
You demonstrate that charming theory; 150
Who knows, you might . . .
ARSINOE   Now, Madam, that will do;
It's time to end this trying interview.
My coach is late in coming to your door,
Or I'd have taken leave of you before.
CELIMENE   Oh, please don't feel that you must rush away; 155
I'd be delighted, Madam, if you'd stay.
However, lest my conversation bore you,
Let me provide some better company for you;
This gentleman, who comes most apropos,
Will please you more than I could do, I know. 160

Scene 6

(ALCESTE, CELIMENE, ARSINOE)

CELIMENE   Alceste, I have a little note to write
Which simply must go out before tonight;
Please entertain *Madame*; I'm sure that she
Will overlook my incivility.

Scene 7

(ALCESTE, ARSINOE)

ARSINOE   Well, Sir, our hostess graciously contrives
For us to chat until my coach arrives;
And I shall be forever in her debt
For granting me this little tête-à-tête.

We women very rightly give our hearts   5
To men of noble character and parts,
And your especial merits, dear Alceste,
Have roused the deepest sympathy in my breast.
Oh, how I wish they had sufficient sense
At court, to recognize your excellence!   10
They wrong you greatly, Sir. How it must hurt you
Never to be rewarded for your virtue!
ALCESTE   Why, Madam, what cause have I to feel aggrieved?
What great and brilliant thing have I achieved?
What service have I rendered to the King   15
That I should look to him for anything?
ARSINOE   Not everyone who's honored by the State
Has done great services. A man must wait
Till time and fortune offer him the chance.
Your merit, Sir, is obvious at a glance,   20
And . . .
ALCESTE   Ah, forget my merit; I'm not neglected.
The court, I think, can hardly be expected
To mine men's souls for merit, and unearth
Our hidden virtues and our secret worth.
ARSINOE   *Some* virtues, though, are far too bright to hide;   25
Yours are acknowledged, Sir, on every side.
Indeed, I've heard you warmly praised of late
By persons of considerable weight.
ALCESTE   This fawning age has praise for everyone,
And all distinctions, Madam, are undone.   30
All things have equal honor nowadays,
And no one should be gratified by praise.
To be admired, one only need exist,
And every lackey's on the honors list.
ARSINOE   I only wish, Sir, that you had your eye   35
On some position at court, however high;
You'd only have to hint at such a notion
For me to set the proper wheels in motion;
I've certain friendships I'd be glad to use
To get you any office you might choose.   40
ALCESTE   Madam, I fear that any such ambition
Is wholly foreign to my disposition.
The soul God gave me isn't of the sort
That prospers in the weather of a court.
It's all too obvious that I don't possess   45

The virtues necessary for success.
My one great talent is for speaking plain;
I've never learned to flatter or to feign;
And anyone so stupidly sincere
Had best not seek a courtier's career.   50
Outside the court, I know, one must dispense
With honors, privilege, and influence;
But still one gains the right, foregoing these,
Not to be tortured by the wish to please.
One needn't live in dread of snubs and slights,   55
Nor praise the verse that every idiot writes,
Nor humor silly Marquesses, nor bestow
Politic sighs on Madam So-and-So.

ARSINOE   Forget the court, then; let the matter rest.
But I've another cause to be distressed   60
About your present situation, Sir.
It's to your love affair that I refer.
She whom you love, and who pretends to love you,
Is, I regret to say, unworthy of you.

ALCESTE   Why, Madam! Can you seriously intend   65
To make so grave a charge against your friend?

ARSINOE   Alas, I must. I've stood aside too long
And let that lady do you grievous wrong;
But now my debt to conscience shall be paid:
I tell you that your love has been betrayed.   70

ALCESTE   I thank you, Madam; you're extremely kind.
Such words are soothing to a lover's mind.

ARSINOE   Yes, though she *is* my friend, I say again
You're very much too good for Célimène.
She's wantonly misled you from the start.   75

ALCESTE   You may be right; who knows another's heart?
But ask yourself if it's the part of charity
To shake my soul with doubts of her sincerity.

ARSINOE   Well, if you'd rather be a dupe than doubt her,
That's your affair. I'll say no more about her.   80

ALCESTE   Madam, you know that doubt and vague suspicion
Are painful to a man in my position;
It's most unkind to worry me this way
Unless you've some real proof of what you say.

ARSINOE   Sir, say no more: all doubt shall be removed,   85
And all that I've been saying shall be proved.

You've only to escort me home, and there
We'll look into the heart of this affair.
I've ocular evidence which will persuade you
Beyond a doubt, that Célimène's betrayed you.   90
Then, if you're saddened by that revelation,
Perhaps I can provide some consolation.

□ WRITING ↔ READING ↔ THINKING ACTIVITIES □
Understanding Act III

1. Scene 1 of act III presents the discussion between Clitandre and Acaste regarding their rivalry for Célimène's favors. What agreement do they reach? Does this agreement cause you to expect any particular event later in the play?
2. In scene 5, what is Arsinoé's purpose in visiting Célimène? What is Célimène's reaction? What is each woman's motive?
3. Look closely at Célimène's speech in scene 5, lines 99–108. She expresses here a view of life that is also found in at least two selections from Chapter 1 of this book. What are those selections, and what are the similarities?
4. What is Arsinoé's reaction to being left alone with Alceste in scene 7? What does she promise Alceste if he will escort her home?
5. What elements in the play so far seem to be peculiar to the setting? Have these aspects puzzled you? What would change if the play were set in twentieth-century America instead of seventeenth-century France?

ACT IV

Scene 1

(ELIANTE, PHILINTE)

PHILINTE   Madam, he acted like a stubborn child;
I thought they never would be reconciled;
In vain we reasoned, threatened, and appealed;
He stood his ground and simply would not yield.
The Marshals, I feel sure, have never heard   5
An argument so splendidly absurd.
"No, gentlemen," said he, "I'll not retract.
His verse is bad: extremely bad, in fact.
Surely it does the man no harm to know it.
Does it disgrace him, not to be a poet?   10

A gentleman may be respected still,
Whether he writes a sonnet well or ill.
That I dislike his verse should not offend him;
In all that touches honor, I commend him;
He's noble, brave, and virtuous—but I fear   15
He can't in truth be called a sonneteer.
I'll gladly praise his wardrobe; I'll endorse
His dancing, or the way he sits a horse;
But, gentlemen, I cannot praise his rhyme.
In fact, it ought to be a capital crime   20
For anyone so sadly unendowed
To write a sonnet, and read the thing aloud."
At length he fell into a gentler mood
And, striking a concessive attitude,
He paid Oronte the following courtesies: 25
"Sir, I regret that I'm so hard to please,
And I'm profoundly sorry that your lyric
Failed to provoke me to a panegyric."
After these curious words, the two embraced,
And then the hearing was adjourned—in haste.   30
ELIANTE   His conduct has been very singular lately;
     Still, I confess that I respect him greatly.
     The honesty in which he takes such pride
     Has—to my mind—its noble, heroic side.
     In this false age, such candor seems outrageous.   35
     But I could wish that it were more contagious.
PHILINTE   What most intrigues me in our friend Alceste
     Is the grand passion that rages in his breast.
     The sullen humors he's compounded of
     Should not, I think, dispose his heart to love;   40
     But since they do, it puzzles me still more
     That he should choose your cousin to adore.
ELIANTE   It does, indeed, belie the theory
     That love is born of gentle sympathy,
     And that the tender passion must be based   45
     On sweet accords of temper and of taste.
PHILINTE   Does she return his love, do you suppose?
ELIANTE   Ah, that's a difficult question, Sir. Who knows?
     How can we judge the truth of her devotion?
     Her heart's a stranger to its own emotion.   50
     Sometimes it thinks it loves, when no love's there;
     At other times it loves quite unaware.

PHILINTE   I rather think Alceste is in for more
    Distress and sorrow than he's bargained for;
    Were he of my mind, Madam, his affection   55
    Would turn in quite a different direction,
    And we would see him more responsive to
    The kind regard which he receives from you.
ELIANTE   Sir, I believe in frankness, and I'm inclined,
    In matters of the heart, to speak my mind.   60
    I don't oppose his love for her; indeed,
    I hope with all my heart that he'll succeed,
    And were it in my power, I'd rejoice
    In giving him the lady of his choice.
    But if, as happens frequently enough   65
    In love affairs, he meets with a rebuff—
    If Célimène should grant some rival's suit—
    I'd gladly play the role of substitute;
    Nor would his tender speeches please me less
    Because they'd once been made without success.   70
PHILINTE   Well, Madam, as for me, I don't oppose
    Your hopes in this affair; and heaven knows
    That in my conversations with the man
    I plead your cause as often as I can.
    But if those two should marry, and so remove   75
    All chance that he will offer you his love,
    Then I'll declare my own, and hope to see
    Your gracious favor pass from him to me.
    In short, should you be cheated of Alceste,
    I'd be most happy to be second best.   80
ELIANTE   Philinte, you're teasing.
PHILINTE   Ah, Madam, never fear;
    No words of mine were ever so sincere,
    And I shall live in fretful expectation
    Till I can make a fuller declaration.

Scene 2

(ALCESTE, ELIANTE, PHILINTE)

ALCESTE   Avenge me, Madam! I must have satisfaction,
    Or this great wrong will drive me to distraction!
ELIANTE   Why, what's the matter? What's upset you so?
ALCESTE   Madam, I've had a mortal, mortal blow.
    If Chaos repossessed the universe,   5

    I swear I'd not be shaken any worse.
    I'm ruined. . . . I can say no more. . . . My soul . . .
ELIANTE   Do try, Sir, to regain your self-control.
ALCESTE   Just heaven! Why were so much beauty and grace
    Bestowed on one so vicious and so base?   10
ELIANTE   Once more, Sir, tell us. . . .
ALCESTE   My world has gone to wrack;
    I'm—I'm betrayed; she's stabbed me in the back:
    Yes, Célimène (who would have thought it of her?)
    Is false to me, and has another lover.
ELIANTE   Are you quite certain? Can you prove these things?   15
PHILINTE   Lovers are prey to wild imaginings
    And jealous fancies. No doubt there's some mistake. . . .
ALCESTE   Mind your own business, Sir, for heaven's sake.

    (*To* ELIANTE)

    Madam, I have the proof that you demand
    Here in my pocket, penned by her own hand.   20
    Yes, all the shameful evidence one could want
    Lies in this letter written to Oronte—
    Oronte! whom I felt sure she couldn't love,
    And hardly bothered to be jealous of.
PHILINTE   Still, in a letter, appearances may deceive;   25
    This may not be so bad as you believe.
ALCESTE   Once more I beg you, Sir, to let me be;
    Tend to your own affairs; leave mine to me.
ELIANTE   Compose yourself; this anguish that you feel . . .
ALCESTE   Is something, Madam, you alone can heal.   30
    My outraged heart, beside itself with grief,
    Appeals to you for comfort and relief.
    Avenge me on your cousin, whose unjust
    And faithless nature has deceived my trust;
    Avenge a crime your pure soul must detest.   35
ELIANTE   But how, Sir?
ALCESTE   Madam, this heart within my breast
    Is yours; pray take it; redeem my heart from her,
    And so avenge me on my torturer.
    Let her be punished by the fond emotion,
    The ardent love, the bottomless devotion,   40
    The faithful worship which this heart of mine
    Will offer up to yours as to a shrine.

ELIANTE   You have my sympathy, Sir, in all you suffer;
    Nor do I scorn the noble heart you offer;
    But I suspect you'll soon be mollified,   45
    And this desire for vengeance will subside.
    When some beloved hand has done us wrong
    We thirst for retribution—but not for long;
    However dark the deed that she's committed,
    A lovely culprit's very soon acquitted.   50
    Nothing's so stormy as an injured lover,
    And yet no storm so quickly passes over.
ALCESTE   No, Madam, no—this is no lovers' spat;
    I'll not forgive her; it's gone too far for that;
    My mind's made up; I'll kill myself before   55
    I waste my hopes upon her any more.
    Ah, here she is. My wrath intensifies.
    I shall confront her with her tricks and lies,
    And crush her utterly, and bring you then
    A heart no longer slave to Célimène.   60

Scene 3

(CELIMENE, ALCESTE)

ALCESTE (*Aside*)   Sweet heaven, help me to control my passion.
CELIMENE (*Aside*)   Oh, Lord.   (*To* ALCESTE)
    Why stand there staring in that fashion?
    And what d'you mean by those dramatic sighs,
    And that malignant glitter in your eyes?
ALCESTE   I mean that sins which cause the blood to freeze   5
    Look innocent beside your treacheries;
    That nothing Hell's or Heaven's wrath could do
    Ever produced so bad a thing as you.
CELIMENE   Your compliments were always sweet and pretty.
ALCESTE   Madam, it's not the moment to be witty.   10
    No, blush and hang your head; you've ample reason,
    Since I've the fullest evidence of your treason.
    Ah, this is what my sad heart prophesied;
    Now all my anxious fears are verified;
    My dark suspicion and my gloomy doubt   15
    Divined the truth, and now the truth is out.
    For all your trickery, I was not deceived;
    It was my bitter stars that I believed.

But don't imagine that you'll go scot-free;
You shan't misuse me with impunity.   20
I know that love's irrational and blind;
I know the heart's not subject to the mind,
And can't be reasoned into beating faster;
I know each soul is free to choose its master;
Therefore had you but spoken from the heart,   25
Rejecting my attentions from the start,
I'd have no grievance, or at any rate
I could complain of nothing but my fate.
Ah, but so falsely to encourage me—
That was a treason and a treachery   30
For which you cannot suffer too severely,
And you shall pay for that behavior dearly.
Yes, now I have no pity, not a shred;
My temper's out of hand; I've lost my head;
Shocked by the knowledge of your double-dealings,   35
My reason can't restrain my savage feelings;
A righteous wrath deprives me of my senses,
And I won't answer for the consequences.
CELIMENE   What does this outburst mean? Will you please explain?
Have you, by any chance, gone quite insane?   40
ALCESTE   Yes, yes, I went insane the day I fell
A victim to your black and fatal spell,
Thinking to meet with some sincerity
Among the treacherous charms that beckoned me.
CELIMENE   Pooh. Of what treachery can you complain?   45
ALCESTE   How sly you are, how cleverly you feign!
But you'll not victimize me any more.
Look: here's a document you've seen before.
This evidence, which I acquired today,
Leaves you, I think, without a thing to say.   50
CELIMENE   Is this what sent you into such a fit?
ALCESTE   You should be blushing at the sight of it.
CELIMENE   Ought I to blush? I truly don't see why.
ALCESTE   Ah, now you're being bold as well as sly;
Since there's no signature, perhaps you'll claim . . .   55
CELIMENE   I wrote it, whether or not it bears my name.
ALCESTE   And you can view with equanimity
This proof of your disloyalty to me!
CELIMENE   Oh, don't be so outrageous and extreme.

ALCESTE   You take this matter lightly, it would seem.   60
　　Was it no wrong to me, no shame to you,
　　That you should send Oronte this billet-doux?
CELIMENE   Oronte! Who said it was for him?
ALCESTE   Why, those
　　Who brought me this example of your prose.
　　But what's the difference? If you wrote the letter   65
　　To someone else, it pleases me no better.
　　My grievance and your guilt remain the same.
CELIMENE   But need you rage, and need I blush for shame,
　　If this was written to a *woman* friend?
ALCESTE   Ah, most ingenious. I'm impressed no end;   70
　　And after that incredible evasion
　　Your guilt is clear. I need no more persuasion.
　　How dare you try so clumsy a deception?
　　D'you think I'm wholly wanting in perception?
　　Come, come, let's see how brazenly you'll try   75
　　To bolster up so palpable a lie:
　　Kindly construe this ardent closing section
　　As nothing more than sisterly affection!
　　Here, let me read it. Tell me, if you dare to,
　　That this is for a woman . . .
CELIMENE   I don't care to.   80
　　What right have you to badger and berate me,
　　And so highhandedly interrogate me?
ALCESTE   Now, don't be angry; all I ask of you
　　Is that you justify a phrase or two . . .
CELIMENE   No, I shall not. I utterly refuse,   85
　　And you may take those phrases as you choose.
ALCESTE   Just show me how this letter could be meant
　　For a woman's eyes, and I shall be content.
CELIMENE   No, no, it's for Oronte; you're perfectly right.
　　I welcome his attentions with delight,   90
　　I prize his character and his intellect,
　　And everything is just as you suspect.
　　Come, do your worst now; give your rage free rein;
　　But kindly cease to bicker and complain.
ALCESTE (*Aside*)   Good God! Could anything be more inhuman?   95
　　Was ever a heart so mangled by a woman?
　　When I complain of how she has betrayed me,
　　She bridles, and commences to upbraid me!

She tries my tortured patience to the limit;
She won't deny her guilt; she glories in it!   100
And yet my heart's too faint and cowardly
To break these chains of passion, and be free,
To scorn her as it should, and rise above
This unrewarded, mad, and bitter love.

(*To* CELIMENE)

Ah, traitress, in how confident a fashion   105
You take advantage of my helpless passion,
And use my weakness for your faithless charms
To make me once again throw down my arms!
But do at least deny this black transgression;
Take back that mocking and perverse confession;   110
Defend this letter and your innocence,
And I, poor fool, will aid in your defense.
Pretend, pretend, that you are just and true,
And I shall make myself believe in you.

CELIMENE   Oh, stop it. Don't be such a jealous dunce,   115
Or I shall leave off loving you at once.
Just why should I *pretend*? What could impel me
To stoop so low as that? And kindly tell me
Why, if I loved another, I shouldn't merely
Inform you of it, simply and sincerely!   120
I've told you where you stand, and that admission
Should altogether clear me of suspicion;
After so generous a guarantee,
What right have you to harbor doubts of me?
Since women are (from natural reticence)   125
Reluctant to declare their sentiments,
And since the honor of our sex requires
That we conceal our amorous desires,
Ought any man for whom such laws are broken
To question what the oracle has spoken?   130
Should he not rather feel an obligation
To trust that most obliging declaration?
Enough, now. Your suspicions quite disgust me;
Why should I love a man who doesn't trust me?
I cannot understand why I continue,   135
Fool that I am, to take an interest in you,
I ought to choose a man less prone to doubt,
And give you something to be vexed about.

ALCESTE   Ah, what a poor enchanted fool I am;   140
  These gentle words, no doubt, were all a sham;
  But destiny requires me to entrust
  My happiness to you, and so I must.
  I'll love you to the bitter end, and see
  How false and treacherous you dare to be.
CELIMENE   No, you don't really love me as you ought.   145
ALCESTE   I love you more than can be said or thought;
  Indeed, I wish you were in such distress
  That I might show my deep devotedness.
  Yes, I could wish that you were wretchedly poor,
  Unloved, uncherished, utterly obscure;   150
  That fate had set you down upon the earth
  Without possession, rank, or gentle birth;
  Then, by the offer of my heart, I might
  Repair the great injustice of your plight;
  I'd raise you from the dust, and proudly prove   155
  The purity and vastness of my love.
CELIMENE   This is a strange benevolence indeed!
  God grant that I may never be in need. . . .
  Ah, here's Monsieur Dubois, in quaint disguise.

Scene 4

(CELIMENE, ALCESTE, DUBOIS)

ALCESTE   Well, why this costume? Why those frightened eyes?
  What ails you?
DUBOIS   Well, Sir, things are most mysterious.
ALCESTE   What do you mean?
DUBOIS   I fear they're very serious.
ALCESTE   What?
DUBOIS   Shall I speak more loudly?
ALCESTE   Yes; speak out.
DUBOIS   Isn't there someone here, Sir?
ALCESTE   Speak, you lout!   5
  Stop wasting time.
DUBOIS   Sir, we must slip away.
ALCESTE   How's that?
DUBOIS   We must decamp without delay.
ALCESTE   Explain yourself.
DUBOIS   I tell you we must fly.

ALCESTE   What for?

DUBOIS   We mustn't pause to say good-by.

ALCESTE   Now what d'you mean by all of this, you clown?   10

DUBOIS   I mean, Sir, that we've got to leave this town.

ALCESTE   I'll tear you limb from limb and joint from joint
   If you don't come more quickly to the point.

DUBOIS   Well, Sir, today a man in a black suit,
   Who wore a black and ugly scowl to boot,   15
   Left us a document scrawled in such a hand
   As even Satan couldn't understand.
   It bears upon your lawsuit, I don't doubt;
   But all hell's devils couldn't make it out.

ALCESTE   Well, well, go on. What then? I fail to see   20
   How this event obliges us to flee.

DUBOIS   Well, Sir: an hour later, hardly more,
   A gentleman who's often called before
   Came looking for you in an anxious way.
   Not finding you, he asked me to convey   25
   (Knowing I could be trusted with the same)
   The following message. . . . Now, what *was* his name?

ALCESTE   Forget his name, you idiot. What did he say?

DUBOIS   Well, it was one of your friends, Sir, anyway.
   He warned you to begone, and he suggested   30
   That if you stay, you may well be arrested.

ALCESTE   What? Nothing more specific? Think, man, think!

DUBOIS   No, Sir. He had me bring him pen and ink,
   And dashed you off a letter which, I'm sure,
   Will render things distinctly less obscure.   35

ALCESTE   Well—let me have it!

CELIMENE   What *is* this all about?

ALCESTE   God knows; but I have hopes of finding out.
   How long am I to wait, you blitherer?

DUBOIS (*After a protracted search for the letter*)
   I must have left it on your table, Sir.

ALCESTE   I ought to . . .

CELIMENE   No, no, keep your self-control;   40
   Go find out what's behind his rigmarole.

ALCESTE   It seems that fate, no matter what I do,
   Has sworn that I may not converse with you;
   But, Madam, pray permit your faithful lover
   To try once more before the day is over.   45

□ WRITING ↔ READING ↔ THINKING ACTIVITIES □
Understanding Act IV

1. In scene 1, line 2, who is the "they" to whom Philinte refers? What conflict has been resolved, according to the rest of his speech?
2. In their conversation in scene 1, Philinte and Eliante reveal much about their feelings. What is your reaction to their exchange? Do you find their characters appealing? humorous? romantic? passionless?
3. Scene 2 follows scene 1 abruptly with Alceste's passionate request that Eliante help him avenge Célimène's faithlessness. How do Philinte and Eliante react in this scene? Does their preceding conversation have any bearing on their responses?
4. Scene 3 opens with Alceste and Célimène speaking their first lines as *asides*, a stage term indicating words spoken by a character which are not heard by any other characters. This convention of "thinking aloud" allows the playwright to give the audience some direct information about what a character is actually feeling or thinking, much as an omniscient narrator may do in a short story. Reread this scene and then write a paragraph or make a list which traces the "thoughts" of Célimène during this scene. To complete this exercise, you will have to make some judgments about Célimène's nature and motives, just as an actress playing the role would have to do in order to decide how to deliver her lines onstage.
5. In scene 3 Alceste's indignant confrontation of Célimène disintegrates into groveling when she berates him for accusing her of misconduct. Explain the irony of his speech in lines 109–114 in light of his frequent outbursts against hypocrisy in the rest of the play.
6. In scene 4, Alceste's avowals of abject devotion to Célimène are interrupted by the arrival of the comical servant Dubois in disguise. What events have triggered Dubois's fears? This scene would be performed with comically exaggerated slapstick onstage, making fun of the inarticulate terror of Dubois and the frustrated rage of Alceste. Write some stage directions indicating how Alceste and Dubois might behave during this scene in order to make the audience laugh.

ACT V

Scene 1

(ALCESTE, PHILINTE)

ALCESTE   No, it's too much. My mind's made up, I tell you.
PHILINTE   Why should this blow, however hard, compel you . . .

ALCESTE   No, no, don't waste your breath in argument;
    Nothing you say will alter my intent;
    This age is vile, and I've made up my mind   5
    To have no further commerce with mankind.
    Did not truth, honor, decency, and the laws
    Oppose my enemy and approve my cause?
    My claims were justified in all men's sight;
    I put my trust in equity and right;   10
    Yet, to my horror and the world's disgrace,
    Justice is mocked, and I have lost my case!
    A scoundrel whose dishonesty is notorious
    Emerges from another lie victorious!
    Honor and right condone his brazen fraud,   15
    While rectitude and decency applaud!
    Before his smirking face, the truth stands charmed,
    And virtue conquered, and the law disarmed!
    His crime is sanctioned by a court decree!
    And not content with what he's done to me,   20
    The dog now seeks to ruin me by stating
    That I composed a book now circulating,
    A book so wholly criminal and vicious
    That even to speak its title is seditious!
    Meanwhile Oronte, my rival, lends his credit   25
    To the same libelous tale, and helps to spread it!
    Oronte! a man of honor and of rank,
    With whom I've been entirely fair and frank;
    Who sought me out and forced me, willy-nilly,
    To judge some verse I found extremely silly;   30
    And who, because I properly refused
    To flatter him, or see the truth abused,
    Abets my enemy in a rotten slander!
    There's the reward of honesty and candor!
    The man will hate me to the end of time   35
    For failing to commend his wretched rhyme!
    And not this man alone, but all humanity
    Do what they do from interest and vanity;
    They prate of honor, truth, and righteousness,
    But lie, betray, and swindle nonetheless.   40
    Come then: man's villainy is too much to bear;
    Let's leave this jungle and this jackal's lair.
    Yes! treacherous and savage race of men,
    You shall not look upon my face again.

PHILINTE Oh, don't rush into exile prematurely; 45
    Things aren't as dreadful as you make them, surely.
    It's rather obvious, since you're still at large,
    That people don't believe your enemy's charge.
    Indeed, his tale's so patently untrue
    That it may do more harm to him than you. 50
ALCESTE Nothing could do that scoundrel any harm:
    His frank corruption is his greatest charm,
    And, far from hurting him, a further shame
    Would only serve to magnify his name.
PHILINTE In any case, his bald prevarication 55
    Has done no injury to your reputation,
    And you may feel secure in that regard.
    As for your lawsuit, it should not be hard
    To have the case reopened, and contest
    This judgment . . .
ALCESTE   No, no, let the verdict rest. 60
    Whatever cruel penalty it may bring,
    I wouldn't have it changed for anything.
    It shows the times' injustice with such clarity
    That I shall pass it down to our posterity
    As a great proof and signal demonstration 65
    Of the black wickedness of this generation.
    It may cost twenty thousand francs; but I
    Shall pay their twenty thousand, and gain thereby
    The right to storm and rage at human evil,
    And send the race of mankind to the devil. 70
PHILINTE Listen to me. . . .
ALCESTE   Why? What can you possibly say?
    Don't argue, Sir; your labor's thrown away.
    Do you propose to offer lame excuses
    For men's behavior and the times' abuses?
PHILINTE No, all you say I'll readily concede: 75
    This is a low, conniving age indeed;
    Nothing but trickery prospers nowadays,
    And people ought to mend their shabby ways.
    Yes, man's a beastly creature; but must we then
    Abandon the society of men? 80
    Here in the world, each human frailty
    Provides occasion for philosophy,
    And that is virtue's noblest exercise;
    If honesty shone forth from all men's eyes,

If every heart were frank and kind and just,   85
What could our virtues do but gather dust
(Since their employment is to help us bear
The villainies of men without despair)?
A heart well-armed with virtue can endure. . . .

ALCESTE   Sir, you're a matchless reasoner, to be sure;   90
Your words are fine and full of cogency;
But don't waste time and eloquence on me.
My reason bids me go, for my own good.
My tongue won't lie and flatter as it should;
God knows what frankness it might next commit,   95
And what I'd suffer on account of it.
Pray let me wait for Célimène's return
In peace and quiet. I shall shortly learn,
By her response to what I have in view,
Whether her love for me is feigned or true.   100

PHILINTE   Till then, let's visit Eliante upstairs.

ALCESTE   No, I am too weighed down with somber cares.
Go to her, do; and leave me with my gloom
Here in the darkened corner of this room.

PHILINTE   Why, that's no sort of company, my friend;   105
I'll see if Eliante will not descend.

Scene 2

(CELIMENE, ORONTE, ALCESTE)

ORONTE   Yes, Madam, if you wish me to remain
Your true and ardent lover, you must deign
To give me some more positive assurance.
All this suspense is quite beyond endurance.
If your heart shares the sweet desires of mine,   5
Show me as much by some convincing sign;
And here's the sign I urgently suggest:
That you no longer tolerate Alceste,
But sacrifice him to my love, and sever
All your relations with the man forever.   10

CELIMENE   Why do you suddenly dislike him so?
You praised him to the skies not long ago.

ORONTE   Madam, that's not the point. I'm here to find
Which way your tender feelings are inclined.
Choose, if you please, between Alceste and me,   15
And I shall stay or go accordingly.

ALCESTE (*Emerging from the corner*)   Yes, Madam, choose; this gentleman's
    demand
  Is wholly just, and I support his stand.
  I too am true and ardent; I too am here
  To ask you that you make your feelings clear.   20
  No more delays, now; no equivocation;
  The time has come to make your declaration.
ORONTE Sir, I've no wish in any way to be
  An obstacle to your felicity.
ALCESTE Sir, I've no wish to share her heart with you;   25
  That may sound jealous, but at least it's true.
ORONTE If, weighing us, she leans in your direction . . .
ALCESTE If she regards you with the least affection . . .
ORONTE I swear I'll yield her to you there and then.
ALCESTE I swear I'll never see her face again.   30
ORONTE Now, Madam, tell us what we've come to hear.
ALCESTE Madam, speak openly and have no fear.
ORONTE Just say which one is to remain your lover.
ALCESTE Just name one name, and it will all be over.
ORONTE What! Is it possible that you're undecided?   35
ALCESTE What! Can your feeling possibly be divided?
CELIMENE Enough: this inquisition's gone too far:
  How utterly unreasonable you are!
  Not that I couldn't make the choice with ease;
  My heart has no conflicting sympathies;   40
  I know full well which one of you I favor,
  And you'd not see me hesitate or waver.
  But how can you expect me to reveal
  So cruelly and bluntly what I feel?
  I think it altogether too unpleasant   45
  To choose between two men when both are present;
  One's heart has means more subtle and more kind
  Of letting its affections be divined,
  Nor need one be uncharitably plain
  To let a lover know he loves in vain.   50
ORONTE No, no, speak plainly; I for one can stand it.
  I beg you to be frank.
ALCESTE   And I demand it.
  The simple truth is what I wish to know,
  And there's no need for softening the blow.
  You've made an art of pleasing everyone,   55
  But now your days of coquetry are done:

You have no choice now, Madam, but to choose,
For I'll know what to think if you refuse;
I'll take your silence for a clear admission
That I'm entitled to my worst suspicion.   60
ORONTE   I thank you for this ultimatum, Sir,
And I may say I heartily concur.
CELIMENE   Really, this foolishness is very wearing:
Must you be so unjust and overbearing?
Haven't I told you why I must demur?   65
Ah, here's Eliante; I'll put the case to her.

Scene 3

(ELIANTE, PHILINTE, CELIMENE, ORONTE, ALCESTE)

CELIMENE   Cousin, I'm being persecuted here
By these two persons, who, it would appear,
Will not be satisfied till I confess
Which one I love the more, and which the less,
And tell the latter to his face that he   5
Is henceforth banished from my company.
Tell me, has ever such a thing been done?
ELIANTE   You'd best not turn to me; I'm not the one
To back you in a matter of this kind:
I'm all for those who frankly speak their mind.   10
ORONTE   Madam, you'll search in vain for a defender.
ALCESTE   You're beaten, Madam, and may as well surrender.
ORONTE   Speak, speak, you must; and end this awful strain.
ALCESTE   Or don't, and your position will be plain.
ORONTE   A single word will close this painful scene.
ALCESTE   But if you're silent, I'll know what you mean.

Scene 4

(ARSINOE, CELIMENE, ELIANTE, ALCESTE, PHILINTE, ACASTE, CLITANDRE, ORONTE)

ACASTE (*To* CELIMENE)   Madam, with all due deference, we two
Have come to pick a little bone with you.
CLITANDRE (*To* ORONTE *and* ALCESTE)   I'm glad you're present,
Sirs; as you'll soon learn,
Our business here is also your concern.

ARSINOE (*To* CELIMENE)   Madam, I visit you so soon again   5
  Only because of these two gentlemen,
  Who came to me indignant and aggrieved
  About a crime too base to be believed.
  Knowing your virtue, having such confidence in it,
  I couldn't think you guilty for a minute,   10
  In spite of all their telling evidence;
  And, rising above our little difference,
  I've hastened here in friendship's name to see
  You clear yourself of this great calumny.
ACASTE   Yes, Madam, let us see with what composure   15
  You'll manage to respond to this disclosure.
  You lately sent Clitandre this tender note.
CLITANDRE   And this one, for Acaste, you also wrote.
ACASTE (*To* ORONTE *and* ALCESTE)   You'll recognize this writing, Sirs, I think;
  The lady is so free with pen and ink   20
  That you must know it all too well, I fear.
  But listen: this is something you should hear.

  "How absurd you are to condemn my lightheartedness in society, and to accuse me
  of being happiest in the company of others. Nothing could be more unjust; and if you
  do not come to me instantly and beg pardon for saying such a thing, I shall never   25
  forgive you as long as I live. Our big bumbling friend the Viscount . . ."

What a shame that he's not here.

  "Our big bumbling friend the Viscount, whose name stands first in your complaint,
  is hardly a man to my taste; and ever since the day I watched him spend three-
  quarters of an hour spitting into a well, so as to make circles in the water, I have   30
  been unable to think highly of him. As for the little Marquess . . ."

In all modesty, gentlemen, that is I.

  "As for the little Marquess, who sat squeezing my hand for such a long while
  yesterday, I find him in all respects the most trifling creature alive; and the only
  things of value about him are his cape and his sword. As for the man with the green   35
  ribbons . . ."

(*To* ALCESTE)

It's your turn now, Sir.

  "As for the man with the green ribbons, he amuses me now and then with his
  bluntness and his bearish ill-humor; but there are many times indeed when I think
  him the greatest bore in the world. And as for the sonneteer . . ."   40

(*To* ORONTE)

Here's your helping.

"And as for the sonneteer, who has taken it into his head to be witty, and insists on being an author in the teeth of opinion, I simply cannot be bothered to listen to him, and his prose wearies me quite as much as his poetry. Be assured that I am not always so well-entertained as you suppose; that I long for your company, more than 45
I dare to say, at all these entertainments to which people drag me; and that the presence of those one loves is the true and perfect seasoning to all one's pleasures."

CLITANDRE   And now for me.

"Clitandre, whom you mention, and who so pesters me with his saccharine speeches, is the last man on earth for whom I could feel any affection. He is quite 50
mad to suppose that I love him, and so are you, to doubt that you are loved. Do come to your senses; exchange your suppositions for his; and visit me as often as possible, to help me bear the annoyance of his unwelcome attentions."

It's a sweet character that these letters show,
And what to call it, Madam, you well know.
Enough. We're off to make the world acquainted   55
With this sublime self-portrait that you've painted.
ACASTE   Madam, I'll make you no farewell oration;
No, you're not worthy of my indignation.
Far choicer hearts than yours, as you'll discover,
Would like this little Marquess for a lover.   60

Scene 5

(CELIMENE, ELIANTE, ARSINOE, ALCESTE, ORONTE, PHILINTE)

ORONTE   So! After all those loving letters you wrote,
You turn on me like this, and cut my throat!
And your dissembling, faithless heart, I find,
Has pledged itself by turns to all mankind!
How blind I've been! But now I clearly see;   5
I thank you, Madam, for enlightening me.
My heart is mine once more, and I'm content;
The loss of it shall be your punishment.

(*To* ALCESTE)

Sir, she is yours; I'll seek no more to stand
Between your wishes and this lady's hand.   10

Scene 6

(CELIMENE, ELIANTE, ARSINOE, ALCESTE, PHILINTE)

ARSINOE (*To* CELIMENE)   Madam, I'm forced to speak. I'm far too stirred
   To keep my counsel, after what I've heard.
   I'm shocked and staggered by your want of morals.
   It's not my way to mix in others' quarrels;
   But really, when this fine and noble spirit,   5
   This man of honor and surpassing merit,
   Laid down the offering of his heart before you,
   How *could* you . . .

ALCESTE   Madam, permit me, I implore you,
   To represent myself in this debate.
   Don't bother, please, to be my advocate.   10
   My heart, in any case, could not afford
   To give your services their due reward;
   And if I chose, for consolation's sake,
   Some other lady, 'twould not be you I'd take.

ARSINOE   What makes you think you could, Sir? And how dare you   15
   Imply that I've been trying to ensnare you?
   If you can for a moment entertain
   Such flattering fancies, you're extremely vain.
   I'm not so interested as you suppose
   In Célimène's discarded gigolos.   20
   Get rid of that absurd illusion, do.
   Women like me are not for such as you.
   Stay with this creature, to whom you're so attached;
   I've never seen two people better matched.

Scene 7

(CELIMENE, ELIANTE, ALCESTE, PHILINTE)

ALCESTE (*To* CELIMENE)   Well, I've been still throughout this exposé,
   Till everyone but me has said his say.
   Come, have I shown sufficient self-restraint?
   And may I now . . .

CELIMENE   Yes, make your just complaint.
   Reproach me freely, call me what you will;   5
   You've every right to say I've used you ill.
   I've wronged you, I confess it; and in my shame
   I'll make no effort to escape the blame.
   The anger of those others I could despise;
   My guilt toward you I sadly recognize.   10

Your wrath is wholly justified, I fear;
I know how culpable I must appear,
I know all things bespeak my treachery,
And that, in short, you've grounds for hating me.
Do so; I give you leave.

ALCESTE   Ah, traitress—how,   15
How should I cease to love you, even now?
Though mind and will were passionately bent
On hating you, my heart would not consent.

(*To* ELIANTE *and* PHILINTE)

Be witness to my madness, both of you;
See what infatuation drives one to;   20
But wait; my folly's only just begun,
And I shall prove to you before I'm done
How strange the human heart is, and how far
From rational we sorry creatures are.

(*To* CELIMENE)

Woman, I'm willing to forget your shame,   25
And clothe your treacheries in a sweeter name;
I'll call them youthful errors, instead of crimes,
And lay the blame on these corrupting times.
My one condition is that you agree
To share my chosen fate, and fly with me   30
To that wild, trackless, solitary place
In which I shall forget the human race.
Only by such a course can you atone
For those atrocious letters; by that alone
Can you remove my present horror of you,   35
And make it possible for me to love you.

CELIMENE   What! *I* renounce the world at my young age,
And die of boredom in some hermitage?

ALCESTE   Ah, if you really loved me as you ought,
You wouldn't give the world a moment's thought;   40
Must you have me, and all the world beside?

CELIMENE   Alas, at twenty one is terrified
Of solitude. I fear I lack the force
And depth of soul to take so stern a course.
But if my hand in marriage will content you,   45
Why, there's a plan which I might well consent to,
And . . .

ALCESTE   No, I detest you now. I could excuse
Everything else, but since you thus refuse
To love me wholly, as a wife should do,
And see the world in me, as I in you,   50
Go! I reject your hand, and disenthrall
My heart from your enchantments, once for all.

Scene 8

(ELIANTE, ALCESTE, PHILINTE)

ALCESTE (*To* ELIANTE)   Madam, your virtuous beauty has no peer;
Of all this world, you only are sincere;
I've long esteemed you highly, as you know;
Permit me ever to esteem you so,
And if I do not now request your hand,   5
Forgive me, Madam, and try to understand.
I feel unworthy of it; I sense that fate
Does not intend me for the married state,
That I should do you wrong by offering you
My shattered heart's unhappy residue,   10
And that in short . . .
ELIANTE   Your argument's well taken:
Nor need you fear that I shall feel forsaken.
Were I to offer him this hand of mine,
Your friend Philinte, I think, would not decline.
PHILINTE   Ah, Madam, that's my heart's most cherished goal,   15
For which I'd gladly give my life and soul.
ALCESTE (*To* ELIANTE *and* PHILINTE)   May you be true to all you now profess,
And so deserve unending happiness.
Meanwhile, betrayed and wronged in everything,
I'll flee this bitter world where vice is king,   20
And seek some spot unpeopled and apart
Where I'll be free to have an honest heart.
PHILINTE   Come, Madam, let's do everything we can
To change the mind of this unhappy man.

□ WRITING ↔ READING ↔ THINKING ACTIVITIES □
Understanding Act V

1. What is the outcome of the lawsuit that had been pending against
    Alceste?

2. In scene 1, Philinte and Alceste argue regarding Alceste's situation. Both men base their arguments on reason in lines 75–96. What are their individual arguments and viewpoints?

3. The action in scenes 2, 3, 4, and 5 exposes the flirtatious Célimène as a coquette. Trace the steps in the revelation of her dishonesty and the subsequent departure of her beaux.

4. In scene 7, what is Alceste's reaction to the revelations? What is Célimène's response to his proposal?

5. The rapid dénouement occurs in the last five speeches. What does Alceste resolve to do? What do Philinte and Eliante decide? What do you make of the last line of the play? Do you think Molière wants us to believe that Philinte will change Alceste's mind? Why or why not?

☐ EXPANDING YOUR WRITING SKILLS ☐
Considering Argument in Dramatic Form

1. In Chapter 3 you were encouraged to ask the question "Whose story is it?" in analyzing fiction. The answer to that question for *The Misanthrope* is clearly "Alceste, the title character." But another important question for a work that presents conflicting ideas is this: "What character, if any, is the reader supposed to agree with?" In order to answer this question for *The Misanthrope*, review the scenes in which Philinte and Alceste argue about the proper way to view the moral weaknesses of human beings. Categorize each character's arguments according to the following types of persuasion set forth in Chapter 3:
   a. Citing evidence
   b. Using logic or reason
   c. Appealing to emotion
   Does either character rely mostly on one type of persuasion? Does either character avoid entirely one or two of the types? Do you find Alceste or Philinte the more convincing? Why?
      Write an essay of approximately 500 words in which you first compare and contrast the views of Alceste and Philinte. Then explain why you find one character's arguments more convincing than the other's. (Your conclusion may well lead to a statement of the play's theme.)

2. Try your hand at writing an argumentative scene in dramatic form. Model your main characters after Alceste and Philinte, but give them modern names, use appropriate modern English dialogue (rhyme if you dare!), and choose a modern social setting and a modern social issue to create conflict. Possible characters:

a. Two college students, one of whom is preparing for an affluent career as a corporate lawyer, while the other is studying to become a social worker in order to help needy people

b. Two married women, one advocating the freedom of spouses to indulge in extramarital flings, the other insisting on total fidelity in marriage

c. Two parents, one insisting that a parent has the right to know everything about a minor child, even to the extent of reading the child's mail, the other maintaining that children have a right to privacy

Family Connections

The childhood view of family members as existing only in relation to one's self generally begins to change with the postadolescent maturation into adulthood. The following article by Leo F. Buscaglia addresses this matter of viewing others—specifically parents—as mere extensions of self rather than as human beings with their own separate existences. Buscaglia says that listening to after-dinner conversations of his parents as they recalled their youth made him realize "that things didn't start with me." He emphasizes a sense of continuity in human existence: "No one exists in isolation. Each of us is a part of a greater story—some of it already written, some that we will write and some that we will pass on to others to complete."

Leo F. Buscaglia (born 1924)

Family History Can Provide
a Sense of Survival

Years ago, when I was teaching at the University of Southern California, I asked my students to write a short history of their parents' lives. They stared blankly at me. "A history of our parents!" They were incredulous. "What do you mean?"

"A short history," I explained, "about where they came from. About the role your grandparents played in their lives, what they did, how they met, their special moments of joy or hurt."

It became painfully apparent that they knew nothing about their family history. When challenged, most of the students didn't even know the exact color of their parents' eyes. It hadn't occurred to them that Mom and Dad had ever courted and loved. It was impossible for some of them to accept the fact that their mother had ever received a first kiss or had gone on dates that may or may not have included their father.

This lack of awareness is not confined to my students. Most of us take those we love for granted. We assume that they are there, and will always be there, when we need them. Not so.

I recall the after-dinner talking time in our home when I was a child. I can't tell you how many times we asked Mama to tell us about her years as a young servant girl to the "padrone" or employer. The indignities. The insults. The inhumane treatment. How vivid were her descriptions of the crowded immigrant ship on which she came to America, her long stay on Ellis Island with her sick child, the train trip to Los Angeles.

Papa's stories of his work at the factory in Italy, of his first days in America, times of extreme poverty and genuine joy were of equal interest. We children sat in rapt attention, full of admiration and wonder that our parents had achieved so much. I learned that things didn't start with me. I was part of an ongoing history—full of pride, survival and love.

No one exists in isolation. Each of us is a part of a greater story—some of it already written, some that we will write and some that we will pass on to others to complete.

At a recent fair I found an interesting soft-cover book. As I recall, it was titled something like *Father Was Quite a Man.* A companion book was called *Mother Was Quite a Woman.* These books comprised a simple series of open-ended questions for Mama and Papa to fill in. Describe your parents. What was the name of your first boyfriend? Who took you to your prom? When completed, these books were to be given to their children as part of their legacy. What a splendid idea! What a long-lasting and valuable gift.

Often we are too concerned with tomorrow to recognize the significance of our yesterdays. Yet they represent the thread of explanation that guides us to who we are now.

I can't tell you the joy my students felt when they went home to complete their assignment. For some it was the best evening the family had experienced together in years: "Did you know my Dad first worked on a railroad?" "My mother waited tables when she was in high school." "My mother was my father's buddy's girlfriend. Dad won a wife but lost a friend." "Mama had a miscarriage which still brings her sorrow." "Dad married his first wife when she was only 17."

We all agreed that it would have been a tragedy to have missed these personal experiences of the past. "It scares me," one student said, "when I think that my parents could have died and I wouldn't have known them at all."

Each generation owes the next a knowledge of the past. It's a shared bond from which we gain the knowledge and strength to face our tomorrows.

The sense of being a part of history is dramatically expressed in a different way in the next selection, which is by Alex Haley. In this essay, Haley describes his listening as a child to his female relatives retelling stories about their ancestors. These vivid stories finally led him to the research which culminated in his discovery of his family origins in Africa and his writing of the immensely popular work *Roots*. Haley's description of the profound emotions he felt upon making the "journey" through his family's past has captured the imagination of millions of readers.

As you read this selection, note elements that might be compared with those of some of the previous selections. For example:

1. A child's attitude toward a grandmother
2. The writer's use of specific details in descriptive passages
3. The writer's persona and tone
4. The writer's use of dialogue or direct quotation

Alex Haley (born 1921)
My Furthest-Back Person—"The African"

My Grandma Cynthia Murray Palmer lived in Henning, Tenn. (pop. 500), about 50 miles north of Memphis. Each summer as I grew up there, we would be visited by several women relatives who were mostly around Grandma's age, such as my Great Aunt Liz Murray who taught in Oklahoma, and Great Aunt Till Merriwether from Jackson, Tenn., or their considerably younger niece, Cousin Georgia Anderson from Kansas City, Kan., and some others. Always after the supper dishes had been washed, they would go out to take seats and talk in the rocking chairs on the front porch, and I would scrunch down, listening, behind Grandma's squeaky chair, with the dusk deepening into the night and the lightning bugs flicking on and off above the now shadowy honeysuckles. Most often they talked about our family—the story had been passed down for generations—until the whistling blur of lights of the southbound Panama Limited train *whooshing* through Henning at 9:05 P.M. signaled our bedtime.

So much of their talking of people, places and events I didn't understand: For instance, what was an "Ol' Massa," an "Ol' Missus" or a "plantation"? But early I gathered that white folks had done lots of bad things to our folks, though I couldn't figure out why. I guessed that all they talked about had happened a long time ago, as now or then Grandma or another, speaking of someone in the past, would excitedly thrust a finger toward me, exclaiming, "Wasn't big as *this* young 'un!" And it would astound me that anyone as old and gray-haired as they could relate to my age. But in time my head began both a recording and picturing of the more graphic scenes they would describe, just as I also visualized David killing Goliath with his slingshot, Old Pharaoh's army drowning, Noah and his ark, Jesus feeding that big multitude with nothing but five loaves and two fishes, and other wonders that I heard in my Sunday school lessons at our New Hope Methodist Church.

The furthest-back person Grandma and the others talked of—always in tones of awe, I noticed—they would call "The African." They said that some ship brought him to a place that they pronounced "'Naplis." They said that then some "Mas' John Waller" bought him for his plantation in "Spotsylvania County, Va." This African kept on escaping, the fourth time trying to kill the "hateful po' cracker" slave-catcher, who gave him the punishment choice of castration or of losing one foot. This African took a foot being chopped off with an ax against a tree stump, they said, and he was about to die. But his life was saved by "Mas' John's" brother—"Mas' William Waller," a doctor, who was so furious about what had happened that he bought the African for himself and gave him the name "Toby."

Crippling about, working in "Mas' William's" house and yard, the African in time met and mated with "the big house cook named Bell," and there was born a girl named Kizzy. As she grew up her African daddy often showed her different kinds of things, telling her what they were in his native tongue. Pointing at a banjo, for example, the African uttered, "*ko*"; or pointing at a river near the plantation, he would say, "*Kamby Bolong.*" Many of his strange words started with a "*k*" sound, and the little, growing Kizzy learned gradually that they identified different things.

When addressed by other slaves as "Toby," the master's name for him, the African said angrily that his name was "*Kin-tay.*" And as he gradually learned English, he told young Kizzy some things about himself—for instance, that he was not far from his village, chopping wood to make himself a drum, when four men had surprised, overwhelmed, and kidnaped him.

So Kizzy's head held much about her African daddy when at age 16 she was sold away onto a much smaller plantation in North Carolina. Her new "Mas' Tom Lea" fathered her first child, a boy she named George. And Kizzy told her boy all about his African grandfather. George grew up to be such a gamecock fighter that he was called "Chicken George," and people would come from all over and "bet big money" on his cockfights. He mated with Matilda, another of Lea's slaves; they had seven children, and he told them the stories and strange sounds of their African great-grandfather. And one of those children, Tom, became a blacksmith who was bought away by a "Mas' Murray" for his tobacco plantation in Alamance County, N.C.

Tom mated there with Irene, a weaver on the plantation. She also bore seven children, and Tom now told them all about their African great-great-grandfather, the faithfully passed-down knowledge of his sounds and stories having become by now the family's prideful treasure.

The youngest of that second set of seven children was a girl, Cynthia, who became my maternal Grandma (which today I can only see as fated). Anyway, all of this is how I was growing up in Henning at Grandma's, listening from behind her rocking chair as she and the other visiting old women talked of that African (never then comprehended as *my* great-great-great-great-grandfather) who said his name was *"Kin-tay,"* and said *"ko"* for banjo, *"Kamby Bolong"* for river, and a jumble of other *"k"*-beginning sounds that Grandma privately muttered, most often while making beds or cooking, and who also said that near his village he was kidnaped while chopping wood to make himself a drum.

The story had become nearly as fixed in my head as in Grandma's by the time Dad and Mama moved me and my two younger brothers, George and Julius, away from Henning to be with them at the small black agricultural and mechanical college in Normal, Ala., where Dad taught.

To compress my next 25 years: When I was 17 Dad let me enlist as a mess boy in the U.S. Coast Guard. I became a ship's cook out in the South Pacific during World War II, and at night down by my bunk I began trying to write sea adventure stories, mailing them off to magazines and collecting rejection slips for eight years before some editors began purchasing and publishing occasional stories. By 1949 the Coast Guard had made me its first "journalist"; finally with 20 years' service, I retired at the age of 37, determined to make a full time career of writing. I wrote mostly magazine articles; my first book was "The Autobiography of Malcolm X."

Then one Saturday in 1965 I happened to be walking past the National Archives building in Washington. Across the interim years I had thought of Grandma's old stories—otherwise I can't think what diverted me up the Archives' steps. And when a main reading room desk attendant asked if he could help me, I wouldn't have dreamed of admitting to him some curiosity hanging on from boyhood about my slave forebears. I kind of bumbled that I was interested in census records of Alamance County, North Carolina, just after the Civil War.

The microfilm rolls were delivered, and I turned them through the machine with a building sense of intrigue, viewing in different census takers' penmanship an endless parade of names. After about a dozen microfilmed rolls, I was beginning to tire, when in utter astonishment I looked upon the names of Grandma's parents: Tom Murray, Irene Murray . . . older sisters of Grandma's as well—every one of them a name that I'd heard countless times on her front porch.

It wasn't that I hadn't believed Grandma. You just *didn't* not believe my Grandma. It was simply so uncanny actually seeing those names in print and in official U.S. Government records.

During the next several months I was back in Washington whenever possible, in the Archives, the Library of Congress, the Daughters of the American Revolution Library. (Whenever black attendants understood the idea of my search, documents I requested reached me with miraculous speed.) In one source or another during 1966 I was able to document at least the highlights of the cherished family story. I would have given anything to have told Grandma, but, sadly, in 1949 she had gone. So I went and told the only survivor of those Henning front-porch storytellers: Cousin Georgia Anderson, now in her 80's in Kansas City, Kan. Wrinkled, bent, not well herself, she was so overjoyed, repeating to me the old stories and sounds; they were like Henning echoes: "Yeah, boy, that African say his name was '*Kin-tay*'; he say the banjo was '*ko*,' an' the river '*Kamby-Bolong*,' an' he was off choppin' some wood to make his drum when they grabbed 'im!" Cousin Georgia grew so excited we had to stop her, calm her down, "You go 'head, boy! Your grandma an' all of 'em—they up there watching what you do!"

That week I flew to London on a magazine assignment. Since by now I was steeped in the old, in the past, scarcely a tour guide missed me—I was awed at so many historical places and treasures I'd heard of and read of. I came upon the Rosetta stone in the British Museum, marveling anew at how Jean Champollion, the French archaeologist, had miraculously deciphered its ancient demotic and hieroglyphic texts. . . .

The thrill of that just kept hanging around in my head. I was on a jet returning to New York when a thought hit me. Those strange, unknown-tongue sounds, always part of our family's old story . . . they were obviously bits of our original African "*Kin-tay*'s" native tongue. What specific tongue? Could I somehow find out?

Back in New York, I began making visits to the United Nations Headquarters lobby; it wasn't hard to spot Africans. I'd stop any I could, asking if my bits of phonetic sounds held any meaning for them. A couple of dozen Africans quickly listened, and took off—understandably dubious about some Tennessean's accent alleging "African" sounds.

My research assistant, George Sims (we grew up together in Henning), brought me some names of ranking scholars of African linguistics. One was particularly intriguing: A Belgian- and English-educated Dr. Jan Vansina; he had spent his early career living in West African villages, studying and tape-recording countless oral histories that were narrated by certain very old African men; he had written a standard textbook, "The Oral Tradition."

So I flew to the University of Wisconsin to see Dr. Vansina. In his living room I told him every bit of the family story in the fullest detail that I could remember it. Then, intensely, he queried me about the story's relay across the generations, about the gibberish of "*k*" sounds Grandma had fiercely muttered to herself while doing her housework, with my brothers and me giggling beyond her hearing at what we had dubbed "Grandma's noises."

Dr. Vansina, his manner very serious, finally said, "These sounds your family has kept sound very probably of the tongue called 'Mandinka.'"

I'd never heard of any "Mandinka." Grandma just told of the African saying "*ko*" for banjo, or "*Kamby Bolong*" for a Virginia river.

Among Mandinka stringed instruments, Dr. Vansina said, one of the oldest was the "*kora.*"

"*Bolong*," he said, was clearly Mandinka for "river." Preceded by "*Kamby*," it very likely meant "Gambia River."

Dr. Vansina telephoned an eminent Africanist colleague, Dr. Philip Curtin. He said that the phonetic "*Kin-tay*" was correctly spelled "*Kinte*," a very old clan that had originated in Old Mali. The Kinte men traditionally were blacksmiths, and the women were potters and weavers.

I knew I must get to the Gambia River.

The first native Gambian I could locate in the U.S. was named Ebou Manga, then a junior attending Hamilton College in upstate Clinton, N.Y. He and I flew to Dakar, Senegal, then took a smaller plane to Yundum Airport, and rode in a van to Gambia's capital, Bathurst. Ebou and his father assembled eight Gambia government officials. I told them Grandma's stories, every detail I could remember, as they listened intently, then reacted. "*'Kamby Bolong'* of course is Gambia River!" I heard. "But more clue is your forefather's saying his name was '*Kinte.*'" Then they told me something I would never even have fantasized—that in places in the back country lived very old men, commonly called *griots*, who could tell centuries of the histories of certain very old family clans. As for *Kintes*, they pointed out to me on a map some family villages, Kinte-Kundah, and Kinte-Kundah Janneh-Ya, for instance.

The Gambian officials said they would try to help me. I returned to New York dazed. It is embarrassing to me now, but despite Grandma's stories, I'd never been concerned much with Africa, and I had the routine images of African people living mostly in exotic jungles. But a compulsion now laid hold of me to learn all I could, and I began devouring books about Africa, especially about the slave trade. Then one Thursday's mail contained a letter from one of the Gambian officials, inviting me to return there.

Monday I was back in Bathurst. It galvanized me when the officials said that a *griot* had been located who told the *Kinte* clan history—his name was Kebba Kanga Fofana. To reach him, I discovered, required a modified safari: renting a launch to get upriver, two land vehicles to carry supplies by a roundabout land route, and employing finally 14 people, including three interpreters and four musicians, since a *griot* would not speak the revered clan histories without background music.

The boat Baddibu vibrated upriver, with me acutely tense: Were these Africans maybe viewing me as but another of the pithhelmets? After about two hours, we put in at James Island, for me to see the ruins of the once British-operated James Fort. Here two centuries of slave ships had loaded thousands of cargoes of Gambian tribespeople. The crumbling stones, the deeply oxidized swivel cannon, even some remnant links of chain seemed all but impossible to believe. Then we continued upriver to the left-bank village of Albreda, and there put ashore to continue on foot to Juffure, village of the *griot*. Once more we stopped, for me to see *toubob kolong*, "the white man's well," now almost filled in, in a swampy area with abundant, tall, saw-toothed grass. It was dug two centuries ago to "17 men's height deep" to insure survival drinking water for long-driven, famishing coffles of slaves.

Walking on, I kept wishing that Grandma could hear how her stories had led me to the "*Kamby Bolong.*" (Our surviving storyteller Cousin Georgia died in a Kansas City hospital during this same morning, I would learn later.) Finally, Juffure village's playing children, sighting us, flashed an alert. The 70-odd people came rushing from their circular, thatch-roofed, mud-walled huts, with goats bounding up and about, and parrots squawking from up in the palms. I sensed him in advance somehow, the small man amid them, wearing a pillbox cap and an off-white robe—the *griot*. Then the interpreters went to him, as the villagers thronged around me.

And it hit me like a gale wind: every one of them, the whole crowd, was *jet black*. An enormous sense of guilt swept me—a sense of being some kind of hybrid . . . a sense of being impure among the pure. It was an awful sensation.

The old *griot* stepped away from my interpreters and the crowd quickly swarmed around him—all of them buzzing. An interpreter named A. B. C. Salla came to me; he whispered: "Why they stare at you so, they have never seen here a black American." And that hit me: I was symbolizing for them twenty-five millions of us they had never seen. What did they think of me—of us?

Then abruptly the old *griot* was briskly walking toward me. His eyes boring into mine, he spoke in Mandinka, as if instinctively I should understand—and A. B. C. Salla translated:

"Yes . . . we have been told by the forefathers . . . that many of us from this place are in exile . . . in that place called America . . . and in other places."

I suppose I physically wavered, and they thought it was the heat; rustling whispers went through the crowd, and a man brought me a low stool. Now the whispering hushed—the musicians had softly begun playing *kora* and *balafon*, and a canvas sling lawn seat was taken by the *griot*, Kebba Kanga Fofana, aged 73 "rains" (one rainy season each year). He seemed to gather himself into a physical rigidity, and he began speaking the *Kinte* clan's ancestral oral history; it came rolling from his mouth across the next hours . . . 17th- and 18th-century *Kinte* lineage details, predominantly what men took wives; the children they "begot," in the order of their births; those children's mates and children.

Events frequently were dated by some proximate singular physical occurrence. It was as if some ancient scroll were printed indelibly within the *griot's* brain. Each few sentences or so, he would pause for an interpreter's translation to me. I distill here the essence:

The *Kinte* clan began in Old Mali, the men generally blacksmiths ". . . who conquered fire," and the women potters and weavers. One large branch of the clan moved to Mauretania from where one son of the clan, Kairaba Kunta Kinte, a Moslem Marabout holy man, entered Gambia. He lived first in the village of Pakali N'Ding; he moved next to Jiffarong village; ". . . and then he came here, into our own village of Juffure."

In Juffure, Kairaba Kunta Kinte took his first wife, ". . . a Mandinka maiden, whose name was Sireng. By her, he begot two sons, whose names were Janneh and Saloum. Then he got a second wife, Yaisa. By her, he begot a son, Omoro."

The three sons became men in Juffure. Janneh and Saloum went off and found a new village, Kinte-Kundah Janneh-Ya. "And then Omoro, the younger son, when he had 30 rains, took as a wife a maiden, Binta Kebba.

"And by her, he begot four sons—Kunta, Lamin, Suwadu, and Madi . . ."

Sometimes, a "begotten," after his naming, would be accompanied by some later-occurring detail, perhaps as ". . . in time of big water buffalo." Having named those four sons, now the *griot* stated such a detail.

"About the time the king's soldiers came, the eldest of these four sons, Kunta, when he had about 16 rains, went away from this village, to chop wood to make a drum . . . and he was never seen again . . ."

Goose-pimples the size of lemons seemed to pop all over me. In my knapsack were my cumulative notebooks, the first of them including how in my boyhood, my Grandma, Cousin Georgia and the others told of the African "*Kin-tay*" who always said he was kidnaped near his village—while chopping wood to make a drum . . .

I showed the interpreter, he showed and told the *griot*, who excitedly told the people; they grew very agitated. Abruptly then they formed a human ring, encircling me, dancing and chanting. Perhaps a dozen of the women carrying their infant babies rushed in toward me, thrusting the infants into my arms—conveying, I would later learn, "the laying on of hands . . . through this flesh which is us, we are you, and you are us." Then men hurried me into their mosque, their Arabic praying later being translated outside: "Thanks be to Allah for returning the long lost from among us." Direct descendants of Kunta Kinte's blood brothers were hastened, some of them from nearby villages, for a family portrait to be taken with me, surrounded by actual ancestral sixth cousins. More symbolic acts filled the remaining day.

When they would let me leave, for some reason I wanted to go away over the African land. Dazed, silent in the bumping Land Rover, I heard the cutting staccato of talking drums. Then when we sighted the next village, its people came thronging to meet us. They were all—little naked ones to wizened elders—waving, beaming, amid a cacophony of crying out; and then my ears identified their words: "*Meester Kinte! Meester Kinte!*"

Let me tell you something: I am a man. But I remember the sob surging up from my feet, flinging up my hands before my face and bawling as I had not done since I was a baby . . . the jet-black Africans were jostling, staring. . . . I didn't care, with the feelings surging. If you really knew the odyssey of us millions of black Americans, if you really knew how we came in the seeds of our forefathers, captured, driven, beaten, inspected, bought, branded, chained in foul ships, if you really knew, you needed weeping. . . .

Back home, I knew that what I must write, really, was our black saga, where any individual's past is the essence of the millions'. Now flat broke, I went to some editors I knew, describing the Gambian miracle, and my desire to pursue the research; Doubleday contracted to publish, and Reader's Digest to condense the projected book; then I had advances to travel further.

What ship brought Kinte to Grandma's "'Naplis" (Annapolis, Md., obviously)? The old *griot*'s time reference to "king's soldiers" sent me flying to London. Feverish searching at last identified, in British Parliament records, "Colonel O'Hare's Forces," dispatched in mid-1767 to protect the then British-held James Fort whose ruins I'd visited. So Kunta Kinte was down in some ship probably sailing later that summer from the Gambia River to Annapolis.

Now I feel it was fated that I had taught myself to write in the U.S. Coast Guard. For the sea dramas I had concentrated on had given me years of experience searching among yellowing old U.S. maritime records. So now in English 18th-century marine records I finally tracked ships reporting themselves in and out of the Commandant of the Gambia River's James Fort. And then early one afternoon I found that a Lord Ligonier under a Captain Thomas Davies had sailed on the Sabbath of July 5, 1767. Her cargo: 3,265 elephants' teeth, 3,700 pounds of beeswax, 800 pounds of cotton, 32 ounces of Gambian gold, and 140 slaves; her destination: "Annapolis."

That night I recrossed the Atlantic. In the Library of Congress the Lord Ligonier's arrival was one brief line in "Shipping In The Port Of Annapolis—1748–1775." I located the author, Vaughan W. Brown, in his Baltimore brokerage office. He drove to Historic Annapolis, the city's historical society, and found me further documentation of her arrival on Sept. 29, 1767. (Exactly two centuries later, Sept. 29, 1967, standing, staring seaward from an Annapolis pier, again I knew tears.) More help came in the Maryland Hall of Records. Archivist Phebe Jacobsen found the Lord Ligonier's arriving customs declaration listing, "98 Negroes"—so in her 86-day crossing, 42 Gambians had died, one among the survivors being 16-year-old Kunta Kinte. Then the microfilmed Oct. 1, 1767, Maryland Gazette contained, on page two, an announcement to prospective buyers from the ship's agents, Daniel of St. Thos. Jenifer and John Ridout (the Governor's secretary): "from the River GAMBIA, in AFRICA . . . a cargo of choice, healthy SLAVES . . ."

□ EXPANDING YOUR WRITING SKILLS □
Writing a Biographical Sketch Based on Interviewing

Alex Haley used his journalistic skills to research and record his family history. This exercise will require you to use your composition skills to do something similar. "Oral history" has become in recent years a popular way to document the past. It consists of interviewing persons who have firsthand knowledge of earlier eras, recording their comments on audio tapes, and then transcribing these spoken memories onto paper.

For this assignment you will need to identify an older person to interview. If possible, select one of your parents, a grandparent, or other relative, and perhaps you will find a satisfaction similar to that described by Buscaglia and Haley in exploring family history. You may either record the interview on tape or simply take notes. Unlike the usual oral history, which is simply transcription of the subject's statements, your finished writing should be a carefully organized narrative or biographical sketch based upon the factual information you gather through one or more interviews.

You may focus on a single incident or a series of related events in the person's life and write a narrative account, or you may write a more general biography of the person. In either case, do *not* try to include everything the person tells you. Your challenge will be to collect ample information; sort and select the best, most relevant items; and then organize the material effectively.

If you write a biographical sketch, you will have to work even harder to make sure that your composition has unity, that it is not simply random facts strung together. Organize the paper around some personal characteristic or central theme. You might, for example, write about your grandmother as "a woman of determination" or about your father as "a man who always sees the silver lining." You would then include only the details from their lives which support the view you have chosen to present.

This assignment will require a good deal of preparation before you actually begin writing. One crucial step will be the formulation of the right questions to ask. "Open-ended questions," those that cannot be answered with a yes or no, serve best. You invite detailed responses when you begin your interview with phrases such as, "Could you describe for me . . ." or "Tell me about the time you. . . ." The more significant information you collect in your interviewing, the richer your finished paper will be, even though you will be able to include only a fraction of all you learn.

Use dialogue—or at least direct quotation of your subject—judiciously but frequently in your paper. The actual words of the person should be used often enough to set the tone, especially for dramatic or humorous incidents in the biographical account, much in the way you use direct quotation from a short story when you write a plot summary. Your own voice or persona should, however, infuse the paper as a whole.

Plan to write a final version of about 500 words. A good test of your success with this biographical writing will be to see if it captures and holds the interest of a reader who is unacquainted with the person you interviewed.

Summary and Review

As you conclude this chapter, you may wish to chart your progress in the three areas of emphasis in this book. In terms of *composition*, you have studied figurative language and its effects in your writing. You have considered the voice and tone of yourself as writer. You have produced increasingly complex writings. In terms of *literature*, you have studied a poetic drama in translation. Here is a list of some important points from the chapter to keep in mind:

☐ You can add force and life to your writing with the appropriate use of figurative language, connotation, and dialogue or direct quotation.

☐ Figurative language includes the simile (a comparison of unlike things using the word *like* or *as*) and the metaphor (an implied comparison).

☐ Connotative diction can appeal to the reader's emotions through words chosen for their positive or negative nuances of meaning.

☐ Dialogue or direct quotation of conversation adds dramatic vigor to your writing.

☐ The purpose, the intended audience, and the form all combine to determine the correct voice or persona for a writing. The attitude projected by that voice creates tone.

☐ Drama is a unique form of writing with its own history, conventions, and terminology.

☐ Drama shares many of the same elements with a short story or novel: plot, character, point of view, setting, and theme.

☐ Any type of writing may use various methods of persuasion.

With respect to the third emphasis of this book, *human experience*, some of you have recognized your current life stage in this chapter. Others who have lived longer will identify with the selections and writing exercises in the next chapter, which emphasizes the later years of adulthood.

5

Coming to Terms
with Life

Something "to look backward to with pride,"
something "to look forward to with hope"*

□ Lyric Poetry   □ Analysis   □ Paraphrase   □ Repetition   □ Assonance
□ Consonance   □ Alliteration   □ Rhyme   □ Argument in Poetry   □ An
Argumentation Checklist

How much of your lifetime lies behind you, and how much lies ahead? Do you see any gray hairs or wrinkles yet when you look in the mirror? Have you reached that stage in your career when the next obvious step is not promotion, but retirement? Have you experienced the conflicting sensations of pleasure at having a precious toddler call you granddad or grandma and amazement and disbelief that you are old enough to be a grandparent? If this advanced stage of life still seems far in your own future, have you seen signs of aging in family members and acquaintances? The focus of this chapter is the period of later adulthood when one day the question occurs, "Am I growing old?" As reader, you will be looking more closely at poetry and at some of

*Robert Frost, "The Death of the Hired Man" (in the Additional Readings for Chapter 5).

its persuasive elements. As writer, you will be considering and practicing some of the techniques of poetry that writers of both poetry and prose can use to advantage.

"The Tears of Things"

"No young man believes he shall ever die," wrote William Hazlitt. In his essay "On the Feeling of Immortality in Youth," he maintains that only gradually, through "time and experience," does one come to acknowledge personal mortality—a realization and admission of what the Roman poet Vergil called "the tears of things."

In the following poem, the writer is dealing with literal tears. Are they also Vergil's "tears of things"?

Gerard Manley Hopkins (1844–1889)

Spring and Fall: To a Young Child

> Márgarét, áre you gríeving
> Over Goldengrove unleaving?
> Leáves, líke the things of man, you
> With your fresh thoughts care for, can you?
> Áh! ás the heart grows older   5
> It will come to such sights colder
> By and by, nor spare a sigh
> Though worlds of wanwood leafmeal lie;
> And yet you *will* weep and know why.
> Now no matter, child, the name: 10
> Sórrow's spríngs áre the same.
> Nor mouth had, no nor mind, expressed
> What heart heard of, ghost guessed:
> It ís the blight man was born for,
> It ís Margaret you mourn for.   15

Lyric Poetry

"Spring and Fall" is a brief poem of the same type as those encountered in earlier chapters. The term for such poems expressing the writers' thoughts and feelings is *lyric* (literally "songlike"). In a *lyric poem*, the writer's purpose is not to tell a story but to record an impression, to express a personal emotion or idea.

In "Spring and Fall," the organization is basically question-and-answer. Hopkins poses the question, elaborates on it, then answers it. What may not seem immediately obvious to a reader is exactly what question he poses and what answer he gives. "If the poet wants me to understand and appreciate what he says as well as how he says it," a perplexed reader may react, "why does he include unexplained, unfamiliar terms like 'Goldengrove' and 'wanwood leafmeal'; why does he use difficult word order, as in lines 3 and 4; what's the purpose and meaning of the accent marks; and how can anyone make sense of a sentence like lines 12 and 13? Furthermore, if writers are supposed to have their audience in mind and write accordingly, whom could Hopkins have been writing for—readers with paranormal powers of perception?"

These legitimate questions about the difficulty of "Spring and Fall" prompt a closer look at the poem for possible answers. But because such questions are apt to arise about *any* difficult reading, perhaps especially poetry, part of the answer may also lie in an observation or two about poetry and difficult writings in general.

Poetry is, first of all, an unfamiliar form of writing to most readers today; twentieth-century readers are primarily readers of prose. And anything unfamiliar is likely to be difficult at first. Poetry is usually a tighter, more condensed form of writing than prose; it requires close, careful reading that many readers are not accustomed to giving and sometimes not willing to give. Furthermore, poems are rather like verbal paintings, with words and sounds and rhythms serving as brush strokes. Sometimes these "paintings" are simple; sometimes they are complex. "Spring and Fall" is more complex than some other poems because this particular poet-artist liked to experiment with language by creating his own rhythm patterns (hence his own accent marks) and by creating new words.

When you encounter such a difficult piece of writing, poetry or prose, specific questions about the content usually lead to a more general question: "Is this piece important enough, or is it sufficiently attractive enough for me to devote the time and effort required to understand it better?" Sometimes the decision has been made for you. If your college instructor or your supervisor at work has assigned some reading and will hold you accountable for it, you will usually give it close and careful attention. Sometimes, though, the choice is yours, and you make the decision according to your own tastes and your own sense of attraction, appreciation, or interest based on what you do comprehend.

In your reading of Hopkins's "Spring and Fall" you probably did not grasp everything, but you did understand the gist of his message about the child's sorrow. Let us assume that you are rather attracted to the message and the sound, and you decide that the poem is worth a closer look. The following exercise provides that opportunity.

□ WRITING ↔ READING ↔ THINKING ACTIVITIES □
Analyzing and Paraphrasing "Spring and Fall"

One way of looking more closely is to *analyze* the writing by first breaking it down into parts. Another is to *paraphrase* the writing, to try to restate its message in your own words. The following exercise combines these two approaches. Taking each sentence of "Spring and Fall," a "perplexed reader" reflects on it, then conveys its meaning in his own words. His observations are an informal recording of his thinking as he considers each sentence. When you are asked to continue these observations, try to record your thinking and analysis in the same informal, personal way. Think aloud on paper.

> Márgarét, áre you gríeving
> Over Goldengrove unleaving?

OBSERVATIONS (*process* of *analysis*): Not too tough, if I can figure out what "Goldengrove unleaving" means. I know from the poem's subtitle that Margaret is "a young child," and this question addressed to her obviously serves as introduction. I'm guessing the poet will later answer the question himself. I can think of two possible meanings for the strange word "unleaving." It could mean "not going anywhere, not leaving," or it could mean "losing its leaves." If "Goldengrove" is the name of a person or animal, it probably means "not leaving," and the thought would be something like "Are you sad because Goldengrove won't go away?" But if "Goldengrove" is the name of a place, perhaps a "grove" of trees, then "unleaving" probably means "losing its leaves." (And maybe it's called "*Golden*grove" because the leaves are dead and yellow.) If I look around in the poem for help in deciding which is the right reading, I see "Leaves" as the first word in the next sentence; since it's used as a noun, not as a verb, I think my "tree leaves" reading is probably right. I think so more strongly because of the "fall" season referred to in the title (I'm not sure about the "spring" part), and also because of the strange phrase "wanwood leafmeal." Whatever else it may mean, I see "wood" and "leaf," so I've worked my way to a fairly confident paraphrase of the poem's opening question:

PARAPHRASE (*product* of *analysis*): "Margaret, are you sad because the leaves are falling in Goldengrove?"

Leáves, líke the things of man, you
With your fresh thoughts care for, can you?

OBSERVATIONS: Not as bad as it first looks, once I realized that this sentence with its scrambled word order is like the "Jumble" puzzle in the newspaper where the challenge is to discover the proper placement of letters, thereby finding the hidden word. It's as though Hopkins wrote the sentence on paper, cut the paper into strips containing phrases, mixed them up, then separated them with commas. If I solve the puzzle by restoring normal English word order, I get "Can you, with your fresh thoughts, care for leaves, like the things of man?" If "fresh" means something like "youthful, unsullied, not weary or worn or jaded," and "the things of man" means "something of more significance or importance than a dead and falling leaf, something man would be expected to value," then I'm probably ready to venture a paraphrase of sentence 2:

PARAPHRASE: "Can you, with your youthful sensitivity of thought and feeling, concern yourself even with dying leaves, as you would with things of greater significance?"

Áh! ás the heart grows older
It will come to such sights colder
By and by, nor spare a sigh
Though worlds of wanwood leafmeal lie;
And yet you *will* weep and know why.

OBSERVATIONS: [*Try your hand at analysis, making the "Observations" simply an account of your thinking as you look closely at the sentence.*]

PARAPHRASE: [*When you have completed your analysis, paraphrase the poet's sentence in a sentence of your own.*]

Now no matter, child, the name:
Sórrow's spríngs áre the same.

OBSERVATIONS and PARAPHRASE: [*Work through this sentence also. Since this is his next-to-last sentence, Hopkins is probably building toward a climactic comment with this thought. Try to capture its meaning clearly in your paraphrase.*]

Nor mouth had, no nor mind, expressed
What heart heard of, ghost guessed:
It ís the blight man was born for,
It ís Margaret you mourn for.

With this last sentence, the "perplexed reader" will work through the Observations; you write the Paraphrase.

OBSERVATIONS: The first part of this sentence seems to me the most difficult section of the poem to understand. For one thing, he's chopping it up with commas, as he did the earlier "Leaves, like the things of man" section. For another, the nouns "mouth," "mind," "heart," and (especially!) "ghost" pose a difficulty. What do they mean, what do they refer to, what do they stand for or symbolize—if they symbolize anything? Another problem is figuring out what the pronoun "It" refers to in the next-to-last line. Since the last two lines of the poem seem to be his all-encompassing conclusion, if I miss "it" I probably go down a wrong road altogether. So much for the obstacles; how many of them can I work my way through?

In the first two lines of the sentence, I think the "Nor . . . nor" construction is really saying "Neither . . . nor"; I've seen other poets—and prose writers—use "nor . . . nor" in this way. And if "mouth" and "mind" are both subjects of the two-part verb "had . . . expressed," then he's saying in the first line "Neither mouth, no, nor mind had expressed." Had expressed *what*? Hopkins seems to be helping me out some in the next line by answering my question with "what heart heard of, [what] ghost guessed." I think he's omitted the second "what" in his two-part direct object. If I'm right about the syntax (that is, the grammatical function and relationship of the words) of the sentence so far, a streamlined version would go like this: "Neither mouth nor mind had expressed what heart had heard of and ghost had guessed." Hopkins may simply intend all these nouns as general references, since he doesn't directly say that he's talking about Margaret's "mouth," "mind," "heart," and "ghost." But *in*directly he does seem to mean Margaret specifically, since earlier he had referred to her "fresh thoughts" (mind?) and her heart, and he both begins and ends the poem referring to her by name. So I'll venture that it's "Neither [Margaret's] mouth nor [Margaret's] mind had expressed what [Margaret's] heart and [Margaret's] ghost had guessed." But what is Margaret's "ghost?" There's no way to be absolutely sure, and there are certainly other possibilities, but my guess is that Hopkins, a nineteenth-century Jesuit priest, is using "ghost" as it was used in earlier versions of the Bible—to mean what is translated in later versions as "spirit." "Spirit" would probably have been clearer even in 1880, when the poem was written. But I'm guessing that as a poet listening to the sounds of his writing he values the repeated "g" sound in "ghost guessed." [*Opting for the effect of sound over clarity of thought or immediacy of reader understanding is a decision all of us as sound-conscious and sense-conscious writers must sometimes make: "Do I please the ear or the mind, or can I somehow combine the* *aesthetic effect and the functional effect in the words I choose?"*] At any rate, if I take a further step and guess that "mouth" and "mind" refer to or stand for conscious thought or realization, and "heart" and "ghost" (spirit) stand for unconscious feelings or sensings, I have worked my way to these two lines saying something like "Margaret had not consciously realized or verbalized what she nevertheless unconsciously felt or sensed as true," or "Margaret's heart and spirit understood what her mind did not yet understand and what she had not yet spoken."

Which is *what?* What is it that she feels but doesn't know? Since Hopkins follows "guessed" with a colon, and a colon directs attention to what follows, I think in his last two lines he is explaining what she knows unconsciously but not consciously. But he sets me an obstacle here, too, when he uses the indefinite pronoun "It"; what does "It" refer to when he says "It is the blight man was born for"? This is another instance in the poem where multiple meanings may be possible, but I think at the close he's reverting to his beginning situation: Margaret mourning the unleaving of Goldengrove. If I'm right, then the dying and falling and rotting of the multitudinous leaves is "the blight man was born for"; that is, it's not only leaves that suffer "blight," that wither and die and fall and decay, but mankind too. And (I think I'm closing in on the meaning of the last line) since Margaret shares that mortal destiny with all humankind, she may think she is mourning falling leaves, but on a deeper, symbolic level of which she is not consciously aware, her heart and spirit see and mourn the fate of Margaret herself—and of us all. Probably more than anywhere else in the poem, there are complexities and possibilities of interpretation here that defy simple explanation or singleness of meaning. But if my thinking—and guesswork—is a logical way of reading this last sentence, then I should be at the point of paraphrasing it with some degree of clarity and confidence.

PARAPHRASE: [*Your turn! Remember, "with . . . clarity and confidence."*]

As a test of how worthwhile this exercise in close reading has been, review the paraphrases of the five sentences, then read aloud "Spring and Fall" once more. Do you see more in the poem now than before?

The Benefits of Close Reading

Perhaps a few additional observations about this analysis-paraphrase process, this close reading of a difficult selection, are in order.

First, obviously it would not work with a long poem like Milton's *Paradise Lost* or with the entirety of Mark Twain's *Life on the Mississippi*. That is, it would not work if you went through such texts sentence by sentence.

But it does work for occasional lines, sentences, or passages, whether the reading is prose or poetry, short or long. And usually it is not every line or sentence that proves difficult—just occasional ones.

Second, each writer-reader approaches close reading in terms of "available light"—you do your best in light of what you know at the time. The initial process and product will reflect your "literacy level" of the moment. As you read more, you learn more about form, style, techniques, and content. With poetry (or any type of literature), it is as Robert Frost said: "We may begin anywhere. We *duff* into our first. We read that imperfectly . . . but the better to read the second. We read the second the better to read the third, the third the better to read the fourth, the fourth the better to read the fifth, the fifth the better to read the first again, or the second if it so happens."*

Third, even allowing for the doctrine of "available light," if you are a commonsensical sort you may question the functional, pragmatic value of putting a poem or any work of imaginative literature under a mental microscope. A monthly budget printout, yes; a critical business report or memo or letter, yes; but a *poem*? On the aesthetic level, no defense of poetry is really needed. It is an art form that attracts through sounds, through emotion, through thought, through artistic creativity with language. Those who are thus attracted delight in such close study and enjoy it as an artistic end in itself. But others, not yet believers in the powers of poetry, may need reassurance in more practical terms. Such close reading of a poem—or of any writing—develops analytical and critical thinking skills, sensitivity to the nuances and possibilities of language, and confidence in the ability to comprehend words and translate their meaning. Usually those who can read poetry with understanding can handle any other form of writing.

□ WRITING ↔ READING ↔ THINKING ACTIVITIES □
Thinking about Hopkins's Symbols and Style

To most observers, a young girl's grieving over falling leaves would be a touching scene. But Hopkins looks more closely, considers more deeply. He sees not only the literal or actual scene, but also perceives its symbolic significance.

1. What are the symbols in this poem? What is the significance of each?
2. What is the significance of the poem's title "Spring and Fall"?
3. If "Spring and Fall" is a typical Hopkins poem, what features would you expect to see in his other poems?

*Robert Frost, "Poetry and School," *The Atlantic* June 1951: 30.

Looking Backward

When the question "Am I growing old?" presents itself, and when the response after glancing in the mirror is "Apparently so," there will probably follow occasional moments or periods of personal inventory. These meditations on the pluses and minuses of one's life will surely include a wistful looking back on "the days that are no more." Sometimes, too, will occur "the tears of things."

Alfred, Lord Tennyson (1809–1892)
Tears, Idle Tears

Tears, idle tears, I know not what they mean;
Tears from the depth of some divine despair
Rise in the heart, and gather to the eyes,
In looking on the happy autumn fields,
And thinking of the days that are no more.   5

Fresh as the first beam glittering on a sail,
That brings our friends up from the underworld,
Sad as the last which reddens over one
That sinks with all we love below the verge;
So sad, so fresh, the days that are no more.   10

Ah, sad and strange as in dark summer dawns
The earliest pipe of half-awakened birds
To dying ears, when unto dying eyes
The casement slowly grows a glimmering square;
So sad, so strange, the days that are no more.   15

Dear as remembered kisses after death,
And sweet as those by hopeless fancy feigned
On lips that are for others; deep as love,
Deep as first love, and wild with all regret;
O Death in Life, the days that are no more!   20

When read thoughtfully, read aloud slowly, this poem creates a strong emotional effect. While under that effect, you would probably agree with the poet Archibald MacLeish that "a poem should not mean, but be," that to interpret or analyze would be to diminish the immediate impact. And so it would. Poetry is often the consummate expression of emotions you recognize and relate to as your own feelings, and the appropriate response lies "in the heart," not in the head.

Repetition

At some point, as the emotional effect subsides, your head—that of a writer interested in *how* effective writing is accomplished, *how* thoughts and feelings are conveyed—will want to know how Tennyson makes you respond so strongly. To satisfy that curiosity, you could analyze and paraphrase, as with "Spring and Fall." If you did analyze "Tears, Idle Tears," you would discover that this writer achieves much of the emotional impact in his poem through the use of repetition.

Repetition is one of the simplest, one of the most common, but one of the most effective devices a writer or speaker can employ. Skillfully used, it can serve in speaking and writing to highlight, to connect, to emphasize. Poorly used, it either grates on your sensitivity or puts you to sleep. This old school bus chant is an example of the latter effect:

> Ninety-nine bottles of beer on the wall,
> Ninety-nine bottles of beer,
> Take one down
> Pass it around,
> Ninety-eight bottles of beer on the wall.
> Ninety-eight bottles of beer on the wall,
> Ninety-eight bottles of beer,
> Take one down. . . .

And so the song goes until you have repetitiously chanted your way to "No more bottles of beer on the wall," or reached home, or have become too hoarse to continue.

Tennyson's repetitions are a bit more subtle and artistic. In his first two lines he repeats "Tears . . . tears . . . / Tears"; in the last line of each stanza he repeats the phrase "the days that are no more." In the second stanza, there are the echoic effects of "Fresh as . . . so fresh" and "Sad as . . . so sad"; in stanza three, there is the slight variation "sad and strange as . . . so sad, so strange"; and in the final stanza, there are the linked "as" phrases, "Dear as . . . sweet as . . . deep as love, / Deep as first love." The repeated words and phrases contribute strongly to the poem's melancholy, mournful tone:

Tears, tears, tears
The days that are no more
Fresh, fresh
Sad, sad
The days that are no more
Sad, sad
Strange, strange
The days that are no more
Deep, deep
The days that are no more.

With the exception of "fresh" and perhaps "deep," the emotional emphasis is on the dark side.

Tennyson repeats words, phrases, almost complete lines. (A line repeated again and again in a poem is called a *refrain.*) Repetition can also be of a pattern, as in these two earlier writings:

A time to be born, and a time to die;
. . . .
A time to kill, and a time to heal;

PATTERN: "a time to . . . and a time to . . . ;"

Never was there such a town, I thought, for the smell of fish and chips on Saturday evenings; for the Saturday afternoon cinema matinees where we shouted and hissed our threepence away; for the crowds in the streets with leeks in their hats on international nights; for the park. . . .

PATTERN: "for the . . . ; for the . . . ; for the. . . ." Such repetition of a pattern is called *parallelism.*

Here are a few additional examples of repetition from earlier chapters:

Sans eyes, sans teeth, sans taste, sans everything.

They pull you out, children. They make you get up and go with them. They make you see the world anew as they are seeing it. They also pull you in, children. They make you lie down and snuggle with them. They make you feel life new and wondrous as they are feeling it.

During your college career, you will take classroom notes and write essay exams, write journals, write critical reviews, write outlines, write lab reports, write case studies, write paraphrases, write summaries, write short essays, write long essays, write research papers; in short, you will *write* in college.

Sometimes, as in Shakespeare's "sans . . . sans . . . sans . . . sans" line, the purpose of repetition is to heighten the audience's emotional response: humankind in the last stage of life is simply without ("sans") anything. At other times, as in the last example above, the purpose is to impress the point strongly upon the reader by repeating "write" twelve times. If the sentence had been written "will write essay exams, journals, critical reviews," and so on, the emphasis on writing would not have been so strong.

☐ WRITING ↔ READING ↔ THINKING ACTIVITIES ☐
Identifying and Evaluating Repetition

Look over earlier writing selections that you particularly enjoyed, prose or poetry, and identify five examples of repetition. Include at least one example each of a repeated word, a repeated phrase, and a repeated pattern. In each case, (1) copy out the example; (2) identify the repetition; and (3) comment on the purpose and effect (good or bad) of the repetition.

☐ EXPANDING YOUR WRITING SKILLS ☐
Using Tone to Create Emotional Effect

Much of the writing in your journal and in response to textbook suggestions has in fact already been based on your recollections of "the days that are no more." Taking your cue this time from Tennyson's poem, identify a "days that are no more" topic from your past life which "Tears, Idle Tears" brings to mind. Write an essay of 500–750 words on the topic. In jotting down ideas, in determining how to introduce, develop, and conclude, in drafting and revising, strive for the creation of a strong emotional effect and a distinct tone. The effect and tone can be dark or light, serious or humorous, tragic or comic. Here are a few words or phrases from the poem which might jog your memory and suggest topics:

"tears"   "remembered kisses"
"despair"   "death"
"happy autumn fields"   "sweet"
"days that are no more"   "hopeless fancy"
"no more"   "lips that are for others"
"friends"   "love"
"sad . . . days"   "deep . . . love"
"fresh . . . days"   "first love"
"The . . . pipe of . . . birds"   "wild"
"dying"   "regret"
"dying ears, . . . dying eyes"   "Death in Life"

As you revise the essay, note your uses of repetition, their purpose, and their effect. Can you revise so as to use repetition more effectively?

"Miles to Go Before I Sleep"

In addition to repetitions of words, phrases, and patterns, writers often employ repetitions of sounds. These sound-repetitions are used in both prose and poetry, but they are associated more closely with poetry. They are, in fact, among the characteristics most readers identify specifically as "poetic": assonance, consonance, alliteration, and rhyme. For purposes of illustration, here is a well-known lyric by Robert Frost.

Robert Frost (1874–1963)

Stopping by Woods on a Snowy Evening

Whose woods these are I think I know.
His house is in the village though;
He will not see me stopping here
To watch his woods fill up with snow.

My little horse must think it queer   5
To stop without a farmhouse near
Between the woods and frozen lake
The darkest evening of the year.

He gives his harness bells a shake
To ask if there is some mistake.   10
The only other sound's the sweep
Of easy wind and downy flake.

The woods are lovely, dark and deep,
But I have promises to keep,
And miles to go before I sleep,   15
And miles to go before I sleep.

Assonance, Consonance, and Alliteration

The last line of this poem is an excellent example of emphasis through repetition of an entire line. (What is Frost's purpose in repeating the line?) Overall, however, the poet leans more heavily on repetition of sounds than repetition of words or phrases.

In order to distinguish the types of sound repetition, recall first of all the distinction between English *vowel* sounds and *consonant* sounds. English vowel sounds are those usually represented by the letters *a, e, i, o,* and *u*. All other sounds in English are consonant sounds: the sounds represented by the letters *b, c, d, f, g, h,* and so on.

Remember also that the irregularities of English spelling are such that sound repetition may not be evident to the eye. *Listen* to detect sound repetitions; don't look for identical spellings. For example, the letter *a* represents different vowel sounds in "may" and "and"; so does the letter *o* in "go," "hot," and "women." And the long *a* vowel sound *ay* is represented differently in "play," "prey," and "sleigh." Sometimes, although less frequently, the same consonant sound will also have variant spellings. So here's an em*ph*atic warning: it's not enou*gh* just to look; listen as well, or you may be *f*ooled.

One type of sound repetition found in Frost's poem is *assonance*, the repetition of a vowel sound or sounds in the same word or in words close to one another. For instance, what assonance do you hear in the second line of the poem:

His house is in the village though;

Or the fourth line:

To watch his woods fill up with snow.

The prominent assonance in these lines is relatively easy to detect, since the repetition in both instances is of the same vowel sound and is represented in spelling each time by the letter *i*.

These same two lines also illustrate *consonance*, the repetition of consonant sounds in the same word or in words close to one another. In each line, most instances of consonance are with the initial sounds of words: "*H*is *h*ouse," "*th*e . . . *th*ough," "*w*atch . . . *w*oods . . . *w*ith."

This repetition at the beginning of words also illustrates *alliteration*. Alliteration is simply the repetition of initial sounds in words, usually—but not always—consonant sounds. Frost's second line, in fact, illustrates alliteration of both consonants (consonance) and vowels (assonance):

*H*is *h*ouse *i*s *i*n *th*e village *th*ough.

□ WRITING ↔ READING ↔ THINKING ACTIVITIES □
Identifying Assonance, Consonance, and Alliteration

Check your understanding and perception of assonance, consonance, and alliteration with these exercises.

1. Read aloud a paragraph from one of your most recent writings. Identify all examples of assonance you hear; then identify consonance; then alliteration.

2. Compose four sentences orally with a classmate. Listen closely to the sounds as you form the sentences.
   a. In the first, attempt to incorporate assonance. (Suggestion: use the same drafting-revising process you use in writing. First, just create a sentence quickly, thinking about including words with vowel sound similarities. Then revise the sentence one or more times to reflect assonance more heavily.)
   b. In the next, incorporate consonance, using the same suggested process.
   c. In the next, incorporate alliteration.
   d. Finally, for the big sound-repetition crescendo, compose a sentence in which all three repetitions are present.

3. How many instances of assonance, consonance, and alliteration do you hear in the following titles, lines, or passages:

   □ "Growing Old"
   □ "There was another world where with my friends I used to dawdle on half holidays along the bent and Devon-facing seashore, hoping for gold watches or the skull of a sheep or a message in a bottle to be washed up with the tide; and another where we used to wander whistling through the packed streets, stale as station sandwiches, round the impressive gasworks and the slaughter house, past by the blackened monuments and the museum that should have been in a museum."
   □ "Nor mouth had, no nor mind, expressed
      What heart heard of, ghost guessed."
   □ "Blood thudded in my ears. I scuffed,
         Steps stubborn, to the telltale booth
      Beyond whose curtained portal coughed
         The robed repositor of truth."
   □ "In a short story, the writer imagines or creates one main incident or closely connected series of events."

□ "Her career mattered more to her than anything—her home, her husband."

□ "We have outlasted other mates, money muddles, and the malaise of monotony."

□ "He gives his harness bells a shake"

These techniques of repetition are usually present to some degree in almost any passage of prose or poetry. Sometimes the repetition is coincidental; since there is a limited number of sounds in English, there will be some repetition any time you string words together in writing or speaking. But often, sound-conscious writers and speakers who *listen* to language and are aware of the effects of sounds and sound repetitions or echoes intentionally use consonance and assonance and alliteration.

For what purpose or purposes? Sometimes such repetitions are used simply as a bonding or linking device, verbal glue to integrate words and make them flow mellifluously from one to the next. This sound-linkage is effective not only in writing poetry but also in writing prose: "The war was the most peaceful period of my life." Often in poetry, sometimes in prose, the writer's intent is to create a certain effect which some sounds evoke. The "oh" sound in Matthew Arnold's poem title "Growing Old" is probably an example (the "oh" a lamentation or a cry of pain); so are the "uh," "d," "sk," and "st" sounds in Kennedy's "Blood thudded in my ears. I scuffed, / Steps stubborn. . . ." The sounds of the pounding blood and the reluctant dragging of the shoes are conveyed not just through the words but through the repeated sounds in the words. Writers often choose words with sounds that reinforce the sense of what they are saying, then echo or stress that sense through repetition.

Rhyme

Perhaps the sound repetition most readily recognizable is the one most closely and exclusively associated with poetry: *rhyme*. Words are said to rhyme when they have the same final vowel sound but the consonants just before those vowel sounds are different:

ag	o	m	e
bl	ow	s	ea
s	o	thr	ee
thr	ow	angr	y

If a consonant sound or sounds follow the final vowel, these consonants must, like the vowel sounds, be the same:

unt	il		t	ooth
st	ill		y	outh
m	ill		sl	euth

In poetry, rhyme usually occurs at the ends of lines, and is called *end rhyme*; rhyme within a line is called *internal rhyme*.

In "Stopping by Woods," three of the first four lines rhyme:

know

though

here

snow

What can you say of the rhyme in the second stanza of that poem? In the first two stanzas considered together? Does the pattern established hold true in the third stanza? What about the fourth?

The pattern of rhyme that a poet establishes is called the *rhyme scheme* of the poem. Sometimes, as in Whitman's poems, there is no rhyme. Sometimes, as in Frost's poem, the poet creates his own rhyme scheme. And sometimes, with certain types of poetry, the poet must make his lines rhyme according to a prescribed pattern. The following poem by Shakespeare was written according to the pattern prescribed for an English or Shakespearean *sonnet*.

William Shakespeare (1564–1616)

Sonnet 73

That time of year thou mayst in me behold
When yellow leaves, or none, or few, do hang
Upon those boughs which shake against the cold,
Bare ruin'd choirs, where late the sweet birds sang.
In me thou see'st the twilight of such day   5
As after sunset fadeth in the west,
Which by and by black night doth take away,
Death's second self, that seals up all in rest.
In me thou see'st the glowing of such fire
That on the ashes of his youth doth lie,   10
As the death-bed whereon it must expire
Consum'd with that which it was nourish'd by.
   This thou perceiv'st, which makes thy love more strong,
   To love that well which thou must leave ere long.

□ WRITING ↔ READING ↔ THINKING ACTIVITIES □

Reading Sonnet 73 Closely

1. What *is* the rhyme scheme in this Shakespearean sonnet? To write it out, simply assign an *a* to the first line. If the second line rhymes with the first, designate it as *a* also; if it does not rhyme with the first line, label it *b*, and so on through the poem. Here is the rhyme scheme for the first half of the poem: a b a b c d c. Determine the rhyme scheme for the last half.
2. Do you see in this poem any instances of metaphor? Connotation? Repetitions in addition to rhyme?
3. What is the structure of the poem? Identify the introduction, development, and conclusion.
4. What is the tone of the poem? How does the writer create the tone?

□ WRITING ↔ READING ↔ THINKING ACTIVITIES □

Enjoying Childhood Rhymes and Limericks

1. Whether or not you like poetry now, as a child you probably enjoyed it greatly in nursery rhymes, childhood songs, or chants associated with games. Part of the pleasure in such songs and rhymes is derived from their heavy repetition of words, sounds, and patterns. Try to recall, from "the days that are no more," three or four of your favorites. For each, identify and classify as many repetitions as you can. If you cannot remember any, here are the first lines of a few to jog your memory.

    "Wynken, Blynken, and Nod one night"
    "Jack be nimble, Jack be quick"
    "Mary, Mary, quite contrary"
    "Three blind mice, three blind mice"
    "The itsy-bitsy spider went up the water spout"
    "Mary had a little lamb"
    "Baa, baa, black sheep"
    "Jack and Jill went up the hill"
    "One potato, two potato, three potato, four"
    "Red Rover, Red Rover, let _____ come over."

2. Write a limerick or two or more. In case you are not familiar with this particular literary form, here is an example (one of the few clean ones):

There was a young lady from Lynn,
Who was so exceedingly thin,
That when she essayed
To drink lemonade,
She slipped through the straw and fell in.

Once you have composed a few, see if you can work out a definition which explains the usual subject matter, number of lines, number of syllables per line, accent patterns in each line, and rhyme scheme. Also identify in your limericks any instances of assonance and consonance and alliteration.

Patterns and repetitions are in large part responsible for the strong effect poetry like Tennyson's, Frost's, and Shakespeare's has on readers. Such repetitions as assonance, consonance, alliteration, and rhyme create the rhythmical, musical qualities of poetry. (And they can make your prose flow musically, too.)

When you use repetition consciously, you do so because it serves a purpose, either a sound-purpose or a sense-purpose or both. These sound and sense purposes, in turn, contribute to your overall purpose in a particular writing.

Looking Forward

Whereas Tennyson in "Tears, Idle Tears" looks backward at "the days that are no more," Matthew Arnold looks forward in "Growing Old" at the aging process. "What is it to grow old?" he asks. Then, like Hopkins, he answers his own question. As you read, consider this question: What is Arnold's primary purpose in this poem?

Matthew Arnold (1822–1888)
Growing Old

What is it to grow old?
Is it to lose the glory of the form,
The luster of the eye?
Is it for beauty to forgo her wreath?
—Yes, but not this alone.   5

Is it to feel our strength—
Not our bloom only, but our strength—decay?
Is it to feel each limb
Grow stiffer, every function less exact,
Each nerve more loosely strung?   10

Yes, this, and more; but not
Ah, 'tis not what in youth we dreamed 'twould be!
'Tis not to have our life
Mellowed and softened as with sunset glow,
A golden day's decline.   15

'Tis not to see the world
As from a height, with rapt prophetic eyes,
And heart profoundly stirred;
And weep, and feel the fullness of the past,
The years that are no more.   20

It is to spend long days
And not once feel that we were ever young;
It is to add, immured
In the hot prison of the present, month
To month with weary pain.   25

It is to suffer this,
And feel but half, and feebly, what we feel.
Deep in our hidden heart
Festers the dull remembrance of a change,
But no emotion—none.   30

It is—last stage of all—
When we are frozen up within, and quite
The phantom of ourselves,
To hear the world applaud the hollow ghost
Which blamed the living man.

□ WRITING ↔ READING ↔ THINKING ACTIVITIES □
Accentuating the Positive

If your attitude toward aging is colored rather darkly by the senescent gloom and doom of Tennyson's "Tears," Shakespeare's "That time of year," and Arnold's "Growing Old," read Robert Browning's "Rabbi Ben Ezra" in the Additional Readings. Browning's "Grow old along with me! / The best is yet to be" outlook will raise your spirits a bit and challenge your reading skills at the same time. (Some critics have maintained that Arnold wrote "Growing Old" as a response to "Rabbi Ben Ezra." Is there also a negative echo of Tennyson's "Tears, Idle Tears" in lines 19–20 of Arnold's poem?)

As for the answer to the question posed before the poem, "What is Arnold's primary purpose?" you probably would agree that he is attempting—very effectively—to convince or persuade his readers that "Growing old is the pits." The poem is basically one of argumentation or persuasion.

In Chapter 3, persuasion or argumentation was described as following one of three paths, with the paths sometimes converging or crossing: argumentation through citing evidence or examples; argumentation through logic or reasoning; and argumentation through appeal to emotion.

Arnold certainly cites examples, but he primarily follows the path poets usually take when arguing—appeal to emotion. He uses language to create the emotional responses he wants. He appeals to the reader's heart, not the reader's head.

☐ WRITING ↔ READING ↔ THINKING ACTIVITIES ☐
Evaluating a Poem's Persuasiveness

To what extent, in what ways, do each of the following techniques contribute to the emotional effectiveness and persuasiveness of "Growing Old":

- ☐ Arnold's use of a question-and-answer organization?
- ☐ His repetition of sounds? of words? of phrases? of patterns?
- ☐ His use of connotative words?
- ☐ His use of similes or metaphors?
- ☐ His choice of examples of aging?
- ☐ The ideas conveyed?
- ☐ The tone?
- ☐ Other techniques?

Persuasion in Everyday Life: A Checklist

Argumentation or persuasion is, simply stated, the attempt to change someone's mind, to convince others of your rightness, to cause a person to act in the way you desire, to prove your point. Persuasion or argumentation in a

more formal mode may be observed in two lawyers prosecuting and defend-
ing in a civil or criminal case, two political candidates debating, a literary
critic arguing that "Young Goodman Brown" is really an allegory, or a minister preaching for or against abortion. In less formal settings, persuasion is
the Dallas tourist in Washington, D.C., trying to convince a cabbie that the
Redskins do not have a chance for the playoffs; the mother arguing against
the daughter's selection of a dress for the party; the principal struggling to
convince the borderline student to remain in school; the English teacher
trying to explain to his class the merits of studying poetry; the Miller Brew-
ing Company creating commercials to sell beer.

Persuasion is also something that you yourself engage in almost daily—
usually verbally, sometimes in writing.

In any of the above cases, including your own use of argumentation, the
individual trying to persuade goes through a mental checklist more or less
along the following lines. Sometimes the process is a conscious, formal one;
sometimes it is instinctive, informal, and abbreviated.

- What is the situation?
- What is the point I want to get across through persuasion?
- Whom am I trying to persuade? An individual? A group? Who is
  my audience?
- What tone do I want to convey? What tone is appropriate for this
  audience?
- What evidence can I use to persuade? What logical arguments?
  What emotional arguments? Which type of persuasion is likely to
  be most effective?
- What is the most effective way to present my persuasive points or
  use my persuasive techniques? Strongest points first? Strongest
  points last? Emotional appeals to begin and conclude?
- Can I use figurative language to make my case more effectively?
  Similes? Metaphors?
- Will repetition of sounds or words or phrases or sentences or
  patterns at the right times reinforce my points or clinch my
  arguments?

Questions such as these represent the kinds of thinking and planning you
engage in, consciously or unconsciously, as a speaker or writer when attempting to persuade. These are the same types of questions that Arnold
surely addressed, consciously or unconsciously, in writing "Growing Old."

□ WRITING ↔ READING ↔ THINKING ACTIVITIES □
Selecting Persuasive Techniques

1. Using the checklist, jot down the arguments or persuasive techniques you would employ if you were indeed one of the following:
    a. A lawyer preparing a case to defend your client against a criminal charge (before you list arguments or techniques, determine the specific crime)
    b. A mother trying to convince her daughter to buy one formal dress rather than another
    c. A marketing writer producing a commercial for a brewing company
    d. A politician arguing for (or against) gay rights
    e. A minister arguing for (or against) legal abortion
2. In your list, which arguments are intellectual, objective reasoning and which are emotional, subjective reasoning? Did you list some which do not fall clearly into either category?
3. Read the first section of "Tell Me a Riddle" in the Additional Readings for Chapter 5. Identify as many arguments by the husband as you can. Which are subjective emotional arguments and which are objective reasoning?

Looking Forward: Three Views of Aging

Suppose we return to Arnold's question, "What is it to grow old?" Here are three poems offering differing responses to that question. As you read, note the point of view employed by each writer.

Alfred, Lord Tennyson (1809–1892)
Ulysses

> It little profits that an idle king,
> By this still hearth, among these barren crags,
> Match'd with an aged wife, I mete and dole
> Unequal laws unto a savage race,
> That hoard, and sleep, and feed, and know not me.   5

I cannot rest from travel: I will drink
Life to the lees: all times I have enjoy'd
Greatly, have suffer'd greatly, both with those
That loved me, and alone; on shore, and when
Thro' scudding drifts the rainy Hyades   10
Vext the dim sea: I am become a name;
For always roaming with a hungry heart
Much have I seen and known; cities of men
And manners, climates, councils, governments,
Myself not least, but honour'd of them all;   15
And drunk delight of battle with my peers,
Far on the ringing plains of windy Troy.

I am a part of all that I have met;
Yet all experience is an arch wherethro'
Gleams that untravell'd world, whose margin fades   20
For ever and for ever when I move.
How dull it is to pause, to make an end,
To rust unburnish'd, not to shine in use!
As tho' to breathe were life. Life piled on life
Were all too little, and of one to me   25
Little remains: but every hour is saved
From that eternal silence, something more,
A bringer of new things; and vile it were
For some three suns to store and hoard myself,
And this gray spirit yearning in desire   30
To follow knowledge like a sinking star,
Beyond the utmost bound of human thought.

   This is my son, mine own Telemachus,
To whom I leave the sceptre and the isle—
Well-loved of me, discerning to fulfil   35
This labour, by slow prudence to make mild
A rugged people, and thro' soft degrees
Subdue them to the useful and the good.
Most blameless is he, centred in the sphere
Of common duties, decent not to fail   40
In offices of tenderness, and pay
Meet adoration to my household gods,
When I am gone. He works his work, I mine.

   There lies the port; the vessel puffs her sail:
There gloom the dark broad seas. My mariners,   45

Souls that have toil'd, and wrought, and thought with me—
That ever with a frolic welcome took
The thunder and the sunshine, and opposed
Free hearts, free foreheads—you and I are old;
Old age hath yet his honour and his toil;   50
Death closes all: but something ere the end,
Some work of noble note, may yet be done,
Not unbecoming men that strove with Gods.
The lights begin to twinkle from the rocks:
The long day wanes: the slow moon climbs: the deep   55
Moans round with many voices. Come, my friends,
'Tis not too late to seek a newer world.
Push off, and sitting well in order smite
The sounding furrows; for my purpose holds
To sail beyond the sunset, and the baths   60
Of all the western stars, until I die.
It may be that the gulfs will wash us down:
It may be we shall touch the Happy Isles,
And see the great Achilles, whom we knew.
Tho' much is taken, much abides; and tho'   65
We are not now that strength which in old days
Moved earth and heaven; that which we are, we are;
One equal temper of heroic hearts,
Made weak by time and fate, but strong in will
To strive, to seek, to find, and not to yield.   70

Ralph Waldo Emerson (1803–1882)

Terminus

It is time to be old,
To take in sail: —
The god of bounds,
Who sets to seas a shore,
Came to me in his fatal rounds,   5

And said: "No more!
No farther shoot
Thy broad ambitious branches, and thy root.
Fancy departs: no more invent;
Contract thy firmament 10
To compass of a tent.
There's not enough for this and that,
Make thy option which of two;
Economize the failing river,
Not the less revere the Giver, 15
Leave the many and hold the few.
Timely wise accept the terms,
Soften the fall with wary foot;
A little while
Still plan and smile, 20
And,—fault of novel germs,—
Mature the unfallen fruit.
Curse, if thou wilt, thy sires,
Bad husbands of their fires,
Who, when they gave thee breath, 25
Failed to bequeath
The needful sinew stark as once,
The Baresark marrow to thy bones,
But left a legacy of ebbing veins,
Inconstant heat and nerveless reins,— 30
Amid the Muses, left thee deaf and dumb,
Amid the gladiators, halt and numb."

As the bird trims her to the gale,
I trim myself to the storm of time,
I man the rudder, reef the sail, 35
Obey the voice at eve obeyed at prime:
"Lowly faithful, banish fear,
Right onward drive unharmed;
The port, well worth the cruise, is near,
And every wave is charmed." 40

Edwin Arlington Robinson (1869–1935)

Mr. Flood's Party

Old Eben Flood, climbing alone one night
Over the hill between the town below
And the forsaken upland hermitage
That held as much as he should ever know
On earth again of home, paused warily.   5
The road was his and not a native near;
And Eben, having leisure, said aloud,
For no man else in Tilbury Town to hear:

"Well, Mr. Flood, we have the harvest moon
Again, and we may not have many more;   10
The bird is on the wing, the poet says,
And you and I have said it here before.
Drink to the bird." He raised up to the light
The jug that he had gone so far to fill,
And answered huskily: "Well, Mr. Flood,   15
Since you propose it, I believe I will."

Alone, as if enduring to the end
A valiant armor of scarred hopes outworn,
He stood there in the middle of the road
Like Roland's ghost winding a silent horn.   20
Below him, in the town among the trees,
Where friends of other days had honored him,
A phantom salutation of the dead
Rang thinly till old Eben's eyes were dim.

Then, as a mother lays her sleeping child   25
Down tenderly, fearing it may awake,
He set the jug down slowly at his feet
With trembling care, knowing that most things break;
And only when assured that on firm earth
It stood, as the uncertain lives of men   30
Assuredly did not, he paced away,
And with his hand extended paused again:

"Well, Mr. Flood, we have not met like this
In a long time; and many a change has come
To both of us, I fear, since last it was   35
We had a drop together. Welcome home!"

Convivially returning with himself,
Again he raised the jug up to the light;
And with an acquiescent quaver said:
"Well, Mr. Flood, if you insist, I might.   40

"Only a very little, Mr. Flood—
For auld lang syne. No more, sir; that will do."
So, for the time, apparently it did,
And Eben evidently thought so too;
For soon amid the silver loneliness   45
Of night he lifted up his voice and sang,
Secure, with only two moons listening,
Until the whole harmonious landscape rang—

"For auld lang syne." The weary throat gave out;
The last word wavered, and the song was done.   50
He raised again the jug regretfully
And shook his head, and was again alone.
There was not much that was ahead of him,
And there was nothing in the town below—
Where strangers would have shut the many doors   55
That many friends had opened long ago.

□ EXPANDING YOUR WRITING SKILLS □
Writing Persuasive Literary Analysis

Jot down some ideas for writing based on your reading of "Ulysses,"
"Terminus," and "Mr. Flood's Party." The topics may deal with ideas expressed, with writing techniques employed or effects created, or with personal concerns or feelings which the poems bring to mind. The only
requirement is that your topic must deal in some way with persuasion. Here
are one writer's journal notes about a few possible topics.

1.   "Ulysses the Egotist" *or* "Ulysses the Seeker"

It seems to me, based on what Ulysses says in this poem about himself and
others, that he can be seen very negatively or very positively. I'll bet he was a
real hit at home when spouse Penelope found out he complained about being
"Match'd with an aged wife," when son Telemachus heard himself described as
"centered in the sphere / Of common duties," and when the folks on the sidewalks
in downtown Ithaca heard that the king thought they were a "savage race."
Also, saying things like "I am become a name," "Myself not least," and "I am a

part of all that I have met" doesn't exactly qualify one for the annual humility award. On the other hand, this never-say-die old warrior is admirable in his boundless energy and enthusiasm and curiosity and spirit of adventure. Life could hardly be dull around this character. Just for the heck of it I'd like to write two persuasive character sketches, one arguing that Ulysses is an insufferable egotist, the other arguing that he's altogether admirable as a person and in his attitude toward old age.

2. "Poetic Effects in 'Ulysses'"

    This poem abounds in the kinds of repetitions studied earlier in this chapter, as well as in vivid figures of speech. I think it would be enlightening to look more closely at these techniques and their effects.

3. "'Ulysses' and 'Terminus': Two Views of Aging"

    These two are a natural for comparison and contrast. They even use the same closing metaphor in reverse: Ulysses setting out to sea, the speaker in "Terminus" putting in to port. Rather than argue myself, I would analyze the arguments set forth in each poem regarding how one should respond to aging.

4. "Tone in 'Mr. Flood's Party'"

    I have an idea how Robinson generates the pathos ("the quality in something experienced or observed which arouses feelings of pity, sorrow, sympathy, or compassion") in this poem. But I'd like to go through it very closely and see if I'm right. Some of the ingredients, I think, are his emphases on "old," "alone," and "home"; his similes; and his many negatives like "no" and "not" and "nothing."

Select one of these topics which interests you or develop your own. Then draft a persuasive essay of about 750 words. In developing your points, work through the earlier checklist of questions about argumentation beginning with "What is the situation?" Jot down your ideas, organize them, and produce a first draft. Then carefully shape and revise until you have a draft you are ready to submit to one or more classmates for peer evaluation. Have the classmates critique your essay using the same set of checklist questions that you used. Review their written critiques and write a final revised version.

Summary and Review

Here (by way of *repetition*) are some of the major points of this chapter.

- □ Poetry written to express the writer's impressions, emotions, or ideas (rather than to tell a story) is called *lyric* poetry.

- ☐ Poetry can be difficult to read because to most readers it is a relatively unfamiliar form of writing; it is also a condensed, compact form of writing; and it usually has an artistic rather than a functional purpose.

- ☐ One way to become more adept at reading poetry is simply to read poetry. Remember Frost's observation: "We may begin anywhere. We *duff* into our first. We read that imperfectly . . . but the better to read the second. We read the second the better to read the third, the third the better to read the fourth, the fourth the better to read the fifth, the fifth the better to read the first again, or the second if it so happens."

- ☐ Another way to deal with difficult writings—poetry or prose—is to use *analysis* and *paraphrase*. To analyze is to break into parts and study closely; to paraphrase is to restate in your own words.

- ☐ When you read a poem closely, you usually discover that the poet uses *repetition* in various ways to create sound-effects or sense-effects. Writers of prose also use repetition for such effects. Words, phrases, lines, or patterns (*parallelism*) may be repeated.

- ☐ Sounds may also be repeated. *Assonance* is the repetition of vowel sounds. *Consonance* is the repetition of consonant sounds. *Alliteration* is repetition of the initial sounds of words.

- ☐ *Rhyme*, a type of repetition associated almost exclusively with poetry, occurs when words have the same final vowel sound but differing consonant sounds preceding those vowel sounds. The pattern of rhyme in a poem is called the *rhyme scheme*.

- ☐ *Argumentation* in poetry usually is through appeal to emotion rather than through citing of evidence or objective reasoning.

- ☐ Any writer or speaker seeking to argue or persuade usually goes through a mental checklist to determine how best to present her or his case. This process may be conscious and extensive, or it may be unconscious and abbreviated.

And finally, to conclude, here is a quotation which looks backward at this chapter and forward to the next:

> Yes, autumn is really the best of the seasons; and I'm not sure that old age isn't the best part of life. But of course, like autumn, it doesn't *last*.*

Letters of C. S. Lewis, ed. W. H. Lewis (New York: Harcourt, Brace and World, Inc., 1966) 308.

6

Coming to Terms with Death

"Dying is the living we do at the end."*

□ Applying and Expanding Your Reading and Writing Skills in Light of Earlier Chapters

Death is a subject most people find painful, something to avoid thinking about, but it is also fascinating. For centuries humans have posed explanations, developed religious doctrines, created myths, and written poems, novels, and plays about the mysteries of death. In this chapter, by focusing your attention on how several different writers treat death, you have another opportunity to test your reading and writing skills. Because these writers have chosen the same general topic, their different approaches to subject, purpose, audience, form, and style are highlighted. As you pull together the literary and compositional threads of earlier chapters, you will be reading and writing in light of what you have already learned.

*Leslie Thompson, "Cultural and Institutional Restrictions on Dying Styles in a Technological Society," in this chapter.

261

Personal Perspectives

☐ WRITING ↔ READING ↔ THINKING ACTIVITIES ☐
Recalling a Personal Reaction to Death

Recall a death that touched your life or the life of someone you know. Describe in your journal how that death affected you or a family member or friend. After you have completed your writing, ask yourself the following questions: Did you find your feelings almost too personal to put on paper? Would you feel comfortable sharing this written recollection with someone else?

The following newspaper column was written by Joyce Maynard about the approaching death of her grandmother. As you read "Four Generations," look for the familiar—in content, form, and style—and note the new: what Maynard contributes to your increasing experience with reading and writing. Do you suppose writing this essay was a painful experience for Maynard? Why would she want to publish this personal account?

Joyce Maynard (born 1954)
Four Generations

My mother called last week to tell me that my grandmother is dying. She has refused an operation that would postpone, but not prevent, her death from pancreatic cancer. She can't eat, she has been hemorrhaging, and she has severe jaundice. "I always prided myself on being different," she told my mother. "Now I *am* different. I'm yellow."

My mother, telling me this news, began to cry. So I became the mother for a moment, reminding her, reasonably, that my grandmother is eighty-seven, she's had a full life, she has all her faculties, and no one who knows her could wish that she live long enough to lose them. Lately my mother has been finding notes in my grandmother's drawers at the nursing home, reminding her, "Joyce's husband's name is Steve. Their daughter is Audrey." In the last few years she hadn't had the strength to cook or garden, and she's begun to say she's had enough of living.

My grandmother was born in Russia, in 1892—the oldest daughter in a large and prosperous Jewish family. But the prosperity didn't last. She tells stories of the pogroms and the cossacks who raped her when she was twelve. Soon after that, her family emigrated to Canada, where she met my grandfather.

Their children were the center of their life. The story I loved best, as a child, was of my grandfather opening every box of Cracker Jack in the general store he ran, in search of the particular tin toy my mother coveted. Though they never had much money, my grandmother saw to it that her daughter had elocution lessons and piano lessons, and assured her that she would go to college.

But while she was at college, my mother met my father, who was blue-eyed and blond-haired and not Jewish. When my father sent love letters to my mother, my grandmother would open and hide them, and when my mother told her parents she was going to marry this man, my grandmother said if that happened, it would kill her.

Not likely, of course. My grandmother is a woman who used to crack Brazil nuts open with her teeth, a woman who once lifted a car off the ground, when there was an accident and it had to be moved. She has been representing her death as imminent ever since I've known her—twenty-five years—and has discussed, at length, the distribution of her possessions and her lamb coat. Every time we said goodbye, after our annual visit to Winnipeg, she'd weep and say she'd never see us again. But in the meantime, while every other relative of her generation, and a good many of the younger ones, has died (nursed usually by her), she has kept making knishes, shopping for bargains, tending the healthiest plants I've ever seen.

After my grandfather died, my grandmother lived, more than ever, through her children. When she came to visit, I would hide my diary. She couldn't understand any desire for privacy. She couldn't bear it if my mother left the house without her.

This possessiveness is what made my mother furious (and then guilt-ridden that she felt that way, when of course she owed so much to her mother). So I harbored the resentment that my mother—the dutiful daughter—would not allow herself. I—who had always performed specially well for my grandmother, danced and sung for her, presented her with kisses and good report cards—stopped writing to her, ceased to visit.

But when I heard that she was dying, I realized I wanted to go to Winnipeg to see her one more time. Mostly to make my mother happy, I told myself (certain patterns being hard to break). But also, I was offering up one more particularly fine accomplishment: my own dark-eyed, dark-skinned, dark-haired daughter, whom my grandmother had never met.

I put on my daughter's best dress for our visit to Winnipeg, the way the best dresses were always put on me, and I filled my pockets with animal crackers, in case Audrey started to cry. I scrubbed her face mercilessly. On the elevator going up to her room, I realized how much I was sweating.

Grandma was lying flat with an IV tube in her arm and her eyes shut, but she opened them when I leaned over to kiss her. "It's Fredelle's daughter, Joyce," I yelled, because she doesn't hear well anymore, but I could see that no explanation was necessary. "You came," she said. "You brought the baby."

Audrey is just one, but she has seen enough of the world to know that people in beds are not meant to be so still and yellow, and she looked frightened. I had never wanted, more, for her to smile.

Then Grandma waved at her—the same kind of slow, finger-flexing wave a baby makes—and Audrey waved back. I spread her toys out on my grandmother's bed and sat her down. There she stayed, most of the afternoon, playing and humming and sipping on her bottle, taking a nap at one point, leaning against my grandmother's leg. When I cranked her Snoopy guitar, Audrey stood up on the bed and danced. Grandma wouldn't talk much anymore, though every once in a while she would say how sorry she was that she wasn't having a better day. "I'm not always like this," she said.

Mostly she just watched Audrey. Sometimes Audrey would get off the bed, inspect the get-well cards, totter down the hall. "Where is she?" Grandma kept asking. "Who's looking after her?" I had the feeling, even then, that if I'd said, "Audrey's lighting matches," Grandma would have shot up to rescue her.

We were flying home that night, and I had dreaded telling her, remembering all those other tearful partings. But in the end, I was the one who cried. She had said she was ready to die. But as I leaned over to stroke her forehead, what she said was, "I wish I had your hair" and "I wish I was well."

On the plane flying home, with Audrey in my arms, I thought about mothers and daughters, and the four generations of the family that I know most intimately. Every one of those mothers loves and needs her daughter more than her daughter will love or need her some day, and we are, each of us, the only person on earth who is quite so consumingly interested in our child.

Sometimes I kiss and hug Audrey so much she starts crying—which is, in effect, what my grandmother was doing to my mother, all her life. And what makes my mother grieve right now, I think, is not simply that her mother will die in a day or two, but that, once her mother dies, there will never again be someone to love her in quite such an unreserved, unquestioning way. No one else who believes that, fifty years ago, she could have put Shirley Temple out of a job, no one else who remembers the moment of her birth. She will only be a mother, then, not a daughter anymore.

Audrey and I have stopped over for a night in Toronto, where my mother lives. Tomorrow she will go to a safe-deposit box at the bank and take out the receipt for my grandmother's burial plot. Then she will fly back to Winnipeg, where, for the first time in anybody's memory, there was waist-high snow on April Fool's Day. But tonight she is feeding me, as she always does when I come, and I am eating more than I do anywhere else. I admire the wedding china (once my grandmother's) that my mother has set on the table. She says (the way Grandma used to say to her, of the lamb coat), "Some day it will be yours."

□ WRITING ↔ READING ↔ THINKING ACTIVITIES □
Analyzing Nonfiction Narrative

1. Begin your analysis of Maynard's nonfiction writing by answering the Who? What? Where? When? How? and Why? questions you would apply to any narrative.

2. What effect does Maynard's use of quotations have on her description of her grandmother? Review the context of each of the following comments. What does each reveal about the grandmother's way of facing life and death?

    a. "I always prided myself on being different. Now I *am* different. I'm yellow."
    b. "You came. . . . You brought the baby."
    c. "I'm not always like this."
    d. "Who's looking after her?"
    e. "I wish I had your hair. . . . I wish I was well."

3. How did you respond to Maynard's first sentence? Did it make you want to read further? What specifically enticed you or discouraged you? a word or phrase? the length of the sentence? the grammatical construction? the meaning? the tone?

4. Identify the selection in this text which begins with each of the following sentences. Do you recall the effect each sentence had on you when you first read it? Can you now identify what specifically created that effect?

    a. "All the trouble began when my grandfather died and my grandmother—my father's mother—came to live with us."
    b. "I like very much people telling me about their childhood, but they'll have to be quick or else I'll be telling them about mine."
    c. "As a child it did not seem strange to me to hear my grandmother speak reverently of her first husband in the presence of her second."
    d. "In 1973, the fifteenth and last year of my marriage to Bill Porterfield, Bill, wanting out, wrote me a letter that began, 'José, why fight it?'"
    e. "After the kings of Great Britain had assumed the right of appointing the colonial governors, the measures of the latter seldom met with the ready and general approbation, which had been paid to those of their predecessors, under the original charters."

5. Look back at the account of a personal experience with death you wrote at the beginning of this chapter. Compose at least three different sentences that could begin your narrative. Try to suggest a different aspect of the experience and a different tone in each sentence. Can you pattern one after Maynard's?

6. What is the effect of Maynard's including four generations in her essay? List other selections you have read which describe members of at least three generations of a family. Compare and contrast these treatments of interactions between generations with Maynard's. What is the point of view in each? the tone?

7. The narrator in Maynard's column views the action from the perspective of a granddaughter who is also a daughter and a mother. Briefly

describe how the narrative would differ if the narrator's mother had written this essay. What might her first sentence be?

Poetic Perspectives

Chapter 2 began with Whitman's describing a child going forth to explore life. As we come to the last stage of human development, we turn again to a Whitman poem about a child. Although the following lines are only a section of a much longer poem, they can be read as a self-contained poetic comment on death.

Walt Whitman (1818–1892)
Song of Myself

6

A child said *What is the grass?* fetching it to me with full hands;
How could I answer the child? I do not know what it is any more than he.

I guess it must be the flag of my disposition, out of hopeful green stuff woven.

Or I guess it is the handkerchief of the Lord,
A scented gift and remembrancer designedly dropt,   5
Bearing the owner's name someway in the corners, that we may see and remark, and
    say *Whose?*

Or I guess the grass is itself a child, the produced babe of the vegetation.

Or I guess it is a uniform hieroglyphic,
And it means, Sprouting alike in broad zones and narrow zones,
Growing among black folks as among white,   10
Kanuck, Tuckahoe, Congressman, Cuff, I give them the same, I receive them the
    same.

And now it seems to me the beautiful uncut hair of graves.

Tenderly will I use you curling grass,
It may be you transpire from the breasts of young men,
It may be if I had known them I would have loved them,   15
It may be you are from old people, or from offspring taken soon out of their mothers'
    laps,
And here you are the mothers' laps.

This grass is very dark to be from the white heads of old mothers,
Darker than the colorless beards of old men,
Dark to come from under the faint red roofs of mouths.   20

O I perceive after all so many uttering tongues,
And I perceive they do not come from the roofs of mouths for nothing.

I wish I could translate the hints about the dead young men and women.
And the hints about old men and mothers, and the offspring taken soon out of their
    laps.

What do you think has become of the young and old men?   25
And what do you think has become of the women and children?

They are alive and well somewhere,
The smallest sprout shows there is really no death,
And if ever there was it led forward life, and does not wait at the end to arrest it,
And ceas'd the moment life appear'd.   30

All goes onward and outward, nothing collapses,
And to die is different from what any one supposed, and luckier.

□ WRITING ↔ READING ↔ THINKING ACTIVITIES □

Considering "Song of Myself"

1. What can you say about the following elements of this poem:

   □ Structure

   □ Voice or persona

   □ Tone

   □ Figurative language

   □ Repetition

   □ Form

   □ Familiar characteristics of Whitman's style

2. Explicate the first twelve lines of the poem.
3. Explicate the last ten lines of the poem.
4. Summarize Whitman's views on death as expressed in this poem.
5. What is your reaction to the metaphor in line twelve?
6. Can you think of an object in nature, like Whitman's grass, which you could employ symbolically as a writer to convey your view of death?

In the next selection, you have an opportunity to compare another poet's treatment of death with Whitman's. See, for example, if Robinson uses a symbol comparable to Whitman's grass. Does he employ figurative language similar to Whitman's? Since you have already read "Mr. Flood's Party," you probably have certain expectations of another Robinson poem. What kind of subject, what tone, and what type of theme do you anticipate?

Edwin Arlington Robinson (1869–1935)

The Man Against the Sky

Between me and the sunset, like a dome
Against the glory of a world on fire,
Now burned a sudden hill,
Bleak, round, and high, by flame-lit height made higher,
With nothing on it for the flame to kill   5
Save one who moved and was alone up there
To loom before the chaos and the glare
As if he were the last god going home
Unto his last desire.

Dark, marvelous, and inscrutable he moved on   10
Till down the fiery distance he was gone,
Like one of those eternal, remote things
That range across a man's imaginings
When a sure music fills him and he knows
What he may say thereafter to few men, —   15
The touch of ages having wrought
An echo and a glimpse of what he thought
A phantom or a legend until then;
For whether lighted over ways that save,
Or lured from all repose,   20
If he go on too far to find a grave,
Mostly alone he goes.

Even he, who stood where I had found him,
On high with fire all round him,
Who moved along the molten west,   25
And over the round hill's crest
That seemed half ready with him to go down,
Flame-bitten and flame-cleft,
As if there were to be no last thing left

Of a nameless unimaginable town, —   30
Even he who climbed and vanished may have taken
Down to the perils of a depth not known,
From death defended though by men forsaken,
The bread that every man must eat alone;
He may have walked while others hardly dared   35
Look on to see him stand where many fell;
And upward out of that, as out of hell,
He may have sung and striven
To mount where more of him shall yet be given,
Bereft of all retreat,   40
To sevenfold heat, —
As on a day when three in Dura shared
The furnace, and were spared
For glory by that king of Babylon
Who made himself so great that God, who heard,   45
Covered him with long feathers, like a bird.

Again, he may have gone down easily,
By comfortable altitudes, and found,
As always, underneath him solid ground
Whereon to be sufficient and to stand   50
Possessed already of the promised land,
Far stretched and fair to see:
A good sight, verily,
And one to make the eyes of her who bore him
Shine glad, with hidden tears.   55
Why question of his ease of who before him,
In one place or another where they left
Their names as far behind them as their bones,
And yet by dint of slaughter toil and theft,
And shrewdly sharpened stones,   60
Carved hard the way for his ascendency
Through deserts of lost years?
Why trouble him now who sees and hears
No more than what his innocence requires,
And therefore to no other height aspires   65
Than one at which he neither quails nor tires?
He may do more by seeing what he sees
Than others eager for iniquities;
He may, by seeing all things for the best,
Incite futurity to do the rest.   70

Or with an even likelihood,
He may have met with atrabilious eyes
The fires of time on equal terms and passed
Indifferently down, until at last
His only kind of grandeur would have been,   75
Apparently, in being seen.
He may have had for evil or for good
No argument; he may have had no care
For what without himself went anywhere
To failure or to glory, and least of all   80
For such a stale, flamboyant miracle;
He may have been the prophet of an art
Immovable to old idolatries;
He may have been a player without a part,
Annoyed that even the sun should have the skies   85
For such a flaming way to advertise;
He may have been a painter sick at heart
With Nature's toiling for a new surprise;
He may have been a cynic, who now, for all
Of anything divine that his effete   90
Negation may have tasted,
Saw truth in his own image, rather small,
Forbore to fever the ephemeral,
Found any barren height a good retreat
From any swarming street,   95
And in the sun saw power superbly wasted;
And when the primitive old-fashioned stars
Came out again to shine on joys and wars
More primitive, and all arrayed for doom,
He may have proved a world a sorry thing   100
In his imagining,
And life a lighted highway to the tomb.

Or, mounting with infirm unsearching tread,
His hopes to chaos led,
He may have stumbled up there from the past,   105
And with an aching strangeness viewed the last
Abysmal conflagration of his dreams,—
A flame where nothing seems
To burn but flame itself, by nothing fed;
And while it all went out,   110
Not even the faint anodyne of doubt

May then have eased a painful going down
From pictured heights of power and lost renown,
Revealed at length to his outlived endeavor
Remote and unapproachable forever;   115
And at his heart there may have gnawed
Sick memories of a dead faith foiled and flawed
And long dishonored by the living death
Assigned alike by chance
To brutes and hierophants;   120
And anguish fallen on those he loved around him
May once have dealt the last blow to confound him.
And so have left him as death leaves a child,
Who sees it all too near;
And he who knows no young way to forget   125
May struggle to the tomb unreconciled.
Whatever suns may rise or set
There may be nothing kinder for him here
Than shafts and agonies;
And under these   130
He may cry out and stay on horribly;
Or, seeing in death too small a thing to fear,
He may go forward like a stoic Roman
Where pangs and terrors in his pathway lie, —
Or, seizing the swift logic of a woman,   135
Curse God and die.

Or maybe there, like many another one
Who might have stood aloft and looked ahead,
Black-drawn against wild red,
He may have built, unawed by fiery gules   140
That in him no commotion stirred,
A living reason out of molecules
Why molecules occurred,
And one for smiling when he might have sighed
Had he seen far enough,   145
And in the same inevitable stuff
Discovered an odd reason too for pride
In being what he must have been by laws
Infrangible and for no kind of cause.
Deterred by no confusion or surprise   150
He may have seen with his mechanic eyes
A world without a meaning, and had room,

Alone amid magnificence and doom,
To build himself an airy monument
That should, or fail him in his vague intent,   155
Outlast an accidental universe—
To call it nothing worse—
Or, by the borrowing guile
Of Time disintegrated and effaced,
Like once-remembered mighty trees go down   160
To ruin, of which by man may now be traced
No part sufficient even to be rotten,
And in the book of things that are forgotten
Is entered as a thing not quite worth while.
He may have been so great   165
That satraps would have shivered at his frown,
And all he prized alive may rule a state
No larger than a grave that holds a clown;
He may have been a master of his fate,
And of his atoms,—ready as another   170
In his emergence to exonerate
His father and his mother;
He may have been a captain of a host,
Self-eloquent and ripe for prodigies,
Doomed here to swell by dangerous degrees,   175
And then give up the ghost.
Nahum's great grasshoppers were such as these,
Sun-scattered and soon lost.

Whatever the dark road he may have taken,
This man who stood on high   180
And faced alone the sky,
Whatever drove or lured or guided him,—
A vision answering a faith unshaken,
An easy trust assumed of easy trials,
A sick negation born of weak denials,   185
A crazed abhorrence of an old condition,
A blind attendance on a brief ambition,—
Whatever stayed him or derided him,
His way was even as ours;
And we, with all our wounds and all our powers,   190
Must each await alone at his own height
Another darkness or another light;
And there, of our poor self dominion reft,
If inference and reason shun

Hell, Heaven, and Oblivion,   195
May thwarted will (perforce precarious,
But for our conservation better thus)
Have no misgiving left
Of doing yet what here we leave undone;
Or if unto the last of these we cleave,   200
Believing or protesting we believe
In such an idle and ephemeral
Florescence of the diabolical,—
If, robbed of two fond old enormities,
Our being had no onward auguries,   205
What then were this great love of ours to say
For launching other lives to voyage again
A little farther into time and pain,
A little faster in a futile chase
For a kingdom and a power and a Race   210
That would have still in sight
A manifest end of ashes and eternal night?
Is this the music of the toys we shake
So loud,—as if there might be no mistake
Somewhere in our indomitable will?   215
Are we no greater than the noise we make
Along one blind atomic pilgrimage
Whereon by crass chance billeted we go
Because our brains and bones and cartilage
Will have it so?   220
If this we say, then let us all be still
About our share in it, and live and die
More quietly thereby.

Where was he going, this man against the sky?
You know not, nor do I.   225
But this we know, if we know anything:
That we may laugh and fight and sing
And of our transience here make offering
To an orient Word that will not be erased,
Or, save in incommunicable gleams   230
Too permanent for dreams,
Be found or known.
No tonic and ambitious irritant
Of increase or of want
Has made an otherwise insensate waste   235
Of ages overthrown

A ruthless, veiled, implacable foretaste
Of other ages that are still to be
Depleted and rewarded variously
Because a few, by fate's economy,   240
Shall seem to move the world the way it goes;
No soft evangel of equality,
Safe-cradled in a communal repose
That huddles into death and may at last
Be covered well with equatorial snows—   245
And all for what, the devil only knows—
Will aggregate an inkling to confirm
The credit of a sage or of a worm,
Or tell us why one man in five
Should have a care to stay alive   250
While in his heart he feels no violence
Laid on his humor and intelligence
When infant Science makes a pleasant face
And waves again that hollow toy, the Race;
No planetary trap where souls are wrought   255
For nothing but the sake of being caught
And sent again to nothing will attune
Itself to any key of any reason
Why man should hunger through another season
To find out why 'twere better late than soon   260
To go away and let the sun and moon
And all the silly stars illuminate
A place for creeping things,
And those that root and trumpet and have wings,
And herd and ruminate,   265
Or dive and flash and poise in rivers and seas,
Or by their loyal tails in lofty trees
Hang screeching lewd victorious derision
Of man's immortal vision.

Shall we, because Eternity records   270
Too vast an answer for the time-born words
We spell, whereof so many are dead that once
In our capricious lexicons
Were so alive and final, hear no more
The Word itself, the living word   275
That none alive has ever heard
Or ever spelt,
And few have ever felt

Without the fears and old surrenderings
And terrors that began   280
When Death let fall a feather from his wings
And humbled the first man?
Because the weight of our humility,
Wherefrom we gain
A little wisdom and much pain,   285
Falls here too sore and there too tedious,
Are we in anguish or complacency,
Nor looking far enough ahead
To see by what mad couriers we are led
Along the roads of the ridiculous,   290
To pity ourselves and laugh at faith
And while we curse life bear it?
And if we see the soul's dead end in death,
Are we to fear it?
What folly is here that has not yet a name   295
Unless we say outright that we are liars?
What have we seen beyond our sunset fires
That lights again the way by which we came?
Why pay we such a price, and one we give
So clamoringly, for each racked empty day   300
That leads one more last human hope away,
As quiet fiends would lead past our crazed eyes
Our children to an unseen sacrifice?
If after all that we have lived and thought,
All comes to Nought, —   305
If there be nothing after Now,
And we be nothing anyhow,
And we know that, —why live?
'Twere sure but weaklings' vain distress
To suffer dungeons where so many doors   310
Will open on the cold eternal shores
That look sheer down
To the tideless floods of Nothingness
Where all who know may drown.

□ WRITING ↔ READING ↔ THINKING ACTIVITIES □
Reading "The Man Against the Sky" More Closely

1.   What is the significance of the title? Why does Robinson use "The" in-
     stead of "A"? Why does he write "Man" instead of "Woman" or "Person"?

Can "Against" be interpreted in more than one way? Why do you suppose Robinson chooses "Sky"? Why did he not say "Man Against the Sun" or "Man on a Hill"?

2. Can you identify three or perhaps four major sections of the poem? Develop a formal outline showing the major divisions and subdivisions of "The Man Against the Sky."

3. How does the image of the man against the sky become significant for the entire poem? How does the last line of the second stanza, "Mostly alone he goes," set the tone and pattern of the rest of the poem? How do assonance and other kinds of sound repetition contribute to tone?

4. In stanzas 3–7, Robinson describes five possible ways of facing life and death. What are they? Sketch in your own words the five types of people the writer associates with these five ways.

5. Beginning with stanza 8, how does the writer emphasize the connections between himself, the "man," and the reader?

6. What is the effect of the writer's concluding with an extended question? What does that question suggest about the theme of the poem? What is the theme?

7. What is the effect of Robinson's use of parallelism, a variation of repetition? Look, for example, at the repeated pattern in his summary of what may have guided the "man against the sky":

> A vision answering a faith unshaken,
> An easy trust assumed of easy trials,
> A sick negation born of weak denials,
> A crazed abhorrence of an old condition,
> A blind attendance on a brief ambition,—

Read through "The Man Against the Sky" one more time looking for other examples of Robinson's parallel structures. Then return to your outline of Robinson's poem and check to be sure you have employed parallel form to express parallel ideas.

☐ EXPANDING YOUR WRITING SKILLS ☐
Analyzing Style and Theme

Develop a 500–700 word essay on one of the following topics:

1. The characteristics of Whitman's writing in "There Was a Child Went Forth," "A Noiseless Patient Spider," and section 6 of "Song of Myself."

2. Characteristics of Robinson's writing in "Mr. Flood's Party," "The Man Against the Sky," and "Richard Cory."

3. Death as viewed by one of the following writers in the Additional Readings:

    ☐ John Donne in "Death Be Not Proud"
    ☐ Dylan Thomas in "Do Not Go Gentle into that Good Night"
    ☐ Emily Dickinson in "Because I Could Not Stop for Death"

4. Read William Faulkner's "A Rose for Emily" in the Additional Readings for Chapter 5. How does the writer's use of symbols reinforce his treatment of death?

Perspectives of Modern Society

Whitman's and Robinson's observations and questions about death and life were individual views expressed in poetic form. To what extent does a person's culture and society shape—or even dictate—those individual views? In the following essay, the writer raises those questions and poses some answers.

Leslie M. Thompson (born 1936)
Cultural and Institutional Restrictions on Dying Styles in a Technological Society

The startling medical advances of this century have created unparalleled opportunities for ill and suffering people, but these same forces have combined to make the experience of dying a terrifying, fearful, lonely vigil for many. Devoid of traditional myths, rituals, and family support, many patients now die in sterile institutional settings often appearing as mere appendages to life-supporting machines. This shift from the moral to the technical order manifests itself in doctors' fascination with gadgets, the emphasis upon parts of the body, and a concomitant blurring of distinctions concerning death, personhood, and individual rights. The patient is reduced to a secondary role in his or her own death, thus engendering a widespread desire for a sudden death. In light of these circumstances, health care personnel need to create circumstances that would give people more opportunities to die in styles commensurate with their life styles. Society must seriously study the implications of the unthinking treatment of people; and routines, policies, and procedures based on matters of mere efficiency and technological convenience must be replaced by those human and humane ceremonies, attitudes, and policies that must assure that technology's magnificent achievements do not obscure the human need for individuality and spiritual growth even during the dying process.

As a society we must consider the various ramifications of what it means to die in a technological age. The startling medical advances of the past hundred years have alleviated pain; they have prolonged life; and they have created new opportunities for countless numbers of people. Nevertheless, these advances, coupled with other forces at work in our urbanized, industrialized world, have also combined to make the experience of dying a terrifying, fearful, lonely vigil for many. Rather than dying as part of an extended family, most people now die in institutions often surrounded only by machines or the professional staff, devoid of meaningful interactions with friends, relatives, and others. Instead of being allowed the opportunity to know the truth about their illness and to die an individualized death, most people are coerced into a restricted death style with limited input concerning treatment and other concerns of most importance to them.

A major factor influencing current death attitudes and death styles is the threat of ultimate destruction which looms over modern technological society. Robert J. Lifton and Eric Olson point out that "meaninglessness has become almost a stereotyped characterization of twentieth-century life, a central theme in modern art, theater, and politics. The roots of this meaninglessness are many. But crucial . . . is the anxiety deriving from the sense that all forms of human associations are perhaps pointless because subject to sudden irrational ends. Cultural life thus becomes still more formless. No one form, no single meaning or style, appears to have any ultimate claim" (1, p. 113).

In addition, modern society has thrown aside most of the myths, rituals, ceremonies, and customs traditionally relied upon to ease the trauma of death, and institutions such as the church and government no longer provide a sense of significance to much of modern life. Unfortunately, these events have occurred at a time when science challenges sacred religious beliefs and replaces spiritual comfort with the scientific method. Thus, both directly and indirectly technology has altered the context, concept, and style of dying. Nevertheless, we must give renewed attention not only to the causes but the styles of dying. Since dying is the living we do at the end, people should be encouraged when possible to die the way they live.

Modern medical technology has without doubt altered the circumstances of dying. Over seventy percent of Americans now die in institutions, and intensive care units best epitomize the impersonal nature of much current death and dying and its likely future course. In these units patients are surrounded by a glittering array of tubing, gadgets, and monitors all under the scrutiny of specially trained nurses and doctors. Iron lungs, respirators, kidney machines, ultrasonic nebulizers, suction pumps—the number of these machines grows by leaps and bounds; and they have the ability to sustain bodies almost indefinitely. At the very least these technological marvels can "keep the body's machinery going long after it might ordinarily have stopped, a tribute not to the healing arts but to the technician" (2, p. 4).

These circumstances have contributed to a shift of society's view of death from the moral to the technical order. In part this movement results from technology's success in increasing life expectancy and in engendering a belief in death as a reversible event. Death thus becomes a technical matter, a failure of technology in rescuing the body from the threat to its functioning and integrity. Eric Cassell asserts that "it does not matter that the death of a person cannot be removed from the moral order by the very nature of personhood; what matters is the mythology of the society. The widespread mythology that things essentially moral can be made technical is reinforced by the effect of technology in altering other events besides death; for example, birth, birth defects or abortion" (3, p. 455). Cassell further points out that the moral order describes those bonds between people based on morality or conscience that indicate what is right; whereas the technical order rests on the usefulness of things, based on expediency and not founded in conceptions of the right. Cassell also states that "the confusion of mechanical events for moral processes creates the further problem of depersonalization of care. And it is seen in the greater attention paid to diseases than to people by doctors and their institutions—a common complaint about physicians and particularly about physicians in their care of the dying" (3, p. 458).

Lay persons and professionals alike question the use of extraordinary means of saving a person, but medical progress may be described as a process of constantly creating ordinary means out of extraordinary ones. Amputations, for example, are now ordinary but once were extraordinary. The same thing is happening with coronary bypasses and other extremely complicated forms of surgery. With such rapid changes there is no way to establish criteria for defining extraordinary treatment.

As medical technology prolongs life, the predominant illnesses become degenerative and chronic, not acute or infectious. In addition, modern medicine has succeeded admirably at resuscitating patients who would have died a decade or two ago and at artificially supporting breathing, heartbeat, and other human functions long after they have ended spontaneously. These medical advances raise the question as to whether we must, because they are accessible, employ all available medical techniques and devices simply in some mad attempt to maintain life at all costs. Mayra Mannes asserts, for example, that in the profession that makes biological continuation the absolute good the price is the loss of dignity of the individual (4, p. 31).

Obviously medical factors play a significant part in a person's ability to develop a death style. Not only must the patient face such matters as poor health, loss of control, and the possibility of ending life as a living vegetable; but some terminal diseases are not socially acceptable. Additionally, a combination of heroic measures now possible may deprive many patients of their desire to have a death of their own. Joseph Fletcher trenchantly says of the fascinating array of surgical, pharmacological, and mechanical devices brought into play to stave off clinical and biological death:

". . . ironically, by their dehumanizing effects these things actually hasten personal death, i.e., loss of self-possession and conscious integrity. They raise in a new form the whole question of 'life' itself, of how we are to understand it and whether the mere minimum presence of vital functions is what we mean by it" (5, p. 355).

A vast majority of people now die in institutions, especially hospitals. Eric Cassell points out that "as medical science, in its effort towards understanding, has taken the body apart system by system, it has departmentalized the intellectual structure of the hospital into medical specialities that represent specific body functions" (3, p. 459). Cassell further asserts that "one can see the hospital, thus compartmentalized, as the concrete expression of the depersonalization resulting from the abstract analytic thought of medical science. Thus, the dying patient in the modern hospital is in an environment ideally suited for the pursuit of knowledge and cure, but representing in its technology and idealized representative—the young doctor—technical values virtually antithetical to the holistic concept of a person" (3, pp. 459–460).

For some patients there is no option about where treatment should take place, but for many others to place them in the hospital is in essence to abandon them. Whenever circumstances permit—and they often do—dying patients need to be removed from hospitals and placed back into the home, amidst family and friends. Unfortunately, the nuclear family and the trend toward smaller families has contracted the space that even middle-class families can spare for the privacy of a chronically ill parent or relative. Families must also recognize that terminal illness and dying may cause psychological mutilation and scars for unprepared family members. Lael Wertenbaker, for example, poignantly stresses the pressure that a dying patient places on the family, and she says of her husband, "Wert refused to despise his flesh even now. He would call me over and spending time at it, we would touch faces and mouths as boys and girls do. What freshness and sweetness there was in that kissing, in the touching of faces above his ruined body" (6, p. 172).

The doctor's important role in death has changed dramatically with general practitioners giving way to specialists who preside over separate parts of the anatomy and who harness their skills to computers and exotic electronic diagnostic equipment. These skills represent great power and give the recommendations and the misconceptions of medical experts the force of law to most patients and families. Even in the case of the dying patients the physician is bound by a network of professional conscience, technical miracles, an accusing society, pleading relatives, and critical colleagues that tend to inhibit his simple humanity. Moreover, if he can use his training, knowledge, and technical skill to add even a week, a month, six months of life to his patient, however tormented or senseless they may be, he will have done his best (4, p. 25). Thus, the forces of technology reduce the patient to a secondary role in his or her own death.

In part this situation results from what Illich calls medical nemesis or the tendency of health care practice to transform human conditions from a personal challenge into a technical condition. "As a result the process of dying becomes a consumer demand for increased technological management" (7, p. 130). This situation differs dramatically from Aries' description of the Middle Ages and Renaissance when ". . . a man insisted upon participating in his own death because he saw in it an exceptional moment—a moment which gave his individuality its definite form. He was only the master of his life to the extent that he was the master of his death. His death belonged to him and to him alone" (8, p. 5).

Death is no longer a grand occasion, and few people today seem to care about a well-crafted death. Nevertheless, an important societal goal would be to create circumstances which allow each person to attain a death style compatible with his or her life style.

Majorie McCoy affirms that "every lifestyle includes an attitude for encountering death in keeping with that style. If we affirm death as part of life and therefore good if life is good, then a covenant with death becomes a vital part of that affirmation" (9, p. 136). Ms. McCoy further notes that each of us has only one death to die, whether that death comes at seventeen or forty-five or ninety. And it is possible to die that death with style—one's own unique and particular style. Whether it is accepting, defiant, sensual, humorous, tragic, questing, or some combination of these, living that style into one's death can add the flair, the verve, the energy by which death is made one's own (9, p. 161).

There is obviously no ideal way to die, but dying people must be given flexibility to adopt a style comfortable to their needs and desires. Lael Tucker Wertenbaker in her sensitive book *Death of a Man* quotes her husband, Wert, as saying "'Dying is the last thing I'll have a chance to do well. I hope to hell I can'" (6, p. 65). In her equally touching book concerning the death of her husband, Gerda Lerner places the same observation in its most basically realistic terms when she despairs, "So what it amounted to was to select one method of dying over another, I thought bitterly. I took a certain satisfaction in stating things in that harsh, barren way—if you were living in hell you might as well forget about decorating it like a rococo salon" (10, p. 152).

This matter forces us once again to face the problem raised earlier that if people live by a variety of styles why as a society should we try to channel dying into one particular style. Like life itself, death can be tragic, angry, raging, and humorous; and we must somehow come to grips with the rising tide of people who consider suicide, euthanasia and other forms of death as acceptable and even honorable. We must obviously continue going about the business of caring for the dying, but somehow we must expand our horizons to allow more individuality on the part of patients. Elizabeth Kübler-Ross once described a woman who said to her, "I've been angry and rebellious my entire life!! Why should you expect me to change when I'm dying?"

In light of the issues discussed above, we must assure that technology's tremendous benefits do not prolong life at the expense of personhood and individuality. We must give serious attention to the ethical and moral problems associated with the unthinking treatment of people without due consideration to the consequences. We must somehow untie the emotional, legal, and ethical knots that bind us down and keep us from a fresh, vigorous, rethinking of the dilemmas of modern medicine and modern dying. We must also reconsider routines, policies, procedures, and attitudes based on matters of mere efficiency and technological convenience and reinstitute those humane and human ceremonies, attitudes, and concerns that permit people to retain their dignity and sense of personal worth even during the process of dying.

REFERENCES

1. Lifton, R. J., & Olson, E. *Living and Dying.* New York: Bantam, 1974.
2. Dempsey, D. *The Way We Die: An Investigation of Death and Dying in America.* New York: McGraw-Hill, 1975.
3. Cassell, E. J. "Dying in a Technological Society." In *The Borzoi College Reader* (3rd ed.). New York: Knopf, 1976.
4. Mannes, M. *Last Rights: A Case for the Good Death.* New York: Signet, 1973.
5. Fletcher, J. "Elective Death." In *Understanding Death and Dying: An Interdisciplinary Approach.* Post Washington, N.Y.: Alfred, 1977.
6. Wertenbaker, L. T. *Death of a Man.* Boston: Beacon, 1974.
7. Sinacore, J. M. "Avoiding the Humanistic Aspect of Death: An Outcome from the Implicit Elements of Health Professions Education." *Death Education* 5 (1981).
8. Illich, I. "Death Inside Out." *Hastings Center Studies* 2 (1974).
9. McCoy, M. C. *To Die with Style.* New York: Abingdon, 1974.
10. Lerner, G. *A Death of One's Own.* New York: Harper, 1978.

Leslie Thompson's article appeared in *Death Education,* a professional journal for educators and health-care professionals whose careers involve a concern for how society deals with death. To communicate with his audience in a way they are accustomed and in a way that most likely will influence them, the writer chooses the style of an academic journal. As you read the essay, you no doubt noticed some of the conventions associated with this kind of writing.

For example, Thompson precedes his article with an *abstract.* In this special kind of summary, each part corresponds in content and proportion to one section of the longer writing it represents. Through the abstract, Thompson offers his readers a brief overview of his argument. If the abstract contains ideas which interest them, then they can read the entire article.

Like the abstract, other features of the article reflect the audience for whom the essay is written. Note, for instance, the formal language and the citations throughout the essay that are keyed to the references at the end. Thompson's audience would expect documentation to support his arguments as well as an indication that he has read others' writings on his topic. If his purpose is to persuade those who care for the dying to consider the value of the patient's choice about where and even how to die, then he must write in the language and convey his arguments in the form those professionals will accept. His purpose and his audience condition the form his article takes.

□ WRITING ↔ READING ↔ THINKING ACTIVITIES □
Reflecting on Form and Ideas

1. How does Thompson's journal article compare with Maynard's newspaper column? Consider how each of the following is significant in contrasting their styles:
    a. Kind of language selected for the title
    b. Use of abstract at the beginning
    c. Inclusion of footnotes
    d. Level of language
    e. Sentence length
    Add your own observations to the list.
2. If you compare Thompson's article with McKeithan's article in Chapter 3 using the list in number 1 above, do you find contrasts or similarities? Are there any obvious differences in audience? in purpose? in form?
3. Select one of your own essays and write an abstract for your classmates.
4. What does Thompson mean by "death styles"? Have you known anyone who died the way he or she lived?
5. Can you summarize Thompson's attitude toward modern technology as it is associated with death?
6. How would you define death? Does Thompson offer a definition?
7. Are your views of death based on your religious beliefs? Summarize those views.
8. What cultural rituals or social customs related to death have you witnessed? Which ones do you approve of? Which do you reject? Why?
9. What do you want your "death style" to be?

Think again of Robinson's poem about death. The poet and the academic writing about the same subject, how people face life and death, offer you a good opportunity to consider how purpose, audience, and form are interconnected.

Perspectives of the Dying

You have discovered that one of the values of literature is the chance to read about events you have not experienced or to learn through what others write that you are not alone in what has happened or will happen to you. Writers like Katherine Anne Porter have been fascinated by what a dying person sees, hears, feels, and thinks in the period just before death. If you have observed someone in this period of the "living they do at the end," you, too, may have wondered about the perspective of the dying. "The Jilting of Granny Weatherall" allows readers to experience vicariously this final period of life.

Katherine Anne Porter (1890–1980)
The Jilting of Granny Weatherall

She flicked her wrist neatly out of Doctor Harry's pudgy careful fingers and pulled the sheet up to her chin. The brat ought to be in knee breeches. Doctoring around the country with spectacles on his nose! "Get along now, take your schoolbooks and go. There's nothing wrong with me."

Doctor Harry spread a warm paw like a cushion on her forehead where the forked green vein danced and made her eyelids twitch. "Now, now, be a good girl, and we'll have you up in no time."

"That's no way to speak to a woman nearly eighty years old just because she's down. I'd have you respect your elders, young man."

"Well, Missy, excuse me." Doctor Harry patted her cheek. "But I've got to warn you, haven't I? You're a marvel, but you must be careful or you're going to be good and sorry."

"Don't tell me what I'm going to be. I'm on my feet now, morally speaking. It's Cornelia. I had to go to bed to get rid of her."

Her bones felt loose, and floated around in her skin, and Doctor Harry floated like a balloon around the foot of the bed. He floated and pulled down his waistcoat and swung his glasses on a cord. "Well, stay where you are, it certainly can't hurt you."

"Get along and doctor your sick," said Granny Weatherall. "Leave a well woman alone. I'll call for you when I want you. . . . Where were you forty years ago when I pulled through milk-leg and double pneumonia? You weren't even born. Don't let Cornelia lead you on," she shouted, because Doctor Harry appeared to float up to the ceiling and out. "I pay my own bills, and I don't throw my money away on nonsense!"

She meant to wave good-by, but it was too much trouble. Her eyes closed of themselves, it was like a dark curtain drawn around the bed. The pillow rose and floated under her, pleasant as a hammock in a light wind. She listened to the leaves rustling outside the window. No, somebody was swishing newspapers: no, Cornelia and Doctor Harry were whispering together. She leaped broad awake, thinking they whispered in her ear.

"She was never like this, *never* like this!" "Well, what can we expect?" "Yes, eighty years old. . . ."

Well, and what if she was? She still had ears. It was like Cornelia to whisper around doors. She always kept things secret in such a public way. She was always being tactful and kind. Cornelia was dutiful; that was the trouble with her. Dutiful and good: "So good and dutiful," said Granny, "that I'd like to spank her." She saw herself spanking Cornelia and making a fine job of it.

"What'd you say, Mother?"

Granny felt her face tying up in hard knots.

"Can't a body think, I'd like to know?"

"I thought you might want something."

"I do. I want a lot of things. First off, go away and don't whisper."

She lay and drowsed, hoping in her sleep that the children would keep out and let her rest a minute. It had been a long day. Not that she was tired. It was always pleasant to snatch a minute now and then. There was always so much to be done, let me see: tomorrow.

Tomorrow was far away and there was nothing to trouble about. Things were finished somehow when the time came; thank God there was always a little margin over for peace: then a person could spread out the plan of life and tuck in the edges orderly. It was good to have everything clean and folded away, with the hair brushes and tonic bottles sitting straight on the white embroidered linen: the day started without fuss and the pantry shelves laid out with rows of jelly glasses and brown jugs and white stone-china jars with blue whirligigs and words painted on them: coffee, tea, sugar, ginger, cinnamon, allspice: and the bronze clock with the lion on top nicely dusted off. The dust that lion could collect in twenty-four hours! The box in the attic with all those letters tied up, well she'd have to go through that tomorrow. All those letters—George's letters and John's letters and her letters to them both—lying around for the children to find afterwards made her uneasy. Yes, that would be tomorrow's business. No use to let them know how silly she had been once.

While she was rummaging around she found death in her mind and it felt clammy and unfamiliar. She had spent so much time preparing for death there was no need for bringing it up again. Let it take care of itself now. When she was sixty she had felt very old, finished, and went around making farewell trips to see her children and grandchildren, with a secret in her mind: This is the very last of your mother, children! Then she made her will and came down with a long fever. That was all just a notion like a lot of other things, but it was lucky too, for she had once for all got over the idea of dying for a long time. Now she couldn't be worried. She hoped she had better sense now. Her father had lived to be one hundred and two years old and had drunk a noggin of strong hot toddy on his last birthday. He told the reporters it was his daily habit, and he owed his long life to that. He had made quite a scandal and was very pleased about it. She believed she'd just plague Cornelia a little.

"Cornelia! Cornelia!" No footsteps, but a sudden hand on her cheek. "Bless you, where have you been?"

"Here, mother."

"Well, Cornelia, I want a noggin of hot toddy."

"Are you cold, darling?"

"I'm chilly, Cornelia. Lying in bed stops the circulation. I must have told you that a thousand times."

Well, she could just hear Cornelia telling her husband that Mother was getting childish and they'd have to humor her. The thing that most annoyed her was that Cornelia thought she was deaf, dumb, and blind. Little hasty glances and tiny gestures tossed around her and over her head saying, "Don't cross her, let her have her way, she's eighty years old," and she sitting there as if she lived in a thin glass cage. Sometimes Granny almost made up her mind to pack up and move back to her own house where nobody could remind her every minute that she was old. Wait, wait, Cornelia, till your own children whisper behind your back!

In her day she had kept a better house and had got more work done. She wasn't too old yet for Lydia to be driving eighty miles for advice when one of the children jumped the track, and Jimmy still dropped in and talked things over: "Now, Mammy, you've a good business head, I want to know what you think of this? . . ." Old Cornelia couldn't change the furniture around without asking. Little things, little things! They had been so sweet when they were little. Granny wished the old days were back again with the children young and everything to be done over. It had been a hard pull, but not too much for her. When she thought of all the food she had cooked, and all the clothes she had cut and sewed, and all the gardens she had made—well, the children showed it. There they were, made out of her, and they couldn't get away from that. Sometimes she wanted to see John again and point to them and say, Well, I didn't do so badly, did I? But that would have to wait. That was for tomorrow. She used to think of him as a man, but now all the children were older than their father, and he would be a child beside her if she saw him now. It seemed strange and there was something wrong in the idea. Why, he couldn't possibly recognize her. She had fenced in a hundred acres once, digging the post holes herself and clamping the wires with just a negro boy to help. That changed a woman. John would be looking for a young woman with the peaked Spanish comb in her hair and the painted fan. Digging post holes changed a woman. Riding country roads in the winter when women had their babies was another thing: sitting up nights with sick horses and sick negroes and sick children and hardly ever losing one. John, I hardly ever lost one of them! John would see that in a minute, that would be something he could understand, she wouldn't have to explain anything!

It made her feel like rolling up her sleeves and putting the whole place to rights again. No matter if Cornelia was determined to be everywhere at once, there were a great many things left undone on this place. She would start tomorrow and do them. It was good to be strong enough for everything, even if all you made melted and changed and slipped under your hands, so that by the time you finished you almost forgot what you were working for. What was it I set out to do? she asked herself intently, but she could not remember. A fog rose over the valley, she saw it marching across the creek swallowing the trees and moving up the hill like an army of ghosts. Soon it would be at the near edge of the orchard, and then it was time to go in and light the lamps. Come in, children, don't stay out in the night air.

Lighting the lamps had been beautiful. The children huddled up to her and breathed like little calves waiting at the bars in the twilight. Their eyes followed the match and watched the flame rise and settle in a blue curve, then they moved away from her. The lamp was lit, they didn't have to be scared and hang on to mother any more. Never, never, never more. God, for all my life I thank Thee. Without Thee, my God, I could never have done it. Hail, Mary, full of grace.

I want you to pick all the fruit this year and see that nothing is wasted. There's always someone who can use it. Don't let good things rot for want of using. You waste life when you waste good food. Don't let things get lost. It's bitter to lose things. Now, don't let me get to thinking, not when I am tired and taking a little nap before supper. . . .

The pillow rose about her shoulders and pressed against her heart and the memory was being squeezed out of it: oh, push down the pillow, somebody: it would smother her if she tried to hold it. Such a fresh breeze blowing and such a green day with no threats in it. But he had not come, just the same. What does a woman do when she has put on the white veil and set out the white cake for a man and he doesn't come? She tried to remember. No, I swear he never harmed me but in that. He never harmed me but in that . . . and what if he did? There was the day, the day, but a whirl of dark smoke rose and covered it, crept up and over into the bright field where everything was planted so carefully in orderly rows. That was hell, she knew hell when she saw it. For sixty years she had prayed against remembering him and against losing her soul in the deep pit of hell, and now the two things were mingled in one and the thought of him was a smoky cloud from hell that moved and crept in her head when she had just got rid of Doctor Harry and was trying to rest a minute. Wounded vanity, Ellen, said a sharp voice in the top of her mind. Don't let your wounded vanity get the upper hand of you. Plenty of girls get jilted. You were jilted, weren't you? Then stand up to it. Her eyelids wavered and let in streamers of blue-gray light like tissue paper over her eyes. She must get up and pull the shades down or she'd never sleep. She was in bed again and the shades were not down. How could that happen? Better turn over, hide from the light, sleeping in the light gave you nightmares. "Mother, how do you feel now?" and a stinging wetness on her forehead. But I don't like having my face washed in cold water!

Hapsy? George? Lydia? Jimmy? No, Cornelia, and her features were swollen and full of little puddles. "They're coming, darling, they'll all be here soon." Go wash your face, child, you look funny.

Instead of obeying, Cornelia knelt down and put her head on the pillow. She seemed to be talking but there was no sound. "Well, are you tongue-tied? Whose birthday is it? Are you going to give a party?"

Cornelia's mouth moved urgently in strange shapes. "Don't do that, you bother me, daughter."

"Oh, no, Mother, Oh, no. . . ."

Nonsense. It was strange about children. They disputed your every word. "No what, Cornelia?"

"Here's Doctor Harry."

"I won't see that boy again. He just left five minutes ago."

"That was this morning, Mother. It's night now. Here's the nurse."

"This is Doctor Harry, Mrs. Weatherall. I never saw you look so young and happy!"

"Ah, I'll never be young again—but I'd be happy if they'd let me lie in peace and get rested."

She thought she spoke up loudly, but no one answered. A warm weight on her forehead, a warm bracelet on her wrist, and a breeze went on whispering, trying to tell her something. A shuffle of leaves in the everlasting hand of God. He blew on them and they danced and rattled. "Mother, don't mind, we're going to give you a little hypodermic." "Look here, daughter, how do ants get in this bed? I saw sugar ants yesterday." Did you send for Hapsy too?

It was Hapsy she really wanted. She had to go a long way back through a great many rooms to find Hapsy standing with a baby on her arm. She seemed to herself to be Hapsy also, and the baby on Hapsy's arm was Hapsy and himself and herself, all at once, and there was no surprise in the meeting. Then Hapsy melted from within and turned flimsy as gray gauze and the baby was a gauzy shadow, and Hapsy came up close and said, "I thought you'd never come," and looked at her very searchingly and said, "You haven't changed a bit!" They leaned forward to kiss, when Cornelia began whispering from a long way off, "Oh, is there anything you want to tell me? Is there anything I can do for you?"

Yes, she had changed her mind after sixty years and she would like to see George. I want you to find George. Find him and be sure to tell him I forgot him. I want him to know I had my husband just the same and my children and my house like any other woman. A good house too and a good husband that I loved and fine children out of him. Better than I hoped for even. Tell him I was given back everything he took away and more. Oh, no, oh, God, no, there was something else besides the house and the man and the children. Oh, surely they were not all? What was it? Something not given back. . . . Her breath crowded down under her ribs and grew into a monstrous frightening shape with cutting edges; it bored up into her head, and the agony was unbelievable: Yes, John, get the doctor now, no more talk, my time has come.

When this one was born it should be the last. The last. It should have been born first, for it was the one she had truly wanted. Everything came in good time. Nothing left out, left over. She was strong, in three days she would be as well as ever. Better. A woman needed milk in her to have her full health.

"Mother, do you hear me?"

"I've been telling you—"

"Mother, Father Connolly's here."

"I went to Holy Communion only last week. Tell him I'm not so sinful as all that."

"Father just wants to speak to you."

He could speak as much as he pleased. It was like him to drop in and inquire about her soul as if it were a teething baby, and then stay on for a cup of tea and a round of cards and gossip. He always had a funny story of some sort, usually about an Irishman who made his little mistakes and confessed them, and the point lay in some absurd thing he would blurt out in the confessional showing his struggles between native piety and original sin. Granny felt easy about her soul. Cornelia, where are your manners? Give Father Connolly a chair. She had her secret comfortable understanding with a few favorite saints who cleared a straight road to God for her. All as surely signed and sealed as the papers for the new Forty Acres. Forever . . . heirs and assigns forever. Since the day the wedding cake was not cut, but thrown out and wasted. The whole bottom dropped out of the world, and there she was blind and sweating with nothing under her feet and the walls falling away. His hand had caught her under the breast, she had not fallen, there was the freshly polished floor with the green rug on it, just as before. He had cursed like a sailor's parrot and said, "I'll kill him for you." Don't lay a hand on him, for my sake leave something to God. "Now, Ellen, you must believe what I tell you. . . ."

So there was nothing, nothing to worry about any more, except sometimes in the night one of the children screamed in a nightmare, and they both hustled out shaking and hunting for the matches and calling, "There, wait a minute, here we are!" John, get the doctor now, Hapsy's time has come. But there was Hapsy standing by the bed in a white cap. "Cornelia, tell Hapsy to take off her cap. I can't see her plain."

Her eyes opened very wide and the room stood out like a picture she had seen somewhere. Dark colors with the shadows rising towards the ceiling in long angles. The tall black dresser gleamed with nothing on it but John's picture, enlarged from a little one, with John's eyes very black when they should have been blue. You never saw him, so how do you know how he looked? But the man insisted the copy was perfect, it was very rich and handsome. For a picture, yes, but it's not my husband. The table by the bed had a linen cover and a candle and a crucifix. The light was blue from Cornelia's silk lampshades. No sort of light at all, just frippery. You had to live forty years with kerosene lamps to appreciate honest electricity. She felt very strong and she saw Doctor Harry with a rosy nimbus around him.

"You look like a saint, Doctor Harry, and I vow that's as near as you'll ever come to it."

"She's saying something."

"I heard you, Cornelia. What's all this carrying-on?"

"Father Connolly's saying—"

Cornelia's voice staggered and bumped like a cart in a bad road. It rounded corners and turned back again and arrived nowhere. Granny stepped up in the cart very lightly and reached for the reins, but a man sat beside her and she knew him by his hands, driving the cart. She did not look in his face, for she knew without seeing, but looked instead down the road where the trees leaned over and bowed to each other and a thousand birds were singing a Mass. She felt like singing too, but she put her hand in the bosom of her dress and pulled out a rosary, and Father Connolly murmured Latin in a very solemn voice and tickled her feet. My God, will you stop that nonsense? I'm a married woman. What if he did run away and leave me to face the priest by myself? I found another a whole world better. I wouldn't have exchanged my husband for anybody except St. Michael himself, and you may tell him that for me with a thank you in the bargain.

Light flashed on her closed eyelids, and a deep roaring shook her. Cornelia, is that lightning? I hear thunder. There's going to be a storm. Close all the windows. Call the children in. . . . "Mother, here we are, all of us." "Is that you, Hapsy?" "Oh, no, I'm Lydia. We drove as fast as we could." Their faces drifted above her, drifted away. The rosary fell out of her hands and Lydia put it back. Jimmy tried to help, their hands fumbled together, and Granny closed two fingers around Jimmy's thumb. Beads wouldn't do, it must be something alive. She was so amazed her thoughts ran round and round. So, my dear Lord, this is my death and I wasn't even thinking about it. My children have come to see me die. But I can't, it's not time. Oh, I always hated surprises. I wanted to give Cornelia the amethyst set—Cornelia, you're to have the amethyst set, but Hapsy's to wear it when she wants, and, Doctor Harry, do shut up. Nobody sent for you. Oh, my dear Lord, do wait a minute. I meant to do something about the Forty Acres, Jimmy doesn't need it and Lydia will later on, with that worthless husband of hers. I meant to finish the altar cloth and send six bottles of wine to Sister Borgia for her dyspepsia. I want to send six bottles of wine to Sister Borgia, Father Connolly, now don't let me forget.

Cornelia's voice made short turns and tilted over and crashed. "Oh, Mother, oh, Mother, oh, Mother. . . ."

"I'm not going, Cornelia. I'm taken by surprise. I can't go."

You'll see Hapsy again. What about her? "I thought you'd never come." Granny made a long journey outward, looking for Hapsy. What if I don't find her? What then? Her heart sank down and down, there was no bottom to death, she couldn't come to the end of it. The blue light from Cornelia's lampshade drew into a tiny point in the center of her brain, it flickered and winked like an eye, quietly it fluttered and dwindled. Granny lay curled down within herself, amazed and watchful, staring at the point of light that was herself; her body was now only a deeper mass of shadow in an endless darkness and this darkness would curl around the light and swallow it up. God, give a sign!

For the second time there was no sign. Again no bridegroom and the priest in the house. She could not remember any other sorrow because this grief wiped them all away. Oh, no, there's nothing more cruel than this—I'll never forgive it. She stretched herself with a deep breath and blew out the light.

Porter's treatment of death depends heavily on point of view. In Robinson's "The Man Against the Sky," the poet talks *about* the "man," but readers can only speculate about his personal thoughts. By contrast, Porter sometimes takes readers *inside* the consciousness of a dying woman and lets them share her thoughts, her concerns, her confusions. At other times, they view her from a distance, imagining how she must appear to other members of her family. This shifting from Granny Weatherall's point of view to the narrator's and back again forms a pattern of interwoven perspectives that makes the reader both a participant in and a spectator of the process of dying.

□ WRITING ↔ READING ↔ THINKING ACTIVITIES □
Concentrating on Point of View

1. To analyze more closely Porter's special use of point of view, focus on paragraphs 8–18, beginning with "She meant to wave good-by" and ending with "She believed she'd just plague Cornelia a little." Note particularly the following:

    □ Pronouns which indicate who is speaking

    □ Questions (without identification of speaker) as means of shifting perspectives

    □ Stream-of-consciousness technique (free flow of thoughts, not necessarily in logical order)

    □ Shifting between present and past

    □ Mingling awareness of death and concern about day-to-day details which need attention

2. How would you rewrite the account of "The Jilting of Granny Weatherall" if you chose a different narrative perspective, perhaps that of one of the following characters:
    a. Doctor Harry
    b. Cornelia
    c. Jimmy or Lydia
    d. Hapsy or George
    e. Father Connolly
    Would you want to add George (the jilter) or John to the list?

3. Porter's story provides insight into the consciousness of a woman of eighty dying at home surrounded by her family. How would this portrayal of death fit into Thompson's concern for death "styles"? Did Granny Weatherall die as she lived? Is there any significance in her name?

4. What particulars do we know about her life? her family? her personal relationships? her values? Can you characterize her way of speaking? What phrases or expressions are part of her verbal style? Does she have a sense of humor?

5. Does Granny Weatherall fit any of Robinson's five categories of people facing death?
6. What is the significance of the title of the story? Why is there no reference to dying in the title?

Perspectives of the Mourners

As we turn from Porter's story focusing on the person dying, we move to a poem by Robert Frost about responses to death by those who remain alive. The death of a child is a subject so personal, so intensely emotional that Frost's poem deeply touches readers, even if they have not experienced his characters' loss.

Robert Frost (1874–1963)
Home Burial

He saw her from the bottom of the stairs
Before she saw him. She was starting down,
Looking back over her shoulder at some fear.
She took a doubtful step and then undid it
To raise herself and look again. He spoke   5
Advancing toward her: "What is it you see
From up there always—for I want to know."

She turned and sank upon her skirts at that,
And her face changed from terrified to dull.
He said to gain time: "What is it you see,"   10
Mounting until she cowered under him.
"I will find out now—you must tell me, dear."
She, in her place, refused him any help
With the least stiffening of her neck and silence.
She let him look, sure that he wouldn't see,   15
Blind creature; and a while he didn't see.
But at last he murmured, "Oh," and again, "Oh."
"What is it—what?" she said.

                              "Just that I see."

"You don't," she challenged. "Tell me what it is."

"The wonder is I didn't see at once.   20
I never noticed it from here before.
I must be wonted to it—that's the reason.
The little graveyard where my people are!
So small the window frames the whole of it.
Not so much larger than a bedroom, is it?   25
There are three stones of slate and one of marble,
Broad-shouldered little slabs there in the sunlight
On the sidehill. We haven't to mind *those*.
But I understand: it is not the stones,
But the child's mound—"

                "Don't, don't, don't, don't," she cried.   30

She withdrew, shrinking from beneath his arm
That rested on the banister, and slid downstairs;
And turned on him with such a daunting look,
He said twice over before he knew himself:
"Can't a man speak of his own child he's lost?"   35

"Not you!—Oh, where's my hat? Oh, I don't need it!
I must get out of here. I must get air.—
I don't know rightly whether any man can."

"Amy! Don't go to someone else this time.
Listen to me. I won't come down the stairs."   40
He sat and fixed his chin between his fists.
"There's something I should like to ask you, dear."

"You don't know how to ask it."

                    "Help me, then."
Her fingers moved the latch for all reply.

"My words are nearly always an offense.   45
I don't know how to speak of anything
So as to please you. But I might be taught,
I should suppose. I can't say I see how.
A man must partly give up being a man
With womenfolk. We could have some arrangement   50
By which I'd bind myself to keep hands off
Anything special you're a-mind to name.
Though I don't like such things 'twixt those that love.
Two that don't love can't live together without them.

But two that do can't live together with them." 55
She moved the latch in a little. "Don't—don't go.
Don't carry it to someone else this time.
Tell me about it if it's something human.
Let me into your grief. I'm not so much
Unlike other folks as your standing there 60
Apart would make me out. Give me my chance.
I do think, though, you overdo it a little.
What was it brought you up to think it the thing
To take your mother-loss of a first child
So inconsolably—in the face of love. 65
You'd think his memory might be satisfied—"

"There you go sneering now!"

       "I'm not, I'm not!
You make me angry. I'll come down to you.
God, what a woman! And it's come to this,
A man can't speak of his own child that's dead." 70

"You can't because you don't know how to speak.
If you had any feelings, you that dug
With your own hand—how could you?—his little grave;
I saw you from that very window there,
Making the gravel leap and leap in air, 75
Leap up, like that, like that, and land so lightly
And roll back down the mound beside the hole.
I thought, Who is that man? I didn't know you.
And I crept down the stairs and up the stairs
To look again, and still your spade kept lifting. 80
Then you came in. I heard your rumbling voice
Out in the kitchen, and I don't know why,
But I went near to see with my own eyes.
You could sit there with the stains on your shoes
Of the fresh earth from your own baby's grave 85
And talk about your everyday concerns.
You had stood the spade up against the wall
Outside there in the entry, for I saw it."

"I shall laugh the worst laugh I ever laughed.
I'm cursed. God, if I don't believe I'm cursed." 90

"I can repeat the very words you were saying.
'Three foggy mornings and one rainy day

Will rot the best birch fence a man can build.'
Think of it, talk like that at such a time!
What had how long it takes a birch to rot   95
To do with what was in the darkened parlour.
You *couldn't* care! The nearest friends can go
With anyone to death, comes so far short
They might as well not try to go at all.
No, from the time when one is sick to death,   100
One is alone, and he dies more alone.
Friends make pretense of following to the grave,
But before one is in it, their minds are turned
And making the best of their way back to life
And living people, and things they understand.   105
But the world's evil. I won't have grief so
If I can change it. Oh, I won't, I won't!"

"There, you have said it all and you feel better.
You won't go now. You're crying. Close the door.
The heart's gone out of it: why keep it up?   110
Amy! There's someone coming down the road!"

"*You*—oh, you think the talk is all. I must go—
Somewhere out of this house. How can I make you—"

"If—you—do!" She was opening the door wider.
"Where do you mean to go? First tell me that.   115
I'll follow and bring you back by force. I *will!*—"

□ WRITING ↔ READING ↔ THINKING ACTIVITIES □
Noting Narrative and Dramatic Elements in Poetry

1. What narrative elements are present in Frost's poem?
2. What is the subject of this poem?
3. What is the meaning and significance of the title?
4. Are there central images or symbols in this poem?
5. Does Frost depict the emotions you would expect in such a situation?
6. Why does the writer choose to reveal this relationship through dialogue?
7. From what perspective or point of view is the poem narrated? Is the point of view objective?
8. What elements of the setting are significant?
9. How would you characterize the husband and wife? List the attitudes each reveals in the poem.

10. What dramatic elements can you identify in the poem?
11. Select one of the "parts" and read the poem aloud with another person. Then switch roles and assume the other part. What did reading the poem aloud reveal to you that you did not notice when reading silently?
12. Chapter 4 dealt with making connections with others. How would you describe this husband-wife connection?

Perspectives of the Dead

Porter's story helps us imagine the "living we do at the end," and Frost's poem deals with those who grieve. Another writer, Edgar Lee Masters, speculates about what those already dead would communicate to the living if they could speak one last time. Masters creates a community, Spoon River, Illinois, and populates the cemetery there with people who have a story to tell. Again the form is poetry, and again you will find narrative and dramatic elements.

Edgar Lee Masters (1869–1950)

The Hill

WHERE *are Elmer, Herman, Bert, Tom and Charley,*
The weak of will, the strong of arm, the clown, the boozer, the fighter?
All, all, are sleeping on the hill.

One passed in a fever,
One was burned in a mine,   5
One was killed in a brawl,
One died in a jail,
One fell from a bridge toiling for children and wife—
All, all are sleeping, sleeping, sleeping on the hill.

Where are Ella, Kate, Mag, Lizzie and Edith,   10
The tender heart, the simple soul, the loud, the proud, the happy one?—
All, all, are sleeping on the hill.

One died in shameful child-birth.
One of a thwarted love,
One at the hands of a brute in a brothel,   15
One of a broken pride, in the search for heart's desire,
One after life in far-away London and Paris
Was brought to her little space by Ella and Kate and Mag—
All, all are sleeping, sleeping, sleeping on the hill.

Where are Uncle Isaac and Aunt Emily,   20
And old Towny Kincaid and Sevigne Houghton,
And Major Walker who had talked
With venerable men of the revolution?—
All, all, are sleeping on the hill.

They brought them dead sons from the war,   25
And daughters whom life had crushed,
And their children fatherless, crying—
All, all are sleeping, sleeping, sleeping on the hill.

Where is Old Fiddler Jones
Who played with life all his ninety years,   30
Braving the sleet with bared breast,
Drinking, rioting, thinking neither of wife nor kin,
Nor gold, nor love, nor heaven?
Lo! he babbles of the fish-frys of long ago,
Of the horse-races of long ago at Clary's Grove,   35
Of what Abe Lincoln said
One time at Springfield.

Pauline Barrett

ALMOST the shell of a woman after the surgeon's knife!
And almost a year to creep back into strength,
Till the dawn of our wedding decennial
Found me my seeming self again.
We walked the forest together,   5
By a path of soundless moss and turf.
But I could not look in your eyes,
And you could not look in my eyes,
For such sorrow was ours—the beginning of gray in your hair,
And I but a shell of myself.   10
And what did we talk of?—sky and water,

Anything, 'most, to hide our thoughts.
And then your gift of wild roses,
Set on the table to grace our dinner.
Poor dear, how bravely you struggled   15
To imagine and live a remembered rapture!
Then my spirit drooped as the night came on,
And you left me alone in my room for a while,
As you did when I was a bride, poor heart.
And I looked in the mirror and something said: 20
"One should be all dead when one is half-dead—"
Nor ever mock life, nor ever cheat love."
And I did it looking there in the mirror—
Dear, have you ever understood?

William and Emily

THERE is something about Death
Like love itself!
If with some one with whom you have known passion,
And the glow of youthful love,
You also, after years of life   5
Together, feel the sinking of the fire,
And thus fade away together,
Gradually, faintly, delicately,
As it were in each other's arms,
Passing from the familiar room—   10
That is a power of unison between souls
Like love itself!

Lucinda Matlock

I WENT to the dances at Chandlerville,
And played snap-out at Winchester.
One time we changed partners,
Driving home in the moonlight of middle June,
And then I found Davis.   5
We were married and lived together for seventy years,
Enjoying, working, raising the twelve children,
Eight of whom we lost

Ere I had reached the age of sixty.
I spun, I wove, I kept the house, I nursed the sick,   10
I made the garden, and for holiday
Rambled over the fields where sang the larks,
And by Spoon River gathering many a shell,
And many a flower and medicinal weed—
Shouting to the wooded hills, singing to the green valleys.   15
At ninety-six I had lived enough, that is all,
And passed to a sweet repose.
What is this I hear of sorrow and weariness,
Anger, discontent and drooping hopes?
Degenerate sons and daughters,   20
Life is too strong for you—
It takes life to love Life.

□ WRITING ↔ READING ↔ THINKING ACTIVITIES □
Responding as Reader, Performing as Writer

1. From the perspective of a reader, answer the following questions:
   a. According to Masters, where are the dead?
   b. What uses does the writer make of parallelism in these poems?
   c. Describe the "connections" in "Pauline Barrett."
   d. What attitudes toward life and death are expressed in "Lucinda Matlock"?
   e. What is the point of view in each of Masters's poems?
   f. What are the characteristics of Masters's writing as reflected in these poems?
   g. How would you compare the poems of Masters and Robinson?
2. To shift from reader to writer, compose a letter, either in prose or poetry, assuming one of the following possible situations:

   □ You are writing a letter for one specific person, to be opened only after you are dead.

   □ You imagine someone already dead wishes to convey a message to you. Write that message.

   □ You are writing a letter to someone you want to communicate with while that person is still alive; you do not want to feel later that you never told him or her how you really felt.

   □ You select some other situation in which the message will be brief but intense (perhaps a love letter or a sympathy letter).

Set yourself the limit of one handwritten page including salutation and closing. Work to achieve the exact tone and message that you want.

Coming to Terms with Death

The final selection in this chapter returns again to the perspective of childhood—and to one child's coming to terms with death by "going forth" into the world and maturing. As you read, decide whether Alice Walker's "To Hell With Dying" is a protest, as the title implies.

Alice Walker (born 1944)
To Hell with Dying

"To hell with dying," my father would say. "These children want Mr. Sweet!"

Mr. Sweet was a diabetic and an alcoholic and a guitar player and lived down the road from us on a neglected cotton farm. My older brothers and sisters got the most benefit from Mr. Sweet, for when they were growing up he had quite a few years ahead of him and so was capable of being called back from the brink of death any number of times—whenever the voice of my father reached him as he lay expiring. "To hell with dying, man," my father would say, pushing the wife away from the bedside (in tears although she knew the death was not necessarily the last one unless Mr. Sweet really wanted it to be). "These children want Mr. Sweet!" And they did want him, for at a signal from Father they would come crowding around the bed and throw themselves on the covers, and whoever was the smallest at the time would kiss him all over his wrinkled brown face and begin to tickle him so that he would laugh all down in his stomach, and his mustache, which was long and sort of straggly, would shake like Spanish moss and was also that color.

Mr. Sweet had been ambitious as a boy, wanted to be a doctor or lawyer or sailor, only to find that black men fare better if they are not. Since he could become none of these things he turned to fishing as his only earnest career and playing the guitar as his only claim to doing anything extraordinarily well. His son, the only one that he and his wife, Miss Mary, had, was shiftless as the day is long and spent money as if he were trying to see the bottom of the mint, which Mr. Sweet would tell him was the clean brown palm of his hand. Miss Mary loved her "baby," however, and worked hard to get him the "li'l necessaries" of life, which turned out mostly to be women.

Mr. Sweet was a tall, thinnish man with thick kinky hair going dead white. He was dark brown, his eyes were very squinty and sort of bluish, and he chewed Brown Mule tobacco. He was constantly on the verge of being blind drunk, for he brewed his own liquor and was not in the least a stingy sort of man, and was always very melancholy and sad, though frequently when he was "feelin' good" he'd dance around the yard with us, usually keeling over just as my mother came to see what the commotion was.

Toward all of us children he was very kind, and had the grace to be shy with us, which is unusual in grown-ups. He had great respect for my mother for she never held his drunkenness against him and would let us play with him even when he was about to fall in the fireplace from drink. Although Mr. Sweet would sometimes lose complete or nearly complete control of his head and neck so that he would loll in his chair, his mind remained strangely acute and his speech not too affected. His ability to be drunk and sober at the same time made him an ideal playmate, for he was as weak as we were and we could usually best him in wrestling, all the while keeping a fairly coherent conversation going.

We never felt anything of Mr. Sweet's age when we played with him. We loved his wrinkles and would draw some on our brows to be like him, and his white hair was my special treasure and he knew it and would never come to visit us just after he had had his hair cut off at the barbershop. Once he came to our house for something, probably to see my father about fertilizer for his crops because, although he never paid the slightest attention to his crops, he liked to know what things would be best to use on them if he ever did. Anyhow, he had not come with his hair since he had just had it shaved off at the barbershop. He wore a huge straw hat to keep off the sun and also to keep his head away from me. But as soon as I saw him I ran up and demanded that he take me up and kiss me with his funny beard which smelled so strongly of tobacco. Looking forward to burying my small fingers into his woolly hair I threw away his hat only to find he had done something to his hair, that it was no longer there! I let out a squall which made my mother think that Mr. Sweet had finally dropped me in the well or something and from that day I've been wary of men in hats. However, not long after, Mr. Sweet showed up with his hair grown out and just as white and kinky and impenetrable as it ever was.

Mr. Sweet used to call me his princess, and I believed it. He made me feel pretty at five and six, and simply outrageously devastating at the blazing age of eight and a half. When he came to our house with his guitar the whole family would stop whatever they were doing to sit around him and listen to him play. He liked to play "Sweet Georgia Brown," that was what he called me sometimes, and also he liked to play "Caldonia" and all sorts of sweet, sad, wonderful songs which he sometimes made up. It was from one of these songs that I learned that he had had to marry Miss Mary when he had in fact loved somebody else (now living in Chi-ca-go, or De-stroy, Michigan). He was not sure that Joe Lee, her "baby," was also his baby. Sometimes he would cry and that was an indication that he was about to die again. And so we would all get prepared, for we were sure to be called upon.

I was seven the first time I remember actually participating in one of Mr. Sweet's "revivals"—my parents told me I had participated before, I had been the one chosen to kiss him and tickle him long before I knew the rite of Mr. Sweet's rehabilitation. He had come to our house, it was a few years after his wife's death, and was very sad, and also, typically, very drunk. He sat on the floor next to me and my older brother, the rest of the children were grown up and lived elsewhere, and began to play his guitar and cry. I held his woolly head in my arms and wished I could have been old enough to have been the woman he loved so much and that I had not been lost years and years ago.

When he was leaving, my mother said to us that we'd better sleep light that night for we'd probably have to go over to Mr. Sweet's before daylight. And we did. For soon after we had gone to bed one of the neighbors knocked on our door and called my father and said that Mr. Sweet was sinking fast and if he wanted to get in a word before the crossover he'd better shake a leg and get over to Mr. Sweet's house. All the neighbors knew to come to our house if something was wrong with Mr. Sweet, but they did not know how we always managed to make him well, or at least stop him from dying, when he was so often near death. As soon as we heard the cry we got up, my brother and I and my mother and father, and put on our clothes. We hurried out of the house and down the road for we were always afraid that we might someday be too late and Mr. Sweet would get tired of dallying.

When we got to the house, a very poor shack really, we found the front room full of neighbors and relatives and someone met us at the door and said it was all very sad that old Mr. Sweet Little (for Little was his family name, although we mostly ignored it) was about to kick the bucket. My parents were advised not to take my brother and me into the "death room," seeing we were so young and all, but we were so much more accustomed to the death room than he that we ignored him and dashed in without giving his warning a second thought. I was almost in tears, for these deaths upset me fearfully, and the thought of how much depended on me and my brother (who was such a ham most of the time) made me very nervous.

The doctor was bending over the bed and turned back to tell us for at least the tenth time in the history of my family that, alas, old Mr. Sweet Little was dying and that the children had best not see the face of implacable death (I didn't know what "implacable" was, but whatever it was, Mr. Sweet was not!). My father pushed him rather abruptly out of the way saying, as he always did and very loudly for he was saying it to Mr. Sweet, "To hell with dying, man, these children want Mr. Sweet"— which was my cue to throw myself upon the bed and kiss Mr. Sweet all around the whiskers and under the eyes and around the collar of his nightshirt where he smelled so strongly of all sorts of things, mostly liniment.

I was very good at bringing him around, for as soon as I saw that he was struggling to open his eyes I knew he was going to be all right, and so could finish my revival sure of success. As soon as his eyes were open he would begin to smile and that way I knew that I had surely won. Once, though, I got a tremendous scare, for he could not open his eyes and later I learned that he had had a stroke and that one side of his face was stiff and hard to get into motion. When he began to smile I could tickle him in earnest because I was sure that nothing would get in the way of his laughter, although once he began to cough so hard that he almost threw me off his stomach, but that was when I was very small, little more than a baby, and my bushy hair had gotten in his nose.

When we were sure he would listen to us we would ask him why he was in bed and when he was coming to see us again and could we play with his guitar, which more than likely would be leaning against the bed. His eyes would get all misty and he would sometimes cry out loud, but we never let it embarrass us, for he knew that we loved him and that we sometimes cried too for no reason. My parents would leave the room to just the three of us; Mr. Sweet, by that time, would be propped up in bed with a number of pillows behind his head and with me sitting and lying on his shoulder and along his chest. Even when he had trouble breathing he would not ask me to get down. Looking into my eyes he would shake his white head and run a scratchy old finger all around my hairline, which was rather low down, nearly to my eyebrows, and made some people say I looked like a baby monkey.

My brother was very generous in all this, he let me do all the revivaling—he had done it for years before I was born and so was glad to be able to pass it on to someone new. What he would do while I talked to Mr. Sweet was pretend to play the guitar, in fact pretend that he was a young version of Mr. Sweet, and it always made Mr. Sweet glad to think that someone wanted to be like him—of course, we did not know this then, we played the thing by ear, and whatever he seemed to like, we did. We were desperately afraid that he was just going to take off one day and leave us.

It did not occur to us that we were doing anything special; we had not learned that death was final when it did come. We thought nothing of triumphing over it so many times, and in fact became a trifle contemptuous of people who let themselves be carried away. It did not occur to us that if our father had been dying we could not have stopped it, that Mr. Sweet was the only person over whom we had power.

When Mr. Sweet was in his eighties I was studying in the university many miles from home. I saw him whenever I went home, but he was never on the verge of dying that I could tell and I began to feel that my anxiety for his health and psychological well-being was unnecessary. By this time he not only had a mustache but a long flowing snow-white beard, which I loved and combed and braided for hours. He was very peaceful, fragile, gentle, and the only jarring note about him was his old steel guitar, which he still played in the old sad, sweet, down-home blues way.

On Mr. Sweet's ninetieth birthday I was finishing my doctorate in Massachusetts and had been making arrangements to go home for several weeks' rest. That morning

I got a telegram telling me that Mr. Sweet was dying again and could I please drop everything and come home. Of course I could. My dissertation could wait and my teachers would understand when I explained to them when I got back. I ran to the phone, called the airport, and within four hours I was speeding along the dusty road to Mr. Sweet's.

The house was more dilapidated than when I was last there, barely a shack, but it was overgrown with yellow roses which my family had planted many years ago. The air was heavy and sweet and very peaceful. I felt strange walking through the gate and up the old rickety steps. But the strangeness left me as I caught sight of the long white beard I loved so well flowing down the thin body over the familiar quilt coverlet. Mr. Sweet!

His eyes were closed tight and his hands, crossed over his stomach, were thin and delicate, no longer scratchy. I remembered how always before I had run and jumped up on him just anywhere; now I knew he would not be able to support my weight. I looked around at my parents, and was surprised to see that my father and mother also looked old and frail. My father, his own hair very gray, leaned over the quietly sleeping man, who, incidentally, smelled still of wine and tobacco, and said, as he'd done so many times, "To hell with dying, man! My daughter is home to see Mr. Sweet!" My brother had not been able to come as he was in the war in Asia. I bent down and gently stroked the closed eyes and gradually they began to open. The closed, wine-stained lips twitched a little, then parted in a warm, slightly embarrassed smile. Mr. Sweet could see me and he recognized me and his eyes looked very spry and twinkly for a moment. I put my head down on the pillow next to his and we just looked at each other for a long time. Then he began to trace my peculiar hairline with a thin, smooth finger. I closed my eyes when his finger halted above my ear (he used to rejoice at the dirt in my ears when I was little), his hand stayed cupped around my cheek. When I opened my eyes, sure that I had reached him in time, his were closed.

Even at twenty-four how could I believe that I had failed? that Mr. Sweet was really gone? He had never gone before. But when I looked at my parents I saw that they were holding back tears. They had loved him dearly. He was like a piece of rare and delicate china which was always being saved from breaking and which finally fell. I looked long at the old face, the wrinkled forehead, the red lips, the hands that still reached out to me. Soon I felt my father pushing something cool into my hands. It was Mr. Sweet's guitar. He had asked them months before to give it to me; he had known that even if I came next time he would not be able to respond in the old way. He did not want me to feel that my trip had been for nothing.

The old guitar! I plucked the strings, hummed "Sweet Georgia Brown." The magic of Mr. Sweet lingered still in the cool steel box. Through the window I could catch the fragrant delicate scent of tender yellow roses. The man on the high old-fashioned bed with the quilt coverlet and the flowing white beard had been my first love.

□ WRITING ↔ READING ↔ THINKING ACTIVITIES □
Considering "To Hell with Dying"

1. Is Walker's story a protest? a tribute? What is the effect of the point of view selected by the author? Can a childhood experience be enhanced by memory so that what might have been vices became virtues when recollected?

2. What is the tone of this story? What specifically accounts for the comic elements? Identify incidents treated humorously that could be tragic in a different context. What words or phrases contribute to the comic tone?

3. Does this story incorporate elements of all the perspectives of death discussed in this chapter? If so, which points of view are represented?

□ EXPANDING YOUR WRITING SKILLS □
Writing about Death

Select one of the following topics and write an essay of 500–700 words:

1. Read all of the poems by Robert Frost or Alfred, Lord Tennyson in this text looking for references to death. Select those you believe deal with death. Discuss the treatment of death in the works you have chosen with special attention to symbolism.

2. Write an essay which shows how two to three people react differently to a death. (Recall Frost's "Home Burial" and review your journal entry about death which you wrote at the beginning of this chapter.) Depict the responses in such a way that the contrast reveals the relationship among the individuals.

3. Select an issue related to death and formulate a topic that can be treated in a persuasive essay, perhaps one of the following: euthanasia, the right to die, hospice care, abortion, legal definition of death, organ donation, suicide. Clearly state a position and then present arguments.

Summary and Review

Expanding your reading and writing abilities, like exploring human experience, means approaching each new opportunity with the accumulated knowledge of what has happened before. In this chapter, you have read various literary treatments of death in light of other literary and compositional experiences offered in this text. With each new author you encounter and each new selection you read, you find much that is familiar and almost always something that is new—some new technique, a different approach, another possibility for developing an idea. All of these become part of your reading and writing skills which you carry with you to your next writing or to the next poem, short story, nonfiction essay, or drama you read. As a reader and as a writer, you increase your capabilities with each additional experience.

In Chapters 1 through 6, you have read and written about the works of others. In Chapter 7, you will become a literary critic of your own writing and gauge the progress you have made.

7

The Literate Mind at Work: Writing as Re-Vision

"The act of looking back,
of seeing with fresh eyes"*

☐ Your Writing as Literature   ☐ Analyzing Your Personal Style   ☐ Improving
Clarity and Forcefulness   ☐ Revising for Conciseness   ☐ Adapting Your Style
for Different Audiences

How does the "you" beginning Chapter 7 differ from the "you" who began Chapter 1? How has your practice in writing, reading, thinking, and exploring human experience affected your personal literacy? Have you achieved the goals set forth in the first chapter of learning to "write better, read the writings of others better, and know a bit more about self and others"?

*Adrienne Rich, "When We Dead Awaken: Writing as Re-Vision," *College English* 34.1 (1972): 18.

In previous chapters you have read and analyzed a wide variety of writings, of "literature." You have also composed writings of many kinds, which now comprise the "literature" you will study in this chapter, measuring the rise in your literacy level since Chapter 1. You will analyze your style, determine its strengths and weaknesses, ascertain which techniques of composition work best for you, and work at further refinement of your writing skills.

As a first step toward analyzing your writings and your personal writing style, think back over your lifetime experiences with written communication. What is the earliest memory you have of writing—not just shaping letters or copying sentences, but writing to communicate? A thank-you note to your grandmother? A letter to Santa Claus? A note to your friend across the classroom? Recall how the demands on your writing abilities became more complex: school reports, letters of application, requests for information, inquiries about your credit card bill, and so on.

What has been your typical response to such demands? Did you welcome the opportunity to put your thoughts on paper, or did you make every effort to avoid doing so? Why? How successful has your writing been so far? (Do not think of "successful" as a grade of A or B in school. Rather, consider whether recipients of your letters, reports, and requests have responded as you wished them to, and whether your audiences have been able to understand and use—and sometimes enjoy—your writings.) Your current level of anxiety at the prospect of writing is probably directly related to how much past success you have experienced with your writing. One quest of this book has been to assist you in slaying the dreaded "fear of writing" dragon.

Now narrow the focus from your lifelong writing experiences to those generated by this book. Take out your portfolio of writing assignments completed for this course: brief exercises, journal entries, notes and drafts, finished essays. Try to examine this material in a detached manner as though it were someone else's work. Review it in chronological order.

□ WRITING ↔ READING ↔ THINKING ACTIVITIES □

Taking Stock of Your Growing Writing Skills

Your individual style in writing manifests itself in various ways: in the forms and topics you choose, in the methods you use to present your ideas, in your organizing principles, in your voice or persona, in your tone, in your sentence and paragraph structures, in your word choice, in your use of punctuation. As you compare your earlier writings with more recent ones, can you detect any changes that have occurred in the style? Has mastery of basics like punctuation and spelling improved? Does the tone suggest greater sophistication? Can you find evidence of a surer grasp of purpose, audience, and structure in your later papers? Ask yourself questions such as the following about your writing processes and products.

1. Have you become more daring in choosing your topics and forms for writing assignments? Have you, for example, tried your hand at poetry or fiction? Have you consciously chosen a more difficult topic over one that offered less challenge in order to stretch yourself a bit?

2. Have you become more aware of alternative ways of organizing your ideas so that they will be presented most clearly and effectively to your audience?

3. Have you developed a keen sensitivity to your own voice or persona? That is, do you adapt your tone to your purpose and audience? What tone seems most prevalent in your writing—lighthearted, earnest, matter-of-fact, enthusiastic? Does the voice generally convey a sense of familiarity with the reader, or a more formal distance?

4. What kinds of sentences appear most often in recent examples of your writing—long, short, simple, complex? Does one type predominate? Are there a great many conjunctions such as *and, but, or*? Do semicolons or colons appear often? How many sentences begin with the subject? with a prepositional phrase? with a subordinate clause? Can you offer reasons for using a particular type of sentence?

5. What about the paragraphs—long or short? What devices connect them—transitional expressions, pronouns with antecedents in the preceding paragraph, repetition of key words? Are most of them organized in one particular way, such as always beginning with a topic sentence? Again, can you give reasons for constructing paragraphs in such a way?

6. Consider the vocabulary in your writing. Do certain phrases or expressions recur frequently? Is the language relatively formal or informal? Are there many adjectives or adverbs?

7. Do you use figurative language frequently? Note any similes and metaphors. Are there many sensory expressions, appealing to the reader's sense of sight, touch, sound, smell, or taste? Do you use words obviously chosen for their connotations?

8. Look for other special characteristics of your style, such as frequent use of parallel structure, repetition, or question-and-answer formats.

9. Your instructor has probably indicated some areas that need improvement in your writing. Do you still need to work on avoiding specific errors in usage, grammar, or punctuation?

10. What do you see as the greatest weakness of your writing? What is its greatest strength?

On the basis of your answers to these questions and others you may think of, consider what your writing style—including the choice of subject matter—reveals about you. Could someone write a character sketch of the "you" revealed in your writings? Are the revelations what you would have them be, or should you work on "correcting" some impression that a casual reader might receive? For instance, accurate spelling and punctuation not only help the reader understand your meaning but also reveal your pride in your work; varied sentence structure suggests maturity of thought; and precise diction denotes precise thinking.

□ EXPANDING YOUR WRITING SKILLS □
Assessing Your Own Writing

After you have studied your writing thoroughly, write a report on your findings. Try to remain detached, as though you were analyzing someone else's style. To encourage this objectivity, refer to yourself in the third person, as "he" or "she." Here is a suggested outline for your report:

   I. Description of writer's early experiences with writing
  II. Analysis of his or her style
      1. Specific characteristics
      2. Greatest weaknesses
      3. Greatest strengths
 III. Speculation as to what makes writer compose as she or he does
  IV. Description of writer's personality as revealed through style

Re-Vision for Clarity and Forcefulness

Now that you have reviewed in detail your writings completed in this course, choose one of those compositions in which you developed a topic rather thoroughly. It should be at least 350 words long. For example, you might decide to use a short story analysis, such as the one below by a student. (If you have not read "A & P" in Chapter 3 of the Additional Readings, you may wish to do so now.)

John Updike's "A & P"

"A & P" is a short story depicting a nineteen-year-old youth's impulsive act of protest against the morality of his boss. The relatively brief story is told very subjectively in the first person by the main character, Sammy. The wealth of detail included in the story and the exuberant, lighthearted tone reveal a great deal about Sammy's personality and background.

The plot is a simple one. The action consists of (1) the arrival in the store of three young girls dressed only in bathing suits, much to the stunned admiration of Sammy and the other young checker; (2) the manager's chastising of the girls for not being properly dressed; and (3) Sammy quits his job in response to the manager's embarrassment of the girls. Upon this slight framework, the author has constructed a well-defined characterization and has created a variation on the theme of initiation.

The setting in a summertime New England is significant primarily for the nearness of the ocean and the season, accounting for the girls' attire. The supermarket milieu, with the youthful checkers and Lengel, the stodgy manager, could be anywhere in the United States, although Lengel's quickness to criticize the girls' appearance openly is probably more credible in a New Englander than in, say, a Californian.

Characterization and point of view are perhaps the strongest elements of "A & P." Sammy's breezy, sometimes breathless tone and his sense of humor are generally very appealing. Although some of his references to the girls suggest a disturbingly sexist viewpoint ("Do you really think it's a mind in there or just a little buzz like a bee in a glass jar?"), his evident good nature and his presumably temporary state of adolescence incline us to forgive him. He seems genuinely goodhearted despite his gibes at the "sheep," as he calls the store's regular customers, and his strong family ties are obvious in the many references to his parents. In the very moment of his grand gesture of quitting his job, he is conscious of using one of his grandmother's favorite expressions, "fiddle-de-doo," and reflects that "she would have been pleased." His interspersing of present-tense verbs ("Lengel sighs and begins to look very patient.") imparts a sense of immediacy to his story and a vividness to his persona.

In the last paragraph of the story is a suggestion that the author's purpose is more serious than merely to present an amusing story. Sammy's tone changes noticeably, becoming almost somber, as he realizes that his impulsiveness will have its repercussions. He has allowed himself to be swept away by his admiration for "Queenie" and the lifestyle she represents, one "from which the crowd that runs the A & P must look pretty crummy," and he does not even get to bask in the gratitude of "his girls," who "flicker across the lot to their car" without taking notice of his "I quit." The theme of the story seems to revolve around the young man's realization that the noblest of motives does not guarantee that others will approve of one's actions. Sammy ends with the morose observation, "My stomach kind of fell as I felt how hard the world was going to be to me hereafter." He is no doubt not only thinking of his parents' reaction to his loss of employment, but also of the times to come in his future when he will again be tempted to take a stand against the enforcers of "policy."

□ WRITING ↔ READING ↔ THINKING ACTIVITIES □
Re-Viewing Your Composition with a Critical Eye

Like the analysis of "A & P" above, your own paper is probably far from perfect. No matter how much time you spent polishing it originally, you no doubt see ways it can be improved now. First, are you still satisfied with the basic organization and the general tone? Have you developed your main idea thoroughly enough to accomplish your purpose? Does the voice suit the form and the intended audience? Once you are happy with these matters, which have been emphasized throughout this textbook, study the following list of suggestions for improving forcefulness and clarity. Edit or rewrite your paper incorporating as many of the suggestions as you can. Remember to exercise your own judgment in completing this activity, however; do not make a change unless you see it as an improvement.

1. Consider changing forms of *to be* and *to have* to more lively and exact verbs.
2. Make sure nouns are as specific as possible.
3. Eliminate any unnecessary passive constructions by rewriting them in the active voice.
4. Examine your diction carefully; have you used the most precise word for the meaning you intend?
5. Be sure that modifiers are placed as close as possible to the words or phrases they are meant to modify. ("They almost walked to town" means something different from "They walked almost to town.")
6. Make sure that parallel ideas are expressed with parallel structure.
7. Consider any other revisions that might enhance the clarity of your paper.

Below is the student's own revision of the paper analyzing "A & P." Revised portions are underlined, and the numbers in brackets refer to the corresponding suggestions enumerated above. Have the revisions improved the paper? Can you suggest other changes that would improve it?

John Updike's "A & P"

The short story "A & P" depicts a nineteen-year-old youth's impulsive [1]
act of protest against what he perceives to be the rigid sense of propriety [4]
exemplified by the manager of the supermarket where he works. The youth, [2]
Sammy, relates the relatively brief story through the use of a very [3]
subjective first-person point of view. The wealth of detail included in the
story and the exuberant, lighthearted tone reveal a great deal about
Sammy's personality and background.

The plot is a simple one. The action consists of (1) the arrival in the store of three young girls dressed only in bathing suits, much to the stunned admiration of Sammy and the other young checker; (2) the manager's chastising of the girls for not being properly dressed; and (3) Sammy's grandly quitting his job in response to the manager's [6] embarrassment of the girls. Upon this slight framework, the author has constructed a well-defined characterization and has created a variation on the theme of initiation.

The very specific setting, a small town north of Boston on a summer's [2] day, allows for the girls' attire, considering the nearness of the beach and [1] the warmth of the season. The supermarket milieu, with the youthful checkers and Lengel, the stodgy manager, could exist anywhere in the United States, but because Lengel is a New Englander, we probably find his quickness to criticize the girls' appearance more believable than if he [3] were, say, a Californian.

Characterization and point of view provide the greatest charms of [1] "A & P." Through his breezy, sometimes breathless tone and his sense of humor Sammy emerges as a likable young man, whose discomfort engages [1] our sympathy. Although some of his references to the girls suggest a disturbingly sexist viewpoint ("Do you really think it's a mind in there or just a little buzz like a bee in a glass jar?"), his evident good nature and his presumably temporary state of adolescence incline us to forgive him. He seems genuinely goodhearted despite his gibes at the "sheep," as he calls the store's regular customers, and references to his family suggest an [4] affectionate nature. In the very moment of his grand gesture of quitting his job, he is conscious of using one of his grandmother's favorite expressions, "fiddle-de-doo," and reflects that "she would have been pleased." His interspersing of present-tense verbs ("Lengel sighs and begins to look very patient.") imparts a sense of immediacy to his story and a vividness to his persona.

The last paragraph of the story leads us to believe that the author's [1] purpose involves more than merely presenting an amusing story. Sammy's [4] tone changes noticeably, becoming almost somber, as he realizes that his impulsiveness will have its repercussions. He has allowed himself to be swept away by his admiration for "Queenie" and the lifestyle she represents, one "from which the crowd that runs the A & P must look pretty crummy," and he is denied even the satisfaction of basking in the gratitude [6] of "his girls," who simply "flicker across the lot to their car" without taking notice of his "I quit." The theme of the story seems to revolve around the young man's learning a lesson about life: the noblest of motives does not guarantee that others will approve of one's actions. Sammy ends with the morose observation, "My stomach kind of fell as I felt how hard the world

was going to be to me hereafter." He is no doubt <u>thinking not only</u> of his   [5]
parents' reaction to his loss of employment, but also of the times to come in
his future when he will again feel obliged to take a stand against the
enforcers of "policy."

Re-Vision for Conciseness

Just as overgrown shrubbery hides the architecture of a building, so
unnecessary words obscure the meaning of your writing. "Pruning," therefore, is a vital step for most writers as they strive for elusive perfection.

□ WRITING ↔ READING ↔ THINKING ACTIVITIES □
Condensing Your Revision

Mark Twain once suggested that any piece of writing could be instantly
improved by simply eliminating every third word. You probably should not
take that advice literally, but as an experiment, take the revised version of
the paper you have been working with, and, whatever its current length,
reduce it by at least one-third; that is, if the paper now contains 600 words,
delete 200 of them. Do your best to cut only the deadwood and to retain
important points. Look for unnecessary repetition and instances in which
one word can be substituted for a phrase.

After you have performed this painful chore (you may have had to cut
some of your favorite passages), compare the two versions. What has been
sacrificed in the condensation? Have you lost anything of real value to the
ideas you develop in the paper? If so, then either shortening was unneeded
or you cut the wrong elements. If you have not lost anything crucial to your
meaning, then the paper has probably been vastly improved. Not one word
should be included if it is not serving a vital purpose to the composition.

Here is the condensed version of the student's essay on "A & P," with
the excised portions and substitutions indicated. Has the paper been improved or damaged by the cutting? Which deleted portions, if any, need to be
restored and why?

John Updike's "A & P"

The short story "A & P" depicts a ~~nineteen-year-old~~ youth's impulsive ~~act of~~ protest against ~~what he perceives to be~~ the rigid sense of propriety exemplified by the manager of ~~the~~ *a* supermarket ~~where he works~~. The youth, Sammy, relates the ~~relatively brief~~ story *in the* ~~through the use of a very subjective~~ first ~~-~~ person ~~point of view~~. The ~~wealth of~~ detail ~~included in the story~~ and the exuberant, ~~lighthearted~~ tone reveal a great deal about Sammy's personality and background.

The plot is ~~a~~ simple ~~one~~. The action consists of (1) the arrival in the store of three young girls dressed only in bathing suits, ~~much to the stunned admiration of Sammy and the other young checker~~; (2) the manager's chastising of the girls ~~for not being properly dressed~~; and (3) Sammy's grandly quitting *because* ~~his job in response to~~ the manager's embarrass ~~ment of~~ *ed* the girls. Upon this slight framework, the author has ~~constructed a well-defined characterization and has~~ created a variation on the theme of initiation.

The ~~very~~ specific setting, a small town north of Boston on a summer's day, *explains* ~~allows for~~ the girls' attire, ~~considering the nearness of the beach and the warmth of the season~~. The supermarket milieu, ~~with the youthful checkers and Lengel, the stodgy manager,~~ could exist anywhere in the United States, ~~but because Lengel is a New Englander, we probably find his quickness to criticize the girls' appearance more believeable than if he were, say, a Californian~~.

Characterization and point of view provide the greatest charms of "A & P." ~~Through his breezy, sometimes breathless tone and his sense of humor,~~ Sammy emerges as a likable young man, whose discomfort engages our sympathy. Although some of his references to the girls suggest a disturbingly sexist viewpoint ~~("Do you really think it's a mind in there or just a little buzz like a bee in a glass jar?"),~~ his ~~evident good nature and~~ his presumably temporary state of adolescence incline us to forgive him. He seems genuinely goodhearted ~~despite his gibes at the "sheep," as he calls the store's regular customers~~, and references to his family suggest an affectionate nature. In ~~the very moment of his grand gesture of~~ quitting his job, he is conscious of using one of his grandmother's favorite expressions, "fiddle-de-doo," and reflects that "she would have been pleased." ~~His interspersing of present-tense verbs ("Lengel sighs and begins to look very patient.") imparts a sense of immediacy to his story and a vividness to his persona.~~

The last paragraph of the story ~~leads us to believe~~ *suggests* that the author's purpose involves more than merely presenting an amusing story. Sammy's tone *becomes* ~~changes noticeably, becoming~~ almost somber, as he realizes that his impulsiveness will have its repercussions. He has *been* ~~allowed himself to be~~

swept away by his admiration for "Queenie" and the lifestyle she represents, one "from which the crowd that runs the A & P must look pretty crummy," and he is denied even the satisfaction of basking in the gratitude of "his girls," who simply "flicker across the lot to their car" without taking notice of his "I quit." The theme of the story seems to revolve around the young man's learning a lesson about life: the noblest of motives does not guarantee that others will approve of one's actions. Sammy ends with the morose observation, "My stomach kind of fell as I felt how hard the world was going to be to me hereafter." He is no doubt thinking not only of his parents' reaction to his loss of employment, but also of the times to come in his future when he will again feel obliged to take a stand against the enforcers of "policy."

Re-Vision for a Different Audience

Consider the audience for whom your original paper was written. Think about the characteristics of that audience which dictated the way you wrote. For example, the paper on "A & P" was written for an audience knowledgeable about literary terms such as point of view and theme. In writing about literature, a writer usually assumes that the audience is acquainted with literary terminology and interested in literary works. The purpose of literary analysis, after all, is to illuminate or explain the work for the audience and to convince the audience that the writer's viewpoint is sound.

However, you might write about a short story for a different audience—perhaps for someone you believe would enjoy the story but who would be put off a bit by literary-sounding terms. The analysis above, for example, might be rewritten as a review for a high school newspaper in this way:

John Updike's "A & P"

"A & P" is a story you won't have to stay up all night to read. It's short and fast-moving. The main character is named Sammy; he's nineteen and works in a supermarket as a checker. He cracks a lot of jokes about his boss and the customers, but he is basically a responsible employee.

His trouble starts when three girls come into the store wearing only bathing suits. They are not bad-looking, so Sammy and the other checker enjoy the view. The manager, Lengel, however, thinks the girls have committed a gross breach of etiquette, and when they are checking out at Sammy's register, Lengel tells them that they should not come in the store unless they are "decently dressed." Sammy, suffering for the girls' embarrassment and swept away by his admiration for the one he calls "Queenie," makes a grand gesture at this point, one which he may later regret.

> You will recognize people you know in this story.

What assumptions has the writer of this version made about the audience? How do these assumptions differ from those made for the original essay?

□ WRITING ↔ READING ↔ THINKING ACTIVITIES □
Revising for a New Audience

As a final exercise in revision, rework your essay one more time for a totally different audience. Whether the writing is about a literary work or something else entirely, you need to ask the same questions about the new audience:

- □ What will make the paper's topic meaningful and interesting to the new audience?
- □ Should the word choice be modified?
- □ Should the tone be changed?

Before you rewrite the paper, write a description of the new audience, listing characteristics which influence the way you will write for that audience. Consider such matters as age, educational level, special interests, and probable experiences that would be relevant to your topic.

Summary and Review

The "you" who began Chapter 1 is now the "you" who has concluded Chapter 7 of this textbook. As an improving writer and reader, you have surveyed and commented upon the various stages of human life, and you have considered lives and experiences and perspectives and thoughts and feelings which, though sometimes different from your own, reflect the shared bases and infinite variety of human experience. You have interacted with other literate minds at work.

The process is ongoing. The "available light" for your efforts will brighten and illuminate more darkness as you continue to write and read and think and talk and listen. Remember "The Chambered Nautilus" from Chapter 1? May the upward spiral of your expanding writing ability, literary knowledge, and human awareness continue.

PART 2

ADDITIONAL
READINGS

1

On Literacy, Literature, and Life

Arthur Hugh Clough (1819–1861)
Life Is Struggle

To wear out heart, and nerves, and brain,
And give oneself a world of pain;
Be eager, angry, fierce, and hot,
Imperious, supple—God knows what,
For what's all one to have or not;   5
O false, unwise, absurd, and vain!
For 'tis not joy, it is not gain,
It is not in itself a bliss,
Only it is precisely this
    That keeps us all alive.   10

To say we truly feel the pain,
And quite are sinking with the strain;—
Entirely, simply, undeceived,
Believe, and say we ne'er believed
The object, e'en were it achieved,   15
A thing we e'er had cared to keep;
With heart and soul to hold it cheap,
And then to go and try it again;

O false, unwise, absurd, and vain!
Oh, 'tis not joy, and 'tis not bliss,   20
Only it is precisely this
    That keeps us still alive.

E. E. Cummings (1894–1962)

anyone lived in a pretty how town

anyone lived in a pretty how town
(with up so floating many bells down)
spring summer autumn winter
he sang his didn't he danced his did.

Women and men(both little and small)   5
cared for anyone not at all
they sowed their isn't they reaped their same
sun moon stars rain

children guessed(but only a few
and down they forgot as up they grew   10
autumn winter spring summer)
that noone loved him more by more

when by now and tree by leaf
she laughed his joy she cried his grief
bird by snow and stir by still   15
anyone's any was all to her

someones married their everyones
laughed their cryings and did their dance
(sleep wake hope and then)they
said their nevers they slept their dream   20

stars rain sun moon
(and only the snow can begin to explain
how children are apt to forget to remember
with up so floating many bells down)

one day anyone died i guess   25
(and noone stooped to kiss his face)
busy folk buried them side by side
little by little and was by was

all by all and deep by deep
and more by more they dream their sleep   30
noone and anyone earth by april
wish by spirit and if by yes.

Women and men(both dong and ding)
summer autumn winter spring
reaped their sowing and went their came   35
sun moon stars rain

Langston Hughes (1902–1967)
Mother to Son

Well, son, I'll tell you:
Life for me ain't been no crystal stair.
It's had tacks in it,
And splinters,
And boards torn up,   5
And places with no carpet on the floor—
Bare.
But all the time
I'se been a-climbin' on,
And reachin' landin's,   10
And turnin' corners,
And sometimes goin' in the dark
Where there ain't been no light.
So, boy, don't you turn back.
Don't you set down on the steps   15
'Cause you finds it kinder hard.
Don't you fall now—
For I'se still climbin',
And life for me ain't been no crystal stair.

Henry Wadsworth Longfellow (1807–1882)
The Tide Rises, the Tide Falls

The tide rises, the tide falls,
The twilight darkens, the curlew calls;
Along the sea-sands damp and brown
The traveller hastens toward the town,
   And the tide rises, the tide falls.   5

Darkness settles on roofs and walls,
But the sea, the sea in the darkness calls;
The little waves, with their soft, white hands,
Efface the footprints in the sands,
   And the tide rises, the tide falls.   10

The morning breaks; the steeds in their stalls
Stamp and neigh, as the hostler calls;
The day returns, but nevermore
Returns the traveller to the shore,
   And the tide rises, the tide falls.   15

Padraic Pearse (1879–1916)
Last Lines—1916
(Written the Night before His Execution)

The beauty of the world hath made me sad,
This beauty that will pass;
Sometimes my heart hath shaken with great joy
To see a leaping squirrel in a tree,
Or a red lady-bird upon a stalk,   5
Or little rabbits in a field at evening,
Lit by a slanting sun,

Or some green hill where shadows drifted by,
Some quiet hill where mountainy man hath sown
And soon would reap, near to the gate of Heaven;   10
Or children with bare feet upon the sands
Of some ebbed sea, or playing on the streets
Of little towns in Connacht,
Things young and happy.
And then my heart hath told me: 15
These will pass,
Will pass and change, will die and be no more,
Things bright and green, things young and happy;
And I have gone upon my way
Sorrowful.   20

Alexander Pope (1688–1744)
An Essay on Man
Epistle II, lines 1–18

    Know then thyself; presume not God to scan:
The proper study of mankind is man.
Placed on this isthmus of a middle state,
A being darkly wise and rudely great:
With too much knowledge for the skeptic side,   5
With too much weakness for the Stoic's pride,
He hangs between, in doubt to act or rest;
In doubt to deem himself a god or beast;
In doubt his mind or body to prefer;
Born but to die, and reas'ning but to err;   10
Alike in ignorance, his reason such,
Whether he thinks too little or too much;
Chaos of thought and passion, all confused;
Still by himself abused or disabused;
Created half to rise, and half to fall;   15
Great lord of all things, yet a prey to all;
Sole judge of truth, in endless error hurled;
The glory, jest, and riddle of the world!

William Shakespeare (1564–1616)
Macbeth
Act 5, Scene 5, lines 19–28

> Tomorrow, and tomorrow, and tomorrow,
> Creeps in this petty pace from day to day,   20
> To the last syllable of recorded time;
> And all our yesterdays have lighted fools
> The way to dusty death. Out, out, brief candle!
> Life's but a walking shadow, a poor player,
> That struts and frets his hour upon the stage,   25
> And then is heard no more. It is a tale
> Told by an idiot, full of sound and fury,
> Signifying nothing.

Percy Bysshe Shelley (1792–1822)
Mutability

> We are as clouds that veil the midnight moon;
>   How restlessly they speed, and gleam, and quiver,
> Streaking the darkness radiantly!—yet soon
>   Night closes round, and they are lost for ever:
>
> Or like forgotten lyres, whose dissonant strings   5
>   Give various response to each varying blast,
> To whose frail frame no second motion brings
>   One mood or modulation like the last.
>
> We rest.—A dream has power to poison sleep;
>   We rise.—One wandering thought pollutes the day;   10
> We feel, conceive or reason, laugh or weep;
>   Embrace fond woe, or cast our cares away:

It is the same!—For, be it joy or sorrow,
　　The path of its departure still is free:
Man's yesterday may ne'er be like his morrow;　　　　　15
　　Nought may endure but Mutability.

William Wordsworth (1770–1850)
My Heart Leaps Up

My heart leaps up when I behold
　　A rainbow in the sky:
So was it when my life began;
So is it now I am a man:
So be it when I shall grow old,　　　　　5
　　Or let me die!
The Child is father of the Man;
And I could wish my days to be
Bound each to each by natural piety.

William Butler Yeats (1865–1939)
The Four Ages of Man

He with body waged a fight,
But body won; it walks upright.

Then he struggled with the heart;
Innocence and peace depart.

Then he struggled with the mind;　　　　　5
His proud heart he left behind.

Now his wars on God begin;
At stroke of midnight God shall win.

Yevgeny Yevtushenko (born 1933)
People

No people are uninteresting.
Their fate is like the chronicle of planets.

Nothing in them is not particular,
and planet is dissimilar from planet.

And if a man lived in obscurity   5
making his friends in that obscurity
obscurity is not uninteresting.

To each his world is private,
and in that world one excellent minute.

And in that world one tragic minute.   10
These are private.

In any man who dies there dies with him
his first snow and kiss and fight.
It goes with him.

They are left books and bridges   15
and painted canvas and machinery.

Whose fate is to survive.
But what has gone is also not nothing:
by the rule of the game something has gone.
Not people die but worlds die in them.   20

Whom we knew as faulty, the earth's creatures.
Of whom, essentially, what did we know?

Brother of a brother? Friend of friends?
Lover of lover?

We who knew our fathers   25
in everything, in nothing.

They perish. They cannot be brought back.
The secret worlds are not regenerated.

And every time again and again
I make my lament against destruction.   30

2

Beginnings

John Berryman (1914–1972)
The Ball Poem

What is the boy now, who has lost his ball,
What what is he to do? I saw it go
Merrily bouncing, down the street, and then
Merrily over—there it is in the water!
No use to say "O there are other balls":   5
An ultimate shaking grief fixes the boy
As he stands rigid, trembling, staring down
All his young days into the harbour where
His ball went. I would not intrude on him,
A dime, another ball, is worthless. Now   10
He senses first his responsibility
In a world of possessions. People will take balls,
Balls will be lost always, little boy,
And no one buys a ball back. Money is external.
He is learning, far behind his desperate eyes,   15
The epistemology of loss, how to stand up.
Knowing what every man must one day know
And most know many days, how to stand up.
And gradually light returns to the street,
A whistle blows, the ball is out of sight,   20
Soon part of me will explore the deep and dark
Floor of the harbour. I am everywhere,

I suffer and move, my mind and my heart move
With all that move me, under the water
Or whistling, I am not a little boy.   25

Elizabeth Bowen (1899–1973)

Tears, Idle Tears

Frederick burst into tears in the middle of Regent's Park. His mother, seeing what was about to happen, had cried: "Frederick, you *can't*—in the middle of Regent's Park!" Really, this was a corner, one of those lively corners just inside a big gate, where two walks meet and a bridge starts across the pretty winding lake. People were passing quickly; the bridge rang with feet. Poplars stood up like delicate green brooms; diaphanous willows whose weeping was not shocking quivered over the lake. May sun spattered gold through the breezy trees; the tulips though falling open were still gay; three girls in a long boat shot under the bridge. Frederick, knees trembling, butted towards his mother a crimson convulsed face, as though he had the idea of burying himself in her. She whipped out a handkerchief and dabbed at him with it under his grey felt hat, exclaiming meanwhile in fearful mortification: "You really haven't got to be such a *baby*!" Her tone attracted the notice of several people, who might otherwise have thought he was having something taken out of his eye.

He was too big to cry: the whole scene was disgraceful. He wore a grey flannel knickerbocker suit and looked like a schoolboy; though in fact he was seven, still doing lessons at home. His mother said to him almost every week: "I don't know what they will think when you go to school!" His tears were a shame of which she could speak to no one; no offensive weakness of body could have upset her more. Once she had got so far as taking her pen up to write to the Mother's Advice Column of a helpful woman's weekly about them. She began: "I am a widow; young, good tempered, and my friends all tell me that I have great control. But my little boy—" She intended to sign herself "Mrs. D., Surrey." But then she had stopped and thought no, no: after all, he is Toppy's son . . . She was a gallant-looking, correct woman, wearing to-day in London a coat and skirt, a silver fox, white gloves and a dark-blue toque put on exactly right—not the sort of woman you ought to see in a Park with a great blubbering boy belonging to her. She looked a mother of sons, but not of a son of this kind, and should more properly, really, have been walking a dog. "Come on!" she said, as though the bridge, the poplars, the people staring were to be borne no longer. She began to walk on quickly, along the edge of the lake, parallel with the park's girdle of trees and the dark, haughty windows of Cornwall Terrace looking at her over the red may. They had meant to go to the Zoo, but now she had changed her mind: Frederick did not deserve the Zoo.

Frederick stumbled along beside her, too miserable to notice. His mother seldom openly punished him, but often revenged herself on him in small ways. He could feel how just this was. His own incontinence in the matter of tears was as shocking to him, as bowing-down, as annulling, as it could be to her. He never knew what happened—a cold black pit with no bottom opened inside himself; a red-hot bellwire jagged up through him from the pit of his frozen belly to the caves of his eyes. Then the hot gummy rush of tears, the convulsion of his features, the terrible square grin he felt his mouth take all made him his own shameful and squalid enemy. Despair howled round his inside like a wind, and through his streaming eyes he saw everything quake. Anyone's being there—and most of all his mother—drove this catastrophe on him. He never cried like this when he was alone.

Crying made him so abject, so outcast from other people that he went on crying out of despair. His crying was not just reflex, like a baby's; it dragged up all unseemliness into view. No wonder everyone was repelled. There is something about an abject person that rouses cruelty in the kindest breast. The plate-glass windows of the lordly houses looked at him through the may-trees with judges' eyes. Girls with their knees crossed, reading on the park benches, looked up with unkind smiles. His apathetic stumbling, his not seeing or caring that they had given up their trip to the Zoo, became more than Mrs. Dickinson, his mother, could bear. She pointed out, in a voice tense with dislike: "I'm not taking you to the Zoo."

"Mmmph-mmph-mmph," sobbed Frederick.

"You know, I so often wonder what your father would think."

"Mmmph-mmph-mmph."

"He used to be so proud of you. He and I used to look forward to what you'd be like when you were a big boy. One of the last things he ever said was: 'Frederick will take care of you.' You almost make me glad he's not here now."

"Oough-oough."

"What do you say?"

"I'm t-t-trying to stop."

"Everybody's looking at you, you know."

She was one of those women who have an unfailing sense of what not to say, and say it: despair, perversity or stubborn virtue must actuate them. She had a horror, also, of the abnormal and had to hit out at it before it could hit at her. Her husband, an R.A.F. pilot who had died two days after a ghastly crash, after two or three harrowing spaces of consciousness, had never made her ashamed or puzzled her. Their intimacies, then even his death, had had a bold naturalness.

"Listen, I shall walk on ahead," said Frederick's mother, lifting her chin with that noble, decided movement so many people liked. "You stay here and look at that duck till you've stopped that noise. Don't catch me up till you have. No, I'm really ashamed of you."

She walked on. He had *not* been making, really, so very much noise. Drawing choppy breaths, he stood still and looked at the duck that sat folded into a sleek white cypher on the green grassy margin of the lake. When it rolled one eye open over a curve, something unseeing in its expression calmed him. His mother walked away under the gay tree-shadows; her step quickened lightly, the tip of her fox fur swung. She thought of the lunch she had had with Major and Mrs. Williams, the party she would be going to at five. First, she must leave Frederick at Aunt Mary's, and what would Aunt Mary say to his bloated face? She walked fast; the gap between her and Frederick widened: she was a charming woman walking by herself.

Everybody had noticed how much courage she had; they said: "How plucky Mrs. Dickinson is." It was five years since her tragedy and she had not remarried, so that her gallantness kept on coming into play. She helped a friend with a little hat shop called *Isobel* near where they lived in Surrey, bred puppies for sale and gave the rest of her time to making a man of Frederick. She smiled nicely and carried her head high. Those two days while Toppy had lain dying she had hardly turned a hair, for his sake: no one knew when he might come conscious again. When she was not by his bed she was waiting about the hospital. The chaplain hanging about her and the doctor had given thanks that there were women like this; another officer's wife who had been her friend had said she was braver than could be good for anyone. When Toppy finally died the other woman had put the unflinching widow into a taxi and driven back with her to the Dickinsons' bungalow. She kept saying: "Cry, dear, cry: you'd feel better." She made tea and clattered about, repeating: "Don't mind me, darling: just have a big cry." The strain became so great that tears streamed down her own face. Mrs. Dickinson looked past her palely, with a polite smile. The empty-feeling bungalow with its rustling curtains still smelt of Toppy's pipe; his slippers were under a chair. Then Mrs. Dickinson's friend, almost tittering with despair, thought of a poem of Tennyson's she had learnt as a child. She said: "Where's Frederick? He's quiet. Do you think he's asleep?" The widow, rising, perfectly automatic, led her into the room where Frederick lay in his cot. A nursemaid rose from beside him, gave them one morbid look and scurried away. The two-year-old baby, flushed, and drawing up his upper lip in his sleep as his father used to do, lay curved under his blue blanket, clenching one fist on nothing. Something suddenly seemed to strike his mother, who, slumping down by the cot, ground her face and forehead into the fluffy blanket, then began winding the blanket round her two fists. Her convulsions, though proper, were fearful: the cot shook. The friend crept away into the kitchen, where she stayed an half-hour, muttering to the maid. They made more tea and waited for Mrs. Dickinson to give full birth to her grief. Then extreme silence drew them back to the cot. Mrs. Dickinson knelt asleep, her profile pressed to the blanket, one arm crooked over the baby's form. Under his mother's arm, as still as an image, Frederick lay wide awake, not making a sound. In conjunction with a certain look in his eyes, the baby's silence gave the two women the horrors. The servant said to the friend: "You would think he knew."

Mrs. Dickinson's making so few demands on pity soon rather alienated her women friends, but men liked her better for it: several of them found in her straight look an involuntary appeal to themselves alone, more exciting than coquetry, deeply, nobly exciting: several wanted to marry her. But courage had given her a new intractable kind of virgin pride: she loved it too much; she could never surrender it. "No, don't ask me that," she would say, lifting her chin and with that calm, gallant smile. "Don't spoil things. You've been splendid to me: such a support. But you see, there's Frederick. He's the man in my life now. I'm bound to put him first. That wouldn't be fair, would it?" After that, she would simply go on shaking her head. She became the perfect friend for men who wished to wish to marry but were just as glad not to, and for married men who liked just a little pathos without being upset.

Frederick had stopped crying. This left him perfectly blank, so that he stared at the duck with abstract intensity, perceiving its moulded feathers and porcelain-smooth neck. The burning, swirling film had cleared away from his eyes, and his diaphragm felt relief, as when retching has stopped. He forgot his focus of grief and forgot his mother, but saw with joy a quivering bough of willow that, dropping into his gaze under his swollen eyelids, looked as pure and strong as something after the Flood. His thought clutched at the willow, weak and wrecked but happy. He knew he was now qualified to walk after his mother, but without feeling either guilty or recalcitrant did not wish to do so. He stepped over the rail—no park keeper being at hand to stop him—and, tenderly and respectfully, attempted to touch the white duck's tail. Without a blink, with automatic uncoyness, the duck slid away from Frederick into the lake. Its lovely white china body balanced on the green glass water as it propelled itself gently round the curve of the bank. Frederick saw with a passion of observation its shadowy webbed feet lazily striking out.

"The keeper'll eat you," said a voice behind him.

Frederick looked cautiously round with his bunged-up eyes. The *individual* who had spoken sat on a park bench; it was a girl with a despatch case beside her. Her big bony knee-joints stuck out through her thin crepe-de-chine dress; she was hatless and her hair made a frizzy, pretty outline, but she wore spectacles, her skin had burnt dull red: her smile and the cock of her head had about them something pungent and energetic, not like a girl's at all. "Whatcher mean, eat me?"

"You're on his grass. And putting salt on his duck's tail."

Frederick stepped back carefully over the low rail. "I haven't got any salt." He looked up and down the walk: his mother was out of sight but from the direction of the bridge a keeper was approaching, still distant but with an awesome gait. "My goodness," the girl said, "what's been biting *you*?" Frederick was at a loss. "Here," she said, "have an apple." She opened her case, which was full of folded grease-paper that must have held sandwiches, and rummaged out an apple with a waxy, bright skin. Frederick came up, tentative as a pony, and finally took the apple. His breath was still hitching and catching; he did not wish to speak.

"Go on," she said, "swallow: it'll settle your chest. Where's your mother gone off to? What's all the noise about?" Frederick only opened his jaws as wide as they would go, then bit slowly, deeply into the apple. The girl re-crossed her legs and tucked her thin crepe-de-chine skirt round the other knee. "What had you done—cheeked her?"

Frederick swept the mouthful of apple into one cheek. "No," he said shortly. "Cried."

"I should say you did. Bellowed. I watched you all down the path." There was something ruminative in the girl's tone that made her remark really not at all offensive; in fact, she looked at Frederick as though she were meeting an artist who had just done a turn. He had been standing about, licking and biting the apple, but now he came and sat down at the other end of the bench. "How do you do it?" she said.

Frederick only turned away: his ears began burning again.

"What gets at you?" she said.

"Don't know."

"Someone coming it over you? I know another boy who cries like you, but he's older. He knots himself up and bellows."

"What's his name?"

"George."

"Does he go to school?"

"Oh, lord, no; he's a boy at the place where I used to work." She raised one arm, leaned back, and watched four celluloid bangles, each of a different colour, slide down it to her elbow joint, where they stuck. "He doesn't know why he does it," she said, "but he's got to. It's as though he saw something. You can't ask him. Some people take him that way: girls do. I never did. It's as if he knew about something he'd better not. I said once, well what just *is* it, and he said if he *could* tell me he wouldn't do it. I said, well, what's the *reason*, and he said, well, what's the reason not to? I knew him well at one time."

Frederick spat out two pips, looked round cautiously for the keeper, then dropped the apple-core down the back of the seat. "Where's George live?"

"I don't know now," she said, "I often wonder. I got sacked from that place where I used to work, and he went right off and I never saw him again. You snap out of that, if you can, before you are George's age. It does you no good. It's all in the way you see things. Look, there's your mother back. Better move, or there'll be *more* trouble." She held out her hand to Frederick, and when he put his in it shook hands so cheerfully, with such tough decision, that the four celluloid bangles danced on her wrist. "You and George," she said. "Funny to meet two of you. Well, good-bye, Henry: cheer up."

"I'm Frederick."

"Well, cheer up, Freddie."

As Frederick walked away, she smoothed down the sandwich papers inside her despatch case and snapped the case shut again. Then she put a finger under her hair at each side, to tuck her spectacles firmly down on her ears. Her mouth, an unreddened line across her harsh-burnt face, still wore the same truculent, homely smile. She crossed her arms under the flat chest, across her stomach, and sat there holding her elbows idly, wagging one foot in its fawn sandal, looking fixedly at the lake through her spectacles wondering about George. She had the afternoon, as she had no work. She saw George's face lifted abjectly from his arms on a table, blotchy over his clerk's collar. The eyes of George and Frederick seemed to her to be wounds in the world's surface, through which its inner, terrible, unassuageable, necessary sorrow constantly bled away and as constantly welled up.

Mrs. Dickinson came down the walk under the band of trees, carefully unanxious, looking lightly at objects to see if Frederick were near them; he had been a long time. Then she saw Frederick shaking hands with a sort of girl on a bench and starting to come her way. So she quickly turned her frank, friendly glance on the lake, down which, as though to greet her, a swan came swimming. She touched her fox fur lightly, sliding it up her shoulder. What a lovely mother to have. "Well, Frederick," she said, as he came into earshot, "coming?" Wind sent a puff of red mayflowers through the air. She stood still and waited for Frederick to come up. She could not think what to do now: they had an hour to put in before they were due at Aunt Mary's. But this only made her manner calmer and more decisive.

Frederick gave a great skip, opened his mouth wide, shouted: "Oo, I say, mother, I nearly caught a duck!"

"Frederick, dear, how silly you are: you couldn't."

"Oo, yes, I could, I could. If I'd had salt for its tail!" Years later, Frederick could still remember, with ease, pleasure and with a sense of lonely shame being gone, that calm white duck swimming off round the bank. But George's friend with the bangles, and George's trouble, fell through a cleft in his memory and were forgotten soon.

E. E. Cummings (1894–1962)
my father moved through dooms of love

> my father moved through dooms of love
> through sames of am through haves of give,
> singing each morning out of each night
> my father moved through depths of height

this motionless forgetful where
turned at his glance to shining here;
that if(so timid air is firm)
under his eyes would stir and squirm   5

newly as from unburied which
floats the first who, his april touch
drove sleeping selves to swarm their fates   10
woke dreamers to their ghostly roots

and should some why completely weep
my father's fingers brought her sleep:
vainly no smallest voice might cry   15
for he could feel the mountains grow.

Lifting the valleys of the sea
my father moved through griefs of joy;
praising a forehead called the moon
singing desire into begin   20

joy was his song and joy so pure
a heart of star by him could steer
and pure so now and now so yes
the wrists of twilight would rejoice

keen as midsummer's keen beyond   25
conceiving mind of sun will stand,
so strictly(over utmost him
so hugely)stood my father's dream

his flesh was flesh his blood was blood:
no hungry man but wished him food;   30
no cripple wouldn't creep one mile
uphill to only see him smile.

Scorning the pomp of must and shall
my father moved through dooms of feel;
his anger was as right as rain   35
his pity was as green as grain

septembering arms of year extend
less humbly wealth to foe and friend
than he to foolish and to wise
offered immeasurable is   40

proudly and(by octobering flame
beckoned)as earth will downward climb,

so naked for immortal work
his shoulders marched against the dark

his sorrow was as true as bread: 45
no liar looked him in the head;
if every friend became his foe
he'd laugh and build a world with snow.

My father moved through theys of we,
singing each new leaf out of each tree   50
(and every child was sure that spring
danced when she heard my father sing)

then let men kill which cannot share,
let blood and flesh be mud and mire,
scheming imagine, passion willed,   55
freedom a drug that's bought and sold

giving to steal and cruel kind,
a heart to fear, to doubt a mind,
to differ a disease of same,
conform the pinnacle of am   60

though dull were all we taste as bright,
bitter all utterly things sweet,
maggoty minus and dumb death
all we inherit, all bequeath

and nothing quite so least as truth   65
—i say though hate were why men breathe—
because my father lived his soul
love is the whole and more than all

William Faulkner (1897–1962)
Barn Burning

The store in which the Justice of the Peace's court was sitting smelled of cheese.
The boy, crouched on his nail keg at the back of the crowded room, knew he smelled
cheese, and more: from where he sat he could see the ranked shelves close-packed
with the solid, squat, dynamic shapes of tin cans whose labels his stomach read, not
from the lettering which meant nothing to his mind but from the scarlet devils and the

silver curve of fish—this, the cheese which he knew he smelled and the hermetic meat which his intestines believed he smelled coming in intermittent gusts momentary and brief between the other constant one, the smell and sense just a little of fear because mostly of despair and grief, the old fierce pull of blood. He could not see the table where the Justice sat and before which his father and his father's enemy (*our enemy* he thought in that despair; *ourn! mine and hisn both! He's my father!*) stood, but he could hear them, the two of them that is, because his father had said no word yet:

"But what proof have you, Mr. Harris?"

"I told you. The hog got into my corn. I caught it up and sent it back to him. He had no fence that would hold it. I told him so, warned him. The next time I put the hog in my pen. When he came to get it I gave him enough wire to patch up his pen. The next time I put the hog up and kept it. I rode down to his house and saw the wire I gave him still rolled on to the spool in his yard. I told him he could have the hog when he paid me a dollar pound fee. That evening a nigger came with the dollar and got the hog. He was a strange nigger. He said, 'He say to tell you wood and hay kin burn.' I said, 'What?' 'That whut he say to tell you,' the nigger said. 'Wood and hay kin burn.' That night my barn burned. I got the stock out but I lost the barn."

"Where is the nigger? Have you got him?"

"He was a strange nigger, I tell you. I don't know what became of him."

"But that's not proof. Don't you see that's not proof?"

"Get that boy up here. He knows." For a moment the boy thought too that the man meant his older brother until Harris said, "Not him. The little one. The boy," and, crouching, small for his age, small and wiry like his father, in patched and faded jeans even too small for him, with straight, uncombed, brown hair and eyes gray and wild as storm scud, he saw the men between himself and the table part and become a lane of grim faces, at the end of which he saw the Justice, a shabby, collarless, graying man in spectacles, beckoning him. He felt no floor under his bare feet; he seemed to walk beneath the palpable weight of the grim turning faces. His father, stiff in his black Sunday coat donned not for the trial but for the moving, did not even look at him. *He aims for me to lie,* he thought, again with that frantic grief and despair. *And I will have to do hit.*

"What's your name, boy?" the Justice said.

"Colonel Sartoris Snopes," the boy whispered.

"Hey?" the Justice said. "Talk louder. Colonel Sartoris? I reckon anybody named for Colonel Sartoris in this country can't help but tell the truth, can they?" The boy said nothing. *Enemy! Enemy!* he thought; for a moment he could not even see, could not see that the Justice's face was kindly or discern that his voice was troubled when he spoke to the man named Harris: "Do you want me to question this boy?" But he could hear, and during those subsequent long seconds while there was absolutely no sound in the crowded little room save that of quiet and intent breathing it was as if he had swung outward at the end of a grape vine, over a ravine, and at the top of the swing had been caught in a prolonged instant of mesmerized gravity, weightless in time.

"No!" Harris said violently, explosively. "Damnation! Send him out of here!" Now time, the fluid world, rushed beneath him again, the voices coming to him again through the smell of cheese and sealed meat, the fear and despair and the old grief of blood:

"This case is closed. I can't find against you, Snopes, but I can give you advice. Leave this country and don't come back to it."

His father spoke for the first time, his voice cold and harsh, level, without emphasis: "I aim to. I don't figure to stay in a country among people who . . ." he said something unprintable and vile, addressed to no one.

"That'll do," the Justice said. "Take your wagon and get out of this country before dark. Case dismissed."

His father turned, and he followed the stiff black coat, the wiry figure walking a little stiffly from where a Confederate provost's man's musket ball had taken him in the heel on a stolen horse thirty years ago, followed the two backs now, since his other brother had appeared from somewhere in the crowd, no taller than the father but thicker, chewing tobacco steadily, between the two lines of grim-faced men and out of the store and across the worn gallery and down the sagging steps and among the dogs and half-grown boys in the mild May dust, where as he passed a voice hissed:

"Barn burner!"

Again he could not see, whirling; there was a face in a red haze, moonlike, bigger than the full moon, the owner of it half again his size, he leaping in the red haze toward the face, feeling no blow, feeling no shock when his head struck the earth, scrabbling up and leaping again, feeling no blow this time either and tasting no blood, scrabbling up to see the other boy in full flight and himself already leaping into pursuit as his father's hand jerked him back, the harsh, cold voice speaking above him: "Go get in the wagon."

It stood in a grove of locusts and mulberries across the road. His two hulking sisters in their Sunday dresses and his mother and her sister in calico and sunbonnets were already in it, sitting on and among the sorry residue of the dozen and more movings which even the boy could remember—the battered stove, the broken beds and chairs, the clock inlaid with mother-of-pearl, which would not run, stopped at some fourteen minutes past two o'clock of a dead and forgotten day and time, which had been his mother's dowry. She was crying, though when she saw him she drew her sleeve across her face and began to descend from the wagon. "Get back," the father said.

"He's hurt. I got to get some water and wash his . . ."

"Get back in the wagon," his father said. He got in too, over the tail-gate. His father mounted to the seat where the older brother already sat and struck the gaunt mules two savage blows with the peeled willow, but without heat. It was not even sadistic; it was exactly that same quality which in later years would cause his descendants to over-run the engine before putting a motor car into motion, striking and reining back in the same movement. The wagon went on, the store with its quiet crowd of grimly watching men dropped behind; a curve in the road hid it. *Forever* he thought. *Maybe he's done satisfied now, now that he has* . . . stopping himself, not to say it aloud even to himself. His mother's hand touched his shoulder.

"Does hit hurt?" she said.

"Naw," he said. "Hit don't hurt. Lemme be."

"Can't you wipe some of the blood off before hit dries?"

"I'll wash to-night," he said. "Lemme be, I tell you."

The wagon went on. He did not know where they were going. None of them ever did or ever asked, because it was always somewhere, always a house of sorts waiting for them a day or two days or even three days away. Likely his father had already arranged to make a crop on another farm before he . . . Again he had to stop himself. He (the father) always did. There was something about his wolflike independence and even courage when the advantage was at least neutral which impressed strangers, as if they got from his latent ravening ferocity not so much a sense of dependability as a feeling that his ferocious conviction in the rightness of his own actions would be of advantage to all whose interest lay with his.

That night they camped, in a grove of oaks and beeches where a spring ran. The nights were still cool and they had a fire against it, of a rail lifted from a nearby fence and cut into lengths—a small fire, neat, niggard almost, a shrewd fire; such fires were his father's habit and custom always, even in freezing weather. Older, the boy might have remarked this and wondered why not a big one; why should not a man who had not only seen the waste and extravagance of war, but who had in his blood an inherent voracious prodigality with material not his own, have burned everything in sight? Then he might have gone a step farther and thought that that was the reason: that niggard blaze was the living fruit of nights passed during those four years in the woods hiding from all men, blue or gray, with his strings of horses (captured horses, he called them). And older still, he might have divined the true reason: that the element of fire spoke to some deep mainspring of his father's being, as the element of steel or of powder spoke to other men, as the one weapon for the preservation of integrity, else breath were not worth the breathing, and hence to be regarded with respect and used with discretion.

But he did not think this now and he had seen those same niggard blazes all his life. He merely ate his supper beside it and was already half asleep over his iron plate when his father called him, and once more he followed the stiff back, the stiff and ruthless limp, up the slope and on to the starlit road where, turning, he could see his father against the stars but without face or depth—a shape black, flat, and bloodless as though cut from tin in the iron folds of the frockcoat which had not been made for him, the voice harsh like tin and without heat like tin:

"You were fixing to tell them. You would have told him." He didn't answer. His father struck him with the flat of his hand on the side of the head, hard but without heat, exactly as he had struck the two mules at the store, exactly as he would strike either of them with any stick in order to kill a horse fly, his voice still without heat or anger: "You're getting to be a man. You got to learn. You got to learn to stick to your own blood or you ain't going to have any blood to stick to you. Do you think either of them, any man there this morning, would? Don't you know all they wanted was a chance to get at me because they knew I had them beat? Eh?" Later, twenty years later, he was to tell himself, "If I had said they wanted only truth, justice, he would have hit me again." But now he said nothing. He was not crying. He just stood there. "Answer me," his father said.

"Yes," he whispered. His father turned.

"Get on to bed. We'll be there tomorrow."

Tomorrow they were there. In the early afternoon the wagon stopped before a paintless two-room house identical almost with the dozen others it had stopped before even in the boy's ten years, and again, as on the other dozen occasions, his mother and aunt got down and began to unload the wagon, although his two sisters and his father and brother had not moved.

"Likely hit ain't fitten for hawgs," one of the sisters said.

"Nevertheless, fit it will and you'll hog it and like it," his father said. "Get out of them chairs and help your Ma unload."

The two sisters got down, big, bovine, in a flutter of cheap ribbons; one of them drew from the jumbled wagon bed a battered lantern, the other a worn broom. His father handed the reins to the older son and began to climb stiffly over the wheel. "When they get unloaded, take the team to the barn and feed them." Then he said, and at first the boy thought he was still speaking to his brother: "Come with me."

"Me?" he said.

"Yes," his father said. "You."

"Abner," his mother said. His father paused and looked back—the harsh level stare beneath the shaggy, graying, irascible brows.

"I reckon I'll have a word with the man that aims to begin tomorrow owning me body and soul for the next eight months."

They went back up the road. A week ago—or before last night, that is—he would have asked where they were going, but not now. His father had struck him before last night but never before had he paused afterward to explain why; it was as if the blow and the following calm, outrageous voice still rang, repercussed, divulging nothing to him save the terrible handicap of being young, the light weight of his few years, just heavy enough to prevent his soaring free of the world as it seemed to be ordered but not heavy enough to keep him footed solid in it, to resist it and try to change the course of its events.

Presently he could see the grove of oaks and cedars and the other flowering trees and shrubs where the house would be, though not the house yet. They walked beside a fence massed with honeysuckle and Cherokee roses and came to a gate swinging open between two brick pillars, and now, beyond a sweep of drive, he saw the house for the first time and at that instant he forgot his father and the terror and despair both, and even when he remembered his father again (who had not stopped) the terror and despair did not return. Because, for all the twelve movings, they had sojourned until now in a poor country, a land of small farms and fields and houses, and he had never seen a house like this before. *Hit's big as a courthouse* he thought quietly, with a surge of peace and joy whose reason he could not have thought into words, being too young for that: *They are safe from him. People whose lives are a part of this peace and dignity are beyond his touch, he no more to them than a buzzing wasp: capable of stinging for a little moment but that's all; the spell of this peace and dignity rendering even the barns and stable and cribs which belong to it impervious to the puny flames he might contrive . . .* this, the peace and joy, ebbing for an instant as he looked again at the stiff black back, the stiff and implacable limp of the figure which was not dwarfed by the house, for the reason that it had never looked big anywhere and which now, against the serene columned backdrop, had more than ever that impervious quality of something cut ruthlessly from tin, depthless, as though, sidewise to the sun, it would cast no shadow. Watching him, the boy remarked the absolutely unde-viating course which his father held and saw the stiff foot come squarely down in a pile of fresh droppings where a horse had stood in the drive and which his father could have avoided by a simple change of stride. But it ebbed only for a moment, though he could not have thought this into words either, walking on in the spell of the house, which he could even want but without envy, without sorrow, certainly never with that ravening and jealous rage which unknown to him walked in the ironlike black coat before him: *Maybe he will feel it too. Maybe it will even change him now from what maybe he couldn't help but be.*

They crossed the portico. Now he could hear his father's stiff foot as it came down on the boards with clocklike finality, a sound out of all proportion to the displace-ment of the body it bore and which was not dwarfed either by the white door before it, as though it had attained to a sort of vicious and ravening minimum not to be dwarfed by anything—the flat, wide, black hat, the formal coat of broadcloth which had once been black but which had now that friction-glazed greenish cast of the bodies of old house flies, the lifted sleeve which was too large, the lifted hand like a curled claw. The door opened so promptly that the boy knew the Negro must have been watching them all the time, an old man with neat grizzled hair, in a linen jacket, who stood barring the door with his body, saying, "Wipe yo foots, white man, fo you come in here. Major ain't home nohow."

"Get out of my way, nigger," his father said, without heat too, flinging the door back and the Negro also and entering, his hat still on his head. And now the boy saw the prints of the stiff foot on the doorjamb and saw them appear on the pale rug behind the machinelike deliberation of the foot which seemed to bear (or transmit) twice the weight which the body compassed. The Negro was shouting "Miss Lula! Miss Lula!" somewhere behind them, then the boy, deluged as though by a warm wave by a suave turn of carpeted stair and a pendant glitter of chandeliers and a mute gleam of gold frames, heard the swift feet and saw her too, a lady—perhaps he had never seen her like before either—in a gray, smooth gown with lace at the throat and an apron tied at the waist and the sleeves turned back, wiping cake or biscuit dough from her hands with a towel as she came up the hall, looking not at his father at all but at the tracks on the blond rug with an expression of incredulous amazement.

"I tried," the Negro cried. "I tole him to . . ."

"Will you please go away?" she said in a shaking voice. "Major de Spain is not at home. Will you please go away?"

His father had not spoken again. He did not speak again. He did not even look at her. He just stood stiff in the center of the rug, in his hat, the shaggy iron-gray brows twitching slightly above the pebble-colored eyes as he appeared to examine the house with brief deliberation. Then with the same deliberation he turned; the boy watched him pivot on the good leg and saw the stiff foot drag round the arc of the turning, leaving a final long and fading smear. His father never looked at it, he never once looked down at the rug. The Negro held the door. It closed behind them, upon the hysteric and indistinguishable woman-wail. His father stopped at the top of the steps and scraped his boot clean on the edge of it. At the gate he stopped again. He stood for a moment, planted stiffly on the stiff foot, looking back at the house. "Pretty and white, ain't it?" he said. "That's sweat. Nigger sweat. Maybe it ain't white enough yet to suit him. Maybe he wants to mix some white sweat with it."

Two hours later the boy was chopping wood behind the house within which his mother and aunt and the two sisters (the mother and aunt, not the two girls, he knew that; even at this distance and muffled by walls the flat loud voices of the two girls emanated an incorrigible idle inertia) were setting up the stove to prepare a meal, when he heard the hooves and saw the linen-clad man on a fine sorrel mare, whom he recognized even before he saw the rolled rug in front of the Negro youth following on a fat bay carriage horse—a suffused, angry face vanishing, still at full gallop, beyond the corner of the house where his father and brother were sitting in the two tilted chairs; and a moment later, almost before he could have put the axe down, he heard the hooves again and watched the sorrel mare go back out of the yard, already galloping again. Then his father began to shout one of the sisters' names, who presently emerged backward from the kitchen door dragging the rolled rug along the ground by one end while the other sister walked behind it.

"If you ain't going to tote, go on and set up the wash pot," the first said.

"You, Sarty!" the second shouted. "Set up the wash pot!" His father appeared at the door, framed against that shabbiness, as he had been against that other bland perfection, impervious to either, the mother's anxious face at his shoulder.

"Go on," the father said. "Pick it up." The two sisters stooped, broad, lethargic; stooping, they presented an incredible expanse of pale cloth and a flutter of tawdry ribbons.

"If I thought enough of a rug to have to git hit all the way from France I wouldn't keep hit where folks coming in would have to tromp on hit," the first said. They raised the rug.

"Abner," the mother said. "Let me do it."

"You go back and git dinner," his father said. "I'll tend to this."

From the woodpile through the rest of the afternoon the boy watched them, the rug spread flat in the dust beside the bubbling wash-pot, the two sisters stooping over it with that profound and lethargic reluctance, while the father stood over them in turn, implacable and grim, driving them though never raising his voice again. He could smell the harsh homemade lye they were using; he saw his mother come to the door once and look toward them with an expression not anxious now but very like despair; he saw his father turn, and he fell to with the axe and saw from the corner of his eye his father raise from the ground a flattish fragment of field stone and examine it and return to the pot, and this time his mother actually spoke: "Abner. Abner. Please don't. Please, Abner."

Then he was done too. It was dusk; the whippoorwills had already begun. He could smell coffee from the room where they would presently eat the cold food remaining from the mid-afternoon meal, though when he entered the house he realized they were having coffee again probably because there was a fire on the hearth, before which the rug now lay spread over the backs of the two chairs. The tracks of his father's foot were gone. Where they had been were now long, water-cloudy scoriations resembling the sporadic course of a lilliputian mowing machine.

It still hung there while they ate the cold food and then went to bed, scattered without order or claim up and down the two rooms, his mother in one bed, where his father would later lie, the older brother in the other, himself, the aunt, and the two sisters on pallets on the floor. But his father was not in bed yet. The last thing the boy remembered was the depthless, harsh silhouette of the hat and coat bending over the rug and it seemed to him that he had not even closed his eyes when the silhouette was standing over him, the fire almost dead behind it, the stiff foot prodding him awake. "Catch up the mule," his father said.

When he returned with the mule his father was standing in the black door, the rolled rug over his shoulder. "Ain't you going to ride?" he said.

"No. Give me your foot."

He bent his knee into his father's hand, the wiry, surprising power flowed smoothly, rising, he rising with it, on to the mule's bare back (they had owned a saddle once; the boy could remember it though not when or where) and with the same effortlessness his father swung the rug up in front of him. Now in the starlight they retraced the afternoon's path, up the dusty road rife with honeysuckle, through the gate and up the black tunnel of the drive to the lightless house, where he sat on the mule and felt the rough warp of the rug drag across his thighs and vanish.

"Don't you want me to help?" he whispered. His father did not answer and now he heard again that stiff foot striking the hollow portico with that wooden and clocklike deliberation, that outrageous overstatement of the weight it carried. The rug, hunched, not flung (the boy could tell that even in the darkness) from his father's shoulder struck the angle of wall and floor with a sound unbelievably loud, thunderous, then the foot again, unhurried and enormous; a light came on in the house and the boy sat, tense, breathing steadily and quietly and just a little fast, though the foot itself did not increase its beat at all, descending the steps now; now the boy could see him.

"Don't you want to ride now?" he whispered. "We kin both ride now," the light within the house altering now, flaring up and sinking. *He's coming down the stairs now*, he thought. He had already ridden the mule up beside the horse block; presently his father was up behind him and he doubled the reins over and slashed the mule across the neck, but before the animal could begin to trot the hard, thin arm came round him, the hard, knotted hand jerking the mule back to a walk.

In the first red rays of the sun they were in the lot, putting plow gear on the mules. This time the sorrel mare was in the lot before he heard it at all, the rider collarless and even bareheaded, trembling, speaking in a shaking voice as the woman in the house had done, his father merely looking up once before stooping again to the hame he was buckling, so that the man on the mare spoke to his stooping back:

"You must realize you have ruined that rug. Wasn't there anybody here, any of your women . . ." he ceased, shaking, the boy watching him, the older brother leaning now in the stable door, chewing, blinking slowly and steadily at nothing apparently. "It cost a hundred dollars. But you never had a hundred dollars. You never will. So I'm going to charge you twenty bushels of corn against your crop. I'll add it in your contract and when you come to the commissary you can sign it. That won't keep Mrs. de Spain quiet but maybe it will teach you to wipe your feet off before you enter her house again."

Then he was gone. The boy looked at his father, who still had not spoken or even looked up again, who was now adjusting the logger-head in the hame.

"Pap," he said. His father looked at him—the inscrutable face, the shaggy brows beneath which the gray eyes glinted coldly. Suddenly the boy went toward him, fast, stopping as suddenly. "You done the best you could!" he cried. "If he wanted hit done different why didn't he wait and tell you how? He won't git no twenty bushels! He won't git none! We'll gether hit and hide hit! I kin watch . . ."

"Did you put the cutter back in that straight stock like I told you?"

"No, sir," he said.

"Then go do it."

That was Wednesday. During the rest of that week he worked steadily, at what was within his scope and some which was beyond it, with an industry that did not need to be driven nor even commanded twice; he had this from his mother, with the difference that some at least of what he did he liked to do, such as splitting wood with the half-size axe which his mother and aunt had earned, or saved money somehow, to present him with at Christmas. In company with the two older women (and on one afternoon, even one of the sisters), he built pens for the shoat and the cow which were a part of his father's contract with the landlord, and one afternoon, his father being absent, gone somewhere on one of the mules, he went to the field.

They were running a middle buster now, his brother holding the plow straight while he handled the reins, and walking beside the straining mule, the rich black soil shearing cool and damp against his bare ankles, he thought *Maybe this is the end of it*.

Maybe even that twenty bushels that seems hard to have to pay for just a rug will be a cheap price for him to stop forever and always from being what he used to be; thinking, dreaming now, so that his brother had to speak sharply to him to mind the mule: *Maybe he even won't collect the twenty bushels. Maybe it will all add up and balance and vanish—corn, rug, fire; the terror and grief, the being pulled two ways like between two teams of horses—gone, done with for ever and ever.*

Then it was Saturday; he looked up from beneath the mule he was harnessing and saw his father in the black coat and hat. "Not that," his father said. "The wagon gear." And then, two hours later, sitting in the wagon bed behind his father and brother on the seat, the wagon accomplished a final curve, and he saw the weathered paintless store with its tattered tobacco- and patent-medicine posters and the tethered wagons and saddle animals below the gallery. He mounted the gnawed steps behind his father and brother, and there again was the lane of quiet, watching faces for the three of them to walk through. He saw the man in spectacles sitting at the plank table and he did not need to be told this was a Justice of the Peace; he sent one glare of fierce, exultant, partisan defiance at the man in collar and cravat now, whom he had seen but twice before in his life, and that on a galloping horse, who now wore on his face an expression not of rage but of amazed unbelief which the boy could not have known was at the incredible circumstance of being sued by one of his own tenants, and came and stood against his father and cried at the Justice: "He ain't done it! He ain't burnt . . ."

"Go back to the wagon," his father said.

"Burnt?" the Justice said. "Do I understand this rug was burned too?"

"Does anybody here claim it was?" his father said. "Go back to the wagon." But he did not, he merely retreated to the rear of the room, crowded as that other had been, but not to sit down this time, instead, to stand pressing among the motionless bodies, listening to the voices:

"And you claim twenty bushels of corn is too high for the damage you did to the rug?"

"He brought the rug to me and said he wanted the tracks washed out of it. I washed the tracks out and took the rug back to him."

"But you didn't carry the rug back to him in the same condition it was in before you made the tracks on it."

His father did not answer, and now for perhaps half a minute there was no sound at all save that of breathing, the faint, steady suspiration of complete and intent listening.

"You decline to answer that, Mr. Snopes?" Again his father did not answer. "I'm going to find against you, Mr. Snopes. I'm going to find that you were responsible for the injury to Major de Spain's rug and hold you liable for it. But twenty bushels of corn seems a little high for a man in your circumstances to have to pay. Major de Spain claims it cost a hundred dollars. October corn will be worth about fifty cents. I figure that if Major de Spain can stand a ninety-five dollar loss on something he paid cash for, you can stand a five-dollar loss you haven't earned yet. I hold you in damages to Major de Spain to the amount of ten bushels of corn over and above your contract with him, to be paid to him out of your crop at gathering time. Court adjourned."

It had taken no time hardly, the morning was but half begun. He thought they would return home and perhaps back to the field, since they were late, far behind all other farmers. But instead his father passed on behind the wagon, merely indicating with his hand for the older brother to follow with it, and crossed the road toward the blacksmith shop opposite, pressing on after his father, overtaking him, speaking, whispering up at the harsh, calm face beneath the weathered hat: "He won't git no ten bushels neither. He won't git one. We'll . . ." until his father glanced for an instant down at him, the face absolutely calm, the grizzled eyebrows tangled above the cold eyes, the voice almost pleasant, almost gentle:

"You think so? Well, we'll wait till October anyway."

The matter of the wagon—the setting of a spoke or two and the tightening of the tires—did not take long either, the business of the tires accomplished by driving the wagon into the spring branch behind the shop and letting it stand there, the mules nuzzling into the water from time to time, and the boy on the seat with the idle reins, looking up the slope and through the sooty tunnel of the shed where the slow hammer rang and where his father sat on an upended cypress bolt, easily, either talking or listening, still sitting there when the boy brought the dripping wagon up out of the branch and halted it before the door.

"Take them on to the shade and hitch," his father said. He did so and returned. His father and the smith and a third man squatting on his heels inside the door were talking, about crops and animals; the boy, squatting too in the ammoniac dust and hoof-parings and scales of rust, heard his father tell a long and unhurried story out of the time before the birth of the older brother even when he had been a professional horsetrader. And then his father came up beside him where he stood before a tattered last year's circus poster on the other side of the store, gazing rapt and quiet at the scarlet horses, the incredible poisings and convolutions of tulle and tights and the painted leers of comedians, and said, "It's time to eat."

But not at home. Squatting beside his brother against the front wall, he watched his father emerge from the store and produce from a paper sack a segment of cheese and divide it carefully and deliberately into three with his pocket knife and produce crackers from the same sack. They all three squatted on the gallery and ate, slowly, without talking; then in the store again, they drank from a tin dipper tepid water smelling of the cedar bucket and of living beech trees. And still they did not go home. It was a horse lot this time, a tall rail fence upon and along which men stood and sat and out of which one by one horses were led, to be walked and trotted and then cantered back and forth along the road while the slow swapping and buying went on and the sun began to slant westward, they—the three of them—watching and listening, the older brother with his muddy eyes and his steady, inevitable tobacco, the father commenting now and then on certain of the animals, to no one in particular.

It was after sundown when they reached home. They ate supper by lamplight, then, sitting on the doorstep, the boy watched the night fully accomplish, listening to the whippoorwills and the frogs, when he heard his mother's voice: "Abner! No! No! Oh, God. Oh, God. Abner!" and he rose, whirled, and saw the altered light through the door where a candle stub now burned in a bottle neck on the table and his father, still in the hat and coat, at once formal and burlesque as though dressed carefully for some shabby and ceremonial violence, emptying the reservoir of the lamp back into the five-gallon kerosene can from which it had been filled, while the mother tugged at his arm until he shifted the lamp to the other hand and flung her back, not savagely or viciously, just hard, into the wall, her hands flung out against the wall for balance, her mouth open and in her face the same quality of hopeless despair as had been in her voice. Then his father saw him standing in the door.

"Go to the barn and get that can of oil we were oiling the wagon with," he said. The boy did not move. Then he could speak.

"What . . ." he cried. "What are you . . ."

"Go get that oil," his father said. "Go."

Then he was moving, running, outside the house, toward the stable: this the old habit, the old blood which he had not been permitted to choose for himself, which had been bequeathed him willy nilly and which had run for so long (and who knew where, battening on what of outrage and savagery and lust) before it came to him. *I could keep on,* he thought. *I could run on and on and never look back, never need to see his face again. Only I can't. I can't,* the rusted can in his hand now, the liquid sploshing in it as he ran back to the house and into it, into the sound of his mother's weeping in the next room, and handed the can to his father.

"Ain't you going to even send a nigger?" he cried. "At least you sent a nigger before!"

This time his father didn't strike him. The hand came even faster than the blow had, the same hand which had set the can on the table with almost excruciating care flashing from the can toward him too quick for him to follow it, gripping him by the back of his shirt and on to tiptoe before he had seen it quit the can, the face stooping at him in breathless and frozen ferocity, the cold, dead voice speaking over him to the older brother who leaned against the table, chewing with that steady, curious, side-wise motion of cows:

"Empty the can into the big one and go on. I'll catch up with you."

"Better tie him up to the bedpost," the brother said.

"Do like I told you," the father said. Then the boy was moving, his bunched shirt and the hard, bony hand between his shoulderblades, his toes just touching the floor, across the room and into the other, past the sisters sitting with spread heavy thighs in the two chairs over the cold hearth, and to where his mother and aunt sat side by side on the bed, the aunt's arms about his mother's shoulders.

"Hold him," the father said. The aunt made a startled movement. "Not you," the father said. "Lennie. Take hold of him. I want to see you do it." His mother took him by the wrist. "You'll hold him better than that. If he gets loose don't you know what he is going to do? He will go up yonder." He jerked his head toward the road. "Maybe I'd better tie him."

"I'll hold him," his mother whispered.

"See you do then." Then his father was gone, the stiff foot heavy and measured upon the boards, ceasing at last.

Then he began to struggle. His mother caught him in both arms, he jerking and wrenching at them. He would be stronger in the end, he knew that. But he had no time to wait for it. "Lemme go!" he cried. "I don't want to have to hit you!"

"Let him go!" the aunt said. "If he don't go, before God, I am going up there myself!"

"Don't you see I can't?" his mother cried. "Sarty! Sarty! No! No! Help me, Lizzie!"

Then he was free. His aunt grasped at him but it was too late. He whirled, running, his mother stumbled forward on to her knees behind him, crying to the nearer sister: "Catch him, Net! Catch him!" But that was too late too, the sister (the sisters were twins, born at the same time, yet either of them now gave the impression of being, encompassing as much living meat and volume and weight as any other two of the family) not yet having begun to rise from the chair, her head, face, alone merely turned, presenting to him in the flying instant an astonishing expanse of young female features untroubled by any surprise even, wearing only an expression of bovine interest. Then he was out of the room, out of the house, in the mild dust of the starlit road and the heavy rifeness of honeysuckle, the pale ribbon unspooling with terrific slowness under his running feet, reaching the gate at last and turning in, running, his heart and lungs drumming, on up the drive toward the lighted house, the lighted door. He did not knock, he burst in, sobbing for breath, incapable for the moment of speech; he saw the astonished face of the Negro in the linen jacket without knowing when the Negro had appeared.

"De Spain!" he cried, panted. "Where's . . ." then he saw the white man too emerging from a white door down the hall. "Barn!" he cried. "Barn!"

"What?" the white man said. "Barn?"

"Yes!" the boy cried. "Barn!"

"Catch him!" the white man shouted.

But it was too late this time too. The Negro grasped his shirt, but the entire sleeve, rotten with washing, carried away, and he was out that door too and in the drive again, and had actually never ceased to run even while he was screaming into the white man's face.

Behind him the white man was shouting, "My horse! Fetch my horse!" and he thought for an instant of cutting across the park and climbing the fence into the road, but he did not know the park nor how high the vine-massed fence might be and he dared not risk it. So he ran on down the drive, blood and breath roaring; presently he was in the road again though he could not see it. He could not hear either: the galloping mare was almost upon him before he heard her, and even then he held his course, as if the very urgency of his wild grief and need must in a moment more find him wings, waiting until the ultimate instant to hurl himself aside and into the weed-choked roadside ditch as the horse thundered past and on, for an instant in furious silhouette against the stars, the tranquil early summer night sky which, even before the shape of the horse and rider vanished, stained abruptly and violently upward: a long, swirling roar incredible and soundless, blotting the stars, and he springing up and into the road again, running again, knowing it was too late yet still running even after he heard the shot and, an instant later, two shots, pausing now without knowing he had ceased to run, crying "Pap! Pap!", running again before he knew he had begun to run, stumbling, tripping over something and scrabbling up again without ceasing to run, looking backward over his shoulder at the glare as he got up, running on among the invisible trees, panting, sobbing, "Father! Father!"

At midnight he was sitting on the crest of a hill. He did not know it was midnight and he did not know how far he had come. But there was no glare behind him now and he sat now, his back toward what he had called home for four days anyhow, his face toward the dark woods which he would enter when breath was strong again, small, shaking steadily in the chill darkness, hugging himself into the remainder of his thin, rotten shirt, the grief and despair now no longer terror and fear but just grief and despair. *Father. My father,* he thought. "He was brave!" he cried suddenly, aloud but not loud, no more than a whisper: "He was! He was in the war! He was in Colonel Sartoris' cav'ry!" not knowing that his father had gone to that war a private in the fine old European sense, wearing no uniform, admitting the authority of and giving fidelity to no man or army or flag, going to war as Malbrouck himself did: for booty—it meant nothing and less than nothing to him if it were enemy booty or his own.

The slow constellations wheeled on. It would be dawn and then sun-up after a while and he would be hungry. But that would be tomorrow and now he was only cold, and walking would cure that. His breathing was easier now and he decided to get up and go on, and then he found that he had been asleep because he knew it was almost dawn, the night almost over. He could tell that from the whippoorwills. They were everywhere now among the dark trees below him, constant and inflectioned and ceaseless, so that, as the instant for giving over to the day birds drew nearer and nearer, there was no interval at all between them. He got up. He was a little stiff, but walking would cure that too as it would the cold, and soon there would be the sun. He went on down the hill, toward the dark woods within which the liquid silver voices of the birds called unceasing—the rapid and urgent beating of the urgent and quiring heart of the late spring night. He did not look back.

Robert Frost (1874–1963)

Birches

When I see birches bend to left and right
Across the lines of straighter darker trees,
I like to think some boy's been swinging them.
But swinging doesn't bend them down to stay
As ice storms do. Often you must have seen them.   5
Loaded with ice a sunny winter morning
After a rain. They click upon themselves
As the breeze rises, and turn many-colored
As the stir cracks and crazes their enamel.
Soon the sun's warmth makes them shed crystal shells   10
Shattering and avalanching on the snow crust—
Such heaps of broken glass to sweep away
You'd think the inner dome of heaven had fallen.
They are dragged to the withered bracken by the load,
And they seem not to break; though once they are bowed   15
So low for long, they never right themselves:
You may see their trunks arching in the woods
Years afterwards, trailing their leaves on the ground
Like girls on hands and knees that throw their hair
Before them over their heads to dry in the sun.   20
But I was going to say when Truth broke in
With all her matter of fact about the ice storm,
I should prefer to have some boy bend them
As he went out and in to fetch the cows—
Some boy too far from town to learn baseball,   25
Whose only play was what he found himself,
Summer or winter, and could play alone.
One by one he subdued his father's trees
By riding them down over and over again
Until he took the stiffness out of them,   30
And not one but hung limp, not one was left
For him to conquer. He learned all there was
To learn about not launching out too soon
And so not carrying the tree away
Clear to the ground. He always kept his poise   35
To the top branches, climbing carefully
With the same pains you use to fill a cup
Up to the brim, and even above the brim.

Then he flung outward, feet first, with a swish,
Kicking his way down through the air to the ground.   40
So was I once myself a swinger of birches.
And so I dream of going back to be.
It's when I'm weary of considerations,
And life is too much like a pathless wood
Where your face burns and tickles with the cobwebs   45
Broken across it, and one eye is weeping
From a twig's having lashed across it open.
I'd like to get away from earth awhile
And then come back to it and begin over.
May no fate willfully misunderstand me   50
And half grant what I wish and snatch me away
Not to return. Earth's the right place for love:
I don't know where it's likely to go better.
I'd like to go by climbing a birch tree,
And climb black branches up a snow-white trunk   55
Toward heaven, till the tree could bear no more,
But dipped its top and set me down again.
That would be good both going and coming back.
One could do worse than be a swinger of birches.

Angelo Gonzalez (born 1943)
Bilingualism, Pro: The Key to Basic Skills

If we accept that a child cannot learn unless taught through the language he speaks and understands; that a child who does not speak or understand English must fall behind when English is the dominant medium of instruction; that one needs to learn English so as to be able to participate in an English-speaking society; that self-esteem and motivation are necessary for effective learning; that rejection of a child's native language and culture is detrimental to the learning process: then any necessary effective educational program for limited or no English-speaking ability must incorporate the following:

- Language arts and comprehensive reading programs taught in the child's native language.
- Curriculum content areas taught in the native language to further comprehension and academic achievement.

- Intensive instruction in English.
- Use of materials sensitive to and reflecting the culture of children within the program.

Most Important Goal

The mastery of basic reading skills is the most important goal in primary education since reading is the basis for much of all subsequent learning. Ordinarily, these skills are learned at home. But where beginning reading is taught in English, only the English-speaking child profits from these early acquired skills that are prerequisites to successful reading development. Reading programs taught in English to children with Spanish as a first language waste their acquired linguistic attributes and also impede learning by forcing them to absorb skills of reading simultaneously with a new language.

Both local and national research data provide ample evidence for the efficacy of well-implemented programs. The New York City Board of Education Report on Bilingual Pupil Services for 1982–83 indicated that in all areas of the curriculum— English, Spanish and mathematics—and at all grade levels, students demonstrated statistically significant gains in tests of reading in English and Spanish and in math. In all but two of the programs reviewed, the attendance rates of students in the program, ranging from 86 to 94 percent, were higher than those of the general school population. Similar higher attendance rates were found among students in high school bilingual programs.

At Yale University, Kenji Hakuta, a linguist, reported recently on a study of working-class Hispanic students in the New Haven bilingual program. He found that children who were the most bilingual, that is, who developed English without the loss of Spanish, were brighter in both verbal and nonverbal tests. Over time, there was an increasing correlation between English and Spanish—a finding that clearly contradicts the charge that teaching in the home language is detrimental to English. Rather the two languages are interdependent within the bilingual child, reinforcing each other.

Essential Contribution

As Jim Cummins of the Ontario Institute for Studies in Education has argued, the use and development of the native language makes an essential contribution to the development of minority children's subject-matter knowledge and academic learning potential. In fact, at least three national data bases—the National Assessment of Educational Progress, National Center for Educational Statistics-High School and Beyond Studies, and the Survey of Income and Education—suggest that there are long-term positive effects among high school students who have participated in bilingual-education programs. These students are achieving higher scores on tests of verbal and mathematics skills.

These and similar findings buttress the argument stated persuasively in the recent joint recommendation of the Academy for Educational Development and the

Hazen Foundation, namely, that America needs to become a more multilingual nation and children who speak a non-English language are a national resource to be nurtured in school.

Unfortunately, the present Administration's educational policies would seem to be leading us in the opposite direction. Under the guise of protecting the common language of public life in the United States, William J. Bennett, the Secretary of Education, unleashed a frontal attack on bilingual education. In a major policy address, he engaged in rhetorical distortions about the nature and effectiveness of bilingual programs, pointing only to unnamed negative research findings to justify the Administration's retrenchment efforts.

Arguing for the need to give local school districts greater flexibility in determining appropriate methodologies in serving limited-English-proficient students, Mr. Bennett fails to realize that, in fact, districts serving large numbers of language-minority students, as is the case in New York City, do have that flexibility. Left to their own devices in implementing legal mandates, many school districts have performed poorly at providing services to all entitled language-minority students.

A Harsh Reality

The harsh reality in New York City for language-minority students was documented comprehensively last month by the Educational Priorities Panel. The panel's findings revealed that of the 113,831 students identified as being limited in English proficiency, as many as 44,000 entitled students are not receiving any bilingual services. The issue at hand is, therefore, not one of choice but rather violation of the rights of almost 40 percent of language-minority children to equal educational opportunity. In light of these findings the Reagan Administration's recent statements only serve to exacerbate existing inequities in the American educational system for linguistic-minority children. Rather than adding fuel to a misguided debate, the Administration would serve these children best by insuring the full funding of the 1984 Bilingual Education Reauthorization Act as passed by the Congress.

Thomas Gray (1716–1771)
Ode on a Distant Prospect of Eton College

Ye distant spires, ye antique towers,
That crown the wat'ry glade,
Where grateful Science still adores
Her Henry's holy shade;

And ye, that from the stately brow   5
Of Windsor's heights th' expanse below
   Of grove, of lawn, of mead survey,
Whose turf, whose shade, whose flowers among
Wanders the hoary Thames along
   His silver-winding way;   10

Ah, happy hills! ah, pleasing shade!
   Ah, fields beloved in vain,
Where once my careless childhood strayed
   A stranger yet to pain!
I feel the gales that from ye blow   15
A momentary bliss bestow,
   As waving fresh their gladsome wing,
My weary soul they seem to sooth,
And, redolent of joy and youth,
   To breathe a second spring.   20

Say, Father Thames, for thou hast seen
   Full many of sprightly race
Disporting on thy margent green
   The paths of pleasure trace,
Who foremost now delight to cleave   25
With pliant arm thy glassy wave?
   The captive linnet which enthrall?
What idle progeny succeed
To chase the rolling circle's speed,
   Or urge the flying ball?   30

While some on earnest business bent
   Their murm'ring labors ply
'Gainst graver hours, that bring constraint
   To sweeten liberty:
Some bold adventurers disdain   35
The limits of their little reign,
   And unknown regions dare descry;
Still as they run they look behind,
They hear a voice in every wind,
   And snatch a fearful joy.   40

Gay hope is theirs by fancy fed,
   Less pleasing when possest;
The tear forgot as soon as shed,
   The sunshine of the breast:

Theirs buxom health of rosy hue,   45
Wild wit, invention ever-new,
   And lively cheer of vigor born;
The thoughtless day, the easy night,
The spirits pure, the slumbers light,
   That fly th' approach of morn.   50

Alas, regardless of their doom,
   The little victims play!
No sense have they of ills to come,
   Nor care beyond today:
Yet see how all around 'em wait   55
The ministers of human fate,
   And black Misfortune's baleful train!
Ah, show them where in ambush stand
To seize their prey the murth'rous band!
   Ah, tell them they are men!   60

These shall the fury Passions tear,
   The vultures of the mind,
Disdainful Anger, pallid Fear,
   And Shame that skulks behind;
Or pining Love shall waste their youth,   65
Or Jealousy with rankling tooth,
   That inly gnaws the secret heart,
And Envy wan, and faded Care,
Grim-visaged comfortless Despair,
   And Sorrow's piercing dart.   70

Ambition this shall tempt to rise,
   Then whirl the wretch from high,
To bitter Scorn a sacrifice,
   And grinning Infamy.
The stings of Falsehood those shall try,   75
And hard Unkindness' altered eye,
   That mocks the tear it forced to flow;
And keen Remorse with blood defiled,
And moody Madness laughing wild
   Amid severest woe.   80

Lo, in the vale of years beneath
   A grisly troop are seen,
The painful family of Death,
   More hideous than their Queen:

This racks the joints, this fires the veins,   85
That every laboring sinew strains,
   Those in the deeper vitals rage:
Lo, Poverty, to fill the band,
That numbs the soul with icy hand,
   And slow-consuming Age.   90

To each his suff'rings: all are men,
   Condemned alike to groan,
The tender for another's pain,
   Th' unfeeling for his own.
Yet, ah! why should they know their fate?   95
Since sorrow never comes too late,
   And happiness too swiftly flies.
Thought would destroy their paradise.
No more; where ignorance is bliss,
   'Tis folly to be wise.   100

Thomas Hood (1799–1845)

I Remember, I Remember

I remember, I remember,
The house where I was born,
The little window where the sun
Came peeping in at morn;
He never came a wink too soon,   5
Nor brought too long a day,
But now, I often wish the night
Had borne my breath away!

I remember, I remember,
The roses, red and white,   10
The violets, and the lily-cups,
Those flowers made of light!
The lilacs where the robin built,
And where my brother set
The laburnum on his birthday, —   15
The tree is living yet!

I remember, I remember,
Where I was used to swing,
And thought the air must rush as fresh
To swallows on the wing   20
My spirit flew in feathers then,
That is so heavy now,
And summer pools could hardly cool
The fever of my brow!

I remember, I remember,   25
The fir trees dark and high;
I used to think their slender tops
Were close against the sky;
It was a childish ignorance,
But now 'tis little joy   30
To know I'm farther off from heaven
Than when I was a boy.

Frank O'Connor (1903–1966)

My Oedipus Complex

Father was in the army all through the war—the first war, I mean—so, up to
the age of five, I never saw much of him, and what I saw did not worry me. Sometimes
I woke and there was a big figure in khaki peering down at me in the candlelight.
Sometimes in the early morning I heard the slamming of the front door and the clatter
of nailed boots down the cobbles of the lane. These were Father's entrances and
exits. Like Santa Claus he came and went mysteriously.

In fact, I rather liked his visits, though it was an uncomfortable squeeze between
Mother and him when I got into the big bed in the early morning. He smoked, which
gave him a pleasant musty smell, and shaved, an operation of astounding interest.
Each time he left a trail of souvenirs—model tanks and Gurkha knives with handles
made of bullet cases, and German helmets and cap badges and button-sticks, and all
sorts of military equipment—carefully stowed away in a long box on top of the
wardrobe, in case they ever came in handy. There was a bit of the magpie about
Father; he expected everything to come in handy. When his back was turned, Mother

let me get a chair and rummage through his treasures. She didn't seem to think so highly of them as he did.

The war was the most peaceful period of my life. The window of my attic faced southeast. My mother had curtained it, but that had small effect. I always woke with the first light and, with all the responsibilities of the previous day melted, feeling myself rather like the sun, ready to illumine and rejoice. Life never seemed so simple and clear and full of possibilities as then. I put my feet out from under the clothes—I called them Mrs. Left and Mrs. Right—and invented dramatic situations for them in which they discussed the problems of the day. At least Mrs. Right did; she was very demonstrative, but I hadn't the same control of Mrs. Left, so she mostly contented herself with nodding agreement.

They discussed what Mother and I should do during the day, what Santa Claus should give a fellow for Christmas, and what steps should be taken to brighten the home. There was that little matter of the baby, for instance. Mother and I could never agree about that. Ours was the only house in the terrace without a new baby, and Mother said we couldn't afford one till Father came back from the war because they cost seventeen and six. That showed how simple she was. The Geneys up the road had a baby, and everyone knew they couldn't afford seventeen and six. It was probably a cheap baby, and Mother wanted something really good, but I felt she was too exclusive. The Geneys' baby would have done us fine.

Having settled my plans for the day, I got up, put a chair under the attic window, and lifted the frame high enough to stick out my head. The window overlooked the front gardens of the terrace behind ours, and beyond these it looked over a deep valley to the tall, red-brick houses terraced up the opposite hillside, which were all still in shadow, while those at our side of the valley were all lit up, though with long strange shadows that made them seem unfamiliar; rigid and painted.

After that I went into Mother's room and climbed into the big bed. She woke and I began to tell her of my schemes. By this time, though I never seem to have noticed it, I was petrified in my nightshirt, and I thawed as I talked until, the last frost melted, I fell asleep beside her and woke again only when I heard her below in the kitchen, making the breakfast.

After breakfast we went into town; heard Mass at St. Augustine's and said a prayer for Father, and did the shopping. If the afternoon was fine we either went for a walk in the country or a visit to Mother's great friend in the convent, Mother St. Dominic. Mother had them all praying for Father, and every night, going to bed, I asked God to send him back safe from the war to us. Little, indeed, did I know what I was praying for!

One morning, I got into the big bed, and there, sure enough, was Father in his usual Santa Claus manner, but later, instead of uniform, he put on his best blue suit, and Mother was as pleased as anything. I saw nothing to be pleased about, because, out of uniform, Father was altogether less interesting, but she only beamed, and explained that our prayers had been answered, and off we went to Mass to thank God for having brought Father safely home.

The irony of it! That very day when he came in to dinner he took off his boots and put on his slippers, donned the dirty old cap he wore about the house to save him from colds, crossed his legs, and began to talk gravely to Mother, who looked anxious. Naturally, I disliked her looking anxious, because it destroyed her good looks, so I interrupted him.

"Just a moment, Larry!" she said gently.

This was only what she said when we had boring visitors, so I attached no importance to it and went on talking.

"Do be quiet, Larry!" she said impatiently. "Don't you hear me talking to Daddy?"

This was the first time I had heard those ominous words, "talking to Daddy," and I couldn't help feeling that if this was how God answered prayers, he couldn't listen to them very attentively.

"Why are you talking to Daddy?" I asked with as great a show of indifference as I could muster.

"Because Daddy and I have business to discuss. Now, don't interrupt again!"

In the afternoon, at Mother's request, Father took me for a walk. This time we went into town instead of out the country, and I thought at first, in my usual optimistic way, that it might be an improvement. It was nothing of the sort. Father and I had quite different notions of a walk in town. He had no proper interest in trams, ships, and horses, and the only thing that seemed to divert him was talking to fellows as old as himself. When I wanted to stop he simply went on, dragging me behind him by the hand; when he wanted to stop I had no alternative but to do the same. I noticed that it seemed to be a sign that he wanted to stop for a long time whenever he leaned against a wall. The second time I saw him do it I got wild. He seemed to be settling himself forever. I pulled him by the coat and trousers, but, unlike Mother who, if you were too persistent, got into a wax and said: "Larry, if you don't behave yourself, I'll give you a good slap," Father had an extraordinary capacity for amiable inattention. I sized him up and wondered would I cry, but he seemed to be too remote to be annoyed even by that. Really, it was like going for a walk with a mountain! He either ignored the wrenching and pummelling entirely, or else glanced down with a grin of amusement from his peak. I had never met anyone so absorbed in himself as he seemed.

At teatime, "talking to Daddy" began again, complicated this time by the fact that he had an evening paper, and every few minutes he put it down and told Mother something new out of it. I felt this was foul play. Man for man, I was prepared to compete with him any time for Mother's attention, but when he had it all made up for him by other people it left me no chance. Several times I tried to change the subject without success.

"You must be quiet while Daddy is reading, Larry," Mother said impatiently.

It was clear that she either genuinely liked talking to Father better than talking to me, or else that he had some terrible hold on her which made her afraid to admit the truth.

"Mummy," I said that night when she was tucking me up, "do you think if I prayed hard God would send Daddy back to the war?"

She seemed to think about that for a moment.

"No, dear," she said with a smile. "I don't think he would."

"Why wouldn't he, Mummy?"

"Because there isn't a war any longer, dear."

"But, Mummy, couldn't God make another war, if He liked?"

"He wouldn't like to, dear. It's not God who makes wars, but bad people."

"Oh!" I said.

I was disappointed about that. I began to think that God wasn't quite what he was cracked up to be.

Next morning I woke at my usual hour, feeling like a bottle of champagne. I put out my feet and invented a long conversation in which Mrs. Right talked of the trouble she had with her own father till she put him in the Home. I didn't quite know what the Home was but it sounded the right place for Father. Then I got my chair and stuck my head out of the attic window. Dawn was just breaking, with a guilty air that made me feel I had caught it in the act. My head bursting with stories and schemes, I stumbled in next door, and in the half-darkness scrambled into the big bed. There was no room at Mother's side so I had to get between her and Father. For the time being I had forgotten about him, and for several minutes I sat bolt upright, racking my brains to know what I could do with him. He was taking up more than his fair share of the bed, and I couldn't get comfortable, so I gave him several kicks that made him grunt and stretch. He made room all right, though. Mother waked and felt for me. I settled back comfortably in the warmth of the bed with my thumb in my mouth.

"Mummy!" I hummed, loudly and contentedly.

"Sssh! dear," she whispered. "Don't wake Daddy!"

This was a new development, which threatened to be even more serious than "talking to Daddy." Life without my early-morning conferences was unthinkable.

"Why?" I asked severely.

"Because poor Daddy is tired."

This seemed to me a quite inadequate reason, and I was sickened by the sentimentality of her "poor Daddy." I never liked that sort of gush; it always struck me as insincere.

"Oh!" I said lightly. Then in my most winning tone: "Do you know where I want to go with you today, Mummy?"

"No, dear," she sighed.

"I want to go down the Glen and fish for thornybacks with my new net, and then I want to go out to the Fox and Hounds, and—"

"Don't-wake-Daddy!" she hissed angrily, clapping her hand across my mouth.

But it was too late. He was awake, or nearly so. He grunted and reached for the matches. Then he stared incredulously at his watch.

"Like a cup of tea, dear?" asked Mother in a meek, hushed voice I had never heard her use before. It sounded almost as though she were afraid.

"Tea?" he exclaimed indignantly. "Do you know what the time is?"

"And after that I want to go up the Rathcooney Road," I said loudly, afraid I'd forget something in all those interruptions.

"Go to sleep at once, Larry!" she said sharply.

I began to snivel. I couldn't concentrate, the way that pair went on, and smothering my early-morning schemes was like burying a family from the cradle.

Father said nothing, but lit his pipe and sucked it, looking out into the shadows without minding Mother or me. I knew he was mad. Every time I made a remark Mother hushed me irritably. I was mortified. I felt it wasn't fair; there was even something sinister in it. Every time I had pointed out to her the waste of making two beds when we could both sleep in one, she had told me it was healthier like that, and now here was this man, this stranger, sleeping with her without the least regard for her health!

He got up early and made tea, but though he brought Mother a cup he brought none for me.

"Mummy," I shouted, "I want a cup of tea, too."

"Yes, dear," she said patiently. "You can drink from Mummy's saucer."

That settled it. Either Father or I would have to leave the house. I didn't want to drink from Mother's saucer; I wanted to be treated as an equal in my own home, so, just to spite her, I drank it all and left none for her. She took that quietly, too.

But that night when she was putting me to bed she said gently:

"Larry, I want you to promise me something."

"What is it?" I asked.

"Not to come in and disturb poor Daddy in the morning. Promise?"

"Poor Daddy" again! I was becoming suspicious of everything involving that quite impossible man.

"Why?" I asked.

"Because poor Daddy is worried and tired and he doesn't sleep well."

"Why doesn't he, Mummy?"

"Well, you know, don't you, that while he was at the war Mummy got the pennies from the Post Office?"

"From Miss MacCarthy?"

"That's right. But now, you see, Miss MacCarthy hasn't any more pennies, so Daddy must go out and find us some. You know what would happen if he couldn't?"

"No," I said, "tell us."

"Well, I think we might have to go out and beg for them like the poor old woman on Fridays. We wouldn't like that, would we?"

"No," I agreed. "We wouldn't."

"So you'll promise not to come in and wake him?"

"Promise."

Mind you, I meant that. I knew pennies were a serious matter, and I was all against having to go out and beg like the old woman on Fridays. Mother laid out all my toys in a complete ring round the bed so that, whatever way I got out, I was bound to fall over one of them.

When I woke I remembered my promise all right. I got up and sat on the floor and played—for hours, it seemed to me. Then I got my chair and looked out the attic window for more hours. I wished it was time for Father to wake; I wished someone would make me a cup of tea. I didn't feel in the least like the sun; instead, I was bored and so very, very cold! I simply longed for the warmth and depth of the big featherbed.

At last I could stand it no longer. I went into the next room. As there was still no room at Mother's side I climbed over her and she woke with a start.

"Larry," she whispered, gripping my arm very tightly, "what did you promise?"

"But I did, Mummy," I wailed, caught in the very act. "I was quiet for ever so long."

"Oh, dear, and you're perished!" she said sadly, feeling me all over. "Now, if I let you stay will you promise not to talk?"

"But I want to talk, Mummy," I wailed.

"That has nothing to do with it," she said with a firmness that was new to me. "Daddy wants to sleep. Now, do you understand that?"

I understood it only too well. I wanted to talk, he wanted to sleep—whose house was it, anyway?

"Mummy," I said with equal firmness, "I think it would be healthier for Daddy to sleep in his own bed."

That seemed to stagger her, because she said nothing for a while.

"Now, once for all," she went on, "you're to be perfectly quiet or go back to your own bed. Which is it to be?"

The injustice of it got me down. I had convicted her out of her own mouth of inconsistency and unreasonableness, and she hadn't even attempted to reply. Full of spite, I gave Father a kick, which she didn't notice but which made him grunt and open his eyes in alarm.

"What time is it?" he asked in a panic-stricken voice, not looking at Mother but at the door, as if he saw someone there.

"It's early yet," she replied soothingly. "It's only the child. Go to sleep again. . . . Now, Larry," she added, getting out of bed, "you've wakened Daddy and you must go back."

This time, for all her quiet air, I knew she meant it, and knew that my principal rights and privileges were as good as lost unless I asserted them at once. As she lifted me, I gave a screech, enough to wake the dead, not to mind Father. He groaned.

"That damn child! Doesn't he ever sleep?"

"It's only a habit, dear," she said quietly, though I could see she was vexed.

"Well, it's time he got out of it," shouted Father, beginning to heave in the bed. He suddenly gathered all the bedclothes about him, turned to the wall, and then looked back over his shoulder with nothing showing only two small, spiteful, dark eyes. The man looked very wicked.

To open the bedroom door, Mother had to let me down, and I broke free and dashed for the farthest corner, screeching. Father sat bolt upright in bed.

"Shut up, you little puppy!" he said in a choking voice.

I was so astonished that I stopped screeching. Never, never had anyone spoken to me in that tone before. I looked at him incredulously and saw his face convulsed with rage. It was only then that I fully realized how God had codded me, listening to my prayers for the safe return of this monster.

"Shut up, you!" I bawled, beside myself.

"What's that you said?" shouted Father, making a wild leap out of the bed.

"Mick, Mick!" cried Mother. "Don't you see the child isn't used to you?"

"I see he's better fed than taught," snarled Father, waving his arms wildly. "He wants his bottom smacked."

All his previous shouting was as nothing to these obscene words referring to my person. They really made my blood boil.

"Smack your own!" I screamed hysterically. "Smack your own! Shut up! Shut up!"

At this he lost his patience and let fly at me. He did it with the lack of conviction you'd expect of a man under Mother's horrified eyes, and it ended up as a mere tap, but the sheer indignity of being struck at all by a stranger, a total stranger who had cajoled his way back from the war into our big bed as a result of my innocent intercession, made me completely dotty. I shrieked and shrieked, and danced in my bare feet, and Father, looking awkward and hairy in nothing but a short gray army shirt, glared down at me like a mountain out for murder. I think it must have been then that I realized he was jealous too. And there stood Mother in her nightdress, looking as if her heart was broken between us. I hoped she felt as she looked. It seemed to me that she deserved it all.

From that morning out my life was a hell. Father and I were enemies, open and avowed. We conducted a series of skirmishes against one another, he trying to steal my time with Mother and I his. When she was sitting on my bed, telling me a story, he took to looking for some pair of old boots which he alleged he had left behind him at the beginning of the war. While he talked to Mother I played loudly with my toys to show my total lack of concern. He created a terrible scene one evening when he came in from work and found me at his box, playing with his regimental badges, Gurkha knives and button-sticks. Mother got up and took the box from me.

"You mustn't play with Daddy's toys unless he lets you, Larry," she said severely. "Daddy doesn't play with yours."

For some reason Father looked at her as if she had struck him and then turned away with a scowl.

"Those are not toys," he growled, taking down the box again to see had I lifted anything. "Some of those curios are very rare and valuable."

But as time went on I saw more and more how he managed to alienate Mother and me. What made it worse was that I couldn't grasp his method or see what attraction he had for Mother. In every possible way he was less winning than I. He had a common accent and made noises at his tea. I thought for a while that it might be the newspapers she was interested in, so I made up bits of news of my own to read to her. Then I thought it might be the smoking, which I personally thought attractive, and took his pipes and went round the house dribbling into them till he caught me. I even made noises at my tea, but Mother only told me I was disgusting. It all seemed to hinge round that unhealthy habit of sleeping together, so I made a point of dropping into their bedroom and nosing around, talking to myself, so that they wouldn't know I was watching them, but they were never up to anything that I could see. In the end it beat me. It seemed to depend on being grown-up and giving people rings, and I realized I'd have to wait.

But at the same time I wanted him to see that I was only waiting, not giving up the fight. One evening when he was being particularly obnoxious, chattering away well above my head, I let him have it.

"Mummy," I said, "do you know what I'm going to do when I grow up?"

"No, dear," she replied. "What?"

"I'm going to marry you," I said quietly.

Father gave a great guffaw out of him, but he didn't take me in. I knew it must only be pretense. And Mother, in spite of everything, was pleased. I felt she was probably relieved to know that one day Father's hold on her would be broken.

"Won't that be nice?" she said with a smile.

"It'll be very nice," I said confidently. "Because we're going to have lots and lots of babies."

"That's right, dear," she said placidly. "I think we'll have one soon, and then you'll have plenty of company."

I was no end pleased about that because it showed that in spite of the way she gave in to Father she still considered my wishes. Besides, it would put the Geneys in their place.

It didn't turn out like that, though. To begin with, she was very preoccupied—I supposed about where she would get the seventeen and six—and though Father took to staying out late in the evenings it did me no particular good. She stopped taking me for walks, became as touchy as blazes, and smacked me for nothing at all. Sometimes I wished I'd never mentioned the confounded baby—I seemed to have a genius for bringing calamity on myself.

And calamity it was! Sonny arrived in the most appalling hullabaloo—even that much he couldn't do without a fuss—and from the first moment I disliked him. He was a difficult child—so far as I was concerned he was always difficult—and demanded far too much attention. Mother was simply silly about him, and couldn't see when he was only showing off. As company he was worse than useless. He slept all day, and I had to go round the house on tiptoe to avoid waking him. It wasn't any longer a question of not waking Father. The slogan now was "Don't-wake-Sonny!" I couldn't understand why the child wouldn't sleep at the proper time, so whenever Mother's back was turned I woke him. Sometimes to keep him awake I pinched him as well. Mother caught me at it one day and gave me a most unmerciful flaking.

One evening, when Father was coming in from work, I was playing trains in the front garden. I let on not to notice him; instead, I pretended to be talking to myself, and said in a loud voice; "If another bloody baby comes into this house, I'm going out."

Father stopped dead and looked at me over his shoulder.

"What's that you said?" he asked sternly.

"I was only talking to myself," I replied, trying to conceal my panic. "It's private."

He turned and went in without a word. Mind you, I intended it as a solemn warning, but its effect was quite different. Father started being quite nice to me. I could understand that, of course. Mother was quite sickening about Sonny. Even at mealtimes she'd get up and gawk at him in the cradle with an idiotic smile, and tell Father to do the same. He was always polite about it, but he looked so puzzled you could see he didn't know what she was talking about. He complained of the way Sonny cried at night, but she only got cross and said that Sonny never cried except when there was something up with him—which was a flaming lie, because Sonny never had anything up with him, and only cried for attention. It was really painful to see how simpleminded she was. Father wasn't attractive, but he had a fine intelligence. He saw through Sonny, and now he knew that I saw through him as well.

One night I woke with a start. There was someone beside me in the bed. For one wild moment I felt sure it must be Mother, having come to her senses and left Father for good, but then I heard Sonny in convulsions in the next room, and Mother saying: "There! There! There!" and I knew it wasn't she. It was Father. He was lying beside me, wide awake, breathing hard and apparently as mad as hell.

After a while it came to me what he was mad about. It was his turn now. After turning me out of the big bed, he had been turned out himself. Mother had no consideration now for anyone but that poisonous pup, Sonny. I couldn't help feeling sorry for Father. I had been through it all myself, and even at that age I was magnanimous. I began to stroke him down and say: "There! There!" He wasn't exactly responsive.

"Aren't you asleep either?" he snarled.

"Ah, come on and put your arm around us, can't you?" I said, and he did, in a sort of way. Gingerly, I suppose is how you'd describe it. He was very bony but better than nothing.

At Christmas he went out of his way to buy me a really nice model railway.

❖

Reynolds Price (born 1933)
The Names and Faces of Heroes

After an hour I believe it and think, "We are people in love. We flee through hard winter night. What our enemies want is to separate us. Will we end together? Will we end alive?" And my lips part to ask him, but seeing his face in dashboard light (his gray eyes set on the road and the dark), I muffle my question and know the reason— "We have not broke silence for an hour by the clock. We must flee on silent. Maybe if we speak even close as we are, we will speak separate tongues after so long a time." I shut my eyes, press hard with the lids till my mind's eye opens, then balloon it light through roof through steel, set it high and cold in January night, staring down to see us whole. First we are one black car on a slim strip of road laid white through pines, drawn slowly west by the hoop of light we cast ahead—the one light burning for fifty miles, it being past eleven, all farms and houses crouched into sleep, all riders but us. Then my eye falls downward, hovers on the roof in the wind we make, pierces steel, sees us close—huddled on the worn mohair of a 1939 Pontiac, he slumped huge at the wheel, I the thin fork of flesh thrust out of his groin on the seat beside him, my dark head the burden in his lap his only hollow that flushes beneath me with rhythm I predict to force blood against my weight through nodes of tissue, squabs of muscle that made me ten years ago, made half anyhow, he being my father and I being nine, we heading towards home not fleeing, silent as I say, my real eyes shut, his eyes on nothing but road. So we are not lovers nor spies nor thieves and speaking for me, my foes are inward not there in the night. My mind's eye enters me calm again, and I brace to look, to say "How much further?" but he drops a hand which stalls me, testing my flannel pajamas for warmth, ringing my ankle and shin and ticklish knee (in earnest, tight not gentle), slipping between two buttons of the coat to brush one breast then out again and down to rest on my hip. His thumb and fingers ride the high saddle bone, the fat of his hand in the hollow *I* have, heavy but still on the dry knots of boyish equipment waiting for life to start. I roll back on my head to see him again, to meet his eyes. He looks on forward so I go blind again and slide my right hand to his, probing with a finger till I find his only wound—a round yellow socket beneath his thumb where he shot himself when he was eight, by surprise, showing off his father's pistol to friends (the one fool thing I know he has done). My finger rests there and we last that way maybe two or three miles while the road is straight. Then a curve begins. He says "Excuse me, Preacher" in his natural voice and takes his hand. My eyes stay blind and I think what I know, "I love you tonight more than all my life before"—think it in *my* natural voice. But I do not say it, and I do not say I excuse him though I do. I open my eyes on his face in dashboard light.

I search it for a hero. For the first time. I have searched nearly every other face since last July, the final Sunday at camp when a minister told us, "The short cut to being a man is finding your hero, somebody who is what you are not but need to be.

What I mean is this. Examine yourself. When you find what your main lack is, seek that in some great man. Say your trouble is fear—you are scared of the dark, scared of that bully in your grade at school, scared of striking out when you come up to bat. Take some great brave, some warrior—Douglas MacArthur, Enos Slaughter. Say your trouble is worse. Say it's telling lies. Take George Washington—personal heroes don't need to be living just so they lived once. Read a book about him. Study his picture. (You may think he looks a little stiff. That is because his teeth were carved out of cypress. A man makes his face and making a good one is as hard a job as laying road through solid rock, and Washington made himself as fine a face as any man since Jesus—and He was not a man.) Then imitate him. Chin yourself on his example and you will be a man before you need a razor." I need to be a man hard as anybody so riding home from camp and that sermon, I sat among lanyards I plaited and whistles I carved and searched my life for the one great lack my foe. He had mentioned lacking courage—that minister. I lack it. I will not try to do what I think I cannot do well such as make friends or play games where somebody hands you a ball and bat and asks the world of you, asks you to launch without thinking some act on the air with natural grace easy as laughing. He had mentioned lying. I lie every day—telling my mother for instance that the weeks at camp were happy when what I did was by day whittle all that trashy equipment, climb through snakes in July sun with brogans grating my heels, swim in ice water with boys that would just as soon drown you as smile and by night pray for three large things—that I not wet the bed, that I choke the homesickness one more day, that these five weeks vanish and leave no sign no memory. But they were only two on a string of lacks which unreeled behind me that Sunday riding home from camp (unseen beyond glass the hateful tan rock turning to round pine hills where Randolph is and home), and on the string were selfishness to Marcia my cousin who is my main friend and gives me whatever she has, envy of my brother who is one year old and whose arms I purposely threw out of joint three months ago, envy of people my age who do so easily things I will not and thus lock together in tangles of friendship, pride in the things I can do which they cannot (but half pride at worst as the things I can do, they do not want to do—drawing, carving, solo singing. I am Randolph's leading boy soprano and was ashamed to be till a Saturday night last August when I sang to a room of sweating soldiers at the U.S.O. I was asked by the hostess for something patriotic, but I thought they would not need that on their weekend off any more than they needed me in Buster Brown collar and white short pants so I sang Brahms' *Lullaby* which you can hum if you forget, and if it was a mistake, they never let on. I do not mean anybody cried. They kept on swallowing Coca-Colas and their boots kept smelling, but they shut up talking and clapped at the end, and as I left the platform and aimed for the door blistered with shame, one long soldier gave me the blue and gold enamel shield off his cap, saying "Here you are"), and far graver things—wishing death nightly on two boys I know, breaking God's law about honoring parents by failing to do simple things they ask such as look at people when I talk, by doubting they can care for me daily (when my mother thinks of little else and Father would no more sleep without kissing me goodnight than he would strike me), sometimes doubting I am theirs at all but just some orphan they took in kindness. I made that list without trying seven months ago, and it has grown since then. Whenever I speak or move these days new faults stare out of my heart. The trouble though is I still do not know my greatest lack, my *mortal* foe. Any one if I stare back long enough seems bound to sink me. So I seek a hero grand enough to take on all my lacks, but for seven months now I have looked—looked hard—and am nowhere near him. Who *is* there these days, who has there ever been broad enough, grand enough to stand day and night and ward off all my foes? Nobody, I begin to think. I have looked everywhere I know to look, first in books I had or bought for the purpose—*Little People Who Became Great* (Abraham Lincoln, Helen Keller, Andrew Carnegie), *Minute Lives of Great Men and Women* (a page and a picture for everybody including Stephen Foster) and a set called *Living Biographies of Great Composers, Philosophers, Prophets, Poets and Statesmen.* I have not read books that do not show faces because I study a man's face first. Then if that calls me on, I read his deeds. I read for three months and taking deeds and faces together, I settled on Caesar Augustus and Alexander the Great as final candidates. They were already great when they were young, and they both wore faces like hard silver medals awarded for lasting—I got that much from *Minute Lives*—so I thought they were safe and that I would read further and then choose one. But as I read they fell in before me— Alexander crushing that boy's head who brought bad news and when they were lost in a desert and famished and his men found one drink of water and gladly brought it to him in a helmet, him pouring it out in the sand to waste, and Augustus leading the wives of his friends into private rooms during public banquets, making them do what they could not refuse. All the dead have failed me. That is why I study my father tonight. He is the last living man I know or can think of that I have not considered, which is no slight to him—you do not seek heroes at home. No, when the dead played out, I turned to my autographs and started there. I have written to famous men for over a year since the war began. I write on Boy Scout stationery (I am not a Scout), give my age and ask for their names in ink. I have got answers from several generals on the battlefield (MacArthur who sent good luck from the Philippines, Mark Clark who typed a note from secret headquarters, Eisenhower who said in his wide leaning hand, "I do not think it would be possible for me to refuse a nine-year-old American anything I could do for him"), from most of Roosevelt's cabinet (but not from him though I have three notes from Miss Grace Tully to say he does not have time and neither does his wife), from Toscanini and a picture of Johnny Weissmuller on a limb crouched with his bare knife to leap, saying "Hello from Tarzan your friend." But studying them I saw I could not know enough to decide. They are surely famous but I cannot see them or watch them move, and until they die and their secrets appear, how can I know they are genuine heroes?—that they do not have yawning holes of their own which they hide? So from them I have turned to men I can watch and hear, and since I seldom travel this means the men I am kin to. I will not think against my blood, but of all my uncles and cousins (my grandfathers died before I was born), the two I love and that seem to love me—that listen when I speak—and that have dark happy faces are the ones who are liable at any time to start drinking and disappear spending money hand over fist in Richmond or Washington until they are broke and wire for my father who drives up and finds them in a bar with a new suit on and a rosebud and some temporary friends and brings them home to their wives. My father has one brother who fought in France in the First World War and was playing cards in a hole one night when a bomb landed, and when he came to, he picked up his best friend who was quiet at his side and crawled with him half a mile before he saw that the friend lacked a head, but later he was gassed and retired from battle so that now, sitting or standing, he slumps round a hole in his chest and scrapes up blood every hour or two even summer nights visiting on our porch from Tennessee his home. My other male kin live even farther away or do not notice me or are fat which is why as I say I have come to my father tonight—my head rolled back on his lap, my ears sunk in his shifting kernels so I cannot hear only see, my eyes strained up through his arms to his face.

It is round as a watch when he does not smile which he does not now, and even in warm yellow light of speedometer-amp meter-oil pressure gauges, it is red as if he was cold, as if there was no plate glass to hold off the wind we make rushing home. It is always red and reddest I know, though I cannot see, under his collar on the back of his neck where the hair leaves off. There is not much hair anywhere on his head. It has vanished two inches back on his forehead, and where it starts it is dark but seems no color or the color of shadows in old photographs. Above his ears it is already white (he is forty-two and the white is real, but five years ago when it was not, I was singing in bed one night "When I Grow Too Old To Dream," and he heard me and went to the toilet and powdered his hair and came and stood in the door ghostly, old with the hall light behind him and said, "I am too old to dream, Preacher." I sang on a minute, looking, and then cried "Stop. Stop" and wept which of course he did not intend), and each morning he wets it and brushes every strand at least five minutes till it lies on his skull like paint and stays all day. It is one of his things you cannot touch. His glasses are another. He treats them kindly as if they were delicate people—unrimmed octagons hooked to gold wires that ride the start of his firm long nose and loop back over his large flat ears—and in return they do not hide his eyes which are gray and wide and which even in the dark draw light to them so he generally seems to be thinking of fun when he may be thinking we have lost our house (we have just done that) or his heart is failing (he thinks his heart stood still last Christmas when he was on a ladder swapping lights in our tree, and whenever I look he is taking his pulse). And with all his worries it mostly *is* fun he thinks because when he opens his mouth, if people are there they generally laugh—with him or at him, he does not mind which. I know a string of his jokes as long as the string of my personal lacks, and he adds on new ones most days he feels well enough. A lot of his jokes of course I do not understand but I no longer ask. I used to ask and he would say, "Wait a little,

Preacher. Your day will come" so I hold them mysterious in my skull till the day they burst into meaning. But most of his fun is open to view, to anybody's eyes that will look because what he mainly loves is turning himself into other people before your eyes. Whenever in the evenings we visit friends, everybody will talk awhile including my father, and then he may go silent and stare into space, pecking his teeth with a fingernail till his eyes come back from where they have been and his long lips stretch straight which is how he smiles, and then whoever we are visiting—if he has been watching my father—will know to say, "Mock somebody for us, Jeff." ("Mocking" is what most people call it. My father calls it "taking people off.") He will look sheepish a minute, then lean forward in his chair—and I sitting on the rug, my heart will rise for I know he has something to give us now—and looking at the floor say, "Remember how Dr. Tucker pulled teeth?" Everybody will grin Yes but somebody (sometimes me) will say "How?" and he will start becoming Dr. Tucker, not lying, just seriously turning himself into that old dentist—greeting his patient at the door, bowing him over to the chair (this is when he shrinks eight inches, dries, goes balder still, hikes his voice up half a scale), talking every step to soothe the patient, sneaking behind him, rinsing his rusty pullers at the tap, cooing "Open your mouth, sweet *thing*," leaping on the mouth like a boa constrictor, holding up the tooth victorious, smiling "*There* he is and you didn't even feel it, did you, darling?" Then he will be Jeff McCraw again, hitching up his trousers with the sides of his wrists, leading us into the laughter. When it starts to die somebody will say, "Jeff, you beat all. You missed your calling. You ought to be in the movies," and if he is not worried that night he may move on through one or two more transformations—Miss Georgie Ballard singing in church with her head like an owl swivelling, Mrs. V. L. Womble on her velvet pillow, President Roosevelt in a "My friends" speech, or on request little pieces of people— Mr. Jim Bender's walk, Miss Amma Godwin's hand on her stomach. But it suits me more when he stops after one. That way I can laugh and take pride in his gifts, but if he continues I may take fright at him spinning on through crowds of old people, dead people, people I do not know as if his own life—his life with us—is not enough. One such night when he was happy and everybody was egging him on I cried to him "Stop" before it was too late and ran from the room. I am not known as a problem so people notice when I cry. My mother came behind me at once and sitting in a cold stairwell, calmed me while I made up a reason for what I had done. She said, "Let your father have a little fun. He does not have much." I remembered how she often warned me against crossing my eyes at school to make children laugh, saying they might get stuck, so I told her he might stick and then we would carry him home as Dr. Tucker or Mrs. Womble or Miss Lula Fleming at the Baptist organ. That was a lie but it was all I knew, all I could offer on such short notice to justify terror, and telling it made us laugh, calmed me, stopped me thinking of reasons. And I did not worry or think of my terror again till several months later when he came in disguise. It was not the first time he had worn disguise (half the stories about him are about his disguises), but he did not wear it often, and though I was seven I had never seen him that way before.

Maybe it is why he came that night, thinking I was old enough and would like the joke since I loved his other fun. Anyhow the joke was not for me but for Uncle Hawk, an old colored man who lived with us. I was just the one who answered the door. It was night of course. I had finished my supper and leaving the others, had gone to the living room and was on the floor by the radio. After a while there came a knock on the panes of the door. I said, "I will get it" to the empty room, thinking they were all in the kitchen, turned on the porch light and opened the door on a tall man heavy-set with white hair, a black derby hat, a black overcoat to his ankles, gray kid gloves, a briefcase, a long white face coiled back under pinch-nose glasses looking down. It was nobody I knew, nobody I had seen and what could he sell at this time of night? My heart seized like a fist and I thought, "He has come for me" (as I say, it is my darkest fear that I am not the blood child of Jeff and Rhew McCraw, that I was adopted at birth, that someday a strange man will come and rightfully claim me). But still looking down he said, "Does an old colored man named Hawk work here?" and I tore to the kitchen for Uncle Hawk who was scraping dishes while my mother cleared table. They were silent a moment. Then my mother said, "Who in the world could it be, Uncle Hawk?" and he said "I wonder myself." I said, "Well, hurry. It is a stranger and the screen door is not even locked." He did not hurry. My mother and I stood and watched him get ready—washing with the Castile soap he keeps for his fine long hands tough as shark hide, adjusting suspenders, the garters on his sleeves, inspecting his shoes. Towards the end I looked at my mother in anxiety. She winked at me and said, "Go on, Uncle Hawk. It certainly is not Jesus *yet.*" Not smiling he said, "I wish it was" and went. Again I looked to my mother and again she winked and beckoned me behind her into the hall where we could watch the door and the meeting. Uncle Hawk said "Good evening" but did not bow, and the man said, "Are you Hawk Reid?" Then he mumbled something about life insurance–did Uncle Hawk have enough life, fire, burial insurance? Uncle Hawk said, "My life is not worth paying on every week. I do not have nothing to insure for fire but a pocket knife and it is iron, and Mr. Jeff McCraw is burying me." The man mumbled some more. Uncle Hawk said "No" and the man reached for the handle to the screen that separated them. Uncle Hawk reached to lock the screen but too slow, and there was the man on us, two feet from Hawk, fifteen from my mother and me. Hawk said, "Nobody asked you to come in here" and drew back his arm (nearly eighty years old) to strike. My mother and I had not made a sound, and I had mostly watched her not the door as she was grinning but then she laughed. Uncle Hawk turned on her, his arm still coiled, then back to the man who was looking up now not moving, and then Hawk laughed, doubled over helpless. The man walked in right past him slowly and stopped six feet from me, holding out his hand to take—he and I the two in the room not laughing. So I knew he had come for me, that I was his and would have to go. His hand stayed out in the glove towards me. There were three lines of careful black stitching down the back of the pale gray leather, the kind of gloves I wanted that are not made for boys. Still I could not take his hand just then, and not for terror. I was really not afraid but suddenly sorry to leave people who had been good to me, the house which I knew. That was what locked me there. I must have stood half a minute that way, and I must have looked worse and worse because my mother said, "Look at his eyes" and pointed me towards the man's face. I looked and at once they were what they had been all along—Jeff McCraw's eyes, the size and color of used nickels, gentle beyond disguising. I said to him then fast and high, "I thought you were my real father and had come to get me." He took off his derby and the old glasses and said, "I *am*, Preacher. I *have*, Preacher," and I ran to circle his thighs with my arms, to hide my tears in the hollow beneath the black overcoat. And I did hide them. When I looked up, everybody thought I had loved the joke like them. But I had not. I had loved my father found at the end with his hand stretched out. But I hoped not to find him again that way under glasses and powder, mumbling, so when he came into my bedroom to kiss me that night, I asked would he do me a favor. He said "What?" and I said, "Please warn me before you dress up ever again." He said he would and then my mother walked in and hearing us said, "You will not need warning. Just stare at his eyes first thing. He cannot hide those." But he always warns me as he promised he would—except at Christmas when he comes in a cheap flannel suit and rayon beard that any baby could see is false—and even though I know in advance that on a certain evening he will arrive as a tramp to scare my Aunt Lola or as a tax collector or a man from the farm office to tell my Uncle Paul he has planted illegal tobacco and must plow it under or suffer, still I fasten on his eyes and hold to them till somebody laughs and he finds time to wink at me.

As I fasten on them now heading home. He travels of course as himself tonight in a brown vested suit and a solid green tie so I see him plain—what is clear in dashboard light—and though I love him, though I rest in his hollow lap now happier than any other place, I know he cannot be my hero. And I list the reasons to myself. Heroes are generally made by war. My father was born in 1900 so the nearest he got to the First World War was the National Guard and in October 1918 an Army camp near Morehead City, N.C. where he spent six weeks in a very wrinkled uniform (my mother has his picture) till peace arrived, so desperately homesick that he saved through the whole six weeks the bones of a chicken lunch his mother gave him on leaving home. And when I woke him a year ago from his Sunday nap to ask what was Pearl Harbor that the radio was suddenly full of, he was well and young enough to sign for the Draft and be nervous but too old to serve. He does own two guns—for protection an Army .45 that his brother brought him from France, never wanting to see it again, and for hunting a double-barreled shotgun with cracked stock—but far as I know he has never shot anything but himself (that time he was a boy) and two or three dozen wharf rats, rabbits and squirrels. Nor is he even in his quiet life what heroes generally must be—physically brave. Not that chances often arise for that class of bravery. I had not seen him face any ordeal worse than a flat tire till a while ago when we had our first mock air raid in Randolph. He took an armband, helmet, blackjack and me, and we drove slowly to the power station which was his post and sat in the cold car thinking it would end soon, but it did not and I began to wonder was it real, were the Germans just beyond hearing, heading towards us? Then he opened his door and we slid out and stood on the hill with great power batteries singing behind us and looked down at the smothered town. I said, "What will we do if the Germans really come?" Not waiting he pointed towards what I guessed was Sunset Avenue (his sense of direction being good) and said, "We would high-tail it there to where your mother is liable to burn down the house any minute with all those candles." He did not laugh but the siren went and lights began and we headed home—the house stinking tallow on through the night and I awake in bed wondering should I tell him, "If you feel that way you ought to resign as warden"? deciding "No, if Hitler comes let him have the power. What could we do anyhow, Father with a blackjack, me with nothing?—hold off steel with our pitiful hands?" (the hand he touches me with again now, his wounded hand but the wrist so whole so full, under its curls so ropey I cannot ring it, trying now I cannot capture it in my hand so I trace one finger through its curls, tracing my name into him as older boys gouge names, gouge love into trees, into posts—gouge proudly. But with all the love I mentioned before, I do not trace proudly. I know him too well, know too many lacks, and my finger stops in the rut where his pulse would be if I could ever find it (I have tried, I cannot find it, maybe could not stand it if I did). I shut my eyes not to see his face for fear he will smile, and continue to name his lacks to myself. He makes people wait—meaning me and my mother. He is a salesman and travels, and sometimes when school is out, I travel with him, hoping each time things will go differently. They start well always (riding and looking though never much talking) till we come to the house where he hopes to sell a stove or refrigerator. We will stop in the yard. He will sit a minute, looking for dangerous dogs, then reach for his briefcase, open his door and say, "Wait here, Preacher. I will be straight back" I will say "All right" and he will turn back to me, "You do not mind that, do you, darling?"—"Not if you remember I am out here and do not spend the day." He of course says he will remember and goes, but before he has gone ten yards I can see that memory rise through his straw hat like steam, and by the time a woman says, "Step in the house," I am out of his mind as if I was part of the car that welcomed this chance to cool and rest. Nothing cool about it (being always summer when I travel with him), and I sit and sweat, shooing out flies and freezing if a yellowjacket comes, and when twenty minutes has gone by the clock, I begin to think, "If this was all the time he meant to give me, why did he bring me along?" And that rushes on into, "Why did he get me, why did he want me at all if he meant to treat me the way he does, giving me as much time each day as it takes to kiss me goodbye when I go to school and again at night in case we die in each other's absence?" And soon I am rushing through ways he neglects me daily. He will not for instance *teach* me. Last fall I ordered an axe from Sears and Roebuck with my own money, asking nobody's permission, and when it came—so beautiful—he acted as if I had ordered mustard gas and finally said I could keep it if I promised not to use it till he showed me the right way. I promised—and kept my promise—and until this day that axe has done nothing but wait on my wall, being taken down every night, having its lovely handle stroked, its dulling edge felt fearfully. And baseball. He has told me how he played baseball when he was my age, making it sound the happiest he ever was, but he cannot make me catch a fly-ball. I have asked him for help, and he went so far as to buy me a glove and spend half an hour in the yard throwing at me, saying "Like this, Preacher" when I threw at him, but when I failed to stop ball after ball, he finally stopped trying and went in the house, not angry or even impatient but never again offering to teach me what he loved when he was my age, what had won him friends. Maybe he thought he was being kind. Maybe he thought he had shamed me, letting me show him my failure. He had, he had. But if he knew how furious I pray when I am the outfield at school recess (pray that flies go any way but mine), how struck, how shrunk, how abandoned I feel when prayer fails and a ball splits hot through my hopeless hand to lie daring me to take it and throw it right while some loud boy no bigger than I, no better made, trots a free homerun—he would try again, do nothing but try. Or maybe there just come stretches when he does not care, when he does not love me or want me in his mind much less his sight—scrambling on the ground like a hungry fice for a white leather ball any third-grade girl could catch, sucking his life, his time, his fun for the food I need, the silly clothes, sucking the joy out of what few hopes he may have seen when his eyes were shut ten years ago, when he and my mother made me late in the night—That is the stuff he makes me think when he goes and leaves me stuck in the car, stuck for an hour many times so that finally sunk in desperation I begin to know he is sick in there—that his heart has seized as he knows it will or that strange woman is wild and has killed him silent with a knife, with poison, or that he has sold his stove and said goodbye and gone out the back in secret across a field into pines to leave us forever, to change his life. And I will say to myself, "You have got to move—run to the road and flag a car and go for the sheriff," but the house door will open and he will be there alive still grinning, then calming his face in the walk through the yard, wiping his forehead, smiling when he sees me again, when he recollects he has a son and I am it (am one anyhow, the one old enough to follow him places and wait). Before I can swallow what has jammed my throat, my heart in the previous hour, he will have us rolling—the cool breeze started and shortly his amends, my reward for waiting. It is always the same, his amends. It is stories about him being my age, especially about his father—Charles McCraw, "Cupe" McCraw who was clerk to the Copeland Register of Deeds, raised six children which were what he left (and a house, a wife, several dozen jokes) when he died sometime before I was born—and he needs no crutch to enter his stories such as "Have I told you this?" He knows he has told me, knows I want it again every time he can spare. He will light a cigarette with a safety match (he threw away the car's lighter long ago out the window down an embankment, thinking *it* was a match) and then say, "No sir. If I live to be ninety, I never want to swallow another cigarette." That is the first of the story about him at my age being sent outdoors by his father to shut off the water when a hard freeze threatened. The valve was sunk in the ground behind the house, and he was squatting over it cursing because it was stiff and pulling on the cigarette he had lit to warm him—when he looked in the frozen grass by his hand and there were black shoes and the ends of trousers. He did not need to look further. It was his father so while he gave one last great turn to the valve, he flipped his lower lip out and up (and here at age forty-two he imitates the flip, swift but credible) and swallowed the cigarette, fire included. Then he may say, "How is your bladder holding out, Preacher? Do you want to run yonder into those bushes?" I will say "No" since I cannot leak in open air, and he will say, "Father had a colored boy named Peter who worked round the house. *Peee-ter*, Peter called it. The first day we had a telephone connected, Father called home from the courthouse to test it. I was home from school—supposed to be sick—and I answered. He did not catch my voice so he said 'Who is this?' I said '*Peee-ter*,' and he thought he would joke a little. He said 'Peter *who?*' I said 'Mr. *McCraw's* Peee-ter,' and he said, 'Hang up, fool, and don't ever answer that thing again!' I waited for him to come home that evening, and he finally came with a box of Grapenuts for me, but he did not mention Peter or the telephone so I didn't either, never mentioned it till the day he died. He died at night . . ."

But *tonight.* This hard winter night in 1942 and he is silent—my father—his eyes on darkness and road to get me safely home as if I was cherished, while I rush on behind shut eyes through all that last—his size, his lacks, his distances—still threading my finger through curls of his wrist, a grander wrist than he needs or deserves. I find his pulse. It rises sudden to my winnowing finger, waylays, appalls, *traps* it. I ride his life with the pad of flesh on my middle finger, and it heaves against me steady and calm as if it did not know I ruled its flow, that poor as I am at games and play, I could press in now, press lightly first so he would not notice, then in and in till his foot would slack on the gas, his head sink heavy to his chest, his eyes shut on me (on what I cause), the car roll still and I be left with what I have made—his permanent death. Towards that picture, that chance, my own pulse rises untouched, unwanted—grunting aloud in the damp stripes under my groins, the tender sides of my windpipe, sides of my heels, the pad of my sinking finger. My finger coils to my side, my whole hand clenches, my eyes clamp tighter, but—innocent surely—he speaks for the first time since begging my pardon. "Am I dying, preacher?"

I look up at him. "No sir. What do you mean?"

"I mean you left my pulse like a bat out of Hell. I wondered did you feel bad news?"

"No sir, it is going fine. I just never felt it before, and it gave me chills." He smiles at the road and we slide on a mile or more till I say, "Are you *scared* of dying?"

He keeps me waiting so I look past him through glass to the sky for a distant point to anchor on—the moon, a planet, Betelgeuse. Nothing is there. All is drowned under cloud but I narrow my eyes and strain to pierce the screen. Then when I am no longer waiting, he says, "It is the main thing I am scared of."

I come back to him. "Everybody is going to die."

"So they tell me. So they tell me. But that is one crowd I would miss if I could. Gladly."

I am not really thinking. "What do people mean when they say somebody is their personal hero?"

It comes sooner than I expect. "Your hero is what you need to be."

"Then is Jesus your hero?"

"Why do you think that?"

"You say you are scared of dying. Jesus is the one that did not die."

He does not take it as funny which is right, and being no Bible scholar he does not name me the others that live on—Enoch, Elijah. I name them to myself but not to him. I have seen my chance. I am aiming now at discovery, and I strike inwards like Balboa mean and brave, not knowing where I go or will end or if I can live with what I find. But the next move is his. He must see me off. And he does. He tells me, "I think your hero has to be a man. Was Jesus a man?"

"No sir. He was God disguised."

"Well, that is it, you see. You would not stand a chance of being God—need to or not—so you pick somebody you have got half a chance of measuring up to."

In all my seeking I have not asked him. I ask him now. "Have you got a hero?"

Again he makes me wait and I *wait*. I look nowhere but at him. I do not think. Then he says, "Yes, I guess I do. But I never called it that to myself."

"What did you call it?"

"I didn't call it nothing. I was too busy trying to get through alive."

"Sir?"

"—Get through some trouble I had. I *had* some troubles and when I did there was generally a person I could visit and talk to till I eased. Then when I left him and the trouble came back, I would press down on *him* in my mind—something he told me or how he shook my hand goodbye. Sometimes that tided me over. Sometimes."

He has still not offered a name. To help him I hold out the first one at hand. "Is it Dr. Truett?" (That is where we are coming from now tonight—a sermon in Raleigh by George W. Truett from Texas.)

The offer is good enough to make him think. (I know how much he admires Dr. Truett. He has one of his books and a sermon on records—"The Need for Encouragement"—that he plays two or three nights a year, standing in the midst of the room, giving what wide curved gestures seem right when Dr. Truett says for instance, "'Yet now be strong, O Zerubbabel, saith the Lord; and be strong O Joshua, son of Josedech, the high priest; and be strong, all ye people of the land, saith the Lord, and work: for I am with you, saith the Lord of hosts: according to the word that I covenanted with you when ye came out of Egypt, so my spirit remaineth among you: fear ye not.'" And here we have come this long way to see him in January with snow due to fall by morning.) But he says—my father, "No, not really. Still you are close." Then a wait—"You are warm."

"Does that mean it is a preacher?"

"Yes."

"Mr. Barden?"

"I guess he is it."

I knew he was—or would have known if I had thought—but I do not know why. He is nothing but the Baptist minister in Copeland, my father's home—half a head shorter than Father, twenty years older, light and dry as kindling with flat bands of gray hair, white skin the day shines through if he stands by windows, Chinese eyes, bird ankles, a long voice for saying things such as "Jeff, I am happy to slide my legs under the same table with yours" and poor digestion (he said that last the one day he ate with us; my mother had cooked all morning, and he ate a cup of warm milk)—but he is one of the people my father loves, one my mother is jealous of, and whenever we visit Copeland (we left there when I was two), there will come a point after dinner on Sunday when my father will stand and without speaking start for the car. If it is winter he may get away unseen, but in summer everybody will be on the porch, and Junie will say, "Jeff is headed to save Brother Barden's soul." My mother will laugh. My father will smile and nod but go and be gone till evening and feel no need to explain when he returns, only grin and agree to people's jokes.

But *tonight*, has he not just offered to explain? and to me who have never asked? So I ask, "Mr. Barden is so skinny. What has he got that you need to be?"

"Before you were born he used to be a lot of things. Still is."

All this time he has not needed his hand on the wheel. It has stayed heavy on me. I slip my hand towards it. I test with my finger, tapping. He turns his palm and takes me, gives me the right to say "Name some things." I fear if he looks at me, we will go back silent (he has not looked down since we started with his pulse), and I roll my face deep into his side, not to take his eyes. But they do not come. He does not look. He does not press my hand in his, and the load of his wrist even lightens. I think it will leave but it lifts a little and settles further on like a folded shield over where I am warmest, takes up guard, and then he is talking the way he must, the best he can, to everything but me—the glass, the hood, the hoop of light we push towards home.

"I have done things you would not believe—and will not believe when you get old enough to do them yourself. I have come home at night where your mother was waiting and said things to her that were worse than a beating, then gone again and left her still waiting till morning, till sometimes night again. And did them knowing I would not do them to a dog. Did them drunk and wild, knowing she loved me and would not leave me even though her sisters said, 'Leave him. He won't change now,' would not even raise her voice. O Preacher, it was Hell. We were both in Hell with the lid screwed down, not a dollar between us except what I borrowed—from Negroes sometimes when friends ran out—to buy my liquor to keep me wild. You were not born yet, were not thought of, God knows not wanted the way I was going. It was 1930. I was thirty years old and my life looked over, and I didn't know why or whether

I wanted it different, but here came Mr. Barden skinny as you say, just sitting by me when I could sit still, talking when I could listen, saying 'Hold up, Jeff. Promise God something before you *die.*' But Preacher, I didn't. I drank up two more years, driving thousands of miles on mirey roads in a model-A Ford to sell little scraps of life insurance to wiped-out farmers that did not have a pot to pee in, giving your mother a dollar or so to buy liver with on a Saturday or a pound of hominy I could not swallow. And then that spring when the bottom looked close, I slipped and started you on the way. When I knew you were coming—Preacher, for days I was out of what mind I had left myself. I do not know what I did but I *did* things, and finally when I had run some sort of course, your mother sent for Mr. Barden and they got me still. He said, 'Jeff, I cherish you, mean as you are. But what can I do if you go on murdering yourself, tormenting your wife?' I told him, 'You can ask the Lord to stop that baby.' I told him that. But you came on every day *every day* like a tumor till late January and she hollered to me you were nearly here. But you were not. You held back twenty-four hours as if you knew who was waiting outside, and Dr. Haskins told me—after he had struggled with your mother all day, all night—'Jeff, one of your family is going to die but I don't know which.' I said, 'Let it be me' and he said he wished he could. I went outdoors to Paul's woodshed and told Jesus, 'If You take Rhew or take that baby, then take me too. But if You can, save her and save that baby, and I make You this promise—I will change my life.' I asked Him, 'Change my life.' So He saved you two and I started trying to change my life, am trying right now God knows. Well, Mr. Barden has helped me out every once in a while—talking to me or just sitting calm, showing me his good heart. Which, Preacher, I need."

I can tell by his voice he is not through, but he stops, leaving raw quiet like a hole beneath us. I feel that because I have stayed awake, and my finger slips to the trough of his wrist where the pulse was before. It is there again awful. I take it, count it long as I can and say, "It feels all right to me, sir" (not knowing of course how right would feel). He says he is glad which frees me to see Mr. Barden again. I call up his face and pick it for anything new. At first it is very much the same—bloodless, old—but I settle on the faded stripes of his lips and strain to picture them years ago saying the things that were just now reported. They move, speak and for a moment I manage to see his face as a wedge—but aimed elsewhere, making no offer to split me clean from my lacks *my* foes. So I let it die and I say to my father, "I still think Jesus is your real hero."

Glad for his rest, he is ready again. "Maybe so. Maybe so. But Mr. Barden was what I could *see.*"

"Who has seen Jesus?"

"Since He died, you mean?"

"Yes sir."

"Several, I guess. Dr. Truett for one."

I know the story—it is why I have come this far to hear an old man tremble for an hour—but I request it again.

"Well, as I understand it, years ago when he was young, he asked a friend to come hunting with him. He came and they went in the woods together, and after a while he shot his friend. By accident but that didn't make him feel any better. He knew some people would always say he killed the man on purpose."

"Maybe he did."

"No he didn't. Hold on."

"How do you know?"

"The same way *he* knew—because after he sweated drops of blood in misery, Jesus came to him one evening in a dream and said not to grieve any more but to live his life and do what he could."

"Does that mean he really saw Jesus?—seeing Him in his sleep?"

"How else could you see Him since He is dead so long?"

I tell him the chance that is one of my hopes, my terrors—"He could walk in your house in daylight. Then you could step around Him. You could put out your hand and He would be there. But in just a dream how would you know? What would keep Him from being a trick?"

"The way He would look. His face, His hands."

"The scars, you mean?"

"They would help. But no—" This is hard for him. He stops and thinks for fully a mile. "I mean whether or not He had the face to say things such as 'Be ye perfect as God is perfect'—not even say '*try* to be,' just '*be*'—a face that could change people's lives."

"People do not *know* what He looks like, Father. That is half the trouble." We are now on one of our oldest subjects. We started three years ago when I first went to vacation Bible school. At the end of that two weeks after we had made our flour-paste model of a Hebrew water hole, they gave us diplomas that were folded leaflets with our name inside and a golden star but on the cover their idea of Jesus—set by a palm under light such as comes after storms (blurred, with piece of a rainbow) and huddled around Him, one each of the earth's children in native dress, two or three inside His arms but all aiming smiles at His face (jellied eyes, tan silk beard, clean silk hair, pink lips that could not call a dog to heel much less children or say to His mother, "Who is my mother?" and call her "Woman" from the bitter cross). I took the picture but at home that night I handed it to my father and asked if he thought that face was possible? He looked and said it was one man's guess, not to worry about it, but I did and later after I had studied picture Bibles and *Christ and the Fine Arts* by Cynthia Pearl Maus full of hairy Jesuses by Germans mostly—Clementz, Deitrich, Hofmann, Lang, Plockhorst, Von Uhde, Wehle—I asked him if in all the guessers, there was one who knew? any Jesus to count on? He said he thought there was but in Student's Bibles, the ones they give to boys studying ministry. I said had he seen one? He had not and I asked if he could buy me one or borrow Mr. Barden's for me to trace? He said he did not think so, that Student's Bibles were confidential, secrets for good men.

So tonight I ask him, "Then how did He look in your mind when I was being born and Mother was dying?"

"He didn't look nohow *that* day. I was not seeing faces. I was doing business. If I saw anything it was rocks underfoot, those smooth little rocks Paul hauled from the creek to spread in his yard."

"I think it is awful."

"What?"

"Him not appearing. Why did Dr. Truett see Him and you could not?"

"Maybe he needed to worse than me. He had killed a man, killed somebody else. I was just killing me, making others watch me do it."

"That is no reason."

"Preacher, if I was as good a man as George W. Truett—half the man—I would be seeing Jesus every day or so, be *fishing* with Him."

"I am not joking, Father. It is awful, I think—Him not helping you better than that."

"Preacher, I didn't mind"—which even with this night's new information is more or less where we always end. It does not worry my father that he is not privileged to see the secret. But it scalds, torments any day of mine in which I think that the face with power to change my life is hid from me and reserved for men who have won their fight (when He Himself claimed He sought the lost), will always be hid, leaving me to work dark. As my father has done, does, must do—not minding, just turning on himself his foe with nothing for hero but Mr. Barden when it could have been Jesus if He had appeared, His gouged hands, His real face, the one He deserved that changes men.

We are quiet again, so quiet I notice the sound of the engine. I have not heard it tonight before. It bores through the floor, crowds my ears, and turning my eyes I take the mileage—sixty-three thousand to round it off. My father travels in his work as I say, and this Pontiac has borne him three times around the earth—the equal of that nearly. It will get us home together, alive, and since in a heavy rush I am tired, I sleep where I am, in his heat, in his hollow. Of course I do not think I am sleeping. I dream I am awake, that I stand on the near side of sleep and yearn, but it *is* a dream and as sudden again I wake—my head laid flat on the mohair seat, blood gathered hot in my eyes that stare up at nothing. My head lifts a little (stiff on my neck), my eyes jerk round collecting terror—the motor runs gentle, the knob of the heater burns red, burns warm, but the car is still and my father is gone. Where he was the dashboard light strikes empty nothing. My head falls back and still half dreaming I think, "They have won at last. They have caught us, come between us. We have ended apart." I say that last aloud and it wakes me fully so I lie on (my head where his loaded lap should be) and think what seems nearer truth—"He has left as I always knew he would to take up his life in secret." Then I plunge towards the heart of my fear—"He knew just now what I thought when I pressed his pulse, and he could not bear my sight any more." Then deeper towards the heart—"God has taken him from me as punishment for causing his death just now in my mind. But why did He not take me?" Still He did not. I am left. So I rise and strain to see out the glass, to know my purpose for being here, what trials lie between me and morning, what vengeance. The first is snow. The headlights shine and in their outward upward hoop there is only flat gobs of snow that saunter into frozen grass and survive. The grass of the shoulder is all but smothered, the weeds of the bank already bent, meaning I have slept long enough for my life to wreck beyond hope—my father vanished and I sealed in a black Pontiac with stiff death held back only long as the draining battery lasts and now too late, no hero to turn to. My forehead presses into the dark windshield. For all the heater's work, the cold crawls in through glass, through flesh, through skull to my blood, my brain.

So I pray. My eyes clamped now, still pressed to the glass, knowing I have not prayed for many weeks past (with things going well), I swallow my shame and naked in fear ask, "Send me my father. Send me help. If You help me now, if You save my life, I will change—be brave, be free with my gifts. Send somebody good." My eyes click open on answered prayer—coming slow from the far edge of light a tall man hunched, his face to the ground hid, head wrapped in black, a black robe bound close about him, his arms inside, bearing towards me borne on the snow as if on water leaving no tracks, his shadow crouched on the snow like a following bird, giant, black (killing? kind?). I stay at the glass, further prayer locked in my throat, waiting only for the sign of my fate. Then the robe spreads open. The man's broad hands are clasped on his heart, turned inward, dark. It is Jesus I see, Jesus I shall touch moments from now—shall lift His face, probe His wounds, kiss His eyes. He is five steps away. I slip from the glass, fall back on my haunches, turn to the driver's door where He already stands, say silent, "If Father could not see Your face, why must I?"—say to the opening door "Thank You, Sir," close my lips to take His unknown kiss.

He says, "Excuse me leaving you asleep," and it is my father come back disguised. "I had to go pee—down that hill in the snow." (He points down the road as if he had covered miles not feet.) "I thought you were dead to the world."

I say, "I *was*"—I laugh—"and I thought you were Jesus, that you had been taken and I was left and Jesus was coming to claim me. I was about to *see* Him."

Standing outside, the warm air rushing towards him, he shrugs the coat from his shoulders, lifts the scarf from his head, lays them in back, slides onto the seat. Shrinking from cold I have crawled almost to the opposite door, but kneeling towards him. He faces me and says, "I am sorry to disappoint you, Preacher."

I say, "Yes sir" and notice he smiles very slow, very deep from his eyes—but ahead at the road. Then he says I had better lie down. I crawl the two steps and lie as before, and we move on so I have no chance to return his smile, to show I share his pleasure. Still I root my head deep in his lap and hope for a chance before sleep returns. The chance never comes. Snow occupies his eyes, his hands. He cannot face me again or test for warmth. Even his mind is surely on nothing but safety. Yet his face is new. Some scraps of the beauty I planned for Jesus hang there—on the corners of the mouth serious now, beneath his glasses in eyes that are no longer simply kind and gray but have darkened and burn new power far back and steady (the power to stop in his tracks and *turn*), on his ears still purple with cold but flared against danger like perfect ugly shells of blind sea life, on his wrists I cannot ring with my hand, stretched from white cuffs at peace on the wheel but shifting with strength beyond soldier's, beyond slave's—and I think, "I will look till I know my father, till all this new disguise falls away leaving him clear as before." I look but his face shows no sign of retreat and still as he is and distant, it is hard to stare, painful then numbing. I feel sleep rise from my feet like blood. When it reaches my head I shut my eyes to flush it back, but it surges again and I know I have lost. My own hands are free—he has not touched me, cannot—so my right hand slips to the gap in my pants, cups itself warm on warmer trinkets long since asleep, soft with blood like new birds nested drowsy. I follow them into darkness, thinking on the threshold, "Now I have lost all hope of knowing my father's life," cupping closer, warmer this hand as I sink.

First in my dream I am only this hand yet have eyes to see—but only this hand and a circle of light around it. It is larger by half than tonight, and black stubble has sprung to shade its back, its new thick veins, its gristly cords showing plain because this hand is cupped too, round like a mold, hiding what it makes. It lifts. What it has molded are the kernels, the knobs of a man still twice the size of mine I held before I slept, but cold, shrunk and shrinking as my hand lifts—their little life pouring out blue through veins gorged like sewers that tunnel and vanish under short lank hairs, grizzled. Then I have ears. I hear the blood rustle like silk as it leaves, retreats, *abandons*, and my hand shuts down, clamps on the blood to turn its race, to warm again, fill again what I hold. But the rustle continues not muffled, and my hand presses harder, squeezes the kernels. Through my fingers green piss streams cold, corrosive. But my hand is locked. It cannot move. I am bound to what I have made, have caused, and seeing only this terror, I find a voice to say, "If I cannot leave may I see what I do?" The light swells in a hoop from my hand filling dimly a room and in that room my whole body standing by a bed—the body I will have as a man—my hand at the core of a man's stripped body laid yellow on the narrow bed. Yet with this new light my original eyes have stayed where they started—on my crushing hand and beneath it. I tear them left to see the rest. So I start at his feet raised parallel now but the soles pressed flat by years of weight, the rims of the heels and the crowded toes guarded by clear callus, the veins of the insteps branching toward shins like blades of antique war polished deadly, marred by sparse hair, the knees like grips to the blades, the thighs ditched inward to what I crush—his hollow his core that streams on thin with no native force but sure as if drained by magnets in the earth. Then his hands at his sides clenched but the little fingers separate, crouched, gathering ridges in the sheet. Then his firm belly drilled deep by the navel, his chest like the hull of a stranded boat, shaved raw, violet paps sunk and from under his left armpit a line traced carefully down his side, curved under his ribs, climbing to the midst of his breast—the letter J perfect, black, cut into him hopeless to dredge out a lung, laced with gut stiff as wire. Then under a tent of soft wrinkled glass his face which of course is my father's—the face he will have when I am this man—turned from me, eyes shut, lips shut, locked in the monstrous stillness of his rest. So he does not watch me, shows no sign of the pain I must cause. Yet I try again to lift my fingers, to set him free, but rocking the heel of my hand, I see our skin has joined maybe past parting. I struggle though—gentle to spare his rest. I step back slowly, hoping this natural movement will peel us clean, but what I have pressed comes with me as if I had given love not pain. I speak again silent to whoever gave me light just now, say, "Set him free. Let me leave him whole in peace." But that prayer fails and turning my eyes I pull against him, ready to wound us both if I must. Our joint holds fast but the rustle beneath my hand swells to scraping, to high short grunts. "Jesus," I say—I speak aloud—"Come again. Come now. I do not ask to see Your face but come in *some* shape now." A shudder begins beneath my hand in his core our core that floods through his belly, his breast to his throat, bearing with it the noise that dims as it enters the tent. I stare through the glass. His head rolls toward me, his yellow lips split to release the noise, his eyes slide open on a quarter-inch of white. The noise scrapes on but behind the tent it is not words—is it rage or pain or wish, is it meant for me? With my free left hand I reach for the tent to throw it back, saying, "Stop. Stop," but I cannot reach so "Father," I say, "I beg your pardon. Pardon me this, I will change my life—will turn in my tracks on myself my foe with you as shield." But he yields no signal. The eyes shut again, the lips shut down on the noise, the shudder runs out as it came, to our core. What my free hand can reach it touches—his wrist. What pulse was there is stopped, and cold succeeds it till with both hands I press hard ice, final as any trapped in the Pole. I can see clearer now, my terror calmed by his grander terror, the peace of his wounds, and facing his abandoned face I say again (to the place, the dream), "Pardon me this, I will change my life. I make this . . ." But pardon comes to stop my speech. My cold hands lift from his hollow, his wrist. My own hot life pours back to claim them. Then those hands fail, those eyes, my dream. A shift of my headrest lifts me from sleep.

I face my live father's present body—my present eyes on his belly but *him*, *tonight*, above me, around me, shifting beneath me. My lips are still open, a trail of spit snails down my cheek, my throat still holds the end of my dream, "I make this promise." So my first thought is fear. Have I spoken aloud what I watched in my dream? Have I warned my father of his waiting death? offered my promise, my life too early? I roll away from his belt to see—and see I am safe. He is what he has been before tonight, been all my life, unchanged by my awful news, my knowledge, undisguised—his ears, his cheeks flushed with healthy blood that also throbs in the broad undersides of his wrists on the wheel, in the wounded fat of his hand, his hollow, even in his eyes which are still ahead on the road for safety, able, unblinking but calm and light as if through snow he watched boys playing skillful games with natural grace.

His legs shift often under me now—braking, turning, accelerating—and we move forward slowly past regular street lamps that soar through the rim of my sight, gold at the ends of green arms. We are in some town. From its lamps, its wires, its hidden sky, I cannot say which—but not home yet I trust, I hope. I am not prepared for home and my mother, the rooms that surround my swelling lacks, direct sight of my doomed father. I need silent time to hoard my secret out of my face deep into my mind, granting my father twelve years fearless to work at his promise, freeing myself to gather in private the strength I will need for my own promise the night he dies, my own first turn on what giant foes I will have as a man. And clamping my eyes I seize my dream and thrust it inward, watching it suck down a blackening funnel, longing to follow it. But his legs shift again, his arms swing left, our wheels strike gravel, stop. Beyond the glass in our stationary light are bare maple limbs accepting snow, limbs of the one tree I climb with ease. Too sudden we are home and my father expels in a seamless shudder the care, the attention that bound him these last three hours. His legs tense once, gather to spring from beneath my weight, then subside, soften. I ride the final surge, then face him—smiling as if just startled from sleep.

He takes my smile, stores it as a gift. "Did you sleep well, Preacher?"

I hunch my shoulders, say "Thank you, sir," and behind my lie floods sudden need—to rise, board him, cherish with my hands, my arms while there still is time this huge gentle body I know like my own, which made my own (made half anyhow) and has hurt nobody since the day I was born.

But he says, "Lift up. Look yonder at the door."

I roll to my knees. Through glass and snow, behind small panes, white curtains, in the center of the house no longer ours stands my mother in a flannel robe, hand raised in welcome the shape of fire. "She waited," I say.

"She waited," he says and reaches for his scarf, his coat, beckons me to him, drapes them around me, steps to the white ground and turning, offers me open arms. Kneeling I ask him, "What do you mean?"

"I mean to save your life, to carry you over this snow."

"Heavy as *I* am?—you and *your* heart?"

But he says no more. His mind is made, his trip is ended. He is nearly home, facing rest, accepting snow like the trees while I stall. Then he claps his palms one time, and I go on my knees out of dry car heat through momentary snow into arms that circle, enfold me, lift me, bear me these last steps home over ice—my legs hung bare down his cooling side, face to his heart, eyes blind again, mind folding in me for years to come his literal death and my own swelling foes, lips against rough brown wool saying to myself as we rise to the porch, to my waiting mother (silent, in the voice I will have as a man), "They did not separate us tonight. We finished alive, together, whole. This one more time."

Richard Rodriguez (born 1944)
Aria

1

I remember to start with that day in Sacramento—a California now nearly thirty years past—when I first entered a classroom, able to understand some fifty stray English words.

The third of four children, I had been preceded to a neighborhood Roman Catholic school by an older brother and sister. But neither of them had revealed very much about their classroom experiences. Each afternoon they returned, as they left in the morning, always together, speaking in Spanish as they climbed the five steps of the porch. And their mysterious books, wrapped in shopping-bag paper, remained on the table next to the door, closed firmly behind them.

An accident of geography sent me to a school where all my classmates were white, many the children of doctors and lawyers and business executives. All my classmates certainly must have been uneasy on that first day of school—as most children are uneasy—to find themselves apart from their families in the first institution of their lives. But I was astonished.

The nun said, in a friendly but oddly impersonal voice, "Boys and girls, this is Richard Rodriguez." (I heard her sound out: *Rich-heard Road-ree-guess.*) It was the first time I had heard anyone name me in English. "Richard," the nun repeated more slowly, writing my name down in her black leather book. Quickly I turned to see my mother's face dissolve in a watery blur behind the pebbled glass door.

Many years later there is something called bilingual education—a scheme proposed in the late 1960s by Hispanic-American social activists, later endorsed by a congressional vote. It is a program that seeks to permit non-English-speaking children, many from lower class homes, to use their family language as the language of school. (Such is the goal its supporters announce.) I hear them and am forced to say no: It is not possible for a child—any child—ever to use his family's language in school. Not to understand this is to misunderstand the public uses of schooling and to trivialize the nature of intimate life—a family's "language."

Memory teaches me what I know of these matters; the boy reminds the adult. I was a bilingual child, a certain kind—socially disadvantaged—the son of working-class parents, both Mexican immigrants.

In the early years of my boyhood, my parents coped very well in America. My father had steady work. My mother managed at home. They were nobody's victims. Optimism and ambition led them to a house (our home) many blocks from the Mexican south side of town. We lived among *gringos* and only a block from the biggest, whitest houses. It never occurred to my parents that they couldn't live wherever they chose. Nor was the Sacramento of the fifties bent on teaching them a contrary lesson. My mother and father were more annoyed than intimidated by those two or three neighbors who tried initially to make us unwelcome. ("Keep your brats away from my sidewalk!") But despite all they achieved, perhaps because they had so much to achieve, any deep feeling of ease, the confidence of "belonging" in public was withheld from them both. They regarded the people at work, the faces in crowds, as very distant from us. They were the others, *los gringos*. That term was interchangeable in their speech with another, even more telling, *los americanos*.

I grew up in a house where the only regular guests were my relations. For one day, enormous families of relatives would visit and there would be so many people that the noise and the bodies would spill out to the backyard and front porch. Then, for weeks, no one came by. (It was usually a salesman who rang the doorbell.) Our house stood apart. A gaudy yellow in a row of white bungalows. We were the people with the noisy dog. The people who raised pigeons and chickens. We were the foreigners on the block. A few neighbors smiled and waved. We waved back. But no one in the family knew the names of the old couple who lived next door; until I was seven years old, I did not know the names of the kids who lived across the street.

In public, my father and mother spoke a hesitant, accented, not always grammatical English. And they would have to strain—their bodies tense—to catch the sense of what was rapidly said by *los gringos*. At home they spoke Spanish. The language of their Mexican past sounded in counterpoint to the English of public society. The words would come quickly, with ease. Conveyed through those sounds was the pleasing, soothing, consoling reminder of being at home.

During those years when I was first conscious of hearing, my mother and father addressed me only in Spanish; in Spanish I learned to reply. By contrast, English (*inglés*), rarely heard in the house, was the language I came to associate with *gringos*. I learned my first words of English overhearing my parents speak to strangers. At five years of age, I knew just enough English for my mother to trust me on errands to stores one block away. No more.

I was a listening child, careful to hear the very different sounds of Spanish and English. Wide-eyed with hearing, I'd listen to sounds more than words. First, there were English (*gringo*) sounds. So many words were still unknown that when the butcher or the lady at the drugstore said something to me, exotic polysyllabic sounds would bloom in the midst of their sentences. Often, the speech of people in public seemed to me very loud, booming with confidence. The man behind the counter would literally ask, "What can I do for you?" But by being so firm and so clear, the sound of his voice said that he was a *gringo*; he belonged in public society.

I would also hear then the high nasal notes of middle-class American speech. The air stirred with sound. Sometimes, even now, when I have been traveling abroad for several weeks, I will hear what I heard as a boy. In hotel lobbies or airports, in

Turkey or Brazil, some Americans will pass, and suddenly I will hear it again—the high sound of American voices. For a few seconds I will hear it with pleasure, for it is now the sound of *my* society—a reminder of home. But inevitably—already on the flight headed for home—the sound fades with repetition. I will be unable to hear it anymore.

When I was a boy, things were different. The accent of *los gringos* was never pleasing nor was it hard to hear. Crowds at Safeway or at bus stops would be noisy with sound. And I would be forced to edge away from the chirping chatter above me.

I was unable to hear my own sounds, but I knew very well that I spoke English poorly. My words could not stretch far enough to form complete thoughts. And the words I did speak I didn't know well enough to make into distinct sounds. (Listeners would usually lower their heads, better to hear what I was trying to say.) But it was one thing for *me* to speak English with difficulty. It was more troubling for me to hear my parents speak in public: their high-whining vowels and guttural consonants; their sentences that got stuck with "eh" and "ah" sounds; the confused syntax; the hesitant rhythm of sounds so different from the way *gringos* spoke. I'd notice, moreover, that my parents' voices were softer than those of *gringos* we'd meet.

I am tempted now to say that none of this mattered. In adulthood I am embarrassed by childhood fears. And, in a way, it didn't matter very much that my parents could not speak English with ease. Their linguistic difficulties had no serious consequences. My mother and father made themselves understood at the county hospital clinic and at government offices. And yet, in another way, it mattered very much—it was unsettling to hear my parents struggle with English. Hearing them, I'd grow nervous, my clutching trust in their protection and power weakened.

There were many times like the night at a brightly lit gasoline station (a blaring white memory) when I stood uneasily, hearing my father. He was talking to a teenaged attendant. I do not recall what they were saying, but I cannot forget the sounds my father made as he spoke. At one point his words slid together to form one word—sounds as confused as the threads of blue and green oil in the puddle next to my shoes. His voice rushed through what he had left to say. And, toward the end, reached falsetto notes, appealing to his listener's understanding. I looked away to the lights of passing automobiles. I tried not to hear anymore. But I heard only too well the calm, easy tones in the attendant's reply. Shortly afterward, walking toward home with my father, I shivered when he put his hand on my shoulder. The very first chance that I got, I evaded his grasp and ran on ahead into the dark, skipping with feigned boyish exuberance.

But then there was Spanish. *Español:* my family's language. *Español:* the language that seemed to me a private language. I'd hear strangers on the radio and in the Mexican Catholic church across town speaking in Spanish, but I couldn't really believe that Spanish was a public language, like English. Spanish speakers, rather, seemed related to me, for I sensed that we shared—through our language—the experience of feeling apart from *los gringos*. It was thus a ghetto Spanish that I heard and I spoke. Like those whose lives are bound by a barrio, I was reminded by Spanish of my separateness from *los otros, los gringos* in power. But more intensely than for most barrio children—because I did not live in a barrio—Spanish seemed to me the language of home. (Most days it was only at home that I'd hear it.) It became the language of joyful return.

A family member would say something to me and I would feel myself specially recognized. My parents would say something to me and I would feel embraced by the sounds of their words. Those sounds said: *I am speaking with ease in Spanish. I am addressing you in words I never use with* los gringos. *I recognize you as someone special, close, like no one outside. You belong with us. In the family.*

(*Ricardo.*)

At the age of five, six, well past the time when most other children no longer easily notice the difference between sounds uttered at home and words spoken in public, I had a different experience. I lived in a world magically compounded of sounds. I remained a child longer than most; I lingered too long, poised at the edge of language—often frightened by the sounds of *los gringos*, delighted by the sounds of Spanish at home. I shared with my family a language that was startlingly different from that used in the great city around us.

For me there were none of the gradations between public and private society so normal to a maturing child. Outside the house was public society; inside the house was private. Just opening or closing the screen door behind me was an important experience. I'd rarely leave home all alone or without reluctance. Walking down the sidewalk, under the canopy of tall trees, I'd warily notice the—suddenly—silent neighborhood kids who stood warily watching me. Nervously, I'd arrive at the grocery store to hear there the sounds of the *gringo*—foreign to me—reminding me that in this world so big, I was a foreigner. But then I'd return. Walking back toward our home, climbing the steps from the sidewalk, when the front door was open in summer, I'd hear voices beyond the screen door talking in Spanish. For a second or two, I'd stay, linger there, listening. Smiling, I'd hear my mother call out, saying in Spanish (words): "Is that you, Richard?" All the while her sounds would assure me: *You are home now; come closer; inside. With us.*

"*Sí,*" I'd reply.

Once more inside the house I would resume (assume) my place in the family. The sounds would dim, grow harder to hear. Once more at home, I would grow less aware of that fact. It required, however, no more than the blurt of the doorbell to alert me to listen to sounds all over again. The house would turn instantly still while my mother went to the door. I'd hear her hard English sounds. I'd wait to hear her voice return to soft-sounding Spanish, which assured me, as surely as did the clicking tongue of the lock on the door, that the stranger was gone.

Plainly, it is not healthy to hear such sounds so often. It is not healthy to distinguish public words from private sounds so easily. I remained cloistered by sounds, timid and shy in public, too dependent on voices at home. And yet it needs to be emphasized: I was an extremely happy child at home. I remember many nights when my father would come back from work, and I'd hear him call out to my mother in Spanish, sounding relieved. In Spanish, he'd sound light and free notes he never could manage in English. Some nights I'd jump up just at hearing his voice. With *mis hermanos* I would come running into the room where he was with my mother. Our laughing (so deep was the pleasure!) became screaming. Like others who know the pain of public alienation, we transformed the knowledge of our public separateness and made it consoling—the reminder of intimacy. Excited, we joined our voices in a celebration of sounds. *We are speaking now the way we never speak out in public. We are alone—together,* voices sounded, surrounded to tell me. Some nights, no one seemed willing to loosen the hold sounds had on us. At dinner, we invented new words. (Ours sounded Spanish, but made sense only to us.) We pieced together new words by taking, say, an English verb and giving it Spanish endings. My mother's instructions at bedtime would be lacquered with mock-urgent tones. Or a word like *sí* would become, in several notes, able to convey added measures of feeling. Tongues explored the edges of words, especially the fat vowels. And we happily sounded that military drum roll, the twirling roar of the Spanish *r*. Family language: my family's sounds. The voices of my parents and sisters and brother. Their voices insisting: *You belong here. We are family members. Related. Special to one another. Listen!* Voices singing and sighing, rising, straining, then surging, teeming with pleasure that burst syllables into fragments of laughter. At times it seemed there was steady quiet only when, from another room, the rustling whispers of my parents faded and I moved closer to sleep.

2

Supporters of bilingual education today imply that students like me miss a great deal by not being taught in their family's language. What they seem not to recognize is that, as a socially disadvantaged child, I considered Spanish to be a private language. What I needed to learn in school was that I had the right—and the obligation—to speak the public language of *los gringos*. The odd truth is that my first-grade classmates could have become bilingual, in the conventional sense of that word, more easily than I. Had they been taught (as upper-middle-class children are often taught early) a second language like Spanish or French, they could have regarded it simply as that: another public language. In my case such bilingualism could not have been so quickly achieved. What I did not believe was that I could speak a single public language.

Without question, it would have pleased me to hear my teachers address me in Spanish when I entered the classroom. I would have felt much less afraid. I would have trusted them and responded with ease. But I would have delayed—for how long postponed?—having to learn the language of public society. I would have evaded—and for how long could I have afforded to delay?—learning the great lesson of school, that I had a public identity.

Fortunately, my teachers were unsentimental about their responsibility. What they understood was that I needed to speak a public language. So their voices would search me out, asking me questions. Each time I'd hear them, I'd look up in surprise to see a nun's face frowning at me. I'd mumble, not really meaning to answer. The nun would persist, "Richard, stand up. Don't look at the floor. Speak up. Speak to the entire class, not just to me!" But I couldn't believe that the English language was mine to use. (In part, I did not want to believe it.) I continued to mumble. I resisted the teacher's demands. (Did I somehow suspect that once I learned public language my pleasing family life would be changed?) Silent, waiting for the bell to sound, I remained dazed, diffident, afraid.

Because I wrongly imagined that English was intrinsically a public language and Spanish an intrinsically private one, I easily noted the difference between classroom language and the language of home. At school, words were directed to a general audience of listeners. ("Boys and girls.") Words were meaningfully ordered. And the point was not self-expression alone but to make oneself understood by many others. The teacher quizzed: "Boys and girls, why do we use that word in this sentence? Could we think of a better word to use there? Would the sentence change its meaning if the words were differently arranged? And wasn't there a better way of saying much the same thing?" (I couldn't say. I wouldn't try to say.)

Three months. Five. Half a year passed. Unsmiling, ever watchful, my teachers noted my silence. They began to connect my behavior with the difficult progress my older sister and brother were making. Until one Saturday morning three nuns arrived at the house to talk to our parents. Stiffly, they sat on the blue living room sofa. From the doorway of another room, spying the visitors, I noted the incongruity—the clash of two worlds, the faces and voices of school intruding upon the familiar setting of home. I overheard one voice gently wondering, "Do your children speak only Spanish at home, Mrs. Rodriguez?" While another voice added, "That Richard especially seems so timid and shy."

That Rich-heard!

With great tact the visitors continued, "Is it possible for you and your husband to encourage your children to practice their English when they are home?" Of course, my parents complied. What would they not do for their children's well-being? And how could they have questioned the Church's authority which those women represented? In an instant, they agreed to give up the language (the sounds) that had revealed and accentuated our family's closeness. The moment after the visitors left, the change was observed. "*Ahora,* speak to us *en inglés,*" my father and mother united to tell us.

At first, it seemed a kind of game. After dinner each night, the family gathered to practice "our" English. (It was still then *inglés,* a language foreign to us, so we felt drawn as strangers to it.) Laughing, we would try to define words we could not pronounce. We played with strange English sounds, often overanglicizing our pronunciations. And we filled the smiling gaps of our sentences with familiar Spanish sounds.

But that was cheating, somebody shouted. Everyone laughed. In school, meanwhile, like my brother and sister, I was required to attend a daily tutoring session. I needed a full year of special attention. I also needed my teachers to keep my attention from straying in class by calling out, *Rich-heard*—their English voices slowly prying loose my ties to my other name, its three notes, *Ri-car-do.* Most of all I needed to hear my mother and father speak to me in a moment of seriousness in broken—suddenly heartbreaking—English. The scene was inevitable: One Saturday morning I entered the kitchen where my parents were talking in Spanish. I did not realize that they were talking in Spanish however until, at the moment they saw me, I heard their voices change to speak English. Those *gringo* sounds they uttered startled me. Pushed me away. In that moment of trivial misunderstanding and profound insight, I felt my throat twisted by unsounded grief. I turned quickly and left the room. But I had no place to escape to with Spanish. (The spell was broken.) My brother and sisters were speaking English in another part of the house.

Again and again in the days following, increasingly angry, I was obliged to hear my mother and father: "Speak to us *en inglés.*" (*Speak.*) Only then did I determine to learn classroom English. Weeks after, it happened: One day in school I raised my hand to volunteer an answer. I spoke out in a loud voice. And I did not think it remarkable when the entire class understood. That day, I moved very far from the disadvantaged child I had been only days earlier. The belief, the calming assurance that I belonged in public, had at last taken hold.

Shortly after, I stopped hearing the high and loud sounds of *los gringos.* A more and more confident speaker of English, I didn't trouble to listen to *how* strangers sounded, speaking to me. And there simply were too many English-speaking people in my day for me to hear American accents anymore. Conversations quickened. Listening to persons who sounded eccentrically pitched voices, I usually noted their sounds for an initial few seconds before I concentrated on *what* they were saying. Conversations became content-full. Transparent. Hearing someone's *tone* of voice— angry or questioning or sarcastic or happy or sad—I didn't distinguish it from the words it expressed. Sound and word were thus tightly wedded. At the end of a day, I was often bemused, always relieved, to realize how "silent," though crowded with words, my day in public had been. (This public silence measured and quickened the change in my life.)

At last, seven years old, I came to believe what had been technically true since my birth: I was an American citizen.

But the special feeling of closeness at home was diminished by then. Gone was the desperate, urgent, intense feeling of being at home; rare was the experience of feeling myself individualized by family intimates. We remained a loving family, but one greatly changed. No longer so close; no longer bound tight by the pleasing and troubling knowledge of our public separateness. Neither my older brother nor sister rushed home after school anymore. Nor did I. When I arrived home there would often be neighborhood kids in the house. Or the house would be empty of sounds.

Following the dramatic Americanization of their children, even my parents grew more publicly confident. Especially my mother. She learned the names of all the people on our block. And she decided we needed to have a telephone installed in the house. My father continued to use the word *gringo*. But it was no longer charged with the old bitterness or distrust. (Stripped of any emotional content, the word simply became a name for those Americans not of Hispanic descent.) Hearing him, sometimes, I wasn't sure if he was pronouncing the Spanish word *gringo* or saying gringo in English.

Matching the silence I started hearing in public was a new quiet at home. The family's quiet was partly due to the fact that, as we children learned more and more English, we shared fewer and fewer words with our parents. Sentences needed to be spoken slowly when a child addressed his mother or father. (Often the parent wouldn't understand.) The child would need to repeat himself. (Still the parent misunderstood.) The young voice, frustrated, would end up saying, "Never mind"—the subject was closed. Dinners would be noisy with the clinking of knives and forks against dishes. My mother would smile softly between her remarks; my father at the other end of the table would chew and chew at his food, while he stared over the heads of his children.

My *mother!* My *father!* After English became my primary language, I no longer knew what words to use in addressing my parents. The old Spanish words (those tender accents of sound) I had used earlier—*mamá* and *papá*—I couldn't use anymore. They would have been too painful reminders of how much had changed in my life. On the other hand, the words I heard neighborhood kids call *their* parents seemed equally unsatisfactory. *Mother* and *Father; Ma, Papa, Pa, Dad, Pop* (how I hated the all-American sound of that last word especially)—all these terms I felt were unsuitable, not really terms of address for *my* parents. As a result, I never used them at home. Whenever I'd speak to my parents, I would try to get their attention with eye contact alone. In public conversations, I'd refer to "my parents" or "my mother and father."

My mother and father, for their part, responded differently, as their children spoke to them less. She grew restless, seemed troubled and anxious at the scarcity of words exchanged in the house. It was she who would question me about my day when I came home from school. She smiled at small talk. She pried at the edges of my sentences to get me to say something more. (What?) She'd join conversations she overheard, but her intrusions often stopped her children's talking. By contrast, my father seemed reconciled to the new quiet. Though his English improved somewhat, he retired into silence. At dinner he spoke very little. One night his children and even his wife helplessly giggled at his garbled English pronunciation of the Catholic Grace before Meals. Thereafter he made his wife recite the prayer at the start of each meal, even on formal occasions, when there were guests in the house. Hers became the public voice of the family. On official business, it was she, not my father, one would usually hear on the phone or in stores, talking to strangers. His children grew so accustomed to his silence that, years later, they would speak routinely of his shyness. (My mother would often try to explain: Both his parents died when he was eight. He was raised by an uncle who treated him like little more than a menial servant. He was never encouraged to speak. He grew up alone. A man of few words.) But my father was not shy, I realized, when I'd watch him speaking Spanish with relatives. Using Spanish, he was quickly effusive. Especially when talking with other men, his voice would spark, flicker, flare alive with sounds. In Spanish, he expressed ideas and feelings he rarely revealed in English. With firm Spanish sounds, he conveyed confidence and authority English would never allow him.

The silence at home, however, was finally more than a literal silence. Fewer words passed between parent and child, but more profound was the silence that resulted from my inattention to sounds. At about the time I no longer bothered to listen with care to the sounds of English in public, I grew careless about listening to the sounds family members made when they spoke. Most of the time I heard someone speaking at home and didn't distinguish his sounds from the words people uttered in public. I didn't even pay much attention to my parents' accented and ungrammatical speech. At least not at home. Only when I was with them in public would I grow alert to their accents. Though, even then, their sounds caused me less and less concern. For I was increasingly confident of my own public identity.

I would have been happier about my public success had I not sometimes recalled what it had been like earlier, when my family had conveyed its intimacy through a set of conveniently private sounds. Sometimes in public, hearing a stranger, I'd hark back to my past. A Mexican farmworker approached me downtown to ask directions to somewhere. "¿Hijito . . . ?" he said. And his voice summoned deep longing. Another time, standing beside my mother in the visiting room of a Carmelite convent, before the dense screen which rendered the nuns shadowy figures, I heard several Spanish-speaking nuns—their busy, singsong overlapping voices—assure us that yes, yes, we were remembered, all our family was remembered in their prayers. (Their voices echoed faraway family sounds.) Another day, a dark-faced old woman—her hand light on my shoulder—steadied herself against me as she boarded a bus. She murmured something I couldn't quite comprehend. Her Spanish voice came near, like the face of a never-before-seen relative in the instant before I was kissed. Her voice, like so many of the Spanish voices I'd hear in public, recalled the golden age of my youth. Hearing Spanish then, I continued to be a careful, if sad, listener to sounds. Hearing a Spanish-speaking family walking behind me, I turned to look. I smiled for an instant, before my glance found the Hispanic-looking faces of strangers in the crowd going by.

Today I hear bilingual educators say that children lose a degree of "individuality" by becoming assimilated into public society. (Bilingual schooling was popularized in the seventies, that decade when middle-class ethnics began to resist the process of assimilation—the American melting pot.) But the bilingualists simplistically scorn the value and necessity of assimilation. They do not seem to realize that there are *two* ways a person is individualized. So they do not realize that while one suffers a diminished sense of *private* individuality by becoming assimilated into public society, such assimilation makes possible the achievement of *public* individuality.

The bilingualists insist that a student should be reminded of his difference from others in mass society, his heritage. But they equate mere separateness with individuality. The fact is that only in private—with intimates—is separateness from the crowd a prerequisite for individuality. (An intimate draws me apart, tells me that I am unique, unlike all others.) In public, by contrast, full individuality is achieved, paradoxically, by those who are able to consider themselves members of the crowd. Thus it happened for me: Only when I was able to think of myself as an American, no longer an alien in *gringo* society, could I seek the rights and opportunities necessary for full public individuality. The social and political advantages I enjoy as a man result from the day that I came to believe that my name, indeed, is *Rich-heard Road-ree-guess.* It is true that my public society today is often impersonal. (My public society is usually mass society.) Yet despite the anonymity of the crowd and despite the fact that the individuality I achieve in public is often tenuous—because it depends on my being one in a crowd—I celebrate the day I acquired my new name. Those middle-class ethnics who scorn assimilation seem to me filled with decadent self-pity, obsessed by the burden of public life. Dangerously, they romanticize public separateness and they trivialize the dilemma of the socially disadvantaged.

My awkward childhood does not prove the necessity of bilingual education. My story discloses instead an essential myth of childhood—inevitable pain. If I rehearse here the changes in my private life after my Americanization, it is finally to emphasize the public gain. The loss implies the gain: The house I returned to each afternoon was quiet. Intimate sounds no longer rushed to the door to greet me. There were other noises inside. The telephone rang. Neighborhood kids ran past the door of the bedroom where I was reading my schoolbooks—covered with shopping-bag paper. Once I learned public language, it would never again be easy for me to hear intimate family voices. More and more of my day was spent hearing words. But that may only be a way of saying that the day I raised my hand in class and spoke loudly to an entire roomful of faces, my childhood started to end.

3

I grew up victim to a disabling confusion. As I grew fluent in English, I no longer could speak Spanish with confidence. I continued to understand spoken Spanish. And in high school, I learned how to read and write Spanish. But for many years I could not pronounce it. A powerful guilt blocked my spoken words; an essential glue was missing whenever I'd try to connect words to form sentences. I would be unable to break a barrier of sound, to speak freely. I would speak, or try to speak, Spanish, and I would manage to utter halting, hiccuping sounds that betrayed my unease.

When relatives and Spanish-speaking friends of my parents came to the house, my brother and sisters seemed reticent to use Spanish, but at least they managed to say a few necessary words before being excused. I never managed so gracefully. I was cursed with guilt. Each time I'd hear myself addressed in Spanish, I would be unable to respond with any success. I'd know the words I wanted to say, but I couldn't manage to say them. I would try to speak, but everything I said seemed to me horribly anglicized. My mouth would not form the words right. My jaw would tremble. After a phrase or two, I'd cough up a warm, silvery sound. And stop.

It surprised my listeners to hear me. They'd lower their heads, better to grasp what I was trying to say. They would repeat their questions in gentle, affectionate voices. But by then I would answer in English. No, no, they would say, we want you to speak to us in Spanish. (". . . *en español.*") But I couldn't do it. *Pocho* then they called me. Sometimes playfully, teasingly, using the tender diminutive—*mi pochito.* Sometimes not so playfully, mockingly, *Pocho.* (A Spanish dictionary defines that word as an adjective meaning "colorless" or "bland." But I heard it as a noun, naming the Mexican-American who, in becoming an American, forgets his native society.) "*¡Pocho!*" the lady in the Mexican food store muttered, shaking her head. I looked up to the counter where red and green peppers were strung like Christmas tree lights and saw the frowning face of the stranger. My mother laughed somewhere behind me. (She said that her children didn't want to practice "our Spanish" after they started going to school.) My mother's smiling voice made me suspect that the lady who faced me was not really angry at me. But, searching her face, I couldn't find the hint of a smile.

Embarrassed, my parents would regularly need to explain their children's inability to speak flowing Spanish during those years. My mother met the wrath of her brother, her only brother, when he came up from Mexico one summer with his family. He saw his nieces and nephews for the very first time. After listening to me, he looked away and said what a disgrace it was that I couldn't speak Spanish, "*su proprio idioma.*" He made that remark to my mother; I noticed, however, that he stared at my father.

I clearly remember one other visitor from those years. A long-time friend of my father from San Francisco would come to stay with us for several days in late August. He took great interest in me after he realized that I couldn't answer his questions in Spanish. He would grab me as I started to leave the kitchen. He would ask me something. Usually he wouldn't bother to wait for my mumbled response. Knowingly, he'd murmur: "*¿Ay Pocho, Pocho, adónde vas?*" And he would press his thumbs into the upper part of my arms, making me squirm with currents of pain. Dumbly, I'd stand there, waiting for his wife to notice us, for her to call him off with a benign smile. I'd giggle, hoping to deflate the tension between us, pretending that I hadn't seen the glittering scorn in his glance.

I remember that man now, but seek no revenge in this telling. I recount such incidents only because they suggest the fierce power Spanish had for many people I met at home; the way Spanish was associated with closeness. Most of those people who called me a *pocho* could have spoken English to me. But they would not. They seemed to think that Spanish was the only language we could use, that Spanish alone permitted our close association. (Such persons are vulnerable always to the ghetto merchant and the politician who have learned the value of speaking their clients' family language to gain immediate trust.) For my part, I felt that I had somehow committed a sin of betrayal by learning English. But betrayal against whom? Not against visitors to the house exactly. No, I felt that I had betrayed my immediate family. I *knew* that my parents had encouraged me to learn English. I *knew* that I had turned to English only with angry reluctance. But once I spoke English with ease, I came to *feel* guilty. (This guilt defied logic.) I felt that I had shattered the intimate bond that had once held the family close. This original sin against my family told whenever anyone addressed me in Spanish and I responded, confounded.

But even during those years of guilt, I was coming to sense certain consoling truths about language and intimacy. I remember playing with a friend in the backyard one day, when my grandmother appeared at the window. Her face was stern with suspicion when she saw the boy (the *gringo*) I was with. In Spanish she called out to me, sounding the whistle of her ancient breath. My companion looked up and watched her intently as she lowered the window and moved, still visible, behind the light curtain, watching us both. He wanted to know what she had said. I started to tell him, to say—to translate her Spanish words into English. The problem was, however, that though I knew how to translate exactly *what* she had told me, I realized that any translation would distort the deepest meaning of her message: It had been directed only to me. This message of intimacy could never be translated because it was not *in* the words she had used but passed *through* them. So any translation would have seemed wrong; her words would have been stripped of an essential meaning. Finally, I decided not to tell my friend anything. I told him that I didn't hear all she had said.

This insight unfolded in time. Making more and more friends outside my house, I began to distinguish intimate voices speaking through *English.* I'd listen at times to a close friend's confidential tone or secretive whisper. Even more remarkable were those instances when, for no special reason apparently, I'd become conscious of the fact that my companion was speaking only to me. I'd marvel just hearing his voice. It was a stunning event: to be able to break through his words, to be able to hear this voice of the other, to realize that it was directed only to me. After such moments of intimacy outside the house, I began to trust hearing intimacy conveyed through my family's English. Voices at home at last punctured sad confusion. I'd hear myself addressed as an intimate at home once again. Such moments were never as raucous with sound as past times had been when we had had "private" Spanish to use. (Our English-sounding house was never to be as noisy as our Spanish-speaking house had been.) Intimate moments were usually soft moments of sound. My mother was in the dining room while I did my homework nearby. And she looked over at me. Smiled. Said something—her words said nothing very important. But her voice sounded to tell me (*We are together*) I was her son.

(*Richard!*)

Intimacy thus continued at home; intimacy was not stilled by English. It is true that I would never forget the great change of my life, the diminished occasions of intimacy. But there would also be times when I sensed the deepest truth about language and intimacy: *Intimacy is not created by a particular language; it is created by intimates.* The great change in my life was not linguistic but social. If, after becoming a successful student, I no longer heard intimate voices as often as I had earlier, it was not because I spoke English rather than Spanish. It was because I used public language for most of the day. I moved easily at last, a citizen in a crowded city of words.

4

This boy became a man. In private now, alone, I brood over language and intimacy—the great themes of my past. In public I expect most of the faces I meet to be the faces of strangers. (How do you do?) If meetings are quick and impersonal, they have been efficiently managed. I rush past the sounds of voices attending only to the words addressed to me. Voices seem planed to an even surface of sound, soundless. A business associate speaks in a deep baritone, but I pass through the timbre to attend to his words. The crazy man who sells me a newspaper every night mumbles something crazy, but I have time only to pretend that I have heard him say hello. Accented versions of English make little impression on me. In the rush-hour crowd a Japanese tourist asks me a question, and I inch past his accent to concentrate on what he is saying. The Eastern European immigrant in a neighborhood delicatessen speaks to me through a marinade of sounds, but I respond to his words. I note for only a second the Texas accent of the telephone operator or the Mississippi accent of the man who lives in the apartment below me.

My city seems silent until some ghetto black teenagers board the bus I am on. Because I do not take their presence for granted, I listen to the sounds of their voices. Of all the accented versions of English I hear in a day, I hear theirs most intently. They are *the* sounds of the outsider. They annoy me for being loud—so self-sufficient and unconcerned by my presence. Yet for the same reason they seem to me glamorous. (A romantic gesture against public acceptance.) Listening to their shouted laughter, I realize my own quiet. Their voices enclose my isolation. I feel envious, envious of their brazen intimacy.

I warn myself away from such envy, however. I remember the black political activists who have argued in favor of using black English in schools. (Their argument varies only slightly from that made by foreign-language bilingualists.) I have heard "radical" linguists make the point that black English is a complex and intricate version of English. And I do not doubt it. But neither do I think that black English should be a language of public instruction. What makes black English inappropriate in classrooms is not something *in* the language. It is rather what lower-class speakers make of it. Just as Spanish would have been a dangerous language for me to have used at the start of my education, so black English would be a dangerous language to use in the schooling of teenagers for whom it reenforces feelings of public separateness.

This seems to me an obvious point. But one that needs to be made. In recent years there have been attempts to make the language of the alien public language. "Bilingual education, two ways to understand . . .," television and radio commercials glibly announce. Proponents of bilingual education are careful to say that they want students to acquire good schooling. Their argument goes something like this: Children permitted to use their family language in school will not be so alienated and will be better able to match the progress of English-speaking children in the crucial first months of instruction. (Increasingly confident of their abilities, such children will be more inclined to apply themselves to their studies in the future.) But then the bilingualists claim another, very different goal. They say that children who use their family language in school will retain a sense of their individuality—their ethnic heritage and cultural ties. Supporters of bilingual education thus want it both ways. They propose bilingual schooling as a way of helping students acquire the skills of the classroom crucial for public success. But they likewise insist that bilingual instruction will give students a sense of their identity apart from the public.

Behind this screen there gleams an astonishing promise: One can become a public person while still remaining a private person. At the very same time one can be both! There need be no tension between the self in the crowd and the self apart from the crowd! Who would not want to believe such an idea? Who can be surprised that the scheme has won the support of many middle-class Americans? If the barrio or ghetto child can retain his separateness even while being publicly educated, then it is almost possible to believe that there is no private cost to be paid for public success. Such is the consolation offered by any of the current bilingual schemes. Consider, for example, the bilingual voters' ballot. In some American cities one can cast a ballot printed in several languages. Such a document implies that a person can exercise that most public of rights—the right to vote—while still keeping apart, unassimilated from public life.

It is not enough to say that these schemes are foolish and certainly doomed. Middle-class supporters of public bilingualism toy with the confusion of those Americans who cannot speak standard English as well as they can. Bilingual enthusiasts, moreover, sin against intimacy. An Hispanic-American writer tells me, "I will never give up my family language; I would as soon give up my soul." Thus he holds to his chest a skein of words, as though it were the source of his family ties. He credits to language what he should credit to family members. A convenient mistake. For as long as he holds on to words, he can ignore how much else has changed in his life.

It has happened before. In earlier decades, persons newly successful and ambitious for social mobility similarly seized upon certain "family words." Working-class men attempting political power took to calling one another "brother." By so doing they escaped oppressive public isolation and were able to unite with many others like themselves. But they paid a price for this union. It was a public union they forged. The word they coined to address one another could never be the sound (*brother*) exchanged by two in intimate greeting. In the union hall the word "brother" became a vague metaphor; with repetition a weak echo of the intimate sound. Context forced the change. Context could not be overruled. Context will always guard the realm of the intimate from public misuse.

Today nonwhite Americans call "brother" to strangers. And white feminists refer to their mass union of "sisters." And white middle-class teenagers continue to prove the importance of context as they try to ignore it. They seize upon the idioms of the black ghetto. But their attempt to appropriate such expressions invariably changes the words. As it becomes a public expression, the ghetto idiom loses its sound—its message of public separateness and strident intimacy. It becomes with public repetition a series of words, increasingly lifeless.

The mystery remains: intimate utterance. The communication of intimacy passes through the word to enliven its sound. But it cannot be held by the word. Cannot be clutched or ever quoted. It is too fluid. It depends not on word but on person.

My grandmother!

She stood among my other relations mocking me when I no longer spoke Spanish. "*Pocho,*" she said. But then it made no difference. (She'd laugh.) Our relationship continued. Language was never its source. She was a woman in her eighties during the first decade of my life. A mysterious woman to me, my only living grandparent. A woman of Mexico. The woman in long black dresses that reached down to her shoes. My one relative who spoke no word of English. She had no interest in *gringo* society. She remained completely aloof from the public. Protected by her daughters. Protected even by me when we went to Safeway together and I acted as her translator. Eccentric woman. Soft. Hard.

When my family visited my aunt's house in San Francisco, my grandmother searched for me among my many cousins. She'd chase them away. Pinching her granddaughters, she'd warn them all away from me. Then she'd take me to her room, where she had prepared for my coming. There would be a chair next to the bed. A dusty jellied candy nearby. And a copy of *Life en Español* for me to examine. "There," she'd say. I'd sit there content. A boy of eight. *Pocho.* Her favorite. I'd sift through the pictures of earthquake-destroyed Latin American cities and blond-wigged Mexican movie stars. And all the while I'd listen to the sound of my grandmother's voice. She'd pace round the room, searching through closets and drawers, telling me stories of her life. Her past. They were stories so familiar to me that I couldn't remember the first time I'd heard them. I'd look up sometimes to listen. Other times she'd look over at me. But she never seemed to expect a response. Sometimes I'd smile or nod. (I understood exactly what she was saying.) But it never seemed to matter to her one way or another. It was enough I was there. The words she spoke were almost irrelevant to that fact—the sounds she made. Content.

The mystery remained: intimate utterance.

I learn little about language and intimacy listening to those social activists who propose using one's family language in public life. Listening to songs on the radio, or hearing a great voice at the opera, or overhearing the woman downstairs singing to herself at an open window, I learn much more. Singers celebrate the human voice. Their lyrics are words. But animated by voice those words are subsumed into sounds. I listen with excitement as the words yield their enormous power to sound—though the words are never totally obliterated. In most songs the drama or tension results from the fact that the singer moves between word (sense) and note (song). At one moment the song simply "says" something. At another moment the voice stretches out the words—the heart cannot contain!—and the voice moves toward pure sound. Words take flight.

Singing out words, the singer suggests an experience of sound most intensely mine at intimate moments. Literally, most songs are about love. (Lost love; celebrations of loving; pleas.) By simply being occasions when sound escapes word, however, songs put me in mind of the most intimate moments of my life.

Finally, among all types of song, it is the song created by lyric poets that I find most compelling. There is no other public occasion of sound so important for me. Written poems exist on a page, at first glance, as a mere collection of words. And yet, despite this, without musical accompaniment, the poet leads me to hear the sounds of the words that I read. As song, the poem passes between sound and sense, never belonging for long to one realm or the other. As public artifact, the poem can never duplicate intimate sound. But by imitating such sound, the poem helps me recall the intimate times of my life. I read in my room—alone—and grow conscious of being alone, sounding my voice, in search of another. The poem serves then as a memory device. It forces remembrance. And refreshes. It reminds me of the possibility of escaping public words, the possibility that awaits me in meeting the intimate.

The poems I read are not nonsense poems. But I read them for reasons which, I imagine, are similar to those that make children play with meaningless rhyme. I have watched them before: I have noticed the way children create private languages to keep away the adult; I have heard their chanting riddles that go nowhere in logic but harken back to some kingdom of sound; I have watched them listen to intricate nonsense rhymes, and I have noted their wonder. I was never such a child. Until I was six years old, I remained in a magical realm of sound. I didn't need to remember that realm because it was present to me. But then the screen door shut behind me as I left home for school. As last I began my movement toward words. On the other side of initial sadness would come the realization that intimacy cannot be held. With time would come the knowledge that intimacy must finally pass.

I would dishonor those I have loved and those I love now to claim anything else. I would dishonor our closeness by holding on to a particular language and calling it my family language. Intimacy is not trapped within words. It passes through words. It passes. The truth is that intimates leave the room. Doors close. Faces move away from the window. Time passes. Voices recede into the dark. Death finally quiets the voice. And there is no way to deny it. No way to stand in the crowd uttering one's family language.

The last time I saw my grandmother I was nine years old. I can tell you some of the things she said to me as I stood by her bed. I cannot, however, quote the message of intimacy she conveyed with her voice. She laughed, holding my hand. Her voice illumined disjointed memories as it passed them again. She remembered her husband, his green eyes, the magic name of Narciso. His early death. She remembered the farm in Mexico. The eucalyptus nearby. (Its scent, she remembered, like incense.) She remembered the family cow, the bell round its neck heard miles away. A dog. She remembered working as a seamstress. How she'd leave her daughters and son for long hours to go into Guadalajara to work. And how my mother would come running toward her in the sun—her bright yellow dress—to see her return. "*Mmmaaammmmmááàá,*" the old lady mimicked her daughter (my mother) to her son. She laughed. There was the snap of a cough. An aunt came into the room and told me it was time I should leave. "You can see her tomorrow," she promised. And so I kissed my grandmother's cracked face. And the last thing I saw was her thin, oddly youthful thigh, as my aunt rearranged the sheet on the bed.

At the funeral parlor a few days after, I knelt with my relatives during the rosary. Among their voices but silent, I traced, then lost, the sounds of individual aunts in the surge of the common prayer. And I heard at that moment what I have since heard often again—the sounds the women in my family make when they are praying in sadness. When I went up to look at my grandmother, I saw her through the haze of a veil draped over the open lid of the casket. Her face appeared calm—but distant and unyielding to love. It was not the face I remembered seeing most often. It was the face she made in public when the clerk at Safeway asked her some question and I would have to respond. It was her public face the mortician had designed with his dubious art.

Bilingualism, Con: Outdated and Unrealistic

How shall we teach the dark-eyed child *inglés?* The debate continues much as it did two decades ago.

Bilingual education belongs to the 1960's, the years of the black civil rights movement. Bilingual education became the official Hispanic demand; as a symbol, the English-only classroom was intended to be analogous to the segregated lunch counter; the locked school door. Bilingual education was endorsed by judges and, of course, by politicians well before anyone knew the answer to the question: Does bilingual education work?

Who knows? *Quien sabe?*

The official drone over bilingual education is conducted by educationists with numbers and charts. Because bilingual education was never simply a matter of pedagogy, it is too much to expect educators to resolve the matter. Proclamations concerning bilingual education are weighted at bottom with Hispanic political grievances and, too, with middle-class romanticism.

No one will say it in public; in private, Hispanics argue with me about bilingual education and every time it comes down to memory. Everyone remembers going to that grammar school where students were slapped for speaking Spanish. Childhood memory is offered as parable; the memory is meant to compress the gringo's long history of offenses against Spanish, Hispanic culture, Hispanics.

It is no coincidence that, although all of America's ethnic groups are implicated in the policy of bilingual education, Hispanics, particularly Mexican-Americans, have been its chief advocates. The English words used by Hispanics in support of bilingual education are words such as "dignity," "heritage," "culture." Bilingualism becomes a way of exacting from gringos a grudging admission of contrition—for the 19th-century theft of the Southwest, the relegation of Spanish to a foreign tongue, the injustice of history. At the extreme, Hispanic bilingual enthusiasts demand that public schools "maintain" a student's sense of separateness.

Hispanics may be among the last groups of Americans who still believe in the 1960's. Bilingual-education proposals still serve the romance of that decade, especially of the late 60's, when the heroic black civil rights movement grew paradoxically wedded to its opposite—the ethnic revival movement. Integration and separatism merged into twin, possible goals.

With integration, the black movement inspired middle-class Americans to imitations—the Hispanic movement; the Gray Panthers; feminism; gay rights. Then there was withdrawal, with black glamour leading a romantic retreat from the anonymous crowd.

Americans came to want it both ways. They wanted in and they wanted out. Hispanics took to celebrating their diversity, joined other Americans in dancing rings around the melting pot.

Mythic Metaphors

More intently than most, Hispanics wanted the romance of their dual cultural allegiance backed up by law. Bilingualism became proof that one could have it both ways, could be a full member of public America and yet also separate, private, Hispanic. "Spanish" and "English" became mythic metaphors, like country and city, describing separate islands of private and public life.

Ballots, billboards, and, of course, classrooms in Spanish. For nearly two decades now, middle-class Hispanics have had it their way. They have foisted a neat ideological scheme on working-class children. What they want to believe about themselves, they wait for the child to prove that it is possible to be two, that one can assume the public language (the public life) of America, even while remaining what one was, existentially separate.

Adulthood is not so neatly balanced. The tension between public and private life is intrinsic to adulthood—certainly middle-class adulthood. Usually the city wins because the city pays. We are mass people for more of the day than we are with our intimates. No Congressional mandate or Supreme Court decision can diminish the loss.

I was talking the other day to a carpenter from Riga, in the Soviet Republic of Latvia. He has been here six years. He told me of his having to force himself to relinquish the "luxury" of reading books in Russian or Latvian so he could begin to read books in English. And the books he was able to read in English were not of a complexity to satisfy him. But he was not going back to Riga.

Beyond any question of pedagogy there is the simple fact that a language gets learned as it gets used. One fills one's mouth, one's mind, with the new names for things.

The civil rights movement of the 1960's taught Americans to deal with forms of discrimination other than economic—racial, sexual. We forget class. We talk about bilingual education as an ethnic issue; we forget to notice that the program mainly touches the lives of working-class immigrant children. Foreign-language acquisition is one thing for the upper-class child in a convent school learning in French to curtsy. Language acquisition can only seem a loss for the ghetto child, for the new language is psychologically awesome, being, as it is, the language of the bus driver and papa's employer. The child's difficulty will turn out to be psychological more than linguistic because what he gives up are symbols of home.

Pain and Guilt

I was that child! I faced the stranger's English with pain and guilt and fear. Baptized to English in school, at first I felt myself drowning—the ugly sounds forced down my throat—until slowly, slowly (held in the tender grip of my teachers), suddenly the conviction took: English was my language to use.

What I yearn for is some candor from those who speak about bilingual education. Which of its supporters dares speak of the price a child pays—the price of adulthood—to make the journey from a working-class home into a middle-class schoolroom? The real story, the silent story of the immigrant child's journey is one of embarrassments in public; betrayal of all that is private; silence at home; and at school the hand tentatively raised.

Bilingual enthusiasts bespeak an easier world. They seek a linguistic solution to a social dilemma. They seem to want to believe that there is an easy way for the child to balance private and public, in order to believe that there is some easy way for themselves.

Ten years ago, I started writing about the ideological implications of bilingual education. Ten years from now some newspaper may well invite me to contribute another Sunday supplement essay on the subject. The debate is going to continue. The bilingual establishment is now inside the door. Jobs are at stake. Politicians can only count heads; growing numbers of Hispanics will insure the compliance of politicians.

Publicly, we will continue the fiction. We will solemnly address this issue as an educational question, a matter of pedagogy. But privately, Hispanics will still seek from bilingual education an admission from the gringo that Spanish has value and presence. Hispanics of middle class will continue to seek the romantic assurance of separateness. Experts will argue. Dark-eyed children will sit in the classroom. Mute.

Theodore Roethke (1908–1963)
Child on Top of a Greenhouse

The wind billowing out the seat of my britches,
My feet crackling splinters of glass and dried putty,
The half-grown chrysanthemums staring up like accusers,
Up through the streaked glass, flashing with sunlight,
A few white clouds all rushing eastward,   5
A line of elms plunging and tossing like horses,
And everyone, everyone pointing up and shouting!

My Papa's Waltz

The whiskey on your breath
Could make a small boy dizzy;
But I hung on like death:
Such waltzing was not easy.

We romped until the pans   5
Slid from the kitchen shelf;
My mother's countenance
Could not unfrown itself.

The hand that held my wrist
Was battered on one knuckle;   10
At every step you missed
My right ear scraped a buckle.

You beat time on my head
With a palm caked hard by dirt,
Then waltzed me off to bed   15
Still clinging to your shirt.

Carl Sagan (born 1934)
The Amniotic Universe

> It is as natural to man to die as to be born; and to a little infant, perhaps, the one is as painful as the other.
>
> —Francis Bacon, *Of Death* (1612)

> The most beautiful thing we can experience is the mysterious. It is the source of all true art and science. He to whom this emotion is a stranger, who can no longer wonder and stand rapt in awe, is as good as dead: his eyes are closed. . . . To know that what is impenetrable to us really exists, manifesting itself as the highest wisdom and the most radiant beauty which our dull facilities can comprehend only in the most primitive forms—this knowledge, this feeling, is at the center of true religiousness. In this sense, and in this sense only, I belong to the ranks of the devoutly religious men.
>
> —Albert Einstein, "What I Believe" (1930)

William Wolcott died and went to heaven. Or so it seemed. Before being wheeled to the operating table, he had been reminded that the surgical procedure would entail a certain risk. The operation was a success, but just as the anaesthesia was wearing off his heart went into fibrillation and he died. It seemed to him that he had somehow left his body and was able to look down upon it, withered and pathetic, covered only by a sheet, lying on a hard and unforgiving surface. He was only a little sad, regarded his body one last time—from a great height, it seemed—and continued a kind of upward journey. While his surroundings had been suffused by a strange permeating darkness, he realized that things were now getting brighter—looking up, you might say. And then he was being illuminated from a distance, flooded with light. He entered a kind of radiant kingdom and there, just ahead of him, he could make out in silhouette, magnificently lit from behind, a great godlike figure whom he was now effortlessly approaching. Wolcott strained to make out His face . . .

And then awoke. In the hospital operating room where the defibrillation machine had been rushed to him, he had been resuscitated at the last possible moment. Actually, his heart had stopped, and by some definitions of this poorly understood process, he had died. Wolcott was certain that he *had* died, that he had been vouchsafed a glimpse of life after death and a confirmation of Judaeo-Christian theology.

Similar experiences, now widely documented by physicians and others, have occurred all over the world. These perithanatic, or near-death, epiphanies have been experienced not only by people of conventional Western religiosity but also by Hindus and Buddhists and skeptics. It seems plausible that many of our conventional ideas about heaven are derived from such near-death experiences, which must have been related regularly over the millennia. No news could have been more interesting or more hopeful than that of the traveler returned, the report that there is a voyage and a life after death, that there is a God who awaits us, and that upon death we feel grateful and uplifted, awed and overwhelmed.

For all I know, these experiences may be just what they seem and a vindication of the pious faith that has taken such a pummeling from science in the past few centuries. Personally, I would be delighted if there were a life after death—especially if it permitted me to continue to learn about this world and others, if it gave me a chance to discover how history turns out. But I am also a scientist, so I think about what other explanations are possible. How could it be that people of all ages, cultures and eschatological predispositions have the *same sort* of near-death experience?

We know that similar experiences can be induced with fair regularity, cross-culturally, by psychedelic drugs.[1] Out-of-body experiences are induced by dissociative anaesthetics such as the ketamines (2-[o-chlorophenyl]-2-[methylamino] cyclo-hexanones). The illusion of flying is induced by atropine and other belladonna alkaloids, and these molecules, obtained, for example, from mandrake or jimson weed, have been used regularly by European witches and North American *curanderos* ("healers") to experience, in the midst of religious ecstasy, soaring and glorious flight. MDA (2,4-methylenedioxyamphetamine) tends to induce age regression, an accessing of experiences from youth and infancy which we had thought entirely forgotten. DMT (N,N-dimethyltryptamine) induces micropsia and macropsia, the sense of the world shrinking or expanding, respectively—a little like what happens to Alice after she obeys instructions on small containers reading "Eat me" or "Drink me." LSD (lysergic acid diethylamide) induces a sense of union with the universe, as in the identification of Brahman with Atman in Hindu religious belief.

Can it really be that the Hindu mystical experience is pre-wired into us, requiring only 200 micrograms of LSD to be made manifest? If something like ketamine is released in times of mortal danger or near-death, and people returning from such an experience always provide the same account of heaven and God, then must there not

---

[1] It is interesting to wonder why psychedelic molecules exist—especially in great abundance—in a variety of plants. The psychedelics are unlikely to provide any immediate benefit for the plant. The hemp plant probably does not get high from its complement of $^1\Delta$ tetrahydrocannabinol. But human beings *cultivate* hemp because the hallucinogenic properties of marijuana are widely prized. There is evidence that in some cultures psychedelic plants are the only domesticated vegetation. It is possible that in such ethnobotany a symbiotic relationship has developed between the plants and the humans. Those plants which by accident provide desired psychedelics are preferentially cultivated. Such artificial selection can exert an extremely powerful influence on subsequent evolution in relatively short time periods—say, tens of thousands of years—as is apparent by comparing many domesticated animals with their wild forebears. Recent work also makes it likely that psychedelic substances work because they are close chemical congeners of natural substances, produced by the brain, which inhibit or enhance neural transmissions, and which may have among their physiological functions the induction of endogenous changes in perception or mood.

be a sense in which Western as well as Eastern religions are hard-wired in the neuronal architecture of our brains?

It is difficult to see why evolution should have selected brains that are predisposed to such experiences, since no one seems to die or fail to reproduce from a want of mystic fervor. Might these drug-inducible experiences as well as the near-death epiphany be due merely to some evolutionarily neutral wiring defect in the brain which, by accident, occasionally brings forth altered perceptions of the world? That possibility, it seems to me, is extremely implausible, and perhaps no more than a desperate rationalist attempt to avoid a serious encounter with the mystical.

The only alternative, so far as I can see, is that every human being, without exception, has already shared an experience like that of those travelers who return from the land of death: the sensation of flight; the emergence from darkness into light; an experience in which, at least sometimes, a heroic figure can be dimly perceived, bathed in radiance and glory. There is only one common experience that matches this description. It is called birth.

His name is Stanislav Grof. In some pronunciations his first and last names rhyme. He is a physician and a psychiatrist who has, for more than twenty years, employed LSD and other psychedelic drugs in psychotherapy. His work long antedates the American drug culture, having begun in Prague, Czechoslovakia, in 1956 and continuing in recent years in the slightly different cultural setting of Baltimore, Maryland. Grof probably has more continuing scientific experience on the effects of psychedelic drugs on patients than anyone else.[2] He stresses that whereas LSD can be used for recreational and aesthetic purposes, it can have other and more profound effects, one of which is the accurate recollection of perinatal experiences. "Perinatal" is a neologism for "around birth," and is intended to apply not just to the time immediately after birth but to the time before as well. (It is a parallel construction to "perithanatic," near-death.) He reports a large number of patients who, after a suitable number of sessions, actually re-experience rather than merely recollect profound experiences, long gone and considered intractable to our imperfect memories, from perinatal times. This is, in fact, a fairly common LSD experience, by no means limited to Grof's patients.

Grof distinguishes four perinatal stages recovered under psychedelic therapy. Stage 1 is the blissful complacency of the child in the womb, free of all anxiety, the center of a small, dark, warm universe—a cosmos in an amniotic sac. In its intrauterine state the fetus seems to experience something very close to the oceanic ecstasy

---

[2] A fascinating description of Grof's work and the entire range of psychedelics can be found in the forthcoming book *Psychedelic Drugs Reconsidered* by Lester Grinspoon and James Bakalar (New York, Basic Books, 1979). Grof's own description of his findings can be found in *Realms of the Human Unconscious* by S. Grof (New York, E. P. Dutton, 1976) and *The Human Encounter with Death* by S. Grof and J. Halifax (New York, E. P. Dutton, 1977).

described by Freud as a fount of the religious sensibility. The fetus is, of course, moving. Just before birth it is probably as alert, perhaps even more alert, than just after birth. It does not seem impossible that we may occasionally and imperfectly remember this Edenic, golden age, when every need—for food, oxygen, warmth and waste disposal—was satisfied before it was sensed, provided automatically by a superbly designed life-support system; and, in dim recollection years later, describe it as "being one with the universe."

In Stage 2, the uterine contractions begin. The walls to which the amniotic sac is anchored, the foundation of the stable intrauterine environment, become traitorous. The fetus is dreadfully compressed. The universe seems to pulsate, a benign world suddenly converted into a cosmic torture chamber. The contractions may last intermittently for hours. As time goes on, they become more intense. No hope of surcease is offered. The fetus has done nothing to deserve such a fate, an innocent whose cosmos has turned upon it, administering seemingly endless agony. The severity of this experience is apparent to anyone who has seen a neonatal cranial distortion that is still evident days after birth. While I can understand a strong motivation to obliterate utterly any trace of this agony, might it not resurface under stress? Might not, Grof asks, the hazy and repressed memory of this experience prompt paranoid fantasies and explain our occasional human predilections for sadism and masochism, for an identification of assailant and victim, for that childlike zest for destruction in a world which, for all we know, may tomorrow become terrifyingly unpredictable and unreliable? Grof finds recollections in the next stage connected with images of tidal waves and earthquakes, the analogues in the physical world of the intrauterine betrayal.

Stage 3 is the end of the birth process, when the child's head has penetrated the cervix and might, even if the eyes are closed, perceive a tunnel illuminated at one end and sense the brilliant radiance of the extrauterine world. The discovery of light for a creature that has lived its entire existence in darkness must be a profound and on some level an unforgettable experience. And there, dimly made out by the low resolution of the newborn's eyes, is some godlike figure surrounded by a halo of light—the Midwife or the Obstetrician or the Father. At the end of a monstrous travail, the baby flies away from the uterine universe, and rises toward the lights and the gods.

Stage 4 is the time immediately after birth when the perinatal apnea has dissipated, when the child is blanketed or swaddled, hugged and given nourishment. If recollected accurately, the contrast between Stages 1 and 2 and 2 and 4, for an infant utterly without other experience, must be very deep and striking and the importance of Stage 3 as the passage between agony and at least a tender simulacrum of the cosmic unity of Stage 1 must have a powerful influence on the child's later view of the world.

There is, of course, room for skepticism in Grof's account and in my expansion upon it. There are many questions to be answered. Do children born before labor by Caesarean section never recall the agonizing Stage 2? Under psychedelic therapy, do they report fewer images of catastrophic earthquakes and tidal waves than those born by normal deliveries? Conversely, are children born after the particularly severe uterine contractions induced in "elective labor" by the hormone oxytocin[3] more likely to acquire the psychological burdens of Stage 2? If the mother is given a strong sedative, will the baby upon maturity recall a very different transition from Stage 1 directly to Stage 4 and never report, in a perithanatic experience, a radiant epiphany? Can neonates resolve an image at the moment of birth or are they merely sensitive to light and darkness? Might the description, in the near-death experience, of a fuzzy and glowing god without hard edges be a perfect recollection of an imperfect neonatal image? Are Grof's patients selected from the widest possible range of human beings or are these accounts restricted to an unrepresentative subset of the human community?

It is easy to understand that there might be more personal objections to these ideas, a resistance perhaps similar to the kind of chauvinism that can be detected in justifications of carnivorous eating habits: the lobsters have no central nervous system; they don't mind being dropped alive into boiling water. Well, maybe. But the lobster-eaters have a vested interest in this particular hypothesis on the neurophysiology of pain. In the same way I wonder if most adults do not have a vested interest in believing that infants possess very limited powers of perception and memory, that there is no way the birth experience could have a profound and, in particular, a profoundly negative influence.

If Grof is right about all this, we must ask why such recollections are possible—why, if the perinatal experience has produced enormous unhappiness, evolution has not selected out the negative psychological consequences. There are some things that newborn infants must do. They must be good at sucking; otherwise they will die. They must, by and large, look cute because at least in previous epochs of human history, infants who in some way seemed appealing were better taken care of. But *must* newborn babies see images of their environment? *Must* they remember the horrors of the perinatal experience? In what sense is there survival value in that? The answer might be that the pros outweigh the cons—perhaps the loss of a universe to which we are perfectly adjusted motivates us powerfully to change the world and improve the human circumstance. Perhaps that striving, questing aspect of the human spirit would be absent if it were not for the horrors of birth.

I am fascinated by the point—which I stress in my book *The Dragons of Eden*— that the pain of childbirth is especially marked in human mothers because of the

---

[3] Astonishingly, oxytocin turns out to be an ergot derivative that is chemically related to psychedelics such as LSD. Since it induces labor, it is at least a plausible hypothesis that some similar natural substance is employed by nature to induce uterine contractions. But this would imply some fundamental connection for the mother—and perhaps for the child—between birth and psychedelic drugs. Perhaps it is therefore not so implausible that, much later in life under the influence of a psychedelic drug, we recall the birth experience—the event during which we first experienced psychedelic drugs.

enormous recent growth of the brain in the last few million years. It would seem that our intelligence is the source of our unhappiness in an almost literal way; but it would also imply that our unhappiness is the source of our strength as a species.

These ideas may cast some light on the origin and nature of religion. Most Western religions long for a life after death; Eastern religions for relief from an extended cycle of deaths and rebirths. But both promise a heaven or satori, an idyllic reunion of the individual and the universe, a return to Stage 1. Every birth is a death—the child leaves the amniotic world. But devotees of reincarnation claim that every death is a birth—a proposition that could have been triggered by perithanatic experiences in which the perinatal memory was recognized as a recollection of birth. ("There was a faint rap on the coffin. We opened it, and it turned out that Abdul had not died. He had awakened from a long illness which had cast its spell upon him, and he told a strange story of being born once again.")

Might not the Western fascination with punishment and redemption be a poignant attempt to make sense of perinatal Stage 2? Is it not better to be punished for something—no matter how implausible, such as original sin—than for nothing? And Stage 3 looks very much like a common experience, shared by all human beings, implanted into our earliest memories and occasionally retrieved in such religious epiphanies as the near-death experience. It is tempting to try to understand other puzzling religious motifs in these terms. *In utero* we know virtually nothing. In Stage 2 the fetus gains experience of what might very well in later life be called evil—and then is forced to leave the uterus. This is entrancingly close to eating the fruit of the tree of knowledge of good and evil and then experiencing the "expulsion" from Eden.[4] In Michelangelo's famous painting on the ceiling of the Sistine Chapel, is the finger of God an obstetrical finger? Why is baptism, especially total-immersion baptism, widely considered a symbolic rebirth? Is holy water a metaphor for amniotic fluid? Is not the entire concept of baptism and the "born again" experience an explicit acknowledgment of the connection between birth and mystical religiosity?

If we study some of the thousands of religions on the planet Earth, we are impressed by their diversity. At least some of them seem stupefyingly harebrained. In doctrinal details, mutual agreement is rare. But many great and good men and women have stated that behind the apparent divergences is a fundamental and important unity; beneath the doctrinal idiocies is a basic and essential truth. There are two very different approaches to a consideration of tenets of belief. On the one hand, there are the believers, who are often credulous, and who accept a received religion literally, even though it may have internal inconsistencies or be in strong variance with what we know reliably about the external world or ourselves. On the other hand, there are the stern skeptics, who find the whole business a farrago of weak-minded

---

[4] A different but not inconsistent hypothesis on the Eden metaphor, in phylogeny rather than ontogeny, is described in *The Dragons of Eden.*

nonsense. Some who consider themselves sober rationalists resist even considering the enormous corpus of recorded religious experience. These mystical insights must mean something. But what? Human beings are, by and large, intelligent and creative, good at figuring things out. If religions are fundamentally silly, why is it that so many people believe in them?

Certainly, bureaucratic religions have throughout human history allied themselves with the secular authorities, and it has frequently been to the benefit of those ruling a nation to inculcate the faith. In India, when the Brahmans wished to keep the "untouchables" in slavery, they proffered divine justification. The same self-serving argument was employed by whites, who actually described themselves as Christians, in the ante-bellum American South to support the enslavement of blacks. The ancient Hebrews cited God's direction and encouragement in the random pillage and murder they sometimes visited on innocent peoples. In medieval times the Church held out the hope of a glorious life after death to those upon whom it urged contentment with their lowly and impoverished station. These examples can be multiplied indefinitely, to include virtually all the world's religions. We can understand why the oligarchy might favor religion when, as is often the case, religion justifies oppression—as Plato, a dedicated advocate of book-burning, did in the *Republic*. But why do the oppressed so eagerly go along with these theocratic doctrines?

The general acceptance of religious ideas, it seems to me, can only be because there is something in them that resonates with our own certain knowledge—something deep and wistful; something every person recognizes as central to our being. And that common thread, I propose, is birth. Religion is fundamentally mystical, the gods inscrutable, the tenets appealing but unsound because, I suggest, blurred perceptions and vague premonitions are the best that the newborn infant can manage. I think that the mystical core of the religious experience is neither literally true nor perniciously wrong-minded. It is rather a courageous if flawed attempt to make contact with the earliest and most profound experience of our lives. Religious doctrine is fundamentally clouded because not a single person has ever at birth had the skills of recollection and retelling necessary to deliver a coherent account of the event. All successful religions seem at their nucleus to make an unstated and perhaps even unconscious resonance with the perinatal experience. Perhaps when secular influences are subtracted, it will emerge that the most successful religions are those which perform this resonance best.

Attempts at rationalistic explanations of religious belief have been resisted vigorously. Voltaire argued that if God did not exist Man would be obliged to invent him, and was reviled for the remark. Freud proposed that a paternalistic God is partly our projection as adults of our perceptions of our fathers when we were infants; he also called his book on religion *The Future of an Illusion*. He was not despised as much as we might imagine for these views, but perhaps only because he had already demonstrated his disreputability by introducing such scandalous notions as infantile sexuality.

Why is the opposition to rational discourse and reasoned argument in religion so strong? In part, I think it is because our common perinatal experiences are real but resist accurate recollection. But another reason, I think, has to do with the fear of death. Human beings and our immediate ancestors and collateral relatives, such as the Neanderthals, are probably the first organisms on this planet to have a clear awareness of the inevitability of our own end. We will die and we fear death. This fear is worldwide and transcultural. It probably has significant survival value. Those who wish to postpone or avoid death can improve the world, reduce its perils, make children who will live after us, and create great works by which they will be remembered. Those who propose rational and skeptical discourse on things religious are perceived as challenging the remaining widely held solution to the human fear of death, the hypothesis that the soul lives on after the body's demise.[5] Since we feel strongly, most of us, about wishing not to die, we are made uncomfortable by those who suggest that death is the end; that the personality and the soul of each of us will not live on. But the soul hypothesis and the God hypothesis are separable; indeed, there are some human cultures in which the one can be found without the other. In any case, we do not advance the human cause by refusing to consider ideas that make us frightened.

Those who raise questions about the God hypothesis and the soul hypothesis are by no means all atheists. An atheist is someone who is certain that God does not exist, someone who has compelling evidence against the existence of God. I know of no such compelling evidence. Because God can be relegated to remote times and places and to ultimate causes, we would have to know a great deal more about the universe than we do now to be sure that no such God exists. To be certain of the existence of God and to be certain of the nonexistence of God seem to me to be the confident extremes in a subject so riddled with doubt and uncertainty as to inspire very little confidence indeed. A wide range of intermediate positions seems admissible, and considering the enormous emotional energies with which the subject is invested, a questing, courageous and open mind seems to be the essential tool for narrowing the range of our collective ignorance on the subject of the existence of God.

When I give lectures on borderline or pseudo or folk science (along the lines of Chapters 5 through 8 of this book) I am sometimes asked if similar criticism should not be applied to religious doctrine. My answer is, of course, yes. Freedom of religion, one of the rocks upon which the United States was founded, is essential for

---

[5] One curious variant is given in Arthur Schnitzler's *Flight Into Darkness:* ". . . at all the moments of death of any nature, one lives over again his past life with a rapidity inconceivable to others. This remembered life must also have a last moment, and this last moment its own last moment, and so on, and hence, dying is itself eternity, and hence, in accordance with the theory of limits, one may approach death but can never reach it." In fact, the sum of an infinite series of this sort is finite, and the argument fails for mathematical as well as other reasons. But it is a useful reminder that we are often willing to accept desperate measures to avoid a serious confrontation with the inevitability of death.

free inquiry. But it does not carry with it any immunity from criticism or reinterpretation for the religions themselves. The words "question" and "quest" are cognates. Only through inquiry can we discover truth. I do not insist that these connections between religion and perinatal experience are correct or original. Many of them are at least implicit in the ideas of Stanislav Grof and the psychoanalytic school of psychiatry, particularly Otto Rank, Sandor Ferenczi and Sigmund Freud. But they are worth thinking about.

There is, of course, a great deal more to the origin of religion that these simple ideas suggest. I do not propose that theology is physiology entirely. But it would be astonishing, assuming we really can remember our perinatal experiences, if they did not affect in the deepest way our attitudes on birth and death, sex and childhood, on purpose and ethics, on causality and God.

And cosmology. Astronomers studying the nature and origin and fate of the universe make elaborate observations, describe the cosmos in differential equations and the tensor calculus, examine the universe from X-rays to radio waves, count the galaxies and determine their motions and distances—and when all is done a choice is to be made between three different views: a Steady State cosmology, blissful and quiet; an Oscillating Universe, in which the universe expands and contracts, painfully and forever; and a Big Bang expanding universe, in which the cosmos is created in a violent event, suffused with radiation ("Let there be light") and then grows and cools, evolves and becomes quiescent, as we saw in the previous chapter. But these three cosmologies resemble with an awkward, almost embarrassing precision the human perinatal experiences of Grof's Stages 1, 2 and 3 plus 4, respectively.

It is easy for modern astronomers to make fun of the cosmologies of other cultures—for example, the Dogon idea that the universe was hatched from a cosmic egg (Chapter 6). But in light of the ideas just presented, I intend to be much more circumspect in my attitudes toward folk cosmologies; their anthropocentrism is just a little bit easier to discern than ours. Might the puzzling Babylonian and Biblical references to waters above and below the firmament, which Thomas Aquinas struggled so painfully to reconcile with Aristotelian physics, be merely an amniotic metaphor? Are we incapable of constructing a cosmology that is not some mathematical encrypting of our own personal origins?

Einstein's equations of general relativity admit a solution in which the universe expands. But Einstein, inexplicably, overlooked such a solution and opted for an absolutely static, nonevolving cosmos. Is it too much to inquire whether this oversight had perinatal rather than mathematical origins? There is a demonstrated reluctance of physicists and astronomers to accept Big Bang cosmologies in which the universe expands forever, although conventional Western theologians are more or less delighted with the prospect. Might this dispute, based almost certainly on psychological predispositions, be understood in Grofian terms?

I do not know how close the analogies are between personal perinatal experiences and particular cosmological models. I suppose it is too much to hope that the originators of the Steady State hypothesis were each born by Caesarean section. But the analogies are very close, and the possible connection between psychiatry and cosmology seems very real. Can it really be that every possible mode of origin and evolution of the universe corresponds to a human perinatal experience? Are we such limited creatures that we are unable to construct a cosmology that differs significantly from one of the perinatal stages?[6] Is our ability to know the universe hopelessly ensnared and enmired in the experiences of birth and infancy? Are we doomed to recapitulate our origins in a pretense of understanding the universe? Or might the emerging observational evidence gradually force us into an accommodation with and an understanding of that vast and awesome universe in which we float, lost and brave and questing?

It is customary in the world's religions to describe Earth as our mother and the sky as our father. This is true of Uranus and Gaea in Greek mythology, and also among Native Americans, Africans, Polynesians, indeed most of the people of the planet Earth. However, the very point of the perinatal experience is that we leave our mothers. We do it first at birth and then again when we set out into the world by ourselves. As painful as those leave-takings are, they are essential for the continuance of the human species. Might this fact have some bearing on the almost mystical appeal that space flight has, at least for many of us? Is it not a leaving of Mother Earth, the world of our origins, to seek our fortune among the stars? This is precisely the final visual metaphor of the film *2001: A Space Odyssey.* Konstantin Tsiolkovsky was a Russian schoolmaster, almost entirely self-educated, who, around the turn of the century, formulated many of the theoretical steps that have since been taken in the development of rocket propulsion and space flight Tsiolkovsky wrote: "The Earth is the cradle of mankind. But one does not live in the cradle forever."

We are set irrevocably, I believe, on a path that will take us to the stars—unless in some monstrous capitulation to stupidity and greed, we destroy ourselves first. And out there in the depths of space, it seems very likely that, sooner or later, we will find other intelligent beings. Some of them will be less advanced than we; some, probably most, will be more. Will all the spacefaring beings, I wonder, be creatures whose births are painful? The beings more advanced than we will have capabilities far beyond our understanding. In some very real sense they will appear to us as godlike.

---

[6] Kangaroos are born when they are little more than embryos and must then make, entirely unassisted, a heroic journey hand over hand from birth canal to pouch. Many fail this demanding test. Those who succeed find themselves once again in a warm, dark and protective environment, this one equipped with teats. Would the religion of a species of intelligent marsupials invoke a stern and implacable god who severely tests marsupialkind? Would marsupial cosmology deduce a brief interlude of radiation in a premature Big Bang followed by a "Second Dark," and then a much more placid emergence into the universe we know?

There will be a great deal of growing up required of the infant human species. Perhaps our descendants in those remote times will look back on us, on the long and wandering journey the human race will have taken from its dimly remembered origins on the distant planet Earth, and recollect our personal and collective histories, our romance with science and religion, with clarity and understanding and love.

Stephen Spender (born 1909)

My Parents Kept Me from Children Who Were Rough

My parents kept me from children who were rough
And who threw words like stones and who wore torn clothes.
Their thighs showed through rags. They ran in the street
And climbed cliffs and stripped by the country streams.

I feared more than tigers their muscles like iron   5
And their jerking hands and their knees tight on my arms.
I feared the salt coarse pointing of those boys
Who copied my lisp behind me on the road.

They were lithe, they sprang out behind hedges
Like dogs to bark at our world. They threw mud   10
And I looked another way, pretending to smile.
I longed to forgive them, yet they never smiled.

Dylan Thomas (1914–1953)

Fern Hill

Now as I was young and easy under the apple boughs
About the lilting house and happy as the grass was green,
    The night above the dingle starry,
        Time let me hail and climb
    Golden in the heydays of his eyes,   5

And honoured among wagons I was prince of the apple towns
And once below a time I lordly had the trees and leaves
  Trail with daisies and barley
 Down the rivers of the windfall light.

And as I was green and carefree, famous among the barns   10
About the happy yard and singing as the farm was home,
 In the sun that is young once only,
  Time let me play and be
 Golden in the mercy of his means,
And green and golden I was huntsman and herdsman, the calves   15
Sang to my horn, the foxes on the hills barked clear and cold,
  And the sabbath rang slowly
 In the pebbles of the holy streams.

All the sun long it was running, it was lovely, the hay-
Fields high as the house, the tunes from the chimneys, it was air   20
 And playing, lovely and watery
  And fire green as grass.
 And nightly under the simple stars
As I rode to sleep the owls were bearing the farm away,
All the moon long I heard, blessed among stables, the night-jars   25
 Flying with the ricks, and the horses
  Flashing into the dark.

And then to awake, and the farm, like a wanderer white
With the dew, come back, the cock on his shoulder: it was all
 Shining, it was Adam and maiden,   30
  The sky gathered again
 And the sun grew round that very day.
So it must have been after the birth of the simple light
In the first, spinning place, the spellbound horses walking warm
 Out of the whinnying green stable   35
 On to the fields of praise.

And honoured among foxes and pheasants by the gay house
Under the new made clouds and happy as the heart was long,
 In the sun born over and over,
  I ran my heedless ways,   40
 My wishes raced through the house-high hay
And nothing I cared, at my sky blue trades, that time allows
In all his tuneful turning so few and such morning songs
 Before the children green and golden
  Follow him out of grace,   45

Nothing I cared, in the lamb white days, that time would take me
Up to the swallow thronged loft by the shadow of my hand,
    In the moon that is always rising,
        Nor that riding to sleep
    I should hear him fly with the high fields   50
And wake to the farm forever fled from the childless land.
Oh as I was young and easy in the mercy of his means,
        Time held me green and dying
    Though I sang in my chains like the sea.

William Wordsworth (1770–1850)
Ode

Intimations of Immortality from Recollections of Early Childhood

> *The Child is father of the Man;*
> *And I could wish my days to be*
> *Bound each to each by natural piety.*

1
There was a time when meadow, grove, and stream,
The earth, and every common sight,
    To me did seem
    Apparelled in celestial light,
The glory and the freshness of a dream.   5
It is not now as it hath been of yore;—
    Turn wheresoe'er I may,
    By night or day,
The things which I have seen I now can see no more.

2
    The Rainbow comes and goes,   10
    And lovely is the Rose,
    The Moon doth with delight
Look round her when the heavens are bare;
    Waters on a starry night
    Are beautiful and fair;   15
The sunshine is a glorious birth;

But yet I know, where'er I go,
That there hath past away a glory from the earth.

3

Now, while the birds thus sing a joyous song,
   And while the young lambs bound   20
      As to the tabor's sound,
To me alone there came a thought of grief:
A timely utterance gave that thought relief,
      And I again am strong:
The cataracts blow their trumpets from the steep;   25
No more shall grief of mine the season wrong;
I hear the Echoes through the mountains throng,
The Winds come to me from the fields of sleep,
      And all the earth is gay;
        Land and sea   30
     Give themselves up to jollity,
      And with the heart of May
Doth every Beast keep holiday; —
      Thou Child of Joy,
Shout round me, let me hear thy shouts, thou
    happy Shepherd-boy!   35

4

Ye blessèd Creatures, I have heard the call
  Ye to each other make; I see
The heavens laugh with you in your jubilee;
   My heart is at your festival,
     My head hath its coronal,   40
The fulness of your bliss, I feel—I feel it all.
     Oh evil day! if I were sullen
     While Earth herself is adorning,
      This sweet May-morning,
     And the Children are culling   45
      On every side,
     In a thousand valleys far and wide,
     Fresh flowers; while the sun shines warm,
And the Babe leaps up on his Mother's arm: —
     I hear, I hear, with joy I hear!   50
     —But there's a Tree, of many, one,
A single Field which I have looked upon,
Both of them speak of something that is gone:

> The Pansy at my feet
> > Doth the same tale repeat: 55
> Whither is fled the visionary gleam?
> Where is it now, the glory and the dream?

5

Our birth is but a sleep and a forgetting:
The Soul that rises with us, our life's Star,
> > Hath had elsewhere its setting,   60
> > And cometh from afar:
> > Not in entire forgetfulness,
> > And not in utter nakedness,
But trailing clouds of glory do we come
> > From God, who is our home: 65
Heaven lies about us in our infancy!
Shades of the prison-house begin to close
> > Upon the growing Boy,
> > > But He
Beholds the light, and whence it flows,   70
> > He sees it in his joy;
The Youth, who daily farther from the east
> > Must travel, still is Nature's Priest,
> > And by the vision splendid
> > Is on his way attended;   75
At length the Man perceives it die away,
And fade into the light of common day.

6

Earth fills her lap with pleasures of her own;
Yearnings she hath in her own natural kind,
And, even with something of a Mother's mind,   80
> > And no unworthy aim,
> > The homely Nurse doth all she can
To make her Foster-child, her Inmate Man,
> > Forget the glories he hath known,
And that imperial palace whence he came.   85

7

Behold the Child among his new-born blisses,
A six years' Darling of a pigmy size!

See, where 'mid work of his own hand he lies,
Fretted by sallies of his mother's kisses,
With light upon him from his father's eyes!   90
See, at his feet, some little plan or chart,
Some fragment from his dream of human life,
Shaped by himself with newly-learnèd art;
    A wedding or a festival,
    A mourning or a funeral;   95
      And this hath now his heart,
      And unto this he frames his song:
        Then will he fit his tongue
To dialogues of business, love, or strife;
      But it will not be long   100
      Ere this be thrown aside,
      And with new joy and pride
The little Actor cons another part;
Filling from time to time his "humorous stage"
With all the Persons, down to palsied Age,   105
That Life brings with her in her equipage;
    As if his whole vocation
    Were endless imitation.

      8
Thou, whose exterior semblance doth belie
    Thy Soul's immensity;   110
Thou best Philosopher, who yet dost keep
Thy heritage, thou Eye among the blind,
That, deaf and silent, read'st the eternal deep,
Haunted for ever by the eternal mind,—
    Mighty Prophet! Seer blest!   115
    On whom those truths do rest,
Which we are toiling all our lives to find,
In darkness lost, the darkness of the grave;
Thou, over whom thy Immortality
Broods like the Day, a Master o'er a Slave,   120
A Presence which is not to be put by;
Thou little Child, yet glorious in the might
Of heaven-born freedom on thy being's height,
Why with such earnest pains dost thou provoke
The years to bring the inevitable yoke,   125
Thus blindly with thy blessedness at strife?

Full soon thy Soul shall have her earthly freight,
And custom lie upon thee with a weight,
Heavy as frost, and deep almost as life!

9

O joy! that in our embers 130
Is something that doth live,
That nature yet remembers
What was so fugitive!
The thought of our past years in me doth breed
Perpetual benediction: not indeed 135
For that which is most worthy to be blest;
Delight and liberty, the simple creed
Of Childhood, whether busy or at rest,
With new-fledged hope still fluttering in his breast: —
Not for these I raise 140
The song of thanks and praise;
But for those obstinate questionings
Of sense and outward things,
Fallings from us, vanishings;
Blank misgivings of a Creature 145
Moving about in worlds not realised,
High instincts before which our mortal Nature
Did tremble like a guilty Thing surprised:
But for those first affections,
Those shadowy recollections, 150
Which, be they what they may,
Are yet the fountain-light of all our day,
Are yet a master-light of all our seeing;
Uphold us, cherish, and have power to make
Our noisy years seem moments in the being 155
Of the eternal Silence: truths that wake,
To perish never:
Which neither listlessness, nor mad endeavour,
Nor Man nor Boy,
Nor all that is at enmity with joy, 160
Can utterly abolish or destroy!
Hence in a season of calm weather
Though inland far we be,
Our Souls have sight of that immortal sea
Which brought us hither, 165
Can in a moment travel thither,

And see the Children sport upon the shore,
And hear the mighty waters rolling evermore.

10

Then sing, ye Birds, sing, sing a joyous song!
  And let the young Lambs bound   170
   As to the tabor's sound!
We in thought will join your throng,
   Ye that pipe and ye that play,
   Ye that through your hearts to-day
   Feel the gladness of the May!   175
What though the radiance which was once so bright
Be now for ever taken from my sight,
 Though nothing can bring back the hour
Of splendour in the grass, of glory in the flower;
   We will grieve not, rather find   180
   Strength in what remains behind;
   In the primal sympathy
   Which having been must ever be;
   In the soothing thoughts that spring
   Out of human suffering;   185
   In the faith that looks through death,
In years that bring the philosophic mind.

11

And O, ye Fountains, Meadows, Hills and Groves,
Forebode not any severing of our loves!
Yet in my heart of hearts I feel your might;   190
I only have relinquished one delight
To live beneath your more habitual sway.
I love the Brooks which down their channels fret,
Even more than when I tripped lightly as they;
The innocent brightness of a new-born Day   195
   Is lovely yet;
The Clouds that gather round the setting sun
Do take a sober colouring from an eye
That hath kept watch o'er man's mortality;
Another race hath been, and other palms are won. 200
Thanks to the human heart by which we live,
Thanks to its tenderness, its joys, and fears,
To me the meanest flower that blows can give
Thoughts that do often lie too deep for tears.

William Butler Yeats (1865–1939)
To a Child Dancing in the Wind

> Dance there upon the shore;
> What need have you to care
> For wind or water's roar?
> And tumble out your hair
> That the salt drops have wet;
> Being young you have not known
> The fool's triumph, nor yet
> Love lost as soon as won,
> Nor the best labourer dead
> And all the sheaves to bind.
> What need have you to dread
> The monstrous crying of the wind?

3

Awakenings

Sherwood Anderson (1876–1941)

I'm a Fool

It was a hard jolt for me, one of the most bitterest I ever had to face. And it all came about through my own foolishness, too. Even yet sometimes, when I think of it, I want to cry or swear or kick myself. Perhaps, even now, after all this time, there will be a kind of satisfaction in making myself look cheap by telling of it.

It began at three o'clock one October afternoon as I sat in the grand stand at the fall trotting and pacing meet at Sandusky, Ohio.

To tell the truth, I felt a little foolish that I should be sitting in the grand stand at all. During the summer before I had left my home town with Harry Whitehead and, with a nigger named Burt, had taken a job as swipe with one of the two horses Harry was campaigning through the fall race meets that year. Mother cried and my sister Mildred, who wanted to get a job as a schoolteacher in our town that fall, stormed and scolded about the house all during the week before I left. They both thought it something disgraceful that one of our family should take a place as a swipe with race horses. I've an idea Mildred thought my taking the place would stand in the way of her getting the job she'd been working so long for.

But after all I had to work, and there was no other work to be got. A big lumbering fellow of nineteen couldn't just hang around the house and I had got too big to mow people's lawns and sell newspapers. Little chaps who could get next to people's sympathies by their sizes were always getting jobs away from me. There was one fellow who kept saying to everyone who wanted a lawn mowed or a cistern cleaned that he was saving money to work his way through college, and I used to lay

425

awake nights thinking up ways to injure him without being found out. I kept thinking of wagons running over him and bricks falling on his head as he walked along the street. But never mind him.

I got the place with Harry and I liked Burt fine. We got along splendid together. He was a big nigger with a lazy sprawling body and soft, kind eyes, and when it came to a fight he could hit like Jack Johnson. He had Bucephalus, a big black pacing stallion that could do 2.09 or 2.10 if he had to, and I had a little gelding named Doctor Fritz that never lost a race all fall when Harry wanted him to win.

We set out from home late in July, in a box car with the two horses and after that, until late November, we kept moving along to the race meets and the fairs. It was a peachy time for me, I'll say that. Sometimes now I think that boys who are raised regular in houses, and never have a fine nigger like Burt for best friend, and go to high schools and college, and never steal anything, or get drunk a little, or learn to swear from fellows who know how, or come walking up in front of a grand stand in their shirt sleeves and with dirty horsy pants on when the races are going on and the grand stand is full of people all dressed up—What's the use of talking about it? Such fellows don't know nothing at all. They've never had no opportunity.

But I did. Burt taught me how to rub down a horse and put the bandages on after a race and steam a horse out and a lot of valuable things for any man to know. He could wrap a bandage on a horse's leg so smooth that if it had been the same color you would think it was his skin, and I guess he'd have been a big driver, too, and got to the top like Murphy and Walter Cox and the others if he hadn't been black.

Gee whizz! it was fun. You got to a county-seat town, maybe say on a Saturday or Sunday, and the fair began the next Tuesday and lasted until Friday afternoon. Doctor Fritz would be, say, in the 2.25 trot on Tuesday afternoon and on Thursday afternoon Bucephalus would knock 'em cold in the "free-for-all" pace. It left you a lot of time to hang around and listen to horse talk, and see Burt knock some yap cold that got too gay, and you'd find out about horses and men and pick up a lot of stuff you could use all the rest of your life, if you had some sense and salted down what you heard and felt and saw.

And then at the end of the week when the race meet was over, and Harry had run home to tend up to his livery-stable business, you and Burt hitched the two horses to carts and drove slow and steady across country, to the place for the next meeting, so as to not overheat the horses, etc., etc., you know.

Gee whizz! Gosh amighty! the nice hickory-nut and beechnut and oaks and other kinds of trees along the roads, all brown and red, and the good smells, and Burt singing a song called "Deep River," and the country girls at the windows of houses and everything. You can stick your colleges up your nose for all me. I guess I know where I got my education.

Why, one of those little burgs of towns you came to on the way, say now on a Saturday afternoon, and Burt says, "Let's lay up here." And you did.

And you took the horses to a livery stable and fed them, and you got your good clothes out of a box and put them on.

And the town was full of farmers gaping, because they could see you were racehorse people, and the kids maybe never see a nigger before and was afraid and run away when the two of us walked down their main street.

And that was before prohibition and all that foolishness, and so you went into a saloon, the two of you, and all the yaps come and stood around, and there was always some one pretended he was horsy and knew things and spoke up and began asking questions, and all you did was to lie and lie all you could about what horses you had, and I said I owned them, and then some fellow said, "Will you have a drink of whisky?" and Burt knocked his eye out the way he could say, offhand like, "Oh, well, all right, I'm agreeable to a little nip. I'll split a quart with you." Gee whizz!

But that isn't what I want to tell my story about. We got home late in November and I promised mother I'd quit the race horses for good. There's a lot of things you've got to promise a mother because she don't know any better.

And so, there not being any work in our town any more than when I left there to go to the races, I went off to Sandusky and got a pretty good place taking care of horses for a man who owned a teaming and delivery and storage and coal and real-estate business there. It was a pretty good place with good eats, and a day off each week, and sleeping on a cot in a big barn, and mostly just shoveling in hay and oats to a lot of big good-enough skates of horses that couldn't have trotted a race with a toad. I wasn't dissatisfied and I could send money home.

And then, as I started to tell you, the fall races come to Sandusky and I got the day off and I went. I left the job at noon and had on my good clothes and my new brown derby hat I'd bought the Saturday before, and a stand-up collar.

First of all I went downtown and walked about with the dudes. I've always thought to myself, "Put up a good front," and so I did it. I had forty dollars in my pockets and so I went into the West House, a big hotel, and walked up to the cigar stand. "Give me three twenty-five cent cigars," I said. There was a lot of horsemen and strangers and dressed-up people from other towns standing around in the lobby and in the bar, and I mingled amongst them. In the bar there was a fellow with a cane and a Windsor tie on, that it made me sick to look at him. I like a man to be a man and dressed up, but not to go put on that kind of airs. So I pushed him aside, kind of rough, and had me a drink of whisky. And then he looked at me, as though he thought maybe he'd get gay, but he changed his mind and didn't say anything. And then I had another drink of whisky, just to show him something, and went out and had a hack out to the races, all to myself, and when I got there I bought myself the best seat I could get up in the grand stand, but didn't go in for any of these boxes. That's putting on too many airs.

And so there I was, sitting up in the grand stand as gay as you please and looking down on the swipes coming out with their horses, and with their dirty horsy pants on and the horseblankets swung over their shoulders, same as I had been doing all the year before. I liked one thing about the same as the other, sitting up there and feeling grand and being down there and looking up at the yaps and feeling grander and more important, too.

One thing's about as good as another, if you take it just right. I've often said that.

Well, right in front of me, in the grand stand that day, there was a fellow with a couple of girls and they was about my age. The young fellow was a nice guy, all right. He was the kind maybe that goes to college and then comes to be a lawyer or maybe a newspaper editor or something like that, but he wasn't stuck on himself. There are some of that kind are all right and he was one of the ones.

He had his sister with him and another girl and the sister looked around over her shoulder, accidental at first, not intending to start anything—she wasn't that kind— and her eyes and mine happened to meet.

You know how it is. Gee, she was a peach! She had on a soft dress, kind of a blue stuff and it looked carelessly made, but was well sewed and made and everything. I knew that much. I blushed when she looked right at me and so did she. She was the nicest girl I've ever seen in my life. She wasn't stuck on herself and could talk proper grammar without being like a schoolteacher or something like that. What I mean is, she was O.K. I think maybe her father was well-to-do, but not rich to make her chesty because she was his daughter, as some are. Maybe he owned a drug store or a dry-goods store in their home town, or something like that. She never told me and I never asked.

My own people are all O.K. too, when you come to that. My grandfather was Welsh and over in the old country, in Wales he was— But never mind that.

The first heat of the first race come off and the young fellow setting there with the two girls left them and went down to make a bet. I knew what he was up to, but he didn't talk big and noisy and let everyone around know he was a sport, as some do. He wasn't that kind. Well, he come back and I heard him tell the two girls what horse he'd bet on, and when the heat trotted they all half got to their feet and acted in the excited, sweaty way people do when they've got money down on a race, and the horse they bet on is up there pretty close at the end, and they think maybe he'll come on with a rush, but he never does because he hasn't got the old juice in him, come right down to it.

And then, pretty soon, the horses came out for the 2.18 pace and there was a horse in it I knew. He was a horse Bob French had in his string but Bob didn't own him. He was a horse owned by a Mr. Mathers down at Marietta, Ohio.

This Mr. Mathers had a lot of money and owned some coal mines or something and he had a swell place out in the country, and he was stuck on race horses, but was a Presbyterian or something, and I think more than likely his wife was one, too, maybe a stiffer one than himself. So he never raced his horses hisself, and the story round the Ohio race tracks was that when one of his horses got ready to go to the races he turned him over to Bob French and pretended to his wife he was sold.

So Bob had the horses and he did pretty much as he pleased and you can't blame Bob, at least, I never did. Sometimes he was out to win and sometimes he wasn't. I never cared much about that when I was swiping a horse. What I did want to know was that my horse had the speed and could go out in front, if you wanted him to.

And, as I'm telling you, there was Bob in this race with one of Mr. Mathers' horses, was named "About Ben Ahem" or something like that, and was fast as a streak. He was a gelding and had a mark of 2.21, but could step in .08 or .09.

Because when Burt and I were out, as I've told you, the year before, there was a nigger Burt knew, worked for Mr. Mathers and we went out there one day when we didn't have no race on at the Marietta Fair and our boss Harry was gone home.

And so everyone was gone to the fair but just this one nigger and he took us all through Mr. Mathers' swell house and he and Burt tapped a bottle of wine Mr. Mathers had hid in his bedroom, back in a closet, without his wife knowing, and he showed us this Ahem horse. Burt was always stuck on being a driver but didn't have much chance to get to the top, being a nigger, and he and the other nigger gulped the whole bottle of wine and Burt got a little lit up.

So the nigger let Burt take this About Ben Ahem and step him a mile in a track Mr. Mathers had all to himself, right there on the farm. And Mr. Mathers had one child, a daughter, kinda sick and not very good looking, and she came home and we had to hustle to get About Ben Ahem stuck back in the barn.

I'm only telling you to get everything straight. At Sandusky, that afternoon I was at the fair, this young fellow with the two girls was fussed, being with the girls and losing his bet. You know how a fellow is that way. One of them was his girl and the other his sister. I had figured that out.

"Gee whizz," I says to myself, "I'm going to give him the dope."

He was mighty nice when I touched him on the shoulder. He and the girls were nice to me right from the start and clear to the end. I'm not blaming them.

And so he leaned back and I give him the dope on About Ben Ahem. "Don't bet a cent on this first heat because he'll go like an oxen hitched to a plow, but when the first heat is over go right down and lay on your pile." That's what I told him.

Well, I never saw a fellow treat any one sweller. There was a fat man sitting beside the little girl, that had looked at me twice by this time, and I at her, and both blushing, and what did he do but have the nerve to turn and ask the fat man to get up and change places with me so I could set with his crowd.

Gee whizz, craps amighty. There I was. What a chump I was to go and get gay up there in the West House bar, and just because that dude was standing there with a cane and that kind of a necktie on, to go and get all balled up and drink that whisky, just to show off.

Of course she would know, me setting right beside her and letting her smell of my breath. I could have kicked myself right down out of that grand stand and all around that race track and made a faster record than most of the skates of horses they had there that year.

Because that girl wasn't any mutt of a girl. What wouldn't I have give right then for a stick of chewing gum to chew, or a lozenger, or some licorice, or most anything. I was glad I had those twenty-five cent cigars in my pocket and right away I give that fellow one and lit one myself. Then that fat man got up and we changed places and there I was, plunked right down beside her.

They introduced themselves and the fellow's best girl, he had with him, was named Miss Elinor Woodbury, and her father was a manufacturer of barrels from a place called Tiffin, Ohio. And the fellow himself was named Wilbur Wessen and his sister was Miss Lucy Wessen.

I suppose it was their having such swell names that got me off my trolley. A fellow, just because he has been a swipe with a race horse, and works taking care of horses for a man in the teaming, delivery, and storage business isn't any better or worse than any one else. I've often thought that, and said it too.

But you know how a fellow is. There's something in that kind of nice clothes, and the kind of nice eyes she had, and the way she had looked at me, awhile before, over her brother's shoulder, and me looking back at her, and both of us blushing.

I couldn't show her up for a boob, could I?

I made a fool of myself, that's what I did. I said my name was Walter Mathers from Marietta, Ohio, and then I told all three of them the smashingest lie you ever heard. What I said was that my father owned the horse About Ben Ahem and that he had let him out to this Bob French for racing purposes, because our family was proud and had never gone into racing that way, in our own name, I mean, and Miss Lucy Wessen's eyes were shining, and I went the whole hog.

I told about our place down at Marietta, and about the big stables and the grand brick house we had on a hill, up above the Ohio River, but I knew enough not to do it in no bragging way. What I did was to start things and then let them drag the rest out of me. I acted just as reluctant to tell as I could. Our family hasn't got any barrel factory, and since I've known us, we've always been pretty poor, but not asking anything of any one at that, and my grandfather, over in Wales—but never mind that.

We set there talking like we had known each other for years and years, and I went and told them that my father had been expecting maybe this Bob French wasn't on the square, and had sent me up to Sandusky on the sly to find out what I could.

And I bluffed it through I had found out all about the 2.18 pace, in which About Ben Ahem was to start.

I said he would lose the first heat by pacing like a lame cow and then he would come back and skin 'em alive after that. And to back up what I said I took thirty dollars out of my pocket and handed it to Mr. Wilbur Wessen and asked him, would he mind, after the first heat, to go down and place it on About Ben Ahem for whatever odds he could get. What I said was that I didn't want Bob French to see me and none of the swipes.

Sure enough the first heat come off and About Ben Ahem went off his stride, up the back stretch, and looked like a wooden horse or a sick one, and come in to be last.

Then this Wilbur Wessen went down to the betting place under the grand stand and there I was with the two girls, and when that Miss Woodbury was looking the other way once, Lucy Wessen kinda, with her shoulder you know, kinda touched me. Not just tucking down, I don't mean. You know how a woman can do. They get close, but not getting gay either. You know what they do. Gee whizz.

And then they give me a jolt. What they had done, when I didn't know, was to get together, and they had decided Wilbur Wessen would bet fifty dollars, and the two girls had gone and put in ten dollars each, of their own money, too. I was sick then, but I was sicker later.

About the gelding, About Ben Ahem, and their winning their money, I wasn't worried a lot about that. It came out O.K. Ahem stepped the next three heats like a bushel of spoiled eggs going to market before they could be found out, and Wilbur Wessen had got nine to two for the money. There was something else eating at me.

Because Wilbur come back, after he had bet the money, and after that he spent most of his time talking to that Miss Woodbury, and Lucy Wessen and I was left alone together like on a desert island. Gee, if I'd only been on the square or if there had been any way of getting myself on the square. There ain't any Walter Mathers, like I said to her and them, and there hasn't ever been one, but if there was, I bet I'd go to Marietta, Ohio, and shoot him tomorrow.

There I was, big boob that I am. Pretty soon the race was over, and Wilbur had gone down and collected our money, and we had a hack downtown, and he stood us a swell supper at the West House, and a bottle of champagne beside.

And I was with the girl and she wasn't saying much, and I wasn't saying much either. One thing I know. She wasn't stuck on me because of the lie about my father being rich and all that. There's a way you know . . . Craps amighty. There's a kind of girl you see just once in your life, and if you don't get busy and make hay, then you're gone for good and all, and might as well go jump off a bridge. They give you a look from inside of them somewhere, and it ain't no vamping, and what it means is—you want that girl to be your wife, and you want nice things around her like flowers and swell clothes, and you want her to have the kids you're going to have, and you want good music played and no ragtime. Gee whizz.

There's a place over near Sandusky, across a kind of bay, and it's called Cedar Point. And after we had supper we went over to it in a launch, all by ourselves. Wilbur and Miss Lucy and that Miss Woodbury had to catch a ten o'clock train back to Tiffin, Ohio, because, when you're out with girls like that you can't get careless and miss any trains and stay out all night, like you can with some kinds of Janes.

And Wilbur blowed himself to the launch and it cost him fifteen cold plunks, but I wouldn't never have knew if I hadn't listened. He wasn't no tin horn kind of a sport.

Over at the Cedar Point place, we didn't stay around where there was a gang of common kind of cattle at all.

There was big dance halls and dining places for yaps, and there was a beach you could walk along and get where it was dark, and we went there.

She didn't talk hardly at all and neither did I, and I was thinking how glad I was my mother was all right, and always made us kids learn to eat with a fork at the table, and not swill soup, and not be noisy and rough like a gang you see around a race track that way.

Then Wilbur and his girl went away up the beach and Lucy and I sat down in a dark place, where there was some roots of old trees the water had washed up, and after that the time, till we had to go back in the launch and they had to catch their trains, wasn't nothing at all. It went like winking your eye.

Here's how it was. The place we were setting in was dark, like I said, and there was the roots from that old stump sticking up like arms, and there was a watery smell, and the night was like—as if you could put your hand out and feel it—so warm and soft and dark and sweet like an orange.

I most cried and I most swore and I most jumped up and danced, I was so mad and happy and sad.

When Wilbur come back from being alone with his girl, and she saw him coming, Lucy she says, "We got to go to the train now," and she was most crying too, but she never knew nothing I knew, and she couldn't be so all busted up. And then, before Wilbur and Miss Woodbury got up to where we was, she put her face up and kissed me quick and put her head up against me and she was all quivering and—Gee whizz.

Sometimes I hope I have cancer and die. I guess you know what I mean. We went in the launch across the bay to the train like that, and it was dark, too. She whispered and said it was like she and I could get out of the boat and walk on water, and it sounded foolish, but I knew what she meant.

And then quick we were right at the depot, and there was a big gang of yaps, the kind that goes to the fairs, and crowded and milling around like cattle, and how could I tell her? "It won't be long because you'll write and I'll write to you." That's all she said.

I got a chance like a hay barn afire. A swell chance I got.

And maybe she would write me, down at Marietta that way, and the letter would come back, and stamped on the front of it by the U.S.A. "there ain't any such guy," or something like that, whatever they stamp on a letter that way.

And me trying to pass myself off for a big-bug and a swell—to her, as decent a little body as God ever made. Craps amighty—swell chance I got!

And then the train come in, and she got on it, and Wilbur Wessen, he come and shook hands with me, and that Miss Woodbury was nice too and bowed to me, and I at her, and the train went and I busted out and cried like a kid.

Gee, I could have run after the train and made Dan Patch look like a freight train after a wreck but, socks amighty, what was the use? Did you ever see such a fool?

I'll bet you what—if I had an arm broke right now or a train had run over my foot—I wouldn't go to no doctor at all. I'd go set down and let her hurt and hurt—that's what I'd do.

I'll bet you what—if I hadn't a drunk that booze I'd never been such a boob as to go tell such a lie—that couldn't never be made straight to a lady like her.

I wish I had that fellow right here that had on a Windsor tie and carried a cane. I'd smash him for fair. Gosh darn his eyes. He's a big fool—that's what he is.

And if I'm not another you just go find me one and I'll quit working and be a bum and give him my job. I don't care nothing for working, and earning money, and saving it for no such boob as myself.

I Want to Know Why

We got up at four in the morning, that first day in the East. On the evening before, we had climbed off a freight train at the edge of town and with the true instinct of Kentucky boys had found our way across town and to the race track and the stables at once. Then we knew we were all right. Hanley Turner right away found a nigger we knew. It was Bildad Johnson, who in the winter works at Ed Becker's livery barn in our home town, Beckersville. Bildad is a good cook as almost all our niggers are and of course he, like everyone in our part of Kentucky who is anyone at all, likes the horses. In the spring Bildad begins to scratch around. A nigger from our country can flatter and wheedle anyone into letting him do most anything he wants. Bildad wheedles the stable men and the trainers from the horse farms in our country around Lexington. The trainers come into town in the evening to stand around and talk and maybe get into a poker game. Bildad gets in with them. He is always doing little favors and telling about things to eat, chicken browned in a pan, and how is the best way to cook sweet potatoes and corn bread. It makes your mouth water to hear him.

When the racing season comes on and the horses go to the races and there is all the talk on the streets in the evenings about the new colts, and everyone says when they are going over to Lexington or to the spring meeting at Churchill Downs or to Latonia, and the horsemen that have been down to New Orleans or maybe at the winter meeting at Havana in Cuba come home to spend a week before they start out again, at such a time when everything talked about in Beckersville is just horses and nothing else and the outfits start out and horse racing is in every breath of air you breathe, Bildad shows up with a job as cook for some outfit. Often when I think about it, his always going all season to the races and working in the livery barn in the winter where horses are and where men like to come and talk about horses, I wish I was a nigger. It's a foolish thing to say, but that's the way I am about being around horses, just crazy. I can't help it.

Well, I must tell you about what we did and let you in on what I'm talking about. Four of us boys from Beckersville, all whites and sons of men who live in Beckersville regular, made up our minds we were going to the races, not just to Lexington or Louisville, I don't mean, but to the big Eastern track we were always hearing our

Beckersville men talk about, to Saratoga. We were all pretty young then. I was just turned fifteen and I was the oldest of the four. It was my scheme. I admit that, and I talked the others into trying it. There was Hanley Turner and Henry Rieback and Tom Tumberton and myself. I had thirty-seven dollars I had earned during the winter working nights and Saturdays in Enoch Myer's grocery. Henry Rieback had eleven dollars and the others, Hanley and Tom, had only a dollar or two each. We fixed it all up and laid low until the Kentucky spring meetings were over and some of our men, the sportiest ones, the ones we envied the most, had cut out. Then we cut out too.

I won't tell you the trouble we had beating our way on freights and all. We went through Cleveland and Buffalo and other cities and saw Niagara Falls. We bought things there, souvenirs and spoons and cards and shells with pictures of the falls on them for our sisters and mothers, but thought we had better not send any of the things home. We didn't want to put the folks on our trail and maybe be nabbed.

We got into Saratoga as I said at night and went to the track. Bildad fed us up. He showed us a place to sleep in hay over a shed and promised to keep still. Niggers are all right about things like that. They won't squeal on you. Often a white man you might meet, when you had run away from home like that, might appear to be all right and give you a quarter or a half dollar or something, and then go right and give you away. White men will do that, but not a nigger. You can trust them. They are squarer with kids. I don't know why.

At the Saratoga meeting that year there were a lot of men from home. Dave Williams and Arthur Mulford and Jerry Myers and others. Then there was a lot from Louisville and Lexington Henry Rieback knew but I didn't. They were professional gamblers and Henry Rieback's father is one too. He is what is called a sheet writer and goes away most of the year to tracks. In the winter when he is home in Beckersville he don't stay there much but goes away to cities and deals faro. He is a nice man and generous, is always sending Henry presents, a bicycle and a gold watch and a boy scout suit of clothes and things like that.

My own father is a lawyer. He's all right, but don't make much money and can't buy me things, and anyway I'm getting so old now I don't expect it. He never said nothing to me against Henry, but Hanley Turner and Tom Tumberton's fathers did. They said to their boys that money so come by is no good and they didn't want their boys brought up to hear gamblers' talk and be thinking about such things and maybe embrace them.

That's all right and I guess the men know what they are talking about, but I don't see what it's got to do with Henry or with horses either. That's what I'm writing this story about. I'm puzzled. I'm getting to be a man and want to think straight and be O.K., and there's something I saw at the race meeting at the Eastern track I can't figure out.

I can't help it, I'm crazy about thoroughbred horses. I've always been that way. When I was ten years old and saw I was growing to be big and couldn't be a rider I was so sorry I nearly died. Harry Hellinfinger in Beckersville, whose father is Postmaster, is grown up and too lazy to work, but likes to stand around in the street and get up jokes on boys like sending them to a hardware store for a gimlet to bore square holes and other jokes like that. He played one on me. He told me that if I would eat a half a cigar I would be stunted and not grow any more and maybe could be a rider. I did it. When father wasn't looking I took a cigar out of his pocket and gagged it down some way. It made me awful sick and the doctor had to be sent for, and then it did no good. I kept right on growing. It was a joke. When I told what I had done and why, most fathers would have whipped me, but mine didn't.

Well, I didn't get stunted and didn't die. It serves Harry Hellinfinger right. Then I made up my mind I would like to be a stableboy, but had to give that up too. Mostly niggers do that work and I knew father wouldn't let me go into it. No use to ask him.

If you've never been crazy about thoroughbreds, it's because you've never been around where they are much and don't know any better. They're beautiful. There isn't anything so lovely and clean and full of spunk and honest and everything as some race horses. On the big horse farms that are all around our town Beckersville there are tracks, and the horses run in the early morning. More than a thousand times I've got out of bed before daylight and walked two or three miles to the tracks. Mother wouldn't of let me go, but father always says, "Let him alone." So I got some bread out of the breadbox and some butter and jam, gobbled it and lit out.

At the tracks you sit on the fence with men, whites and niggers, and they chew tobacco and talk, and then the colts are brought out. It's early and the grass is covered with shiny dew and in another field a man is plowing and they are frying things in a shed where the track niggers sleep, and you know how a nigger can giggle and laugh and say things that make you laugh. A white man can't do it and some niggers can't, but a track nigger can every time.

And so the colts are brought out and some are just galloped by stableboys, but almost every morning on a big track owned by a rich man who lives maybe in New York, there are always, nearly every morning, a few colts and some of the old race horses and geldings and mares that are cut loose.

It brings a lump up into my throat when a horse runs. I don't mean all horses, but some. I can pick them nearly every time. It's in my blood like in the blood of race track niggers and trainers. Even when they just go slop-jogging along with a little nigger on their backs, I can tell a winner. If my throat hurts and it's hard for me to swallow, that's him. He'll run like Sam Hill when you let him out. If he don't win every time it'll be a wonder and because they've got him in a pocket behind another or he was pulled or got off bad at the post or something. If I wanted to be a gambler like Henry Rieback's father I could get rich. I know I could and Henry says so too. All I would have to do is to wait till that hurt comes when I see a horse and then bet every cent. That's what I would do if I wanted to be a gambler, but I don't.

When you're at the tracks in the morning—not the race tracks but the training tracks around Beckersville—you don't see a horse, the kind I've been talking about, very often, but it's nice anyway. Any thoroughbred, that is sired right and out of a good mare and trained by a man that knows how, can run. If he couldn't, what would he be there for and not pulling a plow?

Well, out of the stables they come and the boys are on their backs and it's lovely to be there. You hunch down on top of the fence and itch inside you. Over in the sheds the niggers giggle and sing. Bacon is being fried and coffee made. Everything smells lovely. Nothing smells better than coffee and manure and horses and niggers and bacon frying and pipes being smoked out of doors on a morning like that. It just gets you, that's what it does.

But about Saratoga. We was there six days and not a soul from home seen us and everything came off just as we wanted it to, fine weather and horses and races and all. We beat our way home and Bildad gave us a basket with fried chicken and bread and other eatables in it, and I had eighteen dollars when we got back to Beckersville. Mother jawed and cried, but Pop didn't say much. I told everything we done, except one thing. I did and saw that alone. That's what I'm writing about. It got me upset. I think about it at night. Here it is.

At Saratoga we laid up nights in the hay in the shed Bildad had showed us and ate with the niggers early and at night when the race people had all gone away. The men from home stayed mostly in the grandstand and betting field and didn't come out around the places where the horses are kept except to the paddocks just before a race when the horses are saddled. At Saratoga they don't have paddocks under an open shed as at Lexington and Churchill Downs and other tracks down in our country, but saddle the horses right out in an open place under trees on a lawn as smooth and nice as Banker Bohon's front yard here in Beckersville. It's lovely. The horses are sweaty and nervous and shine and the men come out and smoke cigars and look at them and the trainers are there and the owners, and your heart thumps so you can hardly breathe.

Then the bugle blows for post and the boys that ride come running out with their silk clothes on and you run to get a place by the fence with the niggers.

I always am wanting to be a trainer or owner, and at the risk of being seen and caught and sent home I went to the paddocks before every race. The other boys didn't, but I did.

We got to Saratoga on a Friday, and on Wednesday the next week the big Mulford Handicap was to be run. Middlestride was in it and Sunstreak. The weather was fine and the track fast. I couldn't sleep the night before.

What had happened was that both these horses are the kind it makes my throat hurt to see. Middlestride is long and looks awkward and is a gelding. He belongs to Joe Thompson, a little owner from home who only has a half dozen horses. The Mulford Handicap is for a mile and Middlestride can't untrack fast. He goes away slow and is always way back at the half, then he begins to run and if the race is a mile and a quarter he'll just eat up everything and get there.

Sunstreak is different. He is a stallion and nervous and belongs on the biggest farm we've got in our country, the Van Riddle place that belongs to Mr. Van Riddle of New York. Sunstreak is like a girl you think about sometimes but never see. He is hard all over and lovely too. When you look at his head you want to kiss him. He is trained by Jerry Tillford who knows me and has been good to me lots of times, lets me walk into a horse's stall to look at him close and other things. There isn't anything as sweet as that horse. He stands at the post quiet and not letting on, but he is just burning up inside. Then when the barrier goes up he is off like his name, Sunstreak. It makes you ache to see him. It hurts you. He just lays down and runs like a bird dog. There can't anything I ever see run like him except Middlestride when he gets untraced and stretches himself.

Gee! I ached to see that race and those two horses run, ached and dreaded it too. I didn't want to see either of our horses beaten. We had never sent a pair like that to the races before. Old men in Beckersville said so and the niggers said so. It was a fact.

Before the race, I went over to the paddocks to see. I looked a last look at Middlestride, who isn't such a much standing in a paddock that way, then I went to see Sunstreak.

It was his day. I knew when I seen him. I forgot all about being seen myself and walked right up. All the men from Beckersville were there and no one noticed me except Jerry Tillford. He saw me and something happened. I'll tell you about that.

I was standing looking at that horse and aching. In some way, I can't tell how, I knew just how Sunstreak felt inside. He was quiet and letting the niggers rub his legs and Mr. Van Riddle himself put the saddle on, but he was just a raging torrent inside. He was like the water in the river at Niagara Falls just before it goes plunk down. That horse wasn't thinking about running. He don't have to think about that. He was just thinking about holding himself back till the time for the running came. I knew that. I could just in a way see right inside him. He was going to do some awful running and I knew it. He wasn't bragging or letting on much or prancing or making a fuss, but just waiting. I knew it and Jerry Tillford his trainer knew. I look up, and then that man and I looked into each other's eyes. Something happened to me. I guess I loved the man as much as I did the horse because he knew what I knew. Seemed to me there wasn't anything in the world but that man and the horse and me. I cried and Jerry Tillford had a shine in his eyes. Then I came away to the fence to wait for the race. The horse was better than me, more steadier and, now I know, better than Jerry. He was the quietest and he had to do the running.

Sunstreak ran first of course and he busted the world's record for a mile. I've seen that if I never see anything more. Everthing came out just as I expected. Middlestride got left at the post and was 'way back and closed up to be second, just as I knew he would. He'll get a world's record too some day. They can't skin the Beckersville country on horses.

I watched the race calm because I knew what would happen. I was sure. Hanley Turner and Henry Rieback and Tom Tumberton were all more excited than me.

A funny thing had happened to me. I was thinking about Jerry Tillford the trainer and how happy he was all through the race. I liked him that afternoon even more than I ever liked my own father. I almost forgot the horses thinking that way about him. It was because of what I had seen in his eyes as he stood in the paddocks beside Sunstreak before the race started. I knew he had been watching and working with Sunstreak since the horse was a baby colt, had taught him to run and be patient and when to let himself out and not to quit, never. I knew that for him it was like a mother seeing her child do something brave or wonderful. It was the first time I ever felt for a man like that.

After the race that night I cut out from Tom and Hanley and Henry. I wanted to be by myself and I wanted to be near Jerry Tillford if I could work it. Here is what happened.

The track in Saratoga is near the edge of town. It is all polished up and trees around, the evergreen kind, and grass and everything painted and nice. If you go past the track you get to a hard road made of asphalt for automobiles, and if you go along this for a few miles there is a road turns off to a little rummy-looking farmhouse set in a yard.

That night after the race I went along that road because I had seen Jerry and some other men go that way in an automobile. I didn't expect to find them. I walked for a ways and then sat down by a fence to think. It was the direction they went in. I wanted to be as near Jerry as I could. I felt close to him. Pretty soon I went up the side road—I don't know why—and came to the rummy farmhouse. I was just lonesome to see Jerry, like wanting to see your father at night when you are a young kid. Just then an automobile came along and turned in. Jerry was in it and Henry Rieback's father, and Arthur Bedford from home, and Dave Williams and two other men I didn't know. They got out of the car and went into the house, all but Henry Rieback's father who quarreled with them and said he wouldn't go. It was only about nine o'clock, but they were all drunk and the rummy-looking farmhouse was a place for bad women to stay in. That's what it was. I crept up along a fence and looked through a window and saw.

It's what give me the fantods. I can't make it out. The women in the house were all ugly mean-looking women, not nice to look at or be near. They were homely too, except one who was tall and looked a little like the gelding Middlestride, but not clean like him, but with a hard ugly mouth. She had red hair. I saw everything plain. I got up by an old rosebush by an open window and looked. The women had on loose dresses and sat around in chairs. The men came in and some sat on the women's laps. The place smelled rotten and there was rotten talk, the kind a kid hears around a livery stable in a town like Beckersville in the winter but don't ever expect to hear talked when there are women around. It was rotten. A nigger wouldn't go into such a place.

I looked at Jerry Tillford. I've told you how I had been feeling about him on account of his knowing what was going on inside of Sunstreak in the minute before he went to the post for the race in which he made a world's record.

Jerry bragged in that bad woman house as I know Sunstreak wouldn't never have bragged. He said that he made that horse, that it was him that won the race and made the record. He lied and bragged like a fool. I never heard such silly talk.

And, then, what do you suppose he did! He looked at the woman in there, the one that was lean and hard-mouthed and looked a little like the gelding Middlestride but not clean like him, and his eyes began to shine just as they did when he looked at me and at Sunstreak in the paddocks at the track in the afternoon. I stood there by the window—gee!—but I wished I hadn't gone away from the tracks, but had stayed with the boys and the niggers and the horses. The tall rotten-looking woman was between us just as Sunstreak was in the paddocks in the afternoon.

Then, all of a sudden, I began to hate that man. I wanted to scream and rush in the room and kill him. I never had such a feeling before. I was so mad clean through that I cried and my fists were doubled up so my fingernails cut my hands.

And Jerry's eyes kept shining and he waved back and forth, and then he went and kissed that woman and I crept away and went back to the tracks and to bed and didn't sleep hardly any, and then next day I got the other kids to start home with me and never told them anything I seen.

I been thinking about it ever since. I can't make it out. Spring has come again and I'm nearly sixteen and go to the tracks mornings same as always, and I see Sunstreak and Middlestride and a new colt named Strident I'll bet will lay them all out, but no one thinks so but me and two or three niggers.

But things are different. At the tracks the air don't taste as good or smell as good. It's because a man like Jerry Tillford, who knows what he does, could see a horse like Sunstreak run, and kiss a woman like that the same day. I can't make it out. Darn him, what did he want to do like that for? I keep thinking about it and it spoils looking at horses and smelling things and hearing niggers laugh and everything. Sometimes I'm so mad about it I want to fight someone. It gives me the fantods. What did he do it for? I want to know why.

The Bible (King James Version)
Luke 15: 11–32

The Parable of the Prodigal Son

11 And he said, A certain man had two sons:

12 And the younger of them said to his father, Father, give me the portion of goods that falleth to me. And he divided unto them his living.

13 And not many days after the younger son gathered all together, and took his journey into a far country, and there wasted his substance with riotous living.

14 And when he had spent all, there arose a mighty famine in that land; and he began to be in want.

15 And he went and joined himself to a citizen of that country; and he sent him into his fields to feed swine.

16 And he would fain have filled his belly with the husks that the swine did eat: and no man gave unto him.

17 And when he came to himself, he said, How many hired servants of my father's have bread enough and to spare, and I perish with hunger!

18 I will arise and go to my father, and will say unto him, Father, I have sinned against heaven, and before thee,

19 And am no more worthy to be called thy son: make me as one of thy hired servants.

20 And he arose, and came to his father. But when he was yet a great way off, his father saw him, and had compassion, and ran, and fell on his neck, and kissed him.

21 And the son said unto him, Father, I have sinned against heaven, and in thy sight, and am no more worthy to be called thy son.

22 But the father said to his servants, Bring forth the best robe, and put it on him; and put a ring on his hand, and shoes on his feet:

23 And bring hither the fatted calf, and kill it; and let us eat, and be merry:

24 For this my son was dead, and is alive again; he was lost, and is found. And they began to be merry.

25 Now his elder son was in the field: and as he came and drew nigh to the house, he heard musick and dancing.

26 And he called one of the servants, and asked what these things meant.

27 And he said unto him, Thy brother is come; and thy father hath killed the fatted calf, because he hath received him safe and sound.

28 And he was angry, and would not go in: therefore came his father out, and intreated him.

29 And he answering said to his father, Lo, these many years do I serve thee, neither transgressed I at any time thy commandment: and yet thou never gavest me a kid, that I might make merry with my friends:

30 But as soon as this thy son was come, which hath devoured thy living with harlots, thou has killed for him the fatted calf.

31 And he said unto him, Son, thou art ever with me, and all that I have is thine.

32 It was meet that we should make merry, and be glad: for this thy brother was dead, and is alive again; and was lost, and is found.

David Elkind (born 1931)

Teenagers in Crisis

There is no place for teenagers in American society today—not in our homes, not in our schools, and not in society at large. This was not always the case: barely a decade ago, teenagers had a clearly defined position in the social structure. They were the "next generation," the "future leaders" of America. Their intellectual, social, and moral development was considered important, and therefore it was protected and nurtured. The teenager's occasional foibles and excesses were excused as an expression of youthful spirit, a necessary Mardi Gras before assuming adult responsibility and decorum. Teenagers thus received the time needed to adapt to the remarkable transformations their bodies, minds, and emotions were undergoing. Society recognized that the transition from childhood to adulthood was difficult and that young people needed time, support, and guidance in this endeavor.

In today's rapidly changing society, teenagers have lost their once privileged position. Instead, they have had a premature adulthood thrust upon them. Teenagers now are expected to confront life and its challenges with the maturity once expected only of the middle-aged, without any time for preparation. Many adults are too busy retooling and retraining their own job skills to devote any time to preparing the next generation of workers. And some parents are so involved in reordering their own lives, managing a career, marriage, parenting, and leisure, that they have no time to give their teenagers; other parents simply cannot train a teenager for an adulthood they themselves have yet to attain fully. The media and merchandisers, too, no longer abide by the unwritten rule that teenagers are a privileged group who require special protection and nurturing. They now see teenagers as fair game for all the arts of persuasion and sexual innuendo once directed only to adult audiences and consumers. High schools, which were once the setting for a unique teenage culture and language, have become miniatures of the adult community. Theft, violence, sex, and substance abuse are now as common in the high schools as they are on the streets.

It is true, of course, that many parents and other adults are still committed to giving teenagers the time, protection, and guidance they require to traverse this difficult period. But these well-meaning adults meet almost insurmountable barriers in today's society, and many feel powerless to provide the kind of guidance they believe teenagers need. For example, a mother of a teenager asked me recently what to do with her fourteen-year-old son who was staying up late to watch X-rated movies on cable television. I suggested that if she did not want him to see the movies, she should not permit him to do so and should give him her reasons for the prohibition. Her next question surprised me. She asked me what she should do if he watches them after she goes to bed. It was clear that the mother felt helpless to monitor her son's TV watching. For this youth, as for many others, premature adulthood is gained by default.

In today's society we seem unable to accept the fact of adolescence, that there are young people in transition from childhood to adulthood who need adult guidance and direction. Rather, we assume the teenager is a kind of adult. Whether we confer premature adulthood upon teenagers because we are too caught up in our own lives to give them the time and attention they require or because we feel helpless to provide them with the safe world they need, the end result is the same: teenagers have no place in this society. They are not adults capable of carrying the adult responsibilities we confer upon them. And they are not children whose subservience to adults can be taken for granted. We expect them to be grown up in all those domains where we cannot or do not want to maintain control. But in other domains, such as attending school, we expect our teenagers to behave like obedient children.

Perhaps the best word to describe the predicament of today's teenagers is "unplaced." Teenagers are not displaced in the sense of having been put in a position they did not choose to be in (a state sometimes called anomie). Nor are they misplaced in the sense of having been put in the wrong place (a state sometimes called alienation). Rather, they are unplaced in the sense that there is no place for a young person who needs a measured and controlled introduction to adulthood. In a rapidly changing society, when adults are struggling to adapt to a new social order, few adults are genuinely committed to helping teenagers attain a healthy adulthood. Young people are thus denied the special recognition and protection that society previously accorded their age group. The special stage belonging to teenagers has been excised from the life cycle, and teenagers have been given a pro forma adulthood, an adulthood with all of the responsibilities but few of the prerogatives. Young people today are quite literally all grown up with no place to go.

The imposition of premature adulthood upon today's teenagers affects them in two different but closely related ways. First, because teenagers need a protected period of time within which to construct a personal identity, the absence of that period impairs the formation of that all-important self-definition. Having a personal identity amounts to having an abiding sense of self that brings together, and gives meaning to, the teenager's past while at the same time giving him or her guidance and direction for the future. A secure sense of self, of personal identity, allows the young person to deal with both inner and outer demands with consistency and efficiency. This sense of self is thus one of the teenager's most important defenses against stress. By impairing his or her ability to construct a secure personal identity, today's society leaves the teenager more vulnerable and less competent to meet the challenges that are inevitable in life.

The second effect of premature adulthood is inordinate stress: teenagers today are subject to more stress than were teenagers in previous generations. This stress is of three types. First, teenagers are confronted with many more freedoms today than were available to past generations. Second, they are experiencing losses, to their basic sense of security and expectations for the future, that earlier generations did not encounter. And third, they must cope with the frustration of trying to prepare for their life's work in school settings that hinder rather than facilitate this goal. Any one of these new stresses would put a heavy burden on a young person; taken together, they make a formidable demand on the teenager's ability to adapt to new demands and new situations.

Contemporary American society has thus struck teenagers a double blow. It has rendered them more vulnerable to stress while at the same time exposing them to new and more powerful stresses than were ever faced by previous generations of adolescents. It is not surprising, then, to find that the number of stress-related problems among teenagers has more than trebled in the last decade and a half. Before we examine in more detail the predicament of today's teenagers, we need to look at some of the frightening statistics in order to understand both the seriousness and the magnitude of the problem.

A Generation under Stress

Substance abuse is now the leading cause of death among teenagers and accounts for more than ten thousand deaths each year. Although the use of drugs has leveled off after a threefold rise in the last decade and a half, alcohol use is becoming more widespread and is appearing among younger age groups. According to a recent survey of junior high school students, 65 percent of the thirteen-year-olds had used alcohol at least once that year, some 35 percent used it once a month, and 20 percent used it once a week. Thirty-five percent of the thirteen-year-olds queried said that it was fun and all right to get drunk. The National Institute on Alcohol Abuse and Alcoholism reports, conservatively, that 1.3 million teenagers between the ages of twelve and seventeen have serious drinking problems. According to a 1981 report from the Department of Health, Education and Welfare, more than three million youths nationwide have experienced problems at home, in school, or on the highways as a result of drinking.[1] In my own travels throughout this country I have found that it is commonplace for beer to be available at parties for twelve- and thirteen-year-olds. It is often provided by parents, who, relieved that the youngsters are not into drugs, appear to consider alcohol benign by comparison.

Sexual activity, at least among teenage girls, has more than tripled over the last two decades. In contrast to the 1960s, when only about 10 percent of teenage girls were sexually active, more than 50 percent are sexually active today. By the age of nineteen at least 70 percent of young women have had at least one sexual experience. Among young women who are sexually active, four out of ten will become pregnant before they leave their teens. Currently about 1.3 million teenagers become pregnant each year, and more than a third of them are choosing to have and to keep their babies.[2] Although young women may be able to conceive an infant, the pelvic girdle does not attain its full size until the age of seventeen or eighteen. This puts the young teenage mother and her infant at physical risk. The data also indicate that the infants of teenage mothers are more at risk for child abuse and for emotional problems than are the children of more mature mothers.

Suicide rates for teenagers have climbed at a fearful pace. Five thousand teenagers commit suicide each year, and for each of these suicides fifty to one hundred youngsters make an unsuccessful attempt.[3] Sex differences in mode of suicide are changing. Girls, who in the past resorted to pills and slashing their wrists, are now using the more violent means often employed by boys, namely, hanging and shooting. In addition, many "accidental" teenage deaths are regarded by experts as being, in part at least, suicidal.

Crime rates have increased dramatically among juveniles. For many children, crime is a regular part of their lives, in both the home and the school.

> Every month, secondary schools experience 2.4 million thefts, almost 300,000 assaults and over 100,000 robberies. Criminal behavior starts early, usually in school, and peaks quickly. More 17 to 20 year old males are arrested for virtually every class of crime (including homicide) than males in any other age group. But the record of children under 10 (55,000 arrests in 1980) is itself sobering and it gets seven times worse by age 14.[4]

To these alarming statistics we must add that over one million children run away from home each year, and an indeterminate number of these are forced into prostitution or pornography, or both.[5]

These statistics define the gravity of the problems resulting from teenage stress. Now we need to examine some of the social changes that have taken place in this country and how they have led us to deny, ignore, or abdicate our responsibilities toward youth.

Social Change and Teenage Identity

It is generally agreed today, following the original work of the psychoanalyst Erik Erikson, that the primary task of the teenage years is to construct a sense of personal identity.[6] In Erikson's view, the teenager's task is to bring together all of the various and sometimes conflicting facets of self into a working whole that at once provides continuity with the past and focus and direction for the future. This sense of personal identity includes various roles (son or daughter, student, athlete, musician, artist, and so on), various traits and abilities (quiet, outgoing, timid, generous, high-strung), as well as the teenager's personal tableau of likes and dislikes, political and social attitudes, religious orientation, and much more.

It is clear from this description that the task of forming an identity is a difficult and complex one. It is not undertaken until the teen years in part because the young person has not accumulated all the necessary ingredients until this time, and in part because prior to adolescence young people lack the mental abilities required for the task. The late Jean Piaget demonstrated that it is not until the teen years that young people are capable of constructing theories.[7] And it is not unreasonable to characterize identity as a theory of oneself. Forming an identity, like building a theory, is a creative endeavor that takes much time and concentrated effort. That is why Erikson has suggested that teenagers either make or find a "moratorium," a period of time for themselves during which they can engage in the task of identity formation.

In the past, a clearly demarcated period of development, called adolescence, gave young people the needed respite before assuming adult responsibility and decision making. But this period is no longer available. The current generation of young people is being denied the time needed to put together a workable theory of self. The issue, it should be said, is not one of leisure or free time. Many teenagers today have that. Rather, what is lacking is *pressure-free* time, time that is free of the burdens designated properly for adults. Even at their leisure teenagers carry with them the adult expectation that they will behave as if they were already fully grown and mature. It is because young people today carry with them, and are often preoccupied by, adult issues that they do not have the time to deal with properly teenage concerns, namely, the construction of a personal definition of self.

It is not only time that is missing. Teenagers also need a clearly defined value system against which to test other values and discover their own. But when the important adults in their lives don't know what their own values are and are not sure what is right and what is wrong, what is good and what is bad, the teenagers' task is even more difficult and more time-consuming. The process of constructing an identity is adversely affected because neither the proper time nor the proper ingredients are available. Let us consider how the very process of identity formation is affected by the teenager's being "unplaced" in the society.

Social Change and Parenting

In the last thirty years our society has undergone more change, at a faster rate, than during any other period. We are now moving rapidly from an industrial to a postindustrial or information society:

> Twenty-five years ago, the nation's work force was about equally divided between white-collar and blue-collar jobs, between goods and service industries. There are now more people employed full time in our colleges and universities than are employed in agriculture. In 1981, white-collar jobs outnumbered blue-collar jobs by three to two. And the number of people employed by U.S. Steel is smaller than the number of employees at McDonald's.[8]

The nature of the work force has changed as well. Over half of the 25 million women with children in the United States are working outside the home, compared with 20 percent in 1950.

Although the changes relating to work are significant, even greater changes have come about in our values and social philosophy. Daniel Yankelovich has likened this shift to the major changes in the earth's crust as a result of shifts of the tectonic plates deep in the earth's interior. Yankelovich argues that we are rapidly moving away from the "social role" orientation that once dominated American society.[9] He describes the old "social role" (give-and-take) philosophy this way:

> I give hard work, loyalty and steadfastness, I swallow my frustrations and suppress my impulse to do what I would enjoy, and do what is expected of me instead. I do not put myself first; I put the needs of others ahead of my own. I give a lot, but what I get in return is worth it. I receive an ever growing standard of living, a family life with a devoted spouse and decent kids. Our children will take care of us in our old age if we really need it, which thank goodness we will not. I have a nice home, a good job, the respect of my friends and neighbors, a sense of accomplishment at having made something of my life. Last but not least, as an American I am proud to be a citizen of the finest country in the world.[10]

That is the philosophy most of today's parents grew up with, and it is the one most adults today recognize as familiar and generally their own. But over the last twenty years a new philosophy has emerged to vie with the older social role orientation. This new philosophy has been variously called the "culture of narcissism" or the "me generation" or more kindly by Yankelovich as a "search for self-fulfillment." According to numerous surveys by Yankelovich and others, this new philosophy now fully pervades our society:

> By the late seventies . . . seven out of ten Americans (72 percent) [were] spending a great deal of time thinking about themselves and their inner lives, this in a nation once notorious for its impatience with inwardness. The rage for self-fulfillment . . . has now spread to virtually the entire U.S. population.[11]

The changes we are undergoing today in American society have been described in somewhat different terms by John Naisbitt in his book *Megatrends*.[12] He argues that the "basic building block of the society is shifting from the family to the individual" and that we are changing from a "fixed option" to a "multiple option" society. Choices in the basic areas of family and work have exploded into a multitude of highly individual arrangements and life-styles. And the basic idea of a multiple option society has spilled over into other important areas of our lives: religion, the arts, music, food, entertainment, and, finally, the extent to which cultural, ethnic, and racial diversity are now celebrated in the United States. Both Yankelovich and Naisbitt suggest that there are many pluses and minuses to the new self-fulfillment philosophy, just as there were for the social role orientation. Moreover, it may be, as Naisbitt suggests, that an individual-oriented social philosophy is better suited than a role-oriented social philosophy to the requirements of an information society.

However that may be, the important point here is not that one philosophy is good and the other is bad, but rather that we as adults and parents are caught in the crossfire of these two social philosophies. Sexual values are a case in point. As parents and adults, we have the values we learned as children; as members of a modern society, we recognize that values have changed and a new set of values is followed. The conflict arises when we as adults must confront the new values rather than merely tolerate them. Recently a father admitted to me that his daughter is living with a man. The father grew up when I did, and at that time a young woman who lived with a man would most probably be disowned by her family. But such behavior is the norm today, and though the father may feel deeply that what his daughter is doing is wrong, the contemporary value system supports it. After all, isn't everyone else doing it? This father must now cope with two conflicting value systems—his own and his daughter's.

Parents who, like this father, would like to protect and shield their offspring feel overwhelmed by the pressure to accept the new social code. If they openly challenge the new values, they are sure to be labeled, and dismissed, as old-fashioned and stuffy. Ellen Goodman put the dilemma of the committed parent in a time of changing values this way:

> I belong to a whole generation of people who grew up under traditional rules about sex. We heard all about the rights and wrongs, shoulds and shouldn'ts, do's and don'ts. As adults we have lived through a time when all these rules were questioned, when people were set "free" to discover their own sexuality and their own definition of morality. Whether we observed this change from the outside or were part of it, we were nevertheless affected by it. Now, with all of our ambivalence and confusion, we are the new generation of parents raising the next generation of adults. Our agenda is a complicated one, because we do not want to be the new guardians of sexual repression. Nor are we willing to define sexual freedom as the children's right to do it. We are equally uncomfortable with notions that sex is evil and sex is groovy.[13]

In times of rapid social change, even committed parents are confused about what limits to set and what values to advocate and to enforce. For us adults this is a time to give serious thought to our values and principles, just as it is a time to struggle for greater tolerance. Ironically, our responses may only make matters worse for teenagers. Caught between two value systems, parents become ambivalent, and teenagers perceive their ambivalence as license. Failing to act, we force our teenagers to do so, before they are ready. Because we are reluctant to take a firm stand, we deny teenagers the benefit of our parental concern and we impel them into premature adulthood. We say, honestly, "I don't know," but teenagers hear, "They don't care."

Parents who are themselves awash in the tide of social change and are looking for self-fulfillment may have a different reaction to the teenager. A parent going

448 Awakenings

through a "midlife" crisis may be too self-absorbed with his or her own voyage of personal discovery to appreciate fully and support the needs of a teenage son or daughter. Similarly, parents who are undergoing a divorce (as more than one million couples a year do) may be too caught up in the turbulence of their own lives to be of much help to a teenager with his or her own kind of life change. Other parents, who may be learning new job skills such as those involved in using computers, may look upon teenagers as having the advantage. Such parents may feel that the teenager has more knowledge and technological sophistication than they have and therefore that teenagers have it made. It may be hard for these parents to see the teenager's need for a special time and for support and guidance.

Still other parents and adults find the pace of social change too much to take and are overwhelmed by it. While their mates may have found the new social philosophy liberating and challenging, they find it frightening and isolating. If divorce comes, they feel adrift and alone, lost in a world they did not bargain for and do not want to participate in. It is a great temptation for these parents to reverse roles and look to their teenagers for support and guidance. Here again, the impact of social change is to deny the teenager the time and freedom to be a teenager in order to prepare for adulthood; the teenager is rushed from childhood to adulthood in order to meet the needs of a troubled parent.

Rapid social change, particularly from one social philosophy to another, inevitably affects parental attitudes toward teenagers. Although different parents are affected in different ways, the end result is always the same. For one reason or another, in one way or another, teenagers are denied the protection, guidance, and instruction they desperately need in order to mature. As we shall see in later chapters, it is not only parents but society as a whole that is unplacing teenagers. Perhaps this is why Hermann Hesse in *Steppenwolf* described the plight of youth caught between social philosophies in this way:

> Every age, every culture, every custom and tradition has its own character, its own weaknesses and its own strength, its beauties and ugliness; accepts certain sufferings as matters of course, puts up patiently with certain evils. Human life is reduced to real suffering, to real hell only when two ages, two cultures and religions overlap. . . . Now there are times when a whole generation is caught in this way between two ages, two modes of life with the consequence that it loses all power to understand itself, and has no standard, no security, no simple acquiescence.[14]

If we put Hesse's last sentence in contemporary terms, we would say that youths caught between two cultures have a weak sense of identity (no standard, no security) and self-definition and are thus more vulnerable to stress. Clearly our situation today is not unique; there have been comparable periods in history. But that does not make our present situation any more tolerable. Today's teenager must struggle to achieve a sense of self, a sense of personal identity, if she or he is going to go on to build a full life as a mature and complete adult. But by bestowing a premature mantle of adulthood upon teenagers, we as parents and adults impair the formation of their sense of identity and render them more vulnerable to stress. We thus endanger their future and society's as well.

Two Ways of Growing

When we talk about a "mature" person, we are talking in part about the healthy sense of identity and of self developed during the teen years. This sense of personal identity is constructed by one of two methods, either by differentiation (the process of discriminating or separating out) and higher-order integration (or simply integration) or by substitution. The kind of parenting a teenager receives and the social climate in which he or she grows up are critical in determining which of these two paths of development a young person will follow, and what sort of self-definition he or she will attain.

Growth by *integration* is conflictual, time-consuming, and laborious. A child who is acquiring the concept of squareness, for example, must encounter a variety of different shapes before he or she can separate squareness from roundness or pointedness. In addition, the child must see many different square things such as boxes, dice, sugar cubes, and alphabet blocks before he or she can arrive at a higher-order notion of squareness that will allow him or her to differentiate a square from all other shapes and to integrate all square things, regardless of size, color, or any other features, into the same concept.

The principles of differentiation and integration operate in the social realm as well. To acquire a consistent sense of self, we must encounter a great number of different experiences within which we can discover how our feelings, thoughts, and beliefs are different from those of other people. At the same time, we also need to learn how much we are like other people. We need to discover that other people don't like insults any more than we do and that other people appreciate compliments just as we do. As a result of this slow process of differentiating ourselves from others, in terms of how we are alike and yet different from them, we gradually arrive at a stable and unique perception of our self.

Once growth by integration has occurred, it is difficult if not impossible to break down. After a child has acquired the concept of squareness, for example, he or she will not lose it; the concept becomes a permanent part of the self and a consistent way of seeing reality. The same is true in the social realm. People who have a strong sense of self do not lose it even under the most trying circumstances. Survivors of concentration camps and of brainwashing had such strong concepts of self that even extreme stress, exposure, starvation, torture, did not break them.

Mental structures achieved by differentiation and integration also conserve energy and reduce stress. Once we know what a square is we can identify it immediately; we don't have to go through a laborious process of differentiation and integration in order to recognize it again. In the same way, once we have an integrated sense of self, we know what to do in different situations. A well-defined sense of self and identity provides us with effective strategies for managing psychological stress—the major stress in our society. Later, in Chapter 8, we will look at three basic stress situations and how a healthy sense of self and identity enables us to cope with them effectively and with a minimum expenditure of energy.

The second way in which growth occurs is by *substitution.* Consider the transition we have all made from making a phone call by turning a wheel several times to getting the same number by pushing buttons. Learning to dial a number by turning a wheel is not a preparation for getting that number by pushing buttons. Both actions have the same result, but the first skill is neither required to learn the second nor incorporated within it. Both exist independently and side by side. Either skill can be drawn upon if needed. This type of learning is clearly of value, particularly in a society with a rapidly changing technology. In adapting to new technology, it is an advantage to be able to replace old habits quickly with new ones.

The same principles, again, can be followed in social growth. Indeed, substitution is the kind of growth suggested by the well-known adage "When in Rome do as the Romans do." In some social situations, particularly those in which we don't know the rules, it is generally considered wise to adapt and to follow the example of others who are familiar with the situation. But such learning is not adaptive when it comes to constructing a sense of personal identity. A sense of self constructed by the simple addition of feelings, thoughts, and beliefs copied from others amounts to a *patchwork* self. A person who has constructed a self in this way is not in touch with the deeper core of his or her being. Young people who have a self constructed by substitution are easily swayed and influenced by others because they do not have a clear definition of their own self. In addition, they are more vulnerable to stress than teenagers with an integrated sense of self because each new situation is a new challenge. Teenagers with a patchwork self have not developed an inner core of consistency and stability that allows them to deal with new situations in terms of past experiences.

These two different kinds of growth account for the two quite different types of teenagers we see. Teenagers who have acquired an integrated sense of identity are able to postpone immediate gratification in order to attain long-range goals. They are future-oriented and inner-directed. In contrast, teenagers who have grown by substitution and have only a patchwork self are less able to postpone immediate gratification. They are present-oriented and other-directed, easily influenced by others. By encouraging teenagers to choose growth by substitution and the development of a patchwork self, contemporary society has rendered teenagers more vulnerable to stress and denied them the full development of their personality and character.

. . . There is no place for teenagers in today's society; consequently teenagers are made more vulnerable to stress at the very time when they are being exposed to more powerful stress than ever before. Before elaborating this theme, we need to look at how teenagers have been treated in the past in order to clarify how we are treating them today.

Teenagers Today and Yesterday

The conception of youth as an important and well-marked stage of development dates from antiquity. This idea, however, has had a cyclical history. It seems to have been recognized and emphasized, and then lost and forgotten, only to be rediscovered at a later time. Ancient Greece was one point in history where adolescence was clearly marked. Aristotle, for example, described young people in remarkably familiar terms: "Young men have strong passions and tend to gratify them indiscriminately. Of the bodily desires, it is the sexual to which they are most disposed to give way, and in regard to sexual desire they exercise no self-restraint."

During the Dark Ages the conception of stages of development and of adolescence as a unique stage was lost and a theological theory of human nature was advanced. This theory was that of the homunculus, a "little man" already fully formed in the male sperm. It was believed that when this homunculus was implanted in the woman, the homunculus merely grew in size until the full-term fetal size was attained at the end of nine months. From the standpoint of the homunculus theory, the difference between children and adults was a simple matter of quantity: the adult was larger than the infant and more experienced, but in every other way they were roughly equal.

The homunculus theory was soon challenged by the scientific thinkers of the Renaissance. Once scientific observation came to be a criterion of truth, it was noted that children have both qualitative and quantitative characteristics of their own and are not miniature adults. During this period the stage of adolescence was rediscovered, if not widely accepted and appreciated. During the succeeding period, the age of "Enlightenment," there was a growing appreciation of the stage of youth as a period of *Sturm und Drang,* of "Storm and Stress."

Among the most renowned of the Enlightenment writers was Jean Jacques Rousseau, whose classic *Emile* was the beginning of modern child psychology and progressive education. [15] Rousseau, like Aristotle, believed that development occurred in a sequence of stages. Rousseau's third stage, ages thirteen to fifteen, was concerned with the development of reason and self-consciousness. His notion that youths were inherently decent and were corrupted by an immoral adult society was the opposite of the prevailing religious view that they were, by nature, imbued with original sin and that it was the task of the church and of God-fearing adults to save them. A century later, Charles Darwin added a new dimension to this controversy when he introduced his theory of evolution. By placing humans on the evolutionary ladder with animals, this theory removed humans from their special religious category. Darwin's work thus gave a new scientific legitimacy to the conception of adolescence as a stage, more than two millennia after the idea was articulated by Aristotle.

Darwin's work was the foundation upon which the social sciences were built. As long as human beings were considered outside nature, as part of a religious category, they could not be studied by scientific means any more than religious dogma could be tested empirically. But once humans were regarded as part of nature, their behavior, both individually and collectively, was open to study. Social science, psychology, sociology, and anthropology flourished in the remaining decades of the nineteenth century after Darwin's work was first published. The study of children and adolescents was part of this explosion of new knowledge, which has continued to this day.

Adolescence in America

Belief in the significance of adolescence as a distinct stage in the life cycle emerged in this country when we moved from an agricultural to an industrial economy. On the farm, parents saw children as smaller and weaker adults who could help with the difficult labor of the farm. This notion of children as small adults persisted into the beginning of the industrial revolution when children were used as cheap labor in the factories. But as industrialization and mechanization progressed, children and adolescents were no longer needed in the job market. Parents, who were factory laborers now, began to see children as in need of education and technical training to prepare them for a factory economy. The response of adults to children during the industrial revolution is perhaps the most obvious example of how the economy shapes parental attitudes toward children and youth.

The fact that children were no longer needed in the labor force, along with a more humanistic attitude toward them (reflecting the new view that such handicaps as retardation and mental illness had natural rather than divine causes), led to a series of new child labor laws. By 1914 almost every state in the nation had laws prohibiting the employment of youth below a certain age, usually fourteen. The removal of teenagers from the main labor force was a clear sign of their special estate. As Edgar Friedenberg wrote:

> Adolescence is conceived as a distinct stage of life in those societies so complicated and differentiated that each individual's social role and function takes years to define and to learn. When years of special preparation for adult life are required, these years become a distinguishable period with its own customs, rules and relationships. [16]

The special place of teenagers in society was also recognized by those concerned with education. To function in an industrial society, young people had to know how to read and write and had to have basic information and skills in science and mechanics. In addition, they had to be conditioned to the rhythms of factory work, which is different from farm work. Farm work follows the rhythms of the calendar, the changing seasons. Factory work follows the rhythms of the clock and, with the miracle of artificial lighting, allows work to continue at any time of the day or night. Schools in their schedules—in the taking of the roll, in the sounding of bells to signal entrance time and dismissal, and in the short lunch hour—patterned themselves after factories and in this way prepared young people for the rhythms of factory work. Being a "student" or a "pupil" marked young people as being in a special apprenticeship position in society.

As the years passed and the stage of adolescence became more fully accepted and better understood, more legislation concerning juveniles gradually emerged, this time concerned with drinking (and later driving), voting, and legal responsibilities of all sorts.

The social rediscovery of adolescence in the United States was thus both a reaction to economic needs and a reflection of parental attitudes engendered by the new knowledge about adolescence provided by social science. The result of the rediscovery was the recognition that in a highly industrialized society, young people needed a period between childhood and adulthood, a period before the final assumption of adult responsibilities and decision making. Parents, teachers, the media, the church, the government, and industry all agreed and supported this need of youth and defined the life of the adolescent accordingly.

The recent denial of adolescence as a special stage of life is therefore a denial of more than a century of growth in our understanding of youth. It is, quite literally, a return to the concept of the homunculus theory held during the Dark Ages. We hurry young people as children and then unplace them as teenagers. We cannot, dare not, persist on this dangerous course of denying young people the time, the support, and the guidance they need to arrive at an integrated definition of self. Teenagers are the next generation and the future leaders of this country. Their need is real and pressing. We harm them and endanger the future of our society if we leave them, as our legacy, a patchwork sense of personal identity.

Notes

1. N. Cobb, "Who's Getting High on What?" *Boston Globe*, October 10, 1982.
2. M. Zelnick and J. Kantner, "Sexuality, Contraception and Pregnancy among Young Unwed Females in the United States," *Research Reports*, Commission on Population Growth and the American Future, vol. 1 (Washington, D.C.: Government Printing Office, 1980).
3. C. L. Tishler, "Adolescent Suicide: Prevention, Practice and Treatment," *Feelings and Their Medical Significance* 23, no. 6 (November–December 1981).
4. C. Murphy, "Kids Today," *Wilson Quarterly*, Autumn 1982.

5. "Shelters and Streets Draw Throw-away Kids," *New York Times*, June 3, 1983.
6. E. Erikson, *Childhood and Society* (New York: Norton, 1950).
7. J. Piaget, *The Psychology of Intelligence* (London: Routledge & Kegan Paul, 1950).
8. E. L. Boyer, *Highschool* (New York: Harper & Row, 1983), p. 4.
9. D. Yankelovich, *New Rules* (New York: Bantam, 1981).
10. Ibid., p. 7.
11. Ibid., p. 3.
12. J. Naisbitt, *Megatrends* (New York: Warner, 1982).
13. E. Goodman, "The Turmoil of Teenage Sexuality," *Ms.*, July 1983, pp. 37–41.
14. H. Hesse, *Steppenwolf* (New York: Rinehart, 1963), p. 24.
15. J. J. Rousseau, *Emile* (New York: Basic Books, 1979).
16. E. Z. Friedenberg, *The Vanishing Adolescent* (New York: Dell, 1959), pp. 21–22.

John Updike (born 1932)

A & P

In walks these three girls in nothing but bathing suits. I'm in the third checkout slot, with my back to the door, so I don't see them until they're over by the bread. The one that caught my eye first was the one in the plaid green two-piece. She was a chunky kid, with a good tan and a sweet broad soft-looking can with those two crescents of white just under it, where the sun never seems to hit, at the top of the backs of her legs. I stood there with my hand on a box of HiHo crackers trying to remember if I rang it up or not. I ring it up again and the customer starts giving me hell. She's one of these cash-register-watchers, a witch about fifty with rouge on her cheekbones and no eyebrows, and I know it made her day to trip me up. She'd been watching cash registers for fifty years and probably never seen a mistake before.

By the time I got her feathers smoothed and her goodies into a bag—she gives me a little snort in passing, if she'd been born at the right time they would have burned her over in Salem—by the time I get her on her way the girls had circled around the bread and were coming back, without a pushcart, back my way along the counters, in the aisle between the checkouts and the Special bins. They didn't even have shoes on. There was this chunky one, with the two-piece—it was bright green and the seams on the bra were still sharp and her belly was still pretty pale so I guessed she just got it (the suit)—there was this one, with one of those chubby berry-faces, the lips all bunched together under her nose, this one, and a tall one, with black hair that hadn't quite frizzed right, and one of these sunburns right across under the eyes, and a chin that was too long—you know, the kind of girl other girls think is very "striking" and "attractive" but never quite makes it, as they very well know, which is why they like her so much—and then the third one, that wasn't quite so tall. She was the queen. She kind of led them, the other two peeking around and making their shoulders round. She didn't look around, not this queen, she just walked straight on slowly, on these long white prima-donna legs. She came down a little hard on her heels, as if she didn't walk in her bare feet that much, putting down her heels and then letting the weight move along to her toes as if she was testing the floor with every step, putting a little deliberate extra action into it. You never know for sure how girls' minds work (do you really think it's a mind in there or just a little buzz like a bee in a glass jar?) but you got the idea she had talked the other two into coming in here with her, and now she was showing them how to do it, walk slow and hold yourself straight.

She had on a kind of dirty-pink—beige maybe, I don't know—bathing suit with a little nubble all over it and, what got me, the straps were down. They were off her shoulders looped loose around the cool tops of her arms, and I guess as a result the suit had slipped a little on her, so all around the top of the cloth there was this shining rim. If it hadn't been there you wouldn't have known there could have been anything whiter than those shoulders. With the straps pushed off, there was nothing between the top of the suit and the top of her head except just *her*, this clean bare plane of the top of her chest down from the shoulder bones like a dented sheet of metal tilted in the light. I mean, it was more than pretty.

She had sort of oaky hair that the sun and salt had bleached, done up in a bun that was unravelling, and a kind of prim face. Walking into the A & P with your straps down, I suppose it's the only kind of face you *can* have. She held her head so high her neck, coming up out of those white shoulders, looked kind of stretched, but I didn't mind. The longer her neck was, the more of her there was.

She must have felt in the corner of her eye me and over my shoulder Stokesie in the second slot watching, but she didn't tip. Not this queen. She kept her eyes moving across the racks, and stopped, and turned so slow it made my stomach rub the inside of my apron, and buzzed to the other two, who kind of huddled against her for relief, and then they all three of them went up the cat-and-dog-food-breakfast-cereal-macaroni-rice-raisins-seasonings-spreads-spaghetti-soft-drinks-crackers-and-cookies aisle. From the third slot I look straight up this aisle to the meat counter, and I watched them all the way. The fat one with the tan sort of fumbled with the cookies, but on second thought she put the package back. The sheep pushing their carts down the aisle—the girls were walking against the usual traffic (not that we have one-way signs or anything)—were pretty hilarious. You could see them, when Queenie's white shoulders dawned on them, kind of jerk, or hop, or hiccup, but their eyes snapped back to their own baskets and on they pushed. I bet you could set off dynamite in an A & P and the people would by and large keep reaching and checking oatmeal off their lists and muttering "Let me see, there was a third thing, began with A, asparagus, no, ah, yes, applesauce!" or whatever it is they do mutter. But there was no doubt, this jiggled them. A few houseslaves in pin curlers even looked around after pushing their carts past to make sure what they had seen was correct.

You know, it's one thing to have a girl in a bathing suit down on the beach, where what with the glare nobody can look at each other much anyway, and another thing in the cool of the A & P, under the fluorescent lights, against all those stacked packages, with her feet paddling along naked over our checkerboard green-and-cream rubber-tile floor.

"Oh Daddy," Stokesie said beside me. "I feel so faint."

"Darling," I said. "Hold me tight." Stokesie's married, with two babies chalked up on his fuselage already, but as far as I can tell that's the only difference. He's twenty-two, and I was nineteen this April.

"Is it done?" he asks, the responsible married man finding his voice. I forgot to say he thinks he's going to be manager some sunny day, maybe in 1990 when it's called the Great Alexandrov and Petrooshki Tea Company or something.

What he meant was, our town is five miles from a beach, with a big summer colony out on the Point, but we're right in the middle of town, and the women generally put on a shirt or shorts or something before they get out of the car into the street. And anyway these are usually women with six children and varicose veins mapping their legs and nobody, including them, could care less. As I say, we're right in the middle of town, and if you stand at our front doors you can see two banks and the Congregational church and the newspaper store and three real-estate offices and about twenty-seven old freeloaders tearing up Central Street because the sewer broke again. It's not as if we're on the Cape; we're north of Boston and there's people in this town haven't seen the ocean for twenty years.

The girls had reached the meat counter and were asking McMahon something. He pointed, they pointed, and they shuffled out of sight behind a pyramid of Diet Delight peaches. All that was left for us to see was old McMahon patting his mouth and looking after them sizing up their joints. Poor kids, I began to feel sorry for them, they couldn't help it.

Now here comes the sad part of the story, at least my family says it's sad, but I don't think it's so sad myself. The store's pretty empty, it being Thursday afternoon, so there was nothing much to do except lean on the register and wait for the girls to show up again. The whole store was like a pinball machine and I didn't know which tunnel they'd come out of. After a while they come around out of the far aisle, around the light bulbs, records at discount of the Caribbean Six or Tony Martin Sings or some such gunk you wonder they waste the wax on, sixpacks of candy bars, and plastic toys done up in cellophane that fall apart when a kid looks at them anyway. Around they come, Queenie still leading the way, and holding a little gray jar in her hand. Slots Three through Seven are unmanned and I could see her wondering between Stokes and me, but Stokesie with his usual luck draws an old party in baggy gray pants who stumbles up with four giant cans of pineapple juice (what do these bums *do* with all that pineapple juice? I've often asked myself) so the girls come to me. Queenie puts down the jar and I take it into my fingers icy cold. Kingfish Fancy Herring Snacks in Pure Sour Cream: 49¢. Now her hands are empty, not a ring or a bracelet, bare as God made them, and I wonder where the money's coming from. Still with that prim look she lifts a folded dollar bill out of the hollow at the center of her nubbled pink top. The jar went heavy in my hand. Really, I thought that was so cute.

Then everybody's luck begins to run out. Lengel comes in from haggling with a truck full of cabbages on the lot and is about to scuttle into that door marked MANAGER behind which he hides all day when the girls touch his eye. Lengel's pretty dreary, teaches Sunday school and the rest, but he doesn't miss that much. He comes over and says, "Girls, this isn't the beach."

Queenie blushes, though maybe it's just a brush of sunburn I was noticing for the first time, now that she was so close. "My mother asked me to pick up a jar of herring snacks." Her voice kind of startled me, the way voices do when you see the people first, coming out so flat and dumb yet kind of tony, too, the way it ticked over "pick up" and "snacks." All of a sudden I slid right down her voice into her living room. Her father and the other men were standing around in ice-cream coats and bow ties and the women were in sandals picking up herring snacks on toothpicks off a big glass plate and they were all holding drinks the color of water with olives and sprigs of mint in them. When my parents have somebody over they get lemonade and if it's a real racy affair Schlitz in tall glasses with "They'll Do It Every Time" cartoons stencilled on.

"That's all right," Lengel said. "But this isn't the beach." His repeating this struck me as funny, as if it had just occurred to him, and he had been thinking all these years the A & P was a great big dune and he was the head lifeguard. He didn't like my smiling—as I say he doesn't miss much—but he concentrates on giving the girls that sad Sunday-school-superintendent stare.

Queenie's blush is no sunburn now, and the plump one in plaid, that I liked better from the back—a really sweet can—pipes up, "We weren't doing any shopping. We just came in for the one thing."

"That makes no difference," Lengel tells her, and I could see from the way his eyes went that he hadn't noticed she was wearing a two-piece before. "We want you decently dressed when you come in here."

"We *are* decent," Queenie says suddenly, her lower lip pushing, getting sore now that she remembers her place, a place from which the crowd that runs the A & P must look pretty crummy. Fancy Herring Snacks flashed in her very blue eyes.

"Girls, I don't want to argue with you. After this come in here with your shoulders covered. It's our policy." He turns his back. That's policy for you. Policy is what the kingpins want. What the others want is juvenile delinquency.

All this while, the customers had been showing up with their carts but, you know, sheep, seeing a scene, they had all bunched up on Stokesie, who shook open a paper bag as gently as peeling a peach, not wanting to miss a word. I could feel in the silence everybody getting nervous, most of all Lengel, who asks me, "Sammy, have you rung up their purchase?"

I thought and said "No" but it wasn't about that I was thinking. I go through the punches, 4, 9, GROC, TOT—it's more complicated than you think, and after you do it often enough, it begins to make a little song, that you hear words to, in my case "Hello (*bing*) there, you (*gung*) hap-py *pee*-pul (*splat*)!"—the *splat* being the drawer flying out. I uncrease the bill, tenderly as you may imagine, it just having come from between the two smoothest scoops of vanilla I had ever known were there, and pass a half and a penny into her narrow pink palm, and nestle the herrings in a bag and twist its neck and hand it over, all the time thinking.

The girls, and who'd blame them, are in a hurry to get out, so I say "I quit" to Lengel quick enough for them to hear, hoping they'll stop and watch me, their unsuspected hero. They keep right on going, into the electric eye; the door flies open and they flicker across the lot to their car, Queenie and Plaid and Big Tall Goony-Goony (not that as raw material she was so bad), leaving me with Lengel and a kink in his eyebrow.

"Did you say something, Sammy?"

"I said I quit."

"I thought you did."

"You didn't have to embarrass them."

"It was they who were embarrassing us."

I started to say something that came out "Fiddle-de-doo." It's a saying of my grandmother's, and I know she would have been pleased.

"I don't think you know what you're saying," Lengel said.

"I know you don't," I said. "But I do." I pull the bow at the back of my apron and start shrugging it off my shoulders. A couple customers that had been heading for my slot begin to knock against each other, like scared pigs in a chute.

Lengel sighs and begins to look very patient and old and gray. He's been a friend of my parents for years. "Sammy, you don't want to do this to your Mom and Dad," he tells me. It's true, I don't. But it seems to me that once you begin a gesture it's fatal not to go through with it. I fold the apron, "Sammy" stitched in red on the pocket, and put it on the counter, and drop the bow tie on top of it. The bow tie is theirs, if you've ever wondered. "You'll feel this for the rest of your life," Lengel says, and I know that's true, too, but remembering how he made that pretty girl blush makes me so scrunchy inside I punch the No Sale tab and the machine whirs "pee-pul" and the drawer splats out. One advantage to this scene taking place in summer, I can follow this up with a clean exit, there's no fumbling around getting your coat and galoshes, I just saunter into the electric eye in my white shirt that my mother ironed the night before, and the door heaves itself open, and outside the sunshine is skating around on the asphalt.

I look around for my girls, but they're gone, of course. There wasn't anybody but some young married screaming with her children about some candy they didn't get by the door of a powder-blue Falcon station wagon. Looking back in the big windows, over the bags of peat moss and aluminum lawn furniture stacked on the pavement, I could see Lengel in my place in the slot, checking the sheep through. His face was dark gray and his back stiff, as if he'd just had an injection of iron, and my stomach kind of fell as I felt how hard the world was going to be to me hereafter.

4
Making Connections

Matthew Arnold (1822–1888)
The Buried Life

Light flows our war of mocking words, and yet,
Behold, with tears mine eyes are wet!
I feel a nameless sadness o'er me roll.
Yes, yes, we know that we can jest,
We know, we know that we can smile!   5
But there's a something in this breast,
To which thy light words bring no rest,
And thy gay smiles no anodyne.
Give me thy hand, and hush awhile,
And turn those limpid eyes on mine,   10
And let me read there, love! thy inmost soul.

Alas! is even love too weak
To unlock the heart, and let it speak?
Are even lovers powerless to reveal
To one another what indeed they feel?   15
I knew the mass of men conceal'd
Their thoughts, for fear that if reveal'd
They would by other men be met
With blank indifference, or with blame reproved;

461

I knew they lived and moved   20
Trick'd in disguises, alien to the rest
Of men, and alien to themselves—and yet
The same heart beats in every human breast!

But we, my love!—doth a like spell benumb
Our hearts, our voices?—must we too be dumb?   25

Ah! well for us, if even we,
Even for a moment, can get free
Our heart, and have our lips unchain'd;
For that which seals them hath been deep-ordain'd!

Fate, which foresaw   30
How frivolous a baby man would be—
By what distractions he would be possess'd,
How he would pour himself in every strife,
And well-nigh change his own identity—
That it might keep from his capricious play   35
His genuine self, and force him to obey
Even in his own despite his being's law,
Bade through the deep recesses of our breast
The unregarded river of our life
Pursue with indiscernible flow its way;   40
And that we should not see
The buried stream, and seem to be
Eddying at large in blind uncertainty,
Though driving on with it eternally.

But often, in the world's most crowded streets,   45
But often, in the din of strife,
There rises an unspeakable desire
After the knowledge of our buried life;
A thirst to spend our fire and restless force
In tracking out our true, original course;   50
A longing to inquire
Into the mystery of this heart which beats
So wild, so deep in us—to know
Whence our lives come and where they go.
And many a man in his own breast then delves,   55
But deep enough, alas! none ever mines.
And we have been on many thousand lines,
And we have shown, on each, spirit and power;

But hardly have we, for one little hour,
Been on our own line, have we been ourselves—   60
Hardly had skill to utter one of all
The nameless feelings that course through our breast,
But they course on for ever unexpress'd.
And long we try in vain to speak and act
Our hidden self, and what we say and do   65
Is eloquent, is well—but 'tis not true!
And then we will no more be rack'd
With inward striving, and demand
Of all the thousand nothings of the hour
Their stupefying power;   70
Ah yes, and they benumb us at our call!
Yet still, from time to time, vague and forlorn,
From the soul's subterranean depth upborne
As from an infinitely distant land,
Come airs, and floating echoes, and convey   75
A melancholy into all our day.

Only—but this is rare—
When a belovéd hand is laid in ours,
When, jaded with the rush and glare
Of the interminable hours,   80
Our eyes can in another's eyes read clear,
When our world-deafen'd ear
Is by the tones of a loved voice caress'd—
A bolt is shot back somewhere in our breast,
And a lost pulse of feeling stirs again.   85
The eye sinks inward, and the heart lies plain,
And what we mean, we say, and what we would, we know.
A man becomes aware of his life's flow,
And hears its winding murmur; and he sees
The meadows where it glides, the sun, the breeze.   90

And there arrives a lull in the hot race
Wherein he doth for ever chase
That flying and elusive shadow, rest.
An air of coolness plays upon his face,
And an unwonted calm pervades his breast.   95
And then he thinks he knows
The hills where his life rose,
And the sea where it goes.

Dover Beach

The sea is calm to-night.
The tide is full, the moon lies fair
Upon the straits;—on the French coast the light
Gleams and is gone; the cliffs of England stand,
Glimmering and vast, out in the tranquil bay.   5
Come to the window, sweet is the night-air!
Only, from the long line of spray
Where the sea meets the moon-blanch'd land,
Listen! you hear the grating roar
Of pebbles which the waves draw back, and fling,   10
At their return, up the high strand,
Begin, and cease, and then again begin,
With tremulous cadence slow, and bring
The eternal note of sadness in.

Sophocles long ago   15
Heard it on the Aegean, and it brought
Into his mind the turbid ebb and flow
Of human misery; we
Find also in the sound a thought,
Hearing it by this distant northern sea.   20

The Sea of Faith
Was once, too, at the full, and round earth's shore
Lay like the folds of a bright girdle furl'd.
But now I only hear
Its melancholy, long, withdrawing roar,   25
Retreating, to the breath
Of the night-wind, down the vast edges drear
And naked shingles of the world.

Ah, love, let us be true
To one another! for the world, which seems   30
To lie before us like a land of dreams,
So various, so beautiful, so new,
Hath really neither joy, nor love, nor light,
Nor certitude, nor peace, nor help for pain;
And we are here as on a darkling plain   35
Swept with confused alarms of struggle and flight,
Where ignorant armies clash by night.

W. H. Auden (1907–1973)

Lay Your Sleeping Head, My Love

Lay your sleeping head, my love,
Human on my faithless arm;
Time and fevers burn away
Individual beauty from
Thoughtful children, and the grave   5
Proves the child ephemeral:
But in my arms till break of day
Let the living creature lie,
Mortal, guilty, but to me
The entirely beautiful.   10

Soul and body have no bounds:
To lovers as they lie upon
Her tolerant enchanted slope
In their ordinary swoon,
Grave the vision Venus sends   15
Of supernatural sympathy,
Universal love and hope;
While an abstract insight wakes
Among the glaciers and the rocks
The hermit's sensual ecstasy.   20

Certainty, fidelity
On the stroke of midnight pass
Like vibrations of a bell,
And fashionable madmen raise
Their pedantic boring cry: 25
Every farthing of the cost,
All the dreaded cards foretell,
Shall be paid, but from this night
Not a whisper, not a thought,
Not a kiss nor look be lost.   30

Beauty, midnight, vision dies:
Let the winds of dawn that blow
Softly round your dreaming head
Such a day of sweetness show
Eye and knocking heart may bless,   35
Find the mortal world enough;
Noons of dryness see you fed
By the involuntary powers,
Nights of insult let you pass
Watched by every human love.   40

Louise Bogan (1897–1970)

Women

Women have no wilderness in them,
They are provident instead,
Content in the tight hot cell of their hearts
To eat dusty bread.

They do not see cattle cropping red winter grass,   5
They do not hear
Snow water going down under culverts
Shallow and clear.

They wait, when they should turn to journeys.
They stiffen, when they should bend.   10
They use against themselves that benevolence
To which no man is friend.

They cannot think of so many crops to a field
Or of clean wood cleft by an axe.
Their love is an eager meaninglessness   15
Too tense, or too lax.

They hear in every whisper that speaks to them
A shout and a cry.
As like as not, when they take life over their door-sills
They should let it go by.   20

Anne Bradstreet (1612–1672)
To My Dear and Loving Husband

If ever two were one, then surely we.
If ever man were loved by wife, then thee;
If ever wife was happy in a man,
Compare with me, ye women, if you can.
I prize thy love more than whole mines of gold   5
Or all the riches that the East doth hold.
My love is such that rivers cannot quench,
Nor ought but love from thee, give recompense.
Thy love is such I can no way repay.
The heavens reward thee manifold, I pray.   10
Then while we live, in love let's so persever
That when we live no more, we may live ever.

Robert Browning (1812–1889)
A Woman's Last Word

1
Let's contend no more, Love,
    Strive nor weep:
All be as before, Love,
    —Only sleep!

2
What so wild as words are?   5
    I and thou
In debate, as birds are,
    Hawk on bough!

3
See the creature stalking
    While we speak!   10

Hush and hide the talking,
    Cheek on cheek!

4

What so false as truth is,
    False to thee?
Where the serpent's tooth is   15
    Shun the tree—

5

Where the apple reddens
    Never pry—
Lest we lose our Edens,
    Eve and I.   20

6

Be a god and hold me
    With a charm!
Be a man and fold me
    With thine arm!

7

Teach me, only teach, Love!   25
    As I ought
I will speak thy speech, Love,
    Think thy thought—

8

Meet, if thou require it,
    Both demands,   30
Laying flesh and spirit
    In thy hands.

9

That shall be to-morrow
    Not to night:
I must bury sorrow   35
    Out of sight:

10

—Must a little weep, Love,
    (Foolish me!)
And so fall asleep, Love,
    Loved by thee.

Love among the Ruins

Where the quiet-colored end of evening smiles
      Miles and miles
On the solitary pastures where our sheep
      Half-asleep
Tinkle homeward through the twilight, stray or stop   5
      As they crop—
Was the site once of a city great and gay,
      (So they say)
Of our country's very capital, its prince
      Ages since   10
Held his court in, gathered councils, wielding far
      Peace or war.

Now—the country does not even boast a tree
      As you see,
To distinguish slopes of verdure, certain rills   15
      From the hills
Intersect and give a name to (else they run
      Into one),
Where the domed and daring palace shot its spires
      Up like fires   20
O'er the hundred-gated circuit of a wall
      Bounding all,
Made of marble, men might march on nor be pressed,
      Twelve abreast.

And such plenty and perfection, see, of grass   25
      Never was!
Such a carpet as, this summer-time, o'erspreads
      And embeds
Every vestige of the city, guessed alone,
      Stock or stone—   30
Where a multitude of men breathed joy and woe
      Long ago;
Lust of glory pricked their hearts up, dread of shame
      Struck them tame;
And that glory and that shame alike, the gold   35
      Bought and sold.

Now—the single little turret that remains
   On the plains,
By the caper overrooted, by the gourd
   Overscored,   40
While the patching houseleek's head of blossom winks
   Through the chinks—
Marks the basement whence a tower in ancient time
   Sprang sublime,
And a burning ring, all round, the chariots traced 45
   As they raced,
And the monarch and his minions and his dames
   Viewed the games.

And I know, while thus the quiet-colored eve
   Smiles to leave   50
To their folding, all our many-tinkling fleece
   In such peace,
And the slopes and rills in undistinguished gray
   Melt away—
That a girl with eager eyes and yellow hair   55
   Waits me there
In the turret whence the charioteers caught soul
   For the goal,
When the king looked, where she looks now, breathless, dumb
   Till I come.   60

But he looked upon the city, every side,
   Far and wide,
All the mountains topped with temples, all the glades'
   Colonnades,
All the causeys, bridges, aqueducts—and then, 65
   All the men!
When I do come, she will speak not, she will stand,
   Either hand
On my shoulder, give her eyes the first embrace
   Of my face,   70
Ere we rush, ere we extinguish sight and speech
   Each on each.

In one year they sent a million fighters forth
   South and north,
And they built their gods a brazen pillar high 75
   As the sky,

Yet reserved a thousand chariots in full force—
    Gold, of course.
Oh heart! oh blood that freezes, blood that burns!
    Earth's returns 80
For whole centuries of folly, noise, and sin!
    Shut them in,
With their triumphs and their glories and the rest!
    Love is best.

Truman Capote (1924–1984)

Mojave

At 5 P.M. that winter afternoon she had an appointment with Dr. Bentsen, formerly her psychoanalyst and currently her lover. When their relationship had changed from the analytical to the emotional, he insisted, on ethical grounds, that she cease to be his patient. Not that it mattered. He had not been of much help as an analyst, and as a lover—well, once she had watched him running to catch a bus, two hundred and twenty pounds of shortish, fiftyish, frizzly-haired, hip-heavy, myopic Manhattan Intellectual, and she had laughed: how was it possible that she could love a man so ill-humored, so ill-favored as Ezra Bentsen? The answer was she didn't; in fact, she disliked him. But at least she didn't associate him with resignation and despair. She feared her husband; she was not afraid of Dr. Bentsen. Still, it was her husband she loved.

She was rich; at any rate, had a substantial allowance from her husband, who was rich, and so could afford the studio-apartment hideaway where she met her lover perhaps once a week, sometimes twice, never more. She could also afford gifts he seemed to expect on these occasions. Not that he appreciated their quality: Verdura cuff links, classic Paul Flato cigarette cases, the obligatory Cartier watch, and (more to the point) occasional specific amounts of cash he asked to "borrow."

He had never given *her* a single present. Well, one: a mother-of-pearl Spanish dress comb that he claimed was an heirloom, a mother-treasure. Of course, it was nothing she could wear, for she wore her own hair, fluffy and tobacco colored, like a childish aureole around her deceptively naïve and youthful face. Thanks to dieting, private exercises with Joseph Pilatos, and the dermatological attentions of Dr. Orentreich, she looked in her early twenties; she was thirty-six.

The Spanish comb. Her hair. That reminded her of Jaime Sanchez and something that had happened yesterday. Jaime Sanchez was her hairdresser, and though they had known each other scarcely a year, they were, in their own way, good friends. She confided in him somewhat; he confided in her considerably more. Until recently she had judged Jaime to be a happy, almost overly blessed young man. He shared an apartment with an attractive lover, a young dentist named Carlos. Jaime and Carlos had been schoolmates in San Juan; they had left Puerto Rico together, settling first in New Orleans, then New York, and it was Jaime, working as a beautician, a talented one, who had put Carlos through dental school. Now Carlos had his own office and a clientele of prosperous Puerto Ricans and blacks.

However, during her last several visits she had noticed that Jaime Sanchez's usually unclouded eyes were somber, yellowed, as though he had a hangover, and his expertly articulate hands, ordinarily so calm and capable, trembled a little.

Yesterday, while scissor-trimming her hair, he had stopped and stood gasping, gasping—not as though fighting for air, but as if struggling against a scream.

She had said: "What is it? Are you all right?"

"No."

He had stepped to a washbasin and splashed his face with cold water. While drying himself, he said: "I'm going to kill Carlos." He waited, as if expecting her to ask him why; when she merely stared, he continued: "There's no use talking any more. He understands nothing. My words mean nothing. The only way I can communicate with him is to kill him. Then he will understand."

"I'm not sure that I do, Jaime."

"Have I ever mentioned to you Angelita? My cousin Angelita? She came here six months ago. She has always been in love with Carlos. Since she was, oh, twelve years old. And now Carlos is in love with her. He wants to marry her and have a household of children."

She felt so awkward that all she could think to ask was: "Is she a nice girl?"

"Too nice." He had seized the scissors and resumed clipping. "No, I mean that. She is an excellent girl, very petite, like a pretty parrot, and much too nice; her kindness becomes cruel. Though she doesn't understand that she is being cruel. For example . . ." She glanced at Jaime's face moving in the mirror above the washbasin; it was not the merry face that had often beguiled her, but pain and perplexity exactly reflected. "Angelita and Carlos want me to live with them after they are married, all of us together in one apartment. It was her idea, but Carlos says yes! yes! we must all stay together and from now on he and I will live like brothers. That is the reason I have to kill him. He could never have loved me, not if he could ignore my enduring such hell. He says, 'Yes, I love you, Jaime; but Angelita—this is different.' There is no difference. You love or you do not. You destroy or you do not. But Carlos will never understand that. Nothing reaches him, nothing can—only a bullet or a razor."

She wanted to laugh; at the same time she couldn't because she realized he was serious and also because she well knew how true it was that certain persons could only be made to recognize the truth, be made to *understand*, by subjecting them to extreme punishment.

Nevertheless, she did laugh, but in a manner that Jaime would not interpret as genuine laughter. It was something comparable to a sympathetic shrug. "You could never kill anyone, Jaime."

He began to comb her hair; the tugs were not gentle, but she knew the anger implied was against himself, not her. "Shit!" Then: "No. And that's the reason for most suicides. Someone is torturing you. You want to kill them, but you can't. All that pain is because you love them, and you can't kill them because you love them. So you kill yourself instead."

Leaving, she considered kissing him on the cheek, but settled for shaking his hand. "I know how trite this is, Jaime. And for the moment certainly no help at all. But remember—there's always somebody else. Just don't look for the same person, that's all."

The rendezvous apartment was on East Sixty-fifth Street; today she walked to it from her home, a small town house on Beekman Place. It was windy, there was leftover snow on the sidewalk and a promise of more in the air, but she was snug enough in the coat her husband had given her for Christmas—a sable-colored suede coat that was lined with sable.

A cousin had rented the apartment for her in his own name. The cousin, who was married to a harridan and lived in Greenwich, sometimes visited the apartment with his secretary, a fat Japanese woman who drenched herself in nose-boggling amounts of Mitsouko. This afternoon the apartment reeked of the lady's perfume, from which she deduced that her cousin had lately been dallying here. That meant she would have to change the sheets.

She did so, then prepared herself. On a table beside the bed she placed a small box wrapped in shiny cerulean paper; it contained a gold toothpick she had bought at Tiffany, a gift for Dr. Bentsen, for one of his unpleasing habits was constantly picking his teeth, and, moreover, picking them with an endless series of paper matches. She had thought the gold pick might make the whole process a little less disagreeable. She put a stack of Lee Wiley and Fred Astaire records on a phonograph, poured herself a glass of cold white wine, undressed entirely, lubricated herself, and stretched out on the bed, humming, singing along with the divine Fred and listening for the scratch of her lover's key at the door.

To judge from appearances, orgasms were agonizing events in the life of Ezra Bentsen: he grimaced, he ground his dentures, he whimpered like a frightened mutt. Of course, she was always relieved when she heard the whimper; it meant that soon his lathered carcass would roll off her, for he was not one to linger, whispering tender compliments: he just rolled right off. And today, having done so, he greedily reached for the blue box, knowing it was a present for him. After opening it, he grunted.

She explained: "It's a gold toothpick."

He chuckled, an unusual sound coming from him, for his sense of humor was meager. "That's kind of cute," he said, and began picking his teeth. "You know what happened last night? I slapped Thelma. But good. And I punched her in the stomach, too."

Thelma was his wife; she was a child psychiatrist, and by reputation a fine one.

"The trouble with Thelma is you can't talk to her. She doesn't understand. Sometimes that's the only way you can get the message across. Give her a fat lip."

She thought of Jaime Sanchez.

"Do you know a Mrs. Roger Rhinelander?" Dr. Bentsen said.

"Mary Rhinelander? Her father was my father's best friend. They owned a racing stable together. One of her horses won the Kentucky Derby. Poor Mary, though. She married a real bastard."

"So she tells me."

"Oh? Is Mrs. Rhinelander a new patient?"

"Brand-new. Funny thing. She came to me for more or less the particular reason that brought you; her situation is almost identical."

The particular reason? Actually, she had a number of problems that had contributed to her eventual seduction on Dr. Bentsen's couch, the principal one being that she had not been capable of having a sexual relationship with her husband since the birth of their second child. She had married when she was twenty-four; her husband was fifteen years her senior. Though they had fought a lot, and were jealous of each other, the first five years of their marriage remained in her memory as an unblemished vista. The difficulty started when he asked her to have a child; if she hadn't been so much in love with him, she would never have consented—she had been afraid of children when she herself was a child, and the company of a child still made her uneasy. But she had given him a son, and the experience of pregnancy had traumatized her: when she wasn't actually suffering, she imagined she was, and after the birth she descended into a depression that continued more than a year. Every day she slept fourteen hours of Seconal sleep; as for the other ten, she kept awake by fueling herself with amphetamines. The second child, another boy, had been a drunken accident—though she suspected that really her husband had tricked her. The instant she knew she was pregnant again she had insisted on having an abortion; he had told her that if she went ahead with it, he would divorce her. Well, he had lived to regret that. The child had been born two months prematurely, had nearly died, and because of massive internal hemorrhaging, so had she; they had both hovered above an abyss through months of intensive care. Since then, she had never shared a bed with her husband; she wanted to, but she couldn't, for the naked presence of him, the thought of his body inside hers, summoned intolerable terrors.

Dr. Bentsen wore thick black socks with garters, which he never removed while "making love"; now, as he was sliding his gartered legs into a pair of shiny-seated blue serge trousers, he said: "Let's see. Tomorrow is Tuesday. Wednesday is our anniversary . . ."

"Our anniversary?"

"Thelma's! Our twentieth. I want to take her to . . . Tell me the best restaurant around now?"

"What does it matter? It's very small and very smart and the owner would never give you a table."

His lack of humor asserted itself: "That's a damn strange thing to say. What do you mean, he wouldn't give me a table?"

"Just what I said. One look at you and he'd know you had hairy heels. There are *some* people who won't serve people with hairy heels. He's one of them."

Dr. Bentsen was familiar with her habit of introducing unfamiliar lingo, and he had learned to pretend he knew what it signified; he was as ignorant of her ambience as she was of his, but the shifting instability of his character would not allow him to admit it.

"Well, then," he said, "is Friday all right? Around five?"

She said: "No, thank you." He was tying his tie and stopped; she was still lying on the bed, uncovered, naked; Fred was singing "By Myself." "No, thank you, darling Dr. B. I don't think we'll be meeting here any more."

She could see he was startled. Of course he would miss her—she was beautiful, she was considerate, it never bothered her when he asked her for money. He knelt beside the bed and fondled her breast. She noticed an icy mustache of sweat on his upper lip. "What is this? Drugs? Drink?"

She laughed and said: "All I drink is white wine, and not much of that. No, my friend. It's simply that you have hairy heels."

Like many analysts, Dr. Bentsen was quite literal-minded; just for a second she thought he was going to strip off his socks and examine his feet. Churlishly, like a child, he said: "I *don't* have hairy heels."

"Oh, yes you do. Just like a horse. All ordinary horses have hairy heels. Thoroughbreds don't. The heels of a well-bred horse are flat and glistening. Give my love to Thelma."

"Smart-ass. Friday?"

The Astaire record ended. She swallowed the last of the wine.

"Maybe. I'll call you," she said.

As it happened, she never called, and she never saw him again—except once, a year later, when she sat on a banquette next to him at La Grenouille; he was lunching with Mary Rhinelander, and she was amused to see that Mrs. Rhinelander signed the check.

The promised snow had arrived by the time she returned, again on foot, to the house on Beekman Place. The front door was painted pale yellow and had a brass knocker shaped like a lion's claw. Anna, one of four Irishwomen who staffed the house, answered the door and reported that the children, exhausted from an afternoon of ice-skating at Rockefeller Center, had already had their supper and been put to bed.

Thank God. Now she wouldn't have to undergo the half-hour of playtime and tale-telling and kiss-goodnight that customarily concluded her children's day; she may not have been an affectionate mother, but she was a dutiful one—just as her own mother had been. It was seven o'clock, and her husband had phoned to say he would be home at seven-thirty; at eight they were supposed to go to a dinner party with the Sylvester Hales, friends from San Francisco. She bathed, scented herself to remove memories of Dr. Bentsen, remodeled her makeup, of which she wore the most modest quantity, and changed into a grey silk caftan and grey silk slippers with pearl buckles.

She was posing by the fireplace in the library on the second floor when she heard her husband's footsteps on the stairs. It was a graceful pose, inviting as the room itself, an unusual octagonal room with cinnamon lacquered walls, a yellow lacquered floor, brass bookshelves (a notion borrowed from Billy Baldwin), two huge bushes of brown orchids ensconced in yellow Chinese vases, a Marino Marini horse standing in a corner, a South Seas Gauguin over the mantel, and a delicate fire fluttering in the fireplace. French windows offered a view of a darkened garden, drifting snow, and lighted tugboats floating like lanterns on the East River. A voluptuous couch, upholstered in mocha velvet, faced the fireplace, and in front of it, on a table lacquered the yellow of the floor, rested an ice-filled silver bucket; embedded in the bucket was a carafe brimming with pepper-flavored red Russian vodka.

Her husband hesitated in the doorway, and nodded at her approvingly: he was one of those men who truly noticed a woman's appearance, gathered at a glance the total atmosphere. He was worth dressing for, and it was one of her lesser reasons for loving him. A more important reason was that he resembled her father, a man who had been, and forever would be, the man in her life; her father had shot himself, though no one ever knew why, for he was a gentleman of almost abnormal discretion. Before this happened, she had terminated three engagements, but two months after her father's death she met George, and married him because in both looks and manners he approximated her great lost love.

She moved across the room to meet her husband halfway. She kissed his cheek, and the flesh against her lips felt as cold as the snowflakes at the window. He was a large man, Irish, black-haired and green-eyed, handsome even though he had lately accumulated considerable poundage and had gotten a bit jowly, too. He projected a superficial vitality; both men and women were drawn to him by that alone. Closely observed, however, one sensed a secret fatigue, a lack of any real optimism. His wife was severely aware of it, and why not? She was its principal cause.

She said: "It's such a rotten night out, and you look so tired. Let's stay home and have supper by the fire."

"Really, darling—you wouldn't mind? It seems a mean thing to do to the Haleses. Even if she is a cunt."

"*George!* Don't use that word. You know I hate it."

"Sorry," he said; he was, too. He was always careful not to offend her, just as she took the same care with him: a consequence of the quiet that simultaneously kept them together and apart.

"I'll call and say you're coming down with a cold."

"Well, it won't be a lie. I think I am."

While she called the Haleses, and arranged with Anna for a soup and soufflé supper to be served in an hour's time, he chugalugged a dazzling dose of the scarlet vodka and felt it light a fire in his stomach; before his wife returned, he poured himself a respectable shot and stretched full length on the couch. She knelt on the floor and removed his shoes and began to massage his feet: God knows, *he* didn't have hairy heels.

He groaned. "Hmm. That feels good."

"I love you, George."

"I love you, too."

She thought of putting on a record, but no, the sound of the fire was all the room needed.

"George?"

"Yes, darling."

"What are you thinking about?"

"A woman named Ivory Hunter."

"You really know somebody named Ivory Hunter?"

"Well. That was her stage name. She'd been a burlesque dancer."

She laughed. "What is this, some part of your college adventures?"

"I never knew her. I only heard about her once. It was the summer after I left Yale."

He closed his eyes and drained his vodka. "The summer I hitchhiked out to New Mexico and California. Remember? That's how I got my nose broke. In a bar fight in Needles, California." She liked his broken nose, it offset the extreme gentleness of his face; he had once spoken of having it rebroken and reset, but she had talked him out of it. "It was early September, and that's always the hottest time of the year in Southern California; over a hundred almost every day. I ought to have treated myself to a bus ride, at least across the desert. But there I was like a fool, deep in the Mojave, hauling a fifty-pound knapsack and sweating until there was no sweat in me. I swear it was a hundred and fifty in the shade. Except there wasn't any shade. Nothing but sand and mesquite and this boiling blue sky. Once a big truck drove by, but it wouldn't stop for me. All it did was kill a rattlesnake that was crawling across the road.

"I kept thinking something was bound to turn up somewhere. A garage. Now and then cars passed, but I might as well have been invisible. I began to feel sorry for myself, to understand what it means to be helpless, and to understand why it's a good thing that Buddhists send out their young monks to beg. It's chastening. It rips off that last layer of baby fat.

"And then I met Mr. Schmidt. I thought maybe it was a mirage. An old white-haired man about a quarter mile up the highway. He was standing by the road with heat waves rippling around him. As I got closer I saw that he carried a cane and wore pitch-black glasses, and he was dressed as if headed for church—white suit, white shirt, black tie, black shoes.

"Without looking at me, and while some distance away, he called out: 'My name is George Schmidt.'

"I said: 'Yes. Good afternoon, sir.'

"He said: '*Is* it afternoon?'

" 'After three.'

" 'Then I must have been standing here two hours or more. Would you mind telling me where I am?'

" 'In the Mojave Desert. About eighteen miles west of Needles.'

" 'Imagine that,' he said. 'Leaving a seventy-year-old blind man stranded alone in the desert. Ten dollars in my pocket, and not another rag to my name. Women are like flies: they settle on sugar or shit. I'm not saying I'm sugar, but she's sure settled for shit now. My name is George Schmidt.'

"I said: 'Yes, sir, you told me. I'm George Whitelaw.' He wanted to know where I was going, what I was up to, and when I said I was hitchhiking, heading for New York, he asked if I would take his hand and help him along a bit, maybe until we could catch a ride. I forgot to mention that he had a German accent and was extremely stout, almost fat; he looked as if he'd been lying in a hammock all his life. But when I held his hand I felt the roughness, the immense strength of it. You wouldn't have wanted a pair of hands like that around your throat. He said: 'Yes, I have strong hands. I've worked as a masseur for fifty years, the last twelve in Palm Springs. You got any water?' I gave him my canteen, which was still half full. And he said: 'She left me here without even a drop of water. The whole thing took me by surprise. Though I can't say it should have, knowing Ivory good as I did. That's my wife. Ivory Hunter, she was. A stripper; she played the Chicago World's Fair, 1932, and she would have been a star if it hadn't been for that Sally Rand. Ivory invented this fan-dance thing and that Rand woman stole it off her. So Ivory said. Probably just more of her bullshit. Uh-oh, watch out for that rattler, he's over there someplace, I can hear him really singing. There's two things I'm scared of. Snakes and women. They have a lot in common. One thing they have in common is: the last thing that dies is their tail.'

"A couple of cars passed and I stuck out my thumb and the old man tried to flag them down with his stick, but we must have looked too peculiar—a dirty kid in dungarees and a blind fat man dressed in his city best. I guess we'd still be out there if it hadn't been for this truckdriver. A Mexican. He was parked by the road fixing a flat. He could speak about five words of Tex-Mex, all of them four-letter, but I still remembered a lot of Spanish from the summer with Uncle Alvin in Cuba. So the Mexican told me he was on his way to El Paso, and if that was our direction, we were welcome aboard.

"But Mr. Schmidt wasn't too keen. I had practically to drag him into the caboose. 'I hate Mexicans. Never met a Mexican I liked. If it wasn't for a Mexican . . . Him only nineteen and her I'd say from the touch of her skin, I'd say Ivory was a woman way past sixty. When I married her a couple of years ago, she said she was fifty-two. See, I was living in this trailer camp out on Route 111. One of those trailer camps halfway between Palm Springs and Cathedral City. Cathedral City! Some name for a dump that's nothing but honky-tonks and pool halls and fag bars. The only thing you can say about it is Bing Crosby lives there. If that's saying something. Anyway, living next to me in this other trailer is my friend Hulga. Ever since my wife died—she died the same day Hitler died—Hulga had been driving me to work; she works as a waitress at this Jew club where I'm the masseur. All the waiters and waitresses at the club are big blond Germans. The Jews like that; they really keep them stepping. So one day Hulga tells me she has a cousin coming to visit. Ivory Hunter. I forget her legal name, it was on the marriage certificate, but I forget. She had about three husbands before; she probably didn't remember the name she was born with. Anyway, Hulga tells me that this cousin of hers, Ivory, used to be a famous dancer, but now she's just come out of the hospital and she's lost her last husband on account of she's spent a year in the hospital with TB. That's why Hulga asked her out to Palm Springs. Because of the air. Also, she didn't have any place else to go. The first night she was there, Hulga invited me over, and I liked her cousin right away; we didn't talk much, we listened to the radio mostly, but I liked Ivory. She had a real nice voice, real slow and gentle, she sounded like nurses ought to sound; she said she didn't smoke or drink and she was a member of the Church of God, same as me. After that, I was over at Hulga's almost every night.'"

George lit a cigarette, and his wife tilted out a jigger more of the pepper vodka for him. To her surprise, she poured one for herself. A number of things about her husband's narrative had accelerated her ever-present but usually Librium-subdued anxiety; she couldn't imagine where his memoir was leading, but she knew there was some destination, for George seldom rambled. He had graduated third in his class at Yale Law School, never practiced law but had gone on to top his class at Harvard Business School; within the past decade he had been offered a presidential Cabinet post, and an ambassadorship to England or France or wherever he wanted. However, what had made her feel the need for red vodka, a ruby bauble burning in the firelight, was the disquieting manner in which George Whitelaw had become Mr. Schmidt; her husband was an exceptional mimic. He could imitate certain of their friends with infuriating accuracy. But this was not casual mimicry; he seemed entranced, a man fixed in another man's mind.

"'I had an old Chevy nobody had driven since my wife died. But Ivory got it tuned up, and pretty soon it wasn't Hulga driving me to work and bringing me home, but Ivory. Looking back, I can see it was all a plot between Hulga and Ivory, but I didn't put it together then. Everybody around the trailer park, and everybody that met her, all they said was what a lovely woman she was, big blue eyes and pretty legs. I figured it was just good-heartedness, the Church of God—I figured that was why she was spending her evenings cooking dinner and keeping house for an old blind man. One night we were listening to the *Hit Parade* on the radio, and she kissed me and rubbed her hand along my leg. Pretty soon we were doing it twice a day—once before breakfast and once after dinner, and me a man of sixty-nine. But it seemed like she was as crazy about my cock as I was about her cunt—' "

She tossed her vodka into the fireplace, a splash that made the flames hiss and flourish; but it was an idle protest: Mr. Schmidt would not be reproached.

" 'Yes, sir, Ivory was all cunt. Whatever way you want to use the word. It was exactly one month from the day I met her to the day I married her. She didn't change much, she fed me good, she was always interested to hear about the Jews at the club, and it was me that cut down on the sex—*way* down, what with my blood pressure and all. But she never complained. We read the Bible together, and night after night she would read aloud from magazines, good magazines like *Reader's Digest* and *The Saturday Evening Post*, until I fell asleep. She was always saying she hoped she died before I did because she would be heartbroken and destitute. It was true I didn't have much to leave. No insurance, just some bank-savings that I turned into a joint account, and I had the trailer put in her name. No, I can't say there was a harsh word between us until she had the big fight with Hulga.

" 'For a long time I didn't know what the fight was about. All I knew was that they didn't speak to each other any more, and when I asked Ivory what was going on, she said: "Nothing." As far as she was concerned, she hadn't had any falling-out with Hulga: "But you know how much she drinks." That was true. Well, like I told you, Hulga was a waitress at the club, and one day she comes barging into the massage room. I had a customer on the table, had him there spread out buck-naked, but a lot she cared—she smelled like a Four Roses factory. She could hardly stand up. She told me she had just got fired, and suddenly she started swearing and pissing. She was hollering at me and pissing all over the floor. She said everybody at the trailer park was laughing at me. She said Ivory was an old whore who had latched onto me because she was down and out and couldn't do any better. And she said what kind of a chowderhead was I? Didn't I know my wife was fucking the balls off Freddy Feo since God knows when?

" 'Now, see, Freddy Feo was an itinerant Tex-Mex kid—he was just out of jail somewhere, and the manager of the trailer park had picked him up in one of those fag bars in Cat City and put him to work as a handyman. I don't guess he could have been one-hundred-percent fag because he was giving plenty of the old girls around there a tickle for their money. One of them was Hulga. She was loop-de-do over him. On hot nights him and Hulga used to sit outside her trailer on her swing-seat drinking straight tequila, forget the lime, and he'd play the guitar and sing spic songs. Ivory described it to me as a green guitar with his named spelled out in rhinestone letters. I'll say this, the spic could sing. But Ivory always claimed she couldn't stand him; she said he was a cheap little greaser out to take Hulga for every nickel she had. Myself, I don't remember exchanging ten words with him, but I didn't like him because of the way he smelled. I have a nose like a bloodhound and I could smell him a hundred yards off, he wore so much brilliantine in his hair, and something else that Ivory said was called Evening in Paris.

" 'Ivory swore up and down it wasn't so. Her? *Her* let a Tex-Mex monkey like Freddy Feo put a finger on her? She said it was because Hulga had been dumped by this kid that she was crazy and jealous and thought he was humping everything from Cat City to Indio. She said she was insulted that I'd listen to such lies, even though Hulga was more to be pitied than reviled. And she took off the wedding ring I'd given her—it had belonged to my first wife, but she said that didn't make any difference because she knew I'd loved Hedda and that made it all the better—and she handed it to me and she said if I didn't believe her, then here was the ring and she'd take the next bus going anywhere. So I put it back on her finger and we knelt on the floor and prayed together.

" 'I did believe her; at least I thought I did; but in some way it was like a seesaw in my head—yes, no, yes, no. And Ivory had lost her looseness; before she had an easiness in her body that was like the easiness in her voice. But now it was all wire—tense, like those Jews at the club that keep whining and scolding because you can't rub away all their worries. Hulga got a job at the Miramar, but out at the trailer park I always turned away when I smelled her coming. Once she sort of whispered up beside me: "Did you know that sweet wife of yours gave the greaser a pair of gold earrings! But his boyfriend won't let him wear them." I don't know. Ivory prayed every night with me that the Lord would keep us together, healthy in spirit and body. But I noticed . . . Well, on those warm summer nights when Freddy Feo would be out there somewhere in the dark, singing and playing his guitar, she'd turn off the radio right in the middle of Bob Hope or Edgar Bergen or whatever, and go sit outside and listen. She said she was looking at the stars: "I bet there's no place in the world you can see the stars like here." But suddenly it turned out she hated Cat City and the Springs. The whole desert, the sandstorms, summers with temperatures up to a hundred thirty degrees, and nothing to do if you weren't rich and belonged to the Racquet Club. She just announced this one morning. She said we should pick up the trailer and plant it down anywhere where the air was cool. Wisconsin. Michigan. I felt good about the idea; it set my mind to rest as to what might be going on between her and Freddy Feo.

" 'Well, I had a client there at the club, a fellow from Detroit, and he said he might be able to get me on as a masseur at the Detroit Athletic Club; nothing definite, only one of them maybe deals. But that was enough for Ivory. Twenty-three skidoo, and she's got the trailer uprooted, fifteen years of planting strewn all over the ground, the Chevy ready to roll, and all our savings turned into traveler's checks. Last night she scrubbed me top to bottom and shampooed my hair, and this morning we set off a little after daylight.

"'I realized something was wrong, and I'd have known what it was if I hadn't dozed off soon as we hit the highway. She must have dumped sleeping pills in my coffee.

"'But when I woke up I smelled him. The brilliantine and the dime-store perfume. He was hiding in the trailer. Coiled back there somewhere like a snake. What I thought was: Ivory and the kid are going to kill me and leave me for the buzzards. She said, "You're awake, George." The way she said it, the slight fear, I could tell she knew what was going on in my head. That I'd guessed it all. I told her, *Stop the car.* She wanted to know what for? Because I had to take a leak. She stopped the car, and I could hear she was crying. As I got out, she said: "You been good to me, George, but I didn't know nothing else to do. And you got a profession. There'll always be a place for you somewhere."

"'I got out of the car, and I really did take a leak, and while I was standing there the motor started up and she drove away. I didn't know where I was until you came along, Mr. . . . ?

"'George Whitelaw.' And I told him: 'Jesus, that's just like murder. Leaving a blind man helpless in the middle of nowhere. When we get to El Paso we'll go to the police station.'

"He said: 'Hell, no. She's got enough trouble without the cops. She settled on shit—leave her to it. Ivory's the one out in nowhere. Besides, I love her. A woman can do you like that, and still you love her.'"

George refilled his vodka; she placed a small log on the fire, and the new rush of flame was only a little brighter than the furious red suddenly flushing her cheeks.

"That *women* do," she said, her tone aggressive, challenging. "Only a crazy person . . . Do you think I could do something like that?"

The expression in his eyes, a certain visual silence, shocked her and made her avert her eyes, withdrawing the question. "Well, what happened to him?"

"Mr. Schmidt?"

"Mr. Schmidt."

He shrugged. "The last I saw of him he was drinking a glass of milk in a diner, a truck stop outside El Paso. I was lucky; I got a ride with a trucker all the way to Newark. I sort of forgot about it. But for the last few months I find myself wondering about Ivory Hunter and George Schmidt. It must be age; I'm beginning to feel old myself."

She knelt beside him again; she held his hand, interweaving her fingers with his. "Fifty-two? And you feel *old*?"

He had retreated; when he spoke, it was the wondering murmur of a man addressing himself. "I always had such confidence. Just walking the street, I felt such a *swing.* I could feel people looking at me—on the street, in a restaurant, at a party—envying me, wondering who is that guy. Whenever I walked into a party, I knew I could have half the women in the room if I wanted them. But that's all over. Seems as though old George Whitelaw has become the invisible man. Not a head turns. I called Mimi Stewart twice last week, and she never returned the calls. I didn't tell you, but I stopped at Buddy Wilson's yesterday, he was having a little cocktail thing. There must have been twenty fairly attractive girls, and they all looked right through me; to them I was a tired old guy who smiled too much."

She said: "But I thought you were still seeing Christine."

"I'll tell you a secret. Christine is engaged to that Rutherford boy from Philadelphia. I haven't seen her since November. He's okay for her; she's happy and I'm happy for her."

"Christine! Which Rutherford boy? Kenyon or Paul?"

"The older one."

"That's Kenyon. You knew that and didn't tell me?"

"There's so much I haven't told you, my dear."

Yet that was not entirely true. For when they had stopped sleeping together, they had begun discussing together—indeed, collaborating on—each of his affairs. Alice Kent: five months; ended because she'd demanded he divorce and marry her. Sister Jones: terminated after one year when her husband found out about it. Pat Simpson: A *Vogue* model who'd gone to Hollywood, promised to return and never had. Adele O'Hara: beautiful, an alcoholic, a rambunctious scene-maker; he'd broken that one off himself. Mary Campbell, Mary Chester, Jane Vere-Jones. Others. And now Christine.

A few he had discovered himself; the majority were "romances" she herself had stage-managed, friends she'd introduced him to, confidantes she had trusted to provide him with an outlet but not to exceed the mark.

"Well," she sighed. "I suppose we can't blame Christine. Kenyon Rutherford's rather a catch." Still, her mind was running, searching like the flames shivering through the logs: a name to fill the void. Alice Combs: available, but too dull. Charlotte Finch: too rich, and George felt emasculated by women—or men, for that matter— richer than himself. Perhaps the Ellison woman? The soigné Mrs. Harold Ellison who was in Haiti getting a swift divorce . . .

He said: "Stop frowning."

"I'm not frowning."

"It just means more silicone, more bills from Orentreich. I'd rather see the human wrinkles. It doesn't matter whose fault it is. We all, sometimes, leave each other out there under the skies, and we never understand why."

An echo, caverns resounding: Jaime Sanchez and Carlos and Angelita; Hulga and Freddy Feo and Ivory Hunter and Mr. Schmidt; Dr. Bentsen and George, George and herself, Dr. Bentsen and Mary Rhinelander . . .

He gave a slight pressure to their interwoven fingers, and with his other hand, raised her chin and insisted on their eyes meeting. He moved her hand up to his lips and kissed its palm.

"I love you, Sarah."

"I love you, too."

But the touch of his lips, the insinuated threat, tautened her. Below stairs, she heard the rattle of silver on trays: Anna and Margaret were ascending with the fireside supper.

"I love you, too," she repeated with pretended sleepiness, and with a feigned languor moved to draw the window draperies. Drawn, the heavy silk concealed the night river and the lighted riverboats, so snow-misted that they were as muted as the design in a Japanese scroll of winter night.

"George?" An urgent plea before the supper-laden Irishwomen arrived, expertly balancing their offerings: "*Please*, darling. We'll think of somebody."

Catullus (87?–55? B.C.*)*

"Miserable Catullus, stop being foolish"

Translated by Louis Zukofsky (1904–1978)

8

Miserable Catullus, stop being foolish
And admit it's over,
The sun shone on you those days
When your girl had you
When you gave it to her   5
     like nobody else ever will.
Everywhere together then, always at it
And you liked it and she can't say
     she didn't.
Yes, those days glowed.   10
Now she doesn't want it: why
     should you, washed out,
Want to? Don't trail her,
Don't eat yourself up alive,
Show some spunk, stand up   15
     and take it.
So long, girl. Catullus
     can take it.
He won't bother you, he won't
     be bothered: 20

But you'll be, nights.
What do you want to live for?
Whom will you see?
Who'll say you're pretty?
Who'll give it to you now?   25
Whose name will you have?
Kiss what guy? bite whose
    lips?
Come on, Catullus, you can   30
    take it.

"My woman says she'd prefer to marry no one"

Translated by Gilbert Highet (1906–1978)

70

My woman says she'd prefer to marry no one
but me, even if Jupiter asked for her love.
Ah yes: but what a woman says to an eager lover,
write it on running water, write it on air.

Geoffrey Chaucer (1342–1400)
The Wife of Bath's Tale

Translated by Nevill Coghill (1899–1980)

When good King Arthur ruled in ancient days
(A king that every Briton loves to praise)
This was a land brim-full of fairy folk.
The Elf-Queen and her courtiers joined and broke
Their elfin dance on many a green mead,   5
Or so was the opinion once, I read,
Hundreds of years ago, in days of yore.
But no one now sees fairies any more.
For now the saintly charity and prayer

Of holy friars seem to have purged the air;   10
They search the countryside through field and stream
As thick as motes that speckle a sun-beam,
Blessing the halls, the chambers, kitchens, bowers,
Cities and boroughs, castles, courts and towers,
Thorpes, barns and stables, outhouses and dairies,   15
And that's the reason why there are no fairies.
Wherever there was wont to walk an elf
To-day there walks the holy friar himself
As evening falls or when the daylight springs,
Saying his mattins and his holy things,   20
Walking his limit round from town to town.
Women can now go safely up and down
By every bush or under every tree;
There is no other incubus but he,
So there is really no one else to hurt you   25
And he will do no more than take your virtue.

    Now it so happened, I began to say,
Long, long ago in good King Arthur's day,
There was a knight who was a lusty liver.
One day as he came riding from the river   30
He saw a maiden walking all forlorn
Ahead of him, alone as she was born.
And of that maiden, spite of all she said,
By very force he took her maidenhead.

    This act of violence made such a stir,   35
So much petitioning to the king for her,
That he condemned the knight to lose his head
By course of law. He was as good as dead
(It seems that then the statutes took that view)
But that the queen, and other ladies too,   40
Implored the king to exercise his grace
So ceaselessly, he gave the queen the case
And granted her his life, and she could choose
Whether to show him mercy or refuse.

    The queen returned him thanks with all her might,   45
And then she sent a summons to the knight
At her convenience, and expressed her will:
"You stand, for such is the position still,
In no way certain of your life," said she,
"Yet you shall live if you can answer me: 50
What is the thing that women most desire?

Beware the axe and say as I require.
  "If you can't answer on the moment, though,
I will concede you this: you are to go
A twelvemonth and a day to seek and learn   55
Sufficient answer, then you shall return.
I shall take gages from you to extort
Surrender of your body to the court."
  Sad was the knight and sorrowfully sighed,
But there! All other choices were denied,   60
And in the end he chose to go away
And to return after a year and day
Armed with such answer as there might be sent
To him by God. He took his leave and went.
  He knocked at every house, searched every place,   65
Yes, anywhere that offered hope of grace.
What could it be that women wanted most?
But all the same he never touched a coast,
Country or town in which there seemed to be
Any two people willing to agree.   70
  Some said that women wanted wealth and treasure,
"Honour," said some, some "Jollity and pleasure,"
Some "Gorgeous clothes" and others "Fun in bed,"
"To be oft widowed and remarried," said
Others again, and some that what most mattered   75
Was that we should be cossetted and flattered.
That's very near the truth, it seems to me;
A man can win us best with flattery.
To dance attendance on us, make a fuss,
Ensnares us all, the best and worst of us.   80
  Some say the things we most desire are these:
Freedom to do exactly as we please,
With no one to reprove our faults and lies,
Rather to have one call us good and wise.
Truly there's not a woman in ten score   85
Who has a fault, and someone rubs the sore,
But she will kick if what he says is true;
You try it out and you will find so too.
However vicious we may be within
We like to be thought wise and void of sin.   90
Others assert we women find it sweet
When we are thought dependable, discreet
And secret, firm of purpose and controlled,

Never betraying things that we are told.
But that's not worth the handle of a rake;   95
Women conceal a thing? For Heaven's sake!
Remember Midas? Will you hear the tale?
    Among some other little things, now stale,
Ovid relates that under his long hair
The unhappy Midas grew a splendid pair   100
Of ass's ears; as subtly as he might,
He kept his foul deformity from sight;
Save for his wife, there was not one that knew.
He loved her best, and trusted in her too.
He begged her not to tell a living creature   105
That he possessed so horrible a feature.
And she—she swore, were all the world to win,
She would not do such villainy and sin
As saddle her husband with so foul a name;
Besides to speak would be to share the shame.   110
Nevertheless she thought she would have died
Keeping this secret bottled up inside;
It seemed to swell her heart and she, no doubt,
Thought it was on the point of bursting out.
    Fearing to speak of it to woman or man,   115
Down to a reedy marsh she quickly ran
And reached the sedge. Her heart was all on fire
And, as a bittern bumbles in the mire,
She whispered to the water, near the ground,
"Betray me not, O water, with thy sound!   120
To thee alone I tell it: it appears
My husband has a pair of ass's ears!
Ah! My heart's well again, the secret's out!
I could no longer keep it, not a doubt."
And as you see, although we may hold fast   125
A little while, it must come out at last,
We can't keep secrets; as for Midas, well,
Read Ovid for his story; he will tell.
    This knight that I am telling you about
Perceived at last he never would find out   130
What it could be that women loved the best.
Faint was the soul within his sorrowful breast,
As home he went, he dared no longer stay;
His year was up and now it was the day.

As he rode home in a dejected mood 135
Suddenly, at the margin of a wood,
He saw a dance upon the leafy floor
Of four and twenty ladies, nay, and more.
Eagerly he approached, in hope to learn
Some words of wisdom ere he should return; 140
But lo! Before he came to where they were,
Dancers and dance all vanished into air!
There wasn't a living creature to be seen
Save one old woman crouched upon the green.
A fouler-looking creature I suppose 145
Could scarcely be imagined. She arose
And said, "Sir knight, there's no way on from here.
Tell me what you are looking for, my dear,
For peradventure that were best for you;
We old, old women know a thing or two." 150
      "Dear Mother," said the knight, "alack the day!
I am as good as dead if I can't say
What thing it is that women most desire;
If you could tell me I would pay your hire."
"Give me your hand," she said, "and swear to do 155
Whatever I shall next require of you
—If so to do should lie within your might—
And you shall know the answer before night."
"Upon my honour," he answered, "I agree."
"Then," said the crone, "I dare to guarantee 160
Your life is safe; I shall make good my claim.
Upon my life the queen will say the same.
Show me the very proudest of them all
In costly coverchief or jewelled caul
That dare say no to what I have to teach. 165
Let us go forward without further speech."
And then she crooned her gospel in his ear
And told him to be glad and not to fear.
      They came to court. This knight, in full array,
Stood forth and said, "O Queen, I've kept my day 170
And kept my word and have my answer ready."
      There sat the noble matrons and the heady
Young girls, and widows too, that have the grace
Of wisdom, all assembled in that place,
And there the queen herself was throned to hear 175

And judge his answer. Then the knight drew near
And silence was commanded through the hall.
    The queen gave order he should tell them all
What thing it was that women wanted most.
He stood not silent like a beast or post,   180
But gave his answer with the ringing word
Of a man's voice and the assembly heard:
    "My liege and lady, in general," said he,
"A woman wants the self-same sovereignty
Over her husband as over her lover,   185
And master him; he must not be above her.
That is your greatest wish, whether you kill
Or spare me; please yourself. I wait your will."
    In all the court not one that shook her head
Or contradicted what the knight had said;   190
Maid, wife and widow cried, "He's saved his life!"
    And on the word up started the old wife,
The one the knight saw sitting on the green,
And cried, "Your mercy, sovereign lady queen!
Before the court disperses, do me right!   195
'Twas I who taught this answer to the knight,
For which he swore, and pledged his honour to it,
That the first thing I asked of him he'd do it,
So far as it should lie within his might.
Before this court I ask you then, sir knight,   200
To keep your word and take me for your wife;
For well you know that I have saved your life.
If this be false, deny it on your sword!"
    "Alas!" he said, "Old lady, by the Lord
I know indeed that such was my behest,   205
But for God's love think of a new request,
Take all my goods, but leave my body free."
"A curse on us," she said, "if I agree!
I may be foul, I may be poor and old,
Yet will not choose to be, for all the gold   210
That's bedded in the earth or lies above,
Less than your wife, nay, than your very love!"
    "My love?" said he. "By heaven, my damnation!
Alas that any of my race and station
Should ever make so foul a misalliance!"   215
Yet in the end his pleading and defiance
All went for nothing, he was forced to wed.

He takes his ancient wife and goes to bed.
   Now peradventure some may well suspect
A lack of care in me since I neglect   220
To tell of the rejoicings and display
Made at the feast upon their wedding-day.
I have but a short answer to let fall;
I say there was no joy or feast at all,
Nothing but heaviness of heart and sorrow.   225
He married her in private on the morrow
And all day long stayed hidden like an owl,
It was such torture that his wife looked foul.
   Great was the anguish churning in his head
When he and she were piloted to bed;   230
He wallowed back and forth in desperate style.
His ancient wife lay smiling all the while;
At last she said "Bless us! Is this, my dear,
How knights and wives get on together here?
Are these the laws of good King Arthur's house?   235
Are knights of his all so contemptuous?
I am your own beloved and your wife,
And I am she, indeed, that saved your life;
And certainly I never did you wrong.
Then why, this first of nights, so sad a song?   240
You're carrying on as if you were half-witted
Say, for God's love, what sin have I committed?
I'll put things right if you will tell me how."
   "Put right?" he cried. "That never can be now!
Nothing can ever be put right again!   245
You're old, and so abominably plain,
So poor to start with, so low-bred to follow;
It's little wonder if I twist and wallow!
God, that my heart would burst within my breast!"
   "Is that," said she, "the cause of your unrest?"   250
   "Yes, certainly," he said, "and can you wonder?"
   "I could set right what you suppose a blunder,
That's if I cared to, in a day or two,
If I were shown more courtesy by you.
Just now," she said, "you spoke of gentle birth,   255
Such as descends from ancient wealth and worth.
If that's the claim you make for gentlemen
Such arrogance is hardly worth a hen.
Whoever loves to work for virtuous ends,

Public and private, and who most intends   260
To do what deeds of gentleness he can,
Take him to be the greatest gentleman.
Christ wills we take our gentleness from Him,
Not from a wealth of ancestry long dim,
Though they bequeath their whole establishment   265
By which we claim to be of high descent.
Our fathers cannot make us a bequest
Of all those virtues that became them best
And earned for them the name of gentlemen,
But bade us follow them as best we can.   270
 "Thus the wise poet of the Florentines,
Dante by name, has written in these lines,
For such is the opinion Dante launches:
'Seldom arises by these slender branches
Prowess of men, for it is God, no less,   275
Wills us to claim of Him our gentleness.'
For of our parents nothing can we claim
Save temporal things, and these may hurt and maim.
 "But everyone knows this as well as I;
For if gentility were implanted by   280
The natural course of lineage down the line,
Public or private, could it cease to shine
In doing the fair work of gentle deed?
No vice or villainy could then bear seed.
 "Take fire and carry it to the darkest house   285
Between this kingdom and the Caucasus,
And shut the doors on it and leave it there,
It will burn on, and it will burn as fair
As if ten thousand men were there to see,
For fire will keep its nature and degree,   290
I can assure you, sir, until it dies.
 "But gentleness, as you will recognize,
Is not annexed in nature to possessions.
Men fail in living up to their professions;
But fire never ceases to be fire.   295
God knows you'll often find, if you enquire,
Some lording full of villainy and shame.
If you would be esteemed for the mere name
Of having been by birth a gentleman
And stemming from some virtuous, noble clan,   300
And do not live yourself by gentle deed

Or take your father's noble code and creed,
You are no gentleman, though duke or earl.
Vice and bad manners are what make a churl.
    "Gentility is only the renown   305
For bounty that your fathers handed down,
Quite foreign to your person, not your own;
Gentility must come from God alone.
That we are gentle comes to us by grace
And by no means is it bequeathed with place.   310
    "Reflect how noble (says Valerius)
Was Tullius surnamed Hostilius,
Who rose from poverty to nobleness.
And read Boethius, Seneca no less,
Thus they express themselves and are agreed: 315
'Gentle is he that does a gentle deed.'
And therefore, my dear husband, I conclude
That even if my ancestors were rude,
Yet God on high—and so I hope He will—
Can grant me grace to live in virtue still,   320
A gentlewoman only when beginning
To live in virtue and to shrink from sinning.
    "As for my poverty which you reprove,
Almighty God Himself in whom we move,
Believe and have our being, chose a life   325
Of poverty, and every man or wife
Nay, every child can see our Heavenly King
Would never stoop to choose a shameful thing.
No shame in poverty if the heart is gay,
As Seneca and all the learned say.   330
He who accepts his poverty unhurt
I'd say is rich although he lacked a shirt.
But truly poor are they who whine and fret
And covet what they cannot hope to get.
And he that, having nothing, covets not,   335
Is rich, though you may think he is a sot.
    "True poverty can find a song to sing.
Juvenal says a pleasant little thing:
'The poor can dance and sing in the relief
Of having nothing that will tempt a thief.'   340
Though it be hateful, poverty is good,
A great incentive to a livelihood,
And a great help to our capacity

For wisdom, if accepted patiently.
Poverty is, though wanting in estate,   345
A kind of wealth that none calumniate.
Poverty often, when the heart is lowly,
Brings one to God and teaches what is holy,
Gives knowledge of oneself and even lends
A glass by which to see one's truest friends.   350
And since it's no offence, let me be plain;
Do not rebuke my poverty again.
    "Lastly you taxed me, sir, with being old
Yet even if you never had been told
By ancient books, you gentlemen engage   355
Yourselves in honour to respect old age.
To call an old man 'father' shows good breeding,
And this could be supported from my reading.
    "You say I'm old and fouler than a fen.
You need not fear to be a cuckold, then.   360
Filth and old age, I'm sure you will agree,
Are powerful wardens over chastity.
Nevertheless, well knowing your delights,
I shall fulfil your worldly appetites.
    "You have two choices; which one will you try?   365
To have me old and ugly till I die,
But still a loyal, true, and humble wife
That never will displease you all her life,
Or would you rather I were young and pretty
And chance your arm what happens in a city   370
Where friends will visit you because of me,
Yes, and in other places too, maybe.
Which would you have? The choice is all your own."
    The knight thought long, and with a piteous groan
At last he said, with all the care in life,   375
"My lady and my love, my dearest wife,
I leave the matter to your wise decision.
You make the choice yourself, for the provision
Of what may be agreeable and rich
In honour to us both, I don't care which;   380
Whatever pleases you suffices me."
    "And have I won the mastery?" said she,
"Since I'm to choose and rule as I think fit?"
"Certainly, wife," he answered her, "that's it."

"Kiss me," she cried. "No quarrels! On my oath   385
And word of honour, you shall find me both,
That is, both fair and faithful as a wife;
May I go howling mad and take my life
Unless I prove to be as good and true
As ever wife was since the world was new!   390
And if to-morrow when the sun's above
I seem less fair than any lady-love,
Than any queen or empress east or west,
Do with my life and death as you think best.
Cast up the curtain, husband. Look at me!"   395
   And when indeed the knight had looked to see,
Lo, she was young and lovely, rich in charms.
In ecstasy he caught her in his arms,
His heart went bathing in a bath of blisses
And melted in a hundred thousand kisses,   400
And she responded in the fullest measure
With all that could delight or give him pleasure.
   So they lived ever after to the end
In perfect bliss; and may Christ Jesus send
Us husbands meek and young and fresh in bed,   405
And grace to overbid them when we wed.
And—Jesu hear my prayer!—cut short the lives
Of those who won't be governed by their wives;
And all old, angry niggards of their pence,
God send them soon a very pestilence!   410

John Ciardi (1916–1986)

Most Like an Arch This Marriage

Most like an arch—an entrance which upholds
and shores the stone-crush up the air like lace.
Mass made idea, and idea held in place.
A lock in time. Inside half-heaven unfolds.

Most like an arch—two weaknesses that lean   5
into a strength. Two fallings become firm.
Two joined abeyances become a term
naming the fact that teaches fact to mean.

Not quite that? Not much less. World as it is,
what's strong and separate falters. All I do   10
at piling stone on stone apart from you
is roofless around nothing. Till we kiss

I am no more than upright and unset.
It is by falling in and in we make
the all-bearing point, for one another's sake,   15
in faultless failing, raised by our own weight.

Robert Creeley (born 1926)

A Marriage

The first retainer
he gave to her
was a golden
wedding ring.

The second—late at night   5
he woke up,
leaned over on an elbow,
and kissed her.

The third and the last—
he died with   10
and gave up loving
and lived with her.

John Donne (1573–1631)

A Valediction: Forbidding Mourning

As virtuous men pass mildly away,
    And whisper to their souls to go,
Whilst some of their sad friends do say,
    The breath goes now, and some say, no:

So let us melt, and make no noise,   5
    No tear-floods, nor sigh-tempests move,
'Twere profanation of our joys
    To tell the laity our love.

Moving of the earth brings harms and fears,
    Men reckon what it did and meant,   10
But trepidation of the spheres,
    Though greater far, is innocent.

Dull sublunary lovers' love
    (Whose soul is sense) cannot admit
Absence, because it doth remove   15
    Those things which elemented it.

But we by a love, so much refined
    That our selves know not what it is,
Inter-assurèd of the mind,
    Care less, eyes, lips, and hands to miss.   20

Our two souls, therefore, which are one,
    Though I must go, endure not yet
A breach, but an expansion,
    Like gold to airy thinness beat.

If they be two, they are two so   25
    As stiff twin compasses are two,
Thy soul, the fixed foot, makes no show
    To move, but doth if the other do.

And though it in the center sit,
    Yet when the other far doth roam,   30
It leans and hearkens after it,
    And grows erect as that comes home.

> Such wilt thou be to me, who must,
>   Like the other foot, obliquely run;
> Thy firmness makes my circle just,   35
>   And makes me end where I begun.

Benjamin Franklin (1706–1790)
Advice to a Young Man

PHILADELPHIA, *25 June, 1745.*

TO MY DEAR FRIEND: I know of no Medicine fit to diminish the violent natural Inclinations you mention; and if I did, I think I should not communicate it to you. Marriage is the proper remedy. It is the most natural state of Man, and therefore the State in which you are most likely to find solid Happiness. Your reasons against entering into it at present appear to me to be not well founded. The Circumstantial Advantages you have in View by postponing it, are not only uncertain, but they are small in comparison with that of the Thing itself, the being married and settled. It is the Man and Woman united that makes the complete human Being. Separate, she wants his force of Body and Strength of Reason, he her Softness, Sensibility and acute Discernment. Together they are more likely to succeed in the World. A single Man has not nearly the Value he would have in the State of Union. He is an incomplete Animal. He resembles the odd Half of a pair of Scissors.

If you get a prudent, healthy Wife, your Industry in your Profession, with her good Economy, will be a Fortune sufficient.

But if you will not take this Counsel, and persist in thinking a Commerce with the Sex inevitable, then I repeat my former Advice that in all your Amours you should prefer old Women to young ones. You call this a Paradox, and demand my reasons. They are these:

1. Because they have more Knowledge of the World, and their minds are better stored with Observations, their Conversation is more improving and more lastingly agreeable.

2. Because when Women cease to be handsome, they study to be good. To maintain their Influence over Men, they supply the Diminution of Beauty by an Augmentation of Utility. They learn to do a thousand Services, small and great; and are the most tender and useful of all Friends when you are sick. Thus they continue amiable. And hence there is hardly such a thing to be found as an old Woman who is not a good Woman.

3. Because there is no Hazard of Children, which irregularly produced may be attended with much Inconvenience.

4. Because through more Experience they are more prudent and discreet in conducting an Intrigue to prevent Suspicion. The Commerce with them is therefore safer with regard to your reputation. And with regard to theirs, if the Affair should happen to be known, considerate People might be rather inclined to excuse an old Woman, who would kindly take care of a young Man, form his manners by her good Counsels, and prevent his ruining his Health and Fortune among mercenary Prostitutes.

5. Because in every Animal that walks upright, the Deficiency of the Fluids that fill the Muscles appears first in the highest Part. The Face first grows lank and wrinkled, then the neck, then the Breast and Arms, the lower Parts continuing to the last as plump as ever; so that covering all above with a Basket, and regarding only what is below the Girdle, it is impossible of two Women to know an old one from a young one. And as in the Dark all Cats are grey, the Pleasure of Corporal Enjoyment with an old Woman is at least equal and frequently superior; every Knack being by Practice capable of Improvement.

6. Because the sin is less. The Debauching a Virgin may be her Ruin, and make her for Life unhappy.

7. Because the Compunction is less. The having made a young girl miserable may give you frequent bitter Reflections; none of which can attend making an old Woman happy.

8th, and lastly. They are so grateful!

Thus much for my Paradox. But still I advise you to marry immediately; being sincerely,

Your affectionate Friend,
BENJAMIN FRANKLIN.

Erich Fromm (1900–1980)
The Objects of Love

Love is not primarily a relationship to a specific person; it is an *attitude*, an *orientation* of *character* which determines the relatedness of a person to the world as a whole, not toward one "object" of love. If a person loves only one other person and is indifferent to the rest of his fellow men, his love is not love but a symbiotic attachment, or an enlarged egotism. Yet, most people believe that love is constituted by the object, not by the faculty. In fact, they even believe that it is a proof of the intensity of their love when they do not love anybody except the "loved" person. This is the same fallacy which we have already mentioned above. Because one does not see that love is an activity, a power of the soul, one believes that all that is necessary to find is the right object—and that everything goes by itself afterward. This attitude can be compared to that of a man who wants to paint but who, instead of learning the art, claims that he has just to wait for the right object, and that he will paint beautifully when he finds it. If I truly love one person I love all persons, I love the world, I love life. If I can say to somebody else, "I love you," I must be able to say, "I love in you everybody, I love through you the world, I love in you also myself."

Saying that love is an orientation which refers to all and not to one does not imply, however, the idea that there are no differences between various types of love, which depend on the kind of object which is loved.

a. Brotherly Love

The most fundamental kind of love, which underlies all types of love, is *brotherly love*. By this I mean the sense of responsibility, care, respect, knowledge of any other human being, the wish to further his life. This is the kind of love the Bible speaks of when it says: love thy neighbor as thyself. Brotherly love is love for all human beings; it is characterized by its very lack of exclusiveness. If I have developed the capacity for love, then I cannot help loving my brothers. In brotherly love there is the experience of union with all men, of human solidarity, of human at-onement. Brotherly love is based on the experience that we all are one. The differences in talents, intelligence, knowledge are negligible in comparison with the identity of the human core common to all men. In order to experience this identity it is necessary to penetrate from the periphery to the core. If I perceive in another person mainly the surface, I perceive mainly the differences, that which separates us. If I penetrate to the core, I perceive our identity, the fact of our brotherhood. This relatedness from center to center—instead of that from periphery to periphery—is "central relatedness." Or as Simone Weil expressed it so beautifully: "The same words [e.g., a man says to his wife, "I love you"] can be commonplace or extraordinary according to the manner in which they are spoken. And this manner depends on the depth of the region in a man's being from which they proceed without the will being able to do anything. And by a marvelous agreement they reach the same region in him who hears them. Thus the hearer can discern, if he has any power of discernment, what is the value of the words."[1]

Brotherly love is love between equals: but, indeed, even as equals we are not always "equal"; inasmuch as we are human, we are all in need of help. Today I, tomorrow you. But this need of help does not mean that the one is helpless, the other powerful. Helplessness is a transitory condition; the ability to stand and walk on one's own feet is the permanent and common one.

---

[1] Simone Weil, *Gravity and Grace*, G. P. Putnam's Sons, New York, 1952, p. 117.

Yet, love of the helpless one, love of the poor and the stranger, are the beginning of brotherly love. To love one's flesh and blood is no achievement. The animal loves its young and cares for them. The helpless one loves his master, since his life depends on him; the child loves his parents, since he needs them. Only in the love of those who do not serve a purpose, love begins to unfold. Significantly, in the Old Testament, the central object of man's love is the poor, the stranger, the widow and the orphan, and eventually the national enemy, the Egyptian and the Edomite. By having compassion for the helpless one, man begins to develop love for his brother; and in his love for himself he also loves the one who is in need of help, the frail, insecure human being. Compassion implies the element of knowledge and of identification. "You know the heart of the stranger," says the Old Testament, "for you were strangers in the land of Egypt; . . . *therefore love the stranger!*"[2]

b. Motherly Love

We have already dealt with the nature of motherly love in a previous chapter which discussed the difference between motherly and fatherly love. Motherly love, as I said there, is unconditional affirmation of the child's life and his needs. But one important addition to this description must be made here. Affirmation of the child's life has two aspects; one is the care and responsibility absolutely necessary for the preservation of the child's life and his growth. The other aspect goes further than mere preservation. It is the attitude which instills in the child a love for living, which gives him the feeling: it is good to be alive, it is good to be a little boy or girl, it is good to be on this earth! These two aspects of motherly love are expressed very succinctly in the Biblical story of creation. God creates the world, and man. This corresponds to the simple care and affirmation of existence. But God goes beyond this minimum requirement. On each day after nature—and man—is created, God says: "It is good." Motherly love, in this second step, makes the child feel: it is good to have been born; it instills in the child the *love for life,* and not only the wish to remain alive. The same idea may be taken to be expressed in another Biblical symbolism. The promised land (land is always a mother symbol) is described as "flowing with milk and honey." Milk is the symbol of the first aspect of love, that of care and affirmation. Honey symbolizes the sweetness of life, the love for it and the happiness in being alive. Most mothers are capable of giving "milk," but only a minority of giving "honey" too. In order to be able to give honey, a mother must not only be a "good mother," but a happy person— and this aim is not achieved by many. The effect on the child can hardly be exaggerated. Mother's love for life is as infectious as her anxiety is. Both attitudes have a deep effect on the child's whole personality; one can distinguish indeed, among children—and adults—those who got only "milk" and those who got "milk and honey."

---

[2] The same idea has been expressed by Hermann Cohen in his *Religion der Vernunft aus den Quellen des Judentums,* 2nd edition, J. Kaufmann Verlag, Frankfurt am Main, 1929, p. 168 ff.

In contrast to brotherly love and erotic love which are love between equals, the relationship of mother and child is by its very nature one of inequality, where one needs all the help, and the other gives it. It is for this altruistic, unselfish character that motherly love has been considered the highest kind of love, and the most sacred of all emotional bonds. It seems, however, that the real achievement of motherly love lies not in the mother's love for the small infant, but in her love for the growing child. Actually, the vast majority of mothers are loving mothers as long as the infant is small and still completely dependent on them. Most women want children, are happy with the new-born child, and eager in their care for it. This is so in spite of the fact that they do not "get" anything in return from the child, except a smile or the expression of satisfaction in his face. It seems that this attitude of love is partly rooted in an instinctive equipment to be found in animals as well as in the human female. But, whatever the weight of this instinctive factor may be, there are also specifically human psychological factors which are responsible for this type of motherly love. One may be found in the narcissistic element in motherly love. Inasmuch as the infant is still felt to be a part of herself, her love and infatuation may be a satisfaction of her narcissism. Another motivation may be found in a mother's wish for power, or possession. The child, being helpless and completely subject to her will, is a natural object of satisfaction for a domineering and possessive woman.

Frequent as these motivations are, they are probably less important and less universal than one which can be called the need for transcendence. This need for transcendence is one of the most basic needs of man, rooted in the fact of his self-awareness, in the fact that he is not satisfied with the role of the creature, that he cannot accept himself as dice thrown out of the cup. He needs to feel as the creator, as one transcending the passive role of being created. There are many ways of achieving this satisfaction of creation; the most natural and also the easiest one to achieve is the mother's care and love for her creation. She transcends herself in the infant, her love for it gives her life meaning and significance. (In the very inability of the male to satisfy his need for transcendence by bearing children lies his urge to transcend himself by the creation of man-made things and of ideas.)

But the child must grow. It must emerge from mother's womb, from mother's breast; it must eventually become a completely separate human being. The very essence of motherly love is to care for the child's growth, and that means to want the child's separation from herself. Here lies the basic difference to erotic love. In erotic love, two people who were separate become one. In motherly love, two people who were one become separate. The mother must not only tolerate, she must wish and support the child's separation. It is only at this stage that motherly love becomes such a difficult task, that it requires unselfishness, the ability to give everything and to want nothing but the happiness of the loved one. It is also at this stage that many mothers fail in their task of motherly love. The narcissistic, the domineering, the possessive woman can succeed in being a "loving" mother as long as the child is small. Only the really loving woman, the woman who is happier in giving than in taking, who is firmly rooted in her own existence, can be a loving mother when the child is in the process of separation.

Motherly love for the growing child, love which wants nothing for oneself, is perhaps the most difficult form of love to be achieved, and all the more deceptive because of the ease with which a mother can love her small infant. But just because of this difficulty, a woman can be a truly loving mother only if she can *love*; if she is able to love her husband, other children, strangers, all human beings. The woman who is not capable of love in this sense can be an affectionate mother as long as the child is small, but she cannot be a loving mother, the test of which is the willingness to bear separation—and even after the separation to go on loving.

c. Erotic Love

Brotherly love is love among equals; motherly love is love for the helpless. Different as they are from each other, they have in common that they are by their very nature not restricted to one person. If I love my brother, I love all my brothers; if I love my child, I love all my children; no, beyond that, I love all children, all that are in need of my help. In contrast to both types of love is *erotic love*; it is the craving for complete fusion, for union with one other person. It is by its very nature exclusive and not universal; it is also perhaps the most deceptive form of love there is.

First of all, it is often confused with the explosive experience of "falling" in love, the sudden collapse of the barriers which existed until that moment between two strangers. But, as was pointed out before, this experience of sudden intimacy is by its very nature short-lived. After the stranger has become an intimately known person there are no more barriers to be overcome, there is no more sudden closeness to be achieved. The "loved" person becomes as well known as oneself. Or, perhaps I should better say as little known. If there were more depth in the experience of the other person, if one could experience the infiniteness of his personality, the other person would never be so familiar—and the miracle of overcoming the barriers might occur every day anew. But for most people their own person, as well as others, is soon explored and soon exhausted. For them intimacy is established primarily through sexual contact. Since they experience the separateness of the other person primarily as physical separateness, physical union means overcoming separateness.

Beyond that, there are other factors which to many people denote the overcoming of separateness. To speak of one's own personal life, one's hopes and anxieties, to show oneself with one's childlike or childish aspects, to establish a common interest vis-à-vis the world—all this is taken as overcoming separateness. Even to show one's anger, one's hate, one's complete lack of inhibition is taken for intimacy, and this may explain the perverted attraction married couples often have for each other, who seem intimate only when they are in bed or when they give vent to their mutual hate and rage. But all these types of closeness tend to become reduced more and more as time goes on. The consequence is one seeks love with a new person, with a new stranger. Again the stranger is transformed into an "intimate" person, again the experience of falling in love is exhilarating and intense, and again it slowly becomes less and less intense, and ends in the wish for a new conquest, a new love—always with the illusion that the new love will be different from the earlier ones. These illusions are greatly helped by the deceptive character of sexual desire.

Sexual desire aims at fusion—and is by no means only a physical appetite, the relief of a painful tension. But sexual desire can be stimulated by the anxiety of aloneness, by the wish to conquer or be conquered, by vanity, by the wish to hurt and even to destroy, as much as it can be stimulated by love. It seems that sexual desire can easily blend with and be stimulated by any strong emotion, of which love is only one. Because sexual desire is in the minds of most people coupled with the idea of love, they are easily misled to conclude that they love each other when they want each other physically. Love can inspire the wish for sexual union; in this case the physical relationship is lacking in greediness, in a wish to conquer or to be conquered, but is blended with tenderness. If the desire for physical union is not stimulated by love, if erotic love is not also brotherly love, it never leads to union in more than an orgiastic, transitory sense. Sexual attraction creates, for the moment, the illusion of union, yet without love this "union" leaves strangers as far apart as they were before—sometimes it makes them ashamed of each other, or even makes them hate each other, because when the illusion has gone they feel their estrangement even more markedly than before. Tenderness is by no means, as Freud believed, a sublimation of the sexual instinct; it is the direct outcome of brotherly love, and exists in physical as well as in non-physical forms of love.

In erotic love there is an exclusiveness which is lacking in brotherly love and motherly love. This exclusive character of erotic love warrants some further discussion. Frequently the exclusiveness of erotic love is misinterpreted as meaning possessive attachment. One can often find two people "in love" with each other who feel no love for anybody else. Their love is, in fact, an egotism à deux; they are two people who identify themselves with each other, and who solve the problem of separateness by enlarging the single individual into two. They have the experience of overcoming aloneness, yet, since they are separated from the rest of mankind, they remain separated from each other and alienated from themselves; their experience of union is an illusion. Erotic love is exclusive, but it loves in the other person all of mankind, all that is alive. It is exclusive only in the sense that I can fuse myself fully and intensely with one person only. Erotic love excludes the love for others only in the sense of erotic fusion, full commitment in all aspects of life—but not in the sense of deep brotherly love.

Erotic love, if it is love, has one premise. That I love from the essence of my being—and experience the other person in the essence of his or her being. In essence, all human beings are identical. We are all part of One; we are One. This being so, it should not make any difference whom we love. Love should be essentially an act of will, of decision to commit my life completely to that of one other person. This is, indeed, the rationale behind the idea of the insolubility of marriage, as it is behind the many forms of traditional marriage in which the two partners never choose each other, but are chosen for each other—and yet are expected to love each other. In contemporary Western culture this idea appears altogether false. Love is supposed to be the outcome of a spontaneous, emotional reaction, of suddenly being gripped by an irresistible feeling. In this view, one sees only the peculiarities of the two individuals involved—and not the fact that all men are part of Adam, and all women part of Eve. One neglects to see an important factor in erotic love, that of *will.* To love somebody is not just a strong feeling—it is a decision, it is a judgment, it is a promise. If love were only a feeling, there would be no basis for the promise to love each other forever. A feeling comes and it may go. How can I judge that it will stay forever, when my act does not involve judgment and decision?

Taking these views into account one may arrive at the position that love is exclusively an act of will and commitment, and that therefore fundamentally it does not matter who the two persons are. Whether the marriage was arranged by others, or the result of individual choice, once the marriage is concluded, the act of will should guarantee the continuation of love. This view seems to neglect the paradoxical character of human nature and of erotic love. We are all One—yet every one of us is a unique, unduplicable entity. In our relationships to others the same paradox is repeated. Inasmuch as we are all one, we can love everybody in the same way in the sense of brotherly love. But inasmuch as we are all also different, erotic love requires certain specific, highly individual elements which exist between some people but not between all.

Both views then, that of erotic love as completely individual attraction, unique between two specific persons, as well as the other view that erotic love is nothing but an act of will, are true—or, as it may be put more aptly, the truth is neither this nor that. Hence the idea of a relationship which can be easily dissolved if one is not successful with it is as erroneous as the idea that under no circumstances must the relationship be dissolved.

d. Self-Love[3]

While it raises no objection to apply the concept of love to various objects, it is a widespread belief that, while it is virtuous to love others, it is sinful to love oneself. It is assumed that to the degree to which I love myself I do not love others, that self-

[3] Paul Tillich, in a review of *The Sane Society,* in *Pastoral Psychology,* September, 1955, has suggested that it would be better to drop the ambiguous term "self-love" and to replace it with "natural self-affirmation" or "paradoxical self-acceptance." Much as I can see the merits of this suggestion, I cannot agree with him in this point. In the term "self-love" the paradoxical element in self-love is contained more clearly. The fact is expressed that love is an attitude which is the same toward all objects, including myself. It must also not be forgotten that the term "self-love," in the sense in which it is used here, has a history. The Bible speaks of self-love when it commands to "love thy neighbor *as thyself,*" and Meister Eckhart speaks of self-love in the very same sense.

love is the same as selfishness. This view goes far back in Western thought. Calvin speaks of self-love as "a pest."[4] Freud speaks of self-love in psychiatric terms but, nevertheless, his value judgment is the same as that of Calvin. For him self-love is the same as narcissism, the turning of the libido toward oneself. Narcissism is the earliest stage in human development, and the person who in later life has returned to his narcissistic stage is incapable of love; in the extreme case he is insane. Freud assumes that love is the manifestation of libido, and that the libido is either turned toward others—love; or toward oneself—self-love. Love and self-love are thus mutually exclusive in the sense that the more there is of one, the less there is of the other. If self-love is bad, it follows that unselfishness is virtuous.

These questions arise: Does psychological observation support the thesis that there is a basic contradiction between love for oneself and love for others? Is love for oneself the same phenomenon as selfishness, or are they opposites? Furthermore, is the selfishness of modern man really a *concern for himself* as an individual, with all his intellectual, emotional and sensual potentialities? Has "he" not become an appendage of his socio-economic role? *Is his selfishness identical with self-love or is it not caused by the very lack of it?*

Before we start the discussion of the psychological aspect of selfishness and self-love, the logical fallacy in the notion that love for others and love for oneself are mutually exclusive should be stressed. If it is a virtue to love my neighbor as a human being, it must be a virtue—and not a vice—to love myself, since I am a human being too. There is no concept of man in which I myself am not included. A doctrine which proclaims such an exclusion proves itself to be intrinsically contradictory. The idea expressed in the Biblical "Love thy neighbor as thyself!" implies that respect for one's own integrity and uniqueness, love for and understanding of one's own self, cannot be separated from respect and love and understanding for another individual. The love for my own self is inseparably connected with the love for any other being.

We have come now to the basic psychological premises on which the conclusions of our argument are built. Generally, these premises are as follows: not only others, but we ourselves are the "object" of our feelings and attitudes; the attitudes toward others and toward ourselves, far from being contradictory, are basically *conjunctive*. With regard to the problem under discussion this means: love of others and love of ourselves are not alternatives. On the contrary, an attitude of love toward themselves will be found in all those who are capable of loving others. *Love*, in principle, *is indivisible as far as the connection between "objects" and one's own self is concerned.* Genuine love is an expression of productiveness and implies care, respect, responsibility and knowledge. It is not an "affect" in the sense of being affected by somebody,

---

[4] John Calvin, *Institutes of the Christian Religion*, translated by J. Albau, Presbyterian Board of Christian Education, Philadelphia, 1928, Chap. 7, par. 4, p. 622.

but an active striving for the growth and happiness of the loved person, rooted in one's own capacity to love.

To love somebody is the actualization and concentration of the power to love. The basic affirmation contained in love is directed toward the beloved person as an incarnation of essentially human qualities. Love of one person implies love of man as such. The kind of "division of labor," as William James calls it, by which one loves one's family but is without feeling for the "stranger," is a sign of a basic inability to love. Love of man is not, as is frequently supposed, an abstraction coming after the love for a specific person, but it is its premise, although genetically it is acquired in loving specific individuals.

From this it follows that my own self must be as much an object of my love as another person. *The affirmation of one's own life, happiness, growth, freedom is rooted in one's capacity to love,* i.e., in care, respect, responsibility, and knowledge. If an individual is able to love productively, he loves himself too; if he can love *only* others, he cannot love at all.

Granted that love for oneself and for others in principle is conjunctive, how do we explain selfishness, which obviously excludes any genuine concern for others? The *selfish* person is interested only in himself, wants everything for himself, feels no pleasure in giving, but only in taking. The world outside is looked at only from the standpoint of what he can get out of it; he lacks interest in the needs of others, and respect for their dignity and integrity. He can see nothing but himself; he judges everyone and everything from its usefulness to him; he is basically unable to love. Does not this prove that concern for others and concern for oneself are unavoidable alternatives? This would be so if selfishness and self-love were identical. But that assumption is the very fallacy which has led to so many mistaken conclusions concerning our problem. *Selfishness and self-love, far from being identical, are actually opposites.* The selfish person does not love himself too much but too little; in fact he hates himself. This lack of fondness and care for himself, which is only one expression of his lack of productiveness, leaves him empty and frustrated. He is necessarily unhappy and anxiously concerned to snatch from life the satisfactions which he blocks himself from attaining. He seems to care too much for himself, but actually he only makes an unsuccessful attempt to cover up and compensate for his failure to care for his real self. Freud holds that the selfish person is narcissistic, as if he had withdrawn his love from others and turned it toward his own person. *It is true that selfish persons are incapable of loving others, but they are not capable of loving themselves either.*

It is easier to understand selfishness by comparing it with greedy concern for others, as we find it, for instance, in an oversolicitous mother. While she consciously believes that she is particularly fond of her child, she has actually a deeply repressed hostility toward the object of her concern. She is overconcerned not because she loves the child too much, but because she has to compensate for her lack of capacity to love him at all.

This theory of the nature of selfishness is borne out by psychoanalytic experience with neurotic "unselfishness," a sympton of neurosis observed in not a few people who usually are troubled not by this symptom but by others connected with it, like depression, tiredness, inability to work, failure in love relationships, and so on. Not only is unselfishness not felt as a "symptom"; it is often the one redeeming character trait on which such people pride themselves. The "unselfish" person "does not want anything for himself"; he "lives only for others," is proud that he does not consider himself important. He is puzzled to find that in spite of his unselfishness he is unhappy, and that his relationships to those closest to him are unsatisfactory. Analytic work shows that his unselfishness is not something apart from his other symptoms but one of them, in fact often the most important one; that he is paralyzed in his capacity to love or to enjoy anything; that he is pervaded by hostility toward life and that behind the façade of unselfishness a subtle but not less intense self-centeredness is hidden. This person can be cured only if his unselfishness too is interpreted as a symptom along with the others, so that his lack of productiveness, which is at the root of both his unselfishness *and* his other troubles, can be corrected.

The nature of unselfishness becomes particularly apparent in its effect on others, and most frequently in our culture in the effect the "unselfish" mother has on her children. She believes that by her unselfishness her children will experience what it means to be loved and to learn, in turn, what it means to love. The effect of her unselfishness, however, does not at all correspond to her expectations. The children do not show the happiness of persons who are convinced that they are loved; they are anxious, tense, afraid of the mother's disapproval and anxious to live up to her expectations. Usually, they are affected by their mother's hidden hostility toward life, which they sense rather than recognize clearly, and eventually they become imbued with it themselves. Altogether, the effect of the "unselfish" mother is not too different from that of the selfish one; indeed, it is often worse, because the mother's unselfishness prevents the children from criticizing her. They are put under the obligation not to disappoint her; they are taught, under the mask of virtue, dislike for life. If one has a chance to study the effect of a mother with genuine self-love, one can see that there is nothing more conducive to giving a child the experience of what love, joy and happiness are than being loved by a mother who loves herself.

These ideas on self-love cannot be summarized better than by quoting Meister Eckhart on this topic: "If you love yourself, you love everybody else as you do yourself. As long as you love another person less than you love yourself, you will not really succeed in loving yourself, but if you love all alike, including yourself, you will love them as one person and that person is both God and man. Thus he is a great and righteous person who, loving himself, loves all others equally."[5]

---

[5] *Meister Eckhart*, translated by R. B. Blakney, Harper & Brothers, New York, 1941, p. 204.

Anthony Hecht (born 1922)

The Dover Bitch

A Criticism of Life

So there stood Matthew Arnold and this girl
With the cliffs of England crumbling away behind them,
And he said to her, "Try to be true to me,
And I'll do the same for you, for things are bad
All over, etc., etc."   5
Well now, I knew this girl. It's true she had read
Sophocles in a fairly good translation
And caught that bitter allusion to the sea,
But all the time he was talking she had in mind
The notion of what his whiskers would feel like   10
On the back of her neck. She told me later on
That after a while she got to looking out
At the lights across the channel, and really felt sad,
Thinking of all the wine and enormous beds
And blandishments in French and the perfumes.   15
And then she got really angry. To have been brought
All the way down from London, and then be addressed
As sort of a mournful cosmic last resort
Is really tough on a girl, and she was pretty.
Anyway, she watched him pace the room   20
And finger his watch-chain and seem to sweat a bit,
And then she said one or two unprintable things.
But you mustn't judge her by that. What I mean to say is,
She's really all right. I still see her once in a while
And she always treats me right. We have a drink   25
And I give her a good time, and perhaps it's a year
Before I see her again, but there she is,
Running to fat, but dependable as they come,
And sometimes I bring her a bottle of *Nuit d'Amour.*

❖

James Joyce (1882–1941)
Eveline

She sat at the window watching the evening invade the avenue. Her head was leaned against the window curtains and in her nostrils was the odour of dusty cretonne. She was tired.

Few people passed. The man out of the last house passed on his way home; she heard his footsteps clacking along the concrete pavement and afterwards crunching on the cinder path before the new red houses. One time there used to be a field there in which they used to play every evening with other people's children. Then a man from Belfast bought the field and built houses in it—not like their little brown houses but bright brick houses with shining roofs. The children of the avenue used to play together in that field—the Devines, the Waters, the Dunns, little Keogh the cripple, she and her brothers and sisters. Ernest, however, never played: he was too grown up. Her father used often to hunt them in out of the field with his blackthorn stick; but usually little Keogh used to keep *nix* and call out when he saw her father coming. Still they seemed to have been rather happy then. Her father was not so bad then; and besides, her mother was alive. That was a long time ago; she and her brothers and sisters were all grown up; her mother was dead. Tizzie Dunn was dead, too, and the Waters had gone back to England. Everything changes. Now she was going to go away like the others, to leave her home.

Home! She looked round the room, reviewing all its familiar objects which she had dusted once a week for so many years, wondering where on earth all the dust came from. Perhaps she would never see again those familiar objects from which she had never dreamed of being divided. And yet during all those years she had never found out the name of the priest whose yellowing photograph hung on the wall above the broken harmonium beside the coloured print of the promises made to Blessed Margaret Mary Alacoque. He had been a school friend of her father. Whenever he showed the photograph to a visitor her father used to pass it with a casual word:

"He is in Melbourne now."

She had consented to go away, to leave her home. Was that wise? She tried to weigh each side of the question. In her home anyway she had shelter and food; she had those whom she had known all her life about her. Of course she had to work hard, both in the house and at business. What would they say of her in the Stores when they found out that she had run away with a fellow? Say she was a fool, perhaps; and her place would be filled up by advertisement. Miss Gavan would be glad. She had always had an edge on her, especially whenever there were people listening.

"Miss Hill, don't you see these ladies are waiting?"

"Look lively, Miss Hill, please."

She would not cry many tears at leaving the Stores.

But in her new home, in a distant unknown country, it would not be like that. Then she would be married—she, Eveline. People would treat her with respect then. She would not be treated as her mother had been. Even now, though she was over nineteen, she sometimes felt herself in danger of her father's violence. She knew it was that that had given her the palpitations. When they were growing up he had never gone for her, like he used to go for Harry and Ernest, because she was a girl; but latterly he had begun to threaten her and say what he would do to her only for her dead mother's sake. And now she had nobody to protect her. Ernest was dead and Harry, who was in the church decorating business, was nearly always down somewhere in the country. Besides, the invariable squabble for money on Saturday nights had begun to weary her unspeakably. She always gave her entire wages—seven shillings—and Harry always sent up what he could but the trouble was to get any money from her father. He said she used to squander the money, that she had no head, that he wasn't going to give her his hard-earned money to throw about the streets, and much more, for he was usually fairly bad on Saturday night. In the end he would give her the money and ask her had she any intention of buying Sunday's dinner. Then she had to rush out as quickly as she could and do her marketing, holding her black leather purse tightly in her hand as she elbowed her way through the crowds and returning home later under her load of provisions. She had hard work to keep the house together and to see that the two young children who had been left to her charge went to school regularly and got their meals regularly. It was hard work—a hard life—but now that she was about to leave it she did not find it a wholly undesirable life.

She was about to explore another life with Frank. Frank was very kind, manly, open-hearted. She was to go away with him by the night-boat to be his wife and to live with him in Buenos Ayres where he had a home waiting for her. How well she remembered the first time she had seen him; he was lodging in a house on the main road where she used to visit. It seemed a few weeks ago. He was standing at the gate, his peaked cap pushed back on his head and his hair tumbled forward over a face of bronze. Then they had come to know each other. He used to meet her outside the Stores every evening and see her home. He took her to see *The Bohemian Girl* and she felt elated as she sat in an unaccustomed part of the theatre with him. He was awfully fond of music and sang a little. People knew that they were courting and, when he sang about the lass that loves a sailor, she always felt pleasantly confused. He used to call her Poppens out of fun. First of all it had been an excitement for her to have a fellow and then she had begun to like him. He had tales of distant countries. He had started as a deck boy at a pound a month on a ship of the Allan Line going out to Canada. He told her the names of the ships he had been on and the names of the different services. He had sailed through the Straits of Magellan and he told her stories of the terrible Patagonians. He had fallen on his feet in Buenos Ayres, he said, and had come over to the old country just for a holiday. Of course, her father had found out the affair and had forbidden her to have anything to say to him.

"I know these sailor chaps," he said.

One day he had quarrelled with Frank and after that she had to meet her lover secretly.

The evening deepened in the avenue. The white of two letters in her lap grew indistinct. One was to Harry; the other was to her father. Ernest had been her favourite but she liked Harry too. Her father was becoming old lately, she noticed; he would miss her. Sometimes he could be very nice. Not long before, when she had been laid up for a day, he had read her out a ghost story and made toast for her at the fire. Another day, when their mother was alive, they had all gone for a picnic to the Hill of Howth. She remembered her father putting on her mother's bonnet to make the children laugh.

Her time was running out but she continued to sit by the window, leaning her head against the window curtain, inhaling the odour of dusty cretonne. Down far in the avenue she could hear a street organ playing. She knew the air. Strange that it should come that very night to remind her of the promise to her mother, her promise to keep the home together as long as she could. She remembered the last night of her mother's illness; she was again in the close dark room at the other side of the hall and outside she heard a melancholy air of Italy. The organ-player had been ordered to go away and given sixpence. She remembered her father strutting back into the sickroom saying:

"Damned Italians! coming over here!"

As she mused the pitiful vision of her mother's life laid its spell on the very quick of her being—that life of commonplace sacrifices closing in final craziness. She trembled as she heard again her mother's voice saying constantly with foolish insistence:

"Derevaun Seraun! Derevaun Seraun!"

She stood up in a sudden impulse of terror. Escape! She must escape! Frank would save her. He would give her life, perhaps love, too. But she wanted to live. Why should she be unhappy? She had a right to happiness. Frank would take her in his arms, fold her in his arms. He would save her.

•   •   •

She stood among the swaying crowd in the station at the North Wall. He held her hand and she knew that he was speaking to her, saying something about the passage over and over again. The station was full of soldiers with brown baggages. Through the wide doors of the sheds she caught a glimpse of the black mass of the boat, lying in beside the quay wall, with illumined portholes. She answered nothing. She felt her cheek pale and cold and, out of a maze of distress, she prayed to God to direct her, to show her what was her duty. The boat blew a long mournful whistle into the mist.

If she went, tomorrow she would be on the sea with Frank, steaming towards Buenos Ayres. Their passage had been booked. Could she still draw back after all he had done for her? Her distress awoke a nausea in her body and she kept moving her lips in silent fervent prayer.

A bell clanged upon her heart. She felt him seize her hand:

"Come!"

All the seas of the world tumbled about her heart. He was drawing her into them: he would drown her. She gripped with both hands at the iron railing.

"Come!"

No! No! No! It was impossible. Her hands clutched the iron in frenzy. Amid the seas she sent a cry of anguish.

"Eveline! Evvy!"

He rushed beyond the barrier and called to her to follow. He was shouted at to go on but he still called to her. She set her white face to him, passive, like a helpless animal. Her eyes gave him no sign of love or farewell or recognition.

Garrison Keillor (born 1942)

My Stepmother, Myself

Recently in Weeseville, Pennyslvania, a woman was dismissed from her job as a human-resources coordinator and driven over a cliff by an angry mob of villagers carrying flaming torches and hurling sharp rocks after they learned that she was married to a man who had custody of his three children by a previous marriage.

In California, soon after her marriage to a prince (her first marriage, his seventh), a woman named Sharon Mittel was shut up in a dungeon under the provisions of that state's Cruel and Unnatural Parent Act, which allows the immediate imprisonment of a stepparent upon the complaint of a stepchild. The prince's oldest daughter accused Sharon of slapping her. She was later freed after an appeal to a king, but she now faces a long series of tests to prove her innocence, such as finding a tree of pure gold and a seedless grapefruit. She also must answer some riddles.

Are these merely two isolated incidents? Or are they, as a new and exhaustive report on stepmothers clearly points out, fairly indicative?

"The myth of the evil stepmother is still with us," the report concludes. "Step-mothers are still associated with the words *cruel* and *wicked*, which has made them easy targets for torture and banishment as well as severely limiting their employment, particularly in the so-called 'caring' professions such as nursing, social work, and education. The myth that stepmothers use poisons and potions has virtually barred them from the food and drug industries. In general, stepmothers are not only underpaid and underemployed but also feared and despised."

How cruel is the typical stepmother?

Not very, according to the report, which examines many cases of alleged cruelty and finds almost all of them untrue. "The media have jumped on every little misunderstanding, and have blown it up to outlandish proportions," the report finds.

Recently, three stepdaughters whose relationships with their stepmothers are well known agreed to speak out and set the record straight. Because each has suffered from publicity in the past and is trying to lead as normal a life as possible under the circumstances, only first names will be used.

Snow

The story the press told was that I was in a life-threatening situation as a child and that the primary causal factor was my stepmother's envy. I can see now that there were other factors, and that *I* didn't give *her* much reinforcement—but anyway, the story was that I escaped from her and was taken in by dwarves and she found me and poisoned me with an apple and I was dead and the prince fell in love with me and brought me back to life and we got married, etcetera, etcetera. And that is what *I* believed right up to the day I walked out on him. I felt like I owed my life to Jeff because he had begged the dwarves for my body and carried it away and so the apple was shaken loose from my throat. That's why I married him. Out of gratitude.

As I look back on it, I can see that that was a very poor basis for a relationship. I was traumatized, I had been lying in a coffin under glass for *years*, and I got up and married the first guy I laid eyes on. The big prince. My hero.

Now I can see how sick our marriage was. He was always begging me to lie still and close my eyes and hold my breath. He could only relate to me as a dead person. He couldn't accept me as a living woman with needs and desires of my own. It is terribly hard for a woman to come to terms with the fact that her husband is a necrophiliac, because, of course, when it all starts, you aren't aware of what's going on—you're dead.

In trying to come to terms with myself, I've had to come to terms with my stepmother and her envy of my beauty, which made our relationship so destructive. She was a victim of the male attitude that prizes youth over maturity when it comes to women. Men can't dominate the mature woman, so they equate youth with beauty. In fact, she *was* beautiful, but the mirror (which, of course, reflected that male attitude) presented her with a poor self-image and turned her against me.

But the press never wrote the truth about that.

Or about the dwarves. All I can say is that they should have been named Dopey, Sleepy, Slimy, Sleazy, Dirty, Disgusting, and Sexist. The fact is that I *knew* the apple was poisoned. For me, it was the only way out.

Gretel

When Hansel and I negotiated the sale of book rights to Grimm Bros., he and I retained the right of final approval of the manuscript and agreed to split the proceeds fifty-fifty. We shook hands on it and I thought the deal was set, but then his lawyers put me under a spell, and when I woke up, they had rewritten the contract and the book too! I couldn't believe it! Not only did the new contract cut me out (under the terms, I was to get ten shiny baubles out of the first fortune the book earned and three trinkets for each additional fortune) but the book was pure fiction.

Suddenly he was portrayed as the strong and resourceful one, a regular little knight, and I came off as a weak sister. Dad was shown as a loving father who was talked into abandoning us in the forest by Gladys, our "wicked" stepmother.

Nothing could be further from the truth.

My brother was a basket case from the moment the birds ate his bread crumbs. He lay down in a heap and whimpered, and I had to slap him a couple times *hard* to make him walk. Now the little wiener makes himself out to be the hero who kept telling me, "Don't cry, Gretel." Ha! The only crying I did was from sheer exhaustion carrying him on my back.

As for Dad, he was no bleeding heart. He was very much into that whole woodcutter/peasant/yeoman scene—cockfighting, bullbaiting, going to the village on Saturday to get drunk and watch a garroting or a boiling—don't kid yourself, Gladys couldn't send us to our *rooms* without his say-so. The truth is that he was in favor of the forest idea from the word go.

What I can't understand is why they had to lie about it. Many, *many* parents left their children in the forest in those days. It was nothing unusual.

Nowadays, we tend to forget that famine can be a very difficult experience for a family. For many parents, ditching the kids was not only a solution, it was an act of faith. They believed that ravens would bring morsels of food in their beaks, or that wolves would take care of the kids, or a frog would, or that the fairies would step in. Dwarves, a hermit, a band of pilgrims, a kindly shepherd, *somebody*. And they were right.

And that is why I was never seriously worried for one single moment while we were there. Deep down, I always knew we would make it.

I don't mean to say that it wasn't a trying experience, an *emotional* experience. It was. And yet there isn't a single documented case of a child left in the forest who suffered any lasting damage. You look at those children today and you will find they are better people for having gone through it. Except for my brother, that is. The little jerk. He and my father live in luxurious manors with beautiful tapestries and banners and ballrooms, and I live above an alchemist's shop in a tiny garret they call a condo. As for Gladys, she was kicked out without so much as a property settlement. She didn't even get half of the hut. I guess she is the one who suffered most. Her and the witch.

I often think about the witch—I ask myself, Why did I give her the shove? After all, it wasn't me she was after.

I guess that, back then, I wasn't prepared to understand her type of militance. I couldn't see that she was fattening up Hansel in order to make a very radical statement. If only I had. Not that I necessarily would have joined her in making that statement, but I would have seen that from her point of view it had validity and meaning.

And I would have seen that Gladys, in proposing the forest as a viable alternative, was offering me independence at a very early age.

I wish I had been able to thank her.

Cinderella

A woman in my position does not find it easy to "come out of the palace," so to speak, and to provide intimate details of her personal life. I do so only because I believe it is time to put the Cinderella myth to rest once and for all—the myth that one can escape housework by marrying a prince.

The truth is that I am busier than ever. Supervising a large household staff—cooks, maids, footmen, pages, ladies-in-waiting, minstrels and troubadours, a bard or two—is just plain hard work. Often I find myself longing for the "good old days" when my stepmother made me sweep the hearth.

We see each other almost every day—she comes up here and we play tennis or I go down there for lunch—and we often reminisce and laugh about our little disagreements. She is one of my best friends. Other people treat me like royalty but she treats me like a real person. My husband won't let me touch a broom, but I go to her house and she puts me to work! I love it. I tell her, "Mother, you're the only one who yells at me. Don't ever stop." And I mean it. Anger is real. It's honest.

Honesty is a rare commodity in a palace, and that is why so many "fairy-tale" marriages end up on the rocks. You wouldn't believe the amount of fawning and flattering that goes on! Between the courtiers bowing and scraping and the suppliants and petitioners wheedling and whining, and the scheming of bishops and barons, not to mention the sorcery and witchcraft, the atmosphere is such that it's terribly hard for a man and a woman to establish a loving, trusting, sharing type of relationship.

It's true that we lived happily ever after, but believe me, we have had to work at it!

Christopher Marlowe (1564–1593)
The Passionate Shepherd to His Love

Come live with me and be my love,
And we will all the pleasures prove
That valleys, groves, hills, and fields,
Woods, or steepy mountain yields.

And we will sit upon the rocks,   5
Seeing the shepherds feed their flocks,
By shallow rivers to whose falls
Melodious birds sing madrigals.

And I will make thee beds of roses
And a thousand fragrant posies,   10
A cap of flowers, and a kirtle
Embroidered all with leaves of myrtle;

A gown made of the finest wool
Which from our pretty lambs we pull;
Fair lined slippers for the cold,   15
With buckles of the purest gold;

A belt of straw and ivy buds,
With coral clasps and amber studs:
And if these pleasures may thee move,
Come live with me, and be my love.   20

The shepherds' swains shall dance and sing
For thy delight each May morning:
If these delights thy mind may move,
Then live with me and be my love.

Andrew Marvell (1621–1678)
To His Coy Mistress

Had we but world enough, and time,
This coyness, lady, were no crime.
We would sit down, and think which way

To walk, and pass our long love's day.
Thou by the Indian Ganges' side   5
Should'st rubies find: I by the tide
Of Humber would complain. I would
Love you ten years before the Flood,
And you should, if you please, refuse
Till the conversion of the Jews.   10
My vegetable love should grow
Vaster than empires, and more slow.
An hundred years should go to praise
Thine eyes, and on thy forehead gaze:
Two hundred to adore each breast: 15
But thirty thousand to the rest.
An age at least to every part,
And the last age should show your heart.
For, lady, you deserve this state,
Nor would I love at lower rate.   20
　　But at my back I always hear
Time's wingèd chariot hurrying near;
And yonder all before us lie
Deserts of vast eternity.
Thy beauty shall no more be found,   25
Nor in thy marble vault shall sound
My echoing song; then worms shall try
That long preserved virginity,
And your quaint honor turn to dust,
And into ashes all my lust.   30
The grave's a fine and private place,
But none, I think, do there embrace.
　　Now therefore, while the youthful hue
Sits on thy skin like morning dew,
And while thy willing soul transpires   35
At every pore with instant fires,
Now let us sport us while we may;
And now, like am'rous birds of prey,
Rather at once our time devour,
Than languish in his slow-chapt power,   40
Let us roll all our strength, and all
Our sweetness, up into one ball;
And tear our pleasures with rough strife
Thorough the iron gates of life.
Thus, though we cannot make our sun   45
Stand still, yet we will make him run.

George Meredith (1828–1909)
Modern Love

17

At dinner, she is hostess, I am host.
Went the feast ever cheerfuller? She keeps
The Topic over intellectual deeps
In buoyancy afloat. They see no ghost.
With sparkling surface-eyes we ply the ball: 5
It is in truth a most contagious game:
HIDING THE SKELETON, shall be its name.
Such play as this the devils might appall!
But here's the greater wonder: in that we,
Enamored of an acting naught can tire,   10
Each other, like true hypocrites, admire;
Warm-lighted looks, Love's ephemeridae,
Shoot gayly o'er the dishes and the wine.
We waken envy of our happy lot.
Fast, sweet, and golden, shows the marriage knot.   15
Dear guests, you now have seen Love's corpse-light shine.

Theodore Morrison (born 1901)
Dover Beach Revisited:
A New Fable for Critics

1

Early in the year 1939 a certain Professor of Educational Psychology, occupying a well-paid chair at a large endowed university, conceived a plot. From his desk in the imposing Hall of the Social Sciences where the Research Institute in Education was housed he had long burned with resentment against teachers of literature, especially against English departments. It seemed to him that the professors of English stood square across the path of his major professional ambition. His great desire in life was to introduce into the study, the teaching, the critical evaluation of literature some of the systematic method, some of the "objective procedure" as he liked to call it, some of the certainty of result which he believed to be characteristic of the physical sciences. "You make such a fetish of science," a colleague once said to him, "why aren't you a chemist?"—a question that annoyed him deeply.

If such a poem as Milton's "Lycidas" has a value—and most English teachers, even to-day, would start with that as a cardinal fact—then that value must be measurable and expressible in terms that do not shift and change from moment to moment and person to person with every subjective whim. They would agree, these teachers of literature, these professors of English, that the value of the poem is in some sense objective; they would never agree to undertake any objective procedure to determine what that value is. They would not clearly define what they meant by achievement in the study of literature, and they bridled and snorted when anyone else attempted to define it. He remembered what had happened when he had once been incautious enough to suggest to a professor of English in his own college that it might be possible to establish norms for the appreciation of Milton. The fellow had simply exploded into a peal of histrionic laughter and then had tried to wither him with an equally histrionic look of incredulity and disgust.

He would like to see what would happen if the teachers of English were forced or lured, by some scheme or other, into a public exposure of their position. It would put them in the light of intellectual charlatanism, nothing less . . . and suddenly Professor Chartly (for so he was nicknamed) began to see his way.

It was a simple plan that popped into his head, simple yet bold and practical. It was a challenge that could not be refused. A strategically placed friend in one of the large educational foundations could be counted on: there would be money for clerical expenses, for travel if need be. He took his pipe from his pocket, filled it, and began to puff exultantly. Tomorrow he must broach the scheme to one or two colleagues; tonight, over cheese and beer, would not be too soon. He reached for the telephone.

The plan that he unfolded to his associates that evening aroused considerable skepticism at first, but gradually they succumbed to his enthusiasm. A number of well-known professors of literature at representative colleges up and down the land would be asked to write a critical evaluation of a poem prominent enough to form part of the standard reading in all large English courses. They would be asked to state the criteria on which they based their judgment. When all the answers had been received the whole dossier would be sent to a moderator, a trusted elder statesman of education, known everywhere for his dignity, liberality of intelligence, and long experience. He would be asked to make a preliminary examination of all the documents and to determine from the point of view of a teacher of literature whether they provided any basis for a common understanding. The moderator would then forward all the documents to Professor Chartly, who would make what in his own mind he was frank to call a more scientific analysis. Then the jaws of the trap would be ready to spring.

Once the conspirators had agreed on their plot their first difficulty came in the choice of a poem. Suffice it to say that someone eventually hit on Arnold's "Dover

Beach," and the suggestion withstood all attack. "Dover Beach" was universally known, almost universally praised; it was remote enough so that contemporary jealousies and cults were not seriously involved, yet near enough not to call for any special expertness, historical or linguistic, as a prerequisite for judgment; it was generally given credit for skill as a work of art, yet it contained also, in its author's own phrase, a "criticism of life."

Rapidly in the days following the first meeting the representative teachers were chosen and invited to participate in the plan. Professional courtesy seemed to require the inclusion of an Arnold expert. But the one selected excused himself from producing a value judgment of "Dover Beach" on the ground that he was busy investigating a fresh clue to the identity of "Marguerite." He had evidence that the woman in question, after the episode hinted at in the famous poems, had married her deceased sister's husband, thus perhaps affecting Arnold's views on a social question about which he had said a good deal in his prose writings. The expert pointed out that he had been given a half-year's leave of absence and a research grant to pursue the shadow of Marguerite through Europe, wherever it might lead him. If only war did not break out he hoped to complete his research and solve one of the vexing problems that had always confronted Arnold's biographers. His energies would be too much engaged in this special investigation to deal justly with the more general questions raised by Professor Chartly's invitation. But he asked to be kept informed, since the results of the experiment could not fail to be of interest to him.

After a few hitches and delays from other quarters, the scheme was ripe. The requests were mailed out, and the Professor of Educational Psychology sat back in grim confidence to await the outcome.

2

It chanced that the first of the representative teachers who received and answered Professor Chartly's letter was thought of on his own campus as giving off a distinct though not unpleasant odor of the ivory tower. He would have resented the imputation himself. At forty-five Bradley Dewing was handsome in a somewhat speciously virile style, graying at the temples, but still well-knit and active. He prided himself on being able to beat most of his students at tennis; once a year he would play the third or fourth man on the varsity and go down to creditable defeat with some elegiac phrases on the ravages of time. He thought of himself as a man of the world; it was well for his contentment, which was seldom visibly ruffled, that he never heard the class mimic reproducing at a fraternity house or beer parlor his manner of saying: "After all, gentlemen, it is pure poetry that lasts. We must never forget the staying power of pure art." The class mimic never represents the whole of class opinion but he can usually make everyone within earshot laugh.

Professor Dewing could remember clearly what his own teachers had said about "Dover Beach" in the days when he was a freshman in college himself, phrases rounded with distant professorial unction: faith and doubt in the Victorian era; disturbing influence of Darwin on religious belief; Browning the optimist; Tennyson coming up with firm faith after a long struggle in the waters of doubt; Matthew Arnold, prophet of skepticism. How would "Dover Beach" stack up now as a poem? Pull Arnold down from the shelf and find out.

Ah, yes, how the familiar phrases came back. The sea is calm, the tide is full, the cliffs of England stand . . . And then the lines he particularly liked:

> Come to the window, sweet is the night-air!
> Only, from the long line of spray
> Where the sea meets the moon-blanch'd land,
> Listen! you hear the grating roar
> Of pebbles which the waves draw back, and fling,
> At their return, up the high strand,
> Begin, and cease, and then again begin,
> With tremulous cadence slow . . .

Good poetry, that! No one could mistake it. Onomatopoeia was a relatively cheap effect most of the time. Poe, for instance: "And the silken sad uncertain rustling of each purple curtain." Anyone could put a string of s's together and make them rustle. But these lines in "Dover Beach" were different. The onomatopoeia was involved in the whole scene, and it in turn involved the whole rhythmical movement of the verse, not the mere noise made by the consonants or vowels as such. The pauses—only, listen, draw back, fling, begin, cease—how they infused a subdued melancholy into the moonlit panorama at the same time that they gave it the utmost physical reality by suggesting the endless iteration of the waves! And then the phrase "With tremulous cadence slow" coming as yet one more touch, one "fine excess," when it seemed that every phrase and pause the scene could bear had already been lavished on it: that was Miltonic, Virgilian.

But the rest of the poem?

> The Sea of Faith
> Was once, too, at the full, and round earth's shore
> Lay like the folds of a bright girdle furl'd . . .

Of course Arnold had evoked the whole scene only to bring before us this metaphor of faith in its ebb-tide. But that did not save the figure from triteness and from an even more fatal vagueness. Everything in second-rate poetry is compared to the sea: love is as deep, grief as salty, passion as turbulent. The sea may look like a bright girdle sometimes, though Professor Dewing did not think it particularly impressive to say so. And in what sense is *faith* a bright girdle? Is it the function of faith to embrace, to bind, to hold up a petticoat, or what? And what is the faith that Arnold has in mind? The poet evokes no precise concept of it. He throws us the simple, undifferentiated word, unites its loose emotional connotations with those of the sea, and leaves the whole matter there. And the concluding figure of "Dover Beach":

> we are here as on a darkling plain
> Swept with confused alarms of struggle and flight,
> Where ignorant armies clash by night.

Splendid in itself, this memorable image. But the sea had been forgotten now; the darkling plain had displaced the figure from which the whole poem tacitly promised to evolve. It would not have been so if John Donne had been the craftsman. A single bold yet accurate analogy, with constantly developing implications, would have served him for the whole poem.

Thus mused Professor Dewing, the lines of his verdict taking shape in his head. A critic of poetry of course was not at liberty to pass judgment on a poet's thought; he could only judge whether, in treating of the thought or sensibility he had received from his age, the poet had produced a satisfactory work of art. Arnold, Professor Dewing felt, had not been able to escape from the didactic tone or from a certain commonness and vagueness of expression. With deep personal misgivings about his position in a world both socially and spiritually barbarous, he had sought an image for his emotion, and had found it in the sea—a natural phenomenon still obscured by the drapings of conventional beauty and used by all manner of poets to express all manner of feelings. "Dover Beach" would always remain notable, Professor Dewing decided, as an expression of Victorian sensibility. It contained lines of ever memorable poetic skill. But it could not, he felt, be accepted as a uniformly satisfactory example of poetic art.

3

It was occasionally a source of wonder to those about him just why Professor Oliver Twitchell spent so much time and eloquence urging that man's lower nature must be repressed, his animal instincts kept in bounds by the exertion of the higher will. To the casual observer, Professor Twitchell himself did not seem to possess much animal nature. It seemed incredible that a desperate struggle with powerful bestial passions might be going on at any moment within his own slight frame, behind his delicate white face in which the most prominent feature was the octagonal glasses that focused his eyes on the outside world. Professor Twitchell was a good deal given to discipleship but not much to friendship. He had himself been a disciple of the great Irving Babbitt, and he attracted a small number of disciples among his own more earnest students. But no one knew him well. Only one of his colleagues, who took a somewhat sardonic interest in the mysteries of human nature, possessed a possible clue to the origin of his efforts to repress man's lower nature and vindicate his higher. This colleague had wormed his way sufficiently into Oliver Twitchell's confidence to learn about his family, which he did not often mention. Professor Twitchell, it turned out, had come of decidedly unacademic stock. One of his brothers was the chief salesman for a company that made domestic fire-alarm appliances. At a moment's notice he would whip out a sample from his bag or pocket, plug it into the nearest electric outlet, and while the bystanders waited in terrified suspense, would explain that in the dead of night, if the house caught fire, the thing would go off with a whoop loud enough to warn the soundest sleeper. Lined up with his whole string of brothers and sisters, all older than he, all abounding in spirits, Professor Twitchell looked like the runt of the litter. His colleague decided that he must have had a very hard childhood, and that it was not his own animal nature that he needed so constantly to repress, but his family's.

Whatever the reasons, Professor Twitchell felt no reality in the teaching of literature except as he could extract from it definitions and illustrations of man's moral struggle in the world. For him recent history had been a history of intellectual confusion and degradation, and hence of social confusion and degradation. Western thought had fallen into a heresy. It had failed to maintain the fundamental grounds of a true humanism. It had blurred the distinction between man, God, and nature. Under the influence of the sciences, it has set up a monism in which the moral as well as the physical constitution of man was included within nature and the laws of nature. It had, therefore, exalted man as naturally good, and exalted the free expression of all his impulses. What were the results of this heresy? An age, complained Professor Twitchell bitterly, in which young women talked about sexual perversions at the dinner table; an age in which everyone agreed that society was in dissolution and insisted on the privilege of being dissolute; an age without any common standards of value in morals or art; an age, in short, without discipline, without self-restraint in private life or public.

Oliver Twitchell when he received Professor Chartly's envelope sat down with a strong favorable predisposition toward his task. He accepted whole-heartedly Arnold's attitude toward literature: the demand that poetry should be serious, that it should present us with a criticism of life, that it should be measured by standards not merely personal, but in some sense *real*.

"Dover Beach" had become Arnold's best-known poem, admired as his masterpiece. It would surely contain, therefore, a distillation of his attitude. Professor Twitchell pulled down his copy of Arnold and began to read; and as he read he felt himself overtaken by surprised misgiving. The poem began well enough. The allusion to Sophocles, who had heard the sound of the retreating tide by the Aegean centuries ago, admirably prepared the groundwork of high seriousness for a poem which would culminate in a real criticism of human experience. But did the poem so culminate? It was true that the world

Hath really neither joy, nor love, nor light,
Nor certitude, nor peace, nor help for pain

if one meant the world as the worldling knows it, the man who conducts his life by unreflective natural impulse. Such a man will soon enough encounter the disappointments of ambition, the instability of all bonds and ties founded on nothing firmer than passion or self-interest. But this incertitude of the world, to a true disciple of culture, should become a means of self-discipline. It should lead him to ask how life may be purified and ennobled, how we may by wisdom and self-restraint oppose to the accidents of the world a true human culture based on the exertion of a higher will. No call to such a positive moral will, Professor Twitchell reluctantly discovered, can be heard in "Dover Beach." Man is an ignorant soldier struggling confusedly in a blind battle. Was this the culminating truth that Arnold the poet had given men in his masterpiece? Professor Twitchell sadly revised his value-judgment of the poem. He could not feel that in his most widely admired performance Arnold had seen life steadily or seen it whole; rather he had seen it only on its worldly side, and seen it under an aspect of terror. "Dover Beach" would always be justly respected for its poetic art, but the famous lines of Sophocles better exemplified the poet as a critic of life.

4

As a novelist still referred to in his late thirties as "young" and "promising," Rudolph Mole found himself in a curious relation toward his academic colleagues. He wrote for the public, not for the learned journals; hence he was spared the necessity of becoming a pedant. At the same time the more lucrative fruits of pedantry were denied to him by his quiet exclusion from the guild. Younger men sweating for promotion, living in shabby genteel poverty on yearly appointments, their childless wives mimicking their academic shop-talk in bluestocking phrases, would look up from the stacks of five-by-three cards on which they were constantly accumulating notes and references, and would say to him, "You don't realize how lucky you are, teaching composition. You aren't expected to know anything." Sometimes an older colleague, who had passed through several stages of the mysteries of preferment, would belittle professional scholarship to him with an elaborate show of graciousness and envy. "We are all just pedants," he would say. "You teach the students what they really want and need." Rudolph noticed that the self-confessed pedant went busily on publishing monographs and being promoted, while he himself remained, year by year, the English Department's most eminent poor relation.

He was not embittered. His dealings with students were pleasant and interesting. There was a sense of reality and purpose in trying to elicit from them a better expression of their thoughts, trying to increase their understanding of the literary crafts. He could attack their minds on any front he chose, and he could follow his intellectual hobbies as freely as he liked, without being confined to the artificial boundaries of a professional field of learning.

Freud, for example. When Professor Chartly and his accomplices decided that a teacher of creative writing should be included in their scheme and chose Rudolph Mole for the post, they happened to catch him at the height of his enthusiasm for Freud. Not that he expected to psychoanalyze authors through their works; that, he avowed, was not his purpose. You can't deduce the specific secrets of a man's life, he would cheerfully admit, by trying to fit his works into the text-book patterns of complexes and psychoses. The critic, in any case, is interested only in the man to the extent that he is involved in his work. But everyone agrees, Rudolph maintained, that the man is involved in his work. Some part of the psychic constitution of the author finds expression in every line that he writes. We can't understand the work unless we can understand the psychic traits that have gained expression in it. We may never be able to trace back these traits to their ultimate sources and causes, probably buried deep in the author's childhood. But we need to gain as much light on them as we can, since they appear in the work we are trying to apprehend, and determine its character. This is what criticism has always sought to do. Freud simply brings new light to the old task.

Rudolph was fortunate enough at the outset to pick up at the college bookstore a copy of Mr. Lionel Trilling's recent study of Matthew Arnold. In this volume he found much of his work already done for him. A footnote to Mr. Trilling's text, citing evidence from Professors Tinker and Lowry, made it clear that "Dover Beach" may well have been written in 1850, some seventeen years before it was first published. This, for Rudolph's purposes, was a priceless discovery. It meant that all the traditional talk about the poem was largely null and void. The poem was not a repercussion of the bombshell that Darwin dropped on the religious sensibilities of the Victorians. It was far more deeply personal and individual than that. Perhaps when Arnold published it his own sense of what it expressed or how it would be understood had changed. But clearly the poem came into being as an expression of what Arnold felt to be the particular kind of affection and passion he needed from a woman. It was a love poem, and took its place with utmost naturalness, once the clue had been given, in the group of similar and related poems addressed to "Marguerite." Mr. Trilling summed up in a fine sentence one strain in these poems, and the principal strain in "Dover Beach," when he wrote that for Arnold "fidelity is a word relevant only to those lovers who see the world as a place of sorrow and in their common suffering require the comfort of constancy."

> Ah, love, let us be true
> To one another! for the world . . .
> Hath really neither joy, nor love, nor light . . .

The point was unmistakable. And from the whole group of poems to which "Dover Beach" belonged, a sketch of Arnold as an erotic personality could be derived. The question whether a "real Marguerite" existed was an idle one, for the traits that found expression in the poems were at least "real" enough to produce the poems and to determine their character.

And what an odd spectacle it made, the self-expressed character of Arnold as a lover! The ordinary degree of aggressiveness, the normal joy of conquest and possession, seemed to be wholly absent from him. The love he asked for was essentially a protective love, sisterly or motherly; in its unavoidable ingredient of passion he felt a constant danger, which repelled and unsettled him. He addressed Marguerite as "My sister!" He avowed and deplored his own womanish fits of instability:

> I too have wish'd, no woman more,
> This starting, feverish heart, away.

He emphasized his nervous anguish and contrary impulses. He was a "teas'd o'er-labour'd heart," "an aimless unallay'd Desire." He could not break through his fundamental isolation and submerge himself in another human soul, and he believed that all men shared this plight:

> Yes: in the sea of life enisl'd,
> With echoing straits between us thrown,
> Dotting the shoreless watery wild,
> We mortal millions live *alone*.

He never "without remorse" allowed himself

> To haunt the place where passions reign,

yet it was clear that whether he had ever succeeded in giving himself up wholeheartedly to a passion, he had wanted to. There could hardly be a more telltale phrase than "Once-long'd-for storms of love."

In short much more illumination fell on "Dover Beach" from certain other verses of Arnold's than from Darwin and all his commentators:

> Truth—what is truth? Two bleeding hearts
> Wounded by men, by Fortune tried,
> Outwearied with their lonely parts,
> Vow to beat henceforth side by side.
>
> The world to them was stern and drear;
> Their lot was but to weep and moan.
> Ah, let them keep their faith sincere,
> For neither could subsist alone!

Here was the nub. "Dover Beach" grew directly from and repeated the same emotion, but no doubt generalized and enlarged this emotion, sweeping into one intense and far-reaching conviction of insecurity not only Arnold's personal fortunes in love, but the social and religious faith of the world he lived in. That much could be said for the traditional interpretation.

Of course, as Mr. Trilling did not fail to mention, anguished love affairs, harassed by mysterious inner incompatibilities, formed a well-established literary convention. But the fundamental sense of insecurity in "Dover Beach" was too genuine, too often repeated in other works, to be written off altogether to that account. The same sense of insecurity, the same need for some rock of protection, cried out again and again, not merely in Arnold's love poems but in his elegies, reflective pieces, and fragments of epic as well. Whenever Arnold produced a genuine and striking burst of poetry, with the stamp of true self-expression on it, he seemed always to be in the dumps. Everywhere dejection, confusion, weakness, contention of soul. No adequate cause could be found in the events of Arnold's life for such an acute sense of incertitude; it must have been of psychic origin. Only in one line of effort this fundamental insecurity did not hamper, sadden, or depress him, and that was in the free play of his intelligence as a critic of letters and society. Even there, if it did not hamper his efforts, it directed them. Arnold valiantly tried to erect a barrier of culture against the chaos and squalor of society, against the contentiousness of men. What was this barrier but an elaborate protective device?

The origin of the psychic pattern that expressed itself in Arnold's poems could probably never be discovered. No doubt the influence that Arnold's father exercised over his emotions and his thinking, even though Arnold rebelled to the extent at least of casting off his father's religious beliefs, was of great importance. But much more would have to be known to give a definite clue—more than ever could be known. Arnold was secure from any attempt to spy out the heart of his mystery. But if criticism could not discover the cause, it could assess the result, and could do so (thought Rudolph Mole) with greater understanding by an attempt, with up-to-date psychological aid, to delve a little deeper into the essential traits that manifested themselves in that result.

5

In 1917 Reuben Hale, a young instructor in a Western college, had lost his job and done time in the penitentiary for speaking against conscription and for organizing pacifist demonstrations. In the twenties he had lost two more academic posts for his sympathies with Soviet Russia and his inability to forget his Marxist principles while teaching literature. His contentious, eager, lovable, exasperating temperament tried the patience of one college administration after another. As he advanced into middle age, and his growing family suffered repeated upheavals, his friends began to fear that his robust quarrels with established order would leave him a penniless outcast at fifty. Then he was invited to take a flattering post at a girls' college known for its liberality of views. The connection proved surprisingly durable; in fact it became Professor Hale's turn to be apprehensive. He began to be morally alarmed at his own security, to find that the bourgeois system which he had attacked so valiantly had somehow outwitted him and betrayed him into allegiance. When the C.I.O. made its initial drive and seemed to be carrying everything before it, he did his best to unseat himself again by rushing joyfully to the nearest picket lines and getting himself photographed by an alert press. Even this expedient failed, and he reconciled himself, not without wonder, to apparent academic permanence.

On winter afternoons his voice could be heard booming out through the closed door of his study to girls who came to consult him on all manner of subjects, from the merits of Plekhanov as a Marxist critic to their own most personal dilemmas. They called him Ben; he called them Smith, Jones, and Robinson. He never relaxed his cheerful bombardment of the milieu into which they were born, and of the larger social structure which made bourgeois wealth, bourgeois art, morals, and religion possible. But when a sophomore found herself pregnant it was to Professor Hale that she came for advice. Should she have an abortion or go through with it and heroically bear the social stigma? And it was Professor Hale who kept the affair from the Dean's office and the newspapers, sought out the boy, persuaded the young couple that they were desperately in love with each other, and that pending the revolution a respectable marriage would be the most prudent course, not to say the happiest.

James Joyce remarks of one of his characters that she dealt with moral problems as a cleaver deals with meat. Professor Hale's critical methods were comparably simple and direct. Literature, like the other arts, is in form and substance a product of society, and reflects the structure of society. The structure of society is a class structure: it is conditioned by the mode of production of goods, and by the legal conventions of ownership and control by which the ruling class keeps itself in power and endows itself with the necessary freedom to exploit men and materials for profit. A healthy literature, in a society so constituted, can exist only if writers perceive the essential economic problem and ally themselves firmly with the working class.

Anyone could see the trouble with Arnold. His intelligence revealed to him the chaos that disrupted the society about him; the selfishness and brutality of the ruling class; the ugliness of the world which the industrial revolution had created, and which imperialism and "liberalism" were extending. Arnold was at his best in his critical satire of this world and of the ignorance of those who governed it. But his intelligence far outran his will, and his defect of will finally blinded his intelligence. He was too much a child of his class to disown it and fight his way to a workable remedy for social injustice. He caught a true vision of himself and of his times as standing between "two worlds, one dead, one powerless to be born." But he had not courage or stomach enough to lend his own powers to the birth struggle. Had he thrown in his sympathies unreservedly with the working class, and labored for the inescapable revolution, "Dover Beach" would not have ended in pessimism and confusion. It would have ended in a cheerful, strenuous, and hopeful call to action. But Arnold could not divorce himself from the world of polite letters, of education, of culture, into which he had been born. He did his best to purify them, to make them into an instrument for the reform of society. But instinctively he knew that "culture" as he understood the term was not a social force in the world around him. Instinctively he knew that what he loved was doomed to defeat. And so "Dover Beach" ended in a futile plea for protection against the hideousness of the darkling plain and the confused alarms of struggle and flight.

Professor Chartly's envelope brought Reuben Hale his best opportunity since the first C.I.O. picket lines to vindicate his critical and social principles. He plunged into his answer with complete zest.

6

When Peter Lee Prampton agreed to act as moderator in Professor Chartly's experiment he congratulated himself that this would be his last great academic chore. He had enjoyed his career of scholarship and teaching, no man ever more keenly. But now it was drawing to an end. He was loaded with honors from two continents. The universities of Germany, France, and Britain had first laid their formative hands on his learning and cultivation, then given their most coveted recognition to its fruits. But the honor and the glory seemed a little vague on the June morning when the expressman brought into his library the sizable package of papers which Professor Chartly had boxed and shipped to him. He had kept all his life a certain simplicity of heart. At seventy-four he could still tote a pack with an easy endurance that humiliated men of forty. Now he found himself giving in more and more completely to a lust for trout. Half a century of hastily snatched vacations in Cape Breton or the Scottish Highlands had never allowed him really to fill up that hollow craving to find a wild stream and fish it which would sometimes rise in his throat even in the midst of a lecture.

Well, there would be time left before he died. And meanwhile here was this business of "Dover Beach." Matthew Arnold during one of his American lecture tours had been entertained by neighbors of the Pramptons. Peter Lee Prampton's father had dined with the great man, and had repeated his conversation and imitated his accent at the family table. Peter himself, as a boy of nineteen or so, had gone to hear Arnold lecture. That, he thought with a smile, was probably a good deal more than could be said for any of these poor hacks who had taken Professor Chartly's bait.

At the thought of Arnold he could still hear the carriage wheels grate on the pebbly road as he had driven, fifty odd years ago, to the lecture in town, the prospective Mrs. Prampton beside him. His fishing rod lay under the seat. He chuckled out loud as he remembered how a pound-and-a-half trout had jumped in the pool under the clattering planks of the bridge, and how he had pulled up the horse, jumped out, and tried a cast while Miss Osgood sat scolding in the carriage and shivering in the autumn air. They had been just a little late reaching the lecture, but the trout, wrapped in damp leaves, lay safely beside the rod.

It was queer that "Dover Beach" had not come more recently into his mind. Now that he turned his thoughts in that direction the poem was there in its entirety, waiting to be put on again like a coat that one has worn many times with pleasure and accidentally neglected for a while.

The Sea of Faith
Was once, too, at the full . . .

How those old Victorian battles had raged about the Prampton table when he was a boy! How the names of Arnold, Huxley, Darwin, Carlyle, Morris, Ruskin had been pelted back and forth by the excited disputants! *Literature and Dogma, God and the Bible, Culture and Anarchy.* The familiar titles brought an odd image into his mind: the tall figure of his father stretching up to turn on the gas lamps in the evening as the family sat down to dinner; the terrific pop of the pilot light as it exploded into a net of white flame, shaped like a little beehive; the buzz and whine of a jet turned up too high.

> Ah, love, let us be true
> To one another! for the world, which seems
> To lie before us like a land of dreams,
> So various, so beautiful, so new,
> Hath really neither joy, nor love, nor light,
> Nor certitude, nor peace, nor help for pain . . .

Peter Lee Prampton shivered in the warmth of his sunny library, shivered with that flash of perception into the past which sometimes enables a man to see how all that has happened in his life, for good or ill, turned on the narrowest edge of chance. He lived again in the world of dreams that his own youth had spread before him, a world truly various, beautiful, and new; full of promise, adventure, and liberty of choice, based on the opportunities which his father's wealth provided, and holding out the prospect of a smooth advance into a distinguished career. Then, within six months, a lavish demonstration that the world has neither certitude, nor peace, nor help for pain: his mother's death by cancer, his father's financial overthrow and suicide, the ruin of his own smooth hopes and the prospect instead of a long, hampered, and obscure fight toward his perhaps impossible ambition. He lived again through the night hours when he had tramped out with himself the youthful question whether he could hold Miss Osgood to her promise in the face of such reversals. And he did not forget how she took his long-sleepless face between her hands, kissed him, and smiled away his anxiety with unsteady lips. Surely everyone discovers at some time or other that the world is not a place of certitude; surely everyone cries out to some other human being for the fidelity which alone can make it so. What more could be asked of a poet than to take so profound and universal an experience and turn it into lines that could still speak long after he and his age were dead?

The best of it was that no one could miss the human feeling, the cry from the heart, in "Dover Beach"; it spoke so clearly and eloquently, in a language everyone could understand, in a form classically pure and simple. Or did it? Who could tell what any job-lot of academicians might be trusted to see or fail to see? And this assortment in Chartly's package might be a queer kettle of fish! Peter Lee Prampton had lived through the *Yellow Book* days of Art for Art's sake; he had read the muckrakers, and watched the rise of the Marxists and the Freudians. Could "Dover Beach" be condemned as unsympathetic with labor? Could a neurosis or a complex be discovered in it? His heart sank at the sharp sudden conviction that indeed these and worse discoveries about the poem might be seriously advanced. Well, he had always tried to go on the principle that every school of criticism should be free to exercise any sincere claim on men's interest and attention which it could win for itself. When he actually applied himself to the contents of Professor Chartly's bale he would be as charitable as he could, as receptive to light from any quarter as he could bring himself to be.

But the task could wait. He felt the need of a period of adjustment before he could approach it with reasonable equanimity. And in the meanwhile he could indulge himself in some long-needed editorial work on his dry-fly book.

John Frederick Nims (born 1914)
Love Poem

My clumsiest dear, whose hands shipwreck vases,
At whose quick touch all glasses chip and ring,
Whose palms are bulls in china, burs in linen,
And have no cunning with any soft thing

Except all ill-at-ease fidgeting people: 5
The refugee uncertain at the door
You make at home; deftly you steady
The drunk clambering on his undulant floor.

Unpredictable dear, the taxi drivers' terror,
Shrinking from far headlights pale as a dime   10
Yet leaping before red apoplectic streetcars—
Misfit in any space. And never on time.

A wrench in clocks and the solar system. Only
With words and people and love you move at ease.
In traffic of wit expertly manoeuvre   15
And keep us, all devotion, at your knees.

Forgetting your coffee spreading on our flannel,
Your lipstick grinning on our coat,
So gayly in love's unbreakable heaven
Our souls on glory of spilt bourbon float.   20

Be with me, darling, early and late. Smash glasses—
I will study wry music for your sake.
For should your hands drop white and empty
All the toys of the world would break.

Tillie Olsen (born 1913)
I Stand Here Ironing

I stand here ironing, and what you asked me moves tormented back and forth with the iron.

"I wish you would manage the time to come in and talk with me about your daughter. I'm sure you can help me understand her. She's a youngster who needs help and whom I'm deeply interested in helping."

"Who needs help.". . . Even if I came, what good would it do? You think because I am her mother I have a key, or that in some way you could use me as a key? She has lived for nineteen years. There is all that life that has happened outside of me, beyond me.

And when is there time to remember, to sift, to weigh, to estimate, to total? I will start and there will be an interruption and I will have to gather it all together again. Or I will become engulfed with all I did or did not do, with what should have been and what cannot be helped.

She was a beautiful baby. The first and only one of our five that was beautiful at birth. You do not guess how new and uneasy her tenancy in her now-loveliness. You did not know her all those years she was thought homely, or see her poring over her baby pictures, making me tell her over and over how beautiful she had been—and would be, I would tell her—and was now, to the seeing eye. But the seeing eyes were few or nonexistent. Including mine.

I nursed her. They feel that's important nowadays. I nursed all the children, but with her, with all the fierce rigidity of first motherhood, I did like the books then said. Though her cries battered me to trembling and my breasts ached with swollenness, I waited till the clock decreed.

Why do I put that first? I do not even know if it matters, or if it explains anything.

She was a beautiful baby. She blew shining bubbles of sound. She loved motion, loved light, loved color and music and textures. She would lie on the floor in her blue overalls patting the surface so hard in ecstasy her hands and feet would blur. She was a miracle to me, but when she was eight months old I had to leave her daytimes with the woman downstairs to whom she was no miracle at all, for I worked or looked for work and for Emily's father, who "could no longer endure" (he wrote in his good-bye note) "sharing want with us."

I was nineteen. It was the pre-relief, pre-WPA world of the depression. I would start running as soon as I got off the streetcar, running up the stairs, the place smelling sour, and awake or asleep to startle awake, when she saw me she would break into a clogged weeping that could not be comforted, a weeping I can hear yet.

After a while I found a job hashing at night so I could be with her days, and it was better. But it came to where I had to bring her to his family and leave her.

It took a long time to raise the money for her fare back. Then she got chicken pox and I had to wait longer. When she finally came, I hardly knew her, walking quick and nervous like her father, looking like her father, thin, and dressed in a shoddy red that yellowed her skin and glared at the pockmarks. All the baby loveliness gone.

She was two. Old enough for nursery school they said, and I did not know then what I know now—the fatigue of the long day, and the lacerations of group life in the kinds of nurseries that are only parking places for children.

Except that it would have made no difference if I had known. It was the only place there was. It was the only way we could be together, the only way I could hold a job.

And even without knowing, I knew. I knew the teacher that was evil because all these years it has curdled into my memory, the little boy hunched in the corner, her rasp, "why aren't you outside, because Alvin hits you? that's no reason, go out, scaredy." I knew Emily hated it even if she did not clutch and implore "don't go Mommy" like the other children, mornings.

She always had a reason why we should stay home. Momma, you look sick, Momma. I feel sick. Momma, the teachers aren't there today, they're sick. Momma, we can't go, there was a fire there last night. Momma, it's a holiday today, no school, they told me.

But never a direct protest, never rebellion. I think of our others in their three-, four-year-oldness—the explosions, the tempers, the denunciations, the demands—and I feel suddenly ill. I put the iron down. What in me demanded that goodness in her? And what was the cost, the cost to her of such goodness?

The old man living in the back once said in his gentle way: "You should smile at Emily more when you look at her." What *was* in my face when I looked at her? I loved her. There were all the acts of love.

It was only with the others I remembered what he said, and it was the face of joy, and not of care or tightness or worry I turned to them—too late for Emily. She does not smile easily, let alone almost always as her brothers and sisters do. Her face is closed and sombre, but when she wants, how fluid. You must have seen it in her pantomimes, you spoke of her rare gift for comedy on the stage that rouses a laughter out of the audience so dear they applaud and applaud and do not want to let her go.

Where does it come from, that comedy? There was none of it in her when she came back to me that second time, after I had had to send her away again. She had a new daddy now to learn to love, and I think perhaps it was a better time.

Except when we left her alone nights, telling ourselves she was old enough.

"Can't you go some other time, Mommy, like tomorrow?" she would ask. "Will it be just a little while you'll be gone? Do you promise?"

The time we came back, the front door open, the clock on the floor in the hall. She rigid awake. "It wasn't just a little while. I didn't cry. Three times I called you, just three times, and then I ran downstairs to open the door so you could come faster. The clock talked loud. I threw it away, it scared me what it talked."

She said the clock talked loud again that night I went to the hospital to have Susan. She was delirious with the fever that comes before red measles, but she was fully conscious all the week I was gone and the week after we were home when she could not come near the new baby or me.

She did not get well. She stayed skeleton thin, not wanting to eat, and night after night she had nightmares. She would call for me, and I would rouse from exhaustion to sleepily call back: "You're all right, darling, go to sleep, it's just a dream," and if she still called, in a sterner voice, "now go to sleep, Emily, there's nothing to hurt you." Twice, only twice, when I had to get up for Susan anyhow, I went in to sit with her.

Now when it is too late (as if she would let me hold and comfort her like I do the others) I get up and go to her at once at her moan or restless stirring. "Are you awake, Emily? Can I get you something?" And the answer is always the same: "No, I'm all right, go back to sleep, Mother."

They persuaded me at the clinic to send her away to a convalescent home in the country where "she can have the kind of food and care you can't manage for her, and you'll be free to concentrate on the new baby." They still send children to that place. I see pictures on the society page of sleek young women planning affairs to raise money for it, or dancing at the affairs, or decorating Easter eggs or filling Christmas stockings for the children.

They never have a picture of the children so I do not know if the girls still wear those gigantic red bows and the ravaged looks on the every other Sunday when parents can come to visit "unless otherwise notified"—as we were notified the first six weeks.

Oh it is a handsome place, green lawns and tall trees and fluted flower beds. High up on the balconies of each cottage the children stand, the girls in their red bows and white dresses, the boys in white suits and giant red ties. The parents stand below shrieking up to be heard and the children shriek down to be heard, and between them the invisible wall "Not To Be Contaminated by Parental Germs or Physical Affection."

There was a tiny girl who always stood hand in hand with Emily. Her parents never came. One visit she was gone. "They moved her to Rose Cottage" Emily shouted in explanation. "They don't like you to love anybody here."

She wrote once a week, the labored writing of a seven-year-old. "I am fine. How is the baby. If I write my leter nicly I will have a star. Love." There never was a star. We wrote every other day, letters she could never hold or keep but only hear read—once. "We simply do not have room for children to keep any personal possessions," they patiently explained when we pieced one Sunday's shrieking together to plead how much it would mean to Emily, who loved so to keep things, to be allowed to keep her letters and cards.

Each visit she looked frailer. "She isn't eating," they told us.

(They had runny eggs for breakfast or mush with lumps, Emily said later, I'd hold it in my mouth and not swallow. Nothing ever tasted good, just when they had chicken.)

It took us eight months to get her released home, and only the fact that she gained back so little of her seven lost pounds convinced the social worker.

I used to try to hold and love her after she came back, but her body would stay stiff, and after a while she'd push away. She ate little. Food sickened her, and I think much of life too. Oh she had physical lightness and brightness, twinkling by on skates, bouncing like a ball up and down up and down over the jump rope, skimming over the hill; but these were momentary.

She fretted about her appearance, thin and dark and foreign-looking at a time when every little girl was supposed to look or thought she should look a chubby blonde replica of Shirley Temple. The doorbell sometimes rang for her, but no one seemed to come and play in the house or be a best friend. Maybe because we moved so much.

There was a boy she loved painfully through two school semesters. Months later she told me how she had taken pennies from my purse to buy him candy. "Licorice was his favorite and I brought him some every day, but he still liked Jennifer better'n me. Why, Mommy?" The kind of question for which there is no answer.

School was a worry to her. She was not glib or quick in a world where glibness and quickness were easily confused with ability to learn. To her overworked and exasperated teachers she was an overconscientious "slow learner" who kept trying to catch up and was absent entirely too often.

I let her be absent, though sometimes the illness was imaginary. How different from my now-strictness about attendance with the others. I wasn't working. We had a new baby, I was home anyhow. Sometimes, after Susan grew old enough, I would keep her home from school, too, to have them all together.

Mostly Emily had asthma, and her breathing, harsh and labored, would fill the house with a curiously tranquil sound. I would bring the two old dresser mirrors and her boxes of collections to her bed. She would select beads and single earrings, bottle tops and shells, dried flowers and pebbles, old postcards and scraps, all sorts of oddments; then she and Susan would play Kingdom, setting up landscapes and furniture, peopling them with action.

Those were the only times of peaceful companionship between her and Susan. I have edged away from it, that poisonous feeling between them, that terrible balancing of hurts and needs I had to do between the two, and did so badly, those earlier years.

Oh there are conflicts between the others too, each one human, needing, demanding, hurting, taking—but only between Emily and Susan, no, Emily toward Susan that corroding resentment. It seems so obvious on the surface, yet it is not obvious. Susan, the second child, Susan, golden- and curly-haired and chubby, quick and articulate and assured, everything in appearance and manner Emily was not; Susan, not able to resist Emily's precious things, losing or sometimes clumsily breaking them; Susan telling jokes and riddles to company for applause while Emily sat silent (to say to me later: that was *my* riddle, Mother, I told it to Susan); Susan, who for all the five years' difference in age was just a year behind Emily in developing physically.

I am glad for that slow physical development that widened the difference between her and her contemporaries, though she suffered over it. She was too vulnerable for that terrible world of youthful competition, of preening and parading, of constant measuring of yourself against every other, of envy, "If I had that copper hair," "If I had that skin. . . ." She tormented herself enough about not looking like the others, there was enough of the unsureness, the having to be conscious of words before you speak, the constant caring—what are they thinking of me? without having it all magnified by the merciless physical drives.

Ronnie is calling. He is wet and I change him. It is rare there is such a cry now. That time of motherhood is almost behind me when the ear is not one's own but must always be racked and listening for the child cry, the child call. We sit for a while and I hold him, looking out over the city spread in charcoal with its soft aisles of light. "*Shoogily*," he breathes and curls closer. I carry him back to bed, asleep. *Shoogily*. A funny word, a family word, inherited from Emily, invented by her to say: *comfort*.

In this and other ways she leaves her seal, I say aloud. And startle at my saying it. What do I mean? What did I start to gather together, to try and make coherent? I was at the terrible, growing years. War years. I do not remember them well. I was working, there were four smaller ones now, there was not time for her. She had to help be a mother, and housekeeper, and shopper. She had to set her seal. Mornings of crisis and near hysteria trying to get lunches packed, hair combed, coats and shoes found, everyone to school or Child Care on time, the baby ready for transportation. And always the paper scribbled on by a smaller one, the book looked at by Susan then mislaid, the homework not done. Running out to that huge school where she was one, she was lost, she was a drop; suffering over the unpreparedness, stammering and unsure in her classes.

There was so little time left at night after the kids were bedded down. She would struggle over books, always eating (it was in those years she developed her enormous appetite that is legendary in our family) and I would be ironing, or preparing food for the next day, or writing V-mail to Bill, or tending the baby. Sometimes, to make me laugh, or out of her despair, she would imitate happenings or types at school.

I think I said once: "Why don't you do something like this in the school amateur show?" One morning she phoned me at work, hardly understandable through the weeping: "Mother, I did it. I won, I won; they gave me first prize; they clapped and clapped and wouldn't let me go."

Now suddenly she was Somebody, and as imprisoned in her difference as she had been in anonymity.

She began to be asked to perform at other high schools, even in colleges, then at city and statewide affairs. The first one we went to, I only recognized her that first moment when thin, shy, she almost drowned herself into the curtains. Then: Was this Emily? The control, the command, the convulsing and deadly clowning, the spell, then the roaring, stamping audience, unwilling to let this rare and precious laughter out of their lives.

Afterwards: You ought to do something about her with a gift like that—but without money or knowing how, what does one do? We have left it all to her, and the gift has as often eddied inside, clogged and clotted, as been used and growing.

She is coming. She runs up the stairs two at a time with her light graceful step, and I know she is happy tonight. Whatever it was that occasioned your call did not happen today.

"Aren't you ever going to finish the ironing, Mother? Whistler painted his mother in a rocker. I'd have to paint mine standing over an ironing board." This is one of her communicative nights and she tells me everything and nothing as she fixes herself a plate of food out of the icebox.

She is so lovely. Why did you want me to come in at all? Why were you concerned? She will find her way.

She starts up the stairs to bed. "Don't get me up with the rest in the morning." "But I thought you were having midterms." "Oh, those," she comes back in, kisses me, and says quite lightly, "in a couple of years when we'll all be atom-dead they won't matter a bit."

She has said it before. She *believes* it. But because I have been dredging the past, and all that compounds a human being is so heavy and meaningful in me, I cannot endure it tonight.

I will never total it all. I will never come in to say: She was a child seldom smiled at. Her father left me before she was a year old. I had to work her first six years when there was work, or I sent her home and to his relatives. There were years she had care she hated. She was dark and thin and foreign-looking in a world where the prestige went to blondeness and curly hair and dimples, she was slow where glibness was prized. She was a child of anxious, not proud, love. We were poor and could not afford for her the soil of easy growth. I was a young mother, I was a distracted mother. There were the other children pushing up, demanding. Her younger sister seemed all that she was not. There were years she did not let me touch her. She kept too much in herself, her life has been such she had to keep too much in herself. My wisdom came too late. She has much to her and probably little will come of it. She is a child of her age, of depression, of war, of fear.

Let her be. So all that is in her will not bloom—but in how many does it? There is still enough left to live by. Only help her to know—help make it so there is cause for her to know—that she is more than this dress on the ironing board, helpless before the iron.

Sir Walter Ralegh (1552–1618)
The Nymph's Reply to the Shepherd

If all the world and love were young,
And truth in every shepherd's tongue,
These pretty pleasures might me move
To live with thee and be thy love.

Time drives the flocks from field to fold   5
When rivers rage and rocks grow cold,
And Philomel becometh dumb;
The rest complains of cares to come.

The flowers do fade, and wanton fields
To wayward winter reckoning yields;   10
A honey tongue, a heart of gall,
Is fancy's spring, but sorrow's fall.

Thy gowns, thy shoes, thy beds of roses,
Thy cap, thy kirtle, and thy posies
Soon break, soon wither, soon forgotten—   15
In folly ripe, in reason rotten.

Thy belt of straw and ivy buds,
Thy coral clasps and amber studs,
All these in me no means can move
To come to thee and be thy love.   20

But could youth last and love still breed,
Had joys no date nor age no need,
Then these delights my mind might move
To live with thee and be thy love.

Adrienne Rich (born 1929)
Living in Sin

She had thought the studio would keep itself;
no dust upon the furniture of love.
Half heresy, to wish the taps less vocal,

the panes relieved of grime. A plate of pears,
a piano with a Persian shawl, a cat   5
stalking the picturesque amusing mouse
had risen at his urging.
Not that at five each separate stair would writhe
under the milkman's tramp; that morning light
so coldly would delineate the scraps   10
of last night's cheese and three sepulchral bottles;
that on the kitchen shelf among the saucers
a pair of beetle-eyes would fix her own—
Envoy from some village in the moldings . . .
Meanwhile, he, with a yawn,   15
sounded a dozen notes upon the keyboard,
declared it out of tune, shrugged at the mirror,
rubbed at his beard, went out for cigarettes;
while she, jeered by the minor demons,
pulled back the sheets and made the bed and found   20
a towel to dust the table-top,
and let the coffee-pot boil over on the stove.
By evening she was back in love again,
though not so wholly but throughout the night
she woke sometimes to feel the daylight coming   25
like a relentless milkman up the stairs.

Edwin Arlington Robinson (1869–1935)
Richard Cory

Whenever Richard Cory went down town,
We people on the pavement looked at him:
He was a gentleman from sole to crown,
Clean favored, and imperially slim.

And he was always quietly arrayed,   5
And he was always human when he talked;
But still he fluttered pulses when he said,
"Good-morning," and he glittered when he walked.

And he was rich—yes, richer than a king—
And admirably schooled in every grace: 10
In fine, we thought that he was everything
To make us wish that we were in his place.

So on we worked, and waited for the light,
And went without the meat, and cursed the bread;
And Richard Cory, one calm summer night,   · 15
Went home and put a bullet through his head.

Muriel Rukeyser (born 1913)
Effort at Speech Between Two People

Speak to me. Take my hand. What are you now?
I will tell you all. I will conceal nothing.
When I was three, a little child read a story about a rabbit
who died, in the story, and I crawled under a chair:
a pink rabbit: it was my birthday, and a candle   5
burnt a sore spot on my finger, and I was told to be happy.

Oh, grow to know me. I am not happy. I will be open:
Now I am thinking of white sails against a sky like music,
like glad horns blowing, and birds tilting, and an arm about me.
There was one I loved, who wanted to live, sailing.   10

Speak to me. Take my hand. What are you now?
When I was nine, I was fruitily sentimental,
fluid: and my widowed aunt played Chopin,
and I bent my head on the painted woodwork, and wept.
I want now to be close to you. I would   15
link the minutes of my days close, somehow, to your days.

I am not happy. I will be open.
I have liked lamps in evening corners, and quiet poems.
There has been fear in my life. Sometimes I speculate
On what a tragedy his life was, really.   20

Take my hand. Fist my mind in your hand. What are you now?
When I was fourteen, I had dreams of suicide,

and I stood at a steep window, at sunset, hoping toward death:
if the light had not melted clouds and plains to beauty,
if light had not transformed that day, I would have leapt,   25
I am unhappy. I am lonely. Speak to me.
I will be open. I think he never loved me:
he loved the bright beaches, the little lips of foam
that ride small waves, he loved the veer of gulls:
he said with a gay mouth: I love you. Grow to know me.   30

What are you now? If we could touch one another,
if these our separate entities could come to grips,
clenched like a Chinese puzzle . . . yesterday
I stood in a crowded street that was live with people,
and no one spoke a word, and the morning shone.   35
Everyone silent, moving. . . . . Take my hand. Speak to me.

William Shakespeare (1564–1616)

Hamlet

[DRAMATIS PERSONAE

CLAUDIUS *King of Denmark*

HAMLET *son to the late, and nephew to the present, King*

POLONIUS *Lord Chamberlain*

HORATIO *friend to Hamlet*

LAERTES *son to Polonius*

VOLTEMAND
CORNELIUS
ROSENCRANTZ   } *courtiers*
GUILDENSTERN
OSRIC
A GENTLEMAN

A PRIEST

MARCELLUS } *officers*
BARNARDO

FRANCISCO *a soldier*

REYNALDO *servant to Polonius*

PLAYERS

TWO CLOWNS *gravediggers*

FORTINBRAS *Prince of Norway*

A NORWEGIAN CAPTAIN

ENGLISH AMBASSADORS

GERTRUDE *Queen of Denmark, mother to Hamlet*

OPHELIA *daughter to Polonius*

GHOST OF HAMLET'S FATHER

LORDS, LADIES, OFFICERS,
   SOLDIERS, SAILORS,
   MESSENGERS, ATTENDANTS

Scene. Elsinore]

[ACT I

Scene I. A guard platform of the castle.]

Enter BARNARDO *and* FRANCISCO, *two sentinels.*

BARNARDO	Who's there?	
FRANCISCO	Nay, answer me. Stand and unfold°* yourself.	
BARNARDO	Long live the King!°	
FRANCISCO	Barnardo?	
BARNARDO	He.	5
FRANCISCO	You come most carefully upon your hour.	
BARNARDO	'Tis now struck twelve. Get thee to bed, Francisco.	
FRANCISCO	For this relief much thanks. 'Tis bitter cold,	

And I am sick at heart.

BARNARDO   Have you had quiet guard?

FRANCISCO   Not a mouse stirring.   10

BARNARDO   Well, good night.

If you do meet Horatio and Marcellus,
The rivals° of my watch, bid them make haste.

Enter HORATIO *and* MARCELLUS.

FRANCISCO   I think I hear them. Stand, ho! Who is there?

HORATIO   Friends to this ground.

MARCELLUS   And liegemen to the Dane.°   15

FRANCISCO   Give you° good night.

MARCELLUS   O, farewell, honest soldier.

Who hath relieved you?

FRANCISCO   Barnardo hath my place.

Give you good night.   *Exit* FRANCISCO.

MARCELLUS   Holla, Barnardo!

BARNARDO   Say——

What, is Horatio there?

HORATIO   A piece of him.

BARNARDO   Welcome, Horatio. Welcome, good Marcellus.   20

MARCELLUS   What, has this thing appeared again tonight?

---

* The notes are Edward Hubler's for the Signet edition of *Hamlet*. Superscript numbers in notes refer to line number in which term occurs.   *I.i.* ² **unfold** disclose   ³ **Long live the King** (perhaps a password, perhaps a greeting)   ¹³ **rivals** partners   ¹⁵ **liegemen to the Dane** loyal subjects to the King of Denmark   ¹⁶ **Give you** God give you

BARNARDO   I have seen nothing.
MARCELLUS   Horatio says 'tis but our fantasy,
   And will not let belief take hold of him
   Touching this dreaded sight twice seen of us;   25
   Therefore I have entreated him along
   With us to watch the minutes of this night,
   That, if again this apparition come,
   He may approve° our eyes and speak to it.
HORATIO   Tush, tush, 'twill not appear.
BARNARDO   Sit down awhile,   30
   And let us once again assail your ears,
   That are so fortified against out story,
   What we have two nights seen.
HORATIO   Well, sit we down,
   And let us hear Barnardo speak of this.
BARNARDO   Last night of all,   35
   When yond same star that's westward from the pole°
   Had made his course t' illume that part of heaven
   Where now it burns, Marcellus and myself,
   The bell then beating one——

   Enter GHOST.

MARCELLUS   Peace, break thee off. Look where it comes again.   40
BARNARDO   In the same figure like the king that's dead.
MARCELLUS   Thou art a scholar; speak to it, Horatio.
BARNARDO   Looks 'a not like the king? Mark it, Horatio.
HORATIO   Most like: it harrows me with fear and wonder.
BARNARDO   It would be spoke to.
MARCELLUS   Speak to it, Horatio.   45
HORATIO   What art thou that usurp'st this time of night,
   Together with that fair and warlike form
   In which the majesty of buried Denmark°
   Did sometimes march? By heaven I charge thee, speak.
MARCELLUS   It is offended.
BARNARDO   See, it stalks away.   50
HORATIO   Stay! Speak, speak. I charge thee, speak.   *Exit* GHOST.
MARCELLUS   'Tis gone and will not answer.
BARNARDO   How now, Horatio? You tremble and look pale.
   Is not this something more than fantasy?
   What think you on't?   55

---

²⁹ **approve** confirm   ³⁶ **pole** pole star   ⁴⁸ **buried Denmark** the buried King of Denmark

HORATIO   Before my God, I might not this believe
Without the sensible and true avouch°
Of mine own eyes.
MARCELLUS   Is it not like the King?
HORATIO   As thou art to thyself.
Such was the very armor he had on   60
When he the ambitious Norway° combated:
So frowned he once, when, in an angry parle,°
He smote the sledded Polacks° on the ice.
'Tis strange.
MARCELLUS   Thus twice before, and jump° at this dead hour,   65
With martial stalk hath he gone by our watch.
HORATIO   In what particular thought to work I know not;
But, in the gross and scope° of my opinion,
This bodes some strange eruption to our state.
MARCELLUS   Good now, sit down, and tell me he that knows,   70
Why this same strict and most observant watch
So nightly toils the subject° of the land,
And why such daily cast of brazen cannon
And foreign mart° for implements of war,
Why such impress° of shipwrights, whose sore task   75
Does not divide the Sunday from the week,
What might be toward° that this sweaty haste
Doth make the night joint-laborer with the day?
Who is't that can inform me?
HORATIO   That can I.
At least the whisper goes so: our last king,   80
Whose image even but now appeared to us,
Was, as you know, by Fortinbras of Norway,
Thereto pricked on by a most emulate pride,
Dared to the combat; in which our valiant Hamlet
(For so this side of our known world esteemed him)   85
Did slay this Fortinbras, who, by a sealed compact
Well ratified by law and heraldry,°
Did forfeit, with his life, all those his lands
Which he stood seized° of, to the conqueror;
Against the which a moiety competent°   90

---

⁵⁷ **sensible and true avouch** sensory and true proof   ⁶¹ **Norway** King of Norway   ⁶² **parle** parley
⁶³ **sledded Polacks** Poles in sledges   ⁶⁵ **jump** just   ⁶⁸ **gross and scope** general drift   ⁷² **toils the
subject** makes the subjects toil   ⁷⁴ **mart** trading   ⁷⁵ **impress** forced service   ⁷⁷ **toward** in preparation   ⁸⁷ **law and heraldry** heraldic law (governing the combat)   ⁸⁹ **seized** possessed   ⁹⁰ **moiety
competent** equal portion

Was gagèd° by our King, which had returned
To the inheritance of Fortinbras,
Had he been vanquisher, as, by the same comart°
And carriage of the article designed,°
His fell to Hamlet. Now, sir, young Fortinbras,   95
Of unimprovèd° mettle hot and full,
Hath in the skirts° of Norway here and there
Sharked up° a list of lawless resolutes,°
For food and diet, to some enterprise
That hath a stomach in't;° which is no other,   100
As it doth well appear unto our state,
But to recover of us by strong hand
And terms compulsatory, those forsaid lands
So by his father lost; and this, I take it,
Is the main motive of our preparations,   105
The source of this our watch, and the chief head°
Of this posthaste and romage° in the land.
BARNARDO   I think it be no other but e'en so;
Well may it sort° that this portentous figure
Comes armèd through our watch so like the King   110
That was and is the question of these wars.
HORATIO   A mote it is to trouble the mind's eye:
In the most high and palmy state of Rome,
A little ere the mightiest Julius fell,
The graves stood tenantless, and the sheeted dead   115
Did squeak and gibber in the Roman streets;°
As stars with trains of fire and dews of blood,
Disasters° in the sun; and the moist star,°
Upon whose influence Neptune's empire stands,
Was sick almost to doomsday with eclipse.   120
And even the like precurse° of feared events,
As harbingers° preceding still° the fates
And prologue to the omen° coming on,

---

91 **gagèd** engaged, pledged   93 **comart** agreement   94 **carriage of the article designed** import of the agreement drawn up   96 **unimprovèd** untried   97 **skirts** borders   98 **Sharked up** collected indiscriminately (as a shark gulps its prey)   98 **resolutes** desperadoes   100 **hath a stomach in't** i.e., requires courage   106 **head** fountainhead, origin   107 **romage** bustle   109 **sort** befit   116 **Did squeak . . . Roman streets** (the break in the sense which follows this line suggests that a line has dropped out)   118 **Disasters** threatening signs   118 **moist star** moon   121 **precurse** precursor, foreshadowing   122 **harbingers** forerunners   122 **still** always   123 **omen** calamity

Have heaven and earth together demonstrated
Unto our climatures° and countrymen.   125

Enter GHOST.

But soft, behold, lo where it comes again!
I'll cross it,° though it blast me. —Stay, illusion.

It spreads his° arms.

If thou hast any sound or use of voice,
Speak to me.
If there be any good thing to be done   130
That may to thee do ease and grace to me,
Speak to me.
If thou art privy to thy country's fate,
Which happily° foreknowing may avoid,
O, speak!   135
Or if thou hast uphoarded in thy life
Extorted° treasure in the womb of earth,
For which, they say, you spirits oft walk in death,

The cock crows.

Speak of it. Stay and speak. Stop it, Marcellus.
MARCELLUS   Shall I strike at it with my partisan°?   140
HORATIO   Do, if it will not stand.
BARNARDO   'Tis here.
HORATIO   'Tis here.
MARCELLUS   'Tis gone.   *Exit* GHOST.
We do it wrong, being so majestical,
To offer it the show of violence,
For it is as the air, invulnerable,   145
And our vain blows malicious mockery.
BARNARDO   It was about to speak when the cock crew.
HORATIO   And then it started, like a guilty thing
Upon a fearful summons. I have heard,
The cock, that is the trumpet to the morn,   150
Doth with his lofty and shrill-sounding throat
Awake the god of day, and at his warning,

---

¹²⁵ **climatures** regions   ¹²⁷ **cross it** (1) cross its path, confront it, (2) make the sign of the cross in front of it.   ¹²⁷ˢ·ᵈ· **his** i.e., its, the ghost's (though possibly what is meant is that Horatio spreads his own arms, making a cross of himself)   ¹³⁴ **happily** haply, perhaps   ¹³⁷ **Extorted** ill-won   ¹⁴⁰ **partisan** pike (a long-handled weapon)

Whether in sea or fire, in earth or air,
Th' extravagant and erring° spirit hies
To his confine; and of the truth herein   155
This present object made probation.°
MARCELLUS   It faded on the crowing of the cock.
Some say that ever 'gainst° that season comes
Wherein our Savior's birth is celebrated,
This bird of dawning singeth all night long,   160
And then, they say, no spirit dare stir abroad,
The nights are wholesome, then no planets strike,°
No fairy takes,° nor witch hath power to charm:
So hallowed and so gracious is that time.
HORATIO   So have I heard and do in part believe it.   165
But look, the morn in russet mantle clad
Walks o'er the dew of yon high eastward hill.
Break we our watch up, and by my advice
Let us impart what we have seen tonight
Unto young Hamlet, for upon my life   170
This spirit, dumb to us, will speak to him.
Do you consent we shall acquaint him with it,
As needful in our loves, fitting our duty?
MARCELLUS   Let's do't, I pray, and I this morning know
Where we shall find him most convenient.   *Exeunt.* 175

[*Scene II. The castle.*]

Flourish.° *Enter* CLAUDIUS, *King of Denmark,* GERTRUDE *the Queen, Councilors,*
POLONIUS *and his son* LAERTES, HAMLET, *cum aliis*° [*including* VOLTEMAND *and*
CORNELIUS].

KING   Though yet of Hamlet our dear brother's death
The memory be green, and that it us befitted
To bear our hearts in grief, and our whole kingdom
To be contracted in one brow of woe,
Yet so far hath discretion fought with nature   5
That we with wisest sorrow think on him
Together with remembrance of ourselves.
Therefore our sometime sister,° now our Queen,
Th' imperial jointress° to this warlike state,

---

¹⁵⁴ **extravagant and erring** out of bounds and wandering   ¹⁵⁶ **probation** proof   ¹⁵⁸ **'gainst** just
before   ¹⁶² **strike** exert an evil influence   ¹⁶³ **takes** bewitches   *I.ii.* ˢ·ᵈ· **Flourish** fanfare of trumpets   ˢ·ᵈ· **cum aliis** with others (Latin)   ⁸ **our sometime sister** my (the royal "we") former sister-
in-law   ⁹ **jointress** joint tenant, partner

Have we, as 'twere, with a defeated joy,　　　　　　　　　10
With an auspicious° and a dropping eye,
With mirth in funeral, and with dirge in marriage,
In equal scale weighing delight and dole,
Taken to wife. Nor have we herein barred
Your better wisdoms, which have freely gone　　　　　15
With this affair along. For all, our thanks.
Now follows that you know young Fortinbras,
Holding a weak supposal of our worth,
Or thinking by our late dear brother's death
Our state to be disjoint and out of frame,°　　　　　　20
Colleaguèd with this dream of his advantage,°
He hath not failed to pester us with message,
Importing the surrender of those lands
Lost by his father, with all bands of law,
To our most valiant brother. So much for him.　　　　25
Now for ourself and for this time of meeting.
Thus much the business is: we have here writ
To Norway, uncle of young Fortinbras—
Who, impotent and bedrid, scarcely hears
Of this his nephew's purpose—to suppress　　　　　　30
His further gait° herein, in that the levies,
The lists, and full proportions° are all made
Out of his subject;° and we here dispatch
You, good Cornelius, and you, Voltemand,
For bearers of this greeting to old Norway,　　　　　　35
Giving to you no further personal power
To business with the King, more than the scope
Of these delated articles° allow.
Farewell, and let your haste commend your duty.
CORNELIUS, VOLTEMAND   In that, and all things, will we show our duty.　40
KING   We doubt it nothing. Heartily farewell.
　　　　　　　　　　　　　Exit VOLTEMAND *and* CORNELIUS.

And now, Laertes, what's the news with you?
You told us of some suit. What is't, Laertes?
You cannot speak of reason to the Dane
And lose your voice.° What wouldst thou beg, Laertes,　45
That shall not be my offer, not thy asking?

---

[11] **auspicious** joyful　[20] **frame** order　[21] **advantage** superiority　[31] **gait** proceeding　[32] **propor-**
tions supplies for war　[33] **Out of his subject** i.e., out of old Norway's subjects and realm　[38] **delated**
articles detailed documents　[45] **lose your voice** waste your breath

The head is not more native° to the heart,
The hand more instrumental to the mouth,
Than is the throne of Denmark to thy father.
What wouldst thou have, Laertes?

LAERTES   My dread lord,   50
Your leave and favor to return to France,
From whence, though willingly I came to Denmark
To show my duty in your coronation,
Yet now I must confess, that duty done,
My thoughts and wishes bend again toward France   55
And bow them to your gracious leave and pardon.

KING   Have you your father's leave? What says Polonius?

POLONIUS   He hath, my lord, wrung from me my slow leave
By laborsome petition, and at last
Upon his will I sealed my hard consent.°   60
I do beseech you give him leave to go.

KING   Take thy fair hour, Laertes. Time be thine,
And thy best graces spend it at thy will.
But now, my cousin° Hamlet, and my son——

HAMLET   [aside] A little more than kin, and less than kind!°   65

KING   How is it that the clouds still hang on you?

HAMLET   Not so, my lord. I am too much in the sun.°

QUEEN   Good Hamlet, cast thy nighted color off,
And let thine eye look like a friend on Denmark.
Do not forever with thy vailèd° lids   70
Seek for thy noble father in the dust.
Thou know'st 'tis common; all that lives must die,
Passing through nature to eternity.

HAMLET   Ay, madam, it is common.°

QUEEN   If it be,
Why seems it so particular with thee?   75

HAMLET   Seems, madam? Nay, it is. I know not "seems."
'Tis not alone my inky cloak, good mother,
Nor customary suits of solemn black,
Nor windy suspiration° of forced breath,
No, nor the fruitful river in the eye,   80

---

⁴⁷ **native** related   ⁶⁰ **Upon his . . . hard consent** to his desire I gave my reluctant consent
⁶⁴ **cousin** kinsman   ⁶⁵ **kind** (pun on the meanings "kindly" and "natural"; though doubly related—
more than kin—Hamlet asserts that he neither resembles Claudius in nature or feels kindly toward him)
⁶⁷ **sun** sunshine of royal favor (with a pun on "son")   ⁷⁰ **vailèd** lowered   ⁷⁴ **common** (1) universal,
(2) vulgar   ⁷⁹ **windy suspiration** heavy sighing

Nor the dejected havior of the visage,
Together with all forms, moods, shapes of grief,
That can denote me truly. These indeed seem,
For they are actions that a man might play,
But I have that within which passes show;   85
These but the trappings and the suits of woe.
KING   'Tis sweet and commendable in your nature, Hamlet,
To give these mourning duties to your father,
But you must know your father lost a father,
That father lost, lost his, and the survivor bound   90
In filial obligation for some term
To do obsequious° sorrow. But to persever
In obstinate condolement° is a course
Of impious stubborness. 'Tis unmanly grief.
It shows a will most incorrect to heaven,   95
A heart unfortified, a mind impatient,
An understanding simple and unschooled.
For what we know must be and is as common
As any the most vulgar° thing to sense,
Why should we in our peevish opposition   100
Take it to heart? Fie, 'tis a fault to heaven,
A fault against the dead, a fault to nature,
To reason most absurd, whose common theme
Is death of fathers, and who still hath cried,
From the first corse° till he that died today,   105
"This must be so." We pray you throw to earth
This unprevailing° woe, and think of us
As of a father, for let the world take note
You are the most immediate to our throne,
And with no less nobility of love   110
Than that which dearest father bears his son
Do I impart toward you. For your intent
In going back to school in Wittenberg,
It is most retrograde° to our desire,
And we beseech you, bend you° to remain   115
Here in the cheer and comfort of our eye,
Our chiefest courtier, cousin, and our son.
QUEEN   Let not thy mother lose her prayers, Hamlet. I pray thee stay with us,
go not to Wittenberg.

---

⁹² **obsequious** suitable to obsequies (funerals)   ⁹³ **condolement** mourning   ⁹⁹ **vulgar** common
¹⁰⁵ **corse** corpse   ¹⁰⁷ **unprevailing** unavailing   ¹¹⁴ **retrograde** contrary   ¹¹⁵ **bend you** incline

HAMLET   I shall in all my best obey you, madam.   120
KING   Why, 'tis a loving and a fair reply.
  Be as ourself in Denmark. Madam, come.
  This gentle and unforced accord of Hamlet
  Sits smiling to my heart, in grace whereof
  No jocund health that Denmark drinks today,   125
  But the great cannon to the clouds shall tell,
  And the King's rouse° the heaven shall bruit° again,
  Respeaking earthly thunder. Come away.

Flourish. Exeunt all but HAMLET.

HAMLET   O that this too too sullied° flesh would melt,
  Thaw, and resolve itself into a dew,   130
  Or that the Everlasting had not fixed
  His canon° 'gainst self-slaughter. O God, God,
  How weary, stale, flat, and unprofitable
  Seem to me all the uses of this world!
  Fie on't, ah, fie, 'tis an unweeded garden   135
  That grows to seed. Things rank and gross in nature
  Possess it merely.° That it should come to this:
  But two months dead, nay, not so much, not two,
  So excellent a king, that was to this
  Hyperion° to a satyr, so loving to my mother   140
  That he might not beteem° the winds of heaven
  Visit her face too roughly. Heaven and earth,
  Must I remember? Why, she would hang on him
  As if increase of appetite had grown
  By what it fed on; and yet within a month—   145
  Let me not think on't; frailty, thy name is woman—
  A little month, or ere those shoes were old
  With which she followed my poor father's body
  Like Niobe,° all tears, why she, even she—
  O God, a beast that wants discourse of reason°   150
  Would have mourned longer—married with my uncle,
  My father's brother, but no more like my father
  Than I to Hercules. Within a month,
  Ere yet the salt of most unrighteous tears

[127] **rouse** deep drink   [127] **bruit** announce noisily   [129] **sullied** (Q2 has *sallied*, here modernized to *sullied*, which makes sense and is therefore given; but the Folio reading, *solid*, which fits better with *melt*, is quite possibly correct)   [132] **canon** law   [137] **merely** entirely   [140] **Hyperion** the sun god, a model of beauty   [141] **beteem** allow   [149] **Niobe** (a mother who wept profusely at the death of her children)   [150] **wants discourse of reason** lacks reasoning power

Had left the flushing° in her gallèd eyes,   155
She married. O, most wicked speed, to post°
With such dexterity to incestuous° sheets!
It is not, nor it cannot come to good.
But break my heart, for I must hold my tongue.

Enter HORATIO, MARCELLUS, *and* BARNARDO.

HORATIO   Hail to your lordship!
HAMLET   I am glad to see you well.   160
　Horatio—or I do forget myself.
HORATIO   The same, my lord, and your poor servant ever.
HAMLET   Sir, my good friend, I'll change° that name with you.
　And what make you from Wittenberg, Horatio?
　Marcellus.   165
MARCELLUS   My good lord!
HAMLET   I am very glad to see you. [*To* BARNARDO.] Good even, sir.
　But what, in faith, make you from Wittenberg?
HORATIO   A truant disposition, good my lord.
HAMLET   I would not hear your enemy say so,   170
　Nor shall you do my ear that violence
　To make it truster° of your own report
　Against yourself. I know you are no truant.
　But what is your affair in Elsinore?
　We'll teach you to drink deep ere you depart.   175
HORATIO   My lord, I came to see your father's funeral.
HAMLET   I prithee do not mock me, fellow student.
　I think it was to see my mother's wedding.
HORATIO   Indeed, my lord, it followed hard upon.
HAMLET   Thrift, thrift, Horatio. The funeral baked meats   180
　Did coldly furnish forth the marriage tables.
　Would I had met my dearest° foe in heaven
　Or ever I had seen that day, Horatio!
　My father, methinks I see my father.
HORATIO   Where, my lord?
HAMLET   In my mind's eye, Horatio.   185
HORATIO   I saw him once. 'A° was a goodly king.
HAMLET   'A was a man, take him for all in all,
　I shall not look upon his like again.

---

155 left the flushing stopped reddening   **156 post** hasten   **157 incestuous** (canon law considered marriage with a deceased brother's widow to be incestuous)   **163 change** exchange   **172 truster** believer   **182 dearest** most intensely felt   **186 'A** he

HORATIO   My lord, I think I saw him yesternight.

HAMLET   Saw? Who?   190

HORATIO   My lord, the king your father.

HAMLET   The King my father?

HORATIO   Season your admiration° for a while
With an attent ear till I may deliver
Upon the witness of these gentlemen
This marvel to you.

HAMLET   For God's love let me hear!   195

HORATIO   Two nights together had these gentlemen,
Marcellus and Barnardo, on their watch
In the dead waste and middle of the night
Been thus encountered. A figure like your father,
Armèd at point exactly, cap-a-pe,°   200
Appears before them, and with solemn march
Goes slow and stately by them. Thrice he walked
By their oppressed and fear-surprisèd eyes,
Within his truncheon's length,° whilst they, distilled°
Almost to jelly with the act° of fear,   205
Stand dumb and speak not to him. This to me
In dreadful° secrecy impart they did,
And I with them the third night kept the watch,
Where, as they had delivered, both in time,
Form of the thing, each word made true and good,   210
The apparition comes. I knew your father.
These hands are not more like.

HAMLET   But where was this?

MARCELLUS   My lord, upon the platform where we watched.

HAMLET   Did you not speak to it?

HORATIO   My lord, I did;
But answer made it none. Yet once methought   215
It lifted up it° head and did address
Itself to motion like as it would speak:
But even then the morning cock crew loud,
And at the sound it shrunk in haste away
And vanished from our sight.

HAMLET   'Tis very strange.   220

---

¹⁹² **Season your admiration** control your wonder   ²⁰⁰ **cap-a-pe** head to foot   ²⁰⁴ **truncheon's
length** space of a short staff   ²⁰⁴ **distilled** reduced   ²⁰⁵ **act** action   ²⁰⁷ **dreadful** terrified
²¹⁶ **it** its

HORATIO   As I do live, my honored lord, 'tis true,
And we did think it writ down in our duty
To let you know of it.
HAMLET   Indeed, indeed, sirs, but this troubles me.
Hold you the watch tonight?
ALL   We do, my lord.   225
HAMLET   Armed, say you?
ALL   Armed, my lord.
HAMLET   From top to toe?
ALL   My lord, from head to foot.
HAMLET   Then saw you not his face.
HORATIO   O, yes, my lord. He wore his beaver° up.   230
HAMLET   What, looked he frowningly?
HORATIO   A countenance more in sorrow than in anger.
HAMLET   Pale or red?
HORATIO   Nay, very pale.
HAMLET   And fixed his eyes upon you?
HORATIO   Most constantly.
HAMLET   I would I had been there.   235
HORATIO   It would have much amazed you.
HAMLET   Very like, very like. Stayed it long?
HORATIO   While one with moderate haste might tell° a hundred.
BOTH   Longer, longer.
HORATIO   Not when I saw't.
HAMLET   His beard was grizzled,° no?   240
HORATIO   It was as I have seen it in his life,
A sable silvered.°
HAMLET   I will watch tonight.
Perchance 'twill walk again.
HORATIO   I warr'nt it will.
HAMLET   If it assume my noble father's person,
I'll speak to it though hell itself should gape   245
And bid me hold my peace. I pray you all,
If you have hitherto concealed this sight,
Let it be tenable° in your silence still,
And whatsomever else shall hap tonight,
Give it an understanding but no tongue;   250
I will requite your loves. So fare you well.

---

²³⁰ **beaver** visor, face guard   ²³⁸ **tell** count   ²⁴⁰ **grizzled** gray   ²⁴² **sable silvered** black mingled
with white   ²⁴⁸ **tenable** held

Upon the platform 'twixt eleven and twelve
I'll visit you.
ALL   Our duty to your honor.
HAMLET   Your loves, as mine to you. Farewell.

Exeunt [all but HAMLET].

My father's spirit—in arms? All is not well.   255
I doubt° some foul play. Would the night were come!
Till then sit still, my soul. Foul deeds will rise,
Though all the earth o'erwhelm them, to men's eyes.

Exit.

[*Scene III. A room.*]

Enter LAERTES *and* OPHELIA, *his sister.*

LAERTES   My necessaries are embarked. Farewell.
And, sister, as the winds give benefit
And convoy° is assistant, do not sleep,
But let me hear from you.
OPHELIA   Do you doubt that?
LAERTES   For Hamlet, and the trifling of his favor,   5
Hold it a fashion and a toy° in blood,
A violet in the youth of primy° nature,
Forward,° not permanent, sweet, not lasting,
The perfume and suppliance° of a minute,
No more.
OPHELIA   No more but so?
LAERTES   Think it no more.   10
For nature crescent° does not grow alone
In thews° and bulk, but as this temple° waxes,
The inward service of the mind and soul
Grows wide withal. Perhaps he loves you now,
And now no soil nor cautel° doth besmirch   15
The virtue of his will; but you must fear,
His greatness weighed,° his will is not his own.
For he himself is subject to his birth.
He may not, as unvalued° persons do,
Carve for himself; for on his choice depends   20
The safety and health of this whole state;
And therefore must his choice be circumscribed

---

²⁵⁶ **doubt** suspect   *I.iii.* ³ **convoy** conveyance   ⁶ **toy** idle fancy   ⁷ **primy** springlike   ⁸ **For-**
ward premature   ⁹ **suppliance** diversion   ¹¹ **crescent** growing   ¹² **thews** muscles and sinews
¹² **temple** i.e., the body   ¹⁵ **cautel** deceit   ¹⁷ **greatness weighed** high rank considered
¹⁹ **unvalued** of low rank

Unto the voice and yielding of that body
Whereof he is the head. Then if he says he loves you,
It fits your wisdom so far to believe it   25
As he in his particular act and place
May give his saying deed, which is no further
Than the main voice of Denmark goes withal.
Then weigh what loss your honor may sustain
If with too credent° ear you list his songs,   30
Or lose your heart, or your chaste treasure open
To his unmastered importunity.
Fear it, Ophelia, fear it, my dear sister,
And keep you in the rear of your affection,
Out of the shot and danger of desire.   35
The chariest maid is prodigal enough
If she unmask her beauty to the moon.
Virtue itself scapes not calumnious strokes.
The canker° galls the infants of the spring
Too oft before their buttons° be disclosed,   40
And in the morn and liquid dew of youth
Contagious blastments are most imminent.
Be wary then; best safety lies in fear;
Youth to itself rebels, though none else near.
OPHELIA   I shall the effect of this good lesson keep   45
  As watchman to my heart, but, good my brother,
  Do not, as some ungracious° pastors do,
  Show me the steep and thorny way to heaven,
  Whiles, like a puffed and reckless libertine,
  Himself the primrose path of dalliance treads   50
  And recks not his own rede.°

  Enter POLONIUS.

LAERTES   O, fear me not.
  I stay too long. But here my father comes.
  A double blessing is a double grace;
  Occasion smiles upon a second leave.
POLONIUS   Yet here, Laertes? Aboard, aboard, for shame!   55
  The wind sits in the shoulder of your sail,
  And you are stayed for. There—my blessing with thee,
  And these few precepts in thy memory

---

³⁰ **credent** credulous   ³⁹ **canker** cankerworm   ⁴⁰ **buttons** buds   ⁴⁷ **ungracious** lacking grace
⁵¹ **recks not his own rede** does not heed his own advice

Look thou character.° Give thy thoughts no tongue,
Nor any unproportioned° thought his act.   60
Be thou familiar, but by no means vulgar.
Those friends thou hast, and their adoption tried,
Grapple them unto thy soul with hoops of steel,
But do not dull thy palm with entertainment
Of each new-hatched, unfledged courage.° Beware   65
Of entrance to a quarrel; but being in,
Bear't that th' opposèd may beware of thee.
Give every man thine ear, but few thy voice;
Take each man's censure,° but reserve thy judgment.
Costly thy habits as thy purse can buy,   70
But not expressed in fancy; rich, not gaudy,
For the apparel oft proclaims the man,
And they in France of the best rank and station
Are of a most select and generous, chief in that.°
Neither a borrower nor a lender be,   75
For loan oft loses both itself and friend,
And borrowing dulleth edge of husbandry.°
This above all, to thine own self be true,
And it must follow, as the night the day,
Thou canst not then be false to any man.   80
Farewell. My blessing season this° in thee!
LAERTES   Most humbly do I take my leave, my lord.
POLONIUS   The time invites you. Go, your servants tend.°
LAERTES   Farewell, Ophelia, and remember well
    What I have said to you.
OPHELIA   'Tis in my memory locked,   85
    And you yourself shall keep the key of it.
LAERTES   Farewell.   *Exit* LAERTES.
POLONIUS   What is't, Ophelia, he hath said to you?
OPHELIA   So please you, something touching the Lord Hamlet.
POLONIUS   Marry,° well bethought.   90
    'Tis told me he hath very oft of late
    Given private time to you, and you yourself
    Have of your audience been most free and bounteous.
    If it be so—as so 'tis put on me,
    And that in way of caution—I must tell you   95

---

⁵⁹ **character** inscribe   ⁶⁰ **unproportioned** unbalanced   ⁶⁵ **courage** gallant youth   ⁶⁹ **censure** opinion   ⁷⁴ **Are of . . . in that** show their fine taste and their gentlemanly instincts more in that than in any other point of manners (Kittredge)   ⁷⁷ **husbandry** thrift   ⁸¹ **season this** make fruitful this (advice)   ⁸³ **tend** attend   ⁹⁰ **Marry** (a light oath, from "By the Virgin Mary")

You do not understand yourself so clearly
As it behooves my daughter and your honor.
What is between you? Give me up the truth.
OPHELIA   He hath, my lord, of late made many tenders°
Of his affection to me.   100
POLONIUS   Affection pooh! You speak like a green girl,
Unsifted° in such perilous circumstance.
Do you believe his tenders, as you call them?
OPHELIA   I do not know, my lord, what I should think.
POLONIUS   Marry, I will teach you. Think yourself a baby   105
That you have ta'en these tenders for true pay
Which are not sterling. Tender yourself more dearly,
Or (not to crack the wind of the poor phrase)
Tend'ring it thus you'll tender me a fool.°
OPHELIA   My lord, he hath importuned me with love   110
In honorable fashion.
POLONIUS   Ay, fashion you may call it. Go to, go to.
OPHELIA   And hath given countenance to his speech, my lord,
With almost all the holy vows of heaven.
POLONIUS   Ay, springes to catch woodcocks.° I do know,   115
When the blood burns, how prodigal the soul
Lends the tongue vows. These blazes, daughter,
Giving more light than heat, extinct in both,
Even in their promise, as it is a-making,
You must not take for fire. From this time   120
Be something scanter of your maiden presence.
Set your entreatments° at a higher rate
Than a command to parley. For Lord Hamlet,
Believe so much in him that he is young,
And with a larger tether may he walk   125
Than may be given you. In few, Ophelia,
Do not believe his vows, for they are brokers,°
Not of that dye° which their investments° show,
But mere implorators° of unholy suits,
Breathing like sanctified and pious bonds,°   130
The better to beguile. This is for all:

---

99 **tenders** offers (in line 103 it has the same meaning, but in line 106 Polonius speaks of *tenders* in the sense of counters or chips; in line 109 *Tend'ring* means "holding," and *tender* means "give," "present") 102 **Unsifted** untried   109 **tender me a fool** (1) present me with a fool, (2) present me with a baby   115 **springes to catch woodcocks** snares to catch stupid birds   122 **entreatments** interviews   127 **brokers** procurers   128 **dye** i.e., kind   128 **investments** garments   129 **implorators** solicitors   130 **bonds** pledges

I would not, in plain terms, from this time forth
Have you so slander° any moment leisure
As to give words or talk with the Lord Hamlet.
Look to't, I charge you. Come your ways.   135
OPHELIA   I shall obey, my lord.   *Exeunt.*

[Scene IV. A guard platform.]

Enter HAMLET, HORATIO, *and* MARCELLUS.

HAMLET   The air bites shrewdly;° it is very cold.
HORATIO   It is a nipping and an eager° air.
HAMLET   What hour now?
HORATIO   I think it lacks of twelve.
MARCELLUS   No, it is struck.
HORATIO   Indeed? I heard it not. It then draws near the season   5
  Wherein the spirit held his wont to walk.

A flourish of trumpets, and two pieces go off.

What does this mean, my lord?
HAMLET   The King doth wake° tonight and takes his rouse,°
  Keeps wassail, and the swagg'ring upspring° reels,
  And as he drains his draughts of Rhenish° down   10
  The kettledrum and trumpet thus bray out
  The triumph of his pledge.°
HORATIO   Is it a custom?
HAMLET   Ay, marry, is't,
  But to my mind, though I am native here
  And to the manner born, it is a custom   15
  More honored in the breach than the observance.
  This heavy-headed revel east and west
  Makes us traduced and taxed of° other nations.
  They clepe° us drunkards and with swinish phrase
  Soil our addition,° and indeed it takes   20
  From our achievements, though performed at height,
  The pith and marrow of our attribute.°
  So oft it chances in particular men
  That for some vicious mole° of nature in them,

---

¹³³ **slander** disgrace   *I.iv.* ¹ **shrewdly** bitterly   ² **eager** sharp   ⁸ **wake** hold a revel by night
⁸ **takes his rouse** carouses   ⁹ **upspring** (a dance)   ¹⁰ **Rhenish** Rhine wine   ¹² **The triumph of
his pledge** the achievement (of drinking a wine cup in one draught) of his toast   ¹⁸ **taxed of** blamed by
¹⁹ **clepe** call   ²⁰ **addition** reputation (literally, "title of honor")   ²² **attribute** reputation   ²⁴ **mole**
blemish

As in their birth, wherein they are not guilty, 25
(Since nature cannot choose his origin)
By the o'ergrowth of some complexion,°
Oft breaking down the pales° and forts of reason,
Or by some habit that too much o'erleavens°
The form of plausive° manners, that (these men, 30
Carrying, I say, the stamp of one defect,
Being nature's livery, or fortune's star°)
Their virtues else, be they as pure as grace,
As infinite as man may undergo,
Shall in the general censure° take corruption 35
From that particular fault. The dram of evil
Doth all the noble substance of a doubt,
To his own scandal.°

Enter GHOST.

HORATIO   Look, my lord, it comes.
HAMLET   Angels and ministers of grace defend us!
Be thou a spirit of health° or goblin damned, 40
Bring with thee airs from heaven or blasts from hell,
Be thy intents wicked or charitable,
Thou com'st in such a questionable° shape
That I will speak to thee. I'll call thee Hamlet,
King, father, royal Dane. O, answer me! 45
Let me not burst in ignorance, but tell
Why thy canonized° bones, hearsèd in death,
Have burst their cerements,° why the sepulcher
Wherein we saw thee quietly interred
Hath oped his ponderous and marble jaws 50
To cast thee up again. What may this mean
That thou, dead corse, again in complete steel,
Revisits thus the glimpses of the moon,
Making night hideous, and we fools of nature
So horridly to shake our disposition° 55

---

²⁷ **complexion** natural disposition   ²⁸ **pales** enclosures   ²⁹ **o'erleavens** mixes with, corrupts
³⁰ **plausive** pleasing   ³² **nature's livery, or fortune's star** nature's equipment (i.e., "innate"),
or a person's destiny determined by the stars   ³⁵ **general censure** popular judgment   ³⁶⁻³⁸ **The
dram . . . own scandal** (though the drift is clear, there is no agreement as to the exact meaning of these
lines)   ⁴⁰ **spirit of health** good spirit   ⁴³ **questionable** (1) capable of discourse, (2) dubious
⁴⁷ **canonized** buried according to the canon or ordinance of the church   ⁴⁸ **cerements** waxed linen
shroud   ⁵⁵ **shake our disposition** disturb us

With thoughts beyond the reaches of our souls?
Say, why is this? Wherefore? What should we do?

GHOST *beckons* HAMLET.

HORATIO   It beckons you to go away with it,
As if it some impartment° did desire
To you alone.
MARCELLUS   Look with what courteous action   60
It waves you to a more removèd ground.
But do not go with it.
HORATIO   No, by no means.
HAMLET   It will not speak. Then I will follow it.
HORATIO   Do not, my lord.
HAMLET   Why, what should be the fear?
I do not set my life at a pin's fee,   65
And for my soul, what can it do to that,
Being a thing immortal as itself?
It waves me forth again. I'll follow it.
HORATIO   What if it tempt you toward the flood, my lord,
Or to the dreadful summit of the cliff   70
That beetles° o'er his base into the sea,
And there assume some other horrible form,
Which might deprive your sovereignty of reason°
And draw you into madness? Think of it.
The very place puts toys° of desperation,   75
Without more motive, into every brain
That looks so many fathoms to the sea
And hears it roar beneath.
HAMLET   It waves me still.
Go on; I'll follow thee.
MARCELLUS   You shall not go, my lord.
HAMLET   Hold off your hands.   80
HORATIO   Be ruled. You shall not go.
HAMLET   My fate cries out
And makes each petty artere° in this body
As hardy as the Nemean lion's nerve.°
Still am I called! Unhand me, gentlemen.
By heaven, I'll make a ghost of him that lets° me!   85
I say, away! Go on. I'll follow thee.   *Exit* GHOST, *and* HAMLET.

---

⁵⁹ **impartment** communication   ⁷¹ **beetles** juts out   ⁷³ **deprive your sovereignty of reason**
destroy the sovereignty of your reason   ⁷⁵ **toys** whims, fancies   ⁸² **artere** artery   ⁸³ **Nemean lion's**
nerve sinews of the mythical lion slain by Hercules   ⁸⁵ **lets** hinders

HORATIO   He waxes desperate with imagination.
MARCELLUS   Let's follow. 'Tis not fit thus to obey him.
HORATIO   Have after! To what issue will this come?
MARCELLUS   Something is rotten in the state of Denmark.   90
HORATIO   Heaven will direct it.
MARCELLUS   Nay, let's follow him.   *Exeunt.*

[Scene V. The battlements.]

Enter GHOST *and* HAMLET.

HAMLET   Whither wilt thou lead me? Speak; I'll go no further.
GHOST   Mark me.
HAMLET   I will.
GHOST   My hour is almost come,
   When I to sulf'rous and tormenting flames
   Must render up myself.
HAMLET   Alas, poor ghost.
GHOST   Pity me not, but lend thy serious hearing   5
   To what I shall unfold.
HAMLET   Speak. I am bound to hear.
GHOST   So art thou to revenge, when thou shalt hear.
HAMLET   What?
GHOST   I am thy father's spirit,
   Doomed for a certain term to walk the night,   10
   And for the day confined to fast in fires,
   Till the foul crimes° done in my days of nature
   Are burnt and purged away. But that I am forbid
   To tell the secrets of my prison house,
   I could a tale unfold whose lightest word   15
   Would harrow up thy soul, freeze thy young blood,
   Make thy two eyes like stars start from their spheres,°
   Thy knotted and combinèd locks to part,
   And each particular hair to stand an end
   Like quills upon the fearful porpentine.°   20
   But this eternal blazon° must not be
   To ears of flesh and blood. List, list, O, list!
   If thou didst ever thy dear father love——
HAMLET   O God!
GHOST   Revenge his foul and most unnatural murder.   25

I.v. ¹² **crimes** sins   ¹⁷ **spheres** (in Ptolemaic astronomy, each planet was fixed in a hollow transparent shell concentric with the earth)   ²⁰ **fearful porpentine** timid porcupine   ²¹ **eternal blazon** revelation of eternity

HAMLET   Murder?

GHOST   Murder most foul, as in the best it is,
    But this most foul, strange, and unnatural.

HAMLET   Haste me to know't, that I, with wings as swift
    As meditation° or the thoughts of love,   30
    May sweep to my revenge.

GHOST   I find thee apt,
    And duller shouldst thou be than the fat weed
    That roots itself in ease on Lethe wharf,°
    Wouldst thou not stir in this. Now, Hamlet, hear.
    'Tis given out that, sleeping in my orchard,   35
    A serpent stung me. So the whole ear of Denmark
    Is by a forgèd process° of my death
    Rankly abused. But know, thou noble youth,
    The serpent that did sting thy father's life
    Now wears his crown.

HAMLET   O my prophetic soul!   40
    My uncle?

GHOST   Ay, that incestuous, that adulterate° beast,
    With witchcraft of his wits, with traitorous gifts—
    O wicked wit and gifts, that have the power
    So to seduce!—won to his shameful lust   45
    The will of my most seeming-virtuous queen.
    O Hamlet, what a falling-off was there,
    From me, whose love was of that dignity
    That it went hand in hand even with the vow
    I made to her in marriage, and to decline   50
    Upon a wretch whose natural gifts were poor
    To those of mine.
    But virtue, as it never will be moved,
    Though lewdness° court it in a shape of heaven,
    So lust, though to a radiant angel linked,   55
    Will sate itself in a celestial bed
    And prey on garbage.
    But soft, methinks I scent the morning air;
    Brief let me be. Sleeping within my orchard,
    My custom always of the afternoon,   60
    Upon my secure° hour thy uncle stole

---

³⁰ **meditation** thought   ³³ **Lethe wharf** bank of the river of forgetfulness in Hades   ³⁷ **forgèd process** false account   ⁴² **adulterate** adulterous   ⁵⁴ **lewdness** lust   ⁶¹ **secure** unsuspecting

With juice of cursed hebona° in a vial,
And in the porches of my ears did pour
The leperous distillment, whose effect
Holds such an enmity with blood of man 65
That swift as quicksilver it courses through
The natural gates and alleys of the body,
And with a sudden vigor it doth posset°
And curd, like eager° droppings into milk,
The thin and wholesome blood. So did it mine, 70
And a most instant tetter° barked about
Most lazarlike° with vile and loathsome crust
All my smooth body.
Thus was I, sleeping, by a brother's hand
Of life, of crown, of queen at once dispatched, 75
Cut off even in the blossoms of my sin,
Unhouseled, disappointed, unaneled,°
No reck'ning made, but sent to my account
With all my imperfections on my head.
O, horrible! O, horrible! Most horrible! 80
If thou hast nature in thee, bear it not.
Let not the royal bed of Denmark be
A couch for luxury° and damnèd incest.
But howsomever thou pursues this act,
Taint not thy mind, nor let thy soul contrive 85
Against thy mother aught. Leave her to heaven
And to those thorns that in her bosom lodge
To prick and sting her. Fare thee well at once.
The glowworm shows the matin° to be near
And 'gins to pale his uneffectual fire. 90
Adieu, adieu, adieu. Remember me.   *Exit.*
HAMLET   O all you host of heaven! O earth! What else?
And shall I couple hell? O fie! Hold, hold, my heart,
And you, my sinews, grow not instant old,
But bear me stiffly up. Remember thee? 95
Ay, thou poor ghost, whiles memory holds a seat
In this distracted globe.° Remember thee?
Yea, from the table° of my memory
I'll wipe away all trivial fond° records,

---

⁶² **hebona** a poisonous plant   ⁶⁸ **posset** curdle   ⁶⁹ **eager** acid   ⁷¹ **tetter** scab   ⁷² **lazarlike**
leperlike   ⁷⁷ **Unhouseled, disappointed, unaneled** without the sacrament of communion, unab-
solved, without extreme unction   ⁸³ **luxury** lust   ⁸⁹ **matin** morning   ⁹⁷ **globe** i.e., his head
⁹⁸ **table** tablet, notebook   ⁹⁹ **fond** foolish

All saws° of books, all forms, all pressures° past   100
That youth and observation copied there,
And thy commandment all alone shall live
Within the book and volume of my brain,
Unmixed with baser matter. Yes, by heaven!
O most pernicious woman!   105
O villain, villain, smiling, damnèd villain!
My tables—meet it is I set it down
That one may smile, and smile, and be a villain.
At least I am sure it may be so in Denmark. [*Writes.*]
So, uncle, there you are. Now to my word: 110
It is "Adieu, adieu, remember me."
I have sworn't.
HORATIO and MARCELLUS (*within*)   My lord, my lord!

Enter HORATIO *and* MARCELLUS.

MARCELLUS   Lord Hamlet!
HORATIO   Heavens secure him!
HAMLET   So be it!
MARCELLUS   Illo, ho, ho,° my lord!   115
HAMLET   Hillo, ho, ho, boy! Come, bird, come.
MARCELLUS   How is't, my noble lord?
HORATIO   What news, my lord?
HAMLET   O, wonderful!
HORATIO   Good my lord, tell it.
HAMLET   No, you will reveal it.
HORATIO   Not I, my lord, by heaven.
MARCELLUS   Nor I, my lord.   120
HAMLET   How say you then? Would heart of man once think it?
  But you'll be secret?
BOTH   Ay, by heaven, my lord.
HAMLET   There's never a villain dwelling in all Denmark
  But he's an arrant knave.
HORATIO   There needs no ghost, my lord, come from the grave   125
  To tell us this.
HAMLET   Why, right, you are in the right;
  And so, without more circumstance° at all,
  I hold it fit that we shake hands and part:
  You, as your business and desire shall point you,

---

¹⁰⁰ **saws** maxims   ¹⁰⁰ **pressures** impressions   ¹¹⁵ **Illo, ho, ho** (falconer's call to his hawk)
¹²⁷ **circumstance** details

For every man hath business and desire   130
Such as it is, and for my own poor part,
Look you, I'll go pray.
HORATIO   These are but wild and whirling words, my lord.
HAMLET   I am sorry they offend you, heartily;
Yes, faith, heartily.
HORATIO   There's no offense, my lord.   135
HAMLET   Yes, by Saint Patrick, but there is, Horatio,
And much offense too. Touching this vision here,
It is an honest ghost,° that let me tell you.
For your desire to know what is between us,
O'ermaster't as you may. And now, good friends,   140
As you are friends, scholars, and soldiers,
Give me one poor request.
HORATIO   What is't, my lord? We will.
HAMLET   Never make known what you have seen tonight.
BOTH   My lord, we will not.
HAMLET   Nay, but swear't.
HORATIO   In faith,   145
My lord, not I.
MARCELLUS   Nor I, my lord—in faith.
HAMLET   Upon my sword.
MARCELLUS   We have sworn, my lord, already.
HAMLET   Indeed, upon my sword, indeed.

GHOST *cries under the stage.*

GHOST   Swear.
HAMLET   Ha, ha, boy, say'st thou so? Art thou there, truepenny?°   150
Come on. You hear this fellow in the cellarage.
Consent to swear.
HORATIO   Propose the oath, my lord.
HAMLET   Never to speak of this that you have seen.
Swear by my sword.
GHOST [*beneath*]   Swear.   155
HAMLET   *Hic et ubique?*° Then we'll shift our ground;
Come hither, gentlemen,
And lay your hands again upon my sword.
Swear by my sword
Never to speak of this that you have heard.   160

---

[138] **honest ghost** i.e., not a demon in his father's shape   [150] **truepenny** honest fellow   [156] ***Hic et ubique*** here and everywhere (Latin)

GHOST [*beneath*]   Swear by his sword.
HAMLET   Well said, old mole! Canst work i' th' earth so fast?
   A worthy pioner!° Once more remove, good friends.
HORATIO   O day and night, but this is wondrous strange!
HAMLET   And therefore as a stranger give it welcome.   165
   There are more things in heaven and earth, Horatio,
   Than are dreamt of in your philosophy.
   But come:
   Here as before, never, so help you mercy,
   How strange or odd some'er I bear myself   170
   (As I perchance hereafter shall think meet
   To put an antic disposition° on),
   That you, at such times seeing me, never shall
   With arms encumb'red° thus, or this headshake,
   Or by pronouncing of some doubtful phrase,   175
   As "Well, well, we know," or "We could, an if we would,"
   Or "If we list to speak," or "There be, an if they might,"
   Or such ambiguous giving out, to note
   That you know aught of me—this do swear,
   So grace and mercy at your most need help you.   180
GHOST [*beneath*]   Swear.

   [*They swear.*]

HAMLET   Rest, rest, perturbèd spirit. So, gentlemen,
   With all my love I do commend me° to you,
   And what so poor a man as Hamlet is
   May do t' express his love and friending to you,   185
   God willing, shall not lack. Let us go in together,
   And still your fingers on your lips, I pray.
   The time is out of joint. O cursèd spite,
   That ever I was born to set it right!
   Nay, come, let's go together.   *Exeunt.* 190

[ACT II

Scene I. A room.]

   Enter old POLONIUS, *with his man* REYNALDO.

POLONIUS   Give him this money and these notes, Reynaldo.
REYNALDO   I will, my lord.

---

¹⁶³ **pioner** digger of mines   ¹⁷² **antic disposition** fantastic behavior   ¹⁷⁴ **encumb'red** folded
¹⁸³ **commend me** entrust myself

POLONIUS   You shall do marvell's° wisely, good Reynaldo,
  Before you visit him, to make inquire
  Of his behavior.
REYNALDO   My lord, I did intend it.   5
POLONIUS   Marry, well said, very well said. Look you sir,
  Inquire me first what Danskers° are in Paris,
  And how, and who, what means, and where they keep,°
  What company, at what expense; and finding
  By this encompassment° and drift of question   10
  That they do know my son, come you more nearer
  Than your particular demands° will touch it.
  Take you as 'twere some distant knowledge of him,
  As thus, "I know his father and his friends,
  And in part him." Do you mark this, Reynaldo?   15
REYNALDO   Ay, very well, my lord.
POLONIUS   "And in part him, but," you may say, "not well,
  But if't be he I mean, he's very wild,
  Addicted so and so." And there put on him
  What forgeries° you please; marry, none so rank   20
  As may dishonor him—take heed of that—
  But, sir, such wanton, wild, and usual slips
  As are companions noted and most known
  To youth and liberty.
REYNALDO   As gaming, my lord.
POLONIUS   Ay, or drinking, fencing, swearing, quarreling,   25
  Drabbing.° You may go so far.
REYNALDO   My lord, that would dishonor him.
POLONIUS   Faith, no, as you may season it in the charge.
  You must not put another scandal on him,
  That he is open to incontinency.°   30
  That's not my meaning. But breathe his faults so quaintly°
  That they may seem the taints of liberty,
  The flash and outbreak of a fiery mind,
  A savageness in unreclaimèd blood,
  Of general assault.°
REYNALDO   But, my good lord——   35
POLONIUS   Wherefore should you do this?
REYNALDO   Ay, my lord,
  I would know that.

II.i. ³ **marvell's** marvelous(ly)   ⁷ **Danskers** Danes   ⁸ **keep** dwell   ¹⁰ **encompassment** circling
¹² **demands** questions   ²⁰ **forgeries** inventions   ²⁶ **Drabbing** wenching   ³⁰ **incontinency** habitual licentiousness   ³¹ **quaintly** ingeniously, delicately   ³⁵ **Of general assault** common to all men

POLONIUS   Marry, sir, here's my drift,
And I believe it is a fetch of warrant°
You laying these slight sullies on my son
As 'twere a thing a little soiled i' th' working,   40
Mark you,
Your party in converse, him you would sound,
Having ever seen in the prenominate crimes°
The youth you breathe of guilty, be assured
He closes with you in this consequence:°   45
"Good sir," or so, or "friend," or "gentleman"—
According to the phrase or the addition°
Of man and country—

REYNALDO   Very good, my lord.

POLONIUS   And then, sir, does 'a° this—'a does—
What was I about to say? By the mass, I was about   50
to say something! Where did I leave?

REYNALDO   At "closes in the consequence," at "friend or so," and
     "gentlemen."

POLONIUS   At "closes in the consequence"—Ay, marry!
He closes thus: "I know the gentleman;   55
I saw him yesterday, or t'other day,
Or then, or then, with such or such, and, as you say,
There was 'a gaming, there o'ertook in's rouse,
There falling out at tennis"; or perchance,
"I saw him enter such a house of sale,"   60
Videlicet,° a brothel, or so forth.
See you now—
Your bait of falsehood take this carp of truth,
And thus do we of wisdom and of reach,°
With windlasses° and with assays of bias,°   65
By indirections find directions out.
So, by my former lecture and advice,
Shall you my son. You have me, have you not?

REYNALDO   My lord, I have.

POLONIUS   God bye ye, fare ye well.

REYNALDO   Good my lord.   70

POLONIUS   Observe his inclination in yourself.°

---

38 fetch of warrant justifiable device   **43 Having . . . crimes** if he has ever seen in the aforementioned crimes   **45 He closes . . . this consequence** he falls in with you in this conclusion   **47 addition** title   **49 'a** he   **61 Videlicet** namely   **64 reach** far-reaching awareness (?)   **65 windlasses** circuitous courses   **65 assays of bias** indirect attempts (metaphor from bowling; *bias* = curved course)   **71 in yourself** for yourself

REYNALDO   I shall, my lord.
POLONIUS   And let him ply his music.
REYNALDO   Well, my lord.
POLONIUS   Farewell.   *Exit* REYNALDO.

Enter OPHELIA.

                How now, Ophelia, what's the matter?
OPHELIA   O my lord, my lord, I have been so affrighted!   75
POLONIUS   With what, i' th' name of God?
OPHELIA   My lord, as I was sewing in my closet,°
  Lord Hamlet, with his doublet all unbraced,°
  No hat upon his head, his stockings fouled,
  Ungartered, and down-gyvèd° to his ankle,   80
  Pale as his shirt, his knees knocking each other,
  And with a look so piteous in purport,°
  As if he had been loosèd out of hell
  To speak of horrors—he comes before me.
POLONIUS   Mad for thy love?
OPHELIA   My lord, I do not know,   85
  But truly I do fear it.
POLONIUS   What said he?
OPHELIA   He took me by the wrist and held me hard;
  Then goes he to the length of all his arm,
  And with his other hand thus o'er his brow
  He falls to such perusal of my face   90
  As 'a would draw it. Long stayed he so.
  At last, a little shaking of mine arm,
  And thrice his head thus waving up and down,
  He raised a sigh so piteous and profound
  As it did seem to shatter all his bulk   95
  And end his being. That done, he lets me go,
  And, with his head over his shoulder turned,
  He seemed to find his way without his eyes,
  For out o' doors he went without their helps,
  And to the last bended their light on me.   100
POLONIUS   Come, go with me. I will go seek the King.
  This is the very ecstasy° of love,
  Whose violent property fordoes° itself

---

⁷⁷ **closet** private room   ⁷⁸ **doublet all unbraced** jacket entirely unlaced   ⁸⁰ **down-gyvèd** hanging down like fetters   ⁸² **purport** expression   ¹⁰² **ecstasy** madness   ¹⁰³ **property fordoes** quality destroys

And leads the will to desperate undertakings
As oft as any passions under heaven   105
That does afflict our natures. I am sorry.
What, have you given him any hard words of late?
OPHELIA   No, my good lord; but as you did command,
I did repel his letters and denied
His access to me.
POLONIUS   That hath made him mad.   110
I am sorry that with better heed and judgment
I had not quoted° him. I feared he did but trifle
And meant to wrack thee; but beshrew my jealousy.°
By heaven, it is as proper° to our age
To cast beyond ourselves° in our opinions   115
As it is common for the younger sort
To lack discretion. Come, go we to the King.
This must be known, which, being kept close, might move
More grief to hide than hate to utter love.°
Come.   *Exeunt.* 120

[Scene II. The castle.]

Flourish. Enter KING *and* QUEEN, ROSENCRANTZ, *and* GUILDENSTERN
[*with others*].

KING   Welcome, dear Rosencrantz and Guildenstern.
Moreover that° we much did long to see you,
The need we have to use you did provoke
Our hasty sending. Something have you heard
Of Hamlet's transformation: so call it,   5
Sith° nor th' exterior nor the inward man
Resembles that it was. What it should be,
More than his father's death, that thus hath put him
So much from th' understanding of himself,
I cannot dream of. I entreat you both   10
That, being of so° young days brought up with him,
And sith so neighbored to his youth and havior,°
That you vouchsafe your rest° here in our court
Some little time, so by your companies

[112] **quoted** noted   [113] **beshrew my jealousy** curse on my suspicions   [114] **proper** natural   [115] **To cast beyond ourselves** to be overcalculating   [117–119] **Come, go . . . utter love** (the general meaning is that while telling the King of Hamlet's love may anger the King, more grief would come from keeping it secret)   *II.ii.* [2] **Moreover that** beside the fact that   [6] **Sith** since   [11] **of so** from such   [12] **youth and havior** behavior in his youth   [13] **vouchsafe your rest** consent to remain

To draw him on to pleasures, and to gather   15
So much as from occasion you may glean,
Whether aught to us unknown afflicts him thus,
That opened° lies within our remedy.

QUEEN   Good gentlemen, he hath much talked of you,
And sure I am, two men there is not living   20
To whom he more adheres. If it will please you
To show us so much gentry° and good will
As to expend your time with us awhile
For the supply and profit of our hope,
Your visitation shall receive such thanks   25
As fits a king's remembrance.

ROSENCRANTZ   Both your Majesties
Might, by the sovereign power you have of us,
Put your dread pleasures more into command
Than to entreaty.

GUILDENSTERN   But we both obey,
And here give up ourselves in the full bent°   30
To lay our service freely at your feet,
To be commanded.

KING   Thanks, Rosencrantz and gentle Guildenstern.

QUEEN   Thanks, Guildenstern and gentle Rosencrantz.
And I beseech you instantly to visit   35
My too much changèd son. Go, some of you,
And bring these gentlemen where Hamlet is.

GUILDENSTERN   Heavens make our presence and our practices
Pleasant and helpful to him!

QUEEN   Ay, amen!

                    Exeunt ROSENCRANTZ *and* GUILDENSTERN
                                    [*with some Attendants*].

Enter POLONIUS.

POLONIUS   Th' ambassadors from Norway, my good lord,   40
Are joyfully returned.

KING   Thou still° hast been the father of good news.

POLONIUS   Have I, my lord? Assure you, my good liege,
I hold my duty, as I hold my soul,
Both to my God and to my gracious king;   45
And I do think, or else this brain of mine

---

¹⁸ **opened** revealed   ²² **gentry** courtesy   ³⁰ **in the full bent** entirely (the figure of a bow bent to its capacity)   ⁴² **still** always

Hunts not the trail of policy so sure°
As it hath used to do, that I have found
The very cause of Hamlet's lunacy.
KING   O, speak of that! That do I long to hear.   50
POLONIUS   Give first admittance to th' ambassadors.
   My news shall be the fruit to that great feast.
KING   Thyself do grace to them and bring them in.

                                            [*Exit* POLONIUS.]

He tells me, my dear Gertrude, he hath found
The head and source of all your son's distemper.   55
QUEEN   I doubt° it is no other but the main,°
   His father's death and our o'erhasty marriage.
KING   Well, we shall sift him.

   Enter POLONIUS, VOLTEMAND, *and* CORNELIUS.

                        Welcome, my good friends.
   Say, Voltemand, what from our brother Norway?
VOLTEMAND   Most fair return of greetings and desires.   60
   Upon our first,° he sent out to suppress
   His nephew's levies, which to him appeared
   To be a preparation 'gainst the Polack;
   But better looked into, he truly found
   It was against your Highness, whereat grieved,   65
   That so his sickness, age, and impotence
   Was falsely borne in hand,° sends out arrests
   On Fortinbras; which he, in brief, obeys,
   Receives rebuke from Norway, and in fine,°
   Makes vow before his uncle never more   70
   To give th' assay° of arms against your Majesty.
   Whereon old Norway, overcome with joy,
   Gives him threescore thousand crowns in annual fee
   And his commission to employ those soldiers,
   So levied as before, against the Polack,   75
   With an entreaty, herein further shown, [*gives a paper*]
   That it might please you to give quiet pass
   Through your dominions for this enterprise,
   On such regards of safety and allowance°
   As therein are set down.

---

⁴⁷ **Hunts not . . . so sure** does not follow clues of political doings with such sureness   ⁵⁶ **doubt** suspect   ⁵⁶ **main** principal point   ⁶¹ **first** first audience   ⁶⁷ **borne in hand** deceived   ⁶⁹ **in fine** finally   ⁷¹ **assay** trial   ⁷⁹ **regards of safety and allowance** i.e., conditions

KING   It likes us well;   80
  And at our more considered time° we'll read,
  Answer, and think upon this business.
  Meantime, we thank you for your well-took labor.
  Go to your rest; at night we'll feast together.
  Most welcome home!   *Exeunt* AMBASSADORS.
POLONIUS   This business is well ended.   85
  My liege and madam, to expostulate°
  What majesty should be, what duty is,
  Why day is day, night night, and time is time,
  Were nothing but to waste night, day, and time.
  Therefore, since brevity is the soul of wit,°   90
  And tediousness the limbs and outward flourishes,
  I will be brief. Your noble son is mad.
  Mad call I it, for, to define true madness,
  What is't but to be nothing else but mad?
  But let that go.
QUEEN   More matter, with less art.   95
POLONIUS   Madam, I swear I use no art at all.
  That he's mad, 'tis true: 'tis true 'tis pity,
  And pity 'tis 'tis true—a foolish figure.°
  But farewell it, for I will use no art.
  Mad let us grant him then; and now remains   100
  That we find out the cause of this effect,
  Or rather say, the cause of this defect,
  For this effect defective comes by cause.
  Thus it remains, and the remainder thus.
  Perpend.°   105
  I have a daughter: have, while she is mine,
  Who in her duty and obedience, mark,
  Hath given me this. Now gather, and surmise.

[*Reads*] *the letter.*

  "To the celestial, and my soul's idol, the most
  beautified Ophelia"—   110

That's an ill phrase, a vile phrase; "beautified" is a vile
phrase. But you shall hear. Thus:

  "In her excellent white bosom, these, &c."

---

⁸¹ **considered time** time proper for considering   ⁸⁶ **expostulate** discuss   ⁹⁰ **wit** wisdom, under-standing   ⁹⁸ **figure** figure of rhetoric   ¹⁰⁵ **Perpend** consider carefully

QUEEN   Came this from Hamlet to her?

POLONIUS   Good madam, stay awhile. I will be faithful.   115

> "Doubt thou the stars are fire,
>   Doubt that the sun doth move;
> Doubt° truth to be a liar,
>   But never doubt I love.

O dear Ophelia, I am ill at these numbers.° I have   120
not art to reckon my groans; but that I love thee
best, O most best, believe it. Adieu.

> Thine evermore, most dear lady,
> whilst this machine° is to him, HAMLET."

This in obedience hath my daughter shown me,   125
And more above° hath his solicitings,
As they fell out by time, by means, and place,
All given to mine ear.

KING   But how hath she
   Received his love?

POLONIUS   What do you think of me?

KING   As a man faithful and honorable.   130

POLONIUS   I would fain prove so. But what might you think,
   When I had seen this hot love on the wing
   (As I perceived it, I must tell you that,
   Before my daughter told me), what might you,
   Or my dear Majesty your Queen here, think,   135
   If I had played the desk or table book,°
   Or given my heart a winking,° mute and dumb,
   Or looked upon this love with idle sight?
   What might you think? No, I went round to work
   And my young mistress thus I did bespeak: 140
   "Lord Hamlet is a prince, out of thy star.°
   This must not be." And then I prescripts gave her,
   That she should lock herself from his resort,
   Admit no messengers, receive no tokens.
   Which done, she took the fruits of my advice,   145
   And he, repellèd, a short tale to make,
   Fell into a sadness, then into a fast,
   Thence to a watch,° thence into a weakness,

---

[118] **Doubt** suspect   [120] **ill at these numbers** unskilled in verses   [124] **machine** complex device (here, his body)   [126] **more above** in addition   [136] **played the desk or table book** i.e., been a passive recipient of secrets   [137] **winking** closing of the eyes   [141] **star** sphere   [148] **watch** wakefulness

Thence to a lightness,° and, by this declension,
Into the madness wherein now he raves,   150
    And all we mourn for.
KING   Do you think 'tis this?
QUEEN   It may be, very like.
POLONIUS   Hath there been such a time, I would fain know that,
    That I have positively said "'Tis so,"
    When it proved otherwise?
KING   Not that I know.   155
POLONIUS [*pointing to his head and shoulder*].   Take this from this, if this be
        otherwise.
    If circumstances lead me, I will find
    Where truth is hid, though it were hid indeed
    Within the center.°
KING   How may we try it further?
POLONIUS   You know sometimes he walks four hours together   160
    Here in the lobby.
QUEEN   So he does indeed.
POLONIUS   At such a time I'll loose my daughter to him.
    Be you and I behind an arras° then.
    Mark the encounter. If he love her not,
    And be not from his reason fall'n thereon,   165
    Let me be no assistant for a state
    But keep a farm and carters.
KING   We will try it.

Enter HAMLET *reading on a book.*

QUEEN   But look where sadly the poor wretch comes reading.
POLONIUS   Away, I do beseech you both, away.
                                                              Exit KING *and* QUEEN.

    I'll board him presently.° O, give me leave.   170
    How does my good Lord Hamlet?
HAMLET   Well, God-a-mercy.
POLONIUS   Do you know me, my lord?
HAMLET   Excellent well. You are a fishmonger.°
POLONIUS   Not I, my lord.   175
HAMLET   Then I would you were so honest a man.
POLONIUS   Honest, my lord?

---

¹⁴⁹ **lightness** mental derangement   ¹⁵⁹ **center** center of the earth   ¹⁶³ **arras** tapestry hanging in front of a wall   ¹⁷⁰ **board him presently** accost him at once   ¹⁷⁴ **fishmonger** dealer in fish (slang for a procurer)

HAMLET   Ay, sir. To be honest, as this world goes, is to be one man picked out of
ten thousand.

POLONIUS   That's very true, my lord.   180

HAMLET   For if the sun breed maggots in a dead dog, being a good kissing car-
rion°——Have you a daughter?

POLONIUS   I have, my lord.

HAMLET   Let her not walk i' th' sun. Conception° is a blessing, but as your daughter
may conceive, friend, look to't.   185

POLONIUS [*aside*]   How say you by that? Still harping on my daughter. Yet he knew
me not at first. 'A said I was a fishmonger. 'A is far gone, far gone. And truly in
my youth I suffered much extremity for love, very near this. I'll speak to him
again.—What do you read, my lord?

HAMLET   Words, words, words.   190

POLONIUS   What is the matter,° my lord?

HAMLET   Between who?

POLONIUS   I mean the matter that you read, my lord.

HAMLET   Slanders, sir; for the satirical rogue says here that old men have
gray beards, that their faces are wrinkled, their eyes purging thick amber and   195
plumtree gum, and that they have a plentiful lack of wit, together with most weak
hams. All which, sir, though I most powerfully and potently believe, yet I hold it
not honesty° to have it thus set down; for you yourself, sir, should be old as I am
if, like a crab, you could go backward.

POLONIUS [*aside*]   Though this be madness, yet there is method in't. Will you walk   200
out of the air, my lord?

HAMLET   Into my grave.

POLONIUS   Indeed, that's out of the air. [*Aside.*] How pregnant° sometimes his
replies are! A happiness° that often madness hits on, which reason and sanity
could not so prosperously be delivered of. I will leave him and suddenly contrive 205
the means of meeting between him and my daughter.—My lord, I will take my
leave of you.

HAMLET   You cannot take from me anything that I will more willingly part withal—
except my life, except my life, except my life.

Enter GUILDENSTERN *and* ROSENCRANTZ.

POLONIUS   Fare you well, my lord.   210

HAMLET   These tedious old fools!

POLONIUS   You go to seek the Lord Hamlet? There he is.

ROSENCRANTZ [*to Polonius*]   God save you, sir!   [*Exit* POLONIUS.]

181–182 **a good kissing carrion** (perhaps the meaning is "a good piece of flesh to kiss," but many editors
emend *good* to *god*, taking the word to refer to the sun)   184 **Conception** (1) understanding, (2) becoming
pregnant   191 **matter** (Polonius means "subject matter," but Hamlet pretends to take the word in the
sense of "quarrel")   198 **honesty** decency   203 **pregnant** meaningful   204 **happiness** apt turn of
phrase

GUILDENSTERN   My honored lord!

ROSENCRANTZ   My most dear lord!   215

HAMLET   My excellent good friends! How dost thou, Guildenstern? Ah, Rosencrantz! Good lads, how do you both?

ROSENCRANTZ   As the indifferent° children of the earth.

GUILDENSTERN   Happy in that we are not overhappy. On Fortune's cap we are not
the very button.   220

HAMLET   Nor the soles of her shoe?

ROSENCRANTZ   Neither, my lord.

HAMLET   Then you live about her waist, or in the middle of her favors?

GUILDENSTERN   Faith, her privates° we.

HAMLET   In the secret parts of Fortune? O, most true! She is a strumpet. What 225
news?

ROSENCRANTZ   None, my lord, but that the world's grown honest.

HAMLET   Then is doomsday near. But your news is not true. Let me question more
in particular. What have you, my good friends, deserved at the hands of Fortune
that she sends you to prison hither?   230

GUILDENSTERN   Prison, my lord?

HAMLET   Denmark's a prison.

ROSENCRANTZ   Then is the world one.

HAMLET   A goodly one, in which there are many confines, wards,° and dungeons,
Denmark being one o' th' worst.   235

ROSENCRANTZ   We think not so, my lord.

HAMLET   Why, then 'tis none to you, for there is nothing either good or bad but
thinking makes it so. To me it is a prison.

ROSENCRANTZ   Why then your ambition makes it one. 'Tis too narrow for your mind.

HAMLET   O God, I could be bounded in a nutshell and count myself a king of infinite 240
space, were it not that I have bad dreams.

GUILDENSTERN   Which dreams indeed are ambition, for the very substance of the
ambitious is merely the shadow of a dream.

HAMLET   A dream itself is but a shadow.

ROSENCRANTZ   Truly, and I hold ambition of so airy and light a quality that it is but a 245
shadow's shadow.

HAMLET   Then are our beggars bodies, and our monarchs and outstretched heroes
the beggars' shadows.° Shall we to th' court? For, by my fay,° I cannot reason.

BOTH   We'll wait upon you.

HAMLET   No such matter. I will not sort you with the rest of my servants, for, to 250
speak to you like an honest man, I am most dreadfully attended. But in the
beaten way of friendship, what make you at Elsinore?

ROSENCRANTZ   To visit you, my lord; no other occasion.

---

²¹⁸ **indifferent** ordinary   ²²⁴ **privates** ordinary men (with a pun on "private parts")   ²³⁴ **wards** cells
²⁴⁷⁻²⁴⁸ **Then are . . . beggars' shadows** i.e., by your logic, beggars (lacking ambition) are substantial,
and great men are elongated shadows   ²⁴⁸ **fay** faith

HAMLET Beggar that I am, I am even poor in thanks, but I thank you; and sure, dear
 friends, my thanks are too dear a halfpenny.° Were you not sent for? Is it your 255
 own inclining? Is it a free visitation? Come, come, deal justly with me. Come,
 come; nay, speak.

GUILDENSTERN What should we say, my lord?

HAMLET Why anything—but to th' purpose. You were sent for, and there is a kind
 of confession in your looks, which your modesties have not craft enough to color. 260
 I know the good King and Queen have sent for you.

ROSENCRANTZ To what end, my lord?

HAMLET That you must teach me. But let me conjure you by the rights of our
 fellowship, by the consonancy of our youth, by the obligation of our ever
 preserved love, and by what more dear a better proposer can charge you withal, 265
 be even and direct with me, whether you were sent for or no.

ROSENCRANTZ [*aside to* GUILDENSTERN] What say you?

HAMLET [*aside*] Nay then, I have an eye of you.—If you love me, hold not off.

GUILDENSTERN My lord, we were sent for.

HAMLET I will tell you why; so shall my anticipation prevent your discovery,° and 270
 your secrecy to the King and Queen molt no feather. I have of late, but wherefore
 I know not, lost all my mirth, forgone all custom of exercises; and indeed, it goes
 so heavily with my disposition that this goodly frame, the earth, seems to me a
 sterile promontory; this most excellent canopy, the air, look you, this brave
 o'erhanging firmament, this majestical roof fretted° with golden fire: why, it 275
 appeareth nothing to me but a foul and pestilent congregation of vapors. What a
 piece of work is a man, how noble in reason, how infinite in faculties, in form and
 moving how express° and admirable, in action how like an angel, in apprehension
 how like a god: the beauty of the world, the paragon of animals; and yet to me,
 what is this quintessence of dust? Man delights not me; nor woman neither, 280
 though by your smiling you seem to say so.

ROSENCRANTZ My lord, there was no such stuff in my thoughts.

HAMLET Why did ye laugh then, when I said "Man delights not me"?

ROSENCRANTZ To think, my lord, if you delight not in man, what lenten° entertainment the players shall receive from you. We coted° them on the way, and 285
 hither are they coming to offer you service.

HAMLET He that plays the king shall be welcome; his Majesty shall have tribute of
 me; the adventurous knight shall use his foil and target;° the lover shall not sigh
 gratis; the humorous man° shall end his part in peace; the clown shall make those
 laugh whose lungs are tickle o' th' sere;° and the lady shall say her mind freely, 290
 or° the blank verse shall halt° for't. What players are they?

---

²⁵⁵ **too dear a halfpenny** i.e., not worth a halfpenny   ²⁷⁰ **prevent your discovery** forstall your
disclosure   ²⁷⁵ **fretted** adorned   ²⁷⁸ **express** exact   ²⁸⁴ **lenten** meager   ²⁸⁵ **coted** overtook
²⁸⁸ **target** shield   ²⁸⁹ **humorous man** i.e., eccentric man (among stock characters in dramas were men
dominated by a "humor" or odd trait)   ²⁹⁰ **tickle o' th' sere** on hair trigger (*sere* = part of the gunlock)
²⁹¹ **or** else   ²⁹¹ **halt** limp

ROSENCRANTZ   Even those you were wont to take such delight in, the tragedians of
    the city.

HAMLET   How chances it they travel? Their residence, both in reputation and profit,
    was better both ways.   295

ROSENCRANTZ   I think their inhibition° comes by the means of the late innovation.°

HAMLET   Do they hold the same estimation they did when I was in the city? Are they
    so followed?

ROSENCRANTZ   No indeed, are they not.

HAMLET   How comes it? Do they grow rusty?   300

ROSENCRANTZ   Nay, their endeavor keeps in the wonted pace, but there is, sir, an
    eyrie° of children, little eyases, that cry out on the top of question° and are most
    tyrannically° clapped for't. These are now the fashion, and so berattle the
    common stages° (so they call them) that many wearing rapiers are afraid of
    goosequills° and dare scarce come thither.   305

HAMLET   What, are they children? Who maintains 'em? How are they escoted?° Will
    they pursue the quality° no longer than they can sing? Will they not say
    afterwards, if they should grow themselves to common players (as it is most
    like, if their means are no better), their writers do them wrong to make them
    exclaim against their own succession?°   310

ROSENCRANTZ   Faith, there has been much to-do on both sides, and the nation holds
    it no sin to tarre° them to controversy. There was, for a while, no money bid for
    argument° unless the poet and the player went to cuffs in the question.

HAMLET   Is't possible?

GUILDENSTERN   O, there has been much throwing about of brains.   315

HAMLET   Do the boys carry it away?

ROSENCRANTZ   Ay, that they do, my lord—Hercules and his load° too.

HAMLET   It is not very strange, for my uncle is King of Denmark, and those that
    would make mouths at him while my father lived give twenty, forty, fifty, a
    hundred ducats apiece for his picture in little. 'Sblood,° there is something in this 320
    more than natural, if philosophy could find it out.

A flourish.

GUILDENSTERN   There are the players.

HAMLET   Gentlemen, you are welcome to Elsinore. Your hands, come then. Th'
    appurtenance of welcome is fashion and ceremony. Let me comply° with you in

---

²⁹⁶ **inhibition** hindrance   ²⁹⁶ **innovation** (probably an allusion to the companies of child actors that
had become popular and were offering serious competition to the adult actors)   ³⁰² **eyrie** nest
³⁰² **eyases, that . . . of question** unfledged hawks that cry shrilly above others in matter of debate
³⁰³ **tyrannically** violently   ³⁰⁴ **berattle the common stages** cry down the public theaters (with the
adult acting companies)   ³⁰⁵ **goosequills** pens (of satirists who ridicule the public theaters and their
audiences)   ³⁰⁶ **escoted** financially supported   ³⁰⁷ **quality** profession of acting   ³¹⁰ **succession**
future   ³¹² **tarre** incite   ³¹³ **argument** plot of a play   ³¹⁷ **Hercules and his load** i.e., the whole
world (with a reference to the Globe Theatre, which had a sign that represented Hercules bearing the
globe)   ³²⁰ **'Sblood** by God's blood   ³²⁴ **comply** be courteous

this garb,° lest my extent° to the players (which I tell you must show fairly 325
outwards) should more appear like entertainment than yours. You are welcome.
But my uncle-father and aunt-mother are deceived.

GUILDENSTERN   In what, my dear lord?

HAMLET   I am but mad north-northwest:° when the wind is southerly I know a hawk
from a handsaw.°   330

Enter POLONIUS.

POLONIUS   Well be with you, gentlemen.

HAMLET   Hark you, Guildenstern, and you too; at each ear a hearer. That great baby
you see there is not yet out of his swaddling clouts.

ROSENCRANTZ   Happily° he is the second time come to them, for they say an old man
is twice a child.   335

HAMLET   I will prophesy he comes to tell me of the players. Mark it. —You say right,
sir; a Monday morning, 'twas then indeed.

POLONIUS   My lord, I have news to tell you.

HAMLET   My lord, I have news to tell you. When Roscius° was an actor in
Rome——   340

POLONIUS   The actors are come hither, my lord.

HAMLET   Buzz, buzz.°

POLONIUS   Upon my honor——

HAMLET   Then came each actor on his ass——

POLONIUS   The best actors in the world, either for tragedy, comedy, history, 345
pastoral, pastoral-comical, historical-pastoral, tragical-historical, tragical-
comical-historical-pastoral; scene individable,° or poem unlimited.° Seneca°
cannot be too heavy, nor Plautus° too light. For the law of writ and the liberty,°
these are the only men.

HAMLET   O Jeptha, judge of Israel,° what a treasure hadst thou!   350

POLONIUS   What a treasure had he, my lord?

HAMLET   Why,

> "One fair daughter, and no more,
>   The which he lovèd passing well."

---

³²⁵ **garb** outward show   ³²⁵ **extent** behavior   ³²⁹ **north-northwest** i.e., on one point of the compass
only   ³³⁰ **hawk from a handsaw** (*hawk* can refer not only to a bird but to a kind of pickax; *handsaw*—
a carpenter's tool—may involve a similar pun on "hernshaw," a heron)   ³³⁴ **Happily** perhaps
³³⁹ **Roscius** (a famous Roman comic actor)   ³⁴² **Buzz, buzz** (an interjection, perhaps indicating
that the news is old)   ³⁴⁷ **scene individable** plays observing the unities of time, place, and action
³⁴⁷ **poem unlimited** plays not restricted by the tenets of criticism   ³⁴⁷ **Seneca** (Roman tragic dramatist)   ³⁴⁸ **Plautus** (Roman comic dramatist)   ³⁴⁸ **For the law of writ and liberty** (perhaps "for
sticking to the text and for improvising"; perhaps "for classical plays and for modern loosely written
plays")   ³⁵⁰ **Jeptha, judge of Israel** (the title of a ballad on the Hebrew judge who sacrificed his
daughter; see Judges 11)

POLONIUS [*aside*] Still on my daughter. 355
HAMLET Am I not i' th' right, old Jeptha?
POLONIUS If you call me Jeptha, my lord, I have a daughter that I love passing well.
HAMLET Nay, that follows not.
POLONIUS What follows then, my lord?
HAMLET Why, 360

"As by lot, God wot,"

and then, you know,

"It came to pass, as most like it was."

The first row of the pious chanson° will show you more, for look where my
abridgment° comes. 365

Enter the PLAYERS.

You are welcome, masters, welcome, all. I am glad to see thee well. Welcome,
good friends. O, old friend, why, thy face is valanced° since I saw thee last.
Com'st thou to beard me in Denmark? What, my young lady° and mistress? By'r
Lady, your ladyship is nearer to heaven than when I saw you last by the altitude
of a chopine.° Pray God your voice, like a piece of uncurrent gold, be not cracked 370
within the ring.°—Masters, you are all welcome. We'll e'en to't like French
falconers, fly at anything we see. We'll have a speech straight. Come, give us a
taste of your quality. Come, a passionate speech.
PLAYER What speech, my good lord?
HAMLET I heard thee speak me a speech once, but it was never acted, or if it was, 375
not above once, for the play, I remember, pleased not the million; 'twas caviary
to the general,° but it was (as I received it, and others, whose judgments in such
matters cried in the top of° mine) an excellent play, well digested in the scenes,
set down with as much modesty as cunning.° I remember one said there were no
sallets° in the lines to make the matter savory; nor no matter in the phrase that 380
might indict the author of affectation, but called it an honest method, as
wholesome as sweet, and by very much more handsome than fine.° One speech
in't I chiefly loved. 'Twas Aeneas' tale to Dido, and thereabout of it especially
when he speaks of Priam's slaughter. If it live in your memory, begin at this
line—let me see, let me see: 385

---

³⁶⁴ **row of the pious chanson** stanza of the scriptural song   ³⁶⁵ **abridgment** (1) i.e., entertainers,
who abridge the time, (2) interrupters   ³⁶⁷ **valanced** fringed (with a beard)   ³⁶⁸ **young lady** i.e., boy
for female roles   ³⁷⁰ **chopine** thick-soled shoe   ³⁷⁰⁻³⁷¹ **like a piece . . . the ring** (a coin was unfit
for legal tender if a crack extended from the edge through the ring enclosing the monarch's head. Hamlet,
punning on *ring*, refers to the change of voice that the boy actor will undergo)   ³⁷⁶⁻³⁷⁷ **caviary to the
general** i.e., too choice for the multitude   ³⁷⁸ **in the top of** overtopping   ³⁷⁹ **modesty as cunning**
restraint as art   ³⁸⁰ **sallets** salads, spicy jests   ³⁸² **more handsome than fine** well-proportioned
rather than ornamented

"The rugged Pyrrhus, like th' Hyrcanian beast°—"

'Tis not so; it begins with Pyrrhus:

"The rugged Pyrrhus, he whose sable° arms,
Black as his purpose, did the night resemble
When he lay couchèd in th' ominous horse,° 390
Hath now this dread and black complexion smeared
With heraldry more dismal.° Head to foot
Now is he total gules, horridly tricked°
With blood of fathers, mothers, daughters, sons,
Baked and impasted° with the parching streets, 395
That lend a tyrannous and a damnèd light
To their lord's murder. Roasted in wrath and fire,
And thus o'ersizèd° with coagulate gore,
With eyes like carbuncles, the hellish Pyrrhus
Old grandsire Priam seeks." 400

So, proceed you.

POLONIUS   Fore God, my lord, well spoken, with good accent and good discretion.

PLAYER   "Anon he finds him,
Striking too short at Greeks. His antique sword,
Rebellious to his arm, lies where it falls, 405
Repugnant to command.° Unequal matched,
Pyrrhus at Priam drives, in rage strikes wide,
But with the whiff and wind of his fell sword
Th' unnervèd father falls. Then senseless Ilium,°
Seeming to feel this blow, with flaming top 410
Stoops to his base,° and with a hideous crash
Takes prisoner Pyrrhus' ear. For lo, his sword,
Which was declining on the milky head
Of reverend Priam, seemed i' th' air to stick.
So as a painted tyrant° Pyrrhus stood, 415
And like a neutral to his will and matter°
Did nothing.
But as we often see, against° some storm,
A silence in the heavens, the rack° stand still,

---

[386] **Hyrcanian beast** i.e., tiger (Hyrcania was in Asia)   [388] **sable** black   [390] **ominous horse** i.e.,
wooden horse at the siege of Troy   [392] **dismal** ill-omened   [393] **total gules, horridly tricked** all red,
horridly adorned   [395] **impasted** encrusted   [398] **o'ersizèd** smeared over   [406] **Repugnant to
command** disobedient   [409] **senseless Ilium** insensate Troy   [411] **Stoops to his base** collapses
(*his* = its)   [415] **painted tyrant** tyrant in a picture   [416] **matter** task   [418] **against** just before
[419] **rack** clouds

The bold winds speechless, and the orb below 420
As hush as death, anon the dreadful thunder
Doth rend the region, so after Pyrrhus' pause,
A rousèd vengeance sets him new awork,
And never did the Cyclops' hammers fall
On Mars's armor, forged for proof eterne,° 425
With less remorse than Pyrrhus' bleeding sword
Now falls on Priam.
Out, out, thou strumpet Fortune! All you gods,
In general synod° take away her power,
Break all the spokes and fellies° from her wheel, 430
And bowl the round nave° down the hill of heaven,
As low as to the fiends."
POLONIUS   This is too long.
HAMLET   It shall to the barber's, with your beard. —Prithee say on. He's for a jig or
a tale of bawdry, or he sleeps. Say on; come to Hecuba. 435
PLAYER   "But who (ah woe!) had seen the mobled° queen—"
HAMLET   "The mobled queen"?
POLONIUS   That's good. "Mobled queen" is good.
PLAYER   "Run barefoot up and down, threat'ning the flames
With bisson rheum;° a clout° upon that head 440
Where late the diadem stood, and for a robe,
About her lank and all o'erteemèd° loins,
A blanket in the alarm of fear caught up—
Who this had seen, with tongue in venom steeped
'Gainst Fortune's state would treason have pronounced. 445
But if the gods themselves did see her then,
When she saw Pyrrhus make malicious sport
In mincing with his sword her husband's limbs,
The instant burst of clamor that she made
(Unless things mortal move them not at all) 450
Would have made milch° the burning eyes of heaven
And passion in the gods."

POLONIUS   Look, whe'r° he has not turned his color, and has tears in's eyes. Prithee
no more.
HAMLET   'Tis well. I'll have thee speak out the rest of this soon. Good my lord, will 455
you see the players well bestowed?° Do you hear? Let them be well used, for

---
⁴²⁵ **proof eterne** eternal endurance   ⁴²⁹ **synod** council   ⁴³⁰ **fellies** rims   ⁴³¹ **nave** hub
⁴³⁶ **mobled** muffled   ⁴⁴⁰ **bisson rheum** blinding tears   ⁴⁴⁰ **clout** rag   ⁴⁴² **o'erteemèd** exhausted
with childbearing   ⁴⁵¹ **milch** moist (literally, "milk-giving")   ⁴⁵³ **whe'r** whether   ⁴⁵⁶ **bestowed**
housed

they are the abstract and brief chronicles of the time. After your death you were better have a bad epitaph than their ill report while you live.

POLONIUS   My lord, I will use them according to their desert.

HAMLET   God's bodkin,° man, much better! Use every man after his desert, and 460 who shall scape whipping? Use them after your own honor and dignity. The less they deserve, the more merit is in your bounty. Take them in.

POLONIUS   Come, sirs.

HAMLET   Follow him, friends. We'll hear a play tomorrow. [*Aside to* PLAYER.] Dost thou hear me, old friend? Can you play *The Murder of Gonzago*?   465

PLAYER   Ay, my lord.

HAMLET   We'll ha't tomorrow night. You could for a need study a speech of some dozen or sixteen lines which I would set down and insert in't, could you not?

PLAYER   Ay, my lord.

HAMLET   Very well. Follow that lord, and look you mock him not. My good friends, 470 I'll leave you till night. You are welcome to Elsinore.

Exeunt POLONIUS *and* PLAYERS.

ROSENCRANTZ   Good my lord.

Exeunt [ROSENCRANTZ *and* GUILDENSTERN].

HAMLET   Ay, so, God bye to you. —Now I am alone.
O, what a rogue and peasant slave am I!
Is it not monstrous that this player here,   475
But in a fiction, in a dream of passion,°
Could force his soul so to his own conceit°
That from her working all his visage wanned,
Tears in his eyes, distraction in his aspect,
A broken voice, and his whole function° suiting   480
With forms° to his conceit? And all for nothing!
For Hecuba!
What's Hecuba to him, or he to Hecuba,
That he should weep for her? What would he do
Had he the motive and the cue for passion   485
That I have? He would drown the stage with tears
And cleave the general ear with horrid speech,
Make mad the guilty and appall the free,°
Confound the ignorant, and amaze indeed
The very faculties of eyes and ears.   490
Yet I,
A dull and muddy-mettled° rascal, peak

---

⁴⁶⁰ **God's bodkin** by God's little body   ⁴⁷⁶ **dream of passion** imaginary emotion   ⁴⁷⁷ **conceit** imagination   ⁴⁸⁰ **function** action   ⁴⁸¹ **forms** bodily expressions   ⁴⁸⁸ **appall the free** terrify (make pale?) the guiltless   ⁴⁹² **muddy-mettled** weak-spirited

Like John-a-dreams,° unpregnant of° my cause,
And can say nothing. No, not for a king,
Upon whose property and most dear life   495
A damned defeat was made. Am I a coward?
Who calls me villain? Breaks my pate across?
Plucks off my beard and blows it in my face?
Tweaks me by the nose? Gives me the lie i' th' throat
As deep as to the lungs? Who does me this?   500
Ha, 'swounds,° I should take it, for it cannot be
But I am pigeon-livered° and lack gall
To make oppression bitter, or ere this
I should ha' fatted all the region kites°
With this slave's offal. Bloody, bawdy villain!   505
Remorseless, treacherous, lecherous, kindless° villain!
O, vengeance!
Why, what an ass am I! This is most brave,°
That I, the son of a dear father murdered,
Prompted to my revenge by heaven and hell,   510
Must, like a whore, unpack my heart with words
And fall a-cursing like a very drab,°
A stallion!° Fie upon't, foh! About,° my brains.
Hum——
I have heard that guilty creatures sitting at a play   515
Have by the very cunning of the scene
Been struck so to the soul that presently°
They have proclaimed their malefactions.
For murder, though it have no tongue, will speak
With most miraculous organ. I'll have these players   520
Play something like the murder of my father
Before mine uncle. I'll observe his looks,
I'll tent° him to the quick. If 'a do blench,°
I know my course. The spirit that I have seen
May be a devil, and the devil hath power   525
T' assume a pleasing shape, yea, and perhaps
Out of my weakness and my melancholy,
As he is very potent with such spirits,
Abuses me to damn me. I'll have grounds

492–493 **peak / Like John-a-dreams** mope like a dreamer   493 **unpregnant of** unquickened by   501 **'swounds** by God's wounds   502 **pigeon-livered** gentle as a dove   504 **region kites** kites (scavenger birds) of the sky   506 **kindless** unnatural   508 **brave** fine   512 **drab** prostitute   513 **stallion** male prostitute (perhaps one should adopt the Folio reading, *scullion* = kitchen wench)   513 **About** to work   517 **presently** immediately   523 **tent** probe   523 **blench** flinch

More relative° than this. The play's the thing   530
Wherein I'll catch the conscience of the King.   *Exit.*

[ACT III

Scene I. The castle.]

Enter KING, QUEEN, POLONIUS, OPHELIA, ROSENCRANTZ, GUILDENSTERN, LORDS.

KING   And can you by no drift of conference°
  Get from him why he puts on this confusion,
  Grating so harshly all his days of quiet
  With turbulent and dangerous lunacy?
ROSENCRANTZ   He does confess he feels himself distracted,   5
  But from what cause 'a will by no means speak.
GUILDENSTERN   Nor do we find him forward to be sounded,°
  But with a crafty madness keeps aloof
  When we would bring him on to some confession
  Of his true state.
QUEEN   Did he receive you well?   10
ROSENCRANTZ   Most like a gentleman.
GUILDENSTERN   But with much forcing of his disposition.°
ROSENCRANTZ   Niggard of question,° but of our demands
  Most free in his reply.
QUEEN   Did you assay° him
  To any pastime?   15
ROSENCRANTZ   Madam, it so fell out that certain players
  We o'erraught° on the way; of these we told him,
  And there did seem in him a kind of joy
  To hear of it. They are here about the court,
  And, as I think, they have already order   20
  This night to play before him.
POLONIUS   'Tis most true,
  And he beseeched me to entreat your Majesties
  To hear and see the matter.
KING   With all my heart, and it doth much content me
  To hear him so inclined.   25
  Good gentlemen, give him a further edge
  And drive his purpose into these delights.

---

⁵³⁰ **relative** (probably "pertinent," but possibly "able to be related plausibly")   *III.i.* ¹ **drift of conference** management of conversation   ⁷ **forward to be sounded** willing to be questioned   ¹² **forcing of
his disposition** effort   ¹³ **Niggard of question** uninclined to talk   ¹⁴ **assay** tempt   ¹⁷ **o'erraught**
overtook

ROSENCRANTZ   We shall, my lord.

Exeunt ROSENCRANTZ *and* GUILDENSTERN.

KING   Sweet Gertrude, leave us too,
For we have closely° sent for Hamlet hither,
That he, as 'twere by accident, may here   30
Affront° Ophelia.
Her father and myself (lawful espials°)
Will so bestow ourselves that, seeing unseen,
We may of their encounter frankly judge
And gather by him, as he is behaved,   35
If 't be th' affliction of his love or no
That thus he suffers for.
QUEEN   I shall obey you.
And for your part, Ophelia, I do wish
That your good beauties be the happy cause
Of Hamlet's wildness. So shall I hope your virtues   40
Will bring him to his wonted way again,
To both your honors.
OPHELIA   Madam, I wish it may.   [*Exit* QUEEN.]
POLONIUS   Ophelia, walk you here.—Gracious, so please you,
We will bestow ourselves. [*To* OPHELIA.] Read on this book,
That show of such an exercise may color°   45
Your loneliness. We are oft to blame in this,
'Tis too much proved, that with devotion's visage
And pious action we do sugar o'er
The devil himself.
KING [*aside*]   O, 'tis too true.
How smart a lash that speech doth give my conscience!   50
The harlot's cheek, beautied with plast'ring art,
Is not more ugly to the thing that helps it
Than is my deed to my most painted word.
O heavy burden!
POLONIUS   I hear him coming. Let's withdraw, my lord.   55

[*Exeunt* KING *and* POLONIUS.]

Enter HAMLET

HAMLET   To be, or not to be: that is the question:
Whether 'tis nobler in the mind to suffer
The slings and arrows of outrageous fortune,

___

²⁹ **closely** secretly   ³¹ **Affront** meet face to face   ³² **espials** spies   ⁴⁵ **exercise may color** act of
devotion may give a plausible hue to (the book is one of devotion)

Or to take arms against a sea of troubles,
And by opposing end them. To die, to sleep—   60
No more—and by a sleep to say we end
The heartache, and the thousand natural shocks
That flesh is heir to! 'Tis a consummation
Devoutly to be wished. To die, to sleep—
To sleep—perchance to dream: ay, there's the rub,°   65
For in that sleep of death what dreams may come
When we have shuffled off this mortal coil,°
Must give us pause. There's the respect°
That makes calamity of so long life:°
For who would bear the whips and scorns of time,   70
Th' oppressor's wrong, the proud man's contumely,
The pangs of despised love, the law's delay,
The insolence of office, and the spurns
That patient merit of th' unworthy takes,
When he himself might his quietus° make   75
With a bare bodkin?° Who would fardels° bear,
To grunt and sweat under a weary life,
But that the dread of something after death,
The undiscovered country, from whose bourn°
No traveler returns, puzzles the will,   80
And makes us rather bear those ills we have,
Than fly to others that we know not of?
Thus conscience° does make cowards of us all,
And thus the native hue of resolution
Is sicklied o'er with the pale cast° of thought,   85
And enterprises of great pitch° and moment,
With this regard° their currents turn awry,
And lose the name of action. —Soft you now,
The fair Ophelia!—Nymph, in thy orisons°
Be all my sins remembered.
OPHELIA   Good my lord,   90
How does your honor for this many a day?
HAMLET   I humbly thank you; well, well, well.

---

⁶⁵ **rub** impediment (obstruction to a bowler's ball)   ⁶⁷ **coil** (1) turmoil, (2) a ring of rope (here the flesh encircling the soul)   ⁶⁸ **respect** consideration   ⁶⁹ **makes calamity of so long life** (1) makes calamity so long-lived, (2) makes living so long a calamity   ⁷⁵ **quietus** full discharge (a legal term)   ⁷⁶ **bodkin** dagger   ⁷⁶ **fardels** burdens   ⁷⁹ **bourn** region   ⁸³ **conscience** self-consciousness, introspection   ⁸⁵ **cast** color   ⁸⁶ **pitch** height (a term from falconry)   ⁸⁷ **regard** consideration   ⁸⁹ **orisons** prayers

OPHELIA   My lord, I have remembrances of yours
   That I have longèd long to redeliver.
   I pray you now, receive them.
HAMLET   No, not I,   95
   I never gave you aught.
OPHELIA   My honored lord, you know right well you did,
   And with them words of so sweet breath composed
   As made these things more rich. Their perfume lost,
   Take these again, for to the noble mind   100
   Rich gifts wax poor when givers prove unkind.
   There, my lord.
HAMLET   Ha, ha! Are you honest?°
OPHELIA   My lord?
HAMLET   Are you fair?   105
OPHELIA   What means your lordship?
HAMLET   That if you be honest and fair, your honesty should admit no discourse to
   your beauty.°
OPHELIA   Could beauty, my lord, have better commerce than with honesty?
HAMLET   Ay, truly; for the power of beauty will sooner transform honesty from what 110
   it is to a bawd° than the force of honesty can translate beauty into his likeness.
   This was sometime a paradox, but now the time gives it proof. I did love you
   once.
OPHELIA   Indeed, my lord, you made me believe so.
HAMLET   You should not have believed me, for virtue cannot so inoculate° our old 115
   stock but we shall relish of it.° I loved you not.
OPHELIA   I was the more deceived.
HAMLET   Get thee to a nunnery. Why wouldst thou be a breeder of sinners? I am
   myself indifferent honest,° but yet I could accuse me of such things that it were
   better my mother had not borne me: I am very proud, revengeful, ambitious, 120
   with more offenses at my beck° than I have thoughts to put them in, imagination
   to give them shape, or time to act them in. What should such fellows as I do
   crawling between earth and heaven? We are arrant knaves all; believe none of
   us. Go thy ways to a nunnery. Where's your father?
OPHELIA   At home, my lord.   125
HAMLET   Let the doors be shut upon him, that he may play the fool nowhere but in's
   own house. Farewell.
OPHELIA   O help him, you sweet heavens!

---

103 Are you honest (1) are you modest, (2) are you chaste, (3) have you integrity   **107–108 your honesty . . . to your beauty** your modesty should permit no approach to your beauty   **111 bawd** procurer   **115 inoculate** graft   **116 relish of it** smack of it (our old sinful nature)   **119 indifferent honest** moderately virtuous   **121 beck** call

HAMLET If thou dost marry, I'll give thee this plague for thy dowry: be thou as chaste as ice, as pure as snow, thou shalt not escape calumny. Get thee to a 130 nunnery. Go, farewell. Or if thou wilt needs marry, marry a fool, for wise men know well enough what monsters° you make of them. To a nunnery, go, and quickly too. Farewell.

OPHELIA Heavenly powers, restore him!

HAMLET I have heard of your paintings, well enough. God hath given you one face, 135 and you make yourselves another. You jig and amble, and you lisp; you nickname God's creatures and make your wantonness your ignorance.° Go to, I'll no more on't; it hath made me mad. I say we will have no moe° marriage. Those that are married already—all but one—shall live. The rest shall keep as they are. To a nunnery, go.   *Exit.* 140

OPHELIA O what a noble mind is here o'erthrown!
The courtier's, soldier's, scholar's, eye, tongue, sword,
Th' expectancy and rose° of the fair state,
The glass of fashion, and the mold of form,°
Th' observed of all observers, quite, quite down!   145
And I, of ladies most deject and wretched,
That sucked the honey of his musicked vows,
Now see that noble and most sovereign reason
Like sweet bells jangled, out of time and harsh,
That unmatched form and feature of blown° youth   150
Blasted with ecstasy.° O, woe is me
T' have seen what I have seen, see what I see!

Enter KING *and* POLONIUS.

KING Love? His affections° do not that way tend,
Nor what he spake, though it lacked form a little,
Was not like madness. There's something in his soul   155
O'er which his melancholy sits on brood,
And I do doubt° the hatch and the disclose
Will be some danger; which for to prevent,
I have in quick determination
Thus set it down: he shall with speed to England   160
For the demand of our neglected tribute.
Haply the seas, and countries different,
With variable objects, shall expel
This something-settled° matter in his heart,

---

¹³² **monsters** horned beasts, cuckolds   ¹³⁷ **make your wantonness your ignorance** excuse your wanton speech by pretending ignorance   ¹³⁸ **moe** more   ¹⁴³ **expectancy and rose** i.e., fair hope   ¹⁴⁴ **The glass . . . of form** the mirror of fashion, and the pattern of excellent behavior   ¹⁵⁰ **blown** blooming   ¹⁵¹ **ecstasy** madness   ¹⁵³ **affections** inclinations   ¹⁵⁷ **doubt** fear   ¹⁶⁴ **something-settled** somewhat settled

Whereon his brains still beating puts him thus   165
From fashion of himself. What think you on't?
POLONIUS   It shall do well. But yet do I believe
The origin and commencement of his grief
Sprung from neglected love. How now, Ophelia?
You need not tell us what Lord Hamlet said;   170
We heard it all. My lord, do as you please,
But if you hold it fit, after the play,
Let his queen mother all alone entreat him
To show his grief. Let her be round° with him,
And I'll be placed, so please you, in the ear   175
Of all their conference. If she find him not,°
To England send him, or confine him where
Your wisdom best shall think.
KING   It shall be so.
Madness in great ones must not unwatched go.   *Exeunt.*

[*Scene II. The castle.*]

Enter HAMLET *and three of the* PLAYERS.

HAMLET   Speak the speech, I pray you, as I pronounced it to you, trippingly on the
tongue. But if you mouth it, as many of our players do, I had as lief the town
crier spoke my lines. Nor do not saw the air too much with your hand, thus, but
use all gently, for in the very torrent, tempest, and (as I may say) whirlwind of
your passion, you must acquire and beget a temperance that may give it 5
smoothness. O, it offends me to the soul to hear a robustious periwig-pated°
fellow tear a passion to tatters, to very rags, to split the ears of the groundlings,°
who for the most part are capable of° nothing but inexplicable dumb shows° and
noise. I would have such a fellow whipped for o'erdoing Termagant. It out-herods
Herod.° Pray you avoid it.   10
PLAYER   I warrant your honor.
HAMLET   Be not too tame neither, but let your own discretion be your tutor. Suit
the action to the word, the word to the action, with this special observance, that
you o'erstep not the modesty of nature. For anything so o'erdone is from° the
purpose of playing, whose end, both at the first and now, was and is, to hold, as 15
'twere, the mirror up to nature; to show virtue her own feature, scorn her own
image, and the very age and body of the time his form and pressure.° Now, this

---

¹⁷⁴ **round** blunt   ¹⁷⁶ **find him not** does not find him out   *III.ii.* ⁶ **robustious periwig-pated**
boisterous wig-headed   ⁷ **groundlings** those who stood in the pit of the theater (the poorest and
presumably most ignorant of the audience)   ⁸ **are capable of** are able to understand   ⁸ **dumb shows**
(it had been the fashion for actors to preface plays or parts of plays with silent mime)   ⁹⁻¹⁰ **Terma-**
gant . . . Herod (boisterous characters in the old mystery plays)   ¹⁴ **from** contrary to   ¹⁷ **pressure**
image, impress

overdone, or come tardy off, though it makes the unskillful laugh, cannot but make the judicious grieve, the censure of the which one must in your allowance o'erweigh a whole theater of others. O, there be players that I have seen play, 20 and heard others praise, and that highly (not to speak it profanely), that neither having th' accent of Christians, nor the gait of Christian, pagan, nor man, have so strutted and bellowed that I have thought some of Nature's journeymen° had made men, and not made them well, they imitated humanity so abominably.

PLAYER   I hope we have reformed that indifferently° with us, sir.   25

HAMLET   O, reform it altogether! And let those that play your clowns speak no more than is set down for them, for there be of them that will themselves laugh, to set on some quantity of barren spectators to laugh too, though in the meantime some necessary question of the play be then to be considered. That's villainous and shows a most pitiful ambition in the fool that uses it. Go make you ready.   30

Exit PLAYERS.

Enter POLONIUS, GUILDENSTERN, *and* ROSENCRANTZ.

How now, my lord? Will the King hear this piece of work?

POLONIUS   And the Queen too, and that presently.

HAMLET   Bid the players make haste.   *Exit* POLONIUS.

Will you two help to hasten them?

ROSENCRANTZ   Ay, my lord.   *Exeunt they two.* 35

HAMLET   What, ho, Horatio!

Enter HORATIO.

HORATIO   Here, sweet lord, at your service.

HAMLET   Horatio, thou art e'en as just a man

As e'er my conversation coped withal.°

HORATIO   O, my dear lord——

HAMLET   Nay, do not think I flatter.   40

For what advancement° may I hope from thee,

That no revenue hast but thy good spirits

To feed and clothe thee? Why should the poor be flattered?

No, let the candied° tongue lick absurd pomp,

And crook the pregnant° hinges of the knee   45

Where thrift° may follow fawning. Dost thou hear?

Since my dear soul was mistress of her choice

And could of men distinguish her election,

S' hath sealed thee° for herself, for thou hast been

---

²³ **journeymen** workers not yet masters of their craft   ²⁵ **indifferently** tolerably   ³⁹ **coped withal** met with   ⁴¹ **advancement** promotion   ⁴⁴ **candied** sugared, flattering   ⁴⁵ **pregnant** (1) pliant, (2) full of promise of good fortune   ⁴⁶ **thrift** profit   ⁴⁹ **S'hath sealed thee** she (the soul) has set a mark on you

As one, in suff'ring all, that suffers nothing,   50
And man that Fortune's buffets and rewards
Hast ta'en with equal thanks; and blest are those
Whose blood° and judgment are so well commeddled°
That they are not a pipe for Fortune's finger
To sound what stop she please. Give me that man   55
That is not passion's slave, and I will wear him
In my heart's core, ay, in my heart of heart,
As I do thee. Something too much of this—
There is a play tonight before the King.
One scene of it comes near the circumstance   60
Which I have told thee, of my father's death.
I prithee, when thou seest that act afoot,
Even with the very comment° of thy soul
Observe my uncle. If his occulted° guilt
Do not itself unkennel in one speech,   65
It is a damnèd ghost that we have seen,
And my imaginations are as foul
As Vulcan's stithy.° Give him heedful note,
For I mine eyes will rivet to his face,
And after we will both our judgments join   70
In censure of his seeming.°
HORATIO   Well, my lord.
If 'a steal aught the whilst this play is playing,
And scape detecting, I will pay the theft.

Enter TRUMPETS *and* KETTLEDRUMS, KING, QUEEN, POLONIUS, OPHELIA,
ROSENCRANTZ, GUILDENSTERN, *and other* LORDS *attendant with his* GUARD
carrying torches. Danish March. Sound a Flourish.

HAMLET   They are coming to the play: I must be idle;°
Get you a place.   75
KING   How fares our cousin Hamlet?
HAMLET   Excellent, i' faith, of the chameleon's dish;° I eat the air, promise-
crammed; you cannot feed capons so.
KING   I have nothing with this answer, Hamlet; these words are not mine.
HAMLET   No, nor mine now. [*to* POLONIUS.] My lord, you played once i' th' 80
university, you say?
POLONIUS   That did I, my lord, and was accounted a good actor.
HAMLET   What did you enact?

---

⁵³ **blood** passion   ⁵³ **commeddled** blended   ⁶³ **very comment** deepest wisdom   ⁶⁴ **occulted** hidden   ⁶⁸ **stithy** forge, smithy   ⁷¹ **censure of his seeming** judgment on his looks   ⁷⁴ **be idle** play
the fool   ⁷⁷ **the chameleon's dish** air (on which chameleons were thought to live)

POLONIUS   I did enact Julius Caesar. I was killed i' th' Capitol; Brutus killed me.

HAMLET   It was a brute part of him to kill so capital a calf there. Be the players ready?   85

ROSENCRANTZ   Ay, my lord. They stay upon your patience.

QUEEN   Come hither, my dear Hamlet, sit by me.

HAMLET   No, good mother. Here's metal more attractive.°

POLONIUS [*to the* KING]   O ho! Do you mark that?

HAMLET   Lady, shall I lie in your lap?   90

[*He lies at* OPHELIA'S *feet.*]

OPHELIA   No, my lord.

HAMLET   I mean, my head upon your lap?

OPHELIA   Ay, my lord.

HAMLET   Do you think I meant country matters?°

OPHELIA   I think nothing, my lord.   95

HAMLET   That's a fair thought to lie between maids' legs.

OPHELIA   What is, my lord?

HAMLET   Nothing.

OPHELIA   You are merry, my lord.

HAMLET   Who, I?   100

OPHELIA   Ay, my lord.

HAMLET   O God, your only jig-maker!° What should a man do but be merry? For
look you how cheerfully my mother looks, and my father died within's two hours.

OPHELIA   Nay, 'tis twice two months, my lord.

HAMLET   So long? Nay then, let the devil wear black, for I'll have a suit of sables.° O   105
heavens! Die two months ago, and not forgotten yet? Then there's hope a great
man's memory may outlive his life half a year. But, by'r Lady, 'a must build
churches then, or else shall 'a suffer not thinking on, with the hobbyhorse,°
whose epitaph is "For O, for O, the hobbyhorse is forgot!"

The trumpets sound. Dumb show follows:

Enter a KING *and a* QUEEN *very lovingly, the* QUEEN *embracing him, and he her.
She kneels; and makes show of protestation unto him. He takes her up, and declines
his head upon her neck. He lies him down upon a bank of flowers. She, seeing him
asleep, leaves him. Anon come in another man: takes off his crown, kisses it, pours
poison in the sleeper's ears, and leaves him. The* QUEEN *returns, finds the* KING
*dead, makes passionate action. The poisoner, with some three or four, come in
again, seem to condole with her. The dead body is carried away. The poisoner woos
the* QUEEN *with gifts; she seems harsh awhile, but in the end accepts love.   Exeunt.*

88 attractive magnetic   **94 country matters** rustic doings (with a pun on the vulgar word for the
pudendum)   **102 jig-maker** composer of songs and dances (often a Fool, who performed them)
105 sables (pun on "black" and "luxurious furs")   **108 hobbyhorse** mock horse worn by a performer in
the morris dance

OPHELIA   What means this, my lord?   110

HAMLET   Marry, this is miching mallecho;° it means mischief.

OPHELIA   Belike this show imports the argument° of the play.

Enter PROLOGUE.

HAMLET   We shall know by this fellow. The players cannot keep counsel; they'll
tell all.

OPHELIA   Will 'a tell us what this show meant?   115

HAMLET   Ay, or any show that you will show him. Be not you ashamed to show, he'll
not shame to tell you what it means.

OPHELIA   You are naught,° you are naught; I'll mark the play.

PROLOGUE   For us, and for our tragedy,

  Here stooping to your clemency,   120

  We beg your hearing patiently.   [*Exit.*]

HAMLET   Is this a prologue, or the posy of a ring?°

OPHELIA   'Tis brief, my lord.

HAMLET   As woman's love.

Enter [*two* PLAYERS *as*] KING *and* QUEEN.

PLAYER KING   Full thirty times hath Phoebus' cart° gone round   125

  Neptune's salt wash° and Tellus'° orbèd ground,

  And thirty dozen moons with borrowed sheen

  About the world have times twelve thirties been,

  Since love our hearts, and Hymen did our hands,

  Unite commutual in most sacred bands.   130

PLAYER QUEEN   So many journeys may the sun and moon

  Make us again count o'er ere love be done!

  But woe is me, you are so sick of late,

  So far from cheer and from your former state,

  That I distrust° you. Yet, though I distrust,   135

  Discomfort you, my lord, it nothing must.

  For women fear too much, even as they love,

  And women's fear and love hold quantity,

  In neither aught, or in extremity.°

  Now what my love is, proof° hath made you know,   140

  And as my love is sized, my fear is so.

---

¹¹¹ **miching mallecho** sneaking mischief   ¹¹² **argument** plot   ¹¹⁸ **naught** wicked, improper
¹²² **posy of a ring** motto inscribed in a ring   ¹²⁵ **Phoebus' cart** the sun's chariot   ¹²⁶ **Neptune's salt wash** the sea   ¹²⁶ **Tellus** Roman goddess of the earth   ¹³⁵ **distrust** am anxious about
¹³⁸⁻¹³⁹ **And women's . . . in extremity** (perhaps the idea is that women's anxiety is great or little in
proportion to their love. The previous line, unrhymed, may be a false start that Shakespeare neglected to
delete)   ¹⁴⁰ **proof** experience

Where love is great, the littlest doubts are fear;
Where little fears grow great, great love grows there.
PLAYER KING   Faith, I must leave thee, love, and shortly too;
  My operant° powers their functions leave to do: 145
  And thou shalt live in this fair world behind,
  Honored, beloved, and haply one as kind
  For husband shalt thou——
PLAYER QUEEN   O, confound the rest!
  Such love must needs be treason in my breast.
  In second husband let me be accurst!   150
  None wed the second but who killed the first.
HAMLET [*aside*]   That's wormwood.°
PLAYER QUEEN   The instances° that second marriage move°
  Are base respects of thrift,° but none of love.
  A second time I kill my husband dead   155
  When second husband kisses me in bed.
PLAYER KING   I do believe you think what now you speak,
  But what we do determine oft we break.
  Purpose is but the slave to memory,
  Of violent birth, but poor validity,°   160
  Which now like fruit unripe sticks on the tree,
  But fall unshaken when they mellow be.
  Most necessary 'tis that we forget
  To pay ourselves what to ourselves is debt.
  What to ourselves in passion we propose,   165
  The passion ending, doth the purpose lose.
  The violence of either grief or joy
  Their own enactures° with themselves destroy:
  Where joy most revels, grief doth most lament;
  Grief joys, joy grieves, on slender accident.   170
  This word is not for aye, nor 'tis not strange
  That even our loves should with our fortunes change,
  For 'tis a question left us yet to prove,
  Whether love lead fortune, or else fortune love.
  The great man down, you mark his favorite flies;   175
  The poor advanced makes friends of enemies;
  And hitherto doth love on fortune tend,
  For who not needs shall never lack a friend;
  And who in want a hollow friend doth try,

---

[145] **operant** active   [152] **wormwood** a bitter herb   [153] **instances** motives   [153] **move** induce
[154] **respects of thrift** considerations of profit   [160] **validity** strength   [168] **enactures** acts

Directly seasons him° his enemy.   180
But, orderly to end where I begun,
Our wills and fates do so contrary run
That our devices still are overthrown;
Our thoughts are ours, their ends none of our own.
So think thou wilt no second husband wed,   185
But die thy thoughts when thy first lord is dead.
PLAYER QUEEN   Nor earth to give me food, nor heaven light,
Sport and repose lock from me day and night,
To desperation turn my trust and hope,
An anchor's° cheer in prison be my scope,   190
Each opposite that blanks° the face of joy
Meet what I would have well, and it destroy:
Both here and hence pursue me lasting strife,
If, once a widow, ever I be wife!
HAMLET   If she should break it now!   195
PLAYER KING   'Tis deeply sworn. Sweet, leave me here awhile;
My spirits grow dull, and fain I would beguile
The tedious day with sleep.
PLAYER QUEEN   Sleep rock thy brain,

[*He*] *sleeps.*

And never come mischance between us twain!   *Exit.*
HAMLET   Madam, how like you this play?   200
QUEEN   The lady doth protest too much, methinks.
HAMLET   O, but she'll keep her word.
KING   Have you heard the argument?° Is there no offense in't?
HAMLET   No, no, they do but jest, poison in jest; no offense i' th' world.
KING   What do you call the play?   205
HAMLET   *The Mousetrap.* Marry, how? Tropically.° This play is the image of a
   murder done in Vienna: Gonzago is the Duke's name; his wife, Baptista. You
   shall see anon. 'Tis a knavish piece of work, but what of that? Your Majesty, and
   we that have free° souls, it touches us not. Let the galled jade winch;° our withers
   are unwrung.   210

Enter LUCIANUS.

This is one Lucianus, nephew to the King.
OPHELIA   You are as good as a chorus, my lord.

---

¹⁸⁰ **seasons him** ripens him into   ¹⁹⁰ **anchor's** anchorite's, hermit's   ¹⁹¹ **opposite that blanks**
adverse thing that blanches   ²⁰³ **argument** plot   ²⁰⁶ **Tropically** figuratively (with a pun on "trap")
²⁰⁹ **free** innocent   ²⁰⁹ **galled jade winch** chafed horse wince

HAMLET   I could interpret° between you and your love, if I could see the puppets
   dallying.

OPHELIA   You are keen,° my lord, you are keen.   215

HAMLET   It would cost you a groaning to take off mine edge.

OPHELIA   Still better, and worse.

HAMLET   So you mistake° your husbands.—Begin, murderer. Leave thy damnable
   faces and begin. Come, the croaking raven doth bellow for revenge.

LUCIANUS   Thoughts black, hands apt, drugs fit, and time agreeing,   220
   Confederate season,° else no creature seeing,
   Thou mixture rank, of midnight weeks collected,
   With Hecate's ban° thrice blasted, thrice infected,
   Thy natural magic and dire property°
   On wholesome life usurps immediately.   225

Pours the poison in his ears.

HAMLET   'A poisons him i' th' garden for his estate. His name's Gonzago. The story
   is extant, and written in very choice Italian. You shall see anon how the murderer
   gets the love of Gonzago's wife.

OPHELIA   The King rises.

HAMLET   What, frighted with false fire?°   230

QUEEN   How fares my lord?

POLONIUS   Give o'er the play.

KING   Give me some light. Away!

POLONIUS   Lights, lights, lights!

Exeunt all but HAMLET *and* HORATIO.

HAMLET   Why, let the strucken deer go weep,   235
   The hart ungallèd play:
   For some must watch, while some must sleep;
   Thus runs the world away.

   Would not this, sir, and a forest of feathers°—if the rest of my fortunes turn
   Turk° with me—with two Provincial roses° on my razed° shoes, get me a fellow- 240
   ship in a cry° of players?

HORATIO   Half a share.

HAMLET   A whole one, I.

---

²¹³ **interpret** (like a showman explaining the action of puppets)   ²¹⁵ **keen** (1) sharp, (2) sexually
aroused   ²¹⁸ **mistake** err in taking   ²²¹ **Confederate season** the opportunity allied with me
²²³ **Hecate's ban** the curse of the goddess of sorcery   ²²⁴ **property** nature   ²³⁰ **false fire** blank
discharge of firearms   ²³⁹ **feathers** (plumes were sometimes part of a costume)   ²⁴⁰ **turn Turk** i.e.,
go bad, treat me badly   ²⁴⁰ **Provincial roses** rosettes like the roses of Provence (?)   ²⁴⁰ **razed**
ornamented with slashes   ²⁴¹ **cry** pack, company

> For thou dost know, O Damon dear,
>> This realm dismantled was
> Of Jove himself; and now reigns here
>> A very, very—pajock.°

245

HORATIO You might have rhymed.°

HAMLET O good Horatio, I'll take the ghost's word for a thousand pound. Didst
perceive?

250

HORATIO Very well, my lord.

HAMLET Upon the talk of poisoning?

HORATIO I did very well note him.

HAMLET Ah ha! Come, some music! Come, the recorders!°

> For if the king like not the comedy,
> Why then, belike he likes it not, perdy.°

255

Come, some music!

Enter ROSENCRANTZ *and* GUILDENSTERN.

GUILDENSTERN Good my lord, vouchsafe me a word with you.

HAMLET Sir, a whole history.

GUILDENSTERN The King, sir——

260

HAMLET Ay, sir, what of him?

GUILDENSTERN Is in his retirement marvelous distemp'red.

HAMLET With drink, sir?

GUILDENSTERN No, my lord, with choler.°

HAMLET Your wisdom should show itself more richer to signify this to the doctor, 265
for for me to put him to his purgation would perhaps plunge him into more choler.

GUILDENSTERN Good my lord, put your discourse into some frame,° and start not
so wildly from my affair.

HAMLET I am tame, sir; pronounce.

GUILDENSTERN The Queen, your mother, in most great affliction of spirit hath sent 270
me to you.

HAMLET You are welcome.

GUILDENSTERN Nay, good my lord, this courtesy is not of the right breed. If it shall
please you to make me a wholesome answer, I will do your mother's
commandment: if not, your pardon and my return shall be the end of my 275
business.

HAMLET Sir, I cannot.

---

247 pajock peacock   **248 You might have rhymed** i.e., rhymed "was" with "ass"   **254 recorders**
flutelike instruments   **256 perdy** by God (French: *par dieu*)   **264 choler** anger (but Hamlet pretends to
take the word in its sense of "biliousness")   **267 frame** order, control

ROSENCRANTZ   What, my lord?

HAMLET   Make you a wholesome° answer; my wit's diseased. But, sir, such answer as I can make, you shall command, or rather, as you say, my mother. Therefore 280 no more, but to the matter. My mother, you say——

ROSENCRANTZ   Then thus she says: your behavior hath struck her into amazement and admiration.°

HAMLET   O wonderful son, that can so stonish a mother! But is there no sequel at the heels of this mother's admiration? Impart.   285

ROSENCRANTZ   She desires to speak with you in her closet ere you go to bed.

HAMLET   We shall obey, were she ten times our mother. Have you any further trade with us?

ROSENCRANTZ   My lord, you once did love me.

HAMLET   And do still, by these pickers and stealers.°   290

ROSENCRANTZ   Good my lord, what is your cause of distemper? You do surely bar the door upon your own liberty, if you deny your griefs to your friend.

HAMLET   Sir, I lack advancement.°

ROSENCRANTZ   How can that be, when you have the voice of the King himself for your succession in Denmark?   295

Enter the PLAYERS *with recorders.*

HAMLET   Ay, sir, but "while the grass grows"—the proverb° is something musty. O, the recorders. Let me see one. To withdraw° with you—why do you go about to recover the wind° of me as if you would drive me into a toil?°

GUILDENSTERN   O my lord, if my duty be too bold, my love is too unmannerly.°

HAMLET   I do not well understand that. Will you play upon this pipe?   300

GUILDENSTERN   My lord, I cannot.

HAMLET   I pray you.

GUILDENSTERN   Believe me, I cannot.

HAMLET   I pray you.

GUILDENSTERN   Believe me, I cannot.   305

HAMLET   I do beseech you.

GUILDENSTERN   I know no touch of it, my lord.

HAMLET   It is as easy as lying. Govern these ventages° with your fingers and thumb, give it breath with your mouth, and it will discourse most eloquent music. Look you, these are the stops.   310

---

[279] **wholesome** sane   [283] **admiration** wonder   [290] **pickers and stealers** i.e., hands (with reference to the prayer: "Keep my hands from picking and stealing")   [293] **advancement** promotion   [296] **proverb** ("While the grass groweth, the horse starveth")   [297] **withdraw** speak in private   [298] **recover the wind** get on the windward side (as in hunting)   [298] **toil** snare   [299] **if my duty . . . too unmannerly** i.e., if these questions seem rude, it is because my love for you leads me beyond good manners   [308] **ventages** vents, stops on a recorder

GUILDENSTERN   But these cannot I command to any utt'rance of harmony; I have
    not the skill.

HAMLET   Why, look you now, how unworthy a thing you make of me! You would play
    upon me; you would seem to know my stops; you would pluck out the heart of
    my mystery; you would sound me from my lowest note to the top of my 315
    compass;° and there is much music, excellent voice, in this little organ,° yet
    cannot you make it speak. 'Sblood, do you think I am easier to be played on than
    a pipe? Call me what instrument you will, though you can fret° me, you cannot
    play upon me.

Enter POLONIUS.

God bless you, sir!   320

POLONIUS   My lord, the Queen would speak with you, and presently.

HAMLET   Do you see yonder cloud that's almost in shape of a camel?

POLONIUS   By th' mass and 'tis, like a camel indeed.

HAMLET   Methinks it is like a weasel.

POLONIUS   It is backed like a weasel.   325

HAMLET   Or like a whale.

POLONIUS   Very like a whale.

HAMLET   Then I will come to my mother by and by. [*Aside.*] They fool me to the top
    of my bent.° —I will come by and by.°

POLONIUS   I will say so.   330

HAMLET   "By and by" is easily said. Leave me, friends.

                                                    [*Exeunt all but* HAMLET.]

'Tis now the very witching time of night,
When churchyards yawn, and hell itself breathes out
Contagion to this world. Now could I drink hot blood
And do such bitter business as the day   335
Would quake to look on. Soft, now to my mother.
O heart, lose not thy nature; let not ever
The soul of Nero° enter this firm bosom.
Let me be cruel, not unnatural;
I will speak daggers to her, but use none.   340
My tongue and soul in this be hypocrites:
How in my words somever she be shent,°
To give them seals° never, my soul, consent!   *Exit.*

---

³¹⁶ **compass** range of voice   ³¹⁶ **organ** i.e., the recorder   ³¹⁸ **fret** vex (with a pun alluding to the
frets, or ridges, that guide the fingering on some instruments)   ³²⁸⁻³²⁹ **They fool . . . my bent** they
compel me to play the fool to the limit of my capacity   ³²⁹ **by and by** very soon   ³³⁸ **Nero** (Roman
emperor who had his mother murdered)   ³⁴² **shent** rebuked   ³⁴³ **give them seals** confirm them with
deeds

[Scene III. The castle.]

    Enter KING, ROSENCRANTZ *and* GUILDENSTERN.

KING   I like him not, nor stands it safe with us
  To let his madness range. Therefore prepare you.
  I your commission will forthwith dispatch,
  And he to England shall along with you.
  The terms° of our estate may not endure   5
  Hazard so near's° as doth hourly grow
  Out of his brows.
GUILDENSTERN   We will ourselves provide.
  Most holy and religious fear it is
  To keep those many many bodies safe
  That live and feed upon your Majesty.   10
ROSENCRANTZ   The single and peculiar° life is bound
  With all the strength and armor of the mind
  To keep itself from noyance,° but much more
  That spirit upon whose weal depends and rests
  The lives of many. The cess of majesty°   15
  Dies not alone, but like a gulf° doth draw
  What's near it with it; or it is a massy wheel
  Fixed on the summit of the highest mount,
  To whose huge spokes ten thousand lesser things
  Are mortised and adjoined, which when it falls,   20
  Each small annexment, petty consequence,
  Attends° the boist' rous ruin. Never alone
  Did the King sigh, but with a general groan.
KING   Arm° you, I pray you, to this speedy voyage,
  For we will fetters put about this fear,   25
  Which now goes too free-footed.
ROSENCRANTZ   We will haste us.

                       Exeunt GENTLEMEN.

    Enter POLONIUS.

POLONIUS   My lord, he's going to his mother's closet.°
  Behind the arras I'll convey myself
  To hear the process.° I'll warrant she'll tax him home,°

III.iii. **⁵ terms** conditions   **⁶ near's** near us   **¹¹ peculiar** individual, private   **¹³ noyance** injury
¹⁵ cess of majesty cessation (death) of a king   **¹⁶ gulf** whirlpool   **²² Attends** waits on, participates
in   **²⁴ Arm** prepare   **²⁷ closet** private room   **²⁹ process** proceedings   **²⁹ tax him home** censure
him sharply

And, as you said, and wisely was it said, 30
'Tis meet that some more audience than a mother,
Since nature makes them partial, should o'erhear
The speech of vantage.° Fare you well, my liege.
I'll call upon you ere you go to bed
And tell you what I know.
KING   Thanks, dear my lord. 35

Exit [POLONIUS].

O, my offense is rank, it smells to heaven;
It hath the primal eldest curse° upon't,
A brother's murder. Pray can I not,
Though inclination be as sharp as will.
My stronger guilt defeats my strong intent, 40
And like a man to double business bound
I stand in pause where I shall first begin,
And both neglect. What if this cursèd hand
Were thicker than itself with brother's blood,
Is there not rain enough in the sweet heavens 45
To wash it white as snow? Whereto serves mercy
But to confront° the visage of offense?
And what's in prayer but this twofold force,
To be forestallèd ere we come to fall,
Or pardoned being down? Then I'll look up. 50
My fault is past. But, O, what form of prayer
Can serve my turn? "Forgive me my foul murder"?
That cannot be, since I am still possessed
Of those effects° for which I did the murder,
My crown, mine own ambition, and my queen. 55
May one be pardoned and retain th' offense?
In the corrupted currents of this world
Offense's gilded hand may shove by justice,
And oft 'tis seen the wicked prize itself
Buys out the law. But 'tis not so above. 60
There is no shuffling;° there the action lies
In his true nature, and we ourselves compelled,
Even to the teeth and forehead of our faults,
To give in evidence. What then? What rests?°
Try what repentance can. What can it not? 65

33 of vantage from an advantageous place **37 primal eldest curse** (curse of Cain, who killed Abel)
47 confront oppose **54 effects** things gained **61 shuffling** trickery **64 rests** remains

Yet what can it when one cannot repent?
O wretched state! O bosom black as death!
O limèd° soul, that struggling to be free
Art more engaged!° Help, angels! Make assay.°
Bow, stubborn knees, and, heart with strings of steel,   70
Be soft as sinews of the newborn babe.
All may be well. [*He kneels.*]

Enter HAMLET.

HAMLET   Now might I do it pat, now 'a is a-praying,
    And now I'll do't. And so 'a goes to heaven,
    And so am I revenged. That would be scanned.°   75
    A villain kills my father, and for that
    I, his sole son, do this same villain send
    To heaven.
    Why, this is hire and salary, not revenge.
    'A took my father grossly, full of bread.°   80
    With all his crimes broad blown,° as flush° as May;
    And how his audit° stands, who knows save heaven?
    But in our circumstance and course of thought,
    'Tis heavy with him; and am I then revenged,
    To take him in the purging of his soul,   85
    When he is fit and seasoned for his passage?
    No.
    Up, sword, and know thou a more horrid hent.°
    When he is drunk asleep, or in his rage,
    Or in th' incestuous pleasure of his bed,   90
    At game a-swearing, or about some act
    That has no relish° of salvation in't—
    Then trip him, that his heels may kick at heaven,
    And that his soul may be as damned and black
    As hell, whereto it goes. My mother stays.   95
    This physic° but prolongs thy sickly days.   *Exit.*
KING [*rises*]   My words fly up, my thoughts remain below.
    Words without thoughts never to heaven go.   *Exit.*

---

⁶⁸ **limèd** caught (as with birdlime, a sticky substance spread on boughs to snare birds)   ⁶⁹ **engaged** ensnared   ⁶⁹ **assay** an attempt   ⁷⁵ **would be scanned** ought to be looked into   ⁸⁰ **bread** i.e., wordly gratification   ⁸¹ **crimes broad blown** sins in full bloom   ⁸¹ **flush** vigorous   ⁸² **audit** account   ⁸⁸ **hent** grasp (here, occasion for seizing)   ⁹² **relish** flavor   ⁹⁶ **physic** (Claudius' purgation by prayer, as Hamlet thinks in line 85)

[Scene IV. The Queen's closet.]

Enter [QUEEN] GERTRUDE *and* POLONIUS.

POLONIUS   'A will come straight. Look you lay home° to him.
  Tell him his pranks have been too broad° to bear with,
  And that your Grace hath screened and stood between
  Much heat and him. I'll silence me even here.
  Pray you be round with him.   5
HAMLET *[within]*   Mother, Mother, Mother!
QUEEN   I'll warrant you; fear me not. Withdraw; I hear him coming.

                              [POLONIUS hides behind the arras.]

Enter HAMLET.

HAMLET   Now, Mother, what's the matter?
QUEEN   Hamlet, thou hast thy father much offended.   10
HAMLET   Mother, you have my father much offended.
QUEEN   Come, come, you answer with an idle° tongue.
HAMLET   Go, go, you question with a wicked tongue.
QUEEN   Why, how now, Hamlet?
HAMLET   What's the matter now?
QUEEN   Have you forgot me?
HAMLET   No, by the rood,° not so!   15
  You are the Queen, your husband's brother's wife,
  And, would it were not so, you are my mother.
QUEEN   Nay, then I'll set those to you that can speak.
HAMLET   Come, come, and sit you down. You shall not budge.
  You go not till I set you up a glass°   20
  Where you may see the inmost part of you!
QUEEN   What wilt thou do? Thou wilt not murder me?
  Help, ho!
POLONIUS *[behind]*   What, ho! Help!
HAMLET *[draws]*   How now? A rat? Dead for a ducat, dead!   25

    [Makes a pass through the arras and] kills POLONIUS.

POLONIUS *[behind]*   O, I am slain!
QUEEN   O me, what hast thou done?
HAMLET   Nay, I know not. Is it the King?
QUEEN   O, what a rash and bloody deed is this!

III.iv. ¹ **lay home** thrust (rebuke) him sharply   ² **broad** unrestrained   ¹² **idle** foolish   ¹⁵ **rood** cross   ²⁰ **glass** mirror

HAMLET   A bloody deed—almost as bad, good Mother,
  As kill a king, and marry with his brother.   30
QUEEN   As kill a king?
HAMLET   Ay, lady, it was my word.

  [*Lifts up the arras and sees* POLONIUS.]

  Thou wretched, rash, intruding fool, farewell!
  I took thee for thy better. Take thy fortune.
  Thou find'st to be too busy is some danger.—
  Leave wringing of your hands. Peace, sit you down   35
  And let me wring your heart, for so I shall
  If it be made of penetrable stuff,
  If damnèd custom have not brazed° it so
  That it be proof° and bulwark against sense.°
QUEEN   What have I done that thou dar'st wag thy tongue   40
  In noise so rude against me?
HAMLET   Such an act
  That blurs the grace and blush of modesty,
  Calls virtue hypocrite, takes off the rose
  From the fair forehead of an innocent love,
  And sets a blister° there, makes marriage vows   45
  As false as dicers' oaths. O, such a deed
  As from the body of contraction° plucks
  The very soul, and sweet religion makes
  A rhapsody° of words! Heaven's face does glow
  O'er this solidity and compound mass   50
  With heated visage, as against the doom
  Is thoughtsick at the act.°
QUEEN   Ay me, what act,
  That roars so loud and thunders in the index?°
HAMLET   Look here upon this picture, and on this,
  The counterfeit presentment° of two brothers.   55
  See what a grace was seated on this brow:
  Hyperion's curls, the front° of Jove himself,
  An eye like Mars, to threaten and command,
  A station° like the herald Mercury

---

³⁸ **brazed** hardened like brass   ³⁹ **proof** armor   ³⁹ **sense** feeling   ⁴⁵ **sets a blister** brands (as a harlot)   ⁴⁷ **contraction** marriage contract   ⁴⁹ **rhapsody** senseless string   ⁴⁹–⁵² **Heaven's face . . . the act** i.e., the face of heaven blushes over this earth (compounded of four elements), the face hot, as if Judgment Day were near, and it is thoughtsick at the act   ⁵³ **index** prologue   ⁵⁵ **counterfeit presentment** represented image   ⁵⁷ **front** forehead   ⁵⁹ **station** bearing

New lighted on a heaven-kissing hill—   60
A combination and a form indeed
Where every god did seem to set his seal
To give the world assurance of a man.
This was your husband. Look you now what follows.
Here is your husband, like a mildewed ear   65
Blasting his wholesome brother. Have you eyes?
Could you on this fair mountain leave to feed,
And batten° on this moor? Ha! Have you eyes?
You cannot call it love, for at your age
The heyday° in the blood is tame, it's humble,   70
And waits upon the judgment, and what judgment
Would step from this to this? Sense° sure you have,
Else could you not have motion, but sure that sense
Is apoplexed,° for madness would not err,
Nor sense to ecstasy° was ne'er so thralled   75
But it reserved some quantity of choice
To serve in such a difference. What devil wast
That thus hath cozened you at hoodman-blind?°
Eyes without feeling, feeling without sight,
Ears without hands or eyes, smelling sans° all,   80
Or but a sickly part of one true sense
Could not so mope.°
O shame, where is thy blush? Rebellious hell,
If thou canst mutine in a matron's bones,
To flaming youth let virtue be as wax   85
And melt in her own fire. Proclaim no shame
When the compulsive ardor° gives the charge,
Since frost itself as actively doth burn,
And reason panders will.°
QUEEN   O Hamlet, speak no more.
Thou turn'st mine eyes into my very soul,   90
And there I see such black and grainèd° spots
As will not leave their tinct.°
HAMLET   Nay, but to live
In the rank sweat of an enseamèd° bed,

---

⁶⁸ **batten** feed gluttonously   ⁷⁰ **heyday** excitement   ⁷² **Sense** feeling   ⁷⁴ **apoplexed** paralyzed
⁷⁵ **ecstasy** madness   ⁷⁸ **cozened you at hoodman-blind** cheated you at blindman's b[l]uff   ⁸⁰ **sans**
without   ⁸² **mope** be stupid   ⁸⁷ **compulsive ardor** compelling passion   ⁸⁹ **reason panders will**
reason acts as a procurer for desire   ⁹¹ **grainèd** dyed in grain (fast dyed)   ⁹² **tinct** color
⁹³ **enseamèd** (perhaps "soaked in grease," i.e., sweaty; perhaps "much wrinkled")

Stewed in corruption, honeying and making love
Over the nasty sty——
QUEEN   O, speak to me no more.   95
  These words like daggers enter in my ears.
  No more, sweet Hamlet.
HAMLET   A murderer and a villain,
  A slave that is not twentieth part the tithe°
  Of your precedent lord, a vice° of kings,
  A cutpurse of the empire and the rule,   100
  That from a shelf the precious diadem stole
  And put it in his pocket——
QUEEN   No more.

Enter GHOST.

HAMLET   A king of shreds and patches—
  Save me and hover o'er me with your wings,
  You heavenly guards! What would your gracious figure?   105
QUEEN   Alas, he's mad.
HAMLET   Do you not come your tardy son to chide,
  That, lapsed in time and passion, lets go by
  Th' important acting of your dread command?
  O, say!   110
GHOST   Do not forget. This visitation
  Is but to whet thy almost blunted purpose.
  But look, amazement on thy mother sits.
  O, step between her and her fighting soul!
  Conceit° in weakest bodies strongest works.   115
  Speak to her, Hamlet.
HAMLET   How is it with you, lady?
QUEEN   Alas, how is't with you,
  That you do bend your eye on vacancy,
  And with th' incorporal° air do hold discourse?
  Forth at your eyes your spirits wildly peep,   120
  And as the sleeping soldiers in th' alarm
  Your bedded hair° like life in excrements°
  Start up and stand an end.° O gentle son,
  Upon the heat and flame of thy distemper
  Sprinkle cool patience. Whereon do you look?   125

---

⁹⁸ **tithe** tenth part   ⁹⁹ **vice** (like the Vice, a fool and mischiefmaker in the old morality plays)
¹¹⁵ **Conceit** imagination   ¹¹⁹ **incorporal** bodiless   ¹²² **bedded hair** hairs laid flat   ¹²² **excrements** outgrowths (here, the hair)   ¹²³ **an end** on end

HAMLET   On him, on him! Look you, how pale he glares!
His form and cause conjoined, preaching to stones,
Would make them capable.°—Do not look upon me,
Lest with this piteous action you convert
My stern effects.° Then what I have to do   130
Will want true color; tears perchance for blood.
QUEEN   To whom do you speak this?
HAMLET   Do you see nothing there?
QUEEN   Nothing at all; yet all that is I see.
HAMLET   Nor did you nothing hear?
QUEEN   No, nothing but ourselves.
HAMLET   Why, look you there! Look how it steals away!   135
My father, in his habit° as he lived!
Look where he goes even now at the portal!   *Exit* GHOST.
QUEEN   This is the very coinage of your brain.
This bodiless creation ecstasy
Is very cunning in.
HAMLET   Ecstasy?   140
My pulse as yours doth temperately keep time
And makes as healthful music. It is not madness
That I have uttered. Bring me to the test,
And I the matter will reword, which madness
Would gambol° from. Mother, for love of grace,   145
Lay not that flattering unction° to your soul,
That not your trespass but my madness speaks.
It will but skin and film the ulcerous place
Whiles rank corruption, mining° all within,
Infects unseen. Confess yourself to heaven,   150
Repent what's past, avoid what is to come,
And do not spread the compost° on the weeds
To make them ranker. Forgive me this my virtue.
For in the fatness of these pursy° times
Virtue itself of vice must pardon beg,   155
Yea, curb° and woo for leave to do him good.
QUEEN   O Hamlet, thou hast cleft my heart in twain.
HAMLET   O, throw away the worser part of it,
And live the purer with the other half.

---

¹²⁸ **capable** receptive   ¹²⁹⁻¹³⁰ **convert / My stern effects** divert my stern deeds   ¹³⁶ **habit** garment (Q1, though a "bad" quarto, is probably correct in saying that at line 102 the ghost enters "in his night-gown," i.e., dressing gown)   ¹⁴⁵ **gambol** start away   ¹⁴⁶ **unction** ointment   ¹⁴⁹ **mining** undermining   ¹⁵² **compost** fertilizing substance   ¹⁵⁴ **pursy** bloated   ¹⁵⁶ **curb** bow low

Good night—but go not to my uncle's bed.   160
Assume a virtue, if you have it not.
That monster custom, who all sense doth eat,
Of habits devil, is angel yet in this,
That to the use° of actions fair and good
He likewise gives a frock or livery°   165
That aptly is put on. Refrain tonight,
And that shall lend a kind of easiness
To the next abstinence; the next more easy;
For use almost can change the stamp of nature,
And either° the devil, or throw him out   170
With wondrous potency. Once more, good night,
And when you are desirous to be blest,
I'll blessing beg of you. —For this same lord,
I do repent; but heaven hath pleased it so,
To punish me with this, and this with me,   175
That I must be their° scourge and minister.
I will bestow° him and will answer well
The death I gave him. So again, good night.
I must be cruel only to be kind.
Thus bad begins, and worse remains behind.   180
One word more, good lady.
QUEEN   What shall I do?
HAMLET   Not this, by no means, that I bid you do:
Let the bloat King tempt you again to bed,
Pinch wanton on your cheek, call you his mouse,
And let him, for a pair of reechy° kisses,   185
Or paddling in your neck with his damned fingers,
Make you to ravel° all this matter out,
That I essentially am not in madness,
But mad in craft. 'Twere good you let him know,
For who that's but a queen, fair, sober, wise,   190
Would from a paddock,° from a bat, a gib,°
Such dear concernings hide? Who would do so?
No, in despite of sense and secrecy,
Unpeg the basket on the house's top,
Let the birds fly, and like the famous ape,   195

---

164 **use** practice   165 **livery** characteristic garment (punning on "habits" in line 163)   170 **either** (probably a word is missing after *either;* among suggestions are "master," "curb," and "house"; but possibly *either* is a verb meaning "make easier")   176 **their** i.e., the heavens'   177 **bestow** stow, lodge   185 **reechy** foul (literally "smoky")   187 **ravel** unravel, reveal   191 **paddock** toad   191 **gib** tomcat

To try conclusions,° in the basket creep
And break your own neck down.
QUEEN   Be thou assured, if words be made of breath,
And breath of life, I have no life to breathe
What thou hast said to me.   200
HAMLET   I must to England; you know that?
QUEEN   Alack,
I had forgot. 'Tis so concluded on.
HAMLET   There's letters sealed, and my two school-fellows,
Whom I will trust as I will adders fanged,
They bear the mandate;° they must sweep my way   205
And marshal me to knavery. Let it work;
For 'tis the sport to have the enginer
Hoist with his own petar,° and 't shall go hard
But I will delve one yard below their mines
And blow them at the moon. O, 'tis most sweet   210
When in one line two crafts° directly meet.
This man shall set me packing:
I'll lug the guts into the neighbor room.
Mother, good night. Indeed, this counselor
Is now most still, most secret, and most grave,   215
Who was in life a foolish prating knave.
Come, sir, to draw toward an end with you.
Good night, Mother.

> [*Exit the* QUEEN. *Then*] *exit* HAMLET,
> *tugging in* POLONIUS.

[ACT IV

Scene I. The castle.]

Enter KING *and* QUEEN, *with* ROSENCRANTZ *and* GUILDENSTERN.

KING   There's matter in these sighs. These profound heaves
You must translate; 'tis fit we understand them.
Where is your son?
QUEEN   Bestow this place on us a little while,
> [*Exeunt* ROSENCRANTZ *and* GUILDENSTERN.]
Ah, mine own lord, what have I seen tonight!   5
KING   What, Gertrude? How does Hamlet?

196 **To try conclusions** to make experiments   205 **mandate** command   208 **petar** bomb   211 **crafts**
(1) boats, (2) acts of guile, crafty schemes

QUEEN   Mad as the sea and wind when both contend
    Which is the mightier. In his lawless fit,
    Behind the arras hearing something stir,
    Whips out his rapier, cries, "A rat, a rat!"   10
    And in this brainish apprehension° kills
    The unseen good old man.
KING   O heavy deed!
    It had been so with us, had we been there.
    His liberty is full of threats to all,
    To you yourself, to us, to every one.   15
    Alas, how shall this bloody deed be answered?
    It will be laid to us, whose providence°
    Should have kept short, restrained, and out of haunt°
    This mad young man. But so much was our love
    We would not understand what was most fit,   20
    But, like the owner of a foul disease,
    To keep it from divulging, let it feed
    Even on the pith of life. Where is he gone?
QUEEN   To draw apart the body he hath killed;
    O'er whom his very madness, like some ore   25
    Among a mineral° of metals base,
    Shows itself pure. 'A weeps for what is done.
KING   O Gertrude, come away!
    The sun no sooner shall the mountains touch
    But we will ship him hence, and this vile deed   30
    We must with all our majesty and skill
    Both countenance and excuse. Ho, Guildenstern!

Enter ROSENCRANTZ *and* GUILDENSTERN.

    Friends both, go join you with some further aid:
    Hamlet in madness hath Polonius slain,
    And from his mother's closet hath he dragged him.   35
    Go seek him out; speak fair, and bring the body
    Into the chapel. I pray you haste in this.
                     [*Exeunt* ROSENCRANTZ *and* GUILDENSTERN.]
    Come, Gertrude, we'll call up our wisest friends
    And let them know both what we mean to do
    And what's untimely done . . .°   40

IV.i. **11 brainish apprehension** mad imagination   **17 providence** foresight   **18 out of haunt** away from association with others   **25–26 ore / Among a mineral** vein of gold in a mine   **40 done . . .** (evidently something has dropped out of the text. Cappell's conjecture, "So, haply slander," is usually printed)

Whose whisper o'er the world's diameter,
As level as the cannon to his blank°
Transports his poisoned shot, may miss our name
And hit the woundless° air. O, come away!
My soul is full of discord and dismay.   *Exeunt.* 45

[*Scene II. The castle.*]

Enter HAMLET.

HAMLET   Safely stowed.
GENTLEMEN [*within*]   Hamlet! Lord Hamlet!
HAMLET   But soft, what noise? Who calls on Hamlet?
    O, here they come.

Enter ROSENCRANTZ *and* GUILDENSTERN.

ROSENCRANTZ   What have you done, my lord, with the dead body?   5
HAMLET   Compounded it with dust, whereto 'tis kin.
ROSENCRANTZ   Tell us where 'tis, that we may take it thence
    And bear it to the chapel.
HAMLET   Do not believe it.
ROSENCRANTZ   Believe what?   10
HAMLET   That I can keep your counsel and not mine own. Besides, to be demanded
    of° a sponge, what replication° should be made by the son of a king?
ROSENCRANTZ   Take you me for a sponge, my lord?
HAMLET   Ay, sir, that soaks up the King's countenance,° his rewards, his author-
    ities. But such officers do the King best service in the end. He keeps them, 15
    like an ape, in the corner of his jaw, first mouthed, to be last swallowed. When
    he needs what you have gleaned, it is but squeezing you and, sponge, you shall
    be dry again.
ROSENCRANTZ   I understand you not, my lord.
HAMLET   I am glad of it: a knavish speech sleeps in a foolish ear.   20
ROSENCRANTZ   My lord, you must tell us where the body is and go with us to the
    King.
HAMLET   The body is with the King, but the King is not with the body.° The King is
    a thing——
GUILDENSTERN   A thing, my lord?   25
HAMLET   Of nothing. Bring me to him. Hide fox, and all after.°
                                                          Exeunt.

---

⁴² **blank** white center of a target   ⁴⁴ **woundless** invulnerable   *IV.ii.* ¹² **demanded of** questioned
by   ¹² **replication** reply   ¹⁴ **countenance** favor   ²³ **The body . . . body** i.e., the body of authority
is with Claudius, but spiritually he is not the true king   ²⁶ **Hide fox, and all after** (a cry in a game such
as hide-and-seek; Hamlet runs from the stage)

[Scene III. The castle.]

Enter KING, *and two or three.*

KING   I have sent to seek him and to find the body:
How dangerous is it that this man goes loose!
Yet must not we put the strong law on him:
He's loved of the distracted° multitude,
Who like not in their judgment, but their eyes,   5
And where 'tis so, th' offender's scourge is weighed,
But never the offense. To bear° all smooth and even,
This sudden sending him away must seem
Deliberate pause.° Diseases desperate grown
By desperate appliance are relieved,   10
Or not at all.

Enter ROSENCRANTZ, [GUILDENSTERN,] *and all the rest.*

　　　　　　　How now? What hath befall'n?
ROSENCRANTZ   Where the dead body is bestowed, my lord,
We cannot get from him.
KING   But where is he?
ROSENCRANTZ   Without, my lord; guarded, to know your pleasure.
KING   Bring him before us.
ROSENCRANTZ   Ho! Bring in the lord.   15

They enter.

KING   Now Hamlet, where's Polonius?
HAMLET   At supper.
KING   At supper? Where?
HAMLET   Not where he eats, but where 'a is eaten. A certain convocation of politic°
worms are e'en at him. Your worm is your only emperor for diet. We fat all   20
creatures else to fat us, and we fat ourselves for maggots. Your fat king and your
lean beggar is but variable service°—two dishes, but to one table. That's the
end.
KING   Alas, alas!
HAMLET   A man may fish with the worm that hath eat of a king, and eat of the fish   25
that hath fed of that worm.
KING   What dost thou mean by this?
HAMLET   Nothing but to show you how a king may go a progress° through the guts
of a beggar.

IV.iii. ⁴ **distracted** bewildered, senseless   ⁷ **bear** carry out   ⁹ **pause** planning   ¹⁹ **politic** states-
manlike, shrewd   ²² **variable service** different courses   ²⁸ **progress** royal journey

KING   Where is Polonius?   30

HAMLET   In heaven. Send thither to see. If your messenger find him not there, seek
him i' th' other place yourself. But if indeed you find him not within this month,
you shall nose him as you go up the stairs into the lobby.

KING [*to* ATTENDANTS]   Go seek him there.

HAMLET   'A will stay till you come.   [*Exeunt* ATTENDANTS.] 35

KING   Hamlet, this deed, for thine especial safety,
Which we do tender° as we dearly grieve
For that which thou hast done, must send thee hence
With fiery quickness. Therefore prepare thyself.
The bark is ready and the wind at help,   40
Th' associates tend,° and everything is bent
For England.

HAMLET   For England?

KING   Ay, Hamlet.

HAMLET   Good.

KING   So is it, if thou knew'st our purposes.

HAMLET   I see a cherub° that sees them. But come, for England!
Farewell, dear Mother.   45

KING   Thy loving father, Hamlet.

HAMLET   My mother—father and mother is man and wife, man and wife is one flesh,
and so, my mother. Come, for England!   *Exit.*

KING   Follow him at foot;° tempt him with speed abroad.
Delay it not; I'll have him hence tonight.   50
Away! For everything is sealed and done
That else leans° on th' affair. Pray you make haste.

                                                        [*Exeunt all but the* KING.]

And, England, if my love thou hold'st at aught—
As my great power thereof may give thee sense,
Since yet thy cicatrice° looks raw and red   55
After the Danish sword, and thy free awe°
Pays homage to us—thou mayst not coldly set
Our sovereign process,° which imports at full
By letters congruing to that effect
The present° death of Hamlet. Do it, England,   60
For like the hectic° in my blood he rages,
And thou must cure me. Till I know 'tis done,
How'er my haps,° my joys were ne'er begun.   *Exit.*

---

³⁷ **tender** hold dear   ⁴¹ **tend** wait   ⁴⁴ **cherub** angel of knowledge   ⁴⁹ **at foot** closely   ⁵² **leans**
depends   ⁵⁵ **cicatrice** scar   ⁵⁶ **free awe** uncompelled submission   ⁵⁷⁻⁵⁸ **coldly set / Our sovereign process** regard slightly our royal command   ⁶⁰ **present** instant   ⁶¹ **hectic** fever   ⁶³ **haps**
chances, fortunes

[*Scene IV. A plain in Denmark.*]

Enter FORTINBRAS *with his Army over the stage.*

FORTINBRAS   Go, Captain, from me greet the Danish king.
  Tell him that by his license Fortinbras
  Craves the conveyance of° a promised march
  Over his kingdom. You know the rendezvous.
  If that his Majesty would aught with us,   5
  We shall express our duty in his eye;°
  And let him know so.
CAPTAIN   I will do't, my lord.
FORTINBRAS   Go softly° on.   [*Exeunt all but the* CAPTAIN.]

Enter HAMLET, ROSENCRANTZ, *&c.*

HAMLET   Good sir, whose powers° are these?
CAPTAIN   They are of Norway, sir.   10
HAMLET   How purposed, sir, I pray you?
CAPTAIN   Against some part of Poland.
HAMLET   Who commands them, sir?
CAPTAIN   The nephew to old Norway, Fortinbras.
HAMLET   Goes it against the main° of Poland, sir,   15
  Or for some frontier?
CAPTAIN   Truly to speak, and with no addition,°
  We go to gain a little patch of ground
  That hath in it no profit but the name.
  To pay five ducats, five, I would not farm it,   20
  Nor will it yield to Norway or the Pole
  A ranker° rate, should it be sold in fee.°
HAMLET   Why, then the Polack never will defend it.
CAPTAIN   Yes, it is already garrisoned.
HAMLET   Two thousand souls and twenty thousand ducats   25
  Will not debate° the question of this straw.
  This is th' imposthume° of much wealth and peace,
  That inward breaks, and shows no cause without
  Why the man dies. I humbly thank you, sir.
CAPTAIN   God bye you, sir.   [*Exit.*]
ROSENCRANTZ   Will't please you go, my lord?   30

IV.iv. ³ **conveyance of** escort for   ⁶ **in his eye** before his eyes (i.e., in his presence)   ⁸ **softly**
slowly   ⁹ **powers** forces   ¹⁵ **main** main part   ¹⁷ **with no addition** plainly   ²² **ranker** higher
²² **in fee** outright   ²⁶ **debate** settle   ²⁷ **imposthume** abscess, ulcer

HAMLET   I'll be with you straight. Go a little before.

[*Exeunt all but* HAMLET.]

How all occasions do inform against me
And spur my dull revenge! What is a man,
If his chief good and market° of his time
Be but to sleep and feed? A beast, no more.   35
Sure he that made us with such large discourse,°
Looking before and after, gave us not
That capability and godlike reason
To fust° in us unused. Now, whether it be
Bestial oblivion,° or some craven scruple   40
Of thinking too precisely on th' event°—
A thought which, quartered, hath but one part wisdom
And ever three parts coward—I do not know
Why yet I live to say, "This thing's to do,"
Sith I have cause, and will, and strength, and means   45
To do't. Examples gross° as earth exhort me.
Witness this army of such mass and charge,°
Led by a delicate and tender prince,
Whose spirit, with divine ambition puffed,
Makes mouths at the invisible event,°   50
Exposing what is mortal and unsure
To all that fortune, death, and danger dare,
Even for an eggshell. Rightly to be great
Is not° to stir without great argument,°
But greatly° to find quarrel in a straw   55
When honor's at the stake. How stand I then,
That have a father killed, a mother stained,
Excitements° of my reason and my blood,
And let all sleep, while to my shame I see
The imminent death of twenty thousand men   60
That for a fantasy and trick of fame°
Go to their graves like beds, fight for a plot
Whereon the numbers cannot try the cause,
Which is not tomb enough and continent°
To hide the slain? O, from this time forth,   65
My thoughts be bloody, or be nothing worth!   *Exit.*

---

³⁴ **market** profit   ³⁶ **discourse** understanding   ³⁹ **fust** grow moldy   ⁴⁰ **oblivion** forgetfulness
⁴¹ **event** outcome   ⁴⁶ **gross** large, obvious   ⁴⁷ **charge** expense   ⁵⁰ **Makes mouths at the invisible event** makes scornful faces (is contemptuous of) the unseen outcome   ⁵⁴ **not** (the sense seems to
require "not not")   ⁵⁴ **argument** reason   ⁵⁵ **greatly** i.e., nobly   ⁵⁸ **Excitements** incentives
⁶¹ **fantasy and trick of fame** illusion and trifle of reputation   ⁶⁴ **continent** receptacle, container

[Scene V. The castle.]

Enter HORATIO, [QUEEN] GERTRUDE, *and a* GENTLEMAN.

QUEEN   I will not speak with her.
GENTLEMAN   She is importunate, indeed distract.
Her mood will needs be pitied.
QUEEN   What would she have?
GENTLEMAN   She speaks much of her father, says she hears
There's tricks i' th' world, and hems, and beats her heart,   5
Spurns enviously at straws,° speaks things in doubt°
That carry but half sense. Her speech is nothing,
Yet the unshapèd use of it doth move
The hearers to collection;° they yawn° at it,
And botch the words up fit to their own thoughts,   10
Which, as her winks and nods and gestures yield them,
Indeed would make one think there might be thought,
Though nothing sure, yet much unhappily.
HORATIO   'Twere good she were spoken with, for she may strew
Dangerous conjectures in ill-breeding minds.   15
QUEEN   Let her come in.   [*Exit* GENTLEMAN.]
[*Aside.*] To my sick soul (as sin's true nature is)
Each toy seems prologue to some great amiss;°
So full of artless jealousy° is guilt
It spills° itself in fearing to be spilt.   20

Enter OPHELIA [*distracted*].

OPHELIA   Where is the beauteous majesty of Denmark?
QUEEN   How now, Ophelia?
OPHELIA *(She sings.)*

How should I your truelove know
      From another one?
By his cockle hat° and staff   25
      And his sandal shoon.°

QUEEN   Alas, sweet lady, what imports this song?

IV.v. ⁶ **Spurns enviously at straws** objects spitefully to insignificant matters   ⁶ **in doubt** uncertainly   ⁸⁻⁹ **Yet the . . . to collection** i.e., yet the formless manner of it moves her listeners to gather up some sort of meaning   ⁹ **yawn** gape (?)   ¹⁸ **amiss** misfortune   ¹⁹ **artless jealousy** crude suspicion   ²⁰ **spills** destroys   ²⁵ **cockle hat** (a cockleshell on the hat was the sign of a pilgrim who had journeyed to shrines overseas. The association of lovers and pilgrims was a common one)   ²⁶ **shoon** shoes

OPHELIA Say you? Nay, pray you mark.

> He is dead and gone, lady,   *(Song.)*
>   He is dead and gone;   30
> At his head a grass-green turf,
>   At his heels a stone.

  O, ho!
QUEEN Nay, but Ophelia——
OPHELIA Pray you mark. *(Sings.)*   35

> White his shroud as the mountain snow——

Enter KING.

QUEEN Alas, look here, my lord.
OPHELIA

> Larded° all with sweet flowers   *(Song.)*
> Which bewept to the grave did not go
>   With truelove showers.   40

KING How do you, pretty lady?
OPHELIA Well, God dild° you! They say the owl was a baker's daughter.° Lord, we
    know what we are, but know not what we may be. God be at your table!
KING Conceit° upon her father.
OPHELIA Pray let's have no words of this, but when they ask you what it means, say 45
    you this:

> Tomorrow is Saint Valentine's day.°   *(Song.)*
>   All in the morning betime,
> And I a maid at your window,
>   To be your Valentine.   50

> Then up he rose and donned his clothes
>   And dupped° the chamber door,
> Let in the maid, that out a maid
>   Never departed more.

KING Pretty Ophelia.   55

---

³⁸ **Larded** decorated   ⁴² **dild** yield, i.e., reward   ⁴² **baker's daughter** (an allusion to a tale of a
baker's daughter who begrudged bread to Christ and was turned into an owl)   ⁴⁴ **Conceit** brooding
⁴⁷ **Saint Valentine's day** Feb. 14 (the notion was that a bachelor would become the truelove of the first
girl he saw on this day)   ⁵² **dupped** opened (did up)

OPHELIA   Indeed, la, without an oath, I'll make an end on't:

[*Sings.*]

> By Gis° and by Saint Charity,
>   Alack, and fie for shame!
> Young men will do't if they come to't,
>   By Cock,° they are to blame.   60
> Quoth she, "Before you tumbled me,
>   You promised me to wed."

He answers:

> "So would I 'a' done, by yonder sun,
>   An thou hadst not come to my bed."   65

KING   How long hath she been thus?

OPHELIA   I hope all will be well. We must be patient, but I cannot choose but weep
to think they would lay him i' th' cold ground. My brother shall know of it; and so
I thank you for your good counsel. Come, my coach! Good night, ladies, good
night. Sweet ladies, good night, good night.   70

Exit.

KING   Follow her close; give her good watch, I pray you.

[*Exit* HORATIO.]

> O, this is the poison of deep grief; it springs
> All from her father's death—and now behold!
> O Gertrude, Gertrude,
> When sorrows come, they come not single spies,   75
> But in battalions; first, her father slain;
> Next, your son gone, and he most violent author
> Of his own just remove; the people muddied,°
> Thick and unwholesome in their thoughts and whispers
> For good Polonius' death, and we have done but greenly°   80
> In huggermugger° to inter him; poor Ophelia
> Divided from herself and her fair judgment,
> Without the which we are pictures or mere beasts;
> Last, and as much containing as all these,
> Her brother is in secret come from France,   85
> Feeds on his wonder,° keeps himself in clouds,
> And wants not buzzers° to infect his ear
> With pestilent speeches of his father's death,

---

[57] **Gis** (contraction of "Jesus")   [60] **Cock** (1) God, (2) phallus   [78] **muddied** muddled   [80] **greenly**
foolishly   [81] **huggermugger** secret haste   [86] **wonder** suspicion   [87] **wants not buzzers** does not
lack talebearers

Wherein necessity, of matter beggared,°   90
Will nothing stick° our person to arraign
In ear and ear. O my dear Gertrude, this,
Like a murd'ring piece,° in many places
Gives me superfluous death.   *A noise within.*

Enter a MESSENGER.

QUEEN   Alack, what noise is this?
KING   Attend, where are my Switzers?° Let them guard the door.
   What is the matter?
MESSENGER   Save yourself, my lord.   95
   The ocean, overpeering of his list,°
   Eats not the flats with more impiteous haste
   Than young Laertes, in a riotous head,°
   O'erbears your officers. The rabble call him lord,
   And, as the world were now but to begin,   100
   Antiquity forgot, custom not known,
   The ratifiers and props of every word,
   They cry, "Choose we! Laertes shall be king!"
   Caps, hands, and tongues applaud it to the clouds,
   "Laertes shall be king! Laertes king!"   *A noise within.* 105
QUEEN   How cheerfully on the false trail they cry!
   O, this is counter,° you false Danish dogs!

Enter LAERTES *with others.*

KING   The doors are broke.
LAERTES   Where is this king?—Sirs, stand you all without.
ALL   No, let's come in.
LAERTES   I pray you give me leave.   110
ALL   We will, we will.
LAERTES   I thank you. Keep the door.
                                        [*Exeunt his* FOLLOWERS.]
                          O thou vile King,
   Give me my father.
QUEEN   Calmly, good Laertes.
LAERTES   That drop of blood that's calm proclaims me bastard,
   Cries cuckold° to my father, brands the harlot   115

---

⁸⁹ **of matter beggared** unprovided with facts   ⁹⁰ **Will nothing stick** will not hesitate   ⁹² **murd'r-**
ing piece (a cannon that shot a kind of shrapnel)   ⁹⁴ **Switzers** Swiss guards   ⁹⁶ **list** shore   ⁹⁸ **in a**
riotous head with a rebellious force   ¹⁰⁷ **counter** (a hound runs counter when he follows the scent
backward from the prey)   ¹¹⁵ **cuckold** man whose wife is unfaithful

Even here between the chaste unsmirchèd brow
Of my true mother.

KING   What is the cause, Laertes,
    That thy rebellion looks so giantlike?
    Let him go, Gertrude. Do not fear° our person.
    There's such divinity doth hedge a king   120
    That treason can but peep to° what it would,
    Acts little of his will. Tell me, Laertes,
    Why thou art thus incensed. Let him go, Gertrude.
    Speak, man.

LAERTES   Where is my father?

KING   Dead.

QUEEN   But not by him.   125

KING   Let him demand his fill.

LAERTES   How came he dead? I'll not be juggled with.
    To hell allegiance, vows to the blackest devil,
    Conscience and grace to the profoundest pit!
    I dare damnation. To this point I stand,   130
    That both the worlds I give to negligence,°
    Let come what comes, only I'll be revenged
    Most throughly for my father.

KING   Who shall stay you?

LAERTES   My will, not all the world's.
    And for my means, I'll husband them° so well   135
    They shall go far with little.

KING   Good Laertes,
    If you desire to know the certainty
    Of your dear father, is't writ in your revenge
    That swoopstake° you will draw both friend and foe,
    Winner and loser?   140

LAERTES   None but his enemies.

KING   Will you know them then?

LAERTES   To his good friends thus wide I'll ope my arms
    And like the kind life-rend'ring pelican°
    Repast° them with my blood.

KING   Why, now you speak
    Like a good child and a true gentleman.   145
    That I am guiltless of your father's death,

---

[119] **fear** fear for   [121] **peep to** i.e., look at from a distance   [131] **That both . . . to negligence** i.e., I care not what may happen (to me) in this world or the next   [135] **husband them** use them economically   [139] **swoopstake** in a clean sweep   [143] **pelican** (thought to feed its young with its own blood)   [144] **Repast** feed

And am most sensibly° in grief for it,
It shall as level to your judgment 'pear
As day does to your eye.

A noise within: "Let her come in." 150

LAERTES How now? What noise is that?

Enter OPHELIA.

O heat, dry up my brains; tears seven times salt
Burn out the sense and virtue° of mine eye!
By heaven, thy madness shall be paid with weight
Till our scale turn the beam.° O rose of May,
Dear maid, kind sister, sweet Ophelia! 155
O heavens, is't possible a young maid's wits
Should be as mortal as an old man's life?
Nature is fine° in love, and where 'tis fine,
It sends some precious instance° of itself
After the thing it loves. 160

OPHELIA

> They bore him barefaced on the bier *(Song.)*
>   Hey non nony, nony, hey nony
> And in his grave rained many a tear——

Fare you well, my dove!

LAERTES Hadst thou thy wits, and didst persuade revenge, 165
It could not move thus.

OPHELIA You must sing "A-down a-down, and you call him a-down-a." O, how the
wheel° becomes it! It is the false steward, that stole his master's daughter.

LAERTES This nothing's more than matter.°

OPHELIA There's rosemary, that's for remembrance. Pray you, love, remember. 170
And there is pansies, that's for thoughts.

LAERTES A document° in madness, thoughts and remembrance fitted.

OPHELIA There's fennel° for you, and columbines. There's rue for you, and here's
some for me. We may call it herb of grace o' Sundays. O, you must wear your

---

¹⁴⁷ **sensibly** acutely   ¹⁵² **virtue** power   ¹⁵⁴ **turn the beam** weigh down the bar (of the balance)
¹⁵⁸ **fine** refined, delicate   ¹⁵⁹ **instance** sample   ¹⁶⁸ **wheel** (of uncertain meaning, but probably a turn
or dance of Ophelia's, rather than Fortune's wheel)   ¹⁶⁹ **This nothing's more than matter** this
nonsense has more meaning than matters of consequence   ¹⁷² **document** lesson   ¹⁷³ **fennel** (the
distribution of flowers in the ensuing lines has symbolic meaning, but the meaning is disputed. Perhaps
fennel, flattery; *columbines*, cuckoldry; *rue*, sorrow for Ophelia and repentance for the Queen; *daisy*,
dissembling; *violets*, faithfulness. For other interpretations, see J. W. Lever in *Review of English Studies*,
New Series 3 [1952], pp. 123–29)

rue with a difference. There's a daisy. I would give you some violets, but they 175
withered all when my father died. They say 'a made a good end.   [*Sings.*]

       For bonny sweet Robin is all my joy.

LAERTES   Thought and affliction, passion, hell itself,
  She turns to favor° and to prettiness.
OPHELIA

       And will 'a not come again?   (*Song.*) 180
       And will 'a not come again?
         No, no, he is dead,
         Go to thy deathbed,
       He never will come again.

       His beard was as white as snow,   185
       All flaxen was his poll.°
         He is gone, he is gone,
         And we cast away moan.
       God 'a' mercy on his soul!

    And of all Christian souls, I pray God. God bye you.   190
                                         [*Exit.*]

LAERTES   Do you see this, O God?
KING   Laertes, I must commune with your grief,
  Or you deny me right. Go but apart,
  Make choice of whom your wisest friends you will,
  And they shall hear and judge 'twixt you and me.   195
  If by direct or by collateral° hand
  They find us touched,° we will our kingdom give,
  Our crown, our life, and all that we call ours,
  To you in satisfaction; but if not,
  Be you content to lend your patience to us,   200
  And we shall jointly labor with your soul
  To give it due content.
LAERTES   Let this be so.
  His means of death, his obscure funeral—
  No trophy, sword, nor hatchment° o'er his bones,
  No noble rite nor formal ostentation°—   205

---

¹⁷⁹ **favor** charm, beauty   ¹⁸⁶ **All flaxen was his poll** white as flax was his head   ¹⁹⁶ **collateral**
indirect   ¹⁹⁷ **touched** implicated   ²⁰⁴ **hatchment** tablet bearing the coat of arms of the dead
²⁰⁵ **ostentation** ceremony

Cry to be heard, as 'twere from heaven to earth,
Then I must call't in question.

KING   So you shall;
And where th' offense is, let the great ax fall.
I pray you go with me.   *Exeunt.*

[*Scene VI. The castle.*]

Enter HORATIO *and others.*

HORATIO   What are they that would speak with me?
GENTLEMAN   Seafaring men, sir. They say they have letters for you.
HORATIO   Let them come in.   [*Exit* ATTENDANT.]
  I do not know from what part of the world
  I should be greeted, if not from Lord Hamlet.   5

Enter SAILORS.

SAILOR   God bless you, sir.
HORATIO   Let Him bless thee too.
SAILOR   'A shall, sir, an't please Him. There's a letter for you, sir—it came from th'
    ambassador that was bound for England— if your name be Horatio, as I am let
    to know it is.   10
HORATIO [*reads the letter*].
    "Horatio, when thou shalt have overlooked° this, give these fellows some means
    to the King. They have letters for him. Ere we were two days old at sea, a pirate
    of very warlike appointment° gave us chase. Finding ourselves too slow of sail,
    we put on a compelled valor, and in the grapple I boarded them. On the instant
    they got clear of our ship; so I alone became their prisoner. They have dealt with 15
    me like thieves of mercy, but they knew what they did: I am to do a good turn
    for them. Let the King have the letters I have sent, and repair thou to me with
    as much speed as thou wouldest fly death. I have words to speak in thine ear will
    make thee dumb; yet are they much too light for the bore° of the matter. These
    good fellows will bring thee where I am. Rosencrantz and Guildenstern hold their 20
    course for England. Of them I have much to tell thee. Farewell.
                            He that thou knowest thine, HAMLET."

  Come, I will give you way for these your letters,
  And do't the speedier that you may direct me
  To him from whom you brought them.   *Exeunt.* 25

IV.vi. ¹¹ **overlooked** surveyed   ¹³ **appointment** equipment   ¹⁹ **bore** caliber (here, "importance")

[*Scene VII. The castle.*]

Enter KING *and* LAERTES.

KING Now must your conscience my acquittance seal,
　And you must put me in your heart for friend,
　Sith you have heard, and with a knowing ear,
　That he which hath your noble father slain
　Pursued my life.
LAERTES　　　　　　It well appears. But tell me　　　　　　5
　Why you proceeded not against these feats
　So criminal and so capital° in nature,
　As by your safety, greatness, wisdom, all things else,
　You mainly° were stirred up.
KING　　　　　　　　　　O, for two special reasons,
　Which may to you perhaps seem much unsinewed,°　　　　10
　But yet to me they're strong. The Queen his mother
　Lives almost by his looks, and for myself—
　My virtue or my plague, be it either which—
　She is so conjunctive° to my life and soul,
　That, as the star moves not but in his sphere,　　　　15
　I could not but by her. The other motive
　Why to a public count° I might not go
　Is the great love the general gender° bear him,
　Who, dipping all his faults in their affection,
　Would, like the spring that turneth wood to stone,°　　20
　Convert his gyves° to graces; so that my arrows,
　Too slightly timbered° for so loud a wind,
　Would have reverted to my bow again,
　And not where I had aimed them.
LAERTES　And so have I a noble father lost,　　　　25
　A sister driven into desp'rate terms°
　Whose worth, if praises may go back again,°
　Stood challenger on mount of all the age
　For her perfections. But my revenge will come.
KING　Break not your sleeps for that. You must not think　　30
　That we are made of stuff so flat and dull
　That we can let our beard be shook with danger,

IV.vii. ⁷ **capital** deserving death　⁹ **mainly** powerfully　¹⁰ **unsinewed** weak　¹⁴ **conjunctive** closely united　¹⁷ **count** reckoning　¹⁸ **general gender** common people　²⁰ **spring that turneth wood to stone** (a spring in Shakespeare's county was so charged with lime that it would petrify wood placed in it)　²¹ **gyves** fetters　²² **timbered** shafted　²⁶ **terms** conditions　²⁷ **go back again** revert to what is past

And think it pastime. You shortly shall hear more.
I loved your father, and we love ourself,
And that, I hope, will teach you to imagine——   35

Enter a MESSENGER *with letters.*

How now? What news?
MESSENGER   Letters, my lord, from Hamlet:
These to your Majesty; this to the Queen.
KING   From Hamlet? Who brought them?
MESSENGER   Sailors, my lord, they say; I saw them not.
They were given me by Claudio; he received them   40
Of him that brought them.
KING   Laertes, you shall hear them.——
Leave us. [*Reads.*]   *Exit* MESSENGER.

"High and mighty, you shall know I am set naked° on your kingdom. Tomorrow
shall I beg leave to see your kingly eyes; when I shall (first asking your pardon
thereunto) recount the occasion of my sudden and more strange return.   45
                                                   HAMLET."

What should this mean? Are all the rest come back?
Or is it some abuse,° and no such thing?
LAERTES   Know you the hand?
KING   'Tis Hamlet's character.° "Naked"!
And in a postcript here, he says, "alone."   50
Can you devise° me?
LAERTES   I am lost in it, my lord. But let him come.
It warms the very sickness in my heart
That I shall live and tell him to his teeth,
"Thus did'st thou."
KING   If it be so, Laertes   55
(As how should it be so? How otherwise?),
Will you be ruled by me?
LAERTES   Ay, my lord,
So you will not o'errule me to a peace.
KING   To thine own peace. If he be now returned,
As checking at° his voyage, and that he means   60
No more to undertake it, I will work him
To an exploit now ripe in my device,
Under the which he shall not choose but fall;

---

43 **naked** destitute   48 **abuse** deception   49 **character** handwriting   51 **devise** advise   60 **check-**
ing at turning away from (a term in falconry)

And for his death no wind of blame shall breathe,
But even his mother shall uncharge the practice°   65
And call it accident.
LAERTES   My lord, I will be ruled;
The rather if you could devise it so
That I might be the organ.
KING   It falls right.
You have been talked of since your travel much,
And that in Hamlet's hearing, for a quality   70
Wherein they say you shine. Your sum of parts
Did not together pluck such envy from him
As did that one, and that, in my regard,
Of the unworthiest siege.°
LAERTES   What part is that, my lord?
KING   A very riband in the cap of youth,   75
Yet needful too, for youth no less becomes
The light and careless livery that it wears
Than settled age his sables and his weeds,°
Importing health and graveness. Two months since
Here was a gentleman of Normandy.   80
I have seen myself, and served against, the French,
And they can° well on horseback, but this gallant
Had witchcraft in't. He grew unto his seat,
And to such wondrous doing brought his horse
As had he been incorpsed and deminatured   85
With the brave beast. So far he topped my thought
That I, in forgery° of shapes and tricks,
Come short of what he did.
LAERTES   A Norman was't?
KING   A Norman.
LAERTES   Upon my life, Lamord.
KING   The very same.   90
LAERTES   I know him well. He is the brooch° indeed
And gem of all the nation.
KING   He made confession° of you,
And gave you such a masterly report,
For art and exercise in your defense,   95
And for your rapier most especial,
That he cried out 'twould be a sight indeed

---

⁶⁵ **uncharge the practice** not charge the device with treachery   ⁷⁴ **siege** rank   ⁷⁸ **sables and his weeds** i.e., sober attire   ⁸² **can** do   ⁸⁷ **forgery** invention   ⁹¹ **brooch** ornament   ⁹³ **confession** report

If one could match you. The scrimers° of their nation
He swore had neither motion, guard, nor eye,
If you opposed them. Sir, this report of his   100
Did Hamlet so envenom with his envy
That he could nothing do but wish and beg
Your sudden coming o'er to play with you.
Now, out of this——
LAERTES   What out of this, my lord?
KING   Laertes, was your father dear to you?   105
Or are you like the painting of a sorrow,
A face without a heart?
LAERTES   Why ask you this?
KING   Not that I think you did not love your father,
But that I know love is begun by time,
And that I see, in passages of proof.°   110
Time qualifies° the spark and fire of it.
There lives within the very flame of love
A kind of wick or snuff° that will abate it,
And nothing is at a like goodness still,°
For goodness, growing to a plurisy,°   115
Dies in his own too-much. That we would do
We should do when we would, for this "would" changes,
And hath abatements and delays as many
As there are tongues, are hands, are accidents,
And then this "should" is like a spendthrift sigh,°   120
That hurts by easing. But to the quick° of th' ulcer—
Hamlet comes back; what would you undertake
To show yourself in deed your father's son
More than in words?
LAERTES   To cut his throat i' th' church!
KING   No place indeed should murder sanctuarize;°   125
Revenge should have no bounds. But, good Laertes,
Will you do this? Keep close within your chamber.
Hamlet returned shall know you are come home.
We'll put on those° shall praise your excellence
And set a double varnish on the fame   130
The Frenchman gave you, bring you in fine° together

---

⁹⁸ **scrimers** fencers   ¹¹⁰ **passages of proof** proved cases   ¹¹¹ **qualifies** diminishes   ¹¹³ **snuff** residue of burnt wick (which dims the light)   ¹¹⁴ **still** always   ¹¹⁵ **plurisy** fullness, excess   ¹²⁰ **spendthrift sigh** (sighing provides ease, but because it was thought to thin the blood and so shorten life it was spendthrift)   ¹²¹ **quick** sensitive flesh   ¹²⁵ **sanctuarize** protect   ¹²⁹ **We'll put on those** we'll incite persons who   ¹³¹ **in fine** finally

And wager on your heads. He, being remiss,
Most generous, and free from all contriving,
Will not peruse the foils, so that with ease,
Or with a little shuffling, you may choose   135
A sword unbated,° and, in a pass of practice,°
Requite him for your father.
LAERTES   I will do't,
    And for that purpose I'll anoint my sword.
    I bought an unction of a mountebank,°
    So mortal that, but dip a knife in it,   140
    Where it draws blood, no cataplasm° so rare,
    Collected from all simples° that have virtue°
    Under the moon, can save the thing from death
    That is but scratched withal. I'll touch my point
    With this contagion, that, if I gall him slightly,   145
    It may be death.
    KING   Let's further think of this,
    Weigh what convenience both of time and means
    May fit us to our shape.° If this should fail,
    And that our drift look through° our bad performance,
    'Twere better not assayed. Therefore this project   150
    Should have a back or second, that might hold
    If this did blast in proof° Soft, let me see.
    We'll make a solemn wager on your cunnings—
    I ha't!
    When in your motion you are hot and dry—   155
    As make your bouts more violent to that end—
    And that he calls for drink, I'll have prepared him
    A chalice for the nonce,° whereon but sipping,
    If he by chance escape your venomed stuck,°
    Our purpose may hold there. —But stay, what noise?   160

Enter QUEEN.

QUEEN   One woe doth tread upon another's heel.
    So fast they follow. Your sister's drowned, Laertes.
LAERTES   Drowned! O, where?
QUEEN   There is a willow grows askant° the brook,
    That shows his hoar° leaves in the glassy stream: 165

---

[136] **unbated** not blunted   [136] **pass of practice** treacherous thrust   [139] **mountebank** quack
[141] **cataplasm** poultice   [142] **simples** medicinal herbs   [142] **virtue** power (to heal)   [148] **shape**
role [149] **drift look through** purpose show through   [152] **blast in proof** burst (fail) in performance
[158] **nonce** occasion   [159] **stuck** thrust   [164] **askant** aslant   [165] **hoar** silver-gray

Therewith° fantastic garlands did she make
Of crowflowers, nettles, daisies, and long purples,
That liberal° shepherds give a grosser name,
But our cold maids do dead men's fingers call them.
There on the pendent boughs her crownet° weeds   170
Clamb'ring to hang, an envious sliver° broke,
When down her weedy trophies and herself
Fell in the weeping brook. Her clothes spread wide,
And mermaidlike awhile they bore her up,
Which time she chanted snatches of old lauds,°   175
As one incapable° of her own distress,
Or like a creature native and indued°
Unto that element. But long it could not be
Till that her garments, heavy with their drink,
Pulled the poor wretch from her melodious lay   180
To muddy death.
LAERTES   Alas, then she is drowned?
QUEEN   Drowned, drowned.
LAERTES   Too much of water hast thou, poor Ophelia,
And therefore I forbid my tears; but yet
It is our trick;° nature her custom holds,   185
Let shame say what it will: when these are gone,
The woman° will be out. Adieu, my lord.
I have a speech o' fire, that fain would blaze,
But that this folly drowns it.   *Exit.*
KING   Let's follow, Gertrude.
How much I had to do to calm his rage!   190
Now fear I this will give it start again;
Therefore let's follow.   *Exeunt.*

[ACT V

Scene I. A churchyard.]

Enter two CLOWNS.°

CLOWN   Is she to be buried in Christian burial when she willfully seeks her own
    salvation?
OTHER   I tell thee she is. Therefore make her grave straight.° The crowner° hath
    sate on her, and finds it Christian burial.

---

¹⁶⁶ **Therewith** i.e., with willow twigs   ¹⁶⁸ **liberal** free-spoken, coarse-mouthed   ¹⁷⁰ **crownet** coronet   ¹⁷¹ **envious sliver** malicious branch   ¹⁷⁵ **lauds** hymns   ¹⁷⁶ **incapable** unaware   ¹⁷⁷ **indued** in harmony with   ¹⁸⁵ **trick** trait, way   ¹⁸⁷ **woman** i.e., womanly part of me   *V.i.* ˢ·ᵈ· **Clowns** rustics   ³ **straight** straightway   ³ **crowner** coroner

CLOWN   How can that be, unless she drowned herself in her own defense?   5

OTHER   Why, 'tis found so.

CLOWN   It must be *se offendendo;*° it cannot be else. For here lies the point: if I drown myself wittingly, it argues an act, and an act hath three branches—it is to act, to do, to perform. Argal,° she drowned herself wittingly.

OTHER   Nay, but hear you, Goodman Delver.   10

CLOWN   Give me leave. Here lies the water—good. Here stands the man—good. If the man go to this water and drown himself, it is, will he nill he,° he goes; mark you that. But if the water come to him and drown him, he drowns not himself. Argal, he that is not guilty of his own death, shortens not his own life.

OTHER   But is this law?   15

CLOWN   Ay marry, is't—crowner's quest° law.

OTHER   Will you ha' the truth on't? If this had not been a gentlewoman, she should have been buried out o' Christian burial.

CLOWN   Why, there thou say'st. And the more pity that great folk should have count'nance° in this world to drown or hang themselves more than their even- 20 Christen.° Come, my spade. There is no ancient gentlemen but gard'ners, ditchers, and gravemakers. They hold up° Adam's profession.

OTHER   Was he a gentleman?

CLOWN   'A was the first that ever bore arms.°

OTHER   Why, he had none.   25

CLOWN   What, art a heathen? How dost thou understand the Scripture? The Scripture says Adam digged. Could he dig without arms? I'll put another question to thee. If thou answerest me not to the purpose, confess thyself——

OTHER   Go to.

CLOWN   What is he that builds stronger than either the mason, the shipwright, or 30 the carpenter?

OTHER   The gallowsmaker, for that frame outlives a thousand tenants.

CLOWN   I like thy wit well, in good faith. The gallows does well. But how does it well? It does well to those that do ill. Now thou dost ill to say the gallows is built stronger than the church. Argal, the gallows may do well to thee. To't again, 35 come.

OTHER   Who builds stronger than a mason, a shipwright, or a carpenter?

CLOWN   Ay, tell me that, and unyoke.°

OTHER   Marry, now I can tell.

---

7 se offendendo (blunder for *se defendendo,* a legal term meaning "in self-defense")   **9 Argal** (blunder for Latin *ergo,* "therefore")   **12 will he nill he** will he or will he not (whether he will or will not) **16 quest** inquest   **20 count'nance** privilege   **20–21 even-Christen** fellow Christian   **22 hold up** keep up   **24 bore arms** had a coat of arms (the sign of a gentleman)   **38 unyoke** i.e., stop work for the day

CLOWN To't.   40

OTHER Mass,° I cannot tell.

Enter HAMLET *and* HORATIO *afar off.*

CLOWN Cudgel thy brains no more about it, for your dull ass will not mend his pace
with beating. And when you are asked this question next, say "a gravemaker."
The houses he makes lasts till doomsday. Go, get thee in, and fetch me a stoup°
of liquor.   [*Exit* OTHER CLOWN.] 45

In youth when I did love, did love,   [*Song.*]
  Methought it was very sweet
To contract—O—the time for—a—my behove,°
  O, methought there—a—was nothing—a—meet.

HAMLET Has this fellow no feeling of his business? 'A sings in gravemaking.   50

HORATIO Custom hath made it in him a property of easiness.°

HAMLET 'Tis e'en so. The hand of little employment hath the daintier sense.°

CLOWN

But age with his stealing steps   [*Song.*]
  Hath clawed me in his clutch,
And hath shipped me into the land,   55
  As if I had never been such.

[*Throws up a skull.*]

HAMLET That skull had a tongue in it, and could sing once. How the knave jowls° it
to the ground, as if 'twere Cain's jawbone, that did the first murder! This might
be the pate of a politician, which this ass now o'erreaches,° one that would
circumvent God, might it not?   60

HORATIO It might, my lord.

HAMLET Or of a courtier, which could say "Good morrow, sweet lord! How dost
thou, sweet lord?" This might be my Lord Such-a-one, that praised my Lord
Such-a-one's horse when 'a went to beg it, might it not?

HORATIO Ay, my lord.   65

HAMLET Why, e'en so, and now my Lady Worm's, chapless,° and knocked about
the mazzard° with a sexton's spade. Here's fine revolution, an we had the trick

---

⁴¹ **Mass** by the mass ⁴⁴ **stoup** tankard ⁴⁸ **behove** advantage ⁵¹ **in him a property of easiness**
easy for him ⁵² **hath the daintier sense** is more sensitive (because it is not calloused) ⁵⁷ **jowls**
hurls ⁵⁹ **o'erreaches** (1) reaches over, (2) has the advantage over ⁶⁶ **chapless** lacking the lower
jaw ⁶⁷ **mazzard** head

to see't. Did these bones cost no more than breeding but to play at loggets° with
them? Mine ache to think on't.

CLOWN

> A pickax and a spade, a spade,   [*Song.*] 70
>   For and a shrouding sheet;
> O, a pit of clay for to be made
>   For such a guest is meet.

[*Throws up another skull.*]

HAMLET   There's another. Why may not that be the skull of a lawyer? Where be his
quiddities° now, his quillities,° his cases, his tenures,° and his tricks? Why does 75
he suffer this mad knave now to knock him about the sconce° with a dirty shovel,
and will not tell him of his action of battery? Hum! This fellow might be in's time
a great buyer of land, with his statutes, his recognizances, his fines,° his double
vouchers, his recoveries. Is this the fine° of his fines, and the recovery of his
recoveries, to have his fine pate full of fine dirt? Will his vouchers vouch him no 80
more of his purchases, and double ones too, than the length and breadth of a pair
of indentures?° The very conveyances° of his lands will scarcely lie in this box,
and must th' inheritor himself have no more, ha?

HORATIO   Not a jot more, my lord.

HAMLET   Is not parchment made of sheepskins?   85

HORATIO   Ay, my lord, and of calveskins too.

HAMLET   They are sheep and calves which seek out assurance° in that. I will speak
to this fellow. Whose grave's this, sir-rah?

CLOWN   Mine, sir. [*Sings.*]

> O, a pit of clay for to be made   90
>   For such a guest is meet.

HAMLET   I think it be thine indeed, for thou liest in't.

CLOWN   You lie out on't sir, and therefore 'tis not yours. For my part, I do not lie
in't, yet it is mine.

HAMLET   Thou dost lie in't, to be in't and say it is thine. 'Tis for the dead, not for the 95
quick;° therefore thou liest.

CLOWN   'Tis a quick lie, sir; 'twill away again from me to you.

HAMLET   What man dost thou dig it for?

---

⁶⁸ **loggets** (a game in which small pieces of wood were thrown at an object)   ⁷⁵ **quiddities** subtle
arguments (from Latin *quidditas*, "whatness")   ⁷⁵ **quillities** fine distinctions   ⁷⁵ **tenures** legal means
of holding land   ⁷⁶ **sconce** head   ⁷⁸ **his statutes, his recognizances, his fines** his documents
giving a creditor control of a debtor's land, his bonds of surety, his documents changing an entailed estate
into fee simple (unrestricted ownership)   ⁷⁹ **fine** end   ⁸² **indentures** contracts   ⁸² **conveyances**
legal documents for the transference of land   ⁸⁷ **assurance** safety   ⁹⁶ **quick** living

CLOWN For no man, sir.

HAMLET What woman then? 100

CLOWN For none neither.

HAMLET Who is to be buried in't?

CLOWN One that was a woman, sir; but, rest her soul, she's dead.

HAMLET How absolute° the knave is! We must speak by the card,° or equivocation°
    will undo us. By the Lord, Horatio, this three years I have took note of it, the 105
    age is grown so picked° that the toe of the peasant comes so near the heel of the
    courtier he galls his kibe.° How long hast thou been a gravemaker?

CLOWN Of all the days i' th' year, I came to't that day that our last king Hamlet
    overcame Fortinbras.

HAMLET How long is that since? 110

CLOWN Cannot you tell that? Every fool can tell that. It was that very day that young
    Hamlet was born—he that is mad, and sent into England.

HAMLET Ay, marry, why was he sent into England?

CLOWN Why, because 'a was mad. 'A shall recover his wits there; or, if 'a do not,
    'tis no great matter there. 115

HAMLET Why?

CLOWN 'Twill not be seen in him there. There the men are as mad as he.

HAMLET How came he mad?

CLOWN Very strangely, they say.

HAMLET How strangely? 120

CLOWN Faith, e'en with losing his wits.

HAMLET Upon what ground?

CLOWN Why, here in Denmark. I have been sexton here, man and boy, thirty years.

HAMLET How long will a man lie i' th' earth ere he rot?

CLOWN Faith, if 'a be not rotten before 'a die (as we have many pocky corses° 125
    nowadays that will scarce hold the laying in), 'a will last you some eight year or
    nine year. A tanner will last you nine year.

HAMLET Why he, more than another?

CLOWN Why, sir, his hide is so tanned with his trade that 'a will keep out water a
    great while, and your water is a sore decayer of your whoreson dead body. 130
    Here's a skull now hath lien you i' th' earth three and twenty years.

HAMLET Whose was it?

CLOWN A whoreson mad fellow's it was. Whose do you think it was?

HAMLET Nay, I know not.

CLOWN A pestilence on him for a mad rogue! 'A poured a flagon of Rhenish on my 135
    head once. This same skull, sir, was, sir, Yorick's skull, the King's jester.

---

104 **absolute** positive, decided   104 **by the card** by the compass card, i.e., exactly   104 **equivocation**
ambiguity   106 **picked** refined   107 **kibe** sore on the back of the heel   125 **pocky corses** bodies of
persons who had been infected with the pox (syphilis)

HAMLET   This?

CLOWN   E'en that.

HAMLET   Let me see. [*Takes the skull.*] Alas, poor Yorick! I knew him, Horatio, a
fellow of infinite jest, of most excellent fancy. He hath borne me on his back a   140
thousand times. And now how abhorred in my imagination it is! My gorge rises
at it. Here hung those lips that I have kissed I know not how oft. Where be your
gibes now? Your gambols, your songs, your flashes of merriment that were wont
to set the table on a roar? Not one now to mock your own grinning? Quite
chapfall'n?° Now get you to my lady's chamber, and tell her, let her paint an inch   145
thick, to this favor° she must come. Make her laugh at that. Prithee, Horatio,
tell me one thing.

HORATIO   What's that, my lord?

HAMLET   Dost thou think Alexander looked o' this fashion i' th' earth?

HORATIO   E'en so.   150

HAMLET   And smelt so? Pah! [*Puts down the skull.*]

HORATIO   E'en so, my lord.

HAMLET   To what base uses we may return, Horatio! Why may not imagination trace
the noble dust of Alexander till a' find it stopping a bunghole?

HORATIO   'Twere to consider too curiously,° to consider so.   155

HAMLET   No, faith, not a jot, but to follow him thither with modesty enough,° and
likelihood to lead it; as thus: Alexander died, Alexander was buried. Alexander
returneth to dust; the dust is earth; of earth we make loam; and why of that loam
whereto he was converted might they not stop a beer barrel?

Imperious Caesar, dead and turned to clay.   160
Might stop a hole to keep the wind away.
O, that that earth which kept the world in awe
Should patch a wall t' expel the winter's flaw!°
But soft, but soft awhile! Here comes the King.

Enter KING, QUEEN, LAERTES, *and a coffin, with* LORDS *attendant* [*and a* DOCTOR
OF DIVINITY].

The Queen, the courtiers. Who is this they follow?   165
And with such maimèd° rites? This doth betoken
The corse they follow did with desp'rate hand
Fordo it° own life. 'Twas of some estate.°
Couch° we awhile, and mark.   [*Retires with* HORATIO.]

LAERTES   What ceremony else?

HAMLET   That is Laertes,   170
A very noble youth. Mark.

---

¹⁴⁵ **chapfall'n** (1) down in the mouth, (2) jawless   ¹⁴⁶ **favor** facial appearance   ¹⁵⁵ **curiously** mi-
nutely   ¹⁵⁶ **with modesty enough** without exaggeration   ¹⁶³ **flaw** gust   ¹⁶⁶ **maimèd** incomplete
¹⁶⁸ **Fordo it** destroy its   ¹⁶⁸ **estate** high rank   ¹⁶⁹ **Couch** hide

LAERTES   What ceremony else?

DOCTOR   Her obsequies have been as far enlarged

As we have warranty. Her death was doubtful,°

And, but that great command o'ersways the order,   175

She should in ground unsanctified been lodged

Till the last trumpet. For charitable prayers,

Shards,° flints, and pebbles should be thrown on her.

Yet here she is allowed her virgin crants,°

Her maiden strewments,° and the bringing home   180

Of bell and burial.

LAERTES   Must there no more be done?

DOCTOR   No more be done.

We should profane the service of the dead

To sing a requiem and such rest to her

As to peace-parted souls.

LAERTES   Lay her i' th' earth,   185

And from her fair and unpolluted flesh

May violets spring! I tell thee, churlish priest,

A minist'ring angel shall my sister be

When thou liest howling!

HAMLET   What, the fair Ophelia?

QUEEN   Sweets to the sweet! Farewell. [*Scatters flowers.*]   190

I hoped thou shouldst have been my Hamlet's wife.

I thought thy bride bed to have decked, sweet maid,

And not have strewed thy grave.

LAERTES   O, treble woe

Fall ten times treble on that cursèd head

Whose wicked deed thy most ingenious sense°   195

Deprived thee of! Hold off the earth awhile,

Till I have caught her once more in mine arms.

Leaps in the grave.

Now pile your dust upon the quick and dead

Till of this flat a mountain you have made

T' o'ertop old Pelion° or the skyish head   200

Of blue Olympus.

HAMLET [*coming forward*]   What is he whose grief

Bears such an emphasis, whose phrase of sorrow

---

¹⁷⁴ **doubtful** suspicious   ¹⁷⁸ **Shards** broken pieces of pottery   ¹⁷⁹ **crants** garlands   ¹⁸⁰ **strew-ments** i.e., of flowers   ¹⁹⁵ **most ingenious sense** finely endowed mind   ²⁰⁰ **Pelion** (according to classical legend, giants in their fight with the gods sought to reach heaven by piling Mount Pelion and Mount Ossa on Mount Olympus)

Conjures the wand'ring stars,° and makes them stand
Like wonder-wounded hearers? This is I,   205
Hamlet the Dane.

LAERTES   The devil take thy soul!

[*Grapples with him.*]°

HAMLET   Thou pray'st not well.
I prithee take thy fingers from my throat,
For, though I am not splenitive° and rash,
Yet have I in me something dangerous,   210
Which let thy wisdom fear. Hold off thy hand.

KING   Pluck them asunder.

QUEEN   Hamlet, Hamlet!

ALL   Gentlemen!

HORATIO   Good my lord, be quiet.

[ATTENDANTS *part them.*]

HAMLET   Why, I will fight with him upon this theme
Until my eyelids will no longer wag.   215

QUEEN   O my son, what theme?

HAMLET   I loved Ophelia. Forty thousand brothers
Could not with all their quantity of love
Make up my sum. What wilt thou do for her?

KING   O, he is mad, Laertes.   220

QUEEN   For love of God forbear him.

HAMLET   'Swounds, show me what thou't do.
Woo't weep? Woo't fight? Woo't fast? Woo't tear thyself?
Woo't drink up eisel?° Eat a crocodile?
I'll do't. Dost thou come here to whine?   225
To outface me with leaping in her grave?
Be buried quick with her, and so will I.
And if thou prate of mountains, let them throw
Millions of acres on us, till our ground,
Singeing his pate against the burning zone,°   230

---

²⁰⁴ **wand'ring stars** planets   ^{206 s.d.} **Grapples with him** (Q1, a bad quarto, presumably reporting a version that toured, has a previous direction saying "Hamlet leaps in after Laertes." Possibly he does so, somewhat hysterically. But such a direction—absent from the two good texts, Q2 and F—makes Hamlet the aggressor, somewhat contradicting his next speech. Perhaps Laertes leaps out of the grave to attack Hamlet)   ²⁰⁹ **splenitive** fiery (the spleen was thought to be the seat of anger)   ²²⁴ **eisel** vinegar   ²³⁰ **burning zone** sun's orbit

Make Ossa like a wart! Nay, an thou'lt mouth,
I'll rant as well as thou.
QUEEN   This is mere madness;
  And thus a while the fit will work on him.
  Anon, as patient as the female dove
  When that her golden couplets are disclosed,°   235
  His silence will sit drooping.
HAMLET   Hear you, sir.
  What is the reason that you use me thus?
  I loved you ever. But it is no matter.
  Let Hercules himself do what he may,
  The cat will mew, and dog will have his day.   240
KING   I pray thee, good Horatio, wait upon him.

                             Exit HAMLET *and* HORATIO.

  [*To* LAERTES.] Strengthen your patience in our last night's speech.
  We'll put the matter to the present push.°
  Good Gertrude, set some watch over your son.
  This grave shall have a living° monument.   245
  An hour of quiet shortly shall we see;
  Till then in patience our proceeding be.   *Exeunt.*

[Scene II. The castle.]

Enter HAMLET *and* HORATIO.

HAMLET   So much for this, sir; now shall you see the other.
  You do remember all the circumstance?
HORATIO   Remember it, my lord!
HAMLET   Sir, in my heart there was a kind of fighting
  That would not let me sleep. Methought I lay   5
  Worse than the mutines in the bilboes.° Rashly
  (And praised be rashness for it) let us know,
  Our indiscretion sometime serves us well
  When our deep plots do pall,° and that should learn us
  There's a divinity that shapes our ends,   10
  Rough-hew them how we will.
HORATIO   That is most certain.
HAMLET   Up from my cabin,
  My sea gown scarfed about me, in the dark

---

235 golden couplets are disclosed (the dove lays two eggs, and the newly hatched [*disclosed*] young are covered with golden down)   **243 present push** immediate test   **245 living** lasting (with perhaps also a reference to the plot against Hamlet's life)   *V.ii.* **6 mutines in the bilboes** mutineers in fetters   **9 pall** fail

Groped I to find out them, had my desire,
Fingered° their packet, and in fine° withdrew   15
To mine own room again, making so bold,
My fears forgetting manners, to unseal
Their grand commission; where I found, Horatio—
Ah, royal knavery!—an exact command,
Larded° with many several sorts of reasons,   20
Importing Denmark's health, and England's too,
With, ho, such bugs and goblins in my life,°
That on the supervise,° no leisure bated,°
No, not to stay the grinding of the ax,
My head should be struck off.
HORATIO   Is't possible?   25
HAMLET   Here's the commission; read it at more leisure.
    But wilt thou hear now how I did proceed?
HORATIO   I beseech you.
HAMLET   Being thus benetted round with villains,
    Or° I could make a prologue to my brains,   30
    They had begun the play. I sat me down,
    Devised a new commission, wrote it fair.
    I once did hold it, as our statists° do,
    A baseness to write fair,° and labored much
    How to forget that learning, but, sir, now   35
    It did me yeoman's service. Wilt thou know
    Th' effect° of what I wrote?
HORATIO   Ay, good my lord.
HAMLET   An earnest conjuration from the King,
    As England was his faithful tributary,
    As love between them like the palm might flourish,   40
    As peace should still her wheaten garland wear
    And stand a comma° 'tween their amities,
    And many suchlike as's of great charge,°
    That on the view and knowing of these contents,
    Without debatement further, more or less,   45
    He should those bearers put to sudden death,
    Not shriving° time allowed.
HORATIO   How was this sealed?

---

¹⁵ **Fingered** stole   ¹⁵ **in fine** finally   ²⁰ **Larded** enriched   ²² **such bugs and goblins in my life**
such bugbears and imagined terrors if I were allowed to live   ²³ **supervise** reading   ²³ **leisure bated**
delay allowed   ³⁰ **Or** ere   ³³ **statists** statesmen   ³⁴ **fair** clearly   ³⁷ **effect** purport   ⁴² **comma**
link   ⁴³ **great charge** (1) serious exhortation, (2) heavy burden (punning on *as's* and "asses")
⁴⁷ **shriving** absolution

HAMLET   Why, even in that was heaven ordinant.°
I had my father's signet in my purse,
Which was the model° of that Danish seal,   50
Folded the writ up in the form of th' other,
Subscribed it, gave't th' impression, placed it safely,
The changeling never known. Now, the next day
Was our sea fight, and what to this was sequent
Thou knowest already.   55

HORATIO   So Guildenstern and Rosencrantz go to't.

HAMLET   Why, man, they did make love to this employment.
They are not near my conscience; their defeat
Does by their own insinuation° grow.
'Tis dangerous when the baser nature comes   60
Between the pass° and fell° incensèd points
Of mighty opposites.

HORATIO   Why, what a king is this!

HAMLET   Does it not, think thee, stand me now upon°—
He that hath killed my king, and whored my mother,
Popped in between th' election° and my hopes,   65
Thrown out his angle° for my proper life,°
And with such coz'nage°—is't not perfect conscience
To quit° him with this arm? And is't not to be damned
To let this canker of our nature come
In further evil?   70

HORATIO   It must be shortly known to him from England
What is the issue of the business there.

HAMLET   It will be short; the interim's mine,
And a man's life's no more than to say "one."
But I am very sorry, good Horatio,   75
That to Laertes I forgot myself,
For by the image of my cause I see
The portraiture of his. I'll court his favors.
But sure the bravery° of his grief did put me
Into a tow'ring passion.

HORATIO   Peace, who comes here?   80

Enter young OSRIC, *a courtier.*

OSRIC   Your lordship is right welcome back to Denmark.

---

48 ordinant ruling   **50 model** counterpart   **59 insinuation** meddling   **61 pass** thrust   **61 fell** cruel   **63 stand me now upon** become incumbent upon me   **65 election** (the Danish monarchy was elective)   **66 angle** fishing line   **66 my proper life** my own life   **67 coz'nage** trickery   **68 quit** pay back   **79 bravery** bravado

HAMLET   I humbly thank you, sir. [*Aside to* HORATIO.] Dost know this waterfly?

HORATIO [*aside to* HAMLET]   No, my good lord.

HAMLET [*aside to* HORATIO]   Thy state is the more gracious, for 'tis a vice to know him. He hath much land, and fertile. Let a beast be lord of beasts, and his crib 85 shall stand at the king's mess.° 'Tis a chough,° but, as I say, spacious° in the possession of dirt.

OSRIC   Sweet lord, if your lordship were at leisure, I should impart a thing to you from his Majesty.

HAMLET   I will receive it, sir, with all diligence of spirit. Put your bonnet to his right 90 use. 'Tis for the head.

OSRIC   I thank your lordship, it is very hot.

HAMLET   No, believe me, 'tis very cold; the wind is northerly.

OSRIC   It is indifferent cold, my lord, indeed.

HAMLET   But yet methinks it is very sultry and hot for my complexion.°   95

OSRIC   Exceedingly, my lord; it is very sultry, as 'twere—I cannot tell how. But, my lord, his Majesty bade me signify to you that 'a has laid a great wager on your head. Sir, this is the matter——

HAMLET   I beseech you remember.

[HAMLET *moves him to put on his hat.*]

OSRIC   Nay, good my lord; for my ease, in good faith. Sir, here is newly come to 100 court Laertes—believe me, an absolute gentleman, full of most excellent differences,° of very soft society and great showing. Indeed, to speak feelingly° of him, his is the card° or calendar of gentry; for you shall find in him the continent° of what part a gentleman would see.

HAMLET   Sir, his definement° suffers no perdition° in you, though, I know, to divide 105 him inventorially would dozy° th' arithmetic of memory, and yet but yaw neither in respect of his quick sail.° But, in the verity of extolment, I take him to be a soul of great article,° and his infusion° of such dearth and rareness as, to make true diction° of him, his semblable° is his mirror, and who else would trace him, his umbrage,° nothing more.   110

OSRIC   Your lordship speaks most infallibly of him.

HAMLET   The concernancy,° sir? Why do we wrap the gentleman in our more rawer breath?

---

⁸⁶ **mess** table   ⁸⁶ **chough** jackdaw (here chatterer)   ⁸⁶ **spacious** well off   ⁹⁵ **complexion** temperament   ¹⁰² **differences** distinguishing characteristics   ¹⁰² **feelingly** justly   ¹⁰³ **card** chart   ¹⁰⁴ **continent** summary   ¹⁰⁵ **definement** description   ¹⁰⁵ **perdition** loss   ¹⁰⁶ **dozy** dizzy   ¹⁰⁶⁻¹⁰⁷ **and yet . . . quick sail** i.e., and yet only stagger despite all (*yaw neither*) in trying to overtake his virtues   ¹⁰⁸ **article** (literally, "item," but here perhaps "traits" or "importance")   ¹⁰⁸ **infusion** essential quality   ¹⁰⁹ **diction** description   ¹⁰⁹ **semblable** likeness   ¹¹⁰ **umbrage** shadow ¹¹² **concernancy** meaning

OSRIC   Sir?

HORATIO   Is't not possible to understand in another tongue? You will to't,° sir, really. 115

HAMLET   What imports the nomination of this gentleman?

OSRIC   Of Laertes?

HORATIO [*aside to* HAMLET]   His purse is empty already. All's golden words are
spent.

HAMLET   Of him, sir.   120

OSRIC   I know you are not ignorant——

HAMLET   I would you did, sir; yet, in faith, if you did, it would not much approve°
me. Well, sir?

OSRIC   You are not ignorant of what excellence Laertes is——

HAMLET   I dare not confess that, lest I should compare with him in excellence; but 125
to know a man well were to know himself.

OSRIC   I mean, sir, for his weapon; but in the imputation° laid on him by them, in his
meed° he's unfellowed.

HAMLET   What's his weapon?

OSRIC   Rapier and dagger.   130

HAMLET   That's two of his weapons—but well.

OSRIC   The King, sir, hath wagered with him six Barbary horses, against the which
he has impawned,° as I take it, six French rapiers and poniards, with their
assigns,° as girdle, hangers,° and so. Three of the carriages,° in faith, are very
dear to fancy, very responsive° to the hilts, most delicate carriages, and of very 135
liberal conceit.°

HAMLET   What call you the carriages?

HORATIO [*aside to* HAMLET]   I knew you must be edified by the margent° ere you
had done.

OSRIC   The carriages, sir, are the hangers.   140

HAMLET   The phrase would be more germane to the matter if we could carry a
cannon by our sides. I would it might be hangers till then. But on! Six Barbary
horses against six French swords, their assigns, and three liberal-conceited
carriages—that's the French bet against the Danish. Why is this all impawned,
as you call it?   145

OSRIC   The King, sir, hath laid, sir, that in a dozen passes between yourself and him
he shall not exceed you three hits; he hath laid on twelve for nine, and it would
come to immediate trial if your lordship would vouchsafe the answer.

HAMLET   How if I answer no?

OSRIC   I mean, my lord, the opposition of your person in trial.   150

---

115 **will to't** will get there   122 **approve** commend   127 **imputation** reputation   128 **meed** merit
133 **impawned** wagered   134 **assigns** accompaniments   134 **hangers** straps hanging the sword to the
belt   134 **carriages** (an affected word for hangers)   135 **responsive** corresponding   136 **liberal
conceit** elaborate design   138 **margent** i.e., marginal (explanatory comment)

HAMLET   Sir, I will walk here in the hall. If it please his Majesty, it is the breathing
time of day with me.° Let the foils be brought, the gentleman willing, and the
King hold his purpose, I will win for him an I can; if not, I will gain nothing but
my shame and the odd hits.

OSRIC   Shall I deliver you e'en so?   155

HAMLET   To this effect, sir, after what flourish your nature will.

OSRIC   I commend my duty to your lordship.

HAMLET   Yours, yours.   [*Exit* OSRIC]
He does well to commend it himself; there are no tongues else for's turn.

HORATIO   This lapwing° runs away with the shell on his head.   160

HAMLET   'A did comply, sir, with his dug° before 'a sucked it. Thus has he, and many
more of the same breed that I know the drossy age dotes on, only got the tune
of the time and, out of an habit of encounter,° a kind of yeasty° collection, which
carries them through and through the most fanned and winnowed opinions; and
do but blow them to their trial, the bubbles are out.°   165

Enter a LORD

LORD   My lord, his Majesty commended him to you by young Osric, who brings back
to him that you attend him in the hall. He sends to know if your pleasure hold to
play with Laertes, or that you will take longer time.

HAMLET   I am constant to my purposes; they follow the King's pleasure. If his fitness
speaks, mine is ready; now or whensoever, provided I be so able as now.   170

LORD   The King and Queen and all are coming down.

HAMLET   In happy time.

LORD   The Queen desires you to use some gentle entertainment° to Laertes before
you fall to play.

HAMLET   She well instructs me.   [*Exit* LORD.] 175

HORATIO   You will lose this wager, my lord.

HAMLET   I do not think so. Since he went into France I have been in continual practice.
I shall win at the odds. But thou wouldst not think how ill all's here about my
heart. But it is no matter.

HORATIO   Nay, good my lord——   180

HAMLET   It is but foolery, but it is such a kind of gain-giving° as would perhaps trouble
a woman.

HORATIO   If your mind dislike anything, obey it. I will forestall their repair hither and
say you are not fit.

151–152 breathing time of day with me time when I take exercise   **160 lapwing** (the new-hatched
lapwing was thought to run around with half its shell on its head)   **161 'A did comply, sir, with his dug**
he was ceremoniously polite to his mother's breast   **163 out of an habit of encounter** out of his own
superficial way of meeting and conversing with people   **163 yeasty** frothy   **165 the bubbles are out**
i.e., they are blown away (the reference is to the "yeasty collection")   **173 to use some gentle entertainment** to be courteous   **181 gain-giving** misgiving

HAMLET   Not a whit, we defy augury. There is special providence in the fall of a 185
sparrow.° If it be now, 'tis not to come; if it be not to come, it will be now; if it
be not now, yet it will come. The readiness is all. Since no man of aught he leaves
knows, what is't to leave betimes?° Let be.

A table prepared. [*Enter*] TRUMPETS, DRUMS, *and* OFFICERS *with cushions;* KING,
QUEEN, [OSRIC,] *and all the* STATE, [*with*] *foils, daggers,* [*and stoups of wine
borne in*]; *and* LAERTES.

KING   Come, Hamlet, come, and take this hand from me.

[*The* KING *puts* LAERTES' *hand into* HAMLET'S.]

HAMLET   Give me your pardon, sir. I have done you wrong,   190
But pardon't, as you are a gentleman.
This presence° knows, and you must needs have heard,
How I am punished with a sore distraction.
What I have done
That might your nature, honor, and exception°   195
Roughly awake, I here proclaim was madness.
Was't Hamlet wronged Laertes? Never Hamlet.
If Hamlet from himself be ta'en away,
And when he's not himself does wrong Laertes,
Then Hamlet does it not, Hamlet denies it.   200
Who does it then? His madness. If't be so,
Hamlet is of the faction° that is wronged;
His madness is poor Hamlet's enemy.
Sir, in this audience,
Let my disclaiming from a purposed evil   205
Free me so far in your most generous thoughts
That I have shot my arrow o'er the house
And hurt my brother.
LAERTES   I am satisfied in nature,
Whose motive in this case should stir me most
To my revenge. But in my terms of honor   210
I stand aloof, and will no reconcilement
Till by some elder masters of known honor
I have a voice and precedent° of peace
To keep my name ungored. But till that time

---

^{185–186} **the fall of a sparrow** (cf. Matthew 10:29 "Are not two sparrows sold for a farthing? and one of
them shall not fall on the ground without your Father") ¹⁸⁸ **betimes** early ¹⁹² **presence** royal
assembly ¹⁹⁵ **exception** disapproval ²⁰² **faction** party, side ²¹³ **voice and precedent** authoritative opinion justified by precedent

I do receive your offered love like love,   215
  And will not wrong it.
HAMLET   I embrace it freely,
  And will this brother's wager frankly play.
  Give us the foils. Come on.
LAERTES   Come, one for me.
HAMLET   I'll be your foil,° Laertes. In mine ignorance
  Your skill shall, like a star i' th' darkest night,   220
  Stick fiery off° indeed.
LAERTES   You mock me, sir.
HAMLET   No, by this hand.
KING   Give them the foils, young Osric. Cousin Hamlet,
  You know the wager?
HAMLET   Very well, my lord.
  Your grace has laid the odds o' th' weaker side.   225
KING   I do not fear it, I have seen you both;
  But since he is bettered,° we have therefore odds.
LAERTES   This is too heavy; let me see another.
HAMLET   This likes me well. These foils have all a length?

Prepare to play.

OSRIC   Ay, my good lord.   230
KING   Set me the stoups of wine upon that table.
  If Hamlet give the first or second hit,
  Or quit° in answer of the third exchange,
  Let all the battlements their ordnance fire.
  The King shall drink to Hamlet's better breath,   235
  And in the cup an union° shall he throw
  Richer than that which four successive kings
  In Denmark's crown have worn. Give me the cups,
  And let the kettle° to the trumpet speak,
  The trumpet to the cannoneer without,   240
  The cannons to the heavens, the heaven to earth,
  "Now the King drinks to Hamlet." Come, begin.

Trumpets the while.

  And you, the judges, bear a wary eye.
HAMLET   Come on, sir.
LAERTES   Come, my lord!

---

[219] **foil** (1) blunt sword, (2) background (of metallic leaf) for a jewel   [221] **Stick fiery off** stand out brilliantly   [227] **bettered** has improved (in France)   [233] **quit** repay, hit back   [236] **union** pearl   [239] **kettle** kettledrum

They play.

HAMLET   One!
LAERTES   No.
HAMLET   Judgment?
OSRIC   A hit, a very palpable hit.

Drum, trumpets, and shot. Flourish; a piece goes off.

LAERTES   Well, again.   245
KING   Stay, give me drink. Hamlet, this pearl is thine.
   Here's to thy health. Give him the cup.
HAMLET   I'll play this bout first; set it by a while.
   Come.

[*They play.*]

                 Another hit. What say you?
LAERTES   A touch, a touch; I do confess't.   250
KING   Our son shall win.
QUEEN   He's fat,° and scant of breath.
   Here, Hamlet, take my napkin, rub thy brows.
   The Queen carouses to thy fortune, Hamlet.
HAMLET   Good madam!
KING   Gertrude, do not drink.
QUEEN   I will, my lord; I pray you pardon me. [*Drinks.*]   255
KING [*aside*]   It is the poisoned cup; it is too late.
HAMLET   I dare not drink yet, madam—by and by.
QUEEN   Come, let me wipe thy face.
LAERTES   My lord, I'll hit him now.
KING   I do not think't.
LAERTES [*aside*]   And yet it is almost against my conscience.   260
HAMLET   Come for the third, Laertes. You do but dally.
   I pray you pass with your best violence;
   I am sure you make a wanton° of me.

[*They*] *play.*

LAERTES   Say you so? Come on.
OSRIC   Nothing neither way.   265
LAERTES   Have at you now!

In scuffling they change rapiers, [*and both are wounded*].

KING   Part them. They are incensed.

---

²⁵¹ **fat** (1) sweaty, (2) out of training   ²⁶³ **wanton** spoiled child

HAMLET Nay, come—again!

[*The* QUEEN *falls.*]

OSRIC   Look to the Queen there, ho!
HORATIO They bleed on both sides. How is it, my lord?
OSRIC How is't, Laertes?
LAERTES Why, as a woodcock to my own springe,° Osric.   270
  I am justly killed with mine own treachery.
HAMLET How does the Queen?
KING   She sounds° to see them bleed.
QUEEN No, no, the drink, the drink! O my dear Hamlet!
  The drink, the drink! I am poisoned.   [*Dies.*]
HAMLET O villainy! Ho! Let the door be locked.   275
  Treachery! Seek it out.

[LAERTES *falls.*]

LAERTES It is here, Hamlet. Hamlet, thou art slain;
  No med'cine in the world can do thee good.
  In thee there is not half an hour's life.
  The treacherous instrument is in thy hand,   280
  Unbated and envenomed. The foul practice°
  Hath turned itself on me. Lo, here I lie,
  Never to rise again. Thy mother's poisoned.
  I can no more. The King, the King's to blame.
HAMLET The point envenomed too?   285
  Then, venom, to thy work.   *Hurts the* KING.
ALL Treason! Treason!
KING O, yet defend me, friends. I am but hurt.
HAMLET Here, thou incestuous, murd'rous damnèd Dane,
  Drink off this potion. Is thy union here?   290
  Follow my mother.   KING *dies.*
LAERTES   He is justly served.
  It is a poison tempered° by himself.
  Exchange forgiveness with me, noble Hamlet.
  Mine and my father's death come not upon thee,
  Nor thine on me!   *Dies.* 295
HAMLET Heaven make thee free of it! I follow thee.
  I am dead, Horatio. Wretched Queen, adieu!
  You that look pale and tremble at this chance,
  That are but mutes° or audience to this act,

---

²⁷⁰ **springe** snare   ²⁷² **sounds** swoons   ²⁸¹ **practice** deception   ²⁹² **tempered** mixed
²⁹⁹ **mutes** performers who have no words to speak

Had I but time (as this fell sergeant,° Death,   300
Is strict in his arrest) O, I could tell you—
But let it be. Horatio, I am dead;
Thou livest; report me and my cause aright
To the unsatisfied.°
HORATIO   Never believe it.
I am more an antique Roman° than a Dane.   305
Here's yet some liquor left.
HAMLET   As th' art a man,
Give me the cup. Let go. By heaven, I'll ha't!
O God, Horatio, what a wounded name,
Things standing thus unknown, shall live behind me!
If thou didst ever hold me in thy heart,   310
Absent thee from felicity° awhile,
And in this harsh world draw thy breath in pain,
To tell my story.

                                      A march afar off. [*Exit* OSRIC.]

        What warlike noise is this?

Enter OSRIC.

OSRIC   Young Fortinbras, with conquest come from Poland,
To th' ambassadors of England gives   315
This warlike volley.
HAMLET   O, I die, Horatio!
The potent poison quite o'ercrows° my spirit.
I cannot live to hear the news from England,
But I do prophesy th' election lights
On Fortinbras. He has my dying voice.   320
So tell him, with th' occurrents,° more and less,
Which have solicited°—the rest is silence.   *Dies.*
HORATIO   Now cracks a noble heart. Good night, sweet Prince,
And flights of angels sing thee to thy rest.   [*March within.*]
Why does the drum come hither?   325

Enter FORTINBRAS, *with the* AMBASSADORS *with drum, colors, and* ATTENDANTS.

FORTINBRAS   Where is this sight?
HORATIO   What is it you would see?
If aught of woe or wonder, cease your search.

---

³⁰⁰ **fell sergeant** dread sheriff's officer   ³⁰⁴ **unsatisfied** uninformed   ³⁰⁵ **antique Roman** (with reference to the old Roman fashion of suicide)   ³¹¹ **felicity** i.e., the felicity of death   ³¹⁷ **o'ercrows** overpowers (as a triumphant cock crows over its weak opponent)   ³²¹ **occurrents** occurrences
³²² **solicited** incited

FORTINBRAS   This quarry° cries on havoc.° O proud Death,
    What feast is toward° in thine eternal cell
    That thou so many princes at a shot   330
    So bloodily hast struck?
AMBASSADOR   The sight is dismal;
    And our affairs from England come too late.
    The ears are senseless that should give us hearing
    To tell him his commandment is fulfilled,
    That Rosencrantz and Guildenstern are dead.   335
    Where should we have our thanks?
HORATIO   Not from his° mouth,
    Had it th' ability of life to thank you.
    He never gave commandment for their death.
    But since, so jump° upon this bloody question,
    You from the Polack wars, and you from England,   340
    Are here arrived, give order that these bodies
    High on a stage° be placed to the view,
    And let me speak to th' yet unknowing world
    How these things came about. So shall you hear
    Of carnal, bloody, and unnatural acts,   345
    Of accidental judgments, casual° slaughters,
    Of deaths put on by cunning and forced cause,
    And, in this upshot, purposes mistook
    Fall'n on th' inventors' heads. All this can I
    Truly deliver.
FORTINBRAS   Let us haste to hear it,   350
    And call the noblest to the audience.
    For me, with sorrow I embrace my fortune.
    I have some rights of memory° in this kingdom,
    Which now to claim my vantage doth invite me.
HORATIO   Of that I shall have also cause to speak,   355
    And from his mouth whose voice will draw on° more.
    But let this same be presently performed,
    Even while men's minds are wild, lest more mischance
    On° plots and errors happen.
FORTINBRAS   Let four captains
    Bear Hamlet like a soldier to the stage,   360

---

²²⁸ **quarry** heap of slain bodies   ²²⁸ **cries on havoc** proclaims general slaughter   ²²⁹ **toward** in
preparation   ³³⁶ **his** (Claudius')   ³³⁹ **jump** precisely   ³⁴² **stage** platform   ³⁴⁶ **casual** not humanly
planned, chance   ³⁵³ **rights of memory** remembered claims   ³⁵⁶ **voice will draw on** vote will
influence   ³⁵⁹ **On** on top of

For he was likely, had he been put on,°
To have proved most royal; and for his passage°
The soldiers' music and the rite of war
Speak loudly for him.
Take up the bodies. Such a sight as this   365
Becomes the field,° but here shows much amiss.
Go, bid the soldiers shoot.

Exeunt marching;
after the which a peal of ordnance are shot off.

Finis

Sonnet 116

Let me not to the marriage of true minds
Admit impediments; love is not love
Which alters when it alteration finds,
Or bends with the remover to remove.
O, no, it is an ever-fixèd mark   5
That looks on tempests and is never shaken;
It is the star to every wand'ring bark,
Whose worth's unknown, although his height be taken.
Love's not Time's fool, though rosy lips and cheeks
Within his bending sickle's compass come;   10
Love alters not with his brief hours and weeks
But bears it out even to the edge of doom.
    If this be error and upon me proved,
    I never writ, nor no man ever loved.

Sonnet 130

My mistress' eyes are nothing like the sun;
Coral is far more red than her lips' red;
If snow be white, why then her breasts are dun;
If hairs be wires, black wires grown on her head.
I have seen roses damasked, red and white,   5
But no such roses see I in her cheeks;
And in some perfumes is there more delight

---

361 **put on** advanced (to the throne)   362 **passage** death   366 **field** battlefield

Than in the breath that from my mistress reeks.
I love to hear her speak, yet well I know
That music hath a far more pleasing sound;   10
I grant I never saw a goddess go;
My mistress, when she walks, treads on the ground.
    And yet, by heaven, I think my love as rare
    As any she belied with false compare.

W. D. Snodgrass (born 1926)
Leaving the Motel

Outside, the last kids holler
Near the pool: they'll stay the night.
Pick up the towels; fold your collar
Out of sight.

Check: is the second bed   5
Unrumpled, as agreed?
Landlords have to think ahead
In case of need,

Too. Keep things straight: don't take
The matches, the wrong keyrings—   10
We've nowhere we could keep a keepsake—
Ashtrays, combs, things

That sooner or later others
Would accidentally find.
Check: take nothing of one another's   15
And leave behind

Your license number only,
Which they won't care to trace;
We've paid. Still, should such things get lonely,
Leave in their vase   20

An aspirin to preserve
Our lilacs, the wayside flowers
We've gathered and must leave to serve
A few more hours;

That's all. We can't tell when
We'll come back, can't press claims;
We would no doubt have other rooms then,
Or other names.

May Swenson (born 1919)

Women

Women
  should be
    pedestals
     moving
      pedestals
       moving
        to the
         motions
         of men

Or they
  should be
    little horses
     those wooden
      sweet
       oldfashioned
       painted
        rocking
         horses

the gladdest things in the toyroom

     The
    pegs
    of their
   ears
  so familiar
 and dear
to the trusting
fists
To be chafed

       feelingly
      and then
     unfeelingly
    To be
   joyfully
 ridden
rockingly
ridden until
the restored

egos dismount and the legs stride away

Immobile
  sweetlipped
   sturdy
    and smiling
     women
      should always
       be waiting

willing
to be set
into motion
Women
  should be
   pedestals
    to men

Reed Whittemore (born 1919)
The Bad Daddy

The bad daddy who has been angry with the whole family, one by one,
Now retires to his study to be sullen and think of death.
He has aches in his neck and stomach that he is afraid to see the
        doctor about.
He has a sense of his mind's slopping off into fuzz.
He feels that he is becoming allergic to cigarets,
That he can't digest steak, that he needs glasses, that he is impotent.
He knows he is bored by his friends, bored by novels, Shakespeare,
        youth.
He thinks that if it rains one more day he will kill himself.
He lies on the cot in his study covered by a child's security blanket too
        short to sleep under,
And he improvises idly, a few two-minute commercials for a different
        life, thus:

Dear Son: In the war between the Earthmen and the Martians,
Keep your feet dry, your mess kit clean, your weapons oiled.
Get plenty of sleep, drink not nor fornicate,
Speak when spoken to, write home once a week, get to know your
        chaplain.
If upon your return I should be wandering amid the shades of the
        departed,
Call the president of the bank who will deliver to you a sealed manila
        envelope containing three French hens, two turtle doves
And your further instructions. Vale. Your Sire.

Dear Mathilda: Though we have not spoken a word to each other for
        thirteen years,
We are sympatico, you and I. We commune across the miles; we
        yearn; we dote.
I watch you drive away in your furs in the Rolls to the shoe shop.
I hear you banging pots and pans in the bunker,
And my heart, woman, twitches and the salt tears come, tum-te-tum.
        Your Daddy-o.

Dearest Daughter: It was good, awfully good to have that nice little
    note from you.
Jimmy danced up and down, Mama had tears in her eyes.
We pulled out the scrapbook
And found that the last time you wrote was your fifteenth birthday,
When you were pregnant. Remember?
And now you write that you've won the Insurgent's Prize.
And at Berkeley! Of course we're terribly proud.
But as old-fashioned moralists we doubt the wisdom of compliments,
And anyway you should know that your mother and I really think
    you're a frightful bitch. Love, Dad.

So now the bad Daddy feels much more like himself.
His typewriter pants pleasantly in its shed;
The beast is fed.
Down the long waste of his years he sees, suddenly, Violets.
He picks them and crushes them gently, and is at peace.
Gettem all, bad Daddy, and sleep now.

Margaret Widdemer (1884–1978)

Guidance

The blue limousine checked before the fashionable church on Park Avenue. There was another car, a gray one with a crest on its door, where the chauffeur would have liked to park the limousine.

"Can't you get it any nearer than that?" demanded Mrs. Meriden sharply up the speaking-tube. "Push the other car down."

"What's she doin' here?" murmured her footman to the chauffeur as he lifted a red ear from the hole.

"Askin' for guidance, no doubt," said the chauffeur, with a grin that pointed it out as a good joke.

"Is it guidance?" The handsome young Irish footman snorted softly. "If the young madam got to heaven itself, she'd be telling St. Peter how to handle his job before she'd her halo on straight!" He sprang to open the door, a deferential automaton.

Mrs. Meriden turned a hard, handsome young face to her husband.

"I have to inspect the church furnishing on behalf of the committee," she said. "Fifteen minutes should do it, Allan. We'll get to the Carletons' at exactly the right time."

His tired, gray eyes faced her brilliant black ones with a courteous denial.

"Sorry, Olive. I can just make my own appointment by taking a taxi from here."

"You can't," she said imperiously. "This reception's important."

He smiled a little. "This is more important to me than the reception."

He stepped past her. She heard him speak to a cabby that his upraised cane had summoned.

"Plaza. Fifth Avenue entrance," he said.

She frowned, clicking up the dark aisle. She was too easy with Allan, that was the trouble. She'd have it out with him tonight; once and for all this time. When she had married him six years back he'd been so eager to please, to adjust, to make her happy! And now behaving like this, when everyone knew how much she had forwarded them socially—how good her judgment was.

Her annoyance sharpened to anger when, ending the inspection at her own pew, she found it occupied by a stranger. A slim little girl in a white-collared blue suit, her béreted yellow head bowed on the pew before her, her hands gripping it on either side like a child praying about Santa Claus. Olive touched her on the shoulder, speaking harshly. She had never approved of this high church idea, leaving churches open all day for prayers. It wasn't fair to pew-owners.

"This is my pew. I wish to inspect the cushions. May I ask you to move?"

The girl lifted a soft-blue-eyed face still flushed and intent with prayer. She smiled like a friendly baby.

"Sorry—but—I had to come in and pray for guidance," she said.

"That's nonsense," Olive laid down the law. "What's your problem?" There was a gentleness about the girl that invited dictation. But she rose and moved into the aisle.

"I'd rather not tell you," she said. Then she turned back. "Yes I will! Perhaps you were sent. It's a position I'm offered. An important one. I want it badly. But I have to decide whether it's fair to take it over another girl's head."

Just one of a hundred well-groomed little secretaries, then. Olive had nearly mistaken her for one of her own class. . . . She went on, nevertheless. She felt it was rather fine of her to take time to advise a girl like this.

"Is the other woman giving good service?"

"No. But she thinks so."

"She must be stupid. Are you competent?"

"Yes—oh, yes; I've practically been training for it always!"

"You are weakly sentimental to consider her, then. She'd be sent away anyway. The incompetent must go to the wall."

The girl was not paying attention. Olive felt a sharp contempt for her. . . . Competent! Not likely! She was staring with silly intensity at the pew she had left, at the inconspicuous nameplate.

"Are *you* Mrs. Meriden?" she asked softly.

Olive supposed it was awe in her voice. Perhaps she was trying to make a social contact on the strength of a passing benevolence. Olive called her to account. "Certainly. I told you this was my pew. You asked for advice, listen to it. There is no question of unfairness with incompetents. Take the position before it is given to someone else."

She stood aside, silently dismissing the yellow-haired girl. As she waited, handsome and erect in her furs, she felt regal, complete. . . . Her car waiting without; her ambitions so nearly gained; her handsome, prosperous young husband so nearly broken to her hand, awaiting her shortly at home. . . .

The girl lifted her face, a little strained and pale between the loose golden rings.

"I will do as you advise," she said. She went slowly down the aisle. Mrs. Meriden followed.

From the door of the church she saw the yellow-haired girl speak to the driver of the gray car with the crested panel.

"The Plaza. Fifth Avenue entrance," said the yellow-haired girl in the white-collared blue suit.

5

Coming to Terms with Life

The Bible (King James Version)
Ecclesiastes 11:9–12:8

11

9 Rejoice, O young man, in thy youth; and let thy heart cheer thee in the days of thy youth, and walk in the ways of thine heart, and in the sight of thine eyes: but know thou, that for all these things God will bring thee into judgment. 10 Therefore remove sorrow from thy heart, and put away evil from thy flesh: for childhood and youth are vanity.

12

1 Remember now thy Creator in the days of thy youth, while the evil days come not, nor the years draw nigh, when thou shalt say, I have no pleasure in them; 2 while the sun, or the light, or the moon, or the stars, be not darkened, nor the clouds return after the rain: 3 in the day when the keepers of the house shall tremble, and the strong men shall bow themselves, and the grinders cease because they are few, and those that look out of the windows be darkened, 4 and the doors shall be shut in the streets, when the sound of the grinding is low, and he shall rise up at the voice of the bird, and all the daughters of music shall be brought low; 5 also when they shall be afraid of that which is high, and fears shall be in the way, and the almond tree shall flourish, and the grasshopper shall be a burden, and desire shall fail: because man goeth to his long home, and the mourners go about the streets: 6 or ever the silver cord be loosed, or the golden bowl be broken, or the pitcher be broken at the fountain, or the wheel broken at the cistern. 7 Then shall the dust return to the earth as it was: and the spirit shall return unto God who gave it. 8 Vanity of vanities, saith the Preacher; all is vanity.

Robert Browning (1812–1889)
Rabbi Ben Ezra

1

Grow old along with me!
The best is yet to be,
The last of life, for which the first was made:
Our times are in His hand
Who saith "A whole I planned,
Youth shows but half; trust God: see all nor be afraid!"   5

2

Not that, amassing flowers,
Youth sighed "Which rose make ours,
Which lily leave and then as best recall?"
Not that, admiring stars,
It yearned "Nor Jove, nor Mars;   10
Mine be some figured flame which blends, transcends them all!"

3

Not for such hopes and fears
Annulling youth's brief years,
Do I remonstrate: folly wide the mark!   15
Rather I prize the doubt
Low kinds exist without,
Finished and finite clods, untroubled by a spark.

4

Poor vaunt of life indeed,
Were man but formed to feed   20
On joy, to solely seek and find and feast:
Such feasting ended, then
As sure an end to men;
Irks care the crop-full bird? Frets doubt the maw-crammed beast?

5

Rejoice we are allied   25
To That which doth provide

And not partake, effect and not receive!
    A spark disturbs our clod;
    Nearer we hold of God
Who gives, than of His tribes that take, I must believe.　　　30

6

    Then, welcome each rebuff
    That turns earth's smoothness rough,
Each sting that bids nor sit nor stand but go!
    Be our joys three-parts pain!
    Strive, and hold cheap the strain;　　　35
Learn, nor account the pang; dare, never grudge the throe!

7

    For thence,—a paradox
    Which comforts while it mocks,—
Shall life succeed in that it seems to fail:
    What I aspired to be,　　　40
    And was not, comforts me:
A brute I might have been, but would not sink i' the scale.

8

    What is he but a brute
    Whose flesh has soul to suit,
Whose spirit works lest arms and legs want play?　　　45
    To man, propose this test—
    Thy body at its best,
How far can that project thy soul on its lone way?

9

    Yet gifts should prove their use:
    I own the Past profuse　　　50
Of power each side, perfection every turn:
    Eyes, ears took in their dole,
    Brain treasured up the whole;
Should not the heart beat once "How good to live and learn?"

10

    Not once beat "Praise be Thine!　　　55
    I see the whole design,
I, who saw power, see now love perfect too:
    Perfect I call Thy plan:
    Thanks that I was a man!
Maker, remake, complete,—I trust what Thou shalt do!"　　　60

11

For pleasant in this flesh;
Our soul, in its rose-mesh
Pulled ever to the earth, still yearns for rest;
Would we some prize might hold
To match those manifold
Possessions of the brute, —gain most, as we did best!

65

12

Let us not always say
"Spite of this flesh to-day
I strove, made head, gained ground upon the whole!"
As the bird wings and sings,
Let us cry "All good things
Are ours, nor soul helps flesh more, now, than flesh helps soul!"

70

13

Therefore I summon age
To grant youth's heritage,
Life struggle having so far reached its term:
Thence shall I pass, approved
A man, for aye removed
From the developed brute; a god though in the germ.

75

14

And I shall thereupon
Take rest, ere I be gone
Once more on my adventure brave and new:
Fearless and unperplexed,
When I wage battle next,
What weapons to select, what armour to indue.

80

15

Youth ended, I shall try
My gain or loss thereby;
Leave the fire ashes, what survives is gold:
And I shall weigh the same,
Give life its praise or blame:
Young, all lay in dispute; I shall know, being old.

85

90

16

For note, when evening shuts,
A certain moment cuts
The deed off, calls the glory from the grey:

A whisper from the west
    Shoots—"Add this to the rest,   95
Take it and try its worth: here dies another day."

17

So, still within this life,
    Though lifted o'er its strife,
Let me discern, compare, pronounce at last,
        "This rage was right i' the main,   100
        That acquiescence vain:
The Future I may face now I have proved the Past."

18

For more is not reserved
    To man, with soul just nerved
To act to-morrow what he learns to-day: 105
        Here, work enough to watch
        The Master work, and catch
Hints of the proper craft, tricks of the tool's true play.

19

As it was better, youth
    Should strive, through acts uncouth,   110
Toward making, than repose on aught found made:
        So, better, age, exempt
        From strife, should know, than tempt
Further. Thou waitedest age: wait death nor be afraid!

20

Enough now, if the Right   115
    And Good and Infinite
Be named here, as thou callest thy hand thine own,
        With knowledge absolute,
        Subject to no dispute
From fools that crowded youth, not let thee feel alone.   120

21

Be there, for once and all,
    Severed great minds from small,
Announced to each his station in the Past!
        Was I, the world arraigned,
        Were they, my soul disdained,   125
Right? Let age speak the truth and give us peace at last!

22

Now, who shall arbitrate?
Ten men love what I hate,
Shun what I follow, slight what I receive;
    Ten, who in ears and eyes   130
    Match me: we all surmise,
They this thing, and I that: whom shall my soul believe?

23

Not on the vulgar mass
Called "work," must sentence pass,
Things done, that took the eye and had the price;   135
    O'er which, from level stand,
    The low world laid its hand,
Found straightway to its mind, could value in a trice:

24

But all, the world's coarse thumb
And finger failed to plumb,   140
So passed in making up the main account;
    All instincts immature,
    All purposes unsure,
That weighed not as his work, yet swelled the man's amount:

25

Thoughts hardly to be packed   145
Into a narrow act,
Fancies that broke through language and escaped;
    All I could never be,
    All, men ignored in me,
This, I was worth to God, whose wheel the pitcher shaped.   150

26

Ay, note that Potter's wheel,
That metaphor! and feel
Why time spins fast, why passive lies our clay, —
    Thou, to whom fools propound,
    When the wine makes its round,   155
"Since life fleets, all is change; the Past gone, seize to-day!"

27

Fool! All that is, at all,
Lasts ever, past recall;
Earth changes, but thy soul and God stand sure:

What entered into thee,   160
    That was, is, and shall be:
Time's wheel runs back or stops: Potter and clay endure.

28

He fixed thee mid this dance
    Of plastic circumstance,
This Present, thou, forsooth, wouldst fain arrest: 165
    Machinery just meant
    To give thy soul its bent,
Try thee and turn thee forth, sufficiently impressed.

29

What though the earlier grooves
    Which ran the laughing loves   170
Around thy base, no longer pause and press?
    What though, about thy rim,
    Scull-things in order grim
Grow out, in graver mood, obey the sterner stress?

30

Look not thou down but up!   175
    To uses of a cup,
The festal board, lamp's flash and trumpet's peal,
    The new wine's foaming flow,
    The Master's lips a-glow!
Thou, heaven's consummate cup, what need'st thou with
    earth's wheel?   180

31

But I need, now as then,
    Thee, God, who mouldest men;
And since, not even while the whirl was worst,
    Did I, — to the wheel of life
    With shapes and colours rife,   185
Bound dizzily, — mistake my end, to slake Thy thirst:

32

So, take and use Thy work:
    Amend what flaws may lurk,
What strain o' the stuff, what warpings past the aim!
    My times be in Thy hand!   190
    Perfect the cup as planned!
Let age approve of youth, and death complete the same!

Herbert R. Coursen, Jr. (born 1932)
The Ghost of Christmas Past: "Stopping by Woods on a Snowy Evening"

Much ink has spilled on many pages in exegesis of this little poem. Actually, critical jottings have only obscured what has lain beneath critical noses all these years. To say that the poem means merely that a man stops one night to observe a snowfall, or that the poem contrasts the mundane desire for creature comfort with the sweep of aesthetic appreciation, or that it renders worldly responsibilities paramount, or that it reveals the speaker's latent death-wish is to miss the point rather badly. Lacking has been that mind simple enough to see what is *really* there.

The first line ("Whose woods these are I think I know") shows that the speaker has paused beside a woods of whose ownership he is fairly sure. So much for paraphrase. Uncertainty vanishes with the next two lines ("His house is in the village though; / He will not see me stopping here"). The speaker knows (a) where the owner's home is located, and (b) that the owner won't be out at the woods tonight. Two questions arise immediately: (a) how does the speaker know? and (b) how does the speaker know? As will be made manifest, only one answer exists to each question.

The subsequent two quatrains force more questions to pop up. On auditing the first two lines of the second quatrain ("My little horse must think it queer / To stop without a farmhouse near"), we must ask, "Why does the little 'horse' think oddly of the proceedings?" We must ask also if this *is*, as the speaker claims, the "darkest evening of the year." The calendar date of this occurrence (or lack of occurrence) by an unspecified patch of trees is essential to an apprehension of the poem's true meaning. In the third quatrain, we hear "harness bells" shaken. Is the auditory image really an allusion? Then there is the question of the "horse's" identity. Is this really Equus Caballus? This question links itself to that of the *driver's* identity and reiterates the problem of the animal's untoward attitude toward this evidently unscheduled stop.

The questions have piled up unanswered as we reach the final quatrain and approach the ultimate series of poetic mysteries to be resolved. Clearly, all of the questions asked thus far (save possibly the one about the "horse's" identity) are ones which any normal reader, granted the training in close analysis proved by a survey course in English Literature during his sophomore year in college, might ask. After some extraneous imagery ("The woods are lovely, dark and deep" has either been established or is easily adduced from the dramatic situation), the final three lines hold out the key with which the poem's essence may be released. What, to ask two more questions, are the "promises" which the speaker must "keep," and why are the last two lines so redundant about the distance he must cover before he tumbles into bed? Obviously, the obligations are important, the distance great.

Now, if we swing back to one of the previous questions, the poem will begin to unravel. The "darkest evening of the year" in New England is December 21st, a date near that on which the western world celebrates Christmas. It may be that December 21st *is* the date of the poem, or (and with poets this seems more likely) that this is the closest the poet can come to Christmas without giving it all away. Who has "promises to keep" at or near this date, and who must traverse much territory to fulfill these promises? Yes, and who but St. Nick would know the location of *each* home? Only he would know who had "just settled down for a long winter's nap" (the poem's third line—"He will not see me stopping here"—is clearly a veiled allusion) and would not be out inspecting his acreage this night. The unusual phrase "fill up with snow," in the poem's fourth line, is a transfer of Santa's occupational preoccupation to the countryside; he is mulling the filling of countless stockings hung above countless fireplaces by countless careful children. "Harness bells," of course, alludes to "Sleighing Song," a popular Christmas tune of the time the poem was written, in which the refrain "Jingle Bells! Jingle Bells!" appears; thus again are we put on the Christmas track. The "little horse," like the date, is another attempt at poetic obfuscation. Although the "rein-reindeer" ambiguity has been eliminated from the poem's final version,[1] probably because too obvious, we may speculate that the animal is really a reindeer disguised as a horse by the poet's desire for obscurity, a desire which we must concede has been fulfilled up to now.

The animal is clearly concerned, like the faithful Rudolph—another possible allusion (post facto, hence unconscious)—lest his master fail to complete his mission. Seeing no farmhouse in the second quatrain, but pulling a load of presents, no wonder the little beast wonders! It takes him a full two quatrains to rouse his driver to remember all the empty stockings which hang ahead. And Santa does so reluctantly at that, poor soul, as he ponders the myriad farmhouses and villages which spread between him and his own "winter's nap." The modern St. Nick, lonely and overworked, tosses no "Happy Christmas to all and to all a good night!" into the precipitation. He merely shrugs his shoulders and resignedly plods away.

[1] The original draft contained the following line: "That bid me give the reins a shake" (Stageberg-Anderson, *Poetry as Experience* [New York, 1952], p. 457).

T. S. Eliot (1888–1965)

The Love Song of J. Alfred Prufrock

Let us go then, you and I,
When the evening is spread out against the sky
Like a patient etherised upon a table;
Let us go, through certain half-deserted streets,
The muttering retreats   5
Of restless nights in one-night cheap hotels
And sawdust restaurants with oyster-shells:
Streets that follow like a tedious argument
Of insidious intent
To lead you to an overwhelming question . . .   10
Oh, do not ask, "What is it?"
Let us go and make our visit.

In the room the women come and go
Talking of Michelangelo.

The yellow fog that rubs its back upon the window-panes,   15
The yellow smoke that rubs its muzzle on the window-panes
Licked its tongue into the corners of the evening,
Lingered upon the pools that stand in drains,
Let fall upon its back the soot that falls from chimneys,
Slipped by the terrace, made a sudden leap,   20
And seeing that it was a soft October night,
Curled once about the house, and fell asleep.

And indeed there will be time
For the yellow smoke that slides along the street,
Rubbing its back upon the window-panes;   25
There will be time, there will be time
To prepare a face to meet the faces that you meet;
There will be time to murder and create,
And time for all the works and days of hands
That lift and drop a question on your plate;   30
Time for you and time for me,

And time yet for a hundred indecisions,
And for a hundred visions and revisions,
Before the taking of a toast and tea.

In the room the women come and go   35
Talking of Michelangelo

And indeed there will be time
To wonder, "Do I dare?" and, "Do I dare?"
Time to turn back and descend the stair,
With a bald spot in the middle of my hair—   40
(They will say: "How his hair is growing thin!")
My morning coat, my collar mounting firmly to the chin,
My necktie rich and modest, but asserted by a simple pin—
(They will say: "But how his arms and legs are thin!")
Do I dare   45
Disturb the universe?
In a minute there is time
For decisions and revisions which a minute will reverse.

For I have known them all already, known them all:—
Have known the evenings, mornings, afternoons,   50
I have measured out my life with coffee spoons;
I know the voices dying with a dying fall
Beneath the music from a farther room.
     So how should I presume?

And I have known the eyes already, known them all—   55
The eyes that fix you in a formulated phrase,
And when I am formulated, sprawling on a pin,
When I am pinned and wriggling on the wall,
Then how should I begin
To spit out all the butt-ends of my days and ways?   60
     And how should I presume?

And I have known the arms already, known them all—
Arms that are braceleted and white and bare
(But in the lamplight, downed with light brown hair!)
Is it perfume from a dress   65
That makes me so digress?
Arms that lie along a table, or wrap about a shawl.
     And should I then presume?
     And how should I begin?

                    • • • • •

Shall I say, I have gone at dusk through narrow streets   70
And watched the smoke that rises from the pipes
Of lonely men in shirt-sleeves, leaning out of windows? . . .

I should have been a pair of ragged claws
Scuttling across the floors of silent seas.

• • • • •

And the afternoon, the evening, sleeps so peacefully!   75
Smoothed by long fingers,
Asleep . . . tired . . . or it malingers,
Stretched on the floor, here beside you and me.
Should I, after tea and cakes and ices,
Have the strength to force the moment to its crisis?   80
But though I have wept and fasted, wept and prayed,
Though I have seen my head (grown slightly bald) brought
          in upon a platter,
I am no prophet—and here's no great matter;
I have seen the moment of my greatness flicker,
And I have seen the eternal Footman hold my coat, and snicker,   85
And in short, I was afraid.

And would it have been worth it, after all,
After the cups, the marmalade, the tea,
Among the porcelain, among some talk of you and me,
Would it have been worth while,   90
To have bitten off the matter with a smile,
To have squeezed the universe into a ball
To roll it toward some overwhelming question,
To say: "I am Lazarus, come from the dead,
Come back to tell you all, I shall tell you all"—   95
If one, settling a pillow by her head,
     Should say: "That is not what I meant at all.
     That is not it, at all."

And would it have been worth it, after all,
Would it have been worth while,   100
After the sunsets and the dooryards and the sprinkled streets,
After the novels, after the teacups, after the skirts that trail
          along the floor—
And this, and so much more?—
It is impossible to say just what I mean!
But as if a magic lantern threw the nerves in patterns on a screen: 105
Would it have been worth while

If one, settling a pillow or throwing off a shawl,
And turning toward the window, should say:
   "That is not it at all,
    That is not what I meant, at all."   110

    •   •   •   •   •

No! I am not Prince Hamlet, nor was meant to be;
Am an attendant lord, one that will do
To swell a progress, start a scene or two,
Advise the prince; no doubt, an easy tool,
Deferential, glad to be of use,   115
Politic, cautious, and meticulous;
Full of high sentence, but a bit obtuse;
At times, indeed, almost ridiculous—
Almost, at times, the Fool.

I grow old . . . I grow old . . .   120
I shall wear the bottoms of my trousers rolled.

Shall I part my hair behind? Do I dare to eat a peach?
I shall wear white flannel trousers, and walk upon the beach.
I have heard the mermaids singing, each to each.

I do not think that they will sing to me.   125

I have seen them riding seaward on the waves
Combing the white hair of the waves blown back
When the wind blows the water white and black.

We have lingered in the chambers of the sea
By sea-girls wreathed with seaweed red and brown   130
Till human voices wake us, and we drown.

William Faulkner (1897–1962)
A Rose for Emily

1

When Miss Emily Grierson died, our whole town went to her funeral: the men through a sort of respectful affection for a fallen monument, the women mostly out of curiosity to see the inside of her house, which no one save an old manservant— a combined gardener and cook—had seen in at least ten years.

It was a big, squarish frame house that had once been white, decorated with cupolas and spires and scrolled balconies in the heavily lightsome style of the seventies, set on what had once been our most select street. But garages and cotton gins had encroached and obliterated even the august names of that neighborhood; only Miss Emily's house was left, lifting its stubborn and coquettish decay above the cotton wagons and the gasoline pumps—an eyesore among eyesores. And now Miss Emily had gone to join the representatives of those august names where they lay in the cedar-bemused cemetery among the ranked and anonymous graves of Union and Confederate soldiers who fell at the battle of Jefferson.

Alive, Miss Emily had been a tradition, a duty, and a care; a sort of hereditary obligation upon the town, dating from that day in 1894 when Colonel Sartoris, the mayor—he who fathered the edict that no Negro woman should appear on the streets without an apron—remitted her taxes, the dispensation dating from the death of her father on into perpetuity. Not that Miss Emily would have accepted charity. Colonel Sartoris invented an involved tale to the effect that Miss Emily's father had loaned money to the town, which the town, as a matter of business, preferred this way of repaying. Only a man of Colonel Sartoris' generation and thought could have invented it, and only a woman could have believed it.

When the next generation, with its more modern ideas, became mayors and aldermen, this arrangement created some little dissatisfaction. On the first of the year they mailed her a tax notice. February came, and there was no reply. They wrote her a formal letter, asking her to call at the sheriff's office at her convenience. A week later the mayor wrote her himself, offering to call or to send his car for her, and received in reply a note on paper of an archaic shape, in a thin, flowing calligraphy in faded ink, to the effect that she no longer went out at all. The tax notice was also enclosed, without comment.

They called a special meeting of the Board of Aldermen. A deputation waited upon her, knocked at the door through which no visitor had passed since she ceased giving china-painting lessons eight or ten years earlier. They were admitted by the old Negro into a dim hall from which a stairway mounted into still more shadow. It smelled of dust and disuse—a close, dank smell. The Negro led them into the parlor. It was furnished in heavy, leather-covered furniture. When the Negro opened the blinds of one window, they could see that the leather was cracked; and when they sat down, a faint dust rose sluggishly about their thighs, spinning with slow motes in the single sun-ray. On a tarnished gilt easel before the fireplace stood a crayon portrait of Miss Emily's father.

They rose when she entered—a small, fat woman in black, with a thin gold chain descending to her waist and vanishing into her belt, leaning on an ebony cane with a tarnished gold head. Her skeleton was small and spare; perhaps that was why what would have been merely plumpness in another was obesity in her. She looked bloated, like a body long submerged in motionless water, and of that pallid hue. Her eyes, lost in the fatty ridges of her face, looked like two small pieces of coal pressed into a lump of dough as they moved from one face to another while the visitors stated their errand.

She did not ask them to sit. She just stood in the door and listened quietly until the spokesman came to a stumbling halt. Then they could hear the invisible watch ticking at the end of the gold chain.

Her voice was dry and cold. "I have no taxes in Jefferson. Colonel Sartoris explained it to me. Perhaps one of you can gain access to the city records and satisfy yourselves."

"But we have. We are the city authorities, Miss Emily. Didn't you get a notice from the sheriff, signed by him?"

"I received a paper, yes," Miss Emily said. "Perhaps he considers himself the sheriff . . . I have no taxes in Jefferson."

"But there is nothing on the books to show that, you see. We must go by the—"

"See Colonel Sartoris. I have no taxes in Jefferson."

"But, Miss Emily—"

"See Colonel Sartoris." (Colonel Sartoris had been dead almost ten years.) "I have no taxes in Jefferson. Tobe!" The Negro appeared. "Show these gentlemen out."

2

So she vanquished them, horse and foot, just as she had vanquished their fathers thirty years before about the smell. That was two years after her father's death and a short time after her sweetheart—the one we believed would marry her—had deserted her. After her father's death she went out very little; after her sweetheart went away, people hardly saw her at all. A few of the ladies had the temerity to call, but were not received, and the only sign of life about the place was the Negro man—a young man then—going in and out with a market basket.

"Just as if a man—any man—could keep a kitchen properly," the ladies said; so they were not surprised when the smell developed. It was another link between the gross, teeming world and the high and mighty Griersons.

A neighbor, a woman, complained to the mayor, Judge Stevens, eighty years old.

"But what will you have me do about it, madam?" he said.

"Why, send her word to stop it," the woman said. "Isn't there a law?"

"I'm sure that won't be necessary," Judge Stevens said. "It's probably just a snake or a rat that nigger of hers killed in the yard. I'll speak to him about it."

The next day he received two more complaints, one from a man who came in diffident deprecation. "We really must do something about it, Judge. I'd be the last one in the world to bother Miss Emily, but we've got to do something." That night the Board of Aldermen met—three graybeards and one younger man, a member of the rising generation.

"It's simple enough," he said. "Send her word to have her place cleaned up. Give her a certain time to do it in, and if she don't . . ."

"Dammit, sir," Judge Stevens said, "will you accuse a lady to her face of smelling bad?"

So the next night, after midnight, four men crossed Miss Emily's lawn and slunk about the house like burglars, sniffing along the base of the brickwork and at the cellar openings while one of them performed a regular sowing motion with his hand out of a sack slung from his shoulder. They broke open the cellar door and sprinkled lime there, and in all the outbuildings. As they recrossed the lawn, a window that had been dark was lighted and Miss Emily sat in it, the light behind her, and her upright torso motionless as that of an idol. They crept quietly across the lawn and into the shadow of the locusts that lined the street. After a week or two the smell went away.

That was when people had begun to feel really sorry for her. People in our town, remembering how old lady Wyatt, her great-aunt, had gone completely crazy at last, believed that the Griersons held themselves a little too high for what they really were. None of the young men were quite good enough for Miss Emily and such. We had long thought of them as a tableau, Miss Emily a slender figure in white in the background, her father a spraddled silhouette in the foreground, his back to her and clutching a horsewhip, the two of them framed by the back-flung front door. So when she got to be thirty and was still single, we were not pleased exactly, but vindicated; even with insanity in the family she wouldn't have turned down all of her chances if they had really materialized.

When her father died, it got about that the house was all that was left to her; and in a way, people were glad. At last they could pity Miss Emily. Being left alone, and a pauper, she had become humanized. Now she too would know the old thrill and the old despair of a penny more or less.

The day after his death all the ladies prepared to call at the house and offer condolence and aid, as is our custom. Miss Emily met them at the door, dressed as usual and with no trace of grief on her face. She told them that her father was not dead. She did that for three days, with the ministers calling on her, and the doctors, trying to persuade her to let them dispose of the body. Just as they were about to resort to law and force, she broke down, and they buried her father quickly.

We did not say she was crazy then. We believed she had to do that. We remembered all the young men her father had driven away, and we knew that with nothing left, she would have to cling to that which had robbed her, as people will.

3

She was sick for a long time. When we saw her again, her hair was cut short, making her look like a girl, with a vague resemblance to those angels in colored church windows—sort of tragic and serene.

The town had just let the contracts for paving the sidewalks, and in the summer after her father's death they began the work. The construction company came with

niggers and mules and machinery, and a foreman named Homer Barron, a Yankee—
a big, dark, ready man, with a big voice and eyes lighter than his face. The little boys
would follow in groups to hear him cuss the niggers, and the niggers singing in time
to the rise and fall of picks. Pretty soon he knew everybody in town. Whenever you
heard a lot of laughing anywhere about the square, Homer Barron would be in the
center of the group. Presently we began to see him and Miss Emily on Sunday
afternoons driving in the yellow-wheeled buggy and the matched team of bays from
the livery stable.

At first we were glad that Miss Emily would have an interest, because the ladies
all said, "Of course a Grierson would not think seriously of a Northerner, a day
laborer." But there were still others, older people, who said that even grief could not
cause a real lady to forget *noblesse oblige*—without calling it *noblesse oblige*. They just
said, "Poor Emily. Her kinsfolk should come to her." She had some kin in Alabama;
but years ago her father had fallen out with them over the estate of old lady Wyatt,
the crazy woman, and there was no communication between the two families. They
had not even been represented at the funeral.

And as soon as the old people said, "Poor Emily," the whispering began. "Do
you suppose it's really so?" they said to one another. "Of course it is. What else
could . . ." This behind their hands; rustling of craned silk and satin behind jalousies
closed upon the sun of Sunday afternoon as the thin, swift clop-clop-clop of the
matched team passed: "Poor Emily."

She carried her head high enough—even when we believed that she was fallen.
It was as if she demanded more than ever the recognition of her dignity as the last
Grierson; as if it had wanted that touch of earthiness to reaffirm her imperviousness.
Like when she bought the rat poison, the arsenic. That was over a year after they
had begun to say "Poor Emily," and while the two female cousins were visiting her.

"I want some poison," she said to the druggist. She was over thirty then, still a
slight woman, though thinner than usual, with cold, haughty black eyes in a face the
flesh of which was strained across the temples and about the eyesockets as you
imagine a lighthouse-keeper's face ought to look. "I want some poison," she said.

"Yes, Miss Emily. What kind? For rats and such? I'd recom—"

"I want the best you have. I don't care what kind."

The druggist named several. "They'll kill anything up to an elephant. But what
you want is—"

"Arsenic," Miss Emily said. "Is that a good one?"

"Is . . . arsenic? Yes, ma'am. But what you want—"

"I want arsenic."

The druggist looked down at her. She looked back at him, erect, her face like a
strained flag. "Why, of course," the druggist said. "If that's what you want. But the
law requires you to tell me what you are going to use it for."

Miss Emily just stared at him, her head tilted back in order to look him eye for
eye, until he looked away and went and got the arsenic and wrapped it up. The Negro

delivery boy brought her the package; the druggist didn't come back. When she opened the package at home there was written on the box, under the skull and bones: "For rats."

4

So the next day we all said, "She will kill herself"; and we said it would be the best thing. When she had first begun to be seen with Homer Barron, we had said, "She will marry him." Then we said, "She will persuade him yet," because Homer himself had remarked—he liked men, and it was known that he drank with the younger men in the Elks' Club—that he was not a marrying man. Later we said, "Poor Emily" behind the jalousies as they passed on Sunday afternoon in the glittering buggy, Miss Emily with her head high and Homer Barron with his hat cocked and a cigar in his teeth, reins and whip in a yellow glove.

Then some of the ladies began to say that it was a disgrace to the town and a bad example to the young people. The men did not want to interfere, but at last the ladies forced the Baptist minister—Miss Emily's people were Episcopal—to call upon her. He would never divulge what happened during that interview, but he refused to go back again. The next Sunday they again drove about the streets, and the following day the minister's wife wrote to Miss Emily's relations in Alabama.

So she had blood-kin under her roof again and we sat back to watch developments. At first nothing happened. Then we were sure that they were to be married. We learned that Miss Emily had been to the jeweler's and ordered a man's toilet set in silver, with the letters H. B. on each piece. Two days later we learned that she had bought a complete outfit of men's clothing, including a nightshirt, and we said, "They are married." We were really glad. We were glad because the two female cousins were even more Grierson than Miss Emily had ever been.

So we were not surprised when Homer Barron—the streets had been finished some time since—was gone. We were a little disappointed that there was not a public blowing-off, but we believed that he had gone on to prepare for Miss Emily's coming, or to give her a chance to get rid of the cousins. (By that time it was a cabal, and we were all Miss Emily's allies to help circumvent the cousins.) Sure enough, after another week they departed. And, as we had expected all along, within three days Homer Barron was back in town. A neighbor saw the Negro man admit him at the kitchen door at dusk one evening.

And that was the last we saw of Homer Barron. And of Miss Emily for some time. The Negro man went in and out with the market basket, but the front door remained closed. Now and then we would see her at a window for a moment, as the men did that night when they sprinkled the lime, but for almost six months she did not appear on the streets. Then we knew that this was to be expected too; as if that quality of her father which had thwarted her woman's life so many times had been too virulent and too furious to die.

When we next saw Miss Emily, she had grown fat and her hair was turning gray. During the next few years it grew grayer and grayer until it attained an even pepper-and-salt iron-gray, when it ceased turning. Up to the day of her death at seventy-four it was still that vigorous iron-gray, like the hair of an active man.

From that time on her front door remained closed, save for a period of six or seven years, when she was about forty, during which she gave lessons in china-painting. She fitted up a studio in one of the downstairs rooms, where the daughters and granddaughters of Colonel Sartoris' contemporaries were sent to her with the same regularity and in the same spirit that they were sent to church on Sundays with a twenty-five-cent piece for the collection plate. Meanwhile her taxes had been remitted.

Then the newer generation became the backbone and the spirit of the town, and the painting pupils grew up and fell away and did not send their children to her with boxes of color and tedious brushes and pictures cut from the ladies' magazines. The front door closed upon the last one and remained closed for good. When the town got free postal delivery, Miss Emily alone refused to let them fasten the metal numbers above her door and attach a mailbox to it. She would not listen to them.

Daily, monthly, yearly we watched the Negro grow grayer and more stooped, going in and out with the market basket. Each December we sent her a tax notice, which would be returned by the post office a week later, unclaimed. Now and then we would see her in one of the downstairs windows—she had evidently shut up the top floor of the house—like the carven torso of an idol in a niche, looking or not looking at us, we could never tell which. Thus she passed from generation to generation—dear, inescapable, impervious, tranquil, and perverse.

And so she died. Fell ill in the house filled with dust and shadows, with only a doddering Negro man to wait on her. We did not even know she was sick; we had long since given up trying to get any information from the Negro. He talked to no one, probably not even to her, for his voice had grown harsh and rusty, as if from disuse.

She died in one of the downstairs rooms, in a heavy walnut bed with a curtain, her gray head propped on a pillow yellow and moldy with age and lack of sunlight.

5

The Negro met the first of the ladies at the front door and let them in, with their hushed, sibilant voices and their quick, curious glances, and then he disappeared. He walked right through the house and out the back and was not seen again.

The two female cousins came at once. They held the funeral on the second day, with the town coming to look at Miss Emily beneath a mass of bought flowers, with the crayon face of her father musing profoundly above the bier and the ladies sibilant and macabre; and the very old men—some in their brushed Confederate uniforms—on the porch and the lawn, talking of Miss Emily as if she had been a contemporary of theirs, believing that they had danced with her and courted her perhaps, confusing time with its mathematical progression, as the old do, to whom all the past is not a diminishing road but, instead, a huge meadow which no winter ever quite touches, divided from them now by the narrow bottle-neck of the most recent decade of years.

Already we knew that there was one room in that region above stairs which no one had seen in forty years, and which would have to be forced. They waited until Miss Emily was decently in the ground before they opened it.

The violence of breaking down the door seemed to fill this room with pervading dust. A thin, acrid pall as of the tomb seemed to lie everywhere upon this room decked and furnished as for a bridal: upon the valance curtains of faded rose color, upon the rose-shaded lights, upon the dressing table, upon the delicate array of crystal and the man's toilet things backed with tarnished silver, silver so tarnished that the monogram was obscured. Among them lay collar and tie, as if they had just been removed, which, lifted, left upon the surface a pale crescent in the dust. Upon a chair hung the suit, carefully folded; beneath it the two mute shoes and the discarded socks.

The man himself lay in the bed.

For a long while we just stood there, looking down at the profound and fleshless grin. The body had apparently once lain in the attitude of an embrace, but now the long sleep that outlasts love, that conquers even the grimace of love, had cuckolded him. What was left of him, rotted beneath what was left of the nightshirt, had become inextricable from the bed in which he lay; and upon him and upon the pillow beside him lay that even coating of the patient and biding dust.

Then we noticed that in the second pillow was the indentation of a head. One of us lifted something from it, and leaning forward, that faint and invisible dust dry and acrid in the nostrils, we saw a long strand of iron-gray hair.

Robert Frost (1874–1963)
Bereft

> Where had I heard this wind before
> Change like this to a deeper roar?
> What would it take my standing there for,
> Holding open a restive door,
> Looking down hill to frothy shore?   5
> Summer was past and day was past.
> Somber clouds in the west were massed.

Out in the porch's sagging floor,
Leaves got up in a coil and hissed,
Blindly struck at my knee and missed.   10
Something sinister in the tone
Told me my secret must be known:
Word I was in the house alone
Somehow must have gotten abroad,
Word I was in my life alone,   15
Word I had no one left but God.

The Death of the Hired Man

Mary sat musing on the lamp-flame at the table
Waiting for Warren. When she heard his step,
She ran on tip-toe down the darkened passage
To meet him in the doorway with the news
And put him on his guard. "Silas is back."   5
She pushed him outward with her through the door
And shut it after her. "Be kind" she said.
She took the market things from Warren's arms
And set them on the porch, then drew him down
To sit beside her on the wooden steps.   10

"When was I ever anything but kind to him?
But I'll not have the fellow back," he said.
"I told him so last haying, didn't I?
If he left then, I said, that ended it.
What good is he? Who else will harbor him   15
At his age for the little he can do?
What help he is there's no depending on.
Off he goes always when I need him most.
He thinks he ought to earn a little pay,
Enough at least to buy tobacco with,   20
So he won't have to beg and be beholden.
'All right,' I say, 'I can't afford to pay
Any fixed wages, though I wish I could.'
'Someone else can.' 'Then someone else will have to.'
I shouldn't mind his bettering himself   25
If that was what it was. You can be certain,
When he begins like that, there's someone at him

Trying to coax him off with pocket-money—
In haying time, when any help is scarce.
In winter he comes back to us. I'm done."   30

"Sh! not so loud: he'll hear you," Mary said.

"I want him to: he'll have to soon or late."

"He's worn out. He's asleep beside the stove.
When I came up from Rowe's I found him here,
Huddled against the barn-door fast asleep,   35
A miserable sight, and frightening, too—
You needn't smile—I didn't recognize him—
I wasn't looking for him—and he's changed.
Wait till you see."

                    "Where did you say he'd been?"

"He didn't say, I dragged him to the house,   40
And gave him tea and tried to make him smoke.
I tried to make him talk about his travels.
Nothing would do: he just kept nodding off."

"What did he say? Did he say anything?"

"But little."

                    "Anything? Mary, confess   45
He said he'd come to ditch the meadow for me."

"Warren!"

          "But did he? I just want to know."

"Of course he did. What would you have him say?
Surely you wouldn't grudge the poor old man
Some humble way to save his self-respect.   50
He added, if you really care to know,
He meant to clear the upper pasture, too.
That sounds like something you have heard before?
Warren, I wish you could have heard the way
He jumbled everything. I stopped to look   55
Two or three times—he made me feel so queer—
To see if he was talking in his sleep.
He ran on Harold Wilson—you remember—
The boy you had in haying four years since.
He's finished school, and teaching in his college.   60

Silas declares you'll have to get him back.
He says they two will make a team for work:
Between them they will lay this farm as smooth!
The way he mixed that in with other things.
He thinks young Wilson a likely lad, though daft   65
On education—you know how they fought
All through July under the blazing sun,
Silas up on the cart to build the load,
Harold along beside to pitch it on."

"Yes, I took care to keep well out of earshot."   70

"Well, those days trouble Silas like a dream.
You wouldn't think they would. How some things linger!
Harold's young college boy's assurance piqued him.
After so many years he still keeps finding
Good arguments he sees he might have used.   75
I sympathize. I know just how it feels
To think of the right thing to say too late.
Harold's associated in his mind with Latin.
He asked me what I thought of Harold's saying
He studied Latin like the violin   80
Because he liked it—that an argument!
He said he couldn't make the boy believe
He could find water with a hazel prong—
Which showed how much good school had ever done him.
He wanted to go over that. But most of all   85
He thinks if he could have another chance
To teach him how to build a load of hay—"

"I know, that's Silas' one accomplishment.
He bundles every forkful in its place,
And tags and numbers it for future reference,   90
So he can find and easily dislodge it
In the unloading. Silas does that well.
He takes it out in bunches like big birds' nests.
You never see him standing on the hay
He's trying to lift, straining to lift himself."   95

"He thinks if he could teach him that, he'd be
Some good perhaps to someone in the world.
He hates to see a boy the fool of books.
Poor Silas, so concerned for other folk,

And nothing to look backward to with pride,   100
And nothing to look forward to with hope,
So now and never any different."

Part of a moon was falling down the west,
Dragging the whole sky with it to the hills.
Its light poured softly in her lap. She saw it   105
And spread her apron to it. She put out her hand
Among the harp-like morning-glory strings,
Taut with the dew from garden bed to eaves,
As if she played unheard some tenderness
That wrought on him beside her in the night.   110
"Warren," she said, "he has come home to die:
You needn't be afraid he'll leave you this time."

"Home," he mocked gently.

                    "Yes, what else but home?
It all depends on what you mean by home.
Of course he's nothing to us, any more   115
Than was the hound that came a stranger to us
Out of the woods, worn out upon the trail."

"Home is the place where, when you have to go there,
They have to take you in."

                    "I should have called it
Something you somehow haven't to deserve."   120

Warren leaned out and took a step or two,
Picked up a little stick, and brought it back
And broke it in his hand and tossed it by.
"Silas has better claim on us you think
Than on his brother? Thirteen little miles   125
As the road winds would bring him to his door.
Silas has walked that far no doubt today.
Why doesn't he go there? His brother's rich,
A somebody—director in the bank."

"He never told us that."

                    "We know it though."   130

"I think his brother ought to help, of course.
I'll see to that if there is need. He ought of right
To take him in, and might be willing to—

He may be better than appearances.
But have some pity on Silas. Do you think   135
If he had any pride in claiming kin
Or anything he looked for from his brother,
He'd keep so still about him all this time?"

"I wonder what's between them."

                              "I can tell you.
Silas is what he is—we wouldn't mind him—   140
But just the kind that kinsfolk can't abide.
He never did a thing so very bad.
He don't know why he isn't quite as good
As anybody. Worthless though he is,
He won't be made ashamed to please his brother."   145

"*I* can't think Si ever hurt anyone."

"No, but he hurt my heart the way he lay
And rolled his old head on that sharp-edged chair-back.
He wouldn't let me put him on the lounge.
You must go in and see what you can do.   150
I made the bed up for him there tonight.
You'll be surprised at him—how much he's broken.
His working days are done; I'm sure of it."

"I'd not be in a hurry to say that."

"I haven't been. Go, look, see for yourself.   155
But, Warren, please remember how it is:
He's come to help you ditch the meadow.
He has a plan. You mustn't laugh at him.
He may not speak of it, and then he may.
I'll sit and see if that small sailing cloud   160
Will hit or miss the moon."

                     It hit the moon.
Then there were three there, making a dim row,
The moon, the little silver cloud, and she.

Warren returned—too soon, it seemed to her,
Slipped to her side, caught up her hand and waited.   165

"Warren?" she questioned.

                     "Dead," was all he answered.

They Were Welcome to Their Belief

Grief may have thought it was grief.
Care may have thought it was care.
They were welcome to their belief,
The overimportant pair.

No, it took all the snows that clung   5
To the low roof over his bed,
Beginning when he was young,
To induce the one snow on his head.

But whenever the roof came white
The head in the dark below   10
Was a shade less the color of night
A shade more the color of snow.

Grief may have thought it was grief.
Care may have thought it was care.
But neither one was the thief   15
Of his raven color of hair.

Seamus Heaney (born 1939)
Follower

My father worked with a horse-plough,
His shoulders globed like a full sail strung
Between the shafts and the furrow.
The horses strained at his clicking tongue.

An expert. He would set the wing   5
And fit the bright steel-pointed sock.
The sod rolled over without breaking.
At the headrig, with a single pluck

Of reins, the sweating team turned round
And back into the land. His eye   10

Narrowed and angled at the ground,
Mapping the furrow exactly.

I stumbled in his hob-nailed wake,
Fell sometimes on the polished sod;
Sometimes he rode me on his back   15
Dipping and rising to his plod.

I wanted to grow up and plough,
To close one eye, stiffen my arm.
All I ever did was follow
In his broad shadow round the farm.   20

I was a nuisance, tripping, falling,
Yapping always. But today
It is my father who keeps stumbling
Behind me, and will not go away.

Oliver Wendell Holmes (1809–1894)
The Last Leaf

I saw him once before,
As he passed by the door,
        And again
The pavement stones resound,
As he totters o'er the ground   5
        With his cane.

They say that in his prime,
Ere the pruning-knife of Time
        Cut him down,
Not a better man was found   10
By the Crier on his round
        Through the town.

But now he walks the streets,
And he looks at all he meets
        Sad and wan,   15

And he shakes his feeble head,
That it seems as if he said,
   "They are gone."

The mossy marbles rest
On the lips that he has prest   20
   In their bloom,
And the names he loved to hear
Have been carved for many a year
   On the tomb.

My grandmamma has said—   25
Poor old lady, she is dead
   Long ago—
That he had a Roman nose,
And his cheek was like a rose
   In the snow;   30

But now his nose is thin,
And it rests upon his chin
   Like a staff,
And a crook is in his back,
And a melancholy crack   35
   In his laugh.

I know it is a sin
For me to sit and grin
   At him there;
But the old three-cornered hat,   40
And the breeches, and all that,
   Are so queer!

And if I should live to be
The last leaf upon the tree
   In the spring,   45
Let them smile, as I do now,
At the old forsaken bough
   Where I cling.

Robinson Jeffers (1887–1962)

Age in Prospect

Praise youth's hot blood if you will, I think that happiness
Rather consists in having lived clear through
Youth and hot blood, on to the wintrier hemisphere
Where one has time to wait and to remember.

Youth and hot blood are beautiful, so is peacefulness.   5
Youth had some islands in it, but age is indeed
An island and a peak; age has infirmities,
Not few, but youth is all one fever.

To look around and to love in his appearances,
Though a little calmly, the universal God's   10
Beauty is better I think than to lip eagerly
The mother's breast or another woman's.

And there is no possession more sure than memory's;
But if I reach that gray island, that peak,
My hope is still to possess with eyes the homeliness   15
Of ancient loves, ocean and mountains,

And meditate the sea-mouth of mortality
And the fountain six feet down with a quieter thirst
Than now I feel for old age; a creature progressively
Thirsty for life will be for death too.   20

Charles Lamb (1775–1834)

The Superannuated Man

Sera tamen respexit Libertas.
                              Virgil

A clerk I was in London gay.
                              O'Keefe

If peradventure, reader, it has been thy lot to waste the golden years of thy
life—thy shining youth—in the irksome confinement of an office; to have thy prison
days prolonged through middle age down to decrepitude and silver hairs, without

hope of release or respite; to have lived to forget that there are such things as holidays, or to remember them but as the prerogatives of childhood; then, and then only, will you be able to appreciate my deliverance.

It is now six and thirty years since I took my seat at the desk in Mincing Lane. Melancholy was the transition at fourteen from the abundant playtime, and the frequently intervening vacations of school days, to the eight, nine, and sometimes ten hours' a-day attendance at a counting-house. But time partially reconciles us to anything. I gradually became content—doggedly contented, as wild animals in cages.

It is true I had my Sundays to myself; but Sundays, admirable as the institution of them is for purposes of worship, are for that very reason the very worst adapted for days of unbending and recreation. In particular, there is a gloom for me attendant upon a city Sunday, a weight in the air. I miss the cheerful cries of London, the music, and the ballad-singers—the buzz and stirring murmur of the streets. Those eternal bells depress me. The closed shops repel me. Prints, pictures, all the glittering and endless succession of knacks and gewgaws, and ostentatiously displayed wares of tradesmen, which make a weekday saunter through the less busy parts of the metropolis so delightful—are shut out. No book-stalls deliciously to idle over—no busy faces to recreate the idle man who contemplates them ever passing by—the very face of business a charm by contrast to his temporary relaxation from it. Nothing to be seen but unhappy countenances—or half-happy at best—of emancipated 'prentices and little tradesfolks, with here and there a servant maid that has got leave to go out, who, slaving all the week, with the habit has lost almost the capacity of enjoying a free hour; and livelily expressing the hollowness of a day's pleasuring. The very strollers in the fields on that day look anything but comfortable.

But besides Sundays I had a day at Easter, and a day at Christmas, with a full week in the summer to go and air myself in my native fields of Hertfordshire. This last was a great indulgence; and the prospect of its recurrence, I believe, alone kept me up through the year, and made my durance tolerable. But when the week came round, did the glittering phantom of the distance keep touch with me? or rather was it not a series of seven uneasy days, spent in restless pursuit of pleasure, and a wearisome anxiety to find out how to make the most of them? Where was the quiet, where the promised rest? Before I had a taste of it, it was vanished. I was at the desk again, counting upon the fifty-one tedious weeks that must intervene before such another snatch would come. Still the prospect of its coming threw something of an illumination upon the darker side of my captivity. Without it, as I have said, I could scarcely have sustained my thraldom.

Independently of the rigors of attendance, I have ever been haunted with a sense (perhaps a mere caprice) of incapacity for business. This, during my latter years, had increased to such a degree that it was visible in all the lines of my countenance. My health and my good spirits flagged. I had perpetually a dread of some crisis, to which I should be found unequal. Besides my daylight servitude, I served over again all night in my sleep, and would awake with terrors of imaginary false entries, errors in my accounts, and the like. I was fifty years of age, and no prospect of emancipation presented itself. I had grown to my desk, as it were; and the wood had entered into my soul.

My fellows in the office would sometimes rally me upon the trouble legible in my countenance; but I did not know that it had raised the suspicions of any of my employers, when on the 5th of last month, a day ever to be remembered by me, L——, the junior partner in the firm, calling me on one side, directly taxed me with my bad looks, and frankly inquired the cause of them. So taxed, I honestly made confession of my infirmity, and added that I was afraid I should eventually be obliged to resign his service. He spoke some words of course to hearten me, and there the matter rested. A whole week I remained laboring under the impression that I had acted imprudently in my disclosure; that I had foolishly given a handle against myself, and had been anticipating my own dismissal. A week passed in this manner, the most anxious one, I verily believe, in my whole life, when on the evening of the 12th of April, just as I was about quitting my desk to go home (it might be about eight o'clock) I received an awful summons to attend the presence of the whole assembled firm in the formidable back parlor. I thought, now my time is surely come, I have done for myself, I am going to be told that they have no longer occasion for me. L——, I could see, smiled at the terror I was in, which was a little relief to me,—when to my utter astonishment B——, the eldest partner, began a formal harangue to me on the length of my services, my very meritorious conduct during the whole of the time (the deuce, thought I, how did he find out that? I protest I never had the confidence to think as much). He went on to descant on the expediency of retiring at a certain time of life (how my heart panted!) and asking me a few questions as to the amount of my own property, of which I have a little, ended with a proposal, to which his three partners nodded a grave assent, that I should accept from the house, which I had served so well, a pension for life to the amount of two-thirds of my accustomed salary—a magnificent offer! I do not know what I answered between surprise and gratitude, but it was understood that I accepted their proposal, and I was told that I was free from that hour to leave their service. I stammered out a bow, and at just ten minutes after eight I went home—for ever. This noble benefit—gratitude forbids me to conceal their names—I owe to the kindness of the most munificent firm in the world—the house of Boldero, Merryweather, Bosanquet, and Lacy.

Esto perpetual

For the first day or two I felt stunned, overwhelmed. I could only apprehend my felicity; I was too confused to taste it sincerely. I wandered about, thinking I was happy, and knowing that I was not. I was in the condition of a prisoner in the old Bastille, suddenly let loose after a forty years' confinement. I could scarce trust myself with my self. It was like passing out of time into eternity—for it is a sort of eternity for a man to have his time all to himself. It seemed to me that I had more time on my hands than I could ever manage. From a poor man, poor in time, I was suddenly lifted up into a vast revenue; I could see no end of my possessions; I wanted some steward, or judicious bailiff, to manage my estates in time for me. And here let me caution persons grown old in active business, not lightly, nor without weighing their own resources, to forego their customary employment all at once, for there may be danger in it. I feel it by myself, but I know that my resources are sufficient; and now that those first giddy raptures have subsided, I have a quiet home-feeling of the blessedness of my condition. I am in no hurry. Having all holidays, I am as though I had none. If time hung heavy upon me, I could walk it away; but I do *not* walk all day long, as I used to do in those old transient holidays, thirty miles a day, to make the most of them. If time were troublesome, I could read it away, but I do *not* read in that violent measure, with which, having no time my own but candlelight time, I used to weary out my head and eye-sight in by-gone winters. I walk, read, or scribble (as now), just when the fit seizes me. I no longer hunt after pleasure; I let it come to me. I am like the man

> ——that's born, and has his years come to him / In some green desert.

"Years," you will say; "what is this superannuated simpleton calculating upon? He has already told us he is past fifty."

I have indeed lived nominally fifty years, but deduct out of them the hours which I have lived to other people, and not to myself, and you will find me still a young fellow. For *that* is the only true time, which a man can properly call his own, that which he has all to himself; the rest, though in some sense he may be said to live it, is other people's time, not his. The remnant of my poor days, long or short, is at least multiplied for me threefold. My ten next years, if I stretch so far, will be as long as any preceding thirty. 'Tis a fair rule-of-three sum.

Among the strange fantasies which beset me at the commencement of my freedom, and of which all traces are not yet gone, one was, that a vast tract of time had intervened since I quitted the counting house. I could not conceive of it as an affair of yesterday. The partners, and the clerks with whom I had for so many years, and for so many hours in each day of the year, been closely associated—being suddenly removed from them—they seemed as dead to me. There is a fine passage, which may serve to illustrate this fancy, in a tragedy by Sir Robert Howard, speaking of a friend's death:—

> ——'Twas but just now he went away;
> I have not since had time to shed a tear;
> And yet the distance does the same appear
> As if he had been a thousand years from me,
> Time takes no measure in eternity.

To dissipate this awkward feeling, I have been fain to go among them once or twice since; to visit my old desk-fellows—my co-brethren of the quill—that I had left below in the state militant. Not all the kindness with which they received me could quite restore to me that pleasant familiarity, which I had heretofore enjoyed among them. We cracked some of our old jokes, but methought they went off but faintly. My old desk; the peg where I hung my hat, were appropriated to another. I knew it must be, but I could not take it kindly. D——l take me if I did not feel some remorse— beast, if I had not,—at quitting my old compeers, the faithful partners of my toils for six and thirty years that smoothed for me with their jokes and conundrums the ruggedness of my professional road. Had it been so rugged then after all? or was I a coward simply? Well, it is too late to repent; and I also know that these suggestions are a common fallacy of the mind on such occasions. But my heart smote me. I had violently broken the bands betwixt us. It was at least not courteous. I shall be some time before I get quite reconciled to the separation. Farewell, old cronies, yet not for long, for again and again I will come among ye, if I shall have your leave. Farewell, Ch——, dry, sarcastic, and friendly! Do——, mild, slow to move, and gentlemanly! Pl——, officious to do, and to volunteer, good services!—and thou, thou dreary pile, fit mansion for a Gresham or a Whittington of old, stately house of merchants; with thy labyrinthine passages, and light-excluding, pent-up offices, where candles for one half the year supplied the place of the sun's light; unhealthy contributor to my weal, stern fosterer of my living, farewell! In thee remain, and not in the obscure collection of some wandering bookseller, my "works!" There let them rest, as I do from my labors, piled on thy massy shelves, more MSS. in folio than ever Aquinas left, and full as useful! My mantle I bequeath among ye.

A fortnight has passed since the date of my first communication. At that period I was approaching to tranquillity, but had not reached it. I boasted of a calm indeed, but it was comparative only. Something of the first flutter was left; an unsettling sense of novelty; the dazzle to weak eyes of unaccustomed light. I missed my old chains, forsooth, as if they had been some necessary part of my apparel. I was a poor Carthusian, from strict cellular discipline suddenly by some revolution returned upon the world. I am now as if I had never been other than my own master. It is natural to me to go where I please, to do what I please. I find myself at eleven o'clock in the day in Bond Street, and it seems to me that I have been sauntering there at that very hour for years past. I digress into Soho, to explore a book-stall. Methinks I have been thirty years a collector. There is nothing strange nor new in it. I find myself before a fine picture in the morning. Was it ever otherwise? What is become of Fish Street Hill? Where is Fenchurch Street? Stones of old Mincing Lane which I have worn with my daily pilgrimage for six and thirty years, to the footsteps of what toilworn clerk are your everlasting flints now vocal? I indent the gayer flags of Pall Mall. It is 'change time, and I am strangely among the Elgin marbles. It was no hyperbole when I ventured to compare the change in my condition to a passing into another world. Time stands still in a manner to me. I have lost all distinction of season. I do not know the day of the week, or of the month. Each day used to be individually felt by me in its reference to the foreign post days; in its distance from, or propinquity to the next Sunday. I had my Wednesday feelings, my Saturday nights' sensations. The genius of each day was upon me distinctly during the whole of it, affecting my appetite, spirits, *etc.* The phantom of the next day, with the dreary five to follow, sat as a load upon my poor Sabbath recreations. What charm has washed the Ethiop white?—What is gone of Black Monday? All days are the same. Sunday itself—that unfortunate failure of a holiday as it too often proved, what with my sense of its fugitiveness, and over-care to get the greatest quantity of pleasure out of it—is melted down into a week day. I can spare to go to church now, without grudging the huge cantle which it used to seem to cut out of the holiday. I have time for everything. I can visit a sick friend. I can interrupt the man of much occupation when he is busiest. I can insult over him with an invitation to take a day's pleasure with me to Windsor this fine May-morning. It is Lucretian pleasure to behold the poor drudges, whom I have left behind in the world, carking and caring; like horses in a mill, drudging on in the same eternal round—and what is it all for? A man can never have too much time to himself, nor too little to do. Had I a little son, I would christen him NOTHING-TO-DO; he should do nothing. Man, I verily believe, is out of his element as long as he is operative. I am altogether for the life contemplative. Will no kindly earthquake come and swallow up those accursed cotton mills? Take me that lumber of a desk there, and bowl it down

As low as to the fiends.

I am no longer * * * * * * , clerk to the firm of, *etc.* I am Retired Leisure. I am to be met with in trim gardens. I am already come to be known by my vacant face and careless gesture, perambulating at no fixed pace nor with any settled purpose. I walk about; not to and from. They tell me, a certain *cum dignitate* air, that has been buried so long with my other good parts, has begun to shoot forth in my person. I grow into gentility perceptibly. When I take up a newspaper it is to read the state of the opera. *Opus operatum est.* I have done all that I came into this world to do. I have worked taskwork, and have the rest of the day to myself.

Walter Savage Landor (1775–1864)
On His 75th Birthday

> I strove with none, for none was worth my strife:
>   Nature I loved, and, next to Nature, Art:
> I warmed both hands before the fire of Life;
>   It sinks; and I am ready to depart.

Henry Wadsworth Longfellow (1807–1882)

From Morituri Salutamus

But why, you ask me, should this tale be told
To men grown old, or who are growing old?
It is too late! Ah, nothing is too late
Till the tired heart shall cease to palpitate.
Cato learned Greek at eighty; Sophocles   240
Wrote his grand Œdipus, and Simonides
Bore off the prize of verse from his compeers,
When each had numbered more than four-score years,
And Theophrastus, at fourscore and ten,
Had but begun his "Characters of Men."   245
Chaucer, at Woodstock with the nightingales,
At sixty wrote the Canterbury Tales;
Goethe at Weimar, toiling to the last,
Completed Faust when eighty years were past.
These are indeed exceptions; but they show   250
How far the gulf-stream of our youth may flow
Into the arctic regions of our lives,
Where little else than life itself survives
As the barometer foretells the storm
While still the skies are clear, the weather warm,   255
So something in us, as old age draws near,
Betrays the pressure of the atmosphere.
The nimble mercury, ere we are aware,
Descends the elastic ladder of the air;
The telltale blood in artery and vein   260
Sinks from its higher levels in the brain;
Whatever poet, orator, or sage
May say of it, old age is still old age.
It is the waning, not the crescent moon;
The dusk of evening, not the blaze of noon;   265
It is not strength, but weakness; not desire,
But its surcease; not the fierce heat of fire,
The burning and consuming element,

But that of ashes and of embers spent,
In which some living sparks we still discern,   270
Enough to warm, but not enough to burn.

What then? Shall we sit idly down and say
The night hath come; it is no longer day?
The night hath not yet come; we are not quite
Cut off from labor by the failing light;   275
Something remains for us to do or dare;
Even the oldest tree some fruit may bear;
Not Œdipus Coloneus, or Greek Ode,
Or tales of pilgrims that one morning rode
Out of the gateway of the Tabard Inn,   280
But other something, would we but begin;
For age is opportunity no less
Than youth itself, though in another dress,
And as the evening twilight fades away
The sky is filled with stars, invisible by day.   285

My Lost Youth

Often I think of the beautiful town
   That is seated by the sea;
Often in thought go up and down
The pleasant streets of that dear old town,
   And my youth comes back to me.   5
      And a verse of a Lapland song
      Is haunting my memory still:
      "A boy's will is the wind's will,
And the thoughts of youth are long, long thoughts."

I can see the shadowy lines of its trees,   10
   And catch, in sudden gleams,
The sheen of the far-surrounding seas,
And islands that were the Hesperides
   Of all my boyish dreams.
      And the burden of that old song,   15
      It murmurs and whispers still:
      "A boy's will is the wind's will,
And the thoughts of youth are long, long thoughts."

I remember the black wharves and the slips,
 And the sea-tides tossing free;   20
And Spanish sailors with bearded lips,
And the beauty and mystery of the ships,
 And the magic of the sea.
   And the voice of that wayward song
   Is singing and saying still: 25
   "A boy's will is the wind's will,
And the thoughts of youth are long, long thoughts."

I remember the bulwarks by the shore,
 And the fort upon the hill;
The sunrise gun, with its hollow roar,   30
The drum-beat repeated o'er and o'er,
 And the bugle wild and shrill.
   And the music of that old song
   Throbs in my memory still:
   "A boy's will is the wind's will,   35
And the thoughts of youth are long, long thoughts."

I remember the sea-fight far away,
 How it thundered o'er the tide!
And the dead captains, as they lay
In their graves, o'erlooking the tranquil bay,   40
 Where they in battle died.
   And the sound of that mournful song
   Goes through me with a thrill:
   "A boy's will is the wind's will,
And the thoughts of youth are long, long thoughts."   45

I can see the breezy dome of groves,
 The shadows of Deering's Woods;
And the friendships old and the early loves
Come back with a Sabbath sound, as of doves
 In quiet neighborhoods.   50
   And the verse of that sweet old song,
   It flutters and murmurs still:
   "A boy's will is the wind's will,
And the thoughts of youth are long, long thoughts."

I remember the gleams and glooms that dart   55
 Across the school-boy's brain;
The song and the silence in the heart,

That in part are prophecies, and in part
   Are longings wild and vain.
       And the voice of that fitful song   60
       Sings on, and is never still:
       "A boy's will is the wind's will,
And the thoughts of youth are long, long thoughts."

There are things of which I may not speak;
   There are dreams that cannot die;   65
There are thoughts that make the strong heart weak,
And bring a pallor into the cheek,
   And a mist before the eye.
       And the words of that fatal song
       Come over me like a chill: 70
       "A boy's will is the wind's will,
And the thoughts of youth are long, long thoughts."

Strange to me now are the forms I meet
   When I visit the dear old town;
But the native air is pure and sweet,   75
And the trees that o'ershadow each well-known street,
   As they balance up and down,
       Are singing the beautiful song,
       Are sighing and whispering still:
       "A boy's will is the wind's will,   80
And the thoughts of youth are long, long thoughts."

And Deering's Woods are fresh and fair,
   And with joy that is almost pain
My heart goes back to wander there,
And among the dreams of the days that were,   85
   I find my lost youth again.
       And the strange and beautiful song,
       The groves are repeating it still:
       "A boy's will is the wind's will,
And the thoughts of youth are long, long thoughts."   90

Arthur Miller (Born 1915)
Death of a Salesman

Certain private conversations in two acts and a requiem

CAST

(in order of appearance)

WILLY LOMAN
LINDA
BIFF
HAPPY
BERNARD
THE WOMAN
CHARLEY
UNCLE BEN
HOWARD WAGNER
JENNY
STANLEY
MISS FORSYTHE
LETTA

ACT ONE

(*A melody is heard, played upon a flute. It is small and fine, telling of grass and trees and the horizon. The curtain rises.*

Before us is the Salesman's house. We are aware of towering, angular shapes behind it, surrounding it on all sides. Only the blue light of the sky falls upon the house and forestage; the surrounding area shows an angry glow of orange. As more light appears, we see a solid vault of apartment houses around the small, fragile-seeming home. An air of the dream clings to the place, a dream rising out of reality. The kitchen at center seems actual enough, for there is a kitchen table with three chairs, and a refrigerator. But no other fixtures are seen. At the back of the kitchen there is a draped entrance, which leads to the living-room. To the right of the kitchen, on a level raised two feet, is a bedroom furnished only with a brass bedstead and a straight chair. On a shelf over the bed a silver athletic trophy stands. A window opens onto the apartment house at the side.

Behind the kitchen, on a level raised six and a half feet, is the boys' bedroom, at present barely visible. Two beds are dimly seen, and at the back of the room a dormer window. (This bedroom is above the unseen living-room.) At the left a stairway curves up to it from the kitchen.

The entire setting is wholly or, in some places, partially transparent. The roof-line of the house is one-dimensional; under and over it we see the apartment buildings. Before the house lies an apron, curving beyond the forestage into the orchestra. This forward area serves as the back yard as well as the locale of all WILLY'S *imaginings and of his city scenes. Whenever the action is in the present the actors observe the imaginary wall-lines, entering the house only through its door at the left. But in the scenes of the past these boundaries are broken, and characters enter or leave a room by stepping "through" a wall onto the forestage.*

From the right, WILLY LOMAN, *the Salesman, enters, carrying two large sample cases. The flute plays on. He hears but is not aware of it. He is past sixty years of age, dressed quietly. Even as he crosses the stage to the doorway of the house, his exhaustion is apparent. He unlocks the door, comes into the kitchen, and thankfully lets his burden down, feeling the soreness of his palms. A word-sigh escapes his lips—it might be "Oh, boy, oh, boy." He closes the door, then carries his cases out into the living-room, through the draped kitchen doorway.*

LINDA, *his wife, has stirred in her bed at the right. She gets out and puts on a robe, listening. Most often jovial, she has developed an iron repression of her exceptions to* WILLY'S *behavior—she more than loves him, she admires him, as though his mercurial nature, his temper, his massive dreams and little cruelties, served her only as sharp reminders of the turbulent longings within him, longings which she shares but lacks the temperament to utter and follow to their end.)*

LINDA (*hearing* WILLY *outside the bedroom, calls with some trepidation*)   Willy!

WILLY   It's all right. I came back.

LINDA   Why? What happened? (*Slight pause.*) Did something happen, Willy?

WILLY   No, nothing happened.

LINDA   You didn't smash the car, did you?

WILLY (*with casual irritation*)   I said nothing happened. Didn't you hear me?

LINDA   Don't you feel well?

WILLY   I'm tired to the death. (*The flute has faded away. He sits on the bed beside her, a little numb.*) I couldn't make it. I just couldn't make it, Linda.

LINDA (*very carefully, delicately*)   Where were you all day? You look terrible.

WILLY   I got as far as a little above Yonkers. I stopped for a cup of coffee. Maybe it was the coffee.

LINDA   What?

WILLY (*after a pause*)   I suddenly couldn't drive any more. The car kept going off onto the shoulder, y'know?

LINDA (*helpfully*)   Oh. Maybe it was the steering again. I don't think Angelo knows the Studebaker.

WILLY   No, it's me, it's me. Suddenly I realize I'm goin' sixty miles an hour and I don't remember the last five minutes. I'm—I can't seem to—keep my mind to it.

LINDA   Maybe it's your glasses. You never went for your new glasses.

WILLY   No, I see everything. I came back ten miles an hour. It took me nearly four hours from Yonkers.

LINDA   (*resigned*)   Well, you'll just have to take a rest, Willy, you can't continue this way.

WILLY   I just got back from Florida.

LINDA   But you didn't rest your mind. Your mind is overactive, and the mind is what counts, dear.

WILLY   I'll start out in the morning. Maybe I'll feel better in the morning. (*She is taking off his shoes.*) These goddam arch supports are killing me.

LINDA   Take an aspirin. Should I get you an aspirin? It'll soothe you.

WILLY   (*with wonder*)   I was driving along, you understand? And I was fine. I was even observing the scenery. You can imagine, me looking at scenery, on the road every week of my life. But it's so beautiful up there, Linda, the trees are so thick, and the sun is warm. I opened the windshield and just let the warm air bathe over me. And then all of a sudden I'm goin' off the road! I'm tellin' ya, I absolutely forgot I was driving. If I'd've gone the other way over the white line I might've killed somebody. So I went on again—and five minutes later I'm dreamin' again, and I nearly—(*He presses two fingers against his eyes.*) I have such thoughts, I have such strange thoughts.

LINDA   Willy, dear. Talk to them again. There's no reason why you can't work in New York.

WILLY   They don't need me in New York. I'm the New England man. I'm vital in New England.

LINDA   But you're sixty years old. They can't expect you to keep traveling every week.

WILLY   I'll have to send a wire to Portland. I'm supposed to see Brown and Morrison tomorrow morning at ten o'clock to show the line. Goddammit, I could sell them! (*He starts putting on his jacket.*)

LINDA   (*taking the jacket from him*)   Why don't you go down to the place tomorrow and tell Howard you've simply got to work in New York? You're too accommodating, dear.

WILLY   If old man Wagner was alive I'd a been in charge of New York now! That man was a prince, he was a masterful man. But that boy of his, that Howard, he don't appreciate. When I went north the first time, the Wagner Company didn't know where New England was!

LINDA   Why don't you tell those things to Howard, dear?

WILLY   (*encouraged*)   I will, I definitely will. Is there any cheese?

LINDA   I'll make you a sandwich.

WILLY   No, go to sleep. I'll take some milk. I'll be up right away. The boys in?

LINDA   They're sleeping. Happy took Biff on a date tonight.

WILLY (*interested*)   That so?

LINDA   It was so nice to see them shaving together, one behind the other, in the bathroom. And going out together. You notice? The whole house smells of shaving lotion.

WILLY   Figure it out. Work a lifetime to pay off a house. You finally own it, and there's nobody to live in it.

LINDA   Well, dear, life is a casting off. It's always that way.

WILLY   No, no, some people—some people accomplish something. Did Biff say anything after I went this morning?

LINDA   You shouldn't have criticized him, Willy, especially after he just got off the train. You mustn't lose your temper with him.

WILLY   When the hell did I lose my temper? I simply asked him if he was making any money. Is that a criticism?

LINDA   But, dear, how could he make any money?

WILLY (*worried and angered*)   There's such an undercurrent in him. He became a moody man. Did he apologize when I left this morning?

LINDA   He was crestfallen, Willy. You know how he admires you. I think if he finds himself, then you'll both be happier and not fight any more.

WILLY   How can he find himself on a farm? Is that a life? A farmhand? In the beginning, when he was young, I thought, well, a young man, it's good for him to tramp around, take a lot of different jobs. But it's more than ten years now and he has yet to make thirty-five dollars a week!

LINDA   He's finding himself, Willy.

WILLY   Not finding yourself at the age of thirty-four is a disgrace!

LINDA   Shh!

WILLY   The trouble is he's lazy, goddammit!

LINDA   Willy, please!

WILLY   Biff is a lazy bum!

LINDA   They're sleeping. Get something to eat. Go on down.

WILLY   Why did he come home? I would like to know what brought him home.

LINDA   I don't know. I think he's still lost, Willy. I think he's very lost.

WILLY   Biff Loman is lost. In the greatest country in the world a young man with such—personal attractiveness, gets lost. And such a hard worker. There's one thing about Biff—he's not lazy.

LINDA   Never.

WILLY (*with pity and resolve*)   I'll see him in the morning; I'll have a nice talk with him. I'll get him a job selling. He could be big in no time. My God! Remember how they used to follow him around in high school? When he smiled at one of them their faces lit up. When he walked down the street . . . (*He loses himself in reminiscences.*)

LINDA (*trying to bring him out of it*)   Willy, dear, I got a new kind of American-type cheese today. It's whipped.

WILLY   Why do you get American when I like Swiss?

LINDA   I just thought you'd like a change—

WILLY   I don't want a change! I want Swiss cheese. Why am I always being contradicted?

LINDA (*with a covering laugh*)   I thought it would be a surprise.

WILLY   Why don't you open a window in here, for God's sake?

LINDA (*with infinite patience*)   They're all open, dear.

WILLY   The way they boxed us in here. Bricks and windows, windows and bricks.

LINDA   We should've bought the land next door.

WILLY   The street is lined with cars. There's not a breath of fresh air in the neighborhood. The grass don't grow any more, you can't raise a carrot in the back yard. They should've had a law against apartment houses. Remember those two beautiful elm trees out there? When I and Biff hung the swing between them?

LINDA   Yeah, like being a million miles from the city.

WILLY   They should've arrested the builder for cutting those down. They massacred the neighborhood. (*Lost:*) More and more I think of those days, Linda. This time of year it was lilac and wisteria. And then the peonies would come out, and the daffodils. What fragrance in this room!

LINDA   Well, after all, people had to move somewhere.

WILLY   No, there's more people now.

LINDA   I don't think there's more people. I think—

WILLY   There's more people! That's what's ruining this country! Population is getting out of control. The competition is maddening! Smell the stink from that apartment house! And another one on the other side . . . How can they whip cheese?

(*On* WILLY'S *last line,* BIFF *and* HAPPY *raise themselves up in their beds, listening.*)

LINDA   Go down, try it. And be quiet.

WILLY (*turning to* LINDA, *guiltily*)   You're not worried about me, are you, sweetheart?

BIFF   What's the matter?

HAPPY   Listen!

LINDA   You've got too much on the ball to worry about.

WILLY   You're my foundation and my support, Linda.

LINDA   Just try to relax, dear. You make mountains out of molehills.

WILLY   I won't fight with him any more. If he wants to go back to Texas, let him go.

LINDA   He'll find his way.

WILLY   Sure. Certain men just don't get started till later in life. Like Thomas Edison, I think. Or B. F. Goodrich. One of them was deaf. (*He starts for the bedroom doorway.*) I'll put my money on Biff.

LINDA And Willy—if it's warm Sunday we'll drive in the country. And we'll open the windshield, and take lunch.

WILLY No, the windshields don't open on the new cars.

LINDA But you opened it today.

WILLY Me? I didn't. (*He stops.*) Now isn't that peculiar! Isn't that a remarkable— (*He breaks off in amazement and fright as the flute is heard distantly.*)

LINDA What, darling?

WILLY That is the most remarkable thing.

LINDA What, dear?

WILLY I was thinking of the Chevvy. (*Slight pause.*) Nineteen twenty-eight . . . when I had that red Chevvy—(*Breaks off.*) That funny? I coulda sworn I was driving that Chevvy today.

LINDA Well, that's nothing. Something must've reminded you.

WILLY Remarkable. Ts. Remember those days? The way Biff used to simonize that car? The dealer refused to believe there was eighty thousand miles on it. (*He shakes his head.*) Heh! (*To* LINDA:) Close your eyes, I'll be right up. (*He walks out of the bedroom.*)

HAPPY (*to* BIFF) Jesus, maybe he smashed up the car again!

LINDA (*calling after* WILLY) Be careful on the stairs, dear! The cheese is on the middle shelf! (*She turns, goes over to the bed, takes his jacket, and goes out of the bedroom.*)

(*Light has risen on the boys' room. Unseen,* WILLY *is heard talking to himself, "Eighty thousand miles," and a little laugh.* BIFF *gets out of bed, comes downstage a bit, and stands attentively.* BIFF *is two years older than his brother* HAPPY, *well built, but in these days bears a worn air and seems less self-assured. He has succeeded less, and his dreams are stronger and less acceptable than* HAPPY'S. HAPPY *is tall, powerfully made. Sexuality is like a visible color on him, or a scent that many women have discovered. He, like his brother, is lost, but in a different way, for he has never allowed himself to turn his face toward defeat and is thus more confused and hard-skinned, although seemingly more content.*)

HAPPY (*getting out of bed*) He's going to get his license taken away if he keeps that up. I'm getting nervous about him, y'know, Biff?

BIFF His eyes are going.

HAPPY No, I've driven with him. He sees all right. He just doesn't keep his mind on it. I drove into the city with him last week. He stops at a green light and then it turns red and he goes. (*He laughs.*)

BIFF Maybe he's color-blind.

HAPPY Pop? Why he's got the finest eye for color in the business. You know that.

BIFF (*sitting down on his bed*) I'm going to sleep.

HAPPY You're not still sour on Dad, are you, Biff?

BIFF   He's all right, I guess.

WILLY (*underneath them, in the living-room*)   Yes, sir, eighty thousand miles—eighty-two thousand!

BIFF   You smoking?

HAPPY (*holding out a pack of cigarettes*)   Want one?

BIFF (*taking a cigarette*)   I can never sleep when I smell it.

WILLY   What a simonizing job, heh!

HAPPY (*with deep sentiment*)   Funny, Biff, y'know? Us sleeping in here again? The old beds. (*He pats his bed affectionately.*) All the talk that went across those two beds, huh? Our whole lives.

BIFF   Yeah. Lotta dreams and plans.

HAPPY (*with a deep and masculine laugh*)   About five hundred women would like to know what was said in this room.

(*They share a soft laugh.*)

BIFF   Remember that big Betsy something—what the hell was her name—over on Bushwick Avenue?

HAPPY (*combing his hair*)   With the collie dog!

BIFF   That's the one. I got you in there, remember?

HAPPY   Yeah, that was my first time—I think. Boy, there was a pig! (*They laugh, almost crudely.*) You taught me everything I know about women. Don't forget that.

BIFF   I bet you forgot how bashful you used to be. Especially with girls.

HAPPY   Oh, I still am, Biff.

BIFF   Oh, go on.

HAPPY   I just control it, that's all. I think I got less bashful and you got more so. What happened, Biff? Where's the old humor, the old confidence? (*He shakes* BIFF'S *knee.* BIFF *gets up and moves restlessly about the room.*) What's the matter?

BIFF   Why does Dad mock me all the time?

HAPPY   He's not mocking you, he—

BIFF   Everything I say there's a twist of mockery on his face. I can't get near him.

HAPPY   He just wants you to make good, that's all. I wanted to talk to you about Dad for a long time, Biff. Something's—happening to him. He—talks to himself.

BIFF   I noticed that this morning. But he always mumbled.

HAPPY   But not so noticeable. It got so embarrassing I sent him to Florida. And you know something? Most of the time he's talking to you.

BIFF   What's he say about me?

HAPPY   I can't make it out.

BIFF   What's he say about me?

HAPPY   I think the fact that you're not settled, that you're still kind of up in the air . . .

BIFF   There's one or two other things depressing him, Happy.

HAPPY   What do you mean?

BIFF   Never mind. Just don't lay it all to me.

HAPPY   But I think if you just got started—I mean—is there any future for you out there?

BIFF   I tell ya, Hap, I don't know what the future is. I don't know—what I'm supposed to want.

HAPPY   What do you mean?

BIFF   Well, I spent six or seven years after high school trying to work myself up. Shipping clerk, salesman, business of one kind or another. And it's a measly manner of existence. To get on that subway on the hot mornings in summer. To devote your whole life to keeping stock, or making phone calls, or selling or buying. To suffer fifty weeks of the year for the sake of a two-week vacation, when all you really desire is to be outdoors, with your shirt off. And always to have to get ahead of the next fella. And still—that's how you build a future.

HAPPY   Well, you really enjoy it on a farm? Are you content out there?

BIFF   (*with rising agitation*)   Hap, I've had twenty or thirty different kinds of jobs since I left home before the war, and it always turns out the same. I just realized it lately. In Nebraska when I herded cattle, and the Dakotas, and Arizona, and now in Texas. It's why I came home now, I guess, because I realized it. This farm I work on, it's spring there now, see? And they've got about fifteen new colts. There's nothing more inspiring or—beautiful than the sight of a mare and a new colt. And it's cool there now, see? Texas is cool now, and it's spring. And whenever spring comes to where I am, I suddenly get the feeling, my God, I'm not gettin' anywhere! What the hell am I doing, playing around with horses, twenty-eight dollars a week! I'm thirty-four years old, I oughta be makin' my future. That's when I come running home. And now, I get here, and I don't know what to do with myself. (*After a pause:*) I've always made a point of not wasting my life, and everytime I come back here I know that all I've done is to waste my life.

HAPPY   You're a poet, you know that, Biff? You're a—you're an idealist!

BIFF   No, I'm mixed up very bad. Maybe I oughta get married. Maybe I oughta get stuck into something. Maybe that's my trouble. I'm like a boy. I'm not married, I'm not in business, I just—I'm like a boy. Are you content, Hap? You're a success, aren't you? Are you content?

HAPPY   Hell, no!

BIFF   Why? You're making money, aren't you?

HAPPY   (*moving about with energy, expressiveness*)   All I can do now is wait for the merchandise manager to die. And suppose I get to be merchandise manager? He's a good friend of mine, and he just built a terrific estate on Long Island. And he lived there about two months and sold it, and now he's building another one.

He can't enjoy it once it's finished. And I know that's just what I would do. I don't know what the hell I'm workin' for. Sometimes I sit in my apartment—all alone. And I think of the rent I'm paying. And it's crazy. But then, it's what I always wanted. My own apartment, a car, and plenty of women. And still, goddammit, I'm lonely.

BIFF (*with enthusiasm*)   Listen, why don't you come out West with me?

HAPPY   You and I, heh?

BIFF   Sure, maybe we could buy a ranch. Raise cattle, use our muscles. Men built like us should be working out in the open.

HAPPY (*avidly*)   The Loman Brothers, heh?

BIFF (*with vast affection*)   Sure, we'd be known all over the counties!

HAPPY (*enthralled*)   That's what I dream about, Biff. Sometimes I want to just rip my clothes off in the middle of the store and outbox that goddam merchandise manager. I mean I can outbox, outrun, and outlift anybody in that store, and I have to take orders from those common, petty sons-of-bitches till I can't stand it any more.

BIFF   I'm tellin' you, kid, if you were with me I'd be happy out there.

HAPPY (*enthused*)   See, Biff, everybody around me is so false that I'm constantly lowering my ideals . . .

BIFF   Baby, together we'd stand up for one another, we'd have someone to trust.

HAPPY   If I were around you—

BIFF   Hap, the trouble is we weren't brought up to grub for money. I don't know how to do it.

HAPPY   Neither can I!

BIFF   Then let's go!

HAPPY   The only thing is—what can you make out there?

BIFF   But look at your friend. Builds an estate and then hasn't the peace of mind to live in it.

HAPPY   Yeah, but when he walks into the store the waves part in front of him. That's fifty-two thousand dollars a year coming through the revolving door, and I got more in my pinky finger than he's got in his head.

BIFF   Yeah, but you just said—

HAPPY   I gotta show some of those pompous, self-important executives over there that Hap Loman can make the grade. I want to walk into the store the way he walks in. Then I'll go with you, Biff. We'll be together yet, I swear. But take those two we had tonight. Now weren't they gorgeous creatures?

BIFF   Yeah, yeah, most gorgeous I've had in years.

HAPPY   I get that any time I want, Biff. Whenever I feel disgusted. The only trouble is, it gets like bowling or something. I just keep knockin' them over and it doesn't mean anything. You still run around a lot?

BIFF   Naa. I'd like to find a girl—steady, somebody with substance.

HAPPY   That's what I long for.

BIFF   Go on! You'd never come home.

HAPPY   I would! Somebody with character, with resistance! Like Mom, y'know? You're gonna call me a bastard when I tell you this. That girl Charlotte I was with tonight is engaged to be married in five weeks. (*He tries on his new hat.*)

BIFF   No kiddin'!

HAPPY   Sure, the guy's in line for the vice-presidency of the store. I don't know what gets into me, maybe I just have an overdeveloped sense of competition or something, but I went and ruined her, and furthermore I can't get rid of her. And he's the third executive I've done that to. Isn't that a crummy characteristic? And to top it all, I go to their weddings! (*Indignantly, but laughing:*) Like I'm not supposed to take bribes. Manufacturers offer me a hundred-dollar bill now and then to throw an order their way. You know how honest I am, but it's like this girl, see. I hate myself for it. Because I don't want the girl, and, still, I take it and—I love it!

BIFF   Let's go to sleep.

HAPPY   I guess we didn't settle anything, heh?

BIFF   I just got one idea that I think I'm going to try.

HAPPY   What's that?

BIFF   Remember Bill Oliver?

HAPPY   Sure, Oliver is very big now. You want to work for him again?

BIFF   No, but when I quit he said something to me. He put his arm on my shoulder, and he said, "Biff, if you ever need anything, come to me."

HAPPY   I remember that. That sounds good.

BIFF   I think I'll go to see him. If I could get ten thousand or even seven or eight thousand dollars I could buy a beautiful ranch.

HAPPY   I bet he'd back you. 'Cause he thought highly of you, Biff. I mean, they all do. You're well liked, Biff. That's why I say to come back here, and we both have the apartment. And I'm tellin' you, Biff, any babe you want . . .

BIFF   No, with a ranch I could do the work I like and still be something. I just wonder though. I wonder if Oliver still thinks I stole that carton of basketballs.

HAPPY   Oh, he probably forgot that long ago. It's almost ten years. You're too sensitive. Anyway, he didn't really fire you.

BIFF   Well, I think he was going to. I think that's why I quit. I was never sure whether he knew or not. I know he thought the world of me, though. I was the only one he'd let lock up the place.

WILLY (*below*)   You gonna wash the engine, Biff?

HAPPY   Shh!

(BIFF *looks at* HAPPY, *who is gazing down, listening.* WILLY *is mumbling in the parlor.*)

HAPPY   You hear that?

(*They listen.* WILLY *laughs warmly.*)

BIFF (*growing angry*)   Doesn't he know Mom can hear that?
WILLY   Don't get your sweater dirty, Biff!

(*A look of pain crosses* BIFF'S *face.*)

HAPPY   Isn't that terrible? Don't leave again, will you? You'll find a job here. You
    gotta stick around. I don't know what to do about him, it's getting embarrassing.
WILLY   What a simonizing job!
BIFF   Mom's hearing that!
WILLY   No kiddin', Biff, you got a date? Wonderful!
HAPPY   Go on to sleep. But talk to him in the morning, will you?
BIFF (*reluctantly getting into bed*)   With her in the house. Brother!
HAPPY (*getting into bed*)   I wish you'd have a good talk with him.

(*The light on their room begins to fade.*)

BIFF (*to himself in bed*)   That selfish, stupid . . .
HAPPY   Sh . . . Sleep, Biff.

(*Their light is out. Well before they have finished speaking,* WILLY'S *form is dimly
seen below in the darkened kitchen. He opens the refrigerator, searches in there, and
takes out a bottle of milk. The apartment houses are fading out, and the entire house
and surroundings become covered with leaves. Music insinuates itself as the leaves
appear.*)

WILLY   Just wanna be careful with those girls, Biff, that's all. Don't make any prom-
    ises. No promises of any kind. Because a girl, y'know, they always believe what
    you tell 'em, and you're very young, Biff, you're too young to be talking seriously
    to girls.

(*Light rises on the kitchen.* WILLY, *talking, shuts the refrigerator door and comes
downstage to the kitchen table. He pours milk into a glass. He is totally immersed in
himself, smiling faintly.*)

WILLY   Too young entirely, Biff. You want to watch your schooling first. Then when
    you're all set, there'll be plenty of girls for a boy like you. (*He smiles broadly at a
    kitchen chair.*) That so? The girls pay for you? (*He laughs.*) Boy, you must really
    be makin' a hit.

(WILLY *is gradually addressing—physically—a point offstage, speaking through the
wall of the kitchen, and his voice has been rising in volume to that of a normal
conversation.*)

WILLY   I been wondering why you polish the car so careful. Ha! Don't leave the
    hubcaps, boys. Get the chamois to the hubcaps. Happy, use newspaper on the

windows, it's the easiest thing. Show him how to do it, Biff! You see, Happy? Pad it up, use it like a pad. That's it, that's it, good work. You're doin' all right, Hap. (*He pauses, then nods in approbation for a few seconds, then looks upward.*) Biff, first thing we gotta do when we get time is clip that big branch over the house. Afraid it's gonna fall in a storm and hit the roof. Tell you what. We get a rope and sling her around, and then we climb up there with a couple of saws and take her down. Soon as you finish the car, boys, I wanna see ya. I got a surprise for you, boys.

BIFF (*offstage*) Whatta ya got, Dad?

WILLY No, you finish first. Never leave a job till you're finished—remember that. (*Looking toward the "big trees":*) Biff, up in Albany I saw a beautiful hammock. I think I'll buy it next trip, and we'll hang it right between those two elms. Wouldn't that be something? Just swingin' there under those branches. Boy, that would be . . .

(*Young* BIFF *and Young* HAPPY *appear from the direction* WILLY *was addressing.* HAPPY *carries rags and a pail of water.* BIFF, *wearing a sweater with a block "S," carries a football.*)

BIFF (*pointing in the direction of the car offstage*) How's that, Pop, professional?

WILLY Terrific. Terrific job, boys. Good work, Biff.

HAPPY Where's the surprise, Pop?

WILLY In the back seat of the car.

HAPPY Boy! (*He runs off.*)

BIFF What is it, Dad? Tell me, what'd you buy?

WILLY (*laughing, cuffs him*) Never mind, something I want you to have.

BIFF (*turns and starts off*) What is it, Hap?

HAPPY (*offstage*) It's a punching bag!

BIFF Oh, Pop!

WILLY It's got Gene Tunney's signature on it!

(HAPPY *runs onstage with a punching bag.*)

BIFF Gee, how'd you know we wanted a punching bag?

WILLY Well, it's the finest thing for the timing.

HAPPY (*lies down on his back and pedals with his feet*) I'm losing weight, you notice, Pop?

WILLY (*to* HAPPY) Jumping rope is good too.

BIFF Did you see the new football I got?

WILLY (*examining the ball*) Where'd you get a new ball?

BIFF The coach told me to practice my passing.

WILLY That so? And he gave you the ball, heh?

BIFF Well, I borrowed it from the locker room. (*He laughs confidentially.*)

WILLY (*laughing with him at the theft*)   I want you to return that.

HAPPY   I told you he wouldn't like it!

BIFF (*angrily*)   Well, I'm bringing it back!

WILLY (*stopping the incipient argument, to* HAPPY)   Sure, he's gotta practice with a regulation ball, doesn't he? (*To* BIFF:) Coach'll probably congratulate you on your initiative!

BIFF   Oh, he keeps congratulating my initiative all the time, Pop.

WILLY   That's because he likes you. If somebody else took that ball there'd be an uproar. So what's the report, boys, what's the report?

BIFF   Where'd you go this time, Dad? Gee we were lonesome for you.

WILLY (*pleased, puts an arm around each boy and they come down to the apron*)   Lonesome, heh?

BIFF   Missed you every minute.

WILLY   Don't say? Tell you a secret, boys. Don't breathe it to a soul. Someday I'll have my own business, and I'll never have to leave home any more.

HAPPY   Like Uncle Charley, heh?

WILLY   Bigger than Uncle Charley! Because Charley is not—liked. He's liked, but he's not—well liked.

BIFF   Where'd you go this time, Dad?

WILLY   Well, I got on the road, and I went north to Providence. Met the Mayor.

BIFF   The Mayor of Providence!

WILLY   He was sitting in the hotel lobby.

BIFF   What'd he say?

WILLY   He said, "Morning!" And I said, "You got a fine city here, Mayor." And then he had coffee with me. And then I went to Waterbury. Waterbury is a fine city. Big clock city, the famous Waterbury clock. Sold a nice bill there. And then Boston—Boston is the cradle of the Revolution. A fine city. And a couple of other towns in Mass., and on to Portland and Bangor and straight home!

BIFF   Gee, I'd love to go with you sometime, Dad.

WILLY   Soon as summer comes.

HAPPY   Promise?

WILLY   You and Hap and I, and I'll show you all the towns. America is full of beautiful towns and fine, upstanding people. And they know me, boys, they know me up and down New England. The finest people. And when I bring you fellas up, there'll be open sesame for all of us, 'cause one thing, boys: I have friends. I can park my car in any street in New England, and the cops protect it like their own. This summer, heh?

BIFF and HAPPY (*together*)   Yeah! You bet!

WILLY   We'll take our bathing suits.

HAPPY   We'll carry your bags, Pop!

WILLY   Oh, won't that be something! Me comin' into the Boston stores with you boys carryin' my bags. What a sensation!

(BIFF *is prancing around, practicing passing the ball.*)

WILLY   You nervous, Biff, about the game?

BIFF   Not if you're gonna be there.

WILLY   What do they say about you in school, now that they made you captain?

HAPPY   There's a crowd of girls behind him everytime the classes change.

BIFF (*taking* WILLY'S *hand*)   This Saturday, Pop, this Saturday—just for you, I'm going to break through for a touchdown.

HAPPY   You're supposed to pass.

BIFF   I'm takin' one play for Pop. You watch me, Pop, and when I take off my helmet, that means I'm breakin' out. Then you watch me crash through that line!

WILLY (*kisses* BIFF)   Oh, wait'll I tell this in Boston!

(BERNARD *enters in knickers. He is younger than* BIFF, *earnest and loyal, a worried boy.*)

BERNARD   Biff, where are you? You're supposed to study with me today.

WILLY   Hey, looka Bernard. What're you lookin' so anemic about, Bernard?

BERNARD   He's gotta study, Uncle Willy. He's got Regents next week.

HAPPY (*tauntingly, spinning* BERNARD *around*)   Let's box, Bernard!

BERNARD   Biff! (*He gets away from* HAPPY.) Listen, Biff, I heard Mr. Birnbaum say that if you don't start studyin' math he's gonna flunk you, and you won't graduate. I heard him!

WILLY   You better study with him, Biff. Go ahead now.

BERNARD   I heard him!

BIFF   Oh, Pop, you didn't see my sneakers! (*He holds up a foot for* WILLY *to look at.*)

WILLY   Hey, that's a beautiful job of printing!

BERNARD (*wiping his glasses*)   Just because he printed University of Virginia on his sneakers doesn't mean they've got to graduate him, Uncle Willy!

WILLY (*angrily*)   What're you talking about? With scholarships to three universities they're gonna flunk him?

BERNARD   But I heard Mr. Birnbaum say—

WILLY   Don't be a pest, Bernard! (*To his boys:*) What an anemic!

BERNARD   Okay, I'm waiting for you in my house, Biff.

(BERNARD *goes off. The Lomans laugh.*)

WILLY   Bernard is not well liked, is he?

BIFF   He's liked, but he's not well liked.

HAPPY   That's right, Pop.

WILLY   That's just what I mean. Bernard can get the best marks in school, y'understand, but when he gets out in the business world, y'understand, you are going to be five times ahead of him. That's why I thank Almighty God you're both built like Adonises. Because the man who makes an appearance in the business world, the man who creates personal interest, is the man who gets ahead. Be liked and you will never want. You take me, for instance. I never have to wait in line to see a buyer. "Willy Loman is here!" That's all they have to know, and I go right through.

BIFF   Did you knock them dead, Pop?

WILLY   Knocked 'em cold in Providence, slaughtered 'em in Boston.

HAPPY (*on his back, pedaling again*)   I'm losing weight, you notice, Pop?

(LINDA *enters, as of old, a ribbon in her hair, carrying a basket of washing.*)

LINDA (*with youthful energy*)   Hello, dear!

WILLY   Sweetheart!

LINDA   How'd the Chevvy run?

WILLY   Chevrolet, Linda, is the greatest car ever built. (*To the boys:*) Since when do you let your mother carry wash up the stairs?

BIFF   Grab hold there, boy!

HAPPY   Where to, Mom?

LINDA   Hang them up on the line. And you better go down to your friends, Biff. The cellar is full of boys. They don't know what to do with themselves.

BIFF   Ah, when Pop comes home they can wait!

WILLY (*laughs appreciatively*)   You better go down and tell them what to do, Biff.

BIFF   I think I'll have them sweep out the furnace room.

WILLY   Good work, Biff.

BIFF (*goes through wall-line of kitchen to doorway at back and calls down*)   Fellas! Everybody sweep out the furnace room! I'll be right down!

VOICES   All right! Okay, Biff.

BIFF   George and Sam and Frank, come out back! We're hangin' up the wash! Come on, Hap, on the double! (*He and* HAPPY *carry out the basket.*)

LINDA   The way they obey him!

WILLY   Well, that's training, the training. I'm tellin' you, I was sellin' thousands and thousands, but I had to come home.

LINDA   Oh, the whole block'll be at that game. Did you sell anything?

WILLY   I did five hundred gross in Providence and seven hundred gross in Boston.

LINDA   No! Wait a minute, I've got a pencil. (*She pulls pencil and paper out of her apron pocket.*) That makes your commission . . . Two hundred—my God! Two hundred and twelve dollars!

WILLY   Well, I didn't figure it yet, but . . .

LINDA   How much did you do?

WILLY   Well, I—I did—about a hundred and eighty gross in Providence. Well, no— it came to—roughly two hundred gross on the whole trip.

LINDA (*without hesitation*)   Two hundred gross. That's . . . (*She figures.*)

WILLY   The trouble was that three of the stores were half closed for inventory in Boston. Otherwise I woulda broke records.

LINDA   Well, it makes seventy dollars and some pennies. That's very good.

WILLY   What do we owe?

LINDA   Well, on the first there's sixteen dollars on the refrigerator—

WILLY   Why sixteen?

LINDA   Well, the fan belt broke, so it was a dollar eighty.

WILLY   But it's brand new.

LINDA   Well, the man said that's the way it is. Till they work themselves in, y'know.

(They move through the wall-line into the kitchen.)

WILLY   I hope we didn't get stuck on that machine.

LINDA   They got the biggest ads of any of them!

WILLY   I know, it's a fine machine. What else?

LINDA   Well, there's nine-sixty for the washing machine. And for the vacuum cleaner there's three and a half due on the fifteenth. Then the roof, you got twenty-one dollars remaining.

WILLY   It don't leak, does it?

LINDA   No, they did a wonderful job. Then you owe Frank for the carburetor.

WILLY   I'm not going to pay that man! That goddam Chevrolet, they ought to prohibit the manufacture of that car!

LINDA   Well, you owe him three and a half. And odds and ends, comes to around a hundred and twenty dollars by the fifteenth.

WILLY   A hundred and twenty dollars! My God, if business don't pick up I don't know what I'm gonna do!

LINDA   Well, next week you'll do better.

WILLY   Oh, I'll knock 'em dead next week. I'll go to Hartford. I'm very well liked in Hartford. You know, the trouble is, Linda, people don't seem to take to me.

(They move onto the forestage.)

LINDA   Oh, don't be foolish.

WILLY   I know it when I walk in. They seem to laugh at me.

LINDA   Why? Why would they laugh at you? Don't talk that way, Willy.

(Willy moves to the edge of the stage. LINDA *goes into the kitchen and starts to darn stockings.)*

WILLY   I don't know the reason for it, but they just pass me by. I'm not noticed.

LINDA   But you're doing wonderful, dear. You're making seventy to a hundred dollars a week.

WILLY   But I gotta be at it ten, twelve hours a day. Other men—I don't know—they do it easier. I don't know why—I can't stop myself—I talk too much. A man oughta come in with a few words. One thing about Charley. He's a man of few words, and they respect him.

LINDA   You don't talk too much, you're just lively.

WILLY (*smiling*) Well, I figure, what the hell, life is short, a couple of jokes. (*To himself:*) I joke too much! (*The smile goes.*)

LINDA Why? You're—

WILLY I'm fat. I'm very—foolish to look at, Linda. I didn't tell you, but Christmas time I happened to be calling on F. H. Stewarts, and a salesman I know, as I was going in to see the buyer I heard him say something about—walrus. And I—I cracked him right across the face. I won't take that. I simply will not take that. But they do laugh at me. I know that.

LINDA Darling . . .

WILLY I gotta overcome it. I know I gotta overcome it. I'm not dressing to advantage, maybe.

LINDA Willy, darling, you're the handsomest man in the world—

WILLY Oh, no, Linda.

LINDA To me you are. (*Slight pause.*) The handsomest.

(*From the darkness is heard the laughter of a woman.* WILLY *doesn't turn to it, but it continues through* LINDA'S *lines.*)

LINDA And the boys, Willy. Few men are idolized by their children the way you are.

(*Music is heard as behind a scrim, to the left of the house,* THE WOMAN, *dimly seen, is dressing.*

WILLY (*with great feeling*) You're the best there is, Linda, you're a pal, you know that? On the road—on the road I want to grab you sometimes and just kiss the life outa you.

(*The laughter is loud now, and he moves into a brightening area at the left, where* THE WOMAN *has come from behind the scrim and is standing, putting on her hat, looking into a "mirror" and laughing.*)

WILLY 'Cause I get so lonely—especially when business is bad and there's nobody to talk to. I get the feeling that I'll never sell anything again, that I won't make a living for you, or a business, a business for the boys. (*He talks through* THE WOMAN'S *subsiding laughter;* THE WOMAN *primps at the "mirror."*) There's so much I want to make for—

THE WOMAN Me? You didn't make me, Willy. I picked you.

WILLY (*pleased*) You picked me?

THE WOMAN (*who is quite proper-looking,* WILLY'S *age*) I did. I've been sitting at that desk watching all the salesmen go by, day in, day out. But you've got such a sense of humor, and we do have such a good time together, don't we?

WILLY Sure, sure. (*He takes her in his arms.*) Why do you have to go now?

THE WOMAN It's two o'clock . . .

WILLY No, come on in! (*He pulls her.*)

THE WOMAN . . . my sisters'll be scandalized. When'll you be back?

WILLY   Oh, two weeks about. Will you come up again?

THE WOMAN   Sure thing. You do make me laugh. It's good for me. (*She squeezes his arm, kisses him.*) And I think you're a wonderful man.

WILLY   You picked me, heh?

THE WOMAN   Sure. Because you're so sweet. And such a kidder.

WILLY   Well, I'll see you next time I'm in Boston.

THE WOMAN   I'll put you right through to the buyers.

WILLY (*slapping her bottom*)   Right. Well, bottoms up!

THE WOMAN (*slaps him gently and laughs*)   You just kill me, Willy. (*He suddenly grabs her and kisses her roughly.*) You kill me. And thanks for the stockings. I love a lot of stockings. Well, good night.

WILLY   Good night. And keep your pores open!

THE WOMAN   Oh, Willy!

(THE WOMAN *bursts out laughing, and* LINDA'S *laughter blends in.* THE WOMAN *disappears into the dark. Now the area at the kitchen table brightens.* LINDA *is sitting where she was at the kitchen table, but now is mending a pair of her silk stockings.*)

LINDA   You are, Willy. The handsomest man. You've got no reason to feel that—

WILLY (*coming out of* THE WOMAN'S *dimming area and going over to Linda*)   I'll make it all up to you, Linda, I'll—

LINDA   There's nothing to make up, dear. You're doing fine, better than—

WILLY (*noticing her mending*)   What's that?

LINDA   Just mending my stockings. They're so expensive—

WILLY (*angrily, taking them from her*)   I won't have you mending stockings in this house! Now throw them out!

(LINDA *puts the stockings in her pocket.*)

BERNARD (*entering on the run*)   Where is he? If he doesn't study!

WILLY (*moving to the forestage, with great agitation*)   You'll give him the answers!

BERNARD   I do, but I can't on a Regents! That's a state exam! They're liable to arrest me!

WILLY   Where is he? I'll whip him, I'll whip him!

LINDA   And he'd better give back that football, Willy, it's not nice.

WILLY   Biff! Where is he? Why is he taking everything?

LINDA   He's too rough with the girls, Willy. All the mothers are afraid of him!

WILLY   I'll whip him!

BERNARD   He's driving the car without a license!

(THE WOMAN'S *laugh is heard.*)

WILLY   Shut up!

LINDA   All the mothers—

WILLY   Shut up!

BERNARD (*backing quietly away and out*)   Mr. Birnbaum says he's stuck up.

WILLY   Get outa here!

BERNARD   If he doesn't buckle down he'll flunk math! (*He goes off.*)

LINDA   He's right, Willy, you've gotta—

WILLY (*exploding at her*)   There's nothing the matter with him! You want him to be a worm like Bernard? He's got spirit, personality . . .

(*As he speaks,* LINDA, *almost in tears, exits into the living-room.* WILLY *is alone in the kitchen, wilting and staring. The leaves are gone. It is night again, and the apartment houses look down from behind.*)

WILLY   Loaded with it. Loaded! What is he stealing? He's giving it back, isn't he? Why is he stealing? What did I tell him? I never in my life told him anything but decent things.

(HAPPY *in pajamas has come down the stairs;* WILLY *suddenly becomes aware of* HAPPY'S *presence.*)

HAPPY   Let's go now, come on.

WILLY (*sitting down at the kitchen table*)   Huh! Why did she have to wax the floors herself? Everytime she waxes the floors she keels over. She knows that!

HAPPY   Shh! Take it easy. What brought you back tonight?

WILLY   I got an awful scare. Nearly hit a kid in Yonkers. God! Why didn't I go to Alaska with my brother Ben that time! Ben! That man was a genius, that man was success incarnate! What a mistake! He begged me to go.

HAPPY   Well, there's no use in—

WILLY   You guys! There was a man started with the clothes on his back and ended up with diamond mines!

HAPPY   Boy, someday I'd like to know how he did it.

WILLY   What's the mystery? The man knew what he wanted and went out and got it! Walked into a jungle, and comes out, the age of twenty-one, and he's rich! The world is an oyster, but you don't crack it open on a mattress!

HAPPY   Pop, I told you I'm gonna retire you for life.

WILLY   You'll retire me for life on seventy goddam dollars a week? And your women and your car and your apartment, and you'll retire me for life! Christ's sake, I couldn't get past Yonkers today! Where are you guys, where are you? The woods are burning! I can't drive a car!

(CHARLEY *has appeared in the doorway. He is a large man, slow of speech, laconic, immovable. In all he says, despite what he says, there is pity, and, now, trepidation. He has a robe over pajamas, slippers on his feet. He enters the kitchen.*)

CHARLEY   Everything all right?

HAPPY   Yeah, Charley, everything's . . .

WILLY   What's the matter?

CHARLEY   I heard some noise. I thought something happened. Can't we do something about the walls? You sneeze in here, and in my house hats blow off.

HAPPY   Let's go to bed, Dad. Come on.

(CHARLEY *signals to* HAPPY *to go.*)

WILLY   You go ahead, I'm not tired at the moment.

HAPPY (*to* WILLY)   Take it easy, huh? (*He exits.*)

WILLY   What're you doin' up?

CHARLEY (*sitting down at the kitchen table opposite* WILLY)   Couldn't sleep good. I had a heartburn.

WILLY   Well, you don't know how to eat.

CHARLEY   I eat with my mouth.

WILLY   No, you're ignorant. You gotta know about vitamins and things like that.

CHARLEY   Come on, let's shoot. Tire you out a little.

WILLY (*hesitantly*)   All right. You got cards?

CHARLEY (*taking a deck from his pocket*)   Yeah, I got them. Someplace. What is it with those vitamins?

WILLY (*dealing*)   They build up your bones. Chemistry.

CHARLEY   Yeah, but there's no bones in a heartburn.

WILLY   What are you talkin' about? Do you know the first thing about it?

CHARLEY   Don't get insulted.

WILLY   Don't talk about something you don't know anything about.

(*They are playing. Pause.*)

CHARLEY   What're you doin' home?

WILLY   A little trouble with the car.

CHARLEY   Oh. (*Pause.*) I'd like to take a trip to California.

WILLY   Don't say.

CHARLEY   You want a job?

WILLY   I got a job, I told you that. (*After a slight pause:*) What the hell are you offering me a job for?

CHARLEY   Don't get insulted.

WILLY   Don't insult me.

CHARLEY   I don't see no sense in it. You don't have to go on this way.

WILLY   I got a good job. (*Slight pause.*) What do you keep comin' in here for?

CHARLEY   You want me to go?

WILLY (*after a pause, withering*)   I can't understand it. He's going back to Texas again. What the hell is that?

CHARLEY   Let him go.

WILLY   I got nothin' to give him, Charley, I'm clean, I'm clean.

CHARLEY   He won't starve. None a them starve. Forget about him.

WILLY   Then what have I got to remember?

CHARLEY   You take it too hard. To hell with it. When a deposit bottle is broken you don't get your nickel back.

WILLY   That's easy enough for you to say.

CHARLEY   That ain't easy for me to say.

WILLY   Did you see the ceiling I put up in the living-room?

CHARLEY   Yeah, that's a piece of work. To put up a ceiling is a mystery to me. How do you do it?

WILLY   What's the difference?

CHARLEY   Well, talk about it.

WILLY   You gonna put up a ceiling?

CHARLEY   How could I put up a ceiling?

WILLY   Then what the hell are you bothering me for?

CHARLEY   You're insulted again.

WILLY   A man who can't handle tools is not a man. You're disgusting.

CHARLEY   Don't call me disgusting, Willy.

(UNCLE BEN, *carrying a valise and an umbrella, enters the forestage from around the right corner of the house. He is a stolid man, in his sixties, with a mustache and an authoritative air. He is utterly certain of his destiny, and there is an aura of far places about him. He enters exactly as* WILLY *speaks.*)

WILLY   I'm getting awfully tired, Ben.

(BEN'S *music is heard.* BEN *looks around at everything.*)

CHARLEY   Good, keep playing; you'll sleep better. Did you call me Ben?

(BEN *looks at his watch.*)

WILLY   That's funny. For a second there you reminded me of my brother Ben.

BEN   I only have a few minutes. (*He strolls, inspecting the place.* WILLY *and* CHARLEY *continue playing.*)

CHARLEY   You never heard from him again, heh? Since that time?

WILLY   Didn't Linda tell you? Couple of weeks ago we got a letter from his wife in Africa. He died.

CHARLEY   That so.

BEN (*chuckling*)   So this is Brooklyn, eh?

CHARLEY   Maybe you're in for some of his money.

WILLY   Naa, he had seven sons. There's just one opportunity I had with that man . . .

BEN   I must make a train, William. There are several properties I'm looking at in Alaska.

WILLY   Sure, sure! If I'd gone with him to Alaska that time, everything would've been totally different.

CHARLEY   Go on, you'd froze to death up there.

WILLY   What're you talking about?

BEN   Opportunity is tremendous in Alaska, William. Surprised you're not up there.

WILLY   Sure, tremendous.

CHARLEY   Heh?

WILLY   There was the only man I ever met who knew the answers.

CHARLEY   Who?

BEN   How are you all?

WILLY (*taking a pot, smiling*)   Fine, fine.

CHARLEY   Pretty sharp tonight.

BEN   Is Mother living with you?

WILLY   No, she died a long time ago.

CHARLEY   Who?

BEN   That's too bad. Fine specimen of a lady, Mother.

WILLY (*to* CHARLEY)   Heh?

BEN   I'd hoped to see the old girl.

CHARLEY   Who died?

BEN   Heard anything from Father, have you?

WILLY (*unnerved*)   What do you mean, who died?

CHARLEY (*taking a pot*)   What're you talkin' about?

BEN (*looking at his watch*)   William, it's half-past eight!

WILLY (*as though to dispel his confusion he angrily stops* CHARLEY'S *hand*)   That's my build!

CHARLEY   I put the ace—

WILLY   If you don't know how to play the game I'm not gonna throw my money away on you!

CHARLEY (*rising*)   It was my ace, for God's sake!

WILLY   I'm through, I'm through!

BEN   When did Mother die?

WILLY   Long ago. Since the beginning you never knew how to play cards.

CHARLEY (*picks up the cards and goes to the door*)   All right! Next time I'll bring a deck with five aces.

WILLY   I don't play that kind of game!

CHARLEY (*turning to him*)   You ought to be ashamed of yourself!

WILLY   Yeah?

CHARLEY   Yeah! (*He goes out.*)

WILLY (*slamming the door after him*)   Ignoramus!

BEN (*as* WILLY *comes toward him through the wall-line of the kitchen*)   So you're William.

WILLY (*shaking* BEN'S *hand*)   Ben! I've been waiting for you so long! What's the answer? How did you do it?

BEN   Oh, there's a story in that.

(LINDA *enters the forestage, as of old, carrying the wash basket.*)

LINDA   Is this Ben?

BEN (*gallantly*)   How do you do, my dear.

LINDA   Where've you been all these years? Willy's always wondered why you—

WILLY (*pulling* BEN *away from her impatiently*)   Where is Dad? Didn't you follow him? How did you get started?

BEN   Well, I don't know how much you remember.

WILLY   Well, I was just a baby, of course, only three or four years old—

BEN   Three years and eleven months.

WILLY   What a memory, Ben!

BEN   I have many enterprises, William, and I have never kept books.

WILLY   I remember I was sitting under the wagon in—was it Nebraska?

BEN   It was South Dakota, and I gave you a bunch of wild flowers.

WILLY   I remember you walking away down some open road.

BEN (*laughing*)   I was going to find Father in Alaska.

WILLY   Where is he?

BEN   At that age I had a very faulty view of geography, William. I discovered after a few days that I was heading due south, so instead of Alaska, I ended up in Africa.

LINDA   Africa!

WILLY   The Gold Coast!

BEN   Principally diamond mines.

LINDA   Diamond mines!

BEN   Yes, my dear. But I've only a few minutes—

WILLY   No! Boys! Boys! (*Young* BIFF *and* HAPPY *appear.*) Listen to this. This is your Uncle Ben, a great man! Tell my boys, Ben!

BEN   Why, boys, when I was seventeen I walked into the jungle, and when I was twenty-one I walked out. (*He laughs.*) And by God I was rich.

WILLY (*to the boys*)   You see what I been talking about? The greatest things can happen!

BEN (*glancing at his watch*)   I have an appointment in Ketchikan Tuesday week.

WILLY   No, Ben! Please tell about Dad. I want my boys to hear. I want them to know the kind of stock they spring from. All I remember is a man with a big beard, and I was in Mamma's lap, sitting around a fire, and some kind of high music.

BEN   His flute. He played the flute.

WILLY   Sure, the flute, that's right!

(*New music is heard, a high, rollicking tune.*)

BEN   Father was a very great and a very wild-hearted man. We would start in Boston, and he'd toss the whole family into the wagon, and then he'd drive the team right across the country; through Ohio, and Indiana, Michigan, Illinois, and all the Western states. And we'd stop in the towns and sell the flutes that he'd made on the way. Great inventor, Father. With one gadget he made more in a week than a man like you could make in a lifetime.

WILLY   That's just the way I'm bringing them up, Ben—rugged, well liked, all-around.

BEN   Yeah? (*To* BIFF) Hit that, boy—hard as you can. (*He pounds his stomach.*)

BIFF   Oh, no, sir!

BEN (*taking boxing stance*)   Come on, get to me! (*He laughs.*)

WILLY   Go to it, Biff! Go ahead, show him!

BIFF   Okay! (*He cocks his fists and starts in.*)

LINDA (*to* WILLY)   Why must he fight, dear?

BEN (*sparring with* BIFF)   Good boy! Good boy!

WILLY   How's that, Ben, heh?

HAPPY   Give him the left, Biff!

LINDA   Why are you fighting?

BEN   Good boy! (*Suddenly comes in, trips* BIFF, *and stands over him, the point of his umbrella poised over* BIFF'S *eye.*)

LINDA   Look out, Biff!

BIFF   Gee!

BEN (*patting* BIFF'S *knee*)   Never fight fair with a stranger, boy. You'll never get out of the jungle that way. (*Taking* LINDA'S *hand and bowing:*) It was an honor and a pleasure to meet you, Linda.

LINDA (*withdrawing her hand coldly, frightened*)   Have a nice—trip.

BEN (*to* WILLY)   And good luck with your—what do you do?

WILLY   Selling.

BEN   Yes. Well . . . (*He raises his hand in farewell to all.*)

WILLY   No, Ben, I don't want you to think . . . (*He takes* BEN'S *arm to show him.*) It's Brooklyn, I know, but we hunt too.

BEN   Really, now.

WILLY   Oh, sure, there's snakes and rabbits and—that's why I moved out here. Why, Biff can fell any one of these trees in no time! Boys! Go right over to where they're building the apartment house and get some sand. We're gonna rebuild the entire front stoop right now! Watch this, Ben!

BIFF   Yes, sir! On the double, Hap!

HAPPY (*as he and* BIFF *run off*)   I lost weight, Pop, you notice?

(CHARLEY *enters in knickers, even before the boys are gone.*)

CHARLEY   Listen, if they steal any more from that building the watchman'll put the cops on them!

LINDA (*to* WILLY)   Don't let Biff . . .

(BEN *laughs lustily.*)

WILLY   You shoulda seen the lumber they brought home last week. At least a dozen six-by-tens worth all kinds of money.

CHARLEY   Listen, if that watchman—

WILLY   I gave them hell, understand. But I got a couple of fearless characters there.

CHARLEY   Willy, the jails are full of fearless characters.

BEN (*clapping* WILLY *on the back, with a laugh at* CHARLEY)   And the stock exchange, friend!

WILLY (*joining in* BEN'S *laughter*)   Where are the rest of your pants?

CHARLEY   My wife bought them.

WILLY   Now all you need is a golf club and you can go upstairs and go to sleep. (*To* BEN) Great athlete! Between him and his son Bernard they can't hammer a nail!

BERNARD (*rushing in*)   The watchman's chasing Biff!

WILLY (*angrily*)   Shut up! He's not stealing anything!

LINDA (*alarmed, hurrying off left*)   Where is he? Biff, dear! (*She exits.*)

WILLY (*moving toward the left, away from* BEN)   There's nothing wrong. What's the matter with you?

BEN   Nervy boy. Good!

WILLY (*laughing*)   Oh, nerves of iron, that Biff!

CHARLEY   Don't know what it is. My new England man comes back and he's bleedin', they murdered him up there.

WILLY   It's contacts, Charley, I got important contacts!

CHARLEY (*sarcastically*)   Glad to hear it, Willy. Come in later, we'll shoot a little casino. I'll take some of your Portland money. (*He laughs at* WILLY *and exits.*)

WILLY (*turning to* BEN)   Business is bad, it's murderous. But not for me, of course.

BEN   I'll stop by on my way back to Africa.

WILLY (*longingly*)   Can't you stay a few days? You're just what I need, Ben, because I—I have a fine position here, but I—well, Dad left when I was such a baby and I never had a chance to talk to him and I still feel—kind of temporary about myself.

BEN   I'll be late for my train.

(*They are at opposite ends of the stage.*)

WILLY   Ben, my boys—can't we talk? They'd go into the jaws of hell for me, see, but I—

BEN   William, you're being first-rate with your boys. Outstanding, manly chaps!

WILLY (*hanging on to his words*)   Oh, Ben, that's good to hear! Because sometimes I'm afraid that I'm not teaching them the right kind of— Ben, how should I teach them?

BEN (*giving great weight to each word, and with a certain vicious audacity*)   William, when I walked into the jungle, I was seventeen. When I walked out I was twenty-one. And, by God, I was rich! (*He goes off into darkness around the right corner of the house.*)

WILLY   . . . was rich! That's just the spirit I want to imbue them with! To walk into a jungle! I was right! I was right! I was right!

(BEN *is gone, but* WILLY *is still speaking to him as* LINDA, *in nightgown and robe, enters the kitchen, glances around for* WILLY, *then goes to the door of the house, looks out and sees him. Comes down to his left. He looks at her.*)

LINDA   Willy, dear? Willy?

WILLY   I was right!

LINDA   Did you have some cheese? (*He can't answer.*) It's very late, darling. Come to bed, heh?

WILLY (*looking straight up*)   Gotta break your neck to see a star in this yard.

LINDA   You coming in?

WILLY   Whatever happened to that diamond watch fob? Remember? When Ben came from Africa that time? Didn't he give me a watch fob with a diamond in it?

LINDA   You pawned it, dear. Twelve, thirteen years ago. For Biff's radio correspondence course.

WILLY   Gee, that was a beautiful thing. I'll take a walk.

LINDA   But you're in your slippers.

WILLY (*starting to go around the house at the left*)   I was right! I was! (*Half to* LINDA, *as he goes, shaking his head*) What a man! There was a man worth talking to. I was right!

LINDA (*calling after* WILLY)   But in your slippers, Willy!

(WILLY *is almost gone when* BIFF, *in his pajamas, comes down the stairs and enters the kitchen.*)

BIFF   What is he doing out there?

LINDA   Sh!

BIFF   God Almighty, Mom, how long has he been doing this?

LINDA   Don't, he'll hear you.

BIFF   What the hell is the matter with him?

LINDA   It'll pass by morning.

BIFF   Shouldn't we do anything?

LINDA   Oh, my dear, you should do a lot of things, but there's nothing to do, so go to sleep.

(HAPPY *comes down the stair and sits on the steps.*)

HAPPY   I never heard him so loud, Mom.

LINDA   Well, come around more often; you'll hear him. (*She sits down at the table and mends the lining of* WILLY'S *jacket.*)

BIFF   Why didn't you ever write me about this, Mom?

LINDA   How would I write to you? For over three months you had no address.

BIFF   I was on the move. But you know I thought of you all the time. You know that, don't you, pal?

LINDA   I know, dear, I know. But he likes to have a letter. Just to know that there's still a possibility for better things.

BIFF   He's not like this all the time, is he?

LINDA   It's when you come home he's always the worst.

BIFF   When I come home?

LINDA   When you write you're coming, he's all smiles, and talks about the future, and—he's just wonderful. And then the closer you seem to come, the more shaky he gets, and then, by the time you get here, he's arguing, and he seems angry at you. I think it's just that maybe he can't bring himself to—to open up to you. Why are you so hateful to each other? Why is that?

BIFF (*evasively*)   I'm not hateful, Mom.

LINDA   But you no sooner come in the door than you're fighting!

BIFF   I don't know why. I mean to change. I'm tryin', Mom, you understand?

LINDA   Are you home to stay now?

BIFF   I don't know. I want to look around, see what's doin'.

LINDA   Biff, you can't look around all your life, can you?

BIFF   I just can't take hold, Mom. I can't take hold of some kind of a life.

LINDA   Biff, a man is not a bird, to come and go with the springtime.

BIFF   Your hair . . . (*He touches her hair.*) Your hair got so gray.

LINDA   Oh, it's been gray since you were in high school. I just stopped dyeing it, that's all.

BIFF   Dye it again, will ya? I don't want my pal looking old. (*He smiles.*)

LINDA   You're such a boy! You think you can go away for a year and . . . You've got to get it into your head now that one day you'll knock on this door and there'll be strange people here—

BIFF   What are you talking about? You're not even sixty, Mom.

LINDA   But what about your father?

BIFF (*lamely*)   Well, I meant him too.

HAPPY   He admires Pop.

LINDA   Biff, dear, if you don't have any feeling for him, then you can't have any feeling for me.

BIFF   Sure I can, Mom.

LINDA   No. You can't just come to see me, because I love him. (*With a threat, but only a threat, of tears:*) He's the dearest man in the world to me, and I won't have anyone making him feel unwanted and low and blue. You've got to make up your mind now, darling, there's no leeway any more. Either he's your father and you pay him that respect, or else you're not to come here. I know he's not easy to get along with—nobody knows that better than me—but . . .

WILLY (*from the left, with a laugh*)   Hey, hey, Biffo!

BIFF (*starting to go out after* WILLY)   What the hell is the matter with him? (HAPPY *stops him.*)

LINDA   Don't—don't go near him!

BIFF   Stop making excuses for him! He always, always wiped the floor with you. Never had an ounce of respect for you.

HAPPY   He's always had respect for—

BIFF   What the hell do you know about it?

HAPPY (*surlily*)   Just don't call him crazy!

BIFF   He's got no character—Charley wouldn't do this. Not in his own house— spewing out that vomit from his mind.

HAPPY   Charley never had to cope with what he's got to.

BIFF   People are worse off than Willy Loman. Believe me, I've seen them!

LINDA   Then make Charley your father, Biff. You can't do that, can you? I don't say he's a great man. Willy Loman never made a lot of money. His name was never in the paper. He's not the finest character that ever lived. But he's a human being, and a terrible thing is happening to him. So attention must be paid. He's not to be allowed to fall into his grave like an old dog. Attention, attention must be finally paid to such a person. You called him crazy—

BIFF   I didn't mean—

LINDA   No, a lot of people think he's lost his—balance. But you don't have to be very smart to know what his trouble is. The man is exhausted.

HAPPY   Sure!

LINDA   A small man can be just as exhausted as a great man. He works for a company thirty-six years this March, opens up unheard-of territories to their trademark, and now in his old age they take his salary away.

HAPPY (*indignantly*)   I didn't know that, Mom.

LINDA   You never asked, my dear! Now that you get your spending money some-place else you don't trouble your mind with him.

HAPPY   But I gave you money last—

LINDA   Christmas time, fifty dollars! To fix the hot water it cost ninety-seven fifty! For five weeks he's been on straight commission, like a beginner, an unknown!

BIFF   Those ungrateful bastards!

LINDA   Are they any worse than his sons? When he brought them business, when he was young, they were glad to see him. But now his old friends, the old buyers that loved him so and always found some order to hand him in a pinch—they're all dead, retired. He used to be able to make six, seven calls a day in Boston. Now he takes his valises out of the car and puts them back and takes them out again and he's exhausted. Instead of walking he talks now. He drives seven hundred miles, and when he gets there no one knows him any more, no one welcomes him. And what goes through a man's mind, driving seven hundred miles home without having earned a cent? Why shouldn't he talk to himself? Why? When he has to go to Charley and borrow fifty dollars a week and pretend to me that it's his pay? How long can that go on? How long? You see what I'm sitting here and waiting for? And you tell me he has no character? The man who never worked a day but for your benefit? When does he get the medal for that? Is this his reward—to turn around at the age of sixty-three and find his sons, who he loved better than his life, one a philandering bum—

HAPPY   Mom!

LINDA   That's all you are, my baby! (*To* BIFF:) And you! What happened to the love you had for him? You were such pals! How you used to talk to him on the phone every night! How lonely he was till he could come home to you!

BIFF   All right, Mom. I'll live here in my room, and I'll get a job. I'll keep away from him, that's all.

LINDA   No, Biff. You can't stay here and fight all the time.

BIFF   He threw me out of this house, remember that.

LINDA   Why did he do that? I never knew why.

BIFF   Because I know he's a fake and he doesn't like anybody around who knows!

LINDA   Why a fake? In what way? What do you mean?

BIFF   Just don't lay it all at my feet. It's between me and him—that's all I have to say. I'll chip in from now on. He'll settle for half my pay check. He'll be all right. I'm going to bed. (*He starts for the stairs.*)

LINDA   He won't be all right.

BIFF (*turning on the stairs, furiously*)   I hate this city and I'll stay here. Now what do you want?

LINDA   He's dying, Biff.

(*Happy turns quickly to her, shocked.*)

BIFF (*after a pause*)   Why is he dying?

LINDA   He's been trying to kill himself.

BIFF (*with great horror*)   How?

LINDA   I live from day to day.

BIFF   What're you talking about?

LINDA   Remember I wrote you that he smashed up the car again? In February?

BIFF   Well?

LINDA   The insurance inspector came. He said that they have evidence. That all these accidents in the last year—weren't—weren't—accidents.

HAPPY   How can they tell that? That's a lie.

LINDA   It seems there's a woman . . . (*She takes a breath as*)

⎧ BIFF (*sharply but contained*)   What woman?
⎨
⎩ LINDA (*simultaneously*)   . . . and this woman . . .

LINDA   What?

BIFF   Nothing. Go ahead.

LINDA   What did you say?

BIFF   Nothing. I just said what woman?

HAPPY   What about her?

LINDA   Well, it seems she was walking down the road and saw his car. She says that he wasn't driving fast at all, and that he didn't skid. She says he came to that little bridge, and then deliberately smashed into the railing, and it was only the shallowness of the water that saved him.

BIFF   Oh, no, he probably just fell asleep again.

LINDA   I don't think he fell asleep.

BIFF   Why not?

LINDA   Last month . . . (*with great difficulty:*) Oh, boys, it's so hard to say a thing like this! He's just a big stupid man to you, but I tell you there's more good in him than in many other people. (*She chokes, wipes her eyes.*) I was looking for a fuse. The lights blew out, and I went down the cellar. And behind the fuse box— it happened to fall out—was a length of rubber pipe—just short.

HAPPY   No kidding?

LINDA   There's a little attachment on the end of it. I knew right away. And sure enough, on the bottom of the water heater there's a new little nipple on the gas pipe.

HAPPY   (*angrily*)   That—jerk.

BIFF   Did you have it taken off?

LINDA   I'm—I'm ashamed to. How can I mention it to him? Every day I go down and take away that little rubber pipe. But, when he comes home, I put it back where it was. How can I insult him that way? I don't know what to do. I live from day to day, boys. I tell you, I know every thought in his mind. It sounds so old-fashioned and silly, but I tell you he put his whole life into you and you've turned your backs on him. (*She is bent over in the chair, weeping, her face in her hands.*) Biff, I swear to God! Biff, his life is in your hands!

HAPPY   (*to* BIFF)   How do you like that damned fool!

BIFF   (*kissing her*)   All right, pal, all right. It's all settled now. I've been remiss. I know that, Mom. But now I'll stay, and I swear to you, I'll apply myself. (*Kneeling in front of her, in a fever of self-reproach:*) It's just—you see, Mom, I don't fit in business. Not that I won't try. I'll try, and I'll make good.

HAPPY   Sure you will. The trouble with you in business was you never tried to please people.

BIFF   I know, I—

HAPPY   Like when you worked for Harrison's. Bob Harrison said you were tops, and then you go and do some damn fool thing like whistling whole songs in the elevator like a comedian.

BIFF   (*against* HAPPY)   So what? I like to whistle sometimes.

HAPPY   You don't raise a guy to a responsible job who whistles in the elevator!

LINDA   Well, don't argue about it now.

HAPPY   Like when you'd go off and swim in the middle of the day instead of taking the line around.

BIFF (*his resentment rising*)   Well, don't you run off? You take off sometimes, don't you? On a nice summer day?

HAPPY   Yeah, but I cover myself!

LINDA   Boys!

HAPPY   If I'm going to take a fade the boss can call any number where I'm supposed to be and they'll swear to him that I just left. I'll tell you something that I hate to say, Biff, but in the business world some of them think you're crazy.

BIFF (*angered*)   Screw the business world!

HAPPY   All right, screw it! Great, but cover yourself!

LINDA   Hap, Hap!

BIFF   I don't care what they think! They've laughed at Dad for years, and you know why? Because we don't belong in this nut-house of a city! We should be mixing cement on some open plain, or—or carpenters. A carpenter is allowed to whistle!

(WILLY *walks in from the entrance of the house, at left.*)

WILLY   Even your grandfather was better than a carpenter. (*Pause. They watch him.*) You never grew up. Bernard does not whistle in the elevator, I assure you.

BIFF (*as though to laugh* WILLY *out of it*)   Yeah, but you do, Pop.

WILLY   I never in my life whistled in an elevator! And who in the business world thinks I'm crazy?

BIFF   I didn't mean it like that, Pop. Now don't make a whole thing out of it, will ya?

WILLY   Go back to the West! Be a carpenter, a cowboy, enjoy yourself!

LINDA   Willy, he was just saying—

WILLY   I heard what he said!

HAPPY (*trying to quiet* WILLY)   Hey, Pop, come on now . . .

WILLY (*continuing over* HAPPY'S *line*)   They laugh at me, heh? Go to Filene's, go to the Hub, go to Slattery's, Boston. Call out the name Willy Loman and see what happens! Big shot!

BIFF   All right, Pop.

WILLY   Big!

BIFF   All right!

WILLY   Why do you always insult me?

BIFF   I didn't say a word. (*To* LINDA:) Did I say a word?

LINDA   He didn't say anything, Willy.

WILLY (*going to the doorway of the living-room*)   All right, good night, good night.

LINDA   Willy, dear, he just decided . . .

WILLY (*to* BIFF)   If you get tired hanging around tomorrow, paint the ceiling I put up in the living-room.

BIFF   I'm leaving early tomorrow.

HAPPY   He's going to see Bill Oliver, Pop.

WILLY (*interestedly*)   Oliver? For what?

BIFF (*with reserve, but trying, trying*)   He always said he'd stake me. I'd like to go into business, so maybe I can take him up on it.

LINDA   Isn't that wonderful?

WILLY   Don't interrupt. What's wonderful about it? There's fifty men in the City of New York who'd stake him. (*To* BIFF:) Sporting goods?

BIFF   I guess so. I know something about it and—

WILLY   He knows something about it! You know sporting goods better than Spalding, for God's sake! How much is he giving you?

BIFF   I don't know, I didn't even see him yet, but—

WILLY   Then what're you talkin' about?

BIFF (*getting angry*)   Well, all I said was I'm gonna see him, that's all!

WILLY (turning away)   Ah, you're counting your chickens again.

BIFF (*starting left for the stairs*)   Oh, Jesus, I'm going to sleep!

WILLY (*calling after him*)   Don't curse in this house!

BIFF (*turning*)   Since when did you get so clean?

HAPPY (*trying to stop them*)   Wait a . . .

WILLY   Don't use that language to me! I won't have it!

HAPPY (*grabbing* BIFF, *shouts*)   Wait a minute! I got an idea. I got a feasible idea. Come here, Biff, let's talk this over now, let's talk some sense here. When I was down in Florida last time, I thought of a great idea to sell sporting goods. It just came back to me. You and I, Biff—we have a line, the Loman Line. We train a couple of weeks, and put on a couple of exhibitions, see?

WILLY   That's an idea!

HAPPY   Wait! We form two basketball teams, see? Two water-polo teams. We play each other. It's a million dollars' worth of publicity. Two brothers, see? The Loman Brothers. Displays in the Royal Palms—all the hotels. And banners over the ring and the basketball court: "Loman Brothers." Baby, we could sell sporting goods!

WILLY   That is a one-million-dollar idea!

LINDA   Marvelous!

BIFF   I'm in great shape as far as that's concerned.

HAPPY   And the beauty of it is, Biff, it wouldn't be like a business. We'd be out playin' ball again . . .

BIFF (*enthused*)   Yeah, that's . . .

WILLY   Million-dollar . . .

HAPPY   And you wouldn't get fed up with it, Biff. It'd be the family again. There'd be the old honor, and comradeship, and if you wanted to go off for a swim or somethin'—well, you'd do it! Without some smart cooky gettin' up ahead of you!

WILLY   Lick the world! You guys together could absolutely lick the civilized world.

BIFF   I'll see Oliver tomorrow. Hap, if we could work that out . . .

LINDA   Maybe things are beginning to—

WILLY (*wildly enthused, to* LINDA)   Stop interrupting! (*To* BIFF) But don't wear sport jacket and slacks when you see Oliver.

BIFF   No, I'll—

WILLY   A business suit, and talk as little as possible, and don't crack any jokes.

BIFF   He did like me. Always liked me.

LINDA   He loved you!

WILLY (*to* LINDA)   Will you stop! (*To* BIFF:) Walk in very serious. You are not applying for a boy's job. Money is to pass. Be quiet, fine, and serious. Everybody likes a kidder, but nobody lends him money.

HAPPY   I'll try to get some myself, Biff. I'm sure I can.

WILLY   I see great things for you kids, I think your troubles are over. But remember, start big and you'll end big. Ask for fifteen. How much you gonna ask for?

BIFF   Gee, I don't know—

WILLY   And don't say "Gee." "Gee" is a boy's word. A man walking in for fifteen thousand dollars does not say "Gee!"

BIFF   Ten, I think, would be top though.

WILLY   Don't be so modest. You always started too low. Walk in with a big laugh. Don't look worried. Start off with a couple of your good stories to lighten things up. It's not what you say, it's how you say it—because personality always wins the day.

LINDA   Oliver always thought the highest of him—

WILLY   Will you let me talk?

BIFF   Don't yell at her, Pop, will ya?

WILLY (*angrily*)   I was talking, wasn't I?

BIFF   I don't like you yelling at her all the time, and I'm tellin' you, that's all.

WILLY   What're you, takin' over this house?

LINDA   Willy—

WILLY (*turning on her*)   Don't take his side all the time, goddammit!

BIFF (*furiously*)   Stop yelling at her!

WILLY (*suddenly pulling on his cheek, beaten down, guilt ridden*)   Give my best to Bill Oliver—he may remember me. (*He exits through the living-room doorway.*)

LINDA (*her voice subdued*)   What'd you have to start that for? (BIFF *turns away.*) You see how sweet he was as soon as you talked hopefully? (*She goes over to* BIFF.) Come up and say good night to him. Don't let him go to bed that way.

HAPPY   Come on, Biff, let's buck him up.

LINDA   Please, dear. Just say good night. It takes so little to make him happy. Come. (*She goes through the living-room doorway, calling upstairs from within the living-room:*) Your pajamas are hanging in the bathroom, Willy!

HAPPY (*looking toward where* LINDA *went out*)   What a woman! They broke the mold when they made her. You know that, Biff?

BIFF   He's off salary. My God, working on commission!

HAPPY   Well, let's face it: he's no hot-shot selling man. Except that sometimes, you have to admit, he's a sweet personality.

BIFF (*deciding*)   Lend me ten bucks, will ya? I want to buy some new ties.

HAPPY   I'll take you to a place I know. Beautiful stuff. Wear one of my striped shirts tomorrow.

BIFF   She got gray. Mom got awful old. Gee, I'm gonna go in to Oliver tomorrow and knock him for a—

HAPPY   Come on up. Tell that to Dad. Let's give him a whirl. Come on.

BIFF (*steamed up*)   You know, with ten thousand bucks, boy!

HAPPY (*as they go into the living-room*)   That's the talk, Biff, that's the first time I've heard the old confidence out of you! (*From within the living-room, fading off:*) You're gonna live with me, kid, and any babe you want just say the word . . . (*The last lines are hardly heard. They are mounting the stairs to their parents' bedroom.*)

LINDA (*entering her bedroom and addressing* WILLY, *who is in the bathroom. She is straightening the bed for him*)   Can you do anything about the shower? It drips.

WILLY (*from the bathroom*)   All of a sudden everything falls to pieces! Goddam plumbing, oughta be sued, those people. I hardly finished putting it in and the thing . . . (*His words rumble off.*)

LINDA   I'm just wondering if Oliver will remember him. You think he might?

WILLY (*coming out of the bathroom in his pajamas*)   Remember him? What's the matter with you, you crazy? If he'd've stayed with Oliver he'd be on top by now! Wait'll Oliver gets a look at him. You don't know the average caliber any more. The average young man today—(*he is getting into bed*)—is got a caliber of zero. Greatest thing in the world for him was to bum around.

(BIFF *and* HAPPY *enter the bedroom. Slight pause.*)

WILLY (*stops short, looking at* BIFF)   Glad to hear it, boy.

HAPPY   He wanted to say good night to you, sport.

WILLY (*to* BIFF)   Yeah. Knock him dead, boy. What'd you want to tell me?

BIFF   Just take it easy, Pop. Good night. (*He turns to go.*)

WILLY (*unable to resist*)   And if anything falls off the desk while you're talking to him—like a package or something—don't you pick it up. They have office boys for that.

LINDA   I'll make a big breakfast—

WILLY   Will you let me finish? (*To* BIFF:) Tell him you were in the business in the West. Not farm work.

BIFF   All right, Dad.

LINDA   I think everything—

WILLY (*going right through her speech*)   And don't undersell yourself. No less than fifteen thousand dollars.

BIFF (*unable to bear him*)   Okay. Good night, Mom. (*He starts moving.*)

WILLY   Because you got a greatness in you, Biff, remember that. You got all kinds a greatness . . . (*He lies back, exhausted.* BIFF *walks out.*)

LINDA (*calling after* BIFF)   Sleep well, darling!

HAPPY   I'm gonna get married, Mom. I wanted to tell you.

LINDA   Go to sleep, dear.

HAPPY (*going*)   I just wanted to tell you.

WILLY   Keep up the good work. (HAPPY *exits.*) God . . . remember that Ebbets Field game? The championship of the city?

LINDA   Just rest. Should I sing to you?

WILLY   Yeah. Sing to me. (LINDA *hums a soft lullaby.*) When that team came out—he was the tallest, remember?

LINDA   Oh, yes. And in gold.

(BIFF *enters the darkened kitchen, takes a cigarette, and leaves the house. He comes downstage into a golden pool of light. He smokes, staring at the night.*)

WILLY   Like a young god. Hercules—something like that. And the sun, the sun all around him. Remember how he waved to me? Right up from the field, with the representatives of three colleges standing by? And the buyers I brought, and the cheers when he came out—Loman, Loman, Loman! God Almighty, he'll be great yet. A star like that, magnificent, can never really fade away!

(*The light on* WILLY *is fading. The gas heater begins to glow through the kitchen wall, near the stairs, a blue flame beneath red coils.*)

LINDA (*timidly*)   Willy dear, what has he got against you?

WILLY   I'm so tired. Don't talk any more.

(BIFF *slowly returns to the kitchen. He stops, stares toward the heater.*)

LINDA   Will you ask Howard to let you work in New York?

WILLY   First thing in the morning. Everything'll be all right.

(BIFF *reaches behind the heater and draws out a length of rubber tubing. He is horrified and turns his head toward* WILLY'S *room, still dimly lit, from which the strains of* LINDA'S *desperate but monotonous humming rise.*)

WILLY (*staring through the window into the moonlight*)   Gee, look at the moon moving between the buildings!

(BIFF *wraps the tubing around his hand and quickly goes up the stairs.*)

(*Curtain*)

ACT TWO

(Music is heard, gay and bright. The curtain rises as the music fades away. WILLY, *in shirt sleeves, is sitting at the kitchen table, sipping coffee, his hat in his lap.* LINDA *is filling his cup when she can.)*

WILLY   Wonderful coffee. Meal in itself.

LINDA   Can I make you some eggs?

WILLY   No. Take a breath.

LINDA   You look so rested, dear.

WILLY   I slept like a dead one. First time in months. Imagine, sleeping till ten on a Tuesday morning. Boys left nice and early, heh?

LINDA   They were out of here by eight o'clock.

WILLY   Good work!

LINDA   It was so thrilling to see them leaving together. I can't get over the shaving lotion in this house!

WILLY *(smiling)*   Mmm—

LINDA   Biff was very changed this morning. His whole attitude seemed to be hopeful. He couldn't wait to get downtown to see Oliver.

WILLY   He's heading for a change. There's no question, there simply are certain men that take longer to get—solidified. How did he dress?

LINDA   His blue suit. He's so handsome in that suit. He could be a—anything in that suit!

*(WILLY *gets up from the table.* LINDA *holds his jacket for him.)*

WILLY   There's no question, no question at all. Gee, on the way home tonight I'd like to buy some seeds.

LINDA *(laughing)*   That'd be wonderful. But not enough sun gets back there. Nothing'll grow any more.

WILLY   You wait, kid, before it's all over we're gonna get a little place out in the country, and I'll raise some vegetables, a couple of chickens . . .

LINDA   You'll do it yet, dear.

*(WILLY *walks out of his jacket.* LINDA *follows him.)*

WILLY   And they'll get married, and come for a weekend. I'd build a little guest house. 'Cause I got so many fine tools, all I'd need would be a little lumber and some peace of mind.

LINDA *(joyfully)*   I sewed the lining . . .

WILLY   I could build two guest houses, so they'd both come. Did he decide how much he's going to ask Oliver for?

LINDA (*getting him into the jacket*)   He didn't mention it, but I imagine ten or fifteen thousand. You going to talk to Howard today?

WILLY   Yeah. I'll put it to him straight and simple. He'll just have to take me off the road.

LINDA   And Willy, don't forget to ask for a little advance, because we've got the insurance premium. It's the grace period now.

WILLY   That's a hundred . . . ?

LINDA   A hundred and eight, sixty-eight. Because we're a little short again.

WILLY   Why are we short?

LINDA   Well, you had the motor job on the car . . .

WILLY   That goddam Studebaker!

LINDA   And you got one more payment on the refrigerator . . .

WILLY   But it just broke again!

LINDA   Well, it's old, dear.

WILLY   I told you we should've bought a well-advertised machine. Charley bought a General Electric and it's twenty years old and it's still good, that son-of-a-bitch.

LINDA   But, Willy—

WILLY   Whoever heard of a Hastings refrigerator? Once in my life I would like to own something outright before it's broken! I'm always in a race with the junkyard! I just finished paying for the car and it's on its last legs. The refrigerator consumes belts like a goddam maniac. They time those things. They time them so when you finally paid for them, they're used up.

LINDA (*buttoning up his jacket as he unbuttons it*)   All told, about two hundred dollars would carry us, dear. But that includes the last payment on the mortgage. After this payment, Willy, the house belongs to us.

WILLY   It's twenty-five years!

LINDA   Biff was nine years old when we bought it.

WILLY   Well, that's a great thing. To weather a twenty-five year mortgage is—

LINDA   It's an accomplishment.

WILLY   All the cement, the lumber, the reconstruction I put in this house! There ain't a crack to be found in it any more.

LINDA   Well, it served its purpose.

WILLY   What purpose? Some stranger'll come along, move in, and that's that. If only Biff would take this house, and raise a family . . . (*He starts to go.*) Good-by, I'm late.

LINDA (*suddenly remembering*)   Oh, I forgot! You're supposed to meet them for dinner.

WILLY   Me?

LINDA   At Frank's Chop House on Forty-eighth near Sixth Avenue.

WILLY   Is that so! How about you?

LINDA   No, just the three of you. They're gonna blow you to a big meal!

WILLY   Don't say! Who thought of that?

LINDA   Biff came to me this morning, Willy, and he said, "Tell Dad, we want to blow him to a big meal." Be there six o'clock. You and your two boys are going to have dinner.

WILLY   Gee whiz! That's really somethin'. I'm gonna knock Howard for a loop, kid. I'll get an advance, and I'll come home with a New York job. Goddammit, now I'm gonna do it!

LINDA   Oh, that's the spirit, Willy!

WILLY   I will never get behind a wheel the rest of my life!

LINDA   It's changing, Willy, I can feel it changing!

WILLY   Beyond a question. G'by, I'm late. (*He starts to go again.*)

LINDA   (*calling after him as she runs to the kitchen table for a handkerchief*)   You got your glasses?

WILLY   (*feels for them, then comes back in*)   Yeah, yeah, got my glasses.

LINDA   (*giving him the handkerchief*)   And a handkerchief.

WILLY   Yeah, handkerchief.

LINDA   And your saccharine?

WILLY   Yeah, my saccharine.

LINDA   Be careful on the subway stairs.

(*She kisses him, and a silk stocking is seen hanging from her hand.* WILLY *notices it.*)

WILLY   Will you stop mending stockings? At least while I'm in the house. It gets me nervous. I can't tell you. Please.

(LINDA *hides the stocking in her hand as she follows* WILLY *across the forestage in front of the house.*)

LINDA   Remember, Frank's Chop House.

WILLY   (*passing the apron*)   Maybe beets would grow out there.

LINDA   (*laughing*)   But you tried so many times.

WILLY   Yeah. Well, don't work hard today. (*He disappears around the right corner of the house.*)

LINDA   Be careful!

(*As* WILLY *vanishes,* LINDA *waves to him. Suddenly the phone rings. She runs across the stage and into the kitchen and lifts it.*)

LINDA   Hello? Oh, Biff! I'm so glad you called, I just . . . Yes, sure, I just told him. Yes, he'll be there for dinner at six o'clock, I didn't forget. Listen, I was just dying to tell you. You know that little rubber pipe I told you about? That he connected to the gas heater? I finally decided to go down the cellar this morning and take it away and destroy it. But it's gone! Imagine? He took it away himself, it isn't there! (*She listens.*) When? Oh, then you took it. Oh—nothing, it's just that I'd hoped he'd taken it himself. Oh, I'm not worried, darling, because this morning he left in such high spirits, it was like the old days! I'm not afraid any more. Did Mr. Oliver see you? . . . Well, you wait there then. And make a nice impression on him, darling. Just don't perspire too much before you see him. And have a nice time with Dad. He may have big news too! . . . That's right, a New York job. And be sweet to him tonight, dear. Be loving to him. Because he's only a little boat looking for a harbor. (*She is trembling with sorrow and joy.*) Oh, that's wonderful, Biff, you'll save his life. Thanks, darling. Just put your arm around him when he comes into the restaurant. Give him a smile. That's the boy . . . Good-by, dear. . . . You got your comb? . . . That's fine. Good-by, Biff dear.

(*In the middle of her speech,* HOWARD WAGNER, *thirty-six, wheels on a small typewriter table on which is a wire-recording machine and proceeds to plug it in. This is on the left forestage. Light slowly fades on* LINDA *as it rises on* HOWARD. HOWARD *is intent on threading the machine and only glances over his shoulder as* WILLY *appears.*)

WILLY   Pst! Pst!

HOWARD   Hello, Willy, come in.

WILLY   Like to have a little talk with you, Howard.

HOWARD   Sorry to keep you waiting. I'll be with you in a minute.

WILLY   What's that, Howard?

HOWARD   Didn't you ever see one of these? Wire recorder.

WILLY   Oh. Can we talk a minute?

HOWARD   Records things. Just got delivery yesterday. Been driving me crazy, the most terrific machine I ever saw in my life. I was up all night with it.

WILLY   What do you do with it?

HOWARD   I bought it for dictation, but you can do anything with it. Listen to this. I had it home last night. Listen to what I picked up. The first one is my daughter. Get this. (*He flicks the switch and "Roll out the Barrel" is heard being whistled.*) Listen to that kid whistle.

WILLY   That is lifelike, isn't it?

HOWARD   Seven years old. Get that tone.

WILLY   Ts. ts. Like to ask a little favor if you . . .

(*The whistling breaks off, and the voice of* HOWARD'S *daughter is heard.*)

HIS DAUGHTER   "Now you, Daddy."

HOWARD   She's crazy for me! (*Again the same song is whistled.*) That's me! Ha! (*He winks.*)

WILLY   You're very good!

(*The whistling breaks off again. The machine runs silent for a moment.*)

HOWARD   Sh! Get this now, this is my son.

HIS SON   "The capital of Alabama is Montgomery; the capital of Arizona is Phoenix; the capital of Arkansas is Little Rock; the capital of California is Sacramento . . ." (*and on, and on.*)

HOWARD (*holding up five fingers*)   Five years old, Willy!

WILLY   He'll make an announcer some day!

HIS SON (*continuing*)   "The capital . . ."

HOWARD   Get that—alphabetical order! (*The machine breaks off suddenly.*) Wait a minute. The maid kicked the plug out.

WILLY   It certainly is a—

HOWARD   Sh, for God's sake!

HIS SON   "It's nine o'clock, Bulova watch time. So I have to go to sleep."

WILLY   That really is—

HOWARD   Wait a minute! The next is my wife.

(*They wait.*)

HOWARD'S VOICE   "Go on, say something." (*Pause.*) "Well, you gonna talk?"

HIS WIFE   "I can't think of anything."

HOWARD'S VOICE   "Well, talk—it's turning."

HIS WIFE (*shyly, beaten*)   "Hello." (*Silence.*) "Oh, Howard, I can't talk into this . . ."

HOWARD (*snapping the machine off*)   That was my wife.

WILLY   That is a wonderful machine. Can we—

HOWARD   I tell you, Willy, I'm gonna take my camera, and my bandsaw, and all my hobbies, and out they go. This is the most fascinating relaxation I ever found.

WILLY   I think I'll get one myself.

HOWARD   Sure, they're only a hundred and a half. You can't do without it. Supposing you wanna hear Jack Benny, see? But you can't be at home at that hour. So you tell the maid to turn the radio on when Jack Benny comes on, and this automatically goes on with the radio . . .

WILLY   And when you come home you . . .

HOWARD   You can come home twelve o'clock, one o'clock, any time you like, and you get yourself a Coke and sit yourself down, throw the switch, and there's Jack Benny's program in the middle of the night!

WILLY   I'm definitely going to get one. Because lots of time I'm on the road, and I think to myself, what I must be missing on the radio!

HOWARD   Don't you have a radio in the car?

WILLY   Well, yeah, but who ever thinks of turning it on?

HOWARD   Say, aren't you supposed to be in Boston?

WILLY   That's what I want to talk to you about, Howard. You got a minute? (*He draws a chair in from the wing.*)

HOWARD   What happened? What're you doing here?

WILLY   Well . . .

HOWARD   You didn't crack up again, did you?

WILLY   Oh, no. No . . .

HOWARD   Geez, you had me worried there for a minute. What's the trouble?

WILLY   Well, tell you the truth, Howard. I've come to the decision that I'd rather not travel any more.

HOWARD   Not travel! Well, what'll you do?

WILLY   Remember, Christmas time, when you had the party here? You said you'd try to think of some spot for me here in town.

HOWARD   With us?

WILLY   Well, sure.

HOWARD   Oh, yeah, yeah. I remember. Well, I couldn't think of anything for you, Willy.

WILLY   I tell ya, Howard. The kids are all grown up, y'know. I don't need much any more. If I could take home—well, sixty-five dollars a week, I could swing it.

HOWARD   Yeah, but Willy, see I—

WILLY   I tell ya why, Howard. Speaking frankly and between the two of us, y'know— I'm just a little tired.

HOWARD   Oh, I could understand that, Willy. But you're a road man, Willy, and we do a road business. We've only got a half-dozen salesmen on the floor here.

WILLY   God knows, Howard, I never asked a favor of any man. But I was with the firm when your father used to carry you in here in his arms.

HOWARD   I know that, Willy, but—

WILLY   Your father came to me the day you were born and asked me what I thought of the name of Howard, may he rest in peace.

HOWARD   I appreciate that, Willy, but there just is no spot here for you. If I had a spot I'd slam you right in, but I just don't have a single solitary spot.

(*He lookes for his lighter.* WILLY *has picked it up and gives it to him. Pause.*)

WILLY (*with increasing anger*)   Howard, all I need to set my table is fifty dollars a week.

HOWARD   But where am I going to put you, kid?

WILLY   Look, it isn't a question of whether I can sell merchandise, is it?

HOWARD   No, but it's a business, kid, and everybody's gotta pull his own weight.

WILLY (*desperately*)   Just let me tell you a story, Howard—

HOWARD   'Cause you gotta admit, business is business.

WILLY (*angrily*)   Business is definitely business, but just listen for a minute. You don't understand this. When I was a boy—eighteen, nineteen—I was already on the road. And there was a question in my mind as to whether selling had a future for me. Because in those days I had a yearning to go to Alaska. See, there were three gold strikes in one month in Alaska, and I felt like going out. Just for the ride, you might say.

HOWARD (*barely interested*)   Don't say.

WILLY   Oh, yeah, my father lived many years in Alaska. He was an adventurous man. We've got quite a little streak of self-reliance in our family. I thought I'd go out with my older brother and try to locate him, and maybe settle in the North with the old man. And I was almost decided to go, when I met a salesman in the Parker House. His name was Dave Singleman. And he was eighty-four years old, and he'd drummed merchandise in thirty-one states. And old Dave, he'd go up to his room, y'understand, put on his green velvet slippers—I'll never forget—and pick up his phone and call the buyers, and without ever leaving his room, at the age of eighty-four, he made his living. And when I saw that, I realized that selling was the greatest career a man could want. 'Cause what could be more satisfying than to be able to go, at the age of eighty-four, into twenty or thirty different cities, and pick up a phone, and be remembered and loved and helped by so many different people? Do you know? when he died—and by the way he died the death of a salesman, in his green velvet slippers in the smoker of the New York, New Haven and Hartford, going into Boston—when he died, hundreds of salesmen and buyers were at his funeral. Things were sad on a lotta trains for months after that. (*He stands up. Howard has not looked at him.*) In those days there was personality in it, Howard. There was respect, and comradeship, and gratitude in it. Today, it's all cut and dried, and there's no chance for bringing friendship to bear—or personality. You see what I mean? They don't know me any more.

HOWARD (*moving away, to the right*)   That's just the thing, Willy.

WILLY   If I had forty dollars a week—that's all I'd need. Forty dollars, Howard.

HOWARD   Kid, I can't take blood from a stone, I—

WILLY (*desperation is on him now*)   Howard, the year Al Smith was nominated, your father came to me and—

HOWARD (*starting to go off*)   I've got to see some people, kid.

WILLY (*stopping him*)   I'm talking about your father! There were promises made across this desk! You mustn't tell me you've got people to see—I put thirty-four years into this firm, Howard, and now I can't pay my insurance! You can't eat the orange and throw the peel away—a man is not a piece of fruit! (*After a pause:*) Now pay attention. Your father—in 1928 I had a big year. I averaged a hundred and seventy dollars a week in commissions.

HOWARD (*impatiently*)   Now, Willy, you never averaged—

WILLY (*banging his hand on the desk*)   I averaged a hundred and seventy dollars a week in the year of 1928! And your father came to me—or rather, I was in the office here—it was right over this desk—and he put his hand on my shoulder—

HOWARD (*getting up*)   You'll have to excuse me, Willy, I gotta see some people. Pull yourself together. (*Going out:*) I'll be back in a little while.

(*On* HOWARD'S *exit, the light on his chair grows very bright and strange.*)

WILLY   Pull myself together! What the hell did I say to him? My God, I was yelling at him! How could I! (WILLY *breaks off, staring at the light, which occupies the chair, animating it. He approaches this chair, standing across the desk from it.*) Frank, Frank, don't you remember what you told me that time? How you put your hand on my shoulder, and Frank . . . (*He leans on the desk and as he speaks the dead man's name he accidentally switches on the recorder, and instantly*)

HOWARD'S SON   ". . . of New York is Albany. The capital of Ohio is Cincinnati, the capital of Rhode Island is . . ." (*The recitation continues.*)

WILLY (*leaping away with fright, shouting*)   Ha! Howard! Howard! Howard!

HOWARD (*rushing in*)   What happened?

WILLY (*pointing at the machine, which continues nasally, childishly, with the capital cities*)   Shut it off! Shut it off!

HOWARD (*pulling the plug out*)   Look, Willy . . .

WILLY (*pressing his hands to his eyes*)   I gotta get myself some coffee. I'll get some coffee . . .

(WILLY *starts to walk out.* HOWARD *stops him.*)

HOWARD (*rolling up the cord*)   Willy, look . . .

WILLY   I'll go to Boston.

HOWARD   Willy, you can't go to Boston for us.

WILLY   Why can't I go?

HOWARD   I don't want you to represent us. I've been meaning to tell you for a long time now.

WILLY   Howard, are you firing me?

HOWARD   I think you need a good long rest, Willy.

WILLY   Howard—

HOWARD   And when you feel better, come back, and we'll see if we can work something out.

WILLY   But I gotta earn money, Howard. I'm in no position to—

HOWARD   Where are your sons? Why don't your sons give you a hand?

WILLY   They're working on a very big deal.

HOWARD   This is no time for false pride, Willy. You go to your sons and you tell them that you're tired. You've got two great boys, haven't you?

WILLY   Oh, no question, no question, but in the meantime . . .

HOWARD   Then that's that, heh?

WILLY   All right, I'll go to Boston tomorrow.

HOWARD   No, no.

WILLY   I can't throw myself on my sons. I'm not a cripple!

HOWARD   Look, kid, I'm busy this morning.

WILLY (*grasping* HOWARD'S *arm*)   Howard, you've got to let me go to Boston!

HOWARD (*hard, keeping himself under control*)   I've got a line of people to see this morning. Sit down, take five minutes, and pull yourself together, and then go home, will ya? I need the office, Willy. (*He starts to go, turns, remembering the recorder, starts to push off the table holding the recorder.*) Oh, yeah. Whenever you can this week, stop by and drop off the samples. You'll feel better, Willy, and then come back and we'll talk. Pull yourself together, kid, there's people outside.

(HOWARD *exits, pushing the table off left.* WILLY *stares into space, exhausted. Now the music is heard—*BEN'S *music—first distantly, then closer, closer. As* WILLY *speaks,* BEN *enters from the right. He carries valise and umbrella.*)

WILLY   Oh, Ben, how did you do it? What is the answer? Did you wind up the Alaska deal already?

BEN   Doesn't take much time if you know what you're doing. Just a short business trip. Boarding ship in an hour. Wanted to say good-by.

WILLY   Ben, I've got to talk to you.

BEN (*glancing at his watch*)   Haven't the time, William.

WILLY (*crossing the apron to* BEN)   Ben, nothing's working out. I don't know what to do.

BEN   Now, look here, William. I've bought timberland in Alaska and I need a man to look after things for me.

WILLY   God, timberland! Me and my boys in those grand outdoors!

BEN   You've a continent at your doorstep, William. Get out of these cities, they're full of talk and time payments and courts of law. Screw on your fists and you can fight for a fortune up there.

WILLY   Yes, yes! Linda, Linda!

(LINDA *enters as of old, with the wash.*)

LINDA   Oh, you're back?

BEN   I haven't much time.

WILLY   No, wait! Linda, he's got a proposition for me in Alaska.

LINDA   But you've got—(*To* BEN:) He's got a beautiful job here.

WILLY   But in Alaska, kid, I could—

LINDA   You're doing well enough, Willy!

BEN (*to* LINDA)   Enough for what, my dear?

LINDA (*frightened of* BEN *and angry at him*)   Don't say those things to him! Enough to be happy right here, right now. (*To* WILLY, *while* BEN *laughs:*) Why must everybody conquer the world? You're well liked, and the boys love you, and someday—(*to* BEN)—why, old man Wagner told him just the other day that if he keeps it up he'll be a member of the firm, didn't he, Willy?

WILLY   Sure, sure. I am building something with this firm, Ben, and if a man is building something he must be on the right track, mustn't he?

BEN   What are you building? Lay your hand on it. Where is it?

WILLY (*hesitantly*)   That's true, Linda, there's nothing.

LINDA   Why? (*To* BEN) There's a man eighty-four years old—

WILLY   That's right, Ben, that's right. When I look at that man I say, what is there to worry about?

BEN   Bah!

WILLY   It's true, Ben. All he has to do is go into any city, pick up the phone, and he's making his living and you know why?

BEN (*picking up his valise*)   I've got to go.

WILLY (*holding* BEN *back*)   Look at this boy!

(BIFF, *in his high school sweater, enters carrying suitcase.* HAPPY *carries* BIFF'S *shoulder guards, gold helmet, and football pants.*)

WILLY   Without a penny to his name, three great universities are begging for him, and from there the sky's the limit, because it's not what you do, Ben. It's who you know and the smile on your face! It's contacts, Ben, contacts! The whole wealth of Alaska passes over the lunch table at the Commodore Hotel, and that's the wonder, the wonder of this country, that a man can end with diamonds here on the basis of being liked! (*He turns to* BIFF.) And that's why when you get out on that field today it's important. Because thousands of people will be rooting for you and loving you. (*To* BEN, *who has again begun to leave:*) And Ben! when he walks into a business office his name will sound out like a bell and all the doors will open to him! I've seen it, Ben, I've seen it a thousand times! You can't feel it with your hand like timber, but it's there!

BEN   Good-by, William.

WILLY   Ben, am I right? Don't you think I'm right? I value your advice.

BEN   There's a new continent at your doorstep, William. You could walk out rich. Rich! (*He is gone.*)

WILLY   We'll do it here, Ben! You hear me? We're gonna do it here!

(*Young* BERNARD *rushes in. The gay music of the Boys is heard.*)

BERNARD   Oh, gee, I was afraid you left already!

WILLY   Why? What time is it?

BERNARD   It's half-past one!

WILLY   Well, come on, everybody! Ebbets Field next stop! Where the pennants? (*He rushes through the wall-line of the kitchen and out into the living-room.*)

LINDA (*to* BIFF)   Did you pack fresh underwear?

BIFF (*who has been limbering up*)   I want to go!

BERNARD   Biff, I'm carrying your helmet, ain't I?

HAPPY   No, I'm carrying the helmet.

BERNARD   Oh, Biff, you promised me.

HAPPY   I'm carrying the helmet.

BERNARD   How am I going to get in the locker room?

LINDA   Let him carry the shoulder guards. (*She puts her coat and hat on in the kitchen.*)

BERNARD   Can I, Biff? 'Cause I told everybody I'm going to be in the locker room.

HAPPY   In Ebbets Field it's the clubhouse.

BERNARD   I meant the clubhouse. Biff!

HAPPY   Biff!

BIFF (*grandly, after a slight pause*)   Let him carry the shoulder guards.

HAPPY (*as he gives* BERNARD *the shoulder guards*)   Stay close to us now.

(WILLY *rushes in with the pennants.*)

WILLY (*handing them out*)   Everybody wave when Biff comes out on the field. (HAPPY *and* BERNARD *run off.*) You set now, boy?

(*The music has died away.*)

BIFF   Ready to go, Pop. Every muscle is ready.

WILLY (*at the edge of the apron*)   You realize what this means?

BIFF   That's right, Pop.

WILLY (*feeling* BIFF'S *muscles*)   You're comin' home this afternoon captain of the All-Scholastic Championship Team of the City of New York.

BIFF   I got it, Pop. And remember, pal, when I take off my helmet, that touchdown is for you.

WILLY   Let's go! (*He is starting out, with his arm around* BIFF, *when* CHARLEY *enters, as of old, in knickers.*) I got no room for you, Charley.

CHARLEY   Room? For what?

WILLY   In the car.

CHARLEY   You goin' for a ride? I wanted to shoot some casino.

WILLY (*furiously*)   Casino! (*Incredulously:*) Don't you realize what today is?

LINDA   Oh, he knows, Willy. He's just kidding you.

WILLY   That's nothing to kid about!

CHARLEY   No, Linda, what's goin' on?

LINDA   He's playing in Ebbets Field.

CHARLEY   Baseball in this weather?

WILLY   Don't talk to him. Come on, come on! (*He is pushing them out.*)

CHARLEY   Wait a minute, didn't you hear the news?

WILLY   What?

CHARLEY   Don't you listen to the radio? Ebbets Field just blew up.

WILLY   You go to hell! (CHARLEY *laughs. Pushing them out:*) Come on, come on! We're late.

CHARLEY (*as they go*)   Knock a homer, Biff, knock a homer!

WILLY (*the last to leave, turning to* CHARLEY)   I don't think that was funny, Charley. This is the greatest day of his life.

CHARLEY   Willy, when are you going to grow up?

WILLY   Yeah, heh? When this game is over, Charley, you'll be laughing out of the other side of your face. They'll be calling him another Red Grange. Twenty-five thousand a year.

CHARLEY (*kidding*)   Is that so?

WILLY   Yeah, that's so.

CHARLEY   Well, then, I'm sorry, Willy. But tell me something.

WILLY   What?

CHARLEY   Who is Red Grange?

WILLY   Put up your hands. Goddam you, put up your hands!

(CHARLEY, *chuckling, shakes his head and walks away, around the left corner of the stage.* WILLY *follows him. The music rises to a mocking frenzy.*)

WILLY   Who the hell do you think you are, better than everybody else? You don't know everything, you big, ignorant, stupid . . . Put up your hands!

(*Light rises, on the right side of the forestage, on a small table in the reception room of* CHARLEY'S *office. Traffic sounds are heard.* BERNARD, *now mature, sits whistling to himself. A pair of tennis rackets and an overnight bag are on the floor beside him.*)

WILLY (*offstage*)   What are you walking away for? Don't walk away! If you're going to say something say it to my face! I know you laugh at me behind my back. You'll laugh out of the other side of your goddam face after this game. Touchdown! Touchdown! Eighty thousand people! Touchdown! Right between the goal posts.

(BERNARD *is a quiet, earnest, but self-assured young man.* WILLY'S *voice is coming from right upstage now.* BERNARD *lowers his feet off the table and listens.* JENNY, *his father's secretary, enters.*)

JENNY (*distressed*)   Say, Bernard, will you go out in the hall?

BERNARD   What is that noise? Who is it?

JENNY   Mr. Loman. He just got off the elevator.

BERNARD (*getting up*)   Who's he arguing with?

JENNY   Nobody. There's nobody with him. I can't deal with him any more, and your father gets all upset everytime he comes. I've got a lot of typing to do, and your father's waiting to sign it. Will you see him?

WILLY (*entering*)   Touchdown! Touch—(*He sees* JENNY.) Jenny, Jenny, good to see you. How're ya? Workin'? Or still honest?

JENNY   Fine. How've you been feeling?

WILLY   Not much any more, Jenny. Ha, ha! (*He is surprised to see the rackets.*)

BERNARD   Hello, Uncle Willy.

WILLY (*almost shocked*)   Bernard! Well, look who's here! (*He comes quickly, guiltily, to* BERNARD *and warmly shakes his hand.*)

BERNARD   How are you? Good to see you.

WILLY   What are you doing here?

BERNARD   Oh, just stopped by to see Pop. Get off my feet till my train leaves. I'm going to Washington in a few minutes.

WILLY   Is he in?

BERNARD   Yes, he's in his office with the accountant. Sit down.

WILLY (*sitting down*)   What're you going to do in Washington?

BERNARD   Oh, just a case I've got there, Willy.

WILLY   That so? (*Indicating the rackets:*) You going to play tennis there?

BERNARD   I'm staying with a friend who's got a court.

WILLY   Don't say. His own tennis court. Must be fine people, I bet.

BERNARD   They are, very nice. Dad tells me Biff's in town.

WILLY (*with a big smile*)   Yeah, Biff's in. Working on a very big deal, Bernard.

BERNARD   What's Biff doing?

WILLY   Well, he's been doing very big things in the West. But he decided to establish himself here. Very big. We're having dinner. Did I hear your wife had a boy?

BERNARD   That's right. Our second.

WILLY   Two boys! What do you know!

BERNARD   What kind of a deal has Biff got?

WILLY   Well, Bill Oliver—very big sporting-goods man—he wants Biff very badly. Called him in from the West. Long distance, carte blanche, special deliveries. Your friends have their own private tennis court?

BERNARD   You still with the old firm, Willy?

WILLY (*after a pause*)   I'm—I'm overjoyed to see how you made the grade, Bernard, overjoyed. It's an encouraging thing to see a young man really—really—Looks very good for Biff—very—(*He breaks off, then:*) Bernard— (*He is so full of emotion, he breaks off again.*)

BERNARD   What is it, Willy?

WILLY (*small and alone*)   What—what's the secret?

BERNARD   What secret?

WILLY   How—how did you? Why didn't he ever catch on?

BERNARD   I wouldn't know that, Willy.

WILLY (*confidentially, desperately*)   You were his friend, his boyhood friend. There's something I don't understand about it. His life ended after that Ebbets Field game. From the age of seventeen nothing good ever happened to him.

BERNARD   He never trained himself for anything.

WILLY   But he did, he did. After high school he took so many correspondence courses. Radio mechanics; television; God knows what, and never made the slightest mark.

BERNARD (*taking off his glasses*)   Willy, do you want to talk candidly?

WILLY (*rising, faces* BERNARD)   I regard you as a very brilliant man, Bernard. I value your advice.

BERNARD   Oh, the hell with the advice, Willy. I couldn't advise you. There's just one thing I've always wanted to ask you. When he was supposed to graduate, and the math teacher flunked him—

WILLY   Oh, that son-of-a-bitch ruined his life.

BERNARD   Yeah, but, Willy, all he had to do was go to summer school and make up that subject.

WILLY   That's right, that's right.

BERNARD   Did you tell him not to go to summer school?

WILLY   Me? I begged him to go. I ordered him to go!

BERNARD   Then why wouldn't he go?

WILLY   Why? Why! Bernard, that question has been trailing me like a ghost for the last fifteen years. He flunked the subject, and laid down and died like a hammer hit him!

BERNARD   Take it easy, kid.

WILLY   Let me talk to you—I got nobody to talk to. Bernard, Bernard, was it my fault? Y'see? It keeps going around in my mind, maybe I did something to him. I got nothing to give him.

BERNARD   Don't take it so hard.

WILLY   Why did he lay down? What is the story there? You were his friend!

BERNARD   Willy, I remember, it was June, and our grades came out. And he'd flunked math.

WILLY   That son-of-a-bitch!

BERNARD   No, it wasn't right then. Biff just got very angry, I remember, and he was ready to enroll in summer school.

WILLY   (*surprised*)   He was?

BERNARD   He wasn't beaten by it at all. But then, Willy, he disappeared from the block for almost a month. And I got the idea that he'd gone up to New England to see you. Did he have a talk with you then?

(WILLY *stares in silence.*)

BERNARD   Willy?

WILLY   (*with a strong edge of resentment in his voice*)   Yeah, he came to Boston. What about it?

BERNARD   Well, just that when he came back—I'll never forget this, it always mystifies me. Because I'd thought so well of Biff, even though he'd always taken advantage of me. I loved him, Willy, y'know? And he came back after that month and took his sneakers—remember those sneakers with "University of Virginia" printed on them? He was so proud of those, wore them every day. And he took them down in the cellar, and burned them up in the furnace. We had a fist fight. It lasted at least half an hour. Just the two of us, punching each other down the cellar, and crying right through it. I've often thought of how strange it was that I knew he'd given up his life. What happened in Boston, Willy?

(WILLY *looks at him as at an intruder.*)

BERNARD   I just bring it up because you asked me.

WILLY (*angrily*)   Nothing. What do you mean, "What happened?" What's that got to do with anything?

BERNARD   Well, don't get sore.

WILLY   What are you trying to do, blame it on me? If a boy lays down is that my fault?

BERNARD   Now, Willy, don't get—

WILLY   Well, don't—don't talk to me that way! What does that mean, "What happened?"

(CHARLEY *enters. He is in his vest, and he carries a bottle of bourbon.*)

CHARLEY   Hey, you're going to miss that train. (*He waves the bottle.*)

BERNARD   Yeah, I'm going. (*He takes the bottle.*) Thanks, Pop. (*He picks up his rackets and bag.*) Good-by, Willy, and don't worry about it. You know, "If at first you don't succeed . . ."

WILLY   Yes, I believe in that.

BERNARD   But sometimes, Willy, it's better for a man just to walk away.

WILLY   Walk away?

BERNARD   That's right.

WILLY   But if you can't walk away?

BERNARD (*after a slight pause*)   I guess that's when it's tough. (*Extending his hand:*) Good-by, Willy.

WILLY (*shaking* BERNARD'S *hand*)   Good-by, boy.

CHARLEY (*an arm on* BERNARD'S *shoulder*)   How do you like this kid? Gonna argue a case in front of the Supreme Court.

BERNARD (*protesting*)   Pop!

WILLY (*genuinely shocked, pained, and happy*)   No! The Supreme Court!

BERNARD   I gotta run. 'By, Dad!

CHARLEY   Knock 'em dead, Bernard!

(BERNARD *goes off.*)

WILLY (*as* CHARLEY *takes out his wallet*)   The Supreme Court! And he didn't even mention it!

CHARLEY (*counting out money on the desk*)   He don't have to—he's gonna do it.

WILLY   And you never told him what to do, did you? You never took any interest in him.

CHARLEY   My salvation is that I never took any interest in anything. There's some money—fifty dollars. I got an accountant inside.

WILLY   Charley, look . . . (*With difficulty:*) I got my insurance to pay. If you can manage it—I need a hundred and ten dollars.

(CHARLEY *doesn't reply for a moment; merely stops moving.*)

WILLY   I'd draw it from my bank but Linda would know, and I . . .

CHARLEY   Sit down, Willy.

WILLY (*moving toward the chair*)   I'm keeping an account of everything, remember. I'll pay every penny back. (*He sits.*)

CHARLEY   Now listen to me, Willy.

WILLY   I want you to know I appreciate . . .

CHARLEY (*sitting down on the table*)   Willy, what're you doin'? What the hell is goin' on in your head?

WILLY   Why? I'm simply . . .

CHARLEY   I offered you a job. You can make fifty dollars a week. And I won't send you on the road.

WILLY   I've got a job.

CHARLEY   Without pay? What kind of a job is a job without pay? (*He rises.*) Now, look, kid, enough is enough. I'm no genius but I know when I'm being insulted.

WILLY   Insulted!

CHARLEY   Why don't you want to work for me?

WILLY   What's the matter with you? I've got a job.

CHARLEY   Then what're you walkin' in here every week for?

WILLY (*getting up*)   Well, if you don't want me to walk in here—

CHARLEY   I am offering you a job.

WILLY   I don't want your goddam job!

CHARLEY   When the hell are you going to grow up?

WILLY (*furiously*)   You big ignoramus, if you say that to me again I'll rap you one! I don't care how big you are! (*He's ready to fight.*)

(*Pause.*)

CHARLEY (*kindly, going to him*)   How much do you need, Willy?

WILLY   Charley, I'm strapped, I'm strapped. I don't know what to do. I was just fired.

CHARLEY   Howard fired you?

WILLY   That snotnose. Imagine that? I named him. I named him Howard.

CHARLEY   Willy, when're you gonna realize that them things don't mean anything? You named him Howard, but you can't sell that. The only thing you got in this world is what you can sell. And the funny thing is that you're a salesman, and you don't know that.

WILLY   I've always tried to think otherwise, I guess. I always felt that if a man was impressive, and well liked, that nothing—

CHARLEY   Why must everybody like you? Who liked J. P. Morgan? Was he impressive? In a Turkish bath he'd look like a butcher. But with his pockets on he was very well liked. Now listen, Willy, I know you don't like me, and nobody can say I'm in love with you, but I'll give you a job because—just for the hell of it, put it that way. Now what do you say?

WILLY   I—I just can't work for you, Charley.

CHARLEY   What're you, jealous of me?

WILLY   I can't work for you, that's all, don't ask me why.

CHARLEY (*angered, takes out more bills*)   You been jealous of me all your life, you damned fool! Here, pay your insurance. (*He puts the money in Willy's hand.*)

WILLY   I'm keeping strict accounts.

CHARLEY   I've got some work to do. Take care of yourself. And pay your insurance.

WILLY (*moving to the right*)   Funny, y'know? After all the highways, and the trains, and the appointments, and the years, you end up worth more dead than alive.

CHARLEY   Willy, nobody's worth nothin' dead. (*After a slight pause:*) Did you hear what I said?

(WILLY *stands still, dreaming.*)

CHARLEY   Willy!

WILLY   Apologize to Bernard for me when you see him. I didn't mean to argue with him. He's a fine boy. They're all fine boys, and they'll end up big—all of them. Someday they'll all play tennis together. Wish me luck, Charley. He saw Bill Oliver today.

CHARLEY   Good luck.

WILLY (*on the verge of tears*)   Charley, you're the only friend I got. Isn't that a remarkable thing? (*He goes out.*)

CHARLEY   Jesus!

(CHARLEY *stares after him a moment and follows. All light blacks out. Suddenly raucous music is heard, and a red glow rises behind the screen at right.* STANLEY, *a young waiter, appears, carrying a table, followed by* HAPPY, *who is carrying two chairs.*)

STANLEY (*putting the table down*)   That's all right, Mr. Loman, I can handle it myself. (*He turns and takes the chairs from* HAPPY *and places them at the table.*)

HAPPY (*glancing around*)   Oh, this is better.

STANLEY   Sure, in the front there you're in the middle of all kinds a noise. Whenever you got a party, Mr. Loman, you just tell me and I'll put you back here. Y'know, there's a lotta people they don't like it private, because when they go out they like to see a lotta action around them because they're sick and tired to stay in the house by theirself. But I know you, you ain't from Hackensack. You know what I mean?

HAPPY (*sitting down*)   So how's it coming, Stanley?

STANLEY   Ah, it's a dog's life. I only wish during the war they'd a took me in the Army. I coulda been dead by now.

HAPPY   My brother's back, Stanley.

STANLEY   Oh, he come back, heh? From the Far West.

HAPPY   Yeah, big cattle man, my brother, so treat him right. And my father's coming too.

STANLEY   Oh, your father too!

HAPPY   You got a couple of nice lobsters?

STANLEY   Hundred per cent, big.

HAPPY   I want them with the claws.

STANLEY   Don't worry, I don't give you no mice. (HAPPY *laughs.*) How about some wine? It'll put a head on the meal.

HAPPY   No. You remember, Stanley, that recipe I brought you from overseas? With the champagne in it?

STANLEY   Oh, yeah, sure. I still got it tacked up yet in the kitchen. But that'll have to cost a buck apiece anyways.

HAPPY   That's all right.

STANLEY   What'd you, hit a number or somethin'?

HAPPY   No, it's a little celebration. My brother is—I think he pulled off a big deal today. I think we're going into business together.

STANLEY   Great! That's the best for you. Because a family business, you know what I mean?—that's the best.

HAPPY   That's what I think.

STANLEY   'Cause what's the difference? Somebody steals? It's in the family. Know what I mean? (*Sotto voce:*) Like this bartender here. The boss is goin' crazy what kinda leak he's got in the cash register. You put it in but it don't come out.

HAPPY (*raising his head*)   Sh!

STANLEY   What?

HAPPY   You notice I wasn't lookin' right or left, was I?

STANLEY   No.

HAPPY   And my eyes are closed.

STANLEY   So what's the—?

HAPPY   Strudel's comin'.

STANLEY (*catching on, looks around*)   Ah, no, there's no—

(*He breaks off as a furred, lavishly dressed* GIRL *enters and sits at the next table. Both follow her with their eyes.*)

STANLEY   Geez, how'd ya know?

HAPPY   I got radar or something. (*Staring directly at her profile:*) Ooooooooo . . . Stanley.

STANLEY   I think that's for you, Mr. Loman.

HAPPY   Look at that mouth. Oh, God. And the binoculars.

STANLEY   Geez, you got a life, Mr. Loman.

HAPPY   Wait on her.

STANLEY (*going to the* GIRL'S *table*)   Would you like a menu, ma'am?

GIRL   I'm expecting someone, but I'd like a—

HAPPY   Why don't you bring her—excuse me, miss, do you mind? I sell champagne, and I'd like you to try my brand. Bring her a champagne, Stanley.

GIRL   That's awfully nice of you.

HAPPY   Don't mention it. It's all company money. (*He laughs.*)

GIRL   That's a charming product to be selling, isn't it?

HAPPY   Oh, gets to be like everything else. Selling is selling, y'know.

GIRL   I suppose.

HAPPY   You don't happen to sell, do you?

GIRL   No, I don't sell.

HAPPY   Would you object to a compliment from a stranger? You ought to be on a magazine cover.

GIRL (*looking at him a little archly*)   I have been.

(STANLEY *comes in with a glass of champagne.*)

HAPPY   What'd I say before, Stanley? You see? She's a cover girl.

STANLEY   Oh, I could see, I could see.

HAPPY (*to the* GIRL)   What magazine?

GIRL   Oh, a lot of them. (*She takes the drink.*) Thank you.

HAPPY   You know what they say in France, don't you? "Champagne is the drink of the complexion"—Hya, Biff!

(BIFF *has entered and sits with* HAPPY.)

BIFF   Hello, kid. Sorry I'm late.

HAPPY   I just got here. Uh, Miss—?

GIRL   Forsythe.

HAPPY   Miss Forsythe, this is my brother.

BIFF   Is Dad here?

HAPPY   His name is Biff. You might've heard of him. Great football player.

GIRL   Really? What team?

HAPPY   Are you familiar with football?

GIRL   No, I'm afraid I'm not.

HAPPY   Biff is quarterback with the New York Giants.

GIRL   Well, that is nice, isn't it? (*She drinks.*)

HAPPY   Good health.

GIRL   I'm happy to meet you.

HAPPY   That's my name. Hap. It's really Harold, but at West Point they called me Happy.

GIRL (*now really impressed*)   Oh, I see. How do you do? (*She turns her profile.*)

BIFF   Isn't Dad coming?

HAPPY   You want her?

BIFF   Oh, I could never make that.

HAPPY   I remember the time that idea would never come into your head. Where's the old confidence, Biff?

BIFF   I just saw Oliver—

HAPPY   Wait a minute. I've got to see that old confidence again. Do you want her? She's on call.

BIFF   Oh, no. (*He turns to look at the* GIRL.)

HAPPY   I'm telling you. Watch this. (*Turning to the* GIRL:) Honey? (*She turns to him.*) Are you busy?

GIRL   Well, I am . . . but I could make a phone call.

HAPPY   Do that, will you, honey? And see if you can get a friend. We'll be here for a while. Biff is one of the greatest football players in the country.

GIRL (*standing up*)   Well, I'm certainly happy to meet you.

HAPPY   Come back soon.

GIRL   I'll try.

HAPPY   Don't try, honey, try hard.

(*The* GIRL *exits.* STANLEY *follows, shaking his head in bewildered admiration.*)

HAPPY   Isn't that a shame now? A beautiful girl like that? That's why I can't get married. There's not a good woman in a thousand. New York is loaded with them, kid!

BIFF   Hap, look—

HAPPY   I told you she was on call!

BIFF (*strangely unnerved*)   Cut it out, will ya? I want to say something to you.

HAPPY   Did you see Oliver?

BIFF   I saw him all right. Now look, I want to tell Dad a couple of things and I want you to help me.

HAPPY   What? Is he going to back you?

BIFF   Are you crazy? You're out of your goddam head, you know that?

HAPPY   Why? What happened?

BIFF (*breathlessly*)   I did a terrible thing today, Hap. It's been the strangest day I ever went through. I'm all numb, I swear.

HAPPY   You mean he wouldn't see you?

BIFF   Well, I waited six hours for him, see? All day. Kept sending my name in. Even tried to date his secretary so she'd get me to him, but no soap.

HAPPY   Because you're not showin' the old confidence, Biff. He remembered you, didn't he?

BIFF (*stopping* HAPPY *with a gesture*)   Finally, about five o'clock, he comes out. Didn't remember who I was or anything. I felt like such an idiot, Hap.

HAPPY   Did you tell him my Florida idea?

BIFF   He walked away. I saw him for one minute. I got so mad I could've torn the walls down! How the hell did I ever get the idea I was a salesman there? I even believed myself that I'd been a salesman for him! And then he gave me one look and—I realized what a ridiculous lie my whole life has been! We've been talking in a dream for fifteen years. I was a shipping clerk.

HAPPY   What'd you do?

BIFF (*with great tension and wonder*)   Well, he left, see. And the secretary went out. I was all alone in the waiting-room. I don't know what came over me, Hap. The next thing I know I'm in his office—paneled walls, everything. I can't explain it. I—Hap, I took his fountain pen.

HAPPY   Geez, did he catch you?

BIFF   I ran out. I ran down all eleven flights. I ran and ran and ran.

HAPPY   That was an awful dumb—what'd you do that for?

BIFF (*agonized*)   I don't know, I just—wanted to take something, I don't know. You gotta help me, Hap, I'm gonna tell Pop.

HAPPY   You crazy? What for?

BIFF   Hap, he's got to understand that I'm not the man somebody lends that kind of money to. He thinks I've been spiting him all these years and it's eating him up.

HAPPY   That's just it. You tell him something nice.

BIFF   I can't.

HAPPY   Say you got a lunch date with Oliver tomorrow.

BIFF   So what do I do tomorrow?

HAPPY   You leave the house tomorrow and come back at night and say Oliver is thinking it over. And he thinks it over for a couple of weeks, and gradually it fades away and nobody's the worse.

BIFF   But it'll go on forever!

HAPPY   Dad is never so happy as when he's looking forward to something!

(WILLY *enters.*)

HAPPY   Hello, scout!

WILLY   Gee, I haven't been here in years!

(STANLEY *has followed* WILLY *in and sets a chair for him.* STANLEY *starts off but* HAPPY *stops him.*)

HAPPY   Stanley!

(STANLEY *stands by, waiting for an order.*)

BIFF (*going to* WILLY *with guilt, as to an invalid*)   Sit down, Pop. You want a drink?

WILLY   Sure, I don't mind.

BIFF   Let's get a load on.

WILLY   You look worried.

BIFF   N-no. (*To* STANLEY:) Scotch all around. Make it doubles.

STANLEY   Doubles, right. (*He goes.*)

WILLY   You had a couple already, didn't you?

BIFF   Just a couple, yeah.

WILLY   Well, what happened, boy? (*Nodding affirmatively, with a smile:*) Everything go all right?

BIFF (*takes a breath, then reaches out and grasps* WILLY'S *hand*)   Pal . . . (*He is smiling bravely, and* WILLY *is smiling too.*) I had an experience today.

HAPPY   Terrific, Pop.

WILLY   That so? What happened?

BIFF (*high, slightly alcoholic, above the earth*)   I'm going to tell you everything from first to last. It's been a strange day. (*Silence. He looks around, composes himself as best he can, but his breath keeps breaking the rhythm of his voice.*) I had to wait quite a while for him, and—

WILLY   Oliver?

BIFF   Yeah, Oliver. All day, as a matter of cold fact. And a lot of—instances—facts, Pop, facts about my life came back to me. Who was it, Pop? Who ever said I was a salesman with Oliver?

WILLY   Well, you were.

BIFF   No, Dad, I was a shipping clerk.

WILLY   But you were practically—

BIFF (*with determination*)   Dad, I don't know who said it first, but I was never a salesman for Bill Oliver.

WILLY   What're you talking about?

BIFF   Let's hold on to the facts tonight, Pop. We're not going to get anywhere bullin' around. I was a shipping clerk.

WILLY (*angrily*)   All right, now listen to me—

BIFF   Why don't you let me finish?

WILLY   I'm not interested in stories about the past or any crap of that kind because the woods are burning, boys, you understand? There's a big blaze going on all around. I was fired today.

BIFF (*shocked*)   How could you be?

WILLY   I was fired, and I'm looking for a little good news to tell your mother, because the woman has waited and the woman has suffered. The gist of it is that I haven't got a story left in my head, Biff. So don't give me a lecture about facts and aspects. I am not interested. Now what've you got to say to me?

(STANLEY *enters with three drinks. They wait until he leaves.*)

WILLY   Did you see Oliver?

BIFF   Jesus, Dad!

WILLY   You mean you didn't go up there?

HAPPY   Sure he went up there.

BIFF   I did. I—saw him. How could they fire you?

WILLY (*on the edge of his chair*)   What kind of a welcome did he give you?

BIFF   He won't even let you work on commission?

WILLY   I'm out! (*Driving:*) So tell me, he gave you a warm welcome?

HAPPY   Sure, Pop, sure!

BIFF (*driven*)   Well, it was kind of—

WILLY   I was wondering if he'd remember you. (*To* HAPPY:) Imagine, man doesn't see him for ten, twelve years and gives him that kind of a welcome!

HAPPY   Damn right!

BIFF (*trying to return to the offensive*)   Pop, look—

WILLY   You know why he remembered you, don't you? Because you impressed him in those days.

BIFF   Let's talk quietly and get this down to the facts, huh?

WILLY (*as though* BIFF *had been interrupting*)   Well, what happened? It's great news, Biff. Did he take you into his office or'd you talk in the waiting-room?

BIFF   Well, he came in, see, and—

WILLY (*with a big smile*)   What'd he say? Betcha he threw his arm around you.

BIFF   Well, he kinda—

WILLY   He's a fine man. (*To* HAPPY:) Very hard man to see, y'know.

HAPPY (*agreeing*)   Oh, I know.

WILLY (*to* BIFF)   Is that where you had the drinks?

BIFF   Yeah, he gave me a couple of—no, no!

HAPPY (*cutting in*)   He told him my Florida idea.

WILLY   Don't interrupt. (*To* BIFF:) How'd he react to the Florida idea?

BIFF   Dad, will you give me a minute to explain?

WILLY   I've been waiting for you to explain since I sat down here! What happened? He took you into his office and what?

BIFF   Well—I talked. And—and he listened, see.

WILLY   Famous for the way he listens, y'know. What was his answer?

BIFF   His answer was—(*He breaks off, suddenly angry.*) Dad, you're not letting me tell you what I want to tell you!

WILLY (*accusing, angered*)   You didn't see him, did you?

BIFF   I did see him!

WILLY   What'd you insult him or something? You insulted him, didn't you?

BIFF   Listen, will you let me out of it, will you just let me out of it!

HAPPY   What the hell!

WILLY   Tell me what happened!

BIFF (*to* HAPPY)   I can't talk to him!

(*A single trumpet note jars the ear. The light of green leaves stains the house, which holds the air of night and a dream. Young* BERNARD *enters and knocks on the door of the house.*)

YOUNG BERNARD (*frantically*)   Mrs. Loman, Mrs. Loman!

HAPPY   Tell him what happened!

BIFF (*to* HAPPY)   Shut up and leave me alone!

WILLY   No, no! You had to go and flunk math!

BIFF   What math? What're you talking about?

YOUNG BERNARD   Mrs. Loman, Mrs. Loman!

(LINDA *appears in the house, as of old.*)

WILLY (*wildly*)   Math, math, math!

BIFF   Take it easy, Pop!

YOUNG BERNARD   Mrs. Loman!

WILLY (*furiously*)   If you hadn't flunked you'd've been set by now!

BIFF   Now, look, I'm gonna tell you what happened, and you're going to listen to me.

YOUNG BERNARD   Mrs. Loman!

BIFF   I waited six hours—

HAPPY   What the hell are you saying?

BIFF   I kept sending in my name but he wouldn't see me. So finally he . . . (*He continues unheard as light fades low on the restaurant.*)

YOUNG BERNARD   Biff flunked math!

LINDA   No!

YOUNG BERNARD   Birnbaum flunked him! They won't graduate him!

LINDA   But they have to. He's gotta go to the university. Where is he? Biff! Biff!

YOUNG BERNARD   No, he left. He went to Grand Central.

LINDA   Grand—You mean he went to Boston!

YOUNG BERNARD   Is Uncle Willy in Boston?

LINDA   Oh, maybe Willy can talk to the teacher. Oh, the poor, poor boy!

(*Light on house area snaps out.*)

BIFF (*at the table, now audible, holding up a gold fountain pen*)   . . . so I'm washed up with Oliver, you understand? Are you listening to me?

WILLY (*at a loss*)   Yeah, sure. If you hadn't flunked—

BIFF   Flunked what? What're you talking about?

WILLY   Don't blame everything on me! I didn't flunk math—you did! What pen?

HAPPY   That was awful dumb, Biff, a pen like that is worth—

WILLY (*seeing the pen for the first time*)   You took Oliver's pen?

BIFF (*weakening*)   Dad, I just explained it to you.

WILLY   You stole Bill Oliver's fountain pen!

BIFF   I didn't exactly steal it! That's just what I've been explaining to you!

HAPPY   He had it in his hand and just then Oliver walked in, so he got nervous and stuck it in his pocket!

WILLY   My God, Biff!

BIFF   I never intended to do it, Dad!

OPERATOR'S VOICE   Standish Arms, good evening!

WILLY (*shouting*)   I'm not in my room!

BIFF (*frightened*)   Dad, what's the matter? (*He and* HAPPY *stand up.*)

OPERATOR   Ringing Mr. Loman for you!

WILLY   I'm not there, stop it!

BIFF (*horrified, gets down on one knee before* WILLY)   Dad, I'll make good, I'll make good. (WILLY *tries to get to his feet.* BIFF *holds him down.*) Sit down now.

WILLY   No, you're no good, you're no good for anything.

BIFF   I am, Dad, I'll find something else, you understand? Now don't worry about anything. (*He holds up* WILLY's *face:*) Talk to me, Dad.

OPERATOR   Mr. Loman does not answer. Shall I page him?

WILLY (*attempting to stand, as though to rush and silence the Operator*)   No, no, no!

HAPPY   He'll strike something, Pop.

WILLY   No, no . . .

BIFF (*desperately, standing over* WILLY)   Pop, listen! Listen to me! I'm telling you something good. Oliver talked to his partner about the Florida idea. You listening? He—he talked to his partner, and he came to me . . . I'm going to be all right, you hear? Dad, listen to me, he said it was just a question of the amount!

WILLY   Then you . . . got it?

HAPPY   He's gonna be terrific, Pop!

WILLY (*trying to stand*)   Then you got it, haven't you? You got it! You got it!

BIFF (*agonized, holds* WILLY *down*)   No, no. Look, Pop. I'm supposed to have lunch with them tomorrow. I'm just telling you this so you'll know that I can still make an impression, Pop. And I'll make good somewhere, but I can't go tomorrow, see?

WILLY   Why not? You simply—

BIFF   But the pen, Pop!

WILLY   You give it to him and tell him it was an oversight!

HAPPY   Sure, have lunch tomorrow!

BIFF   I can't say that—

WILLY   You were doing a crossword puzzle and accidentally used his pen!

BIFF   Listen, kid, I took those balls years ago, now I walk in with his fountain pen? That clinches it, don't you see? I can't face him like that! I'll try elsewhere.

PAGE'S VOICE   Paging Mr. Loman!

WILLY   Don't you want to be anything?

BIFF   Pop, how can I go back?

WILLY   You don't want to be anything, is that what's behind it?

BIFF (*now angry at* WILLY *for not crediting his sympathy*)   Don't take it that way! You think it was easy walking into that office after what I'd done to him? A team of horses couldn't have dragged me back to Bill Oliver!

WILLY   Then why'd you go?

BIFF   Why did I go? Why did I go! Look at you! Look at what's become of you!

   (*Off left,* THE WOMAN *laughs.*)

WILLY   Biff, you're going to go to that lunch tomorrow, or—

BIFF   I can't go. I've got no appointment!

HAPPY   Biff, for . . . !

WILLY   Are you spiting me?

BIFF   Don't take it that way! Goddammit!

WILLY (*strikes* BIFF *and falters away from the table*)   You rotten little louse! Are you spiting me?

THE WOMAN   Someone's at the door, Willy!

BIFF   I'm no good, can't you see what I am?

HAPPY (*separating them*)   Hey, you're in a restaurant! Now cut it out, both of you! (*The girls enter.*) Hello, girls, sit down.

(THE WOMAN *laughs, off left.*)

MISS FORSYTHE   I guess we might as well. This is Letta.

THE WOMAN   Willy, are you going to wake up?

BIFF (*ignoring* WILLY)   How're ya, miss, sit down. What do you drink?

MISS FORSYTHE   Letta might not be able to stay long.

LETTA   I gotta get up very early tomorrow. I got jury duty. I'm so excited! Were you fellows ever on a jury?

BIFF   No, but I been in front of them! (*The girls laugh.*) This is my father.

LETTA   Isn't he cute? Sit down with us, Pop.

HAPPY   Sit him down, Biff!

BIFF (*going to him*)   Come on, slugger, drink us under the table. To hell with it! Come on, sit down, pal.

(*On* BIFF'S *last insistence,* WILLY *is about to sit.*)

THE WOMAN (*now urgently*)   Willy, are you going to answer the door!

(THE WOMAN'S *call pulls* WILLY *back. He starts right, befuddled.*)

BIFF   Hey, where are you going?

WILLY   Open the door.

BIFF   The door?

WILLY   The washroom . . . the door . . . where's the door?

BIFF (*leading* WILLY *to the left*)   Just go straight down.

(WILLY *moves left.*)

THE WOMAN   Willy, Willy, are you going to get up, get up, get up, get up?

(WILLY *exits left.*)

LETTA   I think it's sweet you bring your daddy along.

MISS FORSYTHE   Oh, he isn't really your father!

BIFF (*at left, turning to her resentfully*)   Miss Forsythe, you've just seen a prince walk by. A fine, troubled prince. A hard-working, unappreciated prince. A pal, you understand? A good companion. Always for his boys.

LETTA   That's so sweet.

HAPPY   Well, girls, what's the program? We're wasting time. Come on, Biff. Gather round. Where would you like to go?

BIFF   Why don't you do something for him?

HAPPY   Me!

BIFF   Don't you give a damn for him, Hap?

HAPPY   What're you talking about? I'm the one who—

BIFF   I sense it, you don't give a good goddam about him. (*He takes the rolled-up hose from his pocket and puts it on the table in front of* HAPPY.) Look what I found in the cellar, for Christ's sake. How can you bear to let it go on?

HAPPY   Me? Who goes away? Who runs off and—

BIFF   Yeah, but he doesn't mean anything to you. You could help him—I can't! Don't you understand what I'm talking about? He's going to kill himself, don't you know that?

HAPPY   Don't I know it! Me!

BIFF   Hap, help him! Jesus . . . help him . . . Help me, help me, I can't bear to look at his face! (*Ready to weep, he hurries out, up right.*)

HAPPY (*starting after him*)   Where are you going?

MISS FORSYTHE   What's he so mad about?

HAPPY   Come on, girls, we'll catch up with him.

MISS FORSYTHE (*as* HAPPY *pushes her out*)   Say, I don't like that temper of his!

HAPPY   He's just a little overstrung, he'll be all right!

WILLY (*off left, as* THE WOMAN *laughs*)   Don't answer! Don't answer!

LETTA   Don't you want to tell your father—

HAPPY   No, that's not my father. He's just a guy. Come on, we'll catch Biff, and, honey, we're going to paint this town! Stanley, where's the check! Hey, Stanley!

(*They exit.* STANLEY *looks toward left.*)

STANLEY (*calling to* HAPPY *indignantly*)   Mr. Loman! Mr. Loman!

(STANLEY *picks up a chair and follows them off. Knocking is heard off left.* THE WOMAN *enters, laughing.* WILLY *follows her. She is in a black slip; he is buttoning his shirt. Raw, sensuous music accompanies their speech.*)

WILLY   Will you stop laughing? Will you stop?

THE WOMAN   Aren't you going to answer the door? He'll wake the whole hotel.

WILLY   I'm not expecting anybody.

THE WOMAN   Whyn't you have another drink, honey, and stop being so damn self-centered?

WILLY   I'm so lonely.

THE WOMAN   You know you ruined me, Willy? From now on, whenever you come to the office, I'll see that you go right through to the buyers. No waiting at my desk any more, Willy. You ruined me.

WILLY   That's nice of you to say that.

THE WOMAN   Gee, you are self-centered! Why so sad? You are the saddest, self-centeredest soul I ever did see-saw. (*She laughs. He kisses her.*) Come on inside, drummer boy. It's silly to be dressing in the middle of the night. (*As knocking is heard:*) Aren't you going to answer the door?

WILLY   They're knocking on the wrong door.

THE WOMAN   But I felt the knocking. And he heard us talking in here. Maybe the hotel's on fire!

WILLY (*his terror rising*)   It's a mistake.

THE WOMAN   Then tell him to go away!

WILLY   There's nobody there.

THE WOMAN   It's getting on my nerves, Willy. There's somebody standing out there and it's getting on my nerves!

WILLY (*pushing her away from him*)   All right, stay in the bathroom here, and don't come out. I think there's a law in Massachusetts about it, so don't come out. It may be that new room clerk. He looked very mean. So don't come out. It's a mistake, there's no fire.

(*The knocking is heard again. He takes a few steps away from her, and she vanishes into the wing. The light follows him, and now he is facing Young* BIFF, *who carries a suitcase.* BIFF *steps toward him. The music is gone.*)

BIFF   Why didn't you answer?

WILLY   Biff! What are you doing in Boston?

BIFF   Why didn't you answer? I've been knocking for five minutes, I called you on the phone—

WILLY   I just heard you. I was in the bathroom and had the door shut. Did anything happen home?

BIFF   Dad—I let you down.

WILLY   What do you mean?

BIFF   Dad . . .

WILLY   Biffo, what's this about? (*Putting his arm around* BIFF:) Come on, let's go downstairs and get you a malted.

BIFF   Dad, I flunked math.

WILLY   Not for the term?

BIFF   The term. I haven't got enough credits to graduate.

WILLY   You mean to say Bernard wouldn't give you the answers?

BIFF   He did, he tried, but I only got a sixty-one.

WILLY   And they wouldn't give you four points?

BIFF   Birnbaum refused absolutely. I begged him, Pop, but he won't give me those points. You gotta talk to him before they close the school. Because if he saw the kind of man you are, and you just talked to him in your way, I'm sure he'd come through for me. The class came right before practice, see, and I didn't go enough. Would you talk to him? He'd like you, Pop. You know the way you could talk.

WILLY   You're on. We'll drive right back.

BIFF   Oh, Dad, good work! I'm sure he'll change it for you!

WILLY   Go downstairs and tell the clerk I'm checkin' out. Go right down.

BIFF   Yes, sir! See, the reason he hates me, Pop—one day he was late for class so I got up at the blackboard and imitated him. I crossed my eyes and talked with a lithp.

WILLY (*laughing*)   You did? The kids like it?

BIFF   They nearly died laughing!

WILLY   Yeah? What'd you do?

BIFF   The thquare root of thixthy twee is . . . (WILLY *bursts out laughing;* BIFF *joins him.*) And in the middle of it he walked in!

(WILLY *laughs and* THE WOMAN *joins in offstage.*)

BIFF   Somebody in there?

WILLY   No, that was next door.

(THE WOMAN *laughs offstage.*)

BIFF   Somebody got in your bathroom!

WILLY   No, it's the next room, there's a party—

THE WOMAN (*enters, laughing. She lisps this*)   Can I come in? There's something in the bathtub, Willy, and it's moving!

(WILLY *looks at* BIFF, *who is staring open-mouthed and horrified at* THE WOMAN.)

WILLY   Ah—you better go back to your room. They must be finished painting by now. They're painting her room so I let her take a shower here. Go back, go back . . . (*He pushes her.*)

THE WOMAN (*resisting*)   But I've got to get dressed, Willy, I can't—

WILLY   Get out of here! Go back, go back . . . (*Suddenly striving for the ordinary:*) This is Miss Francis, Biff, she's a buyer. They're painting her room. Go back, Miss Francis, go back . . .

THE WOMAN   But my clothes, I can't go out naked in the hall!

WILLY (*pushing her offstage*)   Get outa here! Go back, go back!

(BIFF *slowly sits down on his suitcase as the argument continues offstage.*)

THE WOMAN   Where's my stockings? You promised me stockings, Willy!

WILLY   I have no stockings here!

THE WOMAN   You had two boxes of size nine sheers for me, and I want them!

WILLY   Here, for God's sake, will you get outa here!

THE WOMAN (*enters holding a box of stockings*)   I just hope there's nobody in the hall. That's all I hope. (*To* BIFF:) Are you football or baseball?

BIFF   Football.

THE WOMAN (*angry, humiliated*)   That's me too. G'night. (*She snatches her clothes from* WILLY, *and walks out.*)

WILLY (*after a pause*)   Well, better get going. I want to get to the school first thing in the morning. Get my suits out of the closet. I'll get my valise. (BIFF *doesn't move.*) What's the matter? (BIFF *remains motionless, tears falling.*) She's a buyer. Buys for J. H. Simmons. She lives down the hall—they're painting. You don't imagine—(*He breaks off. After a pause:*) Now listen, pal, she's just a buyer. She sees merchandise in her room and they have to keep it looking just so . . . (*Pause. Assuming command:*) All right, get my suits. (BIFF *doesn't move.*) Now stop crying and do as I say. I gave you an order. Biff, I gave you an order! Is that what you do when I give you an order? How dare you cry! (*Putting his arm around* BIFF:) Now look, Biff, when you grow up you'll understand about these things. You mustn't—you mustn't overemphasize a thing like this. I'll see Birnbaum first thing in the morning.

BIFF   Never mind.

WILLY (*getting down beside* BIFF)   Never mind! He's going to give you those points. I'll see to it.

BIFF   He wouldn't listen to you.

WILLY   He certainly will listen to me. You need those points for the U. of Virginia.

BIFF   I'm not going there.

WILLY   Heh? If I can't get him to change that mark you'll make it up in summer school. You've got all summer to—

BIFF (*his weeping breaking from him*)   Dad . . .

WILLY (*infected by it*)   Oh, my boy . . .

BIFF   Dad . . .

WILLY   She's nothing to me, Biff. I was lonely, I was terribly lonely.

BIFF   You—you gave her Mama's stockings! (*His tears break through and he rises to go.*)

WILLY (*grabbing for* BIFF)   I gave you an order!

BIFF   Don't touch me, you—liar!

WILLY   Apologize for that!

BIFF   You fake! You phony little fake! You fake! (*Overcome, he turns quickly and weeping fully goes out with his suitcase.* WILLY *is left on the floor on his knees.*)

WILLY   I gave you an order! Biff, come back here or I'll beat you! Come back here! I'll whip you!

(STANLEY *comes quickly in from the right and stands in front of* WILLY.)

WILLY (*shouts at* STANLEY)   I gave you an order . . .

STANLEY   Hey, let's pick it up, pick it up, Mr. Loman. (*He helps* WILLY *to his feet.*) Your boys left with the chippies. They said they'll see you home.

(*A second waiter watches some distance away.*)

WILLY   But we were supposed to have dinner together.

(*Music is heard,* WILLY'S *theme.*)

STANLEY   Can you make it?

WILLY   I'll—sure, I can make it. (*Suddenly concerned about his clothes:*) Do I—I look all right?

STANLEY   Sure, you look all right. (*He flicks a speck off* WILLY'S *lapel.*)

WILLY   Here—here's a dollar.

STANLEY   Oh, your son paid me. It's all right.

WILLY (*putting it in* STANLEY'S *hand*)   No, take it. You're a good boy.

STANLEY   Oh, no, you don't have to . . .

WILLY   Here—here's some more, I don't need it any more. (*After a slight pause:*) Tell me—is there a seed store in the neighborhood?

STANLEY   Seeds? You mean like to plant?

(*As* WILLY *turns,* STANLEY *slips the money back into his jacket pocket.*)

WILLY   Yes. Carrots, peas . . .

STANLEY   Well, there's hardware stores on Sixth Avenue, but it may be too late now.

WILLY (*anxiously*)   Oh, I'd better hurry. I've got to get some seeds. (*He starts off to the right.*) I've got to get some seeds, right away. Nothing's planted. I don't have a thing in the ground.

(WILLY *hurries out as the light goes down.* STANLEY *moves over to the right after him, watches him off. The other waiter has been staring at* WILLY.)

STANLEY (*to the waiter*)   Well, whatta you looking at?

(*The waiter picks up the chairs and moves off right.* STANLEY *takes the table and follows him. The light fades on this area. There is a long pause, the sound of the flute coming over. The light gradually rises on the kitchen, which is empty.* HAPPY *appears at the door of the house, followed by* BIFF. HAPPY *is carrying a large bunch of long-stemmed roses. He enters the kitchen, looks around for* LINDA. *Not seeing her, he turns to* BIFF, *who is just outside the house door, and makes a gesture with his hands, indicating "Not here, I guess." He looks into the living-room and freezes. Inside,* LINDA, *unseen, is seated,* WILLY'S *coat on her lap. She rises ominously and quietly and moves toward* HAPPY, *who backs up into the kitchen, afraid.*)

HAPPY   Hey, what're you doing up? (LINDA *says nothing but moves toward him implacably.*) Where's Pop? (*He keeps backing to the right, and now* LINDA *is in full view in the doorway to the living-room.*) Is he sleeping?

LINDA   Where were you?

HAPPY (*trying to laugh it off*)   We met two girls, Mom, very fine types. Here, we brought you some flowers. (*Offering them to her:*) Put them in your room, Ma.

(*She knocks them to the floor at* BIFF'S *feet. He has now come inside and closed the door behind him. She stares at* BIFF, *silent.*)

HAPPY   Now what'd you do that for? Mom, I want you to have some flowers—

LINDA (*cutting* HAPPY *off, violently to* BIFF)   Don't you care whether he lives or dies?

HAPPY (*going to the stairs*)   Come upstairs, Biff.

BIFF (*with a flare of disgust, to* HAPPY)   Go away from me! (*To* LINDA:) What do you mean, lives or dies? Nobody's dying around here, pal.

LINDA   Get out of my sight! Get out of here!

BIFF   I wanna see the boss.

LINDA   You're not going near him!

BIFF   Where is he? (*He moves into the living-room and* LINDA *follows.*)

LINDA (*shouting after* BIFF)   You invite him for dinner. He looks forward to it all day— (BIFF *appears in his parents' bedroom, looks around, and exits*)—and then you desert him there. There's no stranger you'd do that to!

HAPPY   Why? He had a swell time with us. Listen, when I—(LINDA *comes back into the kitchen*)—desert him I hope I don't outlive the day!

LINDA   Get out of here!

HAPPY   Now look, Mom . . .

LINDA   Did you have to go to women tonight? You and your lousy rotten whores!

(BIFF *re-enters the kitchen.*)

HAPPY   Mom, all we did was follow Biff around trying to cheer him up! (*To* BIFF:) Boy, what a night you gave me!

LINDA   Get out of here, both of you, and don't come back! I don't want you tormenting him any more. Go on now, get your things together! (*To* BIFF:) You can sleep in his apartment. (*She starts to pick up the flowers and stops herself.*) Pick up this stuff, I'm not your maid any more. Pick it up, you bum, you!

(HAPPY *turns his back to her in refusal.* BIFF *slowly moves over and gets down on his knees, picking up the flowers.*)

LINDA   You're a pair of animals! Not one, not another living soul would have had the cruelty to walk out on that man in a restaurant!

BIFF (*not looking at her*)   Is that what he said?

LINDA   He didn't have to say anything. He was so humiliated he nearly limped when he came in.

HAPPY   But, Mom, he had a great time with us—

BIFF (*cutting him off violently*)   Shut up!

(*Without another word,* HAPPY *goes upstairs.*)

LINDA   You! You didn't even go in to see if he was all right!

BIFF (*still on the floor in front of* LINDA, *the flowers in his hand; with self-loathing*)   No. Didn't. Didn't do a damned thing. How do you like that, heh? Left him babbling in a toilet.

LINDA   You louse. You . . .

BIFF   Now you hit it on the nose! (*He gets up, throws the flowers in the wastebasket.*) The scum of the earth, and you're looking at him!

LINDA   Get out of here!

BIFF   I gotta talk to the boss, Mom. Where is he?

LINDA   You're not going near him. Get out of this house!

BIFF (*with absolute assurance, determination*)   No. We're gonna have an abrupt conversation, him and me.

LINDA   You're not talking to him!

(*Hammering is heard from outside the house, off right.* BIFF *turns toward the noise.*)

LINDA (*suddenly pleading*)   Will you please leave him alone?

BIFF   What's he doing out there?

LINDA   He's planting the garden!

BIFF (*quietly*)   Now? Oh, my God!

(BIFF *moves outside,* LINDA *following. The light dies down on them and comes up on the center of the apron as* WILLY *walks into it. He is carrying a flashlight, a hoe, and a handful of seed packets. He raps the top of the hoe sharply to fix it firmly, and then moves to the left, measuring off the distance with his foot. He holds the flashlight to look at the seed packets, reading off the instructions. He is in the blue of night.*)

WILLY   Carrots . . . quarter-inch apart. Rows . . . one-foot rows. (*He measures it off.*) One foot. (*He puts down a package and measures off.*) Beets. (*He puts down another package and measures again.*) Lettuce. (*He reads the package, puts it down.*) One foot— (*He breaks off as* BEN *appears at the right and moves slowly down to him.*) What a proposition, ts, ts. Terrific, terrific. 'Cause she's suffered, Ben, the woman has suffered. You understand me? A man can't go out the way he came in, Ben, a man has got to add up to something. You can't, you can't— (BEN *moves toward him as though to interrupt.*) You gotta consider, now. Don't answer so quick. Remember, it's a guaranteed twenty-thousand-dollar proposition. Now look, Ben, I want you to go through the ins and outs of this thing with me. I've got nobody to talk to, Ben, and the woman has suffered, you hear me?

BEN (*standing still, considering*)   What's the proposition?

WILLY   It's twenty thousand dollars on the barrelhead. Guaranteed, gilt-edged, you understand?

BEN   You don't want to make a fool of yourself. They might not honor the policy.

WILLY   How can they dare refuse? Didn't I work like a coolie to meet every premium on the nose? And now they don't pay off? Impossible!

BEN   It's called a cowardly thing, William.

WILLY   Why? Does it take more guts to stand here the rest of my life ringing up a zero?

BEN (*yielding*)   That's a point, William. (*He moves, thinking, turns.*) And twenty thousand—that *is* something one can feel with the hand, it is there.

WILLY (*now assured, with rising power*)   Oh, Ben, that's the whole beauty of it! I see it like a diamond, shining in the dark, hard and rough, that I can pick up and touch in my hand. Not like—like an appointment! This would not be another damned-fool appointment, Ben, and it changes all the aspects. Because he thinks I'm nothing, see, and so he spites me. But the funeral— (*Straightening up:*) Ben, that funeral will be massive! They'll come from Maine, Massachusetts, Vermont, New Hampshire! All the old-timers with the strange license plates—that boy will be thunder-struck, Ben, because he never realized—I am known! Rhode Island, New York, New Jersey—I am known, Ben, and he'll see it with his eyes once and for all. He'll see what I am, Ben! He's in for a shock, that boy!

BEN (*coming down to the edge of the garden*)   He'll call you a coward.

WILLY (*suddenly fearful*)   No, that would be terrible.

BEN   Yes. And a damned fool.

WILLY   No, no, he mustn't, I won't have that! (*He is broken and desperate.*)

BEN   He'll hate you, William.

(*The gay music of the Boys is heard.*)

WILLY   Oh, Ben, how do we get back to all the great times? Used to be so full of light, and comradeship, and sleigh-riding in winter, and the ruddiness on his cheeks. And always some kind of good news coming up, always something nice coming up ahead. And never even let me carry the valises in the house, and simonizing, simonizing that little red car! Why, why can't I give him something and not have him hate me?

BEN   Let me think about it. (*He glances at his watch.*) I still have a little time. Remarkable proposition, but you've got to be sure you're not making a fool of yourself.

(BEN *drifts off upstage and goes out of sight.* BIFF *comes down from the left.*)

WILLY (*suddenly conscious of* BIFF, *turns and looks up at him, then begins picking up the packages of seeds in confusion*)   Where the hell is that seed? (*Indignantly:*) You can't see nothing out here! They boxed in the whole goddam neighborhood!

BIFF   There are people all around here. Don't you realize that?

WILLY   I'm busy. Don't bother me.

BIFF (*taking the hoe from* WILLY)   I'm saying good-by to you, Pop. (WILLY *looks at him, silent, unable to move.*) I'm not coming back any more.

WILLY   You're not going to see Oliver tomorrow?

BIFF   I've got no appointment, Dad.

WILLY   He put his arm around you, and you've got no appointment?

BIFF   Pop, get this now, will you? Everytime I've left it's been a fight that sent me out of here. Today I realized something about myself and I tried to explain it to you and I—I think I'm just not smart enough to make any sense out of it for you. To hell with whose fault it is or anything like that. (*He takes* WILLY'S *arm.*) Let's just wrap it up, heh? Come on in, we'll tell Mom. (*He gently tries to pull* WILLY *to left.*)

WILLY (*frozen, immobile, with guilt in his voice*)   No, I don't want to see her.

BIFF   Come on! (*He pulls again, and* WILLY *tries to pull away.*)

WILLY (*highly nervous*)   No, no, I don't want to see her.

BIFF (*tries to look into* WILLY'S *face, as if to find the answer there*)   Why don't you want to see her?

WILLY (*more harshly now*)   Don't bother me, will you?

BIFF   What do you mean, you don't want to see her? You don't want them calling you yellow, do you? This isn't your fault; it's me, I'm a bum. Now come inside! (WILLY *strains to get away.*) Did you hear what I said to you?

(WILLY *pulls away and quickly goes by himself into the house.* BIFF *follows.*)

LINDA (*to* WILLY)   Did you plant, dear?

BIFF (*at the door, to* LINDA)   All right, we had it out. I'm going and I'm not writing any more.

LINDA (*going to* WILLY *in the kitchen*)   I think that's the best way, dear. 'Cause there's no use drawing it out, you'll just never get along.

(WILLY *doesn't respond.*)

BIFF   People ask where I am and what I'm doing, you don't know, and you don't care. That way it'll be off your mind and you can start brightening up again. All right? That clears it, doesn't it? (WILLY *is silent, and* BIFF *goes to him.*) You gonna wish me luck, scout? (*He extends his hand.*) What do you say?

LINDA   Shake his hand, Willy.

WILLY (*turning to her, seething with hurt*)   There's no necessity to mention the pen at all, y'know.

BIFF (*gently*)   I've got no appointment, Dad.

WILLY (*erupting fiercely*)   He put his arm around . . . ?

BIFF   Dad, you're never going to see what I am, so what's the use of arguing? If I strike oil I'll send you a check. Meantime forget I'm alive.

WILLY (*to* LINDA)   Spite, see?

BIFF   Shake hands, Dad.

WILLY   Not my hand.

BIFF   I was hoping not to go this way.

WILLY   Well, this is the way you're going. Good-by.

(BIFF *looks at him a moment, then turns sharply and goes to the stairs.*)

WILLY (*stops him with*)   May you rot in hell if you leave this house!

BIFF (*turning*)   Exactly what is it that you want from me?

WILLY   I want you to know, on the train, in the mountains, in the valleys, wherever you go, that you cut down your life for spite!

BIFF   No, no.

WILLY   Spite, spite, is the word of your undoing! And when you're down and out, remember what did it. When you're rotting somewhere beside the railroad tracks, remember, and don't you dare blame it on me!

BIFF   I'm not blaming it on you!

WILLY   I won't take the rap for this, you hear?

(HAPPY *comes down the stairs and stands on the bottom step, watching.*)

BIFF   That's just what I'm telling you!

WILLY (*sinking into a chair at the table, with full accusation*)   You're trying to put a knife in me—don't think I don't know what you're doing!

BIFF   All right, phony! Then let's lay it on the line. (*He whips the rubber tube out of his pocket and puts it on the table.*)

HAPPY   You crazy—

LINDA   Biff! (*She moves to grab the hose, but* BIFF *holds it down with his hand.*)

BIFF   Leave it there! Don't move it!

WILLY (*not looking at it*)   What is that?

BIFF   You know goddam well what that is.

WILLY (*caged, wanting to escape*)   I never saw that.

BIFF   You saw it. The mice didn't bring it into the cellar! What is this supposed to do, make a hero out of you? This supposed to make me sorry for you?

WILLY   Never heard of it.

BIFF   There'll be no pity for you, you hear it? No pity!

WILLY (*to* LINDA)   You hear the spite!

BIFF   No, you're going to hear the truth—what you are and what I am!

LINDA   Stop it!

WILLY   Spite!

HAPPY (*coming down toward* BIFF)   You cut it now!

BIFF (*to* HAPPY)   The man don't know who we are! The man is gonna know! (*To* WILLY:) We never told the truth for ten minutes in this house!

HAPPY   We always told the truth!

BIFF (*turning on him*)   You big blow, are you the assistant buyer? You're one of the two assistants to the assistant, aren't you?

HAPPY   Well, I'm practically—

BIFF   You're practically full of it! We all are! And I'm through with it. (*To* WILLY:) Now hear this, Willy, this is me.

WILLY   I know you!

BIFF   You know why I had no address for three months? I stole a suit in Kansas City and I was in jail. (*To* LINDA, *who is sobbing:*) Stop crying. I'm through with it.

(LINDA *turns away from them, her hands covering her face.*)

WILLY   I suppose that's my fault!

BIFF   I stole myself out of every good job since high school!

WILLY   And whose fault is that?

BIFF   And I never got anywhere because you blew me so full of hot air I could never stand taking orders from anybody! That's whose fault it is!

WILLY   I hear that!

LINDA   Don't, Biff!

BIFF   It's goddam time you heard that! I had to be boss big shot in two weeks, and I'm through with it!

WILLY   Then hang yourself! For spite, hang yourself!

BIFF   No! Nobody's hanging himself, Willy! I ran down eleven flights with a pen in my hand today. And suddenly I stopped, you hear me? And in the middle of that office building, do you hear this? I stopped in the middle of that building and I saw—the sky. I saw the things that I love in this world. The work and the food and time to sit and smoke. And I looked at the pen and said to myself, what the hell am I grabbing this for? Why am I trying to become what I don't want to be? What am I doing in an office, making a contemptuous, begging fool of myself, when all I want is out there, waiting for me the minute I say I know who I am! Why can't I say that, Willy? (*He tries to make* WILLY *face him, but* WILLY *pulls away and moves to the left.*)

WILLY   (*with hatred, threateningly*)   The door of your life is wide open!

BIFF   Pop! I'm a dime a dozen, and so are you!

WILLY   (*turning on him now in an uncontrolled outburst*)   I am not a dime a dozen! I am Willy Loman, and you are Biff Loman!

(BIFF *starts for* WILLY, *but is blocked by* HAPPY. *In his fury,* BIFF *seems on the verge of attacking his father.*)

BIFF   I am not a leader of men, Willy, and neither are you. You were never anything but a hard-working drummer who landed in the ash can like all the rest of them! I'm one dollar an hour, Willy! I tried seven states and couldn't raise it. A buck an hour! Do you gather my meaning? I'm not bringing home any prizes any more, and you're going to stop waiting for me to bring them home!

WILLY (*directly to* BIFF)   You vengeful, spiteful mut!

(BIFF *breaks from* HAPPY. WILLY, *in fright, starts up the stairs.* BIFF *grabs him.*)

BIFF (*at the peak of his fury*)   Pop, I'm nothing! I'm nothing, Pop. Can't you understand that? There's no spite in it any more. I'm just what I am, that's all.

(BIFF'S *fury has spent itself, and he breaks down, sobbing, holding on to* WILLY, *who dumbly fumbles for* BIFF'S *face.*)

WILLY (*astonished*) What're you doing? What're you doing? (*To* LINDA:) Why is he crying?

BIFF (*crying, broken*) Will you let me go, for Christ's sake? Will you take that phony dream and burn it before something happens? (*Struggling to contain himself, he pulls away and moves to the stairs.*) I'll go in the morning. Put him—put him to bed. (*Exhausted,* BIFF *moves up the stairs to his room.*)

WILLY (*after a long pause, astonished, elevated*) Isn't that—isn't that remarkable? Biff—he likes me!

LINDA He loves you, Willy!

HAPPY (*deeply moved*) Always did, Pop.

WILLY Oh, Biff! (*Staring wildly:*) He cried! Cried to me. (*He is choking with his love, and now cries out his promise:*) That boy—that boy is going to be magnificent!

(BEN *appears in the light just outside the kitchen.*)

BEN Yes, outstanding, with twenty thousand behind him.

LINDA (*sensing the racing of his mind, fearfully, carefully*) Now come to bed, Willy. It's all settled now.

WILLY (*finding it difficult not to rush out of the house*) Yes, we'll sleep. Come on. Go to sleep, Hap.

BEN And it does take a great kind of a man to crack the jungle.

(*In accents of dread,* BEN'S *idyllic music starts up.*)

HAPPY (*his arm around* LINDA) I'm getting married, Pop, don't forget it. I'm changing everything. I'm gonna run that department before the year is up. You'll see, Mom. (*He kisses her.*)

BEN The jungle is dark but full of diamonds, Willy.

(WILLY *turns, moves, listening to* BEN.)

LINDA Be good. You're both good boys, just act that way, that's all.

HAPPY 'Night, Pop. (*He goes upstairs.*)

LINDA (*to* WILLY) Come, dear.

BEN (*with greater force*) One must go in to fetch a diamond out.

WILLY (*to* LINDA, *as he moves slowly along the edge of the kitchen, toward the door*) I just want to get settled down, Linda. Let me sit alone for a little.

LINDA (*almost uttering her fear*) I want you upstairs.

WILLY (*taking her in his arms*) In a few minutes, Linda. I couldn't sleep right now. Go on, you look awful tired. (*He kisses her.*)

BEN Not like an appointment at all. A diamond is rough and hard to the touch.

WILLY Go on now. I'll be right up.

LINDA   I think this is the only way, Willy.

WILLY   Sure, it's the best thing.

BEN   Best thing!

WILLY   The only way. Everything is gonna be—go on, kid, get to bed. You look so tired.

LINDA   Come right up.

WILLY   Two minutes.

(LINDA *goes into the living-room, then reappears in her bedroom.* WILLY *moves just outside the kitchen door.*)

WILLY   Loves me. (*Wonderingly:*) Always loved me. Isn't that a remarkable thing? Ben, he'll worship me for it!

BEN (*with promise*)   It's dark there, but full of diamonds.

WILLY   Can you imagine that magnificence with twenty thousand dollars in his pocket?

LINDA (*calling from her room*)   Willy! Come up!

WILLY (*calling into the kitchen*)   Yes! Yes. Coming! It's very smart, you realize that, don't you, sweetheart? Even Ben sees it. I gotta go, baby. 'By! 'By! (*Going over to* BEN, *almost dancing*) Imagine? When the mail comes he'll be ahead of Bernard again!

BEN   A perfect proposition all around.

WILLY   Did you see how he cried to me? Oh, if I could kiss him, Ben!

BEN   Time, William, time!

WILLY   Oh, Ben, I always knew one way or another we were gonna make it, Biff and I!

BEN (*looking at his watch*)   The boat. We'll be late. (*He moves slowly off into the darkness.*)

WILLY (*elegiacally, turning to the house*)   Now when you kick off, boy, I want a seventy-yard boot, and get right down the field under the ball, and when you hit, hit low and hit hard, because it's important, boy. (*He swings around and faces the audience.*) There's all kinds of important people in the stands, and the first thing you know . . . (*Suddenly realizing he is alone:*) Ben! Ben, where do I . . . ? (*He makes a sudden movement of search.*) Ben, how do I . . . ?

LINDA (*calling*)   Willy, you coming up?

WILLY (*uttering a gasp of fear, whirling about as if to quiet her*) Sh! (*He turns around as if to find his way; sounds, faces, voices, seem to be swarming in upon him and he flicks at them, crying,*) Sh! Sh! (*Suddenly music, faint and high, stops him. It rises in intensity, almost to an unbearable scream. He goes up and down on his toes, and rushes off around the house.*) Shhh!

LINDA   Willy?

(*There is no answer.* LINDA *waits.* BIFF *gets off his bed. He is still in his clothes.* HAPPY *sits up.* BIFF *stands listening.*)

LINDA (*with real fear*)   Willy, answer me! Willy!

(*There is the sound of a car starting and moving away at full speed.*)

LINDA   No!

BIFF (*rushing down the stairs*)   Pop!

(*As the car speeds off, the music crashes down in a frenzy of sound, which becomes the soft pulsation of a single cello string.* BIFF *slowly returns to his bedroom. He and* HAPPY *gravely don their jackets.* LINDA *slowly walks out of her room. The music has developed into a dead march. The leaves of day are appearing over everything.* CHARLEY *and* BERNARD, *somberly dressed, appear and knock on the kitchen door.* BIFF *and* HAPPY *slowly descend the stairs to the kitchen as* CHARLEY *and* BERNARD *enter. All stop a moment when* LINDA, *in clothes of mourning, bearing a little bunch of roses, comes through the draped doorway into the kitchen. She goes to* CHARLEY *and takes his arm. Now all move toward the audience, through the wall-line of the kitchen. At the limit of the apron,* LINDA *lays down the flowers, kneels, and sits back on her heels. All stare down at the grave.*)

REQUIEM

CHARLEY   It's getting dark, Linda.

(LINDA *doesn't react. She stares at the grave.*)

BIFF   How about it, Mom? Better get some rest, heh? They'll be closing the gate soon.

(LINDA *makes no move. Pause.*)

HAPPY (*deeply angered*)   He had no right to do that. There was no necessity for it. We would've helped him.

CHARLEY (*grunting*)   Hmmm.

BIFF   Come along, Mom.

LINDA   Why didn't anybody come?

CHARLEY   It was a very nice funeral.

LINDA   But where are all the people he knew? Maybe they blame him.

CHARLEY   Naa. It's a rough world, Linda. They wouldn't blame him.

LINDA   I can't understand it. At this time especially. First time in thirty-five years we were just about free and clear. He only needed a little salary. He was even finished with the dentist.

CHARLEY   No man only needs a little salary.

LINDA   I can't understand it.

BIFF   There were a lot of nice days. When he'd come home from a trip; or on Sundays, making the stoop; finishing the cellar; putting on the new porch; when he built the extra bathroom; and put up the garage. You know something, Charley, there's more of him in that front stoop than in all the sales he ever made.

CHARLEY   Yeah. He was a happy man with a batch of cement.

LINDA   He was so wonderful with his hands.

BIFF   He had the wrong dreams. All, all, wrong.

HAPPY (*almost ready to fight* BIFF)   Don't say that!

BIFF   He never knew who he was.

CHARLEY (*stopping* HAPPY'S *movement and reply. To* BIFF)   Nobody dast blame this man. You don't understand: Willy was a salesman. And for a salesman, there is no rock bottom to the life. He don't put a bolt to a nut, he don't tell you the law or give you medicine. He's a man way out there in the blue, riding on a smile and a shoeshine. And when they start not smiling back—that's an earthquake. And then you get yourself a couple of spots on your hat, and you're finished. Nobody dast blame this man. A salesman is got to dream, boy. It comes with the territory.

BIFF   Charley, the man didn't know who he was.

HAPPY (*infuriated*)   Don't say that!

BIFF   Why don't you come with me, Happy?

HAPPY   I'm not licked that easily. I'm staying right in this city, and I'm gonna beat this racket! (*He looks at* BIFF, *his chin set.*) The Loman Brothers!

BIFF   I know who I am, kid.

HAPPY   All right, boy. I'm gonna show you and everybody else that Willy Loman did not die in vain. He had a good dream. It's the only dream you can have—to come out number-one man. He fought it out here, and this is where I'm gonna win it for him.

BIFF (*with a hopeless glance at* HAPPY, *bends toward his mother*)   Let's go, Mom.

LINDA   I'll be with you in a minute. Go on, Charley. (*He hesitates.*) I want to, just for a minute. I never had a chance to say good-by.

(CHARLEY *moves away, followed by* HAPPY. BIFF *remains a slight distance up and left of* LINDA. *She sits there, summoning herself. The flute begins, not far away, playing behind her speech.*)

LINDA   Forgive me, dear. I can't cry. I don't know what it is, but I can't cry. I don't understand it. Why did you ever do that? Help me, Willy, I can't cry. It seems to me that you're just on another trip. I keep expecting you. Willy, dear, I can't cry. Why did you do it? I search and search and I search, and I can't understand it, Willy. I made the last payment on the house today. Today, dear. And there'll be nobody home. (*A sob rises in her throat.*) We're free and clear. (*Sobbing more fully, released:*) We're free. (BIFF *comes slowly toward her.*) We're free . . . We're free . . .

(BIFF *lifts her to her feet and moves out up right with her in his arms.* LINDA *sobs quietly.* BERNARD *and* CHARLEY *come together and follow them, followed by* HAPPY. *Only the music of the flute is left on the darkening stage as over the house the hard towers of the apartment buildings rise into sharp focus, and*

The Curtain Falls)

Tillie Olsen (born 1913)
Tell Me a Riddle

"These Things Shall Be"

1

For forty-seven years they had been married. How deep back the stubborn, gnarled roots of the quarrel reached, no one could say—but only now, when tending to the needs of others no longer shackled them together, the roots swelled up visible, split the earth between them, and the tearing shook even to the children, long since grown.

Why now, why now? wailed Hannah.

As if when we grew up weren't enough, said Paul.

Poor Ma. Poor Dad. It hurts so for both of them, said Vivi. They never had very much; at least in old age they should be happy.

Knock their heads together, insisted Sammy; tell 'em: you're too old for this kind of thing; no reason not to get along now.

Lennie wrote to Clara: They've lived over so much together; what could possibly tear them apart?

Something tangible enough.

Arthritic hands, and such work as he got, occasional. Poverty all his life, and there was little breath left for running. He could not, could not turn away from this desire: to have the troubling of responsibility, the fretting with money, over and done with; to be free, to be *care*free where success was not measured by accumulation, and there was use for the vitality still in him.

There was a way. They could sell the house, and with the money join his lodge's Haven, cooperative for the aged. Happy communal life, and was he not already an official; had he not helped organize it, raise funds, served as a trustee?

But she—would not consider it.

"What do we need all this for?" he would ask loudly, for her hearing aid was turned down and the vacuum was shrilling. "Five rooms" (pushing the sofa so she could get into the corner) "furniture" (smoothing down the rug) "floors and surfaces to make work. Tell me, why do we need it?" And he was glad he could ask in a scream.

"Because I'm use't."

"Because you're use't. This is a reason, Mrs. Word Miser? Used to can get unused!"

"Enough unused I have to get used to already. . . . Not enough words?" turning off the vacuum a moment to hear herself answer. "Because soon enough we'll need only a little closet, no windows, no furniture, nothing to make work, but for worms. Because now I want room. . . . Screech and blow like you're doing, you'll need that closet even sooner. . . . Ha, again!" for the vacuum bag wailed, puffed half up, hung stubbornly limp. "This time fix it so it stays; quick before the phone rings and you get too important-busy."

But while he struggled with the motor, it seethed in him. Why fix it? Why have to bother? And if it can't be fixed, have to wring the mind with how to pay the repair? At the Haven they come in with their own machines to clean your room or your cottage; you fish, or play cards, or make jokes in the sun, not with knotty fingers fight to mend vacuums.

Over the dishes, coaxingly: "For once in your life, to be free, to have everything done for you, like a queen."

"I never liked queens."

"No dishes, no garbage, no towel to sop, no worry what to buy, what to eat."

"And what else would I do with my empty hands? Better to eat at my own table when I want, and to cook and eat how I want."

"In the cottages they buy what you ask, and cook it how you like. *You* are the one who always used to say: better mankind born without mouths and stomachs than always to worry for money to buy, to shop, to fix, to cook, to wash, to clean."

"How cleverly you hid that you heard. I said it then because eighteen hours a day I ran. And you never scraped a carrot or knew a dish towel sops. Now—for you and me—who cares? A herring out of a jar is enough. But when *I* want, and nobody to bother." And she turned off her ear button, so she would not have to hear.

But as *he* had no peace, juggling and rejuggling the money to figure: how will I pay for this now?; prying out the storm windows (there they take care of this); jolting in the streetcar on errands (there I would not have to ride to take care of this or that); fending the patronizing relatives just back from Florida (at the Haven it matters what one is, not what one can afford), he gave *her* no peace.

"Look! In their bulletin. A reading circle. Twice a week it meets."

"Haumm," her answer of not listening.

"A reading circle. Chekhov they read that you like, and Peretz. Cultured people at the Haven that you would enjoy."

"Enjoy!" She tasted the word. "Now, when it pleases you, you find a reading circle for me. And forty years ago when the children were morsels and there was a Circle, did you stay home with them once so I could go? Even once? You trained me well. I do not need others to enjoy. Others!" Her voice trembled. "Because *you* want to be there with others. Already it makes me sick to think of you always around others. Clown, grimacer, floormat, yesman, entertainer, whatever they want of you."

And now it was he who turned on the television loud so he need not hear.

Old scar tissue ruptured and the wounds festered anew. Chekhov indeed. She thought without softness of that young wife, who in the deep night hours while she nursed the current baby, and perhaps held another in her lap, would try to stay awake for the only time there was to read. She would feel again the weather of the outside on his cheek when, coming late from a meeting, he would find her so, and stimulated and ardent, sniffing her skin, coax: "I'll put the baby to bed, and you—put the book away, don't read, don't read."

That had been the most beguiling of all the "don't read, put your book away" her life had been. Chekhov indeed!

"Money?" She shrugged him off. "Could we get poorer than once we were? And in America, who starves?"

But as still he pressed:

"Let me alone about money. Was there ever enough? Seven little ones—for every penny I had to ask—and sometimes, remember, there was nothing. But always *I* had to manage. Now *you* manage. Rub your nose in it good."

But from those years she had had to manage, old humiliations and terrors rose up, lived again, and forced her to relive them. The children's needings; that grocer's face or this merchant's wife she had had to beg credit from when credit was a disgrace; the scenery of the long blocks walked around when she could not pay; school coming, and the desperate going over the old to see what could yet be remade; the soups of meat bones begged "for-the-dog" one winter. . . .

Enough. Now they had no children. Let *him* wrack his head for how they would live. She would not exchange her solitude for anything. *Never again to be forced to move to the rhythms of others.*

For in this solitude she had won to a reconciled peace.

Tranquillity from having the empty house no longer an enemy, for it stayed clean—not as in the days when it was her family, the life in it, that had seemed the enemy: tracking, smudging, littering, dirtying, engaging her in endless defeating battle—and on whom her endless defeat had been spewed.

The few old books, memorized from rereading; the pictures to ponder (the magnifying glass superimposed on her heavy eyeglasses). Or if she wishes, when he is gone, the phonograph, that if she turns up very loud and strains, she can hear: the ordered sounds and the struggling.

Out in the garden, growing things to nurture. Birds to be kept out of the pear tree, and when the pears are heavy and ripe, the old fury of work, for all must be canned, nothing wasted.

And her one social duty (for she will not go to luncheons or meetings) the boxes of old clothes left with her, as with a life-practised eye for finding what is still wearable within the worn (again the magnifying glass superimposed on the heavy glasses) she scans and sorts—this for rag or rummage, that for mending and cleaning, and this for sending away.

Being able at last to live within, and not move to the rhythms of others, as life had forced her to: denying; removing; isolating; taking the children one by one; then deafening, half-blinding—and at last, presenting her solitude.

And in it she had won to a reconciled peace.

Now he was violating it with his constant campaigning: *Sell the house and move to the Haven.* (You sit, you sit—there too you could sit like a stone.) He was making of her a battleground where old grievances tore. (Turn on your ear button—I am talking.) And stubbornly she resisted—so that from wheedling, reasoning, manipulation, it was bitterness he now started with.

And it came to where every happening lashed up a quarrel.

"I will sell the house anyway," he flung at her one night. "I am putting it up for sale. There will be a way to make you sign."

The television blared, as always it did on the evenings he stayed home, and as always it reached her only as noise. She did not know if the tumult was in her or outside. Snap! she turned the sound off. "Shadows," she whispered to him, pointing to the screen, "look, it is only shadows." And in a scream: "Did you say that you will sell the house? Look at me, not at that. I am no shadow. You cannot sell without me."

"Leave on the television. I am watching."

"Like Paulie, like Jenny, a four-year-old. Staring at shadows. *You cannot sell the house.*"

"I will. We are going to the Haven. There you would not hear the television when you do not want it. I could sit in the social room and watch. You could lock yourself up to smell your unpleasantness in a room by yourself—for who would want to come near you?"

"No, no selling." A whisper now.

"The television is shadows. Mrs. Enlightened! Mrs. Cultured! A world comes into your house—and it is shadows. People you would never meet in a thousand lifetimes. Wonders. When you were four years old, yes, like Paulie, like Jenny, did you know of Indian dances, alligators, how they use bamboo in Malaya? No, you scratched in your dirt with the chickens and thought Olshana was the world. Yes, Mrs. Unpleasant, I will sell the house, for there better can we be rid of each other than here."

She did not know if the tumult was outside, or in her. Always a ravening inside, a pull to the bed, to lie down, to succumb.

"Have you thought maybe Ma should let a doctor have a look at her?" asked their son Paul after Sunday dinner, regarding his mother crumpled on the couch, instead of, as was her custom, busying herself in Nancy's kitchen.

"Why not the President too?"

"Seriously, Dad. This is the third Sunday she's lain down like that after dinner. Is she that way at home?"

"A regular love affair with the bed. Every time I start to talk to her."

Good protective reaction, observed Nancy to herself. The workings of hos-til-ity.

"Nancy could take her. I just don't like how she looks. Let's have Nancy arrange an appointment."

"You think she'll go?" regarding his wife gloomily. "All right, we have to have doctor bills, we have to have doctor bills." Loudly: "Something hurts you?"

She startled, looked to his lips. He repeated: "Mrs. Take It Easy, something hurts?"

"Nothing. . . . Only you."

"A woman of honey. That's why you're lying down?"

"Soon I'll get up to do the dishes, Nancy."

"Leave them, Mother, I like it better this way."

"Mrs. Take It Easy, Paul says you should start ballet. You should go to see a doctor and ask: how soon can you start ballet?"

"A doctor?" she begged. "Ballet?"

"We were talking, Ma," explained Paul, "you don't seem any too well. It would be a good idea for you to see a doctor for a checkup."

"I get up now to do the kitchen. Doctors are bills and foolishness, my son. I need no doctors."

"At the Haven," he could not resist pointing out, "a doctor is *not* bills. He lives beside you. You start to sneeze, he is there before you open up a Kleenex. You can be sick there for free, all you want."

"Diarrhea of the mouth, is there a doctor to make you dumb?"

"Ma. Promise me you'll go. Nancy will arrange it."

"It's all of a piece when you think of it," said Nancy, "the way she attacks my kitchen, scrubbing under every cup hook, doing the inside of the oven so I can't enjoy Sunday dinner, knowing that half-blind or not, she's going to find every speck of dirt. . . ."

"Don't, Nancy, I've told you—it's the only way she knows to be useful. What did the *doctor* say?"

"A real fatherly lecture. Sixty-nine is young these days. Go out, enjoy life, find interests. Get a new hearing aid, this one is antiquated. Old age is sickness only if one makes it so. Geriatrics, Inc."

"So there was nothing physical."

"Of course there was. How can you live to yourself like she does without there being? Evidence of a kidney disorder, and her blood count is low. He gave her a diet, and she's to come back for follow-up and lab work. . . . But he was clear enough: Number One prescription—start living like a human being. . . . When I think of your dad, who could really play the invalid with that arthritis of his, as active as a teenager, and twice as much fun. . . .''

"You didn't tell me the doctor says your sickness is in you, how you live." He pushed his advantage. "Life and enjoyments you need better than medicine. And this diet, how can you keep it? To weigh each morsel and scrape away each bit of fat, to make this soup, that pudding. There, at the Haven, they have a dietician, they would do it for you."

She is silent.

"You would feel better there, I know it," he says gently. "There there is life and enjoyments all around."

"What is the matter, Mr. Importantbusy, you have no card game or meeting you can go to?"—turning her face to the pillow.

For a while he cut his meetings and going out, fussed over her diet, tried to wheedle her into leaving the house, brought in visitors:

"I should come to a fashion tea. I should sit and look at pretty babies in clothes I cannot buy. This is pleasure?"

"Always you are better than everyone else. The doctor said you should go out. Mrs. Brem comes to you with goodness and you turn her away."

"Because *you* asked her to, she asked me."

"They won't come back. People you need, the doctor said. Your own cousins I asked; they were willing to come and make peace as if nothing had happened. . . ."

"No more crushers of people, pushers, hypocrites, around me. No more in *my* house. You go to them if you like."

"Kind he is to visit. And you, like ice."

"A babbler. All my life around babblers. Enough!"

"She's even worse, Dad? Then let her stew a while," advised Nancy. "You can't let it destroy you; it's a psychological thing, maybe too far gone for any of us to help."

So he let her stew. More and more she lay silent in bed, and sometimes did not even get up to make the meals. No longer was the tongue-lashing inevitable if he left the coffee cup where it did not belong, or forgot to take out the garbage or mislaid the broom. The birds grew bold that summer and for once pocked the pears, undisturbed.

A bellyful of bitterness and every day the same quarrel in a new way and a different old grievance the quarrel forced her to enter and relive. And the new torment: I am not really sick, the doctor said it, then why do I feel so sick?

One night she asked him: "You have a meeting tonight? Do not go. Stay . . . with me."

He had planned to watch "This Is Your Life," but half sick himself from the heavy heat, and sickening therefore the more after the brooks and woods of the Haven, with satisfaction he grated:

"Hah, Mrs. Live Alone And Like It wants company all of a sudden. It doesn't seem so good the time of solitary when she was a girl exile in Siberia. 'Do not go. Stay with me.' A new song for Mrs. Free As A Bird. Yes, I am going out, and while I am gone chew this aloneness good, and think how you keep us both from where if you want people, you do not need to be alone."

"Go, go. All your life you have gone without me."

After him she sobbed curses he had not heard in years, old-country curses from their childhood: Grow, oh shall you grow like an onion, with your head in the ground. Like the hide of a drum shall you be, beaten in life, beaten in death. Oh shall you be like a chandelier, to hang, and to burn. . . .

She was not in their bed when he came back. She lay on the cot on the sun porch. All week she did not speak or come near him; nor did he try to make peace or care for her.

He slept badly, so used to her next to him. After all the years, old harmonies and dependencies deep in their bodies; she curled to him, or he coiled to her, each warmed, warming, turning as the other turned, the nights a long embrace.

It was not the empty bed or the storm that woke him, but a faint singing. *She* was singing. Shaking off the drops of rain, the lightning riving her lifted face, he saw her so; the cot covers on the floor.

"This is a private concert?" he asked. "Come in, you are wet."

"I can breathe now," she answered; "my lungs are rich." Though indeed the sound was hardly a breath.

"Come in, come in." Loosing the bamboo shades. "Look how wet you are." Half helping, half carrying her, still faint-breathing her song.

A Russian love song of fifty years ago.

He had found a buyer, but before he told her, he called together those children who were close enough to come. Paul, of course, Sammy from New Jersey, Hannah from Connecticut, Vivi from Ohio.

With a kindling of energy for her beloved visitors, she arrayed the house, cooked and baked. She was not prepared for the solemn after-dinner conclave, they too probing in and tearing. Her frightened eyes watched from mouth to mouth as each spoke.

His stories were eloquent and funny of her refusal to go back to the doctor; of the scorned invitations; of her stubborn silence or the bile "like a Niagara"; of her contrariness: "If I clean it's no good how I cleaned; if I don't clean, I'm still a master who thinks he has a slave."

(Vinegar he poured on me all his life; I am well marinated; how can I be honey now?)

Deftly he marched in the rightness for moving to the Haven; their money from social security free for visiting the children, not sucked into daily needs and into the house; the activities in the Haven for him; but mostly the Haven for *her*: her health, her need of care, distraction, amusement, friends who shared her interests.

"This does offer an outlet for Dad," said Paul; "he's always been an active person. And economic peace of mind isn't to be sneezed at, either. I could use a little of that myself."

But when they asked: "And you, Ma, how do you feel about it?" could only whisper:

"For him it is good. It is not for me. I can no longer live between people."

"You lived all your life *for* people," Vivi cried.

"Not with." Suffering doubly for the unhappiness on her children's faces.

"You have to find some compromise," Sammy insisted. "Maybe sell the house and buy a trailer. After forty-seven years there's surely some way you can find to live in peace."

"There is no help, my children. Different things we need."

"Then live alone!" He could control himself no longer. "I have a buyer for the house. Half the money for you, half for me. Either alone or with me to the Haven. You think I can live any longer as we are doing now?"

"Ma doesn't have to make a decision this minute, however you feel, Dad," Paul said quickly, "and you wouldn't want her to. Let's let it lay a few months, and then talk some more."

"I think I can work it out to take Mother home with me for a while," Hannah said. "You both look terrible, but especially you, Mother. I'm going to ask Phil to have a look at you."

"Sure," cracked Sammy. "What's the use of a doctor husband if you can't get free service out of him once in a while for the family? And absence might make the heart . . . you know."

"There was something after all," Paul told Nancy in a colorless voice. "That was Hannah's Phil calling. Her gall bladder. . . . Surgery."

"Her *gall* bladder. If that isn't classic. 'Bitter as gall'—talk of psychosom——"

He stepped closer, put his hand over her mouth, and said in the same colorless, plodding voice. "We have to get Dad. They operated at once. The cancer was everywhere, surrounding the liver, everywhere. They did what they could . . . at best she has a year. Dad . . . we have to tell him."

2

Honest in his weakness when they told him, and that she was not to know. "I'm not an actor. She'll know right away by how I am. Oh that poor woman. I am old too, it will break me into pieces. Oh that poor woman. She will spit on me: 'So my sickness was how I live.' Oh Paulie, how she will be, that poor woman. Only she should not suffer. . . . I can't stand sickness, Paulie, I can't go with you."

But went. And play-acted.

"A grand opening and you did not even wait for me. . . . A good thing Hannah took you with her."

"Fashion teas I needed. They cut out what tore in me; just in my throat something hurts yet. . . . Look! so many flowers, like a funeral. Vivi called, did Hannah tell you? And Lennie from San Francisco, and Clara; and Sammy is coming." Her gnome's face pressed happily into the flowers.

It is impossible to predict in these cases, but once over the immediate effects of the operation, she should have several months of comparative well-being.

The money, where will come the money?

Travel with her, Dad. Don't take her home to the old associations. The other children will want to see her.

The money, where will I wring the money?

Whatever happens, she is not to know. No, you can't ask her to sign papers to sell the house; nothing to upset her. Borrow instead, then after. . . .

I had wanted to leave you each a few dollars to make life easier, as other fathers do. There will be nothing left now. (Failure! you and your "business is exploitation." Why didn't you make it when it could be made?—Is that what you're thinking, Sammy?)

Sure she's unreasonable, Dad—but you have to stay with her; if there's to be any happiness in what's left of her life, it depends on you.

Prop me up, children, think of me, too. Shuffled, chained with her, bitter woman. No Haven, and the little money going. . . . How happy she looks, poor creature.

The look of excitement. The straining to hear everything (the new hearing aid turned full). Why are you so happy, dying woman?

How the petals are, fold on fold, and the gladioli color. The autumn air.

Stranger grandsons, tall above the little gnome grandmother, the little spry grandfather. Paul in a frenzy of picture-taking before going.

She, wandering the great house. Feeling the books; laughing at the maple shoemaker's bench of a hundred years ago used as a table. The ear turned to music.

"Let us go home. See how good I walk now." "One step from the hospital," he answers, "and she wants to fly. Wait till Doctor Phil says."

"Look—the birds too are flying home. Very good Phil is and will not show it, but he is sick of sickness by the time he comes home."

"Mrs. Telepathy, to read minds," he answers; "read mine what it says: when the trunks of medicines become a suitcase, then we will go."

The grandboys, they do not know what to say to us. . . . Hannah, she runs around here, there, when is there time for herself?

Let us go home. Let us go home.

Musing; gentleness—*but for the incidents of the rabbi in the hospital, and of the candles of benediction.*

Of the rabbi in the hospital:

Now tell me what happened, Mother.

From the sleep I awoke, Hannah's Phil, and he stands there like a devil in a dream and calls me by name. I cannot hear. I think he prays. Go away, please, I tell him, I am not a believer. Still he stands, while my heart knocks with fright.

You scared *him*, Mother. He thought you were delirious.

Who sent him? Why did he come to me?

It is a custom. The men of God come to visit those of their religion they might help. The hospital makes up the list for them—race, religion—and you are on the Jewish list.

Not for rabbis. At once go and make them change. Tell them to write: Race, human; Religion, none.

And of the candles of benediction:

Look how you have upset yourself, Mrs. Excited Over Nothing. Pleasant memories you should leave.

Go in, go back to Hannah and the lights. Two weeks I saw candles and said nothing. But she asked me.

So what was so terrible? She forgets you never did, she asks you to light the Friday candles and say the benediction like Phil's mother when she visits. If the candles give her pleasure, why shouldn't she have the pleasure?

Not for pleasure she does it. For emptiness. Because his family does. Because all around her do.

That is not a good reason too? But you did not hear her. For heritage, she told you. For the boys, from the past they should have tradition.

Superstition! From our ancestors, savages, afraid of the dark, of themselves: mumbo words and magic lights to scare away ghosts.

She told you: how it started does not take away the goodness. For centuries, peace in the house it means.

Swindler! does she look back on the dark centuries? Candles bought instead of bread and stuck into a potato for a candlestick? Religion that stifled and said: in Paradise, woman, you will be the footstool of your husband, and in life—poor chosen Jew—ground under, despised, trembling in cellars. And cremated. And cremated.

This is religion's fault? You think you are still an orator of the 1905 revolution? Where are the pills for quieting? Which are they?

Heritage. How have we come from our savage past, how no longer to be savages—this to teach. To look back and learn what humanizes—this to teach. To smash all ghettos that divide us—not to go back, not to go back—this to teach. Learned books in the house, will humankind live or die, and she gives to her boys—superstition.

Hannah that is so good to you. Take your pill, Mrs. Excited For Nothing, swallow.

Heritage! But when did I have time to teach? Of Hannah I asked only hands to help.

Swallow.

Otherwise—musing; gentleness.

Not to travel. To go home.

The children want to see you. We have to show them you are as thorny a flower as ever.

Not to travel.

Vivi wants you should see her new baby. She sent the tickets—airplane tickets—a Mrs. Roosevelt she wants to make of you. To Vivi's we have to go.

A new baby. How many warm, seductive babies. She holds him stiffly, *away* from her, so that he wails. And a long shudder begins, and the sweat beads on her forehead.

"Hush, shush," croons the grandfather, lifting him back. "You should forgive your grandmamma, little prince, she has never held a baby before, only seen them in glass cases. Hush, shush."

"You're tired, Ma," says Vivi. "The travel and the noisy dinner. I'll take you to lie down."

(A long travel from, to, what the feel of a baby evokes.)

In the airplane, cunningly designed to encase from motion (no wind, no feel of flight), she had sat severely and still, her face turned to the sky through which they cleaved and left no scar.

So this was how it looked, the determining, the crucial sky, and this was how man moved through it, remote above the dwindled earth, the concealed human life. Vulnerable life, that could scar.

There was a steerage ship of memory that shook across a great, circular sea: clustered, ill human beings; and through the thick-stained air, tiny fretting waters in a window round like the airplane's—sun round, moon round. (The round thatched roofs of Olshana.) Eye round—like the smaller window that framed distance the solitary year of exile when only her eyes could travel, and no voice spoke. And the polar winds hurled themselves across snows trackless and endless and white—like the clouds which had closed together below and hidden the earth.

Now they put a baby in her lap. Do not ask me, she would have liked to beg. Enough the worn face of Vivi, the remembered grandchildren. I cannot, cannot. . . .

Cannot what? Unnatural grandmother, not able to make herself embrace a baby.

She lay there in the bed of the two little girls, her new hearing aid turned full, listening to the sound of the children going to sleep, the baby's fretful crying and hushing, the clatter of dishes being washed and put away. They thought she slept. Still she rode on.

It was not that she had not loved her babies, her children. The love—the passion of tending—had risen with the need like a torrent; and like a torrent drowned and immolated all else. But when the need was done—oh the power that was lost in the painful damming back and drying up of what still surged, but had nowhere to go. Only the thin pulsing left that could not quiet, suffering over lives one felt, but could no longer hold nor help.

On that torrent she had borne them on their own lives, and the riverbed was desert long years now. Not there would she dwell, a memoried wraith. Surely that was not all, surely there was more. Still the springs, the springs were in her seeking. Somewhere an older power that beat for life. Somewhere coherence, transport, meaning. If they would but leave her in the air now stilled of clamor, in the reconciled solitude, to journey on.

And they put a baby in her lap. Immediacy to embrace, and the breath of *that* past: warm flesh like this that had claims and nuzzled away all else and with lovely mouths devoured; hot-living like an animal—intensely and now; the turning maze; the long drunkenness; the drowning into needing and being needed. Severely she looked back—and the shudder seized her again, and the sweat. Not that way. Not there, not now could she, not yet. . . .

And all that visit, she could not touch the baby.

"Daddy, is it the . . . sickness she's like that?" asked Vivi. "I was so glad to be having the baby—for her. I told Tim, it'll give her more happiness than anything, being around a baby again. And she hasn't played with him once."

He was not listening. "Aahh little seed of life, little charmer," he crooned, "Hollywood should see you. A heart of ice you would melt. Kick, kick. The future you'll have for a ball. In 2050 still kick. Kick for your grandaddy then."

Attentive with the older children; sat through their performances (command performance; we command you to be the audience); helped Ann sort autumn leaves to find the best for a school program; listened gravely to Richard tell about his rock collection, while her lips mutely formed the words to remember: *igneous, sedimen-*

tary, metamorphic; looked for missing socks, books, and bus tickets; watched the children whoop after their grandfather who knew how to tickle, chuck, lift, toss, do tricks, tell secrets, make jokes, match riddle for riddle. (Tell me a riddle, Grammy. I know no riddles, child.) Scrubbed sills and woodwork and furniture in every room; folded the laundry; straightened drawers; emptied the heaped baskets waiting for ironing (while he or Vivi or Tim nagged: You're supposed to rest here, you've been sick) but to none tended or gave food—and could not touch the baby.

After a week she said: "Let us go home. Today call about the tickets."

"You have important business, Mrs. Inahurry? The President waits to consult with you?" He shouted, for the fear of the future raced in him. "The clothes are still warm from the suitcase, your children cannot show enough how glad they are to see you, and you want home. There is plenty of time for home. We cannot be with the children at home."

"Blind to around you as always: the little ones sleep four in a room because we take their bed. We are two more people in a house with a new baby, and no help."

"Vivi is happy so. The children should have their grandparents a while, she told to me. I should have my mommy and daddy. . . ."

"Babbler and blind. Do you look at her so tired? How she starts to talk and she cries? I am not strong enough yet to help. Let us go home."

(To reconciled solitude.)

For it seemed to her the crowded noisy house was listening to her, listening for her. She could feel it like a great ear pressed under her heart. And everything knocked: quick constant raps: let me in, let me in.

How was it that soft reaching tendrils also became blows that knocked?

C'mon, Grandma, I want to show you. . . .

Tell me a riddle, Grandma. (*I know no riddles.*)

Look, Grammy, he's so dumb he can't even find his hands. (Dody and the baby on a blanket over the fermenting autumn mould.)

I made them—for you. (Ann) (Flat paper dolls with aprons that lifted on scalloped skirts that lifted on flowered pants; hair of yarn and great ringed questioning eyes.)

Watch me, Grandma. (Richard snaking up the tree, hanging exultant, free, with one hand at the top. Below Dody hunching over in pretend-cooking.) (*Climb too, Dody, climb and look.*)

Be my nap bed, Grammy. (The "No!" too late.)

Morty's abandoned heaviness, while his fingers ladder up and down her hearing-aid cord to his drowsy chant: eentsiebeentsiespider. (*Children trust.*)

It's to start off your own rock collection, Grandma. That's a trilobite fossil, 200 million years old (millions of years on a boy's mouth) and that one's obsidian, black glass.

Knocked and knocked.

Mother, I *told* you the teacher said we had to bring it back all filled out this morning. Didn't you even ask Daddy? Then tell *me* which plan and I'll check it: evacuate or stay in the city or wait for you to come and take me away. (Seeing the look of straining to hear.) It's for Disaster, Grandma. (*Children trust.*)

Vivi in the maze of the long, the lovely drunkenness. The old old noises: baby sounds; screaming of a mother flayed to exasperation; children quarreling; children playing; singing; laughter.

And Vivi's tears and memories, spilling so fast, half the words not understood.

She had started remembering out loud deliberately, so her mother would know the past was cherished, still lived in her.

Nursing the baby: My friends marvel, and I tell them, oh it's easy to be such a cow. I remember how beautiful my mother seemed nursing my brother, and the milk just flows. . . . Was that Davy? It must have been Davy. . . .

Lowering a hem: How did you ever . . . when I think how you made everything we wore . . . Tim, just think, seven kids and Mommy sewed everything . . . do I remember you sang while you sewed? That white dress with the red apples on the skirt you fixed over for me, was it Hannah's or Clara's before it was mine?

Washing sweaters: Ma, I'll never forget, one of those days so nice you washed clothes outside; one of the first spring days it must have been. The bubbles just danced while you scrubbed, and we chased after, and you stopped to show us how to blow our own bubbles with green onion stalks . . . you always. . . .

"Strong onion, to still make you cry after so many years," her father said, to turn the tears into laughter.

While Richard bent over his homework: Where is it now, do we still have it, the Book of the Martyrs? It always seemed so, well—exalted, when you'd put it on the round table and we'd all look at it together; there was even a halo from the lamp. The lamp with the beaded fringe you could move up and down; they're in style again, pully lamps like that, but without the fringe. You know the book I'm talking about, Daddy, the Book of the Martyrs, the first picture was a bust of Spartacus . . . Socrates? I wish there was something like that for the children, Mommy, to give them what you. . . . (And the tears splashed again.)

(What I intended and did not? Stop it, daughter, stop it, leave that time. And he, the hypocrite, sitting there with tears in his eyes—it was nothing to you then, nothing.)

. . . The time you came to school and I almost died of shame because of your accent and because I knew you knew I was ashamed; how could I? . . . Sammy's harmonica and you danced to it once, yes you did, you and Davy squealing in your arms. . . . That time you bundled us up and walked us down to the railway station to stay the night 'cause it was heated and we didn't have any coal, that winter of the strike, you didn't think I remembered that, did you, Mommy? . . . How you'd call us out to see the sunsets. . . .

Day after day, the spilling memories. Worse now, questions, too. Even the grandchildren: Grandma, in the olden days, when you were little. . . .

It was the afternoons that saved.

While they thought she napped, she would leave the mosaic on the wall (of children's drawings, maps, calendars, pictures, Ann's cardboard dolls with their great ringed questioning eyes) and hunch in the girls' closet on the low shelf where the shoes stood, and the girls' dresses covered.

For that while she would painfully sheathe against the listening house, the tendrils and noises that knocked, and Vivi's spilling memories. Sometimes it helped to braid and unbraid the sashes that dangled, or to trace the pattern on the hoop slips.

Today she had jacks and children under jet trails to forget. Last night, Ann and Dody silhouetted in the window against a sunset of flaming man-made clouds of jet trail, their jacks ball accenting the peaceful noise of dinner being made. Had she told them, yes she had told them of how they played jacks in her village though there was no ball, no jacks. Six stones, round and flat, toss them out, the seventh on the back of the hand, toss, catch and swoop up as many as possible, toss again. . . .

Of stones (repeating Richard) there are three kinds: earth's fire jetting; rock of layered centuries; crucibled new out of the old (*igneous, sedimentary, metamorphic*). But there was that other—frozen to black glass, never to transform or hold the fossil memory . . . (let not my seed fall on stone). There was an ancient man who fought to heights a great rock that crashed back down eternally—eternal labor, freedom, labor . . . (stone will perish, but the word remain). And you, David, who with a stone slew, screaming: Lord, take my heart of stone and give me flesh

Who was screaming? Why was she back in the common room of the prison, the sun motes dancing in the shafts of light, and the informer being brought in, a prisoner now, like themselves. And Lisa leaping, yes, Lisa, the gentle and tender, biting at the betrayer's jugular. Screaming and screaming.

No, it is the children screaming. Another of Paul and Sammy's terrible fights?

In Vivi's house. Severely: you are in Vivi's house.

Blows, screams, a call: "Grandma!" For her? Oh please not for her. Hide, hunch behind the dresses deeper. But a trembling little body hurls itself beside her—surprised, smothered laughter, arms surround her neck, tears rub dry on her cheek, and words too soft to understand whisper into her ear (Is this where you hide too, Grammy? It's my secret place, we have a secret now).

And the sweat beads, and the long shudder seizes.

It seemed the great ear pressed inside now, and the knocking. "We have to go home," she told him, "I grow ill here."

"It's your own fault, Mrs. Bodybusy, you do not rest, you do too much." He raged, but the fear was in his eyes. "It was a serious operation, they told you to take care. . . . All right, we will go to where you can rest."

But where? Not home to death, not yet. He had thought to Lennie's, to Clara's; beautiful visits with each of the children. She would have to rest first, be stronger. If they could but go to Florida—it glittered before him, the never-realized promise of Florida. California: of course. (The money, the money, dwindling!) Los Angeles first for sun and rest, then to Lennie's in San Francisco.

He told her the next day. "You saw what Nancy wrote: snow and wind back home, a terrible winter. And look at you—all bones and a swollen belly. I called Phil: he said: 'A prescription, Los Angeles sun and rest.' "

She watched the words on his lips. "You have sold the house," she cried, "that is why we do not go home. That is why you talk no more of the Haven, why there is money for travel. After the children you will drag me to the Haven."

"The Haven! Who thinks of the Haven any more? Tell her, Vivi, tell Mrs. Suspicious: a prescription, sun and rest, to make you healthy. . . . And how could I sell the house without *you?*"

At the place of farewells and greetings, of winds of coming and winds of going, they say their good-byes.

They look back at her with the eyes of others before them: Richard with her own blue blaze; Ann with the nordic eyes of Tim; Morty's dreaming brown of a great-grandmother he will never know; Dody with the laughing eyes of him who had been her springtide love (who stands beside her now); Vivi's, all tears.

The baby's eyes are closed in sleep.
Good-bye, my children.

3

It is to the back of the great city he brought her, to the dwelling places of the cast-off old. Bounded by two lines of amusement piers to the north and to the south, and between a long straight paving rimmed with black benches facing the sand—sands so wide the ocean is only a far fluting.

In the brief vacation season, some of the boarded stores fronting the sands open, and families, young people and children, may be seen. A little tasselled team shuttles between the piers, and the lights of roller coasters prink and tweak over those who come to have sensation made in them.

The rest of the year it is abandoned to the old, all else boarded up and still; seemingly empty, except the occasional days and hours when the sun, like a tide, sucks them out of the low rooming houses, casts them onto the benches and sandy rim of the walk—and sweeps them into decaying enclosures once again.

A few newer apartments glint among the low bleached squares. It is in one of these Lennie's Jeannie has arranged their rooms. "Only a few miles north and south people pay hundreds of dollars a month for just this gorgeous air, Grandaddy, just this ocean closeness."

She had been ill on the plane, lay ill for days in the unfamiliar room. Several times the doctor came by—left medicine she would not take. Several times Jeannie drove in the twenty miles from work, still in her Visiting Nurse uniform, the lightness and brightness of her like a healing.

"Who can believe it is winter?" he asked one morning. "Beautiful it is outside like an ad. Come, Mrs. Invalid, come to taste it. You are well enough to sit in here, you are well enough to sit outside. The doctor said it too."

But the benches were encrusted with people, and the sands at the sidewalk's edge. Besides, she had seen the far ruffle of the sea: "there take me," and though she leaned against him, it was she who led.

Plodding and plodding, sitting often to rest, he grumbling. Patting the sand so warm. Once she scooped up a handful, cradling it close to her better eye; peered, and flung it back. And as they came almost to the brink and she could see the glistening wet, she sat down, pulled off her shoes and stockings, left him and began to run. "You'll catch cold," he screamed, but the sand in his shoes weighed him down—he who had always been the agile one—and already the white spray creamed her feet.

He pulled her back, took a handkerchief to wipe off the wet and the sand. "Oh no," she said, "the sun will dry," seized the square and smoothed it flat, dropped on it a mound of sand, knotted the kerchief corners and tied it to a bag—"to look at with the strong glass" (for the first time in years explaining an action of hers)—and lay down with the little bag against her cheek, looking toward the shore that nurtured life as it first crawled toward consciousness the millions of years ago.

He took her one Sunday in the evil-smelling bus, past flat miles of blister houses, to the home of relatives. Oh what is this? she cried as the light began to smoke and the houses to dim and recede. Smog, he said, everyone knows but you. . . . Outside he kept his arms about her, but she walked with hands pushing the heavy air as if to open it, whispered: who has done this? sat down suddenly to vomit at the curb and for a long while refused to rise.

One's age as seen on the altered face of those known in youth. Is this they he has come to visit? This Max and Rose, smooth and pleasant, introducing them to polite children, disinterested grandchildren, "the whole family, once a month on Sundays. And why not? We have the room, the help, the food."

Talk of cars, of houses, of success: this son that, that daughter this. And *your* children? Hastily skimped over, the intermarriages, the obscure work—"my doctor son-in-law, Phil"—all he has to offer. She silent in a corner. (Car-sick like a baby, he explains.) Years since he has taken her to visit anyone but the children, and old apprehensions prickle: "no incidents," he silently begs, "no incidents." He itched to tell them. "A very sick woman," significantly, indicating her with his eyes, "a very sick woman." Their restricted faces did not react. "Have you thought maybe she'd do better at Palm Springs?" Rose asked. "Or at least a nicer section of the beach, nicer people, a pool." Not to have to say "money" he said instead: "would she have sand to look at through a magnifying glass?" and went on, detail after detail, the old habit betraying of parading the queerness of her for laughter.

After dinner—the others into the living room in men- or women-clusters, or into the den to watch TV—the four of them alone. She sat close to him, and did not speak. Jokes, stories, people they had known, beginning of reminiscence, Russia fifty-sixty years ago. Strange words across the Duncan Phyfe table: *hunger; secret meetings; human rights; spies; betrayals; prison; escape*—interrupted by one of the grandchildren: "Commercial's on; any Coke left? Gee, you're missing a real hair-raiser." And then a granddaughter (Max proudly: "Look at her, an American queen") drove them home on her way back to U.C.L.A. No incident—except that there had been no incidents.

The first few mornings she had taken with her the magnifying glass, but he would sit only on the benches, so she rested at the foot, where slatted bench shadows fell, and unless she turned her hearing aid down, other voices invaded.

Now on the days when the sun shone and she felt well enough, he took her on the tram to where the benches ranged in oblongs, some with tables for checkers or cards. Again the blanket on the sand in the striped shadows, but she no longer brought the magnifying glass. He played cards, and she lay in the sun and looked towards the waters; or they walked—two blocks down to the scaling hotel, two blocks back— past chili-hamburger stands, open-doored bars, Next-to-new and perpetual rummage sale stores.

Once, out of the aimless walkers, slow and shuffling like themselves, someone ran unevenly towards them, embraced, kissed, wept: "dear friends, old friends." A friend of *hers*, not his: Mrs. Mays who had lived next door to them in Denver when the children were small.

Thirty years are compressed into a dozen sentences; and the present, not even in three. All is told: the children scattered; the husband dead; she lives in a room two blocks up from the sing hall—and points to the domed auditorium jutting before the pier. The leg? phlebitis; the heavy breathing? that, one does not ask. She, too, comes to the benches each day to sit. And tomorrow, tomorrow, are they going to the community sing? Of course he would have heard of it, everybody goes—the big doings they wait for all week. They have never been? She will come to them for dinner tomorrow and they will all go together.

So it is that she sits in the wind of the singing, among the thousand various faces of age.

She had turned off her hearing aid at once they came into the auditorium—as she would have wished to turn off sight.

One by one they streamed by and imprinted on her—and though the savage zest of their singing came voicelessly soft and distant, the faces still roared—the faces densened the air—chorded into

children-chants, mother-croons, singing of the chained
love serenades, Beethoven storms, mad Lucia's scream
drunken joy-songs, keens for the dead, work-singing

> *while from floor to balcony to dome a bare-footed sore-covered little girl threaded the sound-thronged tumult, danced her ecstasy of grimace to flutes that scratched at a cross-roads village wedding*

Yes, faces became sound, and the sound became faces; and faces and sound became weight—pushed, pressed

"Air"—her hands claw his.

"Whenever I enjoy myself. . . ." Then he saw the gray sweat on her face. "Here. Up. Help me, Mrs. Mays," and they support her out to where she can gulp the air in sob after sob.

"A doctor, we should get for her a doctor."

"Tch, it's nothing," says Ellen Mays, "I get it all the time. You've missed the tram; come to my place. Fix your hearing aid, honey . . . close . . . tea. My view. See, she *wants* to come. Steady now, that's how." Adding mysteriously: "Remember your advice, easy to keep your head above water, empty things float. Float."

The singing a fading march for them, tall woman with a swollen leg, weaving little man, and the swollen thinness they help between.

The stench in the hall: mildew? decay? "We sit and rest then climb. My gorgeous view. We help each other and here   we   are."

The stench along into the slab of room. A washstand for a sink, a box with oilcloth tacked around for a cupboard, a three-burner gas plate. Artificial flowers, colorless with dust. Everywhere pictures foaming: wedding, baby, party, vacation, graduation, family pictures. From the narrow couch under a slit of window, sure enough the view: lurching rooftops and a scallop of ocean heaving, preening, twitching under the moon.

"While the water heats. Excuse me . . . down the hall." Ellen Mays has gone.

"You'll live?" he asks mechanically, sat down to feel his fright; tried to pull her alongside.

She pushed him away. "For air," she said; stood clinging to the dresser. Then, in a terrible voice:

After a lifetime of room. Of many rooms.

Shhh.

You remember how she lived. Eight children. And now one room   like a coffin.

She pays rent!

Shrinking the life of her   into one room   like a coffin   Rooms and rooms like this   I lie on the quilt   and hear them talk

Please, Mrs. Orator-without-Breath.

Once you went for coffee   I walked   I saw   A Balzac   a Chekhov to write it   Rummage   Alone   On scraps

Better old here than in the old country!

On scraps   Yet they sang   Wondrous! *Humankind   one has to believe*   So strong   for what? To rot   not grow?

Your poor lungs beg you. They sob between each word.

Singing.   Unused   the life in them.   She   in this poor room   with her pictures   Max   You   The children   Everywhere   unused   the life   And who has meaning?   Century after century   still all in us   not   to grow?

Coffins, rummage, plants: sick woman. Oh lay down. We will get for you the doctor.

"And when will it end. Oh, *the end.*" *That* nightmare thought, and this time she writhed, crumpled against him, seized his hand (for a moment again the weight, the soft distant roaring of humanity) and on the strangled-for breath, begged: "Man . . . we'll destroy ourselves?"

And looking for answer—in the helpless pity and fear for her (for *her*) that distorted his face—she understood the last months, and knew that she was dying.

4

"Let us go home," she said after several days.

"You are in training for a cross-country run? That is why you do not even walk across the room? Here, like a prescription Phil said, till you are stronger from the operation. You want to break doctor's orders?"

She saw the fiction was necessary to him, was silent; then: "At home I will get better. If the doctor here says?"

"And winter? And the visits to Lennie and to Clara? All right," for he saw the tears in her eyes, "I will write Phil, and talk to the doctor."

Days passed. He reported nothing. Jeannie came and took her out for air, past the boarded concessions, the hooded and tented amusement rides, to the end of the pier. They watched the spent waves feeding the new, the gulls in the clouded sky; even up where they sat, the wind-blown sand stung.

She did not ask to go down the crooked steps to the sea.

Back in her bed, while he was gone to the store, she said: "Jeannie, this doctor, he is not one I can ask questions. Ask him for me, can I go home?"

Jeannie looked at her, said quickly: "Of course, poor Granny. You want your own things around you, don't you? I'll call him tonight. . . . Look, I've something to show you," and from her purse unwrapped a large cookie, intricately shaped like a little girl. "Look at the curls—can you hear me well, Granny?—and the darling eyelashes. I just came from a house where they were baking them."

"The dimples, there in the knees," she marveled, holding it to the better light, turning, studying, "like art. Each singly they cut, or a mold?"

"Singly," said Jeannie, "and if it is a child only the mother can make them. Oh Granny, it's the likeness of a real little girl who died yesterday—Rosita. She was three years old. *Pan del Muerto*, the Bread of the Dead. It was the custom in the part of Mexico they came from."

Still she turned and inspected. "Look, the hollow in the throat, the little cross necklace. . . . I think for the mother it is a good thing to be busy with such bread. You know the family?"

Jeannie nodded. "On my rounds. I nursed. . . . Oh Granny, it is like a party; they play songs she liked to dance to. The coffin is lined with pink velvet and she wears a white dress. There are candles. . . ."

"In the house?" Surprised, "They keep her in the house?"

"Yes," said Jeannie, "and it is against the health law. The father said it would be sad to bury her in this country; in Oaxaca they have a feast night with candles each year; everyone picnics on the graves of those they loved until dawn."

"Yes, Jeannie, the living must comfort themselves." And closed her eyes.

"You want to sleep, Granny?"

"Yes, tired from the pleasure of you. I may keep the Rosita? There stand it, on the dresser, where I can see; something of my own around me."

In the kitchenette, helping her grandfather unpack the groceries, Jeannie said in her light voice:

"I'm resigning my job, Grandaddy."

"Ah, the lucky young man. Which one is he?"

"Too late. You're spoken for." She made a pyramid of cans, unstacked, and built again.

"Something is wrong with the job?"

"With me. I can't be"—she searched for the word—"What they call professional enough. I let myself feel things. And tomorrow I have to report a family. . . ." The cans clicked again. "It's not that, either. I just don't know what I want to do, maybe go back to school, maybe go to art school. I thought if you went to San Francisco I'd come along and talk it over with Momma and Daddy. But I don't see how you can go. She wants to go home. She asked me to ask the doctor."

The doctor told her himself. "Next week you may travel, when you are a little stronger." But next week there was the fever of an infection, and by the time that was over, she could not leave the bed—a rented hospital bed that stood beside the double bed he slept in alone now.

Outwardly the days repeated themselves. Every other afternoon and evening he went out to his newfound cronies, to talk and play cards. Twice a week, Mrs. Mays came. And the rest of the time, Jeannie was there.

By the sickbed stood Jeannie's FM radio. Often into the room the shapes of music came. She would lie curled on her side, her knees drawn up, intense in listening (Jeannie sketched her so, coiled, convoluted like an ear), then thresh her hand out and abruptly snap the radio mute—still to lie in her attitude of listening, concealing tears.

Once Jeannie brought in a young Marine to visit, a friend from high-school days she had found wandering near the empty pier. Because Jeannie asked him to, gravely, without self-consciousness, he sat himself cross-legged on the floor and performed for them a dance of his native Samoa.

Long after they left, a tiny thrumming sound could be heard where, in her bed, she strove to repeat the beckon, flight, surrender of his hands, the fluttering foot-beats, and his low plaintive calls.

Hannah and Phil sent flowers. To deepen her pleasure, he placed one in her hair. "Like a girl," he said, and brought the hand mirror so she could see. She looked at the pulsing red flower, the yellow skull face; a desolate, excited laugh shuddered from her, and she pushed the mirror away—but let the flower burn.

The week Lennie and Helen came, the fever returned. With it the excited laugh, and incessant words. She, who in her life had spoken but seldom and then only when necessary (never having learned the easy, social uses of words), now in dying, spoke incessantly.

In a half-whisper: "Like Lisa she is, your Jeannie. Have I told you of Lisa who taught me to read? Of the highborn she was, but noble in herself. I was sixteen; they beat me; my father beat me so I would not go to her. It was forbidden, she was a Tolstoyan. At night, past dogs that howled, terrible dogs, my son, in the snows of winter to the road, I to ride in her carriage like a lady, to books. To her, life was holy, knowledge was holy, and she taught me to read. They hung her. Everything that happens one must try to understand why. She killed one who betrayed many. Because of betrayal, betrayed all she lived and believed. In one minute she killed, before my eyes (there is so much blood in a human being, my son), in prison with me. All that happens, one must try to understand.

"The name?" Her lips would work. "The name that was their pole star; the doors of the death houses fixed to open on it; I read of it my year of penal servitude. Thuban!" very excited. "Thuban, in ancient Egypt the pole star. Can you see, look out to see it, Jeannie, if it swings around *our* pole star that seems to *us* not to move.

"Yes, Jeannie, at your age my mother and grandmother had already buried children . . . yes, Jeannie, it is more than oceans between Olshana and you . . . yes, Jeannie, they danced, and for all the bodies they had they might as well be chickens, and indeed, they scratched and flapped their arms and hopped.

"And Andrei Yefimitch, who for twenty years had never known of it and never wanted to know, said as if he wanted to cry: but why my dear friend this malicious laughter?" Telling to herself half-memorized phrases from her few books. "Pain I answer with tears and cries, baseness with indignation, meanness with repulsion . . . for life may be hated or wearied of, but never despised."

Delirious: "Tell me, my neighbor, Mrs. Mays, the pictures never lived, but what of the flowers? Tell them who ask: no rabbis, no ministers, no priests, no speeches, no ceremonies: ah, false—let the living comfort themselves. Tell Sammy's boy, he who flies, tell him to go to Stuttgart and see where Davy has no grave. And what? . . . And what? where millions have no graves—save air."

In delirium or not, wanting the radio on; not seeming to listen, the words still jetting, wanting the music on. Once, silencing it abruptly as of old, she began to cry, unconcealed tears this time. "You have pain, Granny?" Jeannie asked.

"The music," she said, "still it is there and we do not hear; knocks, and our poor human ears too weak. What else, what else we do not hear?"

Once she knocked his hand aside as he gave her a pill, swept the bottles from her bedside table: "no pills, let me feel what I feel," and laughed as on his hands and knees he groped to pick them up.

Nighttimes her hand reached across the bed to hold his.

A constant retching began. Her breath was too faint for sustained speech now, but still the lips moved:

> *When no longer necessary   to injure others*
> *Pick   pick pick   Blind chicken*
> *As a human being   responsibility*

"David!" imperious, "Basin!" and she would vomit, rinse her mouth, the wasted throat working to swallow, and begin the chant again.

She will be better off in the hospital now, the doctor said.

He sent the telegrams to the children, was packing her suitcase, when her hoarse voice startled. She had roused, was pulling herself to sitting.

"Where now?" she asked. "Where now do you drag me?"

"You do not even have to have a baby to go this time," he soothed, looking for the brush to pack. "Remember, after Davy you told me—worthy to have a baby for the pleasure of the ten-day rest in the hospital?"

"Where now? Not home yet?" Her voice mourned. "Where *is* my home?"

He rose to ease her back. "The doctor, the hospital," he started to explain, but deftly, like a snake, she had slithered out of bed and stood swaying, propped behind the night table.

"Coward," she hissed, "runner."

"You stand," he said senselessly.

"To take me there and run. Afraid of a little vomit."

He reached her as she fell. She struggled against him, half slipped from his arms, pulled herself up again.

"Weakling," she taunted, "to leave me there and run. Betrayer. All your life you have run."

He sobbed, telling Jeannie. "A Marilyn Monroe to run for her virtue. Fifty-nine pounds she weighs, the doctor said, and she beats at me like a Dempsey. Betrayer, she cries, and I running like a dog when she calls; day and night, running to her, her vomit, the bedpan. . . ."

"She needs you, Grandaddy," said Jeannie. "Isn't that what they call love? I'll see if she sleeps, and if she does, poor worn-out darling, we'll have a party, you and I: I brought us rum babas."

They did not move her. By her bed now stood the tall hooked pillar that held the solutions—blood and dextrose—to feed her veins. Jeannie moved down the hall to take over the sickroom, her face so radiant, her grandfather asked her once: "you are in love?" (Shameful the joy, the pure overwhelming joy from being with her grandmother; the peace, the serenity that breathed.) "My darling escape," she answered incoherently, "my darling Granny"—as if that explained.

Now one by one the children came, those that were able. Hannah, Paul, Sammy. Too late to ask: and what did you learn with your living, Mother, and what do we need to know?

Clara, the eldest, clenched:

> *Pay me back, Mother, pay me back for all you took from me. Those others you crowded into your heart. The hands I needed to be for you, the heaviness, the responsibility.*
>
> *Is this she? Noises the dying make, the crablike hands crawling over the covers. The ethereal singing.*
>
> *She hears that music, that singing from childhood; forgotten sound—not heard since, since. . . . And the hardness breaks like a cry: Where did we lose each other, first mother, singing mother?*
>
> *Annulled: the quarrels, the gibing, the harshness between; the fall into silence and the withdrawal.*
>
> *I do not know you, Mother. Mother, I never knew you.*

Lennie, suffering not alone for her who was dying, but for that in her which never lived (for that which in him might never live). From him too, unspoken words: *goodbye Mother who taught me to mother myself.*

Not Vivi, who must stay with her children; not Davy, but he is already here, having to die again with *her* this time, for the living take their dead with them when they die.

Light she grew, like a bird, and, like a bird, sound bubbled in her throat while the body fluttered in agony. Night and day, asleep or awake (though indeed there was no difference now) the songs and the phrases leaping.

And he, who had once dreaded a long dying (from fear of himself, from horror of the dwindling money) now desired her quick death profoundly, for *her* sake. He no longer went out, except when Jeannie forced him; no longer laughed, except when in the bright kitchenette, Jeannie coaxed his laughter (and she, who seemed to hear nothing else, would laugh too, conspiratorial wisps of laughter).

Light, like a bird, the fluttering body, the little claw hands, the beaked shadow on her face; and the throat, bubbling, straining.

He tried not to listen, as he tried not to look on the face in which only the forehead remained familiar, but trapped with her the long nights in that little room, the sounds worked themselves into his consciousness, with their punctuation of death swallows, whimpers, gurglings.

Even in reality (swallow) *life's lack of it*
Slaveships   deathtrains   clubs   eeenough
The bell   summon what enables
78,000 in one minute (whisper of a scream) *78,000 human beings   we'll destroy ourselves?*

"Aah, Mrs. Miserable," he said, as if she could hear, "all your life working, and now in bed you lie, servants to tend, you do not even need to call to be tended, and still you work. Such hard work it is to die? Such hard work?"

The body threshed, her hand clung in his. A melody, ghost-thin, hovered on her lips, and like a guilty ghost, the vision of her bent in listening to it, silencing the record instantly he was near. Now, heedless of his presence, she floated the melody on and on.

"Hid it from me," he complained, "how many times you listened to remember it so?" And tried to think when she had first played it, or first begun to silence her few records when he came near—but could reconstruct nothing. There was only this room with its tall hooked pillar and its swarm of sounds.

No man one   except through others
Strong   with the not yet   in the now
Dogma dead   war dead   one country

"It helps, Mrs. Philosopher, words from books? It helps?" And it seemed to him that for seventy years she had hidden a tape recorder, infinitely microscopic, within her, that it had coiled infinite mile on mile, trapping every song, every melody, every word read, heard, and spoken—and that maliciously she was playing back only what said nothing of him, of the children, of their intimate life together.

"Left us indeed, Mrs. Babbler," he reproached, "you who called others babbler and cunningly saved your words. A lifetime you tended and loved, and now not a word of us, for us. Left us indeed? Left me."

And he took out his solitaire deck, shuffled the cards loudly, slapped them down.
Lift high   banner of reason (tatter of an orator's voice) *justice   freedom   light*
Humankind   life worthy   capacities
Seeks (blur of shudder) *belong   human being*

"Words, words," he accused, "and what human beings did *you* seek around you, Mrs. Live Alone, and what humankind think worthy?"

Though even as he spoke, he remembered she had not always been isolated, had not always wanted to be alone (as he knew there had been a voice before this gossamer one; before the hoarse voice that broke from silence to lash, make incidents, shame him—a girl's voice of eloquence that spoke their holiest dreams). But again he could reconstruct, image, nothing of what had been before, or when, or how, it had changed.

Ace, queen, jack. The pillar shadow fell, so, in two tracks; in the mirror depths glistened a moonlike blob, the empty solution bottle. And it worked in him: *of reason and justice and freedom . . . Dogma dead:* he remembered the full quotation, laughed bitterly. "Hah, good you do not know what you say; good Victor Hugo died and did not see it, his twentieth century."

Deuce, ten, five. Dauntlessly she began a song of their youth of belief:

> *These things shall be, a loftier race*
> *than e'er the world hath known shall rise*
> *with flame of freedom in their souls*
> *and light of knowledge in their eyes*

King, four, jack "In the twentieth century, hah!"

> *They shall be gentle, brave and strong*
> *to spill no drop of blood, but dare*
> *all . . .*
> *   on earth and fire and sea and air*

"To spill no drop of blood, hah! So, cadaver, and you too, cadaver Hugo, 'in the twentieth century ignorance will be dead, dogma will be dead, war will be dead, and for all humankind one country—of fulfilment?' Hah!"

> *And every life* (long strangling cough) *shall be a song*

The cards fell from his fingers. Without warning, the bereavement and betrayal he had sheltered—compounded through the years—hidden even from himself—revealed itself,

uncoiled,

released,

sprung

and with it the monstrous shapes of what had actually happened in the century.

A ravening hunger or thirst seized him. He groped into the kitchenette, switched on all three lights, piled a tray—"you have finished your night snack, Mrs. Cadaver, now I will have mine." And he was shocked at the tears that splashed on the tray.

"Salt tears. For free. I forgot to shake on salt?"

Whispered: "Lost, how much I lost."

Escaped to the grandchildren whose childhoods were childish, who had never hungered, who lived unravaged by disease in warm houses of many rooms, had all the school for which they cared, could walk on any street, stood a head taller than their grandparents, towered above—beautiful skins, straight backs, clear straightforward eyes. "Yes, you in Olshana," he said to the town of sixty years ago, "they would be nobility to you."

And was this not the dream then, come true in ways undreamed? he asked.

And are there no other children in the world? he answered, as if in her harsh voice.

And the flame of freedom, the light of knowledge?

And the drop, to spill no drop of blood?

And he thought that at six Jeannie would get up and it would be his turn to go to her room and sleep, that he could press the buzzer and she would come now; that in the afternoon Ellen Mays was coming, and this time they would play cards and he could marvel at how rouge can stand half an inch on the cheek; that in the evening the doctor would come, and he could beg him to be merciful, to stop the feeding solutions, to let her die.

To let her die, and with her their youth of belief out of which her bright, betrayed words foamed; stained words, that on her working lips came stainless.

Hours yet before Jeannie's turn. He could press the buzzer and wake her to come now; he could take a pill, and with it sleep; he could pour more brandy into his milk glass, though what he had poured was not yet touched.

Instead he went back, checked her pulse, gently tended with his knotty fingers as Jeannie had taught.

She was whimpering; her hand crawled across the covers for his. Compassionately he enfolded it, and with his free hand gathered up the cards again. Still was there thirst or hunger ravening in him.

That world of their youth—dark, ignorant, terrible with hate and disease—how was it that living in it, in the midst of corruption, filth, treachery, degradation, they had not mistrusted man nor themselves; had believed so beautifully, so . . . falsely?

"Aaah, children," he said out loud, "how we believed, how we belonged." And he yearned to package for each of the children, the grandchildren, for everyone, *that joyous certainty, that sense of mattering, of moving and being moved, of being one and indivisible with the great of the past, with all that freed, ennobled.* Package it, stand on corners, in front of stadiums and on crowded beaches, knock on doors, give it as a fabled gift.

"And why not in cereal boxes, in soap packages?" he mocked himself. "Aah. You have taken my senses, cadaver."

Words foamed, died unsounded. Her body writhed; she made kissing motions with her mouth. (Her lips moving as she read, poring over the Book of the Martyrs, the magnifying glass superimposed over the heavy eyeglasses.) *Still she believed?* "Eva!" he whispered. "Still you believed? You lived by it? These Things Shall Be?"

"One pound soup meat," she answered distinctly, "one soup bone."

"My ears heard you. Ellen Mays was witness: 'Humankind . . . one has to believe.'" Imploringly: "Eva!"

"Bread, day-old." She was mumbling. "Please, in a wooden box . . . for kindling. The thread, hah, the thread breaks. Cheap thread"—and a gurgling, enormously loud, began in her throat.

"I ask for stone; she gives me bread—day-old." He pulled his hand away, shouted: "Who wanted questions? Everything you have to wake?" Then dully, "Ah, let me help you turn, poor creature."

Words jumbled, cleared. In a voice of crowded terror:

"Paul, Sammy, don't fight.

"Hannah, have I ten hands?

"How can I give it, Clara, how can I give it if I don't have?"

"You lie," he said sturdily, "there was joy too." Bitterly: "Ah how cheap you speak of us at the last."

As if to rebuke him, as if her voice had no relationship with her flailing body, she sang clearly, beautifully, a school song the children had taught her when they were little; begged:

"Not look   my hair   where they cut. . . ."

(The crown of braids shorn.) And instantly he left the mute old woman poring over the Book of the Martyrs; went past the mother treading at the sewing machine, singing with the children; past the girl in her wrinkled prison dress, hiding her hair with scarred hands, lifting to him her awkward, shamed, imploring eyes of love; and took her in his arms, dear, personal, fleshed, in all the heavy passion he had loved to rouse from her.

"Eva!"

Her little claw hand beat the covers. How much, how much can a man stand? He took up the cards, put them down, circled the beds, walked to the dresser, opened, shut drawers, brushed his hair, moved his hand bit by bit over the mirror to see what of the reflection he could blot out with each move, and felt that at any moment he would die of what was unendurable. Went to press the buzzer to wake Jeannie, looked down, saw on Jeannie's sketch pad the hospital bed, with *her*; the double bed along-side, with him; the tall pillar feeding into her veins, and their hands, his and hers, clasped, feeding each other. And as if he had been instructed he went to his bed, lay down, holding the sketch (as if it could shield against the monstrous shapes of loss, of betrayal, of death) and with his free hand took hers back into his.

So Jeannie found them in the morning.

That last day the agony was perpetual. Time after time it lifted her almost off the bed, so they had to fight to hold her down. He could not endure and left the room; wept as if there never would be tears enough.

Jeannie came to comfort him. In her light voice she said: Grandaddy, Grandaddy don't cry. She is not there, she promised me. On the last day, she said she would go back to when she first heard music, a little girl on the road of the village where she was born. She promised me. It is a wedding and they dance, while the flutes so joyous and vibrant tremble in the air. Leave her there, Grandaddy, it is all right. She promised me. Come back, come back and help her poor body to die.

For two of that generation
Seevya and Genya
Infinite, dauntless, incorruptible

Death deepens the wonder

Edgar Allan Poe (1809–1849)
Eldorado

    Gaily bedight,
    A gallant knight,
In sunshine and in shadow,
    Had journeyed long
    Singing a song,   5
In search of Eldorado.

    But he grew old—
    This knight so bold—
And o'er his heart a shadow
    Fell as he found   10
    No spot of ground
That looked like Eldorado.

    And, as his strength
    Failed him at length,
He met a pilgrim shadow—   15
    "Shadow," said he,
    "Where can it be—
This land of Eldorado?"

    "Over the Mountains
    Of the Moon,   20
Down the Valley of the Shadow,
    Ride, boldly ride,"
    The shade replied,—
"If you seek for Eldorado!"

Edwin Arlington Robinson (1869–1935)

Aunt Imogen

AUNT IMOGEN was coming, and therefore
The children—Jane, Sylvester, and Young George—
Were eyes and ears; for there was only one
Aunt Imogen to them in the whole world,
And she was in it only for four weeks   5
In fifty-two. But those great bites of time
Made all September a Queen's Festival;
And they would strive, informally, to make
The most of them.—The mother understood,
And wisely stepped away. Aunt Imogen   10
Was there for only one month in the year,
While she, the mother,—she was always there;
And that was what made all the difference.
She knew it must be so, for Jane had once
Expounded it to her so learnedly   15
That she had looked away from the child's eyes
And thought; and she had thought of many things.

There was a demonstration every time
Aunt Imogen appeared, and there was more
Than one this time. And she was at a loss   20
Just how to name the meaning of it all:
It puzzled her to think that she could be
So much to any crazy thing alive—
Even to her sister's little savages
Who knew no better than to be themselves;   25
But in the midst of her glad wonderment
She found herself besieged and overcome
By two tight arms and one tumultuous head,
And therewith half bewildered and half pained
By the joy she felt and by the sudden love   30
That proved itself in childhood's honest noise.
Jane, by the wings of sex, had reached her first;
And while she strangled her, approvingly,
Sylvester thumped his drum and Young George howled.
But finally, when all was rectified,   35
And she had stilled the clamor of Young George

By giving him a long ride on her shoulders,
They went together into the old room
That looked across the fields; and Imogen
Gazed out with a girl's gladness in her eyes,   40
Happy to know that she was back once more
Where there were those who knew her, and at last
Had gloriously got away again
From cabs and clattered asphalt for a while;
And there she sat and talked and looked and laughed   45
And made the mother and the children laugh.
Aunt Imogen made everybody laugh.

There was the feminine paradox—that she
Who had so little sunshine for herself
Should have so much for others. How it was   50
That she could make, and feel for making it,
So much of joy for them, and all along
Be covering, like a scar, and while she smiled,
That hungering incompleteness and regret—
That passionate ache for something of her own,   55
For something of herself—she never knew.
She knew that she could seem to make them all
Believe there was no other part of her
Than her persistent happiness; but the why
And how she did not know. Still none of them   60
Could have a thought that she was living down—
Almost as if regret were criminal,
So proud it was and yet so profitless—
The penance of a dream, and that was good.
Her sister Jane—the mother of little Jane,   65
Sylvester, and Young George—might make herself
Believe she knew, for she—well, she was Jane.

Young George, however, did not yield himself
To nourish the false hunger of a ghost
That made no good return. He saw too much: 70
The accumulated wisdom of his years
Had so conclusively made plain to him
The permanent profusion of a world
Where everybody might have everything
To do, and almost everything to eat,   75
That he was jubilantly satisfied
And all unthwarted by adversity.
Young George knew things. The world, he had found out,

Was a good place, and life was a good game—
Particularly when Aunt Imogen   80
Was in it. And one day it came to pass—
One rainy day when she was holding him
And rocking him—that he, in his own right,
Took it upon himself to tell her so;
And something in his way of telling it—   85
The language, or the tone, or something else—
Gripped like insidious fingers on her throat,
And then went foraging as if to make
A plaything of her heart. Such undeserved
And unsophisticated confidence   90
Went mercilessly home; and had she sat
Before a looking glass, the deeps of it
Could not have shown more clearly to her then
Than one thought-mirrored little glimpse had shown
The pang that wrenched her face and filled her eyes   95
With anguish and intolerable mist.
The blow that she had vaguely thrust aside
Like fright so many times had found her now:
Clean-thrust and final it had come to her
From a child's lips at last, as it had come   100
Never before, and as it might be felt
Never again. Some grief, like some delight,
Stings hard but once: to custom after that
The rapture or the pain submits itself,
And we are wiser than we were before.   105
And Imogen was wiser; though at first
Her dream-defeating wisdom was indeed
A thankless heritage: there was no sweet,
No bitter now; nor was there anything
To make a daily meaning for her life—   110
Till truth, like Harlequin, leapt out somehow
From ambush and threw sudden savor to it—
But the blank taste of time. There were no dreams,
No phantoms in her future any more:
One clinching revelation of what was   115
One by-flash of irrevocable chance,
Had acridly but honestly foretold
The mystical fulfilment of a life
That might have once . . . But that was all gone by:
There was no need of reaching back for that: 120

The triumph was not hers: there was no love
Save borrowed love: there was no might have been.

But there was yet Young George—and he had gone
Conveniently to sleep, like a good boy;
And there was yet Sylvester with his drum,   125
And there was frowzle-headed little Jane;
And there was Jane the sister, and the mother,—
Her sister, and the mother of them all.
They were not hers, not even one of them:
She was not born to be so much as that,   130
For she was born to be Aunt Imogen.
Now she could see the truth and look at it;
Now she could make stars out where once had palled
A future's emptiness; now she could share
With others—ah, the others!—to the end   135
The largess of a woman who could smile;
Now it was hers to dance the folly down,
And all the murmuring; now it was hers
To be Aunt Imogen. —So, when Young George
Woke up and blinked at her with his big eyes,   140
And smiled to see the way she blinked at him,
'T was only in old concord with the stars
That she took hold of him and held him close,
Close to herself, and crushed him till he laughed.

Miniver Cheevy

MINIVER CHEEVY, child of scorn,
  Grew lean while he assailed the seasons;
He wept that he was ever born,
  And he had reasons.

Miniver loved the days of old   5
  When swords were bright and steeds were prancing;
The vision of a warrior bold
  Would set him dancing.

Miniver sighed for what was not,
  And dreamed, and rested from his labors;   10
He dreamed of Thebes and Camelot,
  And Priam's neighbors.

Miniver mourned the ripe renown
    That made so many a name so fragrant;
He mourned Romance, now on the town,   15
    And Art, a vagrant.

Miniver loved the Medici,
    Albeit he had never seen one;
He would have sinned incessantly
    Could he have been one.   20

Miniver cursed the commonplace
    And eyed a khaki suit with loathing;
He missed the medieval grace
    Of iron clothing.

Miniver scorned the gold he sought,   25
    But sore annoyed was he without it;
Miniver thought, and thought, and thought,
    And thought about it.

Miniver Cheevy, born too late,
    Scratched his head and kept on thinking;   30
Miniver coughed, and called it fate,
    And kept on drinking.

Edith Wharton (1862–1937)
Roman Fever

1

    From the table at which they had been lunching two American ladies of ripe but well-cared-for middle age moved across the lofty terrace of the Roman restaurant and, leaning on its parapet, looked first at each other, and then down on the outspread glories of the Palatine and the Forum, with the same expression of vague but benevolent approval.

    As they leaned there a girlish voice echoed up gaily from the stairs leading to the court below. "Well, come along, then," it cried, not to them but to an invisible companion, "and let's leave the young things to their knitting"; and a voice as fresh laughed back: "Oh, look here, Babs, not actually *knitting*—" "Well, I mean figuratively," rejoined the first. "After all, we haven't left our poor parents much else to do . . ." and at that point the turn of the stairs engulfed the dialogue.

The two ladies looked at each other again, this time with a tinge of smiling embarrassment, and the smaller and paler one shook her head and coloured slightly.

"Barbara!" she murmured, sending an unheard rebuke after the mocking voice in the stairway.

The other lady, who was fuller, and higher in colour, with a small determined nose supported by vigorous black eyebrows, gave a good-humoured laugh. "That's what our daughters think of us!"

Her companion replied by a deprecating gesture. "Not of us individually. We must remember that. It's just the collective modern idea of Mothers. And you see—" Half guiltily she drew from her handsomely mounted black hand-bag a twist of crimson silk run through by two fine knitting needles. "One never knows," she murmured. "The new system has certainly given us a good deal of time to kill; and sometimes I get tired just looking—even at this." Her gesture was now addressed to the stupendous scene at their feet.

The dark lady laughed again, and they both relapsed upon the view, contemplating it in silence, with a sort of diffused serenity which might have been borrowed from the spring effulgence of the Roman skies. The luncheon-hour was long past, and the two had their end of the vast terrace to themselves. At this opposite extremity a few groups, detained by a lingering look at the outspread city, were gathering up guide-books and fumbling for tips. The last of them scattered, and the two ladies were alone on the air-washed height.

"Well, I don't see why we shouldn't just stay here," said Mrs. Slade, the lady of the high colour and energetic brows. Two derelict basket-chairs stood near, and she pushed them into the angle of the parapet, and settled herself in one, her gaze upon the Palatine. "After all, it's still the most beautiful view in the world."

"It always will be, to me," assented her friend Mrs. Ansley, with so slight a stress on the "me" that Mrs. Slade, though she noticed it, wondered if it were not merely accidental, like the random underlinings of old-fashioned letter-writers.

"Grace Ansley was always old-fashioned," she thought; and added aloud, with a retrospective smile: "It's a view we've both been familiar with for a good many years. When we first met here we were younger than our girls are now. You remember?"

"Oh, yes, I remember," murmured Mrs. Ansley, with the same undefinable stress.—"There's that head-waiter wondering," she interpolated. She was evidently far less sure than her companion of herself and of her rights in the world.

"I'll cure him of wondering," said Mrs. Slade, stretching her hand toward a bag as discreetly opulent-looking as Mrs. Ansley's. Signing to the head-waiter, she explained that she and her friend were old lovers of Rome, and would like to spend the end of the afternoon looking down on the view—that is, if it did not disturb the service? The head-waiter, bowing over her gratuity, assured her that the ladies were most welcome, and would be still more so if they would condescend to remain for dinner. A full moon night, they would remember. . . .

Mrs. Slade's black brows drew together, as though references to the moon were out-of-place and even unwelcome. But she smiled away her frown as the head-waiter retreated. "Well, why not? We might do worse. There's no knowing, I suppose, when the girls will be back. Do you even know back from *where?* I don't!"

Mrs. Ansley again coloured slightly. "I think those young Italian aviators we met at the Embassy invited them to fly to Tarquinia for tea. I suppose they'll want to wait and fly back by moonlight."

"Moonlight—moonlight! What a part it still plays. Do you suppose they're as sentimental as we were?"

"I've come to the conclusion that I don't in the least know what they are," said Mrs. Ansley. "And perhaps we didn't know much more about each other."

"No; perhaps we didn't."

Her friend gave her a shy glance. "I never should have supposed you were sentimental, Alida."

"Well, perhaps I wasn't." Mrs. Slade drew her lids together in retrospect; and for a few moments the two ladies, who had been intimate since childhood, reflected how little they knew each other. Each one, of course, had a label ready to attach to the other's name; Mrs. Delphin Slade, for instance, would have told herself, or any one who asked her, that Mrs. Horace Ansley, twenty-five years ago, had been exquisitely lovely—no, you wouldn't believe it, would you? . . . though, of course, still charming, distinguished . . . Well, as a girl she had been exquisite; far more beautiful than her daughter Barbara, though certainly Babs, according to the new standards at any rate, was more effective—had more edge, as they say. Funny where she got it, with those two nullities as parents. Yes; Horace Ansley was—well, just the duplicate of his wife. Museum specimens of old New York. Good-looking, irre-proachable, exemplary. Mrs. Slade and Mrs. Ansley had lived opposite each other—actually as well as figuratively—for years. When the drawing-room curtains in No. 20 East 73rd Street were renewed, No. 23, across the way, was always aware of it. And of all the movings, buyings, travels, anniversaries, illnesses—the tame chronicle of an estimable pair. Little of it escaped Mrs. Slade. But she had grown bored with it by the time her husband made his big *coup* in Wall Street, and when they bought in upper Park Avenue had already begun to think: "I'd rather live opposite a speak-easy for a change; at least one might see it raided." The idea of seeing Grace raided was so amusing that (before the move) she launched it at a woman's lunch. It made a hit, and went the rounds—she sometimes wondered if it had crossed the street, and reached Mrs. Ansley. She hoped not, but didn't much mind. Those were the days when respectability was at a discount, and it did the irreproachable no harm to laugh at them a little.

A few years later, and not many months apart, both ladies lost their husbands. There was an appropriate exchange of wreaths and condolences, and a brief renewal of intimacy in the half-shadow of their mourning; and now, after another interval, they had run across each other in Rome, at the same hotel, each of them the modest appendage of a salient daughter. The similarity of their lot had again drawn them together, lending itself to mild jokes, and the mutual confession that, if in old days it must have been tiring to "keep up" with daughters, it was now, at times, a little dull not to.

No doubt, Mrs. Slade reflected, she felt her unemployment more than poor Grace ever would. It was a big drop from being the wife of Delphin Slade to being his widow. She had always regarded herself (with a certain conjugal pride) as his equal in social gifts, as contributing her full share to the making of the exceptional couple they were: but the difference after his death was irremediable. As the wife of the famous corporation lawyer, always with an international case or two on hand, every day brought its exciting and unexpected obligation: the impromptu entertaining of eminent colleagues from abroad, the hurried dashes on legal business to London, Paris or Rome, where the entertaining was so handsomely reciprocated; the amusement of hearing in her wake: "What, that handsome woman with the good clothes and eyes is Mrs. Slade—*the* Slade's wife? Really? Generally the wives of celebrities are such frumps."

Yes; being *the* Slade's widow was a dullish business after that. In living up to such a husband all her faculties had been engaged; now she had only her daughter to live up to, for the son who seemed to have inherited his father's gifts had died suddenly in boyhood. She had fought through that agony because her husband was there, to be helped and to help; now, after the father's death, the thought of the boy had become unbearable. There was nothing left but to mother her daughter; and dear Jenny was such a perfect daughter that she needed no excessive mothering. "Now with Babs Ansley I don't know that I *should* be so quiet," Mrs. Slade sometimes half-enviously reflected; but Jenny, who was younger than her brilliant friend, was that rare accident, an extremely pretty girl who somehow made youth and prettiness seem as safe as their absence. It was all perplexing—and to Mrs. Slade a little boring. She wished that Jenny would fall in love—with the wrong man, even; that she might have to be watched, out-maneuvered, rescued. And instead, it was Jenny who watched her mother, kept her out of draughts, made sure that she had taken her tonic . . .

Mrs. Ansley was much less articulate than her friend, and her mental portrait of Mrs. Slade was slighter, and drawn with fainter touches. "Alida Slade's awfully brilliant; but not as brilliant as she thinks," would have summed it up; though she would have added, for the enlightenment of strangers, that Mrs. Slade had been an extremely dashing girl; much more so than her daughter, who was pretty, of course, and clever in a way, but had none of her mother's—well, "vividness," some one had once called it. Mrs. Ansley would take up current words like this, and cite them in quotation marks, as unheard-of audacities. No; Jenny was not like her mother. Some-times Mrs. Ansley thought Alida Slade was disappointed; on the whole she had had a sad life. Full of failures and mistakes; Mrs. Ansley had always been rather sorry for her . . .

So these two ladies visualized each other, each through the wrong end of her little telescope.

2

For a long time they continued to sit side by side without speaking. It seemed as though, to both, there was a relief in laying down their somewhat futile activities in the presence of the vast Memento Mori which faced them. Mrs. Slade sat quite still, her eyes fixed on the golden slope of the Palace of the Cæsars, and after a while Mrs. Ansley ceased to fidget with her bag, and she too sank into meditation. Like many intimate friends, the two ladies had never before had occasion to be silent together, and Mrs. Ansley was slightly embarrassed by what seemed, after so many years, a new stage in their intimacy, and one with which she did not yet know how to deal.

Suddenly the air was full of that deep clangour of bells which periodically covers Rome with a roof of silver. Mrs. Slade glanced at her wrist-watch. "Five o'clock already," she said, as though surprised.

Mrs. Ansley suggested interrogatively: "There's bridge at the Embassy at five." For a long time Mrs. Slade did not answer. She appeared to be lost in contemplation, and Mrs. Ansley thought the remark had escaped her. But after a while she said, as if speaking out of a dream: "Bridge, did you say? Not unless you want to . . . But I don't think I will, you know."

"Oh, no," Mrs. Ansley hastened to assure her. "I don't care to at all. It's so lovely here; and so full of old memories, as you say." She settled herself in her chair, and almost furtively drew forth her knitting. Mrs. Slade took sideway note of this activity, but her own beautifully cared-for hands remained motionless on her knee.

"I was just thinking," she said slowly, "what different things Rome stands for to each generation of travellers. To our grandmothers, Roman fever; to our mothers, sentimental dangers—how we used to be guarded!—to our daughters, no more dangers than the middle of Main Street. They don't know it—but how much they're missing!"

The long golden light was beginning to pale, and Mrs. Ansley lifted her knitting a little closer to her eyes. "Yes; how we were guarded!"

"I always used to think," Mrs. Slade continued, "that our mothers had a much more difficult job than our grandmothers. When Roman fever stalked the streets it must have been comparatively easy to gather in the girls at the danger hour; but when you and I were young, with such beauty calling us, and the spice of disobedience thrown in, and no worse risk than catching cold during the cool hour after sunset, the mothers used to be put to it to keep us in—didn't they?"

She turned again toward Mrs. Ansley, but the latter had reached a delicate point in her knitting. "One, two, three—slip two; yes, they must have been," she assented, without looking up.

Mrs. Slade's eyes rested on her with deepened attention. "She can knit—in the face of *this!* How like her . . ."

Mrs. Slade leaned back, brooding, her eyes ranging from the ruins which faced her to the long green hollow of the Forum, the fading glow of the church fronts beyond it, and the outlying immensity of the Colosseum. Suddenly she thought: "It's all very well to say that our girls have done away with sentiment and moonlight. But if Babs Ansley isn't out to catch that young aviator—the one who's a Marchese—then I don't know anything. And Jenny has no chance beside her. I know that too. I wonder if that's why Grace Ansley likes the two girls to go everywhere together? My poor Jenny as a foil—!" Mrs. Slade gave a hardly audible laugh, and at the sound Mrs. Ansley dropped her knitting.

"Yes—?"

"I—oh, nothing. I was only thinking how your Babs carries everything before her. That Campolieri boy is one of the best matches in Rome. Don't look so innocent, my dear—you know he is. And I was wondering, ever so respectfully, you understand . . . wondering how two such exemplary characters as you and Horace had managed to produce anything quite so dynamic." Mrs. Slade laughed again, with a touch of asperity.

Mrs. Ansley's hands lay inert across her needles. She looked straight out at the great accumulated wreckage of passion and splendour at her feet. But her small profile was almost expressionless. At length she said: "I think you overrate Babs, my dear."

Mrs. Slade's tone grew easier. "No; I don't. I appreciate her. And perhaps envy you. Oh, my girl's perfect; if I were a chronic invalid I'd—well, I think I'd rather be in Jenny's hands. There must be times . . . but there! I always wanted a brilliant daughter . . . and never quite understood why I got an angel instead."

Mrs. Ansley echoed her laugh in a faint murmur. "Babs is an angel too."

"Of course—of course! But she's got rainbow wings. Well, they're wandering by the sea with their young men; and here we sit . . . and it all brings back the past a little too acutely."

Mrs. Ansley had resumed her knitting. One might almost have imagined (if one had known her less well, Mrs. Slade reflected) that, for her also, too many memories rose from the lengthening shadows of those august ruins. But no; she was simply absorbed in her work. What was there for her to worry about? She knew that Babs would almost certainly come back engaged to the extremely eligible Campolieri. "And she'll sell the New York house, and settle down near them in Rome, and never be in their way . . . she's much too tactful. But she'll have an excellent cook, and just the right people in for bridge and cocktails . . . and a perfectly peaceful old age among her grandchildren."

Mrs. Slade broke off this prophetic flight with a recoil of self-disgust. There was no one of whom she had less right to think unkindly than of Grace Ansley. Would she never cure herself of envying her? Perhaps she had begun too long ago.

She stood up and leaned against the parapet, filling her troubled eyes with the tranquillizing magic of the hour. But instead of tranquillizing her the sight seemed to increase her exasperation. Her gaze turned toward the Colosseum. Already its golden flank was drowned in purple shadow, and above it the sky curved crystal clear, without light or colour. It was the moment when afternoon and evening hang balanced in mid-heaven.

Mrs. Slade turned back and laid her hand on her friend's arm. The gesture was so abrupt that Mrs. Ansley looked up, startled.

"The sun's set. You're not afraid, my dear?"

"Afraid—?"

"Of Roman fever or pneumonia? I remember how ill you were that winter. As a girl you had a very delicate throat, hadn't you?"

"Oh, we're all right up here. Down below, in the Forum, it does get deathly cold, all of a sudden . . . but not here."

"Ah, of course you know because you had to be so careful." Mrs. Slade turned back to the parapet. She thought: "I must make one more effort not to hate her." Aloud she said: "Whenever I look at the Forum from up here, I remember that story about a great-aunt of yours, wasn't she? A dreadfully wicked great-aunt?"

"Oh, yes; Great-aunt Harriet. The one who was supposed to have sent her young sister out to the Forum after sunset to gather a night-blooming flower for her album. All our great-aunts and grandmothers used to have albums of dried flowers."

Mrs. Slade nodded. "But she really sent her because they were in love with the same man—"

"Well, that was the family tradition. They said Aunt Harriet confessed it years afterward. At any rate, the poor little sister caught the fever and died. Mother used to frighten us with the story when we were children."

"And you frightened *me* with it, that winter when you and I were here as girls. The winter I was engaged to Delphin."

Mrs. Ansley gave a faint laugh. "Oh, did I? Really frightened you? I don't believe you're easily frightened."

"Not often; but I was then. I was easily frightened because I was too happy. I wonder if you know what that means?"

"I—yes . . ." Mrs. Ansley faltered.

"Well, I suppose that was why the story of your wicked aunt made such an impression on me. And I thought: 'There's no more Roman fever, but the Forum is deathly cold after sunset—especially after a hot day. And the Colosseum's even colder and damper.'"

"The Colosseum—?"

"Yes. It wasn't easy to get in, after the gates were locked for the night. Far from easy. Still, in those days it could be managed; it was managed, often. Lovers met there who couldn't meet elsewhere. You knew that?"

"I—I daresay. I don't remember."

"You don't remember? You don't remember going to visit some ruins or other one evening, just after dark, and catching a bad chill? You were supposed to have gone to see the moon rise. People always said that expedition was what caused your illness."

There was a moment's silence; then Mrs. Ansley rejoined: "Did they? It was all so long ago."

"Yes. And you got well again—so it didn't matter. But I suppose it struck your friends—the reason given for your illness, I mean—because everybody knew you were so prudent on account of your throat, and your mother took such care of you . . . You *had* been out late sightseeing, hadn't you, that night?"

"Perhaps I had. The most prudent girls aren't always prudent. What made you think of it now?"

Mrs. Slade seemed to have no answer ready. But after a moment she broke out: "Because I simply can't bear it any longer—!"

Mrs. Ansley lifted her head quickly. Her eyes were wide and very pale. "Can't bear what?"

"Why—your not knowing that I've always known why you went."

"Why I went—?"

"Yes. You think I'm bluffing, don't you? Well, you went to meet the man I was engaged to—and I can repeat every word of the letter that took you there."

While Mrs. Slade spoke Mrs. Ansley had risen unsteadily to her feet. Her bag, her knitting and gloves, slid in a panic-stricken heap to the ground. She looked at Mrs. Slade as though she were looking at a ghost.

"No, no—don't," she faltered out.

"Why not? Listen, if you don't believe me. 'My one darling, things can't go on like this. I must see you alone. Come to the Colosseum immediately after dark tomorrow. There will be somebody to let you in. No one whom you need fear will suspect'—but perhaps you've forgotten what the letter said?"

Mrs. Ansley met the challenge with an unexpected composure. Steadying herself against the chair she looked at her friend, and replied: "No, I know it by heart too."

"And the signature? 'Only *your* D.S.' Was that it? I'm right, am I? That was the letter that took you out that evening after dark?"

Mrs. Ansley was still looking at her. It seemed to Mrs. Slade that a slow struggle was going on behind the voluntarily controlled mask of her small quiet face. "I shouldn't have thought she had herself so well in hand," Mrs. Slade reflected, almost resentfully. But at this moment Mrs. Ansley spoke. "I don't know how you knew. I burnt that letter at once."

"Yes; you would, naturally—you're so prudent!" The sneer was open now. "And if you burnt the letter you're wondering how on earth I know what was in it. That's it, isn't it?"

Mrs. Slade waited, but Mrs. Ansley did not speak.

"Well, my dear, I know what was in that letter because I wrote it!"

"You wrote it?"

"Yes."

The two women stood for a minute staring at each other in the last golden light. Then Mrs. Ansley dropped back into her chair. "Oh," she murmured, and covered her face with her hands.

Mrs. Slade waited nervously for another word or movement. None came, and at length she broke out: "I horrify you."

Mrs. Ansley's hands dropped to her knee. The face they uncovered was streaked with tears. "I wasn't thinking of you. I was thinking—it was the only letter I ever had from him!"

"And I wrote it. Yes; I wrote it! But I was the girl he was engaged to. Did you happen to remember that?"

Mrs. Ansley's head dropped again. "I'm not trying to excuse myself . . . I remembered . . ."

"And still you went?"

"Still I went."

Mrs. Slade stood looking down on the small bowed figure at her side. The flame of her wrath had already sunk, and she wondered why she had ever thought there would be any satisfaction in inflicting so purposeless a wound on her friend. But she had to justify herself.

"You do understand? I found out—and I hated you, hated you. I knew you were in love with Delphin—and I was afraid; afraid of you, of your quiet ways, your sweetness . . . your . . . well, I wanted you out of the way, that's all. Just for a few weeks; just till I was sure of him. So in a blind fury I wrote that letter . . . I don't know why I'm telling you now."

"I suppose," said Mrs. Ansley slowly, "it's because you've always gone on hating me."

"Perhaps. Or because I wanted to get the whole thing off my mind." She paused. "I'm glad you destroyed the letter. Of course I never thought you'd die."

Mrs. Ansley relapsed into silence, and Mrs. Slade, leaning above her, was conscious of a strange sense of isolation, of being cut off from the warm current of human communion. "You think me a monster!"

"I don't know . . . It was the only letter I had, and you say he didn't write it?"

"Ah, how you care for him still!"

"I cared for that memory," said Mrs. Ansley.

Mrs. Slade continued to look down on her. She seemed physically reduced by the blow—as if, when she got up, the wind might scatter her like a puff of dust. Mrs.

Slade's jealousy suddenly leapt up again at the sight. All these years the woman had been living on that letter. How she must have loved him, to treasure the mere memory of its ashes! The letter of the man her friend was engaged to. Wasn't it she who was the monster?

"You tried your best to get him away from me, didn't you? But you failed; and I kept him. That's all."

"Yes. That's all."

"I wish now I hadn't told you. I'd no idea you'd feel about it as you do; I thought you'd be amused. It all happened so long ago, as you say; and you must do me the justice to remember that I had no reason to think you'd ever taken it seriously. How could I, when you were married to Horace Ansley two months afterward? As soon as you could get out of bed your mother rushed you off to Florence and married you. People were rather surprised—they wondered at its being done so quickly; but I thought I knew. I had an idea you did it out of *pique*—to be able to say you'd got ahead of Delphin and me. Girls have such silly reasons for doing the most serious things. And your marrying so soon convinced me that you'd never really cared."

"Yes, I suppose it would," Mrs. Ansley assented.

The clear heaven overhead was emptied of all its gold. Dusk spread over it, abruptly darkening the Seven Hills. Here and there lights began to twinkle through the foliage at their feet. Steps were coming and going on the deserted terrace—waiters looking out of the doorway at the head of the stairs, then reappearing with trays and napkins and flasks of wine. Tables were moved, chairs straightened. A feeble string of electric lights flickered out. Some vases of faded flowers were carried away, and brought back replenished. A stout lady in a dust-coat suddenly appeared, asking in broken Italian if any one had seen the elastic band which held together her tattered Baedeker. She poked with her stick under the table at which she had lunched, the waiters assisting.

The corner where Mrs. Slade and Mrs. Ansley sat was still shadowy and deserted. For a long time neither of them spoke. At length Mrs. Slade began again: "I suppose I did it as a sort of joke—"

"A joke?"

"Well, girls are ferocious sometimes, you know. Girls in love especially. And I remember laughing to myself all that evening at the idea that you were waiting around there in the dark, dodging out of sight, listening for every sound, trying to get in—. Of course I was upset when I heard you were so ill afterward."

Mrs. Ansley had not moved for a long time. But now she turned slowly toward her companion. "But I didn't wait. He'd arranged everything. He was there. We were let in at once," she said.

Mrs. Slade sprang up from her leaning position. "Delphin there? They let you in?—Ah, now you're lying!" she burst out with violence.

Mrs. Ansley's voice grew clearer, and full of surprise. "But of course he was there. Naturally he came—"

"Came? How did he know he'd find you there? You must be raving!"

Mrs. Ansley hesitated, as though reflecting. "But I answered the letter. I told him I'd be there. So he came."

Mrs. Slade flung her hands up to her face. "Oh, God—you answered! I never thought of your answering . . ."

"It's odd you never thought of it, if you wrote the letter."

"Yes. I was blind with rage."

Mrs. Ansley rose, and drew her fur scarf about her. "It is cold here. We'd better go . . . I'm sorry for you," she said, as she clasped the fur about her throat.

The unexpected words sent a pang through Mrs. Slade. "Yes; we'd better go." She gathered up her bag and cloak. "I don't know why you should be sorry for me," she muttered.

Mrs. Ansley stood looking away from her toward the dusky secret mass of the Colosseum. "Well—because I didn't have to wait that night."

Mrs. Slade gave an unquiet laugh. "Yes; I was beaten there. But I oughtn't to begrudge it to you, I suppose. At the end of all these years. After all, I had everything; I had him for twenty-five years. And you had nothing but that one letter that he didn't write."

Mrs. Ansley was again silent. At length she turned toward the door of the terrace. She took a step, and turned back, facing her companion.

"I had Barbara," she said, and began to move ahead of Mrs. Slade toward the stairway.

William Butler Yeats (1865–1939)
A Last Confession

> What lively lad most pleasured me
> Of all that with me lay?
> I answer that I gave my soul
> And loved in misery,
> But had great pleasure with a lad   5
> That I loved bodily.
>
> Flinging from his arms I laughed
> To think his passion such
> He fancied that I gave a soul
> Did but our bodies touch,   10
> And laughed upon his breast to think
> Beast gave beast as much.

I gave what other women gave
That stepped out of their clothes,
But when this soul, its body off,   15
Naked to naked goes,
He it has found shall find therein
What none other knows,

And give his own and take his own
And rule in his own right;   20
And though it loved in misery
Close and cling so tight,
There's not a bird of day that dare
Extinguish that delight.

Sailing to Byzantium

1
That is no country for old men. The young
In one another's arms, birds in the trees
—Those dying generations—at their song,
The salmon-falls, the mackerel-crowded seas,
Fish, flesh, or fowl, commend all summer long   5
Whatever is begotten, born, and dies.
Caught in that sensual music all neglect
Monuments of unaging intellect.

2
An aged man is but a paltry thing,
A tattered coat upon a stick, unless   10
Soul clap its hands and sing, and louder sing
For every tatter in its mortal dress,
Nor is there singing school but studying
Monuments of its own magnificence;
And therefore I have sailed the seas and come   15
To the holy city of Byzantium.

3
O sages standing in God's holy fire
As in the gold mosaic of a wall,
Come from the holy fire, perne in a gyre,
And be the singing-masters of my soul.   20
Consume my heart away; sick with desire
And fastened to a dying animal

It knows not what it is; and gather me
Into the artifice of eternity.

4

Once out of nature I shall never take   25
My bodily form from any natural thing,
But such a form as Grecian goldsmiths make
Of hammered gold and gold enameling
To keep a drowsy Emperor awake;
Or set upon a golden bough to sing   30
To lords and ladies of Byzantium
Of what is past, or passing, or to come.

The Folly of Being Comforted

One that is ever kind said yesterday:
"Your well-beloved's hair has threads of grey,
And little shadows come about her eyes;
Time can but make it easier to be wise
Though now it seem impossible, and so   5
Patience is all that you have need of."
                                                        No,
I have not a crumb of comfort, not a grain,
Time can but make her beauty over again:
Because of that great nobleness of hers
The fire that stirs about her, when she stirs   10
Burns but more clearly. O she had not these ways,
When all the wild summer was in her gaze.
O heart! O heart! if she'd but turn her head,
You'd know the folly of being comforted.

What Then?

His chosen comrades thought at school
He must grow a famous man;
He thought the same and lived by rule,
All his twenties crammed with toil;
"What then?" sang Plato's ghost. "What then?"   5

Everything he wrote was read,
After certain years he won
Sufficient money for his need,
Friends that have been friends indeed;
"What then?" sang Plato's ghost. "What then?"   10

All his happier dreams came true—
A small old house, wife, daughter, son,
Grounds where plum and cabbage grew,
Poets and Wits about him drew;
"What then?" sang Plato's ghost. "What then?"   15

"The work is done," grown old he thought,
"According to my boyish plan;
Let the fools rage, I swerved in naught,
Something to perfection brought";
But louder sang that ghost, "What then?"   20

Why Should Not Old Men Be Mad?

Why should not old men be mad?
Some have known a likely lad
That had a sound fly-fisher's wrist
Turn to a drunken journalist;
A girl that knew all Dante once   5
Live to bear children to a dunce;
A Helen of social welfare dream,
Climb on a wagonette to scream.
Some think it a matter of course that chance
Should starve good men and bad advance,   10
That if their neighbours figured plain,
As though upon a lighted screen,
No single story would they find
Of an unbroken happy mind,
A finish worthy of the start.   15
Young men know nothing of this sort,
Observant old men know it well;
And when they know what old books tell,
And that no better can be had,
Know why an old man should be mad.   20

6

Coming to Terms with Death

William Cullen Bryant (1794–1878)

Thanatopsis

To him who in the love of Nature holds
Communion with her visible forms, she speaks
A various language; for his gayer hours
She has a voice of gladness, and a smile
And eloquence of beauty, and she glides   5
Into his darker musings, with a mild
And healing sympathy, that steals away
Their sharpness, ere he is aware. When thoughts
Of the last bitter hour come like a blight
Over thy spirit, and sad images   10
Of the stern agony, and shroud, and pall,
And breathless darkness, and the narrow house,
Make thee to shudder, and grow sick at heart;—
Go forth, under the open sky, and list
To Nature's teachings, while from all around—   15
Earth and her waters, and the depths of air—
Comes a still voice—Yet a few days, and thee
The all-beholding sun shall see no more
In all his course; nor yet in the cold ground,
Where thy pale form was laid, with many tears,   20

Nor in the embrace of ocean, shall exist
Thy image. Earth, that nourished thee, shall claim
Thy growth, to be resolved to earth again,
And, lost each human trace, surrendering up
Thine individual being, shalt thou go   25
To mix for ever with the elements,
To be a brother to the insensible rock
And to the sluggish clod, which the rude swain
Turns with his share, and treads upon. The oak
Shall send his roots abroad, and pierce thy mould.   30

    Yet not to thine eternal resting-place
Shalt thou retire alone, nor couldst thou wish
Couch more magnificent. Thou shalt lie down
With patriarchs of the infant world—with kings,
The powerful of the earth—the wise, the good,   35
Fair forms, and hoary seers of ages past,
All in one mighty sepulchre. The hills
Rock-ribbed and ancient as the sun,—the vales
Stretching in pensive quietness between;
The venerable woods—rivers that move   40
In majesty, and the complaining brooks
That make the meadows green; and, poured round all,
Old Ocean's gray and melancholy waste,—
Are but the solemn decorations all
Of the great tomb of man. The golden sun,   45
The planets, all the infinite host of heaven,
Are shining on the sad abodes of death,
Through the still lapse of ages. All that tread
The globe are but a handful to the tribes
That slumber in its bosom.—Take the wings   50
Of morning, pierce the Barcan wilderness,
Or lose thyself in the continuous woods
Where rolls the Oregon, and hears no sound,
Save his own dashings—yet the dead are there:
And millions in those solitudes, since first   55
The flight of years began, have laid them down
In their last sleep—the dead reign there alone.
So shalt thou rest, and what if thou withdraw
In silence from the living, and no friend
Take note of thy departure? All that breathe   60
Will share thy destiny. The gay will laugh

When thou art gone, the solemn brood of care
Plod on, and each one as before will chase
His favorite phantom; yet all these shall leave
Their mirth and their employments, and shall come   65
And make their bed with thee. As the long train
Of ages glide away, the sons of men,
The youth in life's green spring, and he who goes
In the full strength of years, matron and maid,
The speechless babe, and the gray-headed man—   70
Shall one by one be gathered to thy side,
By those, who in their turn shall follow them.

    So live, that when thy summons comes to join
The innumerable caravan, which moves
To that mysterious realm, where each shall take   75
His chamber in the silent halls of death,
Thou go not, like the quarry-slave at night,
Scourged to his dungeon, but, sustained and soothed
By an unfaltering trust, approach thy grave,
Like one who wraps the drapery of his couch   80
About him, and lies down to pleasant dreams.

Emily Dickinson (1830–1886)
Because I could not stop for Death

            Because I could not stop for Death—
            He kindly stopped for me—
            The Carriage held but just Ourselves—
            And Immortality.

            We slowly drove—He knew no haste,   5
            And I had put away
            My labor and my leisure too,
            For His Civility—

            We passed the School, where Children strove
            At Recess—in the Ring—   10

We passed the Fields of Gazing Grain—
We passed the Setting Sun—

Or rather—He passed Us—
The Dews drew quivering and chill—
For only Gossamer, my Gown—   15
My Tippet—only Tulle—

We paused before a House that seemed
A Swelling of the Ground—
The Roof was scarcely visible—
The Cornice—in the Ground—   20

Since then—'tis Centuries—and yet
Feels shorter than the Day
I first surmised the Horses' Heads
Were toward Eternity—

This World is not Conclusion

This World is not Conclusion.
A Species stands beyond—
Invisible, as Music—
But positive, as Sound—
It beckons, and it baffles—   5
Philosophy—don't know—
And through a Riddle, at the last—
Sagacity, must go—
To guess it, puzzles scholars—
To gain it, Men have borne   10
Contempt of Generations
And Crucifixion, shown—
Faith slips—and laughs, and rallies—
Blushes, if any see—
Plucks at a twig of Evidence—   15
And asks a Vane, the way—
Much Gesture, from the Pulpit—
Strong Hallelujahs roll—
Narcotics cannot still the Tooth
That nibbles at the soul—   20

John Donne (1572–1631)
Death, Be Not Proud

Death, be not proud, though some have callèd thee
Mighty and dreadful, for thou art not so;
For those whom thou think'st thou dost overthrow
Die not, poor Death, nor yet canst thou kill me.
From rest and sleep, which but thy pictures be,   5
Much pleasure; then from thee much more must flow,
And soonest our best men with thee do go,
Rest of their bones, and soul's delivery.
Thou art slave to fate, chance, kings, and desperate men,
And dost with poison, war, and sickness dwell,   10
And poppy or charms can make us sleep as well
And better than thy stroke; why swell'st thou then?
One short sleep past, we wake eternally
And death shall be no more; Death, thou shalt die.

Meditation XVII

Now, this bell tolling softly for another, says to me, thou must die.

Perchance he for whom this bell tolls, may be so ill, as that he knows not it tolls for him. And perchance I may think my self so much better than I am, as that they who are about me, and see my state, may have caused it to toll for me, and I know not that. The church is catholic, universal, so are all her actions; all that she does, belongs to all. When she baptizes a child, that action concerns me; for that child is thereby connected to that head, which is my head too, and ingraffed into that body, whereof I am a member. And when she buries a man, that action concerns me; all mankind is of one author, and is one volume; when one man dies, one chapter is not torn out of the book, but translated into a better language; and every chapter must be so translated; God employs several translators; some pieces are translated by age, some by sickness, some by war, some by justice; but God's hand is in every translation; and his hand shall bind up all our scattered leaves again, for that library where every book shall lie open to one another; as therefore the bell that rings to a sermon, calls not upon the preacher only, but upon the congregation to come; so this bell calls us all: but how much more me, who am brought so near the door by this sickness. There was a contention as far as a suit (in which, both piety and dignity, religion and estimation, were mingled) which of the religious orders should ring to prayers first in the morning; and it was determined, that they should ring first that rose earliest. If we understand aright the dignity of this bell, that tolls for our evening prayer, we would be glad to make it ours, by rising early, in that application, that it might be ours, as well as his, whose indeed it is. The bell doth toll for him, that thinks it doth; and though it intermit again, yet from that minute, that that occasion wrought upon him, he is united to God. Who casts not up his eye to the sun when it rises? But who takes off his eye from a comet, when that breaks out? who bends not his ear to any bell, which upon any occasion rings? But who can remove it from that bell, which is passing a piece of himself out of this world? No man is an island, entire of itself; every man is a piece of the continent, a part of the main; if a clod be washed away by the sea, Europe is the less, as well as if a promontory were, as well as if a manor of thy friend's or of thine own were; any man's death diminishes me, because I am involved in mankind, and therefore never send to know for whom the bell tolls; it tolls for thee. Neither can we call this a begging of misery, or a borrowing of misery, as though we were not miserable enough of ourselves, but must fetch in more from the next house, in taking upon us the misery of our neighbours. Truly it were an excusable covetousness, if we did; for affliction is a treasure, and scarce any man hath enough of it. No man hath affliction enough, that is not matured, and ripened by it, and made fit for God by that affliction. If a man carry treasure in bullion or in a wedge of gold, and have none coined into current moneys, his treasure will not defray him as he travels. Tribulation is treasure in the nature of it, but it is not current money in the use of it, except we get nearer and nearer our home, heaven, by it. Another may be sick too, and sick to death, and this affliction may lie in his bowels, as gold in a mine, and be of no use to him; but this bell that tells me of his affliction, digs out, and applies that gold to me: if by this consideration of another's danger, I take mine own into contemplation, and so secure myself, by making my recourse to my God, who is our only security.

Robert Frost (1874–1963)
"Out, Out—"

        The buzz-saw snarled and rattled in the yard
        And made dust and dropped stove-length sticks of wood,
        Sweet-scented stuff when the breeze drew across it.
        And from there those that lifted eyes could count
        Five mountain ranges one behind the other   5
        Under the sunset far into Vermont.
        And the saw snarled and rattled, snarled and rattled,
        As it ran light, or had to bear a load.
        And nothing happened: day was all but done.

Call it a day, I wish they might have said   10
To please the boy by giving him the half hour
That a boy counts so much when saved from work.
His sister stood beside them in her apron
To tell them "Supper." At the word, the saw,
As if to prove saws knew what supper meant,   15
Leaped out at the boy's hand, or seemed to leap—
He must have given the hand. However it was,
Neither refused the meeting. But the hand!
The boy's first outcry was a rueful laugh,
As he swung toward them holding up the hand   20
Half in appeal, but half as if to keep
The life from spilling. Then the boy saw all—
Since he was old enough to know, big boy
Doing a man's work, though a child at heart—
He saw all spoiled. "Don't let him cut my hand off—   25
The doctor, when he comes. Don't let him, sister!"
So. But the hand was gone already.
The doctor put him in the dark of ether.
He lay and puffed his lips out with his breath.
And then—the watcher at his pulse took fright.   30
No one believed. They listened at his heart.
Little—less—nothing!—and that ended it.
No more to build on there. And they, since they
Were not the one dead, turned to their affairs.

Thomas Hardy (1840–1926)

Ah, are you digging on my grave?

"Ah, are you digging on my grave,
      My loved one?—planting rue?"
—"No: yesterday he went to wed
One of the brightest wealth has bred.
'It cannot hurt her now,' he said,   5
      'That I should not be true.'"

"Then who is digging on my grave?
      My nearest dearest kin?"
—"Ah, no: they sit and think, 'What use!

What good will planting flowers produce?   10
No tendance of her mound can loose
    Her spirit from Death's gin.'"

"But some one digs upon my grave?
    My enemy?—prodding sly?"
—"Nay: When she heard you had passed the Gate   15
That shuts on all flesh soon or late,
She thought you no more worth her hate,
    And cares not where you lie."

"Then, who is digging on my grave?
    Say—since I have not guessed!"   20
—"O it is I, my mistress dear,
Your little dog, who still lives near,
And much I hope my movements here
    Have not disturbed your rest?"

"Ah, yes! *You* dig upon my grave . . .   25
    Why flashed it not on me
That one true heart was left behind!
What feeling do we ever find
To equal among human kind
    A dog's fidelity!"   30

"Mistress, I dug upon your grave
    To bury a bone, in case
I should be hungry near this spot
When passing on my daily trot.
I am sorry, but I quite forgot   35
    It was your resting-place."

A. E. Housman (1859–1936)
To an Athlete Dying Young

The time you won your town the race
We chaired you through the market place;
Man and boy stood cheering by,
And home we brought you shoulder-high.

Today, the road all runners come,   5
Shoulder-high we bring you home,
And set you at your threshold down,
Townsman of a stiller town.

Smart lad, to slip betimes away
From fields where glory does not stay   10
And early though the laurel grows
It withers quicker than the rose.

Eyes the shady night has shut
Cannot see the record cut,
And silence sounds no worse than cheers   15
After earth has stopped the ears:

Now you will not swell the rout
Of lads that wore their honors out,
Runners whom renown outran
And the name died before the man.   20

So set, before its echoes fade,
The fleet foot on the sill of shade,
And hold to the low lintel up
The still defended challenge cup.

And round that early laureled head   25
Will flock to gaze the strengthless dead
And find unwithered on its curls
The garland briefer than a girl's.

John Keats (1795–1821)
When I Have Fears

When I have fears that I may cease to be
  Before my pen has gleaned my teeming brain,
Before high-pilèd books, in charact'ry,
  Hold like rich garners the full-ripened grain;
When I behold, upon the night's starred face,   5

>Huge cloudy symbols of a high romance,
>And think that I may never live to trace
>Their shadows, with the magic hand of chance;
>And when I feel, fair creature of an hour,
>That I shall never look upon thee more,   10
>Never have relish in the faery power
>Of unreflecting love!—then on the shore
>Of the wide world I stand alone, and think
>Till Love and Fame to nothingness do sink.

Edna St. Vincent Millay (1892–1950)

Dirge Without Music

I am not resigned to the shutting away of loving hearts in the hard ground.
So it is, and so it will be, for so it has been, time out of mind:
Into the darkness they go, the wise and the lovely. Crowned
With lilies and with laurel they go; but I am not resigned.

Lovers and thinkers, into the earth with you.   5
Be one with the dull, the indiscriminate dust.
A fragment of what you felt, of what you knew,
A formula, a phrase remains,—but the best is lost.

The answers quick and keen, the honest look, the laughter, the love,—
They are gone. They are gone to feed the roses. Elegant and curled   10
Is the blossom. Fragrant is the blossom. I know. But I do not approve.
More precious was the light in your eyes than all the roses in the world.

Down, down, down into the darkness of the grave
Gently they go, the beautiful, the tender, the kind;
Quietly they go, the intelligent, the witty, the brave.   15
I know. But I do not approve. And I am not resigned.

Edwin Arlington Robinson (1869–1935)
How Annandale Went Out

"They called it Annandale—and I was there
To flourish, to find words, and to attend:
Liar, physician, hypocrite, and friend,
I watched him; and the sight was not so fair
As one or two that I have seen elsewhere: 5
An apparatus not for me to mend—
A wreck, with hell between him and the end,
Remained of Annandale; and I was there.

"I knew the ruin as I knew the man;
So put the two together, if you can,   10
Remembering the worst you know of me.
Now view yourself as I was, on the spot—
With a slight kind of engine. Do you see?
Like this—You wouldn't hang me? I thought not."

Christina Rossetti (1830–1894)
Song

When I am dead, my dearest,
    Sing no sad songs for me;
Plant thou no roses at my head,
    Nor shady cypress tree.
Be the green grass above me   5
    With showers and dewdrops wet;
And if thou wilt, remember,
    And if thou wilt, forget.

I shall not see the shadows,
    I shall not feel the rain;   10
I shall not hear the nightingale
    Sing on as if in pain.
And dreaming through the twilight
    That doth not rise nor set,
Haply I may remember,   15
    And haply may forget.

Sophocles (496?–406 B.C.)
Oedipus the King

Translated by Robert Bagg (born 1935)

SPEAKING CHARACTERS

OEDIPUS *King of Thebes*
PRIEST *of Zeus*
KREON *Jocasta's brother*
CHORUS *of older Theban men*
LEADER *of the Chorus*
TIRESIAS *blind prophet of Apollo*
JOCASTA *Oedipus' wife*
MESSENGER *from Corinth*
HERDSMAN *formerly of Laius' house*
SERVANT *from Oedipus' house*

SILENT CHARACTERS

DELEGATION OF THEBANS *mostly young*
ATTENDANTS *and* MAIDS
BOY *to lead* TIRESIAS
ANTIGONE *and* ISMENE, OEDIPUS' *daughters*

Scene

> *Before the Royal Palace in Thebes. The palace has an imposing central double
> door. Two altars stand near it; one is to Apollo. The* DELEGATION OF THEBANS
> *enters carrying olive branches wound with wool strips and gathers by the altars and
> stairs to the palace. The light and atmosphere are oppressive.* OEDIPUS *enters through
> the great doors.*

OEDIPUS   My children, the newest to descend
from ancient Kadmos into my care:
why have you rushed *here*, to these seats,
your wool-strung boughs begging
for god's help? Our city is oppressed—   5
with incense smoke and cries of mourners
and prayers sung to the Healing God.

I thought it wrong to let messengers
speak for you, my sons, I must hear
your words myself, so I have come out, I,   10
Oedipus, the name that all men know.
Speak to me, old man. Yours
is the natural voice for the rest.
What concerns drive you to me?
Fear? Reassurance? Be certain   15
I will give all the help I can.
I would be hard indeed if I didn't
pity those who approach me like this.

PRIEST   You rule my country, Oedipus, and you see
who comes to your altars, how mixed   20
we are in years: children too weak
to travel far, old men worn down by age,
priests like myself, the priest of Zeus,
a picked group of our best young men.
More of us wait with wool-strung boughs   25
in the markets, or at Athena's two temples,
or watch the embers at Ismenus' shrine
for the glow of prophecy.
                              You can see for yourself
our city going under, too weak to lift   30
its head clear of each deadly surge.
Plague is killing our flowering farmland,
it's killing our grazing cattle. Our women
in labor give birth to nothing.
                              A burning god   35
rakes his fire through our city;
he hates us with fever, he empties
the House of Kadmos—but he makes
black Hades rich, with our groans and tears.
We don't believe you are the gods' equal, King,   40
but I, and these children, ask help here,
at your hearth, because we put you first, of all men,
at handling trouble—or confronting gods.
You came to Thebes, you broke us free
of the tax we paid with our lives   45
to the rasping Singer. No one prompted you,
you were not taught by any of us.
We tell ourselves, you had a god's help
when you pulled us back to life.

Once more, Oedipus, we need your power.   50
We beg you, each in our own pain—
find our lost strength!—by learning
what you can from a god's voice
or what some man can tell you.
                        I know this: 55
advice from men proven right in the past
will meet a crisis with the surest force.
Act as our greatest man! Act
as you did when you first seized fame!
Our country believes your nerve saved us then.   60
Don't let us look back on your rule, saying,
once he raised us, but later let us fall.
Lift us to safety!—so that no misstep
ever again will bring Thebes down.

Good luck came with you, a bird from god's will,   65
the day you rescued us. Be that same man now.
If you are going to rule us, King, it's better
to rule the living than a lifeless waste.
A walled city is nothing, a ship is nothing,
when there's no one aboard to man it.   70
OEDIPUS   I do pity you, children. Don't think I'm unaware.
I know what need brings you: this sickness
harms you all. Yet, sick as you are,
not one of you suffers a sickness like mine.
Yours is a private grief, you feel   75
only what touches you. But my heart grieves
for you, for myself, and for our city.
You've come to wake me to all this.
There was truly no need. I haven't been asleep.
I have wept tears enough, for long enough;   80
my thoughts have raced down every twisting path.
The only cure all my thinking found
I've set in motion: I've sent Kreon,
my wife's brother, to Phoebus at Delphi,
to hear what action or what word of mine   85
will save this town. Already, counting what day
this is, I'm anxious: what is Kreon doing?
He takes too long, more than he needs.
But when he comes, I'd be the criminal
not to do all the god shows me to do.   90

PRIEST   Your words have just been made good: your men
  are now signaling me that Kreon's here.
OEDIPUS   O Lord Apollo,
  may the luck he brings save us! Luck so bright
  we can see it—just as we see him now.   95

(KREON *enters from the countryside, wearing a
laurel crown.*)

PRIEST   Only a man whose news is sweet comes home
  wearing a crown of laurel speckled with berries.
OEDIPUS   We'll soon know, he's within earshot. Prince!
  Brother kinsman, son of Menoikeos!
  What kind of answer have you brought from god?   100
KREON   A good one. I call nothing unbearable
  if luck can straighten it, and bless the outcome.
OEDIPUS   But what did the god say? There's nothing in your words—
  so far—to cheer me or to frighten me.
KREON   Will you hear it in front of these men?   105
  If so, I'll speak. Otherwise we go inside.
OEDIPUS   Speak here, to all of us. I suffer more
  for these men than for my own life.
KREON   Then I'll report what I heard from Apollo,
  who did not hide his meaning.   110
  He commands we drive out what corrupts us,
  what makes our land sick. We now harbor
  something incurable. He says: purge it.
OEDIPUS   Tell me the source of our trouble.
  How do we cleanse ourselves?   115
KREON   By banishing a man—or by killing him. It's blood,
  it's kin-murder that brings this storm on our city.
OEDIPUS   Did god name this man whose luck dooms him?
KREON   You know, King, that our city was ruled once
  by Laius, before you came to take the helm?   120
OEDIPUS   So I've heard. Though I never saw him.
KREON   Laius was murdered. Now, to avenge him, god
  wills you to strike down with your own hands
  those men whose hands struck Laius down.
OEDIPUS   Where do I find these men? How do I track   125
  vague footprints from a bygone crime?
KREON   The god said: look here, in our land.
  Nothing's caught that we don't chase—
  what we ignore goes free.

OEDIPUS   Was Laius killed at home? Or in the countryside?   130
  Or did they murder him on foreign ground?
KREON   He said when he left that his journey would take him
  into god's presence. But he never came home.
OEDIPUS   Did none of his troop see and report
  what happened? Is there no one   135
  to question whose answers might help?
KREON   All killed but a single terrified
  survivor, able to tell us but one fact.
OEDIPUS   What fact? One fact might point to many,
  if we had one small clue to raise our hopes.   140
KREON   They had the bad luck, he said, to meet bandits
  who struck them with a force many hands strong.
  It wasn't the violence of one man.
OEDIPUS   What bandit would risk such a huge crime
  unless somebody here hired him to do it?   145
KREON   That was our thought, but fresh trouble
  obsessed us. With Laius dead,
  who was to lead our revenge?
OEDIPUS   But here was your kingship murdered!
  What kind of trouble could have blocked your search?   150
KREON   The Sphinx's song. So wily, so baffling!—
  she forced us to forget the dark past
  to confront what lay at our feet.
OEDIPUS   I will go back, start fresh,
  and clear up all this darkness.   155
  Apollo was exactly right, and so were you,
  to turn our minds back to the murdered man.
  And now it's time I joined your search
  for vengeance, which our land and the god deserve.
  I don't do it to placate any distant kin,   160
  I will dispel this poison for my own sake.
  Laius' killer might one day come for me,
  exacting vengeance with that same hand.
  So to defend the dead man serves my interest.
  Rise, children, quick, up from the altar,   165
  raise those branches that appeal to god.
  Someone go call the people of Kadmos here.
  Tell them I'm ready to do anything.
  If god is with us, we will survive.
  If not, our ruin has already happened.   170

(*Exit* OEDIPUS, *into the palace.*)

PRIEST   Stand, children. The thing we came for
the king himself has promised to do.
Let god Apollo, who commands us to act,
lift this plague off our lives! Apollo our savior!

(*The Theban suppliants leave; the* CHORUS *enters.*)

CHORUS   What will you say to Thebes,   175
Voice from Zeus? What sweet sounds
bring your will from golden Delphi
to our bright city?
We're at the breaking point,
terror ranges through our minds.   180
Our wild cries reach for you,
Healing God from Delos—
in holy dread we ask: does your will
bring a new threat, or an old doom
come back as the years wheel by?   185
Say it, Great Voice,
you who answer us always,
speak as Hope's golden child.

Athena, your help is the first we ask,
immortal daughter of Zeus,   190
then Artemis your sister
who protects our land, sitting throned
in the heart of our marketplace.
And Apollo, whose shots
hit from far off! Our three   195
defenders from death: come now!
If once you fought off destruction
by blowing away the fires of our pain,
come to us now!

The blows I suffer are past count.   200
Plague kills my friends,
thought finds no spear
to keep a man safe.
Our rich earth shrivels what it grows,
our women in labor scream   205
but nothing's born. One life

after another flies,
you see them go
birds driving their strong wings
faster than flash-fire   210
to the shore of the sunset god.

Our city dies as its people die
those countless deaths, her children
rot in the streets, unmourned,
spreading more death.   215
Young wives and gray mothers
wash to our altars, their cries
carry from all sides, sobbing
for help, each lost in her pain.
A hymn shining to the Healer   220
is darkened by a grieving voice,
a flute in a courtyard.
Help us, Goddess,
golden child of Zeus,
send us the bright face   225
we need: Strength.

Force that raging killer, the god Ares,
to turn his back and run from our land.
He murders without armor now
but we, the victims of his fever,   230
shout in the hot blast of his charge.
Blow Ares to the great searoom
of Amphitritè, banish him
under a booming wind
to jagged harbors in the seas   235
roiling off Thrace. If night
doesn't finish the god's black work,
the day will finish it.
The lightning waits
in your fiery will,   240
Zeus, Father. Send its blast
to kill the god killing us.

Apollo,
lord of the morning light, draw back
your curving bowstring   245
of twined gold—fire the sure arrows

that rake our attackers and keep them at bay.
Artemis, carry your radiance
into battle, on bright quick feet
down through the morning hills.   250
I call on the god whose hair
flows through its golden band,
whose name is our country's own,
Bakkhos!—the wine-flushed!—who comes
to the maenads' cries, who runs   255
in their midst: Bakkhos!—
come here on fire,
a pine-torch flaring,
to face with us the one god
all the gods hate: Ares!   260

(OEDIPUS *has entered while the* CHORUS *was singing.*
Now he speaks.)

OEDIPUS   I heard your prayer. Prayer may save you yet—
if you will trust me and do what I say:
work with me toward the one cure
this plague demands of us.
Help will come, the plague will lift.   265
I now outlaw the killer myself, by these words.
I act as a stranger, not familiar
either with this crime or accounts of it.
Unless I can mesh some clue I hold
with something known of the killer,   270
I will be tracking him alone, on a cold trail.
Since I came later to join your ranks,
when the crime itself was past history,
there are some things that you,
the sons of Kadmos, must tell me.   275
If any of you knows how Laius,
son of Labdacus, died, he must
instantly tell me all he knows.
He must not be frightened of naming
himself the guilty one: I swear   280
he'll suffer nothing worse than exile.
Or if you know of someone else,
a foreigner who struck the blow, speak up.

I will reward you now, I will thank you always.
But if you know the killer and don't speak,   285
out of fear, to shield kin or yourself,
listen to what that silence will cost you.
I order everyone in my land
where I hold power and sit as king:
don't let that man under your roof,   290
don't speak with him, no matter who he is.
Don't pray or sacrifice with him,
don't pour purifying water for him.
I say this to all my people:
drive him from your houses.   295
He is our sickness. He poisons us.
This the Pythian god has shown me.
Believe me, I am the ally in this
both of the god and the dead king.
I pray god that the unseen killer,   300
whoever he is, and whether he killed
alone or had help, be cursed with a life
as evil as he is, a life
of utter human deprivation.
I pray this, too: if he's found at my hearth,   305
inside my house, and I know that he's there,
may the curses I aimed at others punish me.
I charge you all—give my words force,
for my sake and the god's, for our dead land
stripped barren of its harvests,   310
forsaken by its gods.
Even if god had not forced the issue,
this crime should not have gone uncleansed.
You should have looked to it!—the dead man
not only being noble, but your king.   315
But as my luck would have it,
I have his power, his bed—a wife
who shares our seed, and had she borne
the children of us both, she
might have linked us closer still. But Laius   320
had no luck fathering children, and fate
itself soon struck a blow at his head.
It's these concerns make me defend Laius
as I would my own father. There is nothing
I won't try, to trace his murder   325

back to the killer's hand.
I act in this for Labdacus and Polydorus,
for Kadmos and Agenor—for our whole line of kings.
I warn those who disobey me:
god make their fields harvest dust, 330
their women's bodies harvest death.
                              O you gods,
kill them with something worse
than this plague killing us now.
For all the rest of us, who are 335
loyal sons of Kadmos:
may Justice fight with us,
the gods be always at our side.
CHORUS   King, your curse forces me to speak.
None of us is the killer. 340
And none of us can point to him.
Apollo ordered us to search,
now *he* must find the killer.
OEDIPUS   So he must. But what man could force
a god against his will? 345
LEADER   Let me suggest a second course of action.
OEDIPUS   Don't stop at two if you have more.
LEADER   Tiresias is the man whose power of seeing
shows him most nearly what Apollo sees.
King, he might make brilliantly clear 350
what you most want to learn.
OEDIPUS   I've acted already not to lose this chance.
At Kreon's urging I've sent for him—twice now.
The fact that he still hasn't come I find strange.
LEADER   There were some old rumors—too faint to help us now. 355
OEDIPUS   I'll study every word. What did those rumors say?
LEADER   That Laius was killed by some travelers.
OEDIPUS   That's something even I have heard. But the man
who actually did it—no one sees.
LEADER   If fear means anything to him 360
he won't linger in Thebes
once he has heard that curse of yours.
OEDIPUS   If murder didn't frighten him, my words won't.
LEADER   There is the man who will convict him:
god's prophet, led here at last. 365
God gave to him what he gave no one else.
The truth is living in his mind.

(*Enter* TIRESIAS, *led by a* BOY.)

OEDIPUS   Tiresias, you are master of the hidden world.
 You can read earth and sky, you know
 what omens to expound, what to keep secret.   370
 Though your eyes can't see it,
 you are aware of the plague
 attacking us. To fight it, we can find
 no savior or defense but you, my Lord.
 For we now have Apollo's answer—   375
 you will have heard it from others:
 to end this plague we must root out Laius' killers
 Find them, then kill them or banish them.
 Help us do it. Don't begrudge us
 what you divine from birdcries, show us   380
 any escape prophecy has shown you.
 Rescue Thebes! Rescue yourself, and me!
 Take charge of our defilement, and stop
 this poison from the murdered man
 which sickens and destroys us.   385
 We're in your hands. To help another
 is the best use a man can make of his powers.
TIRESIAS   The most terrible knowledge is the kind
 it would pay no wise man to use.
 I knew this, but I forgot it.   390
 I should never have come.
OEDIPUS   What's this? You've come—but with no desire to help?
TIRESIAS   Let me go home. Take my advice now. Your life
 will be easier to bear—so will mine.
OEDIPUS   Strange words. And hardly kind—to hold back   395
 god's crucial guidance from your own people.
TIRESIAS   I see that you've spoken out today
 when silence was called for. I'm silent now
 to spare me your mistake.
OEDIPUS   For god's sake do not turn your back   400
 if you understand any of this! We kneel and beg.
TIRESIAS   You beg out of ignorance. I'll never speak.
 If I made my griefs plain, you would see your own.
OEDIPUS   Then you know and won't help us? You intend
 to betray us all and destroy Thebes?   405
TIRESIAS   I'll cause no grief to you or me. Why ask
 futile questions? You'll learn nothing.

OEDIPUS   So the traitor won't answer.
  You would enrage a rock.
                          Still won't speak?   410
  Are you without feelings—or beyond their reach?

TIRESIAS   You blame this rage on me, do you? Rage?
  You haven't seen her yet, the kind
  that's married to your life. *You* find fault with *me*?

OEDIPUS   Who wouldn't be enraged at the words   415
  you're using to insult Thebes?

TIRESIAS   Truth will come. My silence can't hide it.

OEDIPUS   Must it come? Good reason to speak it now.

TIRESIAS   I prefer not to speak. Rage at that, if you like,
  with the most savage fury your heart knows.   420

OEDIPUS   I'm angry enough now to speak my mind.
  I think you helped plot the murder. No,
  you can't have struck the blow itself.
  Had you eyes, though, I would have said
  you alone were the killer.   425

TIRESIAS   That's your truth? Hear mine: I say
  honor the curse your own mouth spoke.
  From today, don't you speak to me,
  or to your people here. You are the plague.
  You ruin your own land.   430

OEDIPUS   So the appalling charge has been at last
  flushed out, into the open.
  Now where will you run?

TIRESIAS   Where you can't reach. To truth, where I'm strong.

OEDIPUS   Who put this truth in your mouth? Not your prophet's trade.   435

TIRESIAS   You did. By forcing me to speak.

OEDIPUS   Speak what? Repeat it so I understand.

TIRESIAS   I made no sense the first time?
  Are you provoking me to use the word?

OEDIPUS   You made no sense at any time. Try once more.   440

TIRESIAS   I say: you are the killer you would find.

OEDIPUS   The second time is even more outrageous.
  You'll wish you'd never spoken.

TIRESIAS   Shall I feed your fury with more words?

OEDIPUS   Say anything. It's all the same worthless noise.   445

TIRESIAS   I say that you are living unaware
  in the most hideous intimacy
  with your nearest and most loving kin.
  You have arrived at evil—which you cannot see.

OEDIPUS   You think you can savage me? Forever? Unscathed?   450
TIRESIAS   Forever. Truth lasts.
OEDIPUS   Truth lasts for some, but your "truth" won't—
   you have blind eyes, blind ears, and a blind brain.
TIRESIAS   And you're a wretched fool, lashing me with taunts
   every man here will soon aim at you.   455
OEDIPUS   You survive in the care of black
   unbroken night! You can't hurt me
   or any man who sees the sunlight.
TIRESIAS   It isn't I who will cause your fall.
   Apollo is enough. You're his concern.   460
OEDIPUS   Did you invent these lies? Or did Kreon?
TIRESIAS   Kreon is not your disease. You are.
OEDIPUS   Wealth, and a king's power,
   the skill that wins every time—
   how much envious malice they provoke!   465
   To rob me of power—power I didn't want,
   but which this city thrust into my hands—
   my oldest friend here, loyal Kreon, worked
   quietly against me—aching to steal my throne.
   He hired for the purpose this fortuneteller—   470
   conniving bogus beggar-priest!—
   who sees the main chance clearly
   but is a blind groper in his art.

   Tell us now, where did you ever
   prove your claim to a seer's power?   475
   Why—when the Sphinx who barked black songs
   was hounding us—why wasn't it *your* answer
   that freed the city? Her riddle wasn't the sort
   just anyone who happened by could solve:
   prophetic skill was needed then,   480
   the kind you didn't have, skill learned
   from birds or from a god. Yet it was Oedipus,
   who knew nothing, that silenced her,
   because my wit seized the answer,
   needing no help from birds.   485
   Now it is I, this same man, for whom you plot
   disgrace and exile, thinking you will
   maneuver close to Kreon's throne.
   But your scheme to rid Thebes of this plague
   will destroy only you—and the man who planned it.   490

You look now so near death—otherwise I'd make you
the first victim of your own plot.
LEADER   He spoke in anger, Oedipus—
but so did you, if you'll hear what we think.
We don't need angry words, we need insight—   495
how best to manage what the god commands.
TIRESIAS   You may be king, but my right
to answer makes me your equal.
In this respect, I am as much
my own master as you are.   500
You do not own my life.
Apollo does. Nor am I Kreon's man.
Hear me out.
Since you have thrown my blindness at me
I will tell you what your eyes don't see: 505
the evil you are mired in.
                    You don't see
where you live or who shares your house.
Do you know your parents?
                              You are their enemy   510
in this life and down there with the dead.
And soon their double curse—
your father's and your mother's lash—
will whip you out of Thebes
on terrorstruck feet.   515
Your eyes will then see darkness
which now see life.
                    Your shriek
will try to hide itself in every cave.
What mountain outcrop on Cithairon   520
won't roar your screaming back at you,
when what your marriage means strikes home,
shows you the house that took you in: you sailed
your lucky wind to a most foul harbor.
Evils you can't guess   525
will level you to what you are,
to what your children are.
Go on, throw muck at Kreon, and at
the warning spoken through my mouth.
But there will never be a man   530
ground into wretchedness as you shall be.
OEDIPUS   Shall I wait for him to attack me more?

May you be damned. Go. Leave my doors
now! Turn your back and go.

TIRESIAS   I'm here only because you sent for me.   535

OEDIPUS   Had I known the madness you would speak
I wouldn't have hurried to get you here.

TIRESIAS   I may seem crazed to you, but your natural
parents thought I had an able mind.

OEDIPUS   My parents? Wait. Who is my father?   540

TIRESIAS   Today, you will be born. Into ruin.

OEDIPUS   You always have a murky riddle in your mouth.

TIRESIAS   Don't you excel us all at finding answers?

OEDIPUS   Sneer at my mind. But you must face the power it won.

TIRESIAS   That very luck is what destroyed you.   545

OEDIPUS   If I save Thebes, I won't care what happens to me.

TIRESIAS   I will leave you to that. Boy, guide me out.

OEDIPUS   Yes, let him take you home.
Here, you are painfully underfoot. Gone,
you'll take away a great source of grief.   550

TIRESIAS   I'll go. But first I must finish
what you brought me to do—
your face won't frighten me.
The man you have been looking for,
the one your curses threaten, the man   555
you had outlawed in Laius' death:
I say that man is here—
                        you think him a foreigner,
but he will prove himself a Theban native,
though he'll find no joy in that news.   560
A blind man who has eyes now,
a beggar who's now rich, he'll jab
his stick, feeling the road to foreign lands.

(OEDIPUS *enters the palace.*)

He will soon be shown father and brother
to his own children, son and husband   565
to the mother who bore him—she took
his father's seed and his seed,
and he took his own father's life.

You go inside. Think through what I have said.
If I have lied, say of me then   570
I am a prophet with no mind.

(*Exit* TIRESIAS.)

CHORUS   Who is the man
  who inspires the rock voice
  of Delphi to speak out?
  This crime that sickens speech   575
  is the work of his red hands.
  Now he will need legs strong enough
  to outrun wild horses of the storm.
  Apollo is ready to strike:
  armed with lightning,   580
  he and the Fates close in,
  grim beings who don't miss.

  From snowfields
  high on Parnassus
  the word blazes out to us all: 585
  track down the man no one sees.
  He takes cover in thick brush,
  he drives up the mountain
  bull-like to its rocks and caves,
  going his bleak and hunted way,   590
  still struggling to escape the doom
  earth from her sacred mouth has spoken:
  but that doom buzzes low,
  never far from his ear.

  Fear is what the man who reads birds   595
  makes us feel, fear we can't fight.
  We can't accept what he says,
  we have no power to challenge.
  We thrash in doubt, we can't see
  even the present clearly,   600
  much less the future.
  And we've heard of no feud
  embittering the House
  of Oedipus in Corinth
  against the House of Laius here,   605
  no past trouble and none now,
  no proof that would make us accuse
  our king's fame, as he works
  to avenge this murder
  done to our royal house.   610

Zeus and Apollo are infallible,
they know what happens to mankind.
But there is no way to prove
whether an earthbound prophet
ever sees more of the future   615
than we do, though in knowledge and skill
one man may surpass another.
But never, not till I see
the charges proved against him,
will I give my credence   620
to a man who blames Oedipus.
All of us saw his brilliance
prevail, when the wingèd virgin
Sphinx came at him: his winning
won him the people.   625
My heart can't find him guilty.

(KREON *enters.*)

KREON   Citizens, I hear that King Oedipus
  has made a fearful charge against me.
  I'm here to prove it false.
  If he thinks anything I've said or done   630
  has made this crisis worse, or injured him—
  then I have no more wish to live.
  This is no minor charge.
  It's the most deadly I could suffer,
  if my city, my own people, you!—   635
  believe I'm a traitor.
LEADER   He could have spoken in a flash
  of anger with no thought behind it.
KREON   Did he say *I* persuaded the prophet to lie?
LEADER   That's what he said. What he meant wasn't clear.   640
KREON   When he announced my guilt—tell me
  how his eyes looked. Did he seem sane?
LEADER   I can't say. I don't question what my rulers do.
  Here he comes, now, out of the palace.

(OEDIPUS *enters.*)

OEDIPUS   So? You would come here? You have the nerve   645
  to face me in my house? When you're
  exposed as its master's murderer?

Caught trying to steal my kingship?
In god's name what weakness did you see
in me—that led you to plot this?   650
Am I a coward or a fool?
Did you suppose I wouldn't notice
your quiet moves? Not fight back if I did?
Aren't you attempting something
downright stupid—to win absolute power   655
without partisans or even friends?
For that you'll need money and a mob.
KREON   Stop!
             Give me time to answer you.
Let me speak before you judge me.   660
OEDIPUS   You're a formidable speaker. But I listen
badly to someone trying to destroy me.
KREON   I'll prove you are mistaken to think that.
OEDIPUS   Your malice is too blatant to deny.
KREON   Why do you prize your perversity?   665
If you think it's a virtue, your mind's deranged.
OEDIPUS   *Your* mind's deranged, if you think a man
can attack a brother kinsman and not suffer.
KREON   I'll grant that. Now: *how* have *I* attacked you?
OEDIPUS   Did you, or did you not, urge me   670
to send for that venerated prophet?
KREON   Yes. I'd give the same advice now.
OEDIPUS   How long ago was it that King Laius . . .
KREON   Laius? Did what? Why speak of him?
OEDIPUS   was lost in that murderous attack?   675
KREON   That was far back in the past.
OEDIPUS   Did this seer practice his craft here, then?
KREON   With the same skill and respect he has now.
OEDIPUS   Back then, did he ever mention my name?
KREON   Not in my hearing.   680
OEDIPUS   You did investigate the murder, though?
KREON   Of course we did. We found out nothing.
OEDIPUS   Why didn't your expert seer accuse me then?
KREON   I don't know. When I've no facts, I don't speak.
OEDIPUS   There's something you know well enough to explain.   685
KREON   What's that. I'm holding nothing back.
OEDIPUS   Just this. If that seer hadn't conspired with you,
he would never have called me Laius' killer.

KREON   If he said that, *you heard him,* I didn't.
   I think I've a right now to some answers from you.   690
OEDIPUS   Question me. *I* have no blood on my hands.
KREON   Did you marry my sister?
OEDIPUS   Do you expect me to deny that?
KREON   You both have equal power in this country?
OEDIPUS   I give her all she asks.   695
KREON   Do I share power with you both as an equal?
OEDIPUS   You shared our power and betrayed us with it.
KREON   You're wrong. Think it through rationally, as I have.
   Who would prefer a king's anxious life
   to one that let him sleep at night—   700
   if his share of power still equaled a king's?
   Nothing in my nature lusts for sheer power.
   It's enough for me to enjoy a king's rights,
   enough for any man who values restraint.
   All I want, you give me—and it comes with no fear.   705
   To be king would rob my life of its ease.
   How could my share of power be more pleasant
   than this painless pre-eminence, this ready
   influence I have? I'm not yet so misguided
   that I go looking for honors that are burdens.   710
   But as things stand, I'm greeted and wished well
   on all sides. Those who want something from you
   come to me, their best hope of gaining it.
   Should I quit this good life for a worse one?
   Treason has no chance to corrupt   715
   a healthy mind like my own:
   I have no love for such exploits.
   Nor would I join someone who did.
   Test me. Go to Delphi yourself. Find out
   whether I brought back the oracle's exact words.   720
   Then if you find I plotted with that omen-reader,
   seize me and kill me—not on your authority
   alone, but on mine too, for I'd vote my own death.
   But don't convict me because of a wild thought
   you can't prove, which only you believe.   725
   And there's no justice in your reckless confusion
   of evil men with good ones, traitors with friends.
   To reject a true friend is like suicide—
   it costs us a life loved as we love our own.
   Time will instruct you in these truths, for time   730

alone is the sure test of a just man,
but you can know a bad man in one day.

LEADER   That's sound advice, King,
for someone anxious not to fall.
Too quick a mind can stumble.   735

OEDIPUS   When a conspirator moves
abruptly and in secret against me,
I must out-plot him and strike first.
If I pause and do nothing
he'll win his purpose   740
while I'm losing mine.

KREON   What is your purpose? My banishment?

OEDIPUS   No. It's your death I want.

KREON   If you will begin by defining "envy" . . .

OEDIPUS   You talk as though you refuse to believe me.   745

KREON   How can I if you won't use reason?

OEDIPUS   I reason in my own interest.

KREON   You ought to reason in mine as well.

OEDIPUS   In a traitor's interest?

KREON   What if you're wrong?   750

OEDIPUS   I must still rule.

KREON   Not if it's selfish rule.

OEDIPUS   Did you hear him, Thebes!

KREON   Thebes isn't just *your* city. It's mine as well!

LEADER   My Lords, stop this. Here's Jocasta   755
leaving the palace—at the right time
to calm you both. She'll see that this feud ends.

(*Enter* JOCASTA *from the palace.*)

JOCASTA   Wretched men. Why are you out here
recklessly yelling at each other?
Aren't you ashamed? With Thebes sick and dying   760
you two fight out some personal grievance?
You go inside, Oedipus. Kreon, go home.
Don't make us all miserable over nothing.

KREON   Sister, it's worse than that. Oedipus your husband
threatens either to drive me   765
from my own country, or have me killed.

OEDIPUS   That's right. I've caught him plotting against my life.
And his technique is lying prophecy.

KREON   I ask the gods to sicken and destroy me
if I did any of the things you charge me with.   770

JOCASTA   Believe what he says, Oedipus.
   Accept that oath he just made to the gods.
   Do it for my sake too, and for these men.
LEADER   Give in to him, Lord, we beg you.
   Do what your mind and instinct tell you.   775
OEDIPUS   What do you want me to do?
LEADER   Believe him. This man was never a fool,
   now he's given himself the force of a great oath.
OEDIPUS   Do you realize what you're asking?
LEADER   I do.   780
OEDIPUS   Then say it to me outright.
LEADER   Groundless rumor shouldn't be used by you
   to dishonor a friend who swears his innocence.
OEDIPUS   Is it clear to you all
   that you ask my exile or my death?   785
LEADER   No! We ask neither. By the god
   outshining all others, the Sun—
   may I die the worst of deaths, die it
   godless and friendless, if I want those things.
   This dying land grinds pain into my soul—   790
   grinds it the more if the bitterness
   you two stir up adds to our misery.
OEDIPUS   Then let him go, though it means my death,
   or my exile from here in disgrace.
   What moves my pity are your words,   795
   not his. My hate goes with him.
KREON   You are as bitter when you yield
   as you are savage in your rage.
   But natures like your own
   punish themselves the most—   800
   which is the way it should be.
OEDIPUS   Leave me alone. Go.
KREON   I'll go. You can see nothing now
   But these men see that I'm right.

(KREON *goes off.*)

LEADER   Lady, what keeps you from taking your man in?   805
JOCASTA   I will, when someone tells me what happened here.
LEADER   Loose talk made one man's suspicion flare up,
   which stung the other's sense of justice.
JOCASTA   Both sides were at fault?
LEADER   Both sides.   810

JOCASTA   What was at issue?

LEADER   Don't ask that. Our land needs no more trouble.
No more trouble! Stop it now where it stands.

OEDIPUS   I know you mean well when you try to calm me,
but do you realize what it does to me?   815

LEADER   King, I have said this more than once.
I would be mad, or have lost my good sense,
if I lost faith in you: you
who wrenched our loved country
back on course when you found her   820
wandering crazed with suffering.
Steer us straight, again—now—
with all your inspired luck.

JOCASTA   In god's name, King, tell me why
you've hardened your mind in this rage.   825

OEDIPUS   I'll tell you, for it's you I respect, not the men.
Kreon caused my rage by his plots against me.

JOCASTA   Go on. Explain what provoked the quarrel.

OEDIPUS   He says I murdered Laius.

JOCASTA   Does he know this himself? Or did someone tell him?   830

OEDIPUS   Neither. He sent that vicious seer to make the charge
so he could keep his own mouth innocent.

JOCASTA   Then you can clear yourself of all his charges.
Listen to me, for I can make you believe
that no man, ever, has mastered prophecy.   835
This one incident will prove it.
A long time back, an oracle reached Laius—
I don't say that Apollo himself sent it,
but the priests who interpret him did—
which said that when Laius came to die   840
his killer would be a son born to him and me.
Yet, as we heard the story, foreign bandits
murdered Laius at a place where three roads meet.

(OEDIPUS *reacts with sudden intensity to her words.*)

But that son of ours was less than three days old
when Laius pierced and yoked its ankle joints,   845
and had it left, by someone else's hands,
on a mountain far from any roads. Apollo failed!
That time Apollo failed to make Laius die
the way he feared—at the hands of his own son.
Does that show you how much sense   850

prophetic voices make of our lives?
You can forget them. When god wants
something to happen, he makes it happen,
then he shows it to us—all with ease.

OEDIPUS Just now, as I listened to you, Lady, my heart raced,   855
something in my memory woke up terrified.

JOCASTA What chilling thought turned you toward me like that?

OEDIPUS I thought you said that Laius
was struck down where three roads meet.

JOCASTA That's what I said—it's the story we still hear.   860

OEDIPUS Tell me the place where it happened.

JOCASTA It happened on a road in Phokis, at the fork
where roads come in from Delphi and from Daulis.

OEDIPUS How much time has passed since it happened?

JOSCASTA We heard the news just before you came to power.   865

OEDIPUS O Zeus! What is this you have willed me to do?

JOCASTA Oedipus, you're heartstricken. What is it?

OEDIPUS Don't ask me yet. Describe Laius to me.
Was he a young man just reaching his prime?

JOCASTA He was tall, with some white showing in his hair.   870
He looked then not very different from you now.

OEDIPUS It's my ruin. I think that savage curse I spoke
in such ignorance is mine—it damns me.

JOCASTA What are you saying? Your face makes me tremble, Lord.

OEDIPUS I have a desperate fear the prophet sees.   875
But there is one more fact you must tell me.

JOCASTA I'm so frightened I can hardly answer.

OEDIPUS Did Laius go with just a few, or the large troop
of armed men one expects of a prince?

JOCASTA There were only five men. One was a herald,   880
there was a wagon for Laius to ride.

OEDIPUS Ah! Now I can see it. Who told you this, Lady?

JOCASTA Our slave. The one man who survived and came home.

OEDIPUS Is he by chance on call here in our house?

JOCASTA No. When he returned here, and saw   885
that you had all dead Laius' power,
he touched my hand and begged me to send him
out to our farmlands and sheepfolds,
so he'd be far away and out of sight.
I sent him. He was deserving—though a slave—   890
of a much larger favor than he asked.

OEDIPUS Can he be sent for immediately?

JOCASTA   Of course. But why do you insist on it?

OEDIPUS   I'm so afraid, Lady, that I've said far
 too much. That's the reason I wish to see him now.   895

JOCASTA   I'll make him come. But I think I've a right
 to know what so deeply disturbs you, Lord.

OEDIPUS   So much of what I dreaded has happened,
 I will tell you everything I fear.
 No one has more right than you do,   900
 to know the risks to which I'm now exposed.
 Polybos of Corinth was my father.
 My mother was Merope, a Dorian.
 I was the leading citizen there
 until this chance happening   905
 challenged me. Shocking enough—
 but I took it much too hard.
 It was this: a drunk man at a feast swore
 that I was not Polybos' real son.
 Though seething, I said nothing. All that day   910
 I barely held it in. But next morning
 I put my question to mother and father.
 They were enraged at this man, and the insult
 he'd shot at me. Their words reassured me.
 Yet, the thing kept pounding in my mind.   915
 It stalked me. So, without telling my parents,
 I traveled to the Pythian oracle.
 But Apollo would not honor me
 with the knowledge I craved.
       Instead,   920
 his words flashed other things—
 horror and disgust—at me:
 that I would be my mother's lover,
 that I would show a kind of children to the world
 it could not bear to look at, that I   925
 would murder the father whose seed I am.
 Once I had heard the god say that, I fled
 far from Corinth, measuring my distance
 from home by its place in the stars. I ran
 for someplace where I'd never see come true   930
 outrages like those predicted for me.
 But my flight carried me to just the place
 where you say that the king was killed.
 Oh, woman, here is the truth.

As I strode toward those joining paths   935
a herald, a colt-drawn wagon, and a man
like the one you describe, met me.
The man out front and the old man himself
tried to crowd me off the roadway.
The driver, who was forcing me aside,   940
I smashed in anger.
                The old man watched me,
he measured my approach, then leaning out
he lunged down with his two-spiked goad
at the center of my skull.   945
                  He was more than repaid:
I hit him so fast with the staff
this hand held, he was knocked back
rolling off the cart, and lay face up.
And then I killed them all.   950

But if this stranger and Laius . . . were the same blood,
whose triumph could be worse than mine?
Is there a man born the gods hate more?
Nobody, no Theban, no foreigner,
can bring me into his home.   955
No one can speak with me.
They must all drive me out.
I am the man who leveled—
no one else!—this curse at myself.
I love his wife with my hands   960
repulsive from her husband's blood.
Has not evil soaked through me
poisoning my whole being?
I must be banished, but I can't
return to my parents, I can't set foot   965
in my homeland, because there—
I would marry my own mother.
I would kill Polybos my father
who gave me birth and brought me up.
If someone said that things like these   970
could only be the work of a savage god,
he would be speaking the truth.
O you perfect and terrifying gods! Never,
never, let the day these things happen
come to me. Let me be wiped from men's eyes   975

before I see my body gripped
by such shame and devastation.
LEADER   What you say terrifies us, Lord. But don't lose hope
until you've heard it from the eyewitness.
OEDIPUS   That is the one hope I have left—   980
to wait for that man to come from the fields.
JOCASTA   When he comes, what will you try to find out?
OEDIPUS   This: if his story matches yours,
then I will have escaped destruction.
JOCASTA   What did you hear that was crucial in mine?   985
OEDIPUS   He told you Laius was killed by bandits.
If he will still claim there were several,
then I cannot be the killer. One man
cannot be many. But if he says: one man,
braving the road alone, did it,   990
there's no more doubt.
The evidence drags me down.
JOCASTA   Never. I told it just as he told me.
Be sure of it. He can't take back what he said—
the whole city heard him, not just me.   995
And even if he does change his story now
he can't show us that Laius' murder
happened as the god predicted.
                                        Apollo
unmistakably said my son would kill Laius.   1000
That poor doomed child never had a chance
to kill his father because he was killed first.
I will never react to an oracle
by fearing everything in sight.
OEDIPUS   You've thought this out well. But you must   1005
still send for that herdsman. Don't fail me.
JOCASTA   I'll send for him now. But come inside.
Would I do anything to displease you?

(OEDIPUS *and* JOCASTA *enter the palace.*)

CHORUS   Let my speech, and all my acts,
prove my love for what's pure.   1010
May my luck hold me, lifelong,
to the great far-reaching laws
who stride through the light-filled
skies they were born to. Olympos

alone was their father,   1015
no human mind conceived them;
those laws never sleep or forget—
a mighty god lives in them
who does not age.
The tyrant is fathered   1020
by his violent will—
violent, and flushed
with wealth and power
which do him no good
but ruin his purpose,   1025
he climbs his city to the ramparts—
then plunges to a sudden doom
where his quick feet are no help.
But there's another fighting will
I ask god never to destroy—   1030
the will that makes our city thrive.
God protects us: I'll never stop
believing that.

If a man goes through life
speaking and showing contempt,   1035
fears no Justice, feels no awe
for stone gods in their shrines,
let a harsh death punish
the doomed indulgence of that man.
For he's dishonest when he wins,   1040
he can't resist disgraceful acts,
his hand reaches for things
too sacred to be touched.
When crimes like these, which god hates,
are not punished—but *honored*—   1045
what good man will think his life safe
from god's arrows winging at his soul?
Why should I dance to *this* holy song?

If prophecies no longer lead
straight to events all men can see,   1050
I will honor no longer
the untouchable holy place,
Earth's navel at Delphi.
I will not go to Olympia
or the temple at Abai.   1055

You, Zeus who hold power, if Zeus
king of all is your right name,
turn your mind to what's happening here:
prophecies made to Laius grow weak,
men are ignoring them,   1060
Apollo is nowhere
glorious with praise:
the gods lose force.

(JOCASTA *enters from the palace carrying a suppliant's branch and some smouldering
incense. She approaches the altar of Apollo near the palace door.*)

JOCASTA   Lords of my country, this thought
came to me: to visit the gods' shrines   1065
with a branch and incense in my hands.
For Oedipus lets alarms of every kind
inflame his mind. He won't let past
experience calm his present fears,
as a man of sense would.   1070
He's at the mercy of everybody's
terrifying words. Since he won't listen to me,
Apollo—you are the nearest god—

(*Enter* MESSENGER *from the countryside.*)

I come praying for your good will
as my branch shows. Cleanse us, cure our sickness.   1075
When we see Oedipus distraught, we all shake,
like sailors catching fear from a nervous helmsman.
MESSENGER   Can you point out to me, strangers,
the house where King Oedipus lives? Or better,
can you tell me where the king is now?   1080
LEADER   He lives in that house, stranger. He's inside.
This woman is the mother of his children.
MESSENGER   I wish her joy, and her family joy,
that comes when a marriage bears fruit.
JOCASTA   No less to you, stranger, for those kind words.   1085
What have you to tell us or to ask us?
MESSENGER   Great news, Lady, for you and your mate.
JOCASTA   What is this news? Who sent you to us?
MESSENGER   I've come from Corinth. My news
should make you very happy—though   1090
it will sadden you some as well.
JOCASTA   What is it? How can it possibly do both?

MESSENGER   They're going to make him king. The people
  of the Isthmus want Oedipus to rule them.
JOCASTA   Isn't old Polybos still in power?   1095
MESSENGER   No more. Death has put him in the tomb.
JOCASTA   Old man, are you saying that Polybos has died?
MESSENGER   Kill me if that's not the truth.

(JOCASTA *turns to a servant girl, who runs inside.*)

JOCASTA   Girl, run to your master with this news.
  You oracles of the gods! Where are you now?   1100
  The man Oedipus feared he would kill,
  the man he ran from, that man's dead.
  Chance killed him, not Oedipus. Chance!

(OEDIPUS *enters quickly from the palace.*)

OEDIPUS   Darling Joscasta, my loving wife,
  why did you ask me to come out?   1105
JOCASTA   Listen to what this man has to say.
  See what it does to god's proud oracle.
OEDIPUS   Where is he from? What is the news he has?
JOCASTA   From Corinth. He says Polybos your father is dead.
OEDIPUS   Say it, old man. I want to hear it from your mouth.   1110
MESSENGER   If the plain fact is what you want first,
  have no doubt he is dead and gone.
OEDIPUS   Was it treason, or did disease bring him down?
MESSENGER   A slight push tips an old man into stillness.
OEDIPUS   Then it was some sickness that killed him?   1115
MESSENGER   That, and the long years he had lived.
OEDIPUS   Oh yes, wife, why should we search Pythian smoke
  or be terrorized by birds screaming up there?
  If signs like these had been telling the truth
  I would have killed my father. But he's dead.   1120
  He's safely in the ground, and I'm here,
  who never raised a spear. Unless—
  he died of longing for me, and that
  is what my killing him means. No more than that.
  This time, Polybos' death has swept   1125
  those worthless oracles with him to Hades.
JOCASTA   Didn't I promise you before they were worthless?
OEDIPUS   You did. But I was too worried to believe you.
JOCASTA   It's time to stop caring about all this.

OEDIPUS   I must care. I must not touch my mother's bed.   1130
JOCASTA   What should a human being fear?
  Chance is what shapes our lives.
  There's no such thing as real foreknowledge.
  The best life is one taken as it comes.
  This marriage with your mother—don't fear it.   1135
  In their very dreams, too, many men
  have slept with their own mothers.
  A man who shrugs off such things
  as meaningless will bear his life best.
OEDIPUS   A brave speech which I would like to believe.   1140
  But how can I if my mother is still living?
  While she lives, I will live in fear,
  though you do your best to reason with me.
JOCASTA   Your father's tomb is a great flood of light.
OEDIPUS   Great, yes! But she's alive—she is my fear.   1145
MESSENGER   What woman do you fear?
OEDIPUS   I dread that oracle from the god, stranger.
MESSENGER   Would it be wrong for someone else to know it?
OEDIPUS   No, you may hear it. Apollo told me
  I would become my mother's lover, that I   1150
  would have my father's blood on these hands.
  I haven't gone near Corinth since I heard that.
  Ever since, I have been lucky—yet,
  what happiness to see
  our parents with our own eyes!   1155
MESSENGER   Did this oracle force you into exile?
OEDIPUS   To keep me from being my father's killer, old man.
MESSENGER   Then let me free you from your fear, King.
  I came here only with helping you in mind.
OEDIPUS   I would give anything to be free of fear.   1160
MESSENGER   I confess I came partly for that reason—
  to be favored by you when you've come home.
OEDIPUS   I'll never live where my parents live.
MESSENGER   My son, you can't possibly know what you're doing.
OEDIPUS   Why is that, old man? In god's name, tell me.   1165
MESSENGER   Is it because of them you won't go home?
OEDIPUS   I am afraid Apollo told the truth.
MESSENGER   Afraid you'd do your parents unforgivable harm?
OEDIPUS   Exactly that, old man. I am in constant fear.
MESSENGER   Your fear is groundless. Do you grasp that?   1170

OEDIPUS   How can it be groundless if I'm their son?
MESSENGER   But Polybos was no relation to you.
OEDIPUS   What? Polybos was not my father?
MESSENGER   No more than I am. The same.
OEDIPUS   How the same? He fathered me and you didn't.   1175
MESSENGER   He didn't father you any more than I did.
OEDIPUS   Why did he say, then, I was his son?
MESSENGER   He took you from my hands as a gift.
OEDIPUS   He loved me so much—knowing I came from you?
MESSENGER   His lack of children taught him to love you.   1180
OEDIPUS   And you? Did you buy me? Or find me somewhere?
MESSENGER   I found you. In the wooded hollows of Cithairon.
OEDIPUS   Why were you traveling out there?
MESSENGER   I had charge of sheep grazing those slopes.
OEDIPUS   A migrant hired to work our flocks?   1185
MESSENGER   I saved your life that day, my son.
OEDIPUS   From what? Was something wrong with me?
MESSENGER   Your ankles might answer that question.
OEDIPUS   You know that? Why do you name my oldest wound?
MESSENGER   I cut the thongs that pierced and laced your feet.   1190
OEDIPUS   From birth I've carried the shame of those scars.
MESSENGER   That luck named you, Oedipus. That's who you are.
OEDIPUS   Did my mother or my father do this?
   Speak the truth for god's sake.
MESSENGER   I don't know. The man who gave you to me   1195
   will know that.
OEDIPUS   You took me from someone?
   You didn't chance on me yourself?
MESSENGER   I took you from another shepherd.
OEDIPUS   Who was he? Tell me as plainly as you can.   1200
MESSENGER   He was known as someone who worked for Laius.
OEDIPUS   The same Laius who was once king *here*?
MESSENGER   The same one. This man worked as his shepherd.
OEDIPUS   Is he alive? Can I see him?
MESSENGER   A native could answer that better.   1205
OEDIPUS   Does anyone here know what's become
   of this shepherd? Has someone seen him
   in town or in the fields? Speak up now.
   The time has come to make all of it known.
LEADER   I believe he means that same herdsman   1210
   you've already sent for. Jocasta
   is the best one to ask.

OEDIPUS   Lady, do you recall the man we ordered here?
Is it that man he speaks of?

JOCASTA   Why ask about him? Don't pursue it, Oedipus,   1215
don't waste a thought on his words. It's nothing.

OEDIPUS   I can't give up with clues like these in my hands.
How can I fail now to solve my birth?

JOCASTA   For god's sake, stop searching if you want to live.
Let my sickness be enough for us both.   1220

OEDIPUS   Accept it! My mother might be from slaves
for three generations back—
would that make you lowborn?

JOCASTA   Please listen to me: do nothing more.

OEDIPUS   I cannot listen. I must have the truth.   1225

JOCASTA   I'm thinking now only of what's best for you.

OEDIPUS   "What's best for me" exasperates me now.

JOCASTA   You poor child! Never find out who you are.

OEDIPUS   Someone bring me that herdsman. Let her
glory in her precious birth.   1230

JOCASTA   Oh you poor doomed child! That is the only name
I can call you now. No other, forever!

(JOCASTA *runs into the palace.*)

LEADER   Why has she gone, Oedipus,
driven out by some savage grief?
Evil is going to burst from this silence.   1235

OEDIPUS   Let it burst! My seed may be base born,
but I will see at last what it is.
It may well be that my birth
humiliates her female pride.
But I, who have always known I am   1240
the child of Luck, whose gifts are always good,
will never know disgrace.
Luck is my mother, my brothers are the months
who measured out the low times
in my life and the great ones.   1245
If these are my true kinsmen,
how could I betray my nature
by giving up the great search
now that will find my birth?

CHORUS   By the gods of Olympos, if I have   1250
a prophet's reach of eye and mind—
tomorrow's moonlight

will shine on you, Cithairon.
Oedipus will honor you—
his native mountain,   1255
his nurse, his mother. Nothing
will keep us from dancing
then, mountain joyful to our king!
We call out to Phoebus Apollo:
be the cause of our joy!   1260

(CHORUS *turns toward* OEDIPUS.)

My son, who was your mother
out there? Which long-lived nymph
loved Pan in his mountain roaming?
Or did Apollo father you
on one of his swift brides   1265
in the pleasing highlands?
Was it Hermes, Lord of Kyllene?
Or did Bakkhos of the mountain peaks
take you—a joyful find—
from the girls whose games he shares: 1270
the nymphs of Helikon?

OEDIPUS   Old men,
if I can recognize a man I've never met,
I think I see the herdsman we've been waiting for.
Our fellow would be old, like the stranger coming.   1275
Those leading him are my own men.
But I expect you'll know him better.
Some of you will know him by sight.

(*Enter* HERDSMAN, *led by* OEDIPUS' *servants.*)

LEADER   I do know him. He is from Laius' house,
a trusted shepherd if he ever had one.   1280

OEDIPUS   I ask you to speak first, Corinthian:
is this the man you mean?

MESSENGER   You're looking at him.

OEDIPUS   Now you, old man. Turn your eyes toward me.
Answer every question I ask you.   1285
Did you once come from Laius' house?

HERDSMAN   I did. I wasn't a bought slave,
I was born and raised in their house.

OEDIPUS   What was your work? How did you spend your time?

HERDSMAN   My life has been spent tending sheep.   1290

OEDIPUS   In what region did you normally work?
HERDSMAN   Mainly Cithairon, and the country around there.

(OEDIPUS *gestures toward the* MESSENGER.)

OEDIPUS   That man. Do you recall ever seeing him . . .
HERDSMAN   Recall him how? Doing what? Which man?

(OEDIPUS *goes to the* MESSENGER *and puts his hand on him.*)

OEDIPUS   This man right here. Have you ever seen him before?   1295
HERDSMAN   Not that I recognize—not right away.
MESSENGER   It's no wonder, master. His memory's faded,
   but I'll revive it for him. I'm sure he knows me.
   We worked the pastures on Cithairon together—
   he with his two flocks, me with one—   1300
   for three whole grazing seasons, from early spring
   until Arcturus rose. When the weather turned cold
   I'd drive my flock home to its winter pens,
   he drove his away to Laius' sheepfolds.
   Do I describe what happened, old friend? Or don't I?   1305
HERDSMAN   That's the truth, but it was so long ago.
MESSENGER   Do you remember giving me a boy
   I was to raise as my own son?
HERDSMAN   What? Why ask me that?
MESSENGER   There, friend, is the man who was that boy.   1310

   (*He nods toward* OEDIPUS.)

HERDSMAN   Damn you! Shut up and say nothing.
OEDIPUS   Don't you attack him for his words, old man.
   Your own ask to be punished far more.
HERDSMAN   Tell me, royal master, what I've done wrong.
OEDIPUS   You didn't answer him about the boy.   1315
HERDSMAN   He's trying to make something out of nothing.
OEDIPUS   Speak willingly, or you'll speak under torture.
HERDSMAN   Dear god! Don't hurt me, I'm an old man.
OEDIPUS   One of you bind his arms behind his back.

   (*Servants approach the* HERDSMAN *and start to seize his arms.*)

HERDSMAN   Why this, you doomed man? What else must you know?   1320
OEDIPUS   Did you give this man the child he claims you gave?
HERDSMAN   I did. I wish I had died that day.
OEDIPUS   You'll die yet if you don't speak the truth.
HERDSMAN   Answering you is what will get me killed.

OEDIPUS   I think this man is determined to stall.   1325
HERDSMAN   No! I've said once that I gave him the boy.
OEDIPUS   Did the boy come from your house? Or someone else's?
HERDSMAN   Not from my house. Someone gave him to me.
OEDIPUS   Name the person! Name the house!
HERDSMAN   Don't ask that of me, master. For god's sake, don't.   1330
OEDIPUS   You will die if I ask one more time.
HERDSMAN   He was a child from the house of Laius.
OEDIPUS   A slave? Or was he born to Laius' own blood?
HERDSMAN   I've come to the terror—which I must speak.
OEDIPUS   And which I must hear. But I will hear it.   1335
HERDSMAN   The child was said to be Laius' own son.
   Your lady in the house would know that best.
OEDIPUS   *She* gave you the child?
HERDSMAN   She gave him, King.
OEDIPUS   To do what?   1340
HERDSMAN   I was to let it die.
OEDIPUS   Kill her own child?
HERDSMAN   She feared prophecies.
OEDIPUS   What prophecies?
HERDSMAN   That this child would kill his father.   1345
OEDIPUS   Why, then, did you give him to this old man?
HERDSMAN   I pitied him, master. The man would take him,
   I hoped, to a new home in another land.
   But that man saved him for this—
   the worst grief of all. If the child   1350
   he speaks of is you, master, you know,
   now, all the evil of your birth and life.
OEDIPUS   All! All! It has all happened,
   it was all true. O light! May this
   be the last time I see you.   1355
   You see now who I am. I am
   the child who must not be born,
   I loved where I must not love,
   I killed where I must not kill.

(OEDIPUS *runs into the palace.*)

CHORUS   Men and women who live and die,   1360
   I set no value on your lives.
   Which one of you ever, who reaches
   for the true blessedness that lasts,

seizes more than what seems blest?
You live in that seeming   1365
a brief time, then you plunge.
Your fate teaches me this, Oedipus,
yours, you suffering man, the story
god spoke through you: praise   1370
no human life, none, for its luck.

O Zeus, no man drew a bow like this man,
he shot his arrow home,
winning power and pleasure and wealth,
he killed the virgin Sphinx
whose talons curl, who sang   1375
the god's black oracles.
He fought death in our land,
he towered against its threat.
I've called you my king since that time,
honoring you mightily, my Oedipus,   1380
who wield the might of Thebes.

But now!—nobody's story
has the sorrow of yours.
O my Oedipus, this is your fame:
the welcome of one harbor was enough   1385
for you, both child and father, when your plow
drove through the room where women love.
How can the furrow your father plowed
not have screamed before now, at you, doomed man?

Time, who sees all, caught you   1390
living a life you never willed.
Time damns this marriage which is
no marriage, where the fathered child
fathered children himself.
O son of Laius, I wish   1395
I'd never seen you. I fill my lungs
to cry with all my power,
to speak the truth in my heart:
you gave me once new breath,
Oedipus, but now you pour   1400
darkness through my eyes.

(*Enter Servant from the palace.*)

SERVANT   Masters, always the most honored men in our land,
  what crushing deeds you will see and hear!—
  whose sorrow you must bear, if you still feel
  a born Theban's love for the House of Labdacus.   1405
  I don't think rivers could wash the evil
  out of this house, not the Danube or the Phasis,
  it hides so much suffering, which is now
  coming to light. But what happened inside
  was not involuntary evil, it was willed.   1410
  The griefs that hurt us worst are those
  we think we've chosen for ourselves.
LEADER   What we already knew made us suffer.
  Do you want to add more?
SERVANT   It is brief news to give or hear.   1415
  Our royal lady Jocasta's dead.
LEADER   That pitiable woman. How did she die?
SERVANT   She killed herself. You will be spared the worst
  because you weren't there to see it.
  But you will hear exactly as I can   1420
  tell it, what that wretched woman suffered.
  She came raging through the courtyard
  straight for her marriage bed, the fists
  of both her hands clenched in her hair.
  Once in, she slammed the doors shut, calling out   1425
  to Laius, so long dead, remembering
  the living seed of long ago, who killed Laius,
  the mother living on to breed with her son
  more ruined children.
                          She grieved for the bed   1430
  where she had loved, and given birth
  to all those doubled lives—
  husband fathered by husband,
  children sired by her child.
  From here on I don't know how she died,   1435
  because Oedipus burst in shouting,
  taking our eyes from her misery.
  We watched him, stunned, as he plowed through us
  feverishly asking each man for his spear,
  demanding his wife who was not a wife,   1440
  but the twice-mothering earth
  out of whom he and his children came.
  He was raving, but some divine hand

drove him toward his wife—none of us near him did.
With a savage yell, as though guided there,
he lunged at the double doors, and wrenching
hollow bolts from their sockets,
he broke through into the room. There we saw her,
the woman above us, hanging by her neck,
twisting there in a noose of tangled cords.
He saw her, anguish roaring from deep inside him,
he reached and loosened the noose that held her.
When the poor lifeless woman was laid on the ground,
this was the terror we saw now: he pulled
the long pins of hammered gold from her gown,
these pins he raised and punched into his eyes
back through the sockets, shouting these words:
"Eyes, now you will never see
the evil I suffered and the evil I caused.
Now you will see blackness! Not those lives
you should never have seen, not those yearned-for
faces you so long failed to know."
While he sang these tortured words,
not once, but many times his raised hands
struck his eyes. And the blood kept coming,
drenching his beard and cheeks, not a few wet drops—
a black storm of bloody hail lashed his face.

What this man and this woman did
broke so much evil loose, that evil joins
the whole of both their lives in grief.
The happiness they once knew was real—
but now that happiness is ruin,
screaming, death, disgrace. Each misery
we have a name for has come here.
LEADER   Has his grief eased at all?
SERVANT   He shouts for someone to open the doorbolts:
   "Show this city its father-killer," he cries,
   "Show it its mother's. . . ." He spoke the word, I can't.
He wants to banish himself from the land,
   not curse this house any longer
   by living here under his own curse.
He's so weak now, though, he needs to be helped.
No one could stand up under a sickness like his.
Look there. The doorbolts are sliding open.

1445
1450
1455
1460
1465
1470
1475
1480

You will witness a vision of suffering   1485
even those it revolts must pity.

(OEDIPUS *emerges from the slowly opening palace doors. He is blinded, with blood on
his face and clothes, but the effect should arouse more awe and pity than shock. He
moves with the aid of a servant.*)

LEADER   An eerie terror fills men's eyes
   at this pure and helpless anguish,
   more moving than any
   my eyes have ever touched.   1490
                                 Man of pain,
   what madness has claimed you?
   Name the god who leapt
   from beyond our knowledge
   to make your naked life his enemy.   1495

   (*Moans.*)

   I cannot look at you—
   though I want so powerfully
   to speak with you, to learn from you,
   though your suffering grips my eyes—
   so strong are the shivers of awe   1500
   you send through me.
OEDIPUS   Ahhh! My whole life,
   my whole being is wretched.
   Where am I?
   Where does my misery lead?   1505
   Is my voice
   fluttering lost out there
   like a stunned bird's?
   Where has my god thrown me down?
LEADER   In a cruel place, unbearable to see or hear.   1510
OEDIPUS   Darkness buries me in her hate, she
   takes me in her black hold.
   It's an unspeakable blackness,
   it can't be fought off,
   it keeps coming,   1515
   blowing evil all over me.
   Ahhh.
   Two things together strike deep in me:
   the pins plunged in my eyes,
   those crimes driving through my mind.   1520

LEADER   It is no wonder you feel
  nothing but pain now
  in both your mind and your flesh.

OEDIPUS   Ah friend, my faithful servant still,   1525
  how gentle you are to the blind man.
  I know you are near me: your voice
  finds me in my darkness.

LEADER   What you did terrifies us. How could you
  kill your eyes? What god raised your hand?

OEDIPUS   Apollo, friends, it was Apollo   1530
  who did this. He made evil,
  perfect evil of my life.
  But the hand
  that struck these eyes
  was my hand.   1535
  It was I in my wretchedness
  who struck, no one else.
  What good was there left for my eyes to see?
  I could see nothing in this world now
  with a glad heart.   1540

LEADER   You are right to say it.

OEDIPUS   Who could I look at? Or love?
  Whose greeting could I
  answer with fondness, friends?
  Drive me quickly from this place,   1545
  the most ruined, most cursed,
  most god-hated man who ever lived.

LEADER   You're broken by what happened, you're broken
  by what's happening in your mind.
  I wish you'd never learned the truth.   1550

OEDIPUS   May the man die
  who found me in the pasture,
  who cut the thongs from my feet,
  who saved me from that death for a worse life,
  a life I cannot thank him for.   1555
  Had I died then, I would have caused
  no great grief to my people and myself.

LEADER   I wish he had let you die.

OEDIPUS   I'd not have come home to kill my father,
  no one could call me lover   1560
  of her from whose body I came.
  I have no god now.

I'm son to a fouled mother,
I fathered children in the bed
where my father gave me   1565
deadly life. If ever an evil
rules all other evils
it is my evil, it is the life
god gave to Oedipus.

LEADER   How can I say you acted wisely? You   1570
  blinded yourself. Why didn't you choose death?

OEDIPUS   There was no other way but mine.
  Don't try to persuade me now. No more advice.
  If I had eyes, how could those eyes
  bear the sight of my father among the dead?   1575
  Or my poor wronged mother—look at her? I've done them
  violence hanging could not justly punish.
  Should I ache to see my children,
  children born to the life that mine must live?
  Never. Not with my eyes. Nor this city,   1580
  its towers, nor the light shining
  from our stone gods. I lost my right to these loves
  when I commanded we outlaw the vile killer—
  myself!—totally wretched, though I won power
  like no other Theban, now proven by the gods   1585
  the defiled son of our dead king.
  Once I found out my own sickness
  how could my eyes look calmly on my people?
  They could not! If I could deafen my ears
  I would, I'd deaden my whole body,   1590
  go blind and deaf to shut those evils out.
  The silence in my mind would be sweet.
  Oh Cithairon, why did you take me in?
  Or once you had me, why didn't you
  kill me instantly? My birth would have left no trace.   1595
  O Polybos and Corinth, I thought you
  were my ancestral strength, the house of my fathers.
  I was their glorious boy growing up,
  but my life there was a fair skin
  over a festering disease. My vile self   1600
  now shows its vile birth.
                          You,
  three roads, and you, darkest ravine,
  you, grove of oaks, you, narrow place

where those three paths drank blood from my hands,   1605
my fathering blood pouring into you.
Do you remember what I did while you watched?
And when I came here, what I did then?
O marriages! You marriages! You made us,
we sprang to life, then from the same seed   1610
you burst fathers, brothers, sons,
kinsmen shedding kinsmen's blood,
brides and mothers and wives—the most loathsome
atrocities that strike mankind.
I must not name what should never have been.   1615
If you love the gods, hide me out there,
kill me, throw me into the sea,
anywhere I will be lost from your eyes.
Come take me. Don't shrink from touching
this ruined man. Believe me. Don't fear me.   1620
I am the only man in all the world
who can carry these sorrows.
LEADER   Kreon will help you. He's come when we need him.
He can act, he can advise you.
He is the only ruler we have left   1625
to protect Thebes in your place.
OEDIPUS   Do I know words that he will listen to?
What would make him believe me?
I wronged him so deeply.
I proved myself so false to him.   1630

(KREON *enters.*)

KREON   I don't come to mock you, Oedipus.
I won't dwell on the wrongs you did me.
Men, even if you are not sensitive
to human feeling, keep some awe
for the nurturing light flaming from the Sun.   1635
Don't leave this stark defilement in the open.
The earth, the holy rain, the light, all hate it.
Take him quickly back to the palace.
If these sorrows are shared
only by our bloodkin,   1640
it will spare us impiety.
OEDIPUS   I feared worse from you. I thank god
you show your noble kindness to me,

who am worthless. I have one thing to ask.
It is for your sake, not mine. 1645
KREON   What do you want, that makes you ask it like that?
OEDIPUS   Expel me quickly to some place
no living person will find me.
KREON   I would have done that. But now I must first
ask the god what I should do. 1650
OEDIPUS   He's given you his command already.
I killed my father. I am unholy. I must die.
KREON   The god did say that. But what has happened
to us is so desperate, we must be
absolutely sure before we act. 1655
OEDIPUS   What else is there to know about me? I'm lost.
KREON   This time, I think even you will trust the god.
OEDIPUS   I will. But there is something I charge you,
yourself, to do. I beg it! Bury her
who's lying inside as you think proper. 1660
Give her the rites due your kinswoman.
As for me, don't doom my father's city
by having me haunt it while I live.
Let me live out my life on the mountain,
on Cithairon, my own famous mountain, 1665
which my father and mother while they lived
had chosen as my rightful tomb. Let me die
out there, just as my parents decreed I die.
And yet, I know this now:
no sickness can kill me, nothing can. 1670
I was saved from that death
to face an evil awesome and unknown.
Let my fate take me now, where it will.

My children, Kreon.
My sons will not need help from you—they're grown. 1675
They'll find a way to live anywhere.
But my poor wretched girls, who never
ate anywhere but at my table—
they've never been without me.
I fed them with my own hands. 1680
                         Care for them.
If you can do it, let me touch them now,
let me give in to my grief.
Grant it Kreon, from your great heart.

Touching them with my hands, I would   1685
imagine them as my eyes once saw them.

(*The gentle sobbing of* OEDIPUS' *two daughters is heard offstage. Soon two small
girls enter.*)

Is it?
O gods, do I hear my children sobbing?
Has Kreon pitied me?
Has he given me my own dear children?   1690
Has he?
KREON   I have. I brought them to you
    because I knew how much joy
    as always, you would take in them.
OEDIPUS   Bless this kindness of yours. Bless your luck.   1695
    May the gods guard you better than they did me.
    Children, where are you? Come to me.
    These are your brother's hands, hands
    of the man who created you, hands that changed
    my once bright eyes to these black sockets.   1700
    He, children, saw nothing, knew nothing,
    he fathered you in his own place of life,
    where his own seed grew. I can still weep
    for you, though I can't see you.

(OEDIPUS *takes his daughters in his arms.*)

I imagine how bitter your lives will be.   1705
I know how men will force you to live.
What great occasions could you join, what festivals,
without being sent home in tears,
forbidden any share in the holy joy?
When it's time for your marriage, my daughters,   1710
what man would risk all the revulsion,
the gods' hatred for me that will wound you,
just as that hatred destroyed my parents?
Do we lack any evil? Your father killed
his father, he started lives where his began,   1715
he took you from the place he was sown,
the place he was born.
                    Those are the insults
you will face. Who will marry you?
No man, my children. You will grow old   1720
unmarried, living a dried-up childless life.

Kreon, you are the only father they have left,
for the parents who conceived them are both lost.
Keep them from rootless wandering,
unmarried and helpless. They are your kin.   1725
Don't bring them down to what I am.
Pity them. They are so young, and but for you,
alone. Touch my hand, kind man,
make that touch your promise.

(KREON *touches him.*)

Children, had you been old enough to comprehend,   1730
I would have taught you more.
My prayer now can be no more than this:
that you live always where people
allow you peace, to make your life
better than your father's was.   1735
KREON   Enough grief. Go inside now.
OEDIPUS   Bitter words, which I must obey.
KREON   Time runs out on all things.
OEDIPUS   Grant my request before I go.
KREON   Tell me, I'll hear you.   1740
OEDIPUS   Banish me from my homeland.
KREON   Ask god to do that, not me.
OEDIPUS   I am the man the gods hate most.
KREON   Then you will have your wish.
OEDIPUS   Do you consent?   1745
KREON   I never promise when I can't be sure.
OEDIPUS   Then lead me inside.
KREON   Come. Let go of your children now.
OEDIPUS   Do not take them from me.
KREON   Let go of your power, too.   1750
    You won power, but it did not
    stay with you all your life.

(KREON *leads* OEDIPUS *into the palace.*)

CHORUS   Thebans, that man is the same Oedipus
    whose great mind solved the famous riddle.
    He was a most powerful man.   1755
    Which of us, seeing his glory,
    did not wish his luck could be ours?
    Now, look at what wreckage the seas
    of savage trouble make of his life.

To know a man's truth, wait   1760
to see his life end.
Look at him on that day.
Don't call a man god's friend
until he has come through life
and crossed over into death   1765
never having been god's victim.

(*Exit.*)

Wallace Stevens (1879–1955)
Sunday Morning

1

Complacencies of the peignoir, and late
Coffee and oranges in a sunny chair,
And the green freedom of a cockatoo
Upon a rug mingle to dissipate
The holy hush of ancient sacrifice.   5
She dreams a little, and she feels the dark
Encroachment of that old catastrophe,
As a calm darkens among water-lights.
The pungent oranges and bright, green wings
Seem things in some procession of the dead,   10
Winding across wide water, without sound.
The day is like wide water, without sound,
Stilled for the passing of her dreaming feet
Over the seas, to silent Palestine,
Dominion of the blood and sepulchre.   15

2

Why should she give her bounty to the dead?
What is divinity if it can come
Only in silent shadows and in dreams?
Shall she not find in comforts of the sun,
In pungent fruit and bright, green wings, or else   20
In any balm or beauty of the earth,
Things to be cherished like the thought of heaven?

Divinity must live within herself:
Passions of rain, or moods in falling snow;
Grievings in loneliness, or unsubdued   25
Elations when the forest blooms; gusty
Emotions on wet roads on autumn nights;
All pleasures and all pains, remembering
The bough of summer and the winter branch.
These are the measures destined for her soul.   30

3

Jove in the clouds had his inhuman birth.
No mother suckled him, no sweet land gave
Large-mannered motions to his mythy mind.
He moved among us, as a muttering king,
Magnificent, would move among his hinds,   35
Until our blood, commingling, virginal,
With heaven, brought such requital to desire
The very hinds discerned it, in a star.
Shall our blood fail? Or shall it come to be
The blood of paradise? And shall the earth   40
Seem all of paradise that we shall know?
The sky will be much friendlier then than now,
A part of labor and a part of pain,
And next in glory to enduring love,
Not this dividing and indifferent blue.   45

4

She says, "I am content when wakened birds,
Before they fly, test the reality
Of misty fields, by their sweet questionings;
But when the birds are gone, and their warm fields
Return no more, where, then, is paradise?"   50
There is not any haunt of prophecy,
Nor any old chimera of the grave,
Neither the golden underground, nor isle
Melodious, where spirits gat them home,
Nor visionary south, nor cloudy palm   55
Remote on heaven's hill, that has endured
As April's green endures; or will endure
Like her remembrance of awakened birds,
Or her desire for June and evening, tipped
By the consummation of the swallow's wings.   60

5

She says, "But in contentment I still feel
The need of some imperishable bliss."
Death is the mother of beauty; hence from her,
Alone, shall come fulfilment to our dreams
And our desires. Although she strews the leaves   65
Of sure obliteration on our paths,
The path sick sorrow took, the many paths
Where triumph rang its brassy phrase, or love
Whispered a little out of tenderness,
She makes the willow shiver in the sun   70
For maidens who were wont to sit and gaze
Upon the grass, relinquished to their feet.
She causes boys to pile new plums and pears
On disregarded plate. The maidens taste
And stray impassioned in the littering leaves.   75

6

Is there no change of death in paradise?
Does ripe fruit never fall? Or do the boughs
Hang always heavy in that perfect sky,
Unchanging, yet so like our perishing earth,
With rivers like our own that seek for seas   80
They never find, the same receding shores
That never touch with inarticulate pang?
Why set the pear upon those river-banks
Or spice the shores with odors of the plum?
Alas, that they should wear our colors there,   85
The silken weavings of our afternoons,
And pick the strings of our insipid lutes!
Death is the mother of beauty, mystical,
Within whose burning bosom we devise
Our earthly mothers waiting, sleeplessly.   90

7

Supple and turbulent, a ring of men
Shall chant in orgy on a summer morn
Their boisterous devotion to the sun,
Not as a god, but as a god might be,
Naked among them, like a savage source.   95
Their chant shall be a chant of paradise,
Out of their blood, returning to the sky;

And in their chant shall enter, voice by voice,
The windy lake wherein their lord delights,
The trees, like serafin, and echoing hills,   100
That choir among themselves long afterward.
They shall know well the heavenly fellowship
Of men that perish and of summer morn.
And whence they came and whither they shall go
The dew upon their feet shall manifest.   105

8

She hears, upon that water without sound,
A voice that cries, "The tomb in Palestine
Is not the porch of spirits lingering.
It is the grave of Jesus, where he lay."
We live in an old chaos of the sun,   110
Or old dependency of day and night,
Or island solitude, unsponsored, free,
Of that wide water, inescapable.
Deer walk upon our mountains, and the quail
Whistle about us their spontaneous cries;   115
Sweet berries ripen in the wilderness;
And, in the isolation of the sky,
At evening, casual flocks of pigeons make
Ambiguous undulations as they sink,
Downward to darkness, on extended wings.   120

Alfred, Lord Tennyson (1809–1892)
Break, Break, Break

Break, break, break,
  On thy cold gray stones, O Sea!
And I would that my tongue could utter
  The thoughts that arise in me.

O, well for the fisherman's boy,   5
  That he shouts with his sister at play!
O, well for the sailor lad,
  That he sings in his boat on the bay!

And the stately ships go on
    To their haven under the hill;   10
But O for the touch of a vanish'd hand,
    And the sound of a voice that is still!

Break, break, break,
    At the foot of thy crags, O Sea!
But the tender grace of a day that is dead   15
    Will never come back to me.

Crossing the Bar

Sunset and evening star,
    And one clear call for me!
And may there be no moaning of the bar,
    When I put out to sea,

But such a tide as moving seems asleep,   5
    Too full for sound and foam,
When that which drew from out the boundless
       deep
    Turns again home.

Twilight and evening bell,
    And after that the dark!   10
And may there be no sadness of farewell,
    When I embark;

For though from out our bourne of Time and Place
    The flood may bear me far,
I hope to see my Pilot face to face   15
    When I have crossed the bar.

From Morte D'Arthur

So all day long the noise of battle rolled
Among the mountains by the winter sea;
Until King Arthur's table, man by man,
Had fallen in Lyonnesse about their Lord,   55
King Arthur: then, because his wound was deep,
The bold Sir Bedivere uplifted him,

Sir Bedivere, the last of all his knights,
And bore him to a chapel nigh the field,
A broken chancel with a broken cross,   60
That stood on a dark strait of barren land.
On one side lay the Ocean, and on one
Lay a great water, and the moon was full.

    Then spake King Arthur to Sir Bedivere:
"The sequel of today unsolders all   65
The goodliest fellowship of famous knights
Whereof this world holds record. Such a sleep
They sleep—the men I loved. I think that we
Shall never more, at any future time,
Delight our souls with talk of knightly deeds,   70
Walking about the gardens and the halls
Of Camelot, as in the days that were.
I perish by this people which I made,—
Though Merlin sware that I should come again
To rule once more—but let what will be, be,   75
I am so deeply smitten through the helm
That without help I cannot last till morn.
Thou therefore take my brand Excalibur,
Which was my pride: for thou rememberest how
In those old days, one summer noon, an arm   80
Rose up from out the bosom of the lake,
Clothed in white samite, mystic, wonderful,
Holding the sword—and how I rowed across
And took it, and have worn it, like a king:
And, wheresoever I am sung or told   85
In aftertime, this also shall be known:
But now delay not: take Excalibur,
And fling him far into the middle mere:
Watch what thou seest, and lightly bring me word."

    To him replied the bold Sir Bedivere: 90
"It is not meet, Sir King, to leave thee thus,
Aidless, alone, and smitten through the helm.
A little thing may harm a wounded man.
Yet I thy hest will all perform at full,
Watch what I see, and lightly bring thee word."   95

    So saying, from the ruined shrine he stept
And in the moon athwart the place of tombs,

Where lay the mighty bones of ancient men,
Old knights, and over them the sea-wind sang
Shrill, chill, with flakes of foam. He, stepping down   100
By zig-zag paths, and juts of pointed rock,
Came on the shining levels of the lake.

   There drew he forth the brand Excalibur,
And o'er him, drawing it, the winter moon,
Brightening the skirts of a long cloud, ran forth   105
And sparkled keen with frost against the hilt:
For all the haft twinkled with diamond sparks,
Myriads of topaz-lights, and jacinth-work
Of subtlest jewellery. He gazed so long
That both his eyes were dazzled, as he stood,   110
This way and that dividing the swift mind,
In act to throw: but at the last it seemed
Better to leave Excalibur concealed
There in the many-knotted waterflags,
That whistled stiff and dry about the marge.   115
So strode he back slow to the wounded King.

   Then spake King Arthur to Sir Bedivere:
"Hast thou performed my mission which I gave?
What is it thou hast seen? or what hast heard?"

   And answer made the bold Sir Bedivere: 120
"I heard the ripple washing in the reeds,
And the wild water lapping on the crag."

   To whom replied King Arthur, faint and pale:
"Thou hast betrayed thy nature and thy name,
Not rendering true answer, as beseemed   125
Thy fealty, nor like a noble knight:
For surer sign had followed, either hand,
Or voice, or else a motion of the mere.
This is a shameful thing for men to lie.
Yet now, I charge thee, quickly go again   130
As thou art lief and dear, and do the thing
I bad thee, watch, and lightly bring me word."

   Then went Sir Bedivere the second time
Across the ridge, and paced beside the mere,
Counting the dewy pebbles, fixed in thought;   135
But when he saw the wonder of the hilt,

How curiously and strangely chased, he smote
His palms together, and he cried aloud,

"And if indeed I cast the brand away,
Surely a precious thing, one worthy note,   140
Should thus be lost for ever from the earth,
Which might have pleased the eyes of many men.
What good should follow this, if this were done?
What harm, undone? deep harm to disobey,
Seeing obedience is the bond of rule.   145
Were it well to obey then, if a king demand
An act unprofitable, against himself?
The King is sick, and knows not what he does.
What record, or what relic of my lord
Should be to aftertime, but empty breath   150
And rumours of a doubt? but were this kept,
Stored in some treasure-house of mighty kings,
Some one might show it at a joust of arms,
Saying, 'King Arthur's sword, Excalibur,
Wrought by the lonely maiden of the Lake.   155
Nine years she wrought it, sitting in the deeps
Upon the hidden bases of the hills.'
So might some old man speak in the aftertime
To all the people, winning reverence.
But now much honour and much fame were lost."   160

So spake he, clouded with his own conceit,
And hid Excalibur the second time,
And so strode back slow to the wounded King.

Then spoke King Arthur, breathing heavily:
"What is it thou hast seen? or what hast heard?"   165

And answer made the bold Sir Bedivere:
"I heard the water lapping on the crag,
And the long ripple washing in the reeds."

To whom replied King Arthur, much in wrath:
"Ah, miserable and unkind, untrue,   170
Unknightly, traitor-hearted! Woe is me!
Authority forgets a dying king,
Laid widowed of the power in his eye
That bowed the will. I see thee what thou art,
For thou, the latest-left of all my knights,   175

In whom should meet the offices of all,
Thou wouldst betray me for the precious hilt;
Either from lust of gold, or like a girl
Valuing the giddy pleasure of the eyes.
Yet, for a man may fail in duty twice,   180
And the third time may prosper, get thee hence:
But, if thou spare to fling Excalibur,
I will arise and slay thee with my hands."

    Then quickly rose Sir Bedivere, and ran,
And, leaping down the ridges lightly, plunged   185
Among the bulrush-beds, and clutched the sword,
And strongly wheeled and threw it. The great brand
Made lightnings in the splendour of the moon,
And flashing round and round, and whirled in an arch,
Shot like a streamer of the northern morn,   190
Seen where the moving isles of winter shock
By night, with noises of the northern sea.
So flashed and fell the brand Excalibur:
But ere he dipt the surface, rose an arm
Clothed in white samite, mystic, wonderful,   195
And caught him by the hilt, and brandished him
Three times, and drew him under in the mere.
And lightly went the other to the King.

    Then spoke King Arthur, drawing thicker breath:
"Now see I by thine eyes that this is done.   200
Speak out: what is it thou hast heard, or seen?"

    And answer made the bold Sir Bedivere:
"Sir King, I closed mine eyelids, lest the gems
Should blind my purpose, for I never saw,
Nor shall see, here or elsewhere, till I die,   205
Not though I live three lives of mortal men,
So great a miracle as yonder hilt.
Then with both hands I flung him, wheeling him;
But when I looked again, behold an arm,
Clothed in white samite, mystic, wonderful,   210
That caught him by the hilt, and brandished him
Three times, and drew him under in the mere."

    And answer made King Arthur, breathing hard:
"My end draws nigh; 'tis time that I were gone.

Make broad thy shoulders to receive my weight,   215
And bear me to the margin; yet I fear
My wound hath taken cold, and I shall die."

So saying, from the pavement he half rose,
Slowly, with pain, reclining on his arm,
And looking wistfully with wide blue eyes   220
As in a picture. Him Sir Bedivere
Remorsefully regarded through his tears,
And would have spoken, but he found not words,
Then took with care, and kneeling on one knee,
O'er both his shoulders drew the languid hands,   225
And rising bore him through the place of tombs.

But, as he walked, King Arthur panted hard,
Like one that feels a nightmare on his bed
When all the house is mute. So sighed the King,
Muttering and murmuring at his ear, "Quick, quick!   230
I fear it is too late, and I shall die."
But the other swiftly strode from ridge to ridge,
Clothed with his breath, and looking, as he walked,
Larger than human on the frozen hills.
He heard the deep behind him, and a cry   235
Before. His own thought drove him, like a goad.
Dry clashed his harness in the icy caves
And barren chasms, and all to left and right
The bare black cliff clanged round him, as he based
His feet on juts of slippery crag that rang   240
Sharp-smitten with the dint of armèd heels—
And on a sudden, lo! the level lake,
And the long glories of the winter moon.

Then saw they how there hove a dusky barge,
Dark as a funeral scarf from stem to stern,   245
Beneath them; and descending they were ware
That all the decks were dense with stately forms
Black-stoled, black-hooded, like a dream—by these
Three Queens with crowns of gold—and from them rose
A cry that shivered to the tingling stars,   250
And, as it were one voice, an agony
Of lamentation, like the wind, that shrills
All night in a waste land, where no one comes,
Or hath come, since the making of the world.

Then murmured Arthur, "Place me in the barge,"   255
And to the barge they came. There those three Queens
Put forth their hands, and took the King, and wept.
But she, that rose the tallest of them all
And fairest, laid his head upon her lap,
And loosed the shattered casque, and chafed his hands,   260
And called him by his name, complaining loud,
And dropping bitter tears against his brow
Striped with dark blood: for all his face was white
And colourless, and like the withered moon
Smote by the fresh beam of the springing east;   265
And all his greaves and cuisses dashed with drops
Of onset; and the light and lustrous curls—
That made his forehead like a rising sun
High from the dais-throne—were parched with dust;
Or, clotted into points and hanging loose,   270
Mixed with the knightly growth that fringed his lips.
So like a shattered column lay the King;
Not like that Arthur who, with lance in rest,
From spur to plume a star of tournament,
Shot through the lists at Camelot, and charged   275
Before the eyes of ladies and of kings.

    Then loudly cried the bold Sir Bedivere,
"Ah! my Lord Arthur, whither shall I go?
Where shall I hide my forehead and my eyes?
For now I see the true old times are dead,   280
When every morning brought a noble chance,
And every chance brought out a noble knight.
Such times have been not since the light that led
The holy Elders with the gift of myrrh.
But now the whole ROUND TABLE is dissolved   285
Which was an image of the mighty world;
And I, the last, go forth companionless,
And the days darken round me, and the years,
Among new men, strange faces, other minds."

    And slowly answered Arthur from the barge: 290
"The old order changeth, yielding place to new,
And God fulfils Himself in many ways,
Lest one good custom should corrupt the world.
Comfort thyself: what comfort is in me?
I have lived my life, and that which I have done   295

May He within Himself make pure! but thou,
If thou shouldst never see my face again,
Pray for my soul. More things are wrought by prayer
Than this world dreams of. Wherefore, let thy voice
Rise like a fountain for me night and day.   300
For what are men better than sheep or goats
That nourish a blind life within the brain,
If, knowing God, they lift not hands of prayer
Both for themselves and those who call them friend?
For so the whole round earth is every way   305
Bound by gold chains about the feet of God.
But now farewell. I am going a long way
With these thou seest—if indeed I go—
(For all my mind is clouded with a doubt)
To the island-valley of Avilion;   310
Where falls not hail, or rain, or any snow,
Nor ever wind blows loudly; but it lies
Deep-meadowed, happy, fair with orchard-lawns
And bowery hollows crowned with summer sea,
Where I will heal me of my grievous wound."   315

    So said he, and the barge with oar and sail
Moved from the brink, like some full-breasted swan
That, fluting a wild carol ere her death,
Ruffles her pure cold plume, and takes the flood
With swarthy webs. Long stood Sir Bedivere   320
Revolving many memories, till the hull
Looked one black dot against the verge of dawn,
And on the mere the wailing died away.

Tithonus

The woods decay, the woods decay and fall,
The vapours weep their burthen to the ground,
Man comes and tills the field and lies beneath,
And after many a summer dies the swan.
Me only cruel immortality   5
Consumes: I wither slowly in thine arms,
Here at the quiet limit of the world,
A white-haired shadow roaming like a dream

The ever-silent spaces of the East,
Far-folded mists, and gleaming halls of morn.   10

    Alas! for this gray shadow, once a man—
So glorious in his beauty and thy choice,
Who madest him thy chosen, that he seemed
To his great heart none other than a God!
I asked thee, "Give me immortality."   15
Then didst thou grant mine asking with a smile,
Like wealthy men who care not how they give.
But thy strong Hours indignant worked their wills,
And beat me down and marred and wasted me,
And though they could not end me, left me maimed   20
To dwell in presence of immortal youth,
Immortal age beside immortal youth,
And all I was, in ashes. Can thy love,
Thy beauty, make amends, though even now
Close over us, the silver star, thy guide,   25
Shines in those tremulous eyes that fill with tears
To hear me? Let me go; take back thy gift;
Why should a man desire in any way
To vary from the kindly race of men,
Or pass beyond the goal of ordinance   30
Where all should pause, as is most meet for all?

    A soft air fans the cloud apart; there comes
A glimpse of that dark world where I was born.
Once more the old mysterious glimmer steals
From thy pure brows, and from thy shoulders pure,   35
And bosom beating with a heart renewed.
Thy cheek begins to redden through the gloom,
Thy sweet eyes brighten slowly close to mine,
Ere yet they blind the stars, and the wild team
Which love thee, yearning for thy yoke, arise,   40
And shake the darkness from their loosened manes,
And beat the twilight into flakes of fire.

    Lo! ever thus thou growest beautiful
In silence, then before thine answer given
Departest, and thy tears are on my cheek.   45
    Why wilt thou ever scare me with thy tears,
And make me tremble lest a saying learnt,
In days far-off, on that dark earth, be true?
"The Gods themselves cannot recall their gifts."

Ay me! ay me! with what another heart   50
In days far-off, and with what other eyes
I used to watch—if I be he that watched—
The lucid outline forming round thee; saw
The dim curls kindle into sunny rings;
Changed with thy mystic change, and felt my blood   55
Glow with the glow that slowly crimsoned all
Thy presence and thy portals, while I lay,
Mouth, forehead, eyelids, growing dewy-warm
With kisses balmier than half-opening buds
Of April, and could hear the lips that kissed   60
Whispering I knew not what of wild and sweet,
Like that strange song I heard Apollo sing,
While Ilion like a mist rose into towers.

   Yet hold me not for ever in thine East:
How can my nature longer mix with thine?   65
Coldly thy rosy shadows bathe me, cold
Are all thy lights, and cold my wrinkled feet
Upon thy glimmering thresholds, when the stream
Floats up from those dim fields about the homes
Of happy men that have the power to die,   70
And grassy barrows of the happier dead.
Release me, and restore me to the ground;
Thou seest all things, thou wilt see my grave:
Thou wilt renew thy beauty morn by morn;
I earth in earth forget these empty courts,   75
And thee returning on thy silver wheels.

Dylan Thomas (1914–1953)
Do Not Go Gentle into That Good Night

Do not go gentle into that good night,
Old age should burn and rave at close of day;
Rage, rage against the dying of the light.

Though wise men at their end know dark is right,
Because their words had forked no lightning they   5
Do not go gentle into that good night.

Good men, the last wave by, crying how bright
Their frail deeds might have danced in a green bay;
Rage, rage against the dying of the light.

Wild men who caught and sang the sun in flight,   10
And learn, too late, they grieved it on its way,
Do not go gentle into that good night.

Grave men, near death, who see with blinding sight
Blind eyes could blaze like meteors and be gay,
Rage, rage against the dying of the light.   15

And you, my father, there on the sad height,
Curse, bless, me now with your fierce tears, I pray.
Do not go gentle into that good night.
Rage, rage against the dying of the light.

William Wordsworth (1770–1850)

We Are Seven

—A simple Child,
That lightly draws its breath,
And feels its life in every limb,
What should it know of death?

I met a little cottage Girl: 5
She was eight years old, she said;
Her hair was thick with many a curl
That clustered round her head.
She had a rustic, woodland air,
And she was wildly clad: 10
Her eyes were fair, and very fair;
—Her beauty made me glad.

"Sisters and brothers, little Maid,
How many may you be?"
"How many? Seven in all," she said,   15
And wondering looked at me.

"And where are they? I pray you tell."
She answered, "Seven are we;

And two of us at Conway dwell,
And two are gone to sea.   20

"Two of us in the churchyard lie,
My sister and my brother;
And, in the churchyard cottage, I
Dwell near them with my mother."

"You say that two at Conway dwell,   25
And two are gone to sea,
Yet ye are seven! I pray you tell,
Sweet Maid, how this may be."

Then did the little Maid reply,
"Seven boys and girls are we;   30
Two of us in the churchyard lie,
Beneath the churchyard tree."

"You run about, my little Maid,
Your limbs they are alive;
If two are in the churchyard laid,   35
Then ye are only five."

"Their graves are green, they may be seen,"
The little Maid replied,
"Twelve steps or more from my mother's door,
And they are side by side.   40

"My stockings there I often knit,
My kerchief there I hem;
And there upon the ground I sit,
And sing a song to them.

"And often after sunset, sir,   45
When it is light and fair,
I take my little porringer,
And eat my supper there.

"The first that died was sister Jane;
In bed she moaning lay,   50
Till God released her of her pain;
And then she went away.

"So in the churchyard she was laid;
And, when the grass was dry,
Together round her grave we played,   55
My brother John and I.

"And when the ground was white with snow,
And I could run and slide,
My brother John was forced to go,   60
And he lies by her side."

"How many are you, then," said I,
"If they two are in heaven?"
Quick was the little Maid's reply,
"O master! we are seven."

"But they are dead; those two are dead!   65
Their spirits are in heaven!"
'Twas throwing words away; for still
The little Maid would have her will,
And say, "Nay, we are seven!"

William Butler Yeats (1865–1939)
Death

Nor dread nor hope attend
A dying animal;
A man awaits his end
Dreading and hoping all;
Many times he died,   5
Many times rose again.
A great man in his pride
Confronting murderous men
Casts derision upon
Supersession of breath;   10
He knows death to the bone—
Man has created death.

APPENDIX:
The Research Paper

Definition

The research paper, a special type of writing often assigned in college courses, is sometimes called an *investigative paper*, a *term paper*, or a *library paper*. Whatever the product is labeled, the process is generally the same. As most of the terms suggest, this type of writing is distinguished by research; the writer locates and incorporates the ideas and discoveries of others into a finished paper that reflects the researcher's own style, sense of organization, and convictions. References to other writings demonstrate that the author has researched the topic well.

In researching and composing such a paper, the writer generally has one of two different purposes: to inform or to persuade, through the presentation of supporting evidence. The intended audiences can vary in levels of knowledge about and interest in the subject. The tone, however, is always relatively formal and objective. Proper mechanics and language usage encourage the reader's confidence in the researcher's judgment and accuracy as an investigator.

Choosing and Narrowing the Subject

Unless your instructor assigns you a specific topic to develop in a specific way, your first task in preparing a research paper is to select a topic which can be adequately researched and developed within the limits of time and space allowed for your project. In an English class, for example, you might be asked to write about one of the authors or works included in this book. If you like the poetry of Robert Frost, you might choose Frost's work as a general subject. Then you might limit that subject to the single poem "Stopping by Woods on a Snowy Evening." You might further narrow the focus by concentrating on the poem's symbolism, its technical characteristics, the circumstances surrounding its composition and publication, or any of several other possibilities.

Primary and Secondary Sources

A writing activity in Chapter 6 involves an examination of the ways one poet approaches the subject of death in different poems. If you completed that assignment, you researched the *primary sources* only; you studied the poems themselves and drew some conclusions about the poet's treatment of death. Had you also consulted articles or books to see what literary critics have said about death in the poet's works, you would have been investigating *secondary* sources, writings about the subject of your paper.

In writing the essay, if you quoted a line or more, the context made it clear that you were citing the poet's work, your primary source. Referring to a secondary source, however, requires the *documentation* of the reference so that the idea or wording is clearly identified as that of someone else and not your own. In the article by D. M. McKeithan in Chapter 3, "Hawthorne's 'Young Goodman Brown': An Interpretation," McKeithan uses footnotes to document both his primary source, "Young Goodman Brown," and his secondary sources. (Different forms of documentation are illustrated in Leslie Thompson's article, "Cultural and Institutional Dying Styles in a Technological Society," in Chapter 6 and in David Elkind's article, "Teenagers in Crisis," in the Additional Readings for Chapter 3.)

Guides to Secondary Sources

How do you go about finding secondary sources relating to "Stopping by Woods on a Snowy Evening"? To locate books on the subject, you may begin by acquainting yourself with the *card catalog* of the library. (The card catalog may actually be a file of individual cards as the name implies, or it may be a computer terminal. In either case, it provides a master listing of the library's holdings.) Checking the card catalog for books about Robert Frost's poetry is a good way to begin your research. You will not necessarily read any books in their entirety; you will study their tables of contents and their indexes for references to "Stopping by Woods on a Snowy Evening." After locating books, you will also need to find articles relating to your subject which have been published in journals, magazines, or other periodicals.

Information about articles can be found in the reference section of the library in listings usually called *bibliographies* or *indexes*. A general listing that you might consult initially, the *Reader's Guide to Periodical Literature*, lists articles, subjects, and authors in general-interest publications; you will probably want to look further to find articles in special-interest journals and magazines. Here are two excellent sources for material on a poem by Frost:

> MHRA (Modern Humanities Research Association). *Annual Bibliography of English Language and Literature.*
>
> MLA (Modern Language Association). *International Bibliography of Books and Articles on the Modern Languages and Literature.*

If you are looking for material in a field of study other than literature, however, you will investigate other listings in the reference section of the library, perhaps the *Art Index, Business Periodical Index, Education Index, Engineering Index,* or *Social Sciences Index.* Such specialized research guides list books and articles from hundreds of publications; their purpose is to guide a researcher to pertinent information. A first step in the use of any research tool such as a bibliography or index is to read the introductory material in order to understand what information is contained and how it is presented.

Locating Secondary Sources

Finding the sources useful in developing your paper will probably take a good deal of time. Combing the indexes for relevant titles, tracking down the periodical issue or the book on the library's shelves, sometimes to discover that the material is not useful after all—this procedure can be frustrating. You must allow time for some dead ends and for locating elusive material, perhaps at a second or even a third library. But the frustration is usually offset by the excitement of discovery. You will find, perhaps, that the subject you wish to pursue has inspired fascinating scholarship.

As you identify probable sources for your paper, be sure to record all the information that you will need to locate the material and, later, to document it in your paper. Many researchers use three- by five-inch note cards for recording the information in the exact form to be used in the list of works cited at the end of the finished paper. You should record the author's full name (last name first for alphabetizing); the full title of the work, including any subtitle; and relevant publication data as specified by the instructor or your handbook. Recording each item on a separate note card offers two advantages: (1) the cards can be arranged in alphabetical order for compiling the final list and (2) the deletion of an inappropriate source is easily accomplished by simply removing a card from the stack. Making these "bibliography cards" is an important step in your research, and your instructor may well ask you to submit them for approval before you proceed with your project.

On the opposite page are two sample bibliography cards, one for a book (A), one for an article (B).

Determining Purpose

Early in the research process, you need to define the purpose of your paper-to-be. Is it to be a *report*, which presents the views and discoveries of others in order to inform? Or is it to be a *thesis paper*, which presents the views and discoveries of others as supporting evidence to persuade the audience to agree with your own thesis or conviction?

Either purpose can lead to an excellent paper, but the choice you make determines the kind of information you collect. If you choose to describe the composition and publication history of "Stopping by Woods on a Snowy Evening," for example, you will probably collect as much factual information as possible to be presented as a report. If you choose to write about the symbolism in the poem, however, you may write a *thesis paper* in support of your own interpretation. In that case, your note-taking will be relatively selective since you will concentrate on the sources that support your own views.

Remember, however, to keep your mind open to new ideas as you investigate. Even though you may develop a tentative thesis (perhaps "All the criticism of 'Stopping by Woods' is pointless since the poem is so easy to understand"), your research may lead you to revise that thesis dramatically.

Taking Notes

When you actually find a book or article which includes significant material for your topic, you are ready for note-taking. The three- by five-inch cards used for the bibliography are too small for recording substantial notes,

Taking Notes 901

A.

Cook, Reginald. Robert Frost: A Living Voice. Amherst: The University of Massachusetts Press, 1974.

B.

Ciardi, John. "Robert Frost: The Way to the Poem." Saturday Review of Literature 12 April 1958: 13-15, 65.

so you may wish to use four- by six-inch cards. First, be sure to identify the source on the note card itself. It is not necessary to repeat all the information from the bibliography card, but you must clearly indicate the source and, when necessary, the exact page numbers for the ideas.

Every step in preparing a research paper requires meticulous attention to detail and accuracy. Carelessly jotting down an incorrect date for a periodical, for instance, can lead to futile searching among library shelves. Nowhere is accuracy more important, however, than in taking notes on your sources. Generally, you should read the entire work or relevant portion of a work before trying to record the ideas. The best procedure is to "digest" the information so that your notes will be written in your own words. Otherwise, you may echo the original writer's phrasing, which may then find its way into your final paper. Notes should be as brief as possible; complete sentences are unnecessary, even undesirable. When you find a phrase or a passage that is so well expressed or so crucial to your thesis that it should be quoted in your paper, be sure to record it exactly and indicate clearly with quotation marks that it is a direct quotation.

On the opposite page are two sample note cards. The first (A) includes a direct quotation; the other (B) summarizes through paraphrase.

Planning the Paper

After you have collected enough material to inform your audience or to support your thesis, you are ready to prepare the first draft. An outline is useful in drafting a research paper. It provides a basic structure and progression for your ideas. Also, managing your note cards is simplified if you arrange them in the order of your outline headings. In generating an outline, think in terms of (1) introduction, (2) presentation of information or of evidence, and (3) conclusion, just as you have done for other types of writing.

The following preliminary outline was created by one student who had collected information on "Stopping by Woods on a Snowy Evening."

"Stopping by Woods on a Snowy Evening":
A Poem of Many Meanings?

Thesis: Despite the seemingly absurd imbalance between the brevity of the poem and the hundreds of pages published about it, studying the variety of possible interpretations helps the literal-minded reader to appreciate the richness of this poem.

A.

Henry, 37-38
       ~~Interpretation~~ of last stanza

Speaker's rejection of beauty in favor
of duty an example of "the <u>little</u>
<u>death</u> of abnegation to which we
sentence ourselves daily "

B.

Cook, 122-123
       Frost's reaction to "death wish "

June 1958 lecture — Frost apparently
making fun of death-wish idea,
but admits that poem could be
about death, though not necessarily

I. Introduction—why so much critical analysis for such a brief poem?
II. Negative responses to "overinterpretation"
  A. Frost's complaints
  B. James Dickey's comment about "mangling"
III. Continued popularity of poem despite "mangling"
IV. "Death wish" idea as example of controversial interpretation
  A. Readers offended by "hidden" meaning
  B. Author not aware of all meanings in his own work
V. Additional critical analyses as enrichment
VI. Conclusion—wealth of published analysis as evidence of poem's significance

Documentation Requirements and Styles

The most obvious difference between a research paper and any other long composition upon a serious topic is the formal acknowledgment of sources. This documentation is the author's way of giving appropriate credit to others for their ideas, arguments, or words. Failure to make such acknowledgment is known as *plagiarism*. Penalties for plagiarism have ranged from loss of credit for a particular class assignment to loss of a university degree and professional standing. Even though plagiarism committed by inexperienced researchers is often unintentional, it is not treated any more gently. Such inadvertent plagiarism usually occurs as a result of careless note-taking.

To avoid plagiarism, identify the source of information on each note card, and scrupulously place quotation marks around direct quotations. Then, when you write your paper, carefully document borrowed material.

The precise method of documentation you use will depend upon your subject and the requirements set forth by your instructor. Although the principles of documentation and the information to be given are similar for all disciplines, the order and format vary from field to field. For example, documentation in scientific fields has for some time been offered in parentheses within the text, whereas works in other areas have featured either footnotes (see D. M. McKeithan's article in Chapter 3) or endnotes (see David Elkind's article in the Additional Readings for Chapter 3). Recently, however, all styles appear to be moving toward a form of parenthetical documentation in which brief reference is made in the text to sources itemized at the end in a list of works cited (see Leslie M. Thompson's article in Chapter 6).

Your instructor will either describe a style for you to follow or ask you to consult a particular handbook or style manual. In either case, follow the prescribed documentation form carefully. This basically mechanical process is critical to the preparation of your final copy and requires close attention to detail, but it is separate from the creative process of defining your topic, gathering your information, and organizing and drafting your paper into a polished composition. Appropriate and accurate documentation, like conventional spelling and punctuation, is necessary for communication with your intended audience, but it is not more important than clear writing and logical organization.

For a detailed guide to documentation, as well as for valuable advice on writing research papers, you may wish to consult one or more of the following books.

Gibaldi, Joseph, and Walter S. Achtert. *MLA Handbook for Writers of Research Papers.* 2nd ed. New York: The Modern Language Association of America, 1984.

Hodges, John C., and Mary E. Whitten. *Harbrace College Handbook.* 10th ed. San Diego: Harcourt Brace Jovanovich, Publishers, 1986.

Publication Manual of the American Psychological Association. 3rd ed. Washington, D.C.: American Psychological Association, 1983.

Turabian, Kate L. *A Manual for Writers of Term Papers, Theses, and Dissertations.* 4th ed. Chicago: The University of Chicago Press, 1973.

Winkler, Anthony C., and Jo Ray McCuen. *Writing the Research Paper: A Handbook.* 2nd ed. San Diego: Harcourt Brace Jovanovich, Publishers, 1985.

A Sample Research Paper

The following research paper was prepared in accordance with the *MLA Handbook*, cited above.

"Stopping by Woods on a Snowy Evening":
A Poem of Many Meanings?

Robert Frost's "Stopping by Woods on a Snowy Evening" is a short, simple poem. The speaker pauses momentarily to observe the beauty of nature, specifically the snow falling quietly among the trees. Then he moves on. Readers can easily recognize and relate to such an incident. The poet has translated a universal experience into the music of poetry using clear, conversational English. Such a straightforward work seems to need no explanation. And yet this sixteen-line lyric has been the subject of an enormous amount of critical analysis since its publication in 1923. Is all this interpretation worthwhile, or does it merely belabor the obvious while reading more into the poem than is actually there?

Frost himself frequently deplored what he considered to be overinterpretation of "Stopping by Woods." In fact he expressed displeasure with literary analysis in general, at least when it prevented a reader from reaching an unassisted understanding. "The heart sinks," he asserted, "when robbed of the chance to see for itself what a poem is all about" (417). Regarding "Stopping by Woods" in particular, he commented after reading the poem to a group in 1954, "That one I've been more bothered with than anybody has ever been with any poem in just the pressing it for more than it should be pressed for. It means enough without its being pressed" (Cook 52). James Dickey, another American poet, echoes Frost's sentiment when he states that poetry "gets mangled and destroyed" by too much interpretation and intellectualizing about its meaning (Greiner 57).

Despite these protests, the "pressing" of analysis and interpretation has continued, but it seems not to have "mangled and destroyed" the poem at all. On the contrary, "Stopping by Woods" has grown in popularity to become what "may be the best-known poem ever written by an American" (Shurr 584). Allen Tate goes so far as to say that "Had Frost written this one short masterpiece and no others, his name would last as long as poetry itself will last" (66). Is this fame because of or in spite of the numerous published analyses? Are Frost and Dickey correct in their disdain for critical analysis, or do varying interpretations add to a poem's ultimate value?

An example of a critical commentary on "Stopping by Woods"—and one which resulted in strongly negative reactions by Frost and others—is John Ciardi's 1958 essay suggesting that the poem expresses a "death wish." Ciardi's explication, printed in the Saturday Review of Literature, resulted in howls of protest from readers who wrote numerous letters to the editor which were printed in subsequent issues of the magazine. Although there were also a few expressions of agreement, most of the letter-writers seemed deeply offended by the suggestion that the poem might contain a "hidden" meaning, especially one so depressing.

On at least one occasion Frost conceded that the analogy to death is present in "Stopping by Woods" (Cook 122–123), but in general he vigorously denied the death-wish interpretation. In fact, he is reported to have growled, "Ciardi says I've got a death wish. No such thing. That's not what the poem was about" (Cifelli 483). Another time, when urged to comment on the possibility of a death wish, he grumbled in exasperation, "All I meant was to get the hell out of there" (Greiner 57).

So the question of interpretation becomes more complex. First, can a poem mean something that the author did not intend it to mean? Second, is it legitimate to "press" a poem for different meanings in spite of its apparent simplicity and in spite of the author's objections?

In discussing Frost's denial of the presence of a death wish in "Stopping by Woods," James Armstrong points out that the author of a work does not necessarily have the final word regarding its meaning:

> Many a poet has publicly refused to admit in his work the presence of an intention or meaning that to any discerning reader is clearly there. It may be that he justly regards his poem as his best and final statement of the matter and dislikes having it diluted or distorted by paraphrase. Or it may

be that he resents having his thoughts and feelings pried at by morbid admirers.... (440)

When a writer has successfully represented an experience, an intelligent and careful reader may well be able to perceive implications that even the author has not, on a conscious level, intended or recognized. Therefore, it is beside the point to argue against any particular interpretation of "Stopping by Woods" on the grounds that Frost said he did not "mean" that.

In spite of occasional excesses of explication, then, the richness of "Stopping by Woods" is revealed by critical analyses which point out the various possibilities for interpretation. For example, later critics have accepted and expanded on Ciardi's original death-wish interpretation. James L. Potter seems to take it for granted that the "temptation" facing the speaker in "Stopping by Woods" is death (137, 166). Marie Borroff refers to the poem's "tacit analogy between the end of one day . . . and the end of all the tasks of a man's life" (28). And Nat Henry suggests that the speaker's leaving the woods represents "the little death of abnegation to which we sentence ourselves daily" when we sacrifice something pleasurable to duty (37–38). The speaker's strong sense of duty has also been commented on by Bernhard Frank. He believes the speaker "embodies at least three facets of the American tragedy: the compulsive adherence to the work-ethic; the preoccupation with the dictates of society; and the terror of facing introspection" (44).

In short, critics have noted that the seemingly straightforward and simple words harbor hints of deeper meanings; as one critic points out, the unspecified "promises" and the unexplained refusal to enter the woods in the "vague last stanza" (Stamper 81) invite the reader to look below the surface meaning of the lines. The very repetition of the last line, according to Ciardi, almost forces the reader to accept "promises" and "sleep" as symbols, thus raising the rest of the poem to the symbolic level as well (15). The "meaning" of the work is therefore much broader than that of a literal reading or a single interpretation such as the "death wish." Even contradictory ideas can be present; the woods can represent the attractions of "both life and death" (Tate 68).

John Ciardi states that poetry at its best is "a reenactment" of life (15). As such, a poem is like a significant incident in a person's life; it cannot be limited to a single "meaning" that can be finally and completely stated. "Stopping by Woods on a Snowy Evening" is an enjoyable poem when it is read literally, but its continued appeal and interest to thoughtful readers reside in Frost's ingenious presentation of symbols which lead the reader to examine the meaning of an everyday human experience. The numerous published analyses of this poem provide evidence of its significance as a work of literature.

Works Cited

Armstrong, James. "The 'Death Wish' in 'Stopping by Woods.'" College English 25 (1964): 440, 445.

Borroff, Marie. "Robert Frost: 'To Earthward.'" Frost: Centennial Essays II. Ed. Jac Tharpe. Jackson: University Press of Mississippi, 1976. 21–39.

Ciardi, John. "Robert Frost: The Way to the Poem." <u>Saturday Review of Literature</u> 12 April 1958: 13–15, 65.

Cifelli, Edward. "Ciardi on Frost: An Interview." <u>Frost: Centennial Essays</u>. Compiled by the Committee on the Frost Centennial of the University of Southern Mississippi. Jackson: University Press of Mississippi, n.d. 471–95.

Cook, Reginald. <u>Robert Frost: A Living Voice</u>. Amherst: The University of Massachusetts Press, 1974.

Frank, Bernhard. "Frost's 'Stopping by Woods on a Snowy Evening.'" <u>Explicator</u> 40.4 (1982): 43–45.

Frost, Robert. <u>Robert Frost, Poetry and Prose</u>. Ed. Edward Connery Lathem and Lawrance Thompson. New York: Holt, Rinehart and Winston, 1972.

Greiner, Donald J. "'That Plain-Speaking Guy': A Conversation with James Dickey on Robert Frost." <u>Frost: Centennial Essays</u>. Compiled by the Committee on the Frost Centennial of the University of Southern Mississippi. Jackson: University Press of Mississippi, n.d. 51–59.

Henry, Nat. "Frost's 'Stopping by Woods on a Snowy Evening.'" <u>Explicator</u> 37.1 (1978): 37–38.

Potter, James L. <u>Robert Frost Handbook</u>. University Park: The Pennsylvania State University Press, 1980.

Shurr, William H. "Once More to the Woods: A New Point of Entry into Frost's Most Famous Poem." <u>New England Quarterly</u> 47 (1974): 584–94.

Stamper, Rexford. "Robert Frost: An Assessment of Criticism, Realism, and Modernity." <u>Frost: Centennial Essays</u>. Compiled by the Committee on the Frost Centennial of the University of Southern Mississippi. Jackson: University Press of Mississippi, n.d. 60–86.

Tate, Allen. "Inner Weather: Robert Frost as a Metaphysical Poet." <u>Robert Frost: Lectures on the Centennial of His Birth</u>. Washington: Library of Congress, 1975. 57–68.

Glossary

abstract A summary in which each part corresponds in content and proportion to one section of the longer writing it represents.

act A major division of a play.

alliteration Repetition of initial sounds in words.

analysis The process of studying a writing closely by dividing it into logical sections or elements and focusing on them individually.

argumentation Writing which attempts to convince a reader by providing evidence through examples or facts.

aside A stage term indicating speech by a character which the audience hears but the other characters on stage do not hear.

assonance Repetition of vowel sounds.

audience Individual or group for whom a writing is created or to whom it is directed.

autobiography The story of a person's life written by that person.

biography The story of a person's life written by another.

character A person in a work of fiction, drama, or poetry; the qualities or traits of that person.
  dynamic character A person in a work of fiction, poetry, or drama whose attitudes or convictions change in some significant way.
  static character A person in a work of fiction, poetry, or drama whose attitudes or convictions remain basically the same.

cliché Overused figure of speech.

climax Turning point or high point of conflict or action in a work of fiction or drama.

comedy of manners A drama in which the conflict and comedy grow out of the customs and morals of a specific cultural setting.

comparison A noting of similarities.

complication Central section of a work of fiction or drama containing incidents which set forth and intensify the conflict.

composition The art and craft of writing.

conclusion The final section of a writing which draws together the threads of the plot, theme, or argument.

conflict A struggle—involving characters, emotions, or ideas—which produces the tension between opposing forces in a plot.
  external conflict Struggle between one character and another person or force.
  internal conflict Struggle between two ideas or emotions within a character.

909

connotation   Positive or negative nuances which a word conveys in addition to its literal definition.

consonance   Repetition of consonant sounds.

contrast   A noting of differences.

dénouement   The concluding section of a work of fiction or drama which reveals the final outcome, literally "untying" or unraveling the threads of the plot.

development   The central section of a writing which expands the topic by example, detail, or evidence.

dialogue   Conversation between two or more people.

draft   An early or rough version of a writing.

drama   A play or writing created to be acted rather than read, usually divided into acts and scenes.

essay   A prose composition of sufficient length to state a thesis and support the main idea with examples, evidence, or arguments.

explication   A close reading or line-by-line analysis of a poem.

exposition   The introduction in a work of fiction, the initial section which provides necessary background information to the reader.

fiction   Prose writing in which an author uses imagined or created material, as in novels and short stories.

figurative language   Metaphors, similes, and other constructions which carry meanings in addition to the literal ones indicated by the words.

form   The arrangement or overall structure of a writing; for example, an essay, letter, poem, short story, or scholarly article.

free verse   Poetry with no conventional meter or rhyme.

introduction   The beginning section of a writing which sets the stage for what is to follow.

irony   The effect created when an event or statement conveys a meaning different from the literal or expected meaning.

   situational irony   The effect created when an event or happening contradicts what is anticipated or seems appropriate.

   irony of statement   The effect created when what is said is the opposite of what is meant.

journal   Personal writing, often a day-by-day account of events and personal impressions.

limerick   A five-line humorous verse with set meter and rhyme.

literacy level   A person's current skillfulness as a writer and reader.

literary criticism   An explanation or interpretation of a work of fiction, poetry, or drama; usually written by a knowledgeable reader who has studied the work in comparison with others of its kind.

literature   All writing in prose and verse; traditionally, imaginative or creative writing, such as fiction, poetry, and drama.

lyric poetry   A songlike poem which expresses the poet's personal emotion or idea.

metaphor   An implied comparison of dissimilar objects.

narration   Narrative relating a happening or an event: someone doing something.

nonfiction   Factual prose writing.

novel   A book-length work of fiction.

oral history   The recording and transcribing of oral interviews as a means of capturing memories and recollections of individuals.

parallelism   Repetition in which words or phrases are of the same grammatical form and contain ideas of equal rank.

paraphrase To restate in your own words.

periodical A magazine, journal, or review which appears at regular intervals.

persona A writer's position, perspective, or voice in a writing; occasionally a character created by a writer to serve as a spokesperson.

persuasion Writing which attempts to convince a reader by providing evidence, by reasoning, or by appealing to emotions.

plagiarism Literary theft; borrowing ideas or language without giving proper credit.

plot The selected cause-and-effect incidents which account for the action in a narrative.

poetry A form of writing organized in lines and stanzas.

point of view The perspective or angle of vision from which events are narrated.

  first-person point of view The perspective of a narrator whose angle of vision is that of "I" and "we."

  third-person point of view The perspective of a narrator describing events and people using "he," "she," and "they."

  omniscient point of view The perspective of an all-knowing narrator.

primary source In literature, the work being studied.

process In writing, the activity of generating ideas, planning, drafting, and revising.

product In writing, the prose or poetry which results from the process of composition.

prose A form of writing organized in sentences and paragraphs.

purpose The reason for writing; provides answers to such questions as "Why am I writing?" and "What am I trying to accomplish?"

refrain A line or stanza that recurs throughout a poem.

repetition The use of a sound, word, phrase, or pattern of language again and again for a desired effect.

revising Improving through clarifying, repositioning, rewriting, and proofreading.

rhyme Repetition of the same final vowel sounds in words preceded by different consonant sounds.

  end rhyme Rhyme occurring at the ends of lines.

  internal rhyme Rhyme within a single line.

  rhyme scheme The pattern of the end rhyme in a poem.

scene The setting of a play; also a division of an act in which one main incident or exchange of dialogue occurs.

secondary source A writing about the selection being studied.

setting The time and place of the action in a narrative.

short story Fiction in which the writer creates or imagines one main incident or closely connected series of events.

simile An explicitly stated comparison of dissimilar objects, usually identified with a phrase such as "is like."

sonnet A fourteen-line poem written according to a set rhyme scheme and meter form.

stanza Lines of poetry organized into a group.

style The traits or characteristics of writing reflected by a writer's choice of form, topic, organization, tone, sentence or stanza structure, word choice, and grammatical conventions.

summary A condensation of a writing, retaining the main thoughts.

symbols   Objects, characters, or actions which have an abstract as well as a literal meaning.

theme   The idea or point which a story or other writing illustrates.

tone   The attitude or perspective of the writer.

transition   The technique of linking parts of a writing by providing logical movement from one sentence, paragraph, or idea to the next.

voice   A writer's position, perspective, or persona in a writing.

Copyrights and Acknowledgments

The authors are grateful to the following publishers and copyright holders for permission to use selections reprinted in this book:

ADDISON-WESLEY PUBLISHING CO.   For "Teenagers in Crisis," pages 3–21 and 219, from *All Grown Up and No Place to Go* by David Elkind, © 1981 Addison-Wesley, Reading, Massachusetts. Reprinted with permission.

ATHENEUM PUBLISHERS, INC.   For "The Dover Bitch," from *The Hard Hours* by Anthony Hecht. Copyright © 1967 by Anthony E. Hecht. For "The Names and Faces of Heroes," excerpted from *The Names and Faces of Heroes* by Reynolds Price. Copyright © 1963 by Reynolds Price. Both reprinted with the permission of Atheneum Publishers, Inc.

JO BRANS   For "A Divorce Made in Heaven" by Jo Brans. Originally appeared in *D Magazine.* Copyright 1981 by Jo Brans. Reprinted by permission of the author.

CURTIS BROWN, LTD.   For "My woman says she'd prefer to marry no one" by Catullus, translated by Gilbert Highet from *Poets in a Landscape* (1957). Copyright © 1957 by Gilbert Highet. Renewed 1985 by Helen Highet. Reprinted by permission of Curtis Brown, Ltd.

THE CHRONICLE OF HIGHER EDUCATION   For "Freshman Writing: It's the Best Course in the University to Teach" by Toby Fulwiler, from *The Chronicle of Higher Education*, February 5, 1986. Copyright 1986 by the Chronicle of Higher Education. Reprinted with permission.

JOHN CIARDI   For "Most Like an Arch This Marriage" by John Ciardi. © 1958 by John Ciardi. Reprinted by permission of the poet.

DALLAS TIMES HERALD   For "Rye Observations" by Bill Porterfield. Appeared in the *Dallas Times Herald*, April 16, 1984. Reprinted by permission.

DELACORTE PRESS   For "I Stand Here Ironing," excerpted from *Tell Me a Riddle* by Tillie Olsen. Copyright © 1956 by Tillie Olsen. For "Tell Me a Riddle," also excerpted from the book *Tell Me a Riddle* by Tillie Olsen. Copyright © 1956, 1957, 1960, 1961 by Tillie Olsen. Both reprinted by permission of Delacorte Press/Seymour Lawrence.

DOUBLEDAY & COMPANY, INC.   For "Youth," from *Youth and Other Stories* by Joseph Conrad. Copyright 1903 by Doubleday & Company, Inc. For "Child on Top of a Greenhouse" by Theodore Roethke. Copyright 1946 by Editorial Publications, Inc., from *The Collected Poems of Theodore Roethke* by Theodore Roethke. For "My

913

Index

A 7
B 8
C 9
D 0
E 1
F 2
G 3
H 4
I 5
J 6